SOME USEFUL FACTS AND FORMULAS

Time Value of Money

Future Value (4.1)

The value to which a $1 investment will grow after t years with compound interest at an annual interest rate of r percent is $FV = (1 + r)^t$

Present Value (4.2)

The value today of $1 to be received in t years is $PV = \dfrac{1}{(1 + r)^t}$

Annuities (4.4)

The present value of a stream of income of $1 per year for t years is $PV = \dfrac{1}{r} - \dfrac{1}{r(1 + r)^t}$

The future value of a stream of income of $1 per year for t years is $FV = \dfrac{(1 + r)^t - 1}{r}$

Real Versus Nominal Quantities (4.5)

The purchasing power of a future cash flow in terms of today's dollars is

$$\text{Real value of cash flow at time } t = \frac{\text{nominal cash flow}}{(1 + \text{inflation rate})^t}$$

The growth of purchasing power from an investment is

$$\text{Real interest rate} = \frac{1 + \text{nominal interest rate}}{1 + \text{inflation rate}} - 1 \approx \text{nominal rate} - \text{inflation rate}$$

Effective Annual Rate (4.6)

The annually compounded rate on a loan given a stated APR and m compounding periods per year is

$$\text{Effective annual rate} = \left(1 + \frac{\text{APR}}{m}\right)^m - 1$$

Stock Valuation

Rate of Return on a Security (6.3)

The rate of return on a stock held for one period equals $\dfrac{\text{Income} + \text{capital gain}}{\text{Initial price}} = \dfrac{\text{DIV}_1 + (P_1 - P_0)}{P_0}$

Dividend Discount Model (6.3)

The value of a share of stock equals the present value of dividends paid until the horizon date, H, plus the present value of the anticipated sales price of the stock, P_H.

$$P_0 = \frac{\text{DIV}_1}{1 + r} + \frac{\text{DIV}_2}{(1 + r)^2} + \cdots + \frac{\text{DIV}_H + P_H}{(1 + r)^H}$$

Constant-Growth Dividend Discount Model (6.4)

If the initial dividend is DIV_1 (paid in 1 year), and if the dividend grows thereafter at a constant rate of g, the present value of the dividend stream is $P_0 = \dfrac{\text{DIV}_1}{r - g}$

(continued inside back cover)

CORPORATE FINANCE
PowerWeb!

McGraw-Hill/Irwin is pleased to provide you access to **Corporate Finance *PowerWeb***, an online site created specifically for finance students to explain both the roots and current events surrounding corporate affairs. It is an effective way to integrate both theoretical and applied corporate finance into the classroom.

The site includes many recent articles from academic and popular press resources, along with an abstract on each article. In addition, there is a news feed that continually updates the site.

Access to the **Corporate Finance *PowerWeb*** gives you:

- Study Tips with Self-Quizzes
- Links to Related Sites for this Course
- Current Readings and News
- Weekly Updates
- Web Research Guide
- And more!

w w w . d u s h k i n . c o m / p o w e r w e b

See other side for your unique access code and details

WITH THE PURCHASE OF A
NEW BOOK *

You Can Access the Real Financial Data that the Experts Use!
*If you purchased a used book, see other side for access information.

This card entitles the purchaser of a new textbook to a semester of access to the Educational Version of Standard & Poor's Market Insight®, a rich online resource featuring hundreds of the most often researched companies in the Market Insight database.

For 1000 companies, this website provides you:

- Access to six years' worth of fundamental financial data from the renowned Standard & Poor's COMPUSTAT® database

- 12 Excel Analytics Reports, including balance sheets, income statements, ratio reports and cash flow statements; adjusted prices reports and profitability; forecasted values and monthly valuation data reports

- Access to Financial Highlights Reports including key ratios

- S & P Stock Reports that offer fundamental, quantitative and technical analysis

- EDGAR reports updated throughout the day and news feeds (updated hourly) for companies and industries

- Industry Surveys, written by S & P's Equity analysts

- Interactive JavaCharts with price and volume data incorporating over 100 different technical studies, user-specific watch lists, easy to customize parameters and drawing tools; delayed real time pricing available

See other side for your unique access code

PowerWeb: CORPORATE FINANCE

Welcome to PowerWeb! This site has been designed to enhance your course—giving you access to readings, up-to-the-minute news, research links, and more!

To access PowerWeb:

1. Use a Web browser to go to **http://register.dushkin.com**.

2. Enter your unique access code in the space provided. You must enter the **entire** code as it appears in the box **below** when you register.

3. After you have entered the "unique access code," click on the "**Register**" button to continue the registration process.

THIS UNIQUE ACCESS CODE WORKS FOR BOTH SITES.

ta162345

Welcome to the EDUCATIONAL VERSION of Market Insight®!

www.mhhe.com/edumarketinsight

Check out your textbook's website for details on how this special offer enhances the value of your purchase!

1. To get started, use your Web browser to go to **www.mhhe.com/edumarketinsight**.
2. Enter your unique access code **exactly** as it appears in the box **above**.
3. You may be prompted to enter the unique access code for future use — *please keep this card.*

*If you purchased a used book, this unique access code may have expired. For new password purchase, please go to **www.mhhe.com/edumarketinsight**. Password activation is good for a 6 month duration.

ISBN-13 978-0-07-301250-6
ISBN-10 0-07-301250-5

FIFTH EDITION

Fundamentals of
Corporate Finance

THE IRWIN/McGRAW-HILL SERIES IN FINANCE, INSURANCE, AND REAL ESTATE

Stephen A. Ross, Franco Modigliani Professor of Finance and Economics, Sloan School of Management, Massachusetts Institute of Technology, Consulting Editor

Financial Management

Adair
Excel Applications for Corporate Finance
First Edition

Benninga and Sarig
Corporate Finance: A Valuation Approach

Block and Hirt
Foundations of Financial Management
Eleventh Edition

Brealey, Myers, and Allen
Principles of Corporate Finance
Eighth Edition

Brealey, Myers, and Marcus
Fundamentals of Corporate Finance
Fifth Edition

Brooks
FinGame Online 4.0

Bruner
Case Studies in Finance: Managing for Corporate Value Creation
Fifth Edition

Chew
The New Corporate Finance: Where Theory Meets Practice
Third Edition

Chew and Gillan
Corporate Governance at the Crossroads: A Book of Readings
First Edition

DeMello
Cases in Finance
Second Edition

Grinblatt and Titman
Financial Markets and Corporate Strategy
Second Edition

Helfert
Techniques of Financial Analysis: A Guide to Value Creation
Eleventh Edition

Higgins
Analysis for Financial Management
Eighth Edition

Kester, Ruback, and Tufano
Case Problems in Finance
Twelfth Edition

Ross, Westerfield, and Jaffe
Corporate Finance
Seventh Edition

Ross, Westerfield, Jaffe, and Jordan
Corporate Finance: Core Principles and Applications
First Edition

Ross, Westerfield, and Jordan
Essentials of Corporate Finance
Fifth Edition

Ross, Westerfield, and Jordan
Fundamentals of Corporate Finance
Seventh Edition

Shefrin
Behavioral Corporate Finance: Decisions That Create Value
First Edition

Smith
The Modern Theory of Corporate Finance
Second Edition

White
Financial Analysis with an Electronic Calculator
Sixth Edition

Investments

Bodie, Kane, and Marcus
Essentials of Investments
Sixth Edition

Bodie, Kane, and Marcus
Investments
Sixth Edition

Cohen, Zinbarg, and Zeikel
Investment Analysis and Portfolio Management
Fifth Edition

Corrado and Jordan
Fundamentals of Investments: Valuation and Management
Third Edition

Hirt and Block
Fundamentals of Investment Management
Eighth Edition

Financial Institutions and Markets

Cornett and Saunders
Fundamentals of Financial Institutions Management

Rose and Hudgins
Bank Management and Financial Services
Sixth Edition

Rose and Marquis
Money and Capital Markets: Financial Institutions and Instruments in a Global Marketplace
Ninth Edition

Santomero and Babbel
Financial Markets, Instruments, and Institutions
Second Edition

Saunders and Cornett
Financial Institutions Management: A Risk Management Approach
Fifth Edition

Saunders and Cornett
Financial Markets and Institutions: An Introduction to the Risk Management Approach
Third Edition

International Finance

Beim and Calomiris
Emerging Financial Markets

Eun and Resnick
International Financial Management
Fourth Edition

Kuemmerle
Case Studies in International Entrepreneurship: Managing and Financing Ventures in the Global Economy
First Edition

Levich
International Financial Markets: Prices and Policies
Second Edition

Real Estate

Brueggeman and Fisher
Real Estate Finance and Investments
Twelfth Edition

Corgel, Ling, and Smith
Real Estate Perspectives: An Introduction to Real Estate
Fourth Edition

Ling and Archer
Real Estate Principles: A Value Approach
First Edition

Financial Planning and Insurance

Allen, Melone, Rosenbloom, and Mahoney
Pension Planning: Pension, Profit-Sharing, and Other Deferred Compensation Plans
Ninth Edition

Altfest
Personal Financial Planning
First Edition

Crawford
Life and Health Insurance Law
Eighth Edition (LOMA)

Harrington and Niehaus
Risk Management and Insurance
Second Edition

Hirsch
Casualty Claim Practice
Sixth Edition

Kapoor, Dlabay, and Hughes
Focus on Personal Finance: An Active Approach to Help You Develop Successful Financial Skills
First Edition

Kapoor, Dlabay, and Hughes
Personal Finance
Eighth Edition

FIFTH EDITION

Fundamentals of
Corporate Finance

Richard A. Brealey
London Business School

Stewart C. Myers
Sloan School of
Management
Massachusetts Institute of
Technology

Alan J. Marcus
Wallace E. Carroll School
of Management
Boston College

McGraw-Hill
Irwin

Boston   Burr Ridge, IL   Dubuque, IA   Madison, WI   New York
San Francisco   St. Louis   Bangkok   Bogotá   Caracas   Kuala Lumpur
Lisbon   London   Madrid   Mexico City   Milan   Montreal   New Delhi
Santiago   Seoul   Singapore   Sydney   Taipei   Toronto

McGraw-Hill
Irwin

FUNDAMENTALS OF CORPORATE FINANCE
Published by McGraw-Hill/Irwin, a business unit of The McGraw-Hill Companies, Inc., 1221 Avenue of the
Americas, New York, NY, 10020. Copyright © 2007 by The McGraw-Hill Companies, Inc. All rights reserved.
No part of this publication may be reproduced or distributed in any form or by any means, or stored in a
database or retrieval system, without the prior written consent of The McGraw-Hill Companies, Inc., including,
but not limited to, in any network or other electronic storage or transmission, or broadcast for distance
learning.

Some ancillaries, including electronic and print components, may not be available to customers
outside the United States.

This book is printed on acid-free paper.

2 3 4 5 6 7 8 9 0 DOW/DOW 0 9 8 7 6

ISBN-13: 978-0-07-301238-4
ISBN-10: 0-07-301238-6

Publisher: *Stephen M. Patterson*
Developmental editor II: *Christina Kouvelis*
Marketing manager: *Julie Phifer*
Media producer: *Jennifer Fisher*
Senior project manager: *Lori Koetters*
Senior production supervisor: *Sesha Bolisetty*
Director of design BR: *Keith J. McPherson*
Photo research coordinator: *Lori Kramer*
Photo researcher: *Keri Johnson*
Lead media project manager: *Becky Szura*
Senior supplement producer: *Carol Loreth*
Cover design: *Chris Bowyer*
Interior design: *Maureen McCutcheon*
Cover Image: *© Gettyimages, The Image Bank Ed Freeman*
Typeface: *10.5/12 Times Roman*
Compositor: *ElectraGraphics, Inc.*
Printer: *R. R. Donnelley*

Library of Congress Cataloging-in-Publication Data
Brealey, Richard A.
    Fundamentals of corporate finance / Richard A. Brealey, Stewart C. Myers, Alan J.
Marcus.—5th ed.
        p. cm.—(The McGraw-Hill/Irwin series in finance, insurance, and real estate)
    Includes bibliographical references and index.
    ISBN-13: 978-0-07-301238-4 (alk. paper)
    ISBN-10: 0-07-301238-6 (alk. paper)
    1. Corporations—Finance. I. Title: Corporate finance. II. Myers, Stewart C. III. Marcus,
Alan J. IV. Title. V. Series.
HG4026.B6668 2007
658.15—dc22
                                                                                2005053133

www.mhhe.com

To Our Wives

About the Authors

Richard A. Brealey

Professor of Finance at the London Business School. He is the former president of the European Finance Association and a former director of the American Finance Association. He is a fellow of the British Academy and has served as a special adviser to the Governor of the Bank of England and as director of a number of financial institutions. Professor Brealey is also the author (with Professor Myers and Franklin Allen) of this book's sister text, *Principles of Corporate Finance*.

Stewart C. Myers

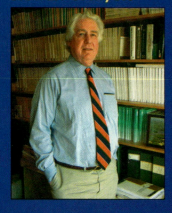

Gordon Y Billard Professor of Finance at MIT's Sloan School of Management. He is past president of the American Finance Association and a research associate of the National Bureau of Economic Research. His research has focused on financing decisions, valuation methods, the cost of capital, and financial aspects of government regulation of business. Dr. Myers is a director of The Brattle Group, Inc., and is active as a financial consultant. He is also the author (with Professor Brealey and Franklin Allen) of this book's sister text, *Principles of Corporate Finance*.

Alan J. Marcus

Professor of Finance in the Wallace E. Carroll School of Management at Boston College. His main research interests are in derivatives and securities markets. He is co-author (with Zvi Bodie and Alex Kane) of the texts *Investments* and *Essentials of Investments*. Professor Marcus has served as a research fellow at the National Bureau of Economic Research. Professor Marcus also spent 2 years at Freddie Mac, where he helped to develop mortgage pricing and credit risk models. He currently serves on the Research Foundation Advisory Board of the CFA Institute.

Preface

This book is about corporate finance. It focuses on how companies invest in real assets and how they raise the money to pay for these investments.

Financial management is important, interesting, and challenging. It is *important* because today's capital investment decisions may determine the businesses that the firm is in 10, 20, or more years ahead. Also, a firm's success or failure depends in large part on its ability to find the capital that it needs.

Finance is *interesting* for several reasons. Financial decisions often involve huge sums of money. Large investment projects or acquisitions may involve billions of dollars. Also, the financial community is international and fast-moving, with colorful heroes and a sprinkling of unpleasant villains.

Finance is *challenging*. Financial decisions are rarely cut and dried, and the financial markets in which companies operate are changing rapidly. Good managers can cope with routine problems, but only the best managers can respond to change. To handle new problems, you need more than rules of thumb; you need to understand why companies and financial markets behave as they do and when common practice may not be best practice. Once you have a consistent framework for making financial decisions, complex problems become more manageable.

This book provides that framework. It is not an encyclopedia of finance. It focuses instead on setting out the basic *principles* of financial management and applying them to the main decisions faced by the financial manager. It explains why the firm's owners would like the manager to increase firm value and shows how managers value investments that may pay off at different points of time or have different degrees of risk. It also describes the main features of financial markets and discusses why companies may prefer a particular source of finance.

Some texts shy away from modern finance, sticking instead with more traditional, procedural, or institutional approaches. These are supposed to be easier or more practical. We disagree emphatically. The concepts of modern finance, properly explained, make the subject simpler, not more difficult. They are also more practical. The tools of financial management are easier to grasp and use effectively when presented in a consistent conceptual framework. Modern finance provides that framework.

Modern financial management is not "rocket science." It is a set of ideas that can be made clear by words, graphs, and numerical examples. The ideas provide the "why" behind the tools that good financial managers use to make investment and financing decisions.

We wrote this book to make financial management clear, useful, interesting, and fun for the beginning student. We set out to show that modern finance and good financial practice go together, even for the financial novice.

Fundamentals and Principles of Corporate Finance

This book is derived in part from its sister text *Principles of Corporate Finance*. The spirit of the two books is similar. Both apply modern finance to give students a working ability to make financial decisions. However, there are also substantial differences between the two books.

First, we provide much more detailed discussion of the principles and mechanics of the time value of money. This material underlies almost all of this text, and we spend a lengthy chapter providing extensive practice with this key concept.

Second, we use numerical examples in this text to a greater degree than in *Principles*. Each chapter presents several detailed numerical examples to help the reader become familiar and comfortable with the material.

Third, we have streamlined the treatment of most topics. Whereas *Principles* has 35 chapters, *Fundamentals* has only 25. The relative brevity of *Fundamentals* necessitates a broader-brush coverage of some topics, but we feel that this is an advantage for a beginning audience.

Fourth, we assume little in the way of background knowledge. While most users will have had an introductory accounting course, we review the concepts of accounting that are important to the financial manager in Chapter 3.

Principles is known for its relaxed and informal writing style, and we continue this tradition in *Fundamentals*. In addition, we use as little mathematical notation as possible. Even when we present an equation, we usually write it in words rather than symbols. This approach has two advantages. It is less intimidating, and it focuses attention on the underlying concept rather than the formula.

Organizational Design

Fundamentals is organized in eight parts.

Part 1 (Introduction)   provides essential background material. In the first chapter we discuss how businesses are organized, the role of the financial manager, and the financial markets in which the manager operates. We explain how shareholders want managers to take actions that increase the value of their investment, and we describe some of the mechanisms that help to align the interests of managers and shareholders. Of course, the task of increasing shareholder value does not justify corrupt and unscrupulous behavior. We therefore discuss some of the ethical issues that confront managers.

Chapter 2 surveys and sets out the functions of financial markets and institutions. It shows how financial managers use these markets and institutions, and it explains how markets provide useful signals to managers concerning the viability of potential investment projects.

A large corporation is a team effort, and so companies produce financial statements to help the players monitor their progress. Chapter 3 provides a brief overview of these financial statements and introduces two key distinctions—between market and book values and between cash flows and profits. This chapter also discusses some of the shortcomings in accounting practice that became apparent in the scandals of 2001–2002. The chapter concludes with a summary of federal taxes.

Part 2 (Value)   is concerned with valuation. In Chapter 4 we introduce the concept of the time value of money, and, since most readers will be more familiar with their own financial affairs than with the big leagues of finance, we motivate our discussion by looking first at some personal financial decisions. We show how to value long-lived streams of cash flows and work through the valuation of perpetuities and annuities. Chapter 4 also contains a short concluding section on inflation and the distinction between real and nominal returns.

Chapters 5 and 6 introduce the basic features of bonds and stocks and give students a chance to apply the ideas of Chapter 4 to the valuation of these securities. We show how to find the value of a bond given its yield, and we show how prices of bonds fluctuate as interest rates change. We look at what determines stock prices and how stock valuation formulas can be used to infer the return that investors expect. Finally, we see how investment opportunities are reflected in the stock price and why analysts focus on the price-earnings multiple. Chapter 6 also introduces the concept of market efficiency. This concept is crucial to interpreting a stock's valuation; it also provides a framework for the later treatment of the issues that arise when firms issue securities or make decisions concerning dividends or capital structure.

The remaining chapters of Part 2 are concerned with the company's investment decision. In Chapter 7 we introduce the concept of net present value and show how to calculate the NPV of a simple investment project. We also look at other measures of an investment's attractiveness—the internal rate of return rule and payback rule. We then turn to more complex investment proposals, including choices between alternative projects, machine replacement decisions, and decisions of when to invest. Finally, we show how the profitability index can be used to choose between investment projects when capital is scarce.

The first step in any NPV calculation is to decide what to discount. Therefore, in Chapter 8 we work through a realistic example of a capital budgeting analysis, showing how the manager needs to recognize the investment in working capital and how taxes and depreciation affect cash flows.

We start Chapter 9 by looking at how companies organize the investment process and ensure everyone works toward a common goal. We then go on to look at various techniques to help managers identify the key assumptions in their estimates, such as sensitivity analysis, scenario analysis, and break-even analysis. We also show how managers can use the notion of economic value added to assess projects. We conclude the chapter by describing how managers try to build future flexibility into projects so that they can capitalize on good luck and mitigate the consequences of bad luck.

Part 3 (Risk)   is concerned with the cost of capital. Chapter 10 starts with a historical survey of returns on bonds and stocks and goes on to distinguish between the unique risk and market risk of individual stocks. Chapter 11 shows how to measure market risk and discusses the relationship between risk and expected return. Chapter 12 introduces the weighted-average cost of capital and provides a practical illustration of how to estimate it.

Part 4 (Financing)   begins our discussion of the financing decision. Chapter 13 looks at the role of shareholders in large corporations and compares corporate governance in the United States and elsewhere. It also provides an overview of the securities that firms issue and their relative importance as sources of finance. In Chapter 14 we look at how firms issue securities, and we follow a firm from its first need for venture capital, through its initial public offering, to its continuing need to raise debt or equity.

Part 5 (Debt and Payout Policy)   focuses on the two classic long-term financing decisions. In Chapter 15 we ask how much the firm should borrow and we summarize bankruptcy procedures that occur when firms can't pay their debts. In Chapter 16 we study how firms should set dividend and payout policy. In each case we start with Modigliani and Miller's (MM's) observation that in well-functioning markets the decision should not matter, but we use this observation to help the reader understand why financial managers in practice do pay attention to these decisions.

Part 6 (Financial Analysis and Planning)   starts with financial statement analysis in Chapter 17 and shows how analysts summarize the large volume of accounting information by calculating some key financial ratios. Long-term financial planning is discussed in Chapter 18, where we look at how the financial manager considers the combined effects of investment and financing decisions on the firm as a whole. We also show how measures of internal and sustainable growth help managers check that the firm's planned growth is consistent with its financing plans. Chapter 19 is an introduction to short-term financial planning. It shows how managers ensure that the firm will have enough cash to pay its bills over the coming year, and describes the principal sources of short-term borrowing. Chapter 20 addresses working capital management. It describes the basic steps of credit management, the principals of inventory management, and how firms handle payments efficiently and put cash to work as quickly as possible.

Part 7 (Special Topics) covers several important but somewhat more advanced topics—mergers (Chapter 21), international financial management (Chapter 22), options (Chapter 23), and risk management (Chapter 24). Some of these topics are touched on in earlier chapters. For example, we introduce the idea of options in Chapter 9, when we show how companies build flexibility into capital projects. However, Chapter 23 generalizes this material, explains at an elementary level how options are valued, and provides some examples of why the financial manager needs to be concerned about options. International finance is also not confined to Chapter 22. As one might expect from a book that is written by an international group of authors, examples from different countries and financial systems are scattered throughout the book. However, Chapter 22 tackles the specific problems that arise when a corporation is confronted by different currencies.

Part 8 (Conclusion) contains a concluding chapter (Chapter 25), in which we review the most important ideas covered in the text. We also introduce some interesting questions that either were unanswered in the text or are still puzzles to the finance profession. Thus the last chapter is an introduction to future finance courses as well as a conclusion to this one.

Routes through the Book

There are about as many effective ways to organize a course in corporate finance as there are teachers. For this reason, we have ensured that the text is modular, so that topics can be introduced in different sequences.

We like to discuss the principles of valuation before plunging into detailed financial statement analysis or issues of financial planning. Nevertheless, we recognize that many instructors will prefer to move directly from Chapter 3 (Accounting and Finance) to Chapter 17 (Financial Statement Analysis) in order to provide a gentler transition from the typical prerequisite accounting course. We have made sure that Part 6 (Financial Analysis and Planning) can easily follow Part 1.

Similarly, we like to discuss working capital after the student is familiar with the basic principles of valuation and financing, but we recognize that here also many instructors prefer to reverse our order. There should be no difficulty in taking Chapter 20 out of order.

When we discuss project valuation in Part 2, we stress that the opportunity cost of capital depends on project risk. But we do not discuss how to measure risk or how return and risk are linked until Part 3. This ordering can easily be modified. For example, the chapters on risk and return can be introduced before, after, or midway through the material on project valuation.

Changes in the Fifth Edition

The most obvious changes in this new edition of *Fundamentals* are the continuing enhancement and use of pedagogical tools such as Internet resources, Excel spreadsheets, and end-of-chapter integrative cases. We have greatly increased our lists of suggested Web sites and have updated and expanded our Internet Insider boxes, which provide students with opportunities to explore the resources available on the Web. In addition, we provide many end-of-chapter student exercises using the recently expanded Web-based educational version of Standard & Poor's Market Insight. This resource provides a wide variety of financial statement data, stock market return history, and analyst coverage of hundreds of stocks, making it well suited for extended student projects on company and industry analysis.

We have also integrated more spreadsheets into the chapter material. These spreadsheets require only a basic knowledge of Excel, but they illustrate the powerful ways in which spreadsheet modeling can facilitate financial analysis. Every spreadsheet in the text is now available on the text Web site at **www.mhhe.com/bmm5e.**

Some of the changes in coverage reflect topics that have been highlighted by recent events. For example, the scandals of 2001–2002 have increased interest in the issues of governance and control, while the dot-com boom has focused attention on behavioral aspects of finance. So you will find more emphasis in this edition on governance and behavioral finance. Other topics that have received increasing emphasis in recent editions include company valuation, real options, and the role of financial institutions and markets.

In revising each chapter we have sought to improve readability and update coverage. Chapters 1 and 2 have been largely rewritten to improve interest and provide a better overview of the financial landscape. We use case histories of real firms such as Apple to show how financial markets help infant firms grow into healthy adults. Along the way, we take a fresh look at agency and reputation issues in the context of recent scandals, and we present a nontechnical introduction to the idea of the opportunity cost of capital that provides context for the later discussion of present value.

Chapter 3 (Accounting and Finance) includes updated discussions of reporting issues informed by the accounting failures and reforms of the last few years.

Chapters 4 to 6 have been updated and rearranged to improve logical flow. We use data on real firms to illustrate the concept and importance of growth opportunities in firm valuation (Google) and to provide an application of valuation using multistage dividend discount models (Pepsi).

The discussion of project analysis in Chapters 7 to 9 has been streamlined and reorganized. The material on project valuation has been rewritten with new spreadsheet material and with more emphasis on each separate component of cash flow.

Chapters 10 to 12 on risk and firm valuation have been updated. In Chapter 12 we work through a practical example showing how the weighted-average cost of capital is used to value entire businesses. The chapter title has been changed to "The Weighted-Average Cost of Capital and Company Valuation."

The overview of financing methods in Part 4 includes an updated discussion of governance issues and Sarbanes-Oxley as well as material on developments in the IPO market.

Part 5 on debt and payout policy also has been updated. The discussion of bankruptcy procedures has now been incorporated into Chapter 15 on debt policy, and Chapter 16 has been renamed "Payout Policy" to reflect its broader focus on share repurchases along with dividend policy.

Material on financial planning in Part 6 has been considerably streamlined. The material on working capital and cash management has been condensed into one chapter. We emphasize new approaches to cash management in particular, and we have correspondingly pruned material that has become obsolete in light of rapid technological advance.

Finally, Part 7 on special topics has been updated with new case studies of mergers (e.g., People Soft–Oracle) and spin-offs (Palm-3Com), as well as additional discussions in the options and risk management chapters on the use of derivatives for hedging.

KEY FEATURES

New and Enhanced Pedagogy

A great deal of effort has gone into expanding and enhancing the features in *Fundamentals of Corporate Finance.*

WALK-THROUGH

Brealey / Myers / Marcus
Your guide through the challenging waters of corporate finance

Key Points
Located throughout the text, these points underscore and summarize the importance of the immediately preceding material, at the same time helping students focus on the most relevant topics critical to their understanding.

Key Terms in the Margin
Key terms are presented in bold and defined in the margin as they are introduced. A glossary is also available at the back of the book.

7.2 Other Investment Criteria

A project with a positive net present value is worth more than it costs. So whenever a firm invests in such a project, it is making its shareholders better off.

These days almost every large corporation calculates the NPV of proposed investments, but management may also consider other criteria when making investment decisions. Most commonly, they may look at the project's payback and its internal rate of return. As we describe these measures, you will see that payback is no better than a very rough guide to an investment's worth. On the other hand, when properly used, the internal rate of return will lead to the same decisions as net present value.

Payback

We suspect that you have often heard conversations that go something like this: "A washing machine costs about $800. But we are currently spending $6 a week, or around $300 a year, at the laundromat. So the washing machine should pay for itself in less than 3 years." You have just encountered the payback rule.

payback period
Time until cash flows recover the initial investment in the project.

A project's **payback period** is the length of time before you recover your initial investment. For the washing machine the payback period was just under 3 years. The *payback rule states that a project should be accepted if its payback period is less than a specified cutoff period.* For example, if the cutoff period is 4 years, the washing machine makes the grade; if the cutoff is 2 years, it doesn't.

As a rough rule of thumb the payback rule may be adequate, but it is easy to see that it can lead to nonsensical decisions. For example, compare projects A and B. Project A has a 2-year payback at a cost of NPV. Project B has a 2-year

Related Web Links
Web citations listed at the beginning of all chapters immediately direct students to the best sources of financial information on the Internet. Since some changes in Web addresses are inevitable, a current list is maintained at the text's Online Learning Center **(www.mhhe.com/bmm5e).**

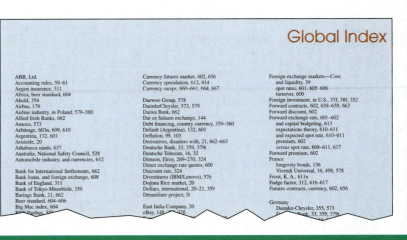

Global Index
The Global Index appears at the end of the text for easy reference to international material.

What makes Brealey/Myers/Marcus such a powerful learning tool?

Internet Insider Boxes

Each chapter includes boxes that highlight particular Web sites and provide students with simple activities to enhance their experience using the Internet.

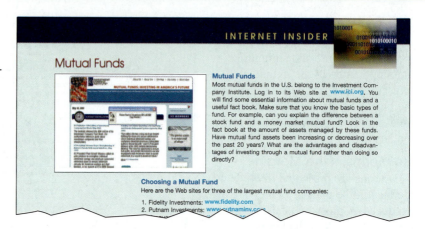

INTERNET INSIDER

Mutual Funds

Mutual Funds

Most mutual funds in the U.S. belong to the Investment Company Institute. Log in to its Web site at www.ici.org. You will find some essential information about mutual funds and a useful fact book. Make sure that you know the basic types of fund. For example, can you explain the difference between a stock fund and a money market mutual fund? Look in the fact book at the amount of assets managed by these funds. Have mutual fund assets been increasing or decreasing over the past 20 years? What are the advantages and disadvantages of investing through a mutual fund rather than doing so directly?

Choosing a Mutual Fund

Here are the Web sites for three of the largest mutual fund companies:

1. Fidelity Investments: www.fidelity.com
2. Putnam Investments: www.putnaminv.com

Spreadsheet Solutions Boxes

These boxes provide the student with detailed examples of how to use Excel spreadsheets when applying financial concepts. Denoted by an icon, these spreadsheets are also available on the student CD and the book Web site at **www.mhhe.com/bmm5e.**

SPREADSHEET SOLUTIONS

Internal Rate of Return

	A	B	C	D	E	F
1		Calculating IRR by using a spreadsheet				
2						
3	Year	Cash Flow				Formula
4	0	-350,000		IRR =	0.1296	=IRR(B4:B7)
5	1	16,000				
6	2	16,000				
7	3	466,000				

eXcel

Please visit us at www.mhhe.com/bmm5e or refer to your Student CD

Calculating internal rate of return in Excel is as easy as listing the project cash flows. For example, to calculate the IRR of the office-block project, you could simply type in its cash flows as in the spreadsheet above, and then calculate IRR as we do in cell E4. As always, the interest rate is returned as a decimal. The spreadsheet is available at www.mhhe.com/bmm5e or on your student CD.

Pitfall 1: Lending or Borrowing? Remember our condition for the IRR rule to work: The project's NPV must fall as the discount rate increases. Now consider the following projects:

Excel Exhibits

Selected exhibits are set as Excel spreadsheets. They are also available on the Student CD and the book Web site at **www.mhhe.com/bmm5e.**

TABLE 8–1 Financial projections for Blooper's magnoosium mine (figures in thousands of dollars)

	A	B	C	D	E	F	G	H
1	Year:	0	1	2	3	4	5	6
2	A. Fixed assets							
3	Investment in fixed assets	10,000						
4	Sales of fixed assets							1,300
5	CF, invest. in fixed assets	−10,000	0	0	0	0	0	1,300
6								
7	B. Working capital							
8	Working capital	1,500	4,075	4,279	4,493	4,717	3,039	0
9	Change in working capital	1,500	2,575	204	214	225	−1,679	−3,039
10	CF, invest. in wk capital	−1,500	−2,575	−204	−214	−225	1,679	3,039
11								
12	C. Operations							
13	Revenues		15,000	15,750	16,538	17,364	18,233	
14	Expenses		10,000	10,500	11,025	11,576	12,155	
15	Depreciation		2,000	2,000	2,000	2,000	2,000	
16	Pretax profit		3,000	3,250	3,513	3,788	4,078	
17	Tax		1,050	1,138	1,229	1,326	1,427	
18	Profit after tax		1,950	2,113	2,283	2,462	2,650	
19	Cash flow from operations		3,950	4,113	4,283	4,462	4,650	
20								
21	D. Project valuation							
22	Total project cash flow	−11,500	1,375	3,909	4,069	4,238	9,329	4,339

eXcel

Please visit us at www.mhhe.com/bmm5e or refer to your Student CD

Finance in Practice Boxes

These are excerpts that appear in most chapters, usually from the financial press, providing real-life illustrations of the chapter's topics, such as ethical choices in finance, disputes about stock valuation, financial planning, and accounting scandals.

Calculator Boxes and Exercises

In a continued effort to help students grasp the critical concept of the time value of money, many pedagogical tools have been added throughout the first section of the text. Financial Calculator boxes provide examples for solving a variety of problems, with directions for the three most popular financial calculators.

FINANCIAL CALCULATOR

Bond Valuation on a Financial Calculator

In Chapter 4 we saw that financial calculators can compute the present values of level annuities as well as the present values of one-time future cash flows. Coupon bonds present both of these characteristics: The coupon payments are level annuities, and the final payment of face value is an additional one-time payment. Thus for the coupon bond we looked at in Example 5.3, you would treat the periodic payment as PMT = $55, the final or future one-time payment as FV = $1,000, the number of periods as $n = 3$ years, and the interest rate as the yield to maturity of the bond, $i = 3.5$ percent. You would thus compute the value of the bond using the following sequence of key strokes. By the way, the order in which the various inputs for the bond valuation problem are entered does not matter.

Your calculator should now display a value of –1,056.03. The minus sign reminds us that the initial cash flow is negative: You have to pay to buy the bond.

You can also use the calculator to find the yield to maturity of a bond. For example, if you buy this bond for $1,056.03, you should find that its yield to maturity is 3.5 percent. Let's check that this is so. You enter the PV as –1,056.03 because you buy the bond for this price. Thus to solve for the interest rate, use the following key strokes:

Hewlett-Packard HP-10B	Sharp EL-733A	Texas Instruments BA II Plus
55 PMT	55 PMT	55 PMT
1000 FV	1000 FV	1000 FV
3 N	3 n	3 N
–1056.03 PV	–1056.03 PV	–1056.03 PV
I/YR	COMP I	CPT I/Y

Hewlett-Packard HP-10B	Sharp EL-733A	Texas Instruments BA II Plus
PMT	55 PMT	5 PMT

Self-Test Questions

Provided in each chapter, these helpful questions enable students to check their understanding as they read. Answers are worked out at the end of each chapter.

- *Liquidation value* is what the company could net by selling its assets and repaying its debts. It does not capture the value of a successful going concern.
- *Market value* is the amount that investors are willing to pay for the shares of the firm. This depends on the earning power of *today's* assets and the expected profitability of *future* investments.

Take a look at the nearby box for more on market versus book values. The next question is, What determines market value?

Self-Test 6.2 In the 1970s, the computer industry was dominated by IBM and was growing rapidly. In the 1980s, many new competitors entered the market, and computer prices fell. Computer makers in the last decade, including IBM, struggled with thinning profit margins and intense competition. How has IBM's market-value balance sheet changed over time? Have assets in place become proportionately more or less important? Do you think this progression is unique to the computer industry?

6.3 Valuing Common Stocks

Today's Price and Tomorrow's Price

The cash payoff to owners of common stocks comes in two forms: (1) cash dividends and (2) capital gains or losses. Usually investors expect to get some of each. Suppose

Quiz, Practice, and Challenge Problems

New end-of-chapter problems are included for even more hands-on practice. Each question is labeled by topic, and questions are separated by level of difficulty. Answers to selected problems are provided at the back of the book.

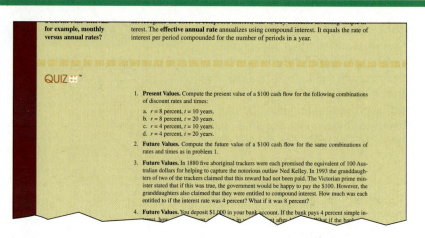

for example, monthly versus annual rates?

... not recognize the effect of compound interest, that is, they annualize assuming simple interest. The **effective annual rate** annualizes using compound interest. It equals the rate of interest per period compounded for the number of periods in a year.

QUIZ

1. **Present Values.** Compute the present value of a $100 cash flow for the following combinations of discount rates and times:

   a. $r = 8$ percent, $t = 10$ years.
   b. $r = 8$ percent, $t = 20$ years.
   c. $r = 4$ percent, $t = 10$ years.
   d. $r = 4$ percent, $t = 20$ years.

2. **Future Values.** Compute the future value of a $100 cash flow for the same combinations of rates and times as in problem 1.

3. **Future Values.** In 1880 five aboriginal trackers were each promised the equivalent of 100 Australian dollars for helping to capture the notorious outlaw Ned Kelley. In 1993 the granddaughters of two of the trackers claimed that this reward had not been paid. The Victorian prime minister stated that if this was true, the government would be happy to pay the $100. However, the granddaughters also claimed that they were entitled to compound interest. How much was each entitled to if the interest rate was 4 percent? What if it was 8 percent?

4. **Future Values.** You deposit $1,000 in your bank account. If the bank pays 4 percent simple interest, how ... in your account after ... What if the bank ...

PRACTICE PROBLEMS

21. **Compound Growth.** In 2004 a pound of apples cost $0.99, while oranges cost $1.14. Ten years earlier the price of apples was only $.72 a pound and that of oranges was $.55 a pound. What was the annual compound rate of growth in the price of the two fruits? If the same rates of growth persist in the future, what will be the price of apples in 2024? What about the price of oranges?

22. **Loan Payments.** If you take out an $8,000 car loan that calls for 48 monthly payments at an APR of 10 percent, what is your monthly payment? What is the effective annual interest rate on the loan?

23. **Annuity Values.**

   a. What is the present value of a 3-year annuity of $100 if the discount rate is 6 percent?
   b. What is the present value of the annuity in (a) if you have to wait 2 years instead of 1 year for the first payment?

24. **Annuities and Interest Rates.** Professor's Annuity Corp. offers a lifetime annuity to retiring professors. For a payment of $80,000 at age 65, the firm will pay the retiring professor $600 a month until death.

   a. If the professor's remaining life expectancy is 20 years, what is the monthly rate on this annuity? What is the effective annual rate?
   b. If the monthly interest rate is 5 percent, what monthly annuity payment can the firm offer ... the ...

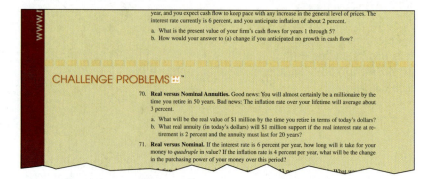

year, and you expect cash flow to keep pace with any increase in the general level of prices. The interest rate currently is 6 percent, and you anticipate inflation of about 2 percent.

a. What is the present value of your firm's cash flows for years 1 through 5?
b. How would your answer to (a) change if you anticipated no growth in cash flow?

CHALLENGE PROBLEMS

70. **Real versus Nominal Annuities.** Good news: You will almost certainly be a millionaire by the time you retire in 50 years. Bad news: The inflation rate over your lifetime will average about 3 percent.

   a. What will be the real value of $1 million by the time you retire in terms of today's dollars?
   b. What real annuity (in today's dollars) will $1 million support if the real interest rate at retirement is 2 percent and the annuity must last for 20 years?

71. **Real versus Nominal.** If the interest rate is 6 percent per year, how long will it take for your money to *quadruple* in value? If the inflation rate is 4 percent per year, what will be the change in the purchasing power of your money over this period?

S&P Problems

Included in each chapter are problems, denoted by an icon, directly incorporating the educational version of Market Insight, a service based on Standard & Poor's renowned Compustat database.

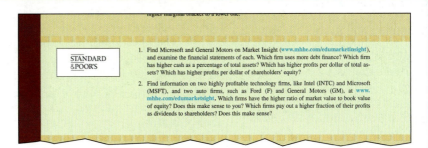

STANDARD &POOR'S

1. Find Microsoft and General Motors on Market Insight (www.mhhe.com/edumarketinsight), and examine the financial statements of each. Which firm uses more debt finance? Which firm has higher cash as a percentage of total assets? Which has higher profits per dollar of total assets? Which has higher profits per dollar of shareholders' equity?

2. Find information on two highly profitable technology firms, like Intel (INTC) and Microsoft (MSFT), and two auto firms, such as Ford (F) and General Motors (GM), at www.mhhe.com/edumarketsight. Which firms have the higher ratio of market value to book value of equity? Does this make sense to you? Which firms pay out a higher fraction of their profits as dividends to shareholders? Does this make sense?

Excel Problems

Most chapters contain problems, denoted by an icon, specifically linked to Excel templates that are available on the student CD and the book Web site at **www.mhhe.com/bmm5e.**

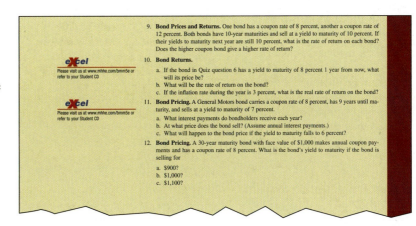

eXcel
Please visit us at www.mhhe.com/bmm5e or refer to your Student CD

9. **Bond Prices and Returns.** One bond has a coupon rate of 8 percent, another a coupon rate of 12 percent. Both bonds have 10-year maturities and sell at a yield to maturity of 10 percent. If their yields to maturity next year are still 10 percent, what is the rate of return on each bond? Does the higher coupon bond give a higher rate of return?

10. **Bond Returns.**

a. If the bond in Quiz question 6 has a yield to maturity of 8 percent 1 year from now, what will its price be?
b. What will be the rate of return on the bond?
c. If the inflation rate during the year is 3 percent, what is the real rate of return on the bond?

eXcel
Please visit us at www.mhhe.com/bmm5e or refer to your Student CD

11. **Bond Pricing.** A General Motors bond carries a coupon rate of 8 percent, has 9 years until maturity, and sells at a yield to maturity of 7 percent.

a. What interest payments do bondholders receive each year?
b. At what price does the bond sell? (Assume annual interest payments.)
c. What will happen to the bond price if the yield to maturity falls to 6 percent?

12. **Bond Pricing.** A 30-year maturity bond with face value of $1,000 makes annual coupon payments and has a coupon rate of 8 percent. What is the bond's yield to maturity if the bond is selling for

a. $900?
b. $1,000?
c. $1,100?

Minicases

Integrative minicases allow students to apply their knowledge to relatively complex, practical problems and typical real-world scenarios.

MINICASE

www.mhhe.com/bmm5

Flowton Products enjoys a steady demand for stainless steel infiltrators used in a number of chemical processes. Revenues from the infiltrator division are $50 million a year and production costs are $47.5 million. However, the 10 high-precision Munster stamping machines that are used in the production process are coming to the end of their useful life. One possibility is simply to replace each existing machine with a new Munster. These machines would cost $800,000 each and would not involve any additional operating costs. The alternative is to buy 10 centrally controlled Skilboro stampers. Skilboros cost $1.25 million each, but compared to the Munster, they would produce a total saving in operator and material costs of $500,000 a year. Moreover, the Skilboro is sturdily built and would last 10 years, compared with an estimated 7-year life for the Munster.

Analysts in the infiltrator division have produced the accompanying summary table, which shows the forecast total cash flows from the infiltrator business over the life of each machine. Flowton's standard procedures for appraising capital investments involve calculating net present value, internal rate of return, and payback, and these measures are also shown in the table.

As usual, Emily Balsam arrived early at Flowton's head office. She had never regretted joining Flowton. Everything about the place, from the mirror windows to the bell fountain in the atrium, suggested a classy outfit. Ms. Balsam sighed happily and reached for the envelope at the top of her in-tray. It was an analysis from the infiltrator division of the replacement options for the stamper machines. Pinned to the paper was the summary table of cash flows and a note from the CFO, which read, "Emily, I have read through 20 pages of excruciating detail and I still don't know which of these machines we should buy. The NPV calculation seems to indicate that the Skilboro is best, while IRR and payback suggest the opposite. Would you take a look and tell me what we should do and why."

Can you help Ms. Balsam by writing a memo to the CFO? You need to justify your solution and also to explain why some or all of the measures in the summary tables are inappropriate.

Supplements

In addition to the overall refinement and improvement of the text material, considerable effort was put into developing a stellar supplement package to provide students and instructors with an abundance of teaching and learning resources.

For the Instructor

Instructor's CD-ROM

ISBN-13: 9780073012438
ISBN-10: 0073012432

This CD contains the Instructor's Manual, the Test Bank, the Computerized Test Bank, the Solutions Manual, PowerPoint slides, Excel templates, video clips, and Web links. We have compiled them in electronic format for easier access and convenience. Print copies are available through your McGraw-Hill/Irwin representative.

Instructor's Manual

Updated and enhanced by Sheen Liu, Youngstown State University, this supplement includes a descriptive preface containing alternative course formats and case teaching methods, a chapter overview and outline, key terms and concepts, video teaching notes, related Web links, and pedagogical ideas.

PowerPoint Presentation System

Prepared by Matt Will, University of Indianapolis, these visually stimulating slides have been fully updated with colorful graphs, charts, and lists. The slides can be edited or manipulated to fit the needs of a particular course.

Test Bank

Ted Fu, Stanford University, has revised and added hundreds of new questions and problems. Over 2,000 true/false, multiple-choice, and discussion questions and problems are available to the instructor at varying levels of difficulty and comprehension. Complete answers are provided for all test questions and problems.

Computerized Test Bank

Utilizing McGraw-Hill's *EZ Test* testing software for Windows to quickly create customized exams, this user-friendly program allows instructors to sort questions by format, edit existing questions or add new ones, and scramble questions for multiple versions of the same test.

Solutions Manual

ISBN-13: 9780073012407
ISBN-10: 0073012408

Bruce Swensen, Aldephi University, has prepared this resource containing solutions to all the end-of-chapter problems.

Excel Spreadsheet Templates

Enhanced by Eric Sandburg of Interactive Learning, these templates allow students to work and gain practice with Excel and are tied to several problems within the text.

Videos

VHS ISBN-13: 9780073012445
ISBN-10: 0073012440
DVD ISBN-13: 9780073257679
ISBN-10: 0073257672

Our professionally produced videos showcase key topics in corporate finance, such as time value of money and capital budgeting. Preview clips are also available on the instructor and student CD-ROMs as well as at the Online Learning Center.

For the Student

Student CD-ROM

ISBN-13: 9780073012414
ISBN-10: 0073012416

Packaged free with the purchase of a new book, this valuable learning tool contains the *Interactive FinSims*, a new series of highly interactive exercises that help students more effectively learn the fundamentals of finance, such as the time value of money, net present value, ratios, leverage, and options. These exercises have been designed for equal applicability in the classroom or as student assignments. The primary focus is on 13 key financial concepts that must be mastered in order to complete most corporate finance course work. The accompanying *Narrated PowerPoints* discuss the concepts in further detail to help students grasp and understand these essential topics.

In addition, the CD contains S&P problems; Internet Insider Activities; and the *Finance Tutor Series,* where students can answer questions and solve problems that assess both the general understanding of the subject and the ability to apply that understanding in the real-world business contexts. Video clips, Excel templates, PowerPoint slides, Web links, and practice quizzes are also included to give the student ample study aids.

Study Guide

ISBN-13: 9780073012421
ISBN-10: 0073012424

Prepared by Matt Will, University of Indianapolis, this helpful asset contains a thorough list of activities for the student, including an introduction to each chapter, sources of business information, key concepts and terms, sample problems with solutions, integrated PowerPoint slides, and related Web links.

Online Support

Online Learning Center
www.mhhe.com/bmm5e

Find a wealth of information online! At this book Web site instructors have access to teaching supports such as electronic files of the ancillary materials. Students have access to study materials created specifically for this text, Interactive Fin-Sims, the Finance Tutor Series, and much more. All Excel spreadsheets, denoted by an icon in the text, are also located at this site. Links to the following support material, as described below, are also included.

Standard & Poor's Version of Market Insight

McGraw-Hill/Irwin has partnered exclusively with Standard & Poor's to bring you the educational version of Market Insight. This rich online resource provides 6 years of financial data for 1,000 companies in the renowned Compustat database. S&P problems can be found at the end of relevant chapters of the text.

Corporate Finance PowerWeb

This password-protected Web site offers professors a turnkey solution to adding the Internet to a course. Included are current articles from the public press, curriculum-based materials, weekly updates with assessment, informative and timely world news, referred Web links, research tools, interactive exercises, and much more.

Corporate Finance Online

An exclusive Web tool from McGraw-Hill/Irwin, this value-added site enables faculty and students to engage in financial exercises and activities for 27 key corporate finance topics. It also allows students to complete challenging exercises and discussion questions that draw on recent articles, company reports, government data, and other Web-based resources. There are also password-protected teaching notes to assist instructors with classroom integration.

Finance around the World

This outstanding global financial resource facilitates researching and exploring corporate finance and investments online. It includes country facts and daily coverage and analysis of financial markets and companies, as well as general finance and business news and articles for over 35 countries.

Packaging Options

 **McGraw-Hill's Homework Manager**

Are you looking for a way to spend less time grading and to have more flexibility with the problems you assign as homework and tests? McGraw-Hill's Homework Manager is an exciting new package option developed for this text. Homework Manager is a Web-based tool that assists instructors and students with delivering, answering, and grading end-of-chapter problems and tests and provides a limitless supply of self-graded practice for students.

All of the book's end-of-chapter Quiz, Practice, and Challenge problems are loaded into Homework Manager, and instructors can choose to assign the problems exactly as stated in the book or to assign algorithmic versions of them so that each student has a unique set of variables for the problems. You create the assignments and control parameters such as whether your students receive hints and whether the assignment is a graded one or practice. The test bank is also available in Homework Manager, giving you the ability to use its questions for online tests. Both the problems and the tests are automatically graded, and the results are stored in a private grade book, which is created when you set up your class. Detailed results let you see at a glance how each student does on an assignment or an individual problem—you can even see how many tries it took the student to solve it. If you order this special package, students will receive a Homework Manager User's Guide and an access code packaged with their text.

Homework Manager Plus

An enhanced version of McGraw-Hill's Homework Manager is available through the Homework Manager Plus package option. If you order the text packaged with Homework Manager Plus, your students will receive Homework Manager as described above, as well as an integrated online text. When students are in Homework Manager and need more help to solve a problem, a link will take them to the section of the online text that explains the concept they are struggling with. All of McGraw-Hill's media assets, such as videos, narrated lectures, and additional online quizzing, are also integrated at the appropriate places of the online text to provide students with a full learning experience. Homework Manager Plus also gives students access to Corporate Finance PowerWeb—current events and articles pertaining to finance linked to appropriate chapters—all accessible with one access code. If you order this special package, students will receive the Homework Manager Plus card packaged with their text, which gives them access to all of these products, as well as an online Homework Manager User's Guide.

McGraw-Hill's Homework Manager is powered by Brownstone.

BusinessWeek Subscription

Your students can subscribe to *BusinessWeek* for a special rate of $8.25 in addition to the price of the text. Students will receive a pass-code card shrink-wrapped with their new text that will refer them to a registration site to begin their subscription. Subscriptions are available in print copy or digital format.

Wall Street Journal Subscription

Your students can subscribe to *The Wall Street Journal* for 15 weeks at a special rate of $20 in addition to the price of the text. Students will receive the "How to Use the *WSJ*" guide plus a subscription card shrink-wrapped with their new text. The subscription also gives students access to **www.wsj.com.**

Financial Times Subscription

Your students can subscribe to the *Financial Times* for 15 weeks at a specially priced rate of $10 in addition to the price of the text. Students will receive a subscription card shrink-wrapped with their new text to fill in and send to the *Financial Times* to start receiving their subscription. Instructors, after ordering the text, can contact their sales representative to receive a complimentary 1-year subscription.

Acknowlegments

We take this opportunity to thank all of the individuals who helped us prepare this fifth edition. We want to express our appreciation to those instructors whose insightful comments and suggestions were invaluable to us during this revision.

John R. Becker Blease
University of New Hampshire

Larry Belcher
Stetson University

Nancy L. Beneda
University of North Dakota

Karan Bhanot
University of Texas—Austin

Timothy Burch
University of Miami

Janice Caudill
Auburn University

Rosita Chang
University of Hawaii

Robert Chatfield
University of Nevada—Las Vegas

Thomas S. Coe
Quinnipiac University

James Colnover
University of North Texas

James Cordeiro
State University of New York—Brockport

Mary Cutler
Central Connecticut State University

Vinay Datar
Seattle University

Ramon DeGennaro
University of Tennessee—Knoxville

Steven A. Dennis
East Tennessee State University

J. David Diltz
University of Texas—Arlington

Robert Dubil
San Jose State University

David Durst
University of Akron

Uchenna Elike
Alabama A&M University

Ahmad Etebari
University of New Hampshire

Hsing Fang
California State University

Sharon Garrison
University of Arizona

Nicholas Gressis
Wright State University

Doreen Grosso
St. Johns University

Pamela Hall
Western Washington University

Yvonne Hall
New Hampshire College

Gordon Hanka
Pennsylvania State University

James Harford
University of Oregon

Robert J. Hartwig
Worcester State College

Hal Heaton
Marriott School of Management, Brigham Young University

George Hruby
University of Akron

Christine Hsu
California State University—Chico

Tom Jackman
Nebraska Wesleyan University

Pankaj K. Jain
University of Memphis

Tim Jares
University of North Florida

Tom Johansen
Fort Hays State University

Chris Jung
University of Colorado—Boulder

Jarl Kallberg
New York University

Kelly Kam
University of Texas—Austin

John Kensinger
University of North Texas

Jim Keys
Florida Atlantic University

Robert Kunkel
University of Wisconsin—Oshkosh

Lynn Leary-Myers
University of Utah

Michael Long
Rutgers University

Robert Lutz
University of Utah

Daniel McConaughy
California State University—Northridge

Gilbert McKee, Jr.
California State Polytechnic University—Pomona

Sunil Mohanty
University of St. Thomas

Carlos A. Molina
University of Texas—San Antonio

Jon Moulton
Oregon State University

Rick Nelson
Carlson School of Management, University of Minnesota

Jeffry Netter
University of Georgia

Jonathan Ohn
Virginia State University

Shalini Perumpral
Radford University

Kathleen Petrie
University of Georgia

Mike Phillips
California State University—Northridge

Peter Poirot
James Madison University

Mary Lou Poloskey
University of Texas—Austin

Chris Pope
University of Georgia

Clarence Rose
Radford University

James Ross
Radford University

Ray Russ
University of Louisville

Burton Schaffer
California State University—Sacramento

Michael Schill
University of California—Riverside

James Sfiridis
Central Connecticut State University

Mike Sibley
Loyola University—New Orleans

John Stansfield
University of Missouri—Columbia

Judy Swisher
Florida Atlantic University

Harry Turtle
Washington State University

Gautam Vora
The University of New Mexico

Doug Waggle	Mark D. Walker	John Wiegel
Berry College	*North Carolina State University*	*California State University—Fullerton*
Joe Walker	Edward Waller	Thomas Zorn
University of Alabama—Birmingham	*University of Houston—Clear Lake*	*University of Nebraska—Lincoln*

In addition, we would like to thank our supplement authors, Sheen Liu (Instructor's Manual), Matt Will (PowerPoints and Study Guide), Bruce Swensen (Solutions Manual), and Ted Fu (Test Bank). Their efforts are much appreciated as they will help both students and instructors. We also appreciate help from Aleijda de Cazenove Balsan and Malcolm Taylor.

We are also grateful to the talented staff at McGraw-Hill/Irwin, especially Steve Patterson, Publisher; Christina Kouvelis, Developmental Editor II; Lori Koetters, Senior Project Manager; Keith McPherson, Design Director; Julie Phifer, Marketing Manager; Jennifer Jelinski, Marketing Coordinator; Lori Kramer, Photo Research Coordinator; Keri Johnson, Photo Researcher; Sesha Bolisetty, Project Supervisor; Carol Loreth, Senior Supplement Producer; Becky Szura, Media Project Manager.

Finally, as was the case with the last four editions, we cannot overstate the thanks due to our wives, Diana, Maureen, and Sheryl.

Richard A. Brealey
Stewart C. Myers
Alan J. Marcus

Contents in Brief

Contents

Part One   Introduction

Part Two   Value

Part Three   Risk

Chapter 12
The Weighted-Average Cost of Capital and Company Valuation 320

Part Four   Financing

Chapter 13
Introduction to Corporate Financing and Governance 348

Chapter 14
Venture Capital, IPOs, and Seasoned Offerings 370

Part Five   Debt and Payout Policy

Part Six   Financial Analysis and Planning

Part Seven   Special Topics

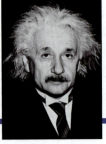

Part Eight   Conclusion

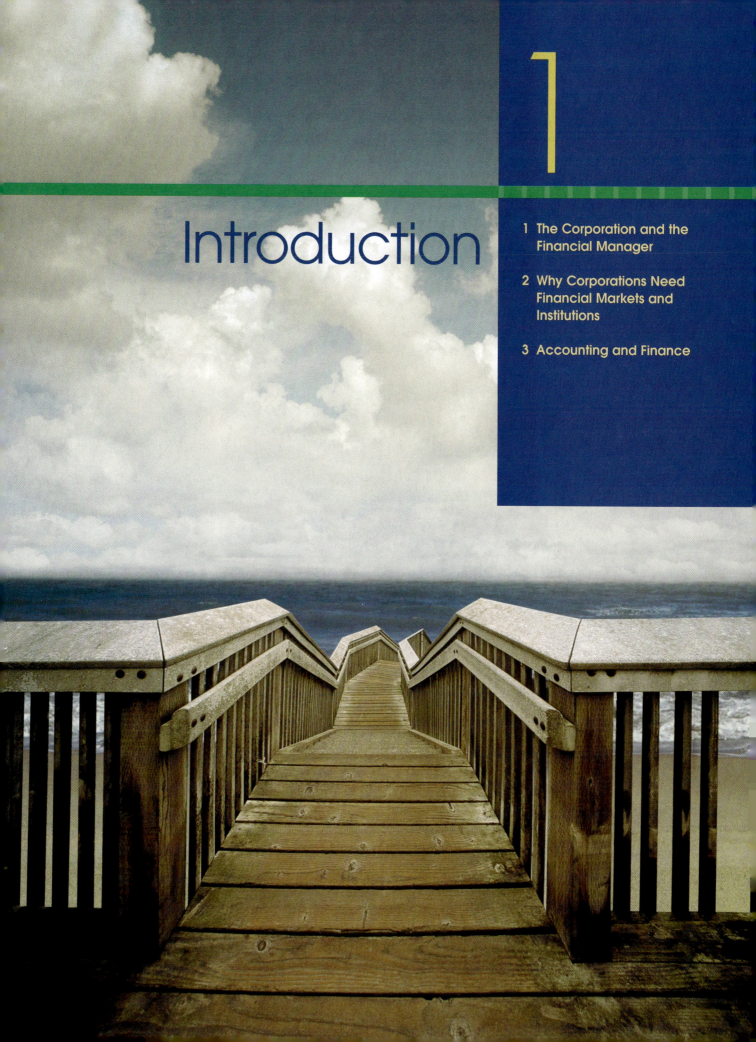

Introduction

1 The Corporation and the Financial Manager

2 Why Corporations Need Financial Markets and Institutions

3 Accounting and Finance

CHAPTER

1

The Corporation and the Financial Manager

RELATED WEB LINKS

www.nolo.com
www.bizfilings.com Information and help in setting up a firm as a corporation, partnership, or proprietorship.
www.business-ethics.com
www.corpgov.net
www.thecorporatelibrary.com Discussions of corporate governance and business ethics.

www.careers-in-finance.com
www.careers.wsj.com
www.wageweb.com
www.financeprofessor.com Career information and salary data.

A meeting of a corporation's directors.
© Susan Moore

Corporate finance boils down to the investment and financing decisions made by corporations. Financial managers in corporations work with other managers to identify investment opportunities, to analyze and value the opportunities, and to decide whether and how much to invest. Financial managers also have to raise the money to finance the corporation's investments. Therefore we start this chapter with examples of recent investment and financing decisions by major U.S. and foreign corporations. We also review what a corporation is and describe the special roles of a corporation's top financial managers, including the chief financial officer (CFO), treasurer, and controller. Later in the chapter we will review several possible career paths in finance.

Next we turn to the financial goals of the corporation. Should it maximize value, or is it enough to survive and avoid bankruptcy? Should it strive to be a good corporate citizen? If the firm maximizes value for its stockholders, can it also be a good corporate citizen? We also consider the conflicts of interest that arise in large corporations and review the mechanisms that align the interests of the firm's managers with the interests of stockholders. Finally, we look ahead to the rest of this book and look back to some entertaining snippets of financial history.

After studying this chapter you should be able to:

- Give examples of the investment and financing decisions that financial managers make, and explain the responsibilities of the CFO, treasurer, and controller.

- Cite some of the advantages and disadvantages of organizing a business as a corporation.

- Explain why maximizing market value is the logical financial goal for the corporation.

- Understand why conflicts of interest arise, especially in large, public corporations.

- Explain how corporations mitigate conflicts and encourage ethical, cooperative behavior.

- Give examples of career paths in finance.

1.1 Investment and Financing Decisions

This book is an introduction to corporate finance and the profession of financial management. Let's begin with a look at some of the decisions that a financial manager is required to make.

Table 1–1 lists nine corporations. Seven are U.S. corporations. Three are foreign: BP's headquarters are in London, LVMH's in Paris,[1] and Toyota's in Japan. We have chosen very large public corporations that you are probably already familiar with. You probably have traveled on a Boeing jet or shopped at Wal-Mart, for example.

What do these companies have to be "good at" in order to succeed in their businesses? The first answers are obvious. For example, Boeing has to produce and sell planes that are technologically advanced, safe, reliable, and efficient. Pfizer has to discover, develop, and sell effective new drugs. Toyota has to make and sell cars that are at least as good as competitive models from GM, Ford, Honda and other manufacturers.

But each of these companies also has to be *good at finance.* This means that each has to make good *investment decisions* and good *financing decisions.* Superior investment and financing decisions could put these companies a step ahead of their competitors. A series of bad investment or financing decisions could cause severe damage.

Table 1–1 gives for each company an example of a recent investment and financing decision. Take a look at the decisions now. We think you will agree that they appear sensible or at least that there is nothing obviously wrong with them. But if you are new to finance, it will be difficult to think about why these companies made these decisions and not others.

Making good investment and financing decisions is the chief task of the financial manager. Let's consider each class of decisions in more detail.

The Investment (Capital Budgeting) Decision

capital budgeting decision or **investment decision** Decision to invest in tangible or intangible assets.

The **investment decision** starts with the identification of investment opportunities, often referred to as *capital investment projects.* The financial manager has to help the firm identify promising projects and decide how much to invest in each project. The investment decision is also called the **capital budgeting decision,** because most firms prepare an annual budget listing authorized capital investments.

In the distant past, "capital investments" included only investments in tangible assets, such as investment in Toyota's automobile plant in Texas or Union Pacific's new locomotives. But you can see from Table 1–1 that the scope of the investment decision is now much broader. It includes investment in intangible assets, for example, investment in research and development (R&D), advertising and marketing of new products, or acquisition of patents and trademarks. Pfizer and other major pharmaceutical companies invest billions every year on R&D for new drugs, for example. Gillette invested about $300 million to advertise the launch of its Mach3 razor. In this case the intangible asset was brand recognition and acceptance.

The world of business can be intensely competitive, and corporations survive and prosper only if they can keep launching new products or services. In some cases the costs and risks of doing so are amazingly large. Boeing is investing more than $7 billion[2] to design, test, build, and sell the new 787 Dreamliner series of aircraft. At the same time its European archrival Airbus is investing more than $12 billion in the new A380 superjumbo aircraft. Each firm is "betting the company" on the success of these investments.

Not all capital investments succeed. The Iridium communications satellite system, which offered its users instant telephone connections worldwide, soaked up $5 billion

---

[1] LVMH (Moët Hennessy Louis Vuitton) markets perfumes and cosmetics, wines and spirits, watches, and other fashion and luxury goods.

[2] Some estimates of the total investment, including investment by suppliers and support from state, local, and national governments, run as high as $13 billion.

TABLE 1-1 Examples of recent investment and financing decisions by major public companies. Revenues, investment costs, and financing proceeds are expressed in U.S. dollars.

Company (2004 revenues in billions)	Recent Investment (Capital Budgeting) Decision	Recent Financing Decision
Boeing ($52.5)	Committed more than $7 billion to design, build, test, and sell the 787 Dreamliner aircraft series.	Negotiated with suppliers to help finance the Dreamliner project. Japanese suppliers, who will build the wing and fuselage, are raising and investing more than $1.5 billion.
Bank of America ($48.9)	Acquired Fleet Boston Financial for $49 billion.	Issued about 600 million new shares to finance the acquisition.
BP ($285)	Invested $600 million to develop the Mad Dog and related oil fields offshore in the Gulf of Mexico.	Announced plans to return surplus cash flow (cash flow not needed for investment and cash dividends) to shareholders. The cash will be returned by repurchasing BP shares from investors.
Citigroup ($86)	Spent $100 million building bank branches and ATMs in Moscow and St. Petersburg, Russia.	Raised $82 billion in debt financing secured by credit card receivables, that is, by outstanding balances on Citigroup-owned credit cards.
LVMH ($17.1)	Acquired Glenmorangie PLC, a producer of scotch malt whiskies.	Issued a 7-year bond in July 2004, raising the euro equivalent of $812 million.
Pfizer ($52.5)	Spent $7.7 billion in 2004 on research and testing of new drugs.	Financed the research and testing with reinvested cash flow generated by sales of pharmaceutical products.
Toyota ($164)	Building an $800 million automobile plant in San Antonio, Texas.	Total borrowing increased by $2.9 billion during 2004, mainly due to issues of short-term debt in the U.S.
Union Pacific ($12.2)	Acquired 400 new locomotives in 2004.	Arranged bank credit lines that will allow Union Pacific to borrow up to $2 billion if needed for its operations.
Wal-Mart ($285)	Plans for 2005 call for up to 530 new retail stores in the U.S. and 165 stores in other countries.	Issued $1,883 million of long-term debt, maturing in 2036 and paying interest at 5.25% per year.

in investment before it started operations in 1998. It needed 400,000 subscribers to break even, but attracted only a small fraction of that target number. Iridium defaulted on its debt and filed for bankruptcy in 1999. The Iridium system was sold a year later for just $25 million.

The investment in Iridium, though it looks stupid with hindsight, may have been rational, given what was known in the early 1990s when the go-ahead decision was made. It may have been a good decision thwarted by bad luck. There are no free guarantees in finance. But you can tilt the odds in your favor if you learn the tools of investment analysis and apply them intelligently. We will cover these tools in detail later in this book.

Today's capital investments generate future returns. Often the returns come in the distant future. Boeing is committing $7 billion to the 787 series because it believes that sales of 787s will generate cash returns for 30 years or more after the planes first enter commercial service. Those cash returns must recover the $7 billion investment and provide at least an adequate profit on that investment. The longer Boeing must wait for cash to flow back, the greater its required profit. Thus the financial manager must pay attention to the timing of project returns, not just their cumulative amount. In addition, these returns are rarely certain. A new project could be a smashing success or a dismal failure, like Iridium.

The financial manager needs a way of placing a *value* on the uncertain future cash inflows generated by capital investment projects. This value should account for the amounts, timing and risk of the future cash flows. If a project's value is greater than its required investment, then the project is attractive financially. An effective financial manager guides his or her firm to invest in projects that add more value than the investment required. In other words, the financial manager helps the firm to invest in projects that are worth more than they cost.

But do not think of financial managers making major investment decisions in solitary confinement. Financial managers may work as part of a team of engineers and managers from manufacturing, marketing, and other business functions. Often the final investment decision is made by senior nonfinancial management.

Also, do not think of the financial manager as making billion-dollar investments on a daily basis. Most investment decisions are smaller and simpler, such as the purchase of a truck, machine tool, or computer system. But the objective is still to add value, that is, to find and make investments that are worth more than they cost. Most firms make thousands of small investment decisions every year. The cumulative value added by the small decisions can be just as large as the value added by occasional big decisions like those shown in Table 1–1.

The Financing Decision

financing decision
The form and amount of financing of a firm's investments.

capital structure
The mix of long-term debt and equity financing.

The financial manager's second main responsibility is to raise the money that the firm needs for its investments and operations. This is the **financing decision.** When a company needs to raise money, it can invite investors to put up cash in exchange for a share of future profits, or it can promise to pay back the investors' cash plus a fixed rate of interest. In the first case, the investors receive shares of stock and become shareholders, part owners of the corporation. The investors in this case are referred to as *equity investors,* who contribute *equity financing.* In the second case, the investors are lenders, that is, *debt investors,* who one day must be repaid. The choice between debt and equity financing is often called the **capital structure** decision. Here "capital" refers to the firm's sources of long-term financing. A firm that is seeking to raise long-term financing is said to be "raising capital."

The financing choices available to large corporations seem almost endless. Suppose the firm decides to borrow. Should it issue debt to investors, or should it borrow from a bank? Should it borrow for 1 year or 20 years? If it borrows for 20 years, should it reserve the right to pay off the debt early if interest rates fall? Should it borrow in Paris, receiving and promising to repay euros, or should it borrow dollars in New York? (As Table 1–1 shows, LVMH borrowed euros, but it could have borrowed dollars instead.) Should it offer specific assets as collateral to back its borrowing? (Note how Citigroup used its credit card receivables as collateral.) We will look at these and other choices in later chapters.

The decision to take out a 20-year loan or to issue new shares of stock obviously has long-term consequences. But the financial manager is also involved in many important short-term decisions. For example, he or she has to make sure that there is enough cash on hand to pay next week's bills and that any spare cash is put to work to earn interest. These are *short-term financing decisions* (how to raise cash to meet a short-term need) and *short-term investment decisions* (how to invest spare cash for brief periods).

The financial manager is involved in many other day-to-day activities that are essential to the smooth operation of the firm but not dramatic enough to show up in Table 1–1. For example, if the firm sells goods or services on credit, the firm has to make sure that its customers pay their bills on time. Corporations that operate internationally must constantly transfer cash from one currency to another. Manufacturing companies must decide how much to invest in inventories of raw materials and finished goods.

Businesses are inherently risky, so the financial manager has to identify risks and make sure they are managed properly. For example, the manager will want to ensure that the firm's operations will not be severely damaged by a rise in oil prices or a fall in the dollar. (Note in Table 1–1 that Toyota has increased short-term debt issues in

U.S. dollars rather than in its home currency. This makes sense because of Toyota's exports to the United States. The exports generate revenues in U.S. dollars.) In later chapters we will look at how managers assess risk and at some of the ways that firms can be protected from nasty surprises.

Self-Test 1.1

Are the following capital budgeting or financing decisions? *Hint:* In one case the answer is "both."

a. Intel decides to spend $1 billion to develop a new microprocessor.
b. Volkswagen borrows 350 million euros (€350 million) from Deutsche Bank.
c. BP constructs a pipeline to bring natural gas onshore from a production platform in the Gulf of Mexico.
d. Budweiser spends €200 million to launch a new brand of beer in European markets.
e. Pfizer issues new shares to buy a small biotech company.

Financing and investment decisions (both long- and short-term) are of course interconnected. The amount of investment determines the amount of financing that has to be raised, and the investors who contribute financing today expect a return on that investment in the future. Thus, the investments that the firm makes today have to generate future returns for payout to investors.

Figure 1–1 traces how money flows from investors to the firm and back to investors again. The flow starts when cash is raised from investors (arrow 1 in the figure). The cash is used to pay for the real assets (investment projects) needed for the firm's operations (arrow 2). Later, if the firm does well, the operations generate enough cash inflow to more than repay the initial investment (arrow 3). Finally, the cash is either reinvested (arrow 4a) or returned to the investors who furnished the money in the first place (arrow 4b). Of course, the choice between arrows 4a and 4b is constrained by the promises made when cash was raised at arrow 1. For example, if the firm borrows money from a bank at arrow 1, it must repay this money plus interest at arrow 4b.

You can see examples of arrows 4a and 4b in Table 1–1. Pfizer finances its drug research and testing by reinvesting earnings (arrow 4a). BP has decided to return cash to shareholders by buying back its stock (arrow 4b). In 2005, a year of very high energy prices, repurchases by BP will probably approach $10 billion.

Notice in Figure 1–1 how the financial manager stands between the firm and outside investors. On the one hand, the financial manager helps manage the firm's operations, particularly by helping to make good investment decisions. On the other, the financial manager deals with investors—not just with shareholders but also with banks and other financial institutions and with financial markets, such as the New York Stock Exchange. We will say more about financial markets and institutions in the next chapter.

Figure 1–1 also distinguishes **real assets** from **financial assets.** Real assets are used to produce the firm's products and services. They include tangible assets such as machinery, factories, and offices and intangible assets such as technical knowledge,

real assets
Assets used to produce goods and services.

financial assets
Financial claims to the income generated by the firm's real assets.

FIGURE 1–1 Flow of cash between investors and the firm's operations. Key: (1) Cash raised by selling financial assets to investors; (2) cash invested in the firm's operations; (3) cash generated by the firm's operations; (4a) cash reinvested; (4b) cash returned to investors.

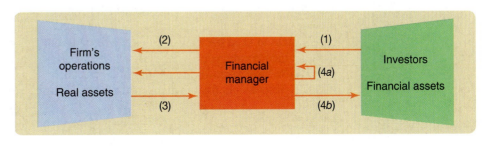

trademarks, and patents. The firm finances its investments in real assets by issuing financial assets to investors. A share of stock is a financial asset, which has value as a claim on the firm's real assets and the income that those assets will produce. A bank loan is a financial asset also. It gives the bank the right to get its money back plus interest. If the firm's operations can't generate enough income to pay what the bank is owed, the bank can force the firm into bankruptcy and stake a claim on its real assets.

Shares of stock and other financial assets that can be purchased and traded by investors are called *securities*.

Self-Test 1.2 ▶ Which of the following are financial assets, and which are real assets?

a. A patent.
b. A share of stock issued by Bank of New York.
c. A blast furnace in a steel-making factory.
d. A mortgage loan taken out to help pay for a new home.
e. After a successful advertising campaign, potential customers believe that your brand of potato chips is extra crispy.
f. An IOU ("I owe you") from your brother-in-law.

1.2 What Is a Corporation?

The nine major corporations in Table 1–1 are a tiny subsample from the list of corporations operating around the world. There are about 8,000 *public companies* in the United States. "Public" means that the corporation's shares are traded in a securities market, such as the New York Stock Exchange, and therefore are available for purchase by any investor. There also are hundreds of thousands of *private corporations* whose shares are closely held by small groups of managers and investors. You can't purchase the shares of these private companies, except by negotiation with existing share owners.

corporation
A business organized as a separate legal entity owned by stockholders.

A **corporation** is a distinct, permanent legal entity. Suppose you decide to create a new corporation. You would work with a lawyer to prepare *articles of incorporation*, which set out the purpose of the business and how it is to be financed, managed, and governed. These articles must conform to the laws of the state in which the business is incorporated. For many purposes, the corporation is considered a resident of its state. For example, it can borrow or lend money and it can sue or be sued. It pays its own taxes (but it cannot vote!).

limited liability
The owners of a corporation are not personally liable for its obligations.

A corporation is legally distinct from its owners, who are called *shareholders* or *stockholders*.[3] A corporation therefore confers **limited liability:** Its owners cannot be held personally responsible for the corporation's debts. When Enron and WorldCom failed in 2002—two of the largest bankruptcies ever—no one demanded that their stockholders put up more money to cover the bankrupt companies' debts. Enron and WorldCom stockholders ended up with worthless shares and lost their entire investment in these firms but had no further liability.

EXAMPLE 1.1 ▶ Business Organization

Suppose you own a commercial building and operate a restaurant in it. You have invested in the building itself, kitchen equipment, dining-room furnishings, a computer system to keep track of supplies and reservations, plus various other assets. If you do not incorporate, you own these assets personally, as the *sole proprietor* of the business. If you have borrowed money from a bank to start the business, then you are personally responsible for this debt. If the business loses money and cannot pay the bank,

---

[3] "Shareholder" and "stockholder" mean exactly the same thing and are used interchangeably.

Other Forms of Business Organization

This book focuses on corporations, which tend to be larger firms with many shareholders. Proprietorships are usually small "mom-and-pop" businesses. What about the middle ground? What about businesses that grow too large for sole proprietorships, but don't want to reorganize as corporations?

Suppose you wish to pool money and expertise with some friends or business associates. You will form a *partnership* and enter into a partnership agreement that sets out how decisions are to be made and how profits are to be split up. Partners, like sole proprietors, face unlimited liability. If the business runs into difficulties, each partner can be held responsible for *all* the business's debts. The moral: Know thy partner.

Partnerships have a tax advantage. Partnerships, unlike corporations, do not have to pay income taxes. The partners simply pay personal income taxes on their shares of the profits.

Some businesses are hybrids that combine the tax advantage of a partnership with the limited liability advantage of a corporation. In a *limited partnership,* partners are clas-sified as general or limited. General partners manage the business and have unlimited personal liability for its debts. Limited partners are liable only for the money they invest and do not participate in management.

Many states allow *limited liability partnerships (LLPs)* or, equivalently, *limited liability companies (LLCs).* These are partnerships in which all partners have limited liability. Another variation on the theme is the *professional corporation (PC),* which is commonly used by doctors, lawyers, and accountants. In this case, the business has limited liability, but the professionals can still be sued personally, for example for malpractice.

Most large investment banks such as Morgan Stanley, Merrill Lynch, and Goldman Sachs started life as partnerships. But eventually these companies and their financing requirements grew too large for them to continue as partnerships, and they reorganized as corporations. The partnership form of organization does not work well when ownership is widespread and separation of ownership and management is essential.

then the bank can demand that you raise cash by selling other assets—your car or house, for example—in order to repay the loan. But if you incorporate the restaurant business, and the corporation borrows from the bank, your other assets are shielded from the restaurant's debts. Of course this also means that the bank will be more cautious in lending if your restaurant is incorporated, because the bank will have no recourse to your other assets.

Notice that if you incorporate your business, you exchange direct ownership of its real assets (the building, kitchen equipment, etc.) for indirect ownership via financial assets (the shares of the new corporation). ◀

Stockholders own the corporation, but they do not usually manage it. Instead, they elect a *board of directors,* who in turn appoint the top managers and monitor their performance. The board represents stockholders and is supposed to ensure that management is acting in their best interests.

This *separation of ownership and management* is one distinctive feature of corporations. (Contrast a sole proprietor, who is both owner and manager.) Separation gives corporations permanence. If managers are fired and replaced, the corporation survives. All of today's stockholders can sell out to new investors without necessarily affecting the conduct of the corporation's business.

Corporations can, in principle, live forever, and in practice they can survive many human lifetimes. One of the oldest corporations is the Hudson's Bay Company, which was formed in 1670 to profit from the fur trade between northern Canada and England, by sea via Hudson's Bay. The company still operates as one of Canada's leading retail chains.

Large, public corporations have thousands of stockholders. An individual may have 100 shares, receive 100 votes, and be entitled to a tiny fraction of the firm's income and value. A pension fund or insurance company may own millions of shares, receive millions of votes, and have a correspondingly large stake in the firm's performance.

Given all these advantages, you may wonder why all businesses are not organized as corporations. One reason is the costs, in both time and money, of managing the corporation's legal machinery. These costs are particularly burdensome for small businesses. There is also an important tax drawback to corporations in the United

States. Because the corporation is a separate legal entity, it is taxed separately. So corporations pay tax on their profits, and shareholders are taxed again when they receive dividends from the company or sell their shares at a profit.[4] By contrast, income generated by businesses that are not incorporated is taxed just once as personal income.

Corporations and proprietorships are not the only ways to organize a business. The nearby box discusses a few alternatives. These options may be especially attractive to growing firms, those too large for a single proprietor but too small to justify corporate organization.

1.3 Who Is the Financial Manager?

In this book we will use the term *financial manager* to refer to anyone responsible for a significant corporate investment or financing decision. But except in the smallest firms, no *single* person is responsible for all the decisions discussed in this book. Responsibility is dispersed throughout the firm. Top management is of course constantly involved in financial decisions. But the engineer who designs a new production facility is also involved: The design determines the kind of real asset the firm will invest in. Likewise the marketing manager who undertakes a major advertising campaign is making an investment decision: The campaign is an investment in an intangible asset that will pay off in future sales and earnings.

treasurer

Responsible for financing, cash management, and relationships with banks and other financial institutions.

Nevertheless, there are managers who specialize in finance, and their functions are summarized in Figure 1–2. The **treasurer** is most directly responsible for looking after the firm's cash, raising new capital, and maintaining relationships with banks and other investors who hold the firm's securities.

For small firms, the treasurer is likely to be the only financial executive. Larger corporations usually also have a **controller,** who prepares the financial statements, manages the firm's internal budgets and accounting, and looks after its tax affairs. You can see that the treasurer and controller have different roles: The treasurer's main function is to obtain and manage the firm's capital, whereas the controller ensures that the money is used efficiently.

controller

Responsible for budgeting, accounting, and taxes.

chief financial officer (CFO)

Oversees the treasurer and controller and sets overall financial strategy.

Large corporations usually appoint a **chief financial officer (CFO)** to oversee both the treasurer's and the controller's work. The CFO is deeply involved in financial policymaking and corporate planning. He or she will have general responsibilities beyond strictly financial issues, and may join the company's board of directors.

In large corporations, a senior financial manager is responsible for organizing and supervising the capital budgeting process. However, major capital investment projects are so closely tied to plans for product development, production, and marketing that managers from these other areas are inevitably drawn into planning and analyzing the projects. If the firm has staff members specializing in corporate planning, they are naturally involved in capital budgeting too.

Because of the importance of many financial issues, ultimate decisions often rest by law or by custom with the board of directors. For example, only the board has the legal power to declare a dividend or to sanction a public issue of securities. Boards usually delegate decision-making authority for small- or medium-sized investment outlays, but the authority to approve large investments is almost never delegated.

Self-Test 1.3

Fritz and Frieda went to business school together 10 years ago. They have just been hired by a midsized corporation that wants to bring in new financial managers. Fritz studied finance, with an emphasis on financial markets and institutions. Frieda majored in accounting and became a CPA 5 years ago. Who is more suited to be treasurer and who controller? Briefly explain.

---

[4] The U.S. tax system is unusual in this respect. To avoid taxing the same income twice, most other countries give shareholders at least some credit for the taxes that the corporation has already paid.

FIGURE 1-2 Financial managers in large corporations

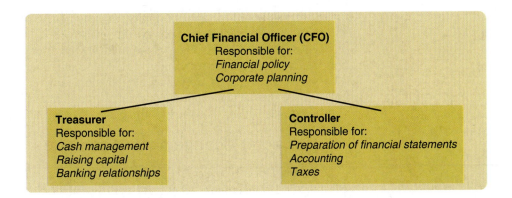

Chief Financial Officer (CFO)
Responsible for:
Financial policy
Corporate planning

Treasurer
Responsible for:
Cash management
Raising capital
Banking relationships

Controller
Responsible for:
Preparation of financial statements
Accounting
Taxes

1.4 Goals of the Corporation

Shareholders Want Managers to Maximize Market Value

For small corporations, shareholders and management may be one and the same. But for large corporations, separation of ownership and management is a practical necessity. For example, Wal-Mart has about 330,000 shareholders. There is no way that these shareholders can be actively involved in management; it would be like trying to run New York City by town meetings. Authority has to be delegated.

How can shareholders decide how to delegate decision making when they all have different tastes, wealth, time horizons, and personal opportunities? Delegation can work only if the shareholders have a common objective. Fortunately there is a natural financial objective on which almost all shareholders can agree: maximize the current *market value* of shareholders' investment in the firm.

A smart and effective financial manager makes decisions that increase the current value of the company's shares and the wealth of its stockholders. That increased wealth can then be put to whatever purposes the shareholders want. They can give their money to charity or spend it in glitzy night clubs; they can save it or spend it now. Whatever their personal tastes or objectives, they can all do more when their shares are worth more.

Sometimes you hear managers speak as if the corporation has other goals. For example, they may say that their job is to "maximize profits." That sounds reasonable. After all, don't shareholders want their company to be profitable? But taken literally, profit maximization is not a well-defined corporate objective. Here are three reasons:

1. Maximize profits? Which year's profits? A corporation may be able to increase current profits by cutting back on outlays for maintenance or staff training, but that will not add value unless the outlays were wasteful in the first place. Shareholders will not welcome higher short-term profits if long-term profits are damaged.
2. A company may be able to increase future profits by cutting this year's dividend and investing the freed-up cash in the firm. That is not in the shareholders' best interest if the company earns only a very low rate of return on the extra investment.
3. Different accountants may calculate profits in different ways. So you may find that a decision that improves profits using one set of accounting rules may reduce them using another.

In a free economy a firm is unlikely to survive if it pursues goals that reduce the firm's value. Suppose, for example, that a firm's only goal is to increase its market share. It aggressively reduces prices to capture new customers, even when the price discounts cause continuing losses. What would happen to such a firm? As losses mount, it will find it more and more difficult to borrow money, and it may not even have sufficient profits to repay existing debts. Sooner or later, however, outside investors would see an opportunity for easy money. They could buy the firm from its current shareholders, toss out existing management, and increase the firm's value by changing its policies. They would profit by the difference between the price paid for the firm and the higher value it would have under new management. Managers who pursue goals that destroy value often land in early retirement.

The natural financial objective of the corporation is to maximize current market value. Managers who consistently ignore this objective are likely to be replaced.

Ethics and Management Objectives

Crime Does Not Pay For a public company, maximizing current market value should also maximize today's stock price. (The firm's market value is the total amount that investors are willing to pay for all of its shares.) Does that objective justify pumping up the stock price by fraud or deception? Of course not. But there will be occasional bad apples in the barrel, companies that attempt to increase market value in unethical ways.

The years 2001 and 2002 revealed an unusual number of bad apples. For example, the telecom giant WorldCom admitted that it failed to report $3.8 billion of operating expenses. (The expenses were classified as investments, contrary to the rules of accounting.) Thus WorldCom's income was overstated by $3.8 billion. In the meantime, WorldCom had run up $41 billion of debt. When the company's true profitability was discovered, it was bankrupt within a month—the largest U.S. bankruptcy ever.

The second-largest bankruptcy was Enron, the energy trading and investment company. In late 2001 it announced over $1.7 billion in losses that had previously been concealed in "special-purpose entities" (SPEs). We need not delve into Enron's SPEs here, except to say that they broke basic rules of accounting and that one of Enron's top financial executives allegedly used SPEs to pocket millions at the expense of Enron and its shareholders. The bad news came out all at once in October and November 2001, and Enron was bankrupt by year-end.

We suspect that WorldCom and Enron's accounting misdeeds were in part a desperate attempt to stave off bankruptcy. In the end these misdeeds were the proximate cause of bankruptcy. Crime, fraud, and deceit do not pay.

The Ethics of Maximizing Value Let us shift the focus back to the great majority of financial managers, who are honest and conscientious. Some idealists say that these managers should not be obliged to act in the selfish interests of their stockholders. Some realists argue that, regardless of what managers ought to do, they in fact look after themselves rather than their shareholders.

Let us respond to the idealists first. Does maximizing value mean that managers must act as greedy mercenaries riding roughshod over the weak and helpless? No, in most instances there is little conflict between doing well (maximizing value) and doing good.

The first step in doing well is doing good by your customers. Here is how Adam Smith put the case in 1776:

> It is not from the benevolence of the butcher, the brewer, or the baker, that we expect our dinner, but from their regard to their own interest. We address ourselves, not to their humanity but to their self-love, and never talk to them of our own necessities but of their advantages.[5]

By striving to enrich themselves and their shareholders, businesspeople have to provide their customers with the products and services they truly desire.

Of course ethical issues do arise in business as in other walks of life. When the stakes are high, competition is intense, and a deadline is looming, it's easy for finan-

---

[5] Adam Smith, *An Inquiry into the Nature and Causes of the Wealth of Nations* (New York: Random House, 1937; first published 1776), p. 14.

The Stock Market Value of a Good Reputation

Are sound business ethics the sign of not only a morally good company but a good investment as well? Jim Huget, the president of Great Companies LLC, a money management firm based in Clearwater, Florida, argues that sticking with companies with sound ethical practices, including transparency, accountability, and a shareholder-friendly corporate governance structure, is a good way to avoid land mines in your portfolio.

The list of companies whose shares have been battered amid accusations of wrongdoing is a who's who of widely held stocks. Among the latest victims has been the insurance giant American International Group (AIG), whose stock has fallen 21 percent between January and April 2005. AIG is being investigated by regulators over transactions that may have masked the company's health. AIG's longtime chairman and chief executive, Maurice R. Greenberg, was forced to step down as a result of the controversy.

And it's not just AIG. The shares of Marsh & McLennan Companies were off 36 percent over the last 12 months; in late January, it agreed to settle a lawsuit by regulators accusing it of cheating customers by rigging prices and steering business to insurers in exchange for incentive payments.

But investors seem willing to give higher valuations to companies that are deemed good citizens. Put another way, investors give some companies with good track records the benefit of the doubt. That may explain in part why Warren Buffet's Berkshire Hathaway has lost only about 1 percent of its value this year. A Berkshire Hathaway subsidiary, General Re, was a party to a transaction that AIG said was accounted for improperly.

Berkshire "is a company with a culture of accountability, and that resonates with investors," said Gavin Anderson, chief executive of GovernanceMetrics International, a firm that grades corporations on governance practices.

Source: Adapted from Paul J. Lim, "Gauging That Other Company Asset: Its Reputation," *New York Times,* April 10, 2005, p. BU6.

cial managers to blunder, and not to inquire as deeply as they should about the legality or morality of their actions.

Written rules and laws can help only so much. In business, as in other day-to-day affairs, there are also unwritten rules of behavior. These work because everyone knows that such rules are in the general interest. But they are reinforced because good managers know that their firm's reputation is one of its most important assets and therefore playing fair and keeping one's word are simply good business practices. Thus huge financial deals are regularly completed on a handshake and each side knows that the other will not renege later if things turn sour. For example, the motto of the London Stock Exchange is "My word is my bond."

Reputation is particularly important in finance. If you buy a well-known brand in a store, you can be fairly sure what you are getting. But in financial transactions the other party often has more information than you and it is less easy to be sure of the quality of what you are buying. The reaction of honest financial firms is to build long-term relationships with their customers and establish a name for fair dealing and financial integrity. Major banks and securities firms protect their reputations by emphasizing their long history and their responsible behavior when seeking new customers. When something happens to undermine that reputation the costs can be enormous.

Take a look at the nearby box on the value to investors of a good corporate reputation. Note particularly the contrast between AIG and Berkshire Hathaway. General Re, a Berkshire Hathaway subsidiary, had sold AIG an insurance contract[6] that AIG accounted for improperly, apparently in an attempt to enhance the company's reported financial strength. The fear that AIG may have been "cooking its books" drove its share price down immediately. Investors shied away from AIG shares even at their new, "bargain" price. "We buy shares that are beat up, but not where we don't understand or trust the accounting," one investment manager said. "It's hard enough figuring out what a business will be in five years, and here you don't even know what it was five years ago."[7]

But Berkshire Hathaway's stock price was not much affected by the AIG controversy, even though its subsidiary General Re did many business deals with AIG.

---

[6] The details of this contract are not public information as we write this, but it seems that the insurance contract was not really insurance but a loan in disguise.

[7] Robert Olson, quoted in "AIG Investors Are Learning a Hard Lesson," *Wall Street Journal,* April 4, 2005, p. C1.

Things Are Not Always Fair in Love or Economics

What constitutes fair behavior by companies? One survey asked a number of individuals to state whether they regarded a particular action as acceptable or unfair. Before we tell you how they responded, think how you would rate each of the following actions:

1a. A small photocopying shop has one employee who has worked in the shop for 6 months and earns $9 per hour. Business continues to be satisfactory, but a factory in the area has closed and unemployment has increased. Other small shops in the area have now hired reliable workers at $7 an hour to perform jobs similar to those done by the photocopying shop employee. The owner of the photocopying shop reduces the employee's wage to $7.

1b. Now suppose that the shop does not reduce the employee's wage but he or she leaves. The owner decides to pay a replacement $7 an hour.

2. A house painter employs two assistants and pays them $9 per hour. The painter decides to quit house painting and go into the business of providing landscape services, where the going wage is lower. He reduces the workers' wages to $7 per hour for the landscaping work.

3a. A small company employs several workers and has been paying them average wages. There is severe unemployment in the area and the company could easily replace its current employees with good workers at a lower wage. The company has been making money. The owners reduce the current workers' wages by 5 percent.

3b. Now suppose instead that the company has been losing money and the owners reduce wages by 5 percent.

4. A grocery store has several months' supply of peanut butter in stock on shelves in the storeroom. The owner hears that the wholesale price of peanut butter has in-creased and immediately raises the price on the current stock of peanut butter.

5. A hardware store has been selling snow shovels for $15. The morning after a large snowstorm, the store raises the price to $20.

6. A store has been sold out of the popular Beanie Baby dolls for a month. A week before Christmas a single doll is discovered in a storeroom. The managers know that many customers would like to buy the doll. They announce over the store's public address system that the doll will be sold by auction to the customer who offers to pay the most.

Now compare your responses with the responses of a random sample of individuals:

Action	Percent Rating the Action As:	
	Acceptable	Unfair
1a	17	83
1b	73	27
2	63	37
3a	23	77
3b	68	32
4	21	79
5	18	82
6	26	74

Source: Adapted from D. Kahneman, J. L. Knetsch, and R. Thaler, "Fairness as a Constraint on Profit Seeking: Entitlements in the Market," *American Economic Review* 76 (September 1986), pp. 728–741. Reprinted by permission of American Economic Association and the authors.

Berkshire Hathaway's reputation for honesty and transparency has so far (as of April 2005) protected it from contamination from AIG's troubles.

It is not always easy to know what is ethical behavior and there can be many gray areas. For example, should the firm be prepared to do business with a corrupt or repressive government? Should it employ child labor in countries where that is the norm? Another nearby box presents several simple situations that call for an ethically based decision, along with survey responses to the proper course of action in each circumstance. Compare your decisions with those of the general public.

Self-Test 1.4

Without knowing anything about the personal ethics of the owners, which company would you better trust to keep its word in a business deal?

a. Harry's Hardware has been in business for 50 years. Harry's grandchildren, now almost adults, plan to take over and operate the business. Hardware stores require considerable investment in customer relations to become established.

b. Victor's Videos just opened for business. It rents a storefront in a strip mall and has financed its inventory with a bank loan. Victor has little of his own money invested in the business. Video shops usually command little customer loyalty.

Do Managers Really Maximize Value?

Owner-managers have no conflicts of interest in their management of the business. They work for themselves, reaping the rewards of good work and suffering the penalties of bad work. Their *personal* well-being is tied to the value of the firm.

In most large corporations the managers are not the owners, and so managers may be tempted to act in ways that are not in the best interests of shareholders. For example, they might buy luxurious corporate jets or overindulge in expense-account dinners. They might shy away from attractive but risky projects because they are worried more about the safety of their jobs than the potential for superior profits. They might engage in empire-building, adding unnecessary capacity or employees. Such problems can arise because the managers of the firm, who are hired as *agents* of the owners, may have their own axes to grind. Therefore they are called **agency problems.**

Think of the company's net revenue as a pie that is divided among a number of claimants. These include the management and the work force as well as the lenders and shareholders who put up the money to establish and maintain the business. The government is a claimant, too, since it gets to tax the profits of the enterprise. It is common to hear these claimants called **stakeholders** in the firm. Each has a stake in the firm. The stakeholders' interests may not coincide.

All these stakeholders are bound together in a complex web of contracts and understandings. For example, when banks lend money to the firm, they insist on a formal contract stating the rate of interest and repayment dates, perhaps placing restrictions on dividends or additional borrowing. Similarly, large companies have carefully worked out personnel policies that establish employees' rights and responsibilities. But you can't devise written rules to cover every possible future event. So the written contracts are supplemented by understandings. For example, managers understand that in return for a fat salary they are expected to work hard and not spend the firm's money on unwarranted personal luxuries.

What enforces these understandings? Is it realistic to expect managers always to act on behalf of the shareholders? The shareholders can't spend their lives watching through binoculars to check that managers are not shirking or dissipating company funds on the latest executive jet.

A closer look reveals several arrangements that help to ensure that the shareholders and managers are working toward common goals.

Compensation Plans Managers are spurred on by incentive schemes that provide big returns if shareholders gain but are valueless if they do not. For example, when Michael Eisner was hired as chief executive officer (CEO) by the Walt Disney Company, his compensation package had three main components: a base annual salary of $750,000; an annual bonus of 2 percent of Disney's net income above a threshold of "normal" profitability; and a 10-year option that allowed him to purchase 2 million shares of stock for $14 per share, which was about the price of Disney stock at the time. Those options would be worthless if Disney's shares were selling for below $14 but highly valuable if the shares were worth more. This gave Eisner a huge personal stake in the success of the firm.

As it turned out, by the end of Eisner's 6-year contract the value of Disney shares had increased by $12 billion, more than sixfold. Eisner's compensation over the period was $190 million.[8] Was he overpaid? We don't know (and we suspect nobody else knows) how much Disney's success was due to Michael Eisner or how hard Eisner would have worked with a different compensation scheme. Our point is that managers often have a strong financial interest in increasing firm value.

But Michael Eisner also found out how much tough pressure investors can muster when they are disappointed. In early 2005, after several years of lagging performance

<hr>

agency problems
Managers, acting as agents for stockholders, may act in their own interests rather than maximizing value.

stakeholder
Anyone with a financial interest in the firm.

<hr>

[8] This discussion is based on Stephen F. O'Byrne, "What Pay for Performance Looks Like: The Case of Michael Eisner," *Journal of Applied Corporate Finance* 5 (Summer 1992), pp. 135–136.

at Disney, Eisner was forced to resign. Eisner had been criticized for adding too many friends and associates to Disney's board of directors, but in the end the board did not protect him.

Well-designed compensation schemes encourage management to maximize shareholder wealth. But some schemes are not well designed and in these cases poorly performing managers may receive large windfall gains. For example, when the CEO of Mattel was ousted after a disastrous $3.6 billion acquisition, she received a farewell payoff of nearly $50 million. Needless to say, shareholders were not impressed by the board's generosity.

The Board of Directors   Boards of directors are often portrayed as passive supporters of top management. But when performance starts to slide and managers don't offer a credible recovery plan, boards do act, as Michael Eisner discovered. The chief executives of Boeing, Fannie Mae,[9] Hewlett Packard, Morgan Stanley, and Eastman Kodak all have been forced out in recent years. Boards in Europe, which traditionally have been more management-friendly, have also become more willing to replace underperforming managers. The list of European departures includes senior management from Deutsche Telekom, Hollinger International, Shell, and Vivendi Universal.

If shareholders believe that the corporation is underperforming and that the board of directors is not sufficiently aggressive in holding the managers to task, they can try to replace the board in the next election. The dissident shareholders will attempt to convince other shareholders to vote for their slate of candidates to the board. If they succeed, a new board will be elected and it can replace the current management team.

Takeovers   Poorly performing companies are also more likely to be taken over by another firm. After the takeover, the old management team may find itself out on the street. We discuss takeovers in Chapter 21.

Specialist Monitoring   Managers are subject to the scrutiny of specialists. Their actions are monitored by the security analysts who advise investors to buy, hold, or sell the company's shares. They are also reviewed by banks, which keep an eagle eye on the progress of firms receiving their loans.

Legal and Regulatory Requirements   CEOs and financial managers have a legal duty to act responsibly and in the interests of investors. For example, the Securities and Exchange Commission (SEC) sets accounting and reporting standards for public companies in order to ensure consistency and transparency. The SEC also prohibits insider trading, that is, the purchase or sale of shares based on information that is not available to public investors. In 2002, in response to Enron, WorldCom, and other debacles of the late 1900s and early 2000s, Congress passed the Sarbanes-Oxley law, which imposed tight new restrictions on corporate financial management. For example, Sarbanes-Oxley requires corporations to have more independent directors on the board, that is, more directors who are not managers or affiliated with managers. Also, Sarbanes-Oxley requires each CFO to sign off personally on the corporation's accounting procedures and results.

We do not want to leave the impression that corporate life is a series of squabbles and endless micromanagement. It isn't, because practical corporate finance has evolved to reconcile personal and corporate interests—to keep everyone working together to increase the value of the whole pie, not merely the size of each person's slice. Agency problems are mitigated in practice in several ways: legal and regulatory standards; compensation plans that tie the fortunes of the managers to the fortunes of the firm; monitoring by lenders, stock market analysts, and investors; and ultimately the threat that poorly performing managers will be fired.

---

[9] The Federal National Mortgage Association (FNMA).

We have covered several types of constraints and incentives designed to mitigate agency costs and ensure cooperative and ethical behavior. All these mechanisms help ensure effective *corporate governance.* When scandals happen, we say that corporate governance has broken down. When corporations compete effectively and ethically and deliver value to shareholders, we are comforted that corporate governance is working properly.

Self-Test 1.5　　　**What is an agency problem? Give two or three examples of decisions by managers that lead to agency costs.**

1.5 Careers in Finance

Well over 1 million people work in the financial services industry in the United States, and many others work as financial managers in corporations. We can't tell you what each one does all day, but we can give you some idea of the variety of careers in finance. The nearby box summarizes the experience of a small sample of recent graduates.[10]

We explained earlier that corporations face two principal financial decisions: the investment decision and the financing decision. Therefore, as a newly recruited financial analyst, you may help to analyze a major new investment project. Or you may instead help to raise the money to pay for it, perhaps by negotiating a bank loan or by arranging to lease the plant and equipment. Other financial analysts work on short-term finance, managing collection and investment of the company's cash or checking whether customers are likely to pay their bills. Financial analysts are also involved in monitoring and controlling risk. For example, they may help to arrange insurance for the firm's plant and equipment, or they may assist with the purchase and sale of options, futures, and other exotic tools for managing risk.

Instead of working in the finance department of a corporation, you may join a financial institution. The largest employers are banks. Banks collect deposits and relend the cash to corporations and individuals. If you join a bank, you may start in a branch office, where individuals and small businesses come to deposit cash or to seek a loan. You could also work in the head office, helping to analyze a $500 million loan to a large corporation.

Banks do many things in addition to lending money, and they probably provide a greater variety of jobs than other financial institutions. For example, individuals and businesses use banks to make payments to each other. So if you work in the cash management department of a large bank, you may help companies electronically transfer huge sums of money as wages, taxes, and payments to suppliers. Banks also buy and sell foreign exchange, so you could find yourself working in front of one of those computer screens in a foreign exchange dealing room. Another glamorous bank job is in the derivatives group, which helps companies to manage their risk by buying and selling options, futures, and so on. This is where the mathematicians and the computer buffs thrive.

Investment banks, such as Merrill Lynch or Goldman Sachs, help companies sell their securities to investors. They also have large corporate finance departments which assist firms in mergers and acquisitions. When firms issue securities or try to take over another firm, a lot of money is at stake and the firms may need to move fast. Thus, working for an investment bank can be a high-pressure activity with long hours. It can also pay very well.

The insurance industry is another large employer. Much of the insurance industry is involved in designing and selling insurance policies on people's lives and property,

---

[10] The careers are fictitious but based on the actual experiences of several of the authors' students.

Working in Finance

Susan Webb, Research Analyst, Mutual Fund Group

After majoring in biochemistry, I joined the research department of a large mutual fund group. Because of my background, I was assigned to work with the senior pharmaceuticals analyst. I start the day by reading *The Wall Street Journal* and reviewing the analyses that come in each day from stockbroking firms. Sometimes we need to revise our earnings forecasts and meet with the portfolio managers to discuss possible trades. The remainder of my day is spent mainly in analyzing companies and developing forecasts of revenues and earnings. I meet frequently with pharmaceutical analysts in stockbroking firms and we regularly visit company management. In the evenings I study for the Chartered Financial Analyst (CFA) exam. Since I did not study finance at college, this is quite challenging. I hope eventually to move from a research role to become a portfolio manager.

Richard Gradley, Project Finance, Large Energy Company

After leaving college, I joined the finance department of a large energy company. I spent my first year helping to analyze capital investment proposals. I then moved to the project finance group, which is responsible for analyzing independent power projects around the world. Recently, I have been involved in a proposal to set up a company that would build and operate a large new electricity plant in southeast Asia. We built a spreadsheet model of the project to make sure that it was viable. We had to check that the contracts with the builders, operators, suppliers, and so on, were all in place before we could arrange bank financing for the project.

Albert Rodriguez, Emerging Markets Group, Major New York Bank

I joined the bank after majoring in finance. I spent the first 6 months in the bank's training program, rotating between departments. I was assigned to the Latin America team just before the 1998 Brazilian crisis when interest rates jumped to nearly 50 percent and the currency fell by 40 percent. There was a lot of activity, with everyone trying to figure out what was likely to happen next and how it would affect our business. My job is largely concerned with analyzing economies and assessing the prospects for bank business. There are plenty of opportunities to work abroad and I hope to spend some time in one of our Latin American offices, such as Argentina or Brazil.

Sherry Solera, Branch Manager, Regional Bank

I took basic finance courses in college, but nothing specific for banking. I started here as a teller. I was able to learn about banking through the bank's training program, and also by evening courses at a local college. Last year I was promoted to branch manager. I oversee the branch's operations and help customers with a wide variety of problems. I'm also spending more time on credit analysis of business loan applications. I want to expand the branch's business customers, but not by making loans to shaky companies.

but businesses are also major customers. So if you work for an insurance company or a large insurance broker, you could find yourself arranging insurance on a Boeing 787 in the United States or an oil rig in Indonesia.

Life insurance companies are major lenders to corporations and to investors in commercial real estate. (Life insurance companies deploy the insurance premiums received from policyholders into medium- or long-term loans; banks specialize in shorter-term financing.) So you could end up negotiating a $50 million loan for construction of a new shopping center or investigating the creditworthiness of a family-owned manufacturing company that has applied for a loan to expand production.

Then there is the business of "managing money," that is, deciding which companies' shares to invest in, or how to balance investment in shares with safer securities, such as the bonds (debt securities) issued by the U.S. Treasury. Take mutual funds, for example. A mutual fund collects money from individuals and invests in a portfolio of stocks or bonds. A financial analyst in a mutual fund analyzes the prospects for the securities and works with the investment manager to decide which should be bought and sold. Many other financial institutions also contain investment management departments. For example, you might work as a financial analyst in the investment department of an insurance company. (Insurance companies also invest in traded securities.) Or you could be a financial analyst in the trust department of a bank that manages money for retirement funds, universities, and charities.

Stockbroking firms help investment management companies and private individuals to invest in securities. They employ sales staff and dealers who make the trades. They also employ financial analysts to analyze the securities and help customers to decide which to buy or sell. Many stockbroking firms are owned by investment banks, such as Merrill Lynch.

Careers in Finance

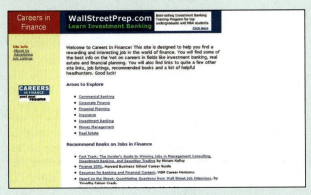

If you would like to learn about careers in finance, log on to **www.careers-in-finance.com**. This site describes jobs in commercial banking, corporate finance, financial planning, insurance, investment banking, money management, and real estate. For each area the site describes the types of jobs available, the skills and talents needed, salary ranges, and so on.

Corporate finance is the focus of this text, so we suggest you start there. Which jobs in corporate finance do you think would best suit you? Now compare the skills needed for these jobs. How do you match up? How will you match up when your education is completed?

The Web site also provides links to the job pages of major financial institutions. Log on to some of these sites and compare their descriptions of the different functions. Are these descriptions consistent with those in careers-in-finance.com?

We have listed several other useful job Web sites at the beginning of this chapter.

Investment banks and stockbroking firms are largely headquartered in New York, as are many of the large commercial banks. Insurance companies and investment management companies tend to be more scattered. For example, some of the largest insurance companies are headquartered in Hartford, Connecticut, and many investment management companies are located in Boston. Of course, some U.S. financial institutions have large businesses outside the United States. Finance is a global business. So you may spend some time working in a branch overseas or making the occasional trip to one of the other major financial centers, such as London, Tokyo, Hong Kong, or Singapore.

Finance professionals tend to be well paid. Starting salaries for new graduates are in the region of $30,000, rather more in a major New York investment bank and somewhat less in a small regional bank. But let us look ahead a little: Table 1–2 gives you an idea of the compensation that you can look forward to when you become a senior financial manager (but don't assume that even department heads of large investment

TABLE 1-2 Representative salaries for jobs in finance

Career	Annual Salary
Commercial Banking	
Loan Officer	$60,000
Department Manager	$100,000
Corporate Finance	
Financial Analyst	$38–47,000
Credit Manager	$30–63,000
Chief Financial Officer	$232–295,000
Investment Banking (bulge bracket)	
First-Year Analyst	$60–110,000
First-Year Associate	$125–235,000
Assistant Vice President	$200–600,000
Director/Principal	$300K–1.2 million
Managing Director/Partner	$400K–20 million
Department Head	$750K–70 million
Money Management	
Portfolio Manager	$500,000+
Bank Trust Department	$100,000

Source: Careers-in-Business, LLC.; **www.careers-in-business.com**. © 2005. All rights reserved.
Note: "Bulge bracket" refers to a few of the largest investment banks.

Finance through the Ages

Date unknown *Compound Growth.* Bacteria start to propagate by subdividing. They thereby demonstrate the power of compound growth. *(Chapter 4)*

c. 1800 B.C. *Interest Rates.* In Babylonia Hammurabi's Code established maximum interest rates on loans. Borrowers often mortgaged their property and sometimes their spouses but in these cases the lender was obliged to return the spouse in good condition within 3 years. *(Chapter 5)*

c. 1000 B.C. *Options.* One of the earliest recorded options is described by Aristotle. The philosopher Thales knew by the stars that there would be a great olive harvest, so, having a little money, he bought options for the use of olive presses. When the harvest came Thales was able to rent the presses at great profit. Today financial managers need to be able to evaluate options to buy or sell a wide variety of assets. *(Chapter 23)*

15th century *International Banking.* Modern international banking has its origins in the great Florentine banking houses. But the entire European network of the Medici empire employed only 57 people in eight offices. Today the London-based bank HSBC has more than 250,000 employees in 77 different countries. *(Chapter 13)*

1650 *Futures.* Futures markets allow companies to protect themselves against fluctuations in commodity prices. During the Tokugawa era in Japan feudal lords collected rents in the form of rice but often they wished to trade their future rice deliveries. Rice futures therefore came to be traded on what was later known as the Dojima Rice Market. Rice futures are still traded but now companies can also trade in futures on a range of items from pork bellies to stock market indexes. *(Chapter 24)*

17th century *Joint Stock Corporations.* Although investors have for a long time combined together as joint owners of an enterprise, the modern corporation with a large number of stockholders originates with the formation in England of the great trading firms like the East India Company (est. 1599). *(Chapter 14)*

17th century *Money.* America has been in the forefront in the development of new types of money. Early settlers often used a shell known as wampum. For example, Peter Stuyvesant raised a loan in wampum and in Massachusetts it was legal tender. Unfortunately, the enterprising settlers found that with a little dye the relatively common white wampum shells could be converted profitably into the more valuable black ones, which confirmed Gresham's law that bad money drives out good. The first issue of paper money in America (and almost in the world) was by the Massachusetts Bay Colony in 1690, and other colonies soon set their printing presses to producing money. In 1862 Congress agreed to an issue of paper money which would be legal tender. These notes, printed in green ink, immediately became known as "greenbacks." *(Chapters 19, 20)*

1720 *New Issue Speculation.* From time to time investors have been tempted by speculative new issues. During the South Sea Bubble in England one company was launched to develop perpetual motion. Another enterprising individual announced a company "for carrying on an undertaking of great advantage but nobody to know what it is." Within 5 hours he had raised £2000; within 6 hours he was on his way out of the country. Readers nearly two centuries later could only wonder at the naïve or foolhardy investors in these ventures—that is, until they had a chance to participate in the dot.com meltdown of 1999–2002. *(Chapter 14)*

1792 *Formation of the New York Stock Exchange.* The New York Stock Exchange (NYSE) was founded in 1792 when a group of brokers met under a buttonwood tree and arranged to trade shares with one another at agreed rates of commission. Today the NYSE is the largest stock exchange in the world, trading on average about a billion shares a day. *(Chapter 6)*

1929 *Stock Market Crashes.* Common stocks are risky investments. In September 1929 stock prices in the United States reached an all-time high and the economist Irving Fisher forecast that they were at "a permanently high plateau." Some 3 years later stock prices were almost 90 percent lower and it was to be a quarter of a century before the prices of September 1929 were seen again. Contrary to popular impression, no Wall Street broker jumped out the window. *(Chapter 10)*

1960s *Eurodollar Market.* In the 1950s the Soviet Union transferred its dollar holdings from the United States to a

---

banking firms typically earn $70 million). The Internet Insider box for this chapter directs you to some Internet sites that provide useful information about careers in finance.

1.6 Topics Covered in This Book

This book covers investment decisions, then financing decisions, and then a variety of planning issues that require an understanding of both investment and financing. But first there are two further introductory chapters that should be helpful to readers making a first acquaintance with financial management. Chapter 2 is an overview of financial markets and institutions. Chapter 3 reviews the basic concepts of accounting.

In Parts 2 and 3 we look at different aspects of the investment decision. The first is the problem of how to value assets, and the second is the link between risk and value. Our discussion of these topics occupies Chapters 4 through 12.

Russian-owned bank in Paris. This bank was best known by its telex address, EUROBANK, and consequently dollars held outside the United States came to be known as eurodollars. In the 1960s U.S. taxes and regulation made it much cheaper to borrow and lend dollars in Europe rather than in the United States, and a huge market in eurodollars arose. *(Chapter 13)*

1971 *Corporate Bankruptcies.* Every generation of investors is shocked and surprised by a major corporate bankruptcy. In 1971 the Penn Central Railroad, a pillar of American industry, suddenly collapsed. Penn Central showed assets of $4.6 billion, about $21 billion in today's dollars. At that time it was the largest corporate bankruptcy in history. Enron and WorldCom have since broken Penn Central's record. *(Chapter 15)*

1972 *Financial Futures.* Financial futures allow companies to protect themselves against fluctuations in interest rates, exchange rates, and so on. It is said that they originated from a remark by the economist Milton Friedman that he was unable to profit from his view that sterling (the U.K. currency) was overpriced. The Chicago Mercantile Exchange founded the first financial futures market. Today futures exchanges in the United States trade 1.4 billion contracts a year of financial futures. *(Chapter 24)*

1986 *Capital Investment Decisions.* The largest investment project undertaken by a private company was the construction of the tunnel under the English Channel. This started in 1986 and was completed in 1994 at a total cost of $15 billion. *(Chapters 7, 8)*

1988 *Mergers.* The 1980s saw a wave of takeovers culminating in the $25 billion takeover of RJR Nabisco. Over a period of 6 weeks three groups battled for control of the company. As one of the contestants put it, "We were charging through the rice paddies, not stopping for anything and taking no prisoners." The takeover was the largest in history and generated almost $1 billion in fees for the banks and advisers. *(Chapter 21)*

1993 *Inflation.* Financial managers need to recognize the effect of inflation on interest rates and on the profitability of the firm's investments. In the United States inflation has been relatively modest, but some countries have suf-fered from hyperinflation. In Hungary after World War II the government issued banknotes worth 1,000 trillion pengoes. In Yugoslavia in October 1993 prices rose by nearly 2,000 percent and a dollar bought 105 million dinars. *(Chapter 4)*

1780 and 1997 *Inflation-Indexed Debt.* In 1780, Massachusetts paid Revolutionary War soldiers with interest-bearing notes rather than its rapidly eroding currency. Interest and principal payments on the notes were tied to the rate of subsequent inflation. After a 217-year hiatus, the United States Treasury issued 10-year inflation-indexed notes. Many other countries, including Britain and Israel, had done so previously. *(Chapter 5)*

1993 *Controlling Risk.* When a company fails to keep close tabs on the risks being taken by its employees, it can get into serious trouble. This was the fate of Barings, a 220-year-old British bank that numbered the queen among its clients. In 1993 it discovered that Nick Leeson, a trader in its Singapore office, had hidden losses of $1.3 billion (£869 million) from unauthorized bets on the Japanese equity market. The losses wiped out Barings and landed Leeson in jail, with a 6-year sentence. *(Chapter 24)*

1999 *The Euro.* Large corporations do business in many currencies. In 1999 a new currency came into existence, when 11 European countries adopted the euro in place of their separate currencies. This was not the first time that different countries have agreed on a common currency. In 1865 France, Belgium, Switzerland, and Italy came together in the Latin Monetary Union, and they were joined by Greece and Romania the following year. Members of the European Monetary Union (EMU) hope that the euro will be a longer-lasting success than earlier experiments. *(Chapter 23)*

2002 *Financial Scandals.* A seemingly endless series of financial and accounting scandals climaxed in this year. Resulting bankruptcies included the icons Enron (and its accounting firm, Arthur Andersen), WorldCom, and the Italian food company Parmalat. Congress passed the Sarbanes-Oxley Act to increase the accountability of corporations and executives. *(Chapters 1, 13)*

Nine chapters devoted to the simple problem of finding real assets that are worth more than they cost may seem excessive, but that problem is not so simple in practice. We will require a theory of how long-lived, risky assets are valued, and that requirement will lead us to basic questions about financial markets. For example:

- How are corporate bonds and stocks valued in capital markets?
- What risks are borne by investors in corporate securities? How can these risks be measured?
- What compensation do investors demand for bearing risk?
- What rate of return can investors in common stocks reasonably expect to receive?
- Do stock prices accurately reflect the underlying value of the firm?

Intelligent capital budgeting and financing decisions require answers to these and other questions about how capital markets work.

Financing decisions occupy Parts 4 and 5. The two chapters in Part 4 describe the kinds of securities corporations use to raise money and explain how and when these securities are issued. Part 5 covers debt policy and dividend policy. We will also describe what happens when firms find themselves in financial distress because of poor operating performance, excessive borrowing, or both.

Part 6 covers financial analysis and planning. We start with the techniques of financial statement analysis, that is, the assessment of a company's financial condition and prospects from analysis of the company's financial reports. Then we cover long- and short-term financial planning and the management of working capital. *Working capital* refers to short-term assets, including cash, inventories, and money due from customers, net of short-term liabilities, such as the money that the firm has promised to pay to suppliers, banks, or other short-term lenders.

Part 7 covers three important problems that require decisions about both investment and financing. First we look at mergers and acquisitions. Then we consider international financial management. All the financial problems of doing business at home are present overseas, but the international financial manager faces the additional complications created by multiple currencies, different tax systems, and special regulations imposed by foreign institutions and governments. Finally, we look at risk management and the specialized securities, including futures and options, that managers can use to hedge or lay off risks.

Part 8 is our conclusion. It also discusses some of the things that we don't know about finance. If you can be the first to solve any of these puzzles, you will be justifiably famous.

Snippets of History

Now let's lighten up a little. In this book we are going to describe how financial decisions are made today. But financial markets also have an interesting history. Look at the nearby box, which lays out bits of this history, starting in prehistoric times, when the growth of bacteria anticipated the mathematics of compound interest, and continuing nearly to the present. We have keyed each of these episodes to the chapter of the book that discusses its topic.

SUMMARY

What are the two major decisions made by financial managers?

Financial management can be broken down into (1) the investment, or capital budgeting, decision and (2) the financing decision. The firm has to decide (1) how much to invest and which real assets to invest in and (2) how to raise the necessary cash.

What does "real asset" mean?

Real assets include all assets used in the production or sale of the firms' products or services. Real assets can be tangible (plant and equipment, for example) or intangible (patents or trademarks, for example).

Who is the financial manager?

Almost all managers are involved to some degree in investment decisions, but some managers specialize in finance, for example, the treasurer, controller, and CFO.

Why does it make sense for corporations to maximize their market value?

Value maximization is the natural financial goal of the firm. Maximizing value maximizes the wealth of the firm's owners, its shareholders. Shareholders can invest or consume that wealth as they wish.

Is value maximization ethical?

Modern finance does not condone attempts to pump up stock price by unethical means. But there need be no conflict between ethics and value maximization. The surest route to maximum value starts with products and services that satisfy customers. A good reputation with customers, employees, and other stakeholders is also important for the firms' long-run profitability and value.

How do corporations ensure that managers' and stockholders' interests coincide?

Conflicts of interest between managers and stockholders can lead to agency problems. These problems are kept in check by compensation plans that link the well-being of employees to that of the firm; by monitoring of management by the board of directors, security analysts, and creditors; and by the threat of takeover.

QUIZ

1. **Financial Decisions.** Give several examples of (a) investment decisions and (b) financing decisions.

2. **Corporations.** What are the key differences between a corporation and a sole proprietorship? What is the difference between a public and a private corporation?

3. **Corporations.** What is the key advantage of separating ownership and management in large corporations?

4. **Limited Liability.** What is limited liability, and who benefits from it?

5. **Corporations.** What do we mean when we say that corporate income is subject to *double taxation?*

6. **Real versus Financial Assets.** Which of the following are real assets, and which are financial?
   a. A share of stock.
   b. A personal IOU.
   c. A trademark.
   d. A truck.
   e. Undeveloped land.
   f. The balance in the firm's checking account.
   g. An experienced and hardworking sales force.
   h. A bank loan agreement.

7. **Financial Managers.** Which of the following statements more accurately describes the treasurer than the controller?
   a. Likely to be the only financial executive in small firms.
   b. Monitors capital expenditures to make sure that they are not misappropriated.
   c. Responsible for investing the firm's spare cash.
   d. Responsible for arranging any issue of common stock.
   e. Responsible for the company's tax affairs.

8. **Value Maximization.** Give an example of an action that might increase short-run profits but at the same time reduce stock price and the market value of the firm.

9. **Agency Costs.** What are agency costs? List some ways by which agency costs are mitigated.

PRACTICE PROBLEMS

10. **Agency Problems.** Many firms have devised defenses that make it much more costly or difficult for other firms to take them over. How might such takeover defenses affect the firm's agency problems? Are managers of firms with formidable takeover defenses more or less likely to act in the firm's interest rather than their own?

11. **Financial Decisions.** What is the difference between capital budgeting decisions and capital structure decisions?

12. **Financial Assets.** Why is a bank loan a financial asset?

13. **Real Assets.** Explain how investment in an R&D program creates a real asset.

14. **Financial Managers.** Explain the differences between the CFO's responsibilities and the treasurer's and controller's responsibilities.

15. **Limited Liability.** Is limited liability always an advantage for a corporation and its shareholders? *Hint:* Could limited liability reduce a corporation's access to financing?

16. **Goals of the Firm.** You may have heard big business criticized for focusing on short-term performance at the expense of long-term results. Explain why a firm that strives to maximize stock price should be *less* subject to an overemphasis on short-term results than one that simply maximizes profits.

17. **Goals of the Firm.** We claim that the goal of the firm is to maximize current market value. Could the following actions be consistent with that goal?
    a. The firm adds a cost-of-living adjustment to the pensions of its retired employees.
    b. The firm reduces its dividend payment, choosing to reinvest more of earnings in the business.
    c. The firm buys a corporate jet for its executives.
    d. The firm drills for oil in a remote jungle. The chance of finding oil is only 1 in 5.

18. **Goals of the Firm.** Explain why each of the following may not be appropriate corporate goals:
    a. Increase market share.
    b. Minimize costs.
    c. Underprice any competitors.
    d. Expand profits.

19. **Agency Issues.** Sometimes lawyers work on a contingency basis. They collect a percentage of their clients' settlements instead of receiving fixed fees. Why might clients prefer this arrangement? Would the arrangement mitigate an agency problem?

20. **Reputation.** As you drive down a deserted highway you are overcome with a sudden desire for a hamburger. Fortunately, just ahead are two hamburger outlets; one is owned by a national brand, the other appears to be owned by "Joe." Which outlet has the greater incentive to serve you catmeat? Why?

21. **Agency Issues.** One of the "Finance through the Ages" episodes that we cited is the 1993 collapse of Barings Bank, when one of its traders lost $1.3 billion. Traders are compensated in large part according to their trading profits. How might this practice have contributed to an agency problem?

22. **Agency Issues.** Discuss which of the following forms of compensation is most likely to align the interests of managers and shareholders:
    a. A fixed salary.
    b. A salary linked to company profits.
    c. A salary that is paid partly in the form of the company's shares.

23. **Agency Issues.** When a company's stock is widely held, it may not pay an individual shareholder to spend time monitoring managers' performance and trying to replace poor performers. Explain why. Do you think that a bank that has made a large loan to the company is in a different position?

24. **Corporate Governance.** How do clear and comprehensive financial reports promote effective corporate governance?

25. **Corporate Governance.** Some commentators have claimed that the U.S. system of corporate governance is "broken" and needs thorough reform. What do you think? Do you see systematic failures in corporate governance or just a few "bad apples" like Enron and WorldCom?

26. **Ethics.** In some countries, such as Japan and Germany, corporations develop close long-term relationships with one bank and rely on that bank for a large part of their financing needs. In the United States companies are more likely to shop around for the best deal. Do you think that this practice is more or less likely to encourage ethical behavior on the part of the corporation?

27. **Ethics.** Is there a conflict between "doing well" and "doing good"? In other words, are policies that increase the value of the firm (doing well) necessarily at odds with socially responsible policies (doing good)? When there are conflicts, how might government regulations or laws tilt the firm toward doing good? For example, how do taxes or fees charged on pollutants affect the firm's decision to pollute? Can you cite other examples of "incentives" used by governments to align private interests with public ones?

28. **Ethics.** The following report appeared in the *Financial Times* (October 28, 1999, p. 1): "Coca-Cola is testing a vending machine that automatically raises the price of the world's favorite soft drink when the temperature increases . . . [T]he new machine, believed to have been tested in Japan, may well create controversy by using hot weather to charge extra. One rival said the idea of charging more when temperatures rose was 'incredible.'" Discuss.

1. This text provides you with access to a very powerful database of company information, called Standard & Poor's Market Insight. You have access via the following link (a password is provided in your book cover) to 6 years of data for 1,000 companies. The site provides 14 different Excel Analytics Reports including financial statements, ratios (6 years of ratios, actual and charted, with comparisons to the firm's industry), stock performance reports, and much more. Industry information (companies and profile) and company business activity are also reported.

   www.mhhe.com/edumarketinsight

   Enter the link above and review the introductions page. Proceed by clicking on the Continue icon, then enter your ID number, and you are in! Carefully review the *Review and Notes* Table of Contents to the right and the profile presented for each area. Take a look at the 1,000 companies in the database by clicking the *Company* icon at the top of the page, then *Population.* Select one company of interest to review. Click on the highlighted link and review the contents available from Market Insight. Look over the reports via the Table of Contents on the left. Throughout the coming chapters we will ask you to review or analyze Market Insight reports.

   The *Company Profile* contains recent market valuation information and a link to the company's Web site. *Financial Highlights* provides current-quarter information on sales, market data, ratios, etc. Click the linked terms, for example, *Employees,* and you will be provided a definition of the term, a very useful feature when getting started.

SOLUTIONS TO SELF-TEST QUESTIONS

1.1 a. The development of a microprocessor is a capital budgeting decision. The investment of $1 billion will purchase a real asset, the microprocessor design and production facilities.
   b. The bank loan is a financing decision. This is how Volkswagen will raise money for its investment.
   c. Capital budgeting.
   d. Capital budgeting. The marketing campaign should generate a real, though intangible, asset.
   e. Both. The acquisition is an investment decision. The decision to issue shares is a financing decision.

1.2 a. A real asset. Real assets can be intangible assets.
   b. Financial.
   c. Real.
   d. Financial.
   e. Real.
   f. Financial.

1.3 Fritz would more likely be the treasurer and Frieda the controller. The treasurer raises money from the financial markets and requires a background in financial institutions. The controller requires a background in accounting.

1.4 Harry's has a far bigger stake in the reputation of its business than Victor's. The store has been in business for a long time. The owners have spent years establishing customer loyalty. In contrast, Victor's has just been established. The owner has little of his own money tied up in the firm, and so has little to lose if the business fails. In addition, the nature of the business results in little customer loyalty. Harry's is probably more reliable.

1.5 Agency problems arise when managers and shareholders have different objectives. Managers may empire-build with excessive investment and growth. Managers may be unduly risk-averse, or they may try to take excessive salaries or perquisites.

Why Corporations Need Financial Markets and Institutions

RELATED WEB LINKS

www.nyse.com

www.nasdaq.com Sites of major U.S. stock markets.

www.rba.co.uk/sources/stocks.htm

www.fibv.com Links to, and comparative statistics on, security markets around the world.

www.ici.org

www.morningstar.com

www.brill.com

biz.yahoo.com/funds Information on mutual funds and the fund industry.

www.americanbanker.com

www.us-banker.com Banking journals with links to related sites.

www.sec.gov

www.cftc.gov/cftc/cftchome.htm

www.federalreserve.gov

www.fmcenter.org Information on regulation of financial markets can be found at these sites.

Read this chapter before you visit the New York Stock Exchange

© James Marshall/CORBIS

If a corporation needs to issue more shares of stock, then its financial manager had better understand how the stock market works. If it wants to take out a bank loan, the financial manager had better understand how banks and other financial institutions work. That much is obvious. But the capital investment decision also requires a broader understanding of financial markets. We have said that a successful investment is one that increases the market value of the firm. How do investors value the firm? What level of profitability do investors require from the firm's capital investments? To answer these questions, we will need to think clearly about the cost of the capital that the firm raises from outside investors.

Financial markets and institutions are the firm's financial environment. You don't have to understand everything about that environment to begin the study of financial management, but a general understanding provides useful context for the work ahead. For example, that context will help you to understand why you are calculating the yield to maturity of a bond in Chapter 5, the net present value of a capital investment in Chapter 8, or the weighted-average cost of capital for a company in Chapter 12.

This chapter does three things. First it surveys financial markets and institutions. We will cover the stock and bond markets, mutual and pension funds, and banks and insurance companies. Second, we will set out the functions of financial markets and institutions. What do they do for corporations and for the economy? Third, it offers another look at why maximizing value is the natural financial objective of the corporation, and it defines the cost of capital for corporate investment.

After studying this chapter you should be able to:

- Understand how financial markets and institutions channel savings to corporate investment.

- Understand the basic structure of mutual funds, pension funds, banks, and insurance companies.

- Enumerate the functions of financial markets and institutions.

- Understand why the cost of capital for corporate investment is determined by investment opportunities in financial markets.

2.1 Why Finance Matters

We saw in the last chapter why a corporation's financing and investment decisions are important to its profitability and growth. Here we shift attention to the corporation's financial environment, particularly to the financial markets and institutions that supply financing for investment by corporations.

It's easy to take modern financial markets and institutions for granted and to miss their contribution to the growth of the firm and the productivity of the overall economy. All large, successful corporations can be traced back to one or a handful of entrepreneurs with just an idea for a new business. For example, both Hewlett-Packard and Apple Computer started up in California garages. But they could not have grown from those humble beginnings without access to well-functioning financial markets and institutions.

One way to appreciate the importance of a modern financial system is to see the plight of businesspeople who have to do without it. Rajan and Zingales give the example of a bamboo stool maker in Bangladesh, who needed to raise 22 cents to buy the raw materials for each stool. That is, each stool required 22 cents of outside financing. She had no access to personal funds or bank loans and had to borrow from middlemen who demanded delivery of the completed stools as repayment of their loans. She was left with a profit of 2 cents per stool and was never able to break out of this cycle of poverty.

Rajan and Zingales contrast the example of two Stanford MBAs, who were able to purchase their own business, an emergency road services company, shortly after graduating. They were able to raise seed money to search for the right acquisition and then additional financing to complete it. They were the beneficiaries of a sophisticated financial system.[1]

Table 2–1 gives examples of the sources of financing tapped by Apple Computer from its start-up garage in 1976 to early in 2005. The initial investment in Apple stock was $250,000. Apple was also able to get short-term financing from parts suppliers who did not demand immediate payment. Apple was able to get the parts, assemble and sell the computers, and then pay off its accounts payable to the suppliers. (We discuss accounts payable in Chapter 19.) Then as Apple grew, it was able to obtain several rounds of financing by selling Apple shares to private venture capital investors. (We discuss venture capital in Chapter 14.) In December 1980, it raised $91 million in an initial public offering (IPO) of its shares to public investors. There was also a follow-up share issue in May 1981.[2]

Once Apple was a public company, it could raise financing from many sources, and it was able to pay for acquisitions by issuing more shares. We have shown a few examples in Table 2–1.

Apple started paying cash dividends to shareholders in 1987, and it also distributed cash to investors by stock repurchases in the early 1990s. But Apple hit a rough patch in 1996 and 1997, and regular dividends were eliminated. The company had to borrow $660 million from a group of private investors in order to finance its recovery plan. Apple was generally profitable, despite the rough years, and it financed growth by plowing back earnings into its operations. Cumulative retained earnings were $3.2 billion by the end of the first quarter of 2005.

Apple is well known for its product innovations, including the Macintosh computer, the iMac, and the iPod. Apple is not special because of financing. In fact, the story of its financing is not too different from that of many other successful companies. But access to financing was vital to Apple's growth and profitability. Would we have iMac

---

[1] R. Rajan and L. Zingales, *Saving Capitalism from the Capitalists* (New York: Crown Business, 2003), pp. 4–8.

[2] Many of the shares sold in the 1981 issue were previously held by Apple employees. Sale of these shares allowed the employees to cash out and diversify some of their Apple holdings but did not raise additional financing for Apple.

TABLE 2-1 Examples of financing decisions by Apple Computer

April 1976: Apple Computer, Inc., founded	Mike Makkula, Apple's first chairman, invests $250,000 in Apple shares.
1976: First 200 computers sold	Parts suppliers give Apple 30 days to pay. (Financing from accounts payable.)
1978–79	Apple raises $3.5 million from venture capital investors.
December 1980: Initial public offering	Apple raises $91 million, after fees and expenses, by selling shares to public investors.
May 1981	Apple sells 2.6 million additional shares at $31.25 per share.
April 1987	Apple pays its first dividend at an annual rate of $.12 per share
Early 1990s	Apple carries out several share repurchase programs.
1994	Apple issues $300 million of debt at an interest rate of 6.5%.
1996–97: Apple reports a $740 million loss in the second quarter of 1996. Lays off 2,700 employees in 1997.	Dividend is suspended in February 1996. Apple sells $661 million of debt to private investors in June 1996. The borrowing provides "sufficient liquidity" to execute Apple's strategic plans and to "return the company to profitability."
September 1997: Acquires assets of Power Computing Corp.	Acquisition is financed with $100 million of Apple stock.
2004: Apple is healthy and profitable, thanks to iMac, iPod, and other products.	Apple pays off the $300 million in long-term debt issued in 1994, leaving the company with no long-term debt outstanding.
Since start-up to the first quarter of 2005	Apple stockholders reinvest $3.2 billion of earnings. Thus Apple's 2004 balance sheet shows cumulative retained earnings of $3.2 billion.

computers or iPods if Apple had been forced to operate in a country with a primitive financial system? Probably not.

A modern financial system offers financing in many different forms, depending on the company's age, its growth rate, and the nature of its business. For example, Apple relied on venture capital financing in its early years and only later floated its shares in public stock markets. Still later, as the company matured, it turned to other forms of financing, including the examples given in Table 2–1. But the table does not begin to cover the range of financing channels open to modern corporations. We will encounter many other channels later in the book, and new channels are opening up regularly. The nearby box describes one recent financial innovation, micro-lending funds that make small loans to businesspeople in the poorer parts of the world. We hope that one of these funds reaches out to the bamboo stool maker in Bangladesh.

2.2 The Flow of Savings to Corporations

The money that corporations invest in real assets comes ultimately from savings by investors. But there can be many stops on the road between savings and corporate investment. The road can pass through financial markets, financial intermediaries, or both.

Let's start with the simplest case of a small, closely held corporation, like Apple in its earliest years. The orange arrows in Figure 2–1 (which we repeat from Chapter 1) show the flow of savings to investment in this simple setting. There are two possible paths: The firm can sell new shares (arrow 1), or it can reinvest cash back into the firm's operations (arrow 4a). Reinvestment means additional savings by existing shareholders. The reinvested cash could have been paid out to those shareholders

Micro Loans, Solid Returns

With about $200 of his own money and a $1,500 loan, Vahid Hujdur rented space in the old section of Sarajevo and started repairing and selling discarded industrial sewing machines. Hujdur now has 10 employees building, installing, and fixing industrial machinery. Hujddur didn't get his initial loan from a local bank. "They were asking for guarantees that were impossible to get," he recalls. Instead the capital came from LOKmicro, a local financial institution specializing in microfinance—the lending of small amounts to the poor in developing nations to help them launch small enterprises.

Microfinance institutions get capital from individual and institutional investors via microfinance funds, which collect the investors' money, vet the local lenders, offer them management assistance, and administer investors' accounts.

The borrowers who take out the micro loans pay relatively high interest rates because the cost of writing and administering such small loans is high and the loans are made in nations with weak currencies. Default rates on the loans run only about 4 percent, however. "There is a deep pride in keeping up with payments," says Deidre Wagner, an executive vice president of Starbucks, who invested $100,000 in a microfinance fund in 2003. "In some instances, when an individual is behind on payments, others in the village may make up the difference." Investors and borrowers know that when the micro loans are repaid, the money gets recycled into new loans, giving still more borrowers a chance to move up the economic ladder.

Source: Adapted from Eric Uhlfelder, "Micro Loans, Solid Returns," *BusinessWeek,* May 9, 2005, pp. 100-102.

(arrow *4b*) and spent by them on personal consumption. By *not* taking and spending the cash, shareholders have reinvested their savings in the corporation. ==Cash retained and reinvested in the firm's operations is cash saved and invested on behalf of the firm's shareholders.==

Of course this small corporation has other financing choices. It could take out a bank loan, for example. The bank in turn may have raised money by attracting savings accounts. In this case investors' savings flow through the bank to the firm.

Now consider a large, public corporation, for example, Apple Computer in 2004. What's different? Scale, for one thing: Apple's annual revenues for 2004 were $8.3 billion, and its balance sheet showed total assets of $8.1 billion. The scope of Apple's activities has also expanded: It now has dozens of products and operates worldwide. Because of this scale and scope, Apple attracts investors' savings by a variety of different routes. It can do so because it is a large, profitable, public firm.

The flow of savings to large public corporations is shown in Figure 2–2. Notice two key differences from Figure 2–1. First, public corporations can draw savings from investors worldwide. Second, the savings flow through financial markets, financial intermediaries, or both. Suppose, for example, that Bank of America raises $300 million by a new issue of shares. An Italian investor buys 1,000 of the new shares for $60 per share. Now Bank of America takes that $60,000, along with money raised by the rest of the issue, and makes a $300 million loan to Apple. The Italian investor's savings end up flowing through financial markets (the stock market), to a financial intermediary (Bank of America), and finally to Apple.

Of course our Italian friend's $60,000 doesn't literally arrive at Apple in an envelope marked "From L. DaVinci." Investments by the purchasers of the Bank of America's stock issue are pooled, not segregated. Sr. DaVinci would own a share of all of Bank of America's assets, not just one loan to Apple. Nevertheless, investors' savings

FIGURE 2-1 Flow of savings to corporate investment (orange arrows) in a closely held corporation. Investors purchase shares with personal savings (1), which are invested (2). The business generates cash (3), which is reinvested (4*a*) or paid out to shareholders (4*b*). Reinvestment (4*a*) represents additional saving on behalf of shareholders.

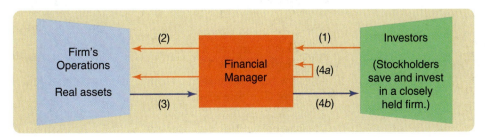

FIGURE 2–2 Flow of savings to a large public corporation (orange arrows). Savings, which can come from investors worldwide, may flow through financial markets or financial intermediaries. Savings may also flow into financial intermediaries through financial markets or into financial markets through financial intermediaries.

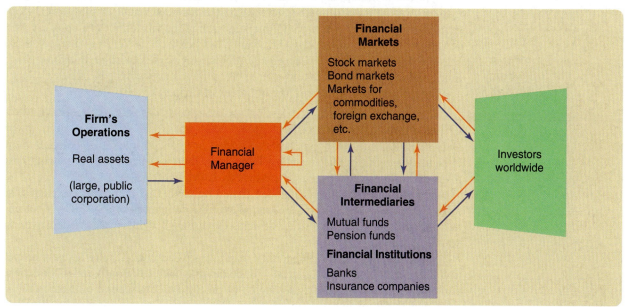

are flowing through the financial markets and the bank to finance Apple's capital investments.

The Stock Market

A **financial market** is a market where securities are issued and traded. A security is just a traded financial asset, such as a share of stock. For a corporation, the stock market is probably the most important financial market.

As corporations grow, their requirements for outside capital can expand dramatically. At some point the firm will decide to "go public" by issuing shares on an organized exchange such as the New York Stock Exchange (NYSE); that first issue is called an *initial public offering* or *IPO*. The buyers of the IPO are helping to finance the firm's investment in real assets. In return, the buyers become part-owners of the firm and share in its future success or failure. (Most investors in the Internet IPOs of 1999 and 2000 are by now sorely disappointed, but many IPOs pay off handsomely. If only we had bought Apple shares on their IPO day in 1980 . . .) Of course a corporation's IPO is not its last chance to issue shares. For example, Bank America went public in the 1930s, but it could make a new issue of shares tomorrow.

A new issue of shares increases both the amount of cash held by the company and the number of shares held by the public. Such an issue is known as a *primary issue,* and it is sold in the **primary market.** But in addition to helping companies raise new cash, financial markets also allow investors to trade securities among themselves. For example, Smith might decide to raise some cash by selling her Apple stock at the same time that Jones invests his spare cash in Apple. The result is simply a transfer of ownership from Smith to Jones, which has no effect on the company itself. Such purchases and sales of existing securities are known as *secondary transactions,* and they take place in the **secondary market.**

Stock markets are also called *equity markets,* since stockholders are said to own the common equity of the firm. You will hear financial managers refer to the capital structure decision as "the choice between debt and equity financing."

Most trading in the shares of large United States corporations takes place on stock exchanges such as the NYSE. There is also a thriving *over-the-counter (OTC)* market

financial market
Market where securities are issued and traded.

primary market
Market for the sale of new securities by corporations.

secondary market
Market in which previously issued securities are traded among investors.

in securities. The over-the-counter market is not a centralized exchange like the NYSE but a network of security dealers who use an electronic system known as NASDAQ to quote prices at which they will buy and sell shares.

Now may be a good point to stress that the financial manager plays on a global stage and needs to be familiar with markets around the world. For example, the stock of Citigroup, one of the largest U.S. banks, is listed in New York but also on several European stock exchanges. Conversely, British Airways, Deutsche Telekom, Nokia, Sony, and 460 other overseas firms have listed their shares on the NYSE.

We return to trading and pricing of shares in Chapter 6.

Other Financial Markets

Debt securities such as bonds are also traded in financial markets. The Apple bond issue in 1994 was a public issue (see Table 2–1). Table 1–1 in the previous chapter also gives examples, including the debt issues by LVMH and Wal-Mart.

A few corporate debt securities are traded on the NYSE and other exchanges, but most corporate debt securities are traded over the counter, not on NASDAQ but on a network of banks and securities dealers. Government debt is also traded over the counter.

A bond is a more complex security than a share of stock. A share is just a proportional ownership claim on the firm, with no definite maturity. Bonds and other debt securities can vary in maturity, the degree of protection or collateral offered by the issuer, and the level and timing of interest payments. Some bonds make "floating" interest payments tied to the future level of interest rates. Many can be "called" (repurchased and retired) by the issuing company before the bonds' stated maturity date. Some bonds can be converted into other securities, usually the stock of the issuing company. You don't need to master these distinctions now; just be aware that the debt or **fixed-income market** is a complicated and challenging place. A corporation must not only decide between debt and equity finance. It must also consider the design of debt. We return to the trading and pricing of debt securities in Chapter 5.

fixed-income market
Market for debt securities.

capital market
Market for long-term financing.

money market
Market for short-term financing (less than 1 year).

The markets for long-term debt and equity are called **capital markets.** A firm's *capital* is its long-run financing. Short-term securities are traded in the **money markets.** "Short term" means less than 1 year. For example, large, creditworthy corporations raise short-term financing by issues of *commercial paper,* which are debt issues with maturities of at most 270 days. Commercial paper is issued in the money market.

Self-Test 2.1

Do you understand the following distinctions? Briefly explain in each case.

a. Primary vs. secondary market.
b. Trading on the NYSE vs. over-the-counter trading on NASDAQ.
c. Capital market vs. money market.
d. Stock market vs. fixed-income market.

The financial manager regularly encounters other financial markets. Here are three examples, with references to the chapters where they are discussed:

- *Foreign-exchange markets* (Chapter 22). Any corporation engaged in international trade must be able to transfer money from dollars to other currencies, or vice versa. Foreign exchange is traded over the counter through a network of the largest international banks.
- *Commodities markets* (Chapter 24). Dozens of commodities are traded on organized exchanges, such as the New York Mercantile Exchange or the Chicago Board of Trade. You can buy or sell corn, wheat, cotton, fuel oil, natural gas, copper, silver, platinum, and so on.

Guessing Games

Talk is cheap, but money speaks the truth. That might be the credo behind the recent rapid rise in the use of novel markets to forecast everything from political events to business successes and failures. During America's recent presidential election, bets on the Iowa Electronic Market, based at the University of Iowa (www.biz.uiowa.edu/iem), and on online exchanges such as www.tradesports.com and www.betfair.com were watched almost as keenly as opinion polls. These and other markets have in recent years been used to forecast, for example, the fate of Saddam Hussein, the outcome of celebrity trials, and the box-office takings of films on their opening weekends.

Markets like these, which are intended to elicit punters' best collective guess about the outcome of some future event, are known as *information, prediction,* or *decision markets.* Take the presidential election: People could bet on George Bush by buying a contract that paid a dollar if he won and nothing if he lost. Anyone certain of a Bush victory should have been willing to pay up to a dollar for the contract. Anyone confident that Bush would lose could have sold such a contract, expecting to pay nothing when the result came. With many participants buying and selling in this way, the market discovered a price for the contract—in effect, its best guess of the probability of a Bush win.

The theory is that the aggregated hunches of many people with money at stake are likely to be more accurate than the opinion of disinterested experts or of whoever happens to be at home when a pollster calls.

Most anecdotal evidence seems to bear this theory out. For instance, one study found that the Iowa Electronic Market, which started life in the late 1980s, predicted the vote shares of candidates in several elections between 1988 and 2001 with an average margin of error of 1.5 percentage points, compared with the polls' average error of 2.1 percentage points. This year the Iowa market and other exchanges predicted a narrow win for Bush.

Businesses have also made good use of information markets. Siemens, a German conglomerate, used an internal market to forecast (correctly) that the firm would fail to deliver a software project on time, even though internal planning methods purportedly showed that the deadline could be met. At Hewlett-Packard, a market did a better job than traditional methods in forecasting printer sales. A joint venture by Goldman Sachs and Deutsche Bank that uses markets to predict economic indicators has been at least as accurate as economists' median forecasts.

• *Markets for options and other derivatives* (Chapters 23 and 24). Derivatives are securities whose payoffs depend on the prices of other securities or commodities. For example, you can buy an option to purchase IBM shares at a fixed price on a fixed future date. The option's payoff depends on the price of IBM shares on that date. Commodities can be traded by a different kind of derivative security called a futures contract.

Commodity and derivative markets are not sources of financing but markets where the financial manager can adjust the firm's exposure to various business risks. For example, an electric generating company may wish to "lock in" the future price of natural gas or fuel oil by trading in commodity markets, thus eliminating the risk of a sudden jump in the price of its raw materials.

Wherever there is uncertainty, investors may be interested in trading, either to speculate or to lay off their risks, and a market may arise to meet that trading demand. In recent years several new markets have been created that allow punters to bet on a single event. The nearby article from *The Economist* discusses how prices in these markets can reveal people's predictions about the future.

Financial Intermediaries

financial intermediary
An organization that raises money from investors and provides financing for individuals, corporations, or other organizations.

A **financial intermediary** is an organization that raises money from investors and provides financing for individuals, companies, and other organizations. For corporations, intermediaries are important sources of financing. Intermediaries are a stop on the road between savings and real investment. We will start with two important classes of intermediaries, mutual funds and pension funds.

mutual fund
An investment company that pools the savings of many investors and invests in a portfolio of securities.

Mutual funds raise money by selling shares to investors. The investors' money is pooled and invested in a portfolio of securities. The Vanguard Windsor Fund, for example, held a portfolio of about 150 stocks with a total market value of $20 billion in May 2005. You could buy additional shares in the fund with an initial investment of as little as $3,000. By doing so, you would contribute $3,000 more to the portfolio and gain a small percentage of the portfolio's subsequent dividends and price appreciation.[3] You could also sell your shares back to the fund if you decide to cash out of your investment.[4]

The advantages of a mutual fund should be clear: Unless you are very wealthy, you cannot buy and manage a 150-stock portfolio on your own, at least not efficiently. ==Mutual funds offer investors low-cost diversification and professional management. For most investors, it's more efficient to buy a mutual fund than to assemble a diversified portfolio of stocks and bonds.==

Mutual fund managers also try their best to "beat the market," that is, to generate superior performance by finding the stocks with better-than-average returns. Whether they can pick winners consistently is another question, which we will address in Chapter 6.

In exchange for their services, the fund's managers take out a management fee. There are also the expenses of running the fund. For Windsor, fees and expenses absorb about .4 percent of portfolio value each year. This seems reasonable, but watch out: The typical mutual fund charges more than Windsor does. In some cases fees and expenses add up to 2 percent per year. That's a big bite out of your investment return.

Mutual funds are a stop on the road from savings to corporate investment. Suppose Windsor purchases part of the new issue of shares by Bank of America. Again we show the flow of savings to investment by orange arrows:

Over 8,000 mutual funds operate in the United States. In fact there are more mutual funds than public companies! The funds pursue a wide variety of investment strategies. Some funds specialize in safe stocks with generous dividend payouts. Some specialize in high-tech growth stocks. Some "balanced" funds offer mixtures of stocks and bonds. Some specialize in particular countries or regions. For example, the Fidelity Investments mutual fund group sponsors funds for Canada, Japan, China, Europe, Latin America, and so on.

pension fund
Investment plan set up by an employer to provide for employees' retirement.

There are other ways of pooling and investing savings. Consider a **pension fund** set up by a corporation or other organization on behalf of its employees. There are several types of pension plan. Here is just one example: In a *defined contribution* plan,[5] a percentage of the employee's monthly paycheck is contributed to a pension fund. (The employer and employee may each contribute 5 percent, for example.) Contributions from all participating employees are pooled and invested in securities or mutual funds. (Usually the employees can choose from a menu of funds with different investment strategies.) Each employee's balance in the plan grows over the years as contributions

---

[3] Mutual funds are not corporations but investment companies. They pay no tax, providing that all income from dividends and price appreciation is passed on to the funds' shareholders. The shareholders pay personal tax on this income.

[4] Windsor, like most mutual funds, is an *open-end* fund. It stands ready to issue shares to new investors in the fund and to buy back existing shares when its shareholders decide to cash out. The purchase and sale prices depend on the fund's net asset value (NAV) on the day of purchase or redemption. *Closed-end* funds have a fixed number of shares traded on an exchange. If you want to invest in a closed-end fund, you must buy shares from another stockholder in the fund.

[5] In a defined contribution plan, each employee owns a portion of the pension fund and accumulates an investment balance to pay for retirement. The amount available for retirement depends on the accumulated contributions and on the rate of return earned on the invested contributions. In a *defined benefit* plan, the employer promises a certain level of retirement benefits (set by a formula) and the *employer* invests in the pension plan. The plan's accumulated investment value has to be large enough to cover the promised benefits. If not, the employer must put in more money.

Mutual Funds

Mutual Funds

Most mutual funds in the U.S. belong to the Investment Company Institute. Log on to its Web site at **www.ici.org.** You will find some essential information about mutual funds and a useful fact book. Make sure that you know the basic types of fund. For example, can you explain the difference between a stock fund and a money market mutual fund? Look in the fact book at the amount of assets managed by these funds. Have mutual fund assets been increasing or decreasing over the past 20 years? What are the advantages and disadvantages of investing through a mutual fund rather than doing so directly?

Choosing a Mutual Fund

Here are the Web sites for three of the largest mutual fund companies:

1. Fidelity Investments: **www.fidelity.com**
2. Putnam Investments: **www.putnam.com**
3. Vanguard Group: **www.vanguard.com**

Pick three or four funds from one of these sites and compare their investment objectives, risks, past returns, fund fees, and so on. Read the prospectuses for each of these funds; they are usually clear and informative. Who do you think should, or should not, invest in each fund? Which one would be most appropriate for a young financial executive saving for retirement?

Mutual Fund Performance

Morningstar provides data on mutual fund performance. Log on to **www. morningstar.com** and click on *Fund Category Returns.* This gives recent returns by category of fund. Which category has performed unusually well or badly? Is it the funds investing in small rather than large company stocks, growth rather than value stocks, or those specializing in a particular industry?

Source: Investment Company Institute Web site.

continue and investment income accumulates. When retirement age arrives, the balance in the plan can be used to finance living expenses.

Pension funds are designed for long-run investment. They provide professional management and diversification. They also have an important tax advantage: Contributions are tax-deductible, and investment returns inside the plan are not taxed until cash is finally withdrawn.[6]

Pension plans are among the most important vehicles for savings. Private pension plans held about $4.4 trillion in assets in 2004.

Self-Test 2.2	Individual investors can buy bonds and stocks directly, or they can put their money in a mutual fund or a defined-contribution pension fund. What are the advantages of the second strategy?

Financial Institutions

financial institution
A bank, insurance company, or similar financial intermediary.

Banks and insurance companies are **financial institutions.**[7] A financial institution is an intermediary that does more than just pool and invest savings. Institutions raise

---

[6] Defined benefit pension plans share these same advantages, except that the employer invests rather than the employees. In a defined benefit plan, the advantage of tax deferral on investment income accrues to the employer. This deferral reduces the cost of funding the plan.

[7] We may be drawing too fine a distinction between financial intermediaries and institutions. A mutual fund could be considered a financial institution. But "financial institution" usually suggests a more complicated intermediary, such as a bank.

Banks

We mentioned in the last chapter that large banks have their fingers in many pies. The Web sites of the very largest banks are equally massive. The Bank of New York (www.bny.com) and Bank of America (www.bankofamerica.com) are examples of banks with relatively straightforward Web sites. Use these Web sites and the company annual reports to find what services banks provide to individuals, small businesses, and large corporations.

Source: The Bank of New York Web site.

financing in special ways, for example, by accepting deposits or selling insurance policies, and they provide additional financial services. Unlike a mutual fund, they not only invest in securities but also loan money directly to individuals, businesses, or other organizations.

Banks lend money to corporations. (In the United States, they are generally not allowed to make equity investments in corporations, although banks in most other countries can do so.) Suppose that a local forest products company negotiates a short-term bank loan for $2.5 million. The flow of savings is:

The bank provides a service to both the company and its depositors. To cover the costs of this service, it charges borrowers a higher interest rate than it pays its depositors.

In the United States, insurance companies are more important than banks for the *long-term* financing of business. They are massive investors in corporate stocks and bonds, and they often make long-term loans directly to corporations.

Suppose a company needs a loan of $2.5 million for 9 years, not 9 months. It could issue a bond directly to investors, or it could negotiate a 9-year loan with an insurance company:

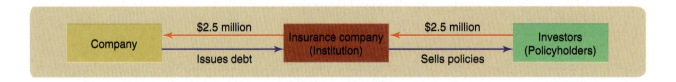

The money to make the loan comes mainly from the sale of insurance policies. Say you buy a fire insurance policy on your home. You pay cash to the insurance company and get a financial asset (the policy) in exchange. You receive no interest payments on this financial asset, but if a fire does strike, the company is obliged to cover the damages up to the policy limit. This is the return on your investment. (Of course, a fire is a sad and dangerous event that you hope to avoid. But if a fire does occur, you are better off getting a return on your investment in insurance than not having insurance at all.)

The company will issue not just one policy but thousands. Normally the incidence of fires "averages out," leaving the company with a predictable obligation to its policyholders as a group. Of course the insurance company must charge enough for its policies to cover selling and administrative costs, pay policyholders' claims, and generate a profit for its stockholders.

Why is a financial intermediary different from a manufacturing corporation? First, it may raise money in different ways, for example, by taking deposits or selling insurance policies. Second, it invests that money in *financial* assets, for example, in stocks, bonds, or loans to businesses or individuals. The manufacturing company's main investments are in plant, equipment, or other *real* assets.

Self-Test 2.3   **What are the key differences between a mutual fund and a bank or an insurance company?**

Total Financing of U.S. Corporations

The pie chart in Figure 2–3 shows the investors in bonds and other debt securities. Notice the importance of institutional investors—mutual funds, pension funds, insurance companies, and banks. Households (individual investors) hold only a small slice of the debt pie. The other slices represent the rest of the world (investors from outside the United States) and various other categories.

The pie chart in Figure 2–4 shows holdings of the shares issued by U.S. corporations. Here households make a stronger showing, about 38 percent of the total. Pension funds, insurance companies, and mutual funds add up to about 48 percent of the total.[8] The rest-of-the-world slice is about 11 percent.

The aggregate amounts represented in these figures are enormous. There is $7.2 trillion of debt behind Figure 2–3 and $17.2 trillion of equity behind Figure 2–4, $17,204,400,000,000, to be more exact.[9]

Chapter 14 reviews corporate financing patterns in more detail.

FIGURE 2–3 Holdings of corporate and foreign bonds, first quarter 2005. The total amount is $7.2 trillion.

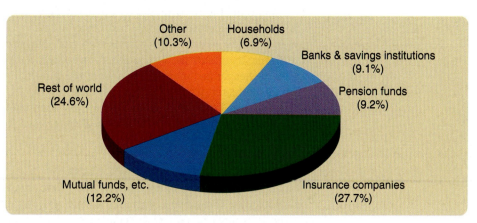

Source: Board of Governors of the Federal Reserve System, Division of Research and Statistics, *Flow of Funds Accounts,* Table L.212 (**www.federalreserve.gov**).

[8] Remember, banks in the United States do not usually hold stock in other companies.

[9] The total market value of shares issued by U.S. *nonfinancial* corporations is $10.8 trillion. "Nonfinancial" excludes financial institutions, such as banks and insurance companies.

FIGURE 2–4 Holdings of corporate equities, first quarter 2005. The total amount is $17.2 trillion.

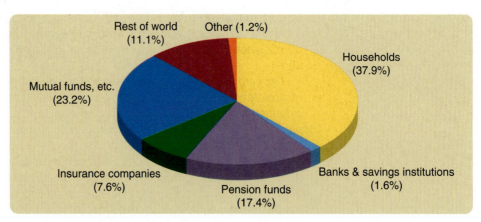

Source: Board of Governors of the Federal Reserve System, Division of Research and Statistics, *Flow of Funds Accounts,* Table L.213 (**www.federalreserve.gov**).

2.3 Functions of Financial Markets and Intermediaries

Financial markets and intermediaries provide financing for business. They channel savings to real investment. That much should be loud and clear from the Sections 2.1 and 2.2 of this chapter. But there are other functions that may not be quite so obvious.

Transporting Cash across Time

Individuals need to transport expenditures in time. If you have money now that you wish to save for a rainy day, you can (for example) put the money in a savings account at a bank and withdraw it with interest later. If you don't have money today, say to buy a car, you can borrow money from the bank and pay off the loan later. Modern finance provides a kind of time machine. Lenders transport money forward in time; borrowers transport it back. Both are happier than if they were forced to spend income as it arrives. Of course, individuals are not alone in needing to raise cash from time to time. Firms with good investment opportunities, but a shortage of internally generated cash, raise cash by borrowing or selling new shares. Many governments run deficits and finance current outlays by issuing debt.

Young people saving for retirement may transport their current earnings 30 or 40 years into the future by means of a pension fund. They may even transport income to their heirs by purchase of a life insurance policy.

In principle, individuals or firms with cash surpluses could take out newspaper advertisements or surf the Net looking for counterparties with cash shortages. But it is usually cheaper and more convenient to use financial markets and intermediaries. It is not just a matter of avoiding the cost of searching for the right counterparty. Follow-up is needed. For example, banks don't just loan money and walk away. They monitor the borrower to make sure that the loan is used for its intended purpose and that the borrower's credit stays solid.

Risk Transfer and Diversification

Financial markets and intermediaries allow investors and businesses to reduce and reallocate risk. Insurance companies are an obvious example. When you buy homeowner's insurance, you greatly reduce the risk of loss from fire, theft, or accidents. But your policy is not a risky bet for the insurance company. It diversifies by issuing thousands of policies, and it expects losses to average out over the policies.[10] The insurance company allows you to pool risk with thousands of other homeowners.

---

[10] Unfortunately for insurance companies, the losses don't always average out. Hurricanes and earthquakes can damage thousands of homes at once. The potential losses are so great that property insurance companies buy *reinsurance* against such catastrophes.

Investors should diversify too. For example, you can buy shares in a mutual fund that holds hundreds of stocks. In fact, you can buy *index funds* that invest in all the stocks in the popular market indexes.[11] For example, the Vanguard Index 500 fund holds the stocks in the Standard & Poor's Composite stock market index. (The "S&P 500" tracks the performance of the largest U.S. stocks. It is the index most used by professional investors.) If you buy this fund, you are insulated from the company-specific risks of the 500 companies in the index. These risks are averaged out by diversification. Of course you are still left with the risk that the level of the stock market as a whole will fall. In fact, we will see in Chapter 10 that investors are mostly concerned with *market risk,* not the specific risks of individual companies.

Financial markets provide other mechanisms for sharing risks. For example, a wheat farmer and a baking company are each exposed to fluctuations in the price of wheat after the harvest. The farmer worries about low prices, the baker about high prices. They can both rest easier if the baker can agree with the farmer to buy wheat in the future at a fixed price. The farmer and baker would not negotiate the trade face-to-face, however. They would each trade in commodity markets, the farmer as a seller and the baker as a buyer.

Liquidity

liquidity
The ability to sell or exchange an asset for cash on short notice.

Markets and intermediaries also provide **liquidity,** that is, the ability to turn an investment back into cash when needed. Suppose you deposit $5,000 in a savings bank on February 1. During that month, the bank uses your deposit and other new deposits to make a 6-month construction loan to a real estate developer. On March 1, you realize that you need your $5,000 back. The bank can give it to you. Because the bank has thousands of depositors, and other sources of financing if necessary, it can make an illiquid loan to the developer financed by liquid deposits made by you and other customers. If you lend out your money for 6 months directly to the real estate developer, you will have a hard time retrieving it 1 month later.

The shares of public companies are liquid because they are traded more or less continuously in the stock market. An Italian investor who puts $60,000 into Bank of America shares can recover that money on short notice. (A $60,000 sell order is a drop in the bucket, compared with the normal trading volume of Bank of America shares.) Mutual funds can redeem their shares for cash on short notice because the funds invest in traded securities, which can be sold as necessary.

Of course liquidity is a matter of degree. Foreign exchange markets for major currencies are exceptionally liquid. Bank of America or Deutsche Bank could buy $200 million worth of yen or euros in the blink of an eye, with hardly any affect on foreign exchange rates. U.S. Treasury securities are also very liquid, and the shares of the largest companies on the major international stock exchanges only slightly less so.

Liquidity is most important when you're in a hurry. If you try to sell $500,000 worth of the shares of a small, thinly traded company all at once, you will probably knock down the price to some extent. If you're patient and don't surprise other investors with a large, sudden sell order, you may be able to unload your shares on better terms. It's the same problem you may face in selling real estate. A house or condominium is not a liquid asset in a panic sale. If you're determined to sell in an afternoon, you're not going to get full value.

The Payment Mechanism

Think how inconvenient life would be if you had to pay for every purchase in cash or if General Motors had to ship truckloads of hundred-dollar bills round the country to pay its suppliers. Checking accounts, credit cards, and electronic transfers allow individuals and firms to send and receive payments quickly and safely over long distances.

---

[11] Index funds don't always own every stock in the index, but they own most of them—enough that the performance of the fund tracks the index almost perfectly.

Banks are the obvious providers of payment services, but they are not alone. For example, if you buy shares in a money market mutual fund, your money is pooled with that of other investors and used to buy safe, short-term securities. You can then write checks on this mutual fund investment, just as if you had a bank deposit.

Information Provided by Financial Markets

In well-functioning financial markets, you can *see* what securities and commodities are worth, and you can see—or at least estimate—the rates of return that investors can expect on their savings. The information provided by financial markets is often essential to a financial manager's job. Here are three examples of how this information can be used.

Commodity Prices   Catalytic converters are used in the exhaust systems of cars and light trucks to reduce pollution. The catalysts include platinum, which is traded on the New York Mercantile Exchange.

In April a manufacturer of catalytic converters is planning production for July. How much per ounce should the company budget for purchases of platinum in that month? Easy: The company's CFO looks up the market price of platinum on the New York Mercantile Exchange—$874 per ounce for delivery in July. (This was the closing price for platinum on April 21, 2005, for delivery in July.) The CFO can lock in that price if she wishes. The details of such a trade are covered in Chapter 24.

Interest Rates   The CFO of Catalytic Concepts has to raise $400 million in new financing. She considers an issue of 10-year bonds. What will the interest rate on the bonds be? To find out, the CFO looks up interest rates on existing bonds traded in financial markets.

The results are shown in Table 2–2. Notice how the interest rate climbs as credit quality deteriorates: the largest, safest companies, which are rated AAA ("triple-A"), can borrow for 10 years at a 4.84 percent interest rate. The interest rates for AA, A, and BBB climb to 4.95, 5.11, and 6.04 percent, respectively. Triple-B companies are still regarded as *investment grade,* that is, good quality, but the next step down takes the investor into *junk bond* territory. The interest rate for double-B companies climbs to 6.68 percent. Single-B companies are riskier still, so investors demand 7.61 percent.

There will be more on bond ratings and interest rates in Chapter 5. But you can see how a financial manager can use information from fixed-income markets to forecast the interest rate on new debt financing. For example, if Catalytic Concepts can qualify as a BBB-rated company, and interest rates are as shown in Table 2–2, it should be able to raise new debt financing for approximately 6 percent.

Company Values   How much was Alaska Air Group worth in April 2005? How about Bob Evans Farms, Callaway Golf, TransCanada Pipelines, or GE? Table 2–3 shows the answers. We simply multiply the number of shares outstanding by the price

TABLE 2–2 Interest rates on 10-year corporate bonds, April 2005. The interest rate is lowest for top-quality (AAA) issuers. The rate rises as credit quality declines.

Credit Rating	Interest Rate
AAA	4.84%
AA	4.95
A	5.11
BBB	6.04
BB	6.68
B	7.61

Source: Bloomberg Composite Corporate Bond Indexes, April 24, 2005.

TABLE 2-3 Calculating the total market values of Alaska Air Group and other companies in April 2005. Shares and market values in millions. Ticker symbols in parentheses.

	Stock Price	×	Number of Shares	=	Market Value
Alaska Air Group (ALK)	28.93	×	27.126	=	$785
Bob Evans Farms (BOBE)	21.04	×	35.36	=	$744
Callaway Golf (ELY)	12.00	×	69.11	=	$829
TransCanada Pipelines (TRP)	23.98	×	484.9	=	$11,628
General Electric (GE)	36.12	×	10,586.4	=	$382,381

Source: Standard & Poor's Market Insight **(www.mhhe.com/edumarketinsight).**

per share in the stock market. Investors valued Alaska Air Group at $785 million, GE at $382 *billion.*

Stock prices and company values summarize investors' collective assessment of how well a company is doing, both its current performance and its future prospects. Thus an increase in stock price sends a positive signal from investors to managers.[12] That is why top management's compensation is linked to stock prices. A manager who owns shares in his or her company will be motivated to increase the company's market value. This reduces agency costs by aligning the interests of managers and stockholders.

This is one important advantage of going public. A private company can't use its stock price as a measure of performance. It can still compensate managers with shares, but the shares will not be valued in a financial market.

Self-Test 2.4   **Which of the functions described in this section require financial markets? Explain briefly.**

2.4 Value Maximization and the Cost of Capital

In Chapter 1 we stated the financial objective of the firm: Maximize the current market value of shareholders' investment. This simple, unqualified goal makes sense when the shareholders have access to well-functioning financial markets and institutions. Access allows them to share risks and transport savings across time. Access gives them the flexibility to manage their own savings and investment plans, leaving the corporation's financial managers with only one task, to increase market value.

A corporation's roster of shareholders will usually include both risk-averse and risk-tolerant investors. You might expect the risk-averse to say, "Sure, maximize value, but don't touch too many high-risk projects." Instead, they say, "Risky projects are OK, *provided* that expected profits are more than enough to offset the risks. If this firm ends up too risky for my taste, I'll adjust my investment portfolio to make it safer." For example, the risk-averse shareholder can shift more of his or her portfolio to safe assets, such as U.S. government bonds. The shareholder can also just say goodbye, selling off shares of the risky firm and buying shares in a safer one. If the risky investments increase market value, the departing shareholder is better off than he or she would be if the risky investments were turned down.

---

[12] We can't claim that investors' assessments of value are always correct. Finance can be a risky and dangerous business—dangerous for your wealth, that is. With hindsight we see horrible mistakes by investors, most recently the gross overvaluation of Internet and telecom companies. On average, however, it appears that financial markets collect and assess information quickly and accurately. We'll discuss this issue again in Chapter 6.

EXAMPLE 2.1 ▶ Value Maximization

Fast-Track Wireless shares trade for $20. It invests $3 per share in a high-risk, but potentially revolutionary, WhyFi technology. Investors note the risk of failure but are even more impressed with the technology's upside. They conclude that the possibility of very high future profits is worth $6 per share. The net value added is $6 − 3 = +$3, and the share price increases from $20 to $23.

Caspar Milquetoast, a thoughtful but timid shareholder, notes the downside risks and decides that it's time for a change. He sells out to more risk-tolerant investors. But he sells at $23 per share, not $20. Thus he captures the value added by the WhyFi project *without having to bear the project's risks.* The risks are transferred to other investors. In a well-functioning stock market, there is always a pool of investors ready to bear downside risks if the upside potential is sufficiently attractive. We know that the upside potential was sufficient in this case, because Fast-Track stock attracted investors willing to pay $23 per share. ◀

The same principles apply to the *timing* of a corporation's cash flows, as the following self-test illustrates.

Self-Test 2.5

Rhonda and Reggie Hotspur are working hard to save for their childrens' college educations. They don't need more cash for current consumption but will face big tuition bills in 2020. Should they therefore avoid investing in stocks that pay generous current cash dividends? Explain briefly.

The Opportunity Cost of Capital

cost of capital
Minimum acceptable rate of return on capital investment.

Financial managers look to financial markets to measure, or at least estimate, the **cost of capital** for the firm's investment projects. The cost of capital is the minimum acceptable rate of return for capital investment. Investment projects offering rates of return higher than the cost of capital add value to the firm. Projects offering rates of return less than the cost of capital actually subtract value and should not be undertaken.[13]

Let's think again about the value added by risky corporate investments, for example, Fast-Track's WhyFi project. That project increased Fast-Track's overall market value and the price of each of its shares. The project was worth more than it cost because it offered a superior rate of return, even after accounting for the risks of failure.

What does "superior rate of return" mean? It means an expected rate of return higher than the return investors could achieve from alternative investments at the same level of risk. For example, suppose that the WhyFi project is just as risky as the shares of other high-tech growth companies, and that the expected return on those companies' shares is 15 percent. If the WhyFi project offers a 20 percent expected return, then the project adds value. If the project offered only 10 percent, investing in it would destroy value, because the project return would be less than the 15 percent return that shareholders could obtain by investing on their own.

When the financial manager invests at a superior rate of return, stockholders applaud and stock price increases. If the financial manager invests at an inferior return, shareholders boo, stock price falls, and stockholders want their money back so that they can invest on their own.

You can see why the rates of return on investments *outside* the corporation set the minimum return for investment projects *inside* the corporation. In other words, the expected rates of return on investments in financial markets determine the cost of capital for corporate investments.

---

[13] Of course, there are exceptions when the corporation invests for other reasons. Think of an investment in pollution control equipment for a factory. The equipment may not generate any significant cash returns, so the rate of return on investment may be negative. But firms still invest in pollution control, not to earn direct profits but to meet legal and ethical obligations.

FIGURE 2–5 The firm can either keep and reinvest cash or return it to investors. (Arrows represent possible cash flows or transfers.) If cash is reinvested, the opportunity cost is the expected rate of return that shareholders could have obtained by investing in financial assets.

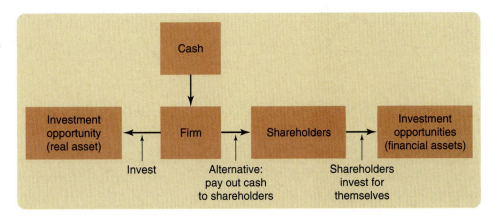

Figure 2–5 summarizes this trade-off. The firm can invest, or it can pay out cash to shareholders. Shareholders can invest for themselves in financial markets. Capital investments by the firm should therefore offer rates of return at least as high as those available in financial markets at the same level of risk. If they do not, the firm should not invest. Therefore, the cost of capital for corporate investment is set by the rates of return on investment opportunities in financial markets.

You can see why financial managers refer to the *opportunity cost* of capital. When the firm invests, shareholders lose the opportunity to invest that cash in financial markets.

For safe investments, you can observe the opportunity cost of capital by looking up current interest rates on safe debt securities. For risky investments, the opportunity cost of capital has to be estimated. That is one of the harder tasks in financial management. We will return to this task in Chapter 5 and in several later chapters.

Notice that the opportunity cost of capital is generally *not* the interest rate that the firm pays on a loan from a bank or insurance company. If the company is making a risky investment, the opportunity cost is the expected return that investors can achieve in financial markets at the same level of risk. The expected return on risky securities will normally be well above the interest rate on corporate borrowing.

Self-Test 2.6

Investing $100,000 in additional raw materials today—mostly in palladium—should allow Cryogenic Concepts to increase production and earn an additional $112,000 next year. This payoff would cover the investment today, plus a 12 percent return. Palladium is traded in commodity markets. The CFO has studied the history of returns on investments in palladium and believes that investors in that precious metal can reasonably expect a 15 percent return. Is Cryogenic's investment in palladium a good idea? Why or why not?

SUMMARY

Where does the financing for corporations come from?

The ultimate source of financing is individuals' savings. The savings may flow through **financial markets** and **intermediaries.** The intermediaries include mutual funds, pension funds, and financial institutions, such as banks and insurance companies.

Why do nonfinancial corporations need modern financial markets and institutions?

It's simple: Corporations need access to financing in order to innovate and grow. A modern financial system offers different types of financing, depending on a corporation's age and the nature of its business. A high-tech start-up will seek venture capital financing, for example. A mature firm will rely more on bond markets.

What if a corporation finances investment by retaining and reinvesting cash generated from its operations?

In that case the corporation is saving on behalf of its shareholders.

What are the key advantages of mutual funds and pension funds?

Mutual and **pension funds** allow investors to diversify in professionally managed portfolios. Pension funds offer an additional tax advantage, because the returns on pension investments are not taxed until withdrawn from the plan.

What are the functions of financial markets?

Financial markets help channel savings to corporate investment, and they help match up borrowers and lenders. They provide **liquidity** and diversification opportunities for investors. Trading in financial markets provides a wealth of useful information for the financial manager.

Do financial institutions have different functions?

Financial institutions carry out a number of similar functions but in different ways. They channel savings to corporate investment, and they serve as **intermediaries** between borrowers and lenders. Banks also provide liquidity for depositors and, of course, play a special role in the economy's payment systems. Insurance companies allow policyholders to pool risks.

How does the financial manager identify the cost of the capital raised by a corporation?

The **cost of capital** is the minimum acceptable rate of return on capital investment. It's an opportunity cost, that is, a rate of return that investors could earn in financial markets. For a safe capital investment, the opportunity cost is the interest rate on safe debt securities, such as high-grade corporate bonds. For riskier capital investments, the opportunity cost is the expected rate of return on risky securities, investments in the stock market, for example.

QUIZ

1. **Corporate Financing.** How can a small, private firm finance its capital investments? Give two or three examples of financing sources.

2. **Corporate Financing.** Is it possible for an individual to save and invest in a corporation without lending money to it or purchasing additional shares? Explain.

3. **Financial Markets.** What is meant by over-the-counter trading? Is this trading mechanism used for stocks, bonds, or both?

4. **Financial Markets.** The stock and bond markets are not the only financial markets. Give two or three additional examples.

5. **Financial Intermediaries.** You are a beginning investor with only $5,000 in savings. How can you achieve a widely diversified portfolio at reasonable cost?

6. **Financial Intermediaries.** What are the key advantages of a defined contribution pension plan as a vehicle for retirement savings?

7. **Financial Intermediaries.** Is an insurance company also a financial intermediary? How does the insurance company channel savings to corporate investment?

8. **Corporate Financing.** What are the largest institutional investors in bonds? In shares?

9. **Financial Markets and Institutions.** List the major functions of financial markets and institutions in a modern financial system.

10. **Financial Markets.** On a mountain trek, you discover a 6-ounce gold nugget. A friend offers to pay you $2,500 for it. How do you check whether this is a fair price?

11. **Financial Markets.** What kinds of useful information can a financial manager obtain from financial markets? Give examples.

12. **Value Maximization.** The objective of value maximization makes sense when stockholders have access to modern financial markets and institutions. Briefly explain why.

13. **Cost of Capital.** Why do financial managers refer to the *opportunity* cost of capital? How would you find the opportunity cost of capital for a safe investment?

PRACTICE PROBLEMS ⊞™

14. **True or False?**
    a. Financing for public corporations must flow through financial markets.
    b. Financing for private corporations must flow through financial intermediaries.
    c. The sale of policies is a source of financing for insurance companies.
    d. Almost all foreign exchange trading occurs on the floors of the FOREX exchanges in New York and London.
    e. The opportunity cost of capital is the capital outlay required to undertake a real investment opportunity.
    f. The cost of capital is the interest rate paid on borrowing from a bank or other financial institution.

15. **Liquidity.** Securities traded in active financial markets are liquid assets. Explain why liquidity is important to individual investors and to mutual funds.

16. **Liquidity.** Bank deposits are liquid; you can withdraw money on demand. How can the bank provide this liquidity, and at the same time make illiquid loans to businesses?

17. **Corporate Financing.** Financial markets and intermediaries channel savings from investors to corporate investment. The savings make this journey by many different routes. Give a specific example for each of the following routes:
    a. Investor to financial intermediary, to financial markets, and to the corporation.
    b. Investor to financial markets, to a financial intermediary, and to the corporation.
    c. Investor to financial markets, to a financial intermediary, back to financial markets, and to the corporation.

18. **Mutual Funds.** Why are mutual funds called financial intermediaries? Why does it make sense for an individual to invest her savings in a mutual fund rather than directly in financial markets?

19. **Value Maximization.** Fritz is risk-averse and is content with a relatively low but safe return on his investments. Frieda is risk-tolerant and seeks a very high rate of return on her invested savings. Yet both shareholders will applaud a low-risk capital investment that offers a superior rate of return. Why? What is meant by "superior"?

20. **Cost of Capital.** British Quince comes across an average-risk investment project that offers a rate of return of 9.5 percent. This is less than the company's normal rate of return, but one of Quince's directors notes that the company can easily borrow the required investment at 7 percent. "It's simple," he says. "If the bank lends us money at 7 percent, then our cost of capital must be 7 percent. The project's return is higher than the cost of capital, so let's move ahead." How would you respond?

21. **Cost of Capital.** In a stroke of good luck, your company has uncovered an opportunity to invest for 10 years at a guaranteed 6 percent rate of return. What is the opportunity cost of capital? Assume interest rates as in Table 2–2.

22. **Cost of Capital.** Pollution Busters, Inc., is considering purchase of 10 additional carbon sequesters for $100,000 apiece. The sequesters only last for 1 year until saturated. Then the carbon is sold to the government.
    a. Suppose the government guarantees the price of carbon. At this price, the payoff after 1 year is $115,000 for sure. How would you determine the opportunity cost of capital for this investment?
    b. Suppose instead that the sequestered carbon has to be sold on the London Carbon Exchange. Carbon prices have been extremely volatile, but Pollution Busters' CFO learns that average rates of return from investment on that exchange have been about 20 percent. She thinks this is a reasonable forecast for the future. What is the opportunity cost of capital in this case? Is purchase of additional sequesters a worthwhile capital investment?

www.mhhe.com/bmm5e

STANDARD
&POOR'S

1. **Information Provided by Financial Markets.** Update Table 2–3. How have these companies' market values changed? Go to Market Insight (**www.mhhe.com/edumarketinsight**), and go to the Financial Highlights page for each company. The companies' ticker symbols are given in Table 2–3.

SOLUTIONS TO SELF-TEST QUESTIONS

2.1 a. Corporations sell securities in the primary market. The securities are later traded in the secondary market.
   b. The NYSE is a formal exchange that centralizes all trades. NASDAQ is an electronic network of traders.
   c. The capital market is for long-term financing, the money market for short-term financing.
   d. The market for stocks versus the market for bonds and other debt securities.

2.2 Efficient diversification and professional management. Pension funds offer an additional advantage, because investment returns are not taxed until withdrawn from the fund.

2.3 Mutual funds pool investor savings and invest in portfolios of traded securities. Financial institutions such as banks or insurance companies raise money in special ways, for example, by accepting deposits or selling insurance policies. They not only invest in securities but also lend directly to businesses. They provide various other financial services.

2.4 Liquidity, risk reduction by investment in diversified portfolios of securities (through a mutual fund, for example), information provided by trading.

2.5 Rhonda and Reggie need not avoid high-dividend stocks. They can reinvest the dividends and keep reinvesting until it's time to pay the tuition bills. (They will have to pay taxes on the dividends, however, which could affect their investment strategy. We discuss dividends and taxes in Chapter 16.)

2.6 It is not a good investment if the opportunity cost of capital is 15 percent. The investment offers only a 12 percent return.

Accounting and Finance

RELATED WEB LINKS

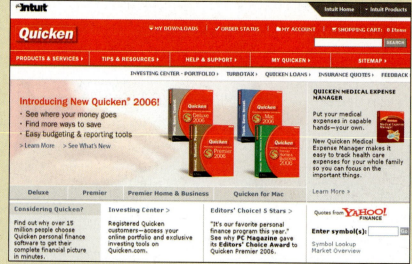

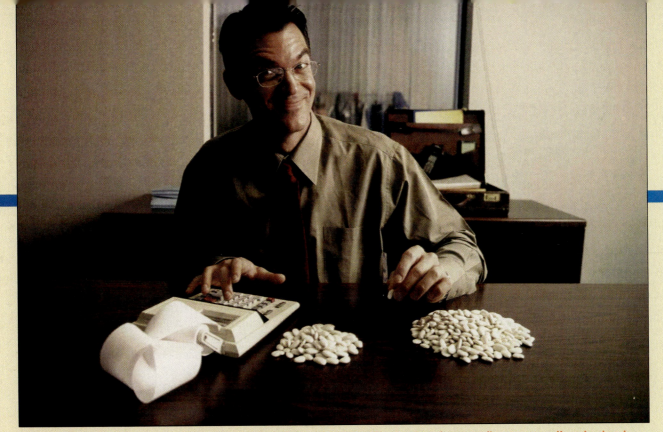

Accounting is not the same as finance, but if you don't understand the basics of accounting, you won't understand finance, either.

© Adamsmith/SuperStock

In Chapter 1 we pointed out that a large corporation is a team effort. All the players—the shareholders, lenders, directors, management, and employees—have a stake in the company's success, and all therefore need to monitor its progress. For this reason the company prepares regular financial accounts and arranges for an independent firm of auditors to certify that these accounts present a "true and fair view."

Until the mid-nineteenth century most businesses were owner-managed and seldom required outside capital beyond personal loans to the proprietor. When businesses were small and there were few outside stakeholders in the firm, accounting could be less formal. But with the industrial revolution and the creation of large railroad and canal companies, the shareholders and bankers demanded information that would help them gauge a firm's financial strength. That was when the accounting profession began to come of age.

We don't want to get lost in the details of accounting practice. But because we will be referring to financial statements throughout this book, it may be useful to review briefly their main features. In this chapter we introduce the major financial statements: the balance sheet, the income statement, and the statement of cash flow. We discuss the important differences between income and cash flow and between book values and market values. We also discuss the federal tax system.

This chapter is our first look at financial statements and is meant primarily to serve as a brief review of your accounting class. It will be far from our last look. For example, we will return (in Chapter 17) to see how managers use financial statements to analyze a firm's performance and assess its financial strength.

After studying this chapter you should be able to

- Interpret the information contained in the balance sheet, income statement, and statement of cash flows.
- Distinguish between market and book values.
- Explain why income differs from cash flow.
- Understand the essential features of the taxation of corporate and personal income.

3.1 The Balance Sheet

balance sheet
Financial statement that shows the firm's assets and liabilities at a particular time.

Firms need to raise cash to acquire the many assets used in their businesses. In the process of raising that cash, they also acquire liabilities to those who provide funding. The **balance sheet** presents a snapshot of the firm's assets and liabilities at one particular moment. The assets—representing the uses of the cash raised—are listed on the left-hand side of the balance sheet. The liabilities—representing the sources of that cash—are listed on the right.

Some assets can be turned more easily into cash than others; these are known as *liquid* assets. The accountant puts the most liquid assets at the top of the list and works down to the least liquid. Look, for example, at Table 3–1, which shows the consolidated balance sheet for PepsiCo, Inc., at the end of 2004.[1] ("Consolidated" simply means that the balance sheet shows the position of PepsiCo and any companies it owns.) You can see that Pepsi had $1,280 million of cash and marketable securities. In addition, it had sold goods worth $2,999 million but had not yet received payment. These payments are due soon and therefore the balance sheet shows the unpaid bills or *accounts receivable* (or simply *receivables*) as an asset. The next asset consists of inventories. These may be (1) raw materials and ingredients that the firm bought from suppliers, (2) work in process, and (3) finished products waiting to be shipped from the warehouse. Of course, there are always some items that don't fit into neat categories. So there is a fourth entry, *other current assets*.

Up to this point all the assets in Pepsi's balance sheet are likely to be used or turned into cash in the near future. They are therefore described as *current assets*. The next assets listed in the balance sheet are longer-lived or *fixed assets* and include items such as buildings, equipment, and vehicles.

The balance sheet shows that the gross value of Pepsi's property, plant, and equipment is $15,930 million. This is what the assets originally cost. But they are unlikely to be worth that now. For example, suppose the company bought a delivery van 2 years ago; that van may be worth far less now than Pepsi paid for it. It might in principle be possible for the accountant to estimate separately the value today of the van, but this would be costly and somewhat subjective. Accountants rely instead on rules of thumb to estimate the *depreciation* in the value of assets and with rare exceptions they stick to these rules. For example, in the case of that delivery van the accountant may deduct a third of the original cost each year to reflect its declining value. So if Pepsi bought the van 2 years ago for $15,000, the balance sheet would show that accumulated depreciation is $2 \times \$5,000 = \$10,000$. Net of depreciation the value is only $5,000. Table 3–1 shows that Pepsi's total accumulated depreciation on fixed assets is $7,781 million. So while the assets cost $15,930 million, their net value in the accounts is only $15,930 - \$7,781 = \$8,149$ million.

In addition to its tangible assets, Pepsi also has valuable intangible assets, such as its brand name, skilled management, and a well-trained labor force. Accountants are generally reluctant to record these intangible assets in the balance sheet unless they can be readily identified and valued.

There is, however, one important exception. When Pepsi has acquired other businesses in the past, it has paid more for their assets than the value shown in the firms' accounts. This difference is shown in Pepsi's balance sheet as "goodwill." Most of the intangible assets on Pepsi's balance sheet consist of goodwill.

Now look at the right-hand portion of Pepsi's balance sheet, which shows where the money to buy the assets came from. The accountant starts by looking at the company's liabilities—that is, the money owed by the company. First come those liabilities that are likely to be paid off most rapidly. For example, Pepsi has borrowed $1,054 million, due to be repaid shortly. It also owes its suppliers $4,594 million for goods that have been delivered but not yet paid for. These unpaid bills are shown as *accounts*

---

[1] We have simplified and eliminated some of the detail in PepsiCo's published financial statements.

TABLE 3–1

CONSOLIDATED BALANCE SHEET FOR PEPSICO, INC. AS OF DECEMBER 31 (millions of dollars)					
Assets	**2004**	**2003**	**Liabilities and Shareholders' Equity**	**2004**	**2003**
Current assets			Current liabilities		
Cash and marketable securities	1,280	820	Debt due for repayment	1,054	591
Receivables	2,999	2,830	Accounts payable	4,594	5,213
Inventories	1,541	1,412	Other current liabilities	1,104	611
Other current assets	2,819	1,868	Total current liabilities	6,752	6,415
Total current assets	8,639	6,930			
			Long-term debt	2,397	1,702
Fixed assets			Deferred income taxes	1,216	1,261
Tangible fixed assets			Other long-term liabilities	4,050	4,075
Property, plant, and equipment	15,930	14,755	Total liabilities	14,415	13,453
Less accumulated depreciation	7,781	6,927			
Net tangible fixed assets	8,149	7,828	Shareholders' equity		
Intangible fixed assets			Common stock and other paid-in capital	648	1,833
Goodwill	3,909	3,796	Retained earnings	12,924	10,041
Other intangible assets	1,531	1,587	Total shareholders' equity	13,572	11,874
Total intangible fixed assets	5,440	5,383	Total liabilities and shareholders' equity	27,987	25,327
Total fixed assets	13,589	13,211			
Other assets	5,759	5,186			
Total assets	27,987	25,327			

Note: Column sums subject to rounding error.
Source: PepsiCo Annual Report, 2004.

payable (or *payables*). Both the borrowings and the payables are debts that Pepsi must repay within the year. They are therefore classified as *current liabilities.*

Pepsi's current assets total $8,639 million; its current liabilities amount to $6,752 million. Therefore the difference between the value of Pepsi's current assets and its current liabilities is $8,639 – $6,752 = $1,887 million. This figure is known as Pepsi's *net current assets or net working capital.* It roughly measures the company's potential reservoir of cash.

Below the current liabilities Pepsi's accountants have listed the firm's long-term liabilities—that is, debts that come due after the end of a year. You can see that banks and other investors have made long-term loans to Pepsi of $2,397 million.

Pepsi's liabilities are financial obligations to various parties. For example, when Pepsi buys goods from its suppliers, it has a liability to pay for them; when it borrows from the bank, it has a liability to repay the loan. Thus the suppliers and the bank have first claim on the firm's assets. What is left over after the liabilities have been paid off belongs to the shareholders. This figure is known as the shareholders' *equity.* For Pepsi the total value of shareholders' equity amounts to $13,572 million. A small part of this sum ($648 million) has resulted from the sale of shares to investors. The remainder ($12,924 million) has come from earnings that Pepsi has retained and invested on shareholders' behalf.

Figure 3–1 shows how the separate items in the balance sheet link together. There are two classes of assets—current assets, which will soon be used or turned into cash, and long-term or "fixed" assets, which may be either tangible or intangible. There are also two classes of liability—current liabilities, which are due for payment shortly, and long-term liabilities.

FIGURE 3-1

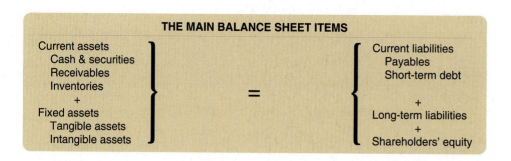

The difference between the assets and the liabilities represents the amount of the shareholders' equity. This is the basic balance sheet identity. Shareholders are sometimes called "residual claimants" on the firm. We mean by this that shareholders' equity is what is left over when the liabilities of the firm are subtracted from its assets:

Shareholders' equity = total assets – total liabilities

Self-Test 3.1   **Suppose that Pepsi borrows $500 million by issuing new long-term bonds. It places $100 million of the proceeds in the bank and uses $400 million to buy new machinery. What items of the balance sheet would change? Would shareholders' equity change?**

By the way, it is easy to obtain the financial statements of almost any publicly traded firm. For example, the Web site **www.reportgallery.com** allows you to access the financial reports of over 2,000 companies. In addition, the Market Insight Web site access that comes with this text provides Excel spreadsheets containing annual financial statements for many firms over several years. See **www. mhhe. com/ edumarketinsight**.

Book Values and Market Values

Throughout this book we will frequently make a distinction between the book values of the assets shown in the balance sheet and their market values.

generally accepted accounting principles (GAAP)
Procedures for preparing financial statements.

Items in the balance sheet are valued according to **generally accepted accounting principles,** commonly called **GAAP.** These state that assets must be shown in the balance sheet at their *historical cost* adjusted for depreciation. **Book values** are therefore "backward-looking" measures of value. They are based on the past cost of the asset, not its current market price or value to the firm. For example, suppose that a printing press cost McGraw-Hill $1 million 2 years ago but that in today's market such presses sell for $1.3 million. The book value of the press would be less than its market value, and the balance sheet would understate the value of McGraw-Hill's assets.

book value
Net worth of the firm according to the balance sheet.

Or consider a specialized plant that Intel develops for producing special-purpose computer chips at a cost of $800 million. The book value of the plant is $800 million less depreciation. But suppose that shortly after the plant is constructed, a new chip makes the existing one obsolete. The market value of Intel's new plant could fall by 50 percent or more. In this case market value would be less than book value.

The difference between book value and market value is greater for some assets than for others. It is zero in the case of cash but potentially very large for fixed assets where the accountant starts with the initial cost of the fixed assets and then depreciates that figure according to a prespecified schedule. The purpose of depreciation is to allocate the original cost of the asset over its life, and the rules governing the depreciation of asset values do not reflect actual loss of market value. As a result, the market value of fixed assets usually is much higher than the book value, but sometimes it is less.

The same goes for the right-hand side of the balance sheet. In the case of liabilities the accountant simply records the amount of money that you have promised to pay. For short-term liabilities this figure is generally close to the market value of that promise. For example, if you owe the bank $1 million tomorrow, the accounts show a book liability of $1 million. As long as you are not bankrupt, that $1 million is also roughly the value to the bank of your promise. But now suppose that $1 million is not due to be repaid for several years. The accounts still show a liability of $1 million, but how much your debt is worth depends on what happens to interest rates. If interest rates rise after you have issued the debt, lenders may not be prepared to pay as much as $1 million for your debt; if interest rates fall, they may be prepared to pay more than $1 million.[2] Thus the market value of a long-term liability may be higher or lower than the book value. Market values of assets and liabilities do not generally equal their book values. Book values are based on historical or *original* values. Market values measure *current* values of assets and liabilities.

The difference between book value and market value is likely to be greatest for shareholders' equity. The book value of equity measures the cash that shareholders have contributed in the past plus the cash that the company has retained and reinvested in the business on their behalf. But this often bears little resemblance to the total market value that investors place on the shares.

If the market price of the firm's shares falls through the floor, don't try telling the shareholders that the book value is satisfactory—they won't want to hear. Shareholders are concerned with the market value of their shares; market value, not book value, is the price at which they can sell their shares. Managers who wish to keep their shareholders happy will focus on market values.

We will often find it useful to think about the firm in terms of a *market-value balance sheet*. Like a conventional balance sheet, a market-value balance sheet lists the firm's assets, but it records each asset at its current market value rather than at historical cost less depreciation. Similarly, each liability is shown at its market value. The difference between the market values of assets and liabilities is the market value of the shareholders' equity claim. The stock price is simply the market value of shareholders' equity divided by the number of outstanding shares.

EXAMPLE 3.1   ▶   Market- versus Book-Value Balance Sheets

Jupiter has developed a revolutionary auto production process that enables it to produce cars 20 percent more efficiently than any rival. It has invested $10 billion in producing its new plant. To finance the investment, Jupiter borrowed $4 billion and raised the remaining funds by selling new shares of stock in the firm. There are currently 100 million shares of stock outstanding. Investors are very excited about Jupiter's prospects. They believe that the flow of profits from the new plant justifies a stock price of $75.

If these are Jupiter's only assets, the book-value balance sheet immediately after it has made the investment is as follows:

BOOK-VALUE BALANCE SHEET FOR JUPITER MOTORS (figures in billions of dollars)			
Assets		**Liabilities and Shareholders' Equity**	
Auto plant	$10	Debt	$4
		Shareholders' equity	6

Investors are placing a *market value* on Jupiter's equity of $7.5 billion ($75 per share times 100 million shares). We assume that the debt outstanding is worth $4

---

[2] We will show you how changing interest rates affect the market value of debt in Chapter 5.

billion.[3] Therefore, if you owned all Jupiter's shares and all its debt, the value of your investment would be $7.5 + $4 = $11.5 billion. In this case you would own the company lock, stock, and barrel and would be entitled to all its cash flows. Because you can buy the entire company for $11.5 billion, the total value of Jupiter's assets must also be $11.5 billion. In other words, the market value of the assets must be equal to the market value of the liabilities plus the market value of the shareholders' equity.

We can now draw up the market-value balance sheet as follows:

MARKET-VALUE BALANCE SHEET FOR JUPITER MOTORS (figures in billions of dollars)			
Assets		**Liabilities and Shareholders' Equity**	
Auto plant	$11.5	Debt	$4
		Shareholders' equity	7.5

Notice that the market value of Jupiter's plant is $1.5 billion more than the plant cost to build. The difference is due to the superior profits that investors expect the plant to earn. Thus in contrast to the balance sheet shown in the company's books, the market-value balance sheet is forward-looking. It depends on the profits that investors expect the assets to provide. ◀

Is it surprising that market value exceeds book value? It shouldn't be. Firms find it attractive to raise money to invest in various projects because they believe the projects will be worth more than they cost. Otherwise, why bother? You will usually find that shares of stock sell for more than the value shown in the company's books.

Self-Test 3.2

a. What would be Jupiter's price per share if the auto plant had a market value of $14 billion?
b. How would you reassess the value of the auto plant if the value of outstanding stock were $8 billion?

3.2 The Income Statement

income statement
Financial statement that shows the revenues, expenses, and net income of a firm over a period of time.

If Pepsi's balance sheet resembles a snapshot of the firm at a particular time, its **income statement** is like a video. It shows how profitable the firm has been during the past year.

Look at the summary income statement in Table 3–2. You can see that during 2004 Pepsi sold goods worth $29,261 million and that the total expenses of producing and selling goods was ($12,142 + $10,142) = $22,284 million. The largest expense item, amounting to $12,142 million, consisted of the raw materials, labor, and so on, that were needed to produce the goods. Almost all the remaining expenses were administrative expenses such as head office costs, advertising, and distribution.

In addition to these out-of-pocket expenses, Pepsi also made a deduction for the value of the plant and equipment used up in producing the goods. In 2004 this charge for depreciation was $1,264 million. Thus Pepsi's *total earnings before interest and taxes* (EBIT) were

$$\text{EBIT} = \text{total revenues} - \text{costs} - \text{depreciation}$$
$$= \quad 29,261 \quad - 22,284 \quad - 1,264$$
$$= \$5,713 \text{ million}$$

---

[3] Jupiter has borrowed $4 billion to finance its investment, but if the interest rate has changed in the meantime, the debt could be worth more or less than $4 billion.

TABLE 3-2

CONSOLIDATED STATEMENT OF INCOME FOR PEPSICO, INC., 2004 (figures in millions of dollars)	
Net sales	+ 29,261
Cost of goods sold	− 12,142
Selling, general & administrative expenses	− 10,142
Depreciation	− 1,264
Earnings before interest and income taxes	5,713
Interest expense	167
Taxable income	5,546
Taxes	1,334
Net income	4,212
Allocation of net income	
Dividends	1,329
Addition to retained earnings	2,883

Source: PepsiCo *Annual Report,* 2004.

The remainder of the income statement shows where these earnings went. As we saw earlier, Pepsi has partly financed its investment in plant and equipment by borrowing. In 2004 it paid $167 million of interest on this borrowing. A further slice of the profit went to the government in the form of taxes. This amounted in 2004 to $1,334 million. The $4,212 million that was left over after paying interest and taxes belonged to the shareholders. Of this sum Pepsi paid out $1,329 million in dividends and reinvested the remaining $2,883 million in the business. Presumably, these reinvested funds made the company more valuable.

The $2,883 of earnings that PepsiCo retained, or reinvested, in the firm in 2004 show up on its balance sheet as an increase in shareholders' equity. Notice that retained earnings in Table 3–1 increased by $2,883 million in 2004, from $10,041 million to $12,924 million.

Profits versus Cash Flow

It is important to distinguish between Pepsi's profits and the cash that the company generates. Here are three reasons why profits and cash are not the same:

1. When Pepsi's accountants prepare the income statement, they do not simply count the cash coming in and the cash going out. Instead the accountant starts with the cash payments but then divides these payments into two groups—current expenditures (such as wages) and capital expenditures (such as the purchase of new machinery). Current expenditures are deducted from current profits. However, rather than deducting the cost of machinery in the year it is purchased, the accountant makes an annual charge for depreciation. Thus the cost of machinery is spread over its forecast life.

   When calculating profits, the accountant does *not* deduct the expenditure on new equipment that year, even though cash is paid out. However, the accountant *does* deduct depreciation on assets previously purchased, even though no cash is currently paid out. For example, suppose a $100,000 investment is depreciated by $10,000 a year.[4] This depreciation is treated as an annual expense, although the cash actually went out of the door when the asset was first purchased. For this reason, the deduction for depreciation is classified as a *noncash* expense. To calculate the cash produced by the business, it is necessary to *add back* the depreciation charge (which is not a cash payment) and to *subtract* the expenditure on new capital equipment (which is a cash payment).

---

[4] We discuss depreciation rules in Chapter 8.

2. Consider the following stages in a manufacturing business. In period 1 the firm produces the goods; it sells them in period 2 for $100; and it is paid for them in period 3. The general rule is to recognize revenue at the time of the sale rather than when the cash is actually received. Therefore, although the cash does not arrive until period 3, the sale is included in the income statement for period 2. However, the accountant does not ignore the fact that the bills have not been paid. When the sale is made in period 2, the figure for accounts receivable in the balance sheet is adjusted to show that the company's customers owe an extra $100 in unpaid bills. Next period, when the customers pay their bills, the firm receives cash and receivables decline by $100. This payment has no impact on profits in that period. The cash that the company *receives* is equal to the sales shown in the income statement less the increase in unpaid bills:

Period:	2	3
Sales	100	0
− Change in receivables	100	(100)
= Cash received	0	+100

3. The accountant also tries to match the costs of producing the goods with the revenues from the sale. For example, suppose that it costs $60 in period 1 to produce the goods that are then sold in period 2 for $100. It would be misleading to say that the business made a loss in period 1 (when it produced the goods) and was very profitable in period 2 (when it sold them). Therefore, to provide a fairer measure of the firm's profitability, the income statement will not show the $60 as an expense of producing the goods until they are sold in period 2. This practice is known as *accrual accounting.* The accountant gathers together all expenses that are associated with a sale and deducts them from the revenues to calculate profit, even though the expenses may have occurred in an earlier period.

   Of course, the accountant cannot ignore the fact that the firm spent money on producing the goods in period 1. So the expenditure will be shown in period 1 as an *investment* in inventories. Subsequently in period 2, when the goods are sold, the inventories would decline again.

   In our example, the cash is paid out when the goods are manufactured in period 1, but this expense is not recognized until period 2 when the goods are sold. The cash *outflow* is equal to the cost of goods sold, which is shown in the income statement, plus the change in inventories:

Period:	1	2
Cost of goods sold	0	60
+ Change in inventories	60	(60)
= Cash paid out	+ 60	0

EXAMPLE 3.2 ▶ Profits versus Cash Flows

Suppose a firm pays $100 in period 1 to produce some goods. It sells those goods for $150 in period 2, but it does not collect payment from its customers until period 3. The firm would "book" a $50 profit in period 2, recognizing both cost ($100) and revenue ($150) when the sale takes place. However, its cash flow in period 2 would be zero, as we see from the following table:

Period:	1	2	3
Sales	0	150	0
− Change in accounts receivable	0	150	(150)
− Cost of goods sold	0	100	0
− Change in inventories	100	(100)	0
= Net cash flow	−100	0	+150

Think about why this makes sense. In period 1, the firm expends $100 to produce the product. The product is not sold then, so the cost of producing the product is not recognized in this period; instead, the expenditure is treated as an investment in inventory, which is a negative cash flow. In period 2, the product is sold, but no cash trades hands. Instead, under accrual accounting, $150 is booked as a sale, with a corresponding investment in accounts receivable. At the same time, the $100 cost of goods sold is recognized in this period, and because the product is sold, the investment in inventories is reversed. Finally, in period 3, the cash is collected. Accounts receivable is reduced by the $150 cash inflow. ◀

Self-Test 3.3   Consider a firm similar to the one in Example 3.2. It spends $200 to produce goods in period 1. In period 2 it sells half of those goods for $150, but it doesn't collect payment until one period later. In period 3, it sells the other half of the goods for $150, and it collects payment on these sales in period 4. Calculate the profits and the cash flows for this firm in periods 1 to 4 by completing a table like that in Example 3.2.

3.3 The Statement of Cash Flows

The firm requires *cash* when it buys new plant and machinery or when it pays interest to the bank and dividends to the shareholders. Therefore, the financial manager needs to keep track of the cash that is coming in and going out.

We have seen that the firm's cash flow can be quite different from its net income. These differences can arise for at least two reasons:

1. The income statement does not recognize capital expenditures as expenses in the year that the capital goods are paid for. Instead, it spreads those expenses over time in the form of an annual deduction for depreciation.
2. The income statement uses the accrual method of accounting, which means that revenues and expenses are recognized when sales are made, rather than when the cash is received or paid out.

statement of cash flows
Financial statement that shows the firm's cash receipts and cash payments over a period of time.

The **statement of cash flows** shows the firm's cash inflows and outflows from operations as well as from its investments and financing activities. Table 3–3 is the cash-flow statement for Pepsi. It contains three sections. The first shows the cash flow from operations. This is the cash generated from Pepsi's normal business activities. Next comes the cash that Pepsi has invested in plant and equipment or in the acquisition of new businesses. The final section reports cash flows from financing activities such as the sale of new debt or stock. We will look at these sections in turn.

The first section, cash flow from operations, starts with net income but adjusts that figure for those parts of the income statement that do not involve cash coming in or going out. Therefore, it adds back the allowance for depreciation because

TABLE 3–3

CONSOLIDATED STATEMENT OF CASH FLOWS FOR PEPSICO	
For the year ended December 31, 2004 (figures in millions)	
Cash Provided by Operations	
Net income	4,212
Noncash expenses	
Depreciation and amortization	854
Changes in working capital	
Decrease (increase) in accounts receivable	(169)
Decrease (increase) in inventories	(129)
Decrease (increase) in other current assets	(951)
Increase (decrease) in accounts payable	(619)
Increase (decrease) in short-term debt	463
Increase (decrease) in other current liabilities	493
Cash provided by operations	4,154
Cash Flows from Investments	
Cash provided by (used for) disposal of (additions to) property, plant, and equipment	(1,175)
Sales (acquisitions) of other investments	(630)
Cash provided by (used for) investments	(1,805)
Cash Provided by (Used for) Financing Activities	
Additions to (reduction in) long-term debt	695
Additions to (reduction in) taxes and other long-term liabilities	(70)
Dividends paid	(1,329)
Net issues (repurchases) of stock	(1,185)
Cash provided by (used for) financing activities	(1,889)
Net increase (decrease) in cash and cash equivalents	460

Note: Column sums subject to rounding error.
Source: PepsiCo Annual Report, 2004.

depreciation is not a cash outflow, even though it is treated as an expense in the income statement.

Any additions to current assets need to be *subtracted* from net income, since these absorb cash but do not show up in the income statement. Conversely, any additions to current liabilities need to be *added* to net income because these release cash. For example, you can see that the increase of $169 million in accounts receivable is subtracted from income, because this represents sales that Pepsi includes in its income statement even though it has not yet received payment from its customers. In addition, Pepsi increased inventories by $129 million. The accountant did not deduct this figure as part of the cost of the goods sold by Pepsi in 2004, even though Pepsi purchased these goods. Thus the $129 million increase in inventories must be subtracted to calculate the cash flow from operations.

We have pointed out that depreciation is not a cash payment; it is simply the accountant's allocation to the current year of the original cost of the capital equipment. However, cash does flow out the door when the firm actually buys and pays for new capital equipment. Therefore, these capital expenditures are set out in the second section of the cash-flow statement. You can see that Pepsi spent $1,175 on new capital equipment. It also spent $630 million on other investments. Total cash used by investments was $1,805 million.

Finally, the third section of the cash-flow statement shows the cash from financing activities. Pepsi increased net long-term debt by $695, and used $70 million to

Understanding Financial Statements

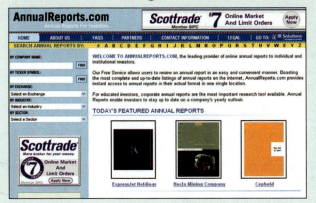

Source: IR Solutions/Annualreports.com, 2005.

You can find a company's financial statements on its home page, but to avoid getting entangled in a web of company promotional material it is usually easier to log on first to www.annualreports.com. Find the latest financial statements for a large nonfinancial company and draw up a simplified balance sheet, income statement, and statement of cash flows as in Tables 3–1, 3–2, and 3–3. Some companies' financial statements can be extremely complex; try to find a relatively straightforward business. Also, as far as possible, use the same headings as in these tables, and don't hesitate to group some items as "other current assets" or "other expenses," etc. Look first at your simplified balance sheet. How much was the company owed by its customers in the form of unpaid bills? What liabilities does the company need to meet within a year? What was the original cost of the company's fixed assets? Now look at the income statement. What were the company's earnings before interest and taxes (EBIT)? Finally, turn to the cash-flow statement. Did changes in working capital add to cash or use it up?

retire other long-term liabilities; it used $1,185 million to buy back its stock and $1,329 million to pay dividends to its stockholders.[5]

To summarize, the cash-flow statement tells us that Pepsi generated $4,154 million from operations, it spent $1,805 million on new investments, and it used $1,889 in financing activities. Pepsi earned and raised more cash than it spent. Therefore, its cash balance rose by $460 million. To calculate this change in cash balance, we subtract the uses of cash from the sources:

	In Millions
Cash flow from operations	$4,154
− Cash flow for new investment	− 1,805
+ Cash provided by new financing	− 1,889
= Change in cash balance	460

Look back at Table 3–1 and you will see that cash accounts on the balance sheet did indeed increase by this amount in 2004.

Self-Test 3.4

Would the following activities increase or decrease the firm's cash balance?

a. Inventories are increased.
b. The firm reduces its accounts payable.
c. The firm issues additional common stock.
d. The firm buys new equipment.

3.4 Accounting Practice and Malpractice

U.S. accounting rules are spelled out by the Financial Accounting Standards Board (FASB) and its generally accepted accounting principles (GAAP). Yet inevitably, rules and principles leave room for discretion. Managers under pressure to perform may be

---

[5] You might think that interest payments also ought to be listed in this section. However, it is usual to include interest in the first section with cash flow from operations. This is because, unlike dividends, interest payments are not discretionary. The firm must pay interest when a payment comes due, so these payments are treated as a business expense rather than as a financing decision.

tempted to take advantage of leeway in how they measure earnings and book values to present their financial statements in the best possible light. And in more extreme cases, some companies simply break the rules.

The years between 2000 and 2004 were filled with a seemingly unending series of accounting scandals. Enron and its auditor Arthur Andersen came to symbolize the crisis in corporate accounting. Enron used so-called special-purpose vehicles to hide debt and inflate profits, and Arthur Andersen was convicted of shredding documents that would have provided evidence concerning Enron's activities. Enron was only the tip of the iceberg, however. Other firms such as Global Crossing, Qwest Communications, and WorldCom misstated profits by billions of dollars. Sunbeam and Xerox used questionable sales assumptions to inflate profits. At the end of 2004, mortgage giant Fannie Mae was found to have improperly accounted for transactions in derivative contracts, reducing its stated profits back to 2001 by $9 billion. Nor was this just a U.S. phenomenon. Parmalat, an Italian dairy company, was dubbed "Europe's Enron" after it falsified the existence of a bank account to the tune of $5.5 billion, eventually entering bankruptcy. The French media and entertainment firm Vivendi Universal nearly ended up in bankruptcy after it was accused of accounting fraud.

In response to these and other scandals, Congress passed the Sarbanes-Oxley Act in 2002. The act attempts to ensure that the firm's financial reports accurately represent its financial condition. The act created the Public Company Accounting Oversight Board to oversee the auditing of public companies, requires CEOs and CFOs to personally sign off on the firm's financial statements, and requires independent financial experts to serve on the audit committee of the board of directors.

However, accounting rules still give firms considerable leeway when preparing their financial statements. Here are a few examples of gray areas that allow for judgment calls.

- *Stock options.* If you pay your employees in cash, that cost is deducted from the company's earnings. But until recently, if you instead gave them options to buy the firm's stock, the value of those options would not show up as an expense, and therefore reported earnings would be correspondingly higher. After more than a decade of contentious debate, FASB decided to require firms to treat stock options as an expense starting in 2005. However, there is no standard means to value these options, so there is still considerable room for discretion in their impact on earnings.
- *Cookie-jar reserves.* Firms know that in the course of business things occasionally will go wrong. For example, some customers who buy on credit may not pay their bills. Firms estimate a fair allowance for these events and create reserve accounts to recognize their expected impact on earnings. But sometimes it can be tempting to take a rosy view of the proportion of bills that will go unpaid, and thereby increase reported earnings. In other cases, some firms have actually overestimated likely future expenses, or "overreserved," so that these reserves could be "released" later in a downturn, thus creating the illusion of smooth and consistent earnings growth. In other words, when extra income is needed, the firm can raid its "cookie-jar reserves."
- *Off-balance-sheet assets and liabilities.* Suppose that one firm guarantees the debt of another firm. This obligation may require payments down the road, but it may not be reported as part of the firm's outstanding debt. This appears to be one way that Enron was able to hide the extent of its debt obligations from the public.
- *Revenue recognition.* As we saw above, firms record a sale when it is made, not when the customer actually pays. But there are occasions when it can be hard to know when a sale occurs. An extreme (and potentially fraudulent) version of this problem is called "channel stuffing." The firm "sells" large quantities of goods to customers, but gives them the right to later refuse delivery or return the product. The revenue from the "sale" is booked immediately, but the likely returns are not

Called to Account

No one becomes an auditor because the job is adventurous. In recent years, however, the profession has been really rather racy. Auditors have been implicated in fraud after fraud. The Enron scandal brought down Arthur Andersen, which had been one of the profession's five giant firms. Now a scandal at Italy's Parmalat that was uncovered in late 2003 threatens Deloitte & Touche, another global giant. And new scandals are still emerging: most recently, financial manipulation was discovered at Fannie Mae, America's quasi-governmental mortgage lender, and at Nortel Networks, a telecoms-equipment group.

Investors depend on the integrity of the auditing profession. In its absence, capital markets would lack a vital base of trust. So it is no surprise that scandals have triggered changes in the profession. In America it has seen self-regulation dissolved in favor of the Public Company Accounting Oversight Board (PCAOB), in effect, a new regulator. It has been deluged with new rules, restrictions and requirements as part of the Sarbanes-Oxley act. In Europe the Eighth Company Law Directive, which, among other things, deals with the auditing profession, is progressing, albeit slowly, toward enactment. Britain's Office of Fair Trading is in the midst of scrutinizing its audit industry.

One consequence of all this change is that audits have become tougher. The requirement introduced by Sarbanes-Oxley that auditors report to independent nonexecutive board directors rather than company management has reduced one overt conflict of interest. The certification of financial reports by chief executives and chief financial officers has focused minds. And the PCAOB has begun its inspections of audit quality and internal controls at auditing firms.

Auditors themselves say they have toughened their standards and beefed up internal controls. Audit committees are taking their roles more seriously and asking tougher questions of management and auditors. Yet despite this flurry of activity, behind the scenes there is a feeling among auditors that they are still a long way from meeting all the challenges they face.

Fearing lawsuits, accounting rules are increasingly interpreted prescriptively rather than based on broad principles that are seen as too fuzzy to hold up in court. Auditors themselves, fearful of lawsuits, are inclined to adopt a "check-the-box" approach, adhering strictly to accounting rules rather than exercising (necessarily subjective) judgment. "Who wants to be a partner in a firm that faces billions of dollars in lawsuits?" asks one company boss.

recognized until they occur in a future accounting period. Channel stuffing hit the headlines in 1997 when the head of Sunbeam Corporation, "Chainsaw" Al Dunlap, allegedly moved millions of dollars of appliances to distributors and retailers to produce record earnings.

Investors worry about the fact that some companies may be particularly tempted to inflate their earnings in such ways. They refer to such firms as having "low-quality" earnings, and they place a correspondingly lower value on the firms' stock.

The nearby box discusses some of the difficult issues currently facing the auditing profession. The box points out that trust in a firm's financial statements is crucial to the operation of capital markets where the firm goes to raise funds. There is a long way to go before that trust is regained.

3.5 Taxes

Taxes often have a major effect on financial decisions. Therefore, we should explain how corporations and investors are taxed.

Corporate Tax

Companies pay tax on their income. Table 3–4 shows that there are special low rates of corporate tax for small companies, but for large companies (those with income over $18.33 million) the corporate tax rate is 35 percent.[6] Thus for every $100 that the firm earns it pays $35 in corporate tax.

When firms calculate taxable income they are allowed to deduct expenses. These expenses include an allowance for depreciation. However, the Internal Revenue Service (IRS) specifies the rates of depreciation that the company can use for different types of equipment.[7] The rates of depreciation that are used to calculate taxes are not the same as the rates that are used when the firm reports its profits to shareholders.

---

[6] In addition, corporations pay state income taxes, which we ignore here for simplicity.

[7] We will tell you more about these allowances in Chapter 8.

TABLE 3–4 Corporate tax rates, 2005

Taxable Income, Dollars	Tax Rate, %
0–50,000	15
50,001–75,000	25
75,001–100,000	34
100,001–18,333,333	Varies between 39 and 34
Over 18,333,333	35

TABLE 3–5 Firms A and B both have earnings before interest and taxes (EBIT) of $100 million, but A pays out part of its profits as debt interest. This reduces the corporate tax paid by A.

	Firm A	Firm B
EBIT	100	100
Interest	40	0
Pretax income	60	100
Tax (35% of pretax income)	21	35
Net income	39	65

Note: Figures in millions of dollars.

The company is also allowed to deduct interest paid to debtholders when calculating its taxable income, but dividends paid to shareholders are not deductible. These dividends are therefore paid out of after-tax income. Table 3–5 provides an example of how interest payments reduce corporate taxes.

The bad news about taxes is that each extra dollar of revenues increases taxable income by $1 and results in 35 cents of extra taxes. The good news is that each extra dollar of expense *reduces* taxable income by $1 and therefore reduces taxes by 35 cents. For example, if the firm borrows money, every dollar of interest it pays on the loan reduces taxes by 35 cents. Therefore, after-tax income is reduced by only 65 cents.

Self-Test 3.5

Recalculate the figures in Table 3–5 assuming that Firm A now has to make interest payments of $60 million. What happens to taxes paid? Does net income fall by the additional $20 million interest payment compared with the case considered in Table 3–5, where interest expense was only $40 million?

When firms make profits, they pay 35 percent of the profits to the Internal Revenue Service. But the process doesn't work in reverse; if the firm makes a loss, the IRS does not simply send it a check for 35 percent of the loss. However, the firm can carry the losses back, deduct them from taxable income in earlier years, and claim a refund of past taxes. Losses can also be carried forward and deducted from taxable income in the future.[8]

Personal Tax

Table 3–6 shows the U.S. rates of personal tax. Notice that as income increases the tax rate also increases. Notice also that the top personal tax rate is higher than the top corporate rate.

marginal tax rate
Additional taxes owed per dollar of additional income.

The tax rates presented in Table 3–6 are **marginal tax rates.** The marginal tax rate is the tax that the individual pays on each *extra* dollar of income. For example, as a single taxpayer, you would pay 10 cents of tax on each extra dollar you earn when your income is below $7,300, but once income exceeds $7,300, you would pay 15 cents of tax on each extra dollar of income up to an income of $29,700. If your total

---

[8] Losses can be carried back for a maximum of 3 years and forward for up to 15 years.

INTERNET INSIDER

1010001
0100
1010100010
11010
00101

Tax Rates

The schedule of tax rates for individuals changes frequently. Check the latest schedules on either **www.irs.gov** or **finance. yahoo.com**. What is your marginal tax rate if you are single with a taxable income of $70,000? What is your average tax rate?

income is $40,000, your tax bill is 10 percent of the first $7,300 of income, 15 percent of the next $22,400 (i.e., 29,700 − 7,300), and 25 percent of the remaining $10,300:

$$\text{Tax} = (.10 \times \$7,300) + (.15 \times \$22,400) + (.25 \times \$10,300) = \$6,665$$

average tax rate
Total taxes owed divided by total income.

The **average tax rate** is simply the total tax bill divided by total income. In this example it is $6,665/$40,000 = .167 = 16.7 percent. Notice that the average rate is below the marginal rate. This is because of the lower rates on the first $29,700.

Self-Test 3.6

What are the average and marginal tax rates for a single taxpayer with a taxable income of $70,000? What are the average and marginal tax rates for married taxpayers filing joint returns if their joint taxable income is also $70,000?

The tax rates in Table 3–6 apply to "ordinary income," primarily income earned as salary or wages. Interest earnings also are treated as ordinary income. Other investment income is treated differently, however.

For example, dividend income for most individual investors in the United States is taxed at a 15 percent rate. Remember that each dollar of income that the company earns is taxed at the corporate tax rate. If the company then pays a dividend out of this after-tax income, the shareholder also pays personal income tax on the dividend, and so the company's original earnings are taxed twice, first as corporate income and then as dividend income. This treatment is commonly dubbed the "double taxation" of corporate earnings. Suppose instead that the company earns a dollar which is paid out as interest. The dollar escapes corporate tax because the interest payment is considered a business expense that reduces the firm's taxable income, but the individual who

TABLE 3–6 Personal tax rates, 2005

Taxable Income (dollars)		
Single Taxpayers	Married Taxpayers Filing Joint Returns	Tax Rate, %
0–7,300	0–14,600	10
7,300–29,700	14,600–59,400	15
29,700–71,950	59,400–119,950	25
71,950–150,150	119,950–182,800	28
150,150–326,450	182,800–326,450	33
326,450 and above	326,450 and above	35

receives the interest must pay personal tax at the rate on ordinary income. Financial managers need to worry about the tax treatment of investment income, because tax policy will affect the prices individuals are willing to pay for the company's stock or bonds. We will return to these issues in Part 5 of the text.

Capital gains are also taxed, but only when the capital gains are realized. For example, suppose that you bought Bio-technics stock when it was selling for 10 cents a share. Its market price is now $1 a share. As long as you hold on to your stock, there is no tax to pay on your gain. But if you sell, the 90 cents of capital gain is taxed. The marginal tax rate on capital gains for most shareholders is 15 percent.

The tax rates in Table 3–6 apply to individuals. But financial institutions are major investors in corporate securities. These institutions often have special tax provisions. For example, pension funds are not taxed on interest or dividend income or on capital gains.

SUMMARY

What information is contained in the balance sheet, income statement, and statement of cash flows?

Investors and other stakeholders in the firm need regular financial information to help them monitor the firm's progress. Accountants summarize this information in a balance sheet, income statement, and statement of cash flows.

The **balance sheet** provides a snapshot of the firm's assets and liabilities. The assets consist of current assets that can be rapidly turned into cash and fixed assets such as plant and machinery. The liabilities consist of current liabilities that are due for payment within a year and long-term debts. The difference between the assets and the liabilities represents the amount of the shareholders' equity.

The **income statement** measures the profitability of the company during the year. It shows the difference between revenues and expenses.

The **statement of cash flows** measures the sources and uses of cash during the year. The change in the company's cash balance is the difference between sources and uses.

What is the difference between market and book value?

It is important to distinguish between the book values that are shown in the company accounts and the market values of the assets and liabilities. **Book values** are historical measures based on the original cost of an asset. For example, the assets in the balance sheet are shown at their historical cost less an allowance for depreciation. Similarly, the figure for shareholders' equity measures the cash that shareholders have contributed in the past or that the company has reinvested on their behalf. In contrast, **market value** is the current price of an asset or liability.

Why does accounting income differ from cash flow?

Income is not the same as cash flow. There are two reasons for this: (1) Investment in fixed assets is not deducted immediately from income but is instead spread over the expected life of the equipment, and (2) the accountant records revenues when the sale is made, rather than when the customer actually pays the bill, and at the same time deducts the production costs even though those costs may have been incurred earlier.

What are the essential features of the taxation of corporate and personal income?

For large companies the **marginal rate of tax** on income is 35 percent. In calculating taxable income the company deducts an allowance for depreciation and interest payments. It cannot deduct dividend payments to the shareholders.

Individuals are also taxed on their income, which includes dividends and interest on their investments. Capital gains are taxed, but only when the investment is sold and the gain realized.

QUIZ

1. **Balance Sheet.** Construct a balance sheet for Sophie's Sofas given the following data. What is shareholders' equity?

   Cash balances = $10,000
   Inventory of sofas = $200,000
   Store and property = $100,000
   Accounts receivable = $22,000
   Accounts payable = $17,000
   Long-term debt = $170,000

2. **Financial Statements.** Earlier in the chapter, we characterized the balance sheet as providing a snapshot of the firm at one point in time and the income statement as providing a video. What did we mean by this? Is the statement of cash flow more like a snapshot or a video?

3. **Income versus Cash Flow.** Explain why accounting income generally will differ from a firm's cash inflows.

4. **Working Capital.** QuickGrow is in an expanding market, and its sales are increasing by 25 percent per year. Would you expect its net working capital to be increasing or decreasing?

5. **Tax Rates.** Using Table 3–6, calculate the marginal and average tax rates for a single taxpayer with the following incomes:
   a. $20,000
   b. $50,000
   c. $300,000
   d. $3,000,000

6. **Tax Rates.** What would be the marginal and average tax rates for a *corporation* with an income level of $100,000?

7. **Taxes.** A married couple earned $95,000 in 2005. How much did they pay in taxes? What were their marginal and average tax brackets?

8. **Cash Flows.** What impact will the following actions have on the firm's cash balance?
   a. The firm sells some goods from inventory.
   b. The firm sells some machinery to a bank and leases it back for a period of 20 years.
   c. The firm buys back 1 million shares of stock from existing shareholders.

PRACTICE PROBLEMS

9. **Balance Sheet/Income Statement.** The year-end 2005 balance sheet of Brandex Inc. listed common stock and other paid-in capital at $1,100,000 and retained earnings at $3,400,000. The next year, retained earnings were listed at $3,700,000. The firm's net income in 2006 was $900,000. There were no stock repurchases during the year. What were the dividends paid by the firm in 2006?

10. **Taxes.** You have set up your tax preparation firm as an incorporated business. You took $70,000 from the firm as your salary. The firm's taxable income for the year (net of your salary) was $30,000. How much taxes must be paid to the federal government, including both your personal taxes and the firm's taxes? Assume you pay personal taxes as an unmarried taxpayer. By how much will you reduce the total tax bill by reducing your salary to $50,000, thereby leaving the firm with taxable income of $50,000? Use the tax rates presented in Tables 3–4 and 3–6.

11. **Market versus Book Values.** The founder of Alchemy Products, Inc., discovered a way to turn lead into gold and patented this new technology. He then formed a corporation and invested $200,000 in setting up a production plant. He believes that he could sell his patent for $50 million.

a. What are the book value and market value of the firm?

b. If there are 2 million shares of stock in the new corporation, what would be the price per share and the book value per share?

12. **Income Statement.** Sheryl's Shingles had sales of $10,000 in 2005. The cost of goods sold was $6,500, general and administrative expenses were $1,000, interest expenses were $500, and depreciation was $1,000. The firm's tax rate is 35 percent.

   a. What is earnings before interest and taxes?
   b. What is net income?
   c. What is cash flow from operations?

13. **Cash Flow.** Can cash flow from operations be positive if net income is negative? Can operating cash flow be negative if net income is positive? Give examples.

14. **Cash Flows.** Ponzi Products produced 100 chain letter kits this quarter, resulting in a total cash outlay of $10 per unit. It will sell 50 of the kits next quarter at a price of $11, and the other 50 kits in two quarters at a price of $12. It takes a full quarter for it to collect its bills from its customers. (Ignore possible sales in earlier or later quarters.)

   a. Prepare an income statement for Ponzi for today and for each of the next three quarters. Ignore taxes.
   b. What are the cash flows for the company today and in each of the next three quarters?
   c. What is Ponzi's net working capital in each quarter?

15. **Profits versus Cash Flow.** During the last year of operations, accounts receivable increased by $10,000, accounts payable increased by $5,000, and inventories decreased by $2,000. What is the total impact of these changes on the difference between profits and cash flow?

16. **Income Statement.** A firm's income statement included the following data. The firm's average tax rate was 20 percent.

Cost of goods sold	$8,000
Income taxes paid	2,000
Administrative expenses	3,000
Interest expense	1,000
Depreciation	1,000

   a. What was the firm's net income?
   b. What must have been the firm's revenues?
   c. What was EBIT?

17. **Profits versus Cash Flow.** Butterfly Tractors had $14 million in sales last year. Cost of goods sold was $8 million, depreciation expense was $2 million, interest payment on outstanding debt was $1 million, and the firm's tax rate was 35 percent.

   a. What was the firm's net income and net cash flow?
   b. What would happen to net income and cash flow if depreciation were increased by $1 million? How do you explain the differing impact of depreciation on income versus cash flow?
   c. Would you expect the change in income and cash flow to have a positive or negative impact on the firm's stock price?
   d. Now consider the impact on net income and cash flow if the firm's interest expense were $1 million higher. Why is this case different from part (b)?

18. **Cash Flow.** Candy Canes, Inc., spends $100,000 to buy sugar and peppermint in April. It produces its candy and sells it to distributors in May for $150,000, but it does not receive payment until June. For each month, find the firm's sales, net income, and net cash flow.

19. **Financial Statements.** Here are the 2005 and 2006 (incomplete) balance sheets for Nobel Oil Corp.

NOBEL OIL CORP. BALANCE SHEET, AS OF END OF YEAR					
Assets	2005	2006	Liabilities and Owners' Equity	2005	2006
Current assets	$ 310	$ 420	Current liabilities	$210	$240
Net fixed assets	1,200	1,420	Long-term debt	830	920

Please visit us at www.mhhe.com/bmm5e or refer to your Student CD

Please visit us at www.mhhe.com/bmm5e or refer to your Student CD

a. What was owners' equity at the end of 2005 and 2006?

b. If Nobel paid dividends of $100 in 2006, and made no stock issues, what must have been net income during the year?

c. If Nobel purchased $300 in fixed assets during the year, what must have been the depreciation charge on the income statement?

d. What was the change in net working capital between 2005 and 2006?

e. If Nobel issued $200 of new long-term debt, how much debt must have been paid off during the year?

20. **Financial Statements.** South Sea Baubles has the following (incomplete) balance sheet and income statement.

BALANCE SHEET, AS OF END OF YEAR (figures in millions of dollars)					
Assets	2005	2006	Liabilities and Shareholders' Equity	2005	2006
Current assets	$ 90	$140	Current liabilities	$ 50	$ 60
Net fixed assets	800	900	Long-term debt	600	750

INCOME STATEMENT, 2006 (figures in millions of dollars)	
Revenue	$1,950
Cost of goods sold	1,030
Depreciation	350
Interest expense	240

a. What is shareholders' equity in 2005 and 2006?

b. What is net working capital in 2005 and 2006?

c. What are taxable income and taxes paid in 2006? Assume the firm pays taxes equal to 35 percent of taxable income.

d. What is cash provided by operations during 2006? Pay attention to changes in net working capital, using Table 3–3 as a guide.

e. Net fixed assets increased from $800 million to $900 million during 2006. What must have been South Sea's *gross* investment in fixed assets during 2006?

f. If South Sea reduced its outstanding accounts payable by $35 million during the year, what must have happened to its other current liabilities?

The following table contains data on Fincorp, Inc., that you should use for Problems 21–28. The balance sheet items correspond to values at year-end of 2005 and 2006, while the income statement items correspond to revenues or expenses during the year ending in either 2005 or 2006. All values are in thousands of dollars.

21. **Balance Sheet.** Construct a balance sheet for Fincorp for 2005 and 2006. What is shareholders' equity?

22. **Working Capital.** What happened to net working capital during the year?

23. **Income Statement.** Construct an income statement for Fincorp for 2005 and 2006. What were reinvested earnings for 2006? How does that compare with the increase in shareholders' equity between the two years?

24. **Earnings per Share.** Suppose that Fincorp has 500,000 shares outstanding. What were earnings per share?

25. **Taxes.** What was the firm's average tax bracket for each year? Do you have enough information to determine the marginal tax bracket?

26. **Balance Sheet.** Examine the values for depreciation in 2006 and net fixed assets in 2005 and 2006. What was Fincorp's gross investment in plant and equipment during 2006?

27. **Cash Flows.** Construct a statement of cash flows for Fincorp for 2006.

Please visit us at www.mhhe.com/bmm5e or refer to your Student CD

	2005	2006
Revenue	$4,000	$4,100
Cost of goods sold	1,600	1,700
Depreciation	500	520
Inventories	300	350
Administrative expenses	500	550
Interest expense	150	150
Federal and state taxes*	400	420
Accounts payable	300	350
Accounts receivable	400	450
Net fixed assets†	5,000	5,800
Long-term debt	2,000	2,400
Notes payable	1,000	600
Dividends paid	410	410
Cash and marketable securities	800	300

* Taxes are paid in their entirety in the year that the tax obligation is incurred.

† Net fixed assets are fixed assets net of accumulated depreciation since the asset was installed.

Please visit us at www.mhhe.com/bmm5e or refer to your Student CD

28. **Book versus Market Value.** Now suppose that the *market value* (in thousands of dollars) of Fincorp's fixed assets in 2006 is $6,000 and that the value of its long-term debt is only $2,400. In addition, the consensus among investors is that Fincorp's past investments in developing the skills of its employees are worth $2,900. This investment of course does not show up on the balance sheet. What will be the price per share of Fincorp stock?

CHALLENGE PROBLEM

29. **Taxes.** Reconsider the data in problem 10 which imply that you have $100,000 of total pretax income to allocate between your salary and your firm's profits. What allocation will minimize the total tax bill? *Hint:* Think about marginal tax rates and the ability to shift income from a higher marginal bracket to a lower one.

STANDARD &POOR'S

1. Find Microsoft and General Motors on Market Insight (www.mhhe.com/edumarketinsight), and examine the financial statements of each. Which firm uses more debt finance? Which firm has higher cash as a percentage of total assets? Which has higher profits per dollar of total assets? Which has higher profits per dollar of shareholders' equity?

2. Find information on two highly profitable technology firms, like Intel (INTC) and Microsoft (MSFT), and two auto firms, such as Ford (F) and General Motors (GM), at www.mhhe.com/edumarketsight. Which firms have the higher ratio of market value to book value of equity? Does this make sense to you? Which firms pay out a higher fraction of their profits as dividends to shareholders? Does this make sense?

SOLUTIONS TO SELF-TEST QUESTIONS

3.1   Cash and equivalents would increase by $100 million. Property, plant, and equipment would increase by $400 million. Long-term debt would increase by $500 million. Shareholders' equity would not increase: assets and liabilities have increased equally, leaving shareholders' equity unchanged.

3.2   a. If the auto plant were worth $14 billion, the equity in the firm would be worth $14 – $4 = $10 billion. With 100 million shares outstanding, each share would be worth $100.

     b. If the outstanding stock were worth $8 billion, we would infer that the market values the auto plant at $8 + $4 = $12 billion.

3.3   The profits for the firm are recognized in periods 2 and 3 when the sales take place. In both of those periods, profits are $150 – $100 = $50. Cash flows are derived as follows.

Period	1	2	3	4
Sales	0	150	150	0
– Change in accounts receivable	0	150	0	(150)
– Cost of goods sold	0	100	100	0
– Change in inventories	200	(100)	(100)	0
= Net cash flow	–200	0	+ 150	+150

In period 2, half the units are sold for $150 but no cash is collected, so the entire $150 is treated as an increase in accounts receivable. Half the $200 cost of production is recognized, and a like amount is taken out of inventory. In period 3, the firm sells another $150 of product but collects $150 from its previous sales, so there is no change in outstanding accounts receivable. Net cash flow is the $150 collected in this period on the sale that occurred in period 2. In period 4, cash flow is again $150, as the accounts receivable from the sale in period 3 are collected.

3.4   a. An increase in inventories uses cash, reducing the firm's net cash balance.

     b. A reduction in accounts payable uses cash, reducing the firm's net cash balance.

     c. An issue of common stock is a source of cash.

     d. The purchase of new equipment is a use of cash, and it reduces the firm's net cash balance.

3.5

	Firm A	Firm B
EBIT	100	100
Interest	60	0
Pretax income	40	100
Tax (35% of pretax income)	14	35
Net income	26	65

Note: Figures in millions of dollars.

Taxes owed by Firm A fall from $21 million to $14 million. The reduction in taxes is 35 percent of the extra $20 million of interest income. Net income does not fall by the full $20 million of extra interest expense. It instead falls by interest expense less the reduction in taxes, or $20 million – $7 million = $13 million.

3.6   For a single taxpayer with taxable income of $70,000, total taxes paid are

$$.10 \times 7,300 + [.15 \times (29,700 - 7,300)] + [.25 \times (70,000 - 29,700)] = \$14,165$$

The marginal tax rate is 25 percent, but the average tax rate is only 14,165/70,000 = .202, or 20.2 percent.

For the married taxpayers filing jointly with taxable income of $70,000, total taxes paid are

$$(.10 \times 14,600) + .15(59,400 - 14,600) + .25(70,000 - 59,400) = \$10,830$$

The marginal tax rate is 25 percent, and the average tax rate is 10,830/70,000 = .155, or 15.5 percent.

2

Value

CHAPTER 4

The Time Value of Money

RELATED WEB LINKS

www.investopedia.com
www.quicken.com
www.smartmoney.com
www.bankrate.com
money.cnn.com Lots of general finance material as well as several interest rate calculators.
www.bls.gov/cpi

www.stlouisfed.org
www.globalfindata.com Data on interest and inflation rates.
www.studyfinance.com
www.teachmefinance.com Includes primers on time value, financial calculators, and use of Excel in finance.

Kangaroo Auto's view of the time value of money Do you truly understand what these percentages mean? Do you realize that the dealership may not be quoting effective annual interest rates? If the dealership quotes a monthly payment on a 4-year, $10,000 car loan, would you be able to double-check the dealership's calculations?

© Myrleen Ferguson Cate/PhotoEdit

Companies invest in lots of things. Some are *tangible assets*—that is, assets you can kick, like factories, machinery, and offices. Others are *intangible assets,* such as patents or trademarks. In each case the company lays out some money now in the hope of receiving even more money later.

Individuals also make investments. For example, your college education may cost you $20,000 per year. That is an investment you hope will pay off in the form of a higher salary later in life. You are sowing now and expecting to reap later.

Companies pay for their investments by raising money and in the process assuming liabilities. For example, they may borrow money from a bank and promise to repay it with interest later. You also may have financed your investment in a college education by borrowing money that you plan to pay back out of that fat salary.

All these financial decisions require comparisons of cash payments at different dates. Will your future salary be sufficient to justify the current expenditure on college tuition? How much will you have to repay the bank if you borrow to finance your education?

In this chapter we take the first steps toward understanding the relationship between the values of dollars today and dollars in the future. We start by looking at how funds invested at a specific interest rate will grow over time. We next ask how much you would need to invest today to produce a specified future sum of money, and we describe some shortcuts for working out the value of a series of cash payments. Then we consider how inflation affects these financial calculations.

There is nothing complicated about these calculations, but if they are to become second nature, you should read the chapter thoroughly, work carefully through the examples (we have provided plenty), and make sure you tackle the self-test questions. We are asking you to make an investment now in return for a payoff later.

4.1 Future Values and Compound Interest

You have $100 invested in a bank account. Suppose banks are currently paying an interest rate of 6 percent per year on deposits. So after a year your account will earn interest of $6:

$$\text{Interest} = \text{interest rate} \times \text{initial investment}$$
$$= .06 \times \$100 = \$6$$

You start the year with $100 and you earn interest of $6, so the value of your investment will grow to $106 by the end of the year:

$$\text{Value of investment after 1 year} = \$100 + \$6 = \$106$$

Notice that the $100 invested grows by the factor $(1 + .06) = 1.06$. In general, for any interest rate r, the value of the investment at the end of 1 year is $(1 + r)$ times the initial investment:

$$\text{Value after 1 year} = \text{initial investment} \times (1 + r)$$
$$= \$100 \times (1.06) = \$106$$

What if you leave this money in the bank for a second year? Your balance, now $106, will continue to earn interest of 6 percent. So

$$\text{Interest in year 2} = .06 \times \$106 = \$6.36$$

You start the second year with $106, on which you earn interest of $6.36. So by the end of the year the value of your account will grow to $106 + $6.36 = $112.36.

In the first year your investment of $100 increases by a factor of 1.06 to $106; in the second year the $106 again increases by a factor of 1.06 to $112.36. Thus the initial $100 investment grows twice by a factor 1.06:

$$\text{Value of investment after 2 years} = \$100 \times 1.06 \times 1.06$$
$$= \$100 \times (1.06)^2 = \$112.36$$

If you keep your money invested for a third year, your investment multiplies by 1.06 each year for 3 years. By the end of the third year it will total $100 \times (1.06)^3 = $119.10, scarcely enough to put you in the millionaire class, but even millionaires have to start somewhere.

Clearly, if you invest your $100 for t years, it will grow to $100 \times (1.06)^t$. For an interest rate of r and a horizon of t years, the **future value** of your investment will be

future value
Amount to which an investment will grow after earning interest.

$$\textbf{Future value of \$100} = \textbf{\$100} \times \textbf{(1 + r)}^t$$

Notice in our example that your interest income in the first year is $6 (6 percent of $100) and in the second year is $6.36 (6 percent of $106). Your income in the second

TABLE 4–1 How your savings grow; the future value of $100 invested to earn 6 percent with compound interest

Year	Balance at Start of Year	Interest Earned during Year	Balance at End of Year
1	$100.00	.06 × $100.00 = $6.00	$106.00
2	$106.00	.06 × $106.00 = $6.36	$112.36
3	$112.36	.06 × $112.36 = $6.74	$119.10
4	$119.10	.06 × $119.10 = $7.15	$126.25
5	$126.25	.06 × $126.25 = $7.57	$133.82

compound interest
Interest earned on interest.

simple interest
Interest earned only on the original investment; no interest is earned on interest.

year is higher because you now earn interest on *both* the original $100 investment *and* the $6 of interest earned in the previous year. Earning interest on interest is called *compounding* or **compound interest.** In contrast, if the bank calculated the interest only on your original investment, you would be paid **simple interest.** With simple interest the value of your investment would grow each year by .06 × $100 = $6.

Table 4–1 and Figure 4–1 illustrate the mechanics of compound interest. Table 4–1 shows that in each year, you start with a greater balance in your account—your savings have been increased by the previous year's interest. As a result, your interest income also is higher.

Obviously, the higher the rate of interest, the faster your savings will grow. Figure 4–2 shows that a few percentage points added to the (compound) interest rate can dramatically affect the future balance of your savings account. For example, after 10 years $100 invested at 10 percent will grow to $100 × (1.10)^{10} = $259.37. If invested at 5 percent, it will grow to only $100 × (1.05)^{10} = $162.89.

Calculating future values is easy using almost any calculator. If you have the patience, you can multiply your initial investment by 1 + r (1.06 in our example) once for each year of your investment. A simpler procedure is to use the power key (the y^x key) on your calculator. For example, to compute (1.06)^{10}, enter 1.06, press the y^x key, enter 10, press =, and discover that the answer is 1.7908. (Try this!)

If you don't have a calculator, you can use a table of future values such as Table 4–2. Check that you can use it to work out the future value of a 10-year investment at 6 percent. First find the row corresponding to 10 years. Now work along that row until you reach the column for a 6 percent interest rate. The entry shows that $1 invested for 10 years at 6 percent grows to $1.7908.

FIGURE 4–1 A plot of the data in Table 4–1, showing the future values of an investment of $100 earning 6 percent with compound interest

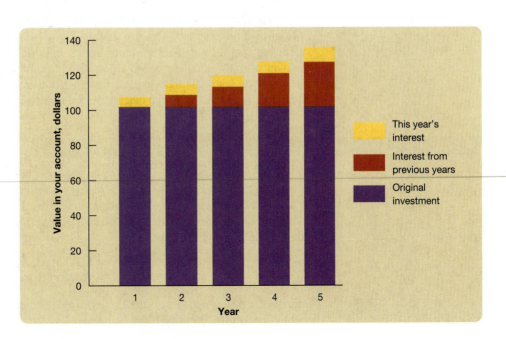

FIGURE 4–2 How an investment of $100 grows with compound interest at different interest rates

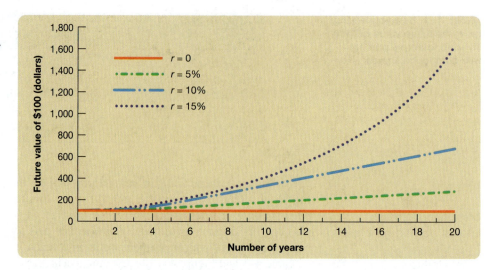

TABLE 4–2 An example of a future value table, showing how an investment of $1 grows with compound interest

Number of Years	Interest Rate per Year					
	5%	6%	7%	8%	9%	10%
1	1.0500	1.0600	1.0700	1.0800	1.0900	1.1000
2	1.1025	1.1236	1.1449	1.1664	1.1881	1.2100
3	1.1576	1.1910	1.2250	1.2597	1.2950	1.3310
4	1.2155	1.2625	1.3108	1.3605	1.4116	1.4641
5	1.2763	1.3382	1.4026	1.4693	1.5386	1.6105
10	1.6289	1.7908	1.9672	2.1589	2.3674	2.5937
20	2.6533	3.2071	3.8697	4.6610	5.6044	6.7275
30	4.3219	5.7435	7.6123	10.0627	13.2677	17.4494

Now try one more example. If you invest $1 for 20 years at 10 percent and do not withdraw any money, what will you have at the end? Your answer should be $6.7275.

Table 4–2 gives futures values for only a small selection of years and interest rates. Table A.1 at the end of the book is a bigger version of Table 4–2. It presents the future value of a $1 investment for a wide range of time periods and interest rates.

Future value tables are tedious, and as Table 4–2 demonstrates, they show future values only for a limited set of interest rates and time periods. For example, suppose that you want to calculate future values using an interest rate of 7.835 percent. The power key on your calculator will be faster and easier than future value tables. A third alternative is to use a financial calculator or a spreadsheet. These are discussed in several boxes later in this chapter.

EXAMPLE 4.1   ▶   Manhattan Island

Almost everyone's favorite example of the power of compound interest is the purchase of Manhattan Island for $24 in 1626 by Peter Minuit. Based on New York real estate prices today, it seems that Minuit got a great deal. But did he? Consider the future value of that $24 if it had been invested for 380 years (2006 minus 1626) at an interest rate of 8 percent per year:

$$\$24 \times (1.08)^{380} = \$120{,}570{,}000{,}000{,}000$$
$$= \$120.57 \text{ trillion}$$

Perhaps the deal wasn't as good as it appeared. The total value of land on Manhattan today is only a fraction of $120.57 trillion.

Though entertaining, this analysis is actually somewhat misleading. First, the 8 percent interest rate we've used to compute future values is quite high by historical standards. At a 3.5 percent interest rate, more consistent with historical experience, the future value of the $24 would be *dramatically* lower, only $24 × (1.035)^{380} = $11,416,794! Second, we have understated the returns to Mr. Minuit and his successors: We have ignored all the rental income that the island's land has generated over the last three or four centuries.

All things considered, if we had been around in 1626, we would have gladly paid $24 for the island. ◀

The power of compounding is not restricted to money. Foresters try to forecast the compound growth rate of trees, demographers the compound growth rate of population. A social commentator once observed that the number of lawyers in the United States is increasing at a higher compound rate than the population as a whole (3.6 versus .9 percent in the 1980s) and calculated that in about two centuries there will be more lawyers than people. In all these cases, the principle is the same: Compound growth means that value increases each period by the factor (1 + growth rate). The value after t periods will equal the initial value times (1 + growth rate)^t. When money is invested at compound interest, the growth rate is the interest rate.

Self-Test 4.1

Suppose that Peter Minuit did not become the first New York real estate tycoon but instead had invested his $24 at a 5 percent interest rate in New Amsterdam Savings Bank. What would have been the balance in his account after 5 years? 50 years?

Self-Test 4.2

In 1973 Gordon Moore, one of Intel's founders, predicted that the number of transistors that could be placed on a single silicon chip would double every 18 months, equivalent to an annual growth of 59 percent (i.e., $1.59^{1.5} = 2.0$). The first microprocessor was built in 1971 and had 2,250 transistors. By 2003 Intel chips contained 410 million transistors, over 182,000 times the number of transistors 32 years earlier. What has been the annual compound rate of growth in processing power? How does it compare with the prediction of Moore's law?

4.2 Present Values

Money can be invested to earn interest. If you are offered the choice between $100,000 now and $100,000 at the end of the year, you naturally take the money now to get a year's interest. Financial managers make the same point when they say that money in hand today has a *time value* or when they quote perhaps the most basic financial principle: A dollar today is worth more than a dollar tomorrow.

present value (PV)
Value today of a future cash flow.

We have seen that $100 invested for 1 year at 6 percent will grow to a future value of 100 × 1.06 = $106. Let's turn this around: How much do we need to invest *now* in order to produce $106 at the end of the year? This is called the **present value (PV)** of the $106 payoff.

To calculate future value, we multiply today's investment by 1 plus the interest rate, .06, or 1.06. To calculate present value, we simply reverse the process and divide the future value by 1.06:

$$\text{Present value} = \text{PV} = \frac{\text{future value}}{1.06} = \frac{\$106}{1.06} = \$100$$

What is the present value of, say, $112.36 to be received 2 years from now? Again we ask, How much would we need to invest now to produce $112.36 after 2 years?

The answer is obviously $100; we've already calculated that at 6 percent $100 grows to $112.36:

$$\$100 \times (1.06)^2 = \$112.36$$

However, if we don't know, or forgot the answer, we just divide future value by $(1.06)^2$:

$$\text{Present value} = \text{PV} = \frac{\$112.36}{(1.06)^2} = \$100$$

In general, for a future value or payment t periods away, present value is

$$\textbf{Present value} = \frac{\textbf{future value after } \textit{t} \textbf{ periods}}{\textbf{(1 + } \textit{r}\textbf{)}^{\textit{t}}}$$

discounted cash flow

Another term for the present value of a future cash flow.

To calculate present value, we *discounted* the future value at the interest rate r. The calculation is therefore termed a **discounted cash-flow (DCF)** calculation, and the interest rate r is known as the **discount rate.**

In this chapter we will be working through a number of more or less complicated DCF calculations. All of them involve a present value, a discount rate, and one or more future cash flows. If ever a DCF problem leaves you confused and flustered, just pause and write down which of these measures you know and which one you need to calculate.

discount rate

Interest rate used to compute present values of future cash flows.

EXAMPLE 4.2

Suppose you need $3,000 next year to buy a new computer. The interest rate is 8 percent per year. How much money should you set aside now in order to pay for the purchase? Just calculate the present value at an 8 percent interest rate of a $3,000 payment at the end of 1 year. To the nearest dollar, this value is

$$\text{PV} = \frac{\$3,000}{1.08} = \$2,778$$

Notice that $2,778 invested for 1 year at 8 percent will prove just enough to buy your computer:

$$\text{Future value} = \$2,778 \times 1.08 = \$3,000$$

The longer the time before you must make a payment, the less you need to invest today. For example, suppose that you can postpone buying that computer until the end of 2 years. In this case we calculate the present value of the future payment by dividing $3,000 by $(1.08)^2$:

$$\text{PV} = \frac{\$3,000}{(1.08)^2} = \$2,572$$

Thus you need to invest $2,778 today to provide $3,000 in 1 year but only $2,572 to provide the same $3,000 in 2 years. ◄

You now know how to calculate future and present values: ==To work out how much you will have in the future if you invest for t years at an interest rate r, *multiply* the initial investment by $(1 + r)^t$. To find the present value of a future payment, run the process in reverse and *divide* by $(1 + r)^t$.==

Present values are always calculated using compound interest. Whereas the ascending lines in Figure 4–2 showed the future value of $1 invested with compound interest, when we calculate present values we move back along the lines from future to present.

Thus present values decline, other things equal, when future cash payments are delayed. The longer you have to wait for money, the less it's worth today, as we see in

FIGURE 4–3 Present value of a future cash flow of $100. Notice that the longer you have to wait for your money, the less it is worth today.

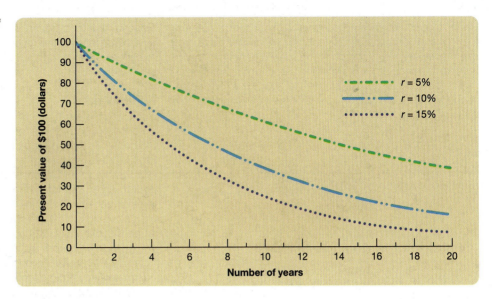

Figure 4–3. Notice how very small variations in the interest rate can have a powerful effect on the value of distant cash flows. At an interest rate of 10 percent, a payment of $100 in year 20 is worth $14.86 today. If the interest rate increases to 15 percent, the value of the future payment falls by about 60 percent to $6.11.

The present value formula is sometimes written differently. Instead of dividing the future payment by $(1 + r)^t$, we could equally well multiply it by $1/(1 + r)^t$:

$$PV = \frac{\text{future payment}}{(1 + r)^t} = \text{future payment} \times \frac{1}{(1 + r)^t}$$

discount factor

Present value of a $1 future payment.

The expression $1/(1 + r)^t$ is called the **discount factor.** It measures the present value of $1 received in year t.

The simplest way to find the discount factor is to use a calculator, but financial managers sometimes find it convenient to use tables of discount factors. For example, Table 4–3 shows discount factors for a small range of years and interest rates. Table A.2 at the end of the book provides a set of discount factors for a wide range of years and interest rates.

Try using Table 4–3 to check our calculations of how much to put aside for that $3,000 computer purchase. If the interest rate is 8 percent, the present value of $1 paid at the end of 1 year is $.9259. So the present value of $3,000 is (to the nearest dollar)

$$PV = \$3,000 \times \frac{1}{1.08} = \$3,000 \times .9259 = \$2,778$$

which matches the value we obtained in Example 4.2.

TABLE 4–3 An example of a present value table, showing the value today of $1 received in the future

Number of Years	Interest Rate per Year					
	5%	6%	7%	8%	9%	10%
1	0.9524	0.9434	0.9346	0.9259	0.9174	0.9091
2	0.9070	0.8900	0.8734	0.8573	0.8417	0.8264
3	0.8638	0.8396	0.8163	0.7938	0.7722	0.7513
4	0.8227	0.7921	0.7629	0.7350	0.7084	0.6830
5	0.7835	0.7473	0.7130	0.6806	0.6499	0.6209
10	0.6139	0.5584	0.5083	0.4632	0.4224	0.3855
20	0.3769	0.3118	0.2584	0.2145	0.1784	0.1486
30	0.2314	0.1741	0.1314	0.0994	0.0754	0.0573

An Introduction to Financial Calculators

Financial calculators are designed with present value and future value formulas already programmed. Therefore, you can readily solve many problems simply by entering the inputs for the problem and punching a key for the solution.

The basic financial calculator uses five keys that correspond to the inputs for common problems involving the time value of money.

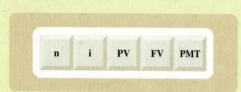

Each key represents the following input:

- *n* is the number of periods. (We have been using *t* to denote the length of time or number of periods. Most calculators use *n* for the same concept.)
- *i* is the interest rate per period, expressed as a percentage (not a decimal). For example, if the interest rate is 8 percent, you would enter 8, not .08. On some calculators this key is written I/Y or I/YR. (We have been using *r* to denote the interest rate or discount rate.)
- *PV* is the present value.
- *FV* is the future value.
- *PMT* is the amount of any recurring payment (called an *annuity*). In single cash-flow problems such as those we have considered so far, *PMT* is zero.

Given any four of these inputs, the calculator will solve for the fifth. (A word of advice: You should get into the habit of

clearing all inputs before beginning any new problem. You don't want leftover inputs to affect your results. Look for the "clear" or CLR key on your calculator.) We will illustrate with several examples.

Future Values

Recall Example 4.1, where we calculated the future value of Peter Minuit's $24 investment. Enter 24 into the *PV* register. (You enter the value by typing 24 and then pushing the *PV* key.) We assumed an interest rate of 8 percent, so enter 8 into the *i* register. Because the $24 had 380 years to compound, enter 380 into the *n* register. Enter 0 into the *PMT* register because there is no recurring payment involved in the calculation. Now ask the calculator to compute *FV*. On some calculators you simply press the *FV* key. On others you need to first press the "compute" key (which may be labeled *COMP* or *CPT*), and then press *FV*. The exact sequences of keystrokes for three popular financial calculators are as follows:*

Hewlett-Packard HP-10B	Sharp EL-733A	Texas Instruments BA II Plus
24 PV	24 PV	24 PV
380 n	380 n	380 n
8 I/YR	8 i	8 I/Y
0 PMT	0 PMT	0 PMT
FV	COMP FV	CPT FV

You should find after hitting the *FV* key that your calculator shows a value of −120.57 trillion, which, except for the minus sign, is the future value of the $24.

What if the computer purchase is postponed until the end of 2 years? Table 4–3 shows that the present value of $1 paid at the end of 2 years is .8573. So the present value of $3,000 is

$$PV = \$3,000 \times \frac{1}{(1.08)^2} = \$3,000 \times .8573 = \$2,572$$

as we found in Example 4.2.

Notice that as you move along the rows in Table 4–3, moving to higher interest rates, present values decline. As you move down the columns, moving to longer discounting periods, present values again decline. (Why does this make sense?)

EXAMPLE 4.3 ▶ Coca-Cola Enterprises Borrows Some Cash

In 1995 Coca-Cola Enterprises needed to borrow about a quarter of a billion dollars for 25 years. It did so by selling IOUs, each of which simply promised to pay the holder $1,000 at the end of 25 years.[1] The market interest rate at the time was 8.53 percent. How much would you have been prepared to pay for one of the company's IOUs?

---

[1] "IOU" means "I owe you." Coca-Cola's IOUs are called *bonds*. Usually, bond investors receive a regular *interest* or *coupon* payment. The Coca-Cola Enterprises bond will make only a single payment at the end of year 25. It was therefore known as a *zero-coupon bond*. More on this in the next chapter.

Why does the minus sign appear? Most calculators treat cash flows as either inflows (shown as positive numbers) or outflows (negative numbers). For example, if you borrow $100 today at an interest rate of 12 percent, you receive money now (a *positive* cash flow), but you will have to pay back $112 in a year, a *negative* cash flow at that time. Therefore, the calculator displays *FV* as a negative number. The following time line of cash flows shows the reasoning employed. The final negative cash flow of $112 has the same present value as the $100 borrowed today.

If, instead of borrowing, you were to *invest* $100 today to reap a future benefit, you would enter *PV* as a negative number (first press 100, then press the +/– key to make the value negative, and finally press *PV* to enter the value into the *PV* register). In this case, *FV* would appear as a positive number, indicating that you will reap a cash inflow when your investment comes to fruition.

Present Values

Suppose your savings goal is to accumulate $10,000 by the end of 30 years. If the interest rate is 8 percent, how much would you need to invest today to achieve your goal? Again, there is no recurring payment involved, so *PMT* is zero. We

therefore enter the following: $n = 30$; $i = 8$; $FV = 10,000$; $PMT = 0$. Now compute *PV*, and you should get an answer of –993.77. The answer is displayed as a negative number because you need to make a cash outflow (an investment) of $993.77 now in order to enjoy a cash inflow of $10,000 in 30 years.

Finding the Interest Rate

The 25-year Coca-Cola Enterprises IOU in Example 4.3 sold at $129.20 and promised a final payment of $1,000. We may obtain the market interest rate by entering $n = 25$, $FV = 1,000$, $PV = -129.20$, and $PMT = 0$. Compute *i* and you will find that the interest rate is 8.53 percent. This is the value we computed directly (but with more work) in the example.

How Long an Investment?

In Example 4.5, we consider how long it would take for an investment to double in value. This sort of problem is easily solved using a calculator. If the investment is to double, we enter $FV = 2$ and $PV = -1$. If the interest rate is 9 percent, enter $i = 9$ and $PMT = 0$. Compute *n* and you will find that $n = 8.04$ years. If the interest rate is 9.05 percent, the doubling period falls to 8 years, as we found in the example.

----

*The BAII Plus requires a little extra work to initialize the calculator. When you buy the calculator, it is set to automatically interpret each period as a year but to assume that interest compounds monthly. In our experience, it is best to change the compounding frequency to once per period. To do so, press [2nd] {P/Y} 1 [ENTER], then press [↓] 1 [ENTER], and finally press [2nd] {QUIT} to return to standard calculator mode. You should need to do this only once, even if the calculator is shut off.

To calculate present value, we multiply the $1,000 future payment by the 25-year discount factor:

$$PV = \$1,000 \times \frac{1}{(1.0853)^{25}}$$
$$= \$1,000 \times .1292 = \$129.20$$

Instead of using a calculator to find the discount factor, we could use Table A.2 at the end of the book. You can see that the 25-year discount factor is .1460 if the interest rate is 8 percent and it is .1160 if the rate is 9 percent. For an interest rate of 8.5 percent the discount factor is roughly halfway between, at .131, a shade higher than the exact figure. ◄

Self-Test 4.3

Suppose that Coca-Cola had promised to pay $1,000 at the end of 10 years. If the market interest rate were 8.53 percent, how much would you have been prepared to pay for a 10-year IOU of $1,000?

EXAMPLE 4.4 ▶ Finding the Value of Free Credit

Kangaroo Autos is offering free credit on a $10,000 car. You pay $4,000 down and then the balance at the end of 2 years. Turtle Motors next door does not offer free

Interest-Rate Functions

Just as financial calculators largely replaced interest rate tables in the 1980s, these calculators are today giving way to spreadsheets. Like financial calculators, spreadsheets provide built-in functions that solve the equations linking the five variables in a time-value-of-money problem: the number of periods, the interest rate per period, the present value, the future value, and any recurring payment (the annuity). For single cash-flow problems such as the ones we've encountered so far, the recurring payment is zero. We will illustrate the use of these spreadsheets by using Microsoft

	A	B	C	D
1	Finding the future value of $24 using a spreadsheet			
2				
3	Present value (PV)	24		
4	Interest rate	0.08		
5	Payment	0		
6	Periods	380		
7				
8	Future value	$120,569,740,656,495		
9				
10				
11	The formula in cell B8 is =FV(B4,B6,B5,-B3). Notice that we enter the present value			
12	as a negative of the value in cell B3, since the "purchase price" is a cash outflow.			
13	The interest rate is entered as a decimal.			
14				
15	You can confirm for yourself that changing the entry in cell B4 to 0.35 will reduce			
16	the value to $11,416,794.			

credit but will give you $500 off the list price. If the interest rate is 10 percent, which company is offering the better deal?

Notice that you pay more in total by buying through Kangaroo, but since part of the payment is postponed, you can keep this money in the bank where it will continue to earn interest. To compare the two offers, you need to calculate the present value of the payments to Kangaroo. The *time line* in Figure 4–4 shows the cash payments to Kangaroo. The first payment, $4,000, takes place today. The second payment, $6,000, takes place at the end of 2 years. To find its present value, we need to multiply by the

FIGURE 4–4 Drawing a time line can help us to calculate the present value of the payments to Kangaroo Autos.

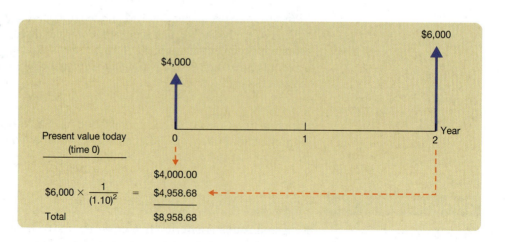

Excel™. An interactive version of this spreadsheet can be found at www.mhhe.com/bmm5e or on the Student CD.

The four Excel functions relevant for single cash-flow problems are:

Future value = FV (rate, nper, pmt, PV)
Present value = PV (rate, nper, pmt, FV)
Interest rate = RATE (nper, pmt, PV, FV)
Number of periods = NPER (rate, pmt, PV, FV)

As you can see, each spreadsheet formula requires four inputs—just as financial calculators require four inputs—and provides the solution for the fifth variable. Also like most calculators, the spreadsheet functions interpret cash inflows as positive values and cash outflows as negative values. Unlike financial calculators, however, most spreadsheets require that interest rates be input as decimals rather than whole numbers (e.g., .06 rather than 6%). Note also the use of = signs in front of the formulas to alert Excel to the fact that these are predefined formulas. In the previous box, we saw how to use calculators to solve several problems. Let's see how we would use spreadsheets to solve the same problems.

Future Values

The figure on the facing page shows a spreadsheet that solves Example 4.1 on the future value of the $24 spent to acquire Manhattan Island. The interest rate is entered as a decimal in cell B4. The formula for future value in cell B8 takes as its last input the negative of cell B3, because the $24 purchase price is treated as cash outflow.

Present Values

We next considered an individual who wishes to accumulate a future value of $10,000 by the end of 30 years. If the interest rate is 8 percent, and there is no recurring payment involved, you can find the necessary investment today (the present value) by entering the formula =PV (.08,30,0,10000). If you try this, you will see that the solution is reported as a negative value: the positive future payoff of $10,000 requires an initial payment (cash outflow) of 993.77. (Notice also that we don't use commas when entering the $10,000 future value. The spreadsheet would think that the comma was being used to separate two inputs to the function.)

Finding the Interest Rate

We showed how to use a calculator to find the interest rate on a 25-year $1,000 IOU sold today for $129.20. In Excel, we can compute =RATE (25,0,−129.20,1000) to confirm again that the interest rate is 8.53 percent.

How Long an Investment?

Example 4.5 asks how long it would take an investment to double if it earned interest at a rate of 9 percent. We treat the present value as a $1 investment (cash outflow) and the future value as a $2 cash payback. Therefore, enter =NPER(.09,0,−1,2) to find that the doubling period is 8.04 years.

2-year discount factor. The total present value of the payments to Kangaroo is therefore

$$PV = \$4{,}000 + \$6{,}000 \times \frac{1}{(1.10)^2}$$
$$= \$4{,}000 + \$4{,}958.68 = \$8{,}958.68$$

Suppose you start with $8,958.68. You make a down payment of $4,000 to Kangaroo Autos and invest the balance of $4,958.68. At an interest rate of 10 percent, this will grow over 2 years to $4,958.68 × $1.10^2 = $6,000, just enough to make the final payment on your automobile. The total cost of $8,958.68 is a better deal than the $9,500 charged by Turtle Motors. ◀

These calculations illustrate how important it is to use present values when comparing alternative patterns of cash payment. You should *never* compare cash flows occurring at different times without first discounting them to a common date. By calculating present values, we see how much cash must be set aside today to pay future bills.

Finding the Interest Rate

When we looked at Coca-Cola's IOUs in Example 4.3, we used the interest rate to compute a fair market price for each IOU. Sometimes, however, you are given the price and have to calculate the interest rate that is being offered.

For example, when Coca-Cola borrowed money, it did not announce an interest rate. It simply offered to sell each IOU for $129.20. Thus we know that

$$PV = \$1,000 \times \frac{1}{(1 + r)^{25}} = \$129.20$$

What is the interest rate?

There are several ways to approach this. First, you might use a table of discount factors. You need to find the interest rate for which the 25-year discount factor = .1292. Look at Table A.2 at the end of the book, and run your finger along the row corresponding to 25 years. You can see that an interest rate of 8 percent gives too high a discount factor and a rate of 9 percent gives too low a discount factor. The interest rate on the Coca-Cola loan was about halfway between, at 8.5 percent.

Second, you can rearrange the equation and use your calculator:

$$\$129.20 \times (1 + r)^{25} = \$1,000$$

$$(1 + r)^{25} = \frac{\$1,000}{\$129.20} = 7.74$$

$$(1 + r) = (7.74)^{1/25} = 1.0853$$

$$r = .0853, \text{ or } 8.53\%$$

In general this is more accurate. You can also use a financial calculator (see the box on pages 80–81).

EXAMPLE 4.5 ▶ Double Your Money

How many times have you heard of an investment adviser who promises to double your money? Is this really an amazing feat? That depends on how long it will take for your money to double. With enough patience, your funds eventually will double even if they earn only a very modest interest rate. Suppose your investment adviser promises to double your money in 8 years. What interest rate is implicitly being promised?

The adviser is promising a future value of $2 for every $1 invested today. Therefore, we find the interest rate by solving for r as follows:

$$\text{Future value} = PV \times (1 + r)^t$$
$$\$2 = \$1 \times (1 + r)^8$$
$$1 + r = 2^{1/8} = 1.0905$$
$$r = .0905, \text{ or } 9.05\%$$ ◀

Self-Test 4.4

An investment of $1,000 in eBay stock at the start of 2000 would have grown to $3,300 five years later. At what annual rate did the investment grow?

4.3 Multiple Cash Flows

So far, we have considered problems involving only a single cash flow. This is obviously limiting. Most real-world investments, after all, will involve many cash flows over time. When there are many payments, you'll hear managers refer to a *stream of cash flows*.

Future Value of Multiple Cash Flows

Recall the computer you hope to purchase in 2 years (see Example 4.2). Now suppose that instead of putting aside one sum in the bank to finance the purchase, you plan to save some amount of money each year. You might be able to put $1,200 in the bank now, and another $1,400 in 1 year. If you earn an 8 percent rate of interest, how much will you be able to spend on a computer in 2 years?

FIGURE 4–5 Drawing a time line can help to calculate the future value of your savings.

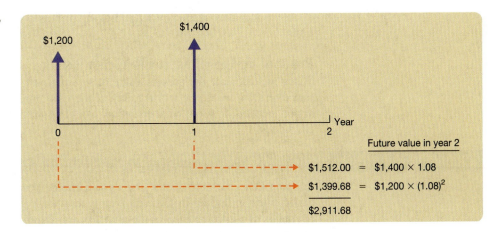

The time line in Figure 4–5 shows how your savings grow. There are two cash inflows into the savings plan. The first cash flow will have 2 years to earn interest and therefore will grow to $1,200 \times (1.08)^2 = \$1,399.68$, while the second deposit, which comes a year later, will be invested for only 1 year and will grow to $1,400 \times (1.08) = \$1,512$. After 2 years, then, your total savings will be the sum of these two amounts, or $2,911.68.

| EXAMPLE 4.6 ▶ | Even More Savings |

Suppose that the computer purchase can be put off for an additional year and that you can make a third deposit of $1,000 at the end of the second year. How much will be available to spend 3 years from now?

Again we organize our inputs using a time line as in Figure 4–6. The total cash available will be the sum of the future values of all three deposits. Notice that when we save for 3 years, the first two deposits each have an extra year for interest to compound:

$$\$1,200 \times (1.08)^3 = \$1,511.65$$
$$\$1,400 \times (1.08)^2 = \quad 1,632.96$$
$$\$1,000 \times (1.08) = \quad \underline{1,080.00}$$
$$\text{Total future value} = \$4,224.61 \quad ◀$$

Our examples show that problems involving multiple cash flows are simple extensions of single cash-flow analysis. ==To find the value at some future date of a stream of cash flows, calculate what each cash flow will be worth at that future date, and then add up these future values.==

FIGURE 4–6 To find the future value of a stream of cash flows, you just calculate the future value of each flow and then add them.

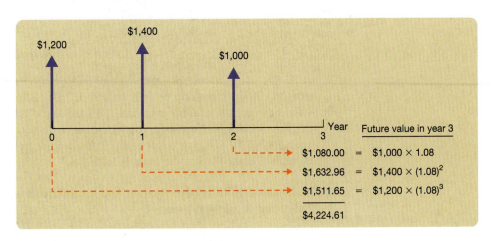

As we will now see, a similar adding-up principle works for present value calculations.

Present Value of Multiple Cash Flows

When we calculate the present value of a future cash flow, we are asking how much that cash flow would be worth today. If there is more than one future cash flow, we simply need to work out what each flow would be worth today and then add these present values.

| EXAMPLE 4.7 ▶ | Cash Up Front versus an Installment Plan |

Suppose that your auto dealer gives you a choice between paying $15,500 for a new car or entering into an installment plan where you pay $8,000 down today and make payments of $4,000 in each of the next 2 years. Which is the better deal? Before reading this chapter, you might have compared the total payments under the two plans: $15,500 versus $16,000 in the installment plan. Now, however, you know that this comparison is wrong, because it ignores the time value of money. For example, the last installment of $4,000 is less costly to you than paying out $4,000 now. The true cost of that last payment is the present value of $4,000.

Assume that the interest rate you can earn on safe investments is 8 percent. Suppose you choose the installment plan. As the time line in Figure 4–7 illustrates, the present value of the plan's three cash flows is:

	Present Value		
Immediate payment	$8,000	=	$ 8,000.00
Second payment	$4,000/1.08	=	3,703.70
Third payment	$4,000/(1.08)²	=	3,429.36
Total present value		=	$15,133.06

Because the present value of the three payments is less than $15,500, the installment plan is in fact the cheaper alternative.

The installment plan's present value is the amount that you would need to invest now to cover the three payments. Let's check.

Here is how your bank balance would change as you make each payment:

Year	Initial Balance	– Payment	= Remaining Balance	+ Interest Earned	= Balance at Year-End
0	$15,133.06	$8,000	$7,133.06	$570.64	$7,703.70
1	7,703.70	4,000	3,703.70	296.30	4,000.00
2	4,000.00	4,000	0	0	0

If you start with the present value of $15,133.06 in the bank, you could make the first $8,000 payment and be left with $7,133.06. After 1 year, your savings account would receive an interest payment of $7,133.06 × .08 = $570.04, bringing your account to $7,703.70. Similarly, you would make the second $4,000 payment and be left with $3,703.70. This sum left in the bank would grow with interest to $4,000, just enough to make the last payment. ◀

The present value of a stream of future cash flows is the amount you need to invest today to generate that stream.

FIGURE 4–7 To find the present value of a stream of cash flows, you just calculate the present value of each flow and then add them.

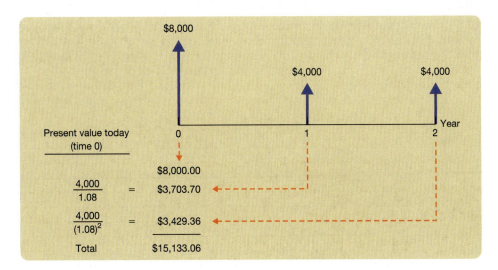

Self-Test 4.5

In order to avoid estate taxes, your rich aunt Frederica will pay you $10,000 per year for 4 years, starting 1 year from now. What is the present value of your benefactor's planned gifts? The interest rate is 7 percent. How much will you have 4 years from now if you invest each gift at 7 percent?

4.4 Level Cash Flows: Perpetuities and Annuities

annuity
Equally spaced level stream of cash flows, with a finite maturity.

perpetuity
Stream of level cash payments that never ends.

Frequently, you may need to value a stream of equal cash flows. For example, a home mortgage might require the homeowner to make equal monthly payments for the life of the loan. For a 30-year loan, this would result in 360 equal payments. A 4-year car loan might require 48 equal monthly payments. Any such sequence of equally spaced, level cash flows is called an **annuity.** If the payment stream lasts forever, it is called a **perpetuity.**

How to Value Perpetuities

Some time ago the British government borrowed by issuing loans known as consols. Consols are perpetuities. In other words, instead of repaying these loans, the British government pays the investors holding these securities a fixed annual payment in perpetuity (forever).

How might we value such a security? Suppose that you could invest $100 at an interest rate of 10 percent. You would earn annual interest of $.10 \times \$100 = \$10$ per year and could withdraw this amount from your investment account each year without ever running down your balance. In other words, a $100 investment could provide a perpetuity of $10 per year. In general,

$$\text{Cash payment from perpetuity} = \text{interest rate} \times \text{present value}$$

$$C = r \times PV$$

We can rearrange this relationship to derive the present value of a perpetuity, given the interest rate r and the cash payment C:

$$\text{PV of perpetuity} = \frac{C}{r} = \frac{\text{cash payment}}{\text{interest rate}}$$

Multiple Cash Flows

While uneven cash-flow problems are conceptually straight-forward, they rapidly become tedious and prone to errors from "typos," even if you use a financial calculator. It really helps to use spreadsheets. The following figure is a spreadsheet solution of Example 4.7.

The spreadsheet lists the time until each payment in column A. This value is used for the number of periods (nper)

in the PV formula in column C. The values for the cash flow in each future period are entered as negative numbers in the PV formula. The present values (column C) therefore appear as positive numbers.

An interactive version of this spreadsheet can be found at **www.mhhe.com/bmm5e** or on the Student CD.

	A	B	C	D	E
1	Finding the present value of multiple cash flows using a spreadsheet				
2					
3	Time until CF	Cash flow	Present value	Formula in Column C	
4	0	8000	$8,000.00	=PV($B$10,A4,0,-B4)	
5	1	4000	$3,703.70	=PV($B$10,A5,0,-B5)	
6	2	4000	$3,429.36	=PV($B$10,A6,0,-B6)	
7					
8	SUM:		$15,133.06	=SUM(C4:C6)	
9					
10	Discount rate:	0.08			
11					
12	Notice that the time until each payment (nper) is found in column A.				
13	Once we enter the formula for present value in cell C4, we can copy it to cells C5 and C6.				
14	The present value for other interest rates can be found by changing the entry in cell B10.				

Suppose some worthy person wishes to endow a chair in finance at your university. If the rate of interest is 10 percent and the aim is to provide $100,000 a year forever, the amount that must be set aside today is

$$\text{Present value of perpetuity} = \frac{C}{r} = \frac{\$100,000}{.10} = \$1,000,000$$

Two warnings about the perpetuity formula. First, at a quick glance you can easily confuse the formula with the present value of a single cash payment. A payment of $1 at the end of 1 year has a present value $1/(1 + r)$. The perpetuity has a value of $1/r$. These are quite different.

Second, the perpetuity formula tells us the value of a regular stream of payments starting one period from now. Thus our endowment of $1 million would provide the university with its first payment of $100,000 one year hence. If the worthy donor wants to provide the university with an additional payment of $100,000 up front, he or she would need to put aside $1,100,000.

Sometimes you may need to calculate the value of a perpetuity that does not start to make payments for several years. For example, suppose that our philanthropist decides to provide $100,000 a year with the first payment 4 years from now. We know that in year 3, this endowment will be an ordinary perpetuity with payments starting at the end of 1 year. So our perpetuity formula tells us that in year 3 the endowment will be worth $100,000/r. But it is not worth that much now. To find today's value we need to multiply by the 3-year discount factor. Thus, the "delayed" perpetuity is worth

$$\$100,000 \times \frac{1}{r} \times \frac{1}{(1 + r)^3} = \$1,000,000 \times \frac{1}{(1.10)^3} = \$751,315$$

Self-Test 4.6

A British government perpetuity pays £4 a year forever and is selling for £48. What is the interest rate?

FIGURE 4–8 The value of an annuity is equal to the difference between the value of two perpetuities.

	Cash Flow							Present Value
Year:	1	2	3	4	5	6 . . .		
1. Perpetuity A	$1	$1	$1	$1	$1	$1 . . .		$\dfrac{1}{r}$
2. Perpetuity B				$1	$1	$1 . . .		$\dfrac{1}{r(1+r)^3}$
3. Three-year annuity	$1	$1	$1					$\dfrac{1}{r} - \dfrac{1}{r(1+r)^3}$

How to Value Annuities

There are two ways to value an annuity, that is, a limited number of cash flows. The slow way is to value each cash flow separately and add up the present values. The quick way is to take advantage of the following simplification. Figure 4–8 shows the cash payments and values of three investments.

Row 1   The investment shown in the first row provides a perpetual stream of $1 payments starting in year 1. We have already seen that this perpetuity has a present value of $1/r$.

Row 2   Now look at the investment shown in the second row of Figure 4–8. It also provides a perpetual stream of $1 payments, but these payments don't start until year 4. This stream of payments is identical to the delayed perpetuity that we just valued. In year 3, the investment will be an ordinary perpetuity with payments starting in 1 year and will therefore be worth $1/r$ in year 3. To find the value today, we simply multiply this figure by the 3-year discount factor. Thus

$$PV = \frac{1}{r} \times \frac{1}{(1+r)^3} = \frac{1}{r(1+r)^3}$$

Row 3   Finally, look at the investment shown in the third-row of Figure 4–8. This provides a level payment of $1 a year for each of 3 years. In other words, it is a 3-year annuity. You can also see that, taken together, the investments in rows 2 and 3 provide exactly the same cash payments as the investment in row 1. Thus the value of our annuity (row 3) must be equal to the value of the row 1 perpetuity less the value of the delayed row 2 perpetuity:

$$\text{Present value of a 3-year \$1 annuity} = \frac{1}{r} - \frac{1}{r(1+r)^3}$$

The general formula for the value of an annuity that pays C dollars a year for each of t years starting in year 1 is

$$\textbf{Present value of } \textit{t}\textbf{-year annuity} = C\left[\frac{1}{r} - \frac{1}{r(1+r)^t}\right]$$

annuity factor
Present value of a $1 annuity.

The expression in square brackets shows the present value of a t-year annuity of $1 a year. It is generally known as the t-year **annuity factor.** Therefore, another way to write the value of an annuity is

$$\textbf{Present value of } \textit{t}\textbf{-year annuity = payment} \times \textbf{annuity factor}$$

Remembering formulas is about as difficult as remembering other people's birthdays. But as long as you bear in mind that an annuity is equivalent to the difference between an immediate and a delayed perpetuity, you shouldn't have any difficulty.

EXAMPLE 4.8   ▶   Back to Kangaroo Autos

Let us return to Kangaroo Autos for (almost) the last time. Most installment plans call for level streams of payments. So let us suppose that this time Kangaroo offers an

FIGURE 4–9 To find the value of an annuity, you can calculate the value of each cash flow. It is usually quicker to use the annuity formula.

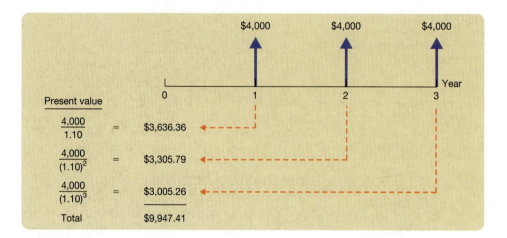

"easy payment" scheme of $4,000 a year at the end of each of the next 3 years. First let's do the calculations the slow way, to show that if the interest rate is 10 percent, the present value of the three payments is $9,947.41. The time line in Figure 4–9 shows these calculations. The present value of each cash flow is calculated and then the three present values are summed. The annuity formula, however, is much quicker:

$$\text{Present value} = \$4,000 \times \left[\frac{1}{.10} - \frac{1}{.10(1.10)^3} \right]$$
$$= \$4,000 \times 2.48685 = \$9,947.41 \quad \blacktriangleleft$$

You can use a calculator or spreadsheet to work out annuity factors (we show you how later in the chapter) or you can use a set of annuity tables. Table 4–4 is an abridged annuity table (an extended version is shown in Table A.3 at the end of the book). Check that you can find the 3-year annuity factor for an interest rate of 10 percent.

Self-Test 4.7

If the interest rate is 8 percent, what is the 4-year discount factor? What is the 4-year annuity factor? What is the relationship between these two numbers? Explain.

EXAMPLE 4.9   ▶   Winning Big at the Lottery

In August 1998 thirteen lucky machinists from Ohio pooled their money to buy Powerball lottery tickets and won a record $295.7 million. (A fourteenth member of the group pulled out at the last minute in order to put in his own numbers.) We suspect

TABLE 4–4 An example of an annuity table, showing the present value today of $1 a year received for each of *t* years

Number of Years	Interest Rate per Year					
	5%	6%	7%	8%	9%	10%
1	0.9524	0.9434	0.9346	0.9259	0.9174	0.9091
2	1.8594	1.8334	1.8080	1.7833	1.7591	1.7355
3	2.7232	2.6730	2.6243	2.5771	2.5313	2.4869
4	3.5460	3.4651	3.3872	3.3121	3.2397	3.1699
5	4.3295	4.2124	4.1002	3.9927	3.8897	3.7908
10	7.7217	7.3601	7.0236	6.7101	6.4177	6.1446
20	12.4622	11.4699	10.5940	9.8181	9.1285	8.5136
30	15.3725	13.7648	12.4090	11.2578	10.2737	9.4269

that the winners received unsolicited congratulations, good wishes, and requests for money from dozens of more or less worthy charities, relations, and newly devoted friends. In response, they could fairly point out that the prize wasn't really worth $295.7 million. That sum was to be paid in 25 equal annual installments of $11.828 million each. Assuming that the first payment occurred at the end of 1 year, what was the present value of the prize? The interest rate at the time was 5.9 percent.

The present value of these payments is simply the sum of the present values of each annual payment. But rather than valuing the payments separately, it is much easier to treat them as a 25-year annuity. To value this annuity, we simply multiply $11.828 million by the 25-year annuity factor:

$$PV = 11.828 \times 25\text{-year annuity factor}$$

$$= 11.828 \times \left[\frac{1}{r} - \frac{1}{r(1 + r)^{25}} \right]$$

At an interest rate of 5.9 percent, the annuity factor is

$$\left[\frac{1}{.059} - \frac{1}{.059(1.059)^{25}} \right] = 12.9057$$

(We could also look up the annuity factor in Table A.3.) The present value of the cash payments is $11.828 \times 12.9057 = 152.6 million, much less than the much-advertised prize, but still not a bad day's haul.

Lottery operators generally make arrangements for winners with big spending plans to take an equivalent lump sum. In our example the winners could either take the $295.7 million spread over 25 years or receive $152.6 million up front. Both arrangements have the same present value. ◀

EXAMPLE 4.10 ▶ How Much Luxury and Excitement Can $46 Billion Buy?

Bill Gates is reputedly the world's richest person, with wealth estimated in 2005 at about $46 billion. We haven't yet met Mr. Gates, and so cannot fill you in on his plans for allocating the $46 billion between charitable good works and the cost of a life of luxury and excitement (L&E). So to keep things simple, we will just ask the following entirely hypothetical question: How much could Mr. Gates spend yearly on 30 more years of L&E if he were to devote the entire $46 billion to those purposes? Assume that his money is invested to earn 9 percent.

The 30-year, 9 percent annuity factor is 10.2737. Thus

$$\text{Present value} = \text{annual spending} \times \text{annuity factor}$$
$$\$46,000,000,000 = \text{annual spending} \times 10.2737$$
$$\text{Annual spending} = \$4,477,000,000, \text{ or about } \$4.5 \text{ billion}$$

Warning to Mr. Gates: We haven't considered inflation. The cost of buying L&E will increase, so $4.5 billion won't buy as much L&E in 30 years as it will today. More on that later. ◀

Self-Test 4.8 Suppose you retire at age 70. You expect to live 20 more years and to spend $55,000 a year during your retirement. How much money do you need to save by age 70 to support this consumption plan? Assume an interest rate of 7 percent.

EXAMPLE 4.11 ▶ Home Mortgages

Sometimes you may need to find the series of cash payments that would provide a given value today. For example, home purchasers typically borrow the bulk of the

Year	Beginning-of-Year Balance	Year-End Interest Due on Balance	Year-End Payment	Amortization of Loan	End-of-Year Balance
1	$1,000.00	$100.00	$315.47	$215.47	$784.53
2	$784.53	$78.45	$315.47	$237.02	$547.51
3	$547.51	$54.75	$315.47	$260.72	$286.79
4	$286.79	$28.68	$315.47	$286.79	$0

house price from a lender. The most common loan arrangement is a 30-year loan that is repaid in equal monthly installments. Suppose that a house costs $125,000 and that the buyer puts down 20 percent of the purchase price, or $25,000, in cash, borrowing the remaining $100,000 from a mortgage lender such as the local savings bank. What is the appropriate monthly mortgage payment?

The borrower repays the loan by making monthly payments over the next 30 years (360 months). The savings bank needs to set these monthly payments so that they have a present value of $100,000. Thus

$$\text{Present value} = \text{mortgage payment} \times \text{360-month annuity factor}$$
$$= \$100,000$$

$$\text{Mortgage payment} = \frac{\$100,000}{\text{360-month annuity factor}}$$

Suppose that the interest rate is 1 percent a month. Then

$$\text{Mortgage payment} = \frac{\$100,000}{\left[\dfrac{1}{.01} - \dfrac{1}{.01(1.01)^{360}}\right]} = \frac{\$100,000}{97.218} = \$1,028.61$$

The mortgage loan in Example 4.11 is an example of an *amortizing loan*. "Amortizing" means that part of the monthly payment is used to pay interest on the loan and part is used to reduce the amount of the loan. Table 4–5 illustrates a 4-year amortizing loan of $1,000 with an interest rate of 10 percent and annual payments starting in 1 year. The annual payment (annuity) that would repay the loan is $315.47. (Confirm this for yourself.) At the end of the first year, the interest payment is 10 percent of $1,000, or $100. So $100 of your first payment is used to pay interest, and the remaining $215.47 is used to reduce (or "amortize") the loan balance to $784.53.

Next year, the outstanding balance is lower, so the interest charge is only $78.45. Therefore, $315.47 – $78.45 = $237.02 can be applied to amortization. Amortization in the second year is higher than in the first, because the amount of the loan has declined and therefore less of the payment is taken up in interest. This procedure continues until the last year, when the amortization is just enough to reduce the outstanding balance on the loan to zero.

Because the loan is progressively paid off, the fraction of each payment devoted to interest steadily falls over time, while the fraction used to reduce the loan (the amortization) steadily increases. Figure 4–10 illustrates the amortization of the mortgage loan in Example 4.11. In the early years, almost all of the mortgage payment is for interest. Even after 15 years, the bulk of the monthly payment is interest.

Self-Test 4.9

What will be the monthly payment if you take out a $100,000 fifteen-year mortgage at an interest rate of 1 percent per month? How much of the first payment is interest, and how much is amortization?

FIGURE 4–10 Mortgage amortization. This figure shows the breakdown of mortgage payments between interest and amortization. Monthly payments within each year are summed, so the figure shows the annual payment on the mortgage.

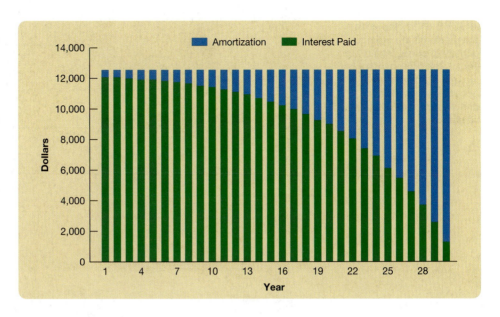

Annuities Due

The perpetuity and annuity formulas assume that the first payment occurs at the end of the period. They tell you the value of a stream of cash payments starting one period hence.

However, streams of cash payments often start immediately. For example, Kangaroo Autos in Example 4.8 might have required three annual payments of $4,000 starting immediately. A level stream of payments starting immediately is known as an **annuity due.**

annuity due

Level stream of cash flows starting immediately.

Figure 4–11 depicts the cash-flow streams of an ordinary annuity and an annuity due. By comparing the two panels of the figure, you can see that each of the three cash flows in the annuity due comes one period earlier than the corresponding cash flow of the ordinary annuity. Therefore,

Present value of an annuity due = $(1 + r) \times$ present value of an annuity

Figure 4–11 shows that the effect of bringing the Kangaroo loan payments forward by 1 year is an increase in their value from $9,947.41 (as an ordinary annuity) to $10,942.15 (as an annuity due). Notice that $10,942.15 = $9,947.41 \times 1.10$.

Self-Test 4.10

When calculating the value of the Powerball lottery prize in Example 4.9, we assumed that the first of the payments occurred at the end of 1 year. However, the winners of the lottery would not in fact have needed to wait a year before receiving their first payment. They would have gotten their first installment of $11.828 million up front and the remaining payments would have been spread over the following 24 years. Recalculate the value of the prize.

Future Value of an Annuity

You are back in savings mode again. This time you are setting aside $3,000 at the end of every year in order to buy a car. If your savings earn interest of 8 percent a year, how much will they be worth at the end of 4 years? We can answer this question with the help of the time line in Figure 4–12. Your first year's savings will earn interest for 3 years, the second will earn interest for 2 years, the third will earn interest for 1 year, and the final savings in year 4 will earn no interest. The sum of the future values of the four payments is

$(\$3,000 \times 1.08^3) + (\$3,000 \times 1.08^2) + (\$3,000 \times 1.08) + \$3,000 = \$13,518$

FIGURE 4-11 The cash payments on the ordinary annuity in panel (*a*) start in year 1. The first payment on the annuity due in panel (*b*) occurs immediately. The annuity due is therefore more valuable.

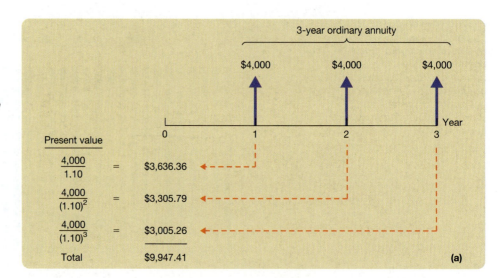

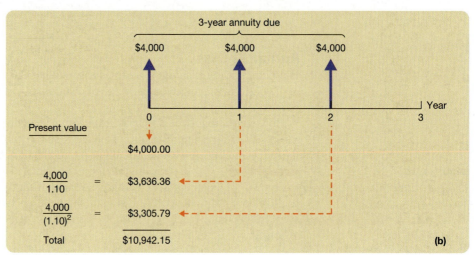

But wait a minute! We are looking here at a level stream of cash flows—an annuity. We have seen that there is a shortcut formula to calculate the *present* value of an annuity. So there ought to be a similar formula for calculating the *future* value of a level stream of cash flows.

FIGURE 4-12 Calculating the future value of an ordinary annuity of $3,000 a year for 4 years (interest rate = 8%)

TABLE 4–6 An example of a table showing the future value of an investment of $1 a year for each of *t* years

Number of Years	Interest Rate per Year					
	5%	6%	7%	8%	9%	10%
1	1.0000	1.0000	1.0000	1.0000	1.0000	1.0000
2	2.0500	2.0600	2.0700	2.0800	2.0900	2.1000
3	3.1525	3.1836	3.2149	3.2464	3.2781	3.3100
4	4.3101	4.3746	4.4399	4.5061	4.5731	4.6410
5	5.5256	5.6371	5.7507	5.8666	5.9847	6.1051
10	12.5779	13.1808	13.8164	14.4866	15.1929	15.9374
20	33.0660	36.7856	40.9955	45.7620	51.1601	57.2750
30	66.4388	79.0582	94.4608	113.2832	136.3075	164.4940

Think first how much your stream of savings is worth today. You are setting aside $3,000 in each of the next 4 years. The *present* value of this 4-year annuity is therefore equal to

$$PV = \$3,000 \times 4\text{-year annuity factor}$$

$$= \$3,000 \times \left[\frac{1}{.08} - \frac{1}{.08(1.08)^4} \right] = \$9,936$$

Now think how much you would have after 4 years if you invested $9,936 today. Simple! Just multiply by $(1.08)^4$:

$$\text{Value at end of year 4} = \$9,936 \times 1.08^4 = \$13,518$$

We calculated the future value of the annuity by first calculating the present value and then multiplying by $(1 + r)^t$. The general formula for the future value of a stream of cash flows of $1 a year for each of *t* years is therefore

Future value of annuity of $1 a year = present value of annuity of $1 a year × $(1 + r)^t$

$$= \left[\frac{1}{r} - \frac{1}{r(1 + r)^t} \right] \times (1 + r)^t = \frac{(1 + r)^t - 1}{r}$$

If you need to find the future value of just four cash flows as in our example, it is a toss up whether it is quicker to calculate the future value of each cash flow separately (as we did in Figure 4–12) or to use the annuity formula. If you are faced with a stream of 10 or 20 cash flows, there is no contest.

You can find the future value of an annuity in Table 4–6 or the more extensive Table A.4 at the end of the book. You can see that in the row corresponding to $t = 4$ and the column corresponding to $r = 8\%$, the future value of an annuity of $1 a year is $4.5061. Therefore, the future value of the $3,000 annuity is $3,000 × 4.5061 = $13,518.

EXAMPLE 4.12   ▶   Saving for Retirement

In only 50 more years, you will retire. (That's right—by the time you retire, the retirement age will be around 70 years. Longevity is not an unmixed blessing.) Have you started saving yet? Suppose you believe you will need to accumulate $500,000 by your retirement date in order to support your desired standard of living. How much must you save *each year* between now and your retirement to meet that future goal? Let's say that the interest rate is 10 percent per year. You need to find how large the annuity in the following figure must be to provide a future value of $500,000:

Interest Rate Calculators

Present and Future Values

There are dozens of Web sites that provide calculators to help with personal finance decisions. Two good examples are **www.quicken.com** and **www.smartmoney.com.** Log on first to the Quicken site, and click on *Bills and Banking* to find a nice savings calculator. Suppose that you invest $1,000 today. How much will you have after 30 years if the interest rate is 6 percent and you don't save another dime? Check your answer with the savings calculator. Now try the same question assuming that you also save $200 a month.

Annuities Due

You can buy a car for $20,000, or you can lease it for 36 monthly payments of $350 each, with the first payment due immediately. At the end of the 36 months the car will be worth $10,000. Which alternative should you prefer if the interest rate is 10 percent? You can check your answer by logging on to the personal finance page of **www.smartmoney.com** and using the auto buy/lease calculator.

Mortgage Payments

In Example 4.11 we showed you how to work out mortgage payments. Log on to the personal finance page of **www.smartmoney.com** and find the mortgage payment calculator. Assume a 20-year mortgage loan of $100,000 and an interest rate of 10 percent. What is the amount of the payment? Check that you get the same answer when using the annuity formula. Now look at how much of the first month's payment goes to reduce the size of the mortgage. How much of the payment by the tenth year? Can you explain why the figure changes? If the interest rate doubles, would you expect the mortgage payment to double? Check whether you are right.

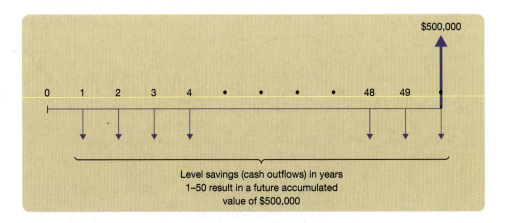

Level savings (cash outflows) in years
1–50 result in a future accumulated
value of $500,000

We know that if you were to save $1 each year your funds would accumulate to

$$\text{Future value of annuity of \$1 a year} = \frac{(1 + r)^t - 1}{r} = \frac{(1.10)^{50} - 1}{.10}$$

$$= \$1,163.91$$

(Rather than compute the future value formula directly, you could look up the future value annuity factor in Table A.4. Alternatively, you can use a financial calculator or spreadsheet as we describe in the nearby boxes.) Therefore, if you save an amount of $C each year, you will accumulate $C × 1,163.91.

We need to choose C to ensure that C × 1,163.91 = $500,000. Thus C = $500,000/1,163.91 = $429.59. This appears to be surprisingly good news. Saving $429.59 a year does not seem to be an extremely demanding savings program. Don't celebrate yet, however. The news will get worse when we consider the impact of inflation. ◀

Self-Test 4.11	**What is the required savings level if the interest rate is only 5 percent? Why has the amount increased?**

Remember that our ordinary annuity formulas assume that the first cash flow does not occur until the end of the first period. If the first cash flow comes immediately, the future value of the cash-flow stream is greater, since each flow has an extra year to earn interest. For example, at an interest rate of 10 percent, the future value of an annuity due would be exactly 10 percent greater than the future value of an ordinary annuity. More generally,

Future value of annuity due = future value of ordinary annuity × (1 + *r*)

EXAMPLE 4.13   ▶   Future Value of Annuities versus Annuities Due

In Example 4.12, we showed that an annual savings stream of $429.59 invested for 50 years at 10 percent would satisfy a savings goal of $500,000. What savings stream would be necessary if we invested our money at the beginning rather than the end of each year?

We know from Example 4.12 that the future value of a $1 ordinary 50-year annuity at an interest rate of 10 percent is $1,163.91. Therefore,

$$\text{FV of \$1 annuity due} = \text{FV of \$1 ordinary annuity} \times (1 + r)$$
$$= \$1,163.91 \times 1.10 = \$1,280.30$$

We need to choose *C* to ensure that *C* × 1,280.30 = $500,000. Thus *C* = $390.53. Notice that $390.53 equals the (ordinary) annuity we found in Example 4.12 divided by 1.10. ◀

The nearby boxes show how to use financial calculators and spreadsheets to solve annuity problems.

4.5 Inflation and the Time Value of Money

When a bank offers to pay 6 percent on a savings account, it promises to pay interest of $60 for every $1,000 you deposit. The bank fixes the number of dollars that it pays, but it doesn't provide any assurance of how much those dollars will buy. If the value of your investment increases by 6 percent while the prices of goods and services increase by 10 percent, you actually lose ground in terms of the goods you can buy.

Real versus Nominal Cash Flows

Prices of goods and services continually change. Textbooks may become more expensive (sorry) while computers become cheaper. An overall general rise in prices is known as **inflation.** If the inflation rate is 5 percent per year, then goods that cost $1.00 a year ago typically cost $1.05 this year. The increase in the general level of prices means that the purchasing power of money has eroded. If a dollar bill bought one loaf of bread last year, the same dollar this year buys only part of a loaf.

inflation

Rate at which prices as a whole are increasing.

Economists track the general level of prices using several different price indexes. The best known of these is the *consumer price index,* or *CPI.* This measures the number of dollars that it takes to buy a specified basket of goods and services that is

Solving Annuity Problems Using a Financial Calculator

The formulas for both the present value and the future value of an annuity are also built into your financial calculator. Again, we can input all but one of the five financial keys, and let the calculator solve for the remaining variable. In these applications, the *PMT* key is used to either enter or solve for the cash payments of the annuity.

Solving for an Annuity

In Example 4.12, we determined the savings stream that would provide a retirement goal of $500,000 after 50 years of saving at an interest rate of 10 percent. To find the required savings each year, enter $n = 50$, $i = 10$, $FV = 500,000$, and $PV = 0$ (because your "savings account" currently is empty). Compute *PMT* and find that it is –$429.59. Again, your calculator is likely to display the solution as –429.59, since the positive $500,000 cash value in 50 years will require 50 cash payments (outflows) of $429.59.

The sequences of key strokes on three popular calculators necessary to solve this problem are as follows:

Hewlett-Packard HP-10B	Sharp EL-733A	Texas Instruments BA II Plus
0 PV	0 PV	0 PV
50 n	50 n	50 n
10 I/YR	10 i	10 I/Y
500,000 FV	500,000 FV	500,000 FV
PMT	COMP PMT	CPT PMT

Present Value of an Annuity

In Example 4.11 we considered a 30-year mortgage with monthly payments of $1,028.61 and a monthly interest rate of 1 percent. Suppose we didn't know the amount of the mortgage loan. Enter $n = 360$ (months), $i = 1$, $PMT = -1,028.61$ (we enter the annuity level paid by the borrower to the lender as a negative number since it is a cash outflow), and $FV = 0$ (the mortgage is wholly paid off after 30 years; there are no final future payments beyond the normal monthly payment). Compute *PV* to find that the value of the loan is $100,000.

What about the balance left on the mortgage after 10 years have passed? This is easy: The monthly payment is still $PMT = -1,028.61$, and we continue to use $i = 1$ and FV

$= 0$. The only change is that the number of monthly payments remaining has fallen from 360 to 240 (20 years are left on the loan). So enter $n = 240$ and compute *PV* as 93,417.76. This is the balance remaining on the mortgage.

Future Value of an Annuity

In Figure 4–12, we showed that a 4-year annuity of $3,000 invested at 8 percent would accumulate to a future value of $13,518. To solve this on your calculator, enter $n = 4$, $i = 8$, $PMT = -3,000$ (we enter the annuity paid by the investor to her savings account as a negative number since it is a cash outflow), and $PV = 0$ (the account starts with no funds). Compute *FV* to find that the future value of the savings account after 3 years is $13,518.

Calculator Self-Test Review (answers follow)

1. Turn back to Kangaroo Autos in Example 4.8. Can you now solve for the present value of the three installment payments using your financial calculator? What key strokes must you use?
2. Now use your calculator to solve for the present value of the three installment payments if the first payment comes immediately, that is, as an annuity due.
3. Find the annual spending available to Bill Gates using the data in Example 4.10 and your financial calculator.

Solutions to Calculator Self-Test Review Questions

1. Inputs are $n = 3$, $i = 10$, $FV = 0$, and $PMT = 4,000$. Compute *PV* to find the present value of the cash flows as $9,947.41, which matches the solution given in the Example.
2. If you put your calculator in BEGIN mode and recalculate *PV* using the same inputs, you will find that *PV* has increased to $10,942.15. Alternatively, you can calculate the value of the annuity due by taking the value of the ordinary annuity, $9,947.41, and multiplying by 1 plus the interest rate, 1.10. The answer is again $9,947.41 × 1.10 = $10,942.15.
3. Inputs are $n = 30$, $i = 9$, $FV = 0$, $PV = -46,000$ million. Compute *PMT* to find that the 30-year annuity with present value of $46 billion is $4,477 million.

supposed to represent the typical family's purchases.[2] Thus the percentage increase in the CPI from one year to the next measures the rate of inflation.

Table 4–7 shows the CPI for selected years. The base period for the index is 1982–1984, so the index shows the price level in each year as a percentage of the average price level during these 3 years. For example, the index in 1950 was 25.0. This means that on average $25 in 1950 would have bought the same quantity of goods and services as $100 in 1982–1984. By the end of 2004, the index had risen to 190.3. In other words, prices in 2004 were 7.61 times their level in 1950 (190.3/25.0 = 7.61).[3]

---

[2] Don't ask how you buy a "basket" of services.

[3] The choice by the Bureau of Labor Statistics of 1982–1984 as a base period is arbitrary. For example, the bureau could have set December 1950 as the base period. In this case the index would have been 100 in 1950 and 761.2 in 2004.

TABLE 4–7 The consumer price index (CPI) shows how inflation has increased the cost of a typical family's purchases.

	CPI	Percent Change since 1950
1950	25.0	
1960	29.8	+ 19.2%
1970	39.8	+ 59.2
1980	86.3	+ 245.2
1990	133.8	+ 435.2
2000	174.0	+ 596.0
2004	190.3	+ 661.2

It is interesting to look at annual inflation rates over a somewhat longer period. These are shown in Figure 4–13. The peak year for inflation was 1918, when prices rose by 20 percent, but you can see that there have also been a few years when prices have fallen quite sharply.

As we write this in early 2005, all is quiet on the inflation front. In the United States inflation is running at about 3 percent a year and a few countries are even experiencing falling prices, or *deflation*. This has led some economists to argue that inflation is dead; others are less sure.

EXAMPLE 4.14 ► The Outrageous Price of Gasoline

In 2004 there was widespread dismay as the price of unleaded gasoline climbed to $2.03 a gallon. Motorists looked back longingly to 20 years earlier when they were paying just $1.19 a gallon. But how much had the real price of gasoline changed over this period? Let's check.

In 2004 the consumer price index was 1.81 times its level in 1984. If the price of gasoline had risen in line with inflation, it would have cost 1.81 × $1.19 = $2.15 a gallon in 2004. That was the cost of gasoline 20 years ago but measured in terms of 2004 dollars rather than 1984 dollars. Thus over the 20 years the real price of gasoline *declined* from $2.15 a gallon to $2.03, a fall of 6 percent. ◄

FIGURE 4–13 Annual rates of inflation in the United States from 1900 to 2004

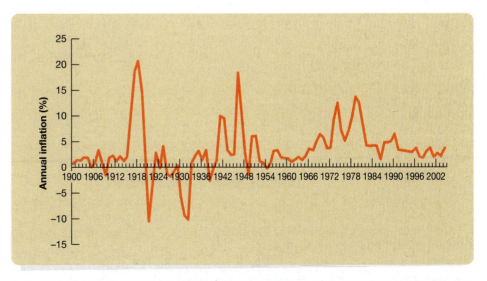

Source: Author's calculations using data from E. Dimson, P. R. Marsh, and M. Staunton, *Triumph of the Optimists: 101 Years of Global Investment Returns* (Princeton, NJ: Princeton University Press, 2002).

Annuities

By now it should be no surprise that the PMT variable in Excel's time-value-of-money functions denotes the level of an annuity. In addition, Excel provides another function to solve for annuity levels given the values of the other variables: PMT (rate, nper, PV, FV). Thus in Example 4.12, we can find the savings stream providing a future retirement goal of $500,000 after 50 years by entering =PMT(.10,50,0,500000), which results in an answer of –$429.59. Notice that we enter 0 for PV because our savings account starts with no funds.

Present Value of an Annuity

Example 4.11 examines a 30-year mortgage loan with 360 monthly payments of $1,028.61 each when the interest rate is 1 percent per month. The present value of this annuity is =PV(.01,360,1028.61,0), which (except for trivial rounding error) is $100,000. We can also find the balance on the loan after 10 years, when there are 240 remaining payments, as =PV(.01,240,1028.61,0) = $93,417.76.

Future Value of an Annuity

We confirmed on our calculators in the previous box that a 4-year annuity of $3,000 invested at 8 percent has a future value of $13,518 (see Figure 4–12). You can also confirm this value on your spreadsheet by entering =FV(.08,4,3000,0).

Annuities Due

Excel will calculate the value of an annuity due rather than an ordinary annuity if you add an extra 1 at the end of the function. For example, we just calculated the present value of 360 monthly mortgage payments. Now assume the first payment comes immediately rather than after 1 month. In other words, the payments are an annuity due. Then the present value is found as =PV(.01,360,1028.61,0,1), which equals $101,000, exactly 1 percent more than the value of the payments as an ordinary annuity. Similarly, the future value of the 4-year, $3,000 annuity that we just looked at also is higher if the first payment is made immediately. As an annuity due, the future value is =FV(.08,4,3000,0,1) = $14,600, which is 8 percent higher than the future value of the ordinary annuity.

Spreadsheet Self-Test Review

In the previous box on page 98, we gave you three self-test review questions for your calculator. Now solve these problems using a spreadsheet program.

Self-Test 4.12

Consider a telephone call to London that currently would cost $5. If the real price of telephone calls does not change in the future, how much will it cost you to make a call to London in 50 years if the inflation rate is 5 percent (roughly its average over the past 30 years)? What if inflation is 10 percent?

Economists sometimes talk about *current* or *nominal dollars* versus *constant* or *real dollars*. Current or nominal dollars refer to the actual number of dollars of the day; constant or real dollars refer to the amount of purchasing power.

Some expenditures are fixed in nominal terms and therefore *decline* in real terms. Suppose you took out a 30-year house mortgage in 1990. The monthly payment was $800. It was still $800 in 2004, even though the CPI increased by a factor of 1.42 over those years (190.3/133.8 = 1.42).

What's the monthly payment for 2004 expressed in real 1990 dollars? The answer is $800/1.42, or $562 per month. The real burden of paying the mortgage was much less in 2004 than in 1990.

Self-Test 4.13

If a family spent $250 a week on their typical purchases in 1950, how much would those purchases have cost in 1980? If your salary in 1980 was $30,000 a year, what would be the real value of that salary in terms of 1950 dollars?

Inflation and Interest Rates

Whenever anyone quotes an interest rate, you can be fairly sure that it is a *nominal,* not a *real,* rate. It sets the actual number of dollars you will be paid with no offset for future inflation.

nominal interest rate
Rate at which money invested grows.

If you deposit $1,000 in the bank at a **nominal interest rate** of 6 percent, you will have $1,060 at the end of the year. But this does not mean you are 6 percent better off. Suppose that the inflation rate during the year is also 6 percent. Then the goods that cost $1,000 last year will now cost $1,000 × 1.06 = $1,060, so you've gained nothing:

$$\text{Real future value of investment} = \frac{\$1,000 \times (1 + \text{nominal interest rate})}{(1 + \text{inflation rate})}$$

$$= \frac{\$1,000 \times 1.06}{1.06} = \$1,000$$

real interest rate
Rate at which the purchasing power of an investment increases.

In this example, the nominal rate of interest is 6 percent, but the **real interest rate** is zero.

The real rate of interest is calculated by

$$\textbf{1 + real interest rate} = \frac{\textbf{1 + nominal interest rate}}{\textbf{1 + inflation rate}}$$

In our example both the nominal interest rate and the inflation rate were 6 percent. So

$$1 + \text{real interest rate} = \frac{1.06}{1.06} = 1$$

$$\text{real interest rate} = \quad 0$$

What if the nominal interest rate is 6 percent but the inflation rate is only 2 percent? In that case the real interest rate is 1.06/1.02 − 1 = .039, or 3.9 percent. Imagine that the price of a loaf of bread is $1, so that $1,000 would buy 1,000 loaves today. If you invest that $1,000 at a nominal interest rate of 6 percent, you will have $1,060 at the end of the year. However, if the price of loaves has risen in the meantime to $1.02, then your money will buy you only 1,060/1.02 = 1,039 loaves. The real rate of interest is 3.9 percent.

Self-Test 4.14

a. Suppose that you invest your funds at an interest rate of 8 percent. What will be your real rate of interest if the inflation rate is zero? What if it is 5 percent?
b. Suppose that you demand a real rate of interest of 3 percent on your investments. What nominal interest rate do you need to earn if the inflation rate is zero? If it is 5 percent?

Here is a useful approximation. The real rate approximately equals the difference between the nominal rate and the inflation rate:[4]

$$\textbf{Real interest rate} \approx \textbf{nominal interest rate − inflation rate}$$

Our example used a nominal interest rate of 6 percent, an inflation rate of 2 percent, and a real rate of 3.9 percent. If we round to 4 percent, the approximation gives the same answer:

$$\text{Real interest rate} \approx \text{nominal interest rate − inflation rate}$$

$$\approx 6 - 2 = 4\%$$

The approximation works best when both the inflation rate and the real rate are small.[5] When they are not small, throw the approximation away and do it right.

EXAMPLE 4.15 ▶ Real and Nominal Rates

In the United States in 2005, long-term high-grade corporate bonds offered a yield of about 5.1 percent. If inflation is expected to stay at about 3 percent, the *real* yield is

$$1 + \text{real interest rate} = \frac{1 + \text{nominal interest rate}}{1 + \text{inflation rate}} = \frac{1.051}{1.03} = 1.0204$$

$$\text{real interest rate} = .0204, \text{ or } 2.04\%$$

---

[4] The squiggle (≈) means "approximately equal to."

[5] When the interest and inflation rates are expressed as decimals (rather than percentages), the approximation error equals the product (real interest rate × inflation rate).

The approximation rule gives a similar value of 5.1 – 3.0 = 2.1 percent. But the approximation would not have worked in the German hyperinflation of 1922–1923, when the inflation rate was well over 100 percent per *month* (at one point you needed 1 million marks to mail a letter), or in Peru in 1990, when prices increased by nearly 7,500 percent.   ◄

Valuing Real Cash Payments

Think again about how to value future cash payments. Earlier in the chapter you learned how to value payments in current dollars by discounting at the nominal interest rate. For example, suppose that the nominal interest rate is 10 percent. How much do you need to invest now to produce $100 in a year's time? Easy! Calculate the present value of $100 by discounting by 10 percent:

$$PV = \frac{\$100}{1.10} = \$90.91$$

You get exactly the same result if you discount the *real* payment by the *real interest rate*. For example, assume that you expect inflation of 7 percent over the next year. The real value of that $100 is therefore only $100/1.07 = $93.46. In one year's time your $100 will buy only as much as $93.46 today. Also with a 7 percent inflation rate the real rate of interest is only about 3 percent. We can calculate it exactly from the formula

$$1 + \text{real interest rate} = \frac{1 + \text{nominal interest rate}}{1 + \text{inflation rate}} = \frac{1.10}{1.07} = 1.028$$

$$\text{real interest rate} = .028, \text{ or } 2.8\%$$

If we now discount the $93.46 real payment by the 2.8 percent real interest rate, we have a present value of $90.91, just as before:

$$PV = \frac{\$93.46}{1.028} = \$90.91$$

The two methods should always give the same answer.[6]

Remember: Current dollar cash flows must be discounted by the nominal interest rate; real cash flows must be discounted by the real interest rate.

Mixing up nominal cash flows and real discount rates (or real rates and nominal flows) is an unforgivable sin. It is surprising how many sinners one finds.

Self-Test 4.15   You are owed $5,000 by a relative who will pay it back in 1 year. The nominal interest rate is 8 percent, and the inflation rate is 5 percent. What is the present value of your relative's IOU? Show that you get the same answer (a) discounting the nominal payment at the nominal rate and (b) discounting the real payment at the real rate.

---

[6] If they don't, there must be an error in your calculations. All we have done in the second calculation is to divide both the numerator (the cash payment) and the denominator (1 plus the nominal interest rate) by the same number (1 plus the inflation rate):

$$PV = \frac{\text{payment in current dollars}}{1 + \text{nominal interest rate}}$$

$$= \frac{(\text{payment in current dollars})/(1 + \text{inflation rate})}{(1 + \text{nominal interest rate})/(1 + \text{inflation rate})}$$

$$= \frac{\text{payment in constant dollars}}{1 + \text{real interest rate}}$$

Inflation

You can find data on the consumer price index (CPI) on the Bureau of Labor Statistics Web site, **www.bls.gov/cpi/home.htm**. Tables of historical data can be formatted to provide either levels of the index or changes in the index (i.e., the rate of inflation). See if you can construct a table of annual inflation rates since 1945. What is the highest level of inflation during this period? Has the USA ever experienced a year of deflation (i.e., falling prices) since 1945? Find the inflation rate in the latest year. Now log on to **www.bloomberg.com**, and on the first page find a measure of the short-term interest rate (e.g., the 2-year rate). Use the recent level of inflation to calculate the *real* interest rate.

The Web site **www.globalfindata.com** is a marvelous source of financial data, which includes a very long-term inflation series. Consider the case of Herbert Protheroe, who in 1830 was an eligible bachelor with an income of $2,000 a year. What is that equivalent to today?

EXAMPLE 4.16 ▶ How Inflation Might Affect Bill Gates

We showed earlier (Example 4.10) that at an interest rate of 9 percent Bill Gates could, if he wished, turn his $46 billion wealth into a 30-year annuity of $4.5 billion per year of luxury and excitement (L&E). Unfortunately, L&E expenses inflate just like gasoline and groceries. Thus Mr. Gates would find the purchasing power of that $4.5 billion steadily declining. If he wants the same luxuries in 2035 as in 2005, he'll have to spend less in 2005 and then increase expenditures in line with inflation. How much should he spend in 2005? Assume the long-run inflation rate is 5 percent.

Mr. Gates needs to calculate a 30-year *real* annuity. The real interest rate is a little less than 4 percent:

$$1 + \text{real interest rate} = \frac{1 + \text{nominal interest rate}}{1 + \text{inflation rate}}$$

$$= \frac{1.09}{1.05} = 1.038$$

so the real rate is 3.8 percent. The 30-year annuity factor at 3.8 percent is 17.720. Therefore, annual spending (in 2005 dollars) should be chosen so that

$$\$46,000,000,000 = \text{annual spending} \times 17.720$$
$$\text{annual spending} = \$2,596,000,000$$

Mr. Gates could spend that amount on L&E in one year's time and 5 percent more (in line with inflation) in each subsequent year. This is only about half the value we calculated when we ignored inflation. Life has many disappointments, even for tycoons. ◀

Self-Test 4.16

You have reached age 60 with a modest fortune of $3 million and are considering early retirement. How much can you spend each year for the next 30 years? Assume that spending is stable in real terms. The nominal interest rate is 10 percent, and the inflation rate is 5 percent.

Real or Nominal?

Any present value calculation done in nominal terms can also be done in real terms, and vice versa. Most financial analysts forecast in nominal terms and discount at nominal rates. However, in some cases real cash flows are easier to deal with. In our example of Bill Gates, the *real* expenditures were fixed. In this case, it was easiest to use real quantities. On the other hand, if the cash-flow stream is fixed in nominal terms (for example, the payments on a loan), it is easiest to use all nominal quantities.

4.6 Effective Annual Interest Rates

Thus far in this chapter we have mainly used *annual* interest rates to value a series of *annual* cash flows. But interest rates may be quoted for days, months, years, or any convenient interval. How should we compare rates when they are quoted for different periods, such as monthly versus annually?

Consider your credit card. Suppose you have to pay interest on any unpaid balances at the rate of 1 percent *per month*. What is it going to cost you if you neglect to pay off your unpaid balance for a year?

Don't be put off because the interest rate is quoted per month rather than per year. The important thing is to maintain consistency between the interest rate and the number of periods. If the interest rate is quoted as a percent per month, then we must define the number of periods in our future value calculation as the number of months. So if you borrow \$100 from the credit card company at 1 percent per month for 12 months, you will need to repay $\$100 \times (1.01)^{12} = \$112.68$. Thus your debt grows after 1 year to \$112.68. Therefore, we can say that the interest rate of 1 percent a month is equivalent to an **effective annual interest rate,** or *annually compounded rate,* of 12.68 percent.

effective annual interest rate

Interest rate that is annualized using compound interest.

In general, the effective annual interest rate is defined as the rate at which your money grows, allowing for the effect of compounding. Therefore, for the credit card,

$$1 + \text{effective annual rate} = (1 + \text{monthly rate})^{12}$$

When comparing interest rates, it is best to use effective annual rates. This compares interest paid or received over a common period (1 year) and allows for possible compounding during the period. Unfortunately, short-term rates are sometimes annualized by multiplying the rate per period by the number of periods in a year. In fact, truth-in-lending laws in the United States *require* that rates be annualized in this manner. Such rates are called annual **percentage rates (APRs).**[7] The interest rate on your credit card loan was 1 percent per month. Since there are 12 months in a year, the APR on the loan is $12 \times 1\% = 12\%$.

annual percentage rate (APR)

Interest rate that is annualized using simple interest.

If the credit card company quotes an APR of 12 percent, how can you find the effective annual interest rate? The solution is simple:

Step 1. Take the quoted APR and divide by the number of compounding periods in a year to recover the rate per period actually charged. In our example, the interest was calculated monthly. So we divide the APR by 12 to obtain the interest rate per month:

$$\text{Monthly interest rate} = \frac{\text{APR}}{12} = \frac{12\%}{1} = 1\%$$

Step 2. Now convert to an annually compounded interest rate:

$$1 + \text{effective annual rate} = (1 + \text{monthly rate})^{12} = (1 + .01)^{12} = 1.1268$$

The effective annual interest rate is .1268, or 12.68 percent.

In general, if an investment is quoted with a given APR and there are m compounding periods in a year, then \$1 will grow to $\$1 \times (1 + \text{APR}/m)^m$ after 1 year. The effective annual interest rate is $(1 + \text{APR}/m)^m - 1$. For example, a credit card loan that charges a monthly interest rate of 1 percent has an APR of 12 percent but an effective annual interest rate of $(1.01)^{12} - 1 = .1268$, or 12.68 percent. To summarize: The effective annual rate is the rate at which invested funds will grow over the course of a year. It equals the rate of interest per period compounded for the number of periods in a year.

---

[7] The truth-in-lending laws apply to credit card loans, auto loans, home improvement loans, and some loans to small businesses. APRs are not commonly used or quoted in the big leagues of finance.

TABLE 4–8 These investments all have an APR of 6 percent, but the more frequently interest is compounded, the higher is the effective annual rate of interest

Compounding Period	Periods per Year (m)	Per-Period Interest Rate	Growth Factor of Invested Funds	Effective Annual Rate
1 year	1	6%	1.06	6.0000%
Semiannually	2	3	$1.03^2 = 1.0609$	6.0900
Quarterly	4	1.5	$1.015^4 = 1.061364$	6.1364
Monthly	12	.5	$1.005^{12} = 1.061678$	6.1678
Weekly	52	.11538	$1.0011538^{52} = 1.061800$	6.1800
Daily	365	.01644	$1.0001644^{365} = 1.061831$	6.1831
Continuous			$e^{.06} = 1.061837$	6.1837

EXAMPLE 4.17 ▶ The Effective Interest Rates on Bank Accounts

Back in the 1960s and 1970s federal regulation limited the (APR) interest rates banks could pay on savings accounts. Banks were hungry for depositors, and they searched for ways to increase the *effective* rate of interest that could be paid within the rules. Their solution was to keep the same APR but to calculate the interest on deposits more frequently. As interest is compounded at shorter and shorter intervals, less time passes before interest can be earned on interest. Therefore, the effective annually compounded rate of interest increases. Table 4–8 shows the calculations assuming that the maximum APR that banks could pay was 6 percent. (Actually, it was a bit less than this, but 6 percent is a nice round number to use for illustration.)

You can see from Table 4–8 how banks were able to increase the effective interest rate simply by calculating interest at more frequent intervals.

The ultimate step was to assume that interest was paid in a continuous stream rather than at fixed intervals. With 1 year's *continuous compounding*, $1 grows to e^{APR}, where $e = 2.718$ (a figure that may be familiar to you as the base for natural logarithms). Thus if you deposited $1 with a bank that offered a continuously compounded rate of 6 percent, your investment would grow by the end of the year to $(2.718)^{.06} =$ $1.061837, just a hair's breadth more than if interest were compounded daily. ◀

Self-Test 4.17

A car loan requiring quarterly payments carries an APR of 8 percent. What is the effective annual rate of interest?

SUMMARY

If you invest money at a given interest rate, what will be the future value of your investment?

An investment of $1 earning an interest rate of r will increase in value each period by the factor $(1 + r)$. After t periods its value will grow to $\$(1 + r)^t$. This is the **future value** of the $1 investment with compound interest.

What is the present value of a cash flow to be received in the future?

The **present value** of a future cash payment is the amount that you would need to invest today to match that future payment. To calculate present value, we divide the cash payment by $(1 + r)^t$ or, equivalently, multiply by the **discount factor** $1/(1 + r)^t$. The discount factor measures the value today of $1 received in period t.

| **How can we calculate present and future values of streams of cash payments?** | A level stream of cash payments that continues indefinitely is known as a **perpetuity;** one that continues for a limited number of years is called an **annuity.** The present value of a stream of cash flows is simply the sum of the present value of each individual cash flow. Similarly, the future value of an annuity is the sum of the future value of each individual cash flow. Shortcut formulas make the calculations for perpetuities and annuities easy. |

What is the difference between real and nominal cash flows and between real and nominal interest rates?

A dollar is a dollar, but the amount of goods that a dollar can buy is eroded by **inflation.** If prices double, the **real value of a dollar** halves. Financial managers and economists often find it helpful to reexpress future cash flows in terms of real dollars—that is, dollars of constant purchasing power.

Be careful to distinguish the **nominal interest rate** and the **real interest rate**—that is, the rate at which the real value of the investment grows. Discount nominal cash flows (that is, cash flows measured in current dollars) at nominal interest rates. Discount real cash flows (cash flows measured in constant dollars) at real interest rates. *Never* mix and match nominal and real.

How should we compare interest rates quoted over different time intervals— for example, monthly versus annual rates?

Interest rates for short time periods are often quoted as annual rates by multiplying the per-period rate by the number of periods in a year. These **annual percentage rates (APRs)** do not recognize the effect of compound interest, that is, they annualize assuming simple interest. The **effective annual rate** annualizes using compound interest. It equals the rate of interest per period compounded for the number of periods in a year.

QUIZ

1. **Present Values.** Compute the present value of a $100 cash flow for the following combinations of discount rates and times:

   a. $r = 8$ percent, $t = 10$ years.
   b. $r = 8$ percent, $t = 20$ years.
   c. $r = 4$ percent, $t = 10$ years.
   d. $r = 4$ percent, $t = 20$ years.

2. **Future Values.** Compute the future value of a $100 cash flow for the same combinations of rates and times as in problem 1.

3. **Future Values.** In 1880 five aboriginal trackers were each promised the equivalent of 100 Australian dollars for helping to capture the notorious outlaw Ned Kelley. In 1993 the granddaughters of two of the trackers claimed that this reward had not been paid. The Victorian prime minister stated that if this was true, the government would be happy to pay the $100. However, the granddaughters also claimed that they were entitled to compound interest. How much was each entitled to if the interest rate was 4 percent? What if it was 8 percent?

4. **Future Values.** You deposit $1,000 in your bank account. If the bank pays 4 percent simple interest, how much will you accumulate in your account after 10 years? What if the bank pays compound interest? How much of your earnings will be interest on interest?

5. **Present Values.** You will require $700 in 5 years. If you earn 5 percent interest on your funds, how much will you need to invest today in order to reach your savings goal?

6. **Calculating Interest Rate.** Find the interest rate implied by the following combinations of present and future values:

Present Value	Years	Future Value
$400	11	$684
$183	4	$249
$300	7	$300

7. **Present Values.** Would you rather receive $1,000 a year for 10 years or $800 a year for 15 years if

   a. the interest rate is 5 percent?
   b. the interest rate is 20 percent?

   Why do your answers to (a) and (b) differ?

8. **Calculating Interest Rate.** Find the annual interest rate.

Present Value	Future Value	Time Period
100	115.76	3 years
200	262.16	4 years
100	110.41	5 years

9. **Present Values.** What is the present value of the following cash-flow stream if the interest rate is 6 percent?

Year	Cash Flow
1	$200
2	$400
3	$300

10. **Number of Periods.** How long will it take for $400 to grow to $1,000 at the interest rate specified?

    a. 4 percent
    b. 8 percent
    c. 16 percent

11. **Calculating Interest Rate.** Find the effective annual interest rate for each case:

APR	Compounding Period
12%	1 month
8%	3 months
10%	6 months

12. **Calculating Interest Rate.** Find the APR (the stated interest rate) for each case:

Effective Annual Interest Rate	Compounding Period
10.00%	1 month
6.09%	6 months
8.24%	3 months

13. **Growth of Funds.** If you earn 6 percent per year on your bank account, how long will it take an account with $100 to double to $200?

14. **Comparing Interest Rates.** Suppose you can borrow money at 8.6 percent per year (APR) compounded semiannually or 8.4 percent per year (APR) compounded monthly. Which is the better deal?

15. **Calculating Interest Rate.** Lenny Loanshark charges "1 point" per week (that is, 1 percent per week) on his loans. What APR must he report to consumers? Assume exactly 52 weeks in a year. What is the effective annual rate?

16. **Compound Interest.** Investments in the stock market have increased at an average compound rate of about 5 percent since 1900. It is now 2005.

a. If you invested $1,000 in the stock market in 1900, how much would that investment be worth today?

b. If your investment in 1900 has grown to $1 million, how much did you invest in 1900?

17. **Compound Interest.** Old Time Savings Bank pays 4 percent interest on its savings accounts. If you deposit $1,000 in the bank and leave it there, how much interest will you earn in the first year? The second year? The tenth year?

18. **Compound Interest.** New Savings Bank pays 4 percent interest on its deposits. If you deposit $1,000 in the bank and leave it there, will it take more or less than 25 years for your money to double? You should be able to answer this without a calculator or interest rate tables.

19. **Calculating Interest Rate.** A zero-coupon bond that will pay $1,000 in 10 years is selling today for $422.41. What interest rate does the bond offer?

20. **Present Values.** A famous quarterback just signed a $15 million contract providing $3 million a year for 5 years. A less famous receiver signed a $14 million 5-year contract providing $4 million now and $2 million a year for 5 years. Who is better paid? The interest rate is 10 percent.

PRACTICE PROBLEMS ™

21. **Compound Growth.** In 2004 a pound of apples cost $0.99, while oranges cost $1.14. Ten years earlier the price of apples was only $.72 a pound and that of oranges was $.55 a pound. What was the annual compound rate of growth in the price of the two fruits? If the same rates of growth persist in the future, what will be the price of apples in 2024? What about the price of oranges?

22. **Loan Payments.** If you take out an $8,000 car loan that calls for 48 monthly payments at an APR of 10 percent, what is your monthly payment? What is the effective annual interest rate on the loan?

23. **Annuity Values.**

a. What is the present value of a 3-year annuity of $100 if the discount rate is 6 percent?

b. What is the present value of the annuity in (a) if you have to wait 2 years instead of 1 year for the first payment?

Please visit us at www.mhhe.com/bmm5e or refer to your Student CD

24. **Annuities and Interest Rates.** Professor's Annuity Corp. offers a lifetime annuity to retiring professors. For a payment of $80,000 at age 65, the firm will pay the retiring professor $600 a month until death.

a. If the professor's remaining life expectancy is 20 years, what is the monthly rate on this annuity? What is the effective annual rate?

b. If the monthly interest rate is .5 percent, what monthly annuity payment can the firm offer to the retiring professor?

25. **Annuity Values.** You want to buy a new car, but you can make an initial payment of only $2,000 and can afford monthly payments of at most $400.

a. If the APR on auto loans is 12 percent and you finance the purchase over 48 months, what is the maximum price you can pay for the car?

b. How much can you afford if you finance the purchase over 60 months?

26. **Calculating Interest Rate.** In a *discount interest loan,* you pay the interest payment up front. For example, if a 1-year loan is stated as $10,000 and the interest rate is 10 percent, the borrower "pays" .10 × $10,000 = $1,000 immediately, thereby receiving net funds of $9,000 and repaying $10,000 in a year.

a. What is the effective interest rate on this loan?

b. If you call the discount d (for example, $d = 10\%$ using our numbers), express the effective annual rate on the loan as a function of d.

c. Why is the effective annual rate always greater than the stated rate d?

27. **Annuity Due.** Recall that an annuity due is like an ordinary annuity except that the first payment is made immediately instead of at the end of the first period.

    a. Why is the present value of an annuity due equal to $(1 + r)$ times the present value of an ordinary annuity?

    b. Why is the future value of an annuity due equal to $(1 + r)$ times the future value of an ordinary annuity?

28. **Rate on a Loan.** If you take out an $8,000 car loan that calls for 48 monthly payments of $240 each, what is the APR of the loan? What is the effective annual interest rate on the loan?

29. **Loan Payments.** Reconsider the car loan in the previous question. What if the payments are made in four annual year-end installments? What annual payment would have the same present value as the monthly payment you calculated? Use the same effective annual interest rate as in the previous question. Why is your answer not simply 12 times the monthly payment?

30. **Annuity Value.** Your landscaping company can lease a truck for $8,000 a year (paid at year-end) for 6 years. It can instead buy the truck for $40,000. The truck will be valueless after 6 years. If the interest rate your company can earn on its funds is 7 percent, is it cheaper to buy or lease?

31. **Annuity-Due Value.** Reconsider the previous problem. What if the lease payments are an annuity due, so that the first payment comes immediately? Is it cheaper to buy or lease?

32. **Annuity Due.** A store offers two payment plans. Under the installment plan, you pay 25 percent down and 25 percent of the purchase price in each of the next 3 years. If you pay the entire bill immediately, you can take a 10 percent discount from the purchase price. Which is a better deal if you can borrow or lend funds at a 5 percent interest rate?

33. **Annuity Value.** Reconsider the previous question. How will your answer change if the payments on the 4-year installment plan do not start for a full year?

34. **Annuity and Annuity-Due Payments.**

    a. If you borrow $1,000 and agree to repay the loan in five equal annual payments at an interest rate of 12 percent, what will your payment be?

    b. What if you make the first payment on the loan immediately instead of at the end of the first year?

35. **Valuing Delayed Annuities.** Suppose that you will receive annual payments of $10,000 for a period of 10 years. The first payment will be made 4 years from now. If the interest rate is 5 percent, what is the present value of this stream of payments?

Please visit us at www.mhhe.com/bmm5e or refer to your Student CD

36. **Mortgage with Points.** Home loans typically involve "points," which are fees charged by the lender. Each point charged means that the borrower must pay 1 percent of the loan amount as a fee. For example, if the loan is for $100,000 and 2 points are charged, the loan repayment schedule is calculated on a $100,000 loan but the net amount the borrower receives is only $98,000. What is the effective annual interest rate charged on such a loan assuming loan repayment occurs over 360 months? Assume the interest rate is 1 percent per month.

37. **Amortizing Loan.** You take out a 30-year $100,000 mortgage loan with an APR of 6 percent and monthly payments. In 12 years you decide to sell your house and pay off the mortgage. What is the principal balance on the loan?

38. **Amortizing Loan.** Consider a 4-year amortizing loan. You borrow $1,000 initially, and repay it in four equal annual year-end payments.

    a. If the interest rate is 8 percent, show that the annual payment is $301.92.

    b. Fill in the following table, which shows how much of each payment is interest versus principal repayment (that is, amortization), and the outstanding balance on the loan at each date.

Time	Loan Balance	Year-End Interest Due on Balance	Year-End Payment	Amortization of Loan
0	$1,000	$80	$301.92	$221.92
1	——	——	301.92	——
2	——	——	301.92	——
3	——	——	301.92	——
4	0	0	—	—

    c. Show that the loan balance after 1 year is equal to the year-end payment of $301.92 times the 3-year annuity factor.

39. **Annuity Value.** You've borrowed $4,248.68 and agreed to pay back the loan with monthly payments of $200. If the interest rate is 12 percent stated as an APR, how long will it take you to pay back the loan? What is the effective annual rate on the loan?

40. **Annuity Value.** The $40 million lottery payment that you just won actually pays $2 million per year for 20 years. If the discount rate is 8 percent and the first payment comes in 1 year, what is the present value of the winnings? What if the first payment comes immediately?

41. **Real Annuities.** A retiree wants level consumption in real terms over a 30-year retirement. If the inflation rate equals the interest rate she earns on her $450,000 of savings, how much can she spend in real terms each year over the rest of her life?

42. **EAR versus APR.** You invest $1,000 at a 6 percent annual interest rate, stated as an APR. Interest is compounded monthly. How much will you have in 1 year? In 1.5 years?

43. **Annuity Value.** You just borrowed $100,000 to buy a condo. You will repay the loan in equal monthly payments of $804.62 over the next 30 years. What monthly interest rate are you paying on the loan? What is the effective annual rate on that loan? What rate is the lender more likely to quote on the loan?

44. **EAR.** If a bank pays 6 percent interest with continuous compounding, what is the effective annual rate?

45. **Annuity Values.** You can buy a car that is advertised for $12,000 on the following terms: (a) pay $12,000 and receive a $1,000 rebate from the manufacturer; (b) pay $250 a month for 4 years for total payments of $12,000, implying zero percent financing. Which is the better deal if the interest rate is 1 percent per month?

46. **Continuous Compounding.** How much will $100 grow to if invested at a continuously compounded interest rate of 10 percent for 8 years? What if it is invested for 10 years at 8 percent?

47. **Future Values.** I now have $20,000 in the bank earning interest of .5 percent per month. I need $30,000 to make a down payment on a house. I can save an additional $100 per month. How long will it take me to accumulate the $30,000?

48. **Perpetuities.** A local bank advertises the following deal: "Pay us $100 a year for 10 years and then we will pay you (or your beneficiaries) $100 a year *forever.*" Is this a good deal if the interest rate available on other deposits is 6 percent?

49. **Perpetuities.** A local bank will pay you $100 a year for your lifetime if you deposit $2,500 in the bank today. If you plan to live forever, what interest rate is the bank paying?

50. **Perpetuities.** A property will provide $10,000 a year forever. If its value is $125,000, what must be the discount rate?

51. **Applying Time Value.** You can buy property today for $3 million and sell it in 5 years for $4 million. (You earn no rental income on the property.)

   a. If the interest rate is 8 percent, what is the present value of the sales price?
   b. Is the property investment attractive to you? Why or why not?
   c. Would your answer to (b) change if you also could earn $200,000 per year rent on the property?

52. **Applying Time Value.** A factory costs $400,000. You forecast that it will produce cash inflows of $120,000 in year 1, $180,000 in year 2, and $300,000 in year 3. The discount rate is 12 percent. Is the factory a good investment? Explain.

53. **Applying Time Value.** You invest $1,000 today and expect to sell your investment for $2,000 in 10 years.

   a. Is this a good deal if the discount rate is 6 percent?
   b. What if the discount rate is 10 percent?

54. **Calculating Interest Rate.** A store will give you a 3 percent discount on the cost of your purchase if you pay cash today. Otherwise, you will be billed the full price with payment due in 1 month. What is the implicit borrowing rate being paid by customers who choose to defer payment for the month?

55. **Quoting Rates.** Banks sometimes quote interest rates in the form of "add-on interest." In this case, if a 1-year loan is quoted with a 20 percent interest rate and you borrow $1,000, then you pay back $1,200. But you make these payments in monthly installments of $100 each. What are the true APR and effective annual rate on this loan? Why should you have known that the true rates must be greater than 20 percent even before doing any calculations?

56. **Compound Interest.** Suppose you take out a $1,000, 3-year loan using add-on interest (see previous problem) with a quoted interest rate of 20 percent per year. What will your monthly payments be? (Total payments are $1,000 + $1,000 × .20 × 3 = $1,600.) What are the true APR and effective annual rate on this loan? Are they the same as in the previous problem?

57. **Calculating Interest Rate.** What is the effective annual rate on a 1-year loan with an interest rate quoted on a discount basis (see problem 26) of 20 percent?

58. **Effective Rates.** First National Bank pays 6.2 percent interest compounded semiannually. Second National Bank pays 6 percent interest, compounded monthly. Which bank offers the higher effective annual rate?

59. **Calculating Interest Rate.** You borrow $1,000 from the bank and agree to repay the loan over the next year in 12 equal monthly payments of $90. However, the bank also charges you a loan-initiation fee of $20, which is taken out of the initial proceeds of the loan. What is the effective annual interest rate on the loan taking account of the impact of the initiation fee?

Please visit us at www.mhhe.com/bmm5e or refer to your Student CD

60. **Retirement Savings.** You believe you will need to have saved $500,000 by the time you retire in 40 years in order to live comfortably. If the interest rate is 6 percent per year, how much must you save each year to meet your retirement goal?

61. **Retirement Savings.** How much would you need in the previous problem if you believe that you will inherit $100,000 in 10 years?

62. **Retirement Savings.** You believe you will spend $40,000 a year for 20 years once you retire in 40 years. If the interest rate is 6 percent per year, how much must you save each year until retirement to meet your retirement goal?

63. **Retirement Planning.** A couple thinking about retirement decide to put aside $3,000 each year in a savings plan that earns 8 percent interest. In 5 years they will receive a gift of $10,000 that also can be invested.

   a. How much money will they have accumulated 30 years from now?

   b. If their goal is to retire with $800,000 of savings, how much extra do they need to save every year?

Please visit us at www.mhhe.com/bmm5e or refer to your Student CD

64. **Retirement Planning.** A couple will retire in 50 years; they plan to spend about $30,000 a year in retirement, which should last about 25 years. They believe that they can earn 8 percent interest on retirement savings.

   a. If they make annual payments into a savings plan, how much will they need to save each year? Assume the first payment comes in 1 year.

   b. How would the answer to part (a) change if the couple also realize that in 20 years, they will need to spend $60,000 on their child's college education?

65. **Real versus Nominal Dollars.** An engineer in 1950 was earning $6,000 a year. Today she earns $60,000 a year. However, on average, goods today cost 6.6 times what they did in 1950. What is her real income today in terms of constant 1950 dollars?

66. **Real versus Nominal Rates.** If investors are to earn a 3 percent real interest rate, what nominal interest rate must they earn if the inflation rate is

   a. zero?

   b. 4 percent?

   c. 6 percent?

67. **Real Rates.** If investors receive a 6 percent interest rate on their bank deposits, what real interest rate will they earn if the inflation rate over the year is

   a. zero?

   b. 3 percent?

   c. 6 percent?

68. **Real versus Nominal Rates.** You will receive $100 from a savings bond in 3 years. The nominal interest rate is 8 percent.

   a. What is the present value of the proceeds from the bond?
   b. If the inflation rate over the next few years is expected to be 3 percent, what will the real value of the $100 payoff be in terms of today's dollars?
   c. What is the real interest rate?
   d. Show that the real payoff from the bond [from part (b)] discounted at the real interest rate [from part (c)] gives the same present value for the bond as you found in part a.

69. **Real versus Nominal Dollars.** Your consulting firm will produce cash flows of $100,000 this year, and you expect cash flow to keep pace with any increase in the general level of prices. The interest rate currently is 6 percent, and you anticipate inflation of about 2 percent.

   a. What is the present value of your firm's cash flows for years 1 through 5?
   b. How would your answer to (a) change if you anticipated no growth in cash flow?

CHALLENGE PROBLEMS

70. **Real versus Nominal Annuities.** Good news: You will almost certainly be a millionaire by the time you retire in 50 years. Bad news: The inflation rate over your lifetime will average about 3 percent.

   a. What will be the real value of $1 million by the time you retire in terms of today's dollars?
   b. What real annuity (in today's dollars) will $1 million support if the real interest rate at retirement is 2 percent and the annuity must last for 20 years?

71. **Real versus Nominal.** If the interest rate is 6 percent per year, how long will it take for your money to *quadruple* in value? If the inflation rate is 4 percent per year, what will be the change in the purchasing power of your money over this period?

72. **Inflation.** Inflation in Brazil in 1992 averaged about 23 percent per month. What was the annual inflation rate?

73. **Perpetuities.** British government 4 percent perpetuities pay £4 interest each year forever. Another bond, $2\frac{1}{2}$ percent perpetuities, pays £2.50 a year forever. What is the value of 4 percent perpetuities if the long-term interest rate is 6 percent? What is the value of $2\frac{1}{2}$ percent perpetuities?

74. **Real versus Nominal Annuities.**

   a. You plan to retire in 30 years and want to accumulate enough by then to provide yourself with $30,000 a year for 15 years. If the interest rate is 10 percent, how much must you accumulate by the time you retire?
   b. How much must you save each year until retirement in order to finance your retirement consumption?
   c. Now you remember that the annual inflation rate is 4 percent. If a loaf of bread costs $1 today, what will it cost by the time you retire?
   d. You really want to consume $30,000 a year in *real* dollars during retirement and wish to save an equal *real* amount each year until then. What is the real amount of savings that you need to accumulate by the time you retire?
   e. Calculate the required preretirement real annual savings necessary to meet your consumption goals. Compare to your answer to (b). Why is there a difference?
   f. What is the nominal value of the amount you need to save during the first year? (Assume the savings are put aside at the end of each year.) The thirtieth year?

75. **Retirement and Inflation.** Redo part (a) of problem 64, but now assume that the inflation rate over the next 50 years will average 4 percent.

   a. What is the real annual savings the couple must set aside?
   b. How much do they need to save in nominal terms in the first year?
   c. How much do they need to save in nominal terms in the last year?
   d. What will be their nominal expenditures in the first year of retirement? The last?

Please visit us at www.mhhe.com/bmm5e or
refer to your Student CD

76. **Perpetuities.** What is the value of a perpetuity that pays $100 every 3 months forever? The discount rate quoted on an APR basis is 6 percent.

77. **Changing Interest Rates.** If the interest rate this year is 8 percent and the interest rate next year will be 10 percent, what is the future value of $1 after 2 years? What is the present value of a payment of $1 to be received in 2 years?

78. **Changing Interest Rates.** Your wealthy uncle established a $1,000 bank account for you when you were born. For the first 8 years of your life, the interest rate earned on the account was 6 percent. Since then, rates have been only 4 percent. Now you are 21 years old and ready to cash in. How much is in your account?

Go to Market Insight (**www.mhhe.com/edumarketinsight**).

STANDARD
&POOR'S

1. Look up Abercrombie & Fitch (ANF). Calculate its 5-year growth rate in sales and net income, using annual income statement data. Next translate these results into the real growth rates. Use the "inflation calculator" provided by the Bureau of Labor Statistics at **www.bls.gov/ cpi/home.htm.** You can find the actual price index data, via the Consumer Price Index link (upper left), then pull down to *Get Detailed Statistics,* and then *All Urban Consumers—Current Series.* What is the increase in the price level in the last 5 years? What is Abercrombie's growth rate of real sales and net income?

2. Look up the most recent stock prices and the prices 5 years earlier for the following firms: E-trade (ET), Sony (SNE), Georgia Pacific (GP), Toyota (TM), and Nordstrom (JWN). What was the compound growth rate of each stock price over the 5-year period? If the stock prices continue to grow at the same rates over the next 5 years, what will they be then?

SOLUTIONS TO SELF-TEST QUESTIONS

4.1   Value after 5 years would have been $24 \times (1.05)^5 = \$30.63$; after 50 years, $24 \times (1.05)^{50} = \$275.22$.

4.2   Call g the annual growth rate of transistors over the 32-year period between 1971 and 2003. Then

$$2,250 \times (1 + g)^{32} = 410,000,000$$
$$(1 + g)^{32} = 182,222$$
$$1 + g = 182,222^{1/32} = 1.46$$

So the actual growth rate was $g = .46$, or 46 percent, not quite as high as Moore's prediction, but not so shabby either.

4.3   Multiply the $1,000 payment by the 10-year discount factor:

$$PV = \$1,000 \times \frac{1}{(1.0853)^{10}} = \$441.06$$

4.4   The $1,000 investment grew to $3,300 in 5 years.

$$FV = PV \times (1 + r)^t$$
$$3,300 = 1,000 \times (1 + r)^5$$
$$(1 + r)^5 = 3.3$$
$$(1 + r) = 3.3^{1/5} = 1.27$$
$$r = .27, \text{ or } 27\%$$

4.5

Gift at Year	Present Value
1	$10,000/(1.07) = \$ 9{,}345.79$
2	$10,000/(1.07)^2 = 8{,}734.39$
3	$10,000/(1.07)^3 = 8{,}162.98$
4	$10,000/(1.07)^4 = 7{,}628.95$
	$\$33{,}872.11$

Gift at Year	Future Value
1	$10,000 \times (1.07)^3 = \$12{,}250.43$
2	$10,000 \times (1.07)^2 = 11{,}449$
3	$10,000 \times (1.07) = 10{,}700$
4	$10,000 = 10{,}000$
	$\$44{,}399.43$

4.6   The rate is $4/48 = .0833$, about 8.3 percent.

4.7   The 4-year discount factor is $1/(1.08)^4 = .7350$. The 4-year annuity factor is $[1/.08 - 1/(.08 \times 1.08^4)] = 3.3121$. This is the difference between the present value of a \$1 perpetuity starting next year and the present value of a \$1 perpetuity starting in year 5:

$$\text{PV (perpetuity starting next year)} = \frac{1}{.08} = 12.50$$

$$- \text{PV (perpetuity starting in year 5)} = \frac{1}{.08} \times \frac{1}{(1.08)^4} = 9.1879$$

$$= \text{PV (4-year annuity)} \qquad = 12.50 - 9.1879 = 3.3121$$

which matches the annuity factor.

4.8   You will need the present value at 7 percent of a 20-year annuity of \$55,000:

$$\text{Present value} = \text{annual spending} \times \text{annuity factor}$$

The annuity factor is $[1/.07 - 1/(.07 \times 1.07^{20})] = 10.5940$. Thus you need $55,000 \times 10.594 = \$582,670$.

4.9   Fifteen years means 180 months. Then

$$\text{Mortgage payment} = \frac{100,000}{\text{180-month annuity factor}}$$

$$= \frac{100,000}{83.32}$$

$$= \$1,200.17 \text{ per month}$$

\$1,000 of the payment is interest. The remainder, \$200.17, is amortization.

4.10   We saw in Example 4.9 that the 25-year annuity factor for an ordinary annuity is 12.9057. Therefore, the 25-year annuity-due factor would be $12.9057 \times 1.059 = 13.6672$. The present value of the winnings would increase to $\$11.828 \times 13.6672 = \$161.7$ million. You can also put your calculator in *begin* mode; enter $n = 25$, $i = 5.9$, FV $= 0$, PMT $= 11.828$; and compute PV. Alternatively, in Excel use the formula =PV(.059,25,11.828,0,1). Starting the 25-year cash-flow stream immediately, rather than waiting 1 year, increases value by about \$9 million.

4.11   If the interest rate is 5 percent, the future value of a 50-year, \$1 annuity will be

$$\frac{(1.05)^{50} - 1}{.05} = 209.348$$

Therefore, we need to choose the cash flow, C, so that $C \times 209.348 = \$500,000$. This requires that $C = \$500,000/209.348 = \$2,388.37$. This required savings level is much higher than we found in Example 4.12. At a 5 percent interest rate, current savings do not grow as rapidly as when the interest rate was 10 percent; with less of a boost from compound interest, we need to set aside greater amounts in order to reach the target of \$500,000.

4.12   The cost in dollars will increase by 5 percent each year, to a value of $\$5 \times (1.05)^{50} = \$57.34$. If the inflation rate is 10 percent, the cost will be $\$5 \times (1.10)^{50} = \$586.95$.

4.13   The CPI in 1980 was 3.452 times its value in 1950 (see Table 4.7). Therefore, purchases that cost $250 in 1950 would have cost $\$250 \times 3.452 = \$863$ in 1980. The value of a 1980 salary of $30,000, expressed in real 1950 dollars, is $\$30,000 \times (1/3.452) = \$8,691$.

4.14   a. If there's no inflation, real and nominal rates are equal at 8 percent. With 5 percent inflation, the real rate is $(1.08/1.05) - 1 = .02857$, a bit less than 3 percent.

      b. If you want a 3 percent *real* interest rate, you need a 3 percent nominal rate if inflation is zero and an 8.15 percent rate if inflation is 5 percent. Note that $1.03 \times 1.05 = 1.0815$.

4.15   The present value is

$$PV = \frac{\$5,000}{1.08} = \$4,629.63$$

The real interest rate is 2.857 percent (see Self-Test 4.14a). The real cash payment is $\$5,000/(1.05) = \$4,761.90$. Thus

$$PV = \frac{\$4,761.90}{1.02857} = \$4,629.63$$

4.16   Calculate the real annuity. The real interest rate is $1.10/1.05 - 1 = .0476$. We'll round to 4.8 percent. The real annuity is

$$\text{Annual payment} = \frac{\$3,000,000}{\text{30-year annuity factor}} = \frac{\$3,000,000}{\dfrac{1}{.048} - \dfrac{1}{.048(1.048)^{30}}} = \frac{\$3,000,000}{15.73} = \$190,728$$

You can spend this much each year in dollars of constant purchasing power. The purchasing power of each dollar will decline at 5 percent per year, so you'll need to spend more in nominal dollars: $\$190,728 \times 1.05 = \$200,264$ in the second year, $\$190,728 \times 1.05^2 = \$210,278$ in the third year, and so on.

4.17   The quarterly rate is 8/4 = 2 percent. The effective annual rate is $(1.02)^4 - 1 = .0824$, or 8.24 percent.

MINICASE

Old Alfred Road, who is well-known to drivers on the Maine Turnpike, has reached his seventieth birthday and is ready to retire. Mr. Road has no formal training in finance but has saved his money and invested carefully.

Mr. Road owns his home—the mortgage is paid off—and does not want to move. He is a widower, and he wants to bequeath the house and any remaining assets to his daughter.

He has accumulated savings of $180,000, conservatively invested. The investments are yielding 9 percent interest. Mr. Road also has $12,000 in a savings account at 5 percent interest. He wants to keep the savings account intact for unexpected expenses or emergencies.

Mr. Road's basic living expenses now average about $1,500 per month, and he plans to spend $500 per month on travel and hobbies. To maintain this planned standard of living, he will have to rely on his investment portfolio. The interest from the portfolio is $16,200 per year (9 percent of $180,000), or $1,350 per month.

Mr. Road will also receive $750 per month in social security payments for the rest of his life. These payments are indexed for inflation. That is, they will be automatically increased in proportion to changes in the consumer price index.

Mr. Road's main concern is with inflation. The inflation rate has been below 3 percent recently, but a 3 percent rate is unusually low by historical standards. His social security payments will increase with inflation, but the interest on his investment portfolio will not.

What advice do you have for Mr. Road? Can he safely spend all the interest from his investment portfolio? How much could he withdraw at year-end from that portfolio if he wants to keep its real value intact?

Suppose Mr. Road will live for 20 more years and is willing to use up all of his investment portfolio over that period. He also wants his monthly spending to increase along with inflation over that period. In other words, he wants his monthly spending to stay the same in real terms. How much can he afford to spend per month?

Assume that the investment portfolio continues to yield a 9 percent rate of return and that the inflation rate will be 4 percent.

Valuing Bonds

RELATED WEB LINKS

bonds.yahoo.com

money.cnn.com/markets/
bondcenter

www.fintools.com

www.smartmoney.com

www.bankrate.com

www.bloomberg.com/markets For current bond rates, glossaries, news, market analysis, and learning centers.

www.nasdbondinfo.com Price data and other trading information on individual bonds.

www.bondsonline.com

www.bondmarkets.com

www.investinginbonds.com

www.bondresources.com

www.finpipe.com Considerable information about bonds and bond markets, with many links to related sites.

www.publicdebt.treas.gov

www.stlouisfed.org

www.federalreserve.gov

www.ustreas.gov Government sites with lots of interest rate data.

www.moodys.com

www.standardandpoors.com

www.fitchratings.com Information on bond ratings.

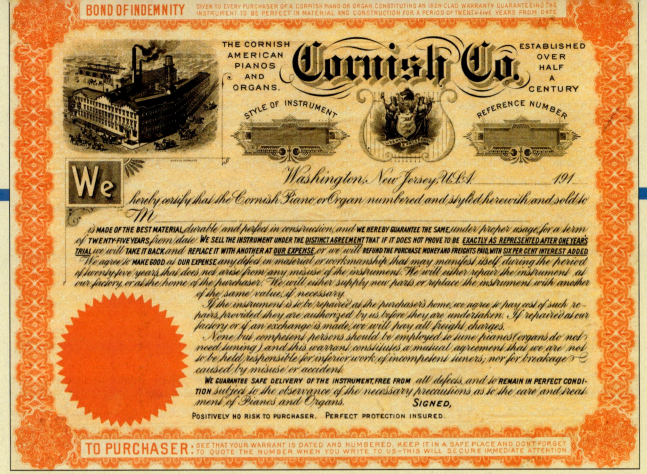

Bondholders once received a beautifully engraved certificate like this one for a bond issued by a piano manufacturer. Nowadays their ownership is simply recorded on an electronic database.

Investment in new plant and equipment requires money—often a lot of money. Sometimes firms may be able to save enough out of previous earnings to cover the cost of investments, but often they need to raise cash from investors. In broad terms, we can think of two ways to raise new money from investors: borrow the cash or sell additional shares of common stock.

If companies need the money only for a short while, they may borrow it from a bank; if they need it to make long-term investments, they generally issue bonds, which are simply long-term loans. When companies issue bonds, they promise to make a series of fixed interest payments and then to repay the debt. As long as the company generates sufficient cash, the payments on a bond are certain. In this case bond valuation involves straightforward time-value-of-money computations. But there is some chance that even the most blue-chip company will fall on hard times and will not be able to repay its debts. Investors take this default risk into account when they price the bonds and demand a higher interest rate to compensate.

Companies are not the only bond issuers. State and local governments also raise money by selling bonds. So does the U.S. Treasury. There is always some risk that a company or municipality will not be able to come up with the cash to repay its bonds, but investors in Treasury issues can be confident that the government will make the promised payments. Therefore, in the first part of this chapter we focus on Treasury bonds and sidestep the issue of default. We show how bond prices are determined by market interest rates and how those prices respond to changes in rates. We also consider the yield to maturity and discuss why a bond's yield may vary with its time to maturity.

Later in the chapter we look at corporate bonds, where there is a possibility of default. We will see how bond ratings provide a guide to the default risk and how low-grade bonds offer higher promised yields.

In Chapter 13 we will look in more detail at the securities that companies issue, and we will see that there are many variations on bond design. But for now, we keep our focus on garden-variety bonds and general principles of bond valuation.

After studying this chapter you should be able to:

- Distinguish among a bond's coupon rate, current yield, and yield to maturity.

- Find the market price of a bond given its yield to maturity, find a bond's yield given its price, and demonstrate why prices and yields vary inversely.

- Show why bonds exhibit interest rate risk.

- Understand why investors pay attention to bond ratings and demand a higher interest rate for bonds with low ratings.

5.1 Bond Characteristics

bond
Security that obligates the issuer to make specified payments to the bondholder.

coupon
The interest payments paid to the bondholder.

face value or **principal**
Payment at the maturity of the bond. Also called par value or maturity value.

coupon rate
Annual interest payment as a percentage of face value.

Governments and corporations borrow money by selling **bonds** to investors. The money they collect when the bond is issued, or sold to the public, is the amount of the loan. In return, they agree to make specified payments to the bondholders, who are the lenders. When you own a bond, you generally receive a fixed interest payment each year until the bond matures. This payment is known as the **coupon** because most bonds used to have coupons that the investors clipped off and mailed to the bond issuer to claim the interest payment. At maturity, the debt is repaid: The borrower pays the bondholder the bond's **face value** (equivalently, its *principal* or *par value*).

How do bonds work? Consider a U.S. Treasury bond as an example. Several years ago, the U.S. Treasury raised money by selling 5.5 percent coupon, 2008 maturity Treasury bonds. Each bond has a face value of $1,000. Because the **coupon rate** is 5.5 percent, the government makes coupon payments of 5.5 percent of $1,000, or $55 each year.[1] When the bond matures in February 2008, the government must pay the $1,000 face value of the bond in addition to the final coupon payment.

Suppose that in 2005 you decided to buy the "5.5s of 2008," that is, the 5.5 percent coupon bonds maturing in 2008. If you planned to hold the bond until maturity, you would then have looked forward to the cash flows shown in Figure 5–1. The initial cash flow is negative and equal to the price you have to pay for the bond. Thereafter, the cash flows equal the annual coupon payment, until the maturity date in 2008, when you receive the $1,000 face value of the bond plus the final coupon payment.

Reading the Financial Pages

The prices at which you can buy and sell bonds are shown each day in the financial press. Figure 5–2 is an excerpt from the bond quotation page of *The Wall Street Journal* and shows the prices of bonds and notes that have been issued by the United States Treasury. (A *note* is just a bond with a maturity of less than 10 years at the time it is issued.[2]) The entry for the 5.5 percent bond maturing in February 2008 that we just looked at is highlighted. The letter *n* indicates that it is a note.

Prices are generally quoted in 32nds rather than decimals. Thus for the 5.5 percent bond the *asked price*—the price investors pay to *buy* the bond from a bond dealer—is shown as 105:23. This means that the price is 105 and 23/32, or 105.719 percent of face value. Therefore each bond costs $1,057.19.

---

[1] In the United States, these coupon payments typically would come in two semiannual installments of $27.50 each. To keep things simple for now, we will assume one coupon payment per year.

[2] The longest bonds that the Treasury issues mature in 30 years, though there was a period between 2001 and 2005 when the longest maturity bond issued was 10 years.

FIGURE 5-1 Cash flows to
an investor in the 5.5 percent
coupon bond maturing in the
year 2008

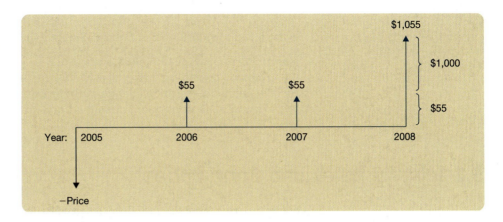

The *bid price* is the price investors receive if they sell the bond to a dealer. Just as the used-car dealer earns his living by reselling cars at higher prices than he paid for them, so the bond dealer needs to charge a *spread* between the bid and the asked price. Notice that the spread for the 5.5 percent bonds is only $\frac{1}{32}$, or about .03 percent, of the bond's value. Don't you wish that used-car dealers charged similar spreads?

The next column in the table shows the change in price since the previous day. The price of the 5.5 percent bonds has fallen by $\frac{1}{32}$. Finally, the column "Ask Yld" stands for *ask yield to maturity,* which measures the return that investors will receive if they buy the bond at the asked price and hold it to maturity in 2008. You can see that the 5.5 percent Treasury bonds offer investors a yield to maturity of 3.47 percent. We will explain shortly how this figure was calculated.

FIGURE 5-2 Treasury bond
quotes from *The Wall Street
Journal,* February 16, 2005

Treasury Bonds, Notes and Bills February 15, 2005

Explanatory Notes

Representative Over-the-Counter quotation based on transactions of $1 million or more. Treasury bond, note and bill quotes are as of mid-afternoon. Colons in bid-and-asked quotes represent 32nds; 101:01 means 101 1/32. Net changes in 32nds. n-Treasury note. i-Inflation-Indexed issue. Treasury bill quotes in hundredths, quoted on terms of a rate of discount. Days to maturity calculated from settlement date. All yields are to maturity and based on the asked quote. Latest 13-week and 26-week bills are boldfaced. For bonds callable prior to maturity, yields are computed to the earliest call date for issues quoted above par and to the maturity date for issues below par. *When issued.

Source: eSpeed/Cantor Fitzgerald

U.S. Treasury strips as of 3 p.m. Eastern time, also based on transactions of $1 million or more. Colons in bid and asked quotes represent 32nds; 99:01 means 99 1/32. Net changes in 32nds. Yields calculated on the asked quotation. ci-stripped coupon interest. bp-Treasury bond, stripped principal. np-Treasury note, stripped principal. For bonds callable prior to maturity, yields are computed to the earliest call date for issues quoted above par and to the maturity date for issues below par.

Source: Bear, Stearns & Co. via Street Software Technology Inc.

RATE	MATURITY MO/YR	BID	ASKED	CHG	ASK YLD	RATE	MATURITY MO/YR	BID	ASKED	CHG	ASK YLD
Government Bonds & Notes						1.875	Jul 13i	103:06	103:07	-16	1.46
1.500	Feb 05n	100:00	100:00	1	1.49	4.250	Aug 13n	101:15	101:16	-6	4.04
1.625	Mar 05n	99:29	99:30	1	2.14	12.000	Aug 13	127:17	127:18	-6	3.55
3.125	May 07n	99:13	99:14	-1	3.38	2.375	Jan 25i	110:00	110:00	-34	1.78
2.750	Aug 07n	98:13	98:14	...	3.41	7.625	Feb 25	140:08	140:09	-20	4.54
3.250	Aug 07n	99:19	99:20	-1	3.41	6.875	Aug 25	130:24	130:25	-19	4.55
6.125	Aug 07n	106:13	106:14	-2	3.41	6.000	Feb 26	119:09	119:10	-18	4.56
3.000	Nov 07n	98:25	98:26	-1	3.46	6.750	Aug 26	129:27	129:28	-18	4.56
3.625	Jan 08i	108:06	108:07	-2	0.77	6.500	Nov 26	126:19	126:20	-18	4.56
3.000	Feb 08n	98:19	98:20	-1	3.48	6.625	Feb 27	128:14	128:15	-19	4.56
5.500	Feb 08n	105:22	105:23	-1	3.47	6.375	Aug 27	125:10	125:11	-19	4.56
3.375	Feb 08n	99:20	99:21	-1	3.49	6.125	Nov 27	122:00	122:01	-18	4.56
2.625	May 08n	97:08	97:09	-2	3.51	3.625	Apr 28i	135:09	135:10	-29	1.76
5.625	May 08n	106:12	106:13	-2	3.51	5.500	Aug 28	113:16	113:17	-17	4.56
3.250	Aug 08n	99:00	99:01	-2	3.54	5.250	Nov 28	110:00	110:00	-17	4.55
3.125	Sep 08n	98:17	98:18	-2	3.56	5.250	Feb 29	110:04	110:05	-18	4.55
3.125	Oct 08n	98:15	98:16	-2	3.56	3.875	Apr 29i	141:16	141:17	-36	1.76
3.375	Nov 08n	99:09	99:10	-1	3.57	6.125	Aug 29	123:04	123:05	-18	4.55
4.750	Nov 08n	104:04	104:05	-2	3.55	6.250	May 30	125:15	125:16	-19	4.54
3.375	Dec 08n	99:08	99:09	-2	3.58	5.375	Feb 31	113:21	113:22	-19	4.48
3.250	Jan 09n	98:25	98:26	-2	3.58	3.375	Apr 32i	137:07	137:08	-32	1.66

Self-Test 5.1   Find the 5.625 May 08 Treasury bond in Figure 5–2.

a. How much does it cost to buy the bond?
b. If you already owned the bond, how much would a bond dealer pay you for it?
c. By how much did the price change from the previous day?
d. What annual interest payment does the bond make?
e. What is the bond's yield to maturity?

5.2 Interest Rates and Bond Prices

In Figure 5–1 we set out the cash flows received by an investor in 5.5 percent Treasury bonds. How much would you have been willing to pay for these cash flows? The value of a security is the present value of the cash flows it will pay to its owners. To find this value, we need to discount each future payment by the current interest rate.

The 5.5s were not the only Treasury bonds that matured in 2008. Almost identical bonds maturing at the same time offered an interest rate of about 3.5 percent. So, if the 5.5s had offered a lower return than 3.5 percent, no one would have been willing to hold them. Equally, if they had offered a *higher* return, everyone would have rushed to sell their other bonds and buy the 5.5s. In other words, if investors were on their toes, the 5.5s had to offer the same 3.5 percent rate of interest as similar Treasury bonds. You might recognize 3.5 percent as the opportunity cost of the funds invested in the bond, as we discussed in Chapter 2. This is the rate that investors could earn by placing their funds in similar securities rather than in this bond.

We can now calculate the present value of the 5.5s of 2008 by discounting the cash flows at 3.5 percent:

$$PV = \frac{\$55}{(1+r)} + \frac{\$55}{(1+r)^2} + \frac{\$1,055}{(1+r)^3}$$

$$= \frac{\$55}{(1.035)} + \frac{\$55}{(1.035)^2} + \frac{\$1,055}{(1.035)^3} = \$1,056.03$$

Bond prices are usually expressed as a percentage of their face value. Thus we can say that our 5.5 percent Treasury bond is worth 105.603 percent of face value, and its price would usually be quoted as 105.603, or about $105^{19}/_{32}$. (The price of the bond shown in Figure 5–2 is $105^{23}/_{32}$, which is slightly higher than our calculation. This is largely due to rounding error in the interest rate we have used to discount the bond's cash flows.)

Did you notice that the coupon payments on the bond are an annuity? In other words, the holder of our 5.5 percent Treasury bond receives a level stream of coupon payments of $55 a year for each of 3 years. At maturity the bondholder gets an additional payment of $1,000. Therefore, you can use the annuity formula to value the coupon payments and then add on the present value of the final payment of face value:

$$\mathbf{PV} = \mathbf{PV(coupons) + PV(face\ value)}$$
$$= \mathbf{(coupon \times annuity\ factor) + (face\ value \times discount\ factor)}$$

$$= \$55 \times \left[\frac{1}{.035} - \frac{1}{.035(1.035)^3}\right] + 1,000 \times \frac{1}{1.035^3}$$
$$= \$154.09 + \$901.94 = \$1,056.03$$

If you need to value a bond with many years to run before maturity, it is usually easiest to value the coupon payments as an annuity and then add on the present value of the final payment.

Self-Test 5.2 Calculate the present value of a 6-year bond with a 9 percent coupon. The interest rate is 12 percent.

EXAMPLE 5.1 ▶ Bond Prices and Semiannual Coupon Payments

Thus far we've assumed that interest payments occur annually. This is the case for bonds in many European countries, but in the United States most bonds make coupon payments *semiannually*. So when you hear that a bond in the United States has a coupon rate of 5.5 percent, you can generally assume that the bond makes a payment of $55/2 = \$27.50$ every 6 months. Similarly, when investors in the United States refer to the bond's interest rate, they usually mean the semiannually compounded interest rate. Thus an interest rate quoted at 3.5 percent really means that the 6-month rate is $3.5/2 = 1.75$ percent.[3] The actual cash flows on the Treasury bond are illustrated in Figure 5–3. To value the bond a bit more precisely, we should have discounted the series of semiannual payments by the semiannual rate of interest as follows:

$$PV = \frac{\$27.50}{(1.0175)} + \frac{\$27.50}{(1.0175)^2} + \frac{\$27.50}{(1.0175)^3} + \frac{\$27.50}{(1.0175)^4} + \frac{\$27.50}{(1.0175)^5} + \frac{\$1,027.50}{(1.0175)^6}$$

$$= \$1,056.49$$

Thus, once we allow for the fact that coupon payments are semiannual, the value of the 5.5s is 105.649 percent of face value, which is slightly higher than the value that we obtained when we assumed annual coupon payments.[4] Since semiannual coupon payments just add to the arithmetic, we will often stick to our simplification and assume annual interest payments. ◀

How Bond Prices Vary with Interest Rates

As interest rates change, so do bond prices. For example, suppose that investors demanded an interest rate of 5.5 percent on 3-year Treasury bonds. What would be the price of the Treasury 5.5s of 2008? Just repeat the last calculation with a discount rate of $r = .055$:

$$PV \text{ at } 5.5\% = \frac{\$55}{(1.055)} + \frac{\$55}{(1.055)^2} + \frac{\$1,055}{(1.055)^3} = \$1,000.00$$

Thus when the interest rate is the same as the coupon rate (5.5 percent in our example), the bond sells for its face value.

We first valued the Treasury bond using an interest rate of 3.5 percent, which is lower than the coupon rate. In that case the price of the bond was *higher* than its face value. We then valued it using an interest rate that is equal to the coupon and found that bond price equaled face value. You have probably already guessed that when the

---

[3] You may have noticed that the semiannually compounded interest rate on the bond is also the bond's APR, although this term is not generally used by bond investors. To find the effective rate, we can use a formula that we presented in Section 4.6:

$$\text{Effective annual rate} = \left(1 + \frac{APR}{m}\right)^m - 1$$

where m is the number of payments each year. In the case of our Treasury bond,

$$\text{Effective annual rate} = \left(1 + \frac{.035}{2}\right)^2 - 1 = 1.0175^2 - 1 = .0353, \text{ or } 3.53\%$$

[4] Why is the present value a bit higher in this case? Because now we recognize that half the annual coupon payment is received only 6 months into the year, rather than at year-end. Since part of the coupon income is received earlier, its present value is higher. The value we find is still a bit below the price shown in *The Wall Street Journal*. This is because we originally rounded the interest rate up to 3.5 percent.

FIGURE 5-3 Cash flows to an investor in the 5.5 percent coupon bond maturing in 2008. The bond pays semiannual coupons, so there are two payments of $27.50 each year.

cash flows are discounted at a rate that is *higher* than the bond's coupon rate, the bond is worth *less* than its face value. The following example confirms that this is the case.

EXAMPLE 5.2 ▶ Interest Rates and Bond Prices

Investors will pay $1,000 for a 5.5 percent, 3-year Treasury bond when the interest rate is 5.5 percent. Suppose that the interest rate is higher than the coupon rate at (say) 15 percent. Now what is the value of the bond? Simple! We just repeat our initial calculation but with $r = .15$:

$$\text{PV at } 15\% = \frac{\$55}{(1.15)} + \frac{\$55}{(1.15)^2} + \frac{\$1,055}{(1.15)^3} = \$783.09$$

The bond sells for 78.31 percent of face value.   ◀

This is a general result. When the market interest rate exceeds the coupon rate, bonds sell for less than face value. When the market interest rate is below the coupon rate, bonds sell for more than face value.

Suppose that interest rates rise. On hearing the news, bond investors appear disconsolate. Why? Don't they like higher interest rates? If you are not sure of the answer, look at Figure 5–4, which shows the present value of the 5.5 percent Treasury bond for different interest rates. For example, imagine yields soar from 3.5 to 10 percent. Our bond would then be worth less than $900, creating a loss to bondholders of some 16 percent. Conversely, bondholders have reason to celebrate when market

FIGURE 5-4 The value of the 5.5 percent bond falls as interest rates rise.

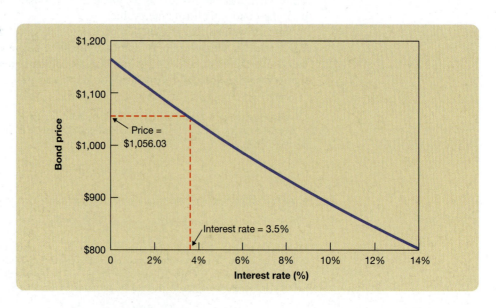

interest rates fall. You can see this also from Figure 5–4. For instance, if interest rates fall to 2 percent, the value of our 5.5 percent bond would increase to $1,100.

Figure 5–4 also illustrates a fundamental relationship between interest rates and bond prices: When the interest rate rises, the present value of the payments to be received by the bondholder falls and bond prices fall. Conversely, declines in the interest rate increase the present value of those payments and result in higher prices.

A warning! People sometimes confuse the interest, or coupon, *payment* on the bond with the *interest rate*—that is, the return that investors require. The $55 coupon payments on our Treasury bond are fixed when the bond is issued. The coupon rate, 5.5 percent, measures the coupon payment ($55) as a percentage of the bond's face value ($1,000) and is therefore also fixed. However, the interest rate changes from day to day. These changes affect the *present value* of the coupon payments but not the payments themselves.

5.3 Current Yield and Yield to Maturity

Suppose you are considering the purchase of a 3-year bond with a coupon rate of 10 percent. Your investment adviser quotes a price for the bond. How do you calculate the rate of return the bond offers?

For bonds priced at face value the answer is easy. The rate of return is the coupon rate. We can check this by setting out the cash flows on your investment:

| You Pay | Cash Paid to You in Year: | | | Rate of Return |
	1	2	3	
$1,000	$100	$100	$1,100	10%

Notice that in each year you earn 10 percent on your money ($100/$1,000). In the final year you also get back your original investment of $1,000. Therefore, your total return is 10 percent, the same as the coupon rate.

Now suppose that the market price of the 3-year bond is $1,136.16. Your cash flows are as follows:

| You Pay | Cash Paid to You in Year: | | | Rate of Return |
	1	2	3	
$1,136.16	$100	$100	$1,100	?

current yield
Annual coupon payments divided by bond price.

What's the rate of return now? Notice that you are paying out $1,136.16 and receiving an annual income of $100. So your income as a proportion of the initial outlay is $100/$1,136.16 = .088, or 8.8 percent. This is sometimes called the bond's **current yield.**

However, total return depends on both interest income and any capital gains or losses. A current yield of 8.8 percent may sound attractive only until you realize that the bond's price must fall. The price today is $1,136.16, but when the bond matures 3 years from now, the bond will sell for its face value, or $1,000. A price decline (i.e., a *capital loss*) of $136.16 is guaranteed, so the overall return over the next 3 years must be less than the 8.8 percent current yield.

Let us generalize. A bond that is priced above its face value is said to sell at a *premium*. Investors who buy a bond at a premium face a capital loss over the life of the bond, so the return on these bonds is always less than the bond's current yield. A bond priced below face value sells at a *discount*. Investors in discount bonds face a capital *gain* over the life of the bond; the return on these bonds is *greater* than the current yield: Because it focuses only on current income and ignores prospective price increases or decreases, the *current* yield does not measure the bond's total rate of return. It overstates the return of premium bonds and understates that of discount bonds.

We need a measure of return that takes account of both coupon payments and the change in a bond's value over its life. The standard measure is called **yield to maturity.** The yield to maturity is the answer to the following question: At what interest rate would the bond be correctly priced? The yield to maturity is defined as the discount rate that makes the present value of the bond's payments equal to its price.

yield to maturity
Interest rate for which the present value of the bond's payments equals the price.

If you can buy the 3-year bond at face value, the yield to maturity is the coupon rate, 10 percent. We can check this by noting that when we discount the cash flows at 10 percent, the present value of the bond is equal to its $1,000 face value:

$$\text{PV at } 10\% = \frac{\$100}{(1.10)} + \frac{\$100}{(1.10)^2} + \frac{\$1,100}{(1.10)^3} = \$1,000.00$$

But suppose the price of the 3-year bond is $1,136.16. In this case the yield to maturity is only 5 percent. At that discount rate, the bond's present value equals its actual market price, $1,136.16:

$$\text{PV at } 5\% = \frac{\$100}{(1.05)} + \frac{\$100}{(1.05)^2} + \frac{\$1,100}{(1.05)^3} = \$1,136.16$$

EXAMPLE 5.3 ▶   Calculating Yield to Maturity for the Treasury Bond

We found the value of the 5.5 percent coupon Treasury bond by discounting at a 3.5 percent interest rate. We could have phrased the question the other way around: If the price of the bond is $1,056.03, what return do investors expect? We need to find the yield to maturity, in other words, the discount rate r, that solves the following equation:

$$\text{Price} = \frac{\$55}{(1 + r)} + \frac{\$55}{(1 + r)^2} + \frac{\$1,055}{(1 + r)^3} = \$1,056.03$$

To find the yield to maturity, most people use either a financial calculator or a spreadsheet. For our Treasury bond you would enter a PV on your calculator of $1,056.03.[5] The bond provides a regular payment of $55, entered as PMT = 55. The bond has a future value of $1,000, so FV = 1,000. The bond life is 3 years, so $n = 3$. Now compute the interest rate, and you will find that the yield to maturity is 3.5 percent. The nearby boxes review the use of spreadsheets and financial calculators in bond valuation problems.   ◀

The yield to maturity is a measure of a bond's total return, including both coupon income and capital gain. If an investor buys the bond today and holds it to maturity, his or her return will be the yield to maturity. Bond investors often refer loosely to a bond's "yield." It's a safe bet that they are talking about its yield to maturity rather than its current yield.

The only *general* procedure for calculating yield to maturity is trial and error. You guess at an interest rate and calculate the present value of the bond's payments. If the present value is greater than the actual price, your discount rate must have been too low, so you try a higher interest rate (since a higher rate results in a lower PV). Conversely, if PV is less than price, you must reduce the interest rate. When a financial

---

[5] Actually, on most calculators you would enter this as a negative number, −1,056.03, because the purchase of the bond represents a cash *outflow.* See the nearby box on financial calculators.

Bond Valuation on a Financial Calculator

In Chapter 4 we saw that financial calculators can compute the present values of level annuities as well as the present values of one-time future cash flows. Coupon bonds present both of these characteristics: The coupon payments are level annuities, and the final payment of face value is an additional one-time payment. Thus for the coupon bond we looked at in Example 5.3, you would treat the periodic payment as PMT = $55, the final or future one-time payment as FV = $1,000, the number of periods as n = 3 years, and the interest rate as the yield to maturity of the bond, i = 3.5 percent. You would thus compute the value of the bond using the following sequence of key strokes. By the way, the order in which the various inputs for the bond valuation problem are entered does not matter.

Hewlett-Packard HP-10B	Sharp EL-733A	Texas Instruments BA II Plus
55 PMT	55 PMT	55 PMT
1000 FV	1000 FV	1000 FV
3 N	3 n	3 N
3.5 I/YR	3.5 i	3.5 I/Y
PV	COMP PV	CPT PV

Your calculator should now display a value of –1,056.03. The minus sign reminds us that the initial cash flow is negative: You have to pay to buy the bond.

You can also use the calculator to find the yield to maturity of a bond. For example, if you buy this bond for $1,056.03, you should find that its yield to maturity is 3.5 percent. Let's check that this is so. You enter the PV as –1,056.03 because you buy the bond for this price. Thus to solve for the interest rate, use the following key strokes:

Hewlett-Packard HP-10B	Sharp EL-733A	Texas Instruments BA II Plus
55 PMT	55 PMT	55 PMT
1000 FV	1000 FV	1000 FV
3 N	3 n	3 N
–1056.03 PV	–1056.03 PV	–1056.03 PV
I/YR	COMP i	CPT I/Y

Your calculator should now display 3.5 percent, the yield to maturity of the bond.

calculator or spreadsheet program finds a bond's yield to maturity, it uses a similar trial-and-error process.

EXAMPLE 5.4 ▶ Yield to Maturity with Semiannual Coupon Payments

Let's redo Example 5.3, but this time we assume the coupons are paid semiannually. Instead of three annual coupons of $55, the bond makes six semiannual payments of $27.50. We can find the *semiannual* yield to maturity on our calculators by using these inputs: n = 6 (semiannual) periods, PV = –1,056.03, FV = 1,000, PMT = 27.50. We then compute the interest rate to find that it is 1.76 percent. This of course is a 6-month, not an annual, rate. Bond dealers typically annualize the semiannual rate by doubling it, so the yield to maturity would be quoted as 1.76×2 = 3.52 percent. [In Excel (see the nearby box), you can confirm that =YIELD(DATE(2005,2,15),DATE (2008,2,15),.055,105.603,100,2) = .0352.] A better way to annualize would be to account for compound interest. A dollar invested at 1.76 percent for two 6-month periods would grow to $1 \times (1.0176)^2$ = $1.0355. The *effective* annual yield is therefore 3.55 percent. ◀

Self-Test 5.3

A 4-year maturity bond with a 14 percent coupon rate can be bought for $1,200. What is the yield to maturity if the coupon is paid annually? What if it is paid semiannually? You will need a spreadsheet or a financial calculator to answer this question.

5.4 Bond Rates of Return

When you invest in a bond, you receive a regular coupon payment. As bond prices change, you may also make a capital gain or loss. For example, suppose you buy the 5.5 percent Treasury bond today for a price of $1,056.03 and sell it next year at a price

Bond Valuation

Excel and most other spreadsheet programs provide built-in functions to compute bond values and yields. They typically ask you to input both the date you buy the bond (called the *settlement date*) and the maturity date of the bond.

The Excel function for bond value is

=PRICE(settlement date, maturity date, annual coupon rate, yield to maturity, final payment, number of coupon payments per year).

An interactive version of this spreadsheet can be found at www.mhhe.com/bmm5e or on the Student CD.

For our 5.5 percent coupon bond, we would enter the values in column B in the spreadsheet below. Alternatively, we could simply enter the following function in Excel:

=PRICE(DATE(2005,02,15),DATE(2008,02,15), .055,.035,100,1).

The DATE function in Excel, which we use for both the settlement and maturity date, uses the format DATE (year,month,day).

Notice that the coupon rate and yield to maturity are expressed as decimals, not percentages. In most cases, final payment will be 100 (i.e., 100 percent of face value), and the resulting price will be expressed as a percent of face value. Occasionally, however, you may encounter bonds that pay off at a premium or discount to face value.

The value of the bond, assuming annual coupon payments, is 105.603 percent of face value, or $1,056.03. If we wanted to assume semiannual coupon payments, we would simply change the entry in cell B12 to 2, and the bond value would change to 105.649 percent of face value, as we found in Example 5.1.

	A	B	C	D	E	F
1						
2		Valuing bonds using a spreadsheet				
3						
4		5.5% coupon		6% coupon		
5		maturing Feb 2008		10-year maturity		
6						
7	Settlement date	2/15/2005		1/1/2000		
8	Maturity date	2/15/2008		1/1/2010		
9	Annual coupon rate	0.055		0.06		
10	Yield to maturity	0.035		0.07		
11	Final payment (% of face value)	100		100		
12	Coupon payments per year	1		1		
13						
14	**Bond price (% of par)**	105.603		92.976		
15						
16						
17		The formula entered here is: =PRICE(B7,B8,B9,B10,B11,B12)				

Please visit us at www.mhhe.com/bmm5e or refer to your Student CD

rate of return

Total income per period per dollar invested.

of $1,080. The return on your investment is the $55 coupon payment plus the price change of ($1,080 − $1,056.03) = $23.97. The **rate of return** on your investment of $1,056.03 is

$$\text{Rate of return} = \frac{\text{coupon income + price change}}{\text{investment}}$$

$$= \frac{\$55 + \$23.97}{\$1,056.03} = .0748, \text{ or } 7.48\%$$

Because bond prices fall when market interest rates rise and rise when market rates fall, the rate of return that you earn on a bond also will fluctuate with market interest rates. This is why we say bonds are subject to interest rate risk.

Do not confuse the bond's rate of return over a particular investment period with its yield to maturity. The yield to maturity is defined as the discount rate that equates the bond's price to the present value of all its promised cash flows. It is a measure of the average rate of return you will earn over the bond's life if you hold it to maturity. In contrast, the rate of return can be calculated for any particular holding period and is based on the actual income and the capital gain or loss on the bond over that period. The difference between yield to maturity and rate of return for a particular period is emphasized in the following example.

In this example, we assume that the first coupon payment comes in exactly one period (either a year or a half-year). In other words, the settlement date is precisely at the beginning of the period. However, the PRICE function will make the necessary adjustments for intraperiod purchase dates.

Suppose now that you wish to find the price of a 10-year maturity bond with a coupon rate of 6 percent (paid annually), selling at a yield to maturity of 7 percent. You are not given a specific settlement or maturity date. You can still use the PRICE function to value the bond. Simply choose an arbitrary settlement date (January 1, 2000 is convenient) and let the maturity date be 10 years hence. The appropriate inputs appear in column D of the spreadsheet on the previous page, with the resulting price, 92.976 percent of face value, appearing in cell D14. You can confirm this value on your calculator using the inputs: $n = 10$, $i = 7$, FV = 1000, PMT = 60.

Excel also provides a function for yield to maturity. It is =YIELD(settlement date, maturity date, annual coupon rate, bond price, final payment as percent of face value, number of coupon payments per year).

For example, to find the yield to maturity in Example 5.3, we would use column B in the spreadsheet below. If the coupons were paid semiannually, as in Example 5.4, we would change the entry for payments per year to 2 (see cell D12), and the yield would increase to 3.52 percent.

	A	B	C	D	E	F	G
1							
2				Finding yield to maturity using a spreadsheet			
3				February 2008 maturity bond, coupon rate = 5.5%, maturity = 3 years			
4							
5		Annual coupons		Semiannual coupons			
6							
7	Settlement date	2/15/2005			2/15/2005		
8	Maturity date	2/15/2008			2/15/2008		
9	Annual coupon rate	0.055			0.055		
10	Bond price	105.603			105.603		
11	Redemption value (% of face value)	100			100		
12	Coupon payments per year	1			2		
13							
14	Yield to maturity (decimal)	0.0350			0.0352		
15							
16							
17			The formula entered here is: =YIELD(B7,B8,B9,B10,B11,B12)				

EXAMPLE 5.5 ▶ **Rate of Return versus Yield to Maturity**

Our 5.5 percent coupon bond with maturity 2008 currently has 3 years left until maturity and sells today for $1,056.03. Its yield to maturity is 3.5 percent. Suppose that by the end of the year, interest rates have fallen and the bond's yield to maturity is now only 2.0 percent. What will be the bond's rate of return?

At the end of the year, the bond will have only 2 years to maturity. If investors then demand an interest rate of 2.0 percent, the value of the bond will be

$$\text{PV at } 2.0\% = \frac{\$55}{(1.020)} + \frac{\$1,055}{(1.020)^2} = \$1,067.95$$

You invested $1,056.03. At the end of the year you receive a coupon payment of $55 and have a bond worth $1,067.95. Your rate of return is therefore

$$\text{Rate of return} = \frac{\$55 + (\$1,067.95 - \$1,056.03)}{\$1,056.03} = .0634, \text{ or } 6.34\%$$

The yield to maturity at the start of the year was 3.5 percent. However, because interest rates fell during the year, the bond price rose and this increased the rate of return. ◀

Suppose that the bond's yield to maturity had risen to 5 percent during the year. Confirm that its rate of return would have been less than the yield to maturity.

Is there *any* connection between yield to maturity and the rate of return during a particular period? Yes: If the bond's yield to maturity remains unchanged during an investment period, its rate of return will equal that yield. We can check this by assuming that the yield on 5.5 percent Treasury bonds stays at 3.5 percent. If investors still demand an interest rate of 3.5 percent at the end of the year, the value of the bond will be

$$PV = \frac{\$55}{(1.035)} + \frac{\$1,055}{(1.035)^2} = \$1,037.99$$

At the end of the year you receive a coupon payment of $55 and have a bond worth $1,037.99, slightly less than you paid for it. Your total profit is $55 + ($1,037.99 − $1,056.03) = $36.96. The return on your investment is therefore $36.96/$1,056.03 = .035, or 3.5 percent, just equal to the yield to maturity.

When interest rates do not change, the bond price changes with time so that the total return on the bond is equal to the yield to maturity. If the bond's yield to maturity increases, the rate of return during the period will be less than that yield. If the yield decreases, the rate of return will be greater than the yield.

Suppose you buy the bond next year for $1,037.99, and hold it for yet another year, so that at the end of that time it has only 1 year to maturity. Show that if the bond's yield to maturity is still 3.5 percent, your rate of return also will be 3.5 percent and the bond price will be $1,019.32.

The solid curve in Figure 5–5 plots the price of a 30-year maturity, 5.5 percent Treasury bond over time assuming that its yield to maturity is currently 3.5 percent and remains at 3.5 percent. The price declines gradually until the maturity date, when it finally reaches face value. In each period, the price decline offsets the coupon income by just enough to reduce total return to 3.5 percent. The dashed curve in Figure 5–5 shows the corresponding price path for a bond with a 2 percent coupon that sells at a discount to face value. In this case, the coupon income would provide less than a competitive rate of return, so the bond sells below face value. Its price gradually approaches face value, however, and the price gain each year brings its total return up to the market interest rate.

FIGURE 5–5 Bond prices over time, assuming an unchanged yield to maturity. Prices of both premium and discount bonds approach face value as their maturity date approaches.

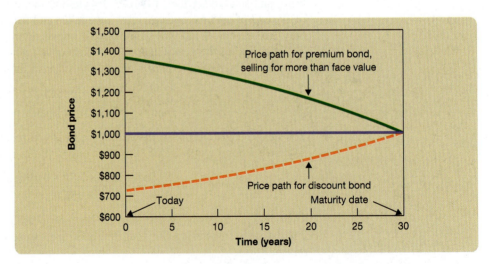

Interest Rate Risk

interest rate risk

The risk in bond prices due to fluctuations in interest rates.

We have seen that bond prices fluctuate as interest rates change. In other words, bonds exhibit **interest rate risk.** Bond investors cross their fingers that market interest rates will fall, so that the price of their bond will rise. If they are unlucky and the market interest rate rises, the value of their investment falls.

But all bonds are not equally affected by changing interest rates. Compare the two curves in Figure 5–6. The green line shows how the value of the 3-year, 5.5 percent coupon bond varies with the level of the interest rate. The purple line shows how the price of a 30-year, 5.5 percent bond varies with the level of interest rates. You can see that the 30-year bond is more sensitive to interest rate fluctuations than the 3-year bond. This should not surprise you. If you buy a 3-year bond when the market interest rate is 5.5 percent and rates then rise, you will be stuck with a bad deal—you have just loaned your money at a lower rate than you could have received if you had waited. However, think how much worse it would be if the loan had been for 30 years rather than 3 years. The longer the loan, the more income you have lost by accepting what turns out to be a low interest rate. This shows up in a bigger decline in the price of the longer-term bond. Of course, there is a flip side to this effect, which you can also see from Figure 5–6. When interest rates fall, the longer-term bond responds with a greater increase in price.

Self-Test 5.6

Suppose that the market interest rate rises overnight from 3.5 percent to 8 percent. Calculate the present values of the 5.5 percent, 3-year bond and of the 5.5 percent, 30-year bond both before and after this change in interest rates. Confirm that your answers correspond with Figure 5–6. Use your financial calculator or a spreadsheet.

5.5 The Yield Curve

yield curve

Graph of the relationship between time to maturity and yield to maturity.

Look back for a moment to Figure 5–2. The U.S. Treasury bonds are arranged in order of their maturity. Notice that the longer the maturity, the higher the yield. This is usually the case, though sometimes long-term bonds offer *lower* yields.

In addition to showing the yields on individual bonds, *The Wall Street Journal* also shows a daily plot of the relationship between bond yields and maturity. This is known as the **yield curve.** You can see from the yield curve in Figure 5–7 that bonds with 3

FIGURE 5–6 Plots of bond prices as a function of the interest rate. Long-term bond prices are more sensitive to the interest rate than prices of short-term bonds.

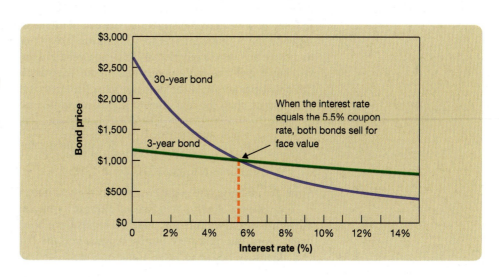

FIGURE 5-7 The yield curve. A plot of yield to maturity as a function of time to maturity for Treasury bonds on February 15, 2005.

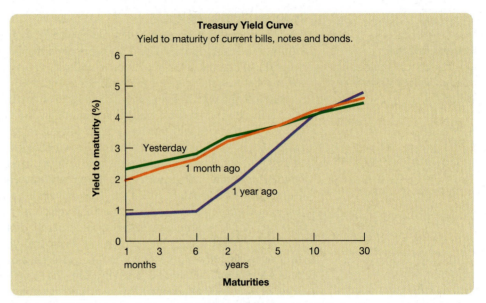

Source: *The Wall Street Journal*, February 16, 2005. © 2005 by Dow Jones & Co. Inc. Reproduced with permission of Dow Jones & Co. Inc. via Copyright Clearance Center.

months to maturity offered a yield of about 2.5 percent; those with 20 years to maturity offered a yield of about 4.5 percent.

Why didn't everyone buy long-maturity bonds and earn an extra 2 percentage points? Who were those investors who put their money into short-term Treasuries at only 2.5 percent?

Even when the yield curve is upward-sloping, investors might rationally stay away from long-term bonds for two reasons. First, the prices of long-term bonds fluctuate much more than prices of short-term bonds. Figure 5–6 illustrates that long-term bond prices are more sensitive to shifting interest rates. A sharp increase in interest rates could easily knock 20 or 30 percent off long-term bond prices. If investors don't like price fluctuations, they will invest their funds in short-term bonds unless they receive a higher yield to maturity on long-term bonds.

Second, short-term investors can profit if interest rates rise. Suppose you hold a 1-year bond. A year from now, when the bond matures, you can reinvest the proceeds and enjoy whatever rates the bond market offers then. Rates may be high enough to offset the first year's relatively low yield on the 1-year bond. Thus you often see an upward-sloping yield curve when future interest rates are expected to rise.

Nominal and Real Rates of Interest

In Chapter 4 we drew a distinction between nominal and real rates of interest. The cash flows on the 5.5 percent Treasury bonds are fixed in nominal terms. Investors are sure to receive an interest payment of $55 each year, but they do not know what that money will buy them. The *real* interest rate on the Treasury bonds depends on the rate of inflation. For example, if the nominal rate of interest is 3.5 percent and the inflation rate is 2 percent, then the real interest rate is calculated as follows:

$$1 + \text{real interest rate} = \frac{1 + \text{nominal interest rate}}{1 + \text{inflation rate}} = \frac{1.035}{1.02} = 1.0147$$

$$\text{Real interest rate} = .0147 = 1.47\%$$

Since the inflation rate is uncertain, so is the real rate of interest on the Treasury bonds.

You *can* nail down a real rate of interest by buying an indexed bond, whose payments are linked to inflation. Indexed bonds have been available in some countries for many years, but they were almost unknown in the United States until 1997 when the U.S. Treasury began to issue inflation-indexed bonds known as *Treasury Inflation-*

Interest Rates and Bond Prices

Bond Calculator

Log on to **www.smartmoney.com** to find a simple bond calculator that shows how prices change as interest rates change. Check whether a change in yield has a greater effect on the price of a long-term or a short-term bond.

Yield Curve

In Figure 5–7 we showed a picture of the Treasury yield curve. When the pros want to see the relationship between yields of bonds with different maturities, they usually look at their Bloomberg terminals. You also can see the current yield curve by logging on to the Web site **www.bloomberg.com** and clicking on *U.S. Treasuries.* Usually yield curves slope upward. Is this still the case? Can you explain why? Notice that the same page also compares the yields on nominal Treasury bonds with those on TIPS. Suppose you are confident that inflation will be 2 percent. Which bonds are the better buy?

Back briefly to yield curves. Log on to **www.smartmoney.com** and find *The Living Yield Curve,* which provides a moving picture of the yield curve. How does today's yield curve compare with yield curves in the past? Do short-term interest rates move more or less than long-term rates?

Treasury Strips

You can also measure the yield curve by looking at the yields on *Treasury strips*. These are government bonds that make only a single payment at maturity. You can find these yields by logging on to the bond screener at **finance.yahoo.com**. Try plotting the yields against maturity. How does the result compare with the Bloomberg yield curve?

Protected Securities, or *TIPS.* The real cash flows on TIPS are fixed, but the nominal cash flows (interest and principal) are increased as the consumer price index increases. For example, suppose the U.S. Treasury issues 3 percent, 2-year TIPS. The **real** cash flows on the 2-year TIPS are therefore

	Year 1	Year 2
Real cash flows	$30	$1,030

The *nominal* cash flows on TIPS depend on the inflation rate. For example, suppose inflation turns out to be 5 percent in year 1 and a further 4 percent in year 2. Then the *nominal* cash flows would be

	Year 1	Year 2
Nominal cash flows	$30 × 1.05 = $31.50	$1,030 × 1.05 × 1.04 = $1,124.76

These cash payments are just sufficient to provide the holder with a 3 percent real rate of interest.

As we write this in early 2005, 5-year TIPS offer a yield of 1.2 percent. This yield is a *real* interest rate. It measures the amount of extra goods your investment will allow you to buy. The 1.2 percent real yield on TIPS is 3.0 percent less than the 4.2 percent yield on nominal 5-year Treasury bonds.[6] If the annual inflation rate proves to be higher than 3.0 percent, you will earn a higher return by holding TIPS; if the

---

[6] You can identify the TIPS bonds in Figure 5–2 by the *i* that appears after the maturity date. You will see that the reported yields to maturity on these bonds are lower than those on the nominal bonds.

FIGURE 5-8 The bottom line shows the real yield on long-term indexed bonds issued by the UK government. The top line shows the yield on UK government long-term nominal bonds. Notice that the real yield has been much more stable than the nominal yield.

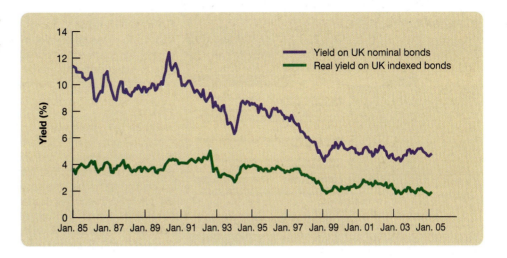

inflation rate is lower than 3.0 percent, the reverse will be true. The nearby box discusses the case for investments in TIPS.

Real interest rates depend on the supply of savings and the demand for new investment. As this supply–demand balance changes, real interest rates change. But they do so gradually. We can see this by looking at the United Kingdom, where the government has issued indexed bonds since 1982. The green line in Figure 5–8 shows that the (real) interest rate on these bonds has fluctuated within a relatively narrow range.

Suppose that investors revise upward their forecast of inflation by 1 percent. How will this affect interest rates? If investors are concerned about the purchasing power of their money, the changed forecast should not affect the real rate of interest. The *nominal* interest rate must therefore rise by 1 percent to compensate investors for the higher inflation prospects.

The blue line in Figure 5–8 shows the nominal rate of interest in the United Kingdom since 1985. You can see that the nominal rate is much more variable than the real rate. When investors were worried about inflation in the late 1980s, the nominal interest rate was about 7 percentage points above the real rate. As we write this in spring 2005, inflation fears have eased and the nominal interest rate in the United Kingdom is less than 3 percentage points above the real rate.

5.6 Corporate Bonds and the Risk of Default

Our focus so far has been on U.S. Treasury bonds. But the federal government is not the only issuer of bonds. State and local governments borrow by selling bonds.[7] So do corporations. Many foreign governments and corporations also borrow in the United States. At the same time U.S. corporations may borrow dollars or other currencies by issuing their bonds in other countries. For example, they may issue dollar bonds in London that are then sold to investors throughout the world.

There is an important distinction between bonds issued by corporations and those issued by the U.S. Treasury. National governments don't go bankrupt—they just print more money.[8] So investors do not worry that the U.S. Treasury will *default* on its

---

[7] These *municipal bonds* enjoy a special tax advantage; investors are exempt from federal income tax on the coupon payments on state and local government bonds. As a result, investors are prepared to accept lower yields on this debt.

[8] But they can't print money of other countries. Therefore, when a foreign government borrows dollars, investors worry that in some future crisis the government may not be able to come up with enough dollars to repay the debt. This worry shows up in the yield that investors demand on such debt. For example, in late 2001, the Argentine government defaulted on over $80 billion of debt. Bondholders were subsequently offered new bonds worth about a third of the face value of the defaulting bonds.

A New Leader in the Bond Derby?

With Wall Street pundits fixated on deflation, the idea of buying Treasury bonds that protect you against inflation seems as crazy as preparing for a communist takeover. But guess what? Treasury Inflation-Indexed Securities are actually a great deal right now. Even if the consumer price index rises only 1.7% annually over the next three decades—a mere tenth of a percentage point above the current rate—buy-and-hold investors will be better off with 30-year inflation-protected securities, commonly known as TIPS, than with conventional Treasuries.

TIPS have yet to catch on with individual investors, who have bought only a fraction of the $75 billion issued so far, says Dan Bernstein, research director at Bridgewater Associates, a Westport (Conn.) money manager. Individuals have shied away from TIPS because they're hard to understand and less liquid than ordinary Treasuries.

If you buy a conventional $1,000, 30-year bond at today's 5.5% rate, you are guaranteed $55 in interest payments each year, no matter what the inflation rate is, until you get your principal back in 2029. Let's say you buy TIPS, now yielding 3.9% plus an adjustment for the consumer price index, and inflation falls to 0.5% from the current 1.6%. Because of the lower inflation rate, you'll get only $44 annually.

Nevertheless, even if the economy falls into deflation, you'll get the face value of the bonds back at maturity.

Less Volatile

But if inflation spikes up, TIPS would outshine conventional bonds. For example, a $1,000, 30-year TIPS with a 4% coupon would yield $40 in its first year. If inflation rises by three points, your principal would be worth $1,030. The $30 gain plus the interest would translate into a 7% total return.

TIPS are attractive for another reason: They're one-quarter to one-third as volatile as conventional Treasuries because of their built-in inflation protection. So investors who use them are less exposed to risk, says Christopher Kinney, a manager at Brown Brothers Harriman. As a result, a portfolio containing TIPS can have a higher percentage of its assets invested in stocks, potentially boosting returns without taking on more risk.

Even so, the price of TIPS can change. If the Federal Reserve hikes interest rates, they'll fall. If it lowers rates, they'll rise. That won't be a concern if you hold the TIPS until maturity, of course.

Source: Anne Tergesen, "A New Leader in the Bond Derby," *BusinessWeek*, April 5, 1999. Reprinted by special permission, copyright © 1999 by The McGraw-Hill Companies, Inc.

---

bonds. However, there is some chance that corporations may get into financial difficulties and may default on their bonds. Thus the payments promised to corporate bondholders represent a best-case scenario: The firm will never pay more than the promised cash flows, but in hard times it may pay less.

default (or credit) risk

The risk that a bond issuer may default on its bonds.

default premium

The additional yield on a bond investors require for bearing credit risk.

The risk that a bond issuer may default on its obligations is called **default risk** (or **credit risk**). It should be no surprise to find that to compensate for this default risk companies need to promise a higher rate of interest than the U.S. Treasury when borrowing money. The difference between the promised yield on a corporate bond and the yield on a U.S. Treasury bond with the same coupon and maturity is called the **default premium.** The greater the chance that the company will get into trouble, the higher the default premium demanded by investors.

The safety of most corporate bonds can be judged from bond ratings provided by Moody's, Standard & Poor's, or other bond-rating firms. Table 5–1 lists the possible

TABLE 5–1 Key to Moody's and Standard & Poor's bond ratings. The highest-quality bonds are rated triple A, then come double-A bonds, and so on.

Moody's	Standard & Poor's	Safety
Aaa	AAA	The strongest rating; ability to repay interest and principal is very strong.
Aa	AA	Very strong likelihood that interest and principal will be repaid.
A	A	Strong ability to repay, but some vulnerability to changes in circumstances.
Baa	BBB	Adequate capacity to repay; more vulnerability to changes in economic circumstances.
Ba	BB	Considerable uncertainty about ability to repay.
B	B	Likelihood of interest and principal payments over sustained periods is questionable.
Caa	CCC	Bonds that may already be in default or in danger of imminent default.
Ca	CC	
C	C	Little prospect for interest or principal on the debt ever to be repaid.

Bond Ratings and Yields

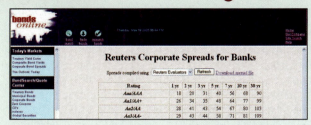

Bond Ratings

You can find the most recent bond rating for any company by logging on to the Web sites of one of the ratings companies. Try www.fitchratings.com (you need to register to use Moody's and Standard & Poor's sites, but not the Fitch Web site). Try finding the bond rating for some sample companies. Were they investment-grade or below?

Default Spreads

In Figure 5–9 we showed how bonds with greater credit risk have promised higher yields to maturity. This yield spread goes up when the economic outlook is particularly uncertain. You can check how much extra yield low-grade bonds offer today by looking at the entry for corporate bond spreads on www.bondsonline.com. Is the yield spread greater for short-term or long-term bonds? Can you explain why? Incidentally, the Bondsonline Web site also offers some useful explanations of bond markets and a facility for searching for bonds with different characteristics.

---

investment grade
Bonds rated Baa or above by Moody's or BBB or above by Standard & Poor's.

junk bond
Bond with a rating below Baa or BBB.

bond ratings in declining order of quality. For example, the bonds that receive the highest Moody's rating are known as *Aaa* (or "triple A") bonds. Then come *Aa* ("double A"), *A, Baa* bonds, and so on. Bonds rated Baa and above are called **investment grade,** while those with a rating of Ba or below are referred to as *speculative grade, high-yield,* or **junk bonds.**

It is rare for highly rated bonds to default. For example, since 1971 fewer than 1 in 1,000 triple-A bonds have defaulted within 10 years of issue. However, when an investment-grade bond does default, the shock waves can be considerable. For example, in May 2001 WorldCom sold $11.8 billion of bonds with an investment-grade rating. Within little more than a year WorldCom filed for bankruptcy, and its bondholders lost more than 80 percent of their investment. For low-grade issues, defaults are less rare. For example, over half of the bonds that were rated CCC by Standard & Poor's at issue have defaulted within 10 years.

As you would expect, the yield on corporate bonds varies with the bond rating. Figure 5–9 shows the extra yield on corporate bonds compared with U.S. Treasuries. You

FIGURE 5–9 Yield spreads between corporate and 10-year Treasury bonds.

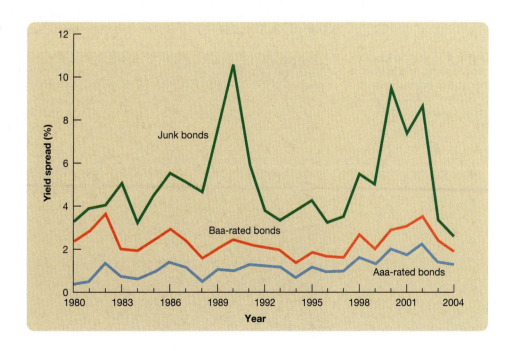

can see that the yield spreads rise as safety falls off. For example, as the economy went into recession in 1990, the promised yield on junk bonds climbed to more than 10 percent higher than the yield on Treasuries. You might have been tempted by the higher promised yields on the lower-grade bonds. But remember, these bonds do not always keep their promises.

EXAMPLE 5.6   ▶   Promised versus Expected Yield to Maturity

Bad Bet Inc. issued bonds several years ago with a coupon rate (paid annually) of 10 percent and face value of $1,000. The bonds are due to mature in 6 years. However, the firm is currently in bankruptcy proceedings, the firm has ceased to pay interest, and the bonds sell for only $200. Based on *promised* cash flow, the yield to maturity on the bond is 63.9 percent. (On your calculator, set PV = –200, FV = 1,000, PMT = 100, *n* = 6, and compute *i*.) But this calculation is based on the very unlikely possibility that the firm will resume paying interest and come out of bankruptcy. Suppose that the most likely outcome is that after 3 years of litigation, during which no interest will be paid, debtholders will receive 27 cents on the dollar—that is, they will receive $270 for each bond with $1,000 face value. In this case the expected return on the bond is 10.5 percent. (On your calculator, set PV = –200, FV = 270, PMT = 0, *n* = 3, and compute *i*.) When default is a real possibility, the promised yield can depart considerably from the expected return. In this example, the default premium is greater than 50 percent.   ◀

Variations in Corporate Bonds

Most corporate bonds are similar to the 5.5 percent Treasury bonds that we examined earlier in the chapter. In other words, they promise to make a fixed nominal coupon payment for each year until maturity, at which point they also promise to repay the face value. However, you will find that there is greater variety in the design of corporate bonds. We will return to this issue in Chapter 13, but here are a few types of corporate bonds that you may encounter.

Zero-Coupon Bonds   Corporations sometimes issue zero-coupon bonds. In this case, investors receive $1,000 face value at the maturity date but do not receive a regular coupon payment. In other words, the bond has a coupon rate of zero. You learned how to value such bonds in Chapter 4. These bonds are issued at prices considerably below face value, and the investor's return comes from the difference between the purchase price and the payment of face value at maturity.

Floating-Rate Bonds   Sometimes the coupon rate can change over time. For example, floating-rate bonds make coupon payments that are tied to some measure of current market rates. The rate might be reset once a year to the current Treasury bill rate plus 2 percent. So if the Treasury bill rate at the start of the year is 6 percent, the bond's coupon rate over the next year would be set at 8 percent. This arrangement means that the bond's coupon rate always approximates current market interest rates.

Convertible Bonds   If you buy a convertible bond, you can choose later to exchange it for a specified number of shares of common stock. For example, a convertible bond that is issued at face value of $1,000 may be convertible into 50 shares of the firm's stock. Because convertible bonds offer the opportunity to participate in any price appreciation of the company's stock, investors will accept lower interest rates on convertible bonds.

Bond issuers are always trying to invent new types of bonds that they hope will appeal to a particular clientele of investors. So, in addition to these fairly common types of bonds, you may also encounter some more peculiar beasts. Here are a couple of examples:

- Managers of insurance companies constantly worry about the possibility of a major hurricane or earthquake that could prompt a flood of costly claims. Some companies therefore shed part of the risk by issuing *catastrophe* (or *Cat*) *bonds.* Cat bonds promise relatively high returns, but the payments on the bond are reduced if a specified type of disaster occurs. Therefore, the bondholders help to provide insurance against catastrophes.
- Most of us hope for a long life. But longevity can create a problem for pension funds that are committed to paying out a regular sum each year until we die. Therefore, pension funds might value an opportunity to protect themselves against an increase in life expectancy. That is the idea behind the *longevity bond* issued by a French bank in 2004. Each year payments on the bond are higher if more of the population survives the extra year. If life expectancy increases, a pension fund may have to pay out for longer than it planned; but if it also owned a longevity bond, it would have the consolation of a boost to its investment income.

Cat bonds are fairly rare and longevity bonds even rarer; most corporate bonds are of the common or garden variety. But bond issuers are always on the lookout for innovative forms of debt that they hope will attract investors.

SUMMARY

www.mhhe.com/bmm5e

What are the differences between the bond's coupon rate, current yield, and yield to maturity?

A bond is a long-term debt of a government or corporation. When you own a bond, you receive a fixed interest payment each year until the bond matures. This payment is known as the coupon. The **coupon rate** is the annual coupon payment expressed as a fraction of the bond's **face value.** At maturity the bond's face value is repaid. In the United States most bonds have a face value of $1,000. The **current yield** is the annual coupon payment expressed as a fraction of the bond's price. The **yield to maturity** measures the average rate of return to an investor who purchases the bond and holds it until maturity, accounting for coupon income as well as the difference between purchase price and face value.

How can one find the market price of a bond given its yield to maturity and find a bond's yield given its price? Why do prices and yields vary inversely?

Bonds are valued by discounting the coupon payments and the final repayment by the yield to maturity on comparable bonds. The bond payments discounted at the bond's yield to maturity equal the bond price. You may also start with the bond price and ask what interest rate the bond offers. The interest rate that equates the present value of bond payments to the bond price is called the yield to maturity. Because present values are lower when discount rates are higher, price and yield to maturity vary inversely.

Why do bonds exhibit interest rate risk?

Bond prices are subject to **interest rate risk,** rising when market interest rates fall and falling when market rates rise. Long-term bonds exhibit greater interest rate risk than short-term bonds.

Why do investors pay attention to bond ratings and demand a higher interest rate for bonds with low ratings?

Investors demand higher promised yields if there is a high probability that the borrower will run into trouble and default. **Credit risk** implies that the promised yield to maturity on the bond is higher than the expected yield. The additional yield investors require for bearing credit risk is called the **default premium.** Bond ratings measure the bond's credit risk.

QUIZ

1. **Bond Yields.** A 30-year Treasury bond is issued with face value of $1,000, paying interest of $60 per year. If market yields increase shortly after the T-bond is issued, what happens to the bond's

   a. coupon rate?
   b. price?
   c. yield to maturity?
   d. current yield?

2. **Bond Yields.** If a bond with face value of $1,000 and a coupon rate of 8 percent is selling at a price of $970, is the bond's yield to maturity more or less than 8 percent? What about the current yield?

3. **Bond Yields.** A bond with face value $1,000 has a current yield of 7 percent and a coupon rate of 8 percent. What is the bond's price?

4. **Bond Pricing.** A 6-year Circular File bond pays interest of $80 annually and sells for $950. What are its coupon rate, current yield, and yield to maturity?

5. **Bond Pricing.** If Circular File (see question 4) wants to issue a new 6-year bond at face value, what coupon rate must the bond offer?

6. **Bond Yields.** A bond has 10 years until maturity, a coupon rate of 8 percent, and sells for $1,100.

   a. What is the current yield on the bond?
   b. What is the yield to maturity?

7. **Coupon Rate.** General Matter's outstanding bond issue has a coupon rate of 10 percent and a current yield of 9.6 percent, and it sells at a yield to maturity of 9.25 percent. The firm wishes to issue additional bonds to the public at face value. What coupon rate must the new bonds offer in order to sell at face value?

8. **Financial Pages.** Turn back to Figure 5–2. What is the current yield of the 5.625 percent, May 2008 maturity bond? What was the closing asked price of the bond on the previous day?

PRACTICE PROBLEMS

9. **Bond Prices and Returns.** One bond has a coupon rate of 8 percent, another a coupon rate of 12 percent. Both bonds have 10-year maturities and sell at a yield to maturity of 10 percent. If their yields to maturity next year are still 10 percent, what is the rate of return on each bond? Does the higher coupon bond give a higher rate of return?

Please visit us at www.mhhe.com/bmm5e or refer to your Student CD

10. **Bond Returns.**

    a. If the bond in Quiz question 6 has a yield to maturity of 8 percent 1 year from now, what will its price be?
    b. What will be the rate of return on the bond?
    c. If the inflation rate during the year is 3 percent, what is the real rate of return on the bond?

Please visit us at www.mhhe.com/bmm5e or refer to your Student CD

11. **Bond Pricing.** A General Motors bond carries a coupon rate of 8 percent, has 9 years until maturity, and sells at a yield to maturity of 7 percent.

    a. What interest payments do bondholders receive each year?
    b. At what price does the bond sell? (Assume annual interest payments.)
    c. What will happen to the bond price if the yield to maturity falls to 6 percent?

12. **Bond Pricing.** A 30-year maturity bond with face value of $1,000 makes annual coupon payments and has a coupon rate of 8 percent. What is the bond's yield to maturity if the bond is selling for

    a. $900?
    b. $1,000?
    c. $1,100?

www.mhhe.com/bmm5e

13. **Bond Pricing.** Repeat the previous problem assuming semiannual coupon payments.

14. **Bond Pricing.** Fill in the table below for the following zero-coupon bonds. The face value of each bond is $1,000.

Price	Maturity (years)	Yield to Maturity
$300	30	—
$300	—	8%
—	10	10%

15. **Consol Bonds.** Perpetual Life Corp. has issued consol bonds with coupon payments of $60. (Consols pay interest forever and never mature. They are perpetuities.) If the required rate of return on these bonds at the time they were issued was 6 percent, at what price were they sold to the public? If the required return today is 10 percent, at what price do the consols sell?

16. **Bond Pricing.** Sure Tea Co. has issued 9 percent annual coupon bonds that are now selling at a yield to maturity of 10 percent and current yield of 9.8375 percent. What is the remaining maturity of these bonds?

17. **Bond Pricing.** Large Industries bonds sell for $1,065.15. The bond life is 9 years, and the yield to maturity is 7 percent. What must be the coupon rate on the bonds?

18. **Bond Prices and Yields.**

    a. Several years ago, Castles in the Sand, Inc., issued bonds at face value at a yield to maturity of 7 percent. Now, with 8 years left until the maturity of the bonds, the company has run into hard times and the yield to maturity on the bonds has increased to 15 percent. What has happened to the price of the bond?

    b. Suppose that investors believe that Castles can make good on the promised coupon payments, but that the company will go bankrupt when the bond matures and the principal comes due. The expectation is that investors will receive only 80 percent of face value at maturity. If they buy the bond today, what yield to maturity do they expect to receive?

19. **Bond Returns.** You buy an 8 percent coupon, 10-year maturity bond for $980. A year later, the bond price is $1,100.

    a. What is the new yield to maturity on the bond?
    b. What is your rate of return over the year?

20. **Bond Returns.** You buy an 8 percent coupon, 20-year maturity bond when its yield to maturity is 9 percent. A year later, the yield to maturity is 10 percent. What is your rate of return over the year?

21. **Interest Rate Risk.** Consider three bonds with 8 percent coupon rates, all selling at face value. The short-term bond has a maturity of 4 years, the intermediate-term bond has maturity 8 years, and the long-term bond has maturity 30 years.

    a. What will happen to the price of each bond if their yields increase to 9 percent?
    b. What will happen to the price of each bond if their yields decrease to 7 percent?
    c. What do you conclude about the relationship between time to maturity and the sensitivity of bond prices to interest rates?

22. **Rate of Return.** A 2-year maturity bond with face value of $1,000 makes annual coupon payments of $80 and is selling at face value. What will be the rate of return on the bond if its yield to maturity at the end of the year is

    a. 6 percent?
    b. 8 percent?
    c. 10 percent?

23. **Rate of Return.** A bond that pays coupons annually is issued with a coupon rate of 4 percent, maturity of 30 years, and a yield to maturity of 7 percent. What rate of return will be earned by an investor who purchases the bond and holds it for 1 year if the bond's yield to maturity at the end of the year is 8 percent?

24. **Bond Risk.** A bond's credit rating provides a guide to its risk. Long-term bonds rated Aa currently offer yields to maturity of 7.5 percent. A-rated bonds sell at yields of 7.8 percent. If a 10-

year bond with a coupon rate of 7 percent is downgraded by Moody's from Aa to A rating, what is the likely effect on the bond price?

25. **Real Returns.** Suppose that you buy a 1-year maturity bond for $1,000 that will pay you back $1,000 plus a coupon payment of $60 at the end of the year. What real rate of return will you earn if the inflation rate is

   a. 2 percent?
   b. 4 percent?
   c. 6 percent?
   d. 8 percent?

26. **Real Returns.** Now suppose that the bond in the previous problem is a TIPS (inflation-indexed) bond with a coupon rate of 4 percent. What will the cash flow provided by the bond be for each of the four inflation rates? What will be the real and nominal rates of return on the bond in each scenario?

27. **Real Returns.** Now suppose the TIPS bond in the previous problem is a 2-year maturity bond. What will be the bondholder's cash flows in each year in each of the inflation scenarios?

CHALLENGE PROBLEM

28. **Interest Rate Risk.** Suppose interest rates increase from 8 to 9 percent. Which bond will suffer the greater percentage decline in price: a 30-year bond paying annual coupons of 8 percent or a 30-year zero-coupon bond? Can you explain intuitively why the zero exhibits greater interest rate risk even though it has the same maturity as the coupon bond?

1. Go to Market Insight (www.mhhe.com/edumarketinsight) and find the bond rating of Toyota (TM) and General Motors (GM) in the *Financial Highlights* section of Market Insight. Why is the bond rating (i.e., S&P Issuer Credit Rating) of Toyota superior to that of GM? Is one firm in better financial health? Compare the ratio of EBIT to interest payments for the two firms. Which has the "healthier" ratio? Which has the lower indebtedness, as measured by the ratio of debt to equity?

SOLUTIONS TO SELF-TEST QUESTIONS

5.1 a. The asked price is $106^{13}/_{32} = 106.40625$ percent of face value, or $1,064.0625.
   b. The bid price is $106^{12}/_{32} = 106.375$ percent of face value, or $1,063.75.
   c. The price decreased by $^2/_{32} = .0625$ percent of face value, or $.625.
   d. The annual coupon is 5.625 percent of face value, or $56.25, paid in two semiannual installments.
   e. The yield to maturity, based on the asked price, is given as 3.51 percent.

5.2 The coupon is 9 percent of $1,000, or $90 a year. First value the 6-year annuity of coupons:

$$\text{PV} = \$90 \times (\text{6-year annuity factor})$$

$$= \$90 \times \left[\frac{1}{.12} - \frac{1}{.12(1.12)^6}\right]$$

$$= \$90 \times 4.11 = \$370.03$$

Then value the final payment and add:

$$\text{PV} = \frac{\$1,000}{(1.12)^6} = \$506.63$$

$$\text{PV of bond} = \$370.03 + \$506.63 = \$876.66$$

5.3   The yield to maturity assuming annual coupons is about 8 percent, because the present value of the bond's cash returns is $1,199 when discounted at 8 percent:

$$PV = PV \text{ (coupons)} + PV \text{ (final payment)}$$

$$= \text{(coupon} \times \text{annuity factor)} + \text{(face value} \times \text{discount factor)}$$

$$= \$140 \times \left[\frac{1}{.08} - \frac{1}{.08(1.08)^4} \right] + \$1,000 \times \frac{1}{1.08^4}$$

$$= \$463.70 + \$735.03 = \$1,199$$

To obtain a more precise solution on your calculator, these would be your inputs:

	Annual Payments	Semiannual Payments
n	4	8
PV	−1,200	−1,200
FV	1000	1000
PMT	140	70

Compute i to find yield to maturity (annual payments) = 7.97 percent. Yield to maturity (semi-annual payments) = 4.026 percent per 6 months, which would be reported in the financial press as 8.05 percent annual yield.

5.4   The 5.5 percent coupon bond with maturity 2008 starts with 3 years left until maturity and sells for $1,056.03. At the end of the year, the bond has only 2 years to maturity and investors demand an interest rate of 5 percent. Therefore, the value of the bond becomes

$$PV \text{ at } 5\% = \frac{\$55}{(1.05)} + \frac{\$1,055}{(1.05)^2} = \$1,009.30$$

You invested $1,056.03. At the end of the year you receive a coupon payment of $55 and have a bond worth $1,009.30. Your rate of return is therefore

$$\text{Rate of return} = \frac{\$55 + (\$1,009.30 - \$1,056.03)}{\$1,056.03} = .0078, \text{ or } .78\%$$

The yield to maturity at the start of the year was 3.5 percent. However, because interest rates rose during the year, the bond price fell and the rate of return was below the yield to maturity.

5.5   By the end of this year, the bond will have only 1 year left until maturity. It will make only one more payment of coupon plus face value, so its price will be $1,055/1.035 = $1,019.32. The rate of return is therefore

$$\frac{\$55 + (\$1,019.32 - \$1,037.99)}{\$1,037.99} = .035, \text{ or } 3.5\%$$

5.6   At an interest rate of 3.5 percent, the 3-year bond sells for $1,056.03. If the interest rate jumps to 8 percent, the bond price falls to $935.57, a decline of 11.4 percent. The 30-year bond sells for $1,367.84 when the interest rate is 3.5 percent, but its price falls to $718.56 at an interest rate of 8 percent, a much larger percentage decline of 47.5 percent.

CHAPTER 6

Valuing Stocks

RELATED WEB LINKS

www.nyse.com

www.nasdaq.com Sites of major U.S. exchanges.

www.rba.co.uk/sources/stocks.htm

www.fibv.com Links to, and comparative statistics on, stock exchanges around the world.

www.djindexes.com

www.spglobal.com

www.msci.com

www.barra.com Information on market indexes.

www.euroland.com Information on European stocks and indexes.

finance.yahoo.com Useful company and market information, with current price quotes.

www.briefing.com

www.thestreet.com

www.fool.com

moneycentral.msn.com/investor/home.asp Company analysis and news.

www.dividenddiscountmodel.com

www.valuepro.com

www.exinfm.com/free_spreadsheets.html Software and downloadable spreadsheets for stock valuation.

www.zacks.com

www.bestcalls.com Conference calls with firms' earnings announcements. Requires a paid subscription.

The floor of the New York Stock Exchange. Watching the hustle and bustle of a trading floor is fun but not informative. How do the buy and sell orders get to the floor? How are the trades actually executed? What underlying factors determine the values of traded stocks and bonds?

© Reuters/CORBIS

Instead of borrowing cash to pay for its investments, a firm can sell new shares of common stock to investors. Whereas bond issues commit the firm to make a series of specified interest payments to the lenders, stock issues are more like taking on new partners. The stockholders all share in the fortunes of the firm according to the number of shares they hold. In this chapter, we will take a first look at stocks, the stock market, and principles of stock valuation.

We start by looking at how stocks are bought and sold. Then we look at what determines stock prices and how stock valuation formulas can be used to infer the rate of return that investors are expecting. We will see how the firm's investment opportunities are reflected in the stock price and why stock market analysts focus so much atten-

tion on the price-earnings, or P/E, ratio of the company.

Why should you care how stocks are valued? After all, if you want to know the value of a firm's stock, you can look up the stock price in *The Wall Street Journal.* But you need to know what determines prices for at least two reasons. First, you may need to value the common stock of a business that is not traded on a stock exchange. Second, in order to make good capital budgeting decisions, corporations need to have some understanding of how the market values firms. A project is attractive if it increases shareholder wealth. But you can't judge that unless you know how shares are valued.

There may be a third reason why you would like to know how stocks are valued. You may be hoping that the knowledge will allow you to make a killing on Wall Street. It's a pleasant thought, but we will see that even professional investors find it difficult to outsmart the competition and earn consistently superior returns.

After studying this chapter you should be able to:

- Understand the stock trading reports in the financial pages of the newspaper.
- Calculate the present value of a stock given forecasts of future dividends and future stock price.
- Use stock valuation formulas to infer the expected rate of return on a common stock.
- Interpret price-earnings ratios.
- Understand what professionals mean when they say that there are no free lunches on Wall Street.

6.1 Stocks and the Stock Market

common stock
Ownership shares in a publicly held corporation.

primary market
Market for the sale of new securities by corporations.

initial public offering (IPO)
First offering of stock to the general public.

secondary market
Market in which previously issued securities are traded among investors.

Firms issue shares of **common stock** to the public when they need to raise money.[1] They typically engage investment banking firms such as Merrill Lynch or Goldman Sachs to help them market these shares. Sales of new stock by the firm are said to occur in the **primary market.** There are two types of primary market issues. In an **initial public offering,** or **IPO,** a company that has been privately owned sells stock to the public for the first time. Some IPOs have proved very popular with investors. For example, the all-time star performer was VA Linux Systems. In 1999, its shares were sold to investors at $30 each; by the end of the first day they had reached $239, a gain of nearly 700 percent.

Established firms that already have issued stock to the public may decide to raise money from time to time by issuing additional shares. Sales of new shares by such firms are also primary market issues and are called *seasoned offerings.* When a firm issues new shares to the public, the previous owners share their ownership of the company with additional shareholders. In this sense, issuing new shares is like having new partners buy into the firm.

Shares of stock can be risky investments. For example, less than 2 years after they were first sold to the public, the shares of VA Linux (now renamed VA Software Corporation) were priced at less than $1 each. If you had bought the shares when they first started trading, you would have lost over 99 percent of your investment. You can understand why investors would be unhappy if forced to tie the knot with a particular company forever. So large companies usually arrange for their stocks to be listed on a stock exchange, which allows investors to trade existing stocks among themselves. Exchanges are really markets for secondhand stocks, but they prefer to describe themselves as **secondary markets,** which sounds more important.

The two principal stock markets in the United States are the New York Stock Exchange (NYSE) and NASDAQ. At the NYSE trades in each stock are handled by a *specialist,* who keeps a record of orders to buy and sell. The specialist ensures that stocks are sold to those investors who are prepared to pay the most and that they are bought from investors who are willing to accept the lowest price.

The NYSE is an example of an *auction market,* in which the specialist acts as the auctioneer. By contrast, NASDAQ operates as a *dealer market.* The NASDAQ exchange provides a screen on which investors can see the prices at which different dealers are prepared to trade. If a price is satisfactory, the investor simply strikes a bargain with the dealer.

Of course, there are stock exchanges in many other countries. Some are midgets, such as the Dar es Salaam exchange in Tanzania, which trades shares in just six companies. Others like the London, Tokyo, and Frankfurt exchanges trade the shares of thousands of firms. Most large exchanges are organized as auction markets.[2] However, the auctioneer on these exchanges is not a specialist but a computer that matches up the best offers to buy or sell shares. This means that there is no stock exchange floor to show on the evening news and no one needs to ring a bell to start trading. In recent years a number of electronic auction markets have also been formed in the United States. These electronic communications networks (or ECNs, as they are called) have captured increasing shares of business from the established exchanges.

Reading the Stock Market Listings

When you read the stock market pages in the newspaper, you are looking at the secondary market. Figure 6–1 is an excerpt from *The Wall Street Journal* of NYSE trad-

---

[1] We use the terms "shares," "stock," and "common stock" interchangeably, as we do "shareholders" and "stockholders."

[2] Although dealer markets are relatively rare for trading equities, dealers are active in trading many other financial instruments. For example, bonds are commonly traded in a dealer market.

FIGURE 6–1 Stock market
listings from *The Wall Street
Journal,* January 17, 2005

YTD % CHG	52-WEEK HI	LO	STOCK (SYM)	DIV	YLD %	PE	VOL 100s	CLOSE	NET CHG
4.4	25.55	18.80	HlthMgt A **HMA**	.16f	.7	18	24278	23.71	0.50
3.2	33.57	21.60	HealthNet **HNT**		...	16	6617	29.78	0.22
-9.9	44.03	32.45	HlthcrRlty **HR**	2.58f	7.0	24	2046	36.69	0.50
-3.0	29.25	22.57◆	HearstArgyl **HTV**	.28f	1.1	21	1330	25.60	0.10
-7.0	9	4.83	HeclaMln **HL**		...	dd	6262	5.42	-0.07
-4.6	23.41	12.90	Heico **HEI**	.05b	.2	27	239	21.54	0.32
-5.8	17.80	9.99	Heico A **HEIA**	.05b	.3	20	240	16.29	0.06
-3.4	40.61	34.53	Heinz **HNZ**	1.14	3.0	17	8784	37.67	...
3.2	9.08	5.74	Hellenic **OTE**	.21e	2.3	...	672	9.08	0.08
-3.1	34.25	23.93	HelmPayne **HP**	.33	1.0	cc	2738	32.98	0.32

KEY
b Annual rate of the cash dividend; indicates that a
   stock dividend was paid.
dd Loss in the most recent four quarters.
f Annual rate, increased on the latest declaration.

Source: "Stock Marketing," *The Wall Street Journal,* January 17,
2005. © 2005 by Dow Jones & Co. Inc. Reproduced with permission
of Dow Jones & Co. Inc. via Copyright Clearance Center.

ing on January 14, 2005. The highlighted bar in the figure shows the listing for Heinz.[3] The first of the three numbers to the left of Heinz shows that the stock price is down 3.4 percent since the start of the year. The next two numbers are the highest and lowest prices at which the stock has traded in the last 52 weeks, $40.61 and $34.53, respectively.

Now skip to the two columns on the right, and you will see the price at which the stock traded on January 14. The closing price was $37.67, which was unchanged from the previous day's close.

dividend
Periodic cash distribution from the firm to its shareholders.

The $1.14 value to the right of Heinz is the annual **dividend** per share paid by the company.[4] In other words, investors in Heinz shares currently receive an annual income of $1.14 on each share. Of course, Heinz is not bound to keep that level of dividend in the future. You hope that earnings and dividends will rise, but it's possible that profits will slump and Heinz will cut its dividend.

The *dividend yield* tells you how much dividend income you receive for each $100 that you invest in the stock. For Heinz the yield is $1.14/$37.67 = .030, or 3 percent. Therefore, for every $100 invested in the stock, you receive annual income of $3. The dividend yield on the stock is like the current yield on a bond: Both look at the current income as a percentage of the price. Both ignore prospective capital gains or losses and therefore do not correspond to total rates of return.

If you scan Figure 6–1, you will see that dividend yields vary widely across companies. While Healthcare Realty Trust has a relatively high yield of 7 percent, Hecla Mining doesn't pay any dividend and therefore has zero yield. Investors are content with a low or zero current yield as long as they can look to higher future dividends and rising share prices.

price-earnings (P/E) multiple
Ratio of stock price to earnings per share.

The **price-earnings (P/E) multiple** for Heinz is reported as 17. This is the ratio of the share price to earnings per share. The P/E ratio is a key tool of stock market analysts. We will have more to say about P/E later in the chapter.

The column headed "Vol 100s" shows that the trading volume in Heinz was 8,784 *round lots.* Each round lot is 100 shares, so 878,400 shares of Heinz traded on this day. A trade of less than 100 shares is an *odd lot.*

Self-Test 6.1   **Explain the entries for Hearst-Argyle Television in Figure 6–1.**

---

[3] The table shows not only the company's name, usually abbreviated, but also the symbol, or ticker, that is used to identify the company on the NYSE price screens. The symbol for Heinz is HNZ; other companies' symbols are not at first glance so obvious.

[4] Actually, it's the last quarterly dividend multiplied by 4.

Stock Exchanges

The major stock exchanges have wonderful Web sites. Look first at the NYSE on **www.nyse.com**. Browse through this Web site. For example, look at how the trading floor works, and make sure you understand how stocks are bought and sold. Click on *Market Information* and *NYSE MarkeTrac,* and click on the DJIA ticker tape, which shows trades for the stocks in the Dow Jones Industrial Average. You can stop the tape at any point and click on the ticker symbol. You will then see a map showing where on the floor the stock is traded and some data about the stock. Check that you know how the dividend yield and price-earnings (P/E) ratio were calculated. Go back to the main page and click on *Market Information.* Here is another place where you can get quotes, dividend yields, P/E ratios, etc. Have a look at *Market Statistics.* (Which are the largest companies traded on the NYSE? What proportion of a company's shares are on average traded each year?). Find the *NYSE Fact Book* and look at who owns shares.

Now log on to **www.nasdaq.com**. Browse through the *Market Activity* pages, and load the NASDAQ ticker tape.

Make Some Trades

And you thought all stock exchanges traded stock! Check out the Hollywood Stock Exchange on **www.hsx.com**. Buy shares of your favorite actors, movies, and music artists and watch their values rise or fall based on the success of their careers and personal life. Stocks soar with a number-one film at the box office and plummet with a stay at the Betty Ford clinic. Join and play for free. It's 90 percent fun, but it will also get you used to some stock market jargon.

Real stock values are established with "votes," just like on the HSX, but the votes cost real money.

6.2 Book Values, Liquidation Values, and Market Values

Why does Heinz sell for $37.67 a share when the stock of Heico is priced at $21.54? And why does it cost $17 to buy a dollar of Heinz's earnings, while Heico is selling at 27 times earnings? Do these numbers imply that one stock is a better buy than the other?

Finding the value of Heinz stock may sound like a simple problem. Each quarter Heinz publishes a balance sheet, which lists the value of the firm's assets and liabilities. The simplified balance sheet in Table 6–1 shows that in October 2004 the book value of all Heinz's assets—plant and machinery, inventories of materials, cash in the bank, and so on—was $10,448 million. Heinz's liabilities—money that it owes the banks, taxes that are due to be paid, and the like—amounted to $8,282 million. The difference between the value of the assets and the liabilities was $2,166 million, about $2.2 billion. This was the **book value** of the firm's equity.[5] Book value records all the money that Heinz has raised from its shareholders plus all the earnings that have been plowed back on their behalf.

book value

Net worth of the firm according to the balance sheet.

TABLE 6–1

BALANCE SHEET FOR H.J. HEINZ CO., OCTOBER 27, 2004 (figures in millions of dollars)			
Assets		**Liabilities and Shareholders' Equity**	
Plant, equipment, and other assets	10,448	Liabilities	8,282
		Equity	2,166

Note: Shares of stock outstanding: 351 million. Book value of equity (per share): 2,166/351 = $6.17.

---

[5] "Equity" is still another word for stock. Thus, stockholders are often referred to as *equity investors.*

146

TABLE 6-2 Market values
versus book values, January
2005

Firm	Stock Price	Book Value per Share	Price-to-Book-Value Ratio
eBay	$114.11	$9.19	12.4
Heinz	37.67	6.17	6.1
Wal-Mart	54.16	10.60	5.1
McDonald's	31.82	10.31	3.1
Pfizer	26.45	9.05	2.9
AT&T	18.81	8.09	2.3
Consolidated Edison	43.30	32.54	1.3
General Motors	40.30	49.19	0.8

Source: Yahoo! Finance Web site, **finance.yahoo.com.**

Book value is a reassuringly definite number. Each year Pricewaterhouse Coopers, one of America's largest accounting firms, tells us:

> In our opinion, the accompanying consolidated balance sheets and the related consolidated statements of income, shareholders' equity and cash flows present fairly, in all material respects, the financial position of H.J. Heinz Company and its subsidiaries (the "Company") . . . , and the results of its operations and its cash flows . . . , in conformity with accounting principles generally accepted in the United States of America.[6]

But does the stock price equal book value? Let's see. Heinz has issued 351 million shares, so the balance sheet suggests that each share was worth $2,166/351 = $6.17.

But in January 2005, Heinz shares actually were selling at $37.67, more than six times their book value. This and the other cases shown in Table 6–2 tell us that investors in the stock market do *not* just buy and sell at book value per share.

Investors know that accountants don't even try to estimate market values. The value of the assets reported on the firm's balance sheet is equal to their original (or "historical") cost less an allowance for depreciation. But that may not be a good guide to what the firm could sell its assets for today.

liquidation value

Net proceeds that could be realized by selling the firm's assets and paying off its creditors.

Well, maybe stock price equals **liquidation value** per share, that is, the amount of cash per share a company could raise if it sold off all its assets in secondhand markets and paid off all its debts. Wrong again. A successful company ought to be worth more than liquidation value. That's the goal of bringing all those assets together in the first place.

The difference between a company's actual value and its book or liquidation value is often attributed to *going-concern value,* which refers to three factors:

1. *Extra earning power.* A company may have the ability to earn more than an adequate rate of return on assets. In this case the value of those assets will be higher than their book value or secondhand value.

2. *Intangible assets.* There are many assets that accountants don't put on the balance sheet. Some of these assets are extremely valuable. Take Pfizer, a pharmaceutical company. As you can see from Table 6–2, it sells at 2.9 times book value per share. Where did all that extra value come from? Largely from the cash flow generated by the drugs it has developed, patented, and marketed. These drugs are the fruits of a research and development (R&D) program that has grown to more than $7 billion per year. But U.S. accountants don't recognize R&D as an investment and don't put it on the company's balance sheet. Successful R&D does show up in stock prices, however.

---

[6] When a major accounting firm makes such a statement and it proves not to be true, there can be hell to pay. Arthur Andersen discovered this when it certified the accounts of Enron Corporation before Enron went bankrupt.

3. *Value of future investments.* If investors believe a company will have the opportunity to make very profitable investments in the future, they will pay more for the company's stock today. When eBay, the Internet auction house, first sold its stock to investors in 1998, the book value of shareholders' equity was about $100 million. Yet 1 day after the issue investors valued the equity at over $6 *billion*. In part, this difference reflected an intangible asset, eBay's unique platform for trading a wide range of goods over the Internet. But investors also judged that eBay was a *growth company*. In other words, they were betting that the company's know-how and brand name would allow it to expand internationally and make it easier for customers to trade and pay online.

Market price is not the same as book value or liquidation value. Market value, unlike book value and liquidation value, treats the firm as a going concern.

It is not surprising that stocks virtually never sell at book or liquidation values. Investors buy shares on the basis of present and *future* earning power. Two key features determine the profits the firm will be able to produce: first, the earnings that can be generated by the firm's current tangible and intangible assets, and second, the opportunities the firm has to invest in lucrative projects that will increase future earnings.

EXAMPLE 6.1 ▶ Amazon.com and Consolidated Edison

Amazon.com, like eBay, is a growth company. By the end of 2002 Amazon had never made a profit and had accumulated losses over its short life of $3 billion. Yet investors at the time were prepared to pay nearly $8 billion for Amazon's common stock. The value of the stock came from the company's market position, its highly regarded distribution system, and the promise of new related products that presumably would lead to future earnings. Amazon was a pure growth firm, because its market value depended wholly on intangible assets and the anticipated profitability of new investments.

Contrast this with Consolidated Edison (Con Ed), the electric utility servicing the New York City area. Con Ed is not a growth company. Its market is limited, and it is expanding capacity at a very deliberate pace. More important, it is a regulated utility, so its returns on present and future investments are constrained. Con Ed's value derives from the stream of income generated by its *existing* assets. Therefore, while Amazon shares at their peak sold for 140 times book value, Con Ed shares have frequently sold for less than book.   ◀

market-value balance sheet

Financial statement that uses the market value of all assets and liabilities.

Financial executives are not bound by generally accepted accounting principles, and they sometimes construct a firm's **market-value balance sheet.** Such a balance sheet helps them to think about and evaluate the sources of firm value. Take a look at Table 6–3. A market-value balance sheet contains two classes of assets: (1) assets already in place, both tangible and intangible, and (2) opportunities to invest in attractive future ventures. Consolidated Edison's stock market value is dominated by tangible assets in place; Amazon's, by the value of future investment opportunities.

Other firms, like Microsoft, seem to have it all. Microsoft earns plenty from its current products. These earnings are part of what makes the stock attractive to investors. In addition, investors are willing to pay for the company's ability to invest profitably in new ventures that will increase future earnings.

TABLE 6–3

A MARKET-VALUE BALANCE SHEET (figures in millions of dollars)	
Assets	**Liabilities and Shareholders' Equity**
Assets in place	Market value of debt and other obligations
Investment opportunities	Market value of shareholders' equity

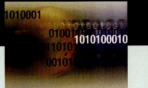

Market versus Book Values

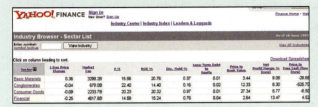

Log on to http://finance.yahoo.com and click on *Stock Research* and then *Sector/Industry Analysis.* You will see some financial ratios for different industries, including the ratio of market price to book value. Is the market value of equity usually higher or lower than book value? Why? Which industries have the highest ratios of market to book? Are there any industries where the market value is on average lower than book value?

Let's summarize. Just remember:

- *Book value* records what a company has paid for its assets, less a deduction for depreciation. It does not capture the true value of a business.
- *Liquidation value* is what the company could net by selling its assets and repaying its debts. It does not capture the value of a successful going concern.
- *Market value* is the amount that investors are willing to pay for the shares of the firm. This depends on the earning power of *today's* assets and the expected profitability of *future* investments.

Take a look at the nearby box for more on market versus book values. The next question is, What determines market value?

> *Self-Test 6.2*
>
> In the 1970s, the computer industry was dominated by IBM and was growing rapidly. In the 1980s, many new competitors entered the market, and computer prices fell. Computer makers in the last decade, including IBM, struggled with thinning profit margins and intense competition. How has IBM's market-value balance sheet changed over time? Have assets in place become proportionately more or less important? Do you think this progression is unique to the computer industry?

6.3 Valuing Common Stocks

Today's Price and Tomorrow's Price

The cash payoff to owners of common stocks comes in two forms: (1) cash dividends and (2) capital gains or losses. Usually investors expect to get some of each. Suppose that the current price of a share is P_0, that the expected price a year from now is P_1, and that the expected dividend per share is DIV_1. The subscript in P_0 denotes time zero, which is today; the subscript in P_1 denotes time 1, which is 1 year hence. We simplify by assuming that dividends are paid only once a year and that the next dividend will come in 1 year. The rate of return that investors expect from this share over the next year is the expected dividend per share DIV_1 plus the expected increase in price $P_1 - P_0$, all divided by the price at the start of the year P_0:

$$\text{Expected return} = r = \frac{DIV_1 + P_1 - P_0}{P_0}$$

Let us now look at how our formula works. Suppose Blue Skies stock is selling for $75 a share ($P_0 = \$75$). Investors expect a $3 cash dividend over the next year ($DIV_1 = \$3$). They also expect the stock to sell for $81 a year hence ($P_1 = \$81$). Then the expected return to stockholders is 12 percent:

$$r = \frac{\$3 + \$81 - \$75}{\$75} = .12, \text{ or } 12\%$$

Notice that this expected return comes in two parts, the dividend and capital gain:

Expected rate of return = expected dividend yield + expected capital gain

$$= \frac{\text{DIV}_1}{P_0} \qquad\qquad + \frac{P_1 - P_0}{P_0}$$

$$= \frac{\$3}{\$75} \qquad\qquad + \frac{\$81 - \$75}{\$75}$$

$$= .04 \qquad\qquad + .08 = .12, \text{ or } 12\%$$

Of course, the *actual* return for Blue Skies may turn out to be more or less than investors expect. For example, one of the best-performing stocks in 2004 was the travel agency Travelzoo. Its price at the end of the year was $100.60, up from $8.70 at the beginning of the year. Since the stock did not pay a dividend during the year, investors earned an actual return of ($0 + $100.60 − $8.70)/$8.70 = 10.56, or 1,056 percent.

This was almost certainly better than investors expected. At the other extreme, the textile company Dan River, which declared bankruptcy during the year, provided a return of −99 percent, well below expectations. Never confuse the actual outcome with the expected outcome.

We saw how to work out the expected return on Blue Skies stock given today's stock price and forecasts of next year's stock price and dividends. You can also explain the market value of the stock in terms of investors' forecasts of dividends and price and the expected return offered by other equally risky stocks. This is just the present value of the cash flows that investors expect to receive:

$$\text{Price today} = P_0 = \frac{\text{DIV}_1 + P_1}{1 + r}$$

For Blue Skies $\text{DIV}_1 = \$3$ and $P_1 = \$81$. If stocks of similar risk offer an expected return of $r = 12$ percent, then 12 percent is the opportunity cost of funds invested in Blue Skies, as we discussed in Chapter 2. Today's price for Blue Skies should be $75:

$$P_0 = \frac{\$3 + \$81}{1.12} = \$75$$

How do we know that $75 is the right price? Because no other price could survive in competitive markets. What if P_0 were above $75? Then the expected rate of return on Blue Skies stock would be *lower* than that on other securities of equivalent risk. (*Check this!*) Investors would bail out of Blue Skies stock and substitute the other securities. In the process they would force down the price of Blue Skies stock. If P_0 were less than $75, Blue Skies stock would offer a *higher* expected rate of return than equivalent-risk securities. (*Check this, too.*) Everyone would rush to buy, forcing the price up to $75. When the stock is priced correctly (that is, price equals present value), the *expected* rate of return on Blue Skies stock is also the rate of return that investors *require* to hold the stock. At each point in time all securities of the same risk are priced to offer the same expected rate of return. This is a fundamental characteristic of prices in well-functioning markets. It is also common sense.

Self-Test 6.3   Androscoggin Copper is increasing next year's dividend to $5 per share. The forecast stock price next year is $105. Equally risky stocks of other companies offer expected rates of return of 10 percent. What should Androscoggin common stock sell for?

The Dividend Discount Model

We have managed to explain today's stock price P_0 in terms of the dividend DIV_1 and the expected stock price next year P_1. But future stock prices are not easy to forecast directly, though you may encounter individuals who claim to be able to do so. A formula that requires tomorrow's stock price to explain today's stock price is not generally helpful.

As it turns out, we can express a stock's value as the present value of all the forecast future dividends paid by the company to its shareholders without referring to the future stock price. This is the **dividend discount model:**

dividend discount model
Discounted cash-flow model which states that today's stock price equals the present value of all expected future dividends.

$$P_0 = \text{present value of } (DIV_1, DIV_2, DIV_3, \ldots, DIV_t, \ldots)$$

$$= \frac{DIV_1}{1+r} + \frac{DIV_2}{(1+r)^2} + \frac{DIV_3}{(1+r)^3} + \cdots + \frac{DIV_t}{(1+r)^t} + \cdots$$

How far out in the future could we look? In principle, 40, 60, or 100 years or more—corporations are potentially immortal. However, far-distant dividends will not have significant present values. For example, the present value of $1 received in 30 years using a 10 percent discount rate is only $.057. Most of the value of established companies comes from dividends to be paid within a person's working lifetime.

How do we get from the one-period formula $P_0 = (DIV_1 + P_1)/(1+r)$ to the dividend discount model? We look at increasingly long investment horizons.

Let's consider investors with different investment horizons. Each investor will value the share of stock as the present value of the dividends that she or he expects to receive plus the present value of the price at which the stock is eventually sold. Unlike bonds, however, the final horizon date for stocks is not specified—stocks do not "mature." Moreover, both dividends and final sales price can only be estimated. But the general valuation approach is the same. For a one-period investor, the valuation formula looks like this:

$$P_0 = \frac{DIV_1 + P_1}{1+r}$$

A 2-year investor would value the stock as

$$P_0 = \frac{DIV_1}{1+r} + \frac{DIV_2 + P_2}{(1+r)^2}$$

and a 3-year investor would use the formula

$$P_0 = \frac{DIV_1}{1+r} + \frac{DIV_2}{(1+r)^2} + \frac{DIV_3 + P_3}{(1+r)^3}$$

In fact we can look as far out into the future as we like. Suppose we call our horizon date H. Then the stock valuation formula would be

$$P_0 = \frac{DIV_1}{1+r} + \frac{DIV_2}{(1+r)^2} + \cdots + \frac{DIV_H + P_H}{(1+r)^H}$$

In words, the value of a stock is the present value of the dividends it will pay over the investor's horizon plus the present value of the expected stock price at the end of that horizon.

Does this mean that investors with different horizons will come to different conclusions about the value of the stock? No! Regardless of the investment horizon, the stock value will be the same. This is because the stock price at the horizon date is determined by expectations of dividends from that date forward. Therefore, as long as the investors agree about a firm's prospects, they will also agree about the same present value. Let's confirm this with an example.

EXAMPLE 6.2 ▶ Valuing Blue Skies Stock

Take Blue Skies. The firm is growing steadily, and investors expect both the stock price and the dividend to increase at 8 percent per year. Now consider three investors,

Erste, Zweiter, and Dritter. Erste plans to hold Blue Skies for 1 year; Zweiter, for 2; and Dritter, for 3. Compare their payoffs:

	Year 1	Year 2	Year 3
Erste	$DIV_1 = 3$		
	$P_1 = 81$		
Zweiter	$DIV_1 = 3$	$DIV_2 = 3.24$	
		$P_2 = 87.48$	
Dritter	$DIV_1 = 3$	$DIV_2 = 3.24$	$DIV_3 = 3.50$
			$P_3 = 94.48$

Remember, we assumed that dividends and stock prices for Blue Skies are expected to grow at a steady 8 percent. Thus $DIV_2 = \$3 \times 1.08 = \$3.24$, $DIV_3 = \$3.24 \times 1.08 = \$3.50$, and so on.

Erste, Zweiter, and Dritter all require the same 12 percent expected return. So we can calculate present value over Erste's 1-year horizon:

$$PV = \frac{DIV_1 + P_1}{1 + r} = \frac{\$3 + \$81}{1.12} = \$75$$

or Zweiter's 2-year horizon:

$$PV = \frac{DIV_1}{1 + r} + \frac{DIV_2 + P_2}{(1 + r)^2}$$

$$= \frac{\$3}{1.12} + \frac{\$3.24 + \$87.48}{(1.12)^2}$$

$$= \$2.68 + \$72.32 = \$75$$

or Dritter's 3-year horizon:

$$PV = \frac{DIV_1}{1 + r} + \frac{DIV_2}{(1 + r)^2} + \frac{DIV_3 + P_3}{(1 + r)^3}$$

$$= \frac{\$3}{1.12} + \frac{\$3.24}{(1.12)^2} + \frac{\$3.50 + \$94.48}{(1.12)^3}$$

$$= \$2.68 + \$2.58 + \$69.74 = \$75$$

All agree the stock is worth $75 per share. This illustrates our basic principle: The value of a common stock equals the present value of dividends received out to the investment horizon plus the present value of the forecast stock price at the horizon. Moreover, when you move the horizon date, the stock's present value should not change. The principle holds for horizons of 1, 3, 10, 20, and 50 years or more. ◄

Self-Test 6.4

Refer to Self-Test 6.3. Assume that Androscoggin Copper's dividend and share price are expected to grow at a constant 5 percent per year. Calculate the current value of Androscoggin stock with the dividend discount model using a 3-year horizon. You should get the same answer as in Self-Test 6.3.

Look at Table 6–4, which continues the Blue Skies example for various time horizons, still assuming that the dividends are expected to increase at a steady 8 percent compound rate. The expected price increases at the same 8 percent rate. Each row in the table represents a present value calculation for a different horizon year. Note that total present value does not depend on the investment horizon. Figure 6–2 presents the

TABLE 6-4 Value of Blue Skies

Horizon, Years	PV (Dividends) +	PV (Terminal Price) =	Value per Share
1	$ 2.68	$72.32	$75
2	5.26	69.74	75
3	7.75	67.25	75
10	22.87	52.13	75
20	38.76	36.24	75
30	49.81	25.19	75
50	62.83	12.17	75
100	73.02	1.98	75

FIGURE 6-2 Value of Blue Skies for different horizons

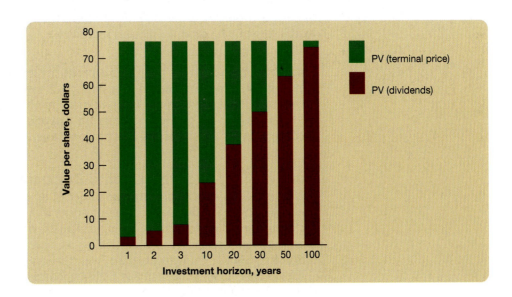

same data in a graph. Each column shows the present value of the dividends up to the horizon and the present value of the price at the horizon. As the horizon recedes, the dividend stream accounts for an increasing proportion of present value but the *total* present value of dividends plus terminal price always equals $75.

If the horizon is infinitely far away, then we can forget about the final horizon price—it has almost no present value—and simply say,

$$\text{Stock price} = \text{PV (all future dividends per share)}$$

This is the dividend discount model.

6.4 Simplifying the Dividend Discount Model

The Dividend Discount Model with No Growth

Consider a company that pays out all its earnings to its common shareholders. Such a company could not grow because it could not reinvest.[7] Stockholders might enjoy a generous immediate dividend, but they could not look forward to higher future dividends. The company's stock would offer a perpetual stream of equal cash payments, $\text{DIV}_1 = \text{DIV}_2 = \cdots = \text{DIV}_t = \cdots$.

The dividend discount model says that these no-growth shares should sell for the present value of a constant, perpetual stream of dividends. We learned how to do that

---

[7] We assume it does not raise money by issuing new shares.

calculation when we valued perpetuities in Chapter 4. Just divide the annual cash payment by the discount rate. The discount rate is the rate of return demanded by investors in other stocks with the same risk:

$$P_0 = \frac{DIV_1}{r}$$

Since our company pays out all its earnings as dividends, dividends and earnings are the same, and we could just as well calculate stock value by

$$\text{Value of a no-growth stock} = P_0 = \frac{EPS_1}{r}$$

where EPS_1 represents next year's earnings per share of stock. Thus some people loosely say, "Stock price is the present value of future earnings," and calculate value by this formula. Be careful—this is a special case.

Self-Test 6.5

Moonshine Industries has produced a barrel per week for the past 20 years but cannot grow because of certain legal hazards. It earns $25 per share per year and pays it all out to stockholders. The stockholders have alternative, equivalent-risk ventures yielding 20 percent per year on average. How much is one share of Moonshine worth? Assume the company can keep going indefinitely.

The Constant-Growth Dividend Discount Model

The dividend discount model requires a forecast of dividends for every year into the future, which poses a bit of a problem for stocks with potentially infinite lives. Unless we want to spend a lifetime forecasting dividends, we must use simplifying assumptions to reduce the number of estimates. As we have just seen, the simplest simplification assumes a no-growth perpetuity, which works only for no-growth shares.

Here's another simplification that finds a good deal of practical use. Suppose forecast dividends grow at a constant rate into the indefinite future. If dividends grow at a steady rate, then instead of forecasting an infinite number of dividends, we need to forecast only the next dividend and the dividend growth rate.

Recall Blue Skies Inc. It will pay a $3 dividend in 1 year. If the dividend grows at a constant rate of $g = .08$ (8 percent) thereafter, then dividends in future years will be

$$
\begin{aligned}
DIV_1 &= \$3 & &= \$3.00 \\
DIV_2 &= \$3 \times (1 + g) = \$3 \times 1.08 & &= \$3.24 \\
DIV_3 &= \$3 \times (1 + g)^2 = \$3 \times 1.08^2 &&= \$3.50
\end{aligned}
$$

Plug these forecasts of future dividends into the dividend discount model:

$$
\begin{aligned}
P_0 &= \frac{D_1}{1 + r} + \frac{D_1(1 + g)}{(1 + r)^2} + \frac{D_1(1 + g)^2}{(1 + r)^3} + \frac{D_1(1 + g)^3}{(1 + r)^4} + \cdots \\
&= \frac{\$3}{1.12} + \frac{\$3.24}{(1.12)^2} + \frac{\$3.50}{(1.12)^3} + \frac{\$3.78}{(1.12)^4} + \cdots \\
&= \$2.68 + \$2.58 + \$2.49 + \$2.40 + \cdots
\end{aligned}
$$

Although there is an infinite number of terms, each term is proportionately smaller than the preceding one as long as the dividend growth rate g is less than the discount rate r. Because the present value of far-distant dividends will be ever closer to zero, the sum of all of these terms is finite despite the fact that an infinite number of dividends will be paid. The sum can be shown to equal

$$P_0 = \frac{DIV_1}{r - g}$$

This equation is called the **constant-growth dividend discount model,** or the *Gordon growth model* after Myron Gordon, who did much to popularize it.[8]

EXAMPLE 6.3 ▶	**Blue Skies Valued by the Constant-Growth Model**

constant-growth dividend discount model

Version of the dividend discount model in which dividends grow at a constant rate.

Let's apply the constant-growth model to Blue Skies. Assume a dividend has just been paid. The next dividend, to be paid in a year, is forecast at $DIV_1 = \$3$, the growth rate of dividends is $g = 8$ percent, and the discount rate is $r = 12$ percent. Therefore, we solve for the stock value as

$$P_0 = \frac{DIV_1}{r - g} = \frac{\$3}{.12 - .08} = \$75$$

◀

The constant-growth formula is close to the formula for the present value of a perpetuity. Suppose you forecast no growth in dividends ($g = 0$). Then the dividend stream is a simple perpetuity, and the valuation formula is $P_0 = DIV_1/r$. This is precisely the formula you used in Self-Test 6.5 to value Moonshine, a no-growth common stock.

The constant-growth model generalizes the perpetuity formula to allow for constant growth in dividends. Notice that as g increases, the stock price also rises. However, the constant-growth formula is valid only when g is less than r. If someone forecasts perpetual dividend growth at a rate greater than investors' required return r, then two things happen:

1. The formula explodes. It gives nutty answers. (Try a numerical example.)
2. You know the forecast is wrong, because far-distant dividends would have incredibly high present values. (Again, try a numerical example. Calculate the present value of a dividend paid after 100 years, assuming $DIV_1 = \$3$, $r = .12$, but $g = .20$.)

Estimating Expected Rates of Return

We argued earlier, in Section 6.3, that in competitive markets, common stocks with the same risk are priced to offer the same expected rate of return. But how do you figure out what that expected rate of return is?

It's not easy. Consensus estimates of future dividends, stock prices, or overall rates of return are not published in *The Wall Street Journal* or reported by TV newscasters. Economists argue about which statistical models give the best estimates. There are nevertheless some useful rules of thumb that can give sensible numbers.

One rule of thumb is based on the constant-growth dividend discount model. Remember that it forecasts a constant growth rate g in both future dividends and stock prices. That means forecast capital gains equal g per year.

We can calculate the expected rate of return by rearranging the constant-growth formula as

$$r = \frac{DIV_1}{P_0} + g$$

= dividend yield + growth rate

For Blue Skies, the expected first-year dividend is $3 and the growth rate is 8 percent. With an initial stock price of $75, the expected rate of return is

---

[8] Notice that the first dividend is assumed to come at the *end* of the first period and is discounted for a full period. If the stock has just paid a dividend DIV_0, then next year's dividend will be $(1 + g)$ times the dividend just paid. So another way to write the valuation formula is

$$P_0 = \frac{DIV_1}{r - g} = \frac{DIV_0 \times (1 + g)}{r - g}$$

$$r = \frac{DIV_1}{P_0} + g$$

$$= \frac{\$3}{\$75} + .08 = .04 + .08 = .12, \text{ or } 12\%$$

Suppose we found another stock with the same risk as Blue Skies. It ought to offer the same expected rate of return even if its immediate dividend or expected growth rate is very different. The required rate of return is not the unique property of Blue Skies or any other company; it is set in the worldwide market for common stocks. Blue Skies cannot change its value of r by paying higher or lower dividends or by growing faster or slower, unless these changes also affect the risk of the stock. When we use the rule-of-thumb formula, $r = DIV_1/P_0 + g$, we are *not* saying that r, the expected rate of return, is *determined by* DIV_1 or g. It is determined by the rate of return offered by other equally risky stocks. That return determines how much investors are willing to pay for Blue Skies' forecast future dividends:

$$\underbrace{\frac{DIV_1}{P_0} + g}_{} = r = \underbrace{\begin{array}{l}\text{expected rate of return offered}\\ \text{by other, equally risky stocks}\end{array}}_{}$$

Given DIV_1 and g, investors set the stock price   so that Blue Skies offers an adequate expected rate of return r

| EXAMPLE 6.4 ▶ | Blue Skies Gets a Windfall |

Blue Skies has won a lawsuit against its archrival, Nasty Manufacturing, which forces Nasty Manufacturing to withdraw as a competitor in a key market. As a result, Blue Skies is able to generate 9 percent per year future growth without sacrificing immediate dividends. Will that increase r, the expected rate of return?

This is very good news for Blue Skies stockholders. The stock price will jump to

$$P_0 = \frac{DIV_1}{r - g} = \frac{\$3}{.12 - .09} = \$100$$

But at the new price Blue Skies will offer the same 12 percent expected return:

$$r = \frac{DIV_1}{P_0} + g$$

$$= \frac{\$3}{\$100} + .09 = .12, \text{ or } 12\%$$

Blue Skies' good news is reflected in a higher stock price today, not in a higher expected rate of return in the future. The unchanged expected rate of return corresponds to Blue Skies' unchanged risk.   ◀

Self-Test 6.6   Androscoggin Copper can grow at 5 percent per year for the indefinite future. It's selling at $100, and next year's dividend is $5. What is the expected rate of return from investing in Carrabasset Mining common stock? Carrabasset and Androscoggin shares are equally risky.

Few real companies are expected to grow in such a regular and convenient way as Blue Skies or Androscoggin Copper. Nevertheless, in some mature industries, growth is reasonably stable and the constant-growth model approximately valid. In such cases the model can be turned around to infer the rate of return expected by investors.

Nonconstant Growth

Many companies grow at rapid or irregular rates for several years before finally settling down. Obviously we can't use the constant-growth dividend discount model in such cases. However, there is an alternative approach. Set the *investment horizon* (year *H*) at the future year by which you expect the company's growth to settle down. Calculate the present value of dividends from now to the horizon year. Forecast the stock price in that year, and discount it also to present value. Then add up to get the total present value of dividends plus the ending stock price. The formula is

$$P_0 = \underbrace{\frac{\mathrm{DIV}_1}{1+r} + \frac{\mathrm{DIV}_2}{(1+r)^2} + \cdots + \frac{\mathrm{DIV}_H}{(1+r)^H}}_{\substack{\text{PV of dividends from} \\ \text{year 1 to horizon}}} + \underbrace{\frac{P_H}{(1+r)^H}}_{\substack{\text{PV of stock price} \\ \text{at horizon}}}$$

The stock price in the horizon year is often called *terminal value*.

EXAMPLE 6.5 ▶ Estimating the Value of PepsiCo Stock

In January 2005 the price of PepsiCo's stock was about $53. The company paid a dividend of $.92 a share. So Pepsi was selling at a dividend yield of $.92/$53 = .017, or 1.7 percent. Let's use the dividend discount model to see if we can make sense of this value.

Investors in 2005 were optimistic about the prospects for Pepsi and were forecasting that earnings would grow over the next 5 years by 10.9 percent a year.[9] This growth rate is almost certainly higher than the return, *r*, that investors required from Pepsi stock, and it is implausible to suppose that such rapid growth could continue indefinitely. Therefore, we cannot use the simple perpetual-growth formula to value Pepsi. Instead, we will break the problem down into three steps:

Step 1. Value Pepsi's dividends over the period of rapid growth.
Step 2. Estimate Pepsi's stock price at the horizon year, when growth should have settled down.
Step 3. Calculate the present value of Pepsi stock by summing the present value of dividends up to the horizon year and the present value of the stock price at the horizon.

Step 1: Our first task is to value Pepsi's dividends over the next 5 years. If dividends keep pace with the growth in earnings, then forecast earnings and dividends are as follows:

Year	1	2	3	4	5
Earnings	$2.52	$2.80	$3.10	$3.44	$3.81
Dividends	1.02	1.13	1.25	1.39	1.54

We estimate that in 2005 investors required a return of about 5.6 percent from Pepsi stock.[10] In this case the present value of the forecast dividends for years 1 to 5 was

$$\text{PV of dividends years 1 to 5} = \frac{\$1.02}{1.056} + \frac{\$1.13}{(1.056)^2} + \frac{\$1.25}{(1.056)^3} + \frac{\$1.39}{(1.056)^4} + \frac{\$1.54}{(1.056)^5} = \$5.33$$

---

[9] Consensus analysts' forecasts are collected by Zack's, First Call, and IBES. They are available on the Web at **moneycentral.com** and **finance.yahoo.com**.

[10] For now, you can take this value purely as an assumption. In Chapter 11, we will show you how to estimate required returns.

Step 2: The trickier task is to estimate the price of Pepsi stock in the horizon year 5. The most likely scenario is that after year 5 growth will gradually settle down to a sustainable rate, but to keep life simple, we will assume that in year 6 the growth rate falls *immediately* to 3.36 percent a year.[11] Thus the forecast dividend in year 6 is

$$DIV_6 = 1.0336 \times DIV_5 = 1.0336 \times \$1.54 = \$1.59$$

and the expected price at the end of year 5 is

$$P_5 = \frac{DIV_6}{r - g} = \frac{\$1.59}{.056 - .0336} = \$70.98$$

Step 3: Remember, the value of Pepsi today is equal to the present value of forecast dividends up to the horizon date plus the present value of the price at the horizon. Thus,

$$P_0 = PV \text{ (dividends years 1–5)} + PV \text{ (price in year 5)}$$
$$= \$5.33 + \frac{\$70.98}{(1.056)^5} = \$59.38$$

◀

A Reality Check   Our estimate of Pepsi's value in Example 6.5 looks reasonable and is not too different from Pepsi's actual market price. But does it make you nervous to note that your estimate of the terminal price accounts for such a large proportion of the stock's value? It should. Only very minor changes in your assumptions about growth beyond year 5 could change your estimate of this terminal price by 10, 20, or 30 percent.

In the case of Pepsi we *know* what the market price really was in January 2005, but suppose that you are using the dividend discount model to value a company that is going public for the first time or that you are wondering whether to buy Blue Skies' concatenator division. In such cases you do not have the luxury of looking up the market price in *The Wall Street Journal*. A valuation error of 30 percent could amount to serious money. Wise managers, therefore, check that their estimate of value is in the right ballpark by looking at what the market is prepared to pay for similar businesses. For example, suppose you can find mature, public companies whose scale, risk, and growth prospects today roughly match those projected for Pepsi at the investment horizon. You discover that their stocks tend to sell at multiples of 17 times recent earnings. Then you can reasonably guess that Pepsi's value in year 5 will be about 17 times current earnings, that is, $17 \times \$3.81 = \$64.77$. This is not too far from the $70.98 horizon value that we obtained from the dividend discount model.

The nearby box contains a link to both constant and nonconstant dividend growth models. Other links are given at the beginning of this chapter.

Self-Test 6.7   Suppose that on further analysis you decide that after year 5 Pepsi's earnings and dividends will grow by a constant 4 percent a year. How does this affect your estimate of the value of Pepsi stock at year 0?

6.5 Growth Stocks and Income Stocks

We often hear investors speak of *growth stocks* and *income stocks*. They seem to buy growth stocks primarily in the expectation of capital gains, and they are interested in the future growth of earnings rather than in next year's dividends. On the other hand,

---

[11] We will show shortly that if a company plows back a constant proportion of earnings and earns a constant return on these new investments, then earnings and dividends will grow by g = plowback ratio × return on new investment. Thus, if from year 5 onward Pepsi continues to reinvest 60 percent of its earnings but earns only the cost of capital on this investment, earnings and dividends will grow by $.6 \times .056 = .0336$, or 3.36 percent.

Dividend Discount Model

Log on to **www.dividenddiscountmodel.com** to value stocks. The program assumes that dividends grow at the same rate as earnings and provides a 5-year consensus forecast of earnings growth (which users are free to change). The "simple model" assumes that dividends continue to grow at this rate for the indefinite future, so stock price equals $\mathrm{DIV}_1/(r - g)$. The "advanced model" assumes that earnings and dividends grow at a constant rate for 5 years only, so you need to forecast the P/E ratio at the end of this time.

Pick a blue-chip stock such as ExxonMobil (XOM) or Heinz (HNZ), and value the stock assuming that the discount rate is equal to the expected return shown in the table. Apart from rounding error, the estimated value should be the same as the current stock price. Now see how the stock price would change if investors decided that they required a 1-percentage-point-higher return from the stock.

they buy income stocks principally for the cash dividends. Let us see whether these distinctions make sense.

Think back once more to Blue Skies. It is expected to pay a dividend next year of $3 ($\mathrm{DIV}_1 = 3$), and this dividend is expected to grow at a steady rate of 8 percent a year ($g = .08$). If investors require a return of 12 percent ($r = .12$), then the price of Blue Skies should be $\mathrm{DIV}_1/(r - g) = \$3/(.12 - .08) = \$75$.

But what determines the rate of dividend growth? Let's check. Suppose that Blue Skies starts year 1 with book equity of $25 a share and earns a return on this equity of 20 percent a year. Then Blue Skies' earnings per share are

Earnings per share = book equity per share × return on equity = $\$25 \times .20 = \$5$

payout ratio
Fraction of earnings paid out as dividends.

Blue Skies proposes to pay a dividend in year 1 of $\mathrm{DIV}_1 = \$3$ a share, which leaves $2 a share to be plowed back in new plant and equipment. The company's **payout ratio** (the fraction of earnings paid out as dividends) is, therefore, $3/$5 = .60, and its **plowback ratio** (the fraction of earnings reinvested in the firm) is $2/$5 = .40.

plowback ratio
Fraction of earnings retained by the firm.

After reinvesting 40 percent of its earnings, Blue Skies will start year 2 with additional equity per share of

> Earnings per share in year 1 × plowback ratio
> = initial equity per share × return on equity × plowback ratio
> = $\$25 \times .20 \times .40 = \$2$

Since Blue Skies started with assets of $25 a share, the *proportionate* growth in Blue Skies' equity is $2/$25 = .08, or 8 percent. The preceding equation reveals that, more generally, the proportionate increase is

> Growth rate = return on equity × plowback ratio

For example, for Blue Skies, the growth rate equals .20 × .40 = .08, or 8 percent.

If Blue Skies continues to earn a return of 20 percent on its equity and plows back 40 percent of its earnings in new plant and equipment, then earnings and dividends will also continue to grow by 8 percent. Financial managers sometimes refer to this as the company's **sustainable growth rate,** because it is the rate of growth that the company can sustain without raising more capital.

sustainable growth rate
Steady rate at which firm can grow; return on equity × plowback ratio.

If a company earns a constant return on its equity and plows back a constant proportion of earnings, then

$$g = \text{sustainable growth rate} = \text{return on equity} \times \text{plowback ratio}$$

What if Blue Skies did not plow back *any* of its earnings into new plant and equipment? In that case it would pay out all of its earnings, $5 a share, but would forego any further growth in earnings and dividends:

g = sustainable growth rate = return on equity × plowback ratio = .20 × 0 = 0

We could recalculate value with $DIV_1 = EPS_1 = \$5$ and $g = 0$:

$$P_0 = \frac{DIV_1}{r - g} = \frac{EPS_1}{r} = \frac{\$5}{.12} = \$41.67$$

Thus, if Blue Skies did not reinvest any of its earnings, its stock price would not be $75 but $41.67. The $41.67 represents the value of earnings from assets that are already in place. The rest of the stock price ($75 − $41.67 = $33.33) is the net present value of the future investments that Blue Skies is expected to make.

What if Blue Skies kept to its policy of reinvesting 40 percent of its profits but the forecast return on new investments was only 12 percent? In that case the sustainable growth rate would also be lower:

g = sustainable growth rate = return on equity × plowback ratio

= .12 × .40 = .048, or 4.8%

If we plug this new figure into our valuation formula, we come up again with a value of $41.67 for Blue Skies stock:

$$P_0 = \frac{\$3}{.12 - .048} = \$41.67$$

Plowing earnings back into new investments may result in growth in earnings and dividends but it does not add to the current stock price if that money is expected to earn only the return that investors require. Plowing earnings back *does* add value if investors believe that the reinvested earnings will earn a higher rate of return.

To repeat, if Blue Skies did not reinvest any of its earnings, the value of its stock would simply derive from the stream of earnings from the existing assets:

$$P_0 = \frac{DIV_1}{r} = \frac{EPS_1}{r} = \frac{\$5}{.12} = \$41.67$$

Equally, if the company *did* reinvest each year but earned only the return that investors require, then those new investments would not add any value. The price of the stock would still be $41.67. Fortunately, investors believe that Blue Skies has the opportunity to earn 20 percent on its new investments, well above the 12 percent return that investors require. This is reflected in the $75 that investors are prepared to pay for the stock. The total value of Blue Skies stock is equal to the value of its assets in place *plus* the **present value of its growth opportunities,** or **PVGO:**

present value of growth opportunities (PVGO)
Net present value of a firm's future investments.

Value of assets in place	$41.67
+ Present value of growth opportunities (PVGO)	33.33
= Total value of Blue Skies stock	$75.00

Of course, valuing stocks is always harder in practice than in principle. Forecasting cash flows and settling on an appropriate discount rate require skill and judgment. The difficulties are often greatest in the case of companies like Blue Skies, whose value comes largely from growth opportunities rather than assets that are already in place. As the nearby box shows, in these cases there is plenty of room for disagreement about value.

Valuing Growth Opportunities

In April 2004 Google, the Internet search-engine provider, announced its plans to go public. Rather than selling shares at a fixed price, Google proposed to auction them to investors. Stock would be allotted to investors who were prepared to pay the most, but all those receiving stock would pay the same price.

The popularity of Google's sophisticated search technology created enormous interest in the issue, and investment managers and their advisers began to debate how much the stock was worth. Google's preliminary prospectus suggested a value of between $108 and $135 a share, which would have valued the equity at $29 billion to $36 billion.

If Google stock was sold at these prices, book value per share would amount to less than $10 and earnings per share would be about $1. Clearly a stock price of $108 or more could not be justified by the stream of earnings generated by existing assets; it would make sense only if investors believed that Google had very valuable growth opportunities that would allow it to earn high returns on future investments. As *The Wall Street Journal* commented, "Sure, the company is making money hand over fist, and it has juicy margins and profits that are expanding rapidly. But . . . in the long run, Google likely will have to prove that it can continue to come up with new ways to profit from its dominant posi-

tion in the Web-search business for its shares to be big winners."

It is notoriously difficult to guess what future opportunities may become available to a high-tech company. Rather than attempting to make detailed growth forecasts, many investors simply compared Google with rival companies such as Yahoo, whose stock was also trading at a price of around 100 times recent earnings.

As the date of the issue approached, a number of financial analysts expressed reservations about Google's suggested price range, and the company announced that it was reducing the number of shares on offer and cutting its estimate of the issue price to $85 to $95 a share. The auction took place in August, and after investors had submitted their bids, Google announced a sale price of $85, somewhat below the point at which the supply of shares equaled demand. It seemed that the pessimists had been right in their criticisms of the price range that Google had originally suggested. However, once trading started, investors rushed to buy. Google stock opened for trading at $100, within 5 months the price had doubled to just over $200, and in mid-2005 the stock was selling at around $300. It seems that valuing growth stocks is far from an exact science.

Self-Test 6.8

Suppose that instead of plowing money back into lucrative ventures, Blue Skies' management is investing at an expected return on equity of 10 percent, which is *below* the return of 12 percent that investors could expect to get from comparable securities.

a. Find the sustainable growth rate of dividends and earnings in these circumstances. Assume a 60 percent payout ratio.

b. Find the new value of its investment opportunities. Explain why this value is negative despite the positive growth rate of earnings and dividends.

c. If you were a corporate raider, would Blue Skies be a good candidate for an attempted takeover?

The Price-Earnings Ratio

The superior prospects of Blue Skies are reflected in its price-earnings ratio. With a stock price of $75 and earnings of $5, the P/E ratio is $75/$5 = 15. If Blue Skies had no growth opportunities, its stock price would be only $41.67 and its P/E would be $41.67/$5 = 8.33. The P/E ratio is, therefore, an indicator of Blue Skies' rosy prospects.

Does this mean that the financial manager should celebrate if the firm's stock sells at a high P/E? The answer is usually yes. The high P/E suggests that investors think that the firm has good growth opportunities. However, firms can have high P/E ratios not because the price is high but because earnings are temporarily depressed. A firm that earns *nothing* in a particular period will have an *infinite* P/E.

6.6 There Are No Free Lunches on Wall Street

We have explained how common stocks are valued. Does that mean that we have just given the game away and told you how to make an instant fortune on the stock market? We are sorry to disappoint you. It is not so easy to beat the market, and even highly paid pros find it very difficult to do so with any consistency.

Look, for example, at Figure 6–3, which shows the average performance of general equity mutual funds over three decades. You can see that in some years these mutual funds did beat the market, but as often as not, it was the other way around. Of course, it would be surprising if some of the managers were not smarter than others and were able to earn superior returns. But it seems hard to spot the smart ones, and the top-performing managers one year have about an average chance of falling on their face the next year.

EXAMPLE 6.6 ▶ Performance of Money Managers

Forbes, a widely read investment magazine, publishes annually an "honor roll" of the most consistently successful mutual funds. Suppose that every year starting in 1975, you invested an equal sum in each of these successful funds when *Forbes* announced its honor roll. You would have outperformed the market in only 5 of the following 16 years, and your average annual return would have been more than 1 percent below the return on the market.[12] ◀

Confronted with this evidence, many large investors have given up the search for superior investment returns, and instead they simply buy and hold a piece of the entire market. Corporate pension funds now invest over a quarter of their U.S. equity holdings in the market index.

Why is it so difficult to beat the market consistently? Let's look at two possible ways that you might attempt to do so.

Method 1: Technical Analysis

Some investors try to achieve superior returns by spotting and exploiting patterns in stock prices. These investors are known as **technical analysts.**

technical analysts
Investors who attempt to identify undervalued stocks by searching for patterns in past stock prices.

Technical analysis sounds plausible. For example, you might hope to beat the market by buying stocks when they are on their way up and by selling them on their way down. Unfortunately, it turns out that such simple rules don't work. A large price rise in one period may be followed by a further rise in the next period, but it is just as likely to be followed by a fall.

Look, for example, at Figure 6–4a. The horizontal axis shows the return on the New York Composite Index in one week (5 business days), while the vertical axis shows the return in the following week. Each point in the chart represents a different week between January 1966 and January 2005. If a market rise one week tended to be followed

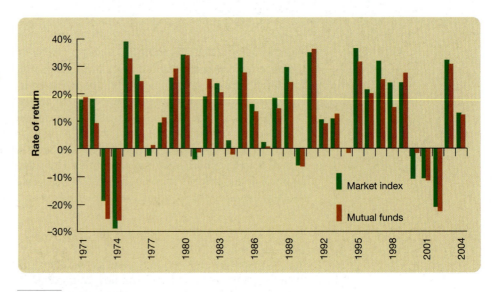

FIGURE 6–3 Annual returns on the Wilshire 5000 Market Index and general equity mutual funds. The market index provided a higher return than the average mutual fund in 23 of the 34 years.

---

[12] See B. G. Malkiel, "Returns from Investing in Equity Mutual Funds 1971 to 1991," *Journal of Finance* 50 (June 1995), pp. 549–572.

FIGURE 6–4a Each dot shows the returns on the New York Composite Index on two successive weeks between January 1966 and January 2005. The circled dot shows a weekly return of +3.4%, followed by +4.9% in the next week. The scatter diagram shows no significant relationship between returns on successive weeks.

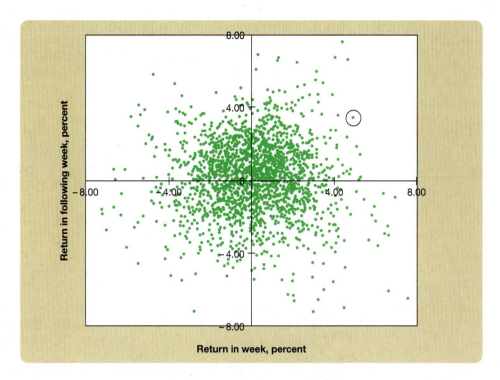

FIGURE 6–4a Each dot shows the returns on the New York Composite Index on two successive weeks between January 1966 and January 2005. The circled dot shows a weekly return of +3.4%, followed by +4.9% in the next week. The scatter diagram shows no significant relationship between returns on successive weeks.

FIGURE 6–4b This scatter diagram shows that there is also no relationship between market returns in successive months.

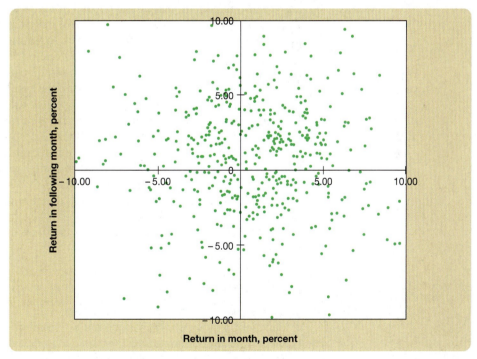

by a rise the next week, the points in the chart would plot along an upward-sloping line. But you can see that there was no such tendency; the points are scattered randomly across the chart. Statisticians sometimes measure the relationship between these changes by the coefficient of correlation. In our example, the correlation between the market movements in successive weeks is –.012—in other words, effectively zero. Figure 6–4b shows a similar plot for monthly (20-business-day) moves. Again you can see that this month's change in the index gives you almost no clue as to the likely change next month. The correlation between successive monthly changes is –.03.

Financial economists and statisticians who have studied stock price movements have concluded that you won't get rich looking for consistent patterns in price changes. This seems to be so regardless of whether you look at the market as a whole (as we did in Figure 6–4) or at individual stocks. Prices appear to wander randomly, virtually equally likely to offer a high or low return on any particular day, *regardless of what has occurred on previous days.* In other words, prices seem to follow a **random walk.**

random walk
Security prices change randomly, with no predictable trends or patterns.

If you are not sure what we mean by "random walk," consider the following example: You are given $100 to play a game. At the end of each week a coin is tossed. If it comes up heads, you win 3 percent of your investment; if it is tails, you lose 2.5 percent. Therefore, your payoff at the end of the first week is either $103 or $97.50. At the end of the second week the coin is tossed again. Now the possible outcomes are as follows:

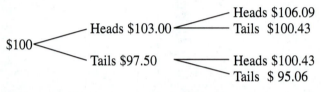

This process is a random walk because successive changes in the value of your stake are independent. That is, the odds of making money each week are the same, regardless of the value at the start of the week or the pattern of heads or tails in the previous weeks.

If a stock's price follows a random walk, the odds of an increase or decrease during any day, month, or year do not depend *at all* on the stock's previous price moves. The historical path of prices gives no useful information about the future—just as a long series of recorded heads and tails gives no information about the next toss.

If you find it difficult to believe that stock prices could behave like our coin-tossing game, then look at the two charts in Figure 6–5. One of these charts shows the outcome from playing our game for 5 years; the other shows the actual performance of the Standard & Poor's Index for a 5-year period. Can you tell which one is which?[13]

Does it surprise you that stocks seem to follow a random walk? If so, imagine that it were not the case and that changes in stock prices were expected to persist for several months. Figure 6–6 provides a hypothetical example of such a predictable cycle. You can see that an upswing in the market started when the index was 1,100 and is expected to carry the price to 1,300 next month. What will happen when investors perceive this bonanza? Since stocks are a bargain at their current level, investors will rush to buy. They will stop buying only when stocks are fairly priced. Thus, as soon as a cycle becomes apparent to investors, they immediately eliminate it by their trading.

Self-Test 6.9   True or false: If stock prices follow a random walk,

a. Successive stock prices are not related.
b. Successive stock price changes are not related.
c. Stock prices fluctuate above and below a normal long-run price.
d. The history of stock prices cannot be used to predict future returns to investors.

Method 2: Fundamental Analysis

You may not be able to earn superior returns just by studying past stock prices, but what about other types of information? After all, most investors don't just look at past

---

[13] The top chart in Figure 6–5 shows the real Standard & Poor's Index for the years 1980 through 1984. The bottom chart was generated by a series of random numbers. You may be among the 50 percent of our readers who guess right, but we bet it was just a guess.

FIGURE 6-5 One of these charts shows the Standard & Poor's Index for a 5-year period. The other shows the results of playing our coin-toss game for 5 years. Can you tell which is which? (The answer is given in footnote 13.)

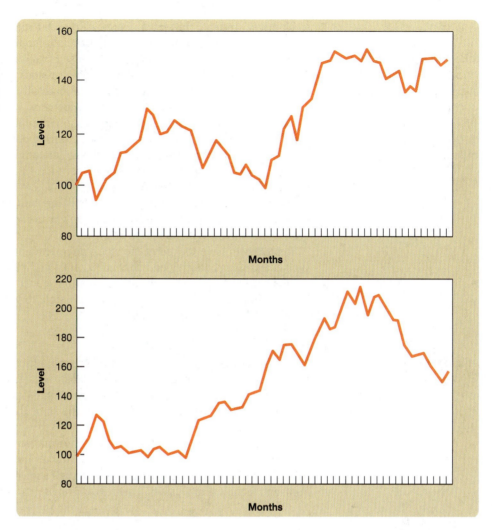

FIGURE 6-6 Cycles self-destruct as soon as they are recognized by investors. The stock price instantaneously jumps to the present value of the expected future price.

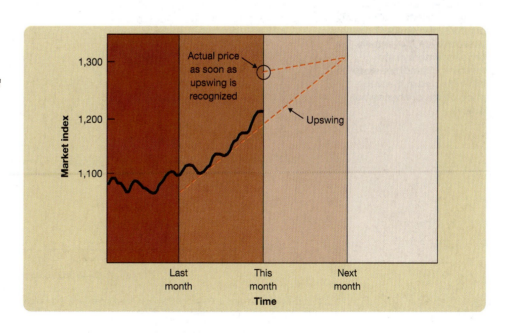

fundamental analysts
Investors who attempt to find mispriced securities by analyzing fundamental information, such as accounting data and business prospects.

stock prices. Instead, they try to gauge a firm's business prospects by studying the financial and trade press, the company's financial accounts, the president's annual statements, and other items of news. These investors are called **fundamental analysts,** in contrast to technical analysts who focus on past stock price movements.

Suppose that you study the financial press carefully and buy a stock when the news about the company is good. Figure 6–7 illustrates why this strategy is unlikely to work. It shows how stock prices react to one particular item of news—the announcement of a takeover. In most takeovers the acquiring company is willing to pay a hefty premium to induce the shareholders of the target company to give up their shares. You can see from Figure 6–7 that the stock price of the target company typically jumps up on the day that the public becomes aware of a takeover attempt (day 0 in the graph). However, this adjustment in the stock price is immediate; thereafter there is no further drift in the stock price, either upward or downward. By the time the acquisition has been made public, it is too late to buy.

Researchers have looked at the stock price reaction to many other types of news, such as earnings and dividend announcements, and plans to issue additional stock or repurchase existing stock. All this information seems to be rapidly and accurately reflected in the price of the stock, so it is impossible to make superior returns by buying or selling after the announcement.

A Theory to Fit the Facts

Economists often refer to the stock market as an **efficient market.** By this they mean that the competition to find misvalued stocks is intense. So when new information comes out, investors rush to take advantage of it and thereby eliminate any profit opportunities. Professional investors express the same idea when they say that there are no free lunches on Wall Street.

It is useful to distinguish three types of information and three degrees of efficiency. The term *weak-form efficiency* describes a market in which prices already reflect all the information contained in past prices. In such a market, share price changes are random, and technical analysis that searches for patterns in past returns is valueless. Fig-

efficient market
Market in which prices reflect all available information.

FIGURE 6–7 The performance of the stocks of target companies compared with that of the market. The prices of target stocks jump up on the announcement day, but from then on there are no unusual price movements. The announcement of the takeover attempt seems to be fully reflected in the stock price on the announcement day.

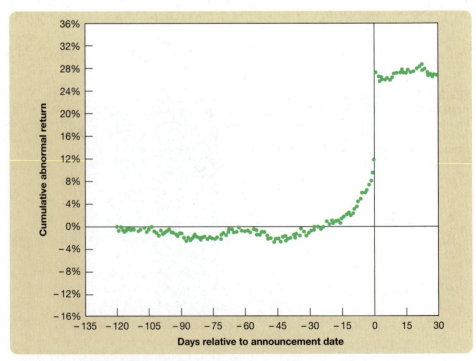

Source: A. Keown and J. Pinkerton, "Merger Announcements and Insider Trading Activity," *Journal of Finance* 36 (September 1981); pp. 855–869.

ure 6–4, which looked at successive weekly and monthly changes in the market index, is evidence in favor of weak-form efficiency.

Semistrong-form efficiency describes a market in which prices reflect not just the information contained in past prices but all publicly available information. In such a market it is impossible to earn consistently superior returns simply by reading the financial press, studying the company's financial statements, and so on. Figure 6–7, which looked at the market reaction to merger announcements, was just one piece of evidence in favor of semistrong efficiency.

Finally, *strong-form efficiency* refers to a market where prices impound all available information. In such a market no investor, however hardworking, could expect to earn superior profits. Figure 6–3, which showed the performance of mutual funds, was consistent with strong-form efficiency.

Self-Test 6.10   Technical analysts and fundamental analysts all try to earn superior returns in the stock market. Explain how their efforts help keep the market efficient.

6.7 Market Anomalies and Behavioral Finance

Market Anomalies
Few simple economic theories are as well supported by the evidence as the efficient-market theory. However, no theory this simple can be universally true; there are always some puzzles or apparent exceptions. Let us look at two examples.

The Earnings Announcement Puzzle   In an efficient stock market, a company's stock price should react instantly at the announcement of unexpectedly good or bad earnings. But Bernard and Thomas found that the stocks with the best earnings news outperformed the stocks with the worst earnings news by more than 4 percent during the 2 months following the earnings announcements.[14] Apparently stock prices did not reflect all available information at the ends of the earnings-announcement days. It seems instead that investors underreacted to the earnings announcement and became aware of the full significance only as further information arrived.

The New-Issue Puzzle   When firms issue stock to the public, investors typically rush to buy. On average, those lucky enough to be awarded stock receive an immediate capital gain. However, researchers have found that these early gains often turn into losses. For example, suppose that you bought stock immediately following each initial public offering and then held that stock for 5 years. Over the period 1970 to 1998 your average annual return would have been 33 percent less than the return on a portfolio of similar-sized stocks.

The jury is still out on these studies of longer-term anomalies. We can't be sure whether they are important exceptions to the efficient-market theory or a coincidence that stems from the efforts of many researchers to find interesting patterns in the data. There may also be other explanations. Take, for example, the new-issue puzzle. Most new issues during the past 30 years have involved growth stocks with high market values and limited book assets. Perhaps the stocks performed badly not because they had just been issued but because all growth stocks happened to perform badly during this period. Of course, if that is true, we need to address another question: Why have growth stocks performed poorly over such a long period of time? We will come back to this question in Chapter 11.

---

[14] See V. L. Bernard and J. K. Thomas, "Post-Earnings-Announcement Drift: Delayed Price Response or Risk Premium?" *Journal of Accounting Research* 27 (Supplement 1989), pp. 1–36.

Behavioral Finance

Investors in technology stocks in the 1990s saw an extraordinary run-up in the value of their holdings. The NASDAQ market index, which is heavily weighted toward high-tech stocks, rose 580 percent from the start of 1995 to March 2000. But then even more rapidly than it began, the boom ended. By October 2002 the NASDAQ index had fallen 78 percent.

Some of the largest price gains and losses were experienced by the new "dot-com stocks." For example, Yahoo shares, which began trading in April 1996, appreciated by 1,400 percent in just 4 years. At this point Yahoo stock was valued at $124 billion, more than that of GM, Heinz, and Boeing combined. It was not, however, to last; just over a year later Yahoo's market capitalization was little more than $6 billion.

What caused the boom in high-tech stocks? Had there been a sharp improvement in the prospects for dividend growth? Or had investors decided that they did not need such high returns from common stocks? Neither explanation seemed capable of explaining the prices that investors were prepared to pay. Could it be that the theory of efficient markets was another casualty of the rise and fall of the dot-coms?

Some scholars believe that the answers to these questions lie in behavioral psychology. People are not 100 percent rational 100 percent of the time. This shows up in two broad areas—their attitudes to risk and the way that they assess probabilities:

1. *Attitudes toward risk.* Psychologists have observed that, when making risky decisions, people are particularly loath to incur losses, even if those losses are small. Losers are liable to regret their actions and kick themselves for having been so foolish. To avoid this unpleasant possibility, individuals will tend to shun those actions that may result in loss.

    The pain of a loss seems to depend on whether it comes on the heels of earlier losses. Once investors have suffered a loss, they may be even more cautious not to risk a further loss. Conversely, just as gamblers are known to be more willing to take large bets when they are ahead, so investors may be more prepared to run the risk of a stock market dip after they have experienced a period of substantial gains. If they do then suffer a small loss, they at least have the consolation of being up on the year.

    You can see how this sort of behavior could lead to a stock price "bubble." The early investors in Amazon and other dot-coms were big winners. They may have stopped worrying about the risk of loss. They may have thrown caution to the winds and piled even more investment into these companies, driving stock prices far above fundamental values. The day of reckoning came when investors woke up and realized how far above fundamental value prices had soared.

2. *Beliefs about probabilities.* Most investors do not have a PhD in probability theory and may make common errors in assessing the probability of uncertain outcomes. Psychologists have found that, when judging the possible future outcomes, individuals commonly look back to what has happened in recent periods and then assume that this is representative of what may occur in the future. The temptation is to project recent experience into the future and to forget the lessons learned from the more distant past. For example, an investor who places too much weight on recent events may judge that glamorous growth companies are very likely to continue to grow rapidly, even though very high rates of growth cannot persist indefinitely.

    A second common bias is that of overconfidence. Most of us believe that we are better-than-average drivers, and most investors think that they are better-than-average stockpickers. We know that two speculators who trade with one another cannot both make money from the deal; for every winner there must be a loser. But presumably investors are prepared to continue trading because each is confident that it is the other one who is the patsy.

    You can see how such behavior may have reinforced the dot-com boom. As the bull market developed, it generated increased optimism about the future and stimulated demand for shares. The more that investors racked up profits on their stocks, the more confident they became in their views and the more willing they became to bear the risk that the next month might not be so good.

Now it is not difficult to believe that your uncle Harry or aunt Hetty may have become caught up in a scatty whirl of irrational exuberance,[15] but why didn't hard-headed professional investors bail out of the overpriced stocks and force their prices down to fair value? Perhaps they felt that it was too difficult to predict when the boom would end and that their jobs would be at risk if they moved aggressively into cash when others were raking up profits. In this case, sales of stock by the pros were simply not large enough to stem the tide of optimism that was sweeping the market.

It is too early to say how far behavioral finance scholars can help to sort out some of the puzzles and explain events like the dot-com boom. One thing, however, seems clear: It is relatively easy for statisticians to spot anomalies with the benefit of hindsight and for psychologists to provide an explanation for them. It is much more difficult for investment managers who are at the sharp end to spot and invest in mispriced securities. And that is the basic message of the efficient-market theory.

---

[15] The term "irrational exuberance" was coined by Alan Greenspan, chairman of the Federal Reserve Board, to describe the dot-com boom. It was also the title of a book by Robert Shiller that examined the boom. See R. Shiller, *Irrational Exuberance* (New York City: Broadway Books, 2001).

SUMMARY

www.mhhe.com/bmm5e

What information about company stocks is regularly reported in the financial pages of the newspaper?

Firms that wish to raise new capital may either borrow money or bring new "partners" into the business by selling shares of **common stock.** Large companies usually arrange for their stocks to be traded on a stock exchange. The stock listings report the stock's **dividend yield,** price, and trading volume.

How can one calculate the present value of a stock given forecasts of future dividends and future stock price?

Stockholders generally expect to receive (1) cash **dividends** and (2) capital gains or losses. The rate of return that they expect over the next year is defined as the expected dividend per share DIV_1 plus the expected increase in price $P_1 - P_0$, all divided by the price at the start of the year P_0.

Unlike the fixed interest payments that the firm promises to bondholders, the dividends that are paid to stockholders depend on the fortunes of the firm. That's why a company's common stock is riskier than its debt. The return that investors expect on any one stock is also the return that they demand on all stocks subject to the same degree of risk. The present value of a stock equals the present value of the forecast future dividends and future stock price, using that expected return as the discount rate.

How can stock valuation formulas be used to infer the expected rate of return on a common stock?

The present value of a share is equal to the stream of expected dividends per share up to some horizon date plus the expected price at this date, all discounted at the return that investors require. If the horizon date is far away, we simply say that stock price equals the present value of all future dividends per share. This is the **dividend discount model.**

If dividends are expected to grow forever at a constant rate g, then the expected return on the stock is equal to the dividend yield (DIV_1/P_0) plus the expected rate of dividend growth. The value of the stock according to this **constant-growth dividend discount model** is $P_0 = DIV_1/(r - g)$.

How should investors interpret price-earnings ratios?

You can think of a share's value as the sum of two parts—the value of the assets in place and the **present value of growth opportunities,** that is, of future opportunities for the firm to invest in high-return projects. The **price-earnings (P/E) ratio** reflects the market's assessment of the firm's growth opportunities.

How does competition among investors lead to efficient markets?

Competition between investors will tend to produce an **efficient market**—that is, a market in which prices rapidly reflect new information and investors have difficulty making consistently superior returns. Of course, we all *hope* to beat the market, but if the market is efficient, all we can rationally *expect* is a return that is sufficient on average to compensate for the time value of money and for the risks we bear.

The efficient-market theory comes in three flavors. The *weak form* states that prices reflect all the information contained in the past series of stock prices. In this case it is impossible to earn superior profits simply by looking for past patterns in stock prices. The *semistrong form* of the theory states that prices reflect all published information, so it is impossible to make consistently superior returns just by reading the newspaper, looking at the company's annual accounts, and so on. The *strong form* states that stock prices effectively impound all available information. This form tells us that private information is hard to come by, because in pursuing it you are in competition with thousands—perhaps millions—of active and intelligent investors. The best you can do in this case is to assume that securities are fairly priced.

The evidence for market efficiency is voluminous, and there is little doubt that skilled professional investors find it difficult to win consistently. Nevertheless, there remain some puzzling instances where markets do not seem to be efficient. Some financial economists attribute these apparent anomalies to behavioral foibles.

QUIZ

1. **Dividend Discount Model.** Amazon.com has never paid a dividend, but in June 2005 the market value of its stock was $13 billion. Does this invalidate the dividend discount model?

2. **Dividend Yield.** Favored stock will pay a dividend this year of $2.40 per share. Its dividend yield is 8 percent. At what price is the stock selling?

3. **Preferred Stock.** Preferred Products has issued preferred stock with an $8 annual dividend that will be paid in perpetuity.
   a. If the discount rate is 12 percent, at what price should the preferred sell?
   b. At what price should the stock sell 1 year from now?
   c. What is the dividend yield, the capital gains yield, and the expected rate of return of the stock?

4. **Constant-Growth Model.** Waterworks has a dividend yield of 8 percent. If its dividend is expected to grow at a constant rate of 5 percent, what must be the expected rate of return on the company's stock?

5. **Dividend Discount Model.** How can we say that price equals the present value of all future dividends when many actual investors may be seeking capital gains and planning to hold their shares for only a year or two? Explain.

6. **Rate of Return.** Steady As She Goes, Inc., will pay a year-end dividend of $3 per share. Investors expect the dividend to grow at a rate of 4 percent indefinitely.
   a. If the stock currently sells for $30 per share, what is the expected rate of return on the stock?
   b. If the expected rate of return on the stock is 16.5 percent, what is the stock price?

7. **Dividend Yield.** BMM Industries pays a dividend of $2 per quarter. The dividend yield on its stock is reported at 4.8 percent. What price is the stock selling at?

8. **Forms of Efficient Markets.** Supply the missing words from the following list: *fundamental, semistrong, strong, technical, weak.*
   There are three forms of the efficient market theory. Tests that have found there are no patterns in share price changes provide evidence for the _____ form of the theory. Evidence for the _____ form of the theory is provided by tests that look at how rapidly markets respond to new public information, and evidence for the _____ form of the theory is provided by tests that look at the performance of professionally managed portfolios. Market effi-

ciency results from competition between investors. Many investors search for information about the company's business that would help them to value the stock more accurately. This is known as _____ analysis. Such research helps to ensure that prices reflect all available information. Other investors study past stock prices for recurrent patterns that would allow them to make superior profits. This is known as _____ analysis. Such research helps to eliminate any patterns.

9. **Information and Efficient Markets.** "It's competition for information that makes securities markets efficient." Is this statement correct? Explain.

10. **Behavioral Finance.** Some finance scholars cite well-documented behavioral biases to explain apparent cases of market inefficiency. Describe some of these biases.

PRACTICE PROBLEMS

Please visit us at www.mhhe.com/bmm5e or refer to your Student CD

11. **Stock Values.** Integrated Potato Chips paid a $1 per share dividend *yesterday*. You expect the dividend to grow steadily at a rate of 4 percent per year.

   a. What is the expected dividend in each of the next 3 years?
   b. If the discount rate for the stock is 12 percent, at what price will the stock sell?
   c. What is the expected stock price 3 years from now?
   d. If you buy the stock and plan to hold it for 3 years, what payments will you receive? What is the present value of those payments? Compare your answer to (b).

12. **Constant-Growth Model.** A stock sells for $40. The next dividend will be $4 per share. If the rate of return earned on reinvested funds is 15 percent and the company reinvests 40 percent of earnings in the firm, what must be the discount rate?

13. **Constant-Growth Model.** Gentleman Gym just paid its annual dividend of $3 per share, and it is widely expected that the dividend will increase by 5 percent per year indefinitely.

   a. What price should the stock sell at? The discount rate is 15 percent.
   b. How would your answer change if the discount rate were only 12 percent? Why does the answer change?

14. **Constant-Growth Model.** Arts and Crafts, Inc., will pay a dividend of $5 per share in 1 year. It sells at $50 a share, and firms in the same industry provide an expected rate of return of 14 percent. What must be the expected growth rate of the company's dividends?

Please visit us at www.mhhe.com/bmm5e or refer to your Student CD

15. **Constant-Growth Model.** Eastern Electric currently pays a dividend of about $1.64 per share and sells for $27 a share.

   a. If investors believe the growth rate of dividends is 3 percent per year, what rate of return do they expect to earn on the stock?
   b. If investors' required rate of return is 10 percent, what must be the growth rate they expect of the firm?
   c. If the sustainable growth rate is 5 percent and the plowback ratio is .4, what must be the rate of return earned by the firm on its new investments?

16. **Constant-Growth Model.** You believe that the Non-stick Gum Factory will pay a dividend of $2 on its common stock next year. Thereafter, you expect dividends to grow at a rate of 6 percent a year in perpetuity. If you require a return of 12 percent on your investment, how much should you be prepared to pay for the stock?

17. **Negative Growth.** Horse and Buggy Inc. is in a declining industry. Sales, earnings, and dividends are all shrinking at a rate of 10 percent per year.

   a. If $r = 15$ percent and $DIV_1 = \$3$, what is the value of a share?
   b. What price do you forecast for the stock next year?
   c. What is the expected rate of return on the stock?
   d. Can you distinguish between "bad stocks" and "bad companies"? Does the fact that the industry is declining mean that the stock is a bad buy?

18. **Constant-Growth Model.** Metatrend's stock will generate earnings of $6 per share this year. The discount rate for the stock is 15 percent, and the rate of return on reinvested earnings also is 15 percent.

   a. Find both the growth rate of dividends and the price of the stock if the company reinvests the following fraction of its earnings in the firm: (i) 0 percent; (ii) 40 percent; (iii) 60 percent.
   b. Redo part (a) now assuming that the rate of return on reinvested earnings is 20 percent. What is the present value of growth opportunities for each reinvestment rate?
   c. Considering your answers to parts (a) and (b), can you briefly state the difference between companies experiencing growth versus companies with growth opportunities?

19. **Nonconstant Growth.** You expect a share of stock to pay dividends of $1.00, $1.25, and $1.50 in each of the next 3 years. You believe the stock will sell for $20 at the end of the third year.

   a. What is the stock price if the discount rate for the stock is 10 percent?
   b. What is the dividend yield?

20. **Constant-Growth Model.** Here are data on two stocks, both of which have discount rates of 15 percent:

	Stock A	Stock B
Return on equity	15%	10%
Earnings per share	$2.00	$1.50
Dividends per share	$1.00	$1.00

   a. What are the dividend payout ratios for each firm?
   b. What are the expected dividend growth rates for each firm?
   c. What is the proper stock price for each firm?

21. **P/E Ratios.** Web Cites Research projects a rate of return of 20 percent on new projects. Management plans to plow back 30 percent of all earnings into the firm. Earnings this year will be $3 per share, and investors expect a 12 percent rate of return on the stock.

   a. What is the sustainable growth rate?
   b. What is the stock price?
   c. What is the present value of growth opportunities?
   d. What is the P/E ratio?
   e. What would the price and P/E ratio be if the firm paid out all earnings as dividends?
   f. What do you conclude about the relationship between growth opportunities and P/E ratios?

22. **Constant-Growth Model.** Fincorp will pay a year-end dividend of $2.40 per share, which is expected to grow at a 4 percent rate for the indefinite future. The discount rate is 12 percent.

   a. What is the stock selling for?
   b. If earnings are $3.10 a share, what is the implied value of the firm's growth opportunities?

23. **P/E Ratios.** No-Growth Industries pays out all of its earnings as dividends. It will pay its next $4 per share dividend in a year. The discount rate is 12 percent.

   a. What is the price-earnings ratio of the company?
   b. What would the P/E ratio be if the discount rate were 10 percent?

24. **Growth Opportunities.** Stormy Weather has no attractive investment opportunities. Its return on equity equals the discount rate, which is 10 percent. Its expected earnings this year are $4 per share. Find the stock price, P/E ratio, and growth rate of dividends for plowback ratios of

   a. zero.
   b. .40.
   c. .80.

25. **Growth Opportunities.** Trend-Line Inc. has been growing at a rate of 6 percent per year and is expected to continue to do so indefinitely. The next dividend is expected to be $5 per share.

   a. If the market expects a 10 percent rate of return on Trend-Line, at what price must it be selling?
   b. If Trend-Line's earnings per share will be $8, what part of Trend-Line's value is due to assets in place, and what part to growth opportunities?

26. **P/E Ratios.** Castles in the Sand generates a rate of return of 20 percent on its investments and maintains a plowback ratio of .30. Its earnings this year will be $4 per share. Investors expect a 12 percent rate of return on the stock.

    a. Find the price and P/E ratio of the firm.

    b. What happens to the P/E ratio if the plowback ratio is reduced to .20? Why?

    c. Show that if plowback equals zero, the earnings-price ratio, E/P, falls to the expected rate of return on the stock.

27. **Dividend Growth.** Grandiose Growth has a dividend growth rate of 20 percent. The discount rate is 10 percent. The end-of-year dividend will be $2 per share.

    a. What is the present value of the dividend to be paid in year 1? Year 2? Year 3?

    b. Could anyone rationally expect this growth rate to continue indefinitely?

Please visit us at www.mhhe.com/bmm5e or refer to your Student CD

28. **Stock Valuation.** Start-Up Industries is a new firm that has raised $200 million by selling shares of stock. Management plans to earn a 24 percent rate of return on equity, which is more than the 15 percent rate of return available on comparable-risk investments. Half of all earnings will be reinvested in the firm.

    a. What will be Start-Up's ratio of market value to book value?

    b. How would that ratio change if the firm can earn only a 10 percent rate of return on its investments?

29. **Nonconstant Growth.** Planned Obsolescence has a product that will be in vogue for 3 years, at which point the firm will close up shop and liquidate the assets. As a result, forecast dividends are $DIV_1 = \$2$, $DIV_2 = \$2.50$, and $DIV_3 = \$18$. What is the stock price if the discount rate is 12 percent?

30. **Nonconstant Growth.** Tattletale News Corp. has been growing at a rate of 20 percent per year, and you expect this growth rate in earnings and dividends to continue for another 3 years.

    a. If the last dividend paid was $2, what will the next dividend be?

    b. If the discount rate is 15 percent and the steady growth rate after 3 years is 4 percent, what should the stock price be today?

31. **Nonconstant Growth.** Reconsider Tattletale News from the previous problem.

    a. What is your prediction for the stock price in 1 year?

    b. Show that the expected rate of return equals the discount rate.

32. **Interpreting the Efficient-Market Theory.** How would you respond to the following comments?

    a. "Efficient market, my eye! I know lots of investors who do crazy things."

    b. "Efficient market? Balderdash! I know at least a dozen people who have made a bundle in the stock market."

    c. "The trouble with the efficient-market theory is that it ignores investors' psychology."

33. **Real versus Financial Investments.** Why do investments in financial markets almost always have zero NPVs, whereas firms can find many investments in their product markets with positive NPVs?

34. **Investment Performance.** It seems that every month we read an article in *The Wall Street Journal* about a stockpicker with a marvelous track record. Do these examples mean that financial markets are not efficient?

35. **Implications of Efficient Markets.** The president of Good Fortunes, Inc., states at a press conference that the company has a 30-year history of ever-increasing dividend payments. Good Fortunes is widely regarded as one of the best-run firms in its industry. Does this make the firm's stock a good buy? Explain.

36. **Implications of Efficient Markets.** "Long-term interest rates are at record highs. Most companies, therefore, find it cheaper to finance with common stock or relatively inexpensive short-term bank loans." Discuss.

37. **Expectations and Efficient Markets.** Geothermal Corp. just announced good news: Its earnings have increased by 20 percent. Most investors had anticipated an increase of 25 percent. Will Geothermal's stock price increase or decrease when the announcement is made?

38. **Behavioral Finance.** In Section 6.7 we gave two examples of market anomalies (the earnings-announcement puzzle and the new-issue puzzle). Do you think that behavioral finance can help to explain these anomalies?

CHALLENGE PROBLEMS

39. **Sustainable Growth.** Computer Corp. reinvests 60 percent of its earnings in the firm. The stock sells for $50, and the next dividend will be $2.50 per share. The discount rate is 15 percent. What is the rate of return on the company's reinvested funds?

40. **Nonconstant Growth.** A company will pay a $2 per share dividend in 1 year. The dividend in 2 years will be $4 per share, and it is expected that dividends will grow at 5 percent per year thereafter. The expected rate of return on the stock is 12 percent.

    a. What is the current price of the stock?
    b. What is the expected price of the stock in a year?
    c. Show that the expected return, 12 percent, equals dividend yield plus capital appreciation.

41. **Nonconstant Growth.** Phoenix Industries has pulled off a miraculous recovery. Four years ago it was near bankruptcy. Today, it announced a $1 per share dividend to be paid a year from now, the first dividend since the crisis. Analysts expect dividends to increase by $1 a year for another 2 years. After the third year (in which dividends are $3 per share) dividend growth is expected to settle down to a more moderate long-term growth rate of 6 percent. If the firm's investors expect to earn a return of 14 percent on this stock, what must be its price?

42. **Nonconstant Growth.** Compost Science, Inc. (CSI), is in the business of converting Boston's sewage sludge into fertilizer. The business is not in itself very profitable. However, to induce CSI to remain in business, the Metropolitan District Commission (MDC) has agreed to pay whatever amount is necessary to yield CSI a 10 percent return on investment. At the end of the year, CSI is expected to pay a $4 dividend. It has been reinvesting 40 percent of earnings and growing at 4 percent a year.

    a. Suppose CSI continues on this growth trend. What is the expected rate of return for an investor who purchases the stock at the market price of $100?
    b. What part of the $100 price is attributable to the present value of growth opportunities?
    c. Now the MDC announces a plan for CSI to also treat Cambridge sewage. CSI's plant will therefore be expanded gradually over 5 years. This means that CSI will have to reinvest 80 percent of its earnings for 5 years. Starting in year 6, however, it will again be able to pay out 60 percent of earnings. What will be CSI's stock price once this announcement is made and its consequences for CSI are known?

Please visit us at www.mhhe.com/bmm5e or refer to your Student CD

43. **Nonconstant Growth.** Better Mousetraps has come out with an improved product, and the world is beating a path to its door. As a result, the firm projects growth of 20 percent per year for 4 years. By then, other firms will have copycat technology, competition will drive down profit margins, and the sustainable growth rate will fall to 5 percent. The most recent annual dividend was $DIV_0 = \$1$ per share.

    a. What are the expected values of DIV_1, DIV_2, DIV_3, and DIV_4?
    b. What is the expected stock price 4 years from now? The discount rate is 10 percent.
    c. What is the stock price today?
    d. Find the dividend yield, DIV_1/P_0.
    e. What will next year's stock price, P_1, be?
    f. What is the expected rate of return to an investor who buys the stock now and sells it in 1 year?

44. **Yield Curve and Efficient Markets.** If the yield curve is downward-sloping, meaning that long-term interest rates are lower than short-term interest rates, what might investors believe about future short-term interest rates?

STANDARD &POOR'S

1. Go to **www.mhhe.com/edumarketinsight.** Review Table 6–2, which lists the market value of several firms. Update the table. Which company's value changed by the greatest percentage since 2005, when the table was created? (Hint: Look for the price per share and the number of shares outstanding. The product of the two is total market capitalization.) Now calculate book value per share. Have the book values for each firm changed? Which seems to be more stable, book or market value? Why?

2. Using the constant dividend growth stock valuation model, estimate the current required rate of return, r, of H.J. Heinz (HNZ). Using the information from the *Company Profile* and *Financial Highlights* reports, estimate next year's dividend DIV_1 by using the current dividend and the 5-year dividend growth rate. Use the current price, DIV_1, and the growth rate to estimate the return required by investors.

3. From the *Financial Highlights* and *Company Profile* tabs of Market Insight, obtain the price-earnings ratios of E*Trade (ET) and Georgia Pacific (GP). Which of these two firms seems to be more of a "growth stock"? Now obtain a forecast of each firm's expected earnings per share in the coming year from a site such as finance.yahoo.com. What is the present value of growth opportunities for each firm as a fraction of the stock price? (Assume, for simplicity, that the required rate of return on the stocks is $r = 12$ percent.) Are the relative values you obtain for PVGO consistent with the P/E ratios?

SOLUTIONS TO SELF-TEST QUESTIONS

6.1 Hearst's stock price currently is 3% lower than its value at the beginning of the year. Its high and low prices over the past 52 weeks have been $29.25 and $22.57 per share. Its annual dividend is $.28 per share, and its dividend yield (annual dividend as a percentage of stock price) is 1.1 percent. The ratio of stock price to earnings per share, the P/E ratio, is 21. Trading volume was 133,000 shares. The closing price was $25.60, which was $.10 higher than the previous day's closing price.

6.2 IBM's forecast future profitability has fallen. Thus the value of future investment opportunities has fallen relative to the value of assets in place. This happens in all growth industries sooner or later, as competition increases and profitable new investment opportunities shrink.

6.3 $P_0 = \dfrac{DIV_1 + P_1}{1 + r} = \dfrac{\$5 + \$105}{1.10} = \$100$

6.4 Since dividends and share price grow at 5 percent,

$$DIV_2 = \$5 \times 1.05 = \$5.25, \quad DIV_3 = \$5 \times 1.05^2 = \$5.51$$

$$P_3 = \$100 \times 1.05^3 = \$115.76$$

$$P_0 = \frac{DIV_1}{1 + r} + \frac{DIV_2}{(1 + r)^2} + \frac{DIV_3 + P_3}{(1 + r)^3}$$

$$= \frac{\$5.00}{1.10} + \frac{\$5.25}{(1.10^2)} + \frac{\$5.51 + \$115.76}{(1.10)^3} = \$100$$

6.5 $P_0 = \dfrac{DIV}{r} = \dfrac{\$25}{.20} = \$125$

6.6 The two firms have equal risk, so we can use the data for Androscoggin to find the expected return on either stock:

$$r = \frac{DIV_1}{P_0} + g = \frac{\$5}{\$100} + .05 = .10, \text{ or } 10\%$$

6.7 We've already calculated the present value of dividends through year 5 as $5.33. We can also forecast the dividend in year 6 as

$$DIV_6 = 1.04 \times DIV_5 = 1.04 \times \$1.54 = \$1.6016$$

Price in year 5 is

$$P_5 = \frac{\$1.6016}{.056 - .04} = \$100.10$$

$$P_0 = PV \text{ (dividends through year 3)} + PV(P_5)$$

$$= \$5.33 + \frac{\$100.10}{(1.056)^5}$$

$$= \$81.56$$

6.8   a. The sustainable growth rate is

$$g = \text{return on equity} \times \text{plowback ratio}$$
$$= 10\% \times .40 = 4\%$$

b. First value the company. At a 60 percent payout ratio, $DIV_1 = \$3$ as before. Using the constant-growth model,

$$P_0 = \frac{\$3}{.12 - .04} = \$37.50$$

which is $4.17 per share less than the company's no-growth value of $41.67. In this example Blue Skies is throwing away $4.17 of potential value by investing in projects with unattractive rates of return.

c. Sure. A raider could take over the company and generate a profit of $4.17 per share just by halting all investments offering less than the 12 percent rate of return demanded by investors. This assumes the raider could buy the shares for $37.50.

6.9   a. False. The *levels* of successive stock prices are related. If a stock is selling for $100 per share today, the best guess of its price tomorrow is $100.

b. True. *Changes* in stock prices are unrelated. Whether a stock price increases or decreases today has no bearing on whether it will do so tomorrow.

c. False. There is no such thing as a "normal" price. If there were, you could make easy profits by buying shares selling below their normal prices (which would tend to be rising back toward those normal levels) and selling shares currently selling above their normal prices. Under a random walk, prices are equally likely to rise or fall.

d. True. Under a random walk, prices are equally likely to over- or underperform regardless of their past history.

6.10 Fundamental analysts ensure that stock prices reflect all publicly available information about the underlying value of the firm. If share prices deviate from their fundamental values, such analysts will generate buying or selling pressure that will return prices to their proper levels. Similarly, technical analysts ensure that if there is useful information in stock price history, it will be reflected in current share prices.

MINICASE

Terence Breezeway, the CEO of Prairie Home Stores, wondered what retirement would be like. It was almost 20 years to the day since his uncle Jacob Breezeway, Prairie Home's founder, had asked him to take responsibility for managing the company. Now it was time to spend more time riding and fishing on the old Lazy Beta Ranch.

Under Mr. Breezeway's leadership Prairie Home had grown slowly but steadily and was solidly profitable. (Table 6–5 shows earnings, dividends, and book asset values for the last 5 years.) Most of the company's supermarkets had been modernized and its brand name was well known.

Mr. Breezeway was proud of this record, although he wished that Prairie Home could have grown more rapidly. He had passed up several opportunities to build new stores in adjacent counties. Prairie Home was still just a family company. Its common stock was distributed among 15 grandchildren and nephews of Jacob Breezeway, most of whom had come to depend on generous regular dividends. The commitment to high dividend payout* had reduced the earnings available for reinvestment and thereby constrained growth.

Mr. Breezeway believed the time had come to take Prairie Home public. Once its shares were traded in the public market, the Breezeway descendants who needed (or just wanted) more cash to spend could sell off part of their holdings. Others with more interest in the business could hold on to their shares and be rewarded by higher future earnings and stock prices.

But if Prairie Home did go public, what should its shares sell for? Mr. Breezeway worried that shares would be sold, either by Breezeway family members or by the company itself, at too low a price. One relative was about to accept a private offer for $200, the current book value per share, but Mr. Breezeway had intervened and convinced the would-be seller to wait.

Prairie Home's value depended not just on its current book value or earnings but on its future prospects, which were good. One financial projection (shown in the top panel of Table 6–6) called for growth in earnings of over 100 percent by 2017. Unfortunately this plan would require reinvestment of all of Prairie Home's earnings from 2011 to 2014. After that the company could resume its normal dividend payout and growth rate. Mr. Breezeway believed this plan was feasible.

He was determined to step aside for the next generation of top management. But before retiring, he had to decide whether to recommend that Prairie Home Stores "go public"—and before that decision he had to know what the company was worth.

*The company traditionally paid out cash dividends equal to 10 percent of start-of-period book value. See Table 6–5.

The next morning he rode thoughtfully to work. He left his horse at the south corral and ambled down the dusty street to Mike Gordon's Saloon, where Francine Firewater, the company's CFO, was having her usual steak-and-beans breakfast. He asked Ms. Firewater to prepare a formal report to Prairie Home stockholders, valuing the company on the assumption that its shares were publicly traded.

Ms. Firewater asked two questions immediately. First, what should she assume about investment and growth? Mr. Breezeway

suggested two valuations, one assuming more rapid expansion (as in the top panel of Table 6–6) and another just projecting past growth (as in the bottom panel of Table 6–6).

Second, what rate of return should she use? Mr. Breezeway said that 15 percent, Prairie Home's usual return on book equity, sounded right to him, but he referred her to an article in the *Journal of Finance* indicating that investors in rural supermarket chains, with risks similar to Prairie Home Stores, expected to earn about 11 percent on average.

TABLE 6–5 Financial data for Prairie Home Stores, 2006–2010 (figures in millions)

	2006	2007	2008	2009	2010
Book value, start of year	$62.7	$66.1	$69.0	$73.9	$76.5
Earnings	9.7	9.5	11.8	11.0	11.2
Dividends	6.3	6.6	6.9	7.4	7.7
Retained earnings	3.4	2.9	4.9	2.6	3.5
Book value, end of year	66.1	69.0	73.9	76.5	80.0

Notes:
1. Prairie Home Stores has 400,000 common shares.
2. The company's policy is to pay cash dividends equal to 10 percent of start-of-year book value.

TABLE 6–6 Financial projections for Prairie Home Stores, 2011–2016 (figures in millions)

	2011	2012	2013	2014	2015	2016
Rapid-Growth Scenario						
Book value, start of year	$80	$ 92	$105.8	$121.7	$139.9	$146.9
Earnings	12	13.8	15.9	18.3	21.0	22.0
Dividends	0	0	0	0	14	14.7
Retained earnings	12	13.8	15.9	18.3	7.0	7.4
Book value, end of year	92	105.8	121.7	139.9	146.9	154.3
Constant-Growth Scenario						
Book value, start of year	$80	$ 84	$88.2	$92.6	$ 97.2	$102.1
Earnings	12	12.6	13.2	13.9	14.6	15.3
Dividends	8	8.4	8.8	9.3	9.7	10.2
Retained earnings	4	4.2	4.4	4.6	4.9	5.1
Book value, end of year	84	88.2	92.6	97.2	102.1	107.2

Notes:
1. Both panels assume earnings equal to 15 percent of start-of-year book value. This profitability rate is constant.
2. The top panel assumes all earnings are reinvested from 2011 to 2014. In 2015 and later years, two-thirds of earnings are paid out as dividends and one-third reinvested.
3. The bottom panel assumes two-thirds of earnings are paid out as dividends in all years.
4. Columns may not add up because of rounding.

Net Present Value and Other Investment Criteria

RELATED WEB LINKS

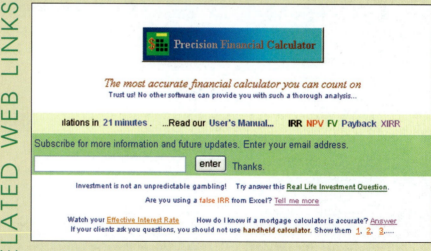

www.datadynamica.com/FinCalc/
FinHome.htm NPV, IRR, and other
financial calculators are available
at this site.

A positive NPV always inspires confidence. This man is not worrying about the payback period.

© Time Life Pictures/Getty Images

The investment decision, also known as *capital budgeting,* is central to the success of the company. We have already seen that capital investments can sometimes absorb substantial amounts of cash; they also have very long-term consequences. The assets you buy today may determine the business you are in many years hence.

For some investment projects "substantial" is an understatement. Consider the following examples:

- Construction of the Channel Tunnel linking England and France cost about $18 billion from 1986 to 1994.
- The cost of bringing one new prescription drug to market is estimated to be $800 million.
- ExxonMobil is developing the Sakhalin Island oil and gas field in eastern Russia with a projected outlay of $12 billion.
- Toyota's research and development costs for its hybrid gas-electric engine have been about $6 billion.
- Production and marketing costs for the movie *Titanic* were about $200 million.

- The development costs of the Airbus A380 jumbo jet are estimated at around $13.5 billion.

Notice from these examples of big capital projects that many projects require heavy investment in intangible assets. For example, almost all the cost of drug development is for research and testing. So is much of the cost of developing the hybrid auto. Any expenditure made in the hope of generating more cash later can be called a *capital investment project,* regardless of whether the cash outlay goes to tangible or intangible assets.

A company's shareholders prefer to be rich rather than poor. Therefore, they want the firm to invest in every project that is worth more than it costs. The difference between a project's value and its cost is termed the *net present value.* Companies can best help their shareholders by investing in projects with a *positive* net present value.

We start this chapter by showing how to calculate the net present value of a simple investment project. We also examine other criteria that companies sometimes consider when evaluating investments. One of these, the payback rule, is little better than a rule of thumb. Although there is a place for rules of thumb in this world, an engineer needs something more accurate when designing a 100-story building, and a financial manager needs more than a rule of thumb when making a substantial capital investment decision.

Instead of calculating a project's net present value, companies sometimes compare the expected rate of return from investing in a project with the return that shareholders could earn on equivalent-risk investments in the capital market. Companies accept only those projects that provide a higher return than shareholders could earn for themselves. This rate of return rule generally gives the same answers as the net present value rule, but, as we shall see, it has some pitfalls.

Next we turn to more complex issues such as project interactions. These occur when a company is obliged to choose between two or more competing proposals; if it accepts one proposal, it cannot take the other. For example, a company may need to choose between buying an expensive, durable machine or buying a cheap and short-lived one. We will show how the net present value criterion can be used to make such choices.

Sometimes the firm may be forced to make choices because it does not have enough money to take on every project that it would like. We will explain how to maximize shareholder wealth when capital is rationed. It turns out that the solution is to pick the projects that have the highest net present value per dollar invested. This measure is known as the *profitability index*.

After studying this chapter you should be able to:

- Calculate the net present value of an investment.
- Calculate the internal rate of return of a project and know what to look out for when using the internal rate of return rule.
- Explain why the payback rule *doesn't* always make shareholders better off.
- Use the net present value rule to analyze three common problems that involve competing projects: (a) when to postpone an investment expenditure, (b) how to choose between projects with unequal lives, and (c) when to replace equipment.
- Calculate the profitability index and use it to choose between projects when funds are limited.

7.1 Net Present Value

In Chapter 4 you learned how to discount future cash payments to find their present value. We now apply these ideas to evaluate a simple investment proposal.

Suppose that you are in the real estate business. You are considering construction of an office block. The land would cost $50,000, and construction would cost a further $300,000. You foresee a shortage of office space and predict that a year from now you will be able to sell the building for $400,000. Thus you would be investing $350,000 now in the expectation of realizing $400,000 at the end of the year. Therefore, projected cash flows may be summarized in a simple time line as follows:

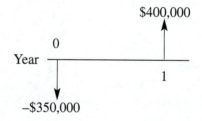

You should go ahead if the present value of the $400,000 payoff is greater than the investment of $350,000.

Assume for the moment that the $400,000 payoff is a sure thing. The office building is not the only way to obtain $400,000 a year from now. You could invest in a 1-year U.S. Treasury note. Suppose the Treasury note offers interest of 7 percent. How much would you have to invest in it in order to receive $400,000 at the end of the year? That's easy: You would have to invest

$$\$400,000 \times \frac{1}{1.07} = \$400,000 \times .9346 = \$373,832$$

Let's assume that as soon as you have purchased the land and laid out the money for construction, you decide to cash in on your project. How much could you sell it for? Since the property will be worth $400,000 in a year, investors would be willing to pay at most $373,832 for it now. That's all it would cost them to get the same $400,000 payoff by investing in a government security. Of course you could always sell your property for less, but why sell for less than the market will bear?

Therefore, at an interest rate of 7 percent, the present value of the $400,000 payoff from the office building is $373,832.

The $373,832 present value is the only price that satisfies both buyer and seller. In general, the present value is the only feasible price, and the present value of the property is also its *market price* or *market value.*

To calculate present value, we discounted the expected future payoff by the rate of return offered by comparable investment alternatives. The discount rate—7 percent in our example—is often known as the **opportunity cost of capital.** It is called the opportunity cost because it is the return that is being given up by investing in the project.

opportunity cost of capital
Expected rate of return given up by investing in a project.

The building is worth $373,832, but this does not mean that you are $373,832 better off. You committed $350,000, and therefore your **net present value (NPV)** is $23,832. Net present value is found by subtracting the required initial investment from the present value of the project cash flows:

net present value (NPV)
Present value of cash flows minus investment.

$$\textbf{NPV} = \textbf{PV} - \textbf{required investment}$$
$$= \$373,832 - \$350,000 = \$23,832$$

In other words, your office development is worth more than it costs—it makes a *net* contribution to value. ==The net present value *rule* states that managers increase shareholders' wealth by accepting all projects that are worth more than they cost. Therefore, they should accept all projects with a positive net present value.==

A Comment on Risk and Present Value

In our discussion of the office development we assumed we knew the value of the completed project. Of course, you will never be *certain* about the future values of office buildings. The $400,000 represents the best *forecast,* but it is not a sure thing.

Therefore, our initial conclusion about how much investors would pay for the building is wrong. Since they could achieve $400,000 risklessly by investing in $373,832 worth of U.S. Treasury notes, they would not buy your building for that amount. You would have to cut your asking price to attract investors' interest.

Here we can invoke a basic financial principle: ==A risky dollar is worth less than a safe one.==

Most investors avoid risk when they can do so without sacrificing return. However, the concepts of present value and the opportunity cost of capital still apply to risky investments. It is still proper to discount the payoff by the rate of return offered by a comparable investment. But we have to think of *expected* payoffs and the *expected* rates of return on other investments.

Not all investments are equally risky. The office development is riskier than a Treasury note but is probably less risky than investing in a start-up biotech company. Suppose you believe the office development is as risky as an investment in the stock market and that you forecast a 12 percent rate of return for stock market investments. Then 12 percent would be the appropriate opportunity cost of capital. That is what you are giving up by not investing in comparable securities. You can now recompute NPV:

$$PV = \$400,000 \times \frac{1}{1.12} = \$400,000 \times .8929 = \$357,143$$

$$NPV = PV - \$350,000 = \$7,143$$

If other investors agree with your forecast of a \$400,000 payoff and with your assessment of a 12 percent opportunity cost of capital, then the property ought to be worth \$357,143 once construction is under way. If you tried to sell for more than that, there would be no takers, because the property would then offer a lower expected rate of return than the 12 percent available in the stock market. The office building still makes a net contribution to value, but it is much smaller than our earlier calculations indicated.

Self-Test 7.1

What is the office development's NPV if construction costs increase to \$355,000? Assume the opportunity cost of capital is 12 percent. Is the development still a worthwhile investment? How high can development costs be before the project is no longer attractive? Now suppose that the opportunity cost of capital is 20 percent with construction costs of \$355,000. Why is the office development no longer an attractive investment?

Valuing Long-Lived Projects

The net present value rule works for projects of any length. For example, suppose that you have identified a possible tenant who would be prepared to rent your office block for 3 years at a fixed annual rent of \$16,000. You forecast that after you have collected the third year's rent the building could be sold for \$450,000. The projected cash flows (denoted C) in each year are now

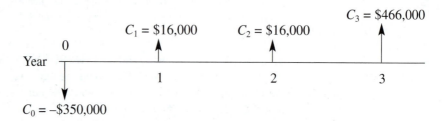

For simplicity, we will again assume that these cash flows are certain and that the opportunity cost of capital is $r = 7$ percent.

Figure 7–1 shows a time line of the cash inflows and their present values. To find the present value of the project, we discount these cash inflows at the 7 percent opportunity cost of capital:

$$PV = \frac{C_1}{1+r} + \frac{C_2}{(1+r)^2} + \frac{C_3}{(1+r)^3}$$

$$= \frac{\$16,000}{1.07} + \frac{\$16,000}{(1.07)^2} + \frac{\$466,000}{(1.07)^3} = \$409,323$$

The net present value of the revised project is NPV = \$409,323 – \$350,000 = \$59,323. Constructing the office block and renting it for 3 years makes a greater addition to your wealth than selling the office block at the end of the first year.

Of course, rather than subtracting the initial investment from the project's present value, you could calculate NPV directly, as in the following equation, where C_0 de-

FIGURE 7-1 Cash flows and their present values for the office block project. Final cash flow of $466,000 is the sum of the rental income in year 3 plus the forecast sales price for the building.

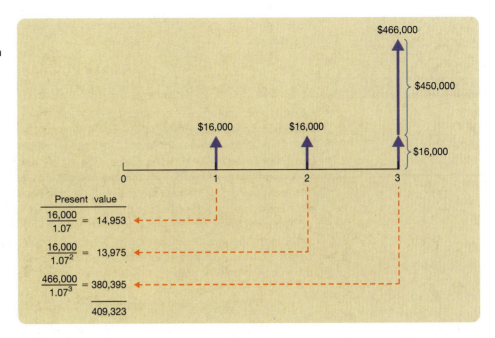

notes the initial cash outflow required to build the office block. (Notice that in this example C_0 is negative, reflecting the fact that it is a cash outflow.)

$$NPV = C_0 + \frac{C_1}{1 + r} + \frac{C_2}{(1 + r)^2} + \frac{C_3}{(1 + r)^3}$$

$$= -\$350,000 + \frac{\$16,000}{1.07} + \frac{\$16,000}{(1.07)^2} + \frac{\$466,000}{(1.07)^3} = \$59,323$$

Let's check that the owners of this project really are better off. Suppose you put up $350,000 of your own money, commit to build the office building, and sign a lease that will bring $16,000 a year for 3 years. Now you can cash in by selling the project to someone else.

Suppose you sell 1,000 shares in the project. Each share represents a claim to 1/1,000 of the future cash flows. Since the cash flows are sure things, and the interest rate offered by other sure things is 7 percent, investors will value the shares for

$$\text{Price per share} = \frac{\$16}{1.07} + \frac{\$16}{(1.07)^2} + \frac{\$466}{(1.07)^3} = \$409.30$$

Thus you can sell the project to outside investors for 1,000 × $409.30 = $409,300, which, save for rounding, is exactly the present value we calculated earlier. Your net gain is

$$\text{Net gain} = \$409,300 - \$350,000 = \$59,300$$

which is the project's NPV. This equivalence should be no surprise, since the present value calculation is *designed* to calculate the value of future cash flows to investors in the capital markets.

Notice that in principle there could be a different opportunity cost of capital for each period's cash flow. In that case we would discount C_1 by r_1, the discount rate for 1-year cash flows; C_2 would be discounted by r_2; and so on. Here we assume that the cost of capital is the same regardless of the date of the cash flow. We do this for one reason only—simplicity. But we are in good company: With only rare exceptions firms decide on an appropriate discount rate and then use it to discount all cash flows from the project.

EXAMPLE 7.1   ▶   Valuing a New Computer System

Obsolete Technologies is considering the purchase of a new computer system to help handle its warehouse inventories. The system costs $50,000, is expected to last 4 years, and should reduce the cost of managing inventories by $22,000 a year. The opportunity cost of capital is 10 percent. Should Obsolete go ahead?

Don't be put off by the fact that the computer system does not generate any sales. If the expected cost savings are realized, the company's cash flows will be $22,000 a year higher as a result of buying the computer. Thus we can say that the computer increases cash flows by $22,000 a year for each of 4 years. To calculate present value, you can discount each of these cash flows by 10 percent. However, it is smarter to recognize that the cash flows are level, and therefore you can use the annuity formula to calculate the present value:

$$PV = \text{cash flow} \times \text{annuity factor} = \$22,000 \times \left[\frac{1}{.10} - \frac{1}{.10(1.10)^4} \right]$$
$$= \$22,000 \times 3.1699 = \$69,738$$

The net present value is

$$NPV = -\$50,000 + \$69,738 = \$19,738$$

The project has a positive NPV of $19,738. Undertaking it would increase the value of the firm by that amount.   ◀

The first two steps in calculating NPVs—forecasting the cash flows and estimating the opportunity cost of capital—are tricky, and we will have a lot more to say about them in later chapters. But once you have assembled the data, the calculation of present value and net present value should be routine. Here is another example.

EXAMPLE 7.2   ▶   Calculating Eurotunnel's NPV

One of the world's largest commercial investment projects was construction of the Channel Tunnel by the Anglo-French company Eurotunnel. Here is a chance to put yourself in the shoes of Eurotunnel's financial manager and find out whether the project looked like it would be a good deal for shareholders. The figures in column C of Table 7–1 are based on the forecasts of construction costs and revenues that the company provided to investors in 1986.

The Channel Tunnel project was not a safe investment. Indeed, the prospectus to the Channel Tunnel share issue cautioned investors that the project "involves significant risk and should be regarded at this stage as speculative. If for any reason the Project is abandoned or Eurotunnel is unable to raise the necessary finance, it is likely that equity investors will lose some or all of their money."

To be induced to invest in the project, investors needed a higher prospective rate of return than they could get on safe government bonds. Suppose investors expected a return of 13 percent from investments in the capital market that had a degree of risk similar to that of the Channel Tunnel. That was what investors were giving up when they provided the capital for the tunnel. To find the project's NPV we therefore discount the cash flows in Table 7–1 at 13 percent.

Since the tunnel was expected to take about 7 years to build, there are 7 years of negative cash flows in Table 7–1. To calculate NPV, you just discount all the cash

TABLE 7–1 Forecast cash flows and present values in 1986 for the Channel Tunnel project. The investment at the time appeared to have a positive NPV of £249.8 million.

	A	B	C	D	E
1			Cash Flow		
2	Year	Time	(£ million)	PV at 13%	Formula in Column D
3	1986	0	−457	−457.0	=C3/1.13^B3
4	1987	1	−476	−421.2	=C4/1.13^B4
5	1988	2	−497	−389.2	=C5/1.13^B5
6	1989	3	−522	−361.8	=C6/1.13^B6
7	1990	4	−551	−337.9	=C7/1.13^B7
8	1991	5	−584	−317.0	=C8/1.13^B8
9	1992	6	−619	−297.3	=C9/1.13^B9
10	1993	7	211	89.7	=C10/1.13^B10
11	1994	8	489	183.9	=C11/1.13^B11
12	1995	9	455	151.5	=C12/1.13^B12
13	1996	10	502	147.9	=C13/1.13^B13
14	1997	11	530	138.2	=C14/1.13^B14
15	1998	12	544	125.5	=C15/1.13^B15
16	1999	13	636	129.8	=C16/1.13^B16
17	2000	14	594	107.3	=C17/1.13^B17
18	2001	15	689	110.2	=C18/1.13^B18
19	2002	16	729	103.2	=C19/1.13^B19
20	2003	17	796	99.7	=C20/1.13^B20
21	2004	18	859	95.2	=C21/1.13^B21
22	2005	19	923	90.5	=C22/1.13^B22
23	2006	20	983	85.3	=C23/1.13^B23
24	2007	21	1,050	80.6	=C24/1.13^B24
25	2008	22	1,113	75.6	=C25/1.13^B25
26	2009	23	1,177	70.8	=C26/1.13^B26
27	2010	24	17,781	946.4	=C27/1.13^B27
28					
29	Sum:			249.8	=SUM(D3:D27)
30					
31	Instead, use Excel's NPV function			249.8	=NPV(0.13,C4:C27) + C3

Note: Cash flow for 2010 includes the value in 2010 of forecast cash flows in all subsequent years. Some of these figures involve guesswork because the prospectus reported accumulated construction costs including interest expenses.

Source: Eurotunnel Equity II Prospectus, October 1986. Reprinted with permission.

flows, positive and negative, at 13 percent and sum the results. Call 1986 "year 0," call 1987 "year 1," and so on. Then

$$\text{NPV} = C_0 + \frac{C_1}{1+r} + \frac{C_2}{(1+r)^2} + \cdots$$

$$= -£457 + \frac{-£476}{1.13} + \frac{-£497}{(1.13)^2} + \cdots + \frac{£17,781}{(1.13)^{24}} = £249.8 \text{ million}$$

We present the calculations in column D. (The nearby box provides additional discussion of how to calculate present values by using spreadsheets.) The net present value of the forecast cash flows is £249.8 million, making the tunnel a worthwhile project, though not by a wide margin, considering the planned investment of nearly £4 billion. ◄

Of course, NPV calculations are only as good as the underlying cash-flow forecasts. The well-known Pentagon Law of Large Projects states that anything big takes longer and costs more than you're originally led to believe. As the law predicted, the tunnel proved much more expensive to build than anticipated in 1986, and the opening was delayed by more than a year. Revenues also have been below forecast, and

Present Values

Computer spreadsheets are tailor-made to calculate the present value of a series of cash flows. For example, the spreadsheet in Table 7–1, available at **www.mhhe. com/bmm5e**, sets up the Eurotunnel problem as an Excel spreadsheet. Cells D3 to D27 calculate the present value of each year's cash flows by discounting at 13 percent for the length of time given in column B. Cell D29 shows the sum of these separate present values.

Excel also provides a built-in function to calculate net present values. The formula is =NPV (discount rate, list of cash flows). So, instead of computing the present value of each cash flow separately and then summing, we could have used the NPV function in cell D31. The first entry in the

function is the discount rate expressed as a decimal, in this case .13. That is followed by a list of the cash flows that appear in column C.

Why is the first entry in the cash-flow list cell C4 rather than C3, which contains the immediate cash flow, −457? It turns out that Excel always assumes the first cash flow comes after one period, the next after two periods, and so on. If the first cash flow actually comes immediately, as in our example, we do not want it discounted, nor do we want the other cash flows discounted for an extra period. Therefore, we don't include the immediate cash flow in the NPV function, instead adding it undiscounted to the present value of the other cash flows (see cells D31 and E31).

Please visit us at www.mhhe.com/bmm5e or refer to your Student CD

Eurotunnel has not even generated enough profits to pay the interest on its debt. Thus, with hindsight, the tunnel was a costly negative-NPV venture. By early 2005, Eurotunnel appeared to be at risk of bankruptcy, and the firm was preparing to negotiate with its creditors over how it might restructure about £6.4 billion of debt.

Using the NPV Rule to Choose among Projects

The simple projects we have considered so far involve take-it-or-leave-it decisions. But almost all real-world decisions are either-or choices. You could build an apartment block, rather than the office block, on that vacant lot. You could build a 7-story office building or a 10-story one. You could heat it with oil or with natural gas. You could build it today or wait a year to start construction. Such choices are said to be **mutually exclusive.** When you need to choose among mutually exclusive projects, the decision rule is simple: Calculate the NPV of each alternative, and choose the highest positive-NPV project.[1]

mutually exclusive projects
Two or more projects that cannot be pursued simultaneously.

EXAMPLE 7.3 ▶	Choosing between Two Projects

It has been several years since your office last upgraded its office networking software. Two competing systems have been proposed. Both have an expected useful life of 3 years, at which point it will be time for another upgrade. One proposal is for an expensive, cutting-edge system, which will cost $800,000 and increase firm cash flows by $350,000 a year through increased productivity. The other proposal is for a cheaper, somewhat slower system. This system would cost only $700,000 but would increase cash flows by only $300,000 a year. If the cost of capital is 7 percent, which is the better option?

The following table summarizes the cash flows and the NPVs of the two proposals:

System	Cash Flows, Thousands of Dollars				NPV at 7%
	C_0	C_1	C_2	C_3	
Faster	−800	+350	+350	+350	+118.5
Slower	−700	+300	+300	+300	+ 87.3

---

[1] Of course, we need to compare the alternatives on a fair basis. For example, if one heating system lasts 10 years and another 15, their different lives must also be considered. More on this later in the chapter.

In both cases, the software systems are worth more than they cost, but the faster system would make the greater contribution to value and therefore should be your preferred choice. ◄

7.2 Other Investment Criteria

A project with a positive net present value is worth more than it costs. So whenever a firm invests in such a project, it is making its shareholders better off.

These days almost every large corporation calculates the NPV of proposed investments, but management may also consider other criteria when making investment decisions. Most commonly, they may look at the project's payback and its internal rate of return. As we describe these measures, you will see that payback is no better than a very rough guide to an investment's worth. On the other hand, when properly used, the internal rate of return will lead to the same decisions as net present value.

Payback

We suspect that you have often heard conversations that go something like this: "A washing machine costs about $800. But we are currently spending $6 a week, or around $300 a year, at the laundromat. So the washing machine should pay for itself in less than 3 years." You have just encountered the payback rule.

payback period
Time until cash flows recover the initial investment in the project.

A project's **payback period** is the length of time before you recover your initial investment. For the washing machine the payback period was just under 3 years. The *payback rule* states that a project should be accepted if its payback period is less than a specified cutoff period. For example, if the cutoff period is 4 years, the washing machine makes the grade; if the cutoff is 2 years, it doesn't.

As a rough rule of thumb the payback rule may be adequate, but it is easy to see that it can lead to nonsensical decisions. For example, compare projects A and B. Project A has a 2-year payback and a large positive NPV. Project B also has a 2-year payback but a negative NPV. Project A is clearly superior, but the payback rule ranks both equally. This is because payback does not consider any cash flows that arrive after the payback period. A firm that uses the payback criterion with a cutoff of 2 or more years would accept both A and B despite the fact that only A would increase shareholder wealth.

Project	Cash Flows, Dollars				Payback Period, Years	NPV at 10%
	C_0	C_1	C_2	C_3		
A	−2,000	+1,000	+1,000	+10,000	2	$7,249
B	−2,000	+1,000	+1,000	0	2	−264
C	−2,000	0	+2,000	0	2	−347

A second problem with payback is that it gives equal weight to all cash flows arriving *before* the cutoff period, despite the fact that the more distant flows are less valuable. For example, look at project C. It also has a payback period of 2 years, but it has an even lower NPV than project B. Why? Because its cash flows arrive later within the payback period.

To use the payback rule, a firm has to decide on an appropriate cutoff period. If it uses the same cutoff regardless of project life, it will tend to accept too many short-lived projects and reject too many long-lived ones. The payback rule will bias the firm against accepting long-term projects because cash flows that arrive after the payback period are ignored.

Earlier in the chapter we evaluated the Channel Tunnel project. Large construction projects of this kind inevitably have long payback periods. The cash flows that we presented in Table 7–1 implied a payback period of just over 14 years. But most firms that employ the payback rule use a much shorter cutoff period than this. If they used the payback rule mechanically, long-lived projects like the Channel Tunnel wouldn't have a chance.

The primary attraction of the payback criterion is its simplicity. But remember that the hard part of project evaluation is forecasting the cash flows, not doing the arithmetic. Today's spreadsheets make discounting a trivial exercise. Therefore, the payback rule saves you only the easy part of the analysis.[2]

We have had little good to say about payback. So why do many companies continue to use it? Senior managers don't truly believe that all cash flows after the payback period are irrelevant. It seems more likely (and more charitable to those managers) that payback survives because the deficiencies are relatively unimportant or because there are some offsetting benefits. Thus managers may point out that payback is the simplest way to *communicate* an idea of project desirability. Investment decisions require discussion and negotiation between people from all parts of the firm, and it is important to have a measure that everyone can understand. Perhaps, also, managers favor quick payback projects even when the projects have lower NPVs because they believe that quicker profits mean quicker promotion. That takes us back to Chapter 1, where we discussed the need to align the objectives of managers with those of the shareholders.

In practice payback is most commonly used when the capital investment is small or when the merits of the project are so obvious that more formal analysis is unnecessary. For example, if a project is expected to produce constant cash flows for 10 years and the payback period is only 2 years, the project in all likelihood has a positive NPV.

Self-Test 7.2   A project costs $5,000 and will generate annual cash flows of $660 for 20 years. What is the payback period? If the interest rate is 6 percent, what is the project NPV? Should the project be accepted?

Internal Rate of Return

Instead of calculating a project's net present value, companies often prefer to ask whether the project's return is higher or lower than the opportunity cost of capital. For example, think back to the original proposal to build the office block. You planned to invest $350,000 to get back a cash flow of $C_1 = \$400,000$ in 1 year. Therefore, you forecast a profit on the venture of $400,000 − $350,000 = $50,000. In a one-period project like this one, it is easy to calculate the rate of return. Simply compute end-of-year profit per dollar invested in the project:

$$\text{Rate of return} = \frac{\text{profit}}{\text{investment}} = \frac{C_1 - \text{investment}}{\text{investment}} = \frac{\$400,000 - \$350,000}{\$350,000}$$

$$= .1429, \text{ or about } 14.3\%$$

---

[2] Sometimes managers calculate the *discounted payback period.* This is the number of periods before the present value of prospective cash flows equals or exceeds the initial investment. Therefore, this rule asks, How long must the project last in order to offer a positive net present value? This surmounts the objection that equal weight is given to all cash flows before the cutoff date. However, the discounted payback rule still takes no account of any cash flows after the cutoff date.

The discounted payback does offer one important advantage over the normal payback criterion. If a project meets a discounted payback cutoff, it must have a positive NPV, because the cash flows that accrue up to the discounted payback period are (by definition) just sufficient to provide a present value equal to the initial investment. Any cash inflows that come after that date tip the balance and ensure positive NPV.

Despite this advantage, the discounted payback has little to recommend it. It still ignores all cash flows occurring after the arbitrary cutoff date and therefore will incorrectly reject some positive NPV opportunities. It is no easier to use than the NPV rule, because it requires determination of both project cash flows and an appropriate discount rate. The best that can be said about it is that it is a better criterion than the even more unsatisfactory ordinary payback rule.

The alternative of investing in a U.S. Treasury note would provide a return of only 7 percent. Thus the return on your office building is higher than the opportunity cost of capital.[3]

This suggests two rules for deciding whether to go ahead with an investment project:

1. *The NPV rule.* Invest in any project that has a positive NPV when its cash flows are discounted at the opportunity cost of capital.
2. *The rate of return rule.* Invest in any project offering a rate of return that is higher than the opportunity cost of capital.

Both rules set the same cutoff point. An investment that is on the knife edge with an NPV of zero will also have a rate of return that is just equal to the cost of capital.

Suppose that the rate of interest on Treasury notes is not 7 percent but 14.3 percent. Since your office project also offers a return of 14.3 percent, the rate of return rule suggests that there is now nothing to choose between taking the project and leaving your money in Treasury notes.

The NPV rule also tells you that if the interest rate is 14.3 percent, the project is evenly balanced with an NPV of zero:

$$NPV = C_0 + \frac{C_1}{1 + r} = -\$350,000 + \frac{\$400,000}{1.143} = 0$$

The project would make you neither richer nor poorer; it is worth what it costs. Thus the NPV rule and the rate of return rule both give the same decision on accepting the project.

A Closer Look at the Rate of Return Rule

We know that if the office project's cash flows are discounted at a rate of 7 percent, the project has a net present value of $23,832. If they are discounted at a rate of 14.3 percent, it has an NPV of zero. In Figure 7–2 the project's NPV for a variety of discount rates is plotted. This is often called the *NPV profile* of the project. Notice two important things about Figure 7–2:

1. The project rate of return (in our example, 14.3 percent) is also the discount rate that would give the project a zero NPV. This gives us a useful definition: The rate of return is the discount rate at which NPV equals zero.[4]
2. If the opportunity cost of capital is less than the project rate of return, then the NPV of your project is positive. If the cost of capital is greater than the project rate of return, then NPV is negative. Thus the rate of return rule and the NPV rule are equivalent.

Calculating the Rate of Return for Long-Lived Projects

There is no ambiguity in calculating the rate of return for an investment that generates a single payoff after one period. Remember that C_0, the time-zero cash flow corresponding to the initial investment, is negative.[5] Thus

$$\text{Rate of return} = \frac{\text{profit}}{\text{investment}} = \frac{C_1 - \text{investment}}{\text{investment}} = \frac{C_1 + C_0}{-C_0}$$

---

[3] Recall that we are assuming the profit on the office building is risk-free. Therefore, the opportunity cost of capital is the rate of return on other risk-free investments.

[4] Check it for yourself. If $NPV = C_0 + C_1/(1 + r) = 0$, then rate of return $= (C_1 + C_0)/-C_0 = r$.

[5] The *investment* in the project is therefore $-C_0 = -(-\$350,000)$, or $350,000.

FIGURE 7–2 The value of the office project is lower when the discount rate is higher. The project has positive NPV if the discount rate is less than 14.3 percent.

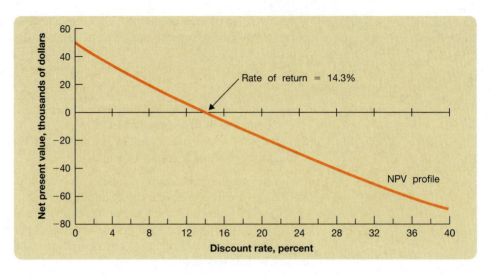

But how do we calculate return when the project produces cash flows in several periods? Just think back to the definition that we introduced above—*the project rate of return is also the discount rate that gives the project a zero NPV*. We can use this idea to find the return on a project that has many cash flows. The discount rate that gives the project a zero NPV is known as the project's **internal rate of return, or IRR.** It is also termed the *discounted cash-flow (DCF) rate of return.*

internal rate of return (IRR)
Discount rate at which project NPV = 0.

Let's calculate the IRR for the revised office project. If you rent out the office block for 3 years, the cash flows are as follows:

Year:	0	1	2	3
Cash flows	–$350,000	+16,000	+16,000	+466,000

The IRR is the discount rate at which these cash flows would have zero NPV. Thus

$$NPV = -\$350,000 + \frac{\$16,000}{1 + IRR} + \frac{\$16,000}{(1 + IRR)^2} + \frac{\$466,000}{(1 + IRR)^3} = 0$$

There is no simple general method for solving this equation. You have to rely on a little trial and error. Let us arbitrarily try a zero discount rate. This gives an NPV of $148,000:

$$NPV = -\$350,000 + \frac{\$16,000}{1.0} + \frac{\$16,000}{(1.0)^2} + \frac{\$466,000}{(1.0)^3} = \$148,000$$

With a zero discount rate the NPV is positive. So the IRR must be greater than zero.

The next step might be to try a discount rate of 50 percent. In this case NPV is –$194,000:

$$NPV = -\$350,000 + \frac{\$16,000}{1.50} + \frac{\$16,000}{(1.50)^2} + \frac{\$466,000}{(1.50)^3} = -\$194,000$$

NPV is now negative. So the IRR must lie somewhere between zero and 50 percent. In Figure 7–3 we have plotted the net present values for a range of discount rates. You can see that a discount rate of 12.96 percent gives an NPV of zero. Therefore, the IRR is 12.96 percent. You can always find the IRR by plotting an NPV profile, as in Figure 7–3, but it is quicker and more accurate to let a spreadsheet or specially programmed

FIGURE 7–3 The internal rate of return is the discount rate for which NPV equals zero.

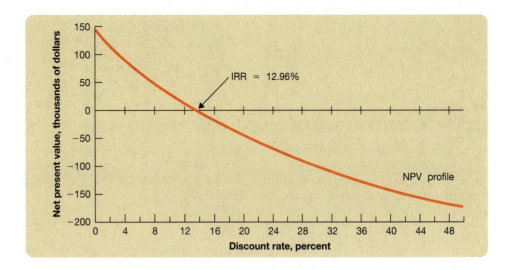

financial calculator do the trial and error for you. The following boxes illustrate how to do so.

The rate of return rule tells you to accept a project if the rate of return exceeds the opportunity cost of capital. You can see from Figure 7–3 why this makes sense. Because the NPV profile is downward-sloping, the project has a positive NPV as long as the opportunity cost of capital is less than the project's 12.96 percent IRR. If the opportunity cost of capital is higher than the 12.96 percent IRR, NPV is negative. Therefore, when we compare the project IRR with the opportunity cost of capital, we are effectively asking whether the project has a positive NPV. This was true for our one-period office project. It is also true for our three-period office project. We conclude that the rate of return rule will give the same answer as the NPV rule *as long as the NPV of a project declines smoothly as the discount rate increases.*

The usual agreement between the net present value and internal rate of return rules should not be a surprise. Both are *discounted cash-flow* methods of choosing between projects. Both are concerned with identifying those projects that make shareholders better off, and both recognize that companies always have a choice: They can invest in a project, or if the project is not sufficiently attractive, they can give the money back to shareholders and let them invest it for themselves in the capital market.

Self-Test 7.3   Suppose the cash flow in year 3 is only $416,000. Redraw Figure 7–3. How would the IRR change?

A Word of Caution

Some people confuse the internal rate of return on a project with the opportunity cost of capital. Remember that the project IRR measures the profitability of the project. It is an *internal* rate of return in the sense that it depends only on the project's own cash flows. The opportunity cost of capital is the standard for deciding whether to accept the project. It is equal to the return offered by equivalent-risk investments in the capital market.

Some Pitfalls with the Internal Rate of Return Rule

Many firms use the internal rate of return rule instead of net present value. We think that this is a pity. When used properly, the two rules lead to the same decision, but the rate of return rule has several pitfalls that can trap the unwary. Here are a couple of examples.

Internal Rate of Return

	A	B	C	D	E	F
1		Calculating IRR by using a spreadsheet				
2						
3	Year	Cash Flow				Formula
4	0	-350,000		IRR =	0.1296	=IRR(B4:B7)
5	1	16,000				
6	2	16,000				
7	3	466,000				

Please visit us at www.mhhe.com/bmm5e or refer to your Student CD

Calculating internal rate of return in Excel is as easy as listing the project cash flows. For example, to calculate the IRR of the office-block project, you could simply type in its cash flows as in the spreadsheet above, and then calculate IRR as we do in cell E4. As always, the interest rate is returned as a decimal. The spreadsheet is available at **www.mhhe. com/bmm5e** or on your student CD.

Pitfall 1: Lending or Borrowing? Remember our condition for the IRR rule to work: The project's NPV must fall as the discount rate increases. Now consider the following projects:

	Cash Flows, Dollars			
Project	C_0	C_1	IRR, %	NPV at 10%
D	−100	+150	+50	+$36.4
E	+100	−150	+50	− 36.4

Each project has an IRR of 50 percent. In other words, if you discount the cash flows at 50 percent, both projects would have zero NPV.

Does this mean that the two projects are equally attractive? Clearly not. In the case of D we are paying out $100 now and getting $150 back at the end of the year. That is better than any bank account. But what about E? Here we are getting paid $100 now but we have to pay out $150 at the end of the year. That is equivalent to borrowing money at 50 percent.

If someone asked you whether 50 percent was a good rate of interest, you could not answer unless you also knew whether that person was proposing to lend or borrow at that rate. Lending money at 50 percent is great (as long as the borrower does not flee the country), but borrowing at 50 percent is not usually a good deal (unless, of course, you plan to flee the country). When you lend money, you want a *high* rate of return; when you borrow, you want a *low* rate of return.

If you plot a graph like Figure 7–2 for project E, you will find the NPV increases as the discount rate increases. *(Try it!)* Obviously, the rate of return rule will not work in this case.

Project E is a fairly obvious trap, but if you want to make sure you don't fall into it, calculate the project's NPV. For example, suppose that the cost of capital is 10 percent. Then the NPV of project D is +$36.4 and the NPV of project E is −$36.4. The NPV rule correctly warns us away from a project that is equivalent to borrowing money at 50 percent.

When NPV rises as the interest rate rises, the rate of return rule is reversed: When NPV is higher as the discount rate increases, a project is acceptable only if its internal rate of return is *less* than the opportunity cost of capital.

Pitfall 2: Multiple Rates of Return Here is a trickier problem. King Coal Corporation is considering a project to strip-mine coal. The project requires an investment of $22 million and is expected to produce a cash inflow of $15 million in each of years 1 through 4. However, the company is obliged in year 5 to reclaim the land at a cost of $40 million. At a 10 percent opportunity cost of capital the project has an NPV of $.7 million.

Using Financial Calculators to Find NPV and IRR

We saw in Chapter 4 that the formulas for the present and future values of level annuities and one-time cash flows are built into financial calculators. However, as the example of the office block illustrates, most investment projects entail multiple cash flows that cannot be expected to remain level over time. Fortunately, many calculators are equipped to handle problems involving a sequence of uneven cash flows. In general, the procedure is quite simple. You enter the cash flows one by one into the calculator, and then you press the IRR key to find the project's internal rate of return. The first cash flow you enter is interpreted as coming immediately, the next cash flow is interpreted as coming at the end of one period, and so on. We can illustrate using the office block as an example. To find the project IRR, you would use the following sequence of keystrokes:

Hewlett-Packard HP-10B		Sharp EL-733A		Texas Instruments BA II Plus	
−350,000	CF/	−350,000	CF/		CF
16,000	CF/	16,000	CF/	2nd	{CLR Work}
16,000	CF/	16,000	CF/	−350,000	ENTER ⬇
466,000	CF/	466,000	CF/	16,000	ENTER ⬇
				16,000	ENTER ⬇
				466,000	ENTER ⬇
☐	{IRR/YR}		IRR		IRR
					CPT

The calculator should display the value 12.96 percent, the project's internal rate of return.

To calculate project NPV, the procedure is similar. You need to enter the discount rate in addition to the project cash flows, and then simply press the NPV key. Here is the specific sequence of keystrokes, assuming that the opportunity cost of capital is 7 percent:

Hewlett-Packard HP-10B		Sharp EL-733A		Texas Instruments BA II Plus	
−350,000	CF/	−350,000	CF/		CF
16,000	CF/	16,000	CF/	2nd	{CLR Work}
16,000	CF/	16,000	CF/	−350,000	ENTER ⬇
466,000	CF/	466,000	CF/	16,000	ENTER ⬇
7	I/YR	7	i	16,000	ENTER ⬇
				466,000	ENTER ⬇
☐	{NPV}		NPV		NPV
				7	ENTER
				⬇	CPT

The calculator should display the value 59,323, the project's NPV when the discount rate is 7 percent.

By the way, you can check the accuracy of our earlier calculations using your calculator. Enter 50 percent for the discount rate (press 50, then press *i*) and then press the NPV key to find that NPV = −194,148. Enter 12.96 (the project's IRR) as the discount rate, and you will find that NPV is just about zero (it is not exactly zero, because we are rounding off the IRR to only two decimal places).

To find the IRR, we have calculated the NPV for various discount rates and plotted the results in Figure 7–4. You can see that there are *two* discount rates at which NPV = 0. That is, *each* of the following statements holds:

$$NPV = -22 + \frac{15}{1.06} + \frac{15}{(1.06)^2} + \frac{15}{(1.06)^3} + \frac{15}{(1.06)^4} - \frac{40}{(1.06)^5} = 0$$

and

$$NPV = -22 + \frac{15}{1.28} + \frac{15}{(1.28)^2} + \frac{15}{(1.28)^3} + \frac{15}{(1.28)^4} - \frac{40}{(1.28)^5} = 0$$

In other words, the investment has an IRR of both 6 percent *and* 28 percent. The reason for this is the double change in the sign of the cash flows. There can be as many different internal rates of return as there are changes in the sign of the cash-flow stream.[6]

Is the coal mine worth developing? The simple IRR rule—accept if the IRR is greater than the cost of capital—won't help. For example, you can see from Figure 7–4 that with a low cost of capital (less than 6 percent) the project has a negative NPV. It has a positive NPV only if the cost of capital is between 6 percent and 28 percent. When there are multiple changes in the sign of the cash flows, the IRR rule does not work. But the NPV rule always does.

---

[6] There may be *fewer* IRRs than the number of sign changes. You may even encounter projects for which there is *no* IRR. For example, there is no IRR for a project that has cash flows of +$1,000 in year 0, −$3,000 in year 1, and +$2,500 in year 2. If you don't believe us, try plotting NPV for different discount rates. Can such a project ever have a negative NPV?

FIGURE 7–4 King Coal's project has two internal rates of return. NPV = 0 when the discount rate is either 6 percent or 28 percent.

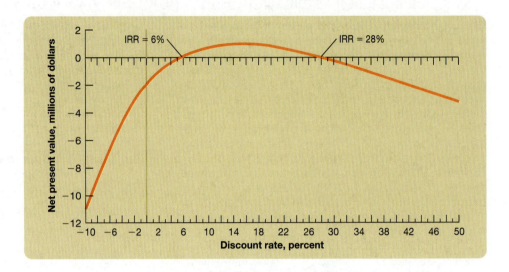

Pitfall 3: Mutually Exclusive Projects   We have seen that firms are seldom faced with take-it-or-leave-it projects. Usually they need to choose from a number of mutually exclusive alternatives. Given a choice between competing projects, you should accept the one that adds most to shareholder wealth. This is the one with the higher NPV.

But what about the rate of return rule? Would it make sense to just choose the project that offers the highest internal rate of return? Unfortunately, no. Mutually exclusive projects involve an additional pitfall for users of the IRR rule.[7]

Think once more about the two office-block proposals from Section 7.1. You initially intended to invest $350,000 in the building and then sell it at the end of the year for $400,000. Under the revised proposal, you planned to rent out the offices for 3 years at a fixed annual rent of $16,000 and then sell the building for $450,000. Here are the cash flows, their IRRs, and their NPVs:

| | Cash Flows, Thousands of Dollars | | | | | |
Project	C_0	C_1	C_2	C_3	IRR	NPV at 7%
Initial proposal	−350	+400			+14.29	+$24,000
Revised proposal	−350	+16	+16	+466	+12.96	+ 59,000

Both projects are good investments; both offer a positive NPV. But the revised proposal has the higher net present value and therefore is the better choice. Unfortunately, the superiority of the revised proposal doesn't show up as a higher rate of return. The IRR rule seems to say you should go for the initial proposal because it has the higher IRR. If you follow the IRR rule, you have the satisfaction of earning a 14.29 percent rate of return; if you use NPV, you are $59,000 richer.

Figure 7–5 shows why the IRR rule gives the wrong signal. The figure plots the NPV of each project as a function of the discount rate. These two NPV profiles cross at an interest rate of 12.26 percent. So if the opportunity cost of capital is higher than 12.26 percent, the initial proposal, with its rapid cash inflow, is the superior investment. If the cost of capital is lower than 12.26 percent, then the revised proposal dominates. Depending on the discount rate, either proposal may be superior. For the 7 percent cost of capital that we have assumed, the revised proposal is the better choice.

Now consider the IRR of each proposal. The IRR is simply the discount rate at which NPV equals zero, that is, the discount rate at which the NPV profile crosses the horizontal axis in Figure 7–5. As noted, these rates are 14.29 percent for the initial pro-

---

[7] The other rule we've considered, payback, gives poor guidance even in the much simpler case of the accept-reject decision of a project considered in isolation. It is of no help in choosing among mutually exclusive projects.

FIGURE 7–5 The initial proposal offers a higher IRR than the revised proposal, but its NPV is lower if the discount rate is less than 12.26 percent.

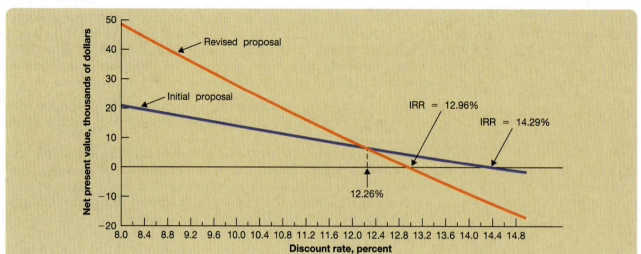

posal and 12.96 percent for the revised proposal. However, as you can see from Figure 7–5, the higher IRR for the initial proposal does not mean that it has a higher NPV.

In our example both projects involved the same outlay, but the revised proposal had the longer life. The IRR rule mistakenly favored the quick payback project with the high percentage return but the lower NPV. Remember, a high IRR is not an end in itself. You want projects that increase the value of the firm. Projects that earn a good rate of return for a long time often have higher NPVs than those that offer high percentage rates of return but die young.

Self-Test 7.4

A rich, friendly, and probably slightly unbalanced benefactor offers you the opportunity to invest $1 million in two mutually exclusive ways. The payoffs are:

a. $2 million after 1 year, a 100 percent return.
b. $300,000 a year forever.

Neither investment is risky, and safe securities are yielding 7.5 percent. Which investment will you take? You can't take both, so the choices are mutually exclusive. Do you want to earn a high percentage return, or do you want to be rich? By the way, if you really had this investment opportunity, you'd have no trouble borrowing the money to undertake it.

Pitfall 3a: Mutually Exclusive Projects Involving Different Outlays A similar misranking also may occur when comparing projects with the same lives but different outlays. In this case the IRR may mistakenly favor small projects with high rates of return but low NPVs.

Self-Test 7.5

Your wacky benefactor (see Self-Test 7.4) now offers you the choice of two opportunities:

a. Invest $1,000 today and quadruple your money—a 300 percent return—in 1 year with no risk.
b. Invest $1 million for 1 year at a guaranteed 50 percent return.

Which will you take? Do you want to earn a wonderful rate of return (300 percent), or do you want to be rich? Safe securities still yield 7.5 percent.

7.3 More Examples of Mutually Exclusive Projects

Although the IRR rule can quickly lead you astray when choosing among mutually exclusive projects, the choice is easy using the NPV rule, at least in principle. As long as at least one project has positive NPV, simply choose the project with the highest NPV. But sometimes comparing project NPVs properly can be surprisingly tricky. Here are three important, but often challenging, decisions:

- *The investment timing decision.* Should you buy a computer now or wait and think again next year? (Here today's investment is competing with possible future investments.)
- *The choice between long- and short-lived equipment.* Should the company save money today by installing cheaper machinery that will not last as long? (Here today's decision would accelerate a later investment in machine replacement.)
- *The replacement decision.* When should existing machinery be replaced? (Using it another year could delay investment in more modern equipment.)

Investment Timing

Let us return to Example 7.1, where Obsolete Technologies was contemplating the purchase of a new computer system. The proposed investment has a net present value of almost $20,000, so it appears that the cost savings would easily justify the expense of the system. However, the financial manager is not persuaded. She reasons that the price of computers is continually falling and therefore proposes postponing the purchase, arguing that the NPV of the system will be even higher if the firm waits until the following year. Unfortunately, she has been making the same argument for 10 years, and the company is steadily losing business to competitors with more efficient systems. Is there a flaw in her reasoning?

This is a problem in investment timing. When is it best to commit to a positive-NPV investment? Investment timing problems all involve choices among mutually exclusive investments. You can either proceed with the project now or do so later. You can't do both.

Table 7–2 lays out the basic data for Obsolete. You can see that the cost of the computer is expected to decline from $50,000 today to $45,000 next year, and so on. The new computer system is expected to last for 4 years from the time it is installed. The present value of the savings *at the time of installation* is expected to be $70,000. Thus if Obsolete invests today, it achieves an NPV of $70,000 – $50,000 = $20,000; if it invests next year, it will have an NPV of $70,000 – $45,000 = $25,000.

Isn't a gain of $25,000 better than one of $20,000? Well, not necessarily—you may prefer to be $20,000 richer *today* rather than $25,000 richer *next year.* The better choice depends on the cost of capital. The fourth column of Table 7–2 shows the value today (year 0) of those net present values at a 10 percent cost of capital. For example, you can see that the discounted value of that $25,000 gain is $25,000/1.10 = $22,700. The financial manager has a point. It is worth postponing investment in the computer,

TABLE 7–2 Obsolete Technologies: The gain from purchase of a computer is rising, but the NPV today is highest if the computer is purchased in year 3 (figures in thousands of dollars).

Year of Purchase	Cost of Computer	PV Savings	NPV at Year of Purchase (r = 10%)	NPV Today	
0	$50	$70	$20	$20.0	
1	45	70	25	22.7	
2	40	70	30	24.8	
3	36	70	34	25.5	←optimal
4	33	70	37	25.3	purchase
5	31	70	39	24.2	date

but it should not be postponed indefinitely. You maximize net present value today by buying the computer in year 3.

Notice that you are involved in a trade-off. The sooner you can capture the $70,000 savings the better, but if it costs you less to realize those savings by postponing the investment, it may pay for you to wait. If you postpone purchase by 1 year, the gain from buying a computer rises from $20,000 to $25,000, an increase of 25 percent. Since the cost of capital is only 10 percent, it pays to postpone at least until year 1. If you postpone from year 3 to year 4, the gain rises from $34,000 to $37,000, a rise of just under 9 percent. Since this is less than the cost of capital, it is not worth waiting any longer. The decision rule for investment timing is to choose the investment date that results in the highest net present value *today.*

Self-Test 7.6

Unfortunately Obsolete Technologies' business is shrinking as the company dithers and dawdles. Its chief financial officer realizes that the savings from installing the new computer will likewise shrink by $4,000 per year, from a present value of $70,000 now, to $66,000 next year, then to $62,000, and so on. Redo Table 7–2 with this new information. When should Obsolete buy the new computer?

Long- versus Short-Lived Equipment

Suppose the firm is forced to choose between two machines, F and G. The two machines are designed differently but have identical capacity and do exactly the same job. Machine F costs $15,000 and will last 3 years. It costs $4,000 per year to run. Machine G is an "economy" model, costing only $10,000, but it will last only 2 years and costs $6,000 per year to run.

Because the two machines produce exactly the same product, the only way to choose between them is on the basis of cost. Suppose we compute the present value of the costs:

	Costs, Thousands of Dollars				
Year:	0	1	2	3	PV at 6%
Machine F	15	4	4	4	$25.69
Machine G	10	6	6	—	21.00

Should we take machine G, the one with the lower present value of costs? Not necessarily. All we have shown is that machine G offers 2 years of service for a lower cost than 3 years of service from machine F. But is the *annual* cost of using G lower than that of F?

Suppose the financial manager agrees to buy machine F and pay for its operating costs out of her budget. She then charges the plant manager an annual amount for use of the machine. There will be three equal payments starting in year 1. Obviously, the financial manager has to make sure that the present value of these payments equals the present value of the costs of machine F, $25,690. When the discount rate is 6 percent, the payment stream with such a present value turns out to be $9,610 a year. In other words, the cost of buying and operating machine F is equivalent to an annual charge of $9,610 a year for 3 years. This figure is therefore termed the **equivalent annual annuity** of operating machine F.

equivalent annual annuity
The cash flow per period with the same present value as the cost of buying and operating a machine.

	Costs, Thousands of Dollars				
Year:	0	1	2	3	PV at 6%
Machine F	15	4	4	4	$25.69
Equivalent annual annuity		9.61	9.61	9.61	25.69

How did we know that an annual charge of $9,610 has a present value of $25,690? The annual charge is a 3-year annuity. So we calculate the value of this annuity and set it equal to $25,690:

Equivalent annual annuity × 3-year annuity factor = PV costs of F = $25,690

If the cost of capital is 6 percent, the 3-year annuity factor is 2.6730. So

$$\textbf{Equivalent annual annuity} = \frac{\textbf{present value of costs}}{\textbf{annuity factor}}$$

$$= \frac{\$25,690}{\text{3-year annuity factor}} = \frac{\$25,690}{2.6730} = \$9,610$$

If we make a similar calculation of costs for machine G, we get:

	Year:	0	1	2	PV at 6%
		Costs, Thousands of Dollars			
Machine G		10	6	6	$21.00
Equivalent 2-year annuity			11.45	11.45	21.00

We see now that machine F is better, because its equivalent annual annuity is less ($9,610 for F versus $11,450 for G). In other words, the financial manager could afford to set a lower *annual* charge for the use of F. We thus have a rule for comparing assets with different lives: *Select the machine that has the lowest equivalent annual annuity.*

Think of the equivalent annual annuity as the level annual charge[8] necessary to recover the present value of investment outlays and operating costs. The annual charge continues for the life of the equipment. Calculate the equivalent annual annuity by dividing the present value by the annuity factor.

EXAMPLE 7.4   ▶   Equivalent Annual Annuity

You need a new car. You can either purchase one outright for $15,000 or lease one for 7 years for $3,000 a year. If you buy the car, it will be worth $500 to you in 7 years. The discount rate is 10 percent. Should you buy or lease? What is the maximum lease payment you would be willing to pay?

The present value of the cost of purchasing is

$$PV = \$15,000 - \frac{\$500}{(1.10)^7} = \$14,743$$

The equivalent annual cost of purchasing the car is therefore the annuity with this present value:

$$\text{Equivalent annual annuity} \times \frac{\text{7-year annuity}}{\text{factor at 10\%}} = \frac{\text{PV costs}}{\text{of buying}} = \$14,743$$

$$\text{Equivalent annual annuity} = \frac{\$14,743}{\text{7-year annuity factor}} = \frac{\$14,743}{4.8684} = \$3,028$$

Therefore, the annual lease payment of $3,000 is less than the equivalent annual annuity of buying the car. You should be willing to pay up to $3,028 annually to lease. ◀

---

[8] We have implicitly assumed that inflation is zero. If that is not the case, it would be better to calculate the equivalent annuities for machines F and G in real terms, using the real rate of interest to calculate the annuity factor.

Replacing an Old Machine

The previous example took the life of each machine as fixed. In practice, the point at which equipment is replaced reflects economics, not physical collapse. We usually decide when to replace. The machine will rarely decide for us.

Here is a common problem: You are operating an old machine that will last 2 more years before it gives up the ghost. It costs $12,000 per year to operate. You can replace it now with a new machine, which costs $25,000 but is much more efficient ($8,000 per year in operating costs) and will last for 5 years. Should you replace now or wait a year? The opportunity cost of capital is 6 percent.

We can calculate the NPV of the new machine and its equivalent annual annuity, that is, the 5-year annuity that has the same present value.

		Costs, Thousands of Dollars					
Year:	0	1	2	3	4	5	PV at 6%
New machine	25	8	8	8	8	8	$58.70
Equivalent 5-year annuity		13.93	13.93	13.93	13.93	13.93	58.70

The cash flows of the new machine are equivalent to an annuity of $13,930 per year. So we can equally well ask at what point you would want to replace your old machine, which costs $12,000 a year to run, with a new one costing $13,930 a year. When the question is posed this way, the answer is obvious. As long as your old machine costs only $12,000 a year, why replace it with a new machine that costs $1,930 a year more?

> ### Self-Test 7.7
>
> Machines H and I are mutually exclusive and have the following investment and operating costs. Note that machine H lasts for only 2 years:
>
> | Year: | 0 | 1 | 2 | 3 |
> |---|---|---|---|---|
> | H | 10,000 | 1,100 | 1,200 | — |
> | I | 12,000 | 1,100 | 1,200 | 1,300 |
>
> Calculate the equivalent annual annuity of each investment by using a discount rate of 10 percent. Which machine is the better buy?
>
> Now suppose you have an existing machine. You can keep it going for 1 more year only, but it will cost $2,500 in repairs and $1,800 in operating costs. Is it worth replacing now with either H or I?

7.4 Capital Rationing

A firm maximizes its shareholders' wealth by accepting every project that has a positive net present value. But this assumes that the firm can raise the funds needed to pay for these investments. This is usually a good assumption, particularly for major firms that can raise very large sums of money on fair terms and short notice. Why then does top management sometimes tell subordinates that capital is limited and that they may not exceed a specified amount of capital spending? There are two reasons.

Soft Rationing

capital rationing
Limit set on the amount of funds available for investment.

For many firms the limits on capital funds are "soft." By this we mean that the **capital rationing** is not imposed by investors. Instead, the limits are imposed by top management. For example, suppose that you are an ambitious, upwardly mobile junior manager. You are keen to expand your part of the business, and as a result you tend to

overstate the investment opportunities. Rather than trying to determine which of your many bright ideas really are worthwhile, upper management may find it simpler to impose a limit on the amount that you and other junior managers can spend. This limit forces you to set your own priorities.

Even if capital is not rationed, other resources may be. For example, very rapid growth can place considerable strains on management and the organization. A somewhat rough-and-ready response to this problem is to ration the amount of capital that the firm spends.

Hard Rationing

Soft rationing should never cost the firm anything. If the limits on investment become so tight that truly good projects are being passed up, then upper management should raise more money and relax the limits it has imposed on capital spending.

But what if there is "hard rationing," meaning that the firm actually *cannot* raise the money it needs? In that case, it may be forced to pass up positive-NPV projects.

With hard rationing you may still be interested in net present value, but you now need to select the package of projects that is within the company's resources and yet gives the highest net present value.

Let us illustrate. Suppose that the opportunity cost of capital is 10 percent, that the company has total resources of $20 million, and that it is presented with the following project proposals:

Project	Cash Flows, Millions of Dollars			PV at 10%	NPV
	C_0	C_1	C_2		
J	−3	+2.2	+2.42	$ 4	$1
K	−5	+2.2	+4.84	6	1
L	−7	+6.6	+4.84	10	3
M	−6	+3.3	+6.05	8	2
N	−4	+1.1	+4.84	5	1

All five projects have a positive NPV. Therefore, if there were no shortage of capital, the firm would like to accept all five proposals. But with only $20 million available, the firm needs to find the package that gives the highest possible NPV within the budget.

The solution is to pick the projects that give the highest net present value *per dollar of investment*. The ratio of net present value to initial investment is known as the **profitability index.**[9]

profitability index

Ratio of net present value to initial investment.

$$\text{Profitability index} = \frac{\text{net present value}}{\text{initial investment}}$$

For our five projects the profitability index is calculated as follows:

Project	PV	Investment	NPV	Profitability Index
J	$ 4	$3	$1	1/3 = 0.33
K	6	5	1	1/5 = 0.20
L	10	7	3	3/7 = 0.43
M	8	6	2	2/6 = 0.33
N	5	4	1	1/4 = 0.25

---

[9] Sometimes the profitability index is defined as the ratio of present value to required investment. By this definition, all the profitability indexes calculated below are increased by 1. For example, project J's index would be PV/investment = 4/3 = 1.33. Note that project rankings under either definition are identical.

Project L offers the highest ratio of net present value to investment (0.43), and therefore L is picked first. Next come projects J and M, which tie with a ratio of 0.33, and after them comes N. These four projects exactly use up the $20 million budget. Between them they offer shareholders the highest attainable gain in wealth.[10]

Self-Test 7.8 **Which projects should the firm accept if its capital budget is only $10 million?**

Pitfalls of the Profitability Index

The profitability index is sometimes used to rank projects even when there is no soft or hard capital rationing. In this case the unwary user may be led to favor small projects over larger projects with higher NPVs. The profitability index was designed to select the projects with the most bang per buck—the greatest NPV per dollar spent. That's the right objective when bucks are limited. When they are not, a bigger bang is always better than a smaller one, even when more bucks are spent. Self-Test 7.9 is a numerical example.

Self-Test 7.9 **Calculate the profitability indexes of the two pairs of mutually exclusive investments in Self-Tests 7.4 and 7.5. Use a 7.5 percent discount rate. Does the profitability index give the right ranking in each case?**

7.5 A Last Look

We've covered several investment criteria, each with its own nuances. If your head is spinning, you might want to take a look at Table 7–3, which gives an overview and summary of these decision rules.

TABLE 7–3 A comparison of investment decision rules

Criterion	Definition	Investment Rule	Comments
Net present value (NPV)	Present value of cash inflows minus present value of cash outflows	Accept project if NPV is positive. For mutually exclusive projects, choose the one with the highest (positive) NPV.	The "gold standard" of investment criteria. Only criterion necessarily consistent with maximizing the value of the firm. Provides proper rule for choosing among mutually exclusive investments. Only pitfall involves capital rationing, when one cannot accept all positive-NPV projects.
Internal rate of return (IRR)	The discount rate at which project NPV equals zero	Accept project if IRR is greater than opportunity cost of capital	Results in same accept-reject decision as NPV in the absence of project interactions. However, beware of the following pitfalls: IRR cannot rank mutually exclusive projects—the project with higher IRR may have lower NPV. The simple IRR rule cannot be used in cases of multiple IRRs or upward-sloping NPV profile.
Payback period	Time until the sum of project cash flows equals the initial investment	Accept project if payback period is less than some specified number of years	A quick and dirty rule of thumb, with several critical pitfalls. Ignores cash flows beyond the acceptable payback period. Ignores discounting. Tends to improperly reject long-lived projects.
Profitability index	Ratio of net present value to initial investment	Accept project if profitability index is greater than 0. In case of capital rationing, accept projects with highest profitability index.	Results in same accept-reject decision as NPV in the absence of project interactions. Useful for ranking projects in case of capital rationing, but misleading in the presence of interactions. Cannot rank mutually exclusive projects.

[10] Unfortunately, when capital is rationed in more than one period, or when personnel, production capacity, or other resources are rationed in addition to capital, it isn't always possible to get the NPV-maximizing package just by ranking projects on their profitability index. Tedious trial and error may be called for, or linear programming methods may be used.

TABLE 7–4 Capital budgeting techniques used in practice

Investment Criterion	Percentage of Firms That Always or Almost Always Use Criterion	Average Score on 0–4 Scale (0 = never use; 4 = always use)		
		All Firms	Small Firms	Large Firms
Internal rate of return	76	3.1	2.9	3.4
Net present value	75	3.1	2.8	3.4
Payback period	57	2.5	2.7	2.3
Profitability index	12	0.8	0.9	0.8

Source: Reprinted from the *Journal of Financial Economics*, Vol. 60, Issue 2-3, J. R. Graham and C. R. Harvey, "The Theory and Practice of Corporate Finance: Evidence from the Field," May 2001, pp. 187–243. © 2001 with permission from Elsevier Science.

Clearly, NPV is the gold standard. It is designed to tell you whether an investment will increase the value of the firm and by how much it will do so. It is the only rule that consistently can be used to rank and choose among mutually exclusive investments. The only instance in which NPV fails as a decision rule occurs when the firm faces capital rationing. In this case, there may not be enough cash to take every project with positive NPV, and the firm must then rank projects by profitability index, that is, net present value per dollar invested.

For managers in the field, discounted cash-flow analysis is in fact the dominant tool for project evaluation. Table 7–4 provides a sample of the results of a large survey of CFOs. Notice that 75 percent of firms either always or almost always use both NPV and IRR to evaluate projects. The dominance of these criteria is even stronger among larger, presumably more sophisticated, firms. Despite the clear advantages of discounted cash-flow methods, however, firms do use other investment criteria to evaluate projects. For example, just over half of corporations always or almost always compute a project's payback period. Profitability index is routinely computed by about 12 percent of firms.

What explains such wide use of presumably inferior decision rules? To some extent, these rules present rough reality checks on the project. As we noted in the introduction to the chapter, managers might want to consider some simple ways to describe project profitability, even if they present obvious pitfalls. For example, managers talk casually about quick-payback projects in the same way that investors talk about high-P/E stocks. The fact that they talk about payback does not mean that the payback rule governs their decisions.

SUMMARY

What is the net present value of an investment, and how do you calculate it?

The **net present value** of a project measures the difference between its value and cost. NPV is therefore the amount that the project will add to shareholder wealth. A company maximizes shareholder wealth by accepting only (and all) projects that have a positive NPV.

How is the internal rate of return of a project calculated, and what must one look out for when using the internal rate of return rule?

Instead of asking whether a project has a positive NPV, many businesses prefer to ask whether it offers a higher return than shareholders could expect to get by investing in the capital market. Return is usually defined as the discount rate that would result in a zero NPV. This is known as the **internal rate of return,** or **IRR.** The project is attractive if the IRR exceeds the **opportunity cost of capital.**

There are some pitfalls in using the internal rate of return rule. Be careful about using the IRR when (1) the early cash flows are positive, (2) there is more than one change in the sign of the cash flows, or (3) you need to choose between two **mutually exclusive projects.**

www.mhhe.com/bmm5e

Why doesn't the payback rule always make shareholders better off?

The net present value rule and the rate of return rule both properly reflect the time value of money. But companies sometimes use rules of thumb to judge projects. One is the **payback rule,** which states that a project is acceptable if you get your money back within a specified period. The payback rule takes no account of any cash flows that arrive after the payback period and fails to discount cash flows within the payback period.

How can the net present value rule be used to analyze three common problems that involve competing projects: when to postpone an investment expenditure; how to choose between projects with equal lives; and when to replace equipment?

Sometimes a project may have a positive NPV if undertaken today but an even higher NPV if the investment is delayed. Choose between these alternatives by comparing their NPVs *today.*

When you have to choose between projects with different lives, you should put them on an equal footing by comparing the **equivalent annual annuity** or benefit of the two projects. When you are considering whether to replace an aging machine with a new one, you should compare the annual cost of operating the old one with the equivalent annual annuity of the new one.

How is the profitability index calculated, and how can it be used to choose between projects when funds are limited?

If there is a shortage of capital, companies need to choose projects that offer the highest net present value per dollar of investment. This measure is known as the **profitability index.**

QUIZ **M**™

Problems 1–8 refer to two projects with the following cash flows:

Year	Project A	Project B
0	–$200	–$200
1	80	100
2	80	100
3	80	100
4	80	

1. **IRR/NPV.** If the opportunity cost of capital is 11 percent, which of these projects is worth pursuing?

2. **Mutually Exclusive Investments.** Suppose that you can choose only one of these projects. Which would you choose? The discount rate is still 11 percent.

3. **IRR/NPV.** Which project would you choose if the opportunity cost of capital were 16 percent?

4. **IRR.** What are the internal rates of return on projects A and B?

5. **Investment Criteria.** In light of your answers to Problems 2–4, is there any reason to believe that the project with the higher IRR is the better project?

6. **Profitability Index.** If the opportunity cost of capital is 11 percent, what is the profitability index for each project? Does the profitability index rank the projects correctly?

7. **Payback.** What is the payback period of each project?

8. **Investment Criteria.** Considering your answers to Problems 2, 3, and 7, is there any reason to believe that the project with the lower payback period is the better project?

9. **NPV and IRR.** A project that costs $3,000 to install will provide annual cash flows of $800 for each of the next 6 years. Is this project worth pursuing if the discount rate is 10 percent? How high can the discount rate be before you would reject the project?

10. **Payback.** A project that costs $2,500 to install will provide annual cash flows of $600 for the next 6 years. The firm accepts projects with payback periods of less than 5 years. Will the project be accepted? *Should* this project be pursued if the discount rate is 2 percent? What if the discount rate is 12 percent? Will the firm's decision change as the discount rate changes?

11. **Profitability Index.** What is the profitability index of a project that costs $10,000 and provides cash flows of $3,000 in years 1 and 2 and $5,000 in years 3 and 4? The discount rate is 9 percent.

12. **NPV.** A proposed nuclear power plant will cost $2.2 billion to build and then will produce cash flows of $300 million a year for 15 years. After that period (in year 15), it must be decommissioned at a cost of $900 million. What is project NPV if the discount rate is 5 percent? What if it is 18 percent?

PRACTICE PROBLEMS ⊞M™

13. **NPV/IRR.** Consider projects A and B:

	Cash Flows, Dollars			
Project	C_0	C_1	C_2	NPV at 10%
A	−30,000	21,000	21,000	+$6,446
B	−50,000	33,000	33,000	+ 7,273

Calculate IRRs for A and B. Which project does the IRR rule suggest is best? Which project is really best?

14. **IRR.** You have the chance to participate in a project that produces the following cash flows:

C_0	C_1	C_2
+$5,000	+$4,000	−$11,000

The internal rate of return is 13.6 percent. If the opportunity cost of capital is 12 percent, would you accept the offer?

15. **NPV/IRR.**

a. Calculate the net present value of the following project for discount rates of 0, 50, and 100 percent:

C_0	C_1	C_2
−$6,750	+$4,500	+$18,000

b. What is the IRR of the project?

16. **IRR.** Marielle Machinery Works forecasts the following cash flows on a project under consideration. It uses the internal rate of return rule to accept or reject projects. Should this project be accepted if the required return is 12 percent?

C_0	C_1	C_2	C_3
−$10,000	0	+$7,500	+$8,500

17. **NPV/IRR.** A new computer system will require an initial outlay of $20,000, but it will increase the firm's cash flows by $4,000 a year for each of the next 8 years. Is the system worth installing if the required rate of return is 9 percent? What if it is 14 percent? How high can the discount rate be before you would reject the project?

18. **Investment Criteria.** If you insulate your office for $10,000, you will save $1,000 a year in heating expenses. These savings will last forever.

    a. What is the NPV of the investment when the cost of capital is 8 percent? 10 percent?
    b. What is the IRR of the investment?
    c. What is the payback period on this investment?

Please visit us at www.mhhe.com/bmm5e or refer to your Student CD

19. **NPV versus IRR.** Here are the cash flows for two mutually exclusive projects:

Project	C_0	C_1	C_2	C_3
A	−$20,000	+$8,000	+$8,000	+$ 8,000
B	− 20,000	0	0	+ 25,000

    a. At what interest rates would you prefer project A to B? *Hint:* Try drawing the NPV profile of each project.
    b. What is the IRR of each project?

20. **Payback and NPV.** A project has a life of 10 years and a payback period of 10 years. What must be true of project NPV?

21. **IRR/NPV.** Consider this project with an internal rate of return of 13.1 percent. Should you accept or reject the project if the discount rate is 12 percent?

Year	Cash Flow
0	+$100
1	−60
2	−60

22. **Payback and NPV.**

    a. What is the payback period on each of the following projects?

Project		Cash Flows, Dollars			
	Year: 0	1	2	3	4
A	−5,000	+1,000	+1,000	+3,000	0
B	−1,000	0	+1,000	+2,000	+3,000
C	−5,000	+1,000	+1,000	+3,000	+5,000

    b. Given that you wish to use the payback rule with a cutoff period of 2 years, which projects would you accept?
    c. If you use a cutoff period of 3 years, which projects would you accept?
    d. If the opportunity cost of capital is 10 percent, which projects have positive NPVs?
    e. "Payback gives too much weight to cash flows that occur after the cutoff date." True or false?

23. **Profitability Index.** Consider the following projects:

Project	C_0	C_1	C_2
A	−$2,100	+$2,000	+$1,200
B	− 2,100	+ 1,440	+ 1,728

a. Calculate the profitability index for A and B assuming a 22 percent opportunity cost of capital.

b. Use the profitability index rule to determine which project(s) you should accept (i) if you could undertake both and (ii) if you could undertake only one.

24. **Capital Rationing.** You are a manager with an investment budget of $8 million. You may invest in the following projects. Investment and cash-flow figures are in millions of dollars.

Project	Discount Rate, %	Investment	Annual Cash Flow	Project Life, Years
A	10	3	1	5
B	12	4	1	8
C	8	5	2	4
D	8	3	1.5	3
E	12	3	1	6

a. Why might these projects have different discount rates?

b. Which projects should the manager choose?

c. Which projects will be chosen if there is no capital rationing?

25. **Profitability Index versus NPV.** Consider these two projects:

Project	C_0	C_1	C_2	C_3
A	–$36	+$20	+$20	+$20
B	– 50	+ 25	+ 25	+ 25

a. Which project has the higher NPV if the discount rate is 10 percent?

b. Which has the higher profitability index?

c. Which project is most attractive to a firm that can raise an unlimited amount of funds to pay for its investment projects? Which project is most attractive to a firm that is limited in the funds it can raise?

26. **Mutually Exclusive Investments.** Here are the cash flow forecasts for two *mutually exclusive* projects:

	Cash Flows, Dollars	
Year	Project A	Project B
0	–100	–100
1	30	49
2	50	49
3	70	49

a. Which project would you choose if the opportunity cost of capital is 2 percent?

b. Which would you choose if the opportunity cost of capital is 12 percent?

c. Why does your answer change?

27. **Equivalent Annual Annuity.** A precision lathe costs $10,000 and will cost $20,000 a year to operate and maintain. If the discount rate is 10 percent and the lathe will last for 5 years, what is the equivalent annual cost of the tool?

28. **Equivalent Annual Annuity.** A firm can lease a truck for 4 years at a cost of $30,000 annually. It can instead buy a truck at a cost of $80,000, with annual maintenance expenses of $10,000. The truck will be sold at the end of 4 years for $20,000. Which is the better option if the discount rate is 10 percent?

29. **Multiple IRR.** Consider the following cash flows:

C_0	C_1	C_2	C_3	C_4
–$22	+$20	+$20	+$20	–$40

a. Confirm that one internal rate of return on this project is (a shade above) 7 percent, and that the other is (a shade below) 34 percent.
b. Is the project attractive if the discount rate is 5 percent?
c. What if it is 20 percent? 40 percent?
d. Why is the project attractive at midrange discount rates but not at very high or very low rates?

Please visit us at www.mhhe.com/bmm5e or refer to your Student CD

30. **Equivalent Annual Cost.** Econo-Cool air conditioners cost $300 to purchase, result in electricity bills of $150 per year, and last for 5 years. Luxury Air models cost $500, result in electricity bills of $100 per year, and last for 8 years. The discount rate is 21 percent.

a. What are the equivalent annual costs of the Econo-Cool and Luxury Air models?
b. Which model is more cost-effective?
c. Now you remember that the inflation rate is expected to be 10 percent per year for the foreseeable future. Redo parts (a) and (b).

31. **Investment Timing.** You can purchase an optical scanner today for $400. The scanner provides benefits worth $60 a year. The expected life of the scanner is 10 years. Scanners are expected to decrease in price by 20 percent per year. Suppose the discount rate is 10 percent. Should you purchase the scanner today or wait to purchase? When is the best purchase time?

32. **Replacement Decision.** You are operating an old machine that is expected to produce a cash inflow of $5,000 in each of the next 3 years before it fails. You can replace it now with a new machine that costs $20,000 but is much more efficient and will provide a cash flow of $10,000 a year for 4 years. Should you replace your equipment now? The discount rate is 15 percent.

33. **Replacement Decision.** A forklift will last for only 2 more years. It costs $5,000 a year to maintain. For $20,000 you can buy a new lift that can last for 10 years and should require maintenance costs of only $2,000 a year.

a. If the discount rate is 4 percent per year, should you replace the forklift?
b. What if the discount rate is 12 percent per year? Why does your answer change?

CHALLENGE PROBLEMS

Please visit us at www.mhhe.com/bmm5e or refer to your Student CD

34. **NPV/IRR.** Growth Enterprises believes its latest project, which will cost $80,000 to install, will generate a perpetual growing stream of cash flows. Cash flow at the end of this year will be $5,000, and cash flows in future years are expected to grow indefinitely at an annual rate of 5 percent.

a. If the discount rate for this project is 10 percent, what is the project NPV?
b. What is the project IRR?

35. **Investment Timing.** A classic problem in management of forests is determining when it is most economically advantageous to cut a tree for lumber. When the tree is young, it grows very rapidly. As it ages, its growth slows down. Why is the NPV-maximizing rule to cut the tree when its growth rate equals the discount rate?

36. **Multiple IRRs.** Strip Mining Inc. can develop a new mine at an initial cost of $5 million. The mine will provide a cash flow of $30 million in 1 year. The land then must be reclaimed at a cost of $28 million in the second year.

a. What are the IRRs of this project?
b. Should the firm develop the mine if the discount rate is 10 percent? 20 percent? 350 percent? 400 percent?

SOLUTIONS TO SELF-TEST QUESTIONS

7.1 Even if construction costs are $355,000, NPV is still positive:

$$NPV = PV - \$355,000 = \$357,143 - \$355,000 = \$2,143$$

Therefore, the project is still worth pursuing. The project is viable as long as construction costs are less than the PV of the future cash flow, that is, as long as construction costs are less than $357,143. However, if the opportunity cost of capital is 20 percent, the PV of the $400,000 sales price is lower and NPV is negative:

$$PV = \$400,000 \times \frac{1}{1.20} = \$333,333$$
$$NPV = PV - \$355,000 = -\$21,667$$

The present value of the future cash flow is not as high when the opportunity cost of capital is higher. The project would need to provide a higher payoff in order to be viable in the face of the higher opportunity cost of capital.

7.2 The payback period is $5,000/$660 = 7.6 years. Calculate NPV as follows. The present value of a $660 annuity for 20 years at 6 percent is

$$PV \text{ annuity} = \$7,570$$
$$NPV = -\$5,000 + \$7,570 = +\$2,570$$

The project should be accepted.

7.3 The IRR is now about 8.9 percent because

$$NPV = -\$350,000 + \frac{\$16,000}{1.089} + \frac{\$16,000}{(1.089)^2} + \frac{\$416,000}{(1.089)^3} = 0$$

Note in Figure 7–6 that NPV falls to zero as the discount rate reaches 8.9 percent.

7.4 You want to be rich. The NPV of the long-lived investment is much larger.

$$\text{Short: } NPV = -\$1 + \frac{\$2}{1.075} = +\$.8605 \text{ million}$$

$$\text{Long: } NPV = -\$1 + \frac{\$.3}{.075} = +\$3 \text{ million}$$

7.5 You want to be richer. The second alternative generates greater value at any reasonable discount rate. For example, suppose other risk-free investments offer 7.5 percent. Then

$$NPV = -\$1,000 + \frac{\$4,000}{1.075} = +\$2,721$$

$$NPV = -\$1,000,000 + \frac{\$1,500,000}{1.075} = +\$395,349$$

7.6

Year of Purchase	Cost of Computer	PV Savings	NPV at Year of Purchase	NPV Today
0	$50	$70	$20	$20
1	45	66	21	19.1
2	40	62	22	18.2
3	36	58	22	16.5
4	33	54	21	14.3
5	31	50	19	11.8

Purchase the new computer now.

FIGURE 7-6 NPV falls to zero at an interest rate of 8.9 percent.

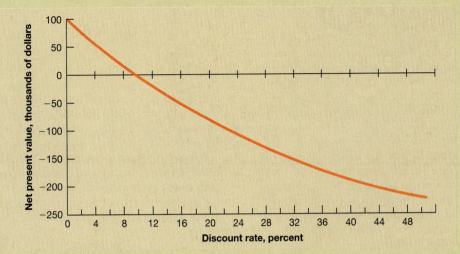

7.7

	Year:	0	1	2	3	PV of Costs
H Cash flows		$10,000	$1,100	$1,200		$11,992
Equivalent annual annuity			6,910	6,910		11,992
I Cash flows		12,000	1,100	1,200	$1,300	14,968
Equivalent annual annuity			6,019	6,019	6,019	14,968

Machine I is the better buy. However, it's still better to keep the old machine going for 1 more year. That costs $4,300, which is less than I's equivalent annual cost, $6,019.

7.8 Rank each project in order of profitability index as in the following table:

Project	Profitability Index	Investment
L	0.43	$7
J	0.33	3
M	0.33	6
N	0.25	4
K	0.20	5

Starting from the top, we run out of funds after accepting projects L and J. While J and M have equal profitability indexes, project M could not be chosen because it would force total investment above the limit of $10 million.

7.9 The profitability index gives the correct ranking for the first pair, but the incorrect ranking for the second:

Project	PV	Investment	NPV	Profitability Index (NPV/Investment)
Short	$1,860,500	$1,000,000	$ 860,500	0.86
Long	4,000,000	1,000,000	3,000,000	3.0
Small	3,721	1,000	2,721	2.7
Large	1,395,349	1,000,000	395,349	0.395

MINICASE

Flowton Products enjoys a steady demand for stainless steel infiltrators used in a number of chemical processes. Revenues from the infiltrator division are $50 million a year and production costs are $47.5 million. However, the 10 high-precision Munster stamping machines that are used in the production process are coming to the end of their useful life. One possibility is simply to replace each existing machine with a new Munster. These machines would cost $800,000 each and would not involve any additional operating costs. The alternative is to buy 10 centrally controlled Skilboro stampers. Skilboros cost $1.25 million each, but compared to the Munster, they would produce a total saving in operator and material costs of $500,000 a year. Moreover, the Skilboro is sturdily built and would last 10 years, compared with an estimated 7-year life for the Munster.

Analysts in the infiltrator division have produced the accompanying summary table, which shows the forecast total cash flows from the infiltrator business over the life of each machine. Flowton's standard procedures for appraising capital investments involve calculating net present value, internal rate of return, and payback, and these measures are also shown in the table.

As usual, Emily Balsam arrived early at Flowton's head office. She had never regretted joining Flowton. Everything about the place, from the mirror windows to the bell fountain in the atrium, suggested a classy outfit. Ms. Balsam sighed happily and reached for the envelope at the top of her in-tray. It was an analysis from the infiltrator division of the replacement options for the stamper machines. Pinned to the paper was the summary table of cash flows and a note from the CFO, which read, "Emily, I have read through 20 pages of excruciating detail and I still don't know which of these machines we should buy. The NPV calculation seems to indicate that the Skilboro is best, while IRR and payback suggest the opposite. Would you take a look and tell me what we should do and why."

Can you help Ms. Balsam by writing a memo to the CFO? You need to justify your solution and also to explain why some or all of the measures in the summary tables are inappropriate.

	Cash Flows, Millions of Dollars				
Year:	0	1–7	8	9	10
Munster					
Investment	−8.0				
Revenues		50.0	0	0	0
Costs		47.5	0	0	0
Net cash flow	−8.0	2.5	0	0	0
NPV at 15%	$2.40 million				
IRR	24.5%				
Payback period	3.2 years				
Skilboro					
Investment	−12.5				
Revenues		50.0	50.0	50.0	50.0
Costs		47.0	47.0	47.0	47.0
Net cash flow	−12.5	3.0	3.0	3.0	3.0
NPV at 15%	$2.56 million				
IRR	20.2%				
Payback period	4.2 years				

Using Discounted Cash-Flow Analysis to Make Investment Decisions

RELATED WEB LINKS

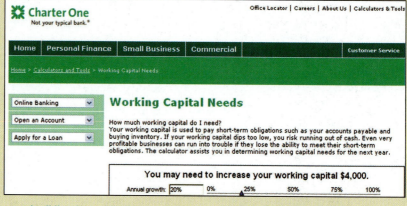

www.toolkit.cch.com/text/ P07_2960.asp Additional depreciation tables and tax rules for various investment classes.

www.charteronebank.com/ calculators/capital.asp A calculator relating growth rates to the need for working capital.

Calculating NPV can be hard work. But you've got to sweat the details and learn to do it right.

© McGraw-Hill Companies/Jill Braaten, photographer

Think of the problems that GM's managers face when considering whether to introduce a new model. How much will we need to invest in new plant and equipment? What will it cost to market and promote the new car? How soon can we get the car into production? What is the projected production cost? What do we need in the way of inventories of raw materials and finished cars? How many cars can we expect to sell each year and at what price? What credit arrangements will we need to give our dealers? How long will the model stay in production? What happens at the end of that time? Can we use the plant and equipment elsewhere in the company? All of these issues affect the level and timing of project cash flows. In this chapter we continue our analysis of the capital budgeting decision by turning our focus to how the financial manager should prepare cash-flow estimates for use in net present value analysis.

In Chapter 7 you used the net present value rule to make a simple capital budgeting decision. You tackled the problem in four steps:

Step 1. Forecast the project cash flows.

Step 2. Estimate the opportunity cost of capital— that is, the rate of return that your shareholders could expect to earn if they invested their money in the capital market.

Step 3. Use the opportunity cost of capital to discount the future cash flows. The project's present value (PV) is equal to the sum of the discounted future cash flows.

Step 4. Net present value (NPV) measures whether the project is worth more than it costs. To calculate NPV, you need to subtract the required investment from the present value of the future payoffs:

$$NPV = PV - \text{required investment}$$

You should go ahead with the project if it has a positive NPV.

We now need to consider how to apply the net present value rule to practical investment problems. The first step is to decide what to discount. We know the answer in principle: discount cash flows. This is why capital budgeting is often referred to as *discounted cash-flow,* or *DCF,* analysis. But useful forecasts of cash flows do not arrive on a silver platter. Often the financial manager has to make do with raw data supplied by specialists in product design, production, marketing, and so on, and must check and combine this information. In addition, most financial forecasts are prepared in accordance with accounting principles that do not necessarily recognize cash flows when they occur. These forecasts must also be adjusted.

We look first at what cash flows should be discounted. We then present an example designed to show how standard accounting information can be used to compute cash flows and why cash flows and accounting income usually differ. The example will lead us to various further points, including the links between depreciation and taxes and the importance of tracking investments in working capital.

After studying this chapter you should be able to:
- Identify the cash flows properly attributable to a proposed new project.

- Calculate the cash flows of a project from standard financial statements.

- Understand how the company's tax bill is affected by depreciation and how this affects project value.

- Understand how changes in working capital affect project cash flows.

8.1 Identifying Cash Flows

Discount Cash Flows, Not Profits

Up to this point we have been concerned mainly with the mechanics of discounting and with the various methods of project appraisal. We have had almost nothing to say about the problem of *what* you should discount. The first and most important point is this: To calculate net present value, you need to discount cash flows, *not* accounting profits.

We stressed the difference between cash flows and profits in Chapter 3. Here we stress it again. Income statements are intended to show how well the firm has performed. They do not track cash flows.

If the firm lays out a large amount of money on a big capital project, you do not conclude that the firm performed poorly that year, even though a lot of cash is going out the door. Therefore, the accountant does not deduct capital expenditure when calculating the year's income but, instead, depreciates it over several years.

That is fine for computing year-by-year profits, but it could get you into trouble when working out net present value. For example, suppose that you are analyzing an investment proposal. It costs $2,000 and is expected to bring in a cash flow of $1,500 in the first year and $500 in the second. You think that the opportunity cost of capital is 10 percent and so calculate the present value of the cash flows as follows:

$$PV = \frac{\$1,500}{1.10} + \frac{\$500}{(1.10)^2} = \$1,776.86$$

The project is worth less than it costs; it has a negative NPV:

$$NPV = \$1,776.86 - \$2,000 = -\$223.14$$

The project costs $2,000 today, but accountants would not treat that outlay as an immediate expense. They would depreciate that $2,000 over 2 years and deduct the depreciation from the cash flow to obtain accounting income:

	Year 1	Year 2
Cash inflow	+$1,500	+$ 500
Less depreciation	− 1,000	− 1,000
Accounting income	+ 500	− 500

Thus an accountant would forecast income of $500 in year 1 and an accounting loss of $500 in year 2.

Suppose you were given this forecast income and loss and naively discounted them. Now NPV *looks* positive:

$$\text{Apparent NPV} = \frac{\$500}{1.10} + \frac{-\$500}{(1.10)^2} = \$41.32$$

Of course we know that this is nonsense. The project is obviously a loser; we are spending money today ($2,000 cash outflow), and we are simply getting our money back ($1,500 in year 1 and $500 in year 2). We are earning a zero return when we could get a 10 percent return by investing our money in the capital market.

The message of the example is this: When calculating NPV, recognize investment expenditures when they occur, not later when they show up as depreciation. Projects are financially attractive because of the cash they generate, either for distribution to shareholders or for reinvestment in the firm. Therefore, the focus of capital budgeting must be on cash flow, not profits.

We saw another example of the distinction between cash flow and accounting profits in Chapter 3. Accountants try to show profit as it is earned, rather than when the company and the customer get around to paying their bills. For example, an income statement will recognize revenue when the sale is made, even if the bill is not paid for months. This practice also results in a difference between accounting profits and cash flow. The sale generates immediate profits, but the cash flow comes later.

EXAMPLE 8.1 ▶ Sales before Cash

Your firm's ace computer salesman closed a $500,000 sale on December 15, just in time to count it toward his annual bonus. How did he do it? Well, for one thing he gave the customer 180 days to pay. The income statement will recognize the sale in December, even though cash will not arrive until June. But a financial analyst tracking cash flows would concentrate on the latter event.

The accountant takes care of the timing difference by adding $500,000 to accounts receivable in December and then reducing accounts receivable when the money arrives in June. (The total of accounts receivable is just the sum of all cash due from customers.)

You can think of the increase in accounts receivable as an investment—it's effectively a 180-day loan to the customer—and therefore a cash outflow. That investment is recovered when the customer pays. Thus financial analysts often find it convenient to calculate cash flow as follows:

December		June	
Sales	$500,000	Sales	0
Less investment in accounts receivable	−500,000	Plus recovery of accounts receivable	+$500,000
Cash flow	0	Cash flow	$500,000

Note that this procedure gives the correct cash flow of $500,000 in June. ◀

It is not always easy to translate accounting data back into actual dollars. If you are in doubt about what is a cash flow, simply count the dollars coming in and take away the dollars going out.

Self-Test 8.1

A regional supermarket chain is deciding whether to install a tewgit machine in each of its stores. Each machine costs $250,000. Projected income per machine is as follows:

Year:	1	2	3	4	5
Sales	$250,000	$300,000	$300,000	$250,000	$250,000
Operating expenses	200,000	200,000	200,000	200,000	200,000
Depreciation	50,000	50,000	50,000	50,000	50,000
Accounting income	0	50,000	50,000	0	0

Why would a store continue to operate a machine in years 4 and 5 if it produces no profits? What are the cash flows from investing in a machine? Assume each tewgit machine is completely depreciated and has no salvage value at the end of its 5-year life.

Discount *Incremental* Cash Flows

A project's present value depends on the *extra* cash flows that it produces. Forecast first the firm's cash flows if you go ahead with the project. Then forecast the cash flows if you *don't* accept the project. Take the difference and you have the extra (or *incremental*) cash flows produced by the project:

$$\text{Incremental cash flow} = \text{cash flow with project} - \text{cash flow without project}$$

EXAMPLE 8.2   ▶   ## Launching a New Product

Consider the decision by Microsoft to develop a new operating system, today code-named Vista. A successful launch could lead to several billion dollars in profits.

But are these profits all incremental cash flows? Certainly not. Our with-versus-without principle reminds us that we need also to think about what the cash flows would be *without* the new system. If Microsoft goes ahead with Vista, demand for Windows XP will be reduced. The incremental cash flows therefore are

Cash flow with Vista
(including lower cash flow   –
from Windows XP)

cash flow without Vista
(with higher cash flow
from Windows XP)   ◀

The trick in capital budgeting is to trace all the incremental flows from a proposed project. Here are some things to look out for.

Include All Indirect Effects   Microsoft's new operating system illustrates a common indirect effect. New products often damage sales of an existing product. Of course, companies frequently introduce new products anyway, usually because they believe that their existing product line is under threat from competition. Even if you don't go ahead with a new product, there is no guarantee that sales of the existing product line will continue at their present level. Sooner or later they will decline.

Sometimes a new project will *help* the firm's existing business. Suppose that you are the financial manager of an airline that is considering opening a new short-haul route from Peoria, Illinois, to Chicago's O'Hare Airport. When considered in isolation, the new route may have a negative NPV. But once you allow for the additional business that the new route brings to your other traffic out of O'Hare, it may be a very worthwhile investment. To forecast incremental cash flow, you must trace out all indirect effects of accepting the project.

Some capital investments have very long lives once all indirect effects are recognized. Consider the introduction of a new jet engine. Engine manufacturers often offer attractive pricing to achieve early sales, because once an engine is installed, 15 years' sales of replacement parts are almost ensured. Also, since airlines prefer to reduce the number of different engines in their fleet, selling jet engines today improves sales tomorrow as well. Later sales will generate further demands for replacement parts. Thus the string of incremental effects from the first sales of a new model engine can run for 20 years or more.

Forget Sunk Costs   Sunk costs are like spilled milk: They are past and irreversible outflows. Sunk costs remain the same whether or not you accept the project. Therefore, they do not affect project NPV.

Unfortunately, managers often are influenced by sunk costs. A classic case occurred in 1971, when Lockheed sought a federal guarantee for a bank loan to continue development of the Tristar airplane. Lockheed and its supporters argued that it would be foolish to abandon a project on which nearly $1 billion had already been spent. This was a poor argument, however, because the $1 billion was sunk. The relevant questions were how much more needed to be invested and whether the finished product warranted the *incremental* investment.

Lockheed's supporters were not the only ones to appeal to sunk costs. Some of its critics claimed that it would be foolish to continue with a project that offered no prospect of a satisfactory return on that $1 billion. This argument too was faulty. The $1 billion was gone, and the decision to continue with the project should have depended only on the return on the incremental investment.

Include Opportunity Costs   Resources are almost never free, even when no cash changes hands. For example, suppose a new manufacturing operation uses land that could otherwise be sold for $100,000. This resource is costly; by using the land, you pass up the opportunity to sell it. There is no out-of-pocket cost, but there is an **opportunity cost,** that is, the value of the forgone alternative use of the land.

opportunity cost
Benefit or cash flow
forgone as a result of an
action.

This example prompts us to warn you against judging projects "before versus after" rather than "with versus without." A manager comparing before versus after might not assign any value to the land because the firm owns it both before and after:

Before	Take Project	After	Cash Flow, Before versus After
Firm owns land	————▶	Firm still owns land	0

The proper comparison, with versus without, is as follows:

Before	Take Project	After	Cash Flow, with Project
Firm owns land	————▶	Firm still owns land	0

Before	Do Not Take Project	After	Cash Flow, without Project
Firm owns land	————▶	Firm sells land for $100,000	$100,000

Comparing the cash flows with and without the project, we see that $100,000 is given up by undertaking the project. The original cost of purchasing the land is irrelevant—that cost is sunk. The opportunity cost equals the cash that could be realized from selling the land now and therefore is a relevant cash flow for project evaluation.

When the resource can be freely traded, its opportunity cost is simply the market price.[1] However, sometimes opportunity costs are difficult to estimate. Suppose that

---

[1] If the value of the land to the firm were less than the market price, the firm would sell it. On the other hand, the opportunity cost of using land in a particular project cannot exceed the cost of buying an equivalent parcel to replace it.

you go ahead with a project to develop Computer Nouveau, pulling your software team off their work on a new operating system that some existing customers are not-so-patiently awaiting. The exact cost of infuriating those customers may be impossible to calculate, but you'll think twice about the opportunity cost of moving the software team to Computer Nouveau.

net working capital
Current assets minus current liabilities.

Recognize the Investment in Working Capital   Net **working capital** (often referred to simply as *working capital*) is the difference between a company's short-term assets and its liabilities. The principal short-term assets are cash, accounts receivable (customers' unpaid bills), and inventories of raw materials and finished goods, and the principal short-term liabilities are accounts payable (bills that *you* have not paid), notes payable, and accruals (liabilities for items such as wages or taxes that have recently been incurred but have not yet been paid).

Most projects entail an additional investment in working capital. For example, before you can start production, you need to invest in inventories of raw materials. Then, when you deliver the finished product, customers may be slow to pay and accounts receivable will increase. (Remember the computer sale described in Example 8.1. It required a $500,000, 6-month investment in accounts receivable.) Next year, as business builds up, you may need a larger stock of raw materials and you may have even more unpaid bills. Investments in working capital, just like investments in plant and equipment, result in cash outflows.

We find that working capital is one of the most common sources of confusion in forecasting project cash flows.[2] Here are the most common mistakes:

1. *Forgetting about working capital entirely.* We hope that you never fall into that trap.
2. *Forgetting that working capital may change during the life of the project.* Imagine that you sell $100,000 of goods per year and customers pay on average 6 months late. You will therefore have $50,000 of unpaid bills. Now you increase prices by 10 percent, so revenues increase to $110,000. If customers continue to pay 6 months late, unpaid bills increase to $55,000, and therefore you need to make an *additional* investment in working capital of $5,000.
3. *Forgetting that working capital is recovered at the end of the project.* When the project comes to an end, inventories are run down, any unpaid bills are (you hope) paid off, and you can recover your investment in working capital. This generates a cash *inflow*.

Beware of Allocated Overhead Costs   We have already mentioned that the accountant's objective in gathering data is not always the same as the project analyst's. A case in point is the allocation of overhead costs such as rent, heat, or electricity. These overhead costs may not be related to a particular project, but they must be paid for nevertheless. Therefore, when the accountant assigns costs to the firm's projects, a charge for overhead is usually made. But our principle of incremental cash flows says that in investment appraisal we should include only the *extra* expenses that would result from the project.

A project may generate extra overhead costs, but then again it may not. We should be cautious about assuming that the accountant's allocation of overhead costs represents the *incremental* cash flow that would be incurred by accepting the project.

Self-Test 8.2   A firm is considering an investment in a new manufacturing plant. The site already is owned by the company, but existing buildings would need to be demolished. Which of the following should be treated as incremental cash flows?

---

[2] If you are not clear *why* working capital affects cash flow, look back to Chapter 3, where we gave a primer on working capital and a couple of simple examples.

a. The market value of the site.
b. The market value of the existing buildings.
c. Demolition costs and site clearance.
d. The cost of a new access road put in last year.
e. Lost cash flows on other projects due to executive time spent on the new facility.
f. Future depreciation of the new plant.

Discount Nominal Cash Flows by the Nominal Cost of Capital

The distinction between nominal and real cash flows and interest rates is crucial in capital budgeting. Interest rates are usually quoted in *nominal* terms. If you invest $100 in a bank deposit offering 6 percent interest, then the bank promises to pay you $106 at the end of the year. It makes no promises about what that $106 will buy. The real rate of interest on the bank deposit depends on inflation. If inflation is 2 percent, that $106 will buy you only 4 percent more goods at the end of the year than your $100 could buy today. The *real* rate of interest is therefore about 4 percent.[3]

If the discount rate is nominal, consistency requires that cash flows be estimated in nominal terms as well, taking account of trends in selling price, labor and materials costs, and so on. This calls for more than simply applying a single assumed inflation rate to all components of cash flow. Some costs or prices increase faster than inflation, some slower. For example, perhaps you have entered into a 5-year fixed-price contract with a supplier. No matter what happens to inflation over this period, this part of your costs is fixed in nominal terms.

Of course, there is nothing wrong with discounting real cash flows at the real interest rate, although this is not commonly done. We saw in Chapter 4 that real cash flows discounted at the real discount rate give exactly the same present values as nominal cash flows discounted at the nominal rate.

It should go without saying that you cannot mix and match real and nominal quantities. Real cash flows must be discounted at a real discount rate, nominal cash flows at a nominal rate. Discounting real cash flows at a nominal rate is a *big* mistake.

While the need to maintain consistency may seem like an obvious point, analysts sometimes forget to account for the effects of inflation when forecasting future cash flows. As a result, they end up discounting real cash flows at a nominal discount rate. This can grossly understate project values.

EXAMPLE 8.3 ▶ Cash Flows and Inflation

City Consulting Services is considering moving into a new office building. The cost of a 1-year lease is $8,000, paid immediately. This cost will increase in future years at the annual inflation rate of 3 percent. The firm believes that it will remain in the building for 4 years. What is the present value of its rental costs if the discount rate is 10 percent?

The present value can be obtained by discounting the nominal cash flows at the 10 percent discount rate as follows:

---

[3] Remember from Chapter 4,

$$\text{Real rate of interest} \approx \text{nominal rate of interest} - \text{inflation rate}$$

The exact formula is

$$1 + \text{real rate of interest} = \frac{1 + \text{nominal rate of interest}}{1 + \text{inflation rate}} = \frac{1.06}{1.02} = 1.0392$$

Therefore, the real interest rate is .0392, or 3.92 percent.

Year	Cash Flow	Present Value at 10% Discount Rate	
0	8,000		8,000
1	$8,000 \times 1.03 = 8,240$	8,240/1.10 =	7,490.91
2	$8,000 \times 1.03^2 = 8,487.20$	$8,487.20/(1.10)^2 =$	7,014.22
3	$8,000 \times 1.03^3 = 8,741.82$	$8,741.82/(1.10)^3 =$	6,567.86
			$29,072.98

Alternatively, the real discount rate can be calculated as $1.10/1.03 - 1 = .067961 = 6.7961$ percent.[4] The present value of the cash flows can also be computed by discounting the real cash flows at the real discount rate as follows:

Year	Real Cash Flow	Present Value at 6.7961% Discount Rate	
0	8,000		8,000
1	8,000	8,000/1.067961 =	7,490.91
2	8,000	$8,000/(1.067961)^2 =$	7,014.22
3	8,000	$8,000/(1.067961)^3 =$	6,567.86
			$29,072.98

Notice the real cash flow is a constant, since the lease payment increases at the rate of inflation. The present value of *each* cash flow is the same regardless of the method used to discount it. The sum of the present values is, of course, also identical.   ◀

Self-Test 8.3

Nasty Industries is closing down an outmoded factory and throwing all of its workers out on the street. Nasty's CEO is enraged to learn that the firm must continue to pay for workers' health insurance for 4 years. The cost per worker next year will be $2,400 per year, but the inflation rate is 4 percent, and health costs have been increasing at 3 percentage points faster than inflation. What is the present value of this obligation? The (nominal) discount rate is 10 percent.

Separate Investment and Financing Decisions

Suppose you finance a project partly with debt. How should you treat the proceeds from the debt issue and the interest and principal payments on the debt? You would *neither* subtract the debt proceeds from the required investment *nor* recognize the interest and prinicpal payments on the debt as cash outflows. Regardless of the actual financing, we should view the project as if it were all equity-financed, treating all cash outflows required for the project as coming from stockholders and all cash inflows as going to them.

This procedure allows us to focus exclusively on the *project* cash flows, not the cash flows associated with alternative financing schemes. By proceeding in this manner, we separate the analysis of the investment decision from that of the financing decision. First, we determine whether the project has a positive net present value, assuming all-equity financing. Then, if the project is viable, we can undertake a separate analysis of the best financing strategy. Financing decisions are considered later in the text.

8.2 Calculating Cash Flow

It is often helpful to think of a project as progressing through three distinct stages. Initially, there is the start-up stage, which typically requires considerable investments in

---

[4] We calculate the real discount rate to four decimal places to avoid confusion from rounding. Such precision is rarely necessary in practice.

plant and equipment. The start-up stage also entails investments in working capital, as the firm builds up inventories of materials and product. In the middle period, projects throw off cash flows from operations as the product is sold for more than its cost of production. There are investments in working capital in this period as well. For example, as we've seen, increasing sales usually entail additions to accounts receivable until the cash is collected. Finally, when the project is liquidated in the terminal or wind-down period, plant and equipment can be sold or moved to other applications. This *dis*investment in fixed assets results in a positive cash flow. As the project comes to its end, there is a similar disinvestment in working capital, which also generates a positive cash flow as inventories are sold off and accounts receivable are collected.

This suggests that cash flow is the sum of three components: investment (or disinvestment) in fixed assets such as plant and equipment, net investment in working capital, and cash flow from operations:

> **Total cash flow = cash flow from investment in fixed assets**
> **+ cash flow from investments in working capital**
> **+ cash flow from operations**

Remember that investments in either fixed assets or working capital result in negative cash flows: The firm uses cash to acquire those assets. Conversely, when the firm disinvests, or sells off these assets, it realizes positive cash flows. Let's now examine each component of cash flow in turn.

Capital Investment

To get a project off the ground, a company will typically need to make considerable up-front investments in plant, equipment, research, marketing, and so on. For example, Gillette spent about $750 million to develop and build the production line for its Mach3 razor cartridge and an additional $300 million in its initial marketing campaign, largely before a single razor was sold. These expenditures are negative cash flows—negative because they represent a cash outflow from the firm.

Conversely, if a piece of machinery can be sold when the project winds down, the sales price (net of any taxes on the sale) represents a positive cash flow to the firm.

EXAMPLE 8.4 ▶	Cash Flow from Investments

Gillette's competitor, Slick, invests $800 million to develop the Mock4 razor blade. The specialized blade factory will run for 7 years, until it is replaced by a more advanced technology. At that point, the machinery will be sold for scrap metal, for a price of $50 million. Taxes of $10 million will be assessed on the sale.

The initial cash flow from investment is –$800 million, and the after-tax cash flow in 7 years from the disinvestment in (equivalently, the sale of) the production line will be $50 million – $10 million = $40 million. ◀

Investment in Working Capital

We pointed out earlier in the chapter that when a company builds up inventories of raw materials or finished product, the company's cash is reduced; the reduction in cash reflects the firm's investment in inventories. Similarly, cash is reduced when customers are slow to pay their bills—in this case, the firm makes an investment in accounts receivable. Investment in working capital, just like investment in plant and equipment, represents a negative cash flow. On the other hand, later in the life of a project, when inventories are sold off and accounts receivable are collected, the firm's investment in working capital is reduced as it converts these assets into cash.

EXAMPLE 8.5 ▶	Cash Flow from Investments in Working Capital

Slick makes an initial (year 0) investment of $10 million in inventories of plastic and steel for its blade plant. Then in year 1 it accumulates an additional $20 million of raw materials. The total level of inventories is now $10 million + $20 million = $30 million, but the cash expenditure in year 1 is simply the $20 million addition to inventory. The $20 million investment in additional inventory results in a cash flow of –$20 million. Notice that the increase in working capital is an *investment* in the project. Like other investments, a buildup of working capital requires cash. Increases in the *level* of working capital therefore show up as *negative* cash flows.

Later on, say, in year 5, the company begins planning for the next-generation blade. At this point, it decides to reduce its inventory of raw material from $20 million to $15 million. This reduction in inventory investment frees up $5 million of cash, which is a positive cash flow. Therefore, the cash flows from inventory investment are –$10 million in year 0, –$20 million in year 1, and +$5 million in year 5.

These calculations can be summarized in a simple table, as follows:

Year:	0	1	2	3	4	5
1. Total working capital, year-end ($ million)	10	30	30	30	30	25
2. Investment in working capital ($ million)	10	20	0	0	0	–5
3. Cash flow from investments in working capital	–10	–20	0	0	0	+5

In years 0 and 1, there is a net investment in working capital (line 2), corresponding to a negative cash flow (line 3), and an increase in the *level* of total working capital (line 1). In years 2 to 4, there is no investment in working capital, so its level remains unchanged at $30 million. But in year 5, as the firm begins to disinvest in working capital, the total declines, which provides a positive cash flow. ◀

In general: An *increase* in working capital is an investment and therefore implies a *negative* cash flow; a decrease in working capital implies a positive cash flow. The cash flow is measured by the *change* in working capital, not the *level* of working capital.

Cash Flow from Operations

The third component of project cash flow is cash flow from operations. There are several ways to work out this component.

Method 1: Dollars In Minus Dollars Out   Take only the items from the income statement that represent actual cash flows. We start with cash revenues and subtract cash expenses and taxes paid. We do not, however, subtract a charge for depreciation because depreciation is just an accounting entry, not a cash expense. Thus,

$$\text{Cash flow from operations} = \text{revenues} - \text{cash expenses} - \text{taxes}$$

Method 2: Adjusted Accounting Profits   Alternatively, you can start with after-tax accounting profits and add back any deductions that were made for noncash expenses such as depreciation. While these noncash expenses reduce accounting profits in the current period, they do not affect cash flows. (Remember from our earlier discussion that you want to discount cash flows, not profits.) By this reasoning,

$$\text{Cash flow from operations} = \text{after-tax profit} + \text{depreciation}$$

Method 3: Tax Shields   Although the depreciation deduction is *not* a cash expense, it does affect net profits and therefore taxes paid, which *is* a cash item. For example, if the firm's tax bracket is 35 percent, each additional dollar of depreciation reduces taxable income by $1. Tax payments therefore fall by $.35, and cash flow increases by the same amount. The total **depreciation tax shield** equals the product of depreciation and the tax rate:

depreciation tax shield
Reduction in taxes attributable to depreciation.

$$\text{Depreciation tax shield} = \text{depreciation} \times \text{tax rate}$$

This suggests a third way to calculate cash flow from operations. First, calculate net profit *assuming* zero depreciation. This item would be (revenues – cash expenses) × (1 – tax rate). Now add back the tax shield created by depreciation. We then calculate operating cash flow as follows:

$$\textbf{Cash flow from operations} = \textbf{(revenues – cash expenses)} \times \textbf{(1 – tax rate)}$$
$$\textbf{+ (depreciation} \times \textbf{tax rate)}$$

The following example confirms that the three methods for estimating cash flow from operations all give the same answer.

EXAMPLE 8.6 ▶ Cash Flow from Operations

A project generates revenues of $1,000, cash expenses of $600, and depreciation charges of $200 in a particular year. The firm's tax bracket is 35 percent. Net income is calculated as follows:

Revenues	1,000
– Cash expenses	600
– Depreciation expense	200
= Profit before tax	200
– Tax at 35%	70
= Net profit	130

Methods 1, 2, and 3 all show that cash flow from operations is $330:

Method 1: Cash flow from operations = revenues – cash expenses – taxes
$$= 1{,}000 - 600 - 70 = 330$$
Method 2: Cash flow from operations = net profit + depreciation
$$= 130 + 200 = 330$$
Method 3: Cash flow from operations = (revenues – cash expenses)
$$\times (1 - \text{tax rate}) + (\text{depreciation} \times \text{tax rate})$$
$$= (1{,}000 - 600) \times (1 - .35) + (200 \times .35) = 330 \blacktriangleleft$$

Self-Test 8.4

A project generates revenues of $600, expenses of $300, and depreciation charges of $200 in a particular year. The firm's tax bracket is 35 percent. Find the operating cash flow of the project by using all three approaches.

In many cases, a project will seek to improve efficiency or cut costs. A new computer system may provide labor savings. A new heating system may be more energy-efficient than the one it replaces. These projects also contribute to the operating cash flow of the firm—not by increasing revenue but by reducing costs. As the next example illustrates, we calculate the addition to operating cash flow on cost-cutting projects just as we would for projects that increase revenues.

EXAMPLE 8.7 ▶ Operating Cash Flow of Cost-Cutting Projects

Suppose the new heating system costs $100,000 but reduces heating costs by $30,000 a year. The system will be depreciated straight-line over a 5-year period, so the annual depreciation charge will be $20,000. The firm's tax rate is 35 percent. We calculate the *incremental* effects on revenues, expenses, and depreciation charges as follows. Notice that the reduction in expenses increases revenues minus cash expenses.

$$
\begin{array}{ll}
\text{Increase in (revenues minus expenses)} & 30,000 \\
- \text{ Additional depreciation expense} & -20,000 \\
= \text{ Incremental profit before tax} & = 10,000 \\
- \text{ Incremental tax at } 35\% & -\ \ 3,500 \\
= \text{ Change in net profit} & =\ \ 6,500
\end{array}
$$

Therefore, the increment to operating cash flow can be calculated by *method 1* as

$$
\begin{array}{c}
\text{Increase in (revenues} - \text{cash expenses)} - \text{additional taxes} \\
= \$30,000 - \$3,500 = \$26,500
\end{array}
$$

or by *method 2:*

$$
\text{Increase in net profit} + \text{additional depreciation} = \$6,500 + \$20,000 = \$26,500
$$

or by *method 3:*

$$
\begin{array}{c}
\text{Increase in (revenues} - \text{cash expenses)} \times (1 - \text{tax rate}) \\
+ \ (\text{additional depreciation} \times \text{tax rate}) = \$30,000 \times (1 - .35) + (\$20,000 \times .35) \\
= \$26,500 \quad \blacktriangleleft
\end{array}
$$

8.3 An Example: Blooper Industries

Now that we have examined many of the pieces of a cash-flow analysis, let's try to put them together into a coherent whole. As the newly appointed financial manager of Blooper Industries, you are about to analyze a proposal for mining and selling a small deposit of high-grade magnoosium ore.[5] You are given the forecasts shown in the spreadsheet in Table 8–1. We will walk through the lines in the table.

Cash-Flow Analysis

Investment in Fixed Assets   Panel A of the spreadsheet details investments and disinvestments in fixed assets. The project requires an investment of $10 million, as shown in cell B3. After 5 years, the ore deposit is exhausted, so the mining equipment may be sold for $2 million, a forecast that already reflects the likely impact of inflation.

When you sell the equipment, the IRS will check to see whether any taxes are due on the sale. Any difference between the sale price ($2 million) and the book value of the equipment will be treated as a taxable gain.

We assume that Blooper depreciates the equipment to a final value of zero. Therefore, the book value of the equipment when it is sold in year 6 will be zero, and you will be subject to taxes on the full $2 million proceeds. Your sale of the equipment will land you with an additional tax bill in year 6 of .35 × $2 million = $.70 million. The net cash flow from the sale in year 6 is therefore

$$
\text{Salvage value} - \text{tax on gain} = \$2 \text{ million} - \$.70 \text{ million} = \$1.30 \text{ million}
$$

This amount is recorded in cell H4.

Row 5 summarizes the cash flows from investments in and sales of fixed assets. The entry in each cell equals the after-tax proceeds from asset sales (row 4) minus the investments in fixed assets (row 3).

---

[5] Readers have inquired whether magnoosium is a real substance. Here, now, are the facts: Magnoosium was created in the early days of television, when a splendid-sounding announcer closed a variety show by saying, "This program has been brought to you by Blooper Industries, proud producer of aleemium, magnoosium, and stool." We forget the company, but the blooper really happened.

TABLE 8-1 Financial projections for Blooper's magnoosium mine (figures in thousands of dollars)

	A	B	C	D	E	F	G	H
1	Year:	0	1	2	3	4	5	6
2	**A. Fixed assets**							
3	Investment in fixed assets	10,000						
4	Sales of fixed assets							1,300
5	CF, invest. in fixed assets	−10,000	0	0	0	0	0	1,300
6								
7	**B. Working capital**							
8	Working capital	1,500	4,075	4,279	4,493	4,717	3,039	0
9	*Change* in working capital	1,500	2,575	204	214	225	−1,679	−3,039
10	CF, invest. in wk capital	−1,500	−2,575	−204	−214	−225	1,679	3,039
11								
12	**C. Operations**							
13	Revenues		15,000	15,750	16,538	17,364	18,233	
14	Expenses		10,000	10,500	11,025	11,576	12,155	
15	Depreciation		2,000	2,000	2,000	2,000	2,000	
16	Pretax profit		3,000	3,250	3,513	3,788	4,078	
17	Tax		1,050	1,138	1,229	1,326	1,427	
18	Profit after tax		1,950	2,113	2,283	2,462	2,650	
19	Cash flow from operations		3,950	4,113	4,283	4,462	4,650	
20								
21	**D. Project valuation**							
22	Total project cash flow	−11,500	1,375	3,909	4,069	4,238	6,329	4,339
23	Discount factor	1.0	0.8929	0.7972	0.7118	0.6355	0.5674	0.5066
24	PV of cash flow	−11,500	1,228	3,116	2,896	2,693	3,591	2,198
25	Net present value	4,223						
26								
27	**E. Other inputs**							
28	Inflation rate	0.05						
29	Discount rate	0.12						
30	Acct receiv. as % of sales	1/6						
31	Inven. as % of expenses	0.15						
32	Tax rate	0.35						

Please visit us at www.mhhe.com/bmm5e or refer to your Student CD

Investments in Working Capital   Row 8 shows the *level* of working capital. As the project gears up in the early years, working capital increases, but later in the project's life, the investment in working capital is recovered and the level declines.

Row 9 shows the *change* in working capital from year to year. Notice that in years 1 to 4 the change is positive; in these years the project requires a continuing investment in working capital. Starting in year 5 the change is negative; there is a disinvestment as working capital is recovered. Cash flow associated with investments in working capital (row 10) is the negative of the change in working capital. Just like investment in plant and equipment, investment in working capital produces a negative cash flow, and disinvestment produces a positive cash flow.

Operating Cash Flow   The company expects to be able to sell 750,000 pounds of magnoosium a year at a price of $20 a pound in year 1. That points to initial revenues of 750,000 × $20 = $15,000,000. But be careful; inflation is running at about 5 percent a year. If magnoosium prices keep pace with inflation, you should increase your forecast of the second-year revenues by 5 percent. Third-year revenues should increase by a further 5 percent, and so on. Row 13 in Table 8–1 shows revenues rising in line with inflation.

The sales forecasts in Table 8–1 are cut off after 5 years. That makes sense if the ore deposit will run out at that time. But if Blooper could make sales for year 6, you should include them in your forecasts. We have sometimes encountered financial managers who assume a project life of (say) 5 years, even when they confidently expect revenues for 10 years or more. When asked the reason, they explain that forecasting beyond 5 years is too hazardous. We sympathize, but you just have to do your best. Do not arbitrarily truncate a project's life.

Expenses in year 1 are $10,000 (cell C14). We assume that the expenses of mining and refining (row 14) also increase in line with inflation at 5 percent a year.

straight-line depreciation
Constant depreciation for each year of the asset's accounting life.

We also assume for now that the company applies **straight-line depreciation** to the mining equipment over 5 years. This means that it deducts one-fifth of the initial $10 million investment from profits. Thus row 15 shows that the annual depreciation deduction is $2 million.

Pretax profit, shown in row 16, equals (revenues – expenses – depreciation). Taxes (row 17) are 35 percent of pretax profit. For example, in year 1,

$$\text{Tax} = .35 \times 3{,}000 = 1{,}050, \text{ or } \$1{,}050{,}000$$

Profit after tax (row 18) equals pretax profit less taxes.

The last row of panel C presents cash flows from operations. We use the adjusted accounting profit approach, calculating cash flow as the sum of after-tax profits plus depreciation. Therefore, row 19 is the sum of rows 18 and 15.

Total Project Cash Flow   Total cash flow is the sum of cash flows from each of the three sources: net investments in fixed assets and working capital, and cash flow from operations. Therefore, total cash flow in row 22 is just the sum of rows 5, 10, and 19.

Calculating the NPV of Blooper's Project

You have now derived (in row 22) the forecast cash flows from Blooper's magnoosium mine. Suppose that investors expect a return of 12 percent from investments in the capital market with the same risk as the magnoosium project. This is the opportunity cost of the shareholders' money that Blooper is proposing to invest in the project. Therefore, to calculate NPV, you need to discount the cash flows at 12 percent.

Rows 23 and 24 set out the calculations. Remember that to calculate the present value of a cash flow in year t you can divide the cash flow by $(1 + r)^t$ or you can multiply by a discount factor that is equal to $1/(1 + r)^t$. Row 23 presents the discount factors for each year, and row 24 is the present value of each cash flow, equal to the cash flow in row 22 times the discount factor. When all cash flows are discounted and added up, the magnoosium project is seen to offer a positive net present value of $4,223 thousand (cell B25), or about $4.2 million.

Now here is a small point that often causes confusion: To calculate the present value of the first year's cash flow, we divide by $(1 + r) = 1.12$. Strictly speaking, this makes sense only if all the sales and all the costs occur exactly 365 days, zero hours, and zero minutes from now. Of course the year's sales don't all take place on the stroke of midnight on December 31. However, when making capital budgeting decisions, companies are usually happy to pretend that all cash flows occur at 1-year intervals. They pretend this for one reason only—simplicity. When sales forecasts are sometimes little more than intelligent guesses, it may be pointless to inquire how the sales are likely to be spread out during the year.[6]

Further Notes and Wrinkles Arising from Blooper's Project

Before we leave Blooper and its magnoosium project, we should cover a few extra wrinkles.

---

[6] Financial managers sometimes assume cash flows arrive in the middle of the calendar year, that is, at the end of June. This midyear convention is roughly equivalent to assuming cash flows are distributed evenly throughout the year. This is a bad assumption for some industries. In retailing, for example, most of the cash flow comes late in the year, as the holiday season approaches.

Forecasting Working Capital   Table 8–1 shows that Blooper expects its magnoo-sium mine to produce revenues of $15,000 in year 1 and $15,750 in year 2. But Blooper will not actually receive these amounts in years 1 and 2, because some of its customers will not pay up immediately. We have assumed that, on average, customers pay with a 2-month lag, so that 2/12 of each year's sales are not paid for until the following year. These unpaid bills show up as accounts receivable. For example, in year 1 Blooper will have accounts receivable of (2/12) × 15,000 = $2,500.[7]

Consider now the mine's expenses. These are forecast at $10,000 in year 1 and $10,500 in year 2. But not all of this cash will go out of the door in these 2 years, for Blooper must produce the magnoosium before selling it. Each year, Blooper mines magnoosium ore, but some of this ore is not sold until the following year. The ore is put into inventory, and the accountant does not deduct the cost of its production until it is taken out of inventory and sold. We assume that 15 percent of each year's ex-penses correspond to an investment in inventory that took place in the previous year. Thus the investment in inventory is forecast at .15 × 10,000 = $1,500 in year 0 and at .15 × $10,500 = $1,575 in year 1.

We can now see how Blooper arrives at its forecast of working capital:

	0	1	2	3	4	5	6
1. Receivables (2/12 × revenues)	$ 0	$2,500	$2,625	$2,756	$2,894	$3,039	0
2. Inventories (.15 × following year's expenses)	1,500	1,575	1,654	1,736	1,823	0	0
3. Working capital (1 + 2)	1,500	4,075	4,279	4,493	4,717	3,039	0

Note: Columns may not sum due to rounding.

Notice that working capital builds up in years 1 to 4, as sales of magnoosium in-crease, and then fall. Year 5 is the last year of sales, so Blooper can reduce its inven-tories to zero in that year. In year 6 the company expects to collect any unpaid bills from year 5 and so in that year receivables also fall to zero. This decline in working capital increases cash flow. For example, in year 6 cash flow is increased as the $3,039 of outstanding bills are paid.

The construction of the Blooper spreadsheet is discussed further in the nearby box. Once the spreadsheet is set up, it is easy to try out different assumptions for working capital. For example, you can adjust the level of receivables and inventories by chang-ing the values in cells B30 and B31.

A Further Note on Depreciation   We warned you earlier not to assume that all cash flows are likely to increase with inflation. The depreciation tax shield is a case in point, because the Internal Revenue Service lets companies depreciate only the amount of the original investment. For example, if you go back to the IRS to explain that inflation mushroomed since you made the investment and you should be allowed to depreciate more, the IRS won't listen. The *nominal* amount of depreciation is fixed, and therefore the higher the rate of inflation, the lower the *real* value of the deprecia-tion that you can claim.

We assumed in our calculations that Blooper could depreciate its investment in mining equipment by $2 million a year. That produced an annual tax shield of $2 mil-lion × .35 = $.70 million per year for 5 years. These tax shields increase cash flows from operations and therefore increase present value. So if Blooper could get those tax shields sooner, they would be worth more, right? Fortunately for corporations, tax law allows them to do just that. It allows *accelerated depreciation.*

[7] For convenience, we assume that, although Blooper's customers pay with a lag, Blooper pays all its bills on the nail. If it didn't, these unpaid bills would be recorded as accounts payable. Working capital would be reduced by the amount of the accounts payable.

TABLE 8–2 Tax depreciation allowed under the modified accelerated cost recovery system (figures in percent of depreciable investment)

Year(s)	Recovery Period Class					
	3 Year	5 Year	7 Year	10 Year	15 Year	20 Year
1	33.33	20.00	14.29	10.00	5.00	3.75
2	44.45	32.00	24.49	18.00	9.50	7.22
3	14.81	19.20	17.49	14.40	8.55	6.68
4	7.41	11.52	12.49	11.52	7.70	6.18
5		11.52	8.93	9.22	6.93	5.71
6		5.76	8.92	7.37	6.23	5.28
7			8.93	6.55	5.90	4.89
8			4.45	6.55	5.90	4.52
9				6.56	5.90	4.46
10				6.55	5.90	4.46
11				3.29	5.90	4.46
12					5.90	4.46
13					5.91	4.46
14					5.90	4.46
15					5.91	4.46
16					2.99	4.46
17–20						4.46
21						2.23

Notes:
1. Tax depreciation is lower in the first year because assets are assumed to be in service for 6 months.
2. Real property is depreciated straight-line over 27.5 years for residential property and 39 years for nonresidential property.

modified accelerated cost recovery system (MACRS) Depreciation method that allows higher tax deductions in early years and lower deductions later.

The rate at which firms are permitted to depreciate equipment is known as the **modified accelerated cost recovery system,** or **MACRS.** MACRS places assets into one of six classes, each of which has an assumed life. Table 8–2 shows the rate of depreciation that the company can use for each of these classes. Most industrial equipment falls into the 5- and 7-year classes. To keep life simple, we will assume that all of Blooper's mining equipment goes into 5-year assets. Thus Blooper can depreciate 20 percent of its $10 million investment in year 1. In the second year it can deduct depreciation of .32 × 10 = $3.2 million, and so on.[8]

How does MACRS depreciation affect the value of the depreciation tax shield for the magnoosium project? Table 8–3 gives the answer. Notice that MACRS does not affect the total amount of depreciation that is claimed. This remains at $10 million just as before. But MACRS allows companies to get the depreciation deduction earlier, which increases the present value of the depreciation tax shield from $2,523,000 to $2,583,000, an increase of $60,000. Before we recognized MACRS depreciation, we calculated project NPV as $4,223,000. When we recognize MACRS, we should increase that figure by $60,000.

All large corporations in the United States keep two sets of books, one for stockholders and one for the Internal Revenue Service. It is common to use straight-line depreciation on the stockholder books and MACRS depreciation on the tax books. Only the tax books are relevant in capital budgeting.

---

[8] You might wonder why the 5-year asset class provides a depreciation deduction in years 1 through 6. This is because the tax authorities assume that the assets are in service for only 6 months of the first year and 6 months of the last year. The total project life is 5 years, but that 5-year life spans parts of 6 calendar years. This assumption also explains why the depreciation is lower in the first year than it is in the second.

MidAmerican's Wind Power Project

In 2005, MidAmerican Energy will bring into operation in Iowa one of the largest wind farms in the world. The wind farm will cost $386 million, contain 257 wind turbines, and have a capacity of 360.5 megawatts (mW). Wind speeds fluctuate, and most wind farms are expected to operate at an average of only 35 percent of their rated capacity. In this case, at an electricity price of $55 per megawatt-hour (mWh), the project will produce revenues in its first year of $60.8 million (i.e., .35 × 8,760 hours × 360.5 mW × $55 per mWh). A reasonable estimate of maintenance and other costs is about $18.9 million in the first year of operation. Thereafter, revenues and costs should increase with inflation by around 3 percent a year. Conventional power stations can be depreciated using 20-year MACRS, and their profits are taxed at 35 percent. A project such as this one might last 25 years and entail a cost of capital of 12 percent.

Wind power is more costly than conventional fossil-fueled power, but to encourage the development of renewable energy sources, the government provides several tax breaks to companies constructing wind farms. How large do these tax breaks need to be to make the wind farm viable for MidAmerican? We estimate that in the absence of any tax breaks the project would have a net present value of –$68 million. So any tax subsidy must have a value of at least $68 million to entice a private firm such as MidAmerican to undertake the project.

You can find our calculations at the Online Learning Center at **www.mhhe.com/bmm5e**. Once you're there, you might consider the following questions. Suppose the government believes that the national security and environmental benefits of being able to generate clean energy domestically is worth 25 percent of the value of the electricity produced. Does the subsidy make economic sense for the government? Some wind farm operators assume a capacity factor of 30 percent rather than 35 percent. If MidAmerican's plant achieves only this level of operation, how much larger would the tax subsidy need to be? If no tax breaks were available for wind farms, how high would electricity prices need to be before this plant would be viable (i.e., have a positive NPV)?

Self-Test 8.5

Suppose that Blooper's mining equipment could be put in the 3-year recovery period class. What is the present value of the depreciation tax shield? Confirm that the change in the value of the depreciation tax shield equals the increase in project NPV from question 1 of the Spreadsheet Solutions box.

More on Salvage Value When you sell equipment, you must pay taxes on the difference between the sales price and the book value of the asset. The book value in turn equals the initial cost minus cumulative charges for depreciation. It is common when figuring tax depreciation to assume a salvage value of zero at the end of the asset's depreciable life.

For reports to shareholders, however, positive expected salvage values are often recognized. For example, Blooper's financial statements might assume that its $10 million investment in mining equipment would be worth $2 million in year 6. In this case, the depreciation reported to shareholders would be based on the difference between the investment and the salvage value, that is, $8 million. Straight-line depreciation then would be $1.6 million annually.

TABLE 8-3 The switch from straight-line to 5-year MACRS depreciation increases the value of Blooper's depreciation tax shield from $2,523,000 to $2,583,000 (figures in thousands of dollars)

	Straight-Line Depreciation			MACRS Depreciation		
Year	Depreciation	Tax Shield	PV Tax Shield at 12%	Depreciation	Tax Shield	PV Tax Shield at 12%
1	2,000	700	625	2,000	700	625
2	2,000	700	558	3,200	1,120	893
3	2,000	700	498	1,920	672	478
4	2,000	700	445	1,152	403	256
5	2,000	700	397	1,152	403	229
6	0	0	0	576	202	102
Totals	10,000	3,500	2,523	10,000	3,500	2,583

Note: Column sums subject to rounding error.

The Blooper Spreadsheet Model

Discounted cash-flow analysis of proposed capital investments is clearly tailor-made for spreadsheet analysis. The formula view of the Excel spreadsheet used in the Blooper example appears below.

Notice that most of the entries in the spreadsheet are formulas rather than specific numbers. Once the relatively few input values are entered, the spreadsheet does most of the work by calculating the formulas. We enter only the initial investment (cell B3), the after-tax salvage value (cell H4), the initial levels of revenues and expenses (cells C13 and C14), and the parameters in panel E (cells B28 to B31).

Revenues and expenses in each year equal the value in the previous year times (1 + inflation rate), which is given in cell B28 as .05. For example, cell D13 equals C13 × 1.05. To make the spreadsheet easier to read, we have defined names for a few cells, such as B28 (named *Inflation*) and B29 (named *Disc_rate*). These names can be assigned using the Insert command in Excel and thereafter can be used to refer to specific cells.

Row 8 sets out the level of working capital, which is the sum of accounts receivable and inventories. To capture the fact that inventories tend to rise with production, we set inventories equal to .15 times expenses recognized in the following year when the product is sold. Similarly, accounts receivable rise with sales, so we assume that they will be 2/12 times the current year's revenues (in other words, that Blooper's customers pay, on average, 2 months after purchasing the product). Each entry in row 8 is the sum of these two quantities.

We calculate the discount factor in row 23 using the discount rate of 12 percent, compute present values of each cash flow in row 24, and add the present value of each cash flow to find project NPV in cell B25.

Once the spreadsheet is up and running, it is easy to do "what if" analyses. Here are a few questions to try your hand.

Formula view

Please visit us at www.mhhe.com/bmm5e or refer to your Student CD

	A	B	C	D	E	F	G	H
1	Year:	0	1	2	3	4	5	6
2	A. Fixed assets							
3	Investment in fixed assets	10000						
4	Sales of fixed assets							=2000*(1-Tax_rate)
5	CF, invest. in fixed assets	=-B3+B4	=-C3+C4	=-D3+D4	=-E3+E4	=-F3+F4	=-G3+G4	=-H3+H4
6								
7	B. Working capital							
8	Working capital	=$B$31*C14+$B$30*B13	=$B$31*D14+$B$30*C13	=$B$31*E14+$B$30*D13	=$B$31*F14+$B$30*E13	=$B$31*G14+$B$30*F13	=$B$31*H14+$B$30*G13	=$B$31*I14+$B$30*H13
9	*Change* in working capital	=B8	=C8-B8	=D8-C8	=E8-D8	=F8-E8	=G8-F8	=H8-G8
10	CF, invest. in wk capital	=-B9	=-C9	=-D9	=-E9	=-F9	=-G9	=-H9
11								
12	C. Operations							
13	Revenues		15000	=C13*(1+Inflation)	=D13*(1+Inflation)	=E13*(1+Inflation)	=F13*(1+Inflation)	
14	Expenses		10000	=C14*(1+Inflation)	=D14*(1+Inflation)	=E14*(1+Inflation)	=F14*(1+Inflation)	
15	Depreciation		=10000/5	=10000/5	=10000/5	=10000/5	=10000/5	
16	Pretax profit		=C13-C14-C15	=D13-D14-D15	=E13-E14-E15	=F13-F14-F15	=G13-G14-G15	
17	Tax		=C16*Tax_rate	=D16*Tax_rate	=E16*Tax_rate	=F16*Tax_rate	=G16*Tax_rate	
18	Profit after tax		=C16-C17	=D16-D17	=E16-E17	=F16-F17	=G16-G17	
19	Cash flow from operations		=C15+C18	=D15+D18	=E15+E18	=F15+F18	=G15+G18	
20								
21	D. Project valuation							
22	Total project cash flow	=B5+B10+B19	=C5+C10+C19	=D5+D10+D19	=E5+E10+E19	=F5+F10+F19	=G5+G10+G19	=H5+H10+H19
23	Discount factor	=1/(1+Disc_rate)^B1	=1/(1+Disc_rate)^C1	=1/(1+Disc_rate)^D1	=1/(1+Disc_rate)^E1	=1/(1+Disc_rate)^F1	=1/(1+Disc_rate)^G1	=1/(1+Disc_rate)^H1
24	PV of cash flow	=B22*B23	=C22*C23	=D22*D23	=E22*E23	=F22*F23	=G22*G23	=H22*H23
25	Net present value	=SUM(B24:H24)						
26								
27	E. Other inputs							
28	Inflation rate	0.05						
29	Discount rate	0.12						
30	Acct receiv. as % of sales	=2/12						
31	Inven. as % of expenses	0.15						
32								

Questions

1. What happens to cash flow in each year and the NPV of the project if the firm uses MACRS depreciation assuming a 3-year recovery period? Assume that year 1 is the first year that depreciation is taken.

2. Suppose the firm can economize on working capital by managing inventories more efficiently. If the firm can reduce inventories from 15 to 10 percent of next year's cost of goods sold, what will be the effect on project NPV?

3. What happens to NPV if the inflation rate falls from 5 percent to zero and the discount rate falls from 12 to 7 percent? Given that the real discount rate is almost unchanged, why does project NPV increase? [To be consistent, you should assume that nominal salvage value will be lower in a zero-inflation environment. If you set (before-tax) salvage value to $1.492 million, you will maintain its real value unchanged.]

Solutions (as well as the full spreadsheet) are available at the Online Learning Center for the text: **www.mhhe.com/bmm5e.**

SUMMARY

How should the cash flows of a proposed new project be calculated?

Here is a checklist to bear in mind when forecasting a project's cash flows:

- Discount cash flows, not profits.
- Estimate the project's *incremental* cash flows—that is, the difference between the cash flows with the project and those without the project.
- Include all indirect effects of the project, such as its impact on the sales of the firm's other products.
- Forget sunk costs.
- Include **opportunity costs,** such as the value of land that you could otherwise sell.
- Beware of allocated overhead charges for heat, light, and so on. These may not reflect the incremental effects of the project on these costs.
- Remember the investment in working capital. As sales increase, the firm may need to make additional investments in working capital, and as the project finally comes to an end, it will recover these investments.
- Treat inflation consistently. If cash flows are forecast in nominal terms (including the effects of future inflation), use a nominal discount rate. Discount real cash flows at a real rate.
- Do not include debt interest or the cost of repaying a loan. When calculating NPV, assume that the project is financed entirely by the shareholders and that they receive all the cash flows. This separates the investment decision from the financing decision.

How can the cash flows of a project be computed from standard financial statements?

Project cash flow does not equal profit. You must allow for changes in working capital as well as noncash expenses such as depreciation. Also, if you use a nominal cost of capital, consistency requires that you forecast *nominal* cash flows—that is, cash flows that recognize the effect of inflation.

How is the company's tax bill affected by depreciation, and how does this affect project value?

Depreciation is not a cash flow. However, because depreciation reduces taxable income, it reduces taxes. This tax reduction is called the **depreciation tax shield. Modified accelerated cost recovery system (MACRS)** depreciation schedules allow more of the depreciation allowance to be taken in early years than is possible under **straight-line depreciation.** This increases the present value of the tax shield.

How do changes in working capital affect project cash flows?

Increases in **net working capital** such as accounts receivable or inventory are investments and therefore use cash—that is, they reduce the net cash flow provided by the project in that period. When working capital is run down, cash is freed up, so cash flow increases.

QUIZ ⠐⠍™

1. **Cash Flows.** A new project will generate sales of $74 million, costs of $42 million, and depreciation expense of $10 million in the coming year. The firm's tax rate is 35 percent. Calculate cash flow for the year by using all three methods discussed in the chapter, and confirm that they are equal.

2. **Cash Flows.** Canyon Tours showed the following components of working capital last year:

	Beginning	End of Year
Accounts receivable	$24,000	$23,000
Inventory	12,000	12,500
Accounts payable	14,500	16,500

   a. What was the change in net working capital during the year?
   b. If sales were $36,000 and costs were $24,000, what was cash flow for the year? Ignore taxes.

3. **Cash Flows.** Tubby Toys estimates that its new line of rubber ducks will generate sales of $7 million, operating costs of $4 million, and a depreciation expense of $1 million. If the tax rate is 35 percent, what is the firm's operating cash flow? Show that you get the same answer using all three methods to calculate operating cash flow.

4. **Cash Flows.** We've emphasized that the firm should pay attention only to cash flows when assessing the net present value of proposed projects. Depreciation is a noncash expense. Why then does it matter whether we assume straight-line or MACRS depreciation when we assess project NPV?

5. **Proper Cash Flows.** Quick Computing currently sells 10 million computer chips each year at a price of $20 per chip. It is about to introduce a new chip, and it forecasts annual sales of 12 million of these improved chips at a price of $25 each. However, demand for the old chip will decrease, and sales of the old chip are expected to fall to 3 million per year. The old chip costs $6 each to manufacture, and the new ones will cost $8 each. What is the proper cash flow to use to evaluate the present value of the introduction of the new chip?

6. **Calculating Net Income.** The owner of a bicycle repair shop forecasts revenues of $160,000 a year. Variable costs will be $50,000, and rental costs for the shop are $30,000 a year. Depreciation on the repair tools will be $10,000. Prepare an income statement for the shop based on these estimates. The tax rate is 35 percent.

7. **Cash Flows.** Calculate the operating cash flow for the repair shop in the previous problem using all three methods suggested in the chapter: (a) net income plus depreciation; (b) cash inflow/cash outflow analysis; and (c) the depreciation tax shield approach. Confirm that all three approaches result in the same value for cash flow.

8. **Cash Flows and Working Capital.** A house painting business had revenues of $16,000 and expenses of $9,000. There were no depreciation expenses. However, the business reported the following changes in working capital:

	Beginning	End
Accounts receivable	$1,200	$4,500
Accounts payable	700	300

   Calculate net cash flow for the business for this period.

9. **Incremental Cash Flows.** A corporation donates a valuable painting from its private collection to an art museum. Which of the following are incremental cash flows associated with the donation?

   a. The price the firm paid for the painting.
   b. The current market value of the painting.
   c. The deduction from income that it declares for its charitable gift.
   d. The reduction in taxes due to its declared tax deduction.

Please visit us at www.mhhe.com/bmm5e or refer to your Student CD

10. **Operating Cash Flows.** Laurel's Lawn Care, Ltd., has a new mower line that can generate revenues of $120,000 per year. Direct production costs are $40,000, and the fixed costs of maintaining the lawn mower factory are $15,000 a year. The factory originally cost $1 million and is being depreciated for tax purposes over 25 years using straight-line depreciation. Calculate the operating cash flows of the project if the firm's tax bracket is 35 percent.

PRACTICE PROBLEMS

11. **Operating Cash Flows.** Talia's Tutus bought a new sewing machine for $40,000 that will be depreciated using the MACRS depreciation schedule for a 5-year recovery period.
    a. Find the depreciation charge each year.
    b. If the sewing machine is sold after 3 years for $22,000, what will be the after-tax proceeds on the sale if the firm's tax bracket is 35 percent?

12. **Proper Cash Flows.** Conference Services Inc. has leased a large office building for $4 million per year. The building is larger than the company needs; two of the building's eight stories are almost empty. A manager wants to expand one of her projects, but this will require using one of the empty floors. In calculating the net present value of the proposed expansion, senior management allocates one-eighth of $4 million of building rental costs (i.e., $.5 million) to the project expansion, reasoning that the project will use one-eighth of the building's capacity.
    a. Is this a reasonable procedure for purposes of calculating NPV?
    b. Can you suggest a better way to assess a cost of the office space used by the project?

13. **Cash Flows and Working Capital.** A firm had after-tax income last year of $1.2 million. Its depreciation expenses were $.4 million, and its total cash flow was $1.2 million. What happened to net working capital during the year?

14. **Cash Flows and Working Capital.** The only capital investment required for a small project is investment in inventory. Profits this year were $10,000, and inventory increased from $4,000 to $5,000. What was the cash flow from the project?

15. **Cash Flows and Working Capital**. A firm's balance sheets for year-end 2006 and 2007 contain the following data. What happened to investment in net working capital during 2007? All items are in millions of dollars.

	Dec. 31, 2006	Dec. 31, 2007
Accounts receivable	32	36
Inventories	25	30
Accounts payable	12	26

16. **Salvage Value.** Quick Computing (from problem 5) installed its previous generation of computer chip manufacturing equipment 3 years ago. Some of that older equipment will become unnecessary when the company goes into production of its new product. The obsolete equipment, which originally cost $40 million, has been depreciated straight-line over an assumed tax life of 5 years, but it can be sold now for $18 million. The firm's tax rate is 35 percent. What is the after-tax cash flow from the sale of the equipment?

17. **Salvage Value.** Your firm purchased machinery with a 7-year MACRS life for $10 million. The project, however, will end after 5 years. If the equipment can be sold for $4.5 million at the completion of the project, and your firm's tax rate is 35 percent, what is the after-tax cash flow from the sale of the machinery?

18. **Depreciation and Project Value.** Bottoms Up Diaper Service is considering the purchase of a new industrial washer. It can purchase the washer for $6,000 and sell its old washer for $2,000. The new washer will last for 6 years and save $1,500 a year in expenses. The opportunity cost of capital is 16 percent, and the firm's tax rate is 40 percent.
    a. If the firm uses straight-line depreciation to an assumed salvage value of zero over a 6-year life, what are the cash flows of the project in years 0 to 6? The new washer will in fact have zero salvage value after 6 years, and the old washer is fully depreciated.
    b. What is project NPV?
    c. What is NPV if the firm uses MACRS depreciation with a 5-year tax life?

19. **Equivalent Annual Cost.** What is the equivalent annual cost of the washer in the previous problem if the firm uses straight-line depreciation?

20. **Cash Flows and NPV.** Johnny's Lunches is considering purchasing a new, energy-efficient grill. The grill will cost $40,000 and will be depreciated according to the 3-year MACRS

schedule. It will be sold for scrap metal after 3 years for $10,000. The grill will have no effect on revenues but will save Johnny's $20,000 in energy expenses. The tax rate is 35 percent.

a. What are the operating cash flows in years 1 to 3?
b. What are total cash flows in years 1 to 3?
c. If the discount rate is 12 percent, should the grill be purchased?

21. **Project Evaluation.** Revenues generated by a new fad product are forecast as follows:

Year	Revenues
1	$40,000
2	30,000
3	20,000
4	10,000
Thereafter	0

Expenses are expected to be 40 percent of revenues, and working capital required in each year is expected to be 20 percent of revenues in the following year. The product requires an immediate investment of $45,000 in plant and equipment.

a. What is the initial investment in the product? Remember working capital.
b. If the plant and equipment are depreciated over 4 years to a salvage value of zero using straight-line depreciation, and the firm's tax rate is 40 percent, what are the project cash flows in each year?
c. If the opportunity cost of capital is 12 percent, what is project NPV?
d. What is project IRR?

22. **Buy versus Lease.** You can buy a car for $25,000 and sell it in 5 years for $5,000. Or you can lease the car for 5 years for $5,000 a year. The discount rate is 12 percent per year.

a. Which option do you prefer?
b. What is the maximum amount you should be willing to pay to lease rather than buy the car?

23. **Project Evaluation.** Kinky Copies may buy a high-volume copier. The machine costs $100,000 and will be depreciated straight-line over 5 years to a salvage value of $20,000. Kinky anticipates that the machine actually can be sold in 5 years for $30,000. The machine will save $20,000 a year in labor costs but will require an increase in working capital, mainly paper supplies, of $10,000. The firm's marginal tax rate is 35 percent, and the discount rate is 8 percent. Should Kinky buy the machine?

24. **Project Evaluation.** Blooper Industries must replace its magnoosium purification system. Quick & Dirty Systems sells a relatively cheap purification system for $10 million. The system will last 5 years. Do-It-Right sells a sturdier but more expensive system for $12 million; it will last for 8 years. Both systems entail $1 million in operating costs; both will be depreciated straight-line to a final value of zero over their useful lives; neither will have any salvage value at the end of its life. The firm's tax rate is 35 percent, and the discount rate is 12 percent. Which system should Blooper install? *Hint:* Check the discussion of equivalent annual annuities in the previous chapter.

25. **Project Evaluation.** The following table presents sales forecasts for Golden Gelt Giftware. The unit price is $40. The unit cost of the giftware is $25.

Year	Unit Sales
1	22,000
2	30,000
3	14,000
4	5,000
Thereafter	0

It is expected that net working capital will amount to 20 percent of sales in the following year. For example, the store will need an initial (year-0) investment in working capital of $.20 \times 22,000 \times \$40 = \$176,000$. Plant and equipment necessary to establish the Giftware business will require an additional investment of $200,000. This investment will be depreciated using MACRS and a 3-year life. After 4 years, the equipment will have an economic and book value of zero. The firm's tax rate is 35 percent. What is the net present value of the project? The discount rate is 20 percent.

26. **Project Evaluation.** Ilana Industries, Inc., needs a new lathe. It can buy a new high-speed lathe for $1 million. The lathe will cost $35,000 to run, will save the firm $125,000 in labor costs, and will be useful for 10 years. Suppose that for tax purposes, the lathe will be depreciated on a straight-line basis over its 10-year life to a salvage value of $100,000. The actual market value of the lathe at that time also will be $100,000. The discount rate is 8 percent, and the corporate tax rate is 35 percent. What is the NPV of buying the new lathe?

CHALLENGE PROBLEMS

27. **Project Evaluation.** The efficiency gains resulting from a just-in-time inventory management system will allow a firm to reduce its level of inventories permanently by $250,000. What is the most the firm should be willing to pay for installing the system?

28. **Project Evaluation.** Better Mousetraps has developed a new trap. It can go into production for an initial investment in equipment of $6 million. The equipment will be depreciated straight-line over 5 years to a value of zero, but in fact it can be sold after 5 years for $500,000. The firm believes that working capital at each date must be maintained at a level of 10 percent of next year's forecast sales. The firm estimates production costs equal to $1.50 per trap and believes that the traps can be sold for $4 each. Sales forecasts are given in the following table. The project will come to an end in 5 years, when the trap becomes technologically obsolete. The firm's tax bracket is 35 percent, and the required rate of return on the project is 12 percent. What is project NPV?

Year:	0	1	2	3	4	5	Thereafter
Sales (millions of traps)	0	.5	.6	1.0	1.0	.6	0

29. **Working Capital Management.** Return to the previous problem. Suppose the firm can cut its requirements for working capital in half by using better inventory control systems. By how much will this increase project NPV?

30. **Project Evaluation.** PC Shopping Network may upgrade its modem pool. It last upgraded 2 years ago, when it spent $115 million on equipment with an assumed life of 5 years and an assumed salvage value of $15 million for tax purposes. The firm uses straight-line depreciation. The old equipment can be sold today for $80 million. A new modem pool can be installed today for $150 million. This will have a 3-year life and will be depreciated to zero using straight-line depreciation. The new equipment will enable the firm to increase sales by $25 million per year and decrease operating costs by $10 million per year. At the end of 3 years, the new equipment will be worthless. Assume the firm's tax rate is 35 percent and the discount rate for projects of this sort is 10 percent.
    a. What is the net cash flow at time 0 if the old equipment is replaced?
    b. What are the incremental cash flows in years 1, 2, and 3?
    c. What are the NPV and IRR of the replacement project?

1. Go to Market Insight (www.mhhe.com/edumarketinsight). Find the net capital expenditures, capital expenditures less sales of plant and equipment, and total sales for General Motors (GM) and Microsoft (MSFT). What were the ratios of net capital expenditure to sales for the last 3 years for both companies? What were the sales and net capital expenditures relative to total

assets? What might explain the variation in these ratios for these two large corporations? Did the company make an investment or disinvestment in working capital in each of the 3 years?

SOLUTIONS TO SELF-TEST QUESTIONS

8.1   Remember, discount cash flows, not profits. Each tewgit machine costs $250,000 right away. Recognize that outlay, but forget accounting depreciation. Cash flows per machine are:

Year:	0	1	2	3	4	5
Investment (outflow)	−250,000					
Sales		250,000	300,000	300,000	250,000	250,000
Operating expenses		−200,000	−200,000	−200,000	−200,000	−200,000
Cash flow	−250,000	+ 50,000	+100,000	+100,000	+ 50,000	+ 50,000

Each machine is forecast to generate $50,000 of cash flow in years 4 and 5. Thus it makes sense to keep operating for 5 years.

8.2   a,b. The site and buildings could have been sold or put to another use. Their values are opportunity costs, which should be treated as incremental cash outflows.
      c. Demolition costs are incremental cash outflows.
      d. The cost of the access road is sunk and not incremental.
      e. Lost cash flows from other projects are incremental cash outflows.
      f. Depreciation is not a cash expense and should not be included, except as it affects taxes. (Taxes are discussed later in this chapter.)

8.3   Actual health costs will be increasing at about 7 percent a year.

Year:	1	2	3	4
Cost per worker	$2,400	$2,568	$2,748	$2,940

The present value at 10 percent is $9,214 if the first payment is made immediately. If it is delayed a year, present value falls to $8,377.

8.4   The tax rate is $T = 35$ percent. Taxes paid will be

$$T \times (\text{revenue} - \text{expenses} - \text{depreciation}) = .35 \times (600 - 300 - 200) = \$35$$

Operating cash flow can be calculated as follows.
    a. Revenue − expenses − taxes = 600 − 300 − 35 = $265
    b. Net profit + depreciation = (600 − 300 − 200 − 35) + 200 = 65 + 200 = 265
    c. (Revenues − cash expenses) × (1 − tax rate) + (depreciation × tax rate)
       = (600 − 300) × (1 − .35) + (200 × .35) = 265

8.5

Year	MACRS 3-Year Depreciation	Tax Shield	PV Tax Shield at 12%
1	3,333	1,167	1,042
2	4,445	1,556	1,240
3	1,481	518	369
4	741	259	165
Totals	10,000	3,500	2,816

The present value increases to 2,816, or $2,816,000.

MINICASE

Jack Tar, CFO of Sheetbend & Halyard, Inc., opened the company confidential envelope. It contained a draft of a competitive bid for a contract to supply duffel canvas to the U.S. Navy. The cover memo from Sheetbend's CEO asked Mr. Tar to review the bid before it was submitted.

The bid and its supporting documents had been prepared by Sheetbend's sales staff. It called for Sheetbend to supply 100,000 yards of duffel canvas per year for 5 years. The proposed selling price was fixed at $30 per yard.

Mr. Tar was not usually involved in sales, but this bid was unusual in at least two respects. First, if accepted by the navy, it would commit Sheetbend to a fixed-price, long-term contract. Second, producing the duffel canvas would require an investment of $1.5 million to purchase machinery and to refurbish Sheetbend's plant in Pleasantboro, Maine.

Mr. Tar set to work and by the end of the week had collected the following facts and assumptions:

- The plant in Pleasantboro had been built in the early 1900s and is now idle. The plant was fully depreciated on Sheetbend's books, except for the purchase cost of the land (in 1947) of $10,000.
- Now that the land was valuable shorefront property, Mr. Tar thought the land and the idle plant could be sold, immediately or in the near future, for $600,000.
- Refurbishing the plant would cost $500,000. This investment would be depreciated for tax purposes on the 10-year MACRS schedule.

- The new machinery would cost $1 million. This investment could be depreciated on the 5-year MACRS schedule.
- The refurbished plant and new machinery would last for many years. However, the remaining market for duffel canvas was small, and it was not clear that additional orders could be obtained once the navy contract was finished. The machinery was custom-built and could be used only for duffel canvas. Its second-hand value at the end of 5 years was probably zero.
- Table 8–4 shows the sales staff's forecasts of income from the navy contract. Mr. Tar reviewed this forecast and decided that its assumptions were reasonable, except that the forecast used book, not tax, depreciation.
- But the forecast income statement contained no mention of working capital. Mr. Tar thought that working capital would average about 10 percent of sales.

Armed with this information, Mr. Tar constructed a spreadsheet to calculate the NPV of the duffel canvas project, assuming that Sheetbend's bid would be accepted by the navy.

He had just finished debugging the spreadsheet when another confidential envelope arrived from Sheetbend's CEO. It contained a firm offer from a Maine real estate developer to purchase Sheetbend's Pleasantboro land and plant for $1.5 million in cash.

Should Mr. Tar recommend submitting the bid to the navy at the proposed price of $30 per yard? The discount rate for this project is 12 percent.

TABLE 8–4 Forecast income statement for the U. S. Navy duffel canvas project (dollar figures in thousands, except price per yard)

Year:	1	2	3	4	5
1. Yards sold	100.00	100.00	100.00	100.00	100.00
2. Price per yard	30.00	30.00	30.00	30.00	30.00
3. Revenue (1 × 2)	3,000.00	3,000.00	3,000.00	3,000.00	3,000.00
4. Cost of goods sold	2,100.00	2,184.00	2,271.36	2,362.21	2,456.70
5. Operating cash flow (3 – 4)	900.00	816.00	728.64	637.79	543.30
6. Depreciation	250.00	250.00	250.00	250.00	250.00
7. Income (5 – 6)	650.00	566.00	478.64	387.79	293.30
8. Tax at 35%	227.50	198.10	167.52	135.72	102.65
9. Net income (7 – 8)	$422.50	$367.90	$311.12	$252.07	$190.65

Notes:
1. Yards sold and price per yard would be fixed by contract.
2. Cost of goods includes fixed cost of $300,000 per year plus variable costs of $18 per yard. Costs are expected to increase at the inflation rate of 4 percent per year.
3. Depreciation: A $1 million investment in machinery is depreciated straight-line over 5 years ($200,000 per year). The $500,000 cost of refurbishing the Pleasantboro plant is depreciated straight-line over 10 years ($50,000 per year).

Project Analysis

RELATED WEB LINKS

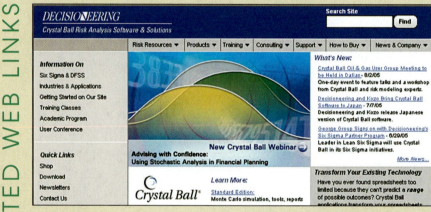

www.jaxworks.com   Illustration of break-even analysis.

www.crystalball.com   Demo of simulation analysis.

www.sternstewart.com

www.valuebasedmanagement.
net/methods_eva.html   Discussions of economic value added, with links to related resources.

When undertaking capital investments, good managers try to keep maximum flexibility.
© Royalty-Free/CORBIS

It helps to use discounted cash-flow techniques to value new projects, but good investment decisions also require good data. Therefore, we start this chapter by thinking about how firms organize the capital budgeting operation to get the kind of information they need. In addition, we look at how they try to ensure that everyone involved works together toward a common goal.

Project evaluation should never be a mechanical exercise in which the financial manager takes a set of cash-flow forecasts and cranks out a net present value. Cash-flow estimates are just that—estimates. Financial managers need to look behind the forecasts to try to understand what makes the project tick and what could go wrong with it. A number of techniques have been developed to help managers identify the key assumptions in their analysis. These techniques involve asking a number of "what-if" questions. What if your market share turns out to be higher or lower than you forecast? What if interest rates rise during the life of the project? In the second part of this chapter we show how managers use the techniques of sensitivity analysis, scenario analysis, and break-even analysis to help answer these what-if questions.

Books about capital budgeting sometimes create the impression that once the manager has made an investment decision, there is nothing to do but sit back and watch the cash flows develop. But since cash flows rarely proceed as anticipated, companies constantly need to modify their operations. If cash flows are better than anticipated, the project may be expanded; if they are worse, it may be scaled back or abandoned altogether. In the third section of this chapter we describe how good managers take account of these options when they analyze a project and why they are willing to pay money today to build in future flexibility.

After studying this chapter you should be able to:

- Appreciate the practical problems of capital budgeting in large corporations.

- Use sensitivity, scenario, and break-even analyses to see how project profitability would be affected by an error in your forecasts and to understand why an overestimate of sales is more serious for projects with high operating leverage.

- Recognize the importance of managerial flexibility in capital budgeting.

9.1 How Firms Organize the Investment Process

In the previous chapter you learned how to evaluate a proposed investment such as the Blooper project. But potential projects and accurate cash-flow forecasts don't fall from the sky. Promising investment opportunities have to be identified, and they must fit in with the firm's strategic goals. To evaluate these opportunities properly, financial managers need unbiased cash-flow forecasts that have not been skewed to "sell" a project to upper management. Large firms in particular need to establish systems that facilitate effective communication across different parts of the organization.

For most sizable firms, investments are evaluated in two separate stages.

Stage 1: The Capital Budget

Once a year, the head office generally asks each of its divisions and plants to provide a list of the investments that they would like to make.[1] These are gathered together into a proposed **capital budget.**

capital budget

List of planned investment projects.

This budget is then reviewed and pruned by senior management and staff specializing in planning and financial analysis. Usually there are negotiations between the firm's senior management and its divisional management, and there may also be special analyses of major outlays or ventures into new areas. Once the budget has been approved, it generally remains the basis for planning over the ensuing year.

Many investment proposals bubble up from the bottom of the organization. But sometimes the ideas are likely to come from higher up. For example, the managers of plants A and B cannot be expected to see the potential benefits of closing their plants and consolidating production at a new plant C. We expect divisional management to propose plant C. Similarly, divisions 1 and 2 may not be eager to give up their own data processing operations to a large central computer. That proposal would come from senior management.

Senior management's concern is to see that the capital budget matches the firm's strategic plans. It needs to ensure that the firm is concentrating its efforts in areas where it has a real competitive advantage. As part of this effort, management must also identify declining businesses that should be sold or allowed to run down.

The firm's capital investment choices should reflect both "bottom-up" and "top-down" processes—capital budgeting and strategic planning, respectively. The two processes should complement each other. Plant and division managers, who do most of the work in bottom-up capital budgeting, may not see the forest for the trees. Strategic planners may have a mistaken view of the forest because they do not look at the trees.

Stage 2: Project Authorizations

The annual budget is important because it allows everybody to exchange ideas before attitudes have hardened and personal commitments have been made. However, the fact that your pet project has been included in the annual budget doesn't mean you have permission to go ahead with it. At a later stage you will need to draw up a detailed proposal describing particulars of the project, engineering analyses, cash-flow forecasts, and present value calculations. If your project is large, this proposal may have to pass a number of hurdles before it is finally approved.

The type of backup information that you need to provide depends on the project category. For example, some firms use a fourfold breakdown:

1. *Outlays required by law or company policy,* for example, for pollution control equipment. These outlays do not need to be justified on financial grounds. The main

---

[1] Large firms may be divided into several divisions. For example, International Paper has divisions that specialize in printing paper, packaging, specialty products, and forest products. Each of these divisions may be responsible for a number of plants.

issue is whether requirements are satisfied at the lowest possible cost. The decision is therefore likely to hinge on engineering analyses of alternative technologies.

2. *Maintenance or cost reduction,* such as machine replacement. Engineering analysis is also important in machine replacement, but new machines have to pay their own way. Here the firm faces the classical capital budgeting problems described in Chapters 7 and 8.

3. *Capacity expansion in existing businesses.* Projects in this category are less straightforward; these decisions may hinge on forecasts of demand, possible shifts in technology, and the reactions of competitors.

4. *Investment for new products.* Projects in this category are most likely to depend on strategic decisions. The first projects in a new area may not have positive NPVs if considered in isolation, but they may give the firm a valuable option to undertake follow-up projects. More about this later in the chapter.

Problems and Some Solutions

Valuing capital investment opportunities is hard enough when you can do the entire job yourself. In most firms, however, capital budgeting is a cooperative effort, and this brings with it some challenges.

Ensuring That Forecasts Are Consistent Inconsistent assumptions often creep into investment proposals. For example, suppose that the manager of the furniture division is bullish (optimistic) on housing starts but the manager of the appliance division is bearish (pessimistic). This inconsistency makes the projects proposed by the furniture division look more attractive than those of the appliance division.

To ensure consistency, many firms begin the capital budgeting process by establishing forecasts of economic indicators, such as inflation and the growth in national income, as well as forecasts of particular items that are important to the firm's business, such as housing starts or the price of raw materials. These forecasts can then be used as the basis for all project analyses.

Eliminating Conflicts of Interest In Chapter 1 we pointed out that while managers want to do a good job, they are also concerned about their own futures. If the interests of managers conflict with those of stockholders, the result is likely to be poor investment decisions. For example, new plant managers naturally want to demonstrate good performance right away. So they might propose quick-payback projects even if NPV is sacrificed. Unfortunately, many firms measure performance and reward managers in ways that encourage such behavior. If the firm always demands quick results, it is unlikely that plant managers will concentrate only on NPV.

Reducing Forecast Bias Someone who is keen to get a project proposal accepted is also likely to look on the bright side when forecasting the project's cash flows. Such overoptimism is a common feature in financial forecasts. For example, think of large public expenditure proposals. How often have you heard of a new missile, dam, or highway that actually cost less than was originally forecast? Think back to the Eurotunnel project introduced in Chapter 7. The final cost of the project was far higher than initial forecasts. It is probably impossible to eliminate bias completely, but if senior management is aware of why bias occurs, it is at least partway to solving the problem.

Project sponsors are likely to overstate their case deliberately only if the head office encourages them to do so. For example, if middle managers believe that success depends on having the largest division rather than the most profitable one, they will propose large expansion projects that they do not believe have the largest possible net present value. Or if divisions must compete for limited resources, they will try to outbid each other for those resources. The fault in such cases is top management's—if lower-level managers are not rewarded on the basis of net present value and contribution to firm value, it should not be surprising that they focus their efforts elsewhere.

Other problems stem from sponsors' eagerness to obtain approval for their favorite projects. As the proposal travels up the organization, alliances are formed. Thus once a division has screened its own plants' proposals, the plants in that division unite in competing against outsiders. The result is that the head office may receive several thousand investment proposals each year, all essentially sales documents presented by united fronts and designed to persuade. The forecasts have been doctored to ensure that NPV appears positive.

Since it is difficult for senior management to evaluate each specific assumption in an investment proposal, capital investment decisions are effectively decentralized whatever the rules say. Some firms accept this; others rely on head office staff to check capital investment proposals.

Sorting the Wheat from the Chaff   Senior managers are continually bombarded with requests for funds for capital expenditures. All these requests are supported with detailed analyses showing that the projects have positive NPVs. How then can managers ensure that only worthwhile projects make the grade? One response of senior managers to this problem of poor information is to impose rigid expenditure limits on individual plants or divisions. These limits force the subunits to choose among projects. The firm ends up using capital rationing not because capital is unobtainable but as a way of decentralizing decisions.[2]

Senior managers might also ask some searching questions about why the project has a positive NPV. After all, if the project is so attractive, why hasn't someone already undertaken it? Will others copy your idea if it is so profitable? Positive NPVs are plausible only if your company has some competitive advantage.

Such an advantage can arise in several ways. You may be smart or lucky enough to be the first to the market with a new or improved product for which customers will pay premium prices. Your competitors eventually will enter the market and squeeze out excess profits, but it may take them several years to do so. Or you may have a proprietary technology or production cost advantage that competitors cannot easily match. You may have a contractual advantage such as the distributorship for a particular region. Or your advantage may be as simple as a good reputation and an established customer list.

Analyzing competitive advantage can also help ferret out projects that incorrectly appear to have a negative NPV. If you are the lowest-cost producer of a profitable product in a growing market, then you should invest to expand along with the market. If your calculations show a negative NPV for such an expansion, then you probably have made a mistake.

9.2 Some "What-If" Questions

"What-if" questions ask what will happen to a project in various circumstances. For example, what will happen if the economy enters a recession? What if a competitor enters the market? What if costs turn out to be higher than anticipated?

You might wonder why one would bother with these sorts of questions. For instance, suppose your project seems to have a positive NPV based on the best available forecasts that have already factored in the chances of both positive and negative surprises. Won't you commit to this project regardless of possible future surprises? If things later don't work out as you had hoped, that is too bad, but would it have changed any of your decisions?

In fact, what-if analysis is crucial to capital budgeting. First recall that cash-flow estimates are just that—estimates. You often have the opportunity to improve on those estimates if you are willing to commit additional resources to the effort. For example, if you wish to improve the precision of an estimate of the demand for a product, you

---
[2] We discussed capital rationing in Chapter 7.

might conduct additional market research. Or if cost uncertainty is a concern, you might commission additional engineering studies to evaluate the feasibility of a novel production process. But how do you know when to keep sharpening your forecasts or where it is best to devote your efforts? What-if analysis can help identify the inputs that are most worth refining before you commit to a project. These will be the ones that have the greatest potential to alter project NPV.

Moreover, managers don't simply turn a key to start a project and then walk away and let the cash flows roll in. There are always surprises, adjustments, and refinements. What-if analysis alerts managers to where the most likely need for adjustments will arise and where to devote the most effort toward contingency planning. In this section, therefore, we examine some of the standard tools managers use when considering important types of what-if questions.

Sensitivity Analysis

sensitivity analysis

Analysis of the effects on project profitability of changes in sales, costs, and so on.

Uncertainty means that more things *can* happen than *will* happen. Therefore, whenever managers are given a cash-flow forecast, they try to determine what else might happen and the implications of those possible events. This is called **sensitivity analysis.**

Put yourself in the well-heeled shoes of the financial manager of the Finefodder supermarket chain. Finefodder is considering opening a new superstore in Gravenstein, and your staff members have prepared the figures shown in Table 9–1. The figures are fairly typical for a new supermarket, except that to keep the example simple we have assumed no inflation. We have also assumed that the entire investment can be depreciated straight-line for tax purposes, we have neglected the working capital requirement, and we have ignored the fact that at the end of the 12 years you could sell off the land and buildings.

fixed costs

Costs that do not depend on the level of output.

Some of the costs of running a supermarket are fixed. For example, regardless of the level of output, you still have to heat and light the store and pay the store manager. These **fixed costs** are forecast to be $2 million per year.

variable costs

Costs that change as the level of output changes.

Other costs vary with the level of sales. In particular, the lower the sales, the less food you need to buy. Also, if sales are lower than forecast, you can operate a lower number of checkouts and reduce the staff needed to restock the shelves. The new superstore's variable costs are estimated at 81.25 percent of sales. Thus **variable costs** = .8125 × $16 million = $13 million (see cells C4 and D4).

The initial investment of $5.4 million will be depreciated on a straight-line basis over the 12-year period, resulting in annual depreciation of $450,000 (cell C6). Profits are taxed at a rate of 40 percent.

Given these inputs, we add after-tax profit plus depreciation to obtain cash flow in periods 1 to 12 of $780,000 (cell C10). As an experienced financial manager, you

TABLE 9–1 Cash-flow forecasts for Finefodder's superstore

Please visit us at www.mhhe.com/bmm5e or refer to your Student CD

	A	B	C	D
1		Year 0	Years 1-12	Formula in column C
2	Initial investment	-5,400,000		
3	1. Sales		16,000,000	16000000
4	2. Variable costs		13,000,000	=$C$12*C3
5	3. Fixed costs		2,000,000	2000000
6	4. Depreciation		450,000	=-B2/12
7	5. Pretax profit		550,000	=C3-C4-C5-C6
8	6. Taxes (at 40%)		220,000	=0.4*C7
9	7. Profit after tax		330,000	=C7-C8
10	8. Cash flow from operations		780,000	=C6+C9
11				
12	Variable costs as % of sales		0.8125	0.8125
13	Discount rate		8%	0.08
14	12-year annuity factor		7.5361	=(1/Rate)*(1 -1 /(1+Rate)^12)
15	Net present value		478,141	=B2+C10*C14

TABLE 9-2 Sensitivity analysis for superstore project

Variable	Range			NPV		
	Pessimistic	Expected	Optimistic	Pessimistic	Expected	Optimistic
Investment	6,200,000	5,400,000	5,000,000	−120,897	+478,141	+777,660
Sales	14,000,000	16,000,000	18,000,000	−1,217,477	+478,141	+2,173,758
Variable cost as percent of sales	83	81.25	80	−787,920	+478,141	+1,382,470
Fixed cost	2,100,000	2,000,000	1,900,000	+25,976	+478,141	+930,306

recognize immediately that these cash flows constitute an annuity, and therefore you calculate the 12-year annuity factor in cell C14. The net present value of the project is calculated in cell C15 as

$$\text{NPV} = -\$5,400,000 + \$780,000 \times 12\text{-year annuity factor} = \$478,141$$

It appears that the project is in fact viable, with a positive net present value. Before you agree to go ahead, however, you want to delve behind these forecasts and identify the key variables that will determine whether the project succeeds or fails.

You seem to have taken account of the important factors that will determine success or failure, but look out for things you may have forgotten. Perhaps there will be delays in obtaining planning permission, or perhaps you will need to undertake costly landscaping. The greatest dangers often lie in these *unknown* unknowns, or "unk-unks," as scientists call them.

Having found no unk-unks (no doubt you'll find them later), you look at how NPV may be affected if you have made a wrong forecast of sales, costs, and so on. To do this, you first obtain optimistic and pessimistic estimates for the underlying variables. These are set out in the left-hand columns of Table 9–2.

Next you see what happens to NPV under the optimistic or pessimistic forecasts for each of these variables. You recalculate project NPV under these various forecasts to determine which variables are most critical to NPV.

EXAMPLE 9.1   ▶   Sensitivity Analysis

The right-hand side of Table 9–2 shows the project's net present value if the variables are set *one at a time* to their optimistic and pessimistic values. For example, suppose fixed costs are $1.9 million rather than the forecast $2 million. To find NPV in this case, we simply substitute $1,900,000 in cell C5 of the spreadsheet, and discover that NPV rises to $930,306, a gain of approximately $452,000. The other entries in the three columns on the right in Table 9–2 similarly show how the NPV of the project changes when each input is changed.

Your project is by no means a sure thing. The principal uncertainties appear to be sales and variable costs. For example, if sales are only $14 million rather than the forecast $16 million (and all other forecasts are unchanged), then the project has an NPV of −$1.217 million. If variable costs are 83 percent of sales (and all other forecasts are unchanged), then the project has an NPV of −$787,920.   ◀

Self-Test 9.1   Recalculate cash flow as in Table 9–1, now assuming that variable costs are 83 percent of sales. Confirm that NPV will be −$787,920.

Value of Information   Now that you know the project could be thrown badly off course by a poor estimate of sales, you might like to see whether it is possible to resolve some of this uncertainty. Perhaps your worry is that the store will fail to attract

sufficient shoppers from neighboring towns. In that case, additional survey data and more careful analysis of travel times may be worthwhile.

On the other hand, there is less value to gathering additional information about fixed costs. Because the project is marginally profitable even under pessimistic assumptions about fixed costs, you are unlikely to be in trouble if you have misestimated that variable.

Limits to Sensitivity Analysis Your analysis of the forecasts for Finefodder's new superstore is known as a sensitivity analysis. Sensitivity analysis expresses cash flows in terms of unknown variables and then calculates the consequences of misestimating those variables. It forces the manager to identify the underlying factors, indicates where additional information would be most useful, and helps to expose confused or inappropriate forecasts.

Of course, there is no law stating which variables you should consider in your sensitivity analysis. For example, you may wish to look separately at labor costs and the costs of the goods sold. Or if you are concerned about a possible change in the corporate tax rate, you may wish to look at the effect of such a change on the project's NPV.

One drawback to sensitivity analysis is that it gives somewhat ambiguous results. For example, what exactly does *optimistic* or *pessimistic* mean? One department may be interpreting the terms in a different way from another. Ten years from now, after hundreds of projects, hindsight may show that one department's pessimistic limit was exceeded twice as often as the other's; but hindsight won't help you now while you're making the investment decision.

Another problem with sensitivity analysis is that the underlying variables are likely to be interrelated. For example, if sales exceed expectations, demand will likely be stronger than you anticipated and your profit margins will be wider. Or, if wages are higher than your forecast, both variable costs and fixed costs are likely to be at the upper end of your range.

Because of these connections, you cannot push *one-at-a-time* sensitivity analysis too far. It is impossible to obtain expected, optimistic, and pessimistic values for total *project* cash flows from the information in Table 9–2. Still, it does give a sense of which variables should be most closely monitored.

Scenario Analysis

scenario analysis
Project analysis given a particular combination of assumptions.

When variables are interrelated, managers often find it helpful to look at how their project would fare under different scenarios. **Scenario analysis** allows them to look at different but *consistent* combinations of variables. Forecasters generally prefer to give an estimate of revenues or costs under a particular scenario rather than to give some absolute optimistic or pessimistic value.

Suppose that you are worried that Stop and Scoff may decide to build a new store in nearby Salome. That would reduce sales in your Gravenstein store by 15 percent, and you might be forced into a price war to keep the remaining business. Prices might be reduced to the point that variable costs equal 82 percent of revenue. Table 9–3 shows that under this scenario of *both* lower sales and smaller margins your new venture would no longer be worthwhile.

simulation analysis
Estimation of the probabilities of different possible outcomes, e.g., from an investment project.

An extension of scenario analysis is called **simulation analysis.** Here, instead of specifying a relatively small number of scenarios, a computer generates several hundred or thousand possible combinations of variables according to probability distributions specified by the analyst. Each combination of variables corresponds to one scenario. Project NPV and other outcomes of interest can be calculated for each combination of variables, and the entire probability distribution of outcomes can be constructed from the simulation results.

Self-Test 9.2   **What is the basic difference between sensitivity analysis and scenario analysis?**

TABLE 9–3 Scenario analysis comparing NPV of superstore with and without competing store

Please visit us at www.mhhe.com/bmm5e or refer to your Student CD

	A	B	C	D
1			Cash flows in years 1-12	
2		Year 0	Base Case	Competing Store Scenario
3	Initial investment	-5,400,000		
4	1. Sales		16,000,000	13,600,000
5	2. Variable costs		13,000,000	11,152,000
6	3. Fixed costs		2,000,000	2,000,000
7	4. Depreciation		450,000	450,000
8	5. Pretax profit		550,000	-2,000
9	6. Taxes (at 40%)		220,000	-800
10	7. Profit after tax		330,000	-1,200
11	8. Cash flow from operations		780,000	448,800
12				
13	Variable costs as % of sales		0.8125	0.8200
14	Discount rate		8%	8%
15	12-year annuity factor		7.5361	7.5361
16	Net present value		478,141	-2,017,808
17				
18	*Assumptions:* Competing store causes (1) a 15 percent decline in sales and (2) variable costs			
19	to increase to 82 percent of sales.			

9.3 Break-Even Analysis

When you undertake a sensitivity analysis of a project or when you look at alternative scenarios, you are asking how serious it would be if we have misestimated sales or costs. Managers sometimes prefer to rephrase this question and ask how far off the estimates could be before the project begins to lose money. This exercise is known as **break-even analysis.**

break-even analysis
Analysis of the level of sales at which the project breaks even.

For many projects, the make-or-break variable is sales volume. Therefore, managers most often focus on the break-even level of sales. However, you might also look at other variables, for example, at how high costs could be before the project goes into the red.

As it turns out, "losing money" can be defined in more than one way. Most often, the break-even condition is defined in terms of accounting profits. More properly, however, it should be defined in terms of net present value. We will start with accounting break-even, show that it can lead you astray, and then show how NPV break-even can be used as an alternative.

Accounting Break-Even Analysis

The *accounting break-even* point is the level of sales at which profits are zero or, equivalently, at which total revenues equal total costs. As we have seen, some costs are fixed regardless of the level of output. Other costs vary with the level of output.

When you first analyzed the superstore project, you came up with the following estimates:

Sales	$16 million
Variable costs	13 million
Fixed costs	2 million
Depreciation	0.45 million

Notice that variable costs are 81.25 percent of sales. So for each additional dollar of sales, costs increase by only $.8125. We can easily determine how much business the superstore needs to attract to avoid losses. If the store sells nothing, the income statement will show fixed costs of $2 million and depreciation of $450,000. Thus there will

TABLE 9–4 Income statement, break-even sales volume

Item	$ Thousand	
Revenues	13,067	
Variable costs	10,617	(81.25% of sales)
Fixed costs	2,000	
Depreciation	450	
Pretax profit	0	
Taxes	0	
Profit after tax	0	

be an accounting *loss* before tax of $2.45 million. Each dollar of sales reduces this loss by $1.00 – $.8125 = $.1875. Therefore, to cover fixed costs plus depreciation, you need sales of 2.45 million/.1875 = $13.067 million. At this sales level, the firm will break even. More generally,

$$\text{Break-even level of revenues} = \frac{\text{fixed costs including depreciation}}{\text{additional profit from each additional dollar of sales}}$$

Table 9–4 shows how the income statement looks with only $13.067 million of sales.

Figure 9–1 shows how the break-even point is determined. The purple 45-degree line shows the store's accounting revenues. The dashed cost line shows how costs vary with sales. If the store doesn't sell a cent, it still incurs fixed costs and depreciation amounting to $2.45 million. Each extra dollar of sales adds $.8125 to these costs. When sales are $13.067 million, the two lines cross, indicating that costs equal revenues. For lower sales, revenues are less than costs and the project is in the red; for higher sales, revenues exceed costs and the project moves into the black.

Is a project that breaks even in accounting terms an acceptable investment? If you are not sure about the answer, here's a possibly easier question: Would you be happy about an investment in a stock that after 5 years gave you a total rate of return of zero? We hope not. You might break even on such a stock, but a zero return does not compensate you for the time value of money or the risk that you have taken. A project that simply breaks even on an accounting basis gives you your money back but does not cover the opportunity cost of the capital tied up in the project. A project that breaks even in accounting terms will surely have a negative NPV.

FIGURE 9–1 Accounting break-even analysis

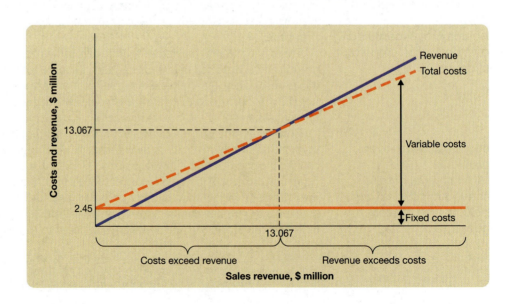

Let's check this with the superstore project. Suppose that in each year the store has sales of $13.067 million—just enough to break even on an accounting basis. What would be the cash flow from operations?

$$\text{Cash flow from operations} = \text{profit after tax} + \text{depreciation}$$
$$= 0 + \$450,000 = \$450,000$$

The initial investment is $5.4 million. In each of the next 12 years, the firm receives a cash flow of $450,000. So the firm gets its money back:

$$\text{Total cash flow from operations} = \text{initial investment}$$
$$12 \times \$450,000 = \$5.4 \text{ million}$$

But revenues are *not* sufficient to repay the *opportunity cost* of that $5.4 million investment. NPV is negative.

Economic Value Added and Break-Even Analysis

A manager who calculates an accounting-based measure of break-even may be tempted to think that any project that earns more than this figure will help shareholders. But projects that only break even on an accounting basis are really making a loss—they are failing to cover the cost of capital employed. Managers who accept such projects are not helping their shareholders.

Accounting earnings are calculated after the deduction of all costs *except the opportunity cost of the capital that is invested in the project.* Think again of how a firm creates value for its investors. It can either invest in new plant and equipment or return the cash to investors, who can then invest the money for themselves by buying stocks and bonds in the capital market. A firm that earns *more* than the cost of capital makes its investors better off: It is earning them a higher return than they could obtain for themselves. Naturally, therefore, financial managers are concerned with whether earnings are positive after deduction of the cost of capital.

If we want managers to account for the opportunity cost of capital when evaluating projects, it is best to account for that cost when measuring their performance. Even aside from giving managers the proper incentives, it makes sense to account for the opportunity cost of capital when calculating a break-even point. A project is not viable unless it covers both explicit costs *and* the opportunity cost of the capital it ties up.

Accounting for the cost of capital is simple, at least in principle—when calculating income, you should deduct the opportunity cost of the capital employed, just as you deduct other costs. Income that is measured after deduction of the cost of capital is often known as *economic profit,* or more commonly, **economic value added** or **EVA.**[3] A project that has a positive EVA adds to firm value; one with a negative EVA reduces firm value.

Think back to our superstore project, which involves an initial investment of $5.4 million and is expected to last for 12 years. Suppose for a moment that the cost of capital is zero. Then the equivalent annual cost of this investment is simply $5.4 million/12 = $450,000. In this case the accountant's deduction for depreciation correctly measures the cost of the capital invested.

However, if the cost of capital is positive, shareholders will not be happy with a project that simply gives them their money back. By ignoring the opportunity cost of capital, the depreciation allowance of $450,000 understates the *true* annual cost of the capital investment. A better measure of that cost is the equivalent annual annuity of the investment. A project that returns a cash flow over its life equal to that equivalent annual annuity will have an NPV of zero. We call the level of sales consistent with this cash flow the **economic break-even** (as opposed to *accounting* break-even) **point.**

economic value added (EVA)
Income that is measured after deduction of the cost of capital.

economic break-even point
Minimum level of sales needed to cover all costs including the cost of capital.

---

[3] The terms are used by Stern-Stewart, the consulting firm, which has done much to promote the measure. With Stern-Stewart's permission, we omit the copyright symbol in what follows.

To find the economic break-even point, we solve for the annual annuity, received over the 12-year life of the project, that will give the project an NPV of zero. For the superstore project, the equivalent annual annuity is

$$\frac{\text{Initial investment}}{\text{12-year annuity factor at 8\%}} = \frac{\$5.4 \text{ million}}{7.536} = \$716{,}553$$

Notice that the accounting depreciation allowance understates the appropriate charge for capital by $716,553 − $450,000 = $266,553. Therefore, the economic profit, or equivalently the economic value added, equals the accounting profit minus this adjustment for the capital charge. For the superstore, economic profit = accounting profit − $266,553. While the superstore is expected to produce an annual after-tax accounting profit of $330,000, each year's profit adds only $330,000 − $266,553 = $63,447 to shareholder value. This is the project's expected annual economic value added.

Now we can perform our break-even calculation, asking how large sales would need to be before the project adds value for the shareholders. The superstore's EVA depends on sales as follows:

1. Variable costs	81.25% of sales
2. Fixed costs	$2 million
3. Depreciation	$450,000
4. Pretax profit	$(.1875 \times \text{sales}) - \$2.45$ million
5. Tax (at 40%)	$.40 \times (.1875 \times \text{sales} - \$2.45 \text{ million})$
6. After-tax accounting profit	$.60 \times (.1875 \times \text{sales} - \$2.45 \text{ million})$
7. Cost of capital *over and above* allowed accounting depreciation*	$266,553
8. Economic value added (EVA) (= line 6 − line 7)	$.60 \times (.1875 \times \text{sales} - \$2.45 \text{ million}) - \$266{,}553$

*Note that the Internal Revenue Service will allow the firm to deduct only the $450,000 cost of the investment. The additional $266,553 that is needed to satisfy shareholders must be earned after payment of tax.

The project will have zero EVA when

$.60 \times (.1875 \times \text{sales} - \$2.45 \text{ million}) - \$266{,}553 = 0$
$.1125 \times \text{sales} = \$1{,}736{,}553$
$\text{Sales} = \$15{,}436{,}027$, or about $15.4 million

This implies that the store needs sales of about $15.4 million a year before it creates value for shareholders, that is, before it achieves economic break-even. This is more than 18 percent higher than the point at which the project has zero accounting profit. These days companies are increasingly aware that capital has an opportunity cost, and therefore they think of break-even in terms of EVA rather than accounting profits.

Self-Test 9.3

A project that has zero EVA creates no value. In other words, it has an NPV of zero. Confirm that if the superstore generates sales of $15.436 million a year, it will also have zero NPV.

Figure 9–2 is a plot of the after-tax cash flow from the superstore as a function of annual sales. The cash flow equals the equivalent annual annuity of the initial investment when sales are $15.4 million. This is the point at which the project has zero EVA.

FIGURE 9–2 NPV break-even analysis

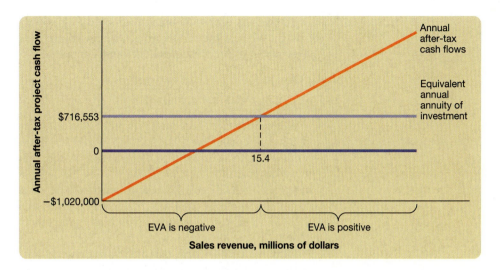

As long as sales are greater than this, the project cash flow exceeds the equivalent annual annuity and the project has a positive EVA.

Self-Test 9.4

What would be the economic break-even level of sales if the capital investment was only $5 million?

EXAMPLE 9.2 ▶ Break-Even Analysis

We have said that projects that break even on an accounting basis are really making a loss—they are losing the opportunity cost of their investment. Here is a dramatic example. Lophead Aviation is contemplating investment in a new passenger aircraft, code-named the Trinova. Lophead's financial staff has gathered together the following estimates:

1. The cost of developing the Trinova is forecast at $900 million, and this investment can be depreciated in six equal annual amounts.
2. Production of the plane is expected to take place at a steady annual rate over the following 6 years.
3. The average price of the Trinova is expected to be $15.5 million.
4. Fixed costs are forecast at $175 million a year.
5. Variable costs are forecast at $8.5 million a plane.
6. The tax rate is 50 percent.
7. The cost of capital is 10 percent.

Lophead's financial manager has used this information to construct a forecast of the profitability of the Trinova program. This is shown in rows 1 to 7 of Table 9–5 (ignore row 8 for a moment).

How many aircraft does Lophead need to sell to break even? The answer depends on what is meant by "break even." In accounting terms the venture will break even when net profit (row 7 in the table) is zero. In this case,

$$(3.5 \times \text{planes sold}) - 162.5 = 0$$
$$\text{Planes sold} = 162.5/3.5 = 46.4$$

Thus Lophead needs to sell about 46 planes a year, or a total of 280 planes over the 6 years to show a profit. With a price of $15.5 million a plane, Lophead will break even in accounting terms with annual revenues of $46.4 \times \$15.5$ million = $719 million.

We would have arrived at the same answer if we had used our formula to calculate the break-even level of revenues. Notice that the variable cost of each plane is $8.5 million, which is 54.8 percent of the $15.5 million sale price. Therefore, each dollar

TABLE 9–5 Forecast profitability for production of the Trinova airliner (figures in millions of dollars)

	Year 0	Years 1–6
Investment	$900	
1. Sales		15.5 × planes sold
2. Variable costs		8.5 × planes sold
3. Fixed costs		175
4. Depreciation		900/6 = 150
5. Pretax profit (1 − 2 − 3 − 4)		(7 × planes sold) − 325
6. Taxes (at 50%)		(3.5 × planes sold) − 162.5
7. Net profit (5 − 6)		(3.5 × planes sold) − 162.5
8. Net cash flow (4 + 7)	−$900	(3.5 × planes sold) − 12.5

of sales increases pretax profits by $1 − $.548 = $.452. Now we use the formula for the accounting break-even point:

$$\text{Break-even revenues} = \frac{\text{fixed costs including depreciation}}{\text{additional profit from each additional dollar of sales}}$$

$$= \frac{\$325 \text{ million}}{.452} = \$719 \text{ million}$$

If Lophead sells about 46 planes a year, it will recover its original investment, but it will not earn any return on the capital tied up in the project. Companies that earn a zero return on their capital can expect some unhappy shareholders. Shareholders will be content only if the company's investments earn at least the cost of the capital invested. True break-even occurs when the projects have zero economic value added.

How many planes must Lophead sell to break even in terms of economic value added? Development of the Trinova costs $900 million. If the cost of capital is 10 percent, the 6-year annuity factor is 4.355. So the equivalent annual annuity of the capital invested in the project is $900 million/4.355 = $206.6 million. This is $56.6 million more than the allowance for depreciation. So the company needs to earn $56.6 million after tax each year just to cover the cost of the capital employed. We can now find how many planes Lophead needs to sell to break even in terms of EVA:

$$\text{EVA} = \text{accounting profit} - \text{additional cost of capital} = 0$$

$$(\$3.5 \times \text{planes sold} - \$162.5) - \$56.6 = 0$$

$$\text{Planes sold} = 219.1/3.5 = 62.6$$

Thus Lophead can recover its initial investment with sales of 46.4 planes a year (about 280 in total), but it needs to sell 62.6 a year (or about 375 in total) to recover the cost of the capital invested in the project. ◀

Our example may seem fanciful, but it is based loosely on reality. In 1971 Lockheed was in the middle of a major program to bring out the L-1011 TriStar airliner. This program was to bring Lockheed to the brink of failure, and it tipped Rolls-Royce (supplier of the TriStar engine) over the brink. In giving evidence to Congress, Lockheed argued that the TriStar program was commercially attractive and that sales would eventually exceed the break-even point of about 200 aircraft. But in calculating this break-even point, Lockheed appears to have ignored the opportunity cost of the huge capital investment in the project. Lockheed probably needed to sell about 500 aircraft to reach a zero net present value.[4]

Self-Test 9.5   **What is the basic difference between sensitivity analysis and break-even analysis?**

---

[4] The true break-even point for the TriStar program is estimated in U. E. Reinhardt, "Break-Even Analysis for Lockheed's TriStar: An Application of Financial Theory," *Journal of Finance* 28 (September 1973), pp. 821–838.

Operating Leverage

A project's break-even point depends on both its *fixed* costs, which do not vary with sales, and the profit on each extra sale. Managers often face a trade-off between these variables. For example, we typically think of rental expenses as fixed costs. But supermarket companies sometimes rent stores with contingent rent agreements. This means that the amount of rent the company pays is tied to the level of sales from the store. Rent rises and falls along with sales. The store thus replaces a fixed cost with a *variable cost* that is linked to sales. Because a greater proportion of the company's expenses will fall when its sales fall, its break-even point is reduced.

Of course, a high proportion of fixed costs is not all bad. The firm whose costs are largely fixed fares poorly when demand is low, but it may make a killing during a boom. Let us illustrate.

Finefodder has a policy of hiring long-term employees who will not be laid off except in the most dire circumstances. For all intents and purposes, these salaries are fixed costs. Its rival, Stop and Scoff, has a much smaller permanent labor force and uses expensive temporary help whenever demand for its product requires extra staff. A greater proportion of its labor expenses are therefore variable costs.

Suppose that if Finefodder adopted its rival's policy, fixed costs in its new superstore would fall from $2 million to $1.56 million but variable costs would rise from 81.25 to 84 percent of sales. Table 9–6 shows that with the normal level of sales, the two policies fare equally. In a slump a store that relies on temporary labor does better since its costs fall along with revenue. In a boom the reverse is true, and the store with the higher proportion of fixed costs has the advantage.

operating leverage
Degree to which costs are fixed.

If Finefodder follows its normal policy of hiring long-term employees, each extra dollar of sales increases pretax profits by $1.00 − $.8125 = $.1875. If it uses temporary labor, an extra dollar of sales increases profits by only $1.00 − $.84 = $.16. As a result, a store with high fixed costs is said to have high **operating leverage**. High operating leverage magnifies the effect on profits of a fluctuation in sales.

degree of operating leverage (DOL)
Percentage change in profits given a 1 percent change in sales.

We can measure a business's operating leverage by asking how much profits change for each 1 percent change in sales. The **degree of operating leverage,** often abbreviated as **DOL,** is this measure:

$$\text{DOL} = \frac{\textbf{percentage change in profits}}{\textbf{percentage change in sales}}$$

For example, Table 9–6 shows that as the store moves from normal conditions to boom, sales increase from $16 million to $19 million, a rise of 18.75 percent. For the policy with high fixed costs, profits increase from $550,000 to $1,112,000, a rise of 102.2 percent. Therefore,

$$\text{DOL} = \frac{102.2}{18.75} = 5.45$$

The percentage change in sales is magnified more than fivefold in terms of the percentage impact on profits.

TABLE 9–6 A store with high operating leverage performs relatively badly in a slump but flourishes in a boom (figures in thousands of dollars)

	High Fixed Costs			High Variable Costs		
	Slump	**Normal**	**Boom**	**Slump**	**Normal**	**Boom**
Sales	13,000	16,000	19,000	13,000	16,000	19,000
− Variable costs	10,563	13,000	15,438	10,920	13,440	15,960
− Fixed costs	2,000	2,000	2,000	1,560	1,560	1,560
− Depreciation	450	450	450	450	450	450
= Pretax profit	−13	550	1,112	70	550	1,030

Now look at the operating leverage of the store if it uses the policy with low fixed costs but high variable costs. As the store moves from normal times to boom, profits increase from $550,000 to $1,030,000, a rise of 87.3 percent. Therefore,

$$DOL = \frac{87.3}{18.75} = 4.65$$

Because some costs remain fixed, a change in sales still generates a large percentage change in profits, but the degree of operating leverage is lower.

In fact, one can show that degree of operating leverage depends on fixed charges (including depreciation) in the following manner:[5]

$$DOL = 1 + \frac{\textbf{fixed costs}}{\textbf{profits}}$$

This relationship makes it clear that operating leverage increases with fixed costs.

EXAMPLE 9.3 ▶ Operating Leverage

Suppose the firm adopts the high-fixed-cost policy. Then fixed costs including depreciation will be 2.00 + .45 = $2.45 million. Since the store produces profits of $.55 million at a normal level of sales, DOL should be

$$DOL = 1 + \frac{\text{fixed costs}}{\text{profits}} = 1 + \frac{2.45}{.55} = 5.45$$

This value matches the one we obtained by comparing the actual percentage changes in sales and profits. ◀

Notice that operating leverage will affect the risk of a project. For example, if the degree of operating leverage is 5.45, every 1 percent drop in sales will decrease profits by 5.45 percent. The greater the degree of operating leverage, the greater the sensitivity of profits to variation in sales. The risk of a project depends on operating leverage. If a large proportion of costs is fixed, a shortfall in sales has a magnified effect on profits.

We will have more to say about risk in the next three chapters.

Self-Test 9.6

Suppose that sales increase by 10 percent from the values in the normal scenario. Compute the percentage change in pretax profits from the normal level for both policies in Table 9–6. Compare your answers to the values predicted by the DOL formula.

9.4 Real Options and the Value of Flexibility

When you use discounted cash flow (DCF) to value a project, you implicitly assume that the firm will hold the assets passively. But managers are not paid to be passive.

---

[5] This formula for DOL can be derived as follows. If sales increase by 1 percent, then variable costs also should increase by 1 percent, and profits will increase by .01 × (sales − variable costs) = .01 × (profits + fixed costs). Now recall the definition of DOL:

$$DOL = \frac{\text{percentage change in profits}}{\text{percentage change in sales}} = \frac{\text{change in profits/level of profits}}{.01}$$

$$= 100 \times \frac{\text{change in profits}}{\text{level of profits}} = 100 \times \frac{.01 \times (\text{profits + fixed costs})}{\text{level of profits}}$$

$$= 1 + \frac{\text{fixed costs}}{\text{profits}}$$

FedEx Buys an Option

In 2000 FedEx placed an order for 10 Airbus A380 super-jumbo transport planes for delivery in the years 2008–2011. Each flight of an A380 freighter will be capable of carrying 200,000 pounds of goods and therefore the plane could have a huge impact on FedEx's worldwide business.

If FedEx's long-haul airfreight business continues to expand and the superjumbo is efficient and reliable, the company will need more superjumbos. But it cannot be sure they will be needed. Therefore, rather than placing further firm orders in 2000, FedEx has secured a place in the Airbus production line by acquiring *options* to buy a "substantial number" of additional aircraft at a predetermined price. These options do not commit the company to expand but give it the flexibility to do so.

After they have invested in a new project, they do not simply sit back and watch the future unfold. If things go well, the project may be expanded; if they go badly, the project may be cut back or abandoned altogether. Projects that can easily be modified in these ways are more valuable than those that don't provide such flexibility. The more uncertain the outlook, the more valuable this flexibility becomes.

The Option to Expand

The scientists at MacCaugh have developed a diet whiskey, and the firm is ready to go ahead with pilot production and test-marketing. The preliminary phase will take a year and cost $200,000. Management feels that there is only a 50-50 chance that the pilot production and market tests will be successful. If they are, then MacCaugh will build a $2 million production plant that will generate an expected annual cash flow in perpetuity of $480,000 after taxes. Given an opportunity cost of capital of 12 percent, project NPV in this case will be –$2 million + $480,000/.12 = $2 million. If the tests are not successful, MacCaugh will discontinue the project and the cost of the pilot production will be wasted.

Notice that MacCaugh's expenditure on the pilot program buys a valuable managerial option. The firm is not obliged to enter full production, but it has the option to do so depending on the outcome of the tests. If there is some doubt as to whether the project will take off, expenditure on the pilot operation could help the firm to avoid a costly mistake. Therefore, when it proposed the expenditure, MacCaugh's management was simply following the fundamental rule of swimmers: If you know the water temperature (and depth) dive in; if you don't, try putting a toe in first.

When faced with projects like this that involve future decisions, it is often helpful to draw a **decision tree** as in Figure 9–3. You can think of the problem as a game between MacCaugh and fate. Each square represents an action or decision by the company. Each circle represents an outcome revealed by fate. MacCaugh starts the play at the left-hand square. If it decides to test, then fate will cast the enchanted dice and decide the results of the test. Once the results are known, MacCaugh faces a second decision: Should it wind up the project, or should it invest $2 million and start full-scale production?

The second-stage decision is obvious: *Invest if the tests indicate that NPV is positive, and stop if they indicate that NPV is negative.* So now MacCaugh can move back to consider whether it should invest in the test program. This first-stage decision boils down to a simple problem: Should MacCaugh invest $200,000 now to obtain a 50 percent chance of a project with an NPV of $2 million a year later? At any reasonable discount rate the test program has a positive NPV.

You can probably now think of many other investments that take on added value because of the options they provide to expand in the future. For example:

- When designing a factory, it can make sense to provide extra land or floor space to reduce the future cost of a second production line.
- When building a four-lane highway, it may pay to build six-lane bridges so that the road can be converted later to six lanes if traffic proves higher than expected.
- An airline may acquire an option to buy a new aircraft (the nearby box explains how Federal Express bought options on the Airbus superjumbo).

decision tree
Diagram of sequential decisions and possible outcomes.

FIGURE 9–3 Decision tree for the diet-whiskey project

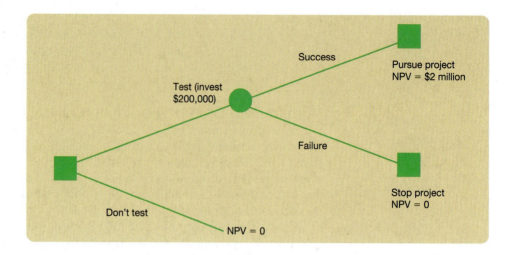

In each of these cases you are paying out money today to give you the option to invest in real assets at some time in the future. Managers therefore often refer to such options as **real options.** These options do not show up in the assets that the company lists in its balance sheet, but investors are very aware of their existence. If a company has valuable real options that allow it to invest in profitable future projects, its market value will be higher than the value of its physical assets now in place. We consider the valuation of options in Chapter 23.

real options

Options to invest in, modify, or dispose of a capital investment project.

A Second Real Option: The Option to Abandon

If the option to expand has value, what about the decision to bail out? Projects don't just go on until assets expire of old age. The decision to terminate a project is usually taken by management, not by nature. Once the project is no longer profitable, the company will cut its losses and exercise its option to abandon the project.

Some assets are simpler to bail out of than others. Tangible assets are usually easier to sell than intangible ones. It helps to have active secondhand markets, which really exist only for standardized items. Real estate, airplanes, trucks, and certain machine tools are likely to be relatively easy to sell. On the other hand, the knowledge accumulated by a software company's research and development program is a specialized intangible asset and probably would not have significant abandonment value. (Some assets, such as old mattresses, even have *negative* abandonment value; you have to pay to get rid of them. It is costly to decommission nuclear power plants or to reclaim land that has been strip-mined.)

EXAMPLE 9.4 ▶ Abandonment Option

Suppose that the Widgeon Company must choose between two technologies for the manufacture of a new product, a Wankel-engined outboard motor:

1. Technology A uses custom-designed machinery to produce the complex shapes required for Wankel engines at low cost. But if the Wankel engine doesn't sell, this equipment will be worthless.
2. Technology B uses standard machine tools. Labor costs are much higher, but the tools can easily be sold if the motor doesn't sell.

Technology A looks better in an NPV analysis of the new product, because it is designed to have the lowest possible cost at the planned production volume. Yet you can sense the advantage of technology B's flexibility if you are unsure whether the new outboard will sink or swim in the marketplace. ◀

Self-Test 9.7

Draw a decision tree showing how the choices open to the Widgeon Company depend on demand for the new product. Pick some plausible numbers to illustrate why it might make sense to adopt the more expensive technology B.

A Third Real Option: The Timing Option

Suppose that you have a project that could be a big winner or a big loser. The project's upside potential outweighs its downside potential, and it has a positive NPV if undertaken today. However, the project is not "now or never." So should you invest right away or wait? It's hard to say. If the project turns out to be a winner, waiting means the loss or deferral of its early cash flows. But if it turns out to be a loser, it may pay to wait and get a better fix on the likely demand.

You can think of any project proposal as giving you the *option* to invest today. You don't have to exercise that option immediately. Instead, you need to weigh the value of the cash flows lost by delaying against the possibility that you will pick up some valuable information. Suppose, for example, you are considering development of a new oil field. At current oil prices the investment has a small positive NPV. But oil prices are highly volatile, occasionally halving or doubling in the space of a couple years. If a small decline in crude prices could push your project into the red, it might be better to wait a little before investing.

Our example illustrates why companies sometimes turn down apparently profitable projects. For example, suppose you approach your boss with a proposed project. It involves spending $1 million and has an NPV of $1,000. You explain to him how carefully you have analyzed the project, but nothing seems to convince him that the company should invest. Is he being irrational to turn down a positive-NPV project?

Faced by such marginal projects, it often makes sense to wait. One year later you may have much better information about the prospects for the project, and it may become clear whether it is really a winner or a loser. In the former case you can go ahead with confidence, but if it looks like a loser, the delay will have helped you to avoid a bad mistake.[6]

A Fourth Real Option: Flexible Production Facilities

A sheep is not a flexible production facility. It produces mutton and wool in roughly fixed proportions. If the price of mutton suddenly rises and that of wool falls, there is little that the farmer with a flock of sheep can do about it. Many manufacturing operations are different, for they have built-in flexibility to vary their output mix as demand changes. Since we have mentioned sheep, we might point to the knitwear industry as a case in which manufacturing flexibility has become particularly important in recent years. Fashion changes have made the pattern of demand in the knitwear industry notoriously difficult to predict, and firms have increasingly invested in computer-controlled knitting machines, which provide an option to vary the product mix as demand changes.

Companies also try to avoid becoming dependent on a single source of raw materials. For example, at current prices gas-fired industrial boilers may be cheaper to operate than oil-fired ones. Yet most companies prefer to buy boilers that can use either oil or natural gas, even though these dual-fired boilers cost more than a gas-fired boiler. The reason is obvious. If gas prices rise relative to oil prices, the dual-fired boiler gives the company a valuable option to exchange one asset (an oil-fired boiler) for another (a gas-fired boiler).

---

[6] Does this conclusion contradict our earlier dictum (see Chapter 7) that the firm should accept all positive-NPV projects? No. Notice that the investment timing problem involves a choice among mutually exclusive alternatives. You can build the project today or next year, but not both. In such cases, we have seen that the right choice is the one with the *highest* NPV. The NPV of the project today, even if positive, may well be less than the NPV of deferring investment and keeping alive the option to invest later.

Self-Test 9.8

Investments in new products or production capacity often include an option to expand. What are other major types of options encountered in capital investment decisions?

SUMMARY

How do large corporations go about selecting positive-NPV projects?

For most large corporations there are two stages in the investment process: the preparation of the **capital budget,** which is a list of planned investments, and the authorization process for individual projects. This process is usually a cooperative effort.

Investment projects should never be selected through a purely mechanical process. Managers need to ask why a project should have a positive NPV. A positive NPV is plausible only if the company has some competitive advantage that prevents its rivals from stealing most of the gains.

How are sensitivity, scenario, and break-even analyses used to see the effect of an error in forecasts on project profitability? Why is an overestimate of sales more serious for projects with high operating leverage?

Good managers realize that the forecasts behind NPV calculations are imperfect. Therefore, they explore the consequences of a poor forecast and check whether it is worth doing some more homework. They use the following principal tools to answer these what-if questions:

- **Sensitivity analysis,** where one variable at a time is changed.
- **Scenario analysis,** where the manager looks at the project under alternative scenarios.
- **Simulation analysis,** an extension of scenario analysis in which a computer generates hundreds or thousands of possible combinations of variables.
- **Break-even analysis,** where the focus is on how far sales could fall before the project begins to lose money. Often the phrase "lose money" is defined in terms of accounting losses, but it makes more sense to define it as "failing to cover the opportunity cost of capital"—in other words, as a negative NPV.
- **Operating leverage,** the degree to which costs are fixed. A project's break-even point will be affected by the extent to which costs can be reduced as sales decline. If the project has mostly **fixed costs,** it is said to have *high operating leverage.* High operating leverage implies that profits are more sensitive to changes in sales.

Why is managerial flexibility important in capital budgeting?

Some projects may take on added value because they give the firm the option to bail out if things go wrong or to capitalize on success by expanding. These options are known as **real options.** Other real options include the possibility to delay a project or to choose flexible production facilities. We showed how **decision trees** may be used to set out the possible choices.

QUIZ

1. **Fixed and Variable Costs.** In a slow year, Deutsche Burgers will produce 2 million hamburgers at a total cost of $3.5 million. In a good year, it can produce 4 million hamburgers at a total cost of $4.5 million. What are the fixed and variable costs of hamburger production?

2. **Average Cost.** Reconsider Deutsche Burgers from Problem 1.
   a. What is the average cost per burger when the firm produces 1 million hamburgers?
   b. What is average cost when the firm produces 2 million hamburgers?
   c. Why is average cost lower when more burgers are produced?

3. **Sensitivity Analysis.** A project currently generates sales of $10 million, variable costs equal to 50 percent of sales, and fixed costs of $2 million. The firm's tax rate is 35 percent. What are the effects of the following changes on after-tax profits and cash flow?

   a. Sales increase from $10 million to $11 million.
   b. Variable costs increase to 65 percent of sales.

PRACTICE PROBLEMS

4. **Sensitivity Analysis.** The project in the preceding problem will last for 10 years. The discount rate is 12 percent.

   a. What is the effect on project NPV of each of the changes considered in the problem?
   b. If project NPV under the base-case scenario is $2 million, how much can fixed costs increase before NPV turns negative?
   c. How much can fixed costs increase before accounting profits turn negative?

5. **Sensitivity Analysis.** Emperor's Clothes Fashions can invest $5 million in a new plant for producing invisible makeup. The plant has an expected life of 5 years, and expected sales are 6 million jars of makeup a year. Fixed costs are $2 million a year, and variable costs are $1 per jar. The product will be priced at $2 per jar. The plant will be depreciated straight-line over 5 years to a salvage value of zero. The opportunity cost of capital is 10 percent, and the tax rate is 40 percent.

   a. What is project NPV under these base-case assumptions?
   b. What is NPV if variable costs turn out to be $1.20 per jar?
   c. What is NPV if fixed costs turn out to be $1.5 million per year?
   d. At what price per jar would project NPV equal zero?

6. **Scenario Analysis.** The most likely outcomes for a particular project are estimated as follows:

Unit price:	$50
Variable cost:	$30
Fixed cost:	$300,000
Expected sales:	30,000 units per year

   However, you recognize that some of these estimates are subject to error. Suppose that each variable may turn out to be either 10 percent higher or 10 percent lower than the initial estimate. The project will last for 10 years and requires an initial investment of $1 million, which will be depreciated straight-line over the project life to a final value of zero. The firm's tax rate is 35 percent and the required rate of return is 12 percent. What is project NPV in the "best-case scenario," that is, assuming all variables take on the best possible value? What about the worst-case scenario?

7. **Scenario Analysis.** Reconsider the best- and worst-case scenarios in the previous problem. Do the best- and worst-case outcomes when each variable is treated independently seem to be reasonable scenarios in terms of the combinations of variables? For example, if price is higher than predicted, is it more or less likely that cost is higher than predicted? What other relationships may exist among the variables?

8. **Break-Even.** The following estimates have been prepared for a project under consideration:

Fixed costs:	$20,000
Depreciation:	$10,000
Price:	$2
Accounting break-even:	60,000 units

   What must be the variable cost per unit?

9. **Break-Even.** Dime a Dozen Diamonds makes synthetic diamonds by treating carbon. Each diamond can be sold for $100. The materials cost for a standard diamond is $40. The fixed costs incurred each year for factory upkeep and administrative expenses are $200,000. The machinery costs $1 million and is depreciated straight-line over 10 years to a salvage value of zero.

a. What is the accounting break-even level of sales in terms of number of diamonds sold?

b. What is the economic break-even level of sales assuming a tax rate of 35 percent, a 10-year project life, and a discount rate of 12 percent?

10. **Break-Even.** Turn back to Problem 9.

a. Would the accounting break-even point in the first year of operation increase or decrease if the machinery were depreciated over a 5-year period?

b. Would the economic break-even point increase or decrease if the machinery were depreciated over a 5-year period?

11. **Break-Even.** You are evaluating a project that will require an investment of $10 million that will be depreciated over a period of 7 years. You are concerned that the corporate tax rate will increase during the life of the project. Would such an increase affect the accounting break-even point? Would it affect the economic break-even point?

12. **Break-Even.** Define the *cash-flow break-even point* as the sales volume (in dollars) at which cash flow equals zero. Is the cash-flow break-even level of sales higher or lower than the zero-profit break-even point?

13. **Break-Even and NPV.** If a project operates at cash-flow break-even (see Problem 12) for its entire life, is its NPV positive or negative?

14. **Economic Break-Even.** Modern Artifacts can produce keepsakes that will be sold for $80 each. Nondepreciation fixed costs are $1,000 per year and variable costs are $60 per unit.

a. If the project requires an initial investment of $3,000 and is expected to last for 5 years and the firm pays no taxes, what are the accounting and economic break-even levels of sales? The initial investment will be depreciated straight-line over 5 years to a final value of zero, and the discount rate is 10 percent.

b. How do your answers change if the firm's tax rate is 35 percent?

15. **Economic Break-Even.** A financial analyst has computed both accounting and economic break-even sales levels for a project using straight-line depreciation over a 6-year period. The project manager wants to know what will happen to these estimates if the firm uses MACRS depreciation instead. The capital investment will be in a 5-year recovery period class under MACRS rules (see Table 8–4). The firm is in a 35 percent tax bracket.

a. What (qualitatively) will happen to the accounting break-even level of sales in the first years of the project?

b. What (qualitatively) will happen to economic break-even level of sales?

c. If you were advising the analyst, would the answer to (a) or (b) be important to you? Specifically, would you say that the switch to MACRS makes the project more or less attractive?

16. **Economic Break-Even.** Reconsider Finefodder's new superstore. Suppose that by investing an additional $600,000 initially in more efficient checkout equipment, Finefodder could reduce variable costs to 80 percent of sales.

a. Using the base-case assumptions (Table 9–1), find the NPV of this alternative scheme. *Hint:* Remember to focus on the incremental cash flows from the project.

b. At what level of sales will accounting profits be unchanged if the firm invests in the new equipment? Assume the equipment receives the same 12-year straight-line depreciation treatment as in the original example. *Hint:* Focus on the project's incremental effects on fixed and variable costs.

c. What is the economic break-even point?

17. **Break-Even and NPV.** If the superstore project (see the previous problem) operates at accounting break-even, will net present value be positive or negative?

18. **Operating Leverage.** You estimate that your cattle farm will generate $1 million of profits on sales of $4 million under normal economic conditions and that the degree of operating leverage is 8. What will profits be if sales turn out to be $3.5 million? What if they are $4.5 million?

19. **Operating Leverage.**

a. What is the degree of operating leverage of Modern Artifacts (in problem 14) when sales are $7,000?

b. What is the degree of operating leverage when sales are $12,000?

c. Why is operating leverage different at these two levels of sales?

www.mhhe.com/bmm5e

Please visit us at www.mhhe.com/bmm5e or refer to your Student CD

Please visit us at www.mhhe.com/bmm5e or refer to your Student CD

20. **Operating Leverage.** What is the lowest possible value for the degree of operating leverage for a profitable firm? Show with a numerical example that if Modern Artifacts (see Problem 14a) has zero fixed costs, then DOL = 1 and in fact sales and profits are directly proportional, so that a 1 percent change in sales results in a 1 percent change in profits.

21. **Operating Leverage.** A project has fixed costs of $1,000 per year, depreciation charges of $500 a year, revenue of $6,000 a year, and variable costs equal to two-thirds of revenues.

    a. If sales increase by 10 percent, what will be the increase in pretax profits?
    b. What is the degree of operating leverage of this project?
    c. Confirm that the percentage change in profits equals DOL times the percentage change in sales.

22. **Project Options.** Your midrange guess as to the amount of oil in a prospective field is 10 million barrels, but in fact there is a 50 percent chance that the amount of oil is 15 million barrels and a 50 percent chance of 5 million barrels. If the actual amount of oil is 15 million barrels, the present value of the cash flows from drilling will be $8 million. If the amount is only 5 million barrels, the present value will be only $2 million. It costs $3 million to drill the well. Suppose that a seismic test that costs $100,000 can verify the amount of oil under the ground. Is it worth paying for the test? Use a decision tree to justify your answer.

23. **Project Options.** A silver mine can yield 10,000 ounces of silver at a variable cost of $8 per ounce. The fixed costs of operating the mine are $10,000 per year. In half the years, silver can be sold for $12 per ounce; in the other years, silver can be sold for only $6 per ounce. Ignore taxes.

    a. What is the average cash flow you will receive from the mine if it is always kept in operation and the silver always is sold in the year it is mined?
    b. Now suppose you can shut down the mine in years of low silver prices. What happens to the average cash flow from the mine?

24. **Project Options.** An auto plant that costs $100 million to build can produce a new line of cars that will produce cash flows with a present value of $140 million if the line is successful but only $50 million if it is unsuccessful. You believe that the probability of success is only about 50 percent. You learn whether the line is successful immediately after building the plant.

    a. Would you build the plant?
    b. Suppose that the plant can be sold for $95 million to another automaker if the auto line is not successful. Now would you build the plant?
    c. Illustrate the option to abandon in (b) using a decision tree.

25. **Production Options.** Explain why options to expand or contract production are most valuable when forecasts about future business conditions are most uncertain.

CHALLENGE PROBLEMS ™

26. **Abandonment Option.** Hit or Miss Sports is introducing a new product this year. If its see-at-night soccer balls are a hit, the firm expects to be able to sell 50,000 units a year at a price of $60 each. If the new product is a bust, only 30,000 units can be sold at a price of $55. The variable cost of each ball is $30, and fixed costs are zero. The cost of the manufacturing equipment is $6 million, and the project life is estimated at 10 years. The firm will use straight-line depreciation over the 10-year life of the project. The firm's tax rate is 35 percent, and the discount rate is 12 percent.

    a. If each outcome is equally likely, what is expected NPV? Will the firm accept the project?
    b. Suppose now that the firm can abandon the project and sell off the manufacturing equipment for $5.4 million if demand for the balls turns out to be weak. The firm will make the decision to continue or abandon after the first year of sales. Does the option to abandon change the firm's decision to accept the project?

27. **Expansion Option.** Now suppose that Hit or Miss Sports from the previous problem can expand production if the project is successful. By paying its workers overtime, it can increase pro-

duction by 25,000 units; the variable cost of each ball will be higher, however, equal to $35 per unit. By how much does this option to expand production increase the NPV of the project?

Go to Market Insight at www.mhhe.com/edumarketinsight.

1. Can you guess Dell's incremental cost for producing one computer? You probably have that amount in your wallet or purse! Let's estimate the sales break-even point and degree of operating leverage for Dell Computer (DELL). Go to the annual income statement. With reference to Table 9–4, treating S&GA and depreciation expense as our proxy for fixed costs, and costs of goods sold as variable costs, estimate the break-even level of sales for Dell for the last year (annual).

2. Estimate Dell's degree of operating leverage (DOL) by calculating the percentage change in operating profits compared to the previous year and dividing that by the percentage change in sales. How does that compare to the result you would obtain for operating leverage using the formula DOL = 1 + fixed costs/profits? Why is there a difference when using these two approaches?

SOLUTIONS TO SELF-TEST QUESTIONS

9.1 Cash-flow forecasts for Finefodder's new superstore:

	Year 0	Years 1–12
Investment	–5,400,000	
1. Sales		16,000,000
2. Variable costs		13,280,000
3. Fixed costs		2,000,000
4. Depreciation		450,000
5. Pretax profit (1 – 2 – 3 – 4)		270,000
6. Taxes (at 40%)		108,000
7. Profit after tax		162,000
8. Cash flow from operations (4 + 7)		612,000
Net cash flow	–5,400,000	612,000

$$\text{NPV} = -\$5.4 \text{ million} + (7.5361 \times \$612,000) = -\$787,907$$

which matches the value in Table 9–2 except for minor rounding error in the annuity factor.

9.2 Both calculate how NPV depends on input assumptions. Sensitivity analysis changes inputs one at a time, whereas scenario analysis changes several variables at once. The changes should add up to a consistent scenario for the project as a whole.

9.3 Cash flow = net income + depreciation. From the table on page 249, we see that net income (i.e., after-tax accounting profit) is $.60 \times (.1875 \times \text{sales} - \$2.45 \text{ million})$ and depreciation is $.45 million. Therefore,

$$\text{Cash flow} = .60 \times (.1875 \times \text{sales} - \$2.45) + .45 = .1125 \times \text{sales} - \$1.02 \text{ million}$$

For a sales level of $15.436 million, cash flow will be $.71655 million. The 12-year annuity factor for an interest rate of 8 percent is 7.536. Therefore, the present value of project cash flows is $.71655 \times 7.536 = \$5.4$ million, just equal to the initial investment. Project NPV = 0.

9.4 With the lower initial investment, depreciation is also lower; it now equals $417,000 per year. Cash flow is now as follows:

1. Variable costs	81.25 percent of sales
2. Fixed costs	$2 million
3. Depreciation	$417,000
4. Pretax profit	$(.1875 \times \text{sales}) - \$2.417$ million
5. Tax (at 40%)	$.4 \times (.1875 \times \text{sales} - \$2.417$ million$)$
6. Profit after tax	$.6 \times (.1875 \times \text{sales} - \$2.417$ million$)$
7. Cash flow (3 + 6)	$.6 \times (.1875 \times \text{sales} - \$2.417$ million$) + \$417,000$ $= .1125 \times \text{sales} - \$1.033$ million

Break-even occurs when

$$\text{PV (cash inflows)} = \text{investment}$$
$$7.536 \times (.1125 \times \text{sales} - \$1.033 \text{ million}) = \$5 \text{ million}$$
$$\text{Sales} = \$15.08 \text{ million}$$

9.5   Break-even analysis finds the level of sales or revenue at which NPV = 0. Sensitivity analysis changes these and other input variables to optimistic and pessimistic values and recalculates NPV.

9.6   Reworking Table 9–6 for the normal level of sales and 10 percent higher sales gives the following:

	High Fixed Costs		**High Variable Costs**	
	Normal	**10% Higher Sales**	**Normal**	**10% Higher Sales**
Sales	16,000	17,600	16,000	17,600
– Variable costs	13,000	14,300	13,440	14,784
– Fixed costs	2,000	2,000	1,560	1,560
– Depreciation	450	450	450	450
= Pretax profit	550	850	550	806

For the high-fixed-cost policy, profits increase by 54.5 percent, from $550,000 to $850,000. For the low-fixed-cost policy, profits increase by 46.5 percent. In both cases the percentage increase in profits equals DOL times the percentage increase in sales. This illustrates that DOL measures the sensitivity of profits to changes in sales.

9.7   See Figure 9–4. Note that while technology A delivers the higher NPV if demand is high, technology B has the advantage of a higher salvage value if demand is unexpectedly low.

9.8   Abandonment options, options due to flexible production facilities, investment timing options.

FIGURE 9–4 **Example of a decision tree for Widgeon Company**

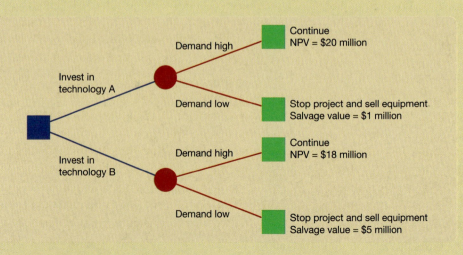

MINICASE

Maxine Peru, the CEO of Peru Resources, hardly noticed the plate of savory quenelles de brochet and the glass of Corton Charlemagne '94 on the table before her. She was absorbed by the engineering report handed to her just as she entered the executive dining room.

The report described a proposed new mine on the North Ridge of Mt. Zircon. A vein of transcendental zirconium ore had been discovered there on land owned by Ms. Peru's company. Test borings indicated sufficient reserves to produce 340 tons per year of transcendental zirconium over a 7-year period.

The vein probably also contained hydrated zircon gemstones. The amount and quality of these zircons were hard to predict, since they tended to occur in "pockets." The new mine might come across one, two, or dozens of pockets. The mining engineer guessed that 150 pounds per year might be found. The current price for high-quality hydrated zircon gemstones was $3,300 per pound.

Peru Resources was a family-owned business with total assets of $45 million, including cash reserves of $4 million. The outlay required for the new mine would be a major commitment. Fortunately, Peru Resources was conservatively financed, and Ms. Peru believed that the company could borrow up to $9 million at an interest rate of about 8 percent.

The mine's operating costs were projected at $900,000 per year, including $400,000 of fixed costs and $500,000 of variable costs. Ms. Peru thought these forecasts were accurate. The big question marks seemed to be the initial cost of the mine and the selling price of transcendental zirconium.

Opening the mine, and providing the necessary machinery and ore-crunching facilities, was supposed to cost $10 million, but cost overruns of 10 or 15 percent were common in the mining business.

In addition, new environmental regulations, if enacted, could increase the cost of the mine by $1.5 million.

There was a cheaper design for the mine, which would reduce its cost by $1.7 million and eliminate much of the uncertainty about cost overruns. Unfortunately, this design would require much higher fixed operating costs. Fixed costs would increase to $850,000 per year at planned production levels.

The current price of transcendental zirconium was $10,000 per ton, but there was no consensus about future prices.[7] Some experts were projecting rapid price increases to as much as $14,000 per ton. On the other hand, there were pessimists saying that prices could be as low as $7,500 per ton. Ms. Peru did not have strong views either way: Her best guess was that price would just increase with inflation at about 3.5 percent per year. (Mine operating costs would also increase with inflation.)

Ms. Peru had wide experience in the mining business, and she knew that investors in similar projects usually wanted a forecasted nominal rate of return of at least 14 percent.

You have been asked to assist Ms. Peru in evaluating this project. Lay out the base-case NPV analysis, and undertake sensitivity, scenario, or break-even analyses as appropriate. Assume that Peru Resources pays tax at a 35 percent rate. For simplicity, also assume that the investment in the mine could be depreciated for tax purposes straight-line over 7 years.

What forecasts or scenarios should worry Ms. Peru the most? Where would additional information be most helpful? Is there a case for delaying construction of the new mine?

---

[7] There were no traded forward or futures contracts on transcendental zirconium. See Chapter 24.

3

Risk

CHAPTER

10

Introduction to Risk, Return, and the Opportunity Cost of Capital

RELATED WEB LINKS

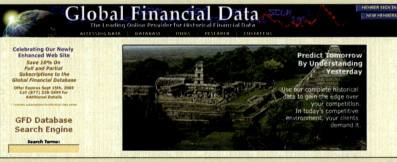

www.globalfindata.com
www.mscidata.com
www.econ.yale.edu/~shiller
pages.stern.nyu.edu/~adamodar
Data on security returns that can be used to assess risk and return history.

www.djindexes.com Data since 1895, and useful bond market data.

"To hell with a balanced portfolio. I want to sell my Fenwick Chemical and sell it now."

More generally, though, investors will want to spread their investments across many securities.

We have thus far skirted the issue of project risk; now it is time to confront it head-on. We can no longer be satisfied with vague statements like "The opportunity cost of capital depends on the risk of the project." We need to know how to measure risk, and we need to understand the relationship between risk and the cost of capital. These are the topics of the next two chapters.

Think for a moment what the cost of capital for a project means. It is the rate of return that shareholders could expect to earn if they invested in equally risky securities. So one way to estimate the cost of capital is to find securities that have the same risk as the project and then estimate the expected rate of return on these securities.

We start our analysis by looking at the rates of return earned in the past from different investments, concentrating on the *extra* return that investors have received for investing in risky rather than safe securities. We then show how to measure the risk of a portfolio by calculating its standard deviation, and we look again at past history

to find out how risky it is to invest in the stock market.

Finally, we explore the concept of diversification. Most investors do not put all their eggs into one basket—they diversify. Thus investors are not concerned with the risk of each security in isolation; instead, they are concerned with how much it contributes to the risk of a diversified portfolio. We therefore need to distinguish between the risk that can be eliminated by diversification and the risk that cannot be eliminated.

After studying this chapter you should be able to:

- Estimate the opportunity cost of capital for an "average-risk" project.
- Calculate the standard deviation of returns for individual common stocks or for a stock portfolio.
- Understand why diversification reduces risk.
- Distinguish between unique risk, which can be diversified away, and market risk, which cannot.

10.1 Rates of Return: A Review

When investors buy a stock or a bond, their return comes in two forms: (1) a dividend or interest payment and (2) a capital gain or a capital loss. For example, suppose you bought the stock of General Electric at the beginning of 2004 when its price was $31.12 a share. By the end of the year the value of that investment had appreciated to $36.59, giving a capital gain of $36.59 – $31.12 = $5.47. In addition, in 2004 GE paid a dividend of $0.82 a share.

The *percentage* return on your investment was therefore

$$\text{Percentage return} = \frac{\text{capital gain + dividend}}{\text{initial share price}}$$

$$= \frac{\$5.47 + \$0.82}{\$31.12} = .202, \text{ or } 20.2\%$$

The percentage return can also be expressed as the sum of the *dividend yield* and *percentage capital gain.* The dividend yield is the dividend expressed as a percentage of the stock price at the beginning of the year:

$$\text{Dividend yield} = \frac{\text{dividend}}{\text{initial share price}}$$

$$= \frac{\$0.82}{\$31.12} = .026, \text{ or } 2.6\%$$

Similarly, the percentage capital gain is

$$\text{Percentage capital gain} = \frac{\text{capital gain}}{\text{initial share price}}$$

$$= \frac{\$5.47}{\$31.12} = 0.176, \text{ or } 17.6\%$$

Thus the total return is the sum of 2.6% + 17.6% = 20.2 percent.

Remember that in Chapter 4 we made a distinction between the *nominal* rate of return and the *real* rate of return. The nominal return measures how much more money you will have at the end of the year if you invest today. The return that we just calculated for GE stock is therefore a nominal return. The real rate of return tells you how much more you will be able to *buy* with your money at the end of the year. To convert from a nominal to a real rate of return, we use the following relationship:

$$1 + \text{real rate of return} = \frac{1 + \text{nominal rate of return}}{1 + \text{inflation rate}}$$

In 2004 inflation was only 3.3 percent. So we calculate the real rate of return on GE stock as follows:

$$1 + \text{real rate of return} = \frac{1.202}{1.033} = 1.164$$

Therefore, the real rate of return equals .164, or 16.4 percent. Fortunately inflation in 2004 was moderate; the real return was not much less than the nominal return.

Self-Test 10.1 Suppose you buy a bond for $1,020 with a 15-year maturity paying an annual coupon of $80. A year later interest rates have dropped and the bond's price has increased to $1,050. What are your nominal and real rates of return? Assume the inflation rate is 4 percent.

10.2 A Century of Capital Market History

When you invest in a stock, you don't know what return you will earn. But by looking at the history of security returns, you can get some idea of the return that investors might reasonably expect from investments in different types of securities and of the risks that they face. Let us look, therefore, at the risks and returns that investors have experienced in the past.

Market Indexes

market index
Measure of the investment performance of the overall market.

Investors can choose from an enormous number of different securities. For example, currently, nearly 3,000 common stocks trade on the New York Stock Exchange, and a further 3,000 are traded by a network of dealers on the NASDAQ Stock Market.[1]

Dow Jones Industrial Average
Index of the investment performance of a portfolio of 30 "blue-chip" stocks.

Financial analysts can't track every stock, so they rely on **market indexes** to summarize the return on different classes of securities. The best-known stock market index in the United States is the **Dow Jones Industrial Average,** generally known as the *Dow*. The Dow tracks the performance of a portfolio that holds one share in each of 30 large firms. For example, suppose that the Dow starts the day at a value of 9,000 and then rises by 90 points to a new value of 9,090. Investors who own one share in each of the 30 companies make a capital gain of 90/9,000 = .01, or 1 percent.[2]

The Dow Jones Industrial Average was first computed in 1896. Most people are used to it and expect to hear it on the 6 o'clock news. However, it is far from the best measure of the performance of the stock market. First, with only 30 large industrial stocks, it is not representative of the performance of stocks generally. Second, investors don't usually hold an equal number of shares in each company. For example, in 2005 there were 10.6 billion shares in General Electric and only 1 billion in Du Pont. So on average investors did *not* hold the same number of shares in the two firms. Instead, they held over 10 times as many shares in General Electric as in Du Pont. It doesn't make sense, therefore, to look at an index that measures the performance of a portfolio with an equal number of shares in the two firms.

Standard & Poor's Composite Index
Index of the investment performance of a portfolio of 500 large stocks. Also called the *S&P 500.*

The **Standard & Poor's Composite Index,** better known as the *S&P 500,* includes the stocks of 500 major companies and is therefore a more comprehensive index than the Dow. Also, it measures the performance of a portfolio that holds shares in each firm in proportion to the number of shares that have been issued to investors. For example, the S&P portfolio would hold 10 times as many shares in General Electric as Du Pont. Thus the S&P 500 shows the *average* performance of investors in the 500 firms.

Only a small proportion of the publicly traded companies are represented in the S&P 500. However, these firms are among the largest in the country, and they account for nearly 80 percent of the stocks traded. Therefore, success for professional investors usually means "beating the S&P."

Some stock market indexes, such as the Wilshire 5000, include an even larger number of stocks, while others focus on special groups of stocks such as the stocks of small companies. There are also stock market indexes for other countries, such as the Nikkei Index for Tokyo and the Financial Times (FT) Index for London. Morgan Stanley Capital International (MSCI) even computes a world stock market index. The Financial Times Company and Standard & Poor's have combined to produce their own world index.

The Historical Record

The historical returns of stock or bond market indexes can give us an idea of the typical performance of different investments. For example, Elroy Dimson, Paul Marsh,

---

[1] This network of dealers is sometimes known as the *over-the-counter market.*

[2] Stock market indexes record the market value of the portfolio. To calculate the total return on the portfolio we need to add in any dividends that are paid.

and Mike Staunton have compiled measures of the investment performance of three portfolios of securities since 1900:

1. A portfolio of 3-month loans issued each week by the U.S. government. These loans are known as *Treasury bills.*
2. A portfolio of long-term *Treasury bonds* issued by the U.S. government and maturing in about 10 years.
3. A diversified portfolio of common stocks.

These portfolios are not equally risky. Treasury bills are about as safe an investment as you can make. Because they are issued by the U.S. government, you can be sure that you will get your money back. Their short-term maturity means that their prices are relatively stable. In fact, investors who wish to lend money for 3 months can achieve a certain payoff by buying 3-month bills. Of course, they can't be sure what that money will buy; there is still some uncertainty about inflation.

Long-term Treasury bonds are also certain to be repaid when they mature, but the prices of these bonds fluctuate more as interest rates vary. When interest rates fall, the value of long-term bonds rises; when rates rise, the value of the bonds falls.

Common stocks are the riskiest of the three groups of securities. When you invest in common stocks, there is no promise that you will get your money back. As a part-owner of the corporation, you receive what is left over after the bonds and any other debts have been repaid.

Figure 10–1 shows the performance of the three groups of securities assuming that all dividends or interest income had been reinvested in the portfolios. You can see that the performance of the portfolios fits our intuitive risk ranking. Common stocks were the riskiest investment, but they also offered the greatest gains. One dollar invested at the start of 1900 in a portfolio of common stocks would have grown to $17,545 by the end of 2004. At the other end of the spectrum, an investment in Treasury bills would have accumulated to only $61.

Table 10–1 shows the average of the annual returns from each of these portfolios. These returns are comparable to the return that we calculated for GE. In other words, they include (1) dividends or interest and (2) any capital gains or losses.

maturity premium
Extra average return from investing in long- versus short-term Treasury securities.

The safest investment, Treasury bills, had the lowest rates of return—they averaged 4 percent a year. Long-term government bonds gave slightly higher returns than Treasury bills. This difference is called the **maturity premium.** Common stocks were in a class by themselves. Investors who accepted the risk of common stocks received on average an extra return of 7.6 percent a year over the return on Treasury bills. This

FIGURE 10–1 How an investment of $1 at the start of 1900 would have grown by the end of 2004 (index values plotted on log scale)

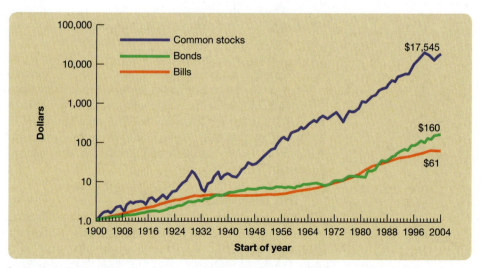

Source: Author's calculations using data from E. Dimson, P. R. Marsh, and M. Staunton, *Triumph of the Optimists: 101 Years of Global Investment Returns* (Princeton, NJ: Princeton University Press, 2002), with updates kindly provided by *Triumph's* authors.

TABLE 10-1 Average rates of return on Treasury bills, government bonds, and common stocks, 1900-2004 (figures in percent per year)

Portfolio	Average Annual Rate of Return	Average Premium (Extra Return versus Treasury Bills)
Treasury bills	4.0	
Treasury bonds	5.3	1.2
Common stocks	11.7	7.6

Source: Authors' calculations using data from Elroy Dimson, Paul Marsh, and Mike Staunton, *Triumph of the Optimists: 101 Years of Global Equity Returns* (Princeton, NJ: Princeton University Press, 2002), with updates kindly provided by *Triumph*'s authors.

risk premium

Expected return in excess of risk-free return as compensation for risk.

compensation for taking on the risk of common stock ownership is known as the market **risk premium:**

$$\text{Rate of return on common stocks} = \text{interest rate on Treasury bills} + \text{market risk premium}$$

The historical record shows that investors have received a risk premium for holding risky assets. Average returns on high-risk assets are higher than those on low-risk assets.

You may ask why we look back over such a long period to measure average rates of return. The reason is that annual rates of return for common stocks fluctuate so much that averages taken over short periods are extremely unreliable. In some years investors in common stocks had a disagreeable shock and received a substantially lower return than they expected. In other years they had a pleasant surprise and received a higher-than-expected return. By averaging the returns across both the rough years and the smooth, we should get a fair idea of the typical return that investors might justifiably expect.

While common stocks have offered the highest average returns, they have also been riskier investments. Figure 10-2 shows the 105 annual rates of return on common stocks. The fluctuations in year-to-year returns on common stocks are remarkably wide. There were 2 years (1933 and 1954) when investors earned a return of more than 50 percent. However, Figure 10-2 shows that you can also lose money by investing in the stock market. The most dramatic case was the stock market crash of 1929-1932. Shortly after President Coolidge joyfully observed that stocks were "cheap at current

FIGURE 10-2 Rates of return on common stocks, 1900-2004

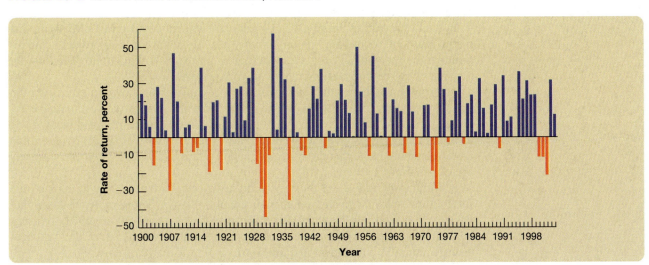

Source: Author's calculations using data from E. Dimson, P. R. Marsh, and M. Staunton, *Triumph of the Optimists: 101 Years of Global Investment Returns* (Princeton, NJ: Princeton University Press, 2002), with updates kindly provided by *Triumph*'s authors.

prices," stocks rapidly became even cheaper. By July 1932 the Dow Jones Industrial Average had fallen in a series of slides by 89 percent.

You don't have to look that far back to see that the stock market is a risky place. Investors who had bought at the stock market peak in March 2000 would have seen little but falling stock prices over the next $2^1/_2$ years. By October 2002 the S&P 500 had declined by 49 percent, while the tech-heavy NASDAQ market fell by 78 percent.

Bond prices also fluctuate, but far less than stock prices. The worst year for investors in our portfolio of Treasury bonds was 1967; their return that year was –9.2 percent.

Self-Test 10.2   Here are the average rates of return for common stocks and Treasury bills for four different periods:

	1900–1924	1925–1949	1950–1975	1976–2004
Stocks	9.5%	10.2%	12.1%	14.0%
Treasury bills	4.9	1.1	3.6	6.2

What was the risk premium on stocks for each of these periods?

Using Historical Evidence to Estimate Today's Cost of Capital

Think back now to Chapter 7, where we showed how firms calculate the present value of a new project by discounting the expected cash flows by the opportunity cost of capital. The opportunity cost of capital is the return that the firm's shareholders are giving up by investing in the project rather than in comparable risk alternatives.

Measuring the cost of capital is easy if the project is a sure thing. Since shareholders can obtain a surefire payoff by investing in a U.S. Treasury bill, the firm should invest in a risk-free project only if it can at least match the rate of interest on such a loan. If the project is risky—and most projects are—then the firm needs to at least match the return that shareholders could expect to earn if they invested in securities of similar risk. It is not easy to put a precise figure on this, but our skim through history provides an idea of the average return an investor might expect to earn from an investment in risky common stocks.

Suppose there is an investment project that you *know*—don't ask how—has the same risk as an investment in a diversified portfolio of U.S. common stocks. We will say that it has the same degree of risk as the *market portfolio.*

Instead of investing in the project, your shareholders could invest directly in this market portfolio. Therefore, the opportunity cost of capital for your project is the return that the shareholders could expect to earn on the market portfolio. This is what they are giving up by investing money in your project.

The problem of estimating the project cost of capital boils down to estimating the currently expected rate of return on the market portfolio. One way to estimate the expected market return is to assume that the future will be like the past and that today's investors expect to receive the average rates of return shown in Table 10–1. In this case, you would judge that the expected market return today is 11.7 percent, the average of past market returns.

Unfortunately, this is *not* the way to do it. Investors are not likely to demand the same return each year on an investment in common stocks. For example, we know that the interest rate on safe Treasury bills varies over time. At their peak in 1981, Treasury bills offered a return of 14 percent, nearly 10 percentage points above the 4 percent average return on bills shown in Table 10–1.

What if you were called upon to estimate the expected return on common stocks in 1981? Would you have said 11.7 percent? That doesn't make sense. Who would invest

Has the Risk Premium Changed?

Long-term data on returns on stocks, bills, and bonds are available on **www.globalfindata.com**. (Choose *Sample Data* in the *Database* pull-down menu.) Copy the data into a spreadsheet. Calculate the average market risk premium for common stocks for successive 10-year periods. Could the fluctuations in the premium be due to chance, or do you think there has been a trend?

in the risky stock market for an expected return of 11.7 percent when you could get a safe 14 percent from Treasury bills?

A better procedure is to take the *current* interest rate on Treasury bills plus 7.6 percent, the average *risk premium* shown in Table 10–1. In 1981, when the rate on Treasury bills was 14 percent, that would have given

$$\text{Expected market return (1981)} = \text{interest rate on Treasury bills (1981)} + \text{normal risk premium}$$

$$= 14 + 7.6 = 21.6\%$$

The first term on the right-hand side tells us the time value of money in 1981; the second term measures the compensation for risk. The expected return on an investment provides compensation to investors both for waiting (the time value of money) and for worrying (the risk of the particular asset).

What about today? As we write this in early 2005, Treasury bills offer a return of only 2.5 percent. This suggests that investors in common stocks are looking for a return of 10.1 percent:[3]

$$\text{Expected market return (2005)} = \text{interest rate on Treasury bills (2005)} + \text{normal risk premium}$$

$$= 2.5 + 7.6 = 10.1\%$$

These calculations assume that there is a normal, stable risk premium on the market portfolio, so the expected *future* risk premium can be measured by the average past risk premium. But even with 100 years of data, we can't estimate the market risk premium exactly; nor can we be sure that investors today are demanding the same reward for risk that they were in the early 1900s. All this leaves plenty of room for argument about what the risk premium *really* is.[4]

Many financial managers and economists believe that long-run historical returns are the best measure available. Others have a gut instinct that investors don't need such a large risk premium to persuade them to hold common stocks. For example, recent surveys of financial economists revealed that they expected a risk premium of between 5.5 and 7 percent, while surveys of chief financial officers have suggested an average risk premium of 5.6 percent.[5]

---

[3] In practice, things might be a bit more complicated. We've mentioned the yield curve, the relationship between bond maturity and yield. When firms consider investments in long-lived projects, they usually think about risk premiums relative to long-term bonds. In this case, the risk-free rate would be taken as the current long-term bond yield less the average maturity premium on such bonds.

[4] Often the disagreements simply reflect the fact that the *risk premium* is defined in different ways. For example, some measure the average difference between stock returns and the returns (or yields) on long-term bonds.

[5] These figures are derived from surveys reported in I. Welch, "Views of Financial Economists on the Equity Premium and on Professional Controversies," *Journal of Business* 73 (2000), pp. 501–537; I. Welch, "The Equity Premium Consensus Forecast Revisited," Cowles Foundation Discussion Paper No. 1325, Yale School of Management, September 2001; and J. R. Graham and C. R. Harvey, "Expectations of Equity Risk Premia, Volatility and Asymmetry from a Corporate Finance Perspective," working paper, Fuqua School of Business, Duke University, July 2003.

FIGURE 10–3 The risk premium in 17 countries, 1900–2004. The return on common stocks has averaged about 7.1 percent more than the interest rate on bills.

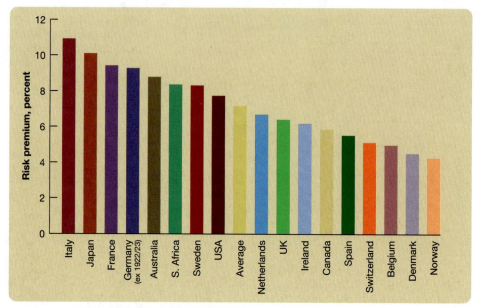

Source: Author's calculations using data from E. Dimson, P. R. Marsh, and M. Staunton, *Triumph of the Optimists: 101 Years of Global Investment Returns* (Princeton, NJ: Princeton University Press, 2002), with updates kindly provided by *Triumph*'s authors.

We may be able to gain some further insights into the question by looking at the experience of other countries. Figure 10–3 shows that the United States is roughly average in terms of the risk premium. Norwegian common stocks come bottom of the league; the average risk premium in Norway is only 4.2 percent. Top of the form is Italy with a premium of 10.8 percent. Some of these variations between countries may reflect differences in risk. For example, Italian stocks have been particularly variable and investors may have required a higher return to compensate. But remember how difficult it is to make precise estimates of what investors expected. You probably would not be too far out if you concluded that the *expected* risk premium was the same in each country.

10.3 Measuring Risk

You now have some benchmarks. You know that the opportunity cost of capital for safe projects must be the rate of return offered by safe Treasury bills, and you know that the opportunity cost of capital for "average-risk" projects must be the expected return on the market portfolio. But you *don't* know how to estimate the cost of capital for projects that do not fit these two simple cases. Before you can do this, you need to understand more about investment risk.

The average fuse time for army hand grenades is 7 seconds, but that average hides a lot of potentially relevant information. If you are in the business of throwing grenades, you need some measure of the variation around the average fuse time.[6] Similarly, if you are in the business of investing in securities, you need some measure of how far the returns may differ from the average.

One way to present the spread of possible investment returns is by using histograms, such as the ones in Figure 10–4. The bars in each histogram show the number of years between 1900 and 2004 that the investment's return fell within a specific range. Look first at the performance of common stocks. Their risk shows up in the wide spread of outcomes. For example, you can see that in one year the return was be-

---

[6] We can reassure you; the variation around the standard fuse time is very small.

FIGURE 10-4 Historical returns on major asset classes, 1900–2004

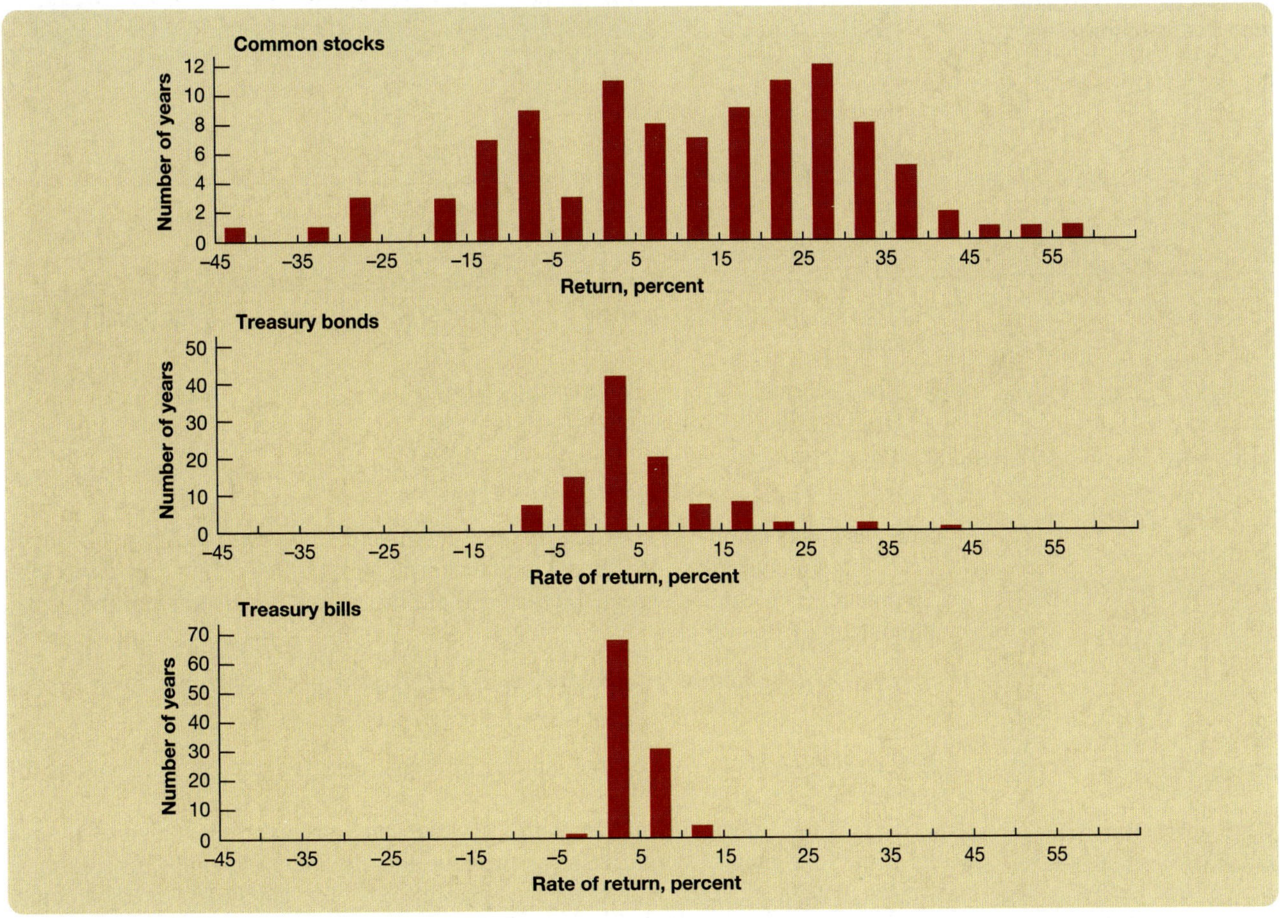

Source: Author's calculations using data from E. Dimson, P. R. Marsh, and M. Staunton, *Triumph of the Optimists: 101 Years of Global Investment Returns* (Princeton, NJ: Princeton University Press, 2002), with updates kindly provided by *Triumph's* authors.

tween +55 percent and +60 percent, but there was also one year that investors lost between 40 percent and 45 percent.

The corresponding histograms for Treasury bonds and bills show that unusually high or low returns are much less common. Investors in these securities could have been much more confident of the outcome than common stockholders.

Variance and Standard Deviation

Investment risk depends on the dispersion or spread of possible outcomes. For example, Figure 10–4 showed that on past evidence there is greater uncertainty about the possible returns from common stocks than about the returns from bills or bonds. Sometimes a picture like Figure 10–4 tells you all you need to know about (past) dispersion. But in general, pictures do not suffice. The financial manager needs a numerical measure of dispersion. The standard measures are **variance** and **standard deviation.** More variable returns imply greater investment risk. This suggests that some measure of dispersion will provide a reasonable measure of risk, and dispersion is precisely what is measured by variance and standard deviation.

Here is a very simple example showing how variance and standard deviation are calculated: Suppose that you are offered the chance to play the following game. You start by investing $100. Then two coins are flipped. For each head that comes up your starting balance will be *increased* by 20 percent, and for each tail that comes up your

variance
Average value of squared deviations from mean. A measure of volatility.

standard deviation
Square root of variance. Another measure of volatility.

TABLE 10–2 The coin-toss game; calculating variance and standard deviation

(1) Percent Rate of Return	(2) Deviation from Expected Return	(3) Squared Deviation
+40	+30	900
+10	0	0
+10	0	0
−20	−30	900

Notes:
1. Variance = average of squared deviations = 1,800/4 = 450.
2. Standard deviation = square root of variance = $\sqrt{450}$ = 21.2, about 21%.

starting balance will be *reduced* by 10 percent. Clearly there are four equally likely outcomes:

- Head + head: You make 20 + 20 = 40%
- Head + tail: You make 20 − 10 = 10%
- Tail + head: You make −10 + 20 = 10%
- Tail + tail: You make −10 − 10 = −20%

There is a chance of 1 in 4, or .25, that you will make 40 percent; a chance of 2 in 4, or .5, that you will make 10 percent; and a chance of 1 in 4, or .25, that you will lose 20 percent. The game's expected return is therefore a weighted average of the possible outcomes:

Expected return = probability-weighted average of possible outcomes
$$= (.25 \times 40) + (.5 \times 10) + (.25 \times -20) = +10\%$$

If you play the game a very large number of times, your average return should be 10 percent.

Table 10–2 shows how to calculate the variance and standard deviation of the returns on your game. Column 1 shows the four equally likely outcomes. In column 2 we calculate the difference between each possible outcome and the expected outcome. You can see that at best the return could be 30 percent higher than expected; at worst it could be 30 percent lower.

These deviations in column 2 illustrate the spread of possible returns. But if we want a measure of this spread, it is no use just averaging the deviations in column 2—the average is always going to be zero. To get around this problem, we *square* the deviations in column 2 before averaging them. These squared deviations are shown in column 3. The variance is the average of these squared deviations and therefore is a natural measure of dispersion:

Variance = average of squared deviations around the average
$$= \frac{1,800}{4} = 450$$

When we squared the deviations from the expected return, we changed the units of measurement from *percentages* to *percentages squared.* Our last step is to get back to percentages by taking the square root of the variance. This is the standard deviation:

Standard deviation = square root of variance
$$= \sqrt{450} = 21\%$$

Because standard deviation is simply the square root of variance, it too is a natural measure of risk. If the outcome of the game had been certain, the standard deviation would have been zero because there would then be no deviations from the expected outcome. The actual standard deviation is positive because we *don't* know what will happen.

TABLE 10-3 The coin-toss game; calculating variance and standard deviation when there are different probabilities of each outcome

(1) Percent Rate of Return	(2) Probability of Return	(3) Deviation from Expected Return	(4) Probability × Squared Deviation
+40	.25	+30	.25 × 900 = 225
+10	.50	0	.50 × 0 = 0
−20	.25	−30	.25 × 900 = 225

Notes:
1. Variance = sum of squared deviations weighted by probabilities = 225 + 0 + 225 = 450.
2. Standard deviation = square root of variance = $\sqrt{450}$ = 21.2, about 21%.

Now think of a second game. It is the same as the first except that each head means a 35 percent gain and each tail means a 25 percent loss. Again there are four equally likely outcomes:

- Head + head: You gain 70%
- Head + tail: You gain 10%
- Tail + head: You gain 10%
- Tail + tail: You lose 50%

For this game, the expected return is 10 percent, the same as that of the first game, but it is more risky. For example, in the first game, the worst possible outcome is a loss of 20 percent, which is 30 percent worse than the expected outcome. In the second game the downside is a loss of 50 percent, or 60 percent below the expected return. This increased spread of outcomes shows up in the standard deviation, which is double that of the first game, 42 percent versus 21 percent. By this measure the second game is twice as risky as the first.

A Note on Calculating Variance

When we calculated variance in Table 10–2 we recorded separately each of the four possible outcomes. An alternative would have been to recognize that in two of the cases the outcomes were the same. Thus there was a 50 percent chance of a 10 percent return from the game, a 25 percent chance of a 40 percent return, and a 25 percent chance of a –20 percent return. We can calculate variance by weighting each squared deviation by the probability and then summing the results. Table 10–3 confirms that this method gives the same answer.

Self-Test 10.3   Calculate the variance and standard deviation of the second (higher-risk) coin-tossing game in the same formats as Tables 10–2 and 10–3.

Measuring the Variation in Stock Returns

When estimating the spread of possible outcomes from investing in the stock market, most financial analysts start by assuming that the spread of returns in the past is a reasonable indication of what could happen in the future. Therefore, they calculate the standard deviation of past returns. To illustrate, suppose that you were presented with the data for stock market returns shown in Table 10–4. The average return over the 6 years from 1999 to 2004 was 4.18 percent. This is just the sum of the returns over the 6 years divided by 6 (25.1/6 = 4.18 percent).

Column 2 in Table 10–4 shows the difference between each year's return and the average return. For example, in 1999 the return of 23.7 percent on common stocks was above the 6-year average by 19.52 percent (23.7 – 4.18 = 19.52 percent). In column 3

TABLE 10-4 The average
return and standard deviation
of stock market returns,
1999-2004

Year	Rate of Return,%	Deviation from Average Return%	Squared Deviation
1999	23.7	19.52	381.03
2000	−10.9	−15.08	227.41
2001	−11.0	−15.18	230.43
2002	−20.9	−25.08	629.01
2003	31.6	27.42	751.86
2004	12.6	8.42	70.90
Total	25.1		2,290.63

Average return = 25.1/6 = 4.18%

Variance = average of squared deviations = 2290.63/6 = 381.77

Standard deviation = square root of variance = 19.54%

Source: Authors' calculations using data from E. Dimson, P. R. Marsh, and M. Staunton, *Triumph of the Optimists: 101 Years of Global Equity Returns* (Princeton, NJ: Princeton University Press, 2002), with updates kindly provided by *Triumph*'s authors.

we square these deviations from the average. The variance is then the average of these squared deviations:[7]

Variance = average of squared deviations

$$= \frac{2,290.63}{6} = 381.77$$

Since standard deviation is the square root of the variance,

Standard deviation = square root of variance

$$= \sqrt{381.77} = 19.54\%$$

It is difficult to measure the risk of securities on the basis of just six past outcomes. Therefore, Table 10–5 lists the annual standard deviations for our three portfolios of securities over the period 1900–2004. As expected, Treasury bills were the least variable security, and common stocks were the most variable. Treasury bonds hold the middle ground.

Of course, there is no reason to believe that the market's variability should stay the same over many years. Indeed many people believe that in recent years the stock market has become more volatile due to irresponsible speculation by . . . (fill in here the name of your preferred guilty party). Figure 10–5 provides a chart of the volatility of

TABLE 10-5 Standard
deviation of returns, 1900-2004

Portfolio	Standard Deviation, %
Treasury bills	2.8
Long-term government bonds	8.3
Common stocks	20.0

Source: Authors' calculations using data from Elroy Dimson, Paul Marsh, and Mike Staunton, *Triumph of the Optimists: 101 Years of Global Equity Returns* (Princeton, NJ: Princeton University Press, 2002), with updates kindly provided by *Triumph*'s authors.

---

[7] *Technical note:* When variance is estimated from a sample of observed returns, it is common to add the squared deviations and divide by $N - 1$, rather than N, where N is the number of observations. This procedure adjusts the estimate for what is called *the loss of a degree of freedom.* We will ignore this fine point, emphasizing the interpretation of variance as an average squared deviation. In any event, the correction for the lost degree of freedom is negligible when there are plentiful observations. For example, with 100 years of data, the difference between dividing by 99 or 100 will affect the estimated variance by only 1 percent (i.e., a factor of 1.01).

FIGURE 10-5 Stock market volatility, 1926-2004

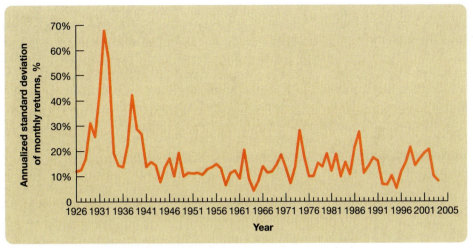

Source: Ibbotson Associates.

the U.S. stock market for each year from 1926 to 2004.[8] You can see that there are periods of unusually high variability, but there is no long-term upward trend.

10.4 Risk and Diversification

Diversification

We can calculate our measures of variability equally well for individual securities and portfolios of securities. Of course, the level of variability over 100 years is less interesting for specific companies than for the market portfolio because it is a rare company that faces the same business risks today as it did a century ago.

Table 10-6 presents estimated standard deviations for 10 well-known common stocks for a recent 5-year period.[9] Do these standard deviations look high to you? They should. Remember that the market portfolio's standard deviation was 20 percent over the entire 1900–2004 period. Of our individual stocks only ExxonMobil had a standard deviation of less than 20 percent. Most stocks are substantially more variable than the market portfolio; only a handful are less variable.

TABLE 10-6 Standard deviations for selected common stocks, January 2001–December 2004

Amazon.com	68.2%
Dell Computer	45.5
Ford	42.7
Boeing	33.8
McDonald's	28.1
General Electric	24.3
Wal-Mart	23.1
H.J. Heinz	21.8
Pfizer	20.4
ExxonMobil	15.7

---

[8] We converted the monthly variance to an annual variance by multiplying by 12. In other words, the variance of annual returns is 12 times that of monthly returns. The longer you hold a security, the more risk you have to bear.

[9] We pointed out earlier that five annual observations are insufficient to give a reliable estimate of variability. Therefore, these estimates are derived from 60 monthly rates of return, and then the monthly variance is multiplied by 12.

diversification
Strategy designed to reduce risk by spreading the portfolio across many investments.

This raises an important question: The market portfolio is made up of individual stocks, so why isn't its variability equal to the average variability of its components? The answer is that **diversification** *reduces variability.*

Selling umbrellas is a risky business; you may make a killing when it rains, but you are likely to lose your shirt in a heat wave. Selling ice cream is no safer; you do well in the heat wave, but business is poor in the rain. Suppose, however, that you invest in both an umbrella shop and an ice cream shop. By diversifying your investment across the two businesses, you make an average level of profit come rain or shine.

Portfolio diversification works because prices of different stocks do not move exactly together. Statisticians make the same point when they say that stock price changes are less than perfectly correlated. Diversification works best when the returns are negatively correlated, as is the case of our umbrella and ice cream businesses. When one business does well, the other does badly. Unfortunately, in practice, stocks that are negatively correlated are as rare as pecan pie in Budapest.

Asset versus Portfolio Risk

The history of returns on different asset classes provides compelling evidence of a risk–return trade-off and suggests that the variability of the rates of return on each asset class is a useful measure of risk. However, volatility of returns can be a misleading measure of risk for an individual asset held as part of a portfolio. To see why, consider the following example.

Suppose there are three equally likely outcomes, or *scenarios,* for the economy: a recession, normal growth, and a boom. An investment in an auto stock will have a rate of return of –8 percent in a recession, 5 percent in a normal period, and 18 percent in a boom. Auto firms are *cyclical:* They do well when the economy does well. In contrast, gold firms are often said to be *countercyclical,* meaning that they do well when other firms do poorly. Suppose that stock in a gold mining firm will provide a rate of return of 20 percent in a recession, 3 percent in a normal period, and –20 percent in a boom. These assumptions are summarized in Table 10–7.

It appears that gold is the more volatile investment. The difference in return across the boom and bust scenarios is 40 percent (–20 percent in a boom versus +20 percent in a recession), compared to a spread of only 26 percent for the auto stock. In fact, we can confirm the higher volatility by measuring the variance or standard deviation of returns of the two assets. The calculations are set out in Table 10–8.

Since all three scenarios are equally likely, the expected return on each stock is simply the average of the three possible outcomes.[10] For the auto stock the expected return is 5 percent; for the gold stock it is 1 percent. The variance is the average of the squared deviations from the expected return, and the standard deviation is the square root of the variance.

Self-Test 10.4 **Suppose the probability of the recession or boom is .30, while the probability of a normal period is .40. Would you expect the variance of returns on these two investments to be higher or lower? Why? Confirm by calculating the standard deviation of the auto stock. (Refer back to "A Note on Calculating Variance" in Section 10.3 if you are unsure of how to do this.)**

The gold mining stock offers a lower expected rate of return than the auto stock and *more* volatility—a loser on both counts, right? Would anyone be willing to hold gold mining stocks in an investment portfolio? The answer is a resounding yes.

---

[10] If the probabilities were not equal, we would need to weight each outcome by its probability in calculating the expected outcome and the variance.

TABLE 10–7 Rate of return assumptions for two stocks

		Rate of Return, %	
Scenario	Probability	Auto Stock	Gold Stock
Recession	1/3	–8	+20
Normal	1/3	+5	+3
Boom	1/3	+18	–20

To see why, suppose you do believe that gold is a lousy asset, and therefore you hold your entire portfolio in the auto stock. Your expected return is 5 percent and your standard deviation is 10.6 percent. We'll compare that portfolio to a partially diversified one, invested 75 percent in autos and 25 percent in gold. For example, if you have a $10,000 portfolio, you could put $7,500 in autos and $2,500 in gold.

First, we need to calculate the return on this portfolio in each scenario. The portfolio return is the weighted average of returns on the individual assets with weights equal to the proportion of the portfolio invested in each asset. For a portfolio formed from only two assets,

$$\begin{aligned}\text{Portfolio rate} \atop \text{of return} = &\left(\begin{matrix}\text{fraction of portfolio} \\ \text{in first asset}\end{matrix} \times \begin{matrix}\text{rate of return} \\ \text{on first asset}\end{matrix}\right) \\ + &\left(\begin{matrix}\text{fraction of portfolio} \\ \text{in second asset}\end{matrix} \times \begin{matrix}\text{rate of return} \\ \text{on second asset}\end{matrix}\right)\end{aligned}$$

For example, autos have a weight of .75 and a rate of return of –8 percent in the recession, and gold has a weight of .25 and a return of 20 percent in a recession. Therefore, the portfolio return in the recession is the following weighted average:[11]

$$\text{Portfolio return in recession} = [.75 \times (-8\%)] + (.25 \times 20\%)$$
$$= -1\%$$

Table 10–9 expands Table 10–7 to include the portfolio of the auto stock and the gold mining stock. The expected returns and volatility measures are summarized at the

TABLE 10–8 Expected return and volatility for two stocks

	Auto Stock			Gold Stock		
Scenario	Rate of Return, %	Deviation from Expected Return, %	Squared Deviation	Rate of Return, %	Deviation from Expected Return, %	Squared Deviation
Recession	–8	–13	169	+20	+19	361
Normal	+5	0	0	+3	+2	4
Boom	+18	+13	169	–20	–21	441
Expected return	$\frac{1}{3}(-8 + 5 + 18) = 5\%$			$\frac{1}{3}(+20 + 3 - 20) = 1\%$		
Variance*	$\frac{1}{3}(169 + 0 + 169) = 112.7$			$\frac{1}{3}(361 + 4 + 441) = 268.7$		
Standard deviation (= √variance)	$\sqrt{112.7} = 10.6\%$			$\sqrt{268.7} = 16.4\%$		

*Variance = average of squared deviations from the expected value.

[11] Let's confirm this. Suppose you invest $7,500 in autos and $2,500 in gold. If the recession hits, the rate of return on autos will be –8 percent, and the value of the auto investment will fall by 8 percent to $6,900. The rate of return on gold will be 20 percent, and the value of the gold investment will rise 20 percent to $3,000. The value of the total portfolio falls from its original value of $10,000 to $6,900 + $3,000 = $9,900, which is a rate of return of –1 percent. This matches the rate of return given by the formula for the weighted average.

TABLE 10–9 Rates of return for two stocks and a portfolio

Scenario	Probability	Rate of Return, %		Portfolio Return, %*
		Auto Stock	**Gold Stock**	
Recession	1/3	−8	+20	−1.0
Normal	1/3	+5	+3	+4.5
Boom	1/3	+18	−20	+8.5
Expected return		5	1	4
Variance		112.7	268.7	15.2
Standard deviation		10.6	16.4	3.9

* Portfolio return = (.75 × auto stock return) + (.25 × gold stock return)

bottom of the table. The surprising finding is this: When you shift funds from the auto stock to the more volatile gold mining stock, your portfolio variability actually *decreases*. In fact, the volatility of the auto-plus-gold stock portfolio is considerably less than the volatility of *either* stock separately. This is the payoff to diversification.

We can understand this more clearly by focusing on asset returns in the two extreme scenarios, boom and recession. In the boom, when auto stocks do best, the poor return on gold reduces the performance of the overall portfolio. However, when auto stocks are stalling in a recession, gold shines, providing a substantial positive return that boosts portfolio performance. The gold stock offsets the swings in the performance of the auto stock, reducing the best-case return but improving the worst-case return. The inverse relationship between the returns on the two stocks means that the addition of the gold mining stock to an all-auto portfolio stabilizes returns.

A gold stock is really a *negative-risk* asset to an investor starting with an all-auto portfolio. Adding it to the portfolio reduces the volatility of returns. The *incremental* risk of the gold stock (that is, the *change* in overall risk when gold is added to the portfolio) is *negative* despite the fact that gold returns are highly volatile.

In general, the incremental risk of a stock depends on whether its returns tend to vary with or against the returns of the other assets in the portfolio. Incremental risk does not just depend on a stock's volatility. If returns do not move closely with those of the rest of the portfolio, the stock will reduce the volatility of portfolio returns.

We can summarize as follows:

1. Investors care about the expected return and risk of their *portfolio* of assets. The risk of the overall portfolio can be measured by the volatility of returns, that is, the variance or standard deviation.
2. The standard deviation of the returns of an individual security measures how risky that security would be if held in isolation. But an investor who holds a portfolio of securities is interested only in how each security affects the risk of the entire portfolio. The contribution of a security to the risk of the portfolio depends on how the security's returns vary with the investor's other holdings. Thus a security that is risky if held in isolation may nevertheless serve to reduce the variability of the portfolio if its returns do not move in lockstep with the rest of the portfolio.

EXAMPLE 10.1 ▶   Ford and Newmont Mining

Our example of the auto and gold mining stocks was entirely fanciful. But we can make the same point by looking at real auto and gold mining companies. For instance, suppose that at the end of 1994 you invested your savings in the stock of Ford Motor Company. The top chart in Figure 10–6 shows how the value of your portfolio would have fluctuated over the following 10 years. The risk shows up in the wide spread of monthly returns. For example, in almost one month in seven you would have lost more than 10 percent of your capital. The standard deviation of Ford's returns during this period amounted to 40.6 percent a year.

FIGURE 10–6 The spread of monthly returns, January 1995–December 2004, on the stocks of Ford Motor, Newmont Mining, and a portfolio evenly divided between the two. Note that diversification reduces the spread of returns.

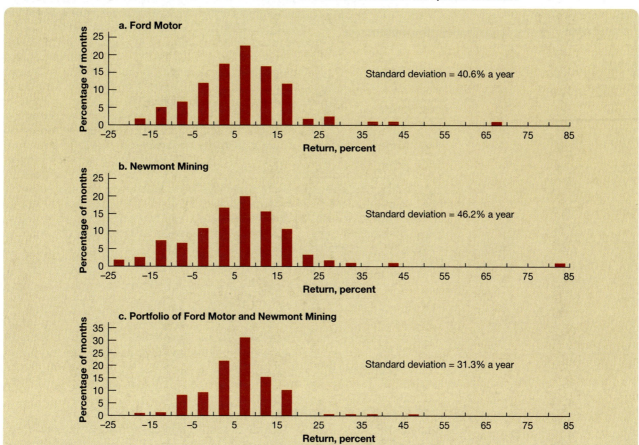

The second chart in Figure 10–6 shows a similar picture of the returns on Newmont Mining stock over the same period. Here the monthly fluctuations are even wider. If you had invested your entire capital in Newmont, you would have lost more than 10 percent of your savings in almost one month in five. The standard deviation of the returns on Newmont stock was 46.2 percent a year.

Although both stocks had their ups and downs, the two stocks have not moved in exact lockstep.[12] As often as not, a decline in the value of Ford stock was offset by a rise in the price of Newmont. So if you had split your portfolio between the two stocks, you could have reduced the monthly fluctuations in the value of your savings. You can see from the bottom chart in Figure 10–6 that if your portfolio had been evenly divided between Ford and Newmont Mining, there would have been many more months when the return was just middling and far fewer cases of extreme returns. By diversifying between the two stocks, you would have reduced the standard deviation of the returns on your investment to 31.3 percent a year. ◄

---

[12] Statisticians calculate a *correlation coefficient* as a measure of how closely two series move together. If Ford's and Newmont's stock moved in perfect lockstep, the correlation coefficient between the returns would be 1.0. If their returns were completely unrelated, the correlation would be zero. If the returns on two stocks tend to move inversely, that is, if one stock usually is up when the other is down, the correlation coefficient will be negative. If returns move in perfect but inverse lockstep, the correlation coefficient will be –1.0. But negative correlations are unusual. Because most firms have a common dependence on the overall economy, correlations between stock returns are typically positive. The average correlation between the returns on the stocks shown in Table 10–6 was .04.

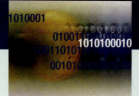

How Diversification Reduces Risk

1. A large mutual fund group such as Fidelity offers a variety of funds. Some, called *sector funds,* specialize in particular industries; others, known as *index funds,* simply invest in the market index. Log on to **www.fidelity.com** and find first the standard deviation of returns on the Fidelity Spartan 500 Index Fund, which replicates the S&P 500. Now find the standard deviation of fund returns for different industry (sector) funds. Are they larger or smaller than the index fund? How do you interpret your findings?

2. The power of diversification depends on the correlation between the assets. You can see this by logging on to Campbell Harvey's home page at **www.duke.edu/~charvey** and following the link from *Finance Tools* to *Two-Assets Mean Variance Graph.* See what happens to portfolio risk if you hold different proportions of two stocks chosen from Table 10–6. Enter the standard deviation for each stock, assuming a different expected return for each. Look first at the levels of portfolio risk if the returns move in perfect lockstep (correlation = 1.0). Now progressively reduce the correlation between the two stocks. You will find that portfolio risk falls. When the correlation is –1 (i.e., the stocks move in exactly opposite directions), diversification can potentially get rid of all risk.

Self-Test 10.5

An investor is currently fully invested in gold mining stocks. Which action would do more to reduce portfolio risk: diversification into silver mining stocks or into automotive stocks? Why?

Market Risk versus Unique Risk

Our examples illustrate that even a little diversification can provide a substantial reduction in variability. Suppose you calculate and compare the standard deviations of randomly chosen one-stock portfolios, two-stock portfolios, five-stock portfolios, and so on. You can see from Figure 10–7 that diversification can cut the variability of returns by about half. But you can get most of this benefit with relatively few stocks: The improvement is slight when the number of stocks is increased beyond, say, 15 or 20.

FIGURE 10–7 The risk (standard deviation) of portfolios containing different numbers of New York Stock Exchange stocks. Notice that diversification reduces risk rapidly at first and then more slowly.

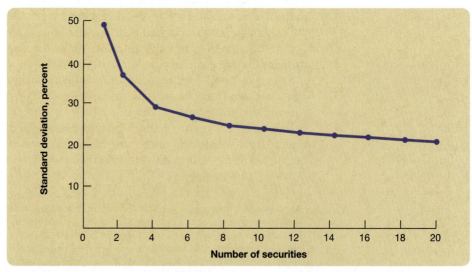

Source: M. Statman, "How Many Stocks Make a Diversified Portfolio?" *Journal of Financial and Quantitative Analysis* 22 (September 1987), pp. 353–363.

FIGURE 10-8 Diversification eliminates unique risk. But there is some risk that diversification cannot eliminate. This is called market risk.

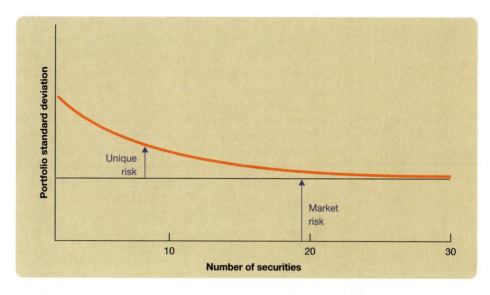

Figure 10–7 also illustrates that no matter how many securities you hold, you cannot eliminate all risk. There remains the danger that the market—including your portfolio—will plummet.

The risk that can be eliminated by diversification is called **unique risk.** The risk that you can't avoid regardless of how much you diversify is generally known as **market risk** or *systematic risk. Unique risk* arises because many of the perils that surround an individual company are peculiar to that company and perhaps its direct competitors. *Market risk* stems from economywide perils that threaten all businesses. Market risk explains why stocks have a tendency to move together, so even well-diversified portfolios are exposed to market movements.

Figure 10–8 divides risk into its two parts—unique risk and market risk. If you have only a single stock, unique risk is very important; but once you have a portfolio of 30 or more stocks, diversification has done most of what it can to eliminate risk. For a reasonably well-diversified portfolio, only market risk matters.

unique risk
Risk factors affecting only that firm. Also called *diversifiable risk.*

market risk
Economywide (macroeconomic) sources of risk that affect the overall stock market. Also called *systematic risk.*

10.5 Thinking about Risk

How can you tell which risks are unique and diversifiable? Where do market risks come from? Here are three messages to help you think clearly about risk.

Message 1: Some Risks Look Big and Dangerous but Really Are Diversifiable

Managers confront risks "up close and personal." They must make decisions about particular investments. The failure of such an investment could cost a promotion, bonus, or otherwise steady job. Yet that same investment may not seem risky to an investor who can stand back and combine it in a diversified portfolio with many other assets or securities.

EXAMPLE 10.2 ▶ Wildcat Oil Wells

You have just been promoted to director of exploration, Western Hemisphere, of MPS Oil. The manager of your exploration team in far-off Costaguana has appealed for $20 million extra to drill in an even steamier part of the Costaguanan jungle. The manager thinks there may be an "elephant" field worth $500 million or more hidden there. But the chance of finding it is at best 1 in 10, and yesterday MPS's CEO sourly commented on the $100 million already "wasted" on Costaguanan exploration.

Is this a risky investment? For you it probably is; you may be a hero if oil is found and a goat otherwise. But MPS drills hundreds of wells worldwide; for the company as a whole, it's the *average* success rate that matters. Geologic risks (is there oil or not?) should average out. The risk of a worldwide drilling program is much less than the apparent risk of any single wildcat well.

Back up one step, and think of the investors who buy MPS stock. The investors may hold other oil companies too, as well as companies producing steel, computers, clothing, cement, and breakfast cereal. They naturally—and realistically—assume that your successes and failures in drilling oil wells will average out with the thousands of independent bets made by the companies in their portfolio.

Therefore, the risks you face in Costaguana do not affect the rate of return they demand for investing in MPS Oil. Diversified investors in MPS stock will be happy if you find that elephant field, but they probably will not notice if you fail and lose your job. In any case, they will not demand a higher *average* rate of return for worrying about geologic risks in Costaguana.   ◄

EXAMPLE 10.3 ► Fire Insurance

Would you be willing to write a $100,000 fire insurance policy on your neighbor's house? The neighbor is willing to pay you $100 for a year's protection, and experience shows that the chance of fire damage in a given year is substantially less than 1 in 1,000. But if your neighbor's house is damaged by fire, you would have to pay up.

Few of us have deep enough pockets to insure our neighbors, even if the odds of fire damage are very low. Insurance seems a risky business if you think policy by policy. But a large insurance company, which may issue a million policies, is concerned only with average losses, which can be predicted with excellent accuracy.   ◄

Self-Test 10.6

Imagine a laboratory at IBM, late at night. One scientist speaks to another.

"You're right, Watson, I admit this experiment will consume all the rest of this year's budget. I don't know what we'll do if it fails. But if this yttrium–magnoosium alloy superconducts, the patents will be worth millions."

Would this be a good or bad investment for IBM? Can't say. But from the ultimate investors' viewpoint this is *not* a risky investment. Explain why.

Message 2: Market Risks Are Macro Risks

We have seen that diversified portfolios are not exposed to the unique risks of individual stocks but are exposed to the uncertain events that affect the entire securities market and the entire economy. These are macroeconomic, or "macro," factors such as changes in interest rates, industrial production, inflation, foreign exchange rates, and energy costs. These factors affect most firms' earnings and stock prices. When the relevant macro risks turn generally favorable, stock prices rise and investors do well; when the same variables go the other way, investors suffer.

You can often assess relative market risks just by thinking through exposures to the business cycle and other macro variables. The following businesses have substantial macro and market risks:

- *Airlines.* Because business travel falls during a recession, and individuals postpone vacations and other discretionary travel, the airline industry is subject to the swings of the business cycle. On the positive side, airline profits really take off when business is booming and personal incomes are rising.
- *Machine tool manufacturers.* These businesses are especially exposed to the business cycle. Manufacturing companies that have excess capacity rarely buy new machine tools to expand. During recessions, excess capacity can be quite high.

Here, on the other hand, are two industries with less than average macro exposures:

- *Food companies.* Companies selling staples, such as breakfast cereal, flour, and dog food, find that demand for their products is relatively stable in good times and bad.
- *Electric utilities.* Business demand for electric power varies somewhat across the business cycle, but by much less than demand for air travel or machine tools. Also, many electric utilities' profits are regulated. Regulation cuts off upside profit potential but also gives the utilities the opportunity to increase prices when demand is slack.

Remember, investors holding diversified portfolios are mostly concerned with macroeconomic risks. They do not worry about microeconomic risks peculiar to a particular company or investment project. Micro risks wash out in diversified portfolios. Company managers may worry about both macro and micro risks, but only the former affect the cost of capital.

Self-Test 10.7

Which company of each of the following pairs would you expect to be more exposed to macro risks?

a. A luxury Manhattan restaurant or an established Burger Queen franchise?
b. A paint company that sells through small paint and hardware stores to do-it-yourselfers or a paint company that sells in large volumes to Ford, GM, and Chrysler?

Message 3: Risk Can Be Measured

Delta Airlines clearly has more exposure to macro risks than food companies such as Kellogg or General Mills. These are easy cases. But is IBM stock a riskier investment than ExxonMobil? That's not an easy question to reason through. We can, however, *measure* the risk of IBM and ExxonMobil by looking at how their stock prices fluctuate.

We've already hinted at how to do this. Remember that diversified investors are concerned with market risks. The movements of the stock market sum up the net effects of all relevant macroeconomic uncertainties. If the market portfolio of all traded stocks is up in a particular month, we conclude that the net effect of macroeconomic news is positive. Remember, the performance of the market is barely affected by a firm-specific event. These cancel out across thousands of stocks in the market.

How do we measure the risk of a single stock, like IBM or ExxonMobil? We do not look at the stocks in isolation, because the risks that loom when you're up close to a single company are often diversifiable. Instead we measure the individual stock's sensitivity to the fluctuations of the overall stock market. We will show you how this works in the next chapter.

SUMMARY

How can one estimate the opportunity cost of capital for an "average-risk" project?

Over the past century the return on the **Standard & Poor's Composite Index** of common stocks has averaged 7.6 percent a year higher than the return on safe Treasury bills. This is the **risk premium** that investors have received for taking on the risk of investing in stocks. Long-term bonds have offered a higher return than Treasury bills but less than stocks.

If the risk premium in the past is a guide to the future, we can estimate the expected return on the market today by adding that 7.6 percent expected risk premium to today's interest rate on Treasury bills. This would be the opportunity cost of capital for an average-risk project, that is, one with the same risk as a typical share of common stock.

How is the standard deviation of returns for individual common stocks or for a stock portfolio calculated?

The spread of outcomes on different investments is commonly measured by the **variance** or **standard deviation** of the possible outcomes. The variance is the average of the squared deviations around the average outcome, and the standard deviation is the square root of the variance. The standard deviation of the returns on a market portfolio of common stocks has averaged 20 percent a year.

Why does diversification reduce risk?

The standard deviation of returns is generally higher on individual stocks than it is on the market. Because individual stocks do not move in exact lockstep, much of their risk can be diversified away. By spreading your portfolio across many investments, you smooth out the risk of your overall position. The risk that can be eliminated through diversification is known as **unique risk.**

What is the difference between unique risk, which can be diversified away, and market risk, which cannot?

Even if you hold a well-diversified portfolio, you will not eliminate all risk. You will still be exposed to macroeconomic changes that affect most stocks and the overall stock market. These macro risks combine to create **market risk**—that is, the risk that the market as a whole will slump.

   Stocks are not all equally risky. But what do we mean by a "high-risk stock"? We don't mean a stock that is risky if held in isolation; we mean a stock that makes an above-average contribution to the risk of a diversified portfolio. In other words, investors don't need to worry much about the risk that they can diversify away; they *do* need to worry about risk that can't be diversified. This depends on the stock's sensitivity to macroeconomic conditions.

QUIZ

1. **Rate of Return.** A stock is selling today for $40 per share. At the end of the year, it pays a dividend of $2 per share and sells for $44. What is the total rate of return on the stock? What are the dividend yield and percentage capital gain?

2. **Rate of Return.** Return to Problem 1. Suppose the year-end stock price after the dividend is paid is $36. What are the dividend yield and percentage capital gain in this case? Why is the dividend yield unaffected?

3. **Real versus Nominal Returns.** You purchase 100 shares of stock for $40 a share. The stock pays a $2 per share dividend at year-end. What is the rate of return on your investment for the end-of-year stock prices listed below? What is your real (inflation-adjusted) rate of return? Assume an inflation rate of 4 percent.
   a. $38
   b. $40
   c. $42

4. **Real versus Nominal Returns.** The Costaguanan stock market provided a rate of return of 95 percent. The inflation rate in Costaguana during the year was 80 percent. In the United States, in contrast, the stock market return was only 12 percent, but the inflation rate was only 2 percent. Which country's stock market provided the higher real rate of return?

5. **Real versus Nominal Returns.** The inflation rate in the United States in the twentieth century averaged around 3 percent. What was the average real rate of return on Treasury bills, Treasury bonds, and common stocks in that period? Use the data in Table 10–1.

6. **Real versus Nominal Returns.** Do you think it is possible for risk-free Treasury bills to offer a negative nominal interest rate? Might they offer a negative real expected rate of return?

7. **Market Indexes.** The accompanying table shows quarterly stock prices on the Dar es Salaam Stock Exchange for 2003–2004. Construct two stock market indexes, one using weights as in

the Dow Jones Industrial Average, the other using weights as in the Standard & Poor's Composite Index.

Quarterly prices in Tanzanian shillings for trading on the Dar es Salaam Stock Exchange. Only six stocks were traded.						
	Tanzania Breweries, 236 million*	TOL, 32 million*	Tanzania Tea Packers, 14 million*	Tanzania Cigarette Company, 100 million*	Simba, 64 million*	Dahaco, 36 million*
Jun. 2003	1,575	265	600	1,775	700	500
Sep. 2003	1,525	265	500	1,700	690	520
Dec. 2003	1,500	260	580	1,720	700	570
Mar. 2004	1,300	260	570	1,720	830	580

*Number of shares outstanding.

8. **Stock Market History.**
    a. What was the average rate of return on large U.S. common stocks from 1900 to 2004?
    b. What was the average risk premium on large stocks?
    c. What was the standard deviation of returns on the market portfolio?

PRACTICE PROBLEMS ℍ𝕄™

9. **Risk Premiums.** Here are stock market and Treasury bill returns between 2000 and 2004:

Year	Stock Market Return	T-Bill Return
2000	−10.89	5.89
2001	−10.97	3.83
2002	−20.86	1.65
2003	31.64	1.02
2004	12.62	1.20

    a. What was the risk premium on common stock in each year?
    b. What was the average risk premium?
    c. What was the standard deviation of the risk premium?

10. **Market Indexes.** In 1990, the Dow Jones Industrial Average was at a level of about 2,600. In 2005, it was about 10,000. Would you expect the Dow in 2005 to be more or less likely to move up or down by more than 40 points in a day than in 1990? Does this mean the market was riskier in 2005 than it was in 1990?

11. **Maturity Premiums.** Investments in long-term government bonds produced a negative average return during the period 1977–1981. How should we interpret this? Did bond investors in 1977 expect to earn a negative maturity premium? What do these 5 years' bond returns tell us about the normal future maturity premium?

12. **Risk Premiums.** What will happen to the opportunity cost of capital if investors suddenly become especially conservative and less willing to bear investment risk?

13. **Risk Premiums and Discount Rates.** You believe that a stock with the same market risk as the S&P 500 will sell at year-end at a price of $50. The stock will pay a dividend at year-end of $2. What price will you be willing to pay for the stock today? *Hint:* Start by checking today's 1-year Treasury rates.

Please visit us at www.mhhe.com/bmm5e or refer to your Student CD

14. **Scenario Analysis.** The common stock of Leaning Tower of Pita, Inc., a restaurant chain, will generate the following payoffs to investors next year:

www.mhhe.com/bmm5e

	Dividend	Stock Price
Boom	$5	$195
Normal economy	2	100
Recession	0	0

The company goes out of business if a recession hits. Calculate the expected rate of return and standard deviation of return to Leaning Tower of Pita shareholders. Assume for simplicity that the three possible states of the economy are equally likely. The stock is selling today for $80.

15. **Portfolio Risk.** Who would view the stock of Leaning Tower of Pita (see Problem 14) as a risk-reducing investment—the owner of a gambling casino or a successful bankruptcy lawyer? Explain.

16. **Scenario Analysis.** The common stock of Escapist Films sells for $25 a share and offers the following payoffs next year:

	Dividend	Stock Price
Boom	0	$18
Normal economy	$1	26
Recession	3	34

Calculate the expected return and standard deviation of Escapist. All three scenarios are equally likely. Then calculate the expected return and standard deviation of a portfolio half invested in Escapist and half in Leaning Tower of Pita (from Problem 14). Show that the portfolio standard deviation is lower than either stock's. Explain why this happens.

17. **Scenario Analysis.** Consider the following scenario analysis:

		Rate of Return	
Scenario	Probability	Stocks	Bonds
Recession	.20	−5%	+14%
Normal economy	.60	+15	+8
Boom	.20	+25	+4

    a. Is it reasonable to assume that Treasury bonds will provide higher returns in recessions than in booms?
    b. Calculate the expected rate of return and standard deviation for each investment.
    c. Which investment would *you* prefer?

18. **Portfolio Analysis.** Use the data in the previous problem and consider a portfolio with weights of .60 in stocks and .40 in bonds.

    a. What is the rate of return on the portfolio in each scenario?
    b. What are the expected rate of return and standard deviation of the portfolio?
    c. Would you prefer to invest in the portfolio, in stocks only, or in bonds only?

19. **Risk Premium.** If the stock market return in 2010 turns out to be −20 percent, what will happen to our estimate of the "normal" risk premium? Does this make sense?

20. **Diversification.** In which of the following situations would you get the largest reduction in risk by spreading your portfolio across two stocks?

    a. The stock returns vary with each other.
    b. The stock returns are independent.
    c. The stock returns vary against each other.

Please visit us at www.mhhe.com/bmm5e or refer to your Student CD

21. **Market Risk.** Which firms of each pair below would you expect to have greater market risk?
    a. General Steel or General Food Supplies.
    b. Club Med or General Cinemas.

22. **Risk and Return.** A stock will provide a rate of return of either –20 percent or +28 percent.
    a. If both possibilities are equally likely, calculate the expected return and standard deviation.
    b. If Treasury bills yield 4 percent and investors believe that the stock offers a satisfactory expected return, what must the market risk of the stock be?

23. **Unique versus Market Risk.** Sassafras Oil is staking all its remaining capital on wildcat exploration off the Côte d'Huile. There is a 10 percent chance of discovering a field with reserves of 50 million barrels. If it finds oil, it will immediately sell the reserves to Big Oil, at a price depending on the state of the economy. Thus the possible payoffs are as follows:

	Value of Reserves, per Barrel	Value of Reserves, 50 Million Barrels	Value of Dryholes
Boom	$4	$200,000,000	0
Normal economy	5	250,000,000	0
Recession	6	300,000,000	0

Is Sassafras Oil a risky investment for a diversified investor in the stock market—compared, say, to the stock of Leaning Tower of Pita, described in Problem 14? Explain.

1. Using Market Insight at **www.mhhe.com/edumarketinsight**, find the monthly rates of return over a 2-year period for five companies of your choice. Now assume you form an equally weighted portfolio of the five firms (i.e., a portfolio with equal investments in each firm). What is the rate of return each month on your portfolio? Compare the standard deviation of the monthly portfolio return to that of each firm and to the average standard deviation across the five firms. What do you conclude about portfolio diversification?

2. Return to the monthly returns of the five companies you chose in the previous question.
   a. Using the Excel functions for average (AVERAGE) and sample standard deviation (STDEV), calculate the average and the standard deviation of the returns for each of the firms.
   b. Using Excel's correlation function (CORREL), find the correlations between each pair of five stocks. What are the highest and lowest correlations?
   c. Try finding correlations between pairs of stocks in the same industry. Are the correlations higher than those you found in part (b)? Is this surprising?

SOLUTIONS TO SELF-TEST QUESTIONS

10.1 The bond price at the end of the year is $1,050. Therefore, the capital gain on each bond is $1,050 – $1,020 = $30. Your dollar return is the sum of the income from the bond, $80, plus the capital gain, $30, or $110. The rate of return is

$$\frac{\text{Income plus capital gain}}{\text{Original price}} = \frac{80 + 30}{1,020} = .108, \text{ or } 10.8\%$$

Real rate of return is

$$\frac{1 + \text{nominal return}}{1 + \text{inflation rate}} - 1 = \frac{1.108}{1.04} - 1 = .065, \text{ or } 6.5\%$$

10.2 The risk premium on stocks is the average return in excess of Treasury bills. It was 4.6 percent in period 1, 9.1 percent in period 2, 8.5 percent in period 3, and 7.8 percent in period 4.

10.3

Rate of Return	Deviation	Squared Deviation
+70%	+60%	3,600
+10	0	0
+10	0	0
−50	−60	3,600
Variance = average of squared deviations = 7,200/4 = 1,800		
Standard deviation = square root of variance = $\sqrt{1,800}$ = 42.4, about 42%		

10.4 The standard deviation should decrease because there is now a lower probability of the more extreme outcomes. The expected rate of return on the auto stock is now

$$[.3 \times (-8\%)] + (.4 \times 5\%) + (.3 \times 18\%) = 5\%$$

The variance is

$$[.3 \times (-8 - 5)^2] + [.4 \times (5 - 5)^2] + [.3 \times (18 - 5)^2] = 101.4$$

The standard deviation is $\sqrt{101.4}$ = 10.07 percent, which is lower than the value assuming equal probabilities of each scenario.

10.5 The gold mining stock's returns are more highly correlated with the silver mining company than with a car company. As a result, the automotive firm will offer a greater diversification benefit. The power of diversification is lowest when rates of return are highly correlated, performing well or poorly in tandem. Shifting the portfolio from one such firm to another has little impact on overall risk.

10.6 The success of this project depends on the experiment. Success does *not* depend on the performance of the overall economy. The experiment creates a diversifiable risk. A portfolio of many stocks will embody "bets" on many such unique risks. Some bets will work out and some will fail. Because the outcomes of these risks do not depend on common factors, such as the overall state of the economy, the risks will tend to cancel out in a well-diversified portfolio.

10.7 a. The luxury restaurant will be more sensitive to the state of the economy because expense account meals will be curtailed in a recession. Burger Queen meals should be relatively recession-proof.

  b. The paint company that sells to the auto producers will be more sensitive to the state of the economy. In a downturn, auto sales fall dramatically as consumers stretch the lives of their cars. In contrast, in a recession, more people "do it themselves," which makes paint sales through small stores more stable and less sensitive to the economy.

Risk, Return, and Capital Budgeting

RELATED WEB LINKS

finance.yahoo.com

moneycentral.msn.com

money.cnn.com

www.bloomberg.com

www.morningstar.com   These sites
present risk and return statistics,

including betas, for both individual
shares and mutual funds.

www.duke.edu/~charvey   Campbell
Harvey's home page includes
simple software illustrating how
diversification reduces risk.

Professor William F. Sharpe receiving the Nobel Prize in Economics. The prize was for Sharpe's development of the capital asset pricing model. This model shows how risk should be measured and provides a formula relating risk to the opportunity cost of capital.

Leif Jansson/Pica Pressfoto

In Chapter 10 we began to come to grips with the topic of risk. We made the distinction between *unique* risk and macro, or *market,* risk. Unique risk arises from events that affect only the individual firm or its immediate competitors; it can be eliminated by diversification. But regardless of how much you diversify, you cannot avoid the macroeconomic events that create market risk. This is why investors do not require a higher rate of return to compensate for unique risk but do need a higher return to persuade them to take on market risk.

How can you measure the market risk of a security or a project? We will see that market risk is usually measured by the sensitivity of the investment's returns to fluctuations in the market. We will also see that the risk premium investors demand should be proportional to this sensitivity. This relationship between risk and return is a useful way to estimate the return that investors expect from investing in common stocks.

Finally, we will distinguish between the risk of the company's securities and the risk of an individual project. We will also consider what managers should do when the risk of the project is different from that of the company's existing business.

After studying this chapter you should be able to:
- Measure and interpret the market risk, or beta, of a security.
- Relate the market risk of a security to the rate of return that investors demand.
- Calculate the opportunity cost of capital for a project.

11.1　Measuring Market Risk

market portfolio
Portfolio of all assets in the economy. In practice a broad stock market index is used to represent the market.

Changes in interest rates, government spending, oil prices, foreign exchange rates, and other macroeconomic events affect almost all companies and the returns on almost all stocks. We can therefore assess the impact of "macro" news by tracking the rate of return on a **market portfolio** of all securities. If the market is up on a particular day, then the net impact of macroeconomic changes must be positive. We know the performance of the market reflects only macro events, because firm-specific events—that is, unique risks—average out when we look at the combined performance of thousands of companies and securities.

In principle the market portfolio should contain all assets in the world economy—not just stocks but bonds, foreign securities, real estate, and so on. In practice, however, financial analysts make do with indexes of the stock market, such as the Standard & Poor's Composite Index (the S&P 500).[1]

Our task here is to define and measure the risk of *individual* common stocks. You can probably see where we are headed. Risk depends on exposure to macroeconomic events and can be measured as the sensitivity of a stock's returns to fluctuations in returns on the market portfolio. This sensitivity is called the stock's **beta.** Beta is often written as the Greek letter β.

beta
Sensitivity of a stock's return to the return on the market portfolio.

Measuring Beta

In the last chapter we looked at the variability of several individual securities. Amazon.com had the highest standard deviation and ExxonMobil the lowest. If you had held Amazon on its own, your returns would have varied over four times as much as if you had held ExxonMobil. But wise investors don't put all their eggs in just one basket: They reduce their risk by diversification. An investor with a diversified portfolio will be interested in the effect each stock has on the risk of the entire portfolio.

Diversification can eliminate the risk that is unique to individual stocks but not the risk that the market as a whole may decline, carrying your stocks with it.

Some stocks are less affected than others by market fluctuations. Investment managers talk about "defensive" and "aggressive" stocks. Defensive stocks are not very sensitive to market fluctuations and therefore have low betas. In contrast, aggressive stocks amplify any market movements and have higher betas. If the market goes up, it is good to be in aggressive stocks; if it goes down, it is better to be in defensive stocks (and better still to have your money in the bank).

Aggressive stocks have high betas, betas greater than 1.0, meaning that their returns tend to respond more than one for one to changes in the return of the overall market. The betas of defensive stocks are less than 1.0. The returns of these stocks vary less than one for one with market returns. The average beta of all stocks is—no surprises here—1.0 exactly.

Now we'll show you how betas are measured.

| EXAMPLE 11.1 ► | Measuring Beta for Turbot-Charged Seafoods |

Suppose we look back at the trading history of Turbot-Charged Seafoods and pick out 6 months when the return on the market portfolio was plus or minus 1 percent.

Month	Market Return, %	Turbot-Charged Seafood's Return, %
1	+1	+ .8
2	+1	+1.8 Average = .8%
3	+1	− .2
4	−1	−1.8
5	−1	+ .2 Average = −.8%
6	−1	− .8

---

[1] We discussed the most popular stock market indexes in Section 10.2.

FIGURE 11-1 This figure is a plot of the data presented in the table in Example 11.1. Each point shows the performance of Turbot-Charged Seafoods stock when the overall market is either up or down by 1 percent. On average, Turbot-Charged moves in the same direction as the market, but not as far. Therefore, Turbot-Charged's beta is less than 1.0. We can measure beta by the slope of a line fitted to the points in the figure. In this case it is .8.

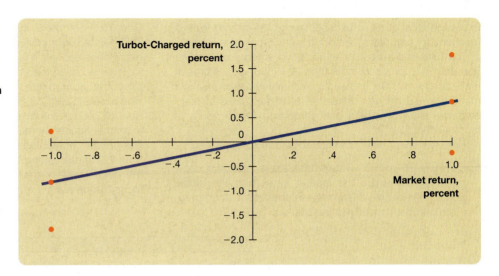

Look at Figure 11–1, where these observations are plotted. We've drawn a line through the average performance of Turbot when the market is up or down by 1 percent. *The slope of this line is Turbot's beta.* You can see right away that the beta is .8, because on average Turbot stock gains or loses .8 percent when the market is up or down by 1 percent. Notice that a 2-percentage-point difference in the market return (−1 to +1) generates on average a 1.6-percentage-point difference for Turbot shareholders (−.8 to +.8). The ratio, 1.6/2 = .8, is beta.

In 4 months, Turbot's returns lie above or below the line in Figure 11–1. The distance from the line shows the response of Turbot's stock returns to news or events that affected Turbot but did *not* affect the overall market. For example, in month 2, investors in Turbot stock benefited from good macroeconomic news (the market was up 1 percent) and also from some favorable news specific to Turbot. The market rise gave a boost of .8 percent to Turbot stock (beta of .8 times the 1 percent market return). Then firm-specific news gave Turbot stockholders an extra 1 percent return, for a total return that month of 1.8 percent.   ◀

As this example illustrates, we can break down common stock returns into two parts: the part explained by market returns and the firm's beta, and the part due to news that is specific to the firm. Fluctuations in the first part reflect market risk; fluctuations in the second part reflect unique risk.

Of course diversification can get rid of the unique risks. That's why wise investors, who don't put all their eggs in one basket, will look to Turbot's less-than-average beta and call its stock "defensive."

Self-Test 11.1

Here are 6 months' returns to stockholders in the Anchovy Queen restaurant chain:

Month	Market Return, %	Anchovy Queen Return, %
1	+1	+2.0
2	+1	+0
3	+1	+1.0
4	−1	−1.0
5	−1	+0
6	−1	−2.0

Draw a figure like Figure 11–1 and check the slope of the fitted line. What is Anchovy Queen's beta?

Calculating Risk

Excel and most other spreadsheet programs provide built-in functions for computing a stock's beta. In columns B and C of the following spreadsheet we have entered returns for Standard & Poor's 500 Index (the S&P 500) and Microsoft for 6 months in 2004. (In practice, estimates based on just 6 months would be *very* unreliable. Most estimates of standard deviation and beta use something like 5 years of monthly data.)

Here are some points to note about the spreadsheet:

1. *Columns B and C.* Notice that these columns show monthly *returns* for the market index and the stock. Sometimes people mistakenly enter prices instead of returns and get nonsensical results.

2. *Row 10.* Footnote 7 in the previous chapter (see page 278) pointed out that in estimating variability from a sample of observations, it is common to make an adjustment for what is called *the loss of a degree of freedom.* In this case the appropriate formula for standard deviation would be STDEV(C3:C8).

3. *Row 11.* We have converted monthly standard deviations to annual figures by multiplying by the square root of 12 (the number of months in a year).

4. *Row 12.* In calculating beta, it is important to enter first the addresses for the stock returns (C3:C8) and then those for the market returns (B3:B8).

Please visit us at www.mhhe.com/bmm5e or refer to your Student CD

	A	B	C	D
1		Returns, percent		Formula used in
2	Month	S&P 500	Microsoft	Column C
3	Dec-04	-0.75	0.07	
4	Nov-04	3.25	-0.34	
5	Oct-04	3.86	6.81	
6	Sep-04	1.40	1.17	
7	Aug-04	0.94	1.31	
8	Jul-04	0.23	-3.92	
9				
10	Standard deviation (monthly)	1.61	3.18	=STDEVP(C3:C8)
11	Standard deviation, annualized	5.59	11.01	=C10*SQRT(12)
12	Beta		1.25	=SLOPE(C3:C8,B3:B8)
13	Correlation		0.63	=CORREL(C3:C8,B3:B8)

Real life doesn't serve up numbers quite as convenient as those in our examples so far. However, the procedure for measuring real companies' betas is exactly the same:

1. Observe rates of return, usually monthly, for the stock and the market.
2. Plot the observations as in Figure 11–1.
3. Fit a line showing the average return to the stock at different market returns.

Beta is the slope of the fitted line.

This may sound like a lot of work, but in practice computers do it for you. The nearby box shows how to use the SLOPE function in Excel to calculate a beta. Here are two real examples.

Betas for Amazon.com and ExxonMobil

Each point in Figure 11–2a shows the return on Amazon.com stock and the return on the market index in a different month. For example, the circled point shows that in September 2002, Amazon stock price rose by 21.5 percent, whereas the market index rose by 8.6 percent. Notice that more often than not Amazon outperformed the market when the index rose and underperformed the market when the index fell. Thus Amazon was a relatively aggressive, high-beta stock.

We have drawn a line of best fit through the points in the figure.[2] The slope of this line is 2.49. For each extra 1 percent rise in the market, Amazon stock price moved on average an extra 2.49 percent. For each extra 1 percent fall in the market, Amazon stock price fell an extra 2.49 percent. Thus Amazon's beta was 2.49.

[2] The line of best fit is usually known as a *regression* line. The slope of the line can be calculated using *ordinary least squares* regression. The dependent variable is the return on the stock (Amazon.com). The independent variable is the return on the market index, in this case the S&P 500.

FIGURE 11-2 (a) Each point in this figure shows the returns on Amazon.com common stock and the overall market in a particular month between January 2000 and December 2004. Amazon's beta is the slope of the line fitted to these points. Amazon has a very high beta of 2.49. (b) In this plot of 60 months' returns for ExxonMobil and the overall market, the slope of the fitted line is much less than Amazon's beta in (a). ExxonMobil has a relatively low beta of .41.

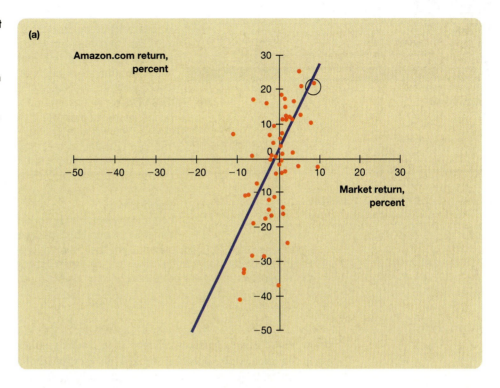

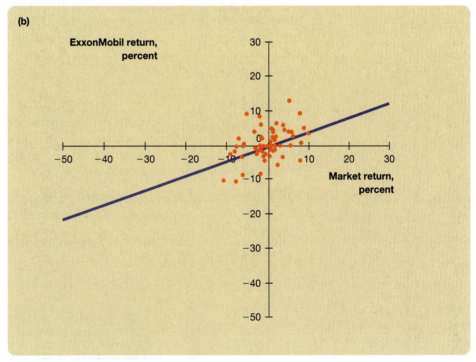

Of course, Amazon's stock returns are not perfectly related to market returns. The company was also subject to unique risk, which shows up in the scatter of points around the line. Sometimes Amazon flew south while the market went north, or vice versa.

Figure 11–2b shows a similar plot of the monthly returns for ExxonMobil. In contrast to Amazon, ExxonMobil was a defensive, low-beta stock. It was not highly sensitive to market movements, usually lagging when the market rose and yet doing better (or less badly) when the market fell. The slope of the line of best fit shows that on

INTERNET INSIDER

Risk and Return

Source: Yahoo! Finance Web site. Reproduced with permission of Yahoo! Inc. © 2005 Yahoo! Inc. Yahoo! and the Yahoo! logo are trademarks of Yahoo! Inc.

Betas and Expected Stock Returns

You can find estimates of stock betas by logging on to **finance.yahoo.com** and looking at a company's profile. Try comparing the stock betas of Eastman Kodak (EK), The Home Depot (HD), Intel (INTC), Altria Group (MO), and Walt Disney (DIS). Once you have read Section 11.2, use the capital asset pricing model to estimate the expected return for each of these stocks. You will need a figure for the current Treasury bill rate. You can find this also on **finance.yahoo.com** by clicking on *Bonds—Rates.* Assume for your estimates a market risk premium of 7 percent.

Fund Betas

Log on to **www.fidelity.com** and look at the list of mutual funds that are managed by Fidelity. Some of these funds, such as *The Aggressive Growth Fund,* appear from their names to be high-risk. Others, such as *The Balanced Fund,* appear to be low-risk. Pick several apparent high- and low-risk funds and then check whether their betas really do match the fund's name.

---

average an extra 1 percent change in the index resulted in an extra .41 percent change in the price of ExxonMobil stock. Thus ExxonMobil's beta was .41.

Estimates of beta can be accessed easily, for example, at **finance.yahoo.com**, but you may find it interesting to look at Table 11–1, which shows how past market movements have affected several well-known stocks. ExxonMobil had the next-to-lowest beta: Its stock return was .41 times as sensitive as the average stock to market movements. Amazon was at the other extreme: Its return was 2.49 times as sensitive as the average stock to market movements.

Portfolio Betas

Diversification decreases variability from unique risk but not from market risk. The beta of a portfolio is just an average of the betas of the securities in the portfolio, weighted by the investment in each security. For example, a portfolio comprising only two stocks would have a beta as follows:

Beta of portfolio = (fraction of portfolio in first stock × beta of first stock)
+ (fraction of portfolio in second stock × beta of second stock)

Thus a portfolio invested 50-50 in Amazon and ExxonMobil would have a beta of (.5 × 2.49) + (.5 × .41) = 1.45.

TABLE 11–1 Betas for selected common stocks, January 2000–December 2004

Amazon.com	2.49
Dell Computer	1.64
Ford	1.34
General Electric	.97
McDonald's	.90
Boeing	.76
Wal-Mart	.51
Pfizer	.46
ExxonMobil	.41
H.J. Heinz	.30

Note: Betas are calculated from 5 years of monthly returns.

A well-diversified portfolio of stocks all with betas of 2.49, like Amazon, would still have a portfolio beta of 2.49. However, most of the individual stocks' unique risk would be diversified away. The market risk would remain, and such a portfolio would end up 2.49 times as variable as the market. For example, if the market has an annual standard deviation of 20 percent (about the historical average reported in Chapter 10), a fully diversified portfolio with beta of 2.49 has a standard deviation of $2.49 \times 20 =$ 49.8 percent.

Portfolios with betas between 0 and 1.0 tend to move in the same direction as the market but not as far. A well-diversified portfolio of low-beta stocks like ExxonMobil, all with betas of .41, has almost no unique risk and is relatively unaffected by market movements. Such a portfolio is .41 times as variable as the market.

Of course, on average stocks have a beta of 1.0. A well-diversified portfolio including all kinds of stocks, with an average beta of 1.0, has the same variability as the market index.

Self-Test 11.2   **Suppose you invested an equal amount in each of the stocks shown in Table 11–1. Calculate the beta of your portfolio.**

EXAMPLE 11.2 ▶   How Risky Are Mutual Funds?

You don't have to be wealthy to own a diversified portfolio. You can buy shares in one of the more than 8,000 mutual funds in the United States.

Investors buy shares of the funds, and the funds use the money to buy portfolios of securities. The returns on the portfolios are passed back to the funds' owners in proportion to their shareholdings. Therefore, the funds act like investment cooperatives, offering even the smallest investors diversification and professional management at low cost.

Let's look at the betas of two mutual funds that invest in stocks. Figure 11–3a plots the monthly returns of Vanguard's Windsor II mutual fund and of the S&P index for 5 years ending in December 2004. You can see that the stocks in the Windsor II fund had below-average sensitivity to market changes: They had on average a beta of .74.

If the Windsor II fund had no unique risk, its portfolio would have been .74 times as variable as the market portfolio. But the fund had not diversified away quite all the

FIGURE 11–3a The slope of the fitted line shows that investors in the Windsor II mutual fund bore market risk below that of the S&P 500 portfolio. Windsor II's beta was .74. This was the average beta of the individual common stocks held by the fund. Investors also bore some unique risk, however; note the scatter of Windsor II's returns above and below the fitted line.

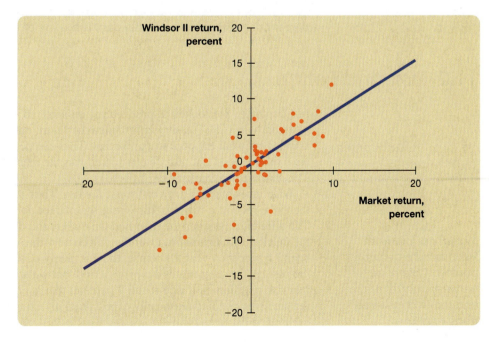

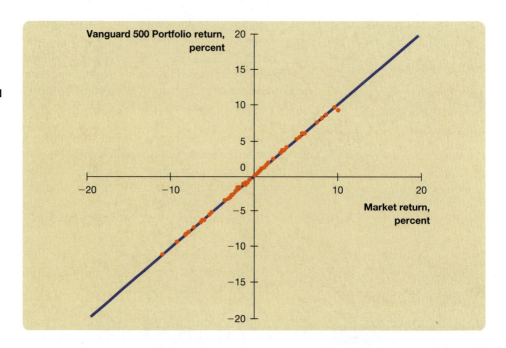

FIGURE 11–3b The Vanguard 500 Portfolio is a fully diversified index fund designed to track the performance of the market. Note the fund's beta (1.0) and the absence of unique risk. The fund's returns lie almost precisely on the fitted line relating its returns to those of the S&P 500 portfolio.

unique risk; there is still some scatter about the line in Figure 11–3a. As a result, the variability of the fund was somewhat more than .74 times that of the market.

Figure 11–3b shows the same sort of plot for Vanguard's Index Trust 500 Portfolio mutual fund. Notice that this fund has a beta of 1.0 and only a tiny residual of unique risk—the fitted line fits almost exactly because an *index fund* is designed to track the market as closely as possible. The managers of the fund do not attempt to pick good stocks but just work to achieve full diversification at very low cost. (The Vanguard index fund takes investments of as little as $3,000 and manages the fund for an annual fee of less than .20 percent of the fund's assets.) The index fund is *fully diversified.* Investors in this fund buy the market as a whole and don't have to worry at all about unique risk.

Self-Test 11.3

Suppose you could achieve full diversification in a portfolio constructed from stocks with an average beta of .5. If the standard deviation of the market is 20 percent per year, what is the standard deviation of the portfolio return?

11.2 Risk and Return

In Chapter 10 we looked at past returns on selected investments. The least risky investment was U.S. Treasury bills. Since the return on Treasury bills is fixed, it is unaffected by what happens to the market. Thus the beta of Treasury bills is zero. The *most* risky investment that we considered was the market portfolio of common stocks. This has average market risk: Its beta is 1.0.

Wise investors don't run risks just for fun. They are playing with real money and therefore require a higher return from the market portfolio than from Treasury bills. The difference between the return on the market and the interest rate on bills is termed the **market risk premium.** Over the past century the average market risk premium has been 7.6 percent a year. Of course, there is plenty of scope for argument as to whether the past century constitutes a typical period, but we will just assume here that the normal risk premium is a nice round 7 percent, that is, 7 percent is the additional return that an investor could reasonably expect from investing in the stock market rather than Treasury bills.

market risk premium
Risk premium of market portfolio. Difference between market return and return on risk-free Treasury bills.

FIGURE 11–4 (a) Here we begin the plot of expected rate of return against beta. The first benchmarks are Treasury bills (beta = 0) and the market portfolio (beta = 1.0). We assume a Treasury bill rate of 3 percent and a market return of 10 percent. The market risk premium is 10 – 3 = 7 percent. (b) A portfolio split evenly between Treasury bills and the market will have beta = .5 and an expected return of 6.5 percent (point X). A portfolio invested 20 percent in the market and 80 percent in Treasury bills has beta = .2 and an expected rate of return of 4.4 percent (point Y). Note that the expected rate of return on any portfolio mixing Treasury bills and the market lies on a straight line. The risk premium is proportional to the portfolio beta.

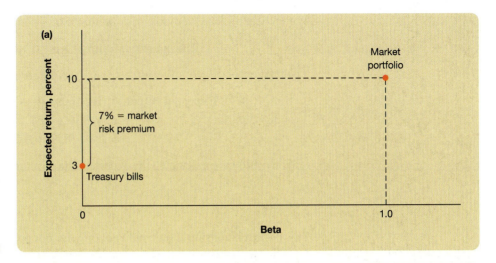

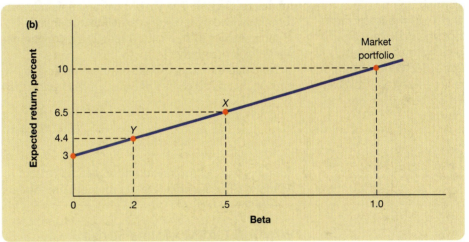

In Figure 11–4*a* we have plotted the risk and expected return from Treasury bills and the market portfolio. You can see that Treasury bills have a beta of zero and a risk-free return; we'll assume that return is 3 percent. The market portfolio has a beta of 1.0 and an assumed expected return of 10 percent.[3]

Now, given these two benchmarks, what expected rate of return should an investor require from a stock or portfolio with a beta of .5? Halfway between, of course. Thus in Figure 11–4*b* we have drawn a straight line through the Treasury bill return and the expected market return and marked with an X the expected return for a beta of .5, that is, 6.5 percent. This includes a risk premium of 3.5 percent above the Treasury bill return of 3 percent.

You can calculate this return as follows: Start with the difference between the expected market return r_m and the Treasury bill rate r_f. This is the expected market risk premium:

$$\text{Market risk premium} = r_m - r_f = 10\% - 3\% = 7\%$$

Beta measures risk relative to the market. Therefore, the expected risk premium equals beta times the market risk premium:

$$\textbf{Risk premium} = r - r_f = \beta(r_m - r_f)$$

---

[3] We assumed that the risk premium on the market is about 7 percent. With a 3 percent Treasury bill rate, the expected market return would be 3 + 7 = 10 percent.

With a beta of .5 and a market risk premium of 7 percent,

$$\text{Risk premium} = \beta(r_m - r_f) = .5 \times 7\% = 3.5\%$$

The total expected rate of return is the sum of the risk-free rate and the risk premium:

Expected return = risk-free rate + risk premium
$$r = r_f + \beta(r_m - r_f)$$
$$= 3\% + 3.5\% = 6.5\%$$

You could have calculated the expected rate of return in one step from this formula:

$$\text{Expected return} = r = r_f + \beta(r_m - r_f)$$
$$= 3\% + (.5 \times 7\%) = 6.5\%$$

capital asset pricing model (CAPM)

Theory of the relationship between risk and return which states that the expected risk premium on any security equals its beta times the market risk premium.

This basic relationship should hold not only for our portfolios of Treasury bills and the market, but for *any* asset. This conclusion is known as the **capital asset pricing model,** or **CAPM.** The CAPM has a simple interpretation: The expected rates of return demanded by investors depend on two things: (1) compensation for the time value of money (the risk-free rate r_f) and (2) a risk premium, which depends on beta and the market risk premium.

Note that the expected rate of return on an asset with $\beta = 1.0$ is just the market return. With a risk-free rate of 3 percent and market risk premium of 7 percent,

$$r = r_f + \beta(r_m - r_f)$$
$$= 3\% + (1 \times 7\%) = 10\%$$

Self-Test 11.4

What are the risk premium and expected rate of return on a stock with $\beta = 1.5$? Assume a Treasury bill rate of 6 percent and a market risk premium of 7 percent.

Why the CAPM Makes Sense

The CAPM assumes that the stock market is dominated by well-diversified investors who are concerned only with market risk. That is reasonable in a stock market where trading is dominated by large institutions and even small fry can diversify at very low cost. The following example shows why in this case the CAPM makes sense.

EXAMPLE 11.3 ▶ How Would You Invest $1 Million?

Have you ever daydreamed about receiving a $1 million check, no strings attached, from an unknown benefactor? Let's daydream about how you would invest it.

We have two good candidates: Treasury bills, which offer an absolutely safe return, and the market portfolio (possibly via the Vanguard index fund discussed earlier in this chapter). The market has generated superior returns on average, but those returns have fluctuated a lot. (Look back to Figure 10–4.) So your investment policy is going to depend on your tolerance for risk.

If you're a wimp, you may invest only part of your money in the market portfolio and lend the remainder to the government by buying Treasury bills. Suppose that you invest 20 percent of your money in the market portfolio and put the other 80 percent in U.S. Treasury bills. Then the beta of your portfolio will be a mixture of the beta of the market ($\beta_{market} = 1.0$) and the beta of the T-bills ($\beta_{T\text{-}bills} = 0$):

$$\text{Beta of portfolio} = \left(\begin{array}{c}\text{proportion}\\\text{in market}\end{array} \times \begin{array}{c}\text{beta of}\\\text{market}\end{array}\right) + \left(\begin{array}{c}\text{proportion}\\\text{in T-bills}\end{array} \times \begin{array}{c}\text{beta of}\\\text{T-bills}\end{array}\right)$$

$$\beta = (.2 \times \beta_{market}) \qquad + (.8 \times \beta_{T\text{-}bills})$$
$$= (.2 \times 1.0) \qquad + (.8 \times 0) = .20$$

The fraction of funds that you invest in the market also affects your expected return. If you invest your entire million in the market portfolio, you earn the full market risk premium. But if you invest only 20 percent of your money in the market, you earn only 20 percent of the risk premium.

$$\begin{aligned} \text{Expected} \\ \text{risk premium} = \\ \text{on portfolio} \end{aligned} \left(\begin{aligned} \text{proportion in} \\ \text{market} \end{aligned} \times \begin{aligned} \text{market risk} \\ \text{premium} \end{aligned} \right) + \left(\begin{aligned} \text{proportion in} \\ \text{T-bills} \end{aligned} \times \begin{aligned} \text{risk premium} \\ \text{on T-bills} \end{aligned} \right)$$

$$= (.2 \times \text{expected market risk premium}) + (.8 \times 0)$$
$$= .2 \times \text{expected market risk premium}$$
$$= .2 \times 7 = 1.4\%$$

The expected return on your portfolio is equal to the risk-free interest rate plus the expected risk premium:

$$\text{Expected portfolio return} = r_{\text{portfolio}} = 3 + 1.4 = 4.4\%$$

In Figure 11–4*b* we show the beta and expected return on this portfolio by the letter *Y*.   ◄

The Security Market Line

security market line
Relationship between expected return and beta.

Example 11.3 illustrates a general point: By investing some proportion of your money in the market portfolio and lending (or borrowing)[4] the balance, you can obtain any combination of risk and expected return along the sloping line in Figure 11–5. This line is generally known as the **security market line.**

Self-Test 11.5

How would you construct a portfolio with a beta of .25? What is the expected return to this strategy? Assume Treasury bills yield 6 percent and the market risk premium is 7 percent.

The security market line describes the expected returns and risks from investing different fractions of your funds in the market. It also sets a standard for other investments. Investors will be willing to hold other investments only if they offer equally good prospects. Thus the required risk premium for *any* investment is given by the security market line:

Risk premium on investment = beta × expected market risk premium

Look back to Figure 11–4*b*, which asserts that an individual common stock with β = .5 must offer a 6.5 percent expected rate of return when Treasury bills yield 3 percent and the market risk premium is 7 percent. You can now see why this has to be so. If that stock offered a lower rate of return, nobody would buy even a little of it—they could get 6.5 percent just by investing 50-50 in Treasury bills and the market. And if nobody wants to hold the stock, its price has to drop. A lower price means a better buy for investors, that is, a higher rate of return. The price will fall until the stock's

---

[4] Notice that the security market line extends above the market return at β = 1.0. How would you generate a portfolio with, say, β = 2.0? It's easy, but it's risky. Suppose you borrow $1 million and invest the loan plus $1 million in the market portfolio. That gives you $2 million invested and a $1 million liability. Your portfolio now has a beta of 2.0:

$$\text{Beta of portfolio} = (\text{proportion in market} \times \text{beta of market}) + (\text{proportion in loan} \times \text{beta of loan})$$
$$\beta = (2 \times \beta_{\text{market}}) + (-1 \times \beta_{\text{loan}})$$
$$= (2 \times 1.0) + (-1 \times 0) = 2$$

Notice that the proportion in the loan is negative because you are borrowing, not lending money.

By the way, borrowing from a bank or stockbroker would not be difficult or unduly expensive as long as you put up your $2 million stock portfolio as security for the loan.

Can you calculate the risk premium and the expected rate of return on this borrow-and-invest strategy?

FIGURE 11–5 The security market line shows how expected rate of return depends on beta. According to the capital asset pricing model, expected rates of return for all securities and all portfolios lie on this line.

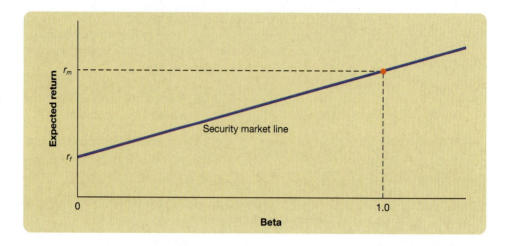

expected rate of return is pushed up to 6.5 percent. At that price and expected return the CAPM holds.

If, on the other hand, our stock offered more than 6.5 percent, diversified investors would want to buy more of it. That would push the price up and the expected return down to the levels predicted by the CAPM.

This reasoning holds for stocks with any beta. That's why the CAPM makes sense, and why the expected risk premium on an investment should be proportional to its beta.

Self-Test 11.6   Suppose you invest $400,000 in Treasury bills and $600,000 in the market portfolio. What is the return on your portfolio if bills yield 6 percent and the expected return on the market is 13 percent? What does the return on this portfolio imply for the expected return on individual stocks with betas of .6?

How Well Does the CAPM Work?

The basic idea behind the capital asset pricing model is that investors expect a reward for both waiting and worrying. The greater the worry, the greater the expected return. If you invest in a risk-free Treasury bill, you just receive the rate of interest. That's the reward for waiting. When you invest in risky stocks, you can expect an extra return or risk premium for worrying. The capital asset pricing model states that this risk premium is equal to the stock's beta times the market risk premium. Therefore,

Expected return on stock = risk-free interest rate + (beta × market risk premium)
$$r = r_f + \beta(r_m - r_f)$$

How well does the CAPM work in practice? Do the returns on stocks with betas of .5 on average lie halfway between the return on the market portfolio and the interest rate on Treasury bills? Unfortunately, the evidence is conflicting. Let's look back to the actual returns earned by investors in low-beta stocks and in high-beta stocks.

Imagine that in 1931 ten investors gathered together in a Wall Street bar and agreed to establish investment trust funds for their children. Each investor decided to follow a different strategy. Investor 1 opted to buy the 10 percent of the New York Stock Exchange stocks with the lowest estimated betas; investor 2 chose the 10 percent with the next-lowest betas; and so on, up to investor 10, who proposed to buy the stocks with the highest betas. They also planned that at the end of each year they would reestimate the betas of all NYSE stocks and reconstitute their portfolios. And so they parted with much cordiality and good wishes.

In time the 10 investors all passed away, but their children agreed to meet in early 2003 in the same bar to compare the performance of their portfolios. Figure 11–6

FIGURE 11–6 The capital asset pricing model states that the expected risk premium from any investment should lie on the security market line. The dots show the actual average risk premium from portfolios with different betas. The high-beta portfolios generated higher returns, just as predicted by the CAPM. But the high-beta portfolios plotted below the market line and four of the five low-beta portfolios plotted above. A line fitted to the 10 portfolio returns would be "flatter" than the security market line.

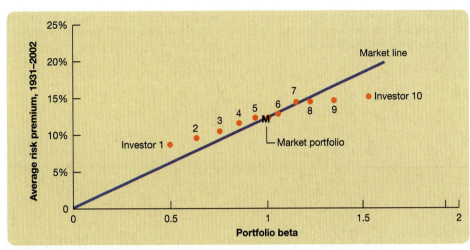

Source: F. Black, "Beta and Return," *Journal of Portfolio Management* 20 (Fall 1993), pp. 8–18. We are grateful to Adam Kolasinski for recalculating and extending the plots.

shows how they fared. Investor 1's portfolio turned out to be much less risky than the market; its beta was only .49. However, investor 1 also realized the lowest return, 9 percent above the risk-free rate of interest. At the other extreme, the beta of investor 10's portfolio was 1.53, about three times that of investor 1's portfolio. But investor 10 was rewarded with the highest return, averaging 15 percent a year above the interest rate. So over this 72-year period returns did indeed increase with beta.

As you can see from Figure 11–6, the market portfolio over the same 72-year period provided an average return of 12.2 percent above the interest rate[5] and (of course) had a beta of 1.0. The CAPM predicts that the risk premium should increase in proportion to beta, so the returns of each portfolio should lie on the upward-sloping security market line in Figure 11–6. Since the market provided a risk premium of 12.2 percent, investor 1's portfolio, with a beta of .49, should have provided a risk premium of about 6 percent and investor 10's portfolio, with a beta of 1.53, should have given a premium of over 18 percent. You can see that, while high-beta stocks performed better than low-beta stocks, the difference was not as great as the CAPM predicts.

Figure 11–6 provides broad support for the CAPM, though it suggests that the line relating return to beta has been too flat. But recent years have been less kind to the CAPM. For example, if the 10 friends had invested their cash in 1966 rather than 1931, there would have been very little relation between their portfolio returns and beta. Does this imply that there has been a fundamental change in the relation between risk and return in the last 35 years, or did high-beta stocks just happen to perform worse during these years than investors expected? It is hard to be sure.

There is little doubt that the CAPM is too simple to capture everything that is going on in the market. For example, look at Figure 11–7. The orange line shows the cumulative difference between the returns on small-firm stocks and large-firm stocks. If you had bought the shares with the smallest market capitalizations and sold those with the largest capitalizations, this is how your wealth would have changed. You can see that small-cap stocks did not always do well, but over the long haul their owners have made substantially higher returns. Since the end of 1926 the average annual difference between the returns on the two groups of stocks has been 3.9 percent. Now look at the purple line in Figure 11–7, which shows the cumulative difference between the returns on value stocks and growth stocks. *Value stocks* here are defined as those with high ratios of book value to market value. *Growth stocks* are those with low

[5] In Figure 11–6 the stocks in the "market portfolio" are weighted equally. Since the stocks of small firms have provided higher average returns than those of large firms, the risk premium on an equally weighted index is higher than that on a value-weighted index. This is one reason for the difference between the 12.2 percent market risk premium in Figure 11–6 and the 7.6 percent premium reported in Table 10–1.

FIGURE 11-7 The orange line shows the cumulative difference between the returns on small-firm and large-firm stocks from 1926 to 2004. The purple line shows the cumulative difference between the returns on high-book-to-market-value stocks and low-book-to-market-value stocks.

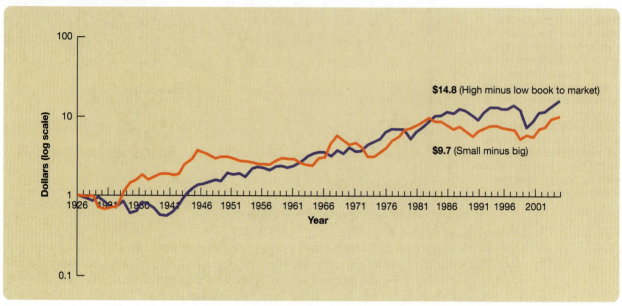

Source: mba.tuck.dartmouth.edu/pages/faculty/ken.french/data_library.html. Used by permission of Kenneth R. French.

ratios of book to market. Notice that value stocks have provided a higher long-run return than growth stocks. Since 1926 the average annual difference between returns on value and growth stocks has been 4.5 percent.

The superior performance of small-firm stocks and value stocks does not fit well with the CAPM, which predicts that beta is the *only* reason that expected returns differ. If investors *expected* the returns to depend on firm size or book-to-market ratios, then the simple version of the capital asset pricing model cannot be the whole truth.

What's going on here? It is hard to say. Defenders of the capital asset pricing model emphasize that it is concerned with *expected* returns, whereas we can observe only *actual* returns. Actual returns reflect expectations, but they also embody lots of "noise"—the steady flow of surprises that conceal whether on average investors have received the returns that they expected. Thus, when we observe that in the past small-firm stocks and value stocks have provided superior performance, we can't be sure whether this was simply a coincidence or whether investors have required a higher return to hold these stocks.

Such debates have prompted headlines like "Is Beta Dead?" in the business press. It is not the first time that beta has been declared dead, but the CAPM remains the leading model for estimating required returns. Only strong theories can have more than one funeral.

The CAPM is not the only model of risk and return. It has several brothers and sisters as well as second cousins. However, the CAPM captures in a simple way two fundamental ideas. First, almost everyone agrees that investors require some extra return for taking on risk. Second, investors appear to be concerned principally with the market risk that they cannot eliminate by diversification. That is why financial managers rely on the capital asset pricing model as a good rule of thumb.

Using the CAPM to Estimate Expected Returns

To calculate the returns that investors are expecting from particular stocks, we need three numbers—the risk-free interest rate, the expected market risk premium, and beta. Suppose that the interest rate on Treasury bills is about 3 percent and that the market risk premium is about 7 percent. Now look back to Table 11–1, where we gave

TABLE 11–2 Expected rates of return

Amazon.com	20.4
Dell Computer	14.5
Ford	12.4
General Electric	9.8
McDonald's	9.3
Boeing	8.3
Wal-Mart	6.6
Pfizer	6.2
ExxonMobil	5.9
H.J. Heinz	5.1

Note: Expected return $= r = r_f + \beta(r_m - r_f) = 3\% + (\beta \times 7\%)$.

you betas of several stocks. Table 11–2 puts these numbers together to give an estimate of the expected return from each stock. Let's take Dell Computer as an example:

$$\text{Expected return on Dell} = \text{risk-free interest rate} + \left(\text{beta} \times \begin{array}{c}\text{expected market}\\ \text{risk premium}\end{array}\right)$$

$$r = 3\% + (1.64 \times 7\%) = 14.5\%$$

You can also use the capital asset pricing model to find the discount rate for a new capital investment. For example, suppose you are asked to analyze a proposal by Dell to expand its operations. At what rate should you discount the forecast cash flows? The capital asset pricing model suggests that investors are looking for a return of 14.5 percent from investments with the risk of Dell stock. That is the opportunity cost of capital for Dell's expansion project.

In practice, choosing a discount rate is seldom this easy. (After all, you can't expect to become a captain of finance simply by plugging numbers into a formula.) For example, you must learn how to estimate the return demanded by the company's investors when the company has issued both equity and debt securities.[6] We will come to such refinements later.

EXAMPLE 11.4 ▶ **Comparing Project Returns and the Opportunity Cost of Capital**

You have forecast the cash flows on a project and calculated that its internal rate of return is 12 percent. Suppose that Treasury bills offer a return of 3 percent and the expected market risk premium is 7 percent. Should you go ahead with the project?

To answer this question you need to figure out the opportunity cost of capital r. This depends on the project's beta. For example, if the project is a sure thing, the beta is zero and the cost of capital equals the interest rate on Treasury bills:

$$r = 3 + (0 \times 7) = 3\%$$

If your project offers a return of 12 percent when the cost of capital is 3 percent, you should obviously go ahead.[7]

---

[6] We could ignore this complication in the case of Dell, because Dell is financed primarily by common stock. Therefore, the risk of its assets equals the risk of its stock. But most companies issue a mix of debt and common stock.

[7] In Chapter 7 we described some special cases where you should prefer projects that offer a *lower* internal rate of return than the cost of capital. We assume here that your project is a "normal" one and that you prefer high IRRs to low ones.

FIGURE 11-8 The expected return of this project is less than the expected return one could earn on stock market investments with the same market risk (beta). Therefore, the project's expected return lies below the security market line, and the project should be rejected.

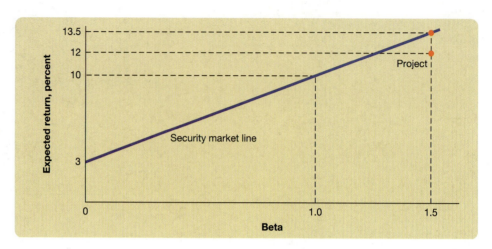

Surefire projects rarely occur outside finance texts. So let's think about the cost of capital if the project has the same risk as the market portfolio. In this case beta is 1.0 and the cost of capital is the expected return on the market:

$$r = 3 + (1.0 \times 7) = 10\%$$

The project appears less attractive than before but still worth doing.

But what if the project has even higher risk? Suppose, for example, that it has a beta of 1.5. What is the cost of capital in this case? To find the answer, we plug a beta of 1.5 into our formula for r:

$$r = 3 + (1.5 \times 7) = 13.5\%$$

A project this risky would need a return of at least 13.5 percent to justify going ahead. The 12 percent project should be rejected.

This rejection occurs because, as Figure 11–8 shows, the project's expected rate of return plots below the security market line. The project offers a lower return than investors can get elsewhere, so it is a negative-NPV investment.   ◄

The security market line provides a standard for project acceptance. If the project's return lies above the security market line, then the return is higher than investors could expect to get by investing their funds in the capital market and therefore is an attractive investment opportunity.

Self-Test 11.7

Suppose that Dell's expansion project is forecast to produce cash flows of $50 million a year for each of 10 years. What is its present value? Use data from Table 11–2. What would the present value be if the beta of the investment were 1.2?

11.3 Capital Budgeting and Project Risk

Company versus Project Risk

company cost of capital
Expected rate of return demanded by investors in a company, determined by the average risk of the company's securities.

Long before the development of modern theories linking risk and return, smart financial managers adjusted for risk in capital budgeting. They realized intuitively that, other things equal, risky projects are less desirable than safe ones and must provide higher rates of return.

Many companies estimate the rate of return required by investors in their securities and use this **company cost of capital** to discount the cash flows on all new projects. Since investors require a higher rate of return from a risky company, risky firms will

How High a Hurdle?

It did raise some eyebrows at first. Two months ago, when Aegon, a Dutch life insurer known for taking care of its shareholders, bought Transamerica, a San Francisco–based insurer, Aegon said it was expecting a return of only 9% from the deal, well below the 11% "hurdle rate" it once proclaimed as its benchmark. Had this darling of the stock market betrayed its devoted investors for the sake of an eye-catching deal?

Not at all. Years of falling interest rates and rising equity valuations have shrunk the cost of capital for firms such as Aegon. So companies that regularly adjust the hurdle rates they use to evaluate potential investment projects and acquisitions are not cheating their shareholders. Far from it: they are doing their investors a service. Unfortunately, such firms are rare in Europe. "I don't know many companies at all who lowered their hurdle rates in line with interest rates, so they're all underinvesting," says Greg Milano, a partner at Stern Stewart, a consultancy that helps companies estimate their cost of capital.

This has a huge impact on corporate strategy. Companies generally make their investment decisions by discounting the net cash flows a project is estimated to generate to their present value. If the net present value is positive, the project should make shareholders better off.

Generally speaking, says Paul Gibbs, an analyst at J.P. Morgan, an American bank, finance directors in America often review their hurdle rates; in continental Europe they do so sometimes; and in Britain, rarely. As a result, the Confederation of British Industry, a big-business lobby, worries about underinvestment, and officials at the Bank of England grumble about firms' reluctance to lower hurdles. This reluctance seems surprising, since companies with high hurdle rates will tend to lose out in bidding for business assets or firms. The hurdle rate should reflect not only interest rates but also the riskiness of each individual project. For instance, Siemens, a German industrial giant, last year started assigning a different hurdle rate to each of its 16 businesses, ranging from household appliances to medical equipment and semiconductors. The hurdle rates—from 8% to 11%—are based on the volatility of shares in rival companies in the relevant industry, and are under constant review.

---

have a higher company cost of capital and will set a higher discount rate for their new investment opportunities. For example, we showed in Table 11–1 that on past evidence Dell has a beta of 1.64 and the corresponding expected rate of return (see Table 11–2) is about 14.5 percent. According to the company cost of capital rule, Dell should use a 14.5 percent cost of capital to calculate project NPVs.

This is a step in the right direction, but we must take care when the firm has issued securities other than equity. Moreover, this approach can get a firm in trouble if its new projects do not have the same risk as its existing business. Dell's beta reflects investors' estimate of the risk of the computer hardware business, and its company cost of capital is the return that investors require for taking on this risk. If Dell is considering an expansion of its regular business, it makes sense to discount the forecast cash flows by the company cost of capital. But suppose that Dell is wondering whether to branch out into production of pharmaceuticals. Its beta tells us nothing about the **project cost of capital.** That depends on the risk of the pharmaceutical business and the return that shareholders require from investing in such a business.

project cost of capital
Minimum acceptable expected rate of return on a project given its risk.

The project cost of capital depends on the use to which that capital is put. Therefore, it depends on the risk of the project and not on the risk of the company. If a company invests in a low-risk project, it should discount the cash flows at a correspondingly low cost of capital. If it invests in a high-risk project, those cash flows should be discounted at a high cost of capital.

The nearby box discusses how companies decide on the discount rate. It notes, for example, that Siemens, a German industrial giant, uses 16 different discount rates, depending on the riskiness of each line of its business.

Self-Test 11.8

The company cost of capital for Dell Computer is about 14.5 percent (see Table 11–2); for Pfizer it is about 6.2 percent. What would be the more reasonable discount rate for Dell to use for a proposed move into pharmaceutical production? Why?

Determinants of Project Risk

We have seen that the company cost of capital is the correct discount rate for projects that have the same risk as the company's existing business but *not* for those projects that are safer or riskier than the company's average. How do we know whether a project is unusually risky? Estimating project risk is never going to be an exact science, but here are two things to bear in mind.

First, we saw in Chapter 9 that operating leverage increases the risk of a project. When a large fraction of your costs is fixed, any change in revenues can have a dramatic effect on earnings. Therefore, projects that involve high fixed costs tend to have higher betas.

Second, many people intuitively associate risk with the variability of earnings. But much of this variability reflects diversifiable risk. Lone prospectors in search of gold look forward to extremely uncertain future earnings, but whether they strike it rich is not likely to depend on the performance of the rest of the economy. These investments have a high standard deviation but a low beta.

What matters is the strength of the relationship between the firm's earnings and the aggregate earnings of all firms. Cyclical businesses, whose revenues and earnings are strongly dependent on the state of the economy, tend to have high betas and a high cost of capital. By contrast, businesses that produce essentials, such as food, beer, and cosmetics, are less affected by the state of the economy. They tend to have low betas and a low cost of capital.

Don't Add Fudge Factors to Discount Rates

Risk to an investor arises because an investment adds to the spread of possible portfolio returns. To a diversified investor, risk is predominantly market risk. But in everyday usage *risk* simply means "bad outcome." People think of the "risks" of a project as the things that can go wrong. For example,

- A geologist looking for oil worries about the risk of a dry hole.
- A pharmaceutical manufacturer worries about the risk that a new drug which reverses balding may not be approved by the Food and Drug Administration.
- The owner of a hotel in a politically unstable part of the world worries about the political risk of expropriation.

Managers sometimes add fudge factors to discount rates to account for worries such as these.

This sort of adjustment makes us nervous. First, the bad outcomes we cited appear to reflect diversifiable risks that would not affect the expected rate of return demanded by investors. Second, the need for an adjustment in the discount rate usually arises because managers fail to give bad outcomes their due weight in cash-flow forecasts. They then try to offset that mistake by adding a fudge factor to the discount rate. For example, if a manager is worried about the possibility of a bad outcome such as a dry hole in oil exploration, he or she may reduce the value of the project by using a higher discount rate. That's not the way to do it. Instead, the possibility of the dry hole should be included in the calculation of the expected cash flows to be derived from the well. Suppose that there is a 50 percent chance of a dry hole and a 50 percent chance that the well will produce oil worth $20 million. Then the *expected* cash flow is not $20 million but $(.5 \times 0) + (.5 \times 20) = \$10$ million. You should discount the $10 million expected cash flow at the opportunity cost of capital; it does not make sense to discount the $20 million using a fudged discount rate.

Expected cash-flow forecasts should already reflect the probabilities of *all* possible outcomes, good and bad. If the cash-flow forecasts are prepared properly, the discount rate should reflect only the market risk of the project. It should not be fudged to offset errors or biases in the cash-flow forecast.

SUMMARY

How can you measure and interpret the market risk, or beta, of a security?

The contribution of a security to the risk of a diversified portfolio depends on its market risk. But not all securities are equally affected by fluctuations in the market. The sensitivity of a stock to market movements is known as **beta.** Stocks with a beta greater than 1.0 are particularly sensitive to market fluctuations. Those with a beta of less than 1.0 are not so sensitive to such movements. The average beta of all stocks is 1.0.

What is the relationship between the market risk of a security and the rate of return that investors demand of that security?

The extra return that investors require for taking risk is known as the risk premium. The **market risk premium**—that is, the risk premium on the **market portfolio**—averaged 7.6 percent between 1900 and 2004. The **capital asset pricing model** states that the expected risk premium of an investment should be proportional to both its beta and the market risk premium. The expected rate of return from any investment is equal to the risk-free interest rate plus the risk premium, so the **CAPM** boils down to

$$r = r_f + \beta(r_m - r_f)$$

The **security market line** is the graphical representation of the CAPM equation. The security market line relates the expected return investors demand of a security to its beta.

How can a manager calculate the opportunity cost of capital for a project?

The opportunity cost of capital is the return that investors give up by investing in the project rather than in securities of equivalent risk. Financial managers use the capital asset pricing model to estimate the opportunity cost of capital. The **company cost of capital** is the expected rate of return demanded by investors in a company. It depends on the *average* risk of the company's assets and operations.

The opportunity cost of capital is determined by the use to which the capital is put. Therefore, required rates of return depend on the risk of the project, not on the risk of the firm's existing business. The **project cost of capital** is the minimum acceptable expected rate of return on a project given its risk.

Your cash-flow forecasts should already factor in the chances of pleasant and unpleasant surprises. Potential bad outcomes should be reflected in the discount rate only to the extent that they affect beta.

QUIZ

1. **Risk and Return.** True or false? Explain or qualify as necessary.
   a. Investors demand higher expected rates of return on stocks with more variable rates of return.
   b. The capital asset pricing model predicts that a security with a beta of zero will provide an expected return of zero.
   c. An investor who puts $10,000 in Treasury bills and $20,000 in the market portfolio will have a portfolio beta of 2.0.
   d. Investors demand higher expected rates of return from stocks with returns that are highly exposed to macroeconomic changes.
   e. Investors demand higher expected rates of return from stocks with returns that are very sensitive to fluctuations in the stock market.

2. **Diversifiable Risk.** In light of what you've learned about market versus diversifiable (unique) risks, explain why an insurance company has no problem in selling life insurance to individuals but is reluctant to issue policies insuring against flood damage to residents of coastal areas. Why don't the insurance companies simply charge coastal residents a premium that reflects the actuarial probability of damage from hurricanes and other storms?

FIGURE 11–9 Monthly rates of return for the Snake Oil mutual fund and the Standard & Poor's Composite Index. See Quiz Problem 3.

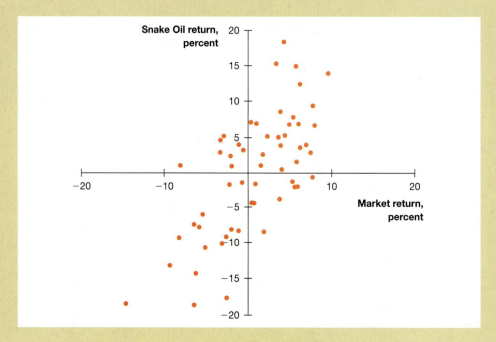

Please visit us at www.mhhe.com/bmm5e or refer to your Student CD

3. **Unique versus Market Risk.** Figure 11–9 plots monthly rates of return from 2000 to 2004 for the Snake Oil mutual fund. Was this fund well-diversified? Explain.

4. **Risk and Return.** Suppose that the risk premium on stocks and other securities did in fact rise with total risk (that is, the variability of returns) rather than just market risk. Explain how investors could exploit the situation to create portfolios with high expected rates of return but low levels of risk.

5. **CAPM and Hurdle Rates.** A project under consideration has an internal rate of return of 14 percent and a beta of .6. The risk-free rate is 4 percent, and the expected rate of return on the market portfolio is 14 percent.
    a. Should the project be accepted?
    b. Should the project be accepted if its beta is 1.6?
    c. Why does your answer change?

PRACTICE PROBLEMS

6. **CAPM and Valuation.** You are considering acquiring a firm that you believe can generate expected cash flows of $10,000 a year forever. However, you recognize that those cash flows are uncertain.
    a. Suppose you believe that the beta of the firm is .4. How much is the firm worth if the risk-free rate is 4 percent and the expected rate of return on the market portfolio is 11 percent?
    b. By how much will you overvalue the firm if its beta is actually .6?

7. **CAPM and Expected Return.** If the risk-free rate is 6 percent and the expected rate of return on the market portfolio is 13 percent, is a security with a beta of 1.25 and an expected rate of return of 16 percent overpriced or underpriced?

8. **Using Beta.** Investors expect the market rate of return this year to be 14 percent. A stock with a beta of .8 has an expected rate of return of 12 percent. If the market return this year turns out to be 10 percent, what is your best guess as to the rate of return on the stock?

9. **Unique versus Market Risk.** Figure 11–10 shows plots of monthly rates of return on three stocks versus the stock market index. The beta and standard deviation of each stock is given beside its plot.

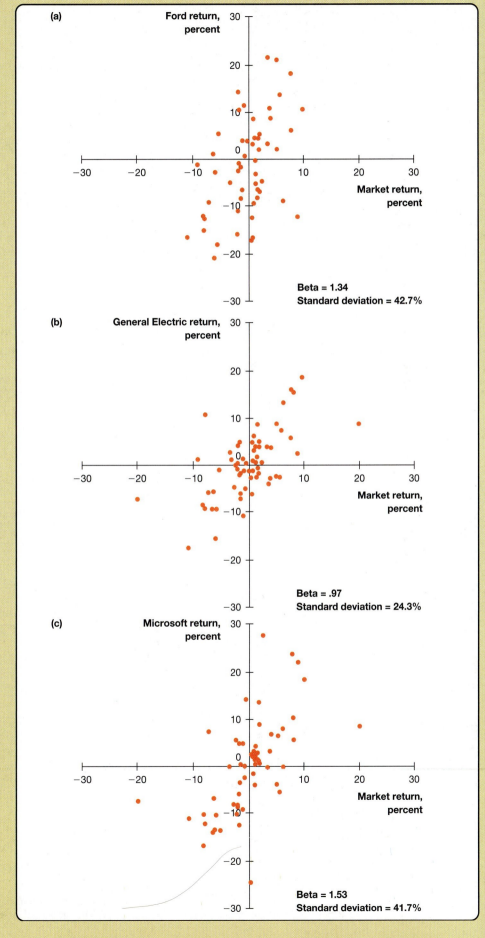

FIGURE 11–10 These plots show monthly rates of return for (a) Ford, (b) General Electric, and (c) Microsoft, plus the market portfolio. See Practice Problem 9.

(a)

Ford return, percent

Market return, percent

Beta = 1.34
Standard deviation = 42.7%

(b)

General Electric return, percent

Market return, percent

Beta = .97
Standard deviation = 24.3%

(c)

Microsoft return, percent

Market return, percent

Beta = 1.53
Standard deviation = 41.7%

a. Which stock is safest for a diversified investor?
b. Which stock is safest for an undiversified investor who puts all her funds in one of these stocks?
c. Consider a portfolio with equal investments in each stock. What would this portfolio's beta have been?
d. Consider a well-diversified portfolio made up of stocks with the same beta as Microsoft. What are the beta and standard deviation of this portfolio's return? The standard deviation of the market portfolio's return is 20 percent.
e. What is the expected rate of return on each stock? Use the capital asset pricing model with a market risk premium of 8 percent. The risk-free rate of interest is 4 percent.

10. **Calculating Beta.** Following are several months' rates of return for Tumblehome Canoe Company. Prepare a plot like Figure 11–1. What is Tumblehome's beta?

Month	Market Return, %	Tumblehome Return, %
1	0	+1
2	0	−1
3	−1	−2.5
4	−1	−0.5
5	+1	+2
6	+1	+1
7	+2	+4
8	+2	+2
9	−2	−2
10	−2	−4

11. **Expected Returns.** Consider the following two scenarios for the economy and the returns in each scenario for the market portfolio, an aggressive stock A, and a defensive stock D.

Scenario	Rate of Return		
	Market	Aggressive Stock A	Defensive Stock D
Bust	−8%	−10%	−6%
Boom	32	38	24

a. Find the beta of each stock. In what way is stock D defensive?
b. If each scenario is equally likely, find the expected rate of return on the market portfolio and on each stock.
c. If the T-bill rate is 4 percent, what does the CAPM say about the fair expected rate of return on the two stocks?
d. Which stock seems to be a better buy on the basis of your answers to (a) through (c)?

12. **CAPM and Cost of Capital.** Draw the security market line when the Treasury bill rate is 4 percent and the market risk premium is 7 percent. What are the project costs of capital for new ventures with betas of .75 and 1.75? Which of the following capital investments have positive NPVs?

Project	Beta	Internal Rate of Return, %
P	1.0	14
Q	0	6
R	2.0	18
S	0.4	7
T	1.6	20

13. **CAPM and Valuation.** You are a consultant to a firm evaluating an expansion of its current business. The cash-flow forecasts (in millions of dollars) for the project are:

Years	Cash Flow
0	−100
1–10	+ 15

On the basis of the behavior of the firm's stock, you believe that the beta of the firm is 1.4. Assuming that the rate of return available on risk-free investments is 4 percent and that the expected rate of return on the market portfolio is 12 percent, what is the net present value of the project?

14. **CAPM and Cost of Capital.** Reconsider the project in the preceding problem. What is the project IRR? What is the cost of capital for the project? Does the accept–reject decision using IRR agree with the decision using NPV?

15. **CAPM and Valuation.** A share of stock with a beta of .75 now sells for $50. Investors expect the stock to pay a year-end dividend of $2. The T-bill rate is 4 percent, and the market risk premium is 7 percent. If the stock is perceived to be fairly priced today, what must be investors' expectation of the price of the stock at the end of the year?

Please visit us at www.mhhe.com/bmm5e or refer to your Student CD

16. **CAPM and Expected Return.** Reconsider the stock in the preceding problem. Suppose investors actually believe the stock will sell for $52 at year-end. Is the stock a good or bad buy? What will investors do? At what point will the stock reach an "equilibrium" at which it again is perceived as fairly priced?

17. **Portfolio Risk and Return.** Suppose that the S&P 500, with a beta of 1.0, has an expected return of 13 percent and T-bills provide a risk-free return of 5 percent.

   a. What would be the expected return and beta of portfolios constructed from these two assets with weights in the S&P 500 of (i) 0; (ii) .25; (iii) .5; (iv) .75; (v) 1.0?
   b. On the basis of your answer to (a), what is the trade-off between risk and return, that is, how does expected return vary with beta?
   c. What does your answer to (b) have to do with the security market line relationship?

18. **Portfolio Risk and Return.** Suppose that the S&P 500, with a beta of 1.0, has an expected return of 10 percent and T-bills provide a risk-free return of 4 percent.

   a. How would you construct a portfolio from these two assets with an expected return of 8 percent?
   b. How would you construct a portfolio from these two assets with a beta of .4?
   c. Show that the risk premiums of the portfolios in (a) and (b) are proportional to their betas.

19. **CAPM and Valuation.** You are considering the purchase of real estate that will provide perpetual income that should average $50,000 per year. How much will you pay for the property if you believe its market risk is the same as the market portfolio's? The T-bill rate is 5 percent, and the expected market return is 12.5 percent.

20. **Risk and Return.** According to the CAPM, would the expected rate of return on a security with a beta less than zero be more or less than the risk-free interest rate? Why would investors be willing to invest in such a security? *Hint:* Look back to the auto and gold example in Chapter 10.

21. **CAPM and Expected Return.** The following table shows betas for several companies. Calculate each stock's expected rate of return using the CAPM. Assume the risk-free rate of interest is 5 percent. Use a 7 percent risk premium for the market portfolio.

Company	Beta
Cisco	2.13
CitiGroup	1.31
Merck	.29
Walt Disney	1.15

22. **CAPM and Expected Return.** Stock A has a beta of .5, and investors expect it to return 5 percent. Stock B has a beta of 1.5, and investors expect it to return 13 percent. Use the CAPM to find the market risk premium and the expected rate of return on the market.

23. **CAPM and Expected Return.** If the expected rate of return on the market portfolio is 13 percent and T-bills yield 6 percent, what must be the beta of a stock that investors expect to return 10 percent?

24. **Project Cost of Capital.** Suppose Cisco is considering a new investment in the common stock of a pharmaceutical company. Which of the betas shown in the table in Problem 21 is most relevant in determining the required rate of return for this venture? Explain why the expected return to Cisco stock is *not* the appropriate required return.

25. **Risk and Return.** True or false? Explain or qualify as necessary.
    a. The expected rate of return on an investment with a beta of 2.0 is twice as high as the expected rate of return of the market portfolio.
    b. The contribution of a stock to the risk of a diversified portfolio depends on the market risk of the stock.
    c. If a stock's expected rate of return plots below the security market line, it is underpriced.
    d. A diversified portfolio with a beta of 2.0 is twice as volatile as the market portfolio.
    e. An undiversified portfolio with a beta of 2.0 is twice as volatile as the market portfolio.

26. **CAPM and Expected Return.** A mutual fund manager expects her portfolio to earn a rate of return of 11 percent this year. The beta of her portfolio is .8. If the rate of return available on risk-free assets is 4 percent and you expect the rate of return on the market portfolio to be 14 percent, should you invest in this mutual fund?

27. **Required Rate of Return.** Reconsider the mutual fund manager in the previous problem. Explain how you would use a stock index mutual fund and a risk-free position in Treasury bills (or a money market mutual fund) to create a portfolio with the same risk as the manager's but with a higher expected rate of return. What is the rate of return on that portfolio?

28. **Required Rate of Return.** In view of your answer to the preceding problem, explain why a mutual fund must be able to provide an expected rate of return in excess of that predicted by the security market line for investors to consider the fund an attractive investment opportunity.

29. **CAPM.** We Do Bankruptcies is a law firm that specializes in providing advice to firms in financial distress. It prospers in recessions when other firms are struggling. Consequently, its beta is negative, –.2.
    a. If the interest rate on Treasury bills is 5 percent and the expected return on the market portfolio is 15 percent, what is the expected return on the shares of the law firm according to the CAPM?
    b. Suppose you invested 90 percent of your wealth in the market portfolio and the remainder of your wealth in the shares in the law firm. What would be the beta of your portfolio?

Please visit us at www.mhhe.com/bmm5e or refer to your Student CD

CHALLENGE PROBLEM

30. **Leverage and Portfolio Risk.** Footnote 4 in the chapter asks you to consider a borrow-and-invest strategy in which you use $1 million of your own money and borrow another $1 million to invest $2 million in a market index fund. If the risk-free interest rate is 4 percent and the expected rate of return on the market index fund is 12 percent, what is the risk premium and expected rate of return on the borrow-and-invest strategy? Why is the risk of this strategy twice that of simply investing your $1 million in the market index fund?

STANDARD &POOR'S

1. Use data from Market Insight (**www.mhhe.com/edumarketinsight**) to calculate the beta of General Motors (GM). Start by obtaining the monthly rates of return of GM and the S&P 500 over the most recent 3 years. Enter these returns in an Excel spreadsheet. Plot the returns and then draw by eye the best line through the points. What is the slope of the line? How much does GM's return increase on average given a 1 percentage point increase in the market return? Now use the regression (SLOPE) function in Excel, calculate a regression with GM's return as the dependent variable and the S&P 500 return as the explanatory variable. What is GM's beta?

2. Go to Market Insight at **www.mhhe.com/edumarketinsight.** Enter the ticker symbol "GE" for General Electric. In the Excel Analytics section, click on *Monthly Valuation Data.* Save the monthly returns for GE and the S&P 500 in a new spreadsheet. Now calculate the beta of GE as in the previous question. Then repeat the procedure to obtain data for Southwest Air (LUV), Ansell (ANSLE), E*Trade (ET), and Georgia Pacific (GP).

   a. Which of the stocks would you classify as defensive? Which would be classified as aggressive?

   b. Do the beta coefficients for the low-beta firms make sense given the industries in which these firms operate? Briefly explain.

SOLUTIONS TO SELF-TEST QUESTIONS

11.1 See Figure 11–11. Anchovy Queen's beta is 1.0.

11.2 A portfolio's beta is just a weighted average of the betas of the securities in the portfolio. In this case the weights are equal, since an equal amount is assumed invested in each of the stocks in Table 11–1. The average beta of these stocks is (2.49 + 1.64 + 1.34 + .97 + .90 + .76 + .51 + .46 + .41 + .30)/10 = .98.

11.3 The standard deviation of a fully diversified portfolio's return is proportional to its beta. The standard deviation in this case is .5 × 20 = 10 percent.

11.4 $r = r_f + \beta(r_m - r_f) = 6 + (1.5 \times 7) = 16.5\%$

11.5 Put 25 percent of your money in the market portfolio and the rest in Treasury bills. The portfolio's beta is .25 and its expected return is

$$r_{\text{portfolio}} = (.75 \times 6) + (.25 \times 13) = 7.75\%$$

The expected return also may be computed as

$$r_f + \beta(r_m - r_f) = 6 + .25 \times 7 = 7.75\%$$

11.6 $r_{\text{portfolio}} = (.4 \times 6) + (.6 \times 13) = 10.2\%$. This portfolio's beta is .6, since $600,000, which is 60 percent of the investment, is in the market portfolio. Investors in a stock with a beta of .6 would not buy it unless it also offered a rate of return of 10.2 percent and would rush to buy if it offered more. The stock price would adjust until the stock's expected rate of return was 10.2 percent.

11.7 Present value = $50 million × 10-year annuity factor at 14.5% = $255.8 million. If $\beta = 1.2$, then the cost of capital is

$$r = 3\% + (1.2 \times 7\%) = 11.4\%$$

and the value of the 10-year annuity increases to $289.6 million.

11.8 Dell should use Pfizer's cost of capital. Dell's company cost of capital tells us what expected rate of return investors demand from the computer hardware business. This is not the appropriate project cost of capital for its proposed venture into pharmaceuticals.

FIGURE 11–11 Each point shows the performance of Anchovy Queen stock when the market is up or down by 1 percent. On average, Anchovy Queen stock follows the market; it has a beta of 1.0.

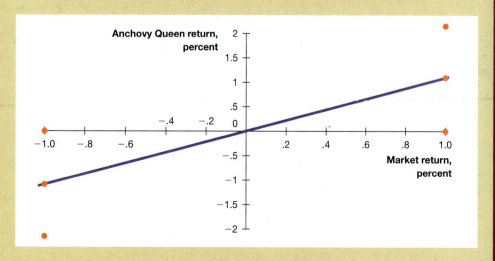

The Weighted-Average Cost of Capital and Company Valuation

RELATED WEB LINKS

www.valuepro.net Software and data for estimating weighted-average cost of capital and valuing companies.

pages.stern.nyu.edu/~adamodar Aswath Damodaran's home page includes estimates of industry asset betas and costs of capital.

www.ibbotson.com Includes sample industry WACCs.

Jo Ann Cox explains the cost of capital to Geothermal's top management.
© McGraw-Hill Companies/Chris Kerrigan, photographer

In the last chapter you learned how to use the capital asset pricing model to estimate the expected return on a company's common stock. If the firm is financed wholly by common stock, then the stockholders own all the firm's assets and are entitled to all the cash flows. In this case, the expected return required by investors in the common stock equals the company cost of capital.[1]

Most companies, however, are financed by a mixture of securities, including common stock, bonds, preferred stock, or other securities. Each of these securities has different risks and therefore investors in them look for different rates of return. In these circumstances, the company cost of capital is no longer the same as the expected return on the common stock. It depends on the expected return from all the securities that the company has issued. It also depends on taxes, because interest payments made by a corporation are tax-deductible expenses.

Therefore, the company cost of capital is usually calculated as a weighted average of the *after-tax* cost of debt interest and the "cost of equity," that is, the expected rate of return on the firm's common stock. The weights are the fractions of debt and equity in the firm's capital structure. Managers refer to the firm's *weighted-average* cost of capital, or *WACC* (rhymes with "quack").

Managers use the weighted-average cost of capital to evaluate average-risk capital investment projects. "Average risk" means that the project's risk matches the risk of the firm's existing assets and operations. This chapter explains how the weighted-average cost of capital is calculated in practice.

After studying this chapter you should be able to:

- Calculate a firm's capital structure.

- Estimate the required rates of return on the securities issued by the firm.

- Calculate the weighted-average cost of capital.

- Understand when the weighted-average cost of capital is—or isn't—the appropriate discount rate for a new project.

---

[1] Investors will invest in the firm's securities only if they offer the same expected return as other equally risky securities. When securities are properly priced, the return that investors can expect from their investments is therefore also the return that they *require*.

- Use the weighted-average cost of capital to value a business given forecasts of its future cash flows.

  Managers calculating WACC can get bogged down in formulas. We want you to understand *why* WACC works, not just how to calculate it. Let's start with "Why?" We'll listen in as a young financial manager struggles to recall the rationale for project discount rates.

12.1 Geothermal's Cost of Capital

Jo Ann Cox, a recent graduate of a prestigious eastern business school, poured a third cup of black coffee and tried again to remember what she once knew about project hurdle rates. Why hadn't she paid more attention in Finance 101? Why had she sold her finance text the day after passing the finance final?

Costas Thermopolis, her boss and CEO of Geothermal Corporation, had told her to prepare a financial evaluation of a proposed expansion of Geothermal's production. She was to report at 9:00 Monday morning. Thermopolis, whose background was geophysics, not finance, not only expected a numerical analysis but also expected her to explain it to him.

Thermopolis had founded Geothermal in 1993 to produce electricity from geothermal energy trapped deep under Nevada. The company had pioneered this business and had been able to obtain perpetual production rights for a large tract on favorable terms from the United States government. When the 2004 oil shock drove up energy prices worldwide, Geothermal became an exceptionally profitable company. It was currently reporting a rate of return on book assets of 25 percent per year.

Now, in 2007, production rights were no longer cheap. The proposed expansion would cost $30 million and should generate a perpetual after-tax cash flow of $4.5 million annually. The projected rate of return was $4.5/30 = .15$, or 15 percent, much less than the profitability of Geothermal's existing assets. However, once the new project was up and running, it would be no riskier than Geothermal's existing business.

Jo Ann realized that 15 percent was not necessarily a bad return—though of course 25 percent would have been better. Fifteen percent might still exceed Geothermal's cost of capital, that is, exceed the expected rate of return that outside investors would demand to invest money in the project. If the cost of capital was less than the 15 percent expected return, expansion would be a good deal and would generate net value for Geothermal and its stockholders.

Jo Ann remembered how to calculate the cost of capital for companies that used only common stock financing. Briefly she sketched the argument.

"I need the expected rate of return investors would require from Geothermal's real assets—the wells, pumps, generators, etc. That rate of return depends on the assets' risk. However, the assets aren't traded in the stock market, so I can't observe how risky they have been. I can only observe the risk of Geothermal's common stock.

"But if Geothermal issues only stock—no debt—then owning the stock means owning the assets, and the expected return demanded by investors in the stock must also be the cost of capital for the assets." She jotted down the following identities:

$$\text{Value of business} = \text{value of stock}$$
$$\text{Risk of business} = \text{risk of stock}$$
$$\text{Rate of return on business} = \text{rate of return on stock}$$
$$\text{Investors' required return from business} = \text{investors' required return from stock}$$

Unfortunately, Geothermal had borrowed a substantial amount of money; its stockholders did *not* have unencumbered ownership of Geothermal's assets. The expansion project would also justify some extra debt finance. Jo Ann realized that she would have to look at Geothermal's **capital structure**—its mix of debt and equity financing—and consider the expected rates of return required by debt as well as equity investors.

capital structure
The mix of long-term debt and equity financing.

Geothermal had issued 22.65 million shares, now trading at $20 each. Thus shareholders valued Geothermal's equity at $20 × 22.65 million = $453 million. In addition, the company had issued bonds with a market value of $194 million. The market value of the company's debt and equity was therefore $194 + $453 = $647 million. Debt was 194/647 = .3, or 30 percent of the total.

"Geothermal's worth more to investors than either its debt or its equity," Jo Ann mused. "But I ought to be able to find the overall value of Geothermal's business by adding up the debt and equity." She sketched a rough balance sheet:

Assets		Liabilities and Shareholders' Equity		
Market value of assets = value of Geothermal's existing business	$647	Market value of debt	$194	(30%)
		Market value of equity	453	(70%)
Total value	$647	Total value	$647	(100%)

"Holy Toledo, I've got it!" Jo Ann exclaimed. "If I bought *all* the securities issued by Geothermal, debt as well as equity, I'd own the entire business. That means . . ." She jotted again:

Value of business = value of portfolio of all the firm's debt and equity securities

Risk of business = risk of portfolio

Rate of return on business = rate of return on portfolio

Investors' required return on business (company cost of capital) = investors' required return on portfolio

"All I have to do is calculate the expected rate of return on a portfolio of all the firm's securities. That's easy. The debt's yielding 8 percent, and Fred, that nerdy banker, says that equity investors want 14 percent. Suppose he's right. The portfolio would contain 30 percent debt and 70 percent equity, so . . ."

$$\text{Portfolio return} = (.3 \times 8\%) + (.7 \times 14\%) = 12.2\%$$

It was all coming back to her now. The company cost of capital is just a weighted average of returns on debt and equity, with weights depending on relative market values of the two securities.

"But there's one more thing. Interest is tax-deductible. If Geothermal pays $1 of interest, taxable income is reduced by $1, and the firm's tax bill drops by 35 cents (assuming a 35 percent tax rate). The net cost is only 65 cents. So the cost of debt is not 8 percent, but .65 × 8 = 5.2 percent.

"Now I can finally calculate the weighted-average cost of capital:

$$\text{WACC} = (.3 \times 5.2\%) + (.7 \times 14\%) = 11.4\%$$

"Looks like the expansion's a good deal. Fifteen's better than 11.4. But I sure need a break."

12.2 The Weighted-Average Cost of Capital

Jo Ann's conclusions were important. It should be obvious by now that the choice of the discount rate can be crucial, especially when the project involves large capital expenditures or is long-lived. The nearby box describes how a major investment in a power station—an investment with both a large capital expenditure and very long life—turned on the choice of the discount rate.

Think again what the company cost of capital is, and what it is used for. We *define* it as the opportunity cost of capital for the firm's existing assets; we *use* it to value new

Choosing the Discount Rate

Shortly before the British government began to sell off the electricity industry to private investors, controversy erupted over the industry's proposal to build a 1,200-megawatt nuclear power station known as Hinkley Point C. The government argued that a nuclear station would both diversify the sources of electricity generation and reduce sulfur dioxide and carbon dioxide emissions. Protesters emphasized the dangers of nuclear accidents and attacked the proposal as "bizarre, dated and irrelevant."

At the public inquiry held to consider the proposal, opponents produced some powerful evidence that the nuclear station was also a very high cost option. Their principal witness, Professor Elroy Dimson, argued that the government-owned power company had employed an unrealistically low figure for the opportunity cost of capital. Had the company used a more plausible figure, the cost of building and operating the nuclear station would have been higher than that of a comparable station based on fossil fuels.

The reason why the choice of discount rate was so important was that nuclear stations are expensive to build but cheap to operate. If capital is cheap (i.e., the discount rate is low), then the high up-front cost is less serious. But if the cost of capital is high, then the high initial cost of nuclear stations made them uneconomic.

Evidence produced at the inquiry suggested that the construction cost of a nuclear station was £1,527 million (or about $2.3 billion), while the cost of a comparable nonnuclear station was only £895 million. However, power stations last about 40 years, and, once built, nuclear stations cost much less to operate than nonnuclear stations. If operated at 75 percent of theoretical capacity, the running costs of the nuclear station would be about £63 million a year, compared with running costs of £168 million a year for the nonnuclear station.

The following table shows the cost advantage of the nuclear power station at different (real) discount rates. At a 5 percent discount rate, which was the figure used by the gov-

ernment, the present value of the costs of the nuclear option was nearly £1 billion lower than that of a station based on fossil fuels. But with a discount rate of 16 percent, which was the figure favored by Professor Dimson, the position was almost exactly reversed, so the government could save nearly £1 billion by refusing the power company permission to build Hinkley Point C and relying instead on new fossil-fuel power stations.

Eight years after the inquiry, the proposal to construct Hinkley Point C continued to gather dust, and British Energy, the privatized electric utility, declared that it had no plans to build a new nuclear power station in the near future.

Present value of the cost advantage to a nuclear rather than a fossil-fuel station (figures in billions of pounds)

Real Discount Rate	Present Value of the Cost Advantage of the Nuclear Station
5%	0.9
8	0.2
10	−0.1
12	−0.4
14	−0.7
16	−0.9
18	−1.2

Technical Notes:
1. Present values are measured at the date that the power station comes into operation.
2. The above table assumes for simplicity that construction costs for nuclear stations are spread evenly over the 8 years before the station comes into operation, while the costs for fossil-fuel stations are assumed to be spread evenly over the 4 years before operation. As a result the present value of the costs of the two stations may differ slightly from the more precise estimates produced by Professor Dimson.

Source: Adapted from *Energy Economics*, Volume 11, Issue 3, E. Dimson, "The Discount Rate for a Power Station," pp. 175–180. © 1989 with permission from Elsevier Science.

assets that have the same risk as the old ones. The company cost of capital is the minimum acceptable rate of return when the firm expands by investing in average-risk projects.

We first introduced the opportunity cost of capital in the last section of Chapter 2. "Opportunity cost" is a shorthand reminder that, when the firm invests rather than returning cash to shareholders, the shareholders lose the opportunity to invest in financial markets. If the corporation acts in the shareholders' interests, it will invest their money only if it can find projects that offer higher rates of return than investors could achieve on their own. Therefore, the expected rates of return on investments in financial markets determine the cost of capital for corporate investments.

The company cost of capital is the opportunity cost of capital for the company as a whole. We discussed the company cost of capital in Chapter 11, but did not explain how to measure it when the firm has raised different types of debt and equity financing or how to adjust it for the tax-deductibility of interest payments. The weighted-average cost of capital formula handles these complications.

Calculating Company Cost of Capital as a Weighted Average

Calculating the company cost of capital is straightforward, though not always easy, when only common stock is outstanding. For example, a financial manager could estimate beta and calculate shareholders' required rate of return using the capital asset pricing model (CAPM). This would be the expected rate of return investors require on the company's existing assets and operations and also the expected return they will require on new investments that do not change the company's market risk.

But most companies issue debt as well as equity. ==The company cost of capital is a *weighted average* of the returns demanded by debt and equity investors. The weighted average is the expected rate of return investors would demand on a portfolio of all the firm's outstanding securities.==

Let's review Jo Ann Cox's calculations for Geothermal. To avoid complications, we'll ignore taxes for the next two or three pages. The total market value of Geothermal, which we denote as V, is the sum of the values of the outstanding debt D and the equity E. Thus firm value is $V = D + E = \$194$ million $+ \$453$ million $= \$647$ million. Debt accounts for 30 percent of the value and equity accounts for the remaining 70 percent. If you held all the shares and all the debt, your investment in Geothermal would be $V = \$647$ million. Between them, the debt- and equityholders own *all* the firm's assets. So V is also the value of these assets—the value of Geothermal's existing business.

Suppose that Geothermal's equity investors require a 14 percent rate of return on their investment in the stock. What rate of return must a new project provide in order that all investors—both debtholders and stockholders—earn a fair rate of return? The debtholders require a rate of return of $r_{debt} = 8$ percent. So each year the firm will need to pay interest of $r_{debt} \times D = .08 \times \$194$ million $= \$15.52$ million. The shareholders, who have invested in a riskier security, require an expected return of $r_{equity} = 14$ percent on their investment of $\$453$ million. Thus in order to keep shareholders happy, the company needs additional income of $r_{equity} \times E = .14 \times \$453$ million $= \$63.42$ million. To satisfy both the debtholders and the shareholders, Geothermal needs to earn $\$15.52$ million $+ \$63.42$ million $= \$78.94$ million. This is equivalent to earning a return of $r_{assets} = 78.94/647 = .122$, or 12.2 percent.

Figure 12–1 illustrates the reasoning behind our calculations. The figure shows the amount of income needed to satisfy the debt and equity investors. Notice that debtholders account for 30 percent of Geothermal's capital structure but receive less than 30 percent of its expected income. On the other hand, they bear less than a 30 percent share of risk, since they have first cut at the company's income and also first claim on its assets if the company gets in trouble. Shareholders expect a return of more than 70 percent of Geothermal's income because they bear correspondingly more risk.

However, if you buy *all* Geothermal's debt and equity, you own its assets lock, stock, and barrel. You receive all the income and bear all the risks. The expected rate of return you'd require on this portfolio of securities is the same return you'd require

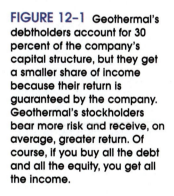

FIGURE 12–1 Geothermal's debtholders account for 30 percent of the company's capital structure, but they get a smaller share of income because their return is guaranteed by the company. Geothermal's stockholders bear more risk and receive, on average, greater return. Of course, if you buy all the debt and all the equity, you get all the income.

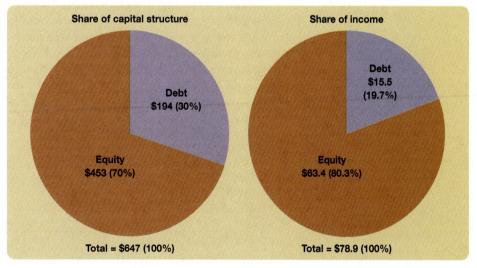

from unencumbered ownership of the business. This rate of return—12.2 percent, ignoring taxes—is therefore the company cost of capital and the required rate of return from an equal-risk expansion of the business.

The bottom line (still ignoring taxes) is

Company cost of capital = weighted average of debt and equity returns

The underlying algebra is simple. Debtholders need income of $(r_{debt} \times D)$, and the equity investors need expected income of $(r_{equity} \times E)$. The *total* income that is needed is $(r_{debt} \times D) + (r_{equity} \times E)$. The amount of their combined existing investment in the company is V. So to calculate the return that is needed on the assets, we simply divide the income by the investment:

$$r_{assets} = \frac{\textbf{total income}}{\textbf{value of investment}}$$

$$= \frac{(D \times r_{debt}) + (E \times r_{equity})}{V} = \left(\frac{D}{V} \times r_{debt}\right) + \left(\frac{E}{V} \times r_{equity}\right)$$

For Geothermal,

$$r_{assets} = (.30 \times 8\%) + (.70 \times 14\%) = 12.2\%$$

This figure is the expected return demanded by investors in the firm's assets.

Self-Test 12.1

Hot Rocks Corp., one of Geothermal's competitors, has issued long-term bonds with a market value of $50 million and an expected return of 9 percent. It has 4 million shares outstanding trading for $10 each. At this price the shares offer an expected return of 17 percent. What is the weighted-average cost of capital for Hot Rocks's assets and operations? Assume Hot Rocks pays no taxes.

Market versus Book Weights

The company cost of capital is the expected rate of return that investors demand from the company's assets and operations. The cost of capital must be based on what investors are actually willing to pay for the company's outstanding securities—that is, based on the securities' *market* values.

Market values usually differ from the values recorded by accountants in the company's books. The book value of Geothermal's equity reflects money raised in the past from shareholders or reinvested by the firm on their behalf. If investors recognize Geothermal's excellent prospects, the market value of equity may be much higher than book, and the debt ratio will be lower when measured in terms of market values rather than book values.

Financial managers use book debt-to-value ratios for various other purposes, and sometimes they unthinkingly look to the book ratios when calculating weights for the company cost of capital. That's a mistake, because the company cost of capital measures what investors want from the company, and it depends on how *they* value the company's securities. That value depends on future profits and cash flows, not on accounting history. Book values, while useful for many other purposes, only measure net cumulative historical outlays; they don't generally measure market values accurately.

Self-Test 12.2

Here is a book balance sheet for Duane S. Burg Associates. Figures are in millions.

Assets		Liabilities and Shareholders' Equity	
Assets (book value)	$75	Debt	$25
		Equity	50
	$75		$75

Unfortunately, the company has fallen on hard times. The 6 million shares are trading for only $4 apiece, and the market value of its debt securities is 20 percent below the face (book) value. Because of the company's large cumulative losses, it will pay no taxes on future income.

Suppose shareholders now demand a 20 percent expected rate of return. The bonds are now yielding 14 percent. What is the weighted-average cost of capital?

Taxes and the Weighted-Average Cost of Capital

Thus far in this section our examples have ignored taxes. Taxes are important because interest payments are deducted from income before tax is calculated. Therefore, the cost to the company of an interest payment is reduced by the amount of this tax saving.

The interest rate on Geothermal's debt is $r_{\text{debt}} = 8$ percent. However, with a corporate tax rate of $T_c = .35$, the government bears 35 percent of the cost of the interest payments. The government doesn't send the firm a check for this amount, but the income tax that the firm pays is reduced by 35 percent of its interest expense.

Therefore, Geothermal's after-tax cost of debt is only $100 - 35 = 65$ percent of the 8 percent pretax cost:

$$\textbf{After-tax cost of debt} = \textbf{pretax cost} \times (1 - \textbf{tax rate})$$
$$= r_{\text{debt}} \times (1 - T_c)$$
$$= 8\% \times (1 - .35) = 5.2\%$$

We can now adjust our calculation of Geothermal's cost of capital to recognize the tax savings associated with interest payments:

$$\text{Company cost of capital, after-tax} = (.3 \times 5.2\%) + (.7 \times 14\%) = 11.4\%$$

Self-Test 12.3

Criss-Cross Industries has earnings before interest and taxes (EBIT) of $10 million. Interest payments are $2 million, and the corporate tax rate is 35 percent. Construct a simple income statement to show that the debt interest reduces the taxes the firm owes to the government. How much more tax would Criss-Cross pay if it were financed solely by equity?

weighted-average cost of capital (WACC)
Expected rate of return on a portfolio of all the firm's securities, adjusted for tax savings due to interest payments.

Now we're back to the **weighted-average cost of capital,** or **WACC.** The general formula is

$$\textbf{WACC} = \left[\frac{D}{V} \times (1 - T_c)r_{\text{debt}}\right] + \left(\frac{E}{V} \times r_{\text{equity}}\right)$$

EXAMPLE 12.1 ▶   Weighted-Average Cost of Capital for McDonald's

In Chapter 11 we showed how the capital asset pricing model can be used to estimate the expected return on McDonald's common stock. We will now use this estimate to figure out the company's weighted-average cost of capital.

Step 1. *Calculate the value of each security as a proportion of firm value.* The company has outstanding 1,260 million shares, which at the beginning of 2005 had a market value of about $31 each. The total market value of

McDonald's equity was $E = 1{,}260 \times \$31 = \$39{,}060$ million. The company's latest balance sheet showed that it had borrowed $D = \$8{,}693$ million. So the total value of McDonald's securities is $V = D + E = \$8{,}693 + \$39{,}060 = \$47{,}753$ million. Debt as a proportion of the total value is $D/V = \$8{,}693/\$47{,}753 = .182$, and equity as a proportion of the total is $\$39{,}060/\$47{,}753 = .818$.

Step 2. *Determine the required rate of return on each security.* In Chapter 11 we estimated that McDonald's shareholders required a return of 9.3 percent. The average yield on McDonald's debt was about 4.1 percent.

Step 3. *Calculate a weighted average of the after-tax return on the debt and the return on the equity.*[2] The weighted-average cost of capital is

$$\text{WACC} = \left[\frac{D}{V} \times (1 - T_c) r_{\text{debt}}\right] + \left(\frac{E}{V} \times r_{\text{equity}}\right)$$

$$= [.182 \times (1 - .35)4.1\%] + (.818 \times 9.3\%) = 8.1\% \quad \blacktriangleleft$$

Self-Test 12.4

Calculate WACC for Hot Rocks (Self-Test 12.1) and Burg Associates (Self-Test 12.2) assuming the companies face a 35 percent corporate income tax rate.

What If There Are Three (or More) Sources of Financing?

We have simplified our discussion of the cost of capital by assuming the firm has only two classes of securities: debt and equity. Even if the firm has issued other classes of securities, our general approach to calculating WACC remains unchanged. We simply calculate the weighted-average after-tax return of each security type.

For example, suppose the firm also has outstanding preferred stock. Preferred stock has some of the characteristics of both common stock and fixed-income securities. Like bonds, preferred stock promises to pay a given, usually level, stream of dividends. Unlike bonds, however, there is no maturity date for the preferred stock. The promised dividends constitute a perpetuity as long as the firm stays in business. Moreover, a failure to come up with the cash to pay the dividends does not push the firm into bankruptcy. Instead, dividends owed simply cumulate; the common stockholders do not receive dividends until the accumulated preferred dividends have been paid. Finally, unlike interest payments, preferred stock dividends are not considered tax-deductible expenses.

How would we calculate WACC for a firm with preferred stock as well as common stock and bonds outstanding? Using P to denote the value of preferred stock, we simply generalize the formula for WACC as follows:

$$\textbf{WACC} = \left[\frac{D}{V} \times (1 - T_c) r_{\textbf{debt}}\right] + \left(\frac{P}{V} \times r_{\textbf{preferred}}\right) + \left(\frac{E}{V} \times r_{\textbf{equity}}\right)$$

Wrapping Up Geothermal

We now turn one last time to Jo Ann Cox and Geothermal's proposed expansion. We want to make sure that she—and you—know how to *use* the weighted-average cost of capital.

Remember that the proposed expansion costs $30 million and should generate a perpetual cash flow of $4.5 million per year. A simple cash-flow worksheet might look like this:[3]

---

[2] Financial managers often use "equity" to refer to common stock, even though a firm's equity strictly includes both common and preferred stock. We continue to use r_{equity} to refer specifically to the expected return on the common stock.

[3] For this example we ignore depreciation, a noncash but tax-deductible expense. (If the project were really perpetual, why depreciate?)

Revenue	$10.00 million
− Operating expenses	− 3.08
= Pretax operating cash flow	6.92
− Tax at 35%	− 2.42
After-tax cash flow	$ 4.50 million

Note that these cash flows do not include the tax benefits of using debt.

Geothermal's managers and engineers forecast revenues, costs, and taxes as if the project were to be all-equity financed. The interest tax shields generated by the project's actual debt financing are not forgotten, however. They are accounted for by using the *after-tax* cost of debt in the weighted-average cost of capital.

Project net present value is calculated by discounting the cash flow (which is a perpetuity) at Geothermal's 11.4 percent weighted-average cost of capital:

$$\text{NPV} = -30 + \frac{4.5}{.114} = +\$9.5 \text{ million}$$

Expansion will thus add $9.5 million to the net wealth of Geothermal's owners.

Checking Our Logic

Any project offering a rate of return more than 11.4 percent will have a positive NPV, assuming that the project has the same risk and financing as Geothermal's business. A project offering exactly 11.4 percent would be just break-even; it would generate just enough cash to satisfy both debtholders and stockholders.

Let's check that out. Suppose the proposed expansion had revenues of only $8.34 million and after-tax cash flows of $3.42 million:

Revenue	$8.34 million
− Operating expenses	− 3.08
= Pretax operating cash flow	5.26
− Tax at 35%	− 1.84
After-tax cash flow	$3.42 million

With an investment of $30 million, the internal rate of return on this perpetuity is exactly 11.4 percent:

$$\text{Rate of return} = \frac{3.42}{30} = .114, \text{ or } 11.4\%$$

and NPV is exactly zero:

$$\text{NPV} = -30 + \frac{3.42}{.114} = 0$$

When we calculated Geothermal's weighted-average cost of capital, we recognized that the company's debt ratio was 30 percent. When Geothermal's analysts use the weighted-average cost of capital to evaluate the new project, they are *assuming* that the $30 million additional investment would support the issue of additional debt equal to 30 percent of the investment, or $9 million. The remaining $21 million is provided by the shareholders.

The following table shows how the cash flows would be shared between the debtholders and shareholders. We start with the pretax operating cash flow of $5.26 million:

Cash flow before tax and interest	$5.26 million
− Interest payment (.08 × $9 million)	− .72
= Pretax cash flow	4.54
− Tax at 35%	− 1.59
After-tax cash flow	$2.95 million

Project cash flows before tax and interest are forecast to be $5.26 million. Out of this figure, Geothermal needs to pay interest of 8 percent of $9 million, which comes to $.72 million. This leaves a pretax cash flow of $4.54 million, on which the company must pay tax. Taxes equal $.35 \times 4.54 = \$1.59$ million. Shareholders are left with $2.95 million, just enough to give them the 14 percent return that they need on their $21 million investment. (Note that $2.95/21 = .14$, or 14 percent.) Therefore, everything checks out.

If a project has zero NPV when the expected cash flows are discounted at the weighted-average cost of capital, then the project's cash flows are just sufficient to give debtholders and shareholders the returns they require.

12.3 Measuring Capital Structure

We have explained the formula for calculating the weighted-average cost of capital. We will now look at some of the practical problems in applying that formula. Suppose that the financial manager of Big Oil has asked you to estimate the firm's weighted-average cost of capital. Your first step is to work out Big Oil's capital structure. But where do you get the data?

Financial managers usually start with the company's accounts, which show the book value of debt and equity, whereas the weighted-average cost of capital formula calls for their *market* values. A little work and a dash of judgment are needed to go from one to the other.

Table 12–1 shows the debt and equity issued by Big Oil. The firm has borrowed $200 million from banks and has issued a further $200 million of long-term bonds. These bonds have a coupon rate of 8 percent and mature at the end of 12 years. Finally, there are 100 million shares of common stock outstanding, each with a par value of $1. But the accounts also recognize that Big Oil has in past years plowed back into the firm $300 million of retained earnings. The total book value of the equity shown in the accounts is $100 million + $300 million = $400 million.

The figures shown in Table 12–1 are taken from Big Oil's annual accounts and are therefore book values. Sometimes the differences between book values and market values are negligible. For example, consider the $200 million that Big Oil owes the bank. The interest rate on bank loans is usually linked to the general level of interest rates. Thus if interest rates rise, the rate charged on Big Oil's loan also rises to maintain the loan's value. As long as Big Oil is reasonably sure to repay the loan, the loan is worth close to $200 million. Most financial managers most of the time are willing to accept the book value of bank debt as a fair approximation of its market value.

What about Big Oil's long-term bonds? Since the bonds were originally issued, long-term interest rates have risen to 9 percent.[4] We can calculate the value today of each bond as follows.[5] There are 12 coupon payments of $.08 \times 200 = \$16$ million and

TABLE 12–1 The *book* values of Big Oil's debt and equity (dollar figures in millions)

Bank debt	$200	25.0%
Long-term bonds (12-year maturity, 8% coupon)	200	25.0
Common stock (100 million shares, par value $1)	100	12.5
Retained earnings	300	37.5
Total	$800	100.0%

---

[4] If Big Oil's bonds are traded, you can simply look up their price. But many bonds are not regularly traded, and in such cases you need to infer their price by calculating the bond's value using the rate of interest offered by similar bonds.

[5] We assume that coupon payments are annual. Most bonds in the United States actually pay interest twice a year.

TABLE 12–2 The market values of Big Oil's debt and equity (dollar figures in millions)

Bank debt	$ 200.0	12.6%
Long-term bonds	185.7	11.7
Total debt	385.7	24.3
Common stock, 100 million shares at $12	1,200.0	75.7
Total	$1,585.7	100.0%

then repayment of face value 12 years out. Thus the final cash payment to the bondholders is $216 million. All the bond's cash flows are discounted back at the *current* interest rate of 9 percent:

$$PV = \frac{16}{1.09} + \frac{16}{(1.09)^2} + \frac{16}{(1.09)^3} + \cdots + \frac{216}{(1.09)^{12}} = \$185.7$$

Therefore, the bonds are worth only $185.7 million, 92.8 percent of their face value.

If you used the book value of Big Oil's long-term debt rather than its market value, you would be a little bit off in your calculation of the weighted-average cost of capital, but probably not seriously so.

The really big errors are likely to arise if you use the book value of equity rather than its market value. The $400 million book value of Big Oil's equity measures the total amount of cash that the firm has raised from shareholders in the past or has retained and invested on their behalf. But perhaps Big Oil has been able to find projects that were worth more than they originally cost, or perhaps the value of the assets has increased with inflation. Perhaps investors see great future investment opportunities for the company. All these considerations determine what investors are willing to pay for Big Oil's common stock.

In September 2004 Big Oil stock was $12 a share. Thus the total *market value* of the stock was

Number of shares × share price = 100 million × $12 = $1,200 million

In Table 12–2 we show the market values of Big Oil's debt and equity. You can see that debt accounts for 24.3 percent of company value ($D/V = .243$) and equity accounts for 75.7 percent ($E/V = .757$). These are the proportions to use when calculating the weighted-average cost of capital. Notice that if you looked only at the book values shown in the company accounts, you would mistakenly conclude that debt and equity each accounted for 50 percent of value.

Self-Test 12.5

Here is the capital structure shown in Executive Fruit's *book* balance sheet:

Debt	$4.1 million	45.0%
Preferred stock	2.2	24.2
Common stock	2.8	30.8
Total	$9.1 million	100.0%

Explain why the percentage weights given above should *not* be used in calculating Executive Fruit's WACC.

12.4 Calculating Required Rates of Return

To calculate Big Oil's weighted-average cost of capital, you also need the rate of return that investors require from each security.

The Expected Return on Bonds

We know that Big Oil's bonds offer a yield to maturity of 9 percent. As long as the company does not go belly-up, that is the rate of return investors can expect to earn from holding Big Oil's bonds. If there is any chance that the firm may be unable to repay the debt, however, the yield to maturity of 9 percent represents the most favorable outcome and the *expected* return is lower than 9 percent.

For most large and healthy firms, the probability of bankruptcy is sufficiently low that financial managers are content to take the promised yield to maturity on the bonds as a measure of the expected return. But beware of assuming that the yield offered on the bonds of Fly-by-Night Corporation is the return that investors could *expect* to receive.

The Expected Return on Common Stock

Estimates Based on the Capital Asset Pricing Model   In the last chapter we showed you how to use the capital asset pricing model to estimate the expected rate of return on common stock. The capital asset pricing model tells us that investors demand a higher rate of return from stocks with high betas. The formula is

$$\text{Expected return on stock} = \text{risk-free interest rate} + \left(\text{stock's beta} \times \text{expected market risk premium} \right)$$

Financial managers and economists measure the risk-free rate of interest by the yield on Treasury bills. To measure the expected market risk premium, they usually look back at capital market history, which suggests that investors have received an extra 7 to 8 percent a year from investing in common stocks rather than Treasury bills. Yet wise financial managers use this evidence with considerable humility, for who is to say whether investors in the past received more or less than they expected or whether investors today require a higher or lower reward for risk than their parents did?

Let's suppose Big Oil's common stock beta is estimated at .85, the risk-free interest rate of r_f is 6 percent, and the expected market risk premium $(r_m - r_f)$ is 7 percent. Then the CAPM would put Big Oil's cost of equity at

$$\text{Cost of equity} = r_{\text{equity}} = r_f + \beta(r_m - r_f)$$
$$= 6\% + .85(7\%) = 12\%$$

Self-Test 12.6   Jo Ann Cox decides to check whether Fred, the nerdy banker, was correct in claiming that Geothermal's cost of equity is 14 percent. She estimates Geothermal's beta at 1.20. The risk-free interest rate in 2007 is 6 percent, and the long-run average market risk premium is 7.6 percent. What is the expected rate of return on Geothermal's common stock, assuming of course that the CAPM is true? Recalculate Geothermal's weighted-average cost of capital.

Estimates Based on the Dividend Discount Model   Whenever you are given an estimate of the expected return on a common stock, always look for ways to check whether it is reasonable. One check on the estimates provided by the CAPM can be obtained from the dividend discount model (DDM). In Chapter 6 we showed you how to use the constant-growth DDM formula to estimate the return that investors expect from different common stocks. Remember the formula: If dividends are expected to grow indefinitely at a constant rate g, then the price of the stock is equal to

$$P_0 = \frac{\text{DIV}_1}{r_{\text{equity}} - g}$$

where P_0 is the current stock price, DIV_1 is the forecast dividend at the end of the year, and r_{equity} is the expected return from the stock. We can rearrange this formula to provide an estimate of r_{equity}:

$$r_{\text{equity}} = \frac{\text{DIV}_1}{P_0} + g$$

In other words, the expected return on equity is equal to the dividend yield (DIV_1/P_0) plus the expected perpetual growth rate in dividends (g).

This constant-growth dividend discount model is widely used in estimating expected rates of return on common stocks of public utilities. Utility stocks have a fairly stable growth pattern and are therefore tailor-made for the constant-growth formula. Remember that the constant-growth formula will get you into trouble if you apply it to firms with very high current rates of growth. Such growth cannot be sustained indefinitely. Using the formula in these circumstances will lead to an overestimate of the expected return.

Beware of False Precision   Do not expect estimates of the cost of equity to be precise. In practice you can't know whether the capital asset pricing model fully explains expected returns or whether the assumptions of the dividend discount model hold exactly. Even if your formulas were right, the required inputs would be noisy and subject to error. Thus a financial analyst who can confidently locate the cost of equity in a band of 2 or 3 percentage points is doing pretty well. In this endeavor it is perfectly OK to conclude that the cost of equity is, say, "about 15 percent" or "somewhere between 14 and 16 percent."[6]

Sometimes accuracy can be improved by estimating the cost of equity or WACC for an industry or a group of comparable companies. This cuts down the "noise" that plagues single-company estimates. Suppose, for example, that Jo Ann Cox is able to identify three companies with investments and operations similar to Geothermal's. The average WACC for these three companies would be a valuable check on her estimate of WACC for Geothermal alone.

Or suppose that Geothermal is contemplating investment in oil refining. For this venture Geothermal's existing WACC is probably not right; it needs a discount rate reflecting the risks of the refining business. It could therefore try to estimate WACC for a sample of oil refining companies. If too few "pure-play" refining companies were available—most oil companies invest in production and marketing as well as refining—an industry WACC for a sample of large oil companies could be a useful check or benchmark.

The Expected Return on Preferred Stock

Preferred stock that pays a fixed annual dividend can be valued from the perpetuity formula:

$$\text{Price of preferred} = \frac{\text{dividend}}{r_{\text{preferred}}}$$

where $r_{\text{preferred}}$ is the appropriate discount rate for the preferred stock. Therefore, we can infer the required rate of return on preferred stock by rearranging the valuation formula to

$$r_{\text{preferred}} = \frac{\textbf{dividend}}{\textbf{price of preferred}}$$

For example, if a share of preferred stock sells for $20 and pays a dividend of $2 per share, the expected return on preferred stock is $r_{\text{preferred}} = \$2/\$20 = 10$ percent, which is simply the dividend yield.

---

[6] The calculations in this chapter have been done to one or two decimal places only to avoid confusion from rounding.

TABLE 12–3 Data needed to calculate Big Oil's weighted-average cost of capital (dollar figures in millions)

Security Type	Capital Structure		Required Rate of Return
Debt	$D = \$\ 385.7$	$D/V = .243$	$r_{debt} = .09$, or 9%
Common stock	$E = \$1{,}200.0$	$E/V = .757$	$r_{equity} = .12$, or 12%
Total	$V = \$1{,}585.7$		

Note: Corporate tax rate = $T_c = .35$.

TABLE 12–4 Calculating the weighted-average cost of capital for selected companies

Company	Expected Return on Equity (r_{equity})	Interest Rate on Debt (r_{debt})	Proportion of Equity (E/V)	Proportion of Debt (D/V)	Weighted-Average Cost of Capital (WACC)
Amazon.com	20.4	8.12	.90	.10	18.9
Dell Computer	14.5	5.04	.99	.01	14.4
Boeing	8.3	5.04	.79	.21	7.2
Pfizer	6.2	4.72	.96	.04	6.1
General Electric	9.8	4.72	.79	.21	7.6
Wal-Mart	6.6	4.86	.91	.09	6.3
ExxonMobil	5.9	4.72	.98	.02	5.9
McDonald's	9.3	4.89	.82	.18	8.2
Ford	12.4	9.68	.13	.87	7.1
H.J. Heinz	5.1	5.04	.74	.26	4.6

Notes:
1. r_{equity} is estimated by using the capital asset pricing model (see estimates in Table 11–2).
2. r_{debt} is calculated from average yields on similarly rated bonds.
3. D is the book value of the firm's debt and E the market value of the equity. (Some small amounts of preferred stock have been lumped in with the debt.)
4. WACC = $(D/V)\ (1 - .35)\ r_{debt} + (E/V)\ r_{equity}$.

12.5 Calculating the Weighted-Average Cost of Capital

Now that you have worked out Big Oil's capital structure and estimated the expected return on its securities, you need only simple arithmetic to calculate the weighted-average cost of capital. Table 12–3 summarizes the necessary data. Now all you need to do is plug the data in Table 12–3 into the weighted-average cost of capital formula:

$$\text{WACC} = \left[\frac{D}{V} \times (1 - T_c)r_{debt}\right] + \left(\frac{E}{V} \times r_{equity}\right)$$

$$= [.243 \times (1 - .35)\ 9\%] + (.757 \times 12\%) = 10.5\%$$

Suppose that Big Oil needed to evaluate a project with the same risk as its existing business that would also support a 24.3 percent debt ratio. The 10.5 percent weighted-average cost of capital is the appropriate discount rate for the cash flows.

Real-Company WACCs

Big Oil is entirely hypothetical. Therefore you might be interested to look at Table 12–4, which gives some estimates of the weighted-average cost of capital for a sample of real companies. As you do so, remember that any estimate of the cost of capital for a single company can be way off the true cost. You should always check your estimate by looking at the cost of capital for a group of similar companies.[7]

---

[7] Notice the low WACC for Ford, which results from the company's very high debt ratio. Should Ford use a WACC of 7.1 percent when valuing a proposal to expand its operations? The answer is yes if an 87 percent debt ratio really is a sensible target capital structure. But if you believe that this debt ratio does not constitute a desirable long-term capital structure for Ford, then you would need to recalculate WACC with a different ratio.

Weighted-Average Cost of Capital

In the Internet Insider box on page 300 we showed how you can estimate expected stock returns for five companies by using the betas shown on finance.yahoo.com. You can now go on to estimate the weighted-average cost of capital for these companies. You need two extra items of data—the relative proportions of equity and debt and the expected return on debt. You can work out the proportions of equity and debt by using finance.yahoo.com and looking at each company's *profile.* Remember, though, to use the market value of the equity, not its book value. Finding the yield on the debt is a little trickier. Log on to www.bondsonline.com to find the current level of Treasury yields and the yield spreads (i.e., the extra yield for bonds with different ratings). As we write this, Moody's ratings for the five companies vary from Baa for Eastman Kodak, Walt Disney, and Altria to A for Intel and Aa for Home Depot.

12.6 Interpreting the Weighted-Average Cost of Capital

When You Can and Can't Use WACC

The weighted-average cost of capital is the rate of return that the firm must expect to earn on its average-risk investments in order to provide a fair expected return to all its security holders. Strictly speaking, the weighted-average cost of capital is an appropriate discount rate only for a project that is a carbon copy of the firm's existing business. But often it is used as a companywide benchmark discount rate; the benchmark is adjusted upward for unusually risky projects and downward for unusually safe ones.

There is a good musical analogy here. Most of us, lacking perfect pitch, need a well-defined reference point, like middle C, before we can sing on key. But anyone who can carry a tune gets *relative* pitches right. Businesspeople have good intuition about *relative* risks, at least in industries they are used to, but not about absolute risk or required rates of return. Therefore, they set a company- or industrywide cost of capital as a benchmark. This is not the right hurdle rate for everything the company does, but judgmental adjustments can be made for more risky or less risky ventures.

Some Common Mistakes

One danger with the weighted-average formula is that it tempts people to make logical errors. Think back to your estimate of the cost of capital for Big Oil:

$$\text{WACC} = \left[\frac{D}{V} \times (1 - T_c)r_{\text{debt}}\right] + \left(\frac{E}{V} \times r_{\text{equity}}\right)$$
$$= [.243 \times (1 - .35)\, 9\%] + (.757 \times 12\%) = 10.5\%$$

Now you might be tempted to say to yourself: "Aha! Big Oil has a good credit rating. It could easily push up its debt ratio to 50 percent. If the interest rate is 9 percent and the required return on equity is 12 percent, the weighted-average cost of capital would be

$$\text{WACC} = [.50 \times (1 - .35)\, 9\%] + (.50 \times 12\%) = 8.9\%$$

At a discount rate of 8.9 percent, we can justify a lot more investment."

That reasoning will get you into trouble. First, if Big Oil increased its borrowing, the lenders would almost certainly demand a higher rate of interest on the debt. Second, as the borrowing increased, the risk of the common stock would also increase and therefore the stockholders would demand a higher return.

There are actually two costs of debt finance. The explicit cost of debt is the rate of interest that bondholders demand. But there is also an implicit cost, because borrowing increases the required return to equity. When you jumped to the conclusion that

335

Big Oil could lower its weighted-average cost of capital to 8.9 percent by borrowing more, you were recognizing only the explicit cost of debt and not the implicit cost.

Self-Test 12.7

Jo Ann Cox's boss has pointed out that Geothermal proposes to finance its expansion entirely by borrowing at an interest rate of 8 percent. He argues that this is therefore the appropriate discount rate for the project's cash flows. Is he right?

How Changing Capital Structure Affects Expected Returns

We will illustrate how changes in capital structure affect expected returns by focusing on the simplest possible case, where the corporate tax rate T_c is zero.

Think back to our earlier example of Geothermal. Geothermal, you may remember, has the following market-value balance sheet:

Assets		Liabilities and Shareholders' Equity		
Assets = value of Geothermal's existing business	$647	Debt	$194	(30%)
		Equity	453	(70%)
Total value	$647	Value	$647	(100%)

Geothermal's debtholders require a return of 8 percent, and the shareholders require a return of 14 percent. Since we assume here that Geothermal pays no corporate tax, its weighted-average cost of capital is simply the expected return on the firm's assets:

$$\text{WACC} = r_{\text{assets}} = (.3 \times 8\%) + (.7 \times 14\%) = 12.2\%$$

This is the return you would expect if you held all Geothermal's securities and therefore owned all its assets.

Now think what will happen if Geothermal borrows an additional $97 million and uses the cash to buy back and retire $97 million of its common stock. The revised market-value balance sheet is

Assets		Liabilities and Shareholders' Equity		
Assets = value of Geothermal's existing business	$647	Debt	$291	(45%)
		Equity	356	(55%)
Total value	$647	Value	$647	(100%)

If there are no corporate taxes, the change in capital structure does not affect the total cash that Geothermal pays out to its security holders and it does not affect the risk of those cash flows. Therefore, if investors require a return of 12.2 percent on the total package of debt and equity before the financing, they must require the same 12.2 percent return on the package afterward. The weighted-average cost of capital is therefore unaffected by the change in the capital structure.

Although the required return on the *package* of the debt and equity is unaffected, the change in capital structure does affect the required return on the individual securities. Since the company has more debt than before, the debt is riskier and debtholders are likely to demand a higher return. Increasing the amount of debt also makes the equity riskier and increases the return that shareholders require. We will return to this point in Chapter 15.

What Happens When the Corporate Tax Rate Is Not Zero

We have shown that when there are no corporate taxes, the weighted-average cost of capital is unaffected by a change in capital structure. Unfortunately, taxes can complicate the picture.[8] For the moment, just remember:

- The weighted-average cost of capital is the right discount rate for average-risk capital investment projects.
- The weighted-average cost of capital is the return the company needs to earn after tax in order to satisfy all its security holders.
- If the firm increases its debt ratio, both the debt and the equity will become more risky. The debtholders and equityholders require a higher return to compensate for the increased risk.

12.7 Valuing Entire Businesses

Investors routinely buy and sell shares of common stock. Companies frequently buy and sell entire businesses. Do the discounted cash-flow formulas that we used in Chapter 6 to value Blue Skies' stock also work for entire businesses?

Sure! As long as the company's debt ratio is expected to remain fairly constant, you can treat the company as one big project and discount its cash flows by the weighted-average cost of capital. The result is the combined value of the company's debt and equity. If you want to know just the value of the equity, you must remember to subtract the value of the debt from the company's total value.

Suppose that you are interested in buying Establishment Industry's concatenator manufacturing operation. The problem is how to figure out what it is worth. Table 12–5 sets out your forecasts for the next 6 years. Row 8 shows the expected cash flow from operations. This is equal to the expected profit after tax plus depreciation. Remember, depreciation is not a cash outflow, and therefore you need to add it back when calculating the operating cash flow. Row 9 in the table shows the forecasted investments in plant and working capital.

free cash flow
Cash flow that is not required for investment in fixed assets or working capital and is therefore available to investors.

The operating cash flow *less* investment expenditures is the amount of cash that the business can pay out to investors after paying for all investments necessary for growth. This is the concatenator division's **free cash flow** (row 10 in the table). Notice that the free cash flow is negative in the early years. Is that a bad sign? Not really. The business is running a cash deficit not because it is unprofitable but because it is growing so fast. Rapid growth is good news, not bad, as long as the business is earning more than the cost of capital on its investments.

The forecast cash flows in Table 12–5 did not include a deduction for debt interest. But we will not forget that acquisition of the concatenator business will support additional debt. We will recognize that fact by discounting the free cash flows by the weighted-average cost of capital, which reflects both the firm's capital structure and the tax deductibility of its interest payments.

Suppose that a sensible capital structure for the concatenator operation is 60 percent equity and 40 percent debt.[9] You estimate that the required rate of return on the

---

[8] There's nothing wrong with our formulas and examples, *provided* that the tax deductibility of interest payments doesn't change the aggregate risk of the debt and equity investors. However, if the tax savings from deducting interest are treated as safe cash flows, the formulas get more complicated. If you really want to dive into the tax-adjusted formulas showing how WACC changes with capital structure, we suggest Chapter 19 in R. A. Brealey, S. C. Myers, and F. Allen, *Principles of Corporate Finance,* 8th ed. (New York: Irwin/McGraw-Hill, 2006).

[9] By this we mean that it makes sense to finance 40 percent of the *present value* of the business by debt. Remember that we use market-value weights to compute WACC. Debt as a proportion of *book value* may be more or less than 40 percent.

TABLE 12–5 Forecasts of operating cash flow and investment for the concatenator manufacturing division (thousands of dollars). Rapid expansion means that free cash flow is negative in the early years, because investment outstrips the cash flow from operations. Free cash flow turns positive when growth slows down.

	Year					
	1	2	3	4	5	6
1. Sales	1,189	1,421	1,700	2,020	2,391	2,510
2. Costs	1,070	1,279	1,530	1,818	2,152	2,260
3. Earnings before interest, taxes, depreciation, and amortization (EBITDA) = 1 − 2	119	142	170	202	239	250
4. Depreciation	45	59	76	99	128	136
5. Profit before tax = 3 − 4	74	83	94	103	111	114
6. Tax at 35%	25.9	29.1	32.9	36.1	38.9	39.9
7. Profit after tax = 5 − 6	48.1	54.0	61.1	67.0	72.2	74.1
8. Operating cash flow = 4 + 7	93.1	113.0	137.1	166.0	200.2	210.1
9. Investment in plant and working capital	166.7	200.0	240.0	200.0	160.0	130.6
10. Free cash flow = 8 − 9	−73.6	−87.1	−102.9	−34.1	40.2	79.5

equity is 12 percent and that the business could borrow at an interest rate of 5 percent. The weighted-average cost of capital is therefore

$$\text{WACC} = \left[\frac{D}{V} \times (1 - T_c)r_{\text{debt}} \right] + \left(\frac{E}{V} \times r_{\text{equity}} \right)$$

$$= [.4 \times (1 - .35)5\%] + (.6 \times 12\%) = 8.5\%$$

Calculating the Value of the Concatenator Business

The value of the concatenator operation is equal to the discounted value of the free cash flows (FCFs) out to a horizon year plus the forecasted value of the business at the horizon, also discounted back to the present. That is,

$$\text{PV} = \underbrace{\frac{\text{FCF}_1}{1 + \text{WACC}} + \frac{\text{FCF}_2}{(1 + \text{WACC})^2} + \cdots + \frac{\text{FCF}_H}{(1 + \text{WACC})^H}}_{\text{PV (free cash flows)}} + \underbrace{\frac{\text{PV}_H}{(1 + \text{WACC})^H}}_{\text{+ PV (horizon value)}}$$

Of course, the concatenator business will continue to grow after the horizon, but it's not practical to forecast free cash flow year by year to infinity. PV_H stands in for the value of free cash flows in periods $H + 1, H + 2$, and so on.

Horizon years are often chosen arbitrarily. Sometimes the boss tells everybody to use 10 years because that'a nice round number. We have picked year 5 as the horizon year because the business is expected to settle down to steady growth of 5 percent a year from then on.

There are several common formulas or rules of thumb for estimating horizon value. Let's try the constant-growth formula that we introduced in Chapter 6:

$$\text{Horizon value} = \frac{\text{free cash flow in year 6}}{r - g} = \frac{79.5}{.085 - .05} = \$2{,}271.4 \text{ thousand}$$

We now have all we need to calculate the value of the concatenator business today. We add up the present values of the free cash flows in the first 5 years and that of the horizon value:

PV (business) = PV (free cash flows years 1–5) + PV (horizon value)

$$= -\frac{73.6}{1.085} - \frac{87.1}{(1.085)^2} - \frac{102.9}{(1.085)^3} - \frac{34.1}{(1.085)^4} + \frac{40.2}{(1.085)^5} + \frac{2{,}271.4}{(1.085)^5}$$

$$= \$1{,}290.4 \text{ thousand}$$

Notice that when we use the weighted-average cost of capital to value a company, we are asking, "What is the combined value of the company's debt and equity?" If you need to value the equity, you must subtract the value of any outstanding debt. Suppose that the concatenator business has been partly financed with $516,000 of debt, 40 percent of the overall value of about $1,290,000. Then the equity in the business is worth only $1,290,000 − 516,000 = $774,000.

Self-Test 12.8

Managers often use rules of thumb to check their estimates of horizon value. Suppose you observe that the value of the debt plus equity of a typical mature concatenator producer is 9 times its EBITDA. (EBITDA is defined at line 3 of Table 12–5.) If your operation sold in year 5 at a similar multiple of EBITDA, how would your estimate of the *present* value of the operation change?

SUMMARY

Why do firms compute weighted-average costs of capital?

They need a standard discount rate for average-risk projects. An "average-risk" project is one that has the same risk as the firm's existing assets and operations.

What about projects that are not average?

The **weighted-average cost of capital** can still be used as a benchmark. The benchmark is adjusted up for unusually risky projects and down for unusually safe ones.

How do firms compute weighted-average costs of capital?

Here's the WACC formula one more time:

$$\text{WACC} = \left[\frac{D}{V} \times (1 - T_c)r_{\text{debt}}\right] + \left(\frac{E}{V} \times r_{\text{equity}}\right)$$

The WACC is the expected rate of return on the portfolio of debt and equity securities issued by the firm. The required rate of return on each security is weighted by its proportion of the firm's total market value (not book value). Since interest payments reduce the firm's income tax bill, the required rate of return on debt is measured after tax, as $r_{\text{debt}} \times (1 - T_c)$.

This WACC formula is usually written assuming the firm's capital structure includes just two classes of securities, debt and equity. If there is another class, say preferred stock, the formula expands to include it. In other words, we would estimate $r_{\text{preferred}}$, the rate of return demanded by preferred stockholders, determine P/V, the fraction of market value accounted for by preferred, and add $r_{\text{preferred}} \times P/V$ to the equation. Of course the weights in the WACC formula always add up to 1. In this case $D/V + P/V + E/V = 1$.

How are the costs of debt and equity calculated?

The cost of debt (r_{debt}) is the market interest rate demanded by bondholders. In other words, it is the rate that the company would pay on *new* debt issued to finance its investment projects. The cost of preferred ($r_{\text{preferred}}$) is just the preferred dividend divided by the market price of a preferred share.

The tricky part is estimating the cost of equity (r_{equity}), the expected rate of return on the firm's shares. Financial managers use the capital asset pricing model to estimate expected return. But for mature, steady-growth companies, it can also make sense to use the constant-growth dividend discount model. Remember, estimates of expected return are less reliable for a single firm's stock than for a sample of comparable-risk firms. Therefore, some managers also consider WACCs calculated for industries.

What happens when capital structure changes?

The rates of return on debt and equity will change. For example, increasing the debt ratio will increase the risk borne by both debt and equity investors and cause them to demand higher returns. However, this does *not* necessarily mean that the overall WACC will increase, because more weight is put on the cost of debt, which is less than the cost of equity. In fact, if we ignore taxes, the overall **cost of capital** will stay constant as the fractions of debt and equity change. This is discussed further in Chapter 15.

Can WACC be used to value an entire business?

Just think of the business as a very large project. Forecast the business's operating cash flows (after-tax profits plus depreciation), and subtract the future investments in plant and equipment and in net working capital. The resulting **free cash flows** can then be discounted back to the present at the weighted-average cost of capital. Of course, the cash flows from a company may stretch far into the future. Financial managers therefore typically produce detailed cash flows only up to some horizon date and then estimate the remaining value of the business at the horizon.

QUIZ

1. **Cost of Debt.** Micro Spinoffs, Inc., issued 20-year debt a year ago at par value with a coupon rate of 8 percent, paid annually. Today, the debt is selling at $1,050. If the firm's tax bracket is 35 percent, what is its after-tax cost of debt?

2. **Cost of Preferred Stock.** Micro Spinoffs also has preferred stock outstanding. The stock pays a dividend of $4 per share, and the stock sells for $40. What is the cost of preferred stock?

3. **Calculating WACC.** Suppose Micro Spinoffs's cost of equity is 12 percent. What is its WACC if equity is 50 percent, preferred stock is 20 percent, and debt is 30 percent of total capital?

4. **Cost of Equity.** Reliable Electric is a regulated public utility, and it is expected to provide steady growth of dividends of 5 percent per year for the indefinite future. Its last dividend was $5 per share; the stock sold for $60 per share just after the dividend was paid. What is the company's cost of equity?

5. **Calculating WACC.** Reactive Industries has the following capital structure. Its corporate tax rate is 35 percent. What is its WACC?

Security	Market Value	Required Rate of Return
Debt	$20 million	6%
Preferred stock	10 million	8
Common stock	50 million	12

6. **Company versus Project Discount Rates.** Geothermal's WACC is 11.4 percent. Executive Fruit's WACC is 12.3 percent. Now Executive Fruit is considering an investment in geothermal power production. Should it discount project cash flows at 12.3 percent? Why or why not?

7. **Company Valuation.** Icarus Airlines is proposing to go public, and you have been given the task of estimating the value of its equity. Management plans to maintain debt at 30 percent of the company's present value, and you believe that at this capital structure the company's debtholders will demand a return of 6 percent and stockholders will require 11 percent. The company is forecasting that next year's operating cash flow (depreciation plus profit after tax at 40 percent) will be $68 million and that investment expenditures will be $30 million. Thereafter, operating cash flows and investment expenditures are forecast to grow by 4 percent a year.
   a. What is the total value of Icarus?
   b. What is the value of the company's equity?

PRACTICE PROBLEMS

8. **WACC.** The common stock of Buildwell Conservation & Construction, Inc., has a beta of .90. The Treasury bill rate is 4 percent, and the market risk premium is estimated at 8 per-

cent. BCCI's capital structure is 30 percent debt, paying a 5 percent interest rate, and 70 percent equity. What is BCCI's cost of equity capital? Its WACC? Buildwell pays tax at 40 percent.

9. **WACC and NPV.** BCCI (see the previous problem) is evaluating a project with an internal rate of return of 12 percent. Should it accept the project? If the project will generate a cash flow of $100,000 a year for 8 years, what is the most BCCI should be willing to pay to initiate the project?

10. **Company Valuation.** You need to estimate the value of Buildwell Conservation (see Problem 8). You have the following forecasts (in millions of dollars) of Buildwell's profits and of its future investments in new plant and working capital:

	Year			
	1	2	3	4 . . .
Earnings before interest, taxes, depreciation, and amortization (EBITDA)	80	100	115	120
Depreciation	20	30	35	40
Pretax profit	60	70	80	80
Investment	12	15	18	20

From year 5 onward, EBITDA, depreciation, and investment are expected to remain unchanged at year-4 levels. Estimate the company's total value and the separate values of its debt and equity.

Please visit us at www.mhhe.com/bmm5e or refer to your Student CD

11. **Calculating WACC.** Find the WACC of William Tell Computers. The total book value of the firm's equity is $10 million; book value per share is $20. The stock sells for a price of $30 per share, and the cost of equity is 15 percent. The firm's bonds have a face value of $5 million and sell at a price of 110 percent of face value. The yield to maturity on the bonds is 9 percent, and the firm's tax rate is 40 percent.

12. **WACC.** Nodebt, Inc., is a firm with all-equity financing. Its equity beta is .80. The Treasury bill rate is 4 percent, and the market risk premium is expected to be 10 percent. What is Nodebt's asset beta? What is Nodebt's weighted-average cost of capital? The firm is exempt from paying taxes.

13. **Cost of Debt.** A financial analyst at Dawn Chemical notes that the firm's total interest payments this year were $10 million while total debt outstanding was $80 million, and he concludes that the cost of debt was 12.5 percent. What is wrong with this conclusion?

14. **Cost of Equity.** Bunkhouse Electronics is a recently incorporated firm that makes electronic entertainment systems. Its earnings and dividends have been growing at a rate of 30 percent, and the current dividend yield is 2 percent. Its beta is 1.2, the market risk premium is 8 percent, and the risk-free rate is 4 percent.
   a. Calculate two estimates of the firm's cost of equity.
   b. Which estimate seems more reasonable to you? Why?

Please visit us at www.mhhe.com/bmm5e or refer to your Student CD

15. **Cost of Debt.** Olympic Sports has two issues of debt outstanding. One is a 9 percent coupon bond with a face value of $20 million, a maturity of 10 years, and a yield to maturity of 10 percent. The coupons are paid annually. The other bond issue has a maturity of 15 years, with coupons also paid annually, and a coupon rate of 10 percent. The face value of the issue is $25 million, and the issue sells for 94 percent of par value. The firm's tax rate is 35 percent.
   a. What is the before-tax cost of debt for Olympic?
   b. What is Olympic's after-tax cost of debt?

Please visit us at www.mhhe.com/bmm5e or refer to your Student CD

16. **Capital Structure.** Examine the following book-value balance sheet for University Products, Inc. What is the capital structure of the firm on the basis of market values? The preferred stock currently sells for $15 per share and the common stock for $20 per share. There are 1 million common shares outstanding.

BOOK VALUE BALANCE SHEET (all values in millions)			
Assets		**Liabilities and Net Worth**	
Cash and short-term securities	$ 1	Bonds, coupon = 8%, paid annually (maturity = 10 years, current yield to maturity = 9%)	$10.0
Accounts receivable	3	Preferred stock (par value $20 per share)	2.0
Inventories	7	Common stock (par value $.10)	.1
Plant and equipment	21	Additional paid-in stockholders' capital	9.9
		Retained earnings	10.0
Total	$32	Total	$32.0

17. **Calculating WACC.** Turn back to University Products's balance sheet from the previous problem. If the preferred stock pays a dividend of $2 per share, the beta of the common stock is .8, the market risk premium is 10 percent, the risk-free rate is 6 percent, and the firm's tax rate is 40 percent, what is University's weighted-average cost of capital?

18. **Project Discount Rate.** University Products is evaluating a new venture into home computer systems (see Problems 16 and 17). The internal rate of return on the new venture is estimated at 13.4 percent. WACCs of firms in the personal computer industry tend to average around 14 percent. Should the new project be pursued? Will University Products make the correct decision if it discounts cash flows on the proposed venture at the firm's WACC?

19. **Cost of Capital.** The total market value of Okefenokee Real Estate Company is $6 million, and the total value of its debt is $4 million. The treasurer estimates that the beta of the stock currently is 1.2 and that the expected risk premium on the market is 10 percent. The Treasury bill rate is 4 percent.

    a. What is the required rate of return on Okefenokee stock?
    b. What is the beta of the company's existing portfolio of assets? The debt is perceived to be virtually risk-free.
    c. Estimate the weighted-average cost of capital assuming a tax rate of 40 percent.
    d. Estimate the discount rate for an expansion of the company's present business.
    e. Suppose the company wants to diversify into the manufacture of rose-colored glasses. The beta of optical manufacturers with no debt outstanding is 1.4. What is the required rate of return on Okefenokee's new venture? (You should assume that the risky project will not enable the firm to issue any additional debt.)

CHALLENGE PROBLEMS

20. **Changes in Capital Structure.** Look again at our calculation of Big Oil's WACC. Suppose Big Oil is excused from paying taxes. How would its WACC change? Now suppose Big Oil makes a large stock issue and uses the proceeds to pay off all its debt. How would the cost of equity change?

21. **Changes in Capital Structure.** Refer again to Challenge Problem 20. Suppose Big Oil starts from the financing mix in Table 12–3, and then borrows an additional $200 million from the bank. It then pays out a special $200 million dividend, leaving its assets and operations unchanged. What happens to Big Oil's WACC, still assuming it pays no taxes? What happens to the cost of equity?

22. **WACC and Taxes.** "The after-tax cost of debt is lower when the firm's tax rate is higher; therefore, the WACC falls when the tax rate rises. Thus, with a lower discount rate, the firm must be worth more if its tax rate is higher." Explain why this argument is wrong.

23. **Cost of Capital.** An analyst at Dawn Chemical notes that its cost of debt is far below that of equity. He concludes that it is important for the firm to maintain the ability to increase its bor-

rowing because if it cannot borrow, it will be forced to use more expensive equity to finance some projects. This might lead it to reject some projects that would have seemed attractive if evaluated at the lower cost of debt. Comment on this reasoning.

STANDARD &POOR'S

Go to Market Insight (www.mhhe.com/edumarketinsight). We will calculate the weighted-average cost of capital for Anheuser-Busch (BUD) using the Market Insight data. First we estimate the required return on the company's long-term debt (bonds) and common stock. (All information is located on the Market Insight reports, except where noted.)

1. Find Anheuser-Busch's S&P credit rating in Market Insight, and then find the current yields on similarly rated bonds at www.bondsonline.com. Find the after-tax cost of debt assuming a tax rate of 40 percent.

2. Use one of these estimates for the cost of equity:
   a. The constant-dividend-growth valuation model, given the current price, current dividend, and the 5-year dividend growth rate.
   b. The CAPM using the U.S. Treasury bill rate as your risk-free rate (www.bondsonline.com). Find the company's beta, and use the historical market risk premium, 7.6%, from Table 10.1.

3. Now find the weights for WACC. Use the book value (from the balance sheet) of long-term debt as an estimate of the market value of debt. Then find total market capitalization (total market value of equity) from *Financial Highlights*. Finally, calculate the proportions of each.

4. Refer to Sections 12.4 and 12.5 of this chapter to calculate the WACC.

SOLUTIONS TO SELF-TEST QUESTIONS

12.1 Hot Rocks' 4 million common shares are worth $40 million. Its market value balance sheet is:

Assets		Liabilities and Shareholders' Equity		
Assets	$90	Debt	$50	(56%)
		Equity	40	(44%)
Value	$90	Value	$90	

$$WACC = (.56 \times 9\%) + (.44 \times 17\%) = 12.5\%$$

We use Hot Rocks' pretax return on debt because the company pays no taxes.

12.2 Burg's 6 million shares are now worth only 6 million × $4 = $24 million. The debt is selling for 80 percent of book, or $20 million. The market value balance sheet is:

Assets		Liabilities and Shareholders' Equity		
Assets	$44	Debt	$20	(45%)
		Equity	24	(55%)
Value	$44	Value	$44	

$$WACC = (.45 \times 14\%) + (.55 \times 20\%) = 17.3\%$$

Note that this question ignores taxes.

12.3 Compare the two income statements, one for Criss-Cross Industries and the other for a firm with identical EBIT but no debt in its capital structure. (All figures in millions.)

	Criss-Cross	Firm with No Debt
EBIT	$10.0	$10.0
Interest expense	2.0	0.0
Taxable income	8.0	10.0
Taxes owed	2.8	3.5
Net income	5.2	6.5
Total income accruing to debt- & equityholders	7.2	6.5

Notice that Criss-Cross pays $.7 million less in taxes than its debt-free counterpart. Accordingly, the total income available to debt- plus equityholders is $.7 million higher.

12.4   For Hot Rocks,

$$WACC = [.56 \times 9 \times (1 - .35)] + (.44 \times 17) = 10.8\%$$

For Burg Associates,

$$WACC = [.45 \times 14 \times (1 - .35)] + (.55 \times 20) = 15.1\%$$

12.5   WACC measures the expected rate of return demanded by debt and equity investors in the firm (plus a tax adjustment capturing the tax-deductibility of interest payments). Thus the calculation must be based on what investors are actually paying for the firm's debt and equity securities. In other words, it must be based on market values.

12.6   From the CAPM:

$$r_{equity} = r_f + \beta_{equity}\,(r_m - r_f)$$
$$= 6\% + 1.20(7.6\%) = 15.1\%$$
$$WACC = .3(1 - .35)\,8\% + .7(15.1\%) = 12.13\%$$

12.7   Jo Ann's boss is wrong. The ability to borrow at 8 percent does not mean that the cost of capital is 8 percent. The firm could not finance a stand-alone project with 8 percent debt. This analysis ignores the side effects of the borrowing, for example, that at the higher indebtedness of the firm the equity will be riskier and, therefore, the equityholders will demand a higher rate of return on their investment.

12.8   Estimated horizon value for the concatenator business is $9 \times$ year-5 EBITDA $= 9 \times 239 =$ $2,151 thousand. PV (horizon value) is $2,151/(1.085)^5 = $1,430.5$ thousand. Adding in the PV of free cash flows for years 1 to 5 gives a present value for the business of $1,210.3 thousand.

MINICASE

Bernice Mountaindog was glad to be back at Sea Shore Salt. Employees were treated well. When she had asked a year ago for a leave of absence to complete her degree in finance, top management promptly agreed. When she returned with an honors degree, she was promoted from administrative assistant (she had been secretary to Joe-Bob Brinepool, the president) to treasury analyst.

Bernice thought the company's prospects were good. Sure, table salt was a mature business, but Sea Shore Salt had grown steadily at the expense of its less well known competitors. The company's brand name was an important advantage, despite the difficulty most customers had in pronouncing it rapidly.

Bernice started work on January 2, 2006. The first 2 weeks went smoothly. Then Mr. Brinepool's cost of capital memo (see Figure 12–2) assigned her to explain Sea Shore Salt's weighted-average cost of capital to other managers. The memo came as a surprise to Bernice, so she stayed late to prepare for the questions that would surely come the next day.

Bernice first examined Sea Shore Salt's most recent balance sheet, summarized in Table 12–6. Then she jotted down the following additional points:

- The company's bank charged interest at current market rates, and the long-term debt had just been issued. Book and market values could not differ by much.
- But the preferred stock had been issued 35 years ago, when interest rates were much lower. The preferred stock was now trading for only $70 per share.
- The common stock traded for $40 per share. Next year's earnings per share would be about $4 and dividends per share probably $2. Sea Shore Salt had traditionally paid out 50

FIGURE 12-2 Mr. Brinepool's cost of capital memo

Sea Shore Salt Company
Spring Vacation Beach, Florida

CONFIDENTIAL MEMORANDUM

DATE: January 15, 2006
TO: S.S.S. Management
FROM: Joe-Bob Brinepool, President
SUBJECT: Cost of Capital

This memo states and clarifies our company's long-standing policy regarding hurdle rates for capital investment decisions. There have been many recent questions, and some evident confusion, on this matter.

Sea Shore Salt evaluates replacement and expansion investments by discounted cash flow. The discount or hurdle rate is the company's after-tax weighted-average cost of capital.

The weighted-average cost of capital is simply a blend of the rates of return expected by investors in our company. These investors include banks, bondholders, and preferred stock investors in addition to common stockholders. Of course many of you are, or soon will be, stockholders of our company.

The following table summarizes the composition of Sea Shore Salt's financing.

	Amount (in millions)	Percent of Total	Rate of Return
Bank loan	$120	20%	8%
Bond issue	80	13.3	7.75
Preferred stock	100	16.7	6
Common stock	300	50	16
	$600	100%	

The rates of return on the bank loan and bond issue are of course just the interest rates we pay. However, interest is tax-deductible, so the after-tax interest rates are lower than shown above. For example, the after-tax cost of our bank financing, given our 35% tax rate, is 8(1 − .35) = 5.2%.

The rate of return on preferred stock is 6%. Sea Shore Salt pays a $6 dividend on each $100 preferred share.

Our target rate of return on equity has been 16% for many years. I know that some newcomers think this target is too high for the safe and mature salt business. But we must all aspire to superior profitability.

Once this background is absorbed, the calculation of Sea Shore Salt's weighted-average cost of capital (WACC) is elementary:

$$\text{WACC} = 8(1 - .35)(.20) + 7.75(1 - .35)(.133) + 6(.167) + 16(.50) = 10.7\%$$

The official corporate hurdle rate is therefore 10.7%.

If you have further questions about these calculations, please direct them to our new Treasury Analyst, Ms. Bernice Mountaindog. It is a pleasure to have Bernice back at Sea Shore Salt after a year's leave of absence to complete her degree in finance.

percent of earnings as dividends and plowed back the rest.

- Earnings and dividends had grown steadily at 6 to 7 percent per year, in line with the company's sustainable growth rate:

$$\text{Sustainable} \atop \text{growth rate} = {\text{return} \atop \text{on equity}} \times {\text{plowback} \atop \text{ratio}}$$

$$= 4/30 \times .5$$

$$= .067, \text{ or } 6.7\%$$

- Sea Shore Salt's beta had averaged about .5, which made sense, Bernice thought, for a stable, steady-growth business. She made a quick cost of equity calculation by using the capital asset pricing model (CAPM). With current interest rates of about 7 percent, and a market risk premium of 7 percent,

$$\text{CAPM cost of equity} = r_E = r_f + \beta(r_m - r_f)$$

$$= 7\% + .5(7\%) = 10.5\%$$

This cost of equity was significantly less than the 16 percent decreed in Mr. Brinepool's memo. Bernice scanned her notes apprehensively. What if Mr. Brinepool's cost of equity was wrong? Was there some other way to estimate the cost of equity as a check on the CAPM calculation? Could there be other errors in his calculations?

Bernice resolved to complete her analysis that night. If necessary, she would try to speak with Mr. Brinepool when he arrived at his office the next morning. Her job was not just finding the right number. She also had to figure out how to explain it all to Mr. Brinepool.

TABLE 12–6 Sea Shore Salt's balance sheet, taken from the company's 2005 balance sheet (figures in millions)

Assets		Liabilities and Net Worth	
Working capital	$200	Bank loan	$120
Plant and equipment	360	Long-term debt	80
Other assets	40	Preferred stock	100
		Common stock, including retained earnings	300
Total	$600	Total	$600

Notes:

1. At year-end 2005, Sea Shore Salt had 10 million common shares outstanding.
2. The company had also issued 1 million preferred shares with book value of $100 per share. Each share receives an annual dividend of $6.

Financing

4

Introduction to Corporate Financing and Governance

RELATED WEB LINKS

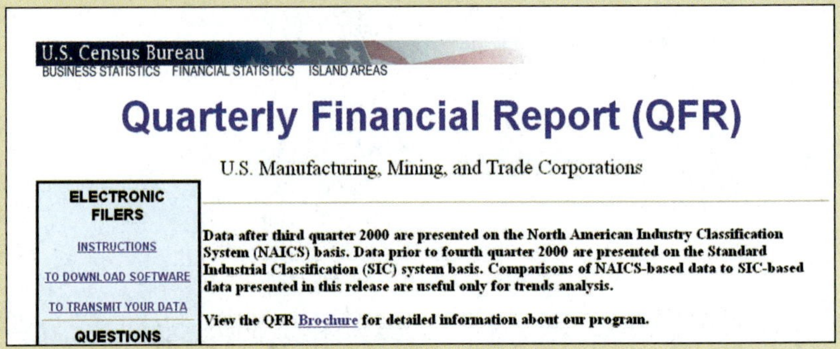

U.S. Census Bureau
BUSINESS STATISTICS   FINANCIAL STATISTICS   ISLAND AREAS

Quarterly Financial Report (QFR)

U.S. Manufacturing, Mining, and Trade Corporations

ELECTRONIC FILERS

INSTRUCTIONS

TO DOWNLOAD SOFTWARE

TO TRANSMIT YOUR DATA

QUESTIONS

Data after third quarter 2000 are presented on the North American Industry Classification System (NAICS) basis. Data prior to fourth quarter 2000 are presented on the Standard Industrial Classification (SIC) system basis. Comparisons of NAICS-based data to SIC-based data presented in this release are useful only for trends analysis.

View the QFR Brochure for detailed information about our program.

www.federalreserve.gov/releases/z1
Statistics on the financing of U.S. industry.

www.census.gov/csd/qfr   Balance sheets and income statements for sectors of the U.S. economy.

There are more than 57 different kinds of securities that a company can issue.

Scott Goodwin Photography

Up to this point we have concentrated almost exclusively on the firm's capital expenditure decision. Now we move to the other side of the balance sheet to look at how the firm can finance those capital expenditures. To put it crudely, you have learned how to spend money; now you must learn how to raise it. In the next few chapters, therefore, we assume that the firm has already decided on which investment projects to accept, and we focus on the best way to finance these projects.

You will find that in some ways financing decisions are more complicated than investment decisions. You'll need to learn about the wide variety of securities that companies can issue and the financial institutions that may buy these securities. But there are also ways in which financing decisions are easier than investment decisions. For example, financing decisions do not have the same degree of finality as investment decisions. When Ford Motor Company decides to issue a bond, it knows that it can buy it back later if second thoughts arise. It would be far more difficult for Ford to dismantle or sell an auto factory that is no longer needed.

In later chapters we will look at some of the classic finance problems, such as how much firms should borrow and what dividends they should pay their shareholders. In this chapter we set the scene with a brief overview of the types of long-term finance.

We begin our discussion of financing with a basic conceptual point. It is easier to make shareholders wealthier through your investment decisions than by your financing decisions. As we explain, competition between investors makes it difficult to find misvalued securities.

We then introduce you to the principal sources of finance, and we show how they are used by corporations. It is customary to classify these sources of finance as debt or equity. However, we will see that a simple division of sources of finance into debt and equity would miss the enormous variety of financing instruments that companies use today. For example, Table 13–1 shows the many long-term securities issued by H.J. Heinz. Yet Heinz has not come close to exhausting the menu of possible securities.

After studying this chapter you should be able to:

- Explain why managers should assume that the securities they issue are fairly priced.

- Describe the major classes of securities sold by the firm.

- Summarize the changing ways that U.S. firms have financed their growth.

13.1 Creating Value with Financing Decisions

Smart investment decisions make shareholders wealthier. So do smart financing decisions. For example, if your company can borrow at 3 percent when the going rate is 4 percent, you have done your shareholders a good turn.

Unfortunately, this is more easily said than done. The problem is that competition in financial markets is more intense than in most product markets. In product markets, companies regularly find competitive advantages that allow positive-NPV investments. For example, a company may have only a few competitors that specialize in the same line of business in the same geographical area. Or it may be able to capitalize on patents or technology or on customer recognition and loyalty. All this opens up the opportunity to make superior profits and find projects with positive NPVs.

But there are few protected niches in *financial* markets. You can't patent the design of a new security. Moreover, in these markets you always face fast-moving competition, including all the other corporations seeking funds, to say nothing of the state, local, and federal governments, financial institutions, individuals, and foreign firms and governments that also come to New York, London, or Tokyo for financing. The investors who supply financing are numerous, and they are smart. Most likely, these investors can assess values of securities at least as well as you can.

Of course, when you borrow, you would like to pay less than the going rate of interest. But if the loan is a good deal for your shareholders, it must be a bad deal for the lenders. So what are the chances that your firm could consistently trick investors into overpaying for its securities? Pretty slim. In general, firms should assume that the securities they issue sell for their true values.

But what do we mean by *true value?* It is a potentially slippery phrase. True value does not mean ultimate future value—we do not expect investors to be fortune-tellers. It means a price that incorporates all the information *currently* available to investors. We came across this idea in Chapter 6, when we introduced the concept of *efficient capital markets* and showed how difficult it is for investors to obtain consistently superior performance. In an efficient capital market all securities are fairly priced given the information available to investors. In that case the sale of securities at their market price can never be a positive-NPV transaction.

All this means that it's harder to make or lose money by smart or stupid financing strategies. It is difficult to make money—that is, to find cheap financing—because the investors who supply the financing demand fair terms. At the same time, it's harder to lose money because competition among investors prevents any one of them from demanding more than fair terms.

Just remember as you read the following chapters: There are no free lunches on Wall Street. . . . and no easy answers for the financial manager who must decide which securities to issue.

TABLE 13–1 Large firms use many different kinds of securities. Look at the variety of sources of finance for H.J. Heinz.

Equity
Common stock
Preferred stock
Debt
Commercial paper
Debentures
Guaranteed notes
Remarketable debt
Euro notes
Sterling notes
New Zealand dollar notes
Bank loans

13.2 Common Stock

We will illustrate the characteristics of different securities by looking at how H.J. Heinz has financed its capital expenditures. We start with common stock.

Most major corporations are far too large to be owned by one investor. For example, you would need to lay your hands on about $13 billion if you wanted to own the whole of Heinz. Heinz is owned by about 48,000 different investors, each of whom holds a number of shares of common stock. These investors are therefore known as *shareholders,* or *stockholders.* Altogether in April 2004 Heinz had outstanding about 352 million shares of common stock. Thus, if you were to buy one Heinz share, you would own 1/352,000,000, or about .0000003 percent, of the company. Of course, a large pension fund might hold many thousands of Heinz shares.

The 352 million shares held by investors are not the only shares that have been issued by Heinz. The company has also issued a further 79 million shares, which it later bought back from investors. These repurchased shares are held in the company's treasury and are known as **treasury stock.** The shares held by investors are said to be **issued and outstanding shares.** By contrast, the 79 million treasury shares are said to be *issued but not outstanding.*

If Heinz wishes to raise more money, it can sell more shares. However, there is a limit to the number that it can issue without getting the approval of the current shareholders. The maximum number of shares that can be issued is known as the **authorized share capital**—for Heinz, this is 600 million shares. Since Heinz has already issued 431 million shares, it can issue 169 million more without shareholders' approval.

Table 13–2 shows how the investment by Heinz's common stockholders is recorded in the company's books. The price at which each share is recorded is known as its **par value.** In Heinz's case each share has a par value of $.25. Thus the total par value of the issued shares is 431 million shares × $.25 per share = $108 million. Par value has little economic significance.[1]

The price at which new shares are sold to investors almost always exceeds par value. The difference is entered into the company's accounts as **additional paid-in capital,** or *capital surplus.* For example, if Heinz sold an additional 1 million shares at $40 a share, the par value of the common stock would increase by 1 million × $.25 = $250,000 and additional paid-in capital would increase by 1 million × ($40 – $.25) = $39,750,000. You can see from this example that the funds raised from the stock issue are divided between par value and additional paid-in capital. Since the choice of par value in the first place was immaterial, so is the allocation between par value and additional paid-in capital.

Besides buying new stock, shareholders also indirectly contribute new capital to the firm whenever profits that could be paid out as dividends are instead plowed back into the company. Table 13–2 shows that the cumulative amount of such **retained earnings** is $4,857 million.

Heinz's books also show the amount that the company has spent to repurchase its own stock. The repurchase of the 79 million shares cost Heinz $2,928 million. This is money that has in effect been returned to shareholders.

The sum of the par value, additional paid-in capital, and retained earnings, less repurchased stock and some miscellaneous other adjustments, is known as the *net common equity* of the firm. It equals the total amount contributed directly by shareholders when the firm issued new stock and indirectly when it plowed back part of its earnings. The book value of Heinz's net common equity is $1,894 million. With 352 million shares outstanding this is equivalent to 1,894/352 = $5.38 a share. But, as we pointed out in Chapter 6, the market value of Heinz's stock is about $38, much higher

treasury stock
Stock that has been repurchased by the company and held in its treasury.

issued shares
Shares that have been issued by the company.

outstanding shares
Shares that have been issued by the company and are held by investors.

authorized share capital
Maximum number of shares that the company is permitted to issue.

par value
Value of security shown in the company's accounts.

additional paid-in capital
Difference between issue price and par value of stock. Also called *capital surplus.*

retained earnings
Earnings not paid out as dividends.

---

[1] Because some states do not allow companies to sell new shares below par value, par value is generally set at a low figure. Some companies even issue shares with no par value, in which case the stock is listed in the accounts at an arbitrarily determined figure.

TABLE 13–2 Book value of common stockholders' equity of H.J. Heinz Company, April 28, 2004 (figures in millions)

Common shares ($.25 par value per share)	$ 108
Additional paid-in capital	403
Retained earnings	4,857
Treasury shares at cost	(2,928)
Other	(546)
Net common equity	1,894
Note:	
Authorized shares	600
Issued shares, of which	431
Outstanding shares	352
Treasury shares	79

than its book value. Evidently investors believe that Heinz's assets are worth much more than they originally cost.

Self-Test 13.1   Generic Products has had one stock issue in which it sold 100,000 shares to the public at $15 per share. Can you fill in the following table?

Common shares ($1 par value per share)	_____
Additional paid-in capital	_____
Retained earnings	_____
Net common equity	$4,500,000

Ownership of the Corporation

A corporation is owned by its common stockholders. Some of its stock is held directly by individual investors, but, as we saw in Chapter 2, the greater proportion belongs to financial institutions such as mutual funds, pension funds, and insurance companies. Their holdings are summarized again in Figure 13–1. You can see that in the United States just over 60 percent of common stock is held by foreign investors or U.S. financial institutions, with pension funds and mutual funds each holding about 20 percent.

What do we mean when we say that the stockholders *own* the corporation? First, the stockholders are entitled to whatever profits are left over after the lenders have received their entitlement. Usually the company pays out part of these profits as dividends and plows back the remainder into new investments. Shareholders hope that these investments will enable the company to earn higher profits and pay higher dividends in the future.

Second, shareholders have the ultimate control over how the company is run. Occasionally, the company must get shareholder approval before it can take certain actions. For example, it needs shareholder agreement to increase the authorized capital or to merge with another company. On most other matters, shareholder control boils down to the right to vote on appointments to the board of directors.

The board of directors usually consists of the company's top management as well as *outside directors,* who are not employed by the firm. The board is there to look after shareholders' interests. It appoints and oversees the management of the firm and meets to vote on such matters as a new share issue or the payment of a dividend. Most of the time the board will go along with the management, but in crisis situations it can be very independent. For example, when the management of RJR Nabisco announced that it wanted to take over the company, the outside directors stepped in to make sure that the company was sold to the highest bidder.

Book Value of Common Equity

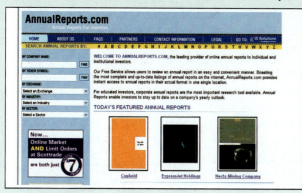

Source: IR Solutions & **Annualreports.com**.

In Table 13–2 we showed the book value of Heinz's common equity. You can construct a similar table for another company by looking up its annual report on the Web. An easy way to do this is to log on to **www.annualreports.com**. What is the difference between the company's outstanding and issued shares? Explain. Has the company in the past raised more money by issuing new shares or by plowing back earnings? Is that typical of U.S. public companies (see Section 13.6)?

Voting Procedures

majority voting
Voting system in which each director is voted on separately.

In most companies stockholders elect directors by a system of **majority voting.** In this case each director is voted on separately, and stockholders can cast one vote for each share they own. In some companies directors are elected by **cumulative voting.** The directors are then voted on jointly, and the stockholders can, if they choose, cast all their votes for just one candidate. For example, suppose that there are five directors to be elected and you own 100 shares. You therefore have a total of $5 \times 100 = 500$ votes.

cumulative voting
Voting system in which all votes that one shareholder is allowed to cast can be cast for one candidate for the board of directors.

Under majority voting you can cast a maximum of 100 votes for any one candidate. With a cumulative voting system you can cast all 500 votes for your favorite candidate. Cumulative voting makes it easier for a minority group of the stockholders to elect a director to represent their interests. That is why minority groups devote so much effort to campaigning for cumulative voting.

On many issues a simple majority of the votes cast is enough to carry the day, but there are some decisions that require a "supermajority" of, say, 75 percent of those eligible to vote. For example, a supermajority vote is sometimes needed to approve a merger. This makes it difficult for the firm to be taken over and therefore helps to protect the incumbent management.

proxy contest
Takeover attempt in which outsiders compete with management for shareholders' votes.

Shareholders can either vote in person or appoint a proxy to vote. The issues on which they are asked to vote are rarely contested, particularly in the case of large publicly traded firms. Occasionally, however, there are **proxy contests** in which outsiders compete with the firm's existing management and directors for control of the corporation. But the odds are stacked against the outsiders, for the insiders can get the firm to pay all the costs of presenting their case and obtaining votes.

FIGURE 13–1 Holdings of corporate equities, first quarter, 2005

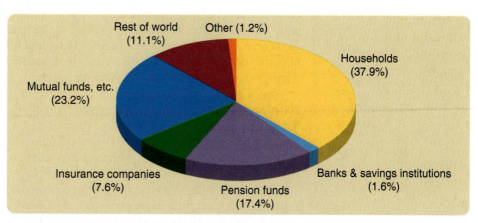

Source: Board of Governors of the Federal Reserve System, Division of Research and Statistics, "Flow of Funds Accounts," table L.213 at **www.federalreserve.gov/releases/z1/current/data.htm**.

Classes of Stock

Most companies in the United States issue just one class of common stock. But a few, such as Ford Motor and Google, have issued two classes of shares with different voting rights. For example, suppose that a firm needs fresh capital, but its management does not want to give up its controlling interest. The existing shares could be labeled "class A," and then "class B" shares with limited voting rights could be issued to outside investors.

In some countries it is fairly common for firms to issue two classes of stock with different voting rights. That may be a good thing if the controlling shareholders then use their influence to improve profitability. However, you can see the dangers here. If an idle or incompetent management has a large block of votes, it may use these votes to stay in control. Or if another corporation has a controlling stake, it may exercise its influence to gain a business advantage.

Corporate Governance in the United States and Elsewhere

Most large businesses in the United States are public corporations with widely dispersed ownership. Each shareholder owns only a small fraction of the shares and can exert little influence on the way the company is run. If shareholders do not like the policies the management team pursues, they can try to vote in another board of directors who will bring about a change in policy. But such attempts are rarely successful, and the shareholders' simplest solution is to sell the shares.

The separation between ownership and management in major U.S. corporations creates a potential conflict of interest between shareholders (the principals who own the company) and managers (the agents who make the decisions). We noted in Chapter 1 several mechanisms that have evolved to mitigate this conflict:

- Shareholders elect a board of directors, which then appoints the managers, oversees them, and on occasion fires them.
- Managers' remuneration is tied to their performance.
- Poorly performing companies are taken over and the management is replaced by a new team.

These mechanisms work only when there is sufficient transparency, so outsiders can judge how well the company is performing. Unfortunately, dishonest managers with creamy option packages may seek to hide the truth from investors. When investors eventually learn the true state of affairs, there can be big trouble. Consider, for example, the case of the telecom giant, WorldCom. Bernie Ebbers, its CEO, was on a generous compensation package that earned him $10 million in bonuses in 2001. Ebbers also owned 17 million shares of WorldCom stock and 8.3 million options and, therefore, had a strong incentive to ensure that the company performed well. Unfortunately, he also had a strong incentive to pump up the price of the stock when the company was not performing so well. In 2002 it emerged that WorldCom had overstated its income over a 3-year period by $11 billion and in the meantime had piled up $41 billion of debt. When the company's true profitability was discovered, it was bankrupt within a month—the largest U.S. bankruptcy ever.

WorldCom has had plenty of company in recent years. In October and November 2001 Enron revealed that it had overstated its earnings by more than $1 billion and had hidden more than $8 billion of debt. By year-end it had become the second-largest bankruptcy ever. Elsewhere, the Italian food processor Parmalat revealed that billions of dollars in assets had simply gone missing, while in Holland the supermarket group Ahold confessed to heavily overstating its profits.

Such scandals led Congress to pass the Sarbanes-Oxley Act, which aims to ensure that companies and their accountants provide directors, lenders, and shareholders with the information that they need to monitor progress. Among other things, the act set up the Public Company Accounting Oversight Board to oversee auditors; it banned accounting firms from offering other services to companies whose accounts they audit;

it prohibited any individual from heading a firm's audit for more than 5 years; and it required that the board's audit committee consist of directors that are independent of the company's management. Sarbanes-Oxley also requires that management (1) certify that the financial statements present a fair view of the firm's financial position and (2) demonstrate that the firm has adequate controls and procedures for financial reporting. All this comes at a price. For example, the CEO of Tennant Company, a mid-sized producer of cleaning products, estimated that complying with the act has led to a doubling of audit fees and added nearly $1 million of other costs.

Self-Test 13.2	**Why do you think that the Sarbanes-Oxley Act prohibits an auditing firm from also providing its clients with consultancy or investment banking services? Why does it not allow an individual to head a firm's audit for more than 5 years?**

Ownership and control are usually separated in U.S. corporations. But a large block of shares may give effective control even when there is no majority owner. For example, Larry Ellison owns over 25 percent of Oracle Corporation as well as being chief executive. Barring some extreme catastrophe, this holding means that he can run the company as he wants to and as long as he wants to. Nevertheless, the concentration of ownership is much less than in some other industrialized countries. The differences are not so apparent in Canada, Britain, Australia, and other English-speaking countries, but there are dramatic differences in Japan and continental Europe.

In Japan major industrial and financial companies have traditionally been linked together in a group called a *keiretsu*. For example, the Mitsubishi keiretsu contains 29 core companies including a bank, two insurance companies, an automobile manufacturer, a brewery, and a steel company. Members of the keiretsu are tied together in several ways. First, managers may sit on the boards of directors of other group companies, and a "president's council" of chief executives meets regularly. Second, each company in the group holds shares in many of the other companies. And third, companies generally borrow from the keiretsu's bank or from elsewhere within the group. These links may have several advantages. Companies can obtain funds from other members of the group without the need to reveal confidential information to the public, and if a member of the group runs into financial heavy weather, its problems can be worked out with other members of the group rather than in the bankruptcy court.

The more stable and concentrated shareholder base of large Japanese corporations may make it easier for them to resist pressures for short-term performance and allow them to focus on securing long-term advantage. But the Japanese system of corporate governance also has its disadvantages, for the lack of market discipline may promote a too-cozy life and allow lagging or inefficient corporations to put off painful surgery. As the Japanese economy languished in the 1990s, these disadvantages became more apparent, the links that bound keiretsus together began to weaken, and companies began to sell their shares in other members of the group.

Keiretsus are found only in Japan. But large companies in continental Europe are linked in some similar ways. For example, banks and other companies often own or control large blocks of stock and can push hard for changes in the management or strategy of poorly performing companies.[2] Thus oversight and control are entrusted largely to banks and other corporations.

In summary, control of large public companies in the United States is exercised through the board of directors and pressure from the stock market. In many other countries the stock market is less important and control shifts to major stockholders, typically banks and other companies.

---

[2] Banks in the United States are prohibited from large or permanent holdings of the stock of nonfinancial corporations.

13.3 Preferred Stock

preferred stock
Stock that takes priority over common stock in regard to dividends.

net worth
Book value of common stockholders' equity plus preferred stock.

Usually when investors talk about equity or stock, they are referring to common stock. But companies may also issue **preferred stock,** and this too is part of the company's equity. The sum of Heinz's common equity and preferred stock is known as its **net worth.**

For most companies preferred stock is much less important than common stock. However, it can be a useful method of financing in mergers and certain other special situations.

Like debt, preferred stock promises a series of fixed payments to the investor and with relatively rare exceptions preferred dividends are paid in full and on time. Nevertheless, preferred stock is legally an equity security. This is because payment of a preferred dividend is within the discretion of the directors. The only obligation is that no dividends can be paid on the common stock until the preferred dividend has been paid.[3] If the company goes out of business, the preferred stockholders get in the queue after the debtholders but before the common stockholders.

Preferred stock rarely confers full voting privileges. This is an advantage to firms that want to raise new money without sharing control of the firm with the new shareholders. However, if there is any matter that affects their place in the queue, preferred stockholders usually get to vote on it. Most issues also provide the holder with some voting power if the preferred dividend is skipped.

Companies cannot deduct preferred dividends when they calculate taxable income. Like common stock dividends, preferred dividends are paid from after-tax income. For most industrial firms this is a serious deterrent to issuing preferred. However, regulated public utilities can take tax payments into account when they negotiate with regulators the rates they charge customers. So they can effectively pass the tax disadvantage of preferred on to the consumer. Preferred stock also has a particular attraction for banks, for regulators allow banks to lump preferred in with common stock when calculating whether they have sufficient equity capital.

Preferred stock does have one tax advantage. If one corporation buys another's stock, only 30 percent of the dividends it receives is taxed. This rule applies to dividends on both common and preferred stock, but it is most important for preferred, for which returns are dominated by dividends rather than capital gains.

Suppose that your firm has surplus cash to invest. If it buys a bond, the interest will be taxed at the company's tax rate of 35 percent. If it buys a preferred share, it owns an asset like a bond (the preferred dividends can be viewed as "interest"), but the effective tax rate is only 30 percent of 35 percent, $.30 \times .35 = .105$, or 10.5 percent. It is no surprise that most preferred shares are held by corporations.

If you invest your firm's spare cash in a preferred stock, you will want to make sure that when it is time to sell the stock, it won't have plummeted in value. One problem with garden-variety preferred stock that pays a fixed dividend is that the preferred's market prices go up and down as interest rates change (because present values fall when rates rise). So one ingenious banker thought up a wrinkle: Why not link the dividend on the preferred stock to interest rates so that it goes up when interest rates rise and vice versa? The result is known as **floating-rate preferred.** If you own floating-rate preferred, you know that any change in interest rates will be counterbalanced by a change in the dividend payment, so the value of your investment is protected.

floating-rate preferred
Preferred stock paying dividends that vary with short-term interest rates.

Self-Test 13.3

A company in a 35 percent tax bracket can buy a bond yielding 10 percent or a preferred stock of the same firm that is priced to yield 8 percent. Which will provide the higher after-tax yield?

---

[3] These days this obligation is usually cumulative. In other words, before the common stockholders get a cent, the firm must pay any preferred dividends that have been missed in the past.

13.4 Corporate Debt

When they borrow money, companies promise to make regular interest payments and to repay the principal (that is, the original amount borrowed). However, corporations have limited liability. By this we mean that the promise to repay the debt is not always kept. If the company gets into deep water, the company has the right to default on the debt and to hand over the company's assets to the lenders.

Clearly it will choose bankruptcy only if the value of the assets is less than the amount of the debt. In practice, when companies go bankrupt, this handover of assets is far from straightforward. For example, when Pacific Gas and Electric filed for bankruptcy in 2004, the bankruptcy court was faced with several thousand creditors all jostling for a better place in the queue. By the time the company had emerged from bankruptcy 3 years later, it had agreed to make 2,100 separate payments resolving $8.4 billion of agreed claims and had set aside a further $1.8 billion for claims that were still under dispute.

Because lenders are not regarded as owners of the firm, they don't normally have any voting power. Also, the company's payments of interest are regarded as a cost and are therefore deducted from taxable income. Thus interest is paid out of *before-tax* income, whereas dividends on common and preferred stock are paid out of *after-tax* income. This means that the government provides a tax subsidy on the use of debt, which it does not provide on stock.

Debt Comes in Many Forms

Some orderly scheme of classification is essential to cope with the almost endless variety of debt issues. We will walk you through the major distinguishing characteristics.

Interest Rate The interest payment, or *coupon,* on most long-term loans is fixed at the time of issue. If a $1,000 bond is issued with a coupon of 10 percent, the firm continues to pay $100 a year regardless of how interest rates change. As we pointed out in Chapter 4, you sometimes encounter zero-coupon bonds. In this case the firm does not make a regular interest payment. It just makes a single payment at maturity. Obviously, investors pay less for zero-coupon bonds.

prime rate
Benchmark interest rate charged by banks.

Most loans from a bank and some long-term loans carry a *floating interest rate.* For example, your firm may be offered a loan at "1 percent over prime." The **prime rate** is the benchmark interest rate charged by banks to large customers with good to excellent credit. (But the largest and most creditworthy corporations can, and do, borrow at *less* than prime.) The prime rate is adjusted up and down with the general level of interest rates. When the prime rate changes, the interest on your floating-rate loan also changes.

Floating-rate loans are not always tied to the prime rate. Often they are tied to the rate at which international banks lend to one another. This is known as the *London Interbank Offered Rate,* or *LIBOR.*

Self-Test 13.4 **Would you expect the price of a 10-year floating-rate bond to be more or less sensitive to changes in interest rates than the price of a 10-year maturity fixed-rate bond?**

funded debt
Debt with more than 1 year remaining to maturity.

Maturity **Funded debt** is any debt repayable more than 1 year from the date of issue. Debt due in less than a year is termed *unfunded* and is carried on the balance sheet as a current liability. Unfunded debt is often described as short-term debt, and funded debt is described as long-term, although it is clearly artificial to call a 364-day debt short-term and a 366-day debt long-term (except in leap years).

There are corporate bonds of nearly every conceivable maturity. For example, Bristol Myers Squibb has issued bonds that do not mature until 2097. Some British banks

have issued perpetuities—that is, bonds which may survive forever. At the other extreme we find firms borrowing literally overnight.

Repayment Provisions   Long-term loans are commonly repaid in a steady regular way, perhaps after an initial grace period. For bonds that are publicly traded, this is done by means of a **sinking fund.** Each year the firm puts aside a sum of cash into a sinking fund that is then used to buy back the bonds. When there is a sinking fund, investors are prepared to lend at a lower rate of interest. They know that they are more likely to be repaid if the company sets aside some cash each year than if the entire loan has to be repaid on one specified day.

Suppose that a company issues a 6 percent, 30-year bond at a price of $1,000. Five years later interest rates have fallen to 4 percent, and the price of the bond has risen dramatically. If you were the company's treasurer, wouldn't you like to be able to retire the bonds and issue some new bonds at the lower interest rate? Well, with some bonds, known as **callable bonds,** the company does have the option to buy them back for the *call price.*[4] Of course, holders of these callable bonds know that the company will wish to buy the issue back if interest rates fall, and therefore the price of the bond will not rise above the call price.

Figure 13–2 shows the risk of a call to the bondholder. The purple line is the value of a 30-year, 6.5 percent "straight," that is, noncallable, bond; the orange line is the value of a bond with the same coupon rate and maturity but callable at $1,060 (i.e., 106 percent of face value). At very high interest rates the risk that the company will call the bonds is negligible, and the values of the two bonds are nearly identical. As rates fall, the straight bond continues to increase steadily in value, but since the capital appreciation of the callable bond is limited by the call price, its capital appreciation will lag behind that of the straight bond.

A callable bond gives the *company* the option to retire the bonds early. But some bonds give the *investor* the right to demand early repayment. During the 1990s many loans to Asian companies gave the lenders a repayment option. Consequently, when the Asian crisis struck in 1997, these companies were faced by a flood of lenders demanding their money back. Needless to say, companies that were already struggling to survive did not appreciate this additional burden.

sinking fund
Fund established to retire debt before maturity.

callable bond
Bond that may be repurchased by firm before maturity at specified call price.

Self-Test 13.5   Suppose Heinz is considering two issues of 20-year maturity coupon bonds; one issue will be callable, the other not. For a given coupon rate, will the callable or noncallable bond sell at the higher price? If the bonds are both to be sold to the public at face value, which bond must have the higher coupon rate?

Seniority   Some debts are **subordinated.** In the event of default the subordinated lender gets in line behind the firm's general creditors. The subordinated lender holds a junior claim and is paid only after all senior creditors are satisfied.

When you lend money to a firm, you can assume that you hold a senior claim unless the debt agreement says otherwise. However, this does not always put you at the front of the line, for the firm may have set aside some of its assets specifically for the protection of other lenders. That brings us to our next classification.

Security   When you borrow to buy your home, the savings and loan company will take out a mortgage on the house. The mortgage acts as security for the loan. If you default on the loan payments, the S&L can seize your home.

When companies borrow, they also may set aside certain assets as security for the loan. These assets are termed *collateral,* and the debt is said to be **secured.** In the event

subordinated debt
Debt that may be repaid in bankruptcy only after senior debt is paid.

secured debt
Debt that has first claim on specified collateral in the event of default.

---

[4] Sometimes callable bonds specify a period during which the firm is not allowed to call the bond if the purpose is simply to issue another bond at a lower interest rate.

FIGURE 13-2 Prices of callable versus straight debt. When interest rates fall, bond prices rise. But the price of the callable bond (orange line) is limited by the call price.

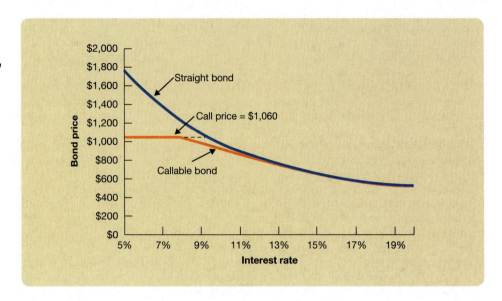

of default, the secured lender has first claim on the collateral; unsecured lenders have a general claim on the rest of the firm's assets but only a junior claim on the collateral.

Default Risk   Seniority and security do not guarantee payment. A debt can be senior and secured but still as risky as a dizzy tightrope walker—it depends on the value and the risk of the firm's assets. In Chapter 5 we showed how the safety of most corporate bonds can be judged from bond ratings provided by Moody's and Standard & Poor's. Bonds that are rated "triple-A" seldom default. At the other extreme, many speculative-grade (or "junk") bonds may be teetering on the brink.

As you would expect, investors demand a high return from low-rated bonds. We saw evidence of this in Chapter 5, where Figure 5–9 showed yields on default-free U.S. Treasury bonds as well as on corporate bonds in various rating classes. The lower-rated bonds did in fact offer higher promised yields to maturity.

Country and Currency   These days capital markets know few national boundaries and many large firms in the United States borrow abroad. For example, an American company may choose to finance a new plant in Switzerland by borrowing Swiss francs from a Swiss bank, or it may expand its Dutch operation by issuing a bond in Holland. Also many foreign companies come to the United States to borrow dollars, which are then used to finance their operations throughout the world.

In addition to these national capital markets, there is also an international capital market centered mainly in London. Banks from all over the world have branches in London. They include such giants as Citicorp, UBS, Deutsche Bank, Bank of Tokyo–Mitsubishi, HSBC, and BNP Paribas. One reason they are there is to collect deposits in the major currencies. For example, suppose an Arab sheikh has just received payment in dollars for a large sale of oil to the United States. Rather than depositing the check in the United States, he may choose to open a dollar account with a bank in London. Dollars held in a bank outside the United States came to be known as **eurodollars.** Similarly, yen held outside Japan were termed euroyen, and so on.

eurodollars

Dollars held on deposit in a bank outside the United States.

The London bank branch that is holding the sheikh's dollar deposit may temporarily lend those dollars to a company, in the same way that a bank in the United States may relend dollars that have been deposited with it. Thus a company can either borrow dollars from a bank in the United States or borrow dollars from a bank in London.[5]

---

[5] Because the Federal Reserve requires banks in the United States to keep interest-free reserves, there is in effect a tax on dollar deposits in the United States. Overseas dollar deposits are free of this tax and therefore banks can afford to charge the borrower slightly lower interest rates.

Marriott Plan Enrages Holders of Its Bonds

Marriott Corp. has infuriated bond investors with a restructuring plan that may be a new way for companies to pull the rug out from under bondholders.

Prices of Marriott's existing bonds have plunged as much as 30% in the past two days in the wake of the hotel and food-services company's announcement that it plans to separate into two companies, one burdened with virtually all of Marriott's debt.

On Monday, Marriott said that it will divide its operations into two separate businesses. One, Marriott International Inc., is a healthy company that will manage Marriott's vast hotel chain; it will get most of the old company's revenue, a larger share of the cash flow and will be nearly debt-free.

The second business, called Host Marriott Corp., is a debt-laden company that will own Marriott hotels along with other real estate and retain essentially all of the old Marriott's $3 billion of debt.

The announcement stunned and infuriated bondholders, who watched nervously as the value of their Marriott bonds tumbled and as Moody's Investors Service Inc. downgraded the bond to the junk-bond category from investment-grade.

Price Plunge

In trading, Marriott's 10% bonds that mature in 2012, which Marriott sold to investors just six months ago, were quoted yesterday at about 80 cents on the dollar, down from 110 Friday. The price decline translates into a stunning loss of $300 for a bond with a $1,000 face amount.

Marriott officials concede that the company's spinoff plan penalizes bondholders. However, the company notes that, like all public corporations, its fiduciary duty is to stockholders, not bondholders. Indeed, Marriott's stock jumped 12% Monday. (It fell a bit yesterday.)

Bond investors and analysts worry that if the Marriott spinoff goes through, other companies will soon follow suit by separating debt-laden units from the rest of the company. "Any company that fears it has underperforming divisions that are dragging down its stock price is a possible candidate" for such a restructuring, says Dorothy K. Lee, an assistant vice president at Moody's.

If the trend heats up, investors said, the Marriott restructuring could be the worst news for corporate bondholders since RJR Nabisco Inc.'s managers shocked investors in 1987 by announcing they were taking the company private in a record $25 billion leveraged buy-out. The move, which loaded RJR with debt and tanked the value of RJR bonds, triggered a deep slump in prices of many investment-grade corporate bonds as investors backed away from the market.

Strong Covenants May Re-Emerge

Some analysts say the move by Marriott may trigger the re-emergence of strong covenants, or written protections, in future corporate bond issues to protect bondholders against such restructurings as the one being engineered by Marriott. In the wake of the RJR buy-out, many investors demanded stronger covenants in new corporate bond issues.

Some investors blame themselves for not demanding stronger covenants. "It's our own fault," said Robert Hickey, a bond fund manager at Van Kampen Merritt. In their rush to buy bonds in an effort to lock in yields, many investors have allowed companies to sell bonds with covenants that have been "slim to none," Mr. Hickey said.

---

eurobond
Bond that is marketed internationally.

If a firm wants to make an issue of long-term bonds, it can choose to do so in the United States. Alternatively, it can sell the bonds to investors in several countries. Because these international issues have usually been marketed by the London branches of international banks, they have traditionally been known as **eurobonds.** A eurobond may be denominated in dollars, yen, or any other currency. Unfortunately, when the single European currency was established it was called the *euro.* It is easy, therefore, to confuse a *eurobond* (a bond that is sold internationally) with a bond that is denominated in *euros.*

Public versus Private Placements   Publicly issued bonds are sold to anyone who wishes to buy, and once they have been issued, they can be freely traded in the securities markets. In a **private placement,** the issue is sold directly to a small number of banks, insurance companies, or other investment institutions. Privately placed bonds cannot be resold to individuals in the United States but can be resold only to other qualified institutional investors. However, there is increasingly active trading *among* these investors.

private placement
Sale of securities to a limited number of investors without a public offering.

We will have more to say about the difference between public issues and private placements in the next chapter.

Protective Covenants   When investors lend to a company, they know that they might not get their money back. But they expect that the company will use their money well and not take unreasonable risks. To help ensure this, lenders usually impose a

protective covenant
Restriction on a firm to protect bondholders.

number of conditions, or **protective covenants,** on companies that borrow from them. An honest firm is willing to accept these conditions because it knows that they enable the firm to borrow at a reasonable rate of interest.

Companies that borrow in moderation are less likely to get into difficulties than those that are up to the gunwales in debt. So lenders usually restrict the amount of extra debt that the firm can issue. Lenders are also eager to prevent others from pushing ahead of them in the queue if trouble occurs. So they will not allow the company to create new debt that is senior to them or to put aside assets for other lenders.

Another possible hazard for lenders is that the company will pay a bumper dividend to the shareholders, leaving no cash for the debtholders. Therefore, lenders sometimes limit the size of the dividends that can be paid.

The story of Marriott in the nearby box shows what can happen when bondholders are not sufficiently careful about the conditions they impose.

Self-Test 13.6

In 1987 RJR Nabisco, the food and tobacco giant, had $5 billion of A-rated debt outstanding. In that year the company was taken over, and $19 billion of debt was issued and used to buy back equity. The debt ratio skyrocketed, and the debt was downgraded to a BB rating. The holders of the previously issued debt were furious, and one filed a lawsuit claiming that RJR had violated an *implicit* obligation not to undertake major financing changes at the expense of existing bondholders. Why did these bondholders believe they had been harmed by the massive issue of new debt? What type of *explicit* restriction would you have wanted if you had been one of the original bondholders?

A Debt by Any Other Name   The word *debt* sounds straightforward, but companies enter into a number of financial arrangements that look suspiciously like debt yet are treated differently in the accounts. Some of these obligations are easily identifiable. For example, accounts payable are simply obligations to pay for goods that have already been delivered and are therefore like a short-term debt.

Other arrangements are not so easy to spot. For example, instead of borrowing money to buy equipment, many companies **lease** or rent it on a long-term basis. In this case the firm promises to make a series of payments to the lessor (the owner of the equipment). This is just like the obligation to make payments on an outstanding loan. What if the firm can't make the payments? The lessor can then take back the equipment, which is precisely what would happen if the firm had *borrowed* money from the lessor, using the equipment as collateral for the loan.

There is nothing underhanded about entering into long-term leases. They are clearly shown on the company's balance sheet as a liability. Sometimes, however, companies go to considerable lengths to ensure that investors do not know how much they have borrowed. For example, Enron was able to borrow $658 million by setting up *special-purpose entities (SPEs),* which raised cash by a mixture of equity and debt and then used that debt to help fund the parent company. None of this debt showed up on Enron's balance sheet.

lease
Long-term rental agreement.

EXAMPLE 13.1 ▶ The Terms of Heinz's Bond Issue

Now that you are familiar with some of the jargon, you might like to look at an example of a bond issue. Table 13–3 is a summary of the terms of a bond issue by Heinz taken from *Mergent's Industrial Manual.* We have added some explanatory notes. ◀

Innovation in the Debt Market

We have discussed domestic bonds and eurobonds, fixed-rate and floating-rate loans, secured and unsecured loans, senior and junior loans, and much more. You might think

TABLE 13–3 Heinz's bond issue

Comment	Description of Bond
1. A debenture is an unsecured bond.	**H.J. Heinz Company 6.375% debentures, due 2028**
2. Coupon is 6.375 percent. Thus each bond makes an annual interest payment of .06375 × $1,000 = $63.75.	
3. Moody's bond rating is A, the third-highest quality rating.	**Rating—A**
4. Heinz is authorized to issue (and has outstanding) $250 million of the bonds.	AUTH. $250,000,000: outstg. $250,000,000.
5. The bond was issued in July 1998 and is to be repaid in July 2028.	DATED July 10, 1998. DUE July 15, 2028.
6. Interest is payable at 6-month intervals on January and July 15.	INTEREST J&J 15.
7. A trustee is appointed to look after the bondholders' interest.	TRUSTEE First National Bank of Chicago.
8. The bonds are registered. The registrar keeps a record of who owns the bonds.	DENOMINATION Fully registered. $1,000 and integral multiples thereof. Transferable and exchangable without service charge.
9. The bond can be held in multiples of $1,000.	
10. Unlike some bond issues, the Heinz issue does not give the company an option to call (i.e., repurchase) the bonds before maturity at specified prices. Also Heinz does not set aside money each year in a sinking fund that is then used to redeem the bonds.	EARLY REDEMPTION The debentures are not redeemable prior to maturity.
11. The bonds are not secured, that is, no assets have been set aside to protect the bondholders in the event of default.	SECURITY Not secured. Ranks equally with all other unsecured and unsubordinated indebtedness of the Company. Company or any affiliate will not create as security for any indebtedness for borrowed money, any mortgage, pledge, security interest, or lien on any stock or any indebtedness of any affiliate . . . without effectively providing that the debentures shall be secured equally and ratably with such indebtedness, unless such secured debt would not exceed 10% of Consolidated Net Assets.
12. However, if Heinz sets aside assets to protect any other bondholders, the debenture will also be secured on these assets. This is termed a *negative pledge clause*.	
13. The bonds were sold at a price of 99.549 percent of face value. After deducting the payment to the underwriters the company received $986.74 per bond. The bonds could be bought from the listed underwriters.	OFFERED $250,000,000 at 99.549 plus accrued interest (proceeds to Company 98.674) thru Goldman, Sachs & Co., J. P. Morgan & Co., Warburg Dillon Read LLC.

that this gives you all the choice you need. Yet almost every day companies and their advisers dream up new types of debt. We described some unusual bonds in Chapter 5. Here are a couple more examples.

Indexed Bonds   We saw in Chapter 5 how the United States government has issued bonds whose payments rise in line with inflation. Occasionally borrowers have linked the payments on their bonds to the price of a particular commodity. For example, Mexico, which is a large oil producer, has issued billions of dollars worth of bonds that provide an extra payoff if oil prices rise. Mexico reasons that oil-linked bonds reduce its risk. If the price of oil is high, it can afford the higher payments on the bond. If oil prices are low, its interest payments will also be lower. The Swiss insurance company Winterthur has also issued an unusual bond with varying interest payments. The payments on the bonds are reduced if there is a hailstorm in Switzerland that damages at least 6,000 cars that have been insured by Winterthur.[6] The bondholders receive a higher interest rate but take on some of the company's risk.

---

[6] The Winterthur bond is an example of a *catastrophe* (or *CAT*) bond. Its payments are linked to the occurrence of a natural catastrophe. CAT bonds are discussed in M. S. Cantor, J. B. Cole, and R. L. Sandor, "Insurance Derivatives: A New Asset Class for the Capital Markets and a New Hedging Tool for the Insurance Industry," *Journal of Applied Corporate Finance* 10 (Fall 1997), pp. 69–83.

Asset-Backed Bonds   The rock star David Bowie earns royalties from a number of successful albums such as *The Rise and Fall of Ziggy Stardust* and *Diamond Dogs.* But instead of waiting to receive these royalties, Bowie decided that he would prefer the money up front. The solution was to issue $55 million of 10-year bonds and to set aside the future royalty payments from the singer's albums to make the payments on these bonds. Such bonds are known as *asset-backed securities;* the borrower sets aside a group of assets and the income from these assets is then used to service the debt. The Bowie bonds are an unusual example of an asset-backed security, but billions of dollars of house mortgages and credit card loans are packaged each year and resold as asset-backed bonds.

These two examples illustrate the great variety of potential security designs. As long as you can convince investors of its attractions, you can issue a callable, subordinated, floating-rate bond denominated in euros. Rather than combining features of existing securities, you may be able to create an entirely new one. We can imagine a copper mining company issuing preferred shares on which the dividend fluctuates with the world copper price. We know of no such security, but it is perfectly legal to issue it and—who knows?—it might generate considerable interest among investors.

Variety is intrinsically good. People have different tastes, levels of wealth, rates of tax, and so on. Why not offer them a choice? Of course, the problem is the expense of designing and marketing new securities. But if you can think of a new security that will appeal to investors, you may be able to issue it on especially favorable terms and thus increase the value of your company.

13.5 Convertible Securities

warrant
Right to buy shares from a company at a stipulated price before a set date.

We have seen that companies sometimes have the option to repay an issue of bonds before maturity. There are also cases in which *investors* have an option. The most dramatic case is provided by a **warrant,** which is *nothing but* an option. Companies often issue warrants and bonds in a package.

EXAMPLE 13.2 ▶	Warrants

Macaw Bill wishes to make a bond issue, which could include some warrants as a "sweetener." Each warrant might allow you to purchase one share of Macaw stock at a price of $50 any time during the next 5 years. If Macaw's stock performs well, that option could turn out to be very valuable. For instance, if the stock price at the end of the 5 years is $80, then you pay the company $50 and receive in exchange a share worth $80. Of course, an investment in warrants also has its perils. If the price of Macaw stock fails to rise above $50, then the warrants expire worthless.   ◀

convertible bond
Bond that the holder may exchange for a specified amount of another security

A **convertible bond** gives its owner the option to exchange the bond for a predetermined number of common shares. The convertible bondholder hopes that the company's share price will zoom up so that the bond can be converted at a big profit. But if the shares zoom down, there is no obligation to convert; the bondholder remains just that. Not surprisingly, investors value this option to keep the bond or exchange it for shares, and therefore a convertible bond sells at a higher price than a comparable bond that is not convertible.

The convertible is rather like a package of a bond and a warrant. But there is an important difference: When the owners of a convertible wish to exercise their options to buy shares, they do not pay cash—they just exchange the bond for shares of the stock.

Companies may also issue convertible preferred stock. In this case the investor receives preferred stock with fixed dividend payments but has the option to exchange this preferred stock for the company's common stock. The preferred stock issued by Heinz is convertible into common stock.

These examples do not exhaust the options encountered by the financial manager. In fact, once you read Chapter 23 and learn how to analyze options, you will find that they are all around you.

13.6 Patterns of Corporate Financing

Firms have two broad sources of cash: They can raise money from external sources by an issue of shares or debt, or they can plow back part of their profits. Shareholders are happy for companies to plow this money back into the firm, so long as it goes to positive-NPV investments. Every positive-NPV investment generates a higher price for their shares.

internally generated funds
Cash reinvested in the firm: depreciation plus earnings not paid out as dividends

Figure 13–3 summarizes the sources of capital for U.S. corporations. Notice the importance of **internally generated funds,** defined as depreciation plus earnings that are not paid out as dividends.[7] Over these 15 years, internally generated cash covered nearly 90 percent of firms' capital requirements.

Do Firms Rely Too Heavily on Internal Funds?

Some observers worry that companies rely so much on internal funds. They argue that managers might think more carefully about spending money if they have to ask investors for it. Think back to Chapter 1, where we pointed out that a firm is a team, consisting of managers, shareholders, debtholders, and so on. The shareholders and debtholders would like to monitor management to make sure that it is pulling its weight and truly maximizing market value, but it is costly for individual investors to keep check on management. However, large financial institutions are specialists in monitoring, so when the firm goes to the bank for a large loan or makes a public issue of stock or bonds, managers know that they had better have all the answers. If they want a quiet life, they will avoid going to the capital market to raise money and they will retain sufficient earnings to be able to meet unanticipated demands for cash.

We do not mean to paint managers as loafers. There are also rational reasons for relying on internally generated funds. For example, the costs of issuing new securities

FIGURE 13–3 Sources of funds for U.S. nonfinancial corporations, 1989–2004

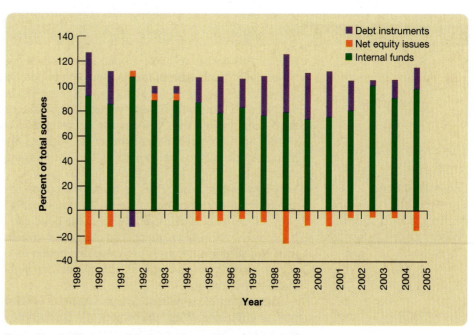

Source: Board of Governors of the Federal Reserve System, Division of Research and Statistics, "Flow of Funds Accounts," Table F.102 at **www.federalreserve.gov/releases/z1/current/data.htm.**

---

[7] Remember that depreciation is a noncash expense.

Patterns of Corporate Financing

In Figure 13–3 we summarized the sources and uses of funds for U.S. nonfinancial corporations. The data for this figure can be found on **www.federalreserve.gov/releases/z1/current/data.htm**. Look at Table F.102 for the latest year. Don't be put off by its complexity. Just find "total internal funds" (which appeared in row 9 at the time we last looked) and "net funds raised in markets" (row 36). What proportion of the funds that companies needed in the latest year was generated internally, and how much had to be raised on the financial markets? Is this the usual pattern? Now look at "net new equity issues" (row 37). Were companies on average issuing new equity or buying their shares back?

are avoided. Moreover, the announcement of a new equity issue is usually bad news for investors, who worry that management may be trying to sell overpriced stock.[8] Raising equity capital from internal sources, then, avoids the costs and the bad omens associated with equity issues.

Self-Test 13.7 — "Since internal funds provide the bulk of industry's needs for capital, the securities markets serve little function." Does the speaker have a point?

External Sources of Capital

Of course, firms don't rely exclusively on internal funds. In most years there is a gap between the cash that companies need and the cash that they generate internally. This gap is the **financial deficit.** To make up the deficit, companies must either sell new equity or borrow.

Look again at Figure 13–3, which shows how corporate America has made up the deficit. Notice that for most of this period firms were making large issues of debt and using the money to buy back common stock. In Figure 13–3 these repurchases show up as negative issues of equity.

financial deficit
Difference between the cash companies need and the amount generated internally.

FIGURE 13–4 The ratio of debt to debt plus equity for the nonfinancial corporate sector

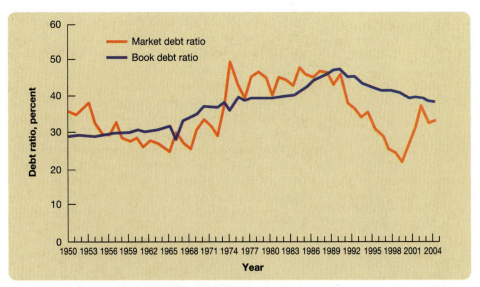

Source: Board of Governors of the Federal Reserve System, Division of Research and Statistics, "Flow of Funds Accounts," Table B.102 at **www.federalreserve.gov/releases/z1/current/data.htm**.

---

[8] Managers do have insiders' insights and naturally are tempted to issue stock when the stock price looks good to them, that is, when they are less optimistic than outside investors. The outside investors realize all this and will buy a new issue only at a discount from the preannouncement price. Stock issues are discussed further in the next chapter.

Has this policy resulted in an increase in the proportion of debt that companies use? Figure 13–4 shows that the answer partly depends on how you measure the debt ratio. You can see that in book-value terms the debt ratio has crept fairly steadily upward over the last 50 years (though it actually dipped a little during the 1990s). However, the picture is rather different in terms of market values. Booming stock prices until 1999 ensured that for two decades the amount of long-term debt grew less rapidly than the market value of equity.

Should we be worried that book debt ratios are higher today than they were 50 years ago? It is true that high debt ratios mean that more companies are likely to fall into financial distress when a serious recession hits the economy. But all companies live with this to some degree, and it does not always follow that less risk is better. Finding the optimal debt ratio is like finding the optimal speed limit; we can agree that accidents at 30 miles per hour are less dangerous, other things being equal, than accidents at 60 miles per hour, but we do not therefore set the national speed limit at 30. Speed has benefits as well as risks. So does debt, as we will see in Chapter 15.

SUMMARY

Why should firms assume that the securities they issue are fairly priced?

Managers want to raise money at the lowest possible cost, but their ability to find cheap financing is limited by the intense competition between investors. As a result of this competition, securities are likely to be fairly priced given the information available to investors. Such a market is said to be *efficient.*

What are the major classes of securities issued by firms to raise capital?

A company can issue a variety of securities such as common stock, preferred stock, and bonds. The **common stockholders** own the company. By this we mean that they are entitled to whatever profits are left over after other investors have been paid and that they have the ultimate control over how the company is run. Because shareholdings in the United States are usually widely dispersed, managers get to make most of the decisions. Managers may be given strong financial incentives to perform well, and their actions are monitored by the board of directors. Nevertheless, the U.S. devolved system of corporate governance breaks down when a company's performance is not transparent. Laws such as the recent Sarbanes-Oxley Act have tried to ensure that managers cannot draw a veil over the company's true profitability.

Preferred stock offers a fixed dividend but the company has the discretion not to pay it. It can't, however, then pay a dividend on the common stock. Despite its name, preferred stock is not a popular source of finance, but it is useful in special situations.

When companies issue **bonds,** they promise to make a series of interest payments and to repay the principal. However, this liability is limited. Stockholders have the right to default on their obligation and to hand over the assets to the debtholders. Unlike dividends on common stock and preferred stock, the interest payments on debt are regarded as a cost and therefore they are paid out of before-tax income. Here are some forms of debt:

- *Fixed-rate* and *floating-rate* debt.
- *Funded (long-term)* and *unfunded (short-term)* debt.
- *Callable* and *sinking-fund* debt.
- *Senior* and *subordinated* debt.
- *Secured* and *unsecured* debt.
- *Investment grade* and *junk* debt.
- *Domestic bonds* and *eurobonds.*
- *Publicly traded* debt and *private placements.*

The fourth source of finance consists of options and optionlike securities. The simplest option is a **warrant,** which gives its holder the right to buy a share from the firm at a set

price by a set date. Warrants are often sold in combination with other securities. **Convertible bonds** give their holder the right to convert the bond to shares. They therefore resemble a package of straight debt and a warrant.

What are recent trends in firms' use of different sources of finance?

Internally generated cash is the principal source of company funds. Some people worry about that; they think that if management does not go to the trouble of raising money, it may be profligate in spending it.

In recent years, net equity issues have often been negative; that is, companies have repurchased more equity than they have issued. At the same time companies have issued large quantities of debt. However, large levels of **internally generated funds** in this period allowed book equity to increase despite the share repurchases, with the result that the ratio of long-term debt to book value of equity was fairly stable.

QUIZ

1. **Equity Accounts.** The authorized share capital of the Alfred Cake Company is 100,000 shares. The equity is currently shown in the company's books as follows:

Common stock ($1 par value)	$ 60,000
Additional paid-in capital	10,000
Retained earnings	30,000
Common equity	100,000
Treasury stock (2,000 shares)	5,000
Net common equity	$ 95,000

   a. How many shares are issued?
   b. How many are outstanding?
   c. How many more shares can be issued without the approval of shareholders?

2. **Equity Accounts.**

   a. Look back at Problem 1. Suppose that the company issues 10,000 shares at $4 a share. Which of the above figures would change?
   b. What would happen to the company's books if instead it bought back 1,000 shares at $4 per share?

3. **Financing Terms.** Fill in the blanks by choosing the appropriate term from the following list: *lease, funded, floating-rate, eurobond, convertible, subordinated, call, sinking fund, prime rate, private placement, public issue, senior, unfunded, eurodollar rate, warrant, debentures, term loan.*

   a. Debt maturing in more than 1 year is often called _____ debt.
   b. An issue of bonds that is sold simultaneously in several countries is traditionally called a(n) _____.
   c. If a lender ranks behind the firm's general creditors in the event of default, the loan is said to be _____.
   d. In many cases a firm is obliged to make regular contributions to a(n) _____, which is then used to repurchase bonds.
   e. Most bonds give the firm the right to repurchase or _____ the bonds at specified prices.
   f. The benchmark interest rate that banks charge to their customers with good credit is generally termed the _____.
   g. The interest rate on bank loans is often tied to short-term interest rates. These loans are usually called _____ loans.
   h. Where there is a(n) _____, securities are sold directly to a small group of institutional investors. These securities cannot be resold to individual investors. In the case of a(n) _____, debt can be freely bought and sold by individual investors.
   i. A long-term rental agreement is called a(n) _____.
   j. A(n) _____ bond can be exchanged for shares of the issuing corporation.

k. A(n) _____ gives its owner the right to buy shares in the issuing company at a predetermined price.

4. **Financing Trends.** True or false? Explain.

a. In several recent years, nonfinancial corporations in the United States have repurchased
more stock than they have issued.

b. A corporation pays tax on only 30 percent of the common or preferred dividends it receives
from other corporations.

c. Because of the tax advantage, a large fraction of preferred shares is held by corporations.

5. **Preferred Stock.** In what ways is preferred stock like long-term debt? In what ways is it like
common stock?

PRACTICE PROBLEMS

6. **Voting for Directors.** If there are 10 directors to be elected and a shareholder owns 100 shares,
indicate the maximum number of votes that he or she can cast for a favorite candidate under

a. majority voting.
b. cumulative voting.

Please visit us at www.mhhe.com/bmm5e or
refer to your Student CD

7. **Voting for Directors.** The shareholders of the Pickwick Paper Company need to elect five directors. There are 400,000 shares outstanding. How many shares do you need to own to *ensure*
that you can elect at least one director if the company has

a. majority voting?
b. cumulative voting?

Hint: How many votes in total will be cast? How many votes are required to ensure that at least
one-fifth of votes are cast for your choice?

Please visit us at www.mhhe.com/bmm5e or
refer to your Student CD

8. **Equity Accounts.** Look back at Table 13–2.

a. Suppose that Heinz issues 10 million shares at $40 a share. Rework Table 13–2 to show the
company's equity after the issue.

b. Suppose that Heinz *subsequently* repurchased 500,000 shares at $50 a share. Rework part
(a) to show the effect of the further change.

9. **Equity Accounts.** Common Products has just made its first issue of stock. It raised $2 million
by selling 200,000 shares of stock to the public. These are the only shares outstanding. The par
value of each share was $2. Fill in the following table:

Common shares (par value)	_____
Additional paid-in capital	_____
Retained earnings	_____
Net common equity	$2,500,000

10. **Protective Covenants.** Why might a bond agreement limit the amount of assets that the firm
can lease?

11. **Bond Yields.** Other things equal, will the following provisions increase or decrease the yield to
maturity at which a firm can issue a bond?

a. A call provision.
b. A restriction on further borrowing.
c. A provision of specific collateral for the bond.
d. An option to convert the bonds into shares.

12. **Income Bonds.** *Income bonds* are unusual. Interest payments on such bonds may be skipped or
deferred if the firm's income is insufficient to make the payment. In what way are these bonds
like preferred stock? Why might a firm choose to issue an income bond instead of preferred
stock?

13. **Preferred Stock.** Preferred stock of financially strong firms sometimes sells at lower yields
than the bonds of those firms. For weaker firms, the preferred stock has a higher yield. What
might explain this pattern?

STANDARD
&POOR'S

1. Go to Market Insight at www.mhhe.com/edumarketinsight. Anheuser-Busch Inc. (BUD) used internal and external sources to fund its recent growth. Examine Anheuser-Busch's internal and external sources of funds, and then compare your findings with Figure 13–3 in this chapter. (See Annual Cash Flow Statement.) What was Anheuser-Busch's primary use of funds?

2. What has happened to the book debt ratios (Ratios Report) of Anheuser-Busch Inc. (BUD) in the last few years? How has the debt ratio changed if one calculates debt ratios using the market value of equity?

3. Compare the major sources and uses of funds (Annual Cash Flow Report and Balance Sheet) for General Mills (GIS) and Heinz (HNZ). What factors might explain the differences in financing patterns for the two companies?

SOLUTIONS TO SELF-TEST QUESTIONS

13.1 Par value of common shares must be $1 × 100,000 shares = $100,000. Additional paid-in capital is ($15 − $1) × 100,000 = $1,400,000. Since book value is $4,500,000, retained earnings must be $3,000,000. Therefore, the accounts look like this:

Common shares ($1 par value per share)	$100,000
Additional paid-in capital	1,400,000
Retained earnings	3,000,000
Net common equity	$4,500,000

13.2 The Sarbanes-Oxley Act tried to prevent damaging conflicts of interest. If auditing firms earn substantial business from other services to their clients, they may be more forgiving about the firm's transgressions. (E.g., many believe that Enron's auditors, Arthur Andersen, might have been tougher on the company had it not also earned substantial fees from providing Enron with accounting services.) The requirement for rotation of auditors is prompted by the view that the relationship between company and auditor may become unduly cozy.

13.3 The corporation's after-tax yield on the bonds is 10% − (.35 × 10%) = 6.5%. The after-tax yield on the preferred is 8% − [.35 × (.30 × 8%)] = 7.16%. The preferred stock provides the higher after-tax rate despite its lower before-tax rate.

13.4 Because the coupon on floating-rate debt adjusts periodically to current market conditions, the bondholder is less vulnerable to changes in market yields. The coupon rate paid by the bond is not locked in for as long a period of time. Therefore, prices of floaters should be less sensitive to changes in market interest rates.

13.5 The callable bond will sell at a lower price. Investors will not pay as much for the callable bond since they know that the firm may call it away from them if interest rates fall. Thus they know that their capital gains potential is limited, which makes the bond less valuable. If both bonds are to sell at face value, the callable bond must pay a higher coupon rate as compensation to the investor for the firm's right to call the bond.

13.6 The extra debt makes it more likely that the firm will not be able to make good on its promised payments to its creditors. If the new debt is not junior to the already-issued debt, then the original bondholders suffer a loss when their bonds become more susceptible to default risk. A protective covenant limiting the amount of new debt that the firm can issue would have prevented this problem. Investors, having witnessed the problems of the RJR bondholders, generally demanded the covenant on future debt issues.

13.7 Capital markets provide liquidity for investors. Because individual stockholders can always lay their hands on cash by selling shares, they are prepared to invest in companies that retain earnings rather than pay them out as dividends. Well-functioning capital markets allow the firm to serve all its stockholders simply by maximizing value. Capital markets also provide managers with information. Without this information, it would be very difficult to determine opportunity costs of capital or to assess financial performance.

CHAPTER

14

Venture Capital, IPOs, and Seasoned Offerings

RELATED WEB LINKS

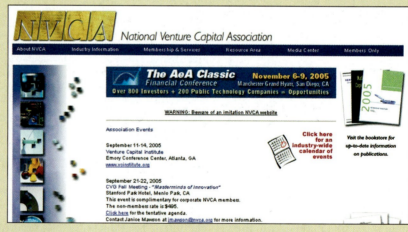

www.ventureeconomics.com

www.vnpartners.com

www.v1.com News and statistics on the venture capital industry.

www.nvca.org Home page of the National Venture Capital Association.

biz.yahoo.com/ipo

www.ipodata.com

www.ipohome.com

www.hoovers.com

www.marketwatch.com News and analysis concerning IPOs. For latter sites, click on tab for IPOs.

www.dealflow.com

www.vfinance.com Sites that help match up entrepreneurs and venture capitalists.

thomson.com/financial Information on underwriting activity.

bear.cba.ufl.edu/ritter Jay Ritter's home page includes extensive data on IPOs.

www.edgaronline.com A comprehensive database of issue prospectuses.

www.edgarscan.pwcglobal.com Easy to navigate list of current IPOs.

Trading opens on NASDAQ for shares in Google.
© Getty Images

Bill Gates and Paul Allen founded Microsoft in 1975, when both were around 20 years old. Eleven years later Microsoft shares were sold to the public for $21 a share and immediately zoomed to $35. The largest shareholder was Bill Gates, whose shares in Microsoft then were worth $350 million.

In 1976 two college dropouts, Steve Jobs and Steve Wozniak, sold their most valuable possessions, a van and a couple of calculators, and used the cash to start manufacturing computers in a garage. In 1980, when Apple Computer went public, the shares were offered to investors at $22 and jumped to $36. At that point, the shares owned by the company's two founders were worth $414 million.

In 1996 two Stanford computer science students, Larry Page and Sergey Brin, decided to collaborate to develop a Web search engine. To help turn their idea into a commercial product, the two friends succeeded in raising almost $1 million from several wealthy investors (known as *angel investors*), and this was later supplemented by funding from two *venture capital* firms that specialized in helping young start-up businesses. The company, now named Google, went public

in 2004 at a price of $85 a share, putting a value on the enterprise of $23 billion.

Such stories illustrate that the most important asset of a new firm may be a good idea. But that is not all you need. To take an idea from the drawing board to a prototype and through to large-scale production requires ever greater amounts of capital.

To get a new company off the ground, entrepreneurs may rely on their own savings and personal bank loans. But this is unlikely to be sufficient to build a successful enterprise. *Venture capital* firms specialize in providing new equity capital to help firms over the awkward adolescent period before they are large enough to "go public." In the first part of this chapter we will explain how venture capital firms do this.

If the firm continues to be successful, there is likely to come a time when it needs to tap a wider source of capital. At this point it will make its first public issue of common stock. This is known as an *initial public offering*, or *IPO*. In the second section of the chapter we will describe what is involved in an IPO.

A company's initial public offering is seldom its last. In Chapter 13 we saw that internally generated cash is not usually sufficient to satisfy the firm's needs. Established companies make up the deficit by issuing more equity or debt. The remainder of this chapter looks at this process.

After studying this chapter you should be able to:
- Understand how venture capital firms design successful deals.
- Understand how firms make initial public offerings and the costs of such offerings.
- Know what is involved when established firms make a general cash offer or a private placement of securities.
- Explain the role of the underwriter in an issue of securities.

14.1 Venture Capital

You have taken a big step. With a couple of friends, you have formed a corporation to open a number of fast-food outlets, offering innovative combinations of national dishes such as sushi with sauerkraut, curry Bolognese, and chow mein with Yorkshire pudding. Breaking into the fast-food business costs money, but, after pooling your savings and borrowing to the hilt from the bank, you have raised $100,000 and purchased 1 million shares in the new company. At this *zero-stage* investment, your company's assets are $100,000 plus the *idea* for your new product.

That $100,000 is enough to get the business off the ground, but if the idea takes off, you will need more capital to pay for new restaurants. Many start-ups continue to grow with funds provided directly by managers or by their friends and families. Some thrive using bank loans and reinvested earnings. But, particularly if your start-up combines high-risk, sophisticated technology and substantial investment, you will probably need to find an investor who is prepared to back an untried company in return for part of the profits. Equity capital in young businesses is known as **venture capital,** and it is provided by specialist venture capital firms, wealthy individuals, and investment institutions such as pension funds.

venture capital

Money invested to finance a new firm.

Most entrepreneurs are able to spin a plausible yarn about their company. But it is as hard to convince a venture capitalist to invest in your business as it is to get a first novel published. Your first step is to prepare a *business plan.* This describes your product, the potential market, the production method, and the resources—time, money, employees, plant, and equipment—needed for success. It helps if you can point to the fact that you are prepared to put your money where your mouth is. By staking all your savings in the company, you *signal* your faith in the business.

The venture capital company knows that the success of a new business depends on the effort its managers put in. Therefore, it will try to structure any deal so that you have a strong incentive to work hard. For example, if you agree to accept a modest salary (and look forward instead to increasing the value of your investment in the company's stock), the venture capital company knows you will be committed to working hard. However, if you insist on a watertight employment contract and a fat salary, you won't find it easy to raise venture capital.

You are unlikely to persuade a venture capitalist to give you all at once as much money as you need. Rather, the firm will probably offer you enough to reach the next major checkpoint. Suppose you can convince the venture capital company to buy 1 million new shares for $.50 each. This will give it one-half ownership of the firm: It owns 1 million shares, and you and your friends also own 1 million shares. Because the venture capitalist is paying $500,000 for a claim to half your firm, it is placing a $1 million value on the business. After this *first-stage* financing, your company's balance sheet looks like this:

FIRST-STAGE MARKET-VALUE BALANCE SHEET (figures in millions)			
Assets		**Liabilities and Shareholders' Equity**	
Cash from new equity	$ .5	New equity from venture capital	$ .5
Other assets	.5	Your original equity	.5
Value	$1.0	Value	$1.0

Self-Test 14.1

Why might the venture capital company prefer to put up only part of the funds up front? Would this affect the amount of effort put in by you, the entrepreneur? Is your willingness to accept only part of the venture capital that will eventually be needed a good signal of the likely success of the venture?

Suppose that 2 years later your business has grown to the point at which it needs a further injection of equity. This *second-stage* financing might involve the issue of a further 1 million shares at $1 each. Some of these shares might be bought by the original backers and some by other venture capital firms. The balance sheet after the new financing would then be as follows:

SECOND-STAGE MARKET-VALUE BALANCE SHEET (figures in millions)			
Assets		**Liabilities and Shareholders' Equity**	
Cash from new equity	$1	New equity from second-stage financing	$1
Other assets	2	Equity from first stage	1
		Your original equity	1
Value	$3	Value	$3

Notice that the value of the initial 1 million shares owned by you and your friends has now been marked up to $1 million. Does this begin to sound like a money machine? It was so only because you have made a success of the business and new investors are prepared to pay $1 to buy a share in the business. When you started out, it wasn't clear that sushi and sauerkraut would catch on. If it hadn't caught on, the venture capital firm could have refused to put up more funds.

You are not yet in a position to cash in on your investment, but your gain is real. The second-stage investors have paid $1 million for a one-third share in the company. (There are now 3 million shares outstanding, and the second-stage investors hold 1 million shares.) Therefore, at least these impartial observers—who are willing to back up their opinions with a large investment—must have decided that the company was worth at least $3 million. Your one-third share is therefore also worth $1 million.

Venture capital firms are not passive investors. They are usually represented on each company's board of directors, they help to recruit senior managers for the company, and they provide ongoing advice. This advice can be very valuable to businesses in their early years and helps them to bring their products more quickly to market.

For every 10 first-stage venture capital investments, only 2 or 3 may survive as successful, self-sufficient businesses, and only 1 may pay off big. From these statistics come two rules of success in venture capital investment. First, don't shy away from uncertainty; accept a low probability of success. But don't buy into a business unless you can see the *chance* of a big, public company in a profitable market. There's no sense taking a big risk unless the reward is big if you win. Second, cut your losses;

Venture Capital

To find out what is happening in the venture capital industry, look at the recent news on **www.ventureeconomics.com**. Now click on *Statistics* and look at the recent national data. How does the level of deals compare with levels in recent years? Which industries are attracting the most venture capital? Is the money going into new start-ups or expansion of existing businesses?

identify losers early, and if you can't fix the problem—by replacing management, for example—don't throw good money after bad.

Very few new businesses make it big, but those that do can be very profitable. For example, an investor who provided $1,000 of first-stage financing for Intel would have reaped over $25 million by 2005. So venture capitalists keep sane by reminding themselves of the success stories—those who got in on the ground floor of firms like Genentech, Sun Microsystems, and Federal Express.[1]

14.2 The Initial Public Offering

initial public offering (IPO)
First offering of stock to the general public.

Some very large companies, such as Levi Strauss or Cargill, have been able to continue and prosper as independent, private businesses. But for many other successful start-ups there comes a time when they need more capital than can comfortably be provided by a small number of individuals or venture capitalists. At this point one solution is to sell the business to a larger firm. But many entrepreneurs do not fit easily into a corporate bureaucracy and would prefer instead to remain the boss. In this case, the company may choose to raise money by selling shares to the public. A firm is said to *go public* when it sells its first issue of shares in a general offering to investors. This first sale of stock is called an **initial public offering, or IPO.**

An IPO is called a *primary* offering when new shares are sold to raise additional cash for the company. It is a *secondary* offering when the company's founders and the venture capitalist cash in on some of their gains by selling shares. A secondary offer therefore is no more than a sale of shares from the early investors in the firm to new investors, and the cash raised in a secondary offer does not flow to the company. Of course, IPOs can be and commonly are both primary and secondary: The firm raises new cash at the same time that some of the already existing shares in the firm are sold to the public. Some of the biggest secondary offerings have involved governments selling off stock in nationalized enterprises. For example, the Japanese government raised $12.6 billion by selling its stock in Nippon Telegraph and Telephone, and the British government took in $9 billion from its sale of British Gas. The world's largest IPO took place in 1999 when the Italian government raised $19.3 billion from the sale of shares in the state-owned electricity company, Enel.

Arranging a Public Issue

underwriter
Firm that buys an issue of securities from a company and resells it to the public.

Once a firm decides to go public, the first task is to select the underwriters. **Underwriters** are investment banking firms that act as financial midwives to a new issue. Usually they play a triple role—first providing the company with procedural and financial advice, then buying the stock, and finally reselling it to the public.

A small IPO may have only one underwriter, but larger issues usually require a syndicate of underwriters who buy the issue and resell it. For example, the initial public offering by Microsoft involved a total of 114 underwriters.

---

[1] Fortunately, the successes seem to have outweighed the failures. The National Venture Capital Association (NVCA) estimated that net returns on early-stage venture capital funds averaged nearly 16 percent a year for the 20 years ending in September 2004.

spread
Difference between public offer price and price paid by underwriter.

In the typical underwriting arrangement, called a *firm commitment,* the underwriters buy the securities from the firm and then resell them to the public. The underwriters receive payment in the form of a **spread**—that is, they are allowed to sell the shares at a slightly higher price than they paid for them. But the underwriters also accept the risk that they won't be able to sell the stock at the agreed offering price. If that happens, they will be stuck with unsold shares and must get the best price they can for them. In the more risky cases, the underwriter may not be willing to enter into a firm commitment and handles the issue on a *best efforts* basis. In this case the underwriter agrees to sell as much of the issue as possible but does not guarantee the sale of the entire issue.

Before any stock can be sold to the public, the company must register the stock with the Securities and Exchange Commission (SEC). This involves preparation of a detailed and sometimes cumbersome registration statement, which contains information about the proposed financing and the firm's history, existing business, and plans for the future. The SEC does not evaluate the wisdom of an investment in the firm, but it does check the registration statement for accuracy and completeness. The firm must also comply with the "blue-sky" laws of each state, so named because they seek to protect the public against firms that fraudulently promise the blue sky to investors.[2]

prospectus
Formal summary that provides information on an issue of securities.

The first part of the registration statement is distributed to the public in the form of a preliminary **prospectus.** One function of the prospectus is to warn investors about the risks involved in any investment in the firm. Some investors have joked that if they read prospectuses carefully, they would never dare buy any new issue. In the following Internet Insider box we show how you can find real IPO prospectuses on the Web. However, if you find the prospect intimidating, you can instead turn to the appendix to this chapter, which provides a streamlined version of a possible prospectus for your restaurant business.

The company and its underwriters also need to set the issue price. To gauge how much the stock is worth, they may undertake discounted cash-flow calculations like those described in Chapter 6. They also look at the price-earnings ratios of the shares of the firm's principal competitors.

Before settling on the issue price, the underwriters generally arrange a "roadshow," which gives the underwriters and the company's management an opportunity to talk to potential investors. These investors may then offer their reaction to the issue, suggest what they think is a fair price, and indicate how much stock they would be prepared to buy. This allows the underwriters to build up a book of likely orders. Although investors are not bound by their indications, they know that if they want to remain in the underwriters' good books, they must be careful not to renege on their expressions of interest.

underpricing
Issuing securities at an offering price set below the true value of the security.

The managers of the firm are eager to secure the highest possible price for their stock, but the underwriters are likely to be cautious because they will be left with any unsold stock if they overestimate investor demand. As a result, underwriters typically try to underprice the initial public offering. **Underpricing,** they argue, is needed to tempt investors to buy stock and to reduce the cost of marketing the issue to customers. Underpricing represents a cost to the existing owners since the new investors are allowed to buy shares in the firm at a favorable price.

Sometimes new issues are dramatically underpriced. For example, when the prospectus for the IPO of eBay was first published, the underwriters indicated that the company would sell 3.5 million shares at a price between $14 and $16 each. However, the enthusiasm for eBay's Web-based auction system was such that the underwriters increased the issue price to $18. The next morning dealers were flooded with orders to

---

[2] Sometimes states go beyond blue-sky laws in their efforts to protect their residents. In 1980 when Apple Computer Inc. made its first public issue, the Massachusetts state government decided the offering was too risky for its residents and therefore banned the sale of the shares to investors in the state. The state relented later, after the issue was out and the price had risen. Massachusetts investors obviously did not appreciate this "protection."

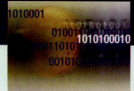

INTERNET INSIDER

Initial Public Offerings (IPOs)

1. In the appendix to this chapter we provide a flavor of an IPO prospectus, but you can see what an actual prospectus or registration statement looks like by using the SEC's huge database on **www.edgaronline.com**. Edgar can be a bit complicated, however. We suggest instead that you first log on to **finance.yahoo.com** to find a recent IPO and then click on *Filings,* which will take you to the correct SEC form. (Registration statements are shown as SEC Form S-1.) On the basis of this prospectus, do you think the stock looks like an attractive investment? Which parts of the statement appear most useful? Which seem the least useful?

2. When markets are booming, there tend to be more IPOs. Find out what has been happening to the market for IPOs recently by logging on to **www.ipohome.com**. Has there been an unusually large volume of IPOs recently? What have been the largest issues? How have IPOs performed recently?

3. We described underpricing as part of the costs of a new issue. Jay Ritter's home page (**bear.cba.ufl.edu/ritter**) is a mine of information on IPO underpricing. Look up his table of underpricing by year. Is underpricing now less of a problem than in the boom IPO years of 1998–2000? Now look at Jay Ritter's table of "money-left-on-the-table." Which company provided the greatest 1-day dollar gains to investors?

buy eBay; over 4.5 million shares traded, and the stock closed the day at a price of $47.375.

We admit that the experience of eBay is not typical, but it is common to see the stock price increase significantly from the issue price in the days following the sale. For example, one study of over 2,000 new issues between 1990 and 2004 found an average first-day price rise of 23 percent.[3] Such immediate price jumps suggest that investors would have been prepared to pay much more than they did for the shares.

EXAMPLE 14.1 ▶	Underpricing of IPOs

Suppose an IPO is a secondary issue and the firm's founders sell part of their holding to investors. Clearly, if the shares are sold for less than their true worth, the founders will suffer an opportunity loss.

But what if the IPO is a primary issue that raises new cash for the company? Do the founders care whether the shares are sold for less than their market value? The following example illustrates that they do care.

Suppose Cosmos.com has 2 million shares outstanding and now offers a further 1 million shares to investors at $50. On the first day of trading the share price jumps to $80, so the shares that the company sold for $50 million are now worth $80 million. The total market capitalization of the company is 3 million × $80 = $240 million.

The value of the founders' shares is equal to the total value of the company less the value of the shares that have been sold to the public—in other words, $240 million – $80 million = $160 million. The founders might justifiably rejoice at their good fortune. However, if the company had issued shares at a higher price, it would have needed to sell fewer shares to raise the $50 million that it needs and the founders would have retained a larger share of the company. For example, suppose that the outside investors, who put up $50 million, received shares that were *worth* only $50 million. In that case the value of the founders' shares would be $240 million – $50 million = $190 million.

The effect of selling shares below their true value is to transfer $30 million of value from the founders to the investors who buy the new shares. ◀

---

[3] These figures are provided on Jay Ritter's home page, **bear.cba.ufl.edu/ritter**.

Unfortunately, underpricing does not mean that anyone can become wealthy by buying stock in IPOs. If an issue is underpriced, everybody will want to buy it and the underwriters will not have enough stock to go around. You are therefore likely to get only a small share of these hot issues. If it is overpriced, other investors are unlikely to want it and the underwriter will be only too delighted to sell it to you. This phenomenon is known as the *winner's curse*.[4] It implies that, unless you can spot which issues are underpriced, you are likely to receive a small proportion of the cheap issues and a large proportion of the expensive ones. Since the dice are loaded against uninformed investors, they will play the game only if there is substantial underpricing on average.

EXAMPLE 14.2 ▶ Underpricing of IPOs and Investor Returns

Suppose that an investor will earn an immediate 10 percent return on underpriced IPOs and lose 5 percent on overpriced IPOs. But because of high demand, you may get only half the shares you bid for when the issue is underpriced. Suppose you bid for $1,000 of shares in two issues, one overpriced and the other underpriced. You are awarded the full $1,000 of the overpriced issue but only $500 worth of shares in the underpriced issue. The net gain on your two investments is $(.10 \times \$500) - (.05 \times \$1,000) = 0$. Your net profit is zero, despite the fact that, on average, IPOs are underpriced. You have suffered the winner's curse: You "win" a larger allotment of shares when they are overpriced.   ◀

Self-Test 14.2   **What is the percentage profit earned by an investor who can identify the underpriced issues in Example 14.2? Who are such investors likely to be?**

---

flotation costs
The costs incurred when a firm issues new securities to the public.

The costs of a new issue are termed **flotation costs.** Underpricing is not the only flotation cost. In fact, when people talk about the cost of a new issue, they often think only of the *direct costs* of the issue. For example, preparation of the registration statement and prospectus involves management, legal counsel, and accountants, as well as underwriters and their advisers. There is also the underwriting spread. (Remember, underwriters make their profit by selling the issue at a higher price than they paid for it.)

Look at the green bars (corresponding to IPOs) in Figure 14–1. These show the direct costs of going public.[5] For a small IPO of no more than $10 million, the underwriting spread and administrative costs are likely to absorb 15 to 20 percent of the proceeds from the issue. For the very largest IPOs, these direct costs may amount to only 5 percent of the proceeds.

EXAMPLE 14.3 ▶ Costs of an IPO

When the investment bank Goldman Sachs went public in 1999, the sale was partly a primary issue (the company sold new shares to raise cash) and partly a secondary one (two large existing shareholders cashed in some of their shares). The underwriters acquired a total of 69 million Goldman Sachs shares for $50.75 each and sold them to the public at an offering price of $53.[6] The underwriters' spread was therefore $53 − $50.75 = $2.25. The firm and its shareholders also paid a total of $9.2 million in legal

---

[4] The highest bidder in an auction is the participant who places the highest value on the auctioned object. Therefore, it is likely that the winning bidder has an overly optimistic assessment of true value. Winning the auction suggests that you have overpaid for the object—this is the winner's curse. In the case of IPOs, your ability to "win" an allotment of shares may signal that the stock is overpriced.

[5] These figures do not capture all administrative costs. For example, they do not include management time spent on the issue.

[6] No prizes for guessing which investment bank acted as lead underwriter.

FIGURE 14-1 Total direct costs as a percentage of gross proceeds. The total direct costs for initial public offerings (IPOs), seasoned equity offerings (SEOs), convertible bonds, and straight bonds are composed of underwriter spreads and other direct expenses.

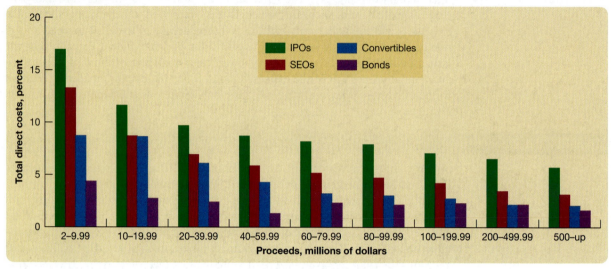

Source: Immoo Lee, Scott Lochhead, Jay Ritter, and Quanshui Zhao, "The Costs of Raising Capital," *Journal of Financial Research* 19 (Spring 1996), pp. 59–74. Copyright © 1996. Reprinted by permission.

fees and other costs. By the end of the first day's trading Goldman's stock price had risen to $70.

Here are the direct costs of the Goldman Sachs issue:

Direct Expenses	
Underwriting spread	69 million × $2.25 = $155.25 million
Other expenses	9.2
Total direct expenses	$164.45 million

The total amount of money raised by the issue was 69 million × $53 = $3,657 million. Of this sum 4.5 percent was absorbed by direct expenses (that is, 164.45/3,657 = .045).

In addition to these direct costs, there was underpricing. The market valued each share of Goldman Sachs at $70, so the cost of underpricing was 69 million × ($70 − $53) = $1,173 million, resulting in total costs of $164.45 + $1,173 = $1,337.45 million. Therefore, while the total market value of the issued shares was 69 million × $70 = $4,830 million, direct costs and the costs of underpricing absorbed nearly 28 percent of the market value of the shares. ◀

Self-Test 14.3   Suppose that the underwriters acquired Goldman Sachs shares for $60 and sold them to the public at an offering price of $64. If all other features of the offer were unchanged (and investors still valued the stock at $70 a share), what would have been the direct costs of the issue and the costs of underpricing? What would have been the total costs as a proportion of the market value of the shares?

14.3 The Underwriters

We have described underwriters as playing a triple role—providing advice, buying a new issue from the company, and reselling it to investors. Underwriters don't just help the company to make its initial public offering; they are called in whenever a company wishes to raise cash by selling securities to the public.

TABLE 14-1 Top 10 underwriters of global debt and equity issues (figures in billions)

Underwriter	Value of Issues	Market Share
Citigroup	$ 534	9.4%
Morgan Stanley	414	7.3
J. P. Morgan	386	6.8
Lehman Brothers	370	6.5
Credit Suisse First Boston (CSFB)	362	6.4
Deutsche Bank	335	5.9
UBS	300	5.3
Goldman Sachs	286	5.0
Banc of America Securities	204	3.6
Totals	$3,564	62.6%

Source: **thomson.com.**

Successful underwriting requires considerable experience and financial muscle. If a large issue fails to sell, the underwriters may be left with a loss of several hundred million dollars and some very red faces. Underwriting in the United States is therefore dominated by the major investment banking firms, which specialize in underwriting new issues, dealing in securities, and arranging mergers. Large commercial banks, including a number of foreign banks, are also heavily involved in underwriting. Table 14–1 lists some of the largest firms, ranked by total volume of issues in 2004. Citigroup, the winner, raised a total of $534 billion. Of course, only a small proportion of this sum involved companies that were coming to the market for the first time.

Underwriting is not always fun. On October 15, 1987, the British government finalized arrangements to sell its holding of British Petroleum (BP) shares at £3.30 a share. This huge issue involving more than $12 billion was underwritten by an international group of underwriters and simultaneously marketed in a number of countries. Four days after the underwriting arrangement was finalized, the October stock market crash occurred and stock prices nose-dived. The underwriters appealed to the British government to cancel the issue, but the government hardened its heart and pointed out that the underwriters knew the risks when they agreed to handle the sale.[7] By the closing date of the offer, the price of BP stock had fallen to £2.96 and the underwriters had lost more than $1 billion.

Companies get to make only one IPO, but underwriters are in the business all the time. Wise underwriters, therefore, realize that their reputation is on the line and will not handle an issue unless they believe the facts have been presented fairly to investors. If a new issue goes wrong and the stock price crashes, the underwriters can find themselves very unpopular with their clients. For example, in 1999 the software company VA Linux went public at $30 a share. The next day trading opened at $299 a share, but then the price began to sag. Within 2 years it had fallen below $2. Disgruntled VA Linux investors sued the underwriters for overhyping the issue. VA Linux investors were not the only ones to feel aggrieved. As the nearby box explains, investment banks soon found themselves embroiled in a major scandal as evidence emerged that they had deliberately oversold many of the issues that they underwrote during the dot-com boom years. The underwriter's seal of approval for a new issue no longer seemed as valuable as it once had.

---

[7] The government's only concession was to put a floor on the underwriters' losses by giving them the option to resell their stock to the government at £2.80 a share. The BP offering is described and analyzed in C. Muscarella and M. Vetsuypens, "The British Petroleum Stock Offering: An Application of Option Pricing," *Journal of Applied Corporate Finance* 1 (1989), pp. 74–80.

FINANCE IN PRACTICE

How Scandal Hit the Investment Banking Industry

For investment banks, 1999 looked like a wonderful year. Not only did they underwrite a near-record number of IPOs, but the stocks that they sold leaped by an average of 71 percent on their first day of trading, earning the underwriters some very grateful clients. Just 3 years later the same investment banks were in disgrace. Probing by the New York State attorney general, Eliot Spitzer, uncovered a chronicle of unethical and shameful behavior during the boom years.

As the dot-com stock market boom developed, investment banking analysts had begun to take on the additional role of promoters of the shares they analyzed, in the process becoming celebrities with salaries to match. The early run-up in the stock price of dot-com IPOs therefore owed much to hype by the underwriters' analysts, who strongly promoted stocks that they sometimes privately thought were overpriced. One superstar Internet analyst was revealed in internal e-mails to have believed that stocks he was peddling to investors were "junk" and "a piece of crap." In many cases the stocks were indeed junk, and the underwriters who had puffed the IPOs soon found themselves sued by disgruntled investors who had bought at the inflated prices.

The underwriters' troubles deepened further when it was disclosed that in a number of cases they had allocated stock in hot new issues to the personal brokerage accounts of the CEOs of major corporate clients. This stock could then be sold, or "spun," for quick profits. Five senior executives of leading telecom companies were disclosed to have received a total of $28 million in profits from their allocation of stocks in IPOs underwritten by one bank. Over the same period the bank received over $100 million of business from these five companies. Eliot Spitzer argued that such lucrative perks were really attempts by the banks to buy future business and that the profits therefore belonged to the companies' shareholders rather than the executives. Soon top executives of several other companies were facing demands from disgruntled shareholders that they return to their companies the profits they had pocketed from hot initial public offerings.

These scandals that engulfed the investment banking industry resulted in a $1.4 billion payout by the banks and an agreement to separate investment banking and research departments, hire independent consultants, and select independent research providers. But the revelations also raised troubling questions about ethical standards and the pressures that can lead employees to unscrupulous behavior.

14.4 General Cash Offers by Public Companies

seasoned offering
Sale of securities by a firm that is already publicly traded.

rights issue
Issue of securities offered only to current stockholders.

After the initial public offering a successful firm will continue to grow, and from time to time it will need to raise more money by issuing stock or bonds. An issue of additional stock by a company whose stock already is publicly traded is called a **seasoned offering.** Any issue of securities needs to be formally approved by the firm's board of directors. If a stock issue requires an increase in the company's authorized capital, it also needs the consent of the stockholders.

Public companies can issue securities either by making a general cash offer to investors at large or by making a **rights issue,** which is limited to existing shareholders. In the latter case, the company offers the shareholders the opportunity, or *right,* to buy more shares at an "attractive" price. For example, if the current stock price is $100, the company might offer investors an additional share at $50 for each share they hold. Suppose that before the issue an investor has one share worth $100 and $50 in the bank. If the investor takes up the offer of a new share, that $50 of cash is transferred from the investor's bank account to the company's. The investor now has two shares that are a claim on the original assets worth $100 and on the $50 cash that the company has raised. So the two shares are worth a total of $150, or $75 each.

EXAMPLE 14.4 ▶ Rights Issues

Easy Writer Word Processing Company has 1 million shares outstanding, selling at $20 a share. To finance the development of a new software package, it plans a rights issue, allowing 1 new share to be purchased for each 10 shares currently held. The purchase price will be $10 a share. How many shares will be issued? How much money will be raised? What will be the stock price after the rights issue?

The firm will issue 1 new share for every 10 old ones, or 100,000 shares. So shares outstanding will rise to 1.1 million. The firm will raise $10 × 100,000 = $1 million. Therefore, the total value of the firm will increase from $20 million to $21 million, and the stock price will fall to $21 million/1.1 million shares = $19.09 per share. ◀

In some countries the rights issue is the most common or only method for issuing stock, but in the United States rights issues are now very rare. We therefore will concentrate on the mechanics of the general cash offer.

General Cash Offers and Shelf Registration

general cash offer

Sale of securities open to all investors by an already-public company.

When a public company makes a **general cash offer** of debt or equity, it essentially follows the same procedure used when it first went public. This means that it must first register the issue with the SEC and draw up a prospectus.[8] Before settling on the issue price, the underwriters will usually contact potential investors and build up a book of likely orders. The company will then sell the issue to the underwriters, and they in turn will offer the securities to the public.

Companies do not need to prepare a separate registration statement every time they issue new securities. Instead, they are allowed to file a single registration statement covering financing plans for up to 2 years into the future. The actual issues can then be sold to the public with scant additional paperwork, whenever the firm needs cash or thinks it can issue securities at an attractive price. This is called **shelf registration**—the registration is put "on the shelf," to be taken down, dusted off, and used as needed.

shelf registration

A procedure that allows firms to file one registration statement for several issues of the same security.

Think of how you might use shelf registration when you are a financial manager. Suppose that your company is likely to need up to $200 million of new long-term debt over the next year or so. It can file a registration statement for that amount. It now has approval to issue up to $200 million of debt, but it isn't obliged to issue any. Nor is it required to work through any *particular* underwriters—the registration statement may name the underwriters the firm thinks it may work with, but others can be substituted later.

Now you can sit back and issue debt as needed, in bits and pieces if you like. Suppose Merrill Lynch comes across an insurance company with $10 million ready to invest in corporate bonds, priced to yield, say, 7.3 percent. If you think that's a good deal, you say OK and the deal is done, subject to only a little additional paperwork. Merrill Lynch then resells the bonds to the insurance company, hoping for a higher price than it paid for them.

Here is another possible deal. Suppose you think you see a window of opportunity in which interest rates are "temporarily low." You invite bids for $100 million of bonds. Some bids may come from large investment bankers acting alone, others from ad hoc syndicates. But that's not your problem; if the price is right, you just take the best deal offered.

Thus shelf registration offers several advantages:

1. Securities can be issued in dribs and drabs without incurring excessive costs.
2. Securities can be issued on short notice.
3. Security issues can be timed to take advantage of "market conditions" (although any financial manager who can reliably identify favorable market conditions could make a lot more money by quitting and becoming a bond or stock trader instead).
4. The issuing firm can make sure that underwriters compete for its business.

Not all companies eligible for shelf registration actually use it for all their public issues. Sometimes they believe they can get a better deal by making one large issue through traditional channels, especially when the security to be issued has some unusual feature or when the firm believes it needs the investment banker's counsel or stamp of approval on the issue. Thus shelf registration is less often used for issues of common stock than for garden-variety corporate bonds.

---

[8] The procedure is similar when a company makes an international issue of bonds or equity, but as long as these issues are not sold publicly in the United States, they do not need to be registered with the SEC.

Costs of the General Cash Offer

Whenever a firm makes a cash offer, it incurs substantial administrative costs. Also, the firm needs to compensate the underwriters by selling them securities below the price that they expect to receive from investors. Look back at Figure 14–1, which shows the average underwriting spread and administrative costs for several types of security issues in the United States.

The figure clearly shows that the costs are proportionately smaller for large issues. Costs may absorb 13 percent of a $5 million seasoned equity issue but less than 4 percent of a $500 million issue.

Figure 14–1 also shows that issue costs are higher for equity than for debt securities. Issue costs are higher for equity than for debt because administrative costs are somewhat higher and also because underwriting stock is riskier than underwriting bonds. The underwriters demand additional compensation for the greater risk they take in buying and reselling equity.

Self-Test 14.4   Use Figure 14–1 to compare the costs of 10 issues of $15 million of stock in a seasoned offering versus 1 issue of $150 million.

Market Reaction to Stock Issues

Because stock issues usually throw a sizable number of new shares onto the market, it is widely believed that they must temporarily depress the stock price. If the proposed issue is very large, this price pressure may, it is thought, be so severe as to make it almost impossible to raise money.

This belief in price pressure implies that a new issue depresses the stock price temporarily below its true value. However, that view doesn't appear to fit very well with the notion of market efficiency. If the stock price falls solely because of increased supply, then that stock would offer a higher return than comparable stocks and investors would be attracted to it as ants to a picnic.

Economists who have studied new issues of common stock have generally found that the announcement of the issue does result in a decline in the stock price. For industrial issues in the United States this decline amounts to about 3 percent.[9] While this may not sound overwhelming, such a price drop can be a large fraction of the money raised. Suppose that a company with a market value of equity of $5 billion announces its intention to issue $500 million of additional equity and thereby causes the stock price to drop by 3 percent. The loss in value is .03 × $5 billion, or $150 million. That's 30 percent of the amount of money raised (.30 × $500 million = $150 million).

What's going on here? Is the price of the stock simply depressed by the prospect of the additional supply? Possibly, but here is an alternative explanation.

Suppose managers (who have better information about the firm than outside investors) know that their stock is undervalued. If the company sells new stock at this low price, it will give the new shareholders a good deal at the expense of the old shareholders. In these circumstances managers might be prepared to forgo the new investment rather than sell shares at too low a price.

If managers know that the stock is *overvalued,* the position is reversed. If the company sells new shares at the high price, it will help its existing shareholders at the expense of the new ones. Managers might be prepared to issue stock even if the new cash were just put in the bank.

---

[9] See, for example, P. Asquith and D. W. Mullins, "Equity Issues and Offering Dilution," *Journal of Financial Economics* 15 (January–February 1986), pp. 61–90; R. W. Masulis and A. N. Korwar, "Seasoned Equity Offerings: An Empirical Investigation," *Journal of Financial Economics* 15 (January–February 1986), pp. 91–118; and W. H. Mikkelson and M. M. Partch, "Valuation Effects of Security Offerings and the Issuance Process," *Journal of Financial Economics* 15 (January–February 1986), pp. 31–60.

Of course investors are not stupid. They can predict that managers are more likely to issue stock when they think it is overvalued, and therefore they mark the price of the stock down accordingly. The tendency for stock prices to decline at the time of an issue may have nothing to do with increased supply. Instead, the stock issue may simply be a *signal* that well-informed managers believe the market has overpriced the stock.[10]

14.5 The Private Placement

private placement
Sale of securities to a limited number of investors without a public offering.

Whenever a company makes a public offering, it must register the issue with the SEC. It could avoid this costly process by selling the issue privately. There are no hard-and-fast definitions of a **private placement,** but the SEC has insisted that the security should be sold to no more than a dozen or so knowledgeable investors.

One disadvantage of a private placement is that the investor cannot easily resell the security. This is less important to institutions such as life insurance companies, which invest huge sums of money in corporate debt for the long haul. In 1990 the SEC relaxed its restrictions on who could buy unregistered issues. Under the new rule, Rule 144a, large financial institutions can trade unregistered securities among themselves.

As you would expect, it costs less to arrange a private placement than to make a public issue. That might not be so important for the very large issues where costs are less significant, but it is a particular advantage for companies making smaller issues.

Another advantage of the private placement is that the debt contract can be custom-tailored for firms with special problems or opportunities. Also, if the firm wishes later to change the terms of the debt, it is much simpler to do this with a private placement where only a few investors are involved.

Therefore, it is not surprising that private placements occupy a particular niche in the corporate debt market, namely, loans to small and medium-sized firms. These are the firms that face the highest costs in public issues, that require the most detailed investigation, and that may require specialized, flexible loan arrangements.

We do not mean that large, safe, and conventional firms should rule out private placements. Enormous amounts of capital are sometimes raised by this method. For example, in 2005, Berkshire Hathaway, the investment company controlled by Warren Buffett, borrowed $3.75 billion in a private placement. Nevertheless, the advantages of private placement—avoiding registration costs and establishing a direct relationship with the lender—are generally more important to smaller firms.

Of course these advantages are not free. Lenders in private placements have to be compensated for the risks they face and for the costs of research and negotiation. They also have to be compensated for holding an asset that is not easily resold. All these factors are rolled into the interest rate paid by the firm. It is difficult to generalize about the differences in interest rates between private placements and public issues, but a typical yield differential is on the order of half a percentage point.

---

[10] This explanation was developed in S. C. Myers and N. S. Majluf, "Corporate Financing and Investment Decisions When Firms Have Information That Investors Do Not Have," *Journal of Financial Economics* 13 (1984), pp. 187–222.

SUMMARY

How do venture capital firms design successful deals?

Infant companies raise **venture capital** to carry them through to the point at which they can make their first public issue of stock. Venture capital firms try to structure the financing to avoid conflicts of interest. If both the entrepreneur and the venture capital investors have an important equity stake in the company, they are likely to pull in the same direction. The entrepreneur's willingness to take that stake also *signals* management's confidence in the company's future. In addition, most venture capital is provided in stages that keep the firm on a short leash and force it to prove at each stage that it deserves the additional funds.

How do firms make initial public offerings, and what are the costs of such offerings?

The **initial public offering** is the first sale of shares in a general offering to investors. The sale of the securities is usually managed by an underwriting firm that buys the shares from the company and resells them to the public. The **underwriter** helps to prepare a **prospectus,** which describes the company and its prospects. The costs of an IPO include direct costs, such as legal and administrative fees, as well as the **underwriting spread**—the difference between the price the underwriter pays to acquire the shares from the firm and the price the public pays the underwriter for those shares. Another major implicit cost is the **underpricing** of the issue—that is, shares are typically sold to the public somewhat below the true value of the security. This discount is reflected in abnormally high average returns to new issues on the first day of trading.

What are some of the significant issues that arise when established firms make a general cash offer or a private placement of securities?

There are always economies of scale in issuing securities. It is cheaper to go to the market once for $100 million than to make two trips for $50 million each. Consequently, firms "bunch" security issues. This may mean relying on short-term financing until a large issue is justified. Or it may mean issuing more than is needed at the moment to avoid another issue later.

A **seasoned offering** may depress the stock price. The extent of this price decline varies, but for issues of common stocks by industrial firms the fall in the value of the existing stock may amount to a significant proportion of the money raised. The likely explanation for this pressure is the information the market reads into the company's decision to issue stock.

Shelf registration often makes sense for debt issues by blue-chip firms. Shelf registration reduces the time taken to arrange a new issue, it increases flexibility, and it may cut underwriting costs. It seems best suited for debt issues by large firms that are happy to switch between investment banks. It seems least suited for issues of unusually risky securities or for issues by small companies that most need a close relationship with an investment bank.

Private placements are well-suited for small, risky, or unusual firms. The special advantages of private placement stem from avoiding registration expenses and a more direct relationship with the lender. These are not worth as much to blue-chip borrowers.

What is the role of the underwriter in an issue of securities?

Underwriters manage the sale of the securities and advise on the price at which the issue is sold. They then buy the securities from the issuing company, and resell them to the public. The difference between the price at which the underwriter buys the securities and the price at which they are resold is the underwriter's spread. Underwriting firms have expertise in such sales because they are in the business all the time, whereas the company raises capital only occasionally.

QUIZ ⊞™

1. **Underwriting.**
    a. Is a rights issue more likely to be used for an initial public offering or for subsequent issues of stock?
    b. Is a private placement more likely to be used for issues of seasoned stock or seasoned bonds by an industrial company?
    c. Is shelf registration more likely to be used for issues of unseasoned stocks or bonds by a large industrial company?

2. **Underwriting.** Each of the following terms is associated with one of the events beneath. Can you match them up?

   a. Shelf registration
   b. Firm commitment
   c. Rights issue
   A. The underwriter agrees to buy the issue from the company at a fixed price.
   B. The company offers to sell stock to existing stockholders.
   C. Several issues of the same security may be sold under the same registration.

3. **Underwriting Costs.** State for each of the following pairs of issues which you would expect to involve the lower proportionate underwriting and administrative costs, other things equal:

   a. A large issue/a small issue.
   b. A bond issue/a common stock issue.
   c. A small private placement of bonds/a small general cash offer of bonds.

4. **IPO Costs.** Why are the issue costs for debt issues generally less than those for equity issues?

5. **Venture Capital.** Why do venture capital companies prefer to advance money in stages?

6. **IPOs.** Your broker calls and says that you can get 500 shares of an imminent IPO at the offering price. Should you buy? Are you worried about the fact that your broker called *you*?

PRACTICE PROBLEMS

7. **IPO Underpricing.** Having heard about IPO underpricing, I put in an order to my broker for 1,000 shares of every IPO he can get for me. After 3 months, my investment record is as follows:

IPO	Shares Allocated to Me	Price per Share	Initial Return
A	500	$10	7%
B	200	20	12
C	1,000	8	−2
D	0	12	23

   a. What is the average underpricing of this sample of IPOs?
   b. What is the average initial return on my "portfolio" of shares purchased from the four IPOs I bid on? Calculate the average initial return, weighting by the amount of money invested in each issue.
   c. Why have I performed so poorly relative to the average initial return on the full sample of IPOs? What lessons do you draw from my experience?

8. **IPO Costs.** Moonscape has just completed an initial public offering. The firm sold 3 million shares at an offer price of $8 per share. The underwriting spread was $.50 a share. The price of the stock closed at $12 per share at the end of the first day of trading. The firm incurred $100,000 in legal, administrative, and other costs. What were flotation costs as a fraction of funds raised? Were flotation costs for Moonscape higher or lower than is typical for IPOs of this size (see Figure 14–1)?

9. **IPO Costs.** Look at the illustrative new issue prospectus in the appendix.

   a. Is this issue a primary offering, a secondary offering, or both?
   b. What are the direct costs of the issue as a percentage of the total proceeds? Are these more than the average for an issue of this size?
   c. Suppose that on the first day of trading the price of Hotch Pot stock is $15 a share. What are the *total* costs of the issue as a percentage of the market price?

d. After paying her share of the expenses, how much will the firm's president, Emma Lucullus, receive from the sale? What will be the value of the shares that she retains in the company?

10. **Flotation Costs.** "For small issues of common stock, the costs of flotation amount to about 15 percent of the proceeds. This means that the opportunity cost of external equity capital is about 15 percentage points higher than that of retained earnings." Does this follow?

Please visit us at www.mhhe.com/bmm5e or refer to your Student CD

11. **Flotation Costs.** When Microsoft went public, the company sold 2 million new shares (the primary issue). In addition, existing shareholders sold .8 million shares (the secondary issue) and kept 21.1 million shares. The new shares were offered to the public at $21, and the underwriters received a spread of $1.31 a share. At the end of the first day's trading the market price was $35 a share.

a. How much money did the company receive before paying its portion of the direct costs?
b. How much did the existing shareholders receive from the sale before paying their portion of the direct costs?
c. If the issue had been sold to the underwriters for $30 a share, how many shares would the company have needed to sell to raise the same amount of cash?
d. How much better off would the existing shareholders have been?

12. **Flotation Costs.** The market value of the marketing research firm Fax Facts is $600 million. The firm issues an additional $100 million of stock, but as a result the stock price falls by 2 percent. What is the cost of the price drop to existing shareholders as a fraction of the funds raised?

13. **Flotation Costs.** Young Corporation stock currently sells for $30 per share. There are 1 million shares currently outstanding. The company announces plans to raise $3 million by offering shares to the public at a price of $30 per share.

a. If the underwriting spread is 6 percent, how many shares will the company need to issue in order to be left with net proceeds of $3 million?
b. If other administrative costs are $60,000, what is the dollar value of the total direct costs of the issue?
c. If the share price falls by 3 percent at the announcement of the plans to proceed with a seasoned offering, what is the dollar cost of the announcement effect?

14. **Private Placements.** You need to choose between the following types of issues:

- *A public issue of $10 million face value of 10-year debt.* The interest rate on the debt would be 8.5 percent, and the debt would be issued at face value. The underwriting spread would be 1.5 percent, and other expenses would be $80,000.
- *A private placement of $10 million face value of 10-year debt.* The interest rate on the private placement would be 9 percent, but the total issuing expenses would be only $30,000.

a. What is the difference in the proceeds to the company net of expenses?
b. Other things equal, which is the better deal?
c. What other factors beyond the interest rate and issue costs would you wish to consider before deciding between the two offers?

15. **Rights.** In 2005 Pandora, Inc., makes a rights issue at a subscription price of $5 a share. One new share can be purchased for every four shares held. Before the issue there were 10 million shares outstanding and the share price was $6.

a. What is the total amount of new money raised?
b. What is the expected stock price after the rights are issued?

16. **Rights.** Problem 15 contains details of a rights offering by Pandora. Suppose that the company had decided to issue the new stock at $4 instead of $5 a share. How many new shares would it have needed to raise the same sum of money? Recalculate the answers to Problem 15. Show that Pandora's shareholders are just as well off if it issues the shares at $4 a share rather than the $5 assumed in Problem 15.

Please visit us at www.mhhe.com/bmm5e or refer to your Student CD

17. **Rights.** Consolidated Jewels needs to raise $2 million to pay for its Diamonds in the Rough campaign. It will raise the funds by offering 200,000 rights, each of which entitles the owner to buy one new share. The company currently has outstanding 1 million shares priced at $20 each.

    a. What must be the subscription price on the rights the company plans to offer?

    b. What will be the share price after the rights issue?

    c. What is the value of a right to buy one share?

    d. How many rights would be issued to an investor who currently owns 1,000 shares?

    e. Show that the investor who currently holds 1,000 shares is unaffected by the rights issue. Specifically, show that the value of the rights plus the value of the 1,000 shares after the rights issue equals the value of the 1,000 shares before the rights issue.

18. **Rights.** Associated Breweries is planning to market unleaded beer. To finance the venture, it proposes to make a rights issue with a subscription price of $10. One new share can be purchased for each two shares held. The company currently has outstanding 100,000 shares priced at $40 a share. Assuming that the new money is invested to earn a fair return, give values for the

    a. number of new shares.

    b. amount of new investment.

    c. total value of company after issue.

    d. total number of shares after issue.

    e. share price after the issue.

CHALLENGE PROBLEM

Please visit us at www.mhhe.com/bmm5e or refer to your Student CD

19. **Venture Capital.** Here is a difficult question. Pickwick Electronics is a new high-tech company financed entirely by 1 million ordinary shares, all of which are owned by George Pickwick. The firm needs to raise $1 million now for stage 1 and, assuming all goes well, a further $1 million at the end of 5 years for stage 2.

    First Cookham Venture Partners is considering two possible financing schemes:

- Buying 2 million shares now at their current valuation of $1.
- Buying 1 million shares at the current valuation and investing a further $1 million at the end of 5 years at whatever the shares are worth.

The outlook for Pickwick is uncertain, but as long as the company can secure the additional finance for stage 2, it will be worth either $2 million or $12 million after completing stage 2. (The company will be valueless if it cannot raise the funds for stage 2.) Show the possible payoffs for Mr. Pickwick and First Cookham, and explain why one scheme might be preferred. Assume an interest rate of zero.

SOLUTIONS TO SELF-TEST QUESTIONS

14.1 Unless the firm can secure second-stage financing, it is unlikely to succeed. If the entrepreneur is going to reap any reward on his own investment, he needs to put in enough effort to get further financing. By accepting only part of the necessary venture capital, management increases its own risk and reduces that of the venture capitalist. This decision would be costly and foolish if management lacked confidence that the project would be successful enough to get past the first stage. A credible signal by management is one that only managers who are truly confident can afford to provide. However, words are cheap and there is little to be lost by saying that you are confident (although if you are proved wrong, you may find it difficult to raise money a second time).

14.2 If an investor can distinguish between overpriced and underpriced issues, she will bid only on the underpriced ones. In this case she will purchase only issues that provide a 10 percent gain. However, the ability to distinguish these issues requires considerable insight and research. The return to the informed IPO participant may be viewed as a return on the resources expended to become informed.

14.3   Direct expenses:

Underwriting spread = 69 million × $4	$ 276.0 million
Other expenses	9.2
Total direct expenses	$ 285.2 million
Underpricing = 69 million × ($70 − $64)	414.0
Total expenses	$ 699.2 million
Market value of issue = 69 million × $70	$ 4,830.0 million

Expenses as proportion of market value = 699.2/4,830 = .145 = 14.5%.

14.4   Ten issues of $15 million each will cost about 9 percent of proceeds, or .09 × $150 million = $13.5 million. One issue of $150 million will cost only about 4 percent of $150 million, or $6 million.

MINICASE

Mutt.Com was founded in 2003 by two graduates of the University of Wisconsin with help from Georgina Sloberg, who had built up an enviable reputation for backing new start-up businesses. Mutt.Com's user-friendly system was designed to find buyers for unwanted pets. Within 3 years the company was generating revenues of $3.4 million a year and, despite racking up sizable losses, was regarded by investors as one of the hottest new e-commerce businesses. The news that the company was preparing to go public therefore generated considerable excitement.

The company's entire equity capital of 1.5 million shares was owned by the two founders and Ms. Sloberg. The initial public offering involved the sale of 500,000 shares by the three existing shareholders, together with the sale of a further 750,000 shares by the company in order to provide funds for expansion.

The company estimated that the issue would involve legal fees, auditing, printing, and other expenses of $1.3 million, which would be shared proportionately between the selling shareholders and the company. In addition, the company agreed to pay the underwriters a spread of $1.25 per share (this cost also would be shared).

The roadshow had confirmed the high level of interest in the issue, and indications from investors suggested that the entire issue could be sold at a price of $24 a share. The underwriters, however, cautioned about being too greedy on price. They pointed out that indications from investors were not the same as firm orders. Also, they argued, it was much more important to have a successful issue than to have a group of disgruntled shareholders. They therefore suggested an issue price of $18 a share.

That evening Mutt.Com's financial manager decided to run through some calculations. First, she worked out the net receipts to the company and the existing shareholders assuming that the stock was sold for $18 a share. Next, she looked at the various costs of the IPO and tried to judge how they stacked up against the typical costs for similar IPOs. That brought her up against the question of underpricing. When she had raised the matter with the underwriters that morning, they had dismissed the notion that the initial day's return on an IPO should be considered part of the issue costs. One of the members of the underwriting team had asked: "The underwriters want to see a high return and a high stock price. Would Mutt.Com prefer a low stock price? Would that make the issue less costly?" Mutt.Com's financial manager was not convinced but felt that she should have a good answer. She wondered whether underpricing was only a problem because the existing shareholders were selling part of their holdings. Perhaps the issue price would not matter if they had not planned to sell.

APPENDIX   Hotch Pot's New-Issue Prospectus[11]

Prospectus

800,000 Shares
Hotch Pot, Inc.
Common Stock ($.01 par value)

Of the 800,000 shares of Common Stock offered hereby, 500,000 shares are being sold by the Company and 300,000 shares are being sold by the Selling Stockholders. See "Principal and Selling Stockholders." The Company will not receive any of the proceeds from the sale of shares by the Selling Stockholders.

Before this offering there has been no public market for the Common Stock. **These securities involve a high degree of risk. See "Certain Factors."**

THESE SECURITIES HAVE NOT BEEN APPROVED OR DISAPPROVED BY THE SECURITIES AND EXCHANGE COMMISSION NOR HAS THE COMMISSION PASSED ON THE ACCURACY OR ADEQUACY OF THIS PROSPECTUS. ANY REPRESENTATION TO THE CONTRARY IS A CRIMINAL OFFENSE.

	Price to Public	Underwriting Discount	Proceeds to Company*	Proceeds to Selling Shareholders
Per share	$12.00	$1.30	$10.70	$10.70
Total	$9,600,000	$1,040,000	$5,350,000	$3,210,000

* Before deducting expenses payable by the Company estimated at $400,000, of which $250,000 will be paid by the Company and $150,000 by the Selling Stockholders.

The Common Stock is offered, subject to prior sale, when, as, and if delivered to and accepted by the Underwriters and subject to approval of certain legal matters by their counsel and by counsel for the Company and the Selling Shareholders. The Underwriters reserve the right to withdraw, cancel, or modify such offer and reject orders in whole or in part.

Silverman Pinch Inc.   April 1, 2006

No person has been authorized to give any information or to make any representations, other than as contained therein, in connection with the offer contained in this Prospectus, and, if given or made, such information or representations must not be relied upon. This Prospectus does not constitute an offer of any securities other than the registered securities to which it relates or an offer to any person in any jurisdiction where such an offer would be unlawful. The delivery of this Prospectus at any time does not imply that information herein is correct as of any time subsequent to its date.

IN CONNECTION WITH THIS OFFERING, THE UNDERWRITER MAY OVERALLOT OR EFFECT TRANSACTIONS WHICH STABILIZE OR MAINTAIN THE MARKET PRICE OF THE COMMON STOCK OF THE COMPANY AT A LEVEL ABOVE THAT WHICH MIGHT OTHERWISE PREVAIL IN THE OPEN MARKET. SUCH STABILIZING, IF COMMENCED, MAY BE DISCONTINUED AT ANY TIME.

Prospectus Summary

The following summary information is qualified in its entirety by the detailed information and financial statements appearing elsewhere in this Prospectus.

---

[11] Real prospectuses would be much longer than our simple example. You can get a better impression of the contents of a prospectus by looking at some real ones. These are available on the SEC's site **www.sec.gov/edgar/searchedgar/webusers.htm** and are shown as Form S-1. For example, take a look at the prospectus dated 11/14/01 for the IPO of Bam!Entertainment, the publisher of games software. Notice the mixture of useful information and redundant qualification.

The Company: Hotch Pot, Inc., operates a chain of 140 fast-food outlets in the United States offering unusual combinations of dishes.

The Offering: Common Stock offered by the Company 500,000 shares;
   Common Stock offered by the Selling Stockholders 300,000 shares;
   Common Stock to be outstanding after this offering 3,500,000 shares.

Use of Proceeds: For the construction of new restaurants and to provide working capital.

The Company

Hotch Pot, Inc., operates a chain of 140 fast-food outlets in Illinois, Pennsylvania, and Ohio. These restaurants specialize in offering an unusual combination of foreign dishes.

The Company was organized in Delaware in 1996.

Use of Proceeds

The Company intends to use the net proceeds from the sale of 500,000 shares of Common Stock offered hereby, estimated at approximately $5 million, to open new outlets in midwest states and to provide additional working capital. It has no immediate plans to use any of the net proceeds of the offering for any other specific investment.

Dividend Policy

The Company has not paid cash dividends on its Common Stock and does not anticipate that dividends will be paid on the Common Stock in the foreseeable future.

Certain Factors

Investment in the Common Stock involves a high degree of risk. The following factors should be carefully considered in evaluating the Company:

Substantial Capital Needs The Company will require additional financing to continue its expansion policy. The Company believes that its relations with its lenders are good, but there can be no assurance that additional financing will be available in the future.

Competition The Company is in competition with a number of restaurant chains supplying fast food. Many of these companies are substantially larger and better capitalized than the Company.

Capitalization

The following table sets forth the capitalization of the Company as of December 31, 2005, and as adjusted to reflect the sale of 500,000 shares of Common Stock by the Company.

	Actual	As Adjusted
		(in thousands)
Long-term debt	$ —	$ —
Stockholders' equity	30	35
Common stock—$.01 par value, 3,000,000 shares outstanding, 3,500,000 shares outstanding, as adjusted		
Paid-in capital	1,970	7,315
Retained earnings	3,200	3,200
Total stockholders' equity	5,200	10,550
Total capitalization	$5,200	$10,550

Selected Financial Data

[The Prospectus typically includes a summary income statement and balance sheet.]

Management's Analysis of Results of Operations and Financial Condition

Revenue growth for the year ended December 31, 2005, resulted from the opening of ten new restaurants in the Company's existing geographic area and from sales of a new range of desserts, notably crepe suzette with custard. Sales per customer increased by 20% and this contributed to the improvement in margins.

During the year the Company borrowed $600,000 from its banks at an interest rate of 2% above the prime rate.

Business

Hotch Pot, Inc., operates a chain of 140 fast-food outlets in Illinois, Pennsylvania, and Ohio. These restaurants specialize in offering an unusual combination of foreign dishes. 50% of company's revenues derived from sales of two dishes, sushi and sauerkraut and curry bolognese. All dishes are prepared in three regional centers and then frozen and distributed to the individual restaurants.

Management

The following table sets forth information regarding the Company's directors, executive officers, and key employees:

Name	Age	Position
Emma Lucullus	28	President, Chief Executive Officer, & Director
Ed Lucullus	33	Treasurer & Director

Emma Lucullus   Emma Lucullus established the Company in 1996 and has been its Chief Executive Officer since that date.

Ed Lucullus   Ed Lucullus has been employed by the Company since 1996.

Executive Compensation

The following table sets forth the cash compensation paid for services rendered for the year 2005 by the executive officers:

Name	Capacity	Cash Compensation
Emma Lucullus	President and Chief Executive Officer	$130,000
Ed Lucullus	Treasurer	$ 95,000

Certain Transactions

At various times between 1996 and 2005 First Cookham Venture Partners invested a total of $1.5 million in the Company. In connection with this investment, First Cookham Venture Partners was granted certain rights to registration under the Securities Act of 1933, including the right to have their shares of Common Stock registered at the Company's expense with the Securities and Exchange Commission.

Principal and Selling Stockholders

The following table sets forth certain information regarding the beneficial ownership of the Company's voting Common Stock as of the date of this prospectus by (i) each person known by the Company to be the beneficial owner of more than 5% of its voting Common Stock, and (ii) each director of the Company who beneficially owns voting Common Stock. Unless otherwise indicated, each owner has sole voting and dispositive power over his shares.

Name of Beneficial Owner	Shares Beneficially Owned prior to Offering		Shares to Be Sold	Shares Beneficially Owned after Offering	
	Number	Percent		Number	Percent
Emma Lucullus	400,000	13.3	25,000	375,000	12.9
Ed Lucullus	400,000	13.3	25,000	375,000	12.9
First Cookham Venture Partners	1,700,000	66.7	250,000	1,450,000	50.0
Hermione Kraft	200,000	6.7	—	200,000	6.9

Description of Capital Stock

The Company's authorized capital stock consists of 10,000,000 shares of voting Common Stock.

As of the date of this Prospectus, there are 4 holders of record of the Common Stock.

Under the terms of one of the Company's loan agreements, the Company may not pay cash dividends on Common Stock except from net profits without the written consent of the lender.

Underwriting

Subject to the terms and conditions set forth in the Underwriting Agreement, the Underwriter, Silverman Pinch Inc., has agreed to purchase from the Company and the Selling Stockholders 800,000 shares of Common Stock.

There is no public market for the Common Stock. The price to the public for the Common Stock was determined by negotiation between the Company and the Underwriter and was based on, among other things, the Company's financial and operating history and condition, its prospects, and the prospects for its industry in general, the management of the Company, and the market prices of securities for companies in businesses similar to that of the Company.

Legal Matters

The validity of the shares of Common Stock offered by the Prospectus is being passed on for the Company by Blair, Schroder, and Chirac and for the Underwriter by Chretien Howard.

Legal Proceedings

Hotch Pot was served in January 2006 with a summons and complaint in an action commenced by a customer who alleges that consumption of the Company's products caused severe nausea and loss of feeling in both feet. The Company believes that the complaint is without foundation.

Experts

The consolidated financial statements of the Company have been so included in reliance on the reports of Hooper Firebrand, independent accountants, given on the authority of that firm as experts in auditing and accounting.

Financial Statements

[*Text and tables omitted.*]

5

Debt and Payout Policy

Debt Policy

RELATED WEB LINKS

finance.yahoo.com

moneycentral.msn.com Information on the capital structure of individual firms and industries.

edgarscan.pwcglobal.com Use the Benchmarking Assistant to compare capital structures and the way they have changed.

www.bankruptcydata.com Systematic coverage of bankruptcy filings and general trends.

www.abiworld.org

www.bankrupt.com Information and news about bankruptcy and bankruptcy procedures.

www.turnaround.org The Turnaround Management Association, providing information and resources for firms in financial distress.

"Neither a borrower nor a lender be." So says Polonius in Shakespeare's *Hamlet*. Is this sound advice for the modern corporation?

Everett Collection

A firm's basic financial resource is the stream of cash flows produced by its assets and operations. When the firm is financed entirely by common stock, all those cash flows belong to the stockholders. When it issues both debt and equity, the firm splits the cash flows into two streams, a relatively safe stream that goes to the debtholders and a more risky one that goes to the stockholders.

The firm's mix of securities is known as its *capital structure*. Look at Table 15–1. You can see that in some industries companies borrow much more heavily than in others. Most high-tech firms, such as Intel and Microsoft, rely almost wholly on equity finance. So do most biotech, software, and Internet companies. At the other extreme, debt accounts for a substantial part of the market value of airlines, food and drink producers, and utilities.

Capital structure is not immutable. Firms change their capital structure, sometimes almost overnight. Later in the chapter you will see how Sealed Air Corporation did just that.

Shareholders want management to choose the mix of securities that maximizes firm value. But is there an optimal capital structure? We must consider the possibility that no combination has any greater appeal than any other. Perhaps the really important decisions concern the company's assets, and decisions about capital structure are mere details—matters to be attended to but not worried about.

In the first part of the chapter we will look at examples in which capital structure *doesn't* matter. After that we will put back some of the things that do make a difference, such as taxes, bankruptcy, and the signals that your financing decisions may send to investors. We will then draw up a checklist for financial managers who need to decide on the firm's capital structure. We conclude the chapter with a brief discussion of what happens when firms cannot pay their debts and enter bankruptcy proceedings.

- Analyze the effect of debt finance on the risk and required return of equityholders.

- Appreciate the advantages and disadvantages of debt finance.

- Cite the various costs of financial distress.

- Explain why the debt-equity mix varies across firms and across industries.

- Summarize the bankruptcy procedures for firms that cannot pay their creditors.

15.1 How Borrowing Affects Value in a Tax-Free Economy

It is after the ball game and the pizza man is delivering a pizza to Yogi Berra. "Should I cut it into four slices as usual, Yogi?" asks the pizza man. "No," replies Yogi, "Cut it into eight; I'm hungry tonight."

capital structure
The mix of long-term debt and equity financing.

If you understand why more slices won't sate Yogi's appetite, you will have no difficulty understanding why a company's choice of **capital structure** can't increase the underlying value of the firm.

Think of a simple balance sheet, with all entries expressed as current market values:

Assets	Liabilities and Stockholders' Equity
Value of cash flows from the firm's real assets and operations	Market value of debt
	Market value of equity
Value of firm	Value of firm

The right- and left-hand sides of a balance sheet are always equal. (Balance sheets have to balance!) Therefore, if you add up the market values of all the firm's debt and equity securities, you can calculate the value of the future cash flows from the real assets and operations.

TABLE 15–1 Average book debt ratios for a sample of nonfinancial industries

Industry	Debt Ratio
Software and programming	.06
Semiconductors	.09
Communications equipment	.13
Biotech	.28
Retail	.34
Hotels and motels	.41
Chemical manufacturing	.47
Airlines	.54
Electric utilities	.65
Real estate operations	.67
Beverages (alcoholic)	.70
Average for U.S. companies	.51

Note: Debt ratio = $D/(D + E)$, where D = book value of long-term debt and E = book value of equity.
Source: **finance.yahoo.com**.

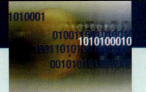
Book- and Market-Value Balance Sheets

Log on to finance.yahoo.com and find the key statistics for Pfizer (PFE) and Anheuser-Busch (BUD). Construct the debt ratio, debt/(debt + equity), for both firms. Now calculate their debt ratios by using the market value of equity, but assuming that book value of debt approximates its market value. How does debt as a proportion of firm value change as you switch from book to market values?

Source: Yahoo! Finance Web site. Reproduced with permission of Yahoo! Inc. Yahoo! and the Yahoo! logo are trademarks of Yahoo! Inc.

In fact, the value of those cash flows *determines* the value of the firm and therefore determines the aggregate value of all the firm's outstanding debt and equity securities. If the firm changes its capital structure, say, by using more debt and less equity financing, overall value should not change.

Think of the left-hand side of the balance sheet as the size of the pizza; the right-hand side determines how it is sliced. A company can slice its cash flow into as many parts as it likes, but the value of those parts will always sum back to the value of the unsliced cash flow. (Of course, we have to make sure that none of the cash-flow stream is lost in the slicing. We cannot say "The value of a pizza is independent of how it is sliced" if the slicer is also a nibbler.)

The basic idea here (the value of a pizza does not depend on how it is sliced) has various applications. Yogi Berra got friendly chuckles for his misapplication. Franco Modigliani and Merton Miller received Nobel Prizes for applying it to corporate financing. Modigliani and Miller, always referred to as "MM," showed in 1958 that the value of a firm does not depend on how its cash flows are "sliced." More precisely, they demonstrated the following proposition: When there are no taxes and capital markets function well, the market value of a company does not depend on its capital structure. In other words, financial managers cannot increase value by changing the mix of securities used to finance the company.

Of course, this MM proposition rests on some important simplifying assumptions. For example, capital markets have to be "well functioning." This means that investors can trade securities without restrictions and can borrow or lend on the same terms as the firm. It also means that capital markets are efficient, so securities are fairly priced given the information available to investors. (We discussed market efficiency in Chapter 6.) MM's proposition also assumes that there are no distorting taxes, and it ignores the costs encountered if a firm borrows too much and lands in financial distress.

The firm's capital structure decision can matter if these assumptions are not true or if other practical complications are encountered. But the best way to *start* thinking about capital structure is to work through MM's argument. *To keep things as simple as possible, we will ignore taxes until further notice.*

MM's Argument

Cleo, the president of River Cruises, is reviewing that firm's capital structure with Antony, the financial manager. Table 15–2 shows the current position. The company has no debt and all its operating income is paid as dividends to the shareholders. The *expected* earnings and dividends per share are $1.25, but this figure is by no means certain—it could turn out to be more or less than $1.25. For example, earnings could fall to $.75 in a slump or they could jump to $1.75 in a boom.

397

TABLE 15–2 River Cruises is entirely equity-financed. Although it expects to have an income of $125,000 in perpetuity, this income is not certain. This table shows the return to the stockholder under different assumptions about operating income. We assume no taxes.

Data			
Number of shares	100,000		
Price per share	$10		
Market value of shares	$1 million		

	State of the Economy		
	Slump	**Normal**	**Boom**
Operating income	$75,000	125,000	175,000
Earnings per share	$.75	1.25	1.75
Return on shares	7.5%	12.5%	17.5%
		Expected outcome	

The price of each share is $10. The firm expects to produce a level stream of earnings and dividends in perpetuity. With no growth forecast, stockholders' expected return is equal to the dividend yield—that is, the expected dividend per share divided by the price, $1.25/$10.00 = .125, or 12.5 percent.

Cleo has come to the conclusion that shareholders would be better off if the company had equal proportions of debt and equity. She therefore proposes to issue $500,000 of debt at an interest rate of 10 percent and to use the proceeds to repurchase 50,000 shares. This is called a **restructuring.** Notice that the $500,000 raised by the new borrowing does not stay in the firm. It goes right out the door to shareholders in order to repurchase and retire 50,000 shares. Therefore, the assets and investment policy of the firm are not affected. Only the financing mix changes.

restructuring
Process of changing the firm's capital structure without changing its assets.

What would MM say about this new capital structure? Suppose the change is made. Operating income is the same, so the value of the "pie" is fixed at $1 million. With $500,000 in new debt outstanding, the remaining common shares must be worth $500,000, that is, 50,000 shares at $10 per share. The total value of the debt and equity is still $1 million.

Since the value of the firm is the same, common shareholders are no better or worse off than before. River Cruises shares still trade at $10 each. The overall value of River Cruises's equity falls from $1 million to $500,000, but shareholders have also received $500,000 in cash.

Antony points all this out: "The restructuring doesn't make our stockholders any richer or poorer, Cleo. Why bother? Capital structure doesn't matter."

Self-Test 15.1   Suppose River Cruises issues $350,000 of new debt (rather than $500,000) and uses the proceeds to repurchase and retire common stock. How does this affect price per share? How many shares will be left outstanding?

How Borrowing Affects Earnings per Share

Cleo is unconvinced. She prepares Table 15–3 and Figure 15–1 to show how borrowing $500,000 could increase earnings per share. Comparison of Tables 15–2 and 15–3 shows that "normal" earnings per share increase to $1.50 (versus $1.25) after the restructuring. Table 15–3 also shows more "upside" (earnings per share of $2.50 versus $1.75) and more "downside" ($.50 versus $.75).

The orange line in Figure 15–1 shows how earnings per share would vary with operating income under the firm's current all-equity financing. It is therefore simply a plot of the data in Table 15–2. The purple line shows how earnings per share would vary if the company moves to equal proportions of debt and equity. It is therefore a plot of the data in Table 15–3.

TABLE 15–3 River Cruises is wondering whether to issue $500,000 of debt at an interest rate of 10 percent and repurchase 50,000 shares. This table shows the return to the shareholder under different assumptions about operating income. Returns to shareholders are increased in normal and boom times but fall more in slumps.

Data	
Number of shares	50,000
Price per share	$10
Market value of shares	$500,000
Market value of debt	$500,000

Outcomes			
	State of the Economy		
	Slump	**Normal**	**Boom**
Operating income	$75,000	125,000	175,000
Interest	$50,000	50,000	50,000
Equity earnings	$25,000	75,000	125,000
Earnings per share	$.50	1.50	2.50
Return on shares	5%	15%	25%
		Expected outcome	

Cleo reasons as follows: "It is clear that debt could either increase or reduce the return to the equityholder. In a slump the return to the equityholder is reduced by the use of debt, but otherwise it is *increased*. We could be heading for a recession but it doesn't look likely. Maybe we could help our shareholders by going ahead with the debt issue."

As financial manager, Antony replies as follows: "I agree that borrowing will increase earnings per share as long as there's no slump. But we're not really doing anything for shareholders that they can't do on their own. Suppose River Cruises does *not* borrow. In that case an investor could go to the bank, borrow $10, and then invest $20 in two shares. Such an investor would put up only $10 of her own money. Table 15–4 shows how the payoffs on this $10 investment vary with River Cruises's operating income. You can see that these payoffs are exactly the same as the investor would get by buying one share in the company after the restructuring. (Compare the last two lines of Tables 15–3 and 15–4.) It makes no difference whether shareholders borrow directly or whether River Cruises borrows on their behalf. Therefore, if River Cruises goes ahead and borrows, it will not allow investors to do anything that they could not do already, and so it cannot increase the value of the firm.

"We can run the same argument in reverse and show that investors also won't be any *worse* off after the restructuring. Imagine an investor who owns two shares in the company before the restructuring. If River Cruises borrows money, there is some

FIGURE 15–1 Borrowing increases River Cruises's earnings per share (EPS) when operating income is greater than $100,000 but reduces it when operating income is less than $100,000. Expected EPS rises from $1.25 to $1.50.

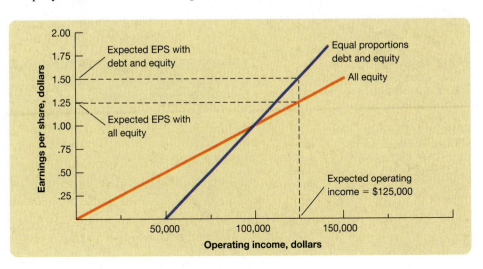

TABLE 15–4 Individual investors can replicate River Cruises's borrowing by borrowing on their own. In this example we assume that River Cruises has not restructured. However, the investor can put up $10 of her own money, borrow $10 more, and buy two shares at $10 apiece. This generates the same rates of return as in Table 15–3.

TABLE 15–4 Individual investors can replicate River Cruises's borrowing by borrowing on their own. In this example we assume that River Cruises has not restructured. However, the investor can put up $10 of her own money, borrow $10 more, and buy two shares at $10 apiece. This generates the same rates of return as in Table 15–3.

	State of the Economy		
	Slump	Normal	Boom
Earnings on two shares	$1.50	2.50	3.50
Less interest at 10%	$1.00	1.00	1.00
Net earnings on investment	$.50	1.50	2.50
Return on $10 investment	5%	15%	25%
		Expected outcome	

chance that the return on the shares will be lower than before. If that possibility is not to our investor's taste, he can buy one share in the restructured company and also invest $10 in the firm's debt. Table 15–5 shows how the payoff on this investment varies with River Cruises's operating income. You can see that these payoffs are exactly the same as the investor got before the restructuring. (Compare the last lines of Tables 15–2 and 15–5.) By lending half of his capital (by investing in River Cruises's debt), the investor exactly offsets the company's borrowing. So if River Cruises goes ahead and borrows, it won't *stop* investors from doing anything that they could previously do."

This re-creates MM's original argument.[1] As long as investors can borrow or lend on their own account on the same terms as the firm, they are not going to pay more for a firm that has borrowed on their behalf. The value of the firm after the restructuring must be the same as before. In other words, the value of the firm must be unaffected by its capital structure.

MM's proposition I (debt irrelevance proposition) The value of a firm is unaffected by its capital structure.

This conclusion is widely known as **MM's proposition I.** It is also called the **MM debt irrelevance proposition,** because it shows that under ideal conditions the firm's debt policy shouldn't matter to shareholders.

Self-Test 15.2

Suppose that River Cruises had issued $750,000 of debt, using the proceeds to buy back stock.

a. What would be the impact of a $50,000 change in operating income on earnings per share?
b. Show how a conservative investor could "undo" the change in River Cruises's capital structure by varying the investment strategy shown in Table 15–5. *Hint:* The investor will have to lend $3 for every dollar invested in River Cruises's stock.

TABLE 15–5 Individual investors can also undo the effects of River Cruises's borrowing. Here the investor buys one share for $10 and lends out $10 more. Compare these rates of return to the original returns of River Cruises in Table 15–2.

	State of the Economy		
	Slump	Normal	Boom
Earnings on one share	$.50	1.50	2.50
Plus interest at 10%	$1.00	1.00	1.00
Net earnings on investment	$1.50	2.50	3.50
Return on $20 investment	7.5%	12.5%	17.5%
		Expected outcome	

---

[1] There are many more general—and technical—proofs of the MM proposition. We will not pursue them here.

How Borrowing Affects Risk and Return

Figure 15–2 summarizes the implications of MM's debt irrelevance proposition for River Cruises. The upper circles represent firm value; the lower circles, expected, or "normal," operating income. Restructuring does not affect the size of the circles, because the amount and risk of operating income are unchanged. Thus if the firm raises $500,000 in debt and uses the proceeds to repurchase and retire shares, the remaining shares *must* be worth $500,000, and the total value of debt and equity *must* stay at $1 million.

The two bottom circles in Figure 15–2 are also the same size. But notice that the bottom right circle shows that shareholders can expect to earn more than half of River Cruises's normal operating income. They get more than half of the expected income "pie." Does that mean shareholders are better off? MM say no. Why? Because shareholders bear more risk.

Look again at Tables 15–2 and 15–3. Restructuring does not affect operating income, regardless of the state of the economy. Therefore, debt financing does not affect the **operating risk** or, equivalently, the **business risk** of the firm. But with less equity outstanding, a change in operating income has a greater impact on earnings per share. Suppose operating income drops from $125,000 to $75,000. Under all-equity financing, there are 100,000 shares; so earnings per share fall by $.50. With 50 percent debt, there are only 50,000 shares outstanding; so the same drop in operating income reduces earnings per share by $1.

You can see now why the use of debt finance is known as **financial leverage** and a firm that has issued debt is described as a *levered firm.* The debt increases the uncertainty about percentage stock returns. If the firm is financed entirely by equity, a decline of $50,000 in operating income reduces the return on the shares by 5 percentage points. If the firm issues debt, then the same decline of $50,000 in operating income reduces the return on the shares by 10 percentage points. (Compare Tables 15–2 and 15–3.) In other words, the effect of leverage is to double the magnitude of the upside and downside in the return on River Cruises's shares. Whatever the beta of the firm's shares before the restructuring, it would be twice as high afterward.

operating risk, business risk
Risk in firm's operating income.

financial leverage
Debt financing to amplify the effects of changes in operating income on the returns to stockholders.

FIGURE 15–2 "Slicing the pie" for River Cruises. The circles on the left assume the company has no debt. The circles on the right reflect the proposed restructuring. The restructuring splits firm value (top circles) 50–50. Shareholders get more than 50 percent of expected, or "normal," operating income (bottom circles), but only because they bear financial risk. Note that restructuring does not affect total firm value or operating income.

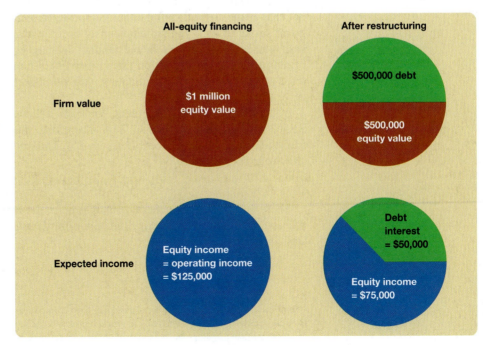

financial risk

Risk to shareholders resulting from the use of debt.

Debt finance does not affect the operating risk but it does add **financial risk.** With only half the equity to absorb the same amount of operating risk, risk per share must double.[2]

Consider now the implications of MM's proposition I for the expected return on River Cruises's stock. Before the proposed debt issue, the expected stream of earnings and dividends per share is $1.25. Since investment in the shares is risky, the shareholders require a return of 12.5 percent, or 2.5 percent above the interest rate. So the share price (which for a perpetuity is equal to the expected dividend divided by the required return) is $1.25/.125 = $10. The good news is that after the debt issue, expected earnings and dividends rise to $1.50. The bad news is that the risk of the shares has now doubled. So instead of being content with a return of 2.5 percent above the interest rate, shareholders now demand a return of 5 percent more than the interest rate—that is, a required return of 10 + 5 = 15 percent. The benefit from the rise in dividends is exactly canceled out by the rise in the required return. The share price after the debt issue is $1.50/.15 = $10—exactly the same as before.

	Current Structure: All Equity	Proposed Structure: Equal Debt and Equity
Expected earnings per share	$1.25	$1.50
Share price	$10	$10
Expected return on share	12.5%	15.0%

Thus leverage increases the expected return to shareholders, but it also increases the risk. The two effects cancel, leaving shareholder value unchanged.

Debt and the Cost of Equity

What is River Cruises's cost of capital? With all-equity financing, the answer is easy. Stockholders pay $10 per share and expect earnings per share of $1.25. If the earnings per share are paid out in a perpetual stream, the expected return is $1.25/10 = .125, or 12.5 percent. This is the cost of equity capital, r_{equity}, and also r_{assets}, the expected return and cost of capital for the firm's assets.

Since the restructuring does not change operating earnings or firm value, it should not change the cost of capital either. Suppose the restructuring takes place. Also, by a grand stroke of luck you simultaneously become a real estate billionaire. Flush with cash, you decide to buy *all* the outstanding debt and equity of River Cruises. What rate of return should you expect on this investment? The answer is 12.5 percent, because once you own all the debt and equity, you will effectively own all the assets and receive all the operating income.

You will indeed get 12.5 percent. Table 15–3 shows expected earnings per share of $1.50, and share price is still $10. Therefore, the expected return on equity is $1.50/$10 = .15, or 15 percent (r_{equity} = .15). The return on debt is 10 percent (r_{debt} = .10). Your overall return is

$$(.5 \times .10) + (.5 \times .15) = .125 = r_{assets}$$

There is obviously a general principle here: the appropriate weighted average of r_{debt} and r_{equity} takes you to r_{assets}, the opportunity cost of capital for the company's assets. The formula is

$$r_{assets} = (r_{debt} \times D/V) + (r_{equity} \times E/V)$$

---

[2] Think back to Section 9.3, where we showed that fixed costs increase the variability in a firm's profits. These fixed costs are said to provide *operating leverage*. It is exactly the same with debt. Debt interest is a fixed cost, and therefore debt magnifies the variability of profits after interest. These fixed interest charges create financial leverage.

where D and E are the amounts of outstanding debt and equity and V equals overall firm value, the sum of D and E. Remember that D, E, and V are market values, not book values.

This formula does not match the weighted-average cost of capital (WACC) formula presented in Chapter 12.[3] Don't worry, we'll get to WACC in a moment. (Remember, we're still ignoring taxes.) First let's look at the implications of MM's debt irrelevance proposition for the cost of equity.

MM's proposition I states that the firm's choice of capital structure does not affect the firm's operating income or the value of its assets. So r_{assets}, the expected return on the package of debt and equity, is unaffected.

However, we have just seen that leverage does increase the risk of the equity and the return that shareholders demand. To see how the expected return on equity varies with leverage, we simply rearrange the formula for the company cost of capital as follows:

$$r_{equity} = r_{assets} + \frac{D}{E}(r_{assets} - r_{debt})$$

which in words says that

$$
\begin{matrix}
\text{Expected} \\
\text{return} \\
\text{on equity}
\end{matrix}
=
\begin{matrix}
\text{expected} \\
\text{return} \\
\text{on assets}
\end{matrix}
+
\left[
\begin{matrix}
\text{debt-} \\
\text{equity} \\
\text{ratio}
\end{matrix}
\times
\left(
\begin{matrix}
\text{expected} \\
\text{return on} \\
\text{assets}
\end{matrix}
-
\begin{matrix}
\text{expected} \\
\text{return on} \\
\text{debt}
\end{matrix}
\right)
\right]
$$

MM's proposition II
The required rate of return on equity increases as the firm's debt-equity ratio increases.

This is **MM's proposition II.** It states that the expected rate of return on the common stock of a levered firm increases in proportion to the debt-equity ratio (D/E), expressed in market values. Note that $r_{equity} = r_{assets}$ if the firm has no debt.

EXAMPLE 15.1 ▶ River Cruises's Cost of Equity

We can check out MM's proposition II for River Cruises. Before the decision to borrow,

$$r_{equity} = r_{assets} = \frac{\text{expected operating income}}{\text{market value of all securities}}$$

$$= \frac{125,000}{1,000,000} = .125, \text{ or } 12.5\%$$

If the firm goes ahead with its plan to borrow, the expected return on assets, r_{assets}, is still 12.5 percent. So the expected return on equity is

$$r_{equity} = r_{assets} + \frac{D}{E}(r_{assets} - r_{debt})$$

$$= .125 + \frac{500,000}{500,000}(.125 - .10)$$

$$= .15, \text{ or } 15\% \qquad ◀$$

We pointed out in Chapter 12 that you can think of a debt issue as having an explicit cost and an implicit cost. The explicit cost is the rate of interest charged on the firm's debt. But debt also increases financial risk and causes shareholders to demand a higher return on their investment. Once you recognize this implicit cost, debt is no cheaper than equity—the return that investors require on their assets is unaffected by the firm's borrowing decision.

Self-Test 15.3

When the firm issues debt, why does r_{assets}, the company cost of capital, remain fixed while the expected return on equity, r_{equity}, changes? Why is it not the other way around?

---

[3] See Sections 12.1 and 12.2.

FIGURE 15-3 MM's proposition II with a fixed interest rate on debt. The expected return on River Cruises's equity rises in line with the debt-equity ratio. The weighted average of the expected returns on debt and equity is constant, equal to the expected return on assets.

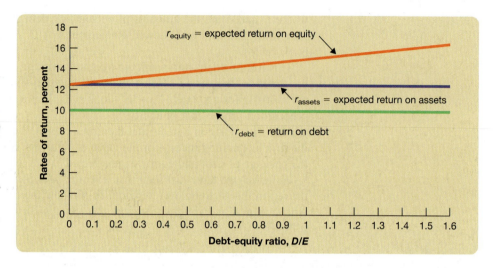

The implications of MM's proposition II are shown in Figure 15-3. No matter how much the firm borrows, the expected return on the package of debt and equity, r_{assets}, is unchanged, but the expected rate of return on the separate parts of the package does change. How is this possible? Because the proportions of debt and equity in the package are also changing. More debt means that the cost of equity increases, but at the same time the *amount* of equity is less.

In Figure 15-3 we have drawn the rate of interest on the debt as constant no matter how much the firm borrows. That is not wholly realistic. It is true that most large, conservative companies could borrow a little more or less without noticeably affecting the interest rate that they pay. But at higher debt levels lenders become concerned that they may not get their money back and they demand higher rates of interest. Figure 15-4 modifies Figure 15-3 to take account of this. You can see that as the firm borrows more, the risk of default increases and the firm has to pay higher rates of interest. Proposition II continues to predict that the expected return on the package of debt and equity does not change. However, the slope of the r_{equity} line now tapers off as D/E increases. Why? Essentially because holders of risky debt begin to bear part of the firm's operating risk. As the firm borrows more, more of that risk is transferred from stockholders to bondholders.

Figures 15-3 and 15-4 wrap up our discussion of MM's leverage irrelevance proposition. Because overall firm value is constant, the average return on the firm's debt and equity securities is also constant, regardless of the fraction of debt financing. This result follows from MM's assumptions that capital markets are well functioning and taxes are absent. Now it's time to put taxes back into the picture.

FIGURE 15-4 MM's proposition II when debt is not risk-free. As the debt-equity ratio increases, debtholders demand a higher expected rate of return to compensate for the risk of default. The expected return on equity increases more slowly when debt is risky because the debtholders take on part of the risk. The expected return on the package of debt and equity, r_{assets}, remains constant.

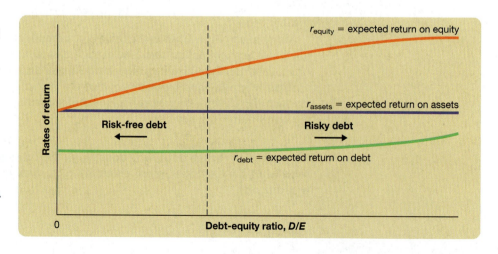

15.2 Capital Structure and Corporate Taxes

The MM propositions suggest that debt policy should not matter. Yet financial managers do worry about debt policy, and for good reasons. Now we are ready to see why.

If debt policy were *completely* irrelevant, actual debt ratios would vary randomly from firm to firm and from industry to industry. Yet almost all airlines, utilities, and real estate development companies rely heavily on debt. And so do many firms in capital-intensive industries like steel, aluminum, chemicals, and mining. On the other hand, it is rare to find a drug or software company that is not predominantly equity-financed. Glamorous growth companies seldom use much debt, despite rapid expansion and often heavy requirements for capital.

The explanation of these patterns lies partly in the things that we have so far left out of our discussion. Now we will put all these things back in, starting with taxes.

Debt and Taxes at River Cruises

Debt financing has one important advantage: The interest that the company pays is a tax-deductible expense, but equity income is subject to corporate tax.

To see the advantage of debt finance, let's look once again at River Cruises. Table 15–6 shows how expected income is reduced if profits are taxed at a rate of 35 percent. The left-hand column sets out the position if River Cruises is financed entirely by equity. The right-hand column shows what happens if the firm issues $500,000 of debt at an interest rate of 10 percent.

Notice that the combined income of the debtholders and equityholders is higher by $17,500 when the firm is levered. This is because the interest payments are tax-deductible. Thus every dollar of interest reduces taxes by $.35. The total amount of tax savings is simply .35 × interest payments. In the case of River Cruises, the **interest tax shield** is .35 × $50,000 = $17,500 each year. In other words, the "pie" of after-tax income that is shared by debt and equity investors increases by $17,500 relative to the zero-debt case. Since the debtholders receive no more than the going rate of interest, all the benefit of this interest tax shield is captured by the shareholders.

interest tax shield
Tax savings resulting from deductibility of interest payments.

The interest tax shield is a valuable asset. Let's see how much it could be worth. Suppose that River Cruises plans to replace its bonds when they mature and to keep "rolling over" the debt indefinitely. It therefore looks forward to a permanent stream of tax savings of $17,500 per year. These savings depend only on the corporate tax rate and on the ability of River Cruises to earn enough to cover interest payments. So the risk of the tax shield is likely to be small. Therefore, if we wish to compute the present value of all the future tax savings associated with permanent debt, we should discount the interest tax shields at a relatively low rate.

But what rate? The most common assumption is that the risk of the tax shields is the same as that of the interest payments generating them. Thus we discount, at 10 percent, the expected rate of return demanded by investors who are holding the firm's

TABLE 15–6 Since debt interest is tax-deductible, River Cruises's debtholders and equityholders expect to receive a higher combined income when the firm is leveraged

	Zero Debt	$500,000 of Debt
Expected operating income	$125,000	$125,000
Debt interest at 10%	0	50,000
Before-tax income	125,000	75,000
Tax at 35%	43,750	26,250
After-tax income	81,250	48,750
Combined debt and equity income (debt interest + after-tax income)	81,250	98,750

debt. If the debt is permanent, then the firm can look forward to annual savings of $17,500 in perpetuity. Their present value is

$$\text{PV tax shield} = \frac{\$17,500}{.10} = \$175,000$$

This is what the tax savings are worth to River Cruises.

How does company value change? We continue to assume that if the firm is all-equity-financed, the shareholders will demand a 12.5 percent return and therefore the company will be valued at $81,250/.125 = $650,000.[4] But if River Cruises issues $500,000 of permanent debt, the package of all the firm's securities increases by the value of the tax shield to $650,000 + $175,000 = $825,000.

Let us generalize. The interest payment each year equals the rate of interest times the amount borrowed, or $r_{debt} \times D$. The annual tax saving is the corporate tax rate T_c times the interest payment. Therefore,

$$\text{Annual tax shield} = \text{corporate tax rate} \times \text{interest payment}$$
$$= T_c \times (r_{debt} \times D)$$

If the tax shield is perpetual, we use the perpetuity formula to calculate its present value:

$$\textbf{PV tax shields} = \frac{\textbf{annual tax shield}}{r_{debt}} = \frac{T_c \times (r_{debt} \times D)}{r_{debt}} = T_c D$$

Of course the present value of the tax shield is less if the firm does not plan to borrow permanently or if it may not be able to use the tax shields in the future. This present value (T_cD) is actually the maximum possible value. However, we will continue to use this value in the rest of this chapter in order to keep the argument and illustrations simple.

Self-Test 15.4

In the year ending January 2004, Wal-Mart paid out $996 million as debt interest. How much more tax would Wal-Mart have paid if the firm had been entirely equity-financed? What would be the present value of Wal-Mart's interest tax shield if the company planned to keep its borrowing permanently at the 2004 level? Assume an interest rate of 6 percent and a corporate tax rate of 35 percent.

How Interest Tax Shields Contribute to the Value of Stockholders' Equity

MM's proposition I amounts to saying that "the value of the pizza does not depend on how it is sliced." The pizza is the firm's assets, and the slices are the debt and equity claims. If we hold the pizza constant, then a dollar more of debt means a dollar less of equity value.

But there is really a third slice—the government's. MM would still say that the value of the pizza—in this case the company value *before* taxes—is not changed by slicing. But anything the firm can do to reduce the size of the government's slice obviously leaves more for the others. One way to do this is to borrow money. This reduces the firm's tax bill and increases the cash payments to the investors. The value of their investment goes up by the present value of the tax savings.

In a no-tax world, MM's proposition I states that the value of the firm is unaffected by capital structure. But MM also modified proposition I to recognize corporate taxes:

Value of levered firm = value if all-equity-financed + present value of tax shield

---

[4] The firm was worth $1 million when the corporate tax rate was zero (see Table 15–2). It is worth only $650,000 when all-equity-financed because 35 percent of income is lost to taxes.

FIGURE 15–5 The heavy purple line shows how the availability of interest tax shields affects the market value of the firm. Additional borrowing decreases corporate income tax payments and increases the cash flows available to investors. Thus market value increases.

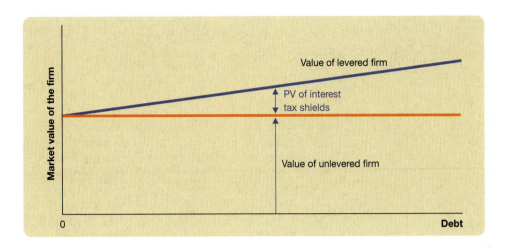

In the special case of permanent debt,

Value of levered firm = value if all-equity-financed + $T_c D$

This "corrected" formula is illustrated in Figure 15–5. It implies that borrowing increases firm value and shareholders' wealth.

Corporate Taxes and the Weighted-Average Cost of Capital

We have shown that when there are corporate taxes, debt provides the company with a valuable tax shield. Few companies explicitly calculate the present value of interest tax shields associated with a particular borrowing policy. The tax shields are not forgotten, however, because they show up in the discount rate used to evaluate capital investments.

Since debt interest is tax-deductible, the government in effect pays 35 percent of the interest cost. So to keep its investors happy, the firm has to earn the *after-tax* rate of interest on its debt and the return required by shareholders. Once we recognize the tax benefit of debt, the weighted-average cost of capital formula (see Chapter 12 for a review if you need one) becomes

$$\text{WACC} = (1 - T_c)\, r_{\text{debt}} \left(\frac{D}{D + E} \right) + r_{\text{equity}} \left(\frac{E}{D + E} \right)$$

Notice that when we allow for the tax advantage of debt, the weighted-average cost of capital depends on the *after-tax* rate of interest $(1 - T_c) \times r_{\text{debt}}$.

EXAMPLE 15.2 ▶   WACC and Debt Policy

We can use the weighted-average cost of capital formula to see how leverage affects River Cruises's cost of capital if the company pays corporate tax. When a company has no debt, the weighted-average cost of capital and the return required by shareholders are identical. In the case of River Cruises the WACC with all-equity financing is 12.5 percent, and the value of the firm is $650,000.

Now let us calculate the weighted-average cost of capital if River Cruises issues $500,000 of permanent debt ($D = \$500,000$). Company value increases by PV tax shield = $175,000, from $650,000 to $825,000 (meaning that $D + E = \$825,000$). Therefore the value of equity must be $825,000 − $500,000 = $325,000 ($E = \$325,000$).

Table 15–6 shows that when River Cruises borrows, the expected equity income is $48,750. So the expected return to shareholders is 48,750/325,000 = 15 percent (r_{equity} = .15). The interest rate is 10 percent (r_{debt} = .10), and the corporate tax rate is 35 percent (T_c = .35). This is all the information we need to see how leverage affects River Cruises's weighted-average cost of capital:

$$\text{WACC} = (1 - T_c)r_{\text{debt}}\left(\frac{D}{D+E}\right) + r_{\text{equity}}\left(\frac{E}{D+E}\right)$$

$$= (1 - .35)\,.10\left(\frac{500{,}000}{825{,}000}\right) + .15\left(\frac{325{,}000}{825{,}000}\right) = .0985,\text{ or }9.85\%$$

We saw earlier that if there are no corporate taxes, the weighted-average cost of capital is unaffected by borrowing. But when there are corporate taxes, debt provides the company with a new benefit—the interest tax shield. In this case leverage reduces the weighted-average cost of capital (in River Cruises's case from 12.5 to 9.85 percent).

Figure 15–6 repeats Figure 15–3 except that now we have allowed for the effect of taxes on River Cruises's cost of capital. You can see that as the company borrows more, the expected return on equity rises, but the rise is less rapid than in the absence of taxes. The after-tax cost of debt is only 6.5 percent. As a result, the weighted-average cost of capital declines. For example, if the company has debt of $500,000, the equity is worth $325,000 and the debt/equity ratio (*D/E*) is $500,000/$325,000 = 1.54. Figure 15–6 shows that with this amount of debt the weighted-average cost of capital is 9.85 percent, the same figure that we calculated above.   ◄

The Implications of Corporate Taxes for Capital Structure

If borrowing provides an interest tax shield, the implied optimal debt policy appears to be embarrassingly extreme: All firms should borrow to the hilt. This maximizes firm value and minimizes the weighted-average cost of capital.

MM were not that fanatical about it. No one would expect the gains to apply at extreme debt ratios. For example, if a firm borrows heavily, all its operating income may go to pay interest and therefore there are no corporate taxes to be paid. There is no point in such firms borrowing any more.

There may also be some tax *disadvantages* to borrowing, for bondholders have to pay personal income tax on any interest they receive. The top rate of tax on bond interest is 35 percent. Stockholders, on the other hand, are taxed at only 15 percent on both dividends and capital gains. Capital gains have the additional advantage that they are not taxed until the stock is sold.[5]

All this suggests that there may come a point at which the tax savings from debt level off and may even decline. But it doesn't explain why highly profitable companies with large tax bills often thrive with little or no debt. There are clearly factors besides tax to consider. One such factor is the likelihood of financial distress.

FIGURE 15–6 Changes in River Cruises's cost of capital with increased leverage when there are corporate taxes. The after-tax cost of debt is assumed to be constant at (1 − .35)10 = 6.5 percent. With increased borrowing the cost of equity rises, but more slowly than in the no-tax case (see Figure 15–3). The weighted-average cost of capital (WACC) declines as the firm borrows more.

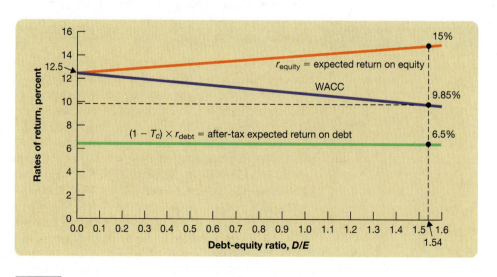

[5] The delay reduces the present value of the tax payment.

15.3 Costs of Financial Distress

costs of financial distress
Costs arising from bankruptcy or distorted business decisions before bankruptcy.

Financial distress occurs when promises to creditors are broken or honored with difficulty. Sometimes financial distress leads to bankruptcy. Sometimes it means only skating on thin ice.

As we will see, financial distress is costly. Investors know that levered firms may run into financial difficulty, and they worry about the **costs of financial distress.** That worry is reflected in the current market value of the levered firm's securities. Even if the firm is not now in financial distress, investors factor the potential for future distress into their assessment of current value. This means that the overall value of the firm is

$$\text{Overall market value} = \text{value if all-equity-financed} + \text{PV tax shield} - \text{PV costs of financial distress}$$

The present value of the costs of financial distress depends both on the probability of distress and on the magnitude of the costs encountered if distress occurs.

Figure 15–7 shows how the trade-off between the tax benefits of debt and the costs of distress determines optimal capital structure. Think of a firm like River Cruises, which starts with no debt but considers moving to higher and higher debt levels, holding its assets and operations constant. At moderate debt levels the probability of financial distress is trivial, and therefore the tax advantages of debt dominate. But at some point additional borrowing causes the probability of financial distress to increase rapidly and the potential costs of distress begin to take a substantial bite out of firm value. The theoretical optimum is reached when the present value of tax savings from further borrowing is just offset by increases in the present value of costs of distress.

trade-off theory
Debt levels are chosen to balance interest tax shields against the costs of financial distress.

This is called the **trade-off theory** of optimal capital structure. The theory says that managers will try to increase debt levels to the point where the value of additional interest tax shields is exactly offset by the additional costs of financial distress.

Now let's take a closer look at financial distress.

Bankruptcy Costs

In principle, bankruptcy is merely a legal mechanism for allowing creditors (that is, lenders) to take over the firm when the decline in the value of its assets triggers a default on outstanding debt. If the company cannot pay its debts, the company is turned over to the creditors, who become the new owners; the old stockholders are left with nothing. Bankruptcy is not the *cause* of the decline in the value of the firm. It is the result.

FIGURE 15–7 The trade-off theory of capital structure. The curved orange line shows how the market value of the firm at first increases as the firm borrows but finally decreases as the costs of financial distress become more and more important. The optimal capital structure balances the costs of financial distress against the value of the interest tax shields generated by borrowing.

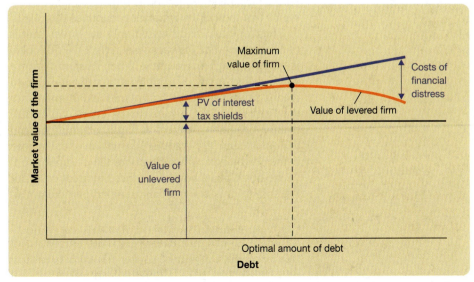

In practice, of course, anything involving courts and lawyers cannot be free. The fees involved in a bankruptcy proceeding are paid out of the remaining value of the firm's assets. Creditors end up with only what is left after paying the lawyers and other court expenses. If there is a possibility of bankruptcy, the current market value of the firm is reduced by the present value of these potential costs.

It is easy to see how increased leverage affects the costs of financial distress. The more the firm owes, the higher the chance of default and therefore the greater the expected value of the associated costs. This reduces the current market value of the firm.

Creditors foresee the costs and realize that if default occurs, the bankruptcy costs will come out of the value of the firm. For this they demand compensation in advance in the form of a higher promised interest rate. This reduces the possible payoffs to stockholders and reduces the current market value of their shares.

Self-Test 15.5   **Suppose investors foresee $2 million of legal costs if the firm defaults on its bonds. How does this affect the value of the firm's bonds if bankruptcy occurs? How does the possibility of default affect the interest rate demanded by bond- holders *today*? How does this possibility affect today's value of the firm's com- mon stock?**

When large firms file for bankruptcy, they usually do so under an arrangement called *Chapter 11*. The purpose of Chapter 11 is to nurse the firm back to health and enable it to face the world again. This requires approval of a reorganization plan for who gets what; under the plan each class of creditors needs to give up its claim in ex- change for new securities or a mixture of new securities and cash. The challenge is to design a new capital structure that will satisfy the creditors and allow the firm to solve the business problems that got it into trouble in the first place. Sometimes it proves possible to satisfy both demands and the patient emerges fit and healthy. Often, how- ever, the proceedings involve costly delays and legal tangles, and the business contin- ues to deteriorate.

Bankruptcy costs can add up fast. Failed energy giant Enron has estimated that its total legal and accounting costs since entering bankruptcy may reach $1 billion by 2006. And WorldCom paid between $800 million and $1 billion in fees during the 21 months that it spent in Chapter 11.[6]

Of course, these are exceptional cases, for only the largest firms can lay their hands on a billion dollars when bankrupt. But daunting as such numbers may seem, bank- ruptcy costs average only about 3 percent of the value of a firm in the year before bankruptcy.[7] The proportion is typically higher for small firms than for large ones; it seems that there are significant economies of scale in going bankrupt.

Thus far we have discussed only the *direct* (that is, legal and administrative) costs of bankruptcy. The *indirect* costs reflect the difficulties of running a company while it is going through bankruptcy. When Eastern Airlines entered bankruptcy in 1989, it was in severe financial trouble but it still had some valuable, profit-making routes and readily salable assets such as planes and terminal facilities. After nearly 2 years under the "protection" of a bankruptcy court, which allowed Eastern to continue loss- making operations, there was hardly anything of value left when it was finally forced to liquidate in 1991. Another illustration of the indirect costs of bankruptcy is provided in the nearby box, which describes the disruption to Penn Central Railroad's business.

We don't know how much these indirect costs add to the expenses of bankruptcy. We suspect it is a significant number, particularly when bankruptcy proceedings are

---

[6] See "Enron Bankruptcy Specialist to File for Additional Payment," *Wall Street Journal,* September 3, 2004, p. A2, and "Weil Gotshal Leads Pack as Firms Gobble $50 Million MCI Fees," *The Lawyer,* April 26, 2004, p. 5.

[7] See, for example, L. A. Weiss, "Bankruptcy Resolution: Direct Costs and Violation of Priority of Claims," *Jour- nal of Financial Economics* 27 (October 1990), pp. 285–314.

Penn Central's Bankruptcy

The Penn Central Railroad went under in June 1970. It was the largest and most dramatic corporate failure up to that time. Four years later, with bankruptcy proceedings nowhere near completion, *BusinessWeek* published an article called "Why the Penn Central Is Falling Apart." Here are some excerpts.

The article noted:

Although the railroad needed to invest huge sums of money to rebuild its facilities and continue operations, its creditors were more concerned with getting their own money back, even if that meant shutting down the railroad. In a chicken-and-egg type of problem, the capital necessary to make the railroad viable would not be forthcoming unless Penn Central could convince investors that it could be reorganized as a viable corporation.

Penn Central could have raised money by selling off some of its assets, but its creditors naturally opposed this. As the *BusinessWeek* article put it:

Agonizingly for everyone on the Penn Central, there is a tremendous source of capital that cannot be touched. For example, just about every abandoned mine branch in the Allegheny Mountains is chock full of old Penn Central cars destined for scrap. With today's scrap prices, they are a potential gold mine. But the creditors will not allow this asset to be turned into cash that will be reinvested in the estate, since that estate is eroding everyday.

Penn Central's problems show that some of the most important costs of bankruptcy are difficult to measure. The disruption of business activity is less visible but can be far more costly than the firm's legal bills.

Source: Excerpts from "Why the Penn Central Is Falling Apart," *Business-Week,* October 12, 1974. Reprinted by special permission. © 1974 The McGraw-Hill Companies, Inc.

prolonged. Perhaps the best evidence is the reluctance of creditors to force a firm into bankruptcy. In principle, they would be better off to end the agony and seize the assets as soon as possible. But, instead, creditors often overlook defaults in the hope of nursing the firm over a difficult period. They do this in part to avoid the costs of bankruptcy. There is an old financial saying, "Borrow $1,000 and you've got a banker. Borrow $10,000,000 and you've got a partner."

Financial Distress without Bankruptcy

Not every firm that gets into trouble goes bankrupt. As long as the firm can scrape up enough cash to pay the interest on its debt, it may be able to postpone bankruptcy for many years. Eventually the firm may recover, pay off its debt, and escape bankruptcy altogether.

A narrow escape from bankruptcy does *not* mean that costs of financial distress are avoided. When a firm is in trouble, suppliers worry that they may not be paid, potential customers fear that the firm will not be able to honor its warranties, and employees start slipping out for job interviews. The firm's bondholders and stockholders both want it to recover, but in other respects their interests may be in conflict. In times of financial distress the security holders are like many political parties—united on generalities but threatened by squabbling on any specific issue. Financial distress is costly when conflicts get in the way of running the business. Stockholders are tempted to forsake the usual objective of maximizing the overall market value of the firm and to pursue narrower self-interest instead. They are tempted to play games at the expense of their creditors. These games add to the costs of financial distress.

Think of a company—call it Double-R Nutting—which is teetering on the brink of bankruptcy. It has large debts and large losses. Double-R's assets have little value, and if its debts were due today, Double-R would default, leaving the firm bankrupt. The debtholders would perhaps receive a few cents on the dollar, and the shareholders would be left with nothing.

But suppose the debts are not due yet. That grace period explains why Double-R's shares still have value. There could be a stroke of luck that will rescue the firm and allow it to pay off its debts with something left over. That's a long shot—unless firm value increases sharply, the stock will be valueless. But the owners have a secret weapon: They control investment and operating strategy.

The First Game: Bet the Bank's Money   Suppose Double-R has the opportunity to take a wild gamble. If it does not come off, the shareholders will be no worse off; the company will probably go under anyway. But if the gamble does succeed, there will be more than enough assets to pay off the debt and the surplus will go into the shareholders' pockets. You can see why management might want to take the chance. In taking the gamble, they are essentially betting the debtholders' money, but if Double-R does hit the jackpot, the equityholders get most of the loot.

One owner-manager of a small bankrupt company called KenDavis Industries put the point this way: "Everyone agrees there is no shareholder equity—so *we've* got *nothing* to lose. The *banks* have it all on the line now—not us." In another case, the managers of the failing firm took the incentive to gamble literally. They went to Las Vegas and bet the company's money, hoping to win enough to pay off the creditors. The effects of such distorted incentives to take on risk are usually not this blatant, but the results can be the same. For example, Sambo's Restaurants borrowed against unencumbered assets while in bankruptcy proceedings and used the funds to pay for a risky marketing initiative, changing the name and concept of its restaurants. When the gamble failed, unsecured creditors suffered most of the loss: They received only 11 cents of each dollar owed them.[8]

These kinds of warped capital investment strategies clearly are costly for the bondholders and for the firm as a whole. Why do we say they create costs of financial distress? Because the temptation to follow such strategies is strongest when the odds of default are high. A healthy firm would never invest in Double-R's negative-NPV gamble, since it would be gambling with its own money, not the bondholders'. A healthy firm's creditors would not be vulnerable to this type of game.

The Second Game: Don't Bet Your Own Money   We have just seen how shareholders, acting in their narrow self-interest, may take on risky, unprofitable projects. These are errors of commission. We will now illustrate how conflicts of interest may also lead to errors of omission.

Suppose Double-R uncovers a relatively safe project with a positive NPV. Unfortunately, the project requires a substantial investment. Double-R will need to raise this extra cash from its shareholders. Although the project has a positive NPV, the profits may not be sufficient to rescue the company from bankruptcy. If that is so, all the profits from the new project will be used to help pay off the company's debt, and the shareholders will get no return on the cash they put up. Although it is in the firm's interest to go ahead with the project, it is not in the *owners'* interest, and the project will be passed up.

Again, our example illustrates a general point. The value of any investment opportunity to the firm's *stockholders* is reduced because project benefits must be shared with the bondholders. Thus it may not be in the stockholders' self-interest to contribute fresh equity capital even if that means forgoing positive-NPV opportunities.

These two games illustrate potential conflicts of interest between stockholders and debtholders. These conflicts, which theoretically affect all levered firms, become much more serious when firms are staring bankruptcy in the face. If the probability of default is high, managers and stockholders will be tempted to take on excessively risky projects. At the same time, stockholders may refuse to contribute more equity capital even if the firm has safe, positive-NPV opportunities. Stockholders would rather take money out of the firm than put new money in.

The more the firm borrows, the greater the temptation to play such games. The increased odds of poor decisions in the future prompt investors to reduce today's assessment of the market value of the firm. Potential lenders, realizing that games may be played at their expense in the future, protect themselves by demanding better terms on the money they lend today. So the fall in value comes out of stockholders' pockets.

[8] These cases are cited in Lynn M. LoPucki, "The Trouble with Chapter 11," *Wisconsin Law Review*, 1993, pp. 729–760.

This is the reason that it is ultimately in the stockholders' interest to avoid temptation. The easiest way to do this is to limit borrowing to levels at which the firm's debt is safe or close to it.

We do not mean to leave the impression that managers and stockholders always succumb to temptation unless restrained. Usually they refrain voluntarily, not only because of a sense of fair play but also on pragmatic grounds: A firm or individual that makes a killing today at the expense of a creditor will be coldly received when the time comes to borrow again. Aggressive game playing is done only by out-and-out crooks and by firms in extreme financial distress. Firms limit borrowing precisely because they don't wish to land in distress and be exposed to the temptation to play.

Self-Test 15.6   We have described two games that might be played by firms in financial distress. Why are the games costly? How does the possibility that the game might be played at some point in the future affect today's capital structure decisions?

Costs of Distress Vary with Type of Asset

Suppose your firm's only asset is a large downtown hotel, mortgaged to the hilt. A recession hits, occupancy rates fall, and the mortgage payments cannot be met. The lender takes over and sells the hotel to a new owner and operator. The stock is worthless and you use the firm's stock certificates for wallpaper.

What is the cost of bankruptcy? In this example, probably very little. The value of the hotel is, of course, much less than you hoped, but that is due to the lack of guests, not to bankruptcy. Bankruptcy does not damage the hotel itself. The direct bankruptcy costs are restricted to items such as legal and court fees, real estate commissions, and the time the lender spends sorting things out.

Suppose we repeat the story of Heartbreak Hotel for Fledgling Electronics. Everything is the same, except for the underlying assets. Fledgling is a high-tech going concern, and much of its value reflects investors' belief that its research team will come up with profitable ideas. Fledgling is a "people business"; its most important assets go down in the elevator and into the parking lot every night.

If Fledgling gets into trouble, the stockholders may be reluctant to put up money to cash in on those profitable ideas—why should they put up cash which will simply go to pay off the banks? Failure to invest is likely to be much more serious for Fledgling than for a company like Heartbreak Hotel.

If Fledgling finally defaults on its debt, the lender would find it much more difficult to cash in by selling off the assets. In fact, if trouble comes, many of those assets may drive into the sunset and never come back.

Some assets, like good commercial real estate, can pass through bankruptcy and reorganization largely unscathed; the values of other assets are likely to be considerably diminished. The losses are greatest for intangible assets that are linked to the continuing prosperity of the firm. That may be why debt ratios are low in the pharmaceutical industry, where company values depend on continued success in research and development. It may also explain the low debt ratios in many service companies, whose main asset is their skilled labor. The moral of these examples is this: Do not think only about whether borrowing is likely to bring trouble. Think also of the value that may be lost if trouble comes.

Self-Test 15.7   For which of the following companies would the costs of financial distress be most serious? Why?

- A 3-year-old biotech company. So far the company has no products approved for sale, but its scientists are hard at work developing a breakthrough drug.
- An oil production company with 50 producing wells and 20 million barrels of proven oil reserves.

We have now completed our review of the building blocks of the trade-off theory of optimal capital structure. In the next section we will sum up that theory and briefly cover a competing "pecking order" theory.

15.4 Explaining Financing Choices

The Trade-Off Theory

Financial managers often think of the firm's debt-equity decision as a trade-off between interest tax shields and the costs of financial distress. Of course, there is controversy about how valuable interest tax shields are and what kinds of financial trouble are most threatening, but these disagreements are only variations on a theme. Thus Figure 15–7 illustrates the debt-equity trade-off.

This trade-off theory predicts that target debt ratios will vary from firm to firm. Companies with safe, tangible assets and plenty of taxable income to shield ought to have high target ratios. Unprofitable companies with risky, intangible assets ought to rely primarily on equity financing.

All in all, this trade-off theory of capital structure tells a comforting story. It avoids extreme predictions and rationalizes moderate debt ratios. But what are the facts? Can the trade-off theory of capital structure explain how companies actually behave?

The answer is yes and no. On the yes side, the trade-off theory successfully explains many industry differences in capital structure. For example, high-tech growth companies, whose assets are risky and mostly intangible, normally use relatively little debt. Utilities or retailers can and do borrow heavily because their assets are tangible and relatively safe.

On the no side, there are other things the trade-off theory cannot explain. It cannot explain why some of the most successful companies thrive with little debt. Consider, for example, the large pharmaceutical company Johnson & Johnson, which is basically all-equity-financed. Granted, Johnson & Johnson's most valuable assets are intangible: the fruits of its research and development. We know that intangible assets and conservative capital structures should go together. But Johnson & Johnson also has a very large corporate income tax bill ($4.3 billion in 2004) and the highest possible credit rating. It could borrow enough to save tens of millions of tax dollars without raising a whisker of concern about possible financial distress.

Our example illustrates an odd fact about real-life capital structures: The most profitable companies generally borrow the least. Here the trade-off theory fails, for it predicts exactly the reverse. Under the trade-off theory, high profits should mean more debt-servicing capacity and more taxable income to shield and therefore should give a *higher* debt ratio.

Self-Test 15.8   Rank these industries in order of predicted debt ratios under the trade-off theory of capital structure: (a) Internet software; (b) auto manufacturing; (c) regulated electric utilities.

A Pecking Order Theory

There is an alternative theory which could explain why profitable companies borrow less. It is based on *asymmetric information*—managers know more than outside investors about the profitability and prospects of the firm. Thus investors may not be able to assess the true value of a new issue of securities by the firm. They may be especially reluctant to buy newly issued common stock, because they worry that the new shares will turn out to be overpriced.

Such worries can explain why the announcement of a stock issue can drive down the stock price.[9] If managers know more than outside investors, they will be tempted

---

[9] We described this "announcement effect" in Chapter 14.

Capital Structure

1. On finance.yahoo.com find the Profile for PepsiCo (PEP) and IBM (IBM), and then look at each firm's annual balance sheet and income statement under *Highlights*. Calculate the present value of the interest tax shield contributed by each company's long-term debt. Now suppose that each issues $3 billion more of long-term debt and uses the proceeds to repurchase equity. How would the interest tax shield change?
2. While you are logged on to the Yahoo! page for PepsiCo or IBM, move down and click on the word *Industry* in the left-hand column. This will give you a table of financial ratios for different industries. Compare the debt-equity ratios for different industries. Can you account for the differences? Are they better explained by the trade-off theory or the pecking order theory?

Source: Yahoo! Finance Web site. Reproduced with permission of Yahoo! Inc. © 2005 by Yahoo! Inc. Yahoo! and the Yahoo! logo are trademarks of Yahoo! Inc.

to time stock issues when their companies' stock is *overpriced*—in other words, when the managers are relatively pessimistic. On the other hand, optimistic managers will see their companies' shares as *underpriced* and decide *not* to issue. You can see why investors would learn to interpret the announcement of a stock issue as a "pessimistic manager" signal and mark down the stock price accordingly. You can also see why optimistic financial managers—and most managers *are* optimistic!—would view a common stock issue as a relatively expensive source of financing.

All these problems are avoided if the company can finance with internal funds, that is, with earnings retained and reinvested. But if external financing is required, the path of least resistance is debt, not equity. Issuing debt seems to have a trifling effect on stock prices. There is less scope for debt to be misvalued and therefore a debt issue is a less worrisome signal to investors.

pecking order theory
Firms prefer to issue debt rather than equity if internal finance is insufficient.

These observations suggest a **pecking order theory** of capital structure. It goes like this:

1. Firms prefer internal finance, since these funds are raised without sending any adverse signals that may lower the stock price.
2. If external finance is required, firms issue debt first and issue equity only as a last resort. This pecking order arises because an issue of debt is less likely than an equity issue to be interpreted by investors as a bad omen.

In this story, there is no clear target debt-equity mix, because there are two kinds of equity, internal and external. The first is at the top of the pecking order, and the second is at the bottom. The pecking order explains why the most profitable firms generally borrow less; it is not because they have low target debt ratios but because they don't need outside money. Less profitable firms issue debt because they do not have sufficient internal funds for their capital investment program and because debt is first in the pecking order for *external* finance.

The pecking order theory does not deny that taxes and financial distress can be important factors in the choice of capital structure. However, the theory says that these factors are less important than managers' preference for internal over external funds and for debt financing over new issues of common stock.

For most U.S. corporations, internal funds finance the majority of new investment, and most external financing comes from debt. These aggregate financing patterns are consistent with the pecking order theory. Yet the pecking order seems to work best for mature firms. Fast-growing high-tech firms often resort to a series of common stock issues to finance their investments. For this type of firm common stock often comes at the *top* of the pecking order. The reasons why the pecking order theory works for some firms and not others are not well understood.

The Two Faces of Financial Slack

Other things equal, it's better to be at the top of the pecking order than at the bottom. Firms that have worked down the pecking order and need external equity may end up living with excessive debt or bypassing good investments because shares can't be sold at what managers consider a fair price.

financial slack
Ready access to cash or debt financing.

In other words, **financial slack** is valuable. Having financial slack means having cash, marketable securities, readily salable real assets, and ready access to the debt markets or to bank financing. Ready access basically requires conservative financing so that potential lenders see the company's debt as a safe investment.

In the long run, a company's value rests more on its capital investment and operating decisions than on financing. Therefore, you want to make sure your firm has sufficient financial slack so that financing is quickly available for good investments. Financial slack is most valuable to firms with plenty of positive-NPV growth opportunities. That is another reason why growth companies usually aspire to conservative capital structures.

However, there is also a dark side to financial slack. Too much of it may encourage managers to take it easy, expand their perks, or empire-build with cash that should be paid back to stockholders. Michael Jensen has stressed the tendency of managers with ample free cash flow (or unnecessary financial slack) to plow too much cash into mature businesses or ill-advised acquisitions. "The problem," Jensen says, "is how to motivate managers to disgorge the cash rather than investing it below the cost of capital or wasting it in organizational inefficiencies."[10]

If that's the problem, then maybe debt is an answer. Scheduled interest and principal payments are contractual obligations of the firm. Debt forces the firm to pay out cash. Perhaps the best debt level would leave just enough cash in the bank, after debt service, to finance all positive-NPV projects, with not a penny left over.

We do not recommend this degree of fine-tuning, but the idea is valid and important. For some firms, the threat of financial distress may have a good effect on managers' incentives. After all, skating on thin ice can be useful if it makes the skater concentrate. Likewise, managers of highly levered firms are more likely to work harder, run a leaner operation, and think more carefully before they spend money.

The nearby box tells the story of how Sealed Air Corporation borrowed more than $300 million, using the proceeds of the loan to pay a special cash dividend to shareholders. The net effect was an increase in debt from a trivial level to fully 65 percent of the total value of the firm. The dramatic increase in debt committed the firm to pay out large sums of money as interest, leaving it with little opportunity to fritter its cash away in pursuit of a comfortable life. Sealed Air showed great improvements in efficiency after the change in capital structure.

15.5 Bankruptcy Procedures

Firms that issue debt always bear at least a small risk that when the debt comes due, they will not be able to pay their creditors. At that point, the firm may be forced into bankruptcy. We conclude this chapter with a brief overview of the bankruptcy process.

workout
Agreement between a company and its creditors establishing the steps the company must take to avoid bankruptcy.

A corporation that cannot pay its debts will often try to come to an informal agreement with its creditors. This is known as a **workout.** A workout may take several forms. For example, the firm may negotiate an *extension,* that is, an agreement with its creditors to delay payments. Or the firm may negotiate a *composition,* in which the firm makes partial payments to its creditors in exchange for relief of its debts.

---

[10] M. C. Jensen, "Agency Costs of Free Cash Flow, Corporate Finance and Takeovers," *American Economic Review* 26 (May 1986), p. 323.

How Sealed Air's Change in Capital Structure Acted as a Catalyst to Organizational Change

Sealed Air Corporation manufactures a wide variety of packaging materials such as plastic packing bubbles and Jiffy padded envelopes.

As it entered 1989, Sealed Air was very conservatively financed with $33 million in total debt and over $54 million in cash. Thus, rather than borrowing cash, the company was actually a net lender. However, in June of that year Sealed Air dramatically changed its capital structure by paying a special one-time dividend of $40 a share. With about 8.25 million shares trading, the total cash payout amounted to almost $330 million, or close to 90 percent of the total market value of the firm's common stock. To help finance this special dividend, the company borrowed a total of $307 million. Thus, the company went overnight from being a net lender to being a very heavy borrower. Debt now amounted to 125 percent of the book value of the assets and 65 percent of their market value.

Until the change in capital structure Sealed Air's performance was no better than that of the industry as a whole. But the change was a prelude to a sharp improvement in the company's operating performance. In the following 5 years, operating profit increased by 70 percent while the asset base grew by only 9 percent. This improvement in profitability was more than matched by the company's stock market performance. The initial effect of Sealed Air's announced change in capital structure was a jump of 10 percent in the stock price. Over the next 5½ years the stock outperformed the market by 400 percent.

What then motivated the change in capital structure and what role, if any, did this change play in the company's subsequent performance?

Some of the gains from the change in capital structure may have come from the fact that the company was able to offset the interest payments against tax. But this does not appear to have been a primary motive. Instead, the change appears to have been management's response to the realization that life at Sealed Air was in many respects too comfortable. For years patents had insulated the company from competition. Cash was plentiful. So the company never needed to think hard about requests to invest in new projects, and there was no sense of urgency in removing inefficiencies. In the management's view it would take nothing less than a "crisis" to shake employees out of their complacency. The change in capital structure was just such a crisis.

The sharp increase in debt levels meant that cash was no longer abundant for it was now needed to pay the debtholders and was literally essential to the company's survival. Thus managers now felt under pressure to make those efficiency gains that previously had not seemed worthwhile. As employees became aware of the need for more effective operations, it was possible to decentralize decision making within the company and to install a more effective system of performance measurement and compensation. The result was a sharp increase in profit margins and a reduction in the working capital and fixed assets employed to generate each dollar of sales. It seemed that the capital structure change had succeeded in kickstarting a remarkable improvement in Sealed Air's performance.

Source: Adapted from K. H. Wruck, "Financial Policy as a Catalyst for Organizational Change: Sealed Air Corporation's Leveraged Special Dividend," *Journal of Applied Corporate Finance* 7 (Winter 1995), pp. 20–37. Used with permission.

The advantage of a negotiated agreement is that the costs and delays of formal bankruptcy are avoided. However, the larger the firm and the more complicated its capital structure, the less likely it is that a negotiated settlement can be reached. (For example, Wickes Corp. tried—and failed—to reach a negotiated settlement with its 250,000 creditors.)

If the firm cannot get an agreement, then it may have no alternative but to file for **bankruptcy.**[11] Under the federal bankruptcy system the firm has a choice of procedures. In about two-thirds of the cases a firm will file for, or be forced into, bankruptcy under Chapter 7 of the 1978 Bankruptcy Reform Act. Then the firm's assets are **liquidated**—that is, sold—and the proceeds are used to pay creditors.

There is a pecking order of unsecured creditors.[12] First come claims for expenses that arise after bankruptcy is filed, such as attorney's fees or employee compensation earned after the filing. If such postfiling claims did not receive priority, no firm in bankruptcy proceedings could continue to operate. Next come claims for wages and employee benefits earned in the period immediately prior to the filing. Taxes are next in line, together with debts to some government agencies such as the Small Business

bankruptcy

The reorganization or liquidation of a firm that cannot pay its debts.

liquidation

Sale of bankrupt firm's assets.

---

[11] Occastionally creditors will allow the firm to petition for bankruptcy after it has reached an agreement with the creditors. This is known as a *prepackaged bankruptcy*. The court simply approves the agreed workout plan.

[12] Secured creditors have the first priority to the collateral pledged for their loans.

reorganization
Restructuring of financial claims on failing firm to allow it to keep operating.

Administration or the Pension Benefit Guarantee Corporation. Finally come general unsecured claims such as bonds or unsecured trade debt.

The alternative to a liquidation is to seek a **reorganization,** which keeps the firm as a going concern and usually compensates creditors with new securities in the reorganized firm. Such reorganizations are generally in the shareholders' interests—they have little to lose if things deteriorate further and everything to gain if the firm recovers.

Firms attempting reorganization seek refuge under Chapter 11 of the Bankruptcy Reform Act. Chapter 11 is designed to keep the firm alive and operating and to protect the value of its assets while a plan of reorganization is worked out. During this period, other proceedings against the firm are halted and the company is operated by existing management or by a court-appointed trustee.

The responsibility for developing a plan of reorganization may fall on the debtor firm. If no trustee is appointed, the firm has 120 days to present a plan to creditors. If this deadline is *not* met, or if a trustee is appointed, anyone can submit a plan—the trustee, for example, or a committee of creditors.

The reorganization plan is basically a statement of who gets what; each class of creditors gives up its claim in exchange for new securities. (Sometimes creditors receive cash as well.) The problem is to design a new capital structure for the firm that will (1) satisfy the creditors and (2) allow the firm to solve the *business* problems that got the firm into trouble in the first place. Sometimes only a plan of baroque complexity can satisfy these two requirements. When the Penn Central Corporation was finally reorganized in 1978 (7 years after it became the largest railroad bankruptcy ever), more than a dozen new securities were created and parceled out among 15 classes of creditors.

The reorganization plan goes into effect if it is accepted by creditors and confirmed by the court. Acceptance requires approval by a majority of each class of creditor. Once a plan is accepted, the court normally approves it, provided that *each* class of creditors has approved it and that the creditors will be better off under the plan than if the firm's assets were liquidated and distributed. The court may, under certain conditions, confirm a plan even if one or more classes of creditors vote against it. This is known as a *cram-down.*

The interests of the different classes of creditors do not always coincide. For example, unsecured creditors may threaten to slow the process as a way of extracting concessions from secured creditors. The secured creditors may take less than 100 cents on the dollar and give something to unsecured creditors in order to expedite the process and reach an agreement.

Chapter 11 proceedings are often successful, and the patient emerges fit and healthy. But in other cases cure proves impossible and the assets are liquidated. Sometimes the firm may emerge from Chapter 11 for a brief period before it is once again submerged by disaster and back in bankruptcy. For example, TWA came out of bankruptcy at the end of 1993 and was back again less than 2 years later, prompting jokes about "Chapter 22." TWA has plenty of company in this regard. In recent years, about 80 percent of large firms have emerged from bankruptcy proceedings with a second life, but nearly one-third of those reorganized firms met with failure within 5 years.[13] Among other notable "serial failures" are Planet Hollywood, Grand Union, Memorex, Continental Airlines, and Harvard Industries, which had the rare distinction of achieving a "Chapter 44."

The Choice between Liquidation and Reorganization

Here is an idealized view of the bankruptcy decision. Whenever a payment is due to creditors, management checks the value of the firm. If the firm is worth more than the promised payment, the firm pays up (if necessary, raising the cash by an issue of

[13] "The Firms That Can't Stop Failing," *The Economist,* September 7, 2002.

shares). If not, the equity is worthless, and the firm defaults on its debt and petitions for bankruptcy. If in the court's judgment the assets of the bankrupt firm can be put to better use elsewhere, the firm is liquidated and the proceeds are used to pay off the creditors. Otherwise, the creditors simply become the new owners and the firm continues to operate.

In practice, matters are rarely so simple. For example, we observe that firms often petition for bankruptcy even when the equity has a positive value. Moreover, the bankruptcy court may decide to keep the firm on life support even when the assets could be used more efficiently elsewhere. There are several reasons for this.

First, although the reorganized firm is legally a new entity, it is entitled to any tax-loss carry-forwards belonging to the old firm. If the firm is liquidated rather than reorganized, any tax-loss carry-forwards disappear. Thus there is an incentive to continue in operation even if assets are better used by another firm.

Second, if the firm's assets are sold off, it is easy to determine what is available to pay the creditors. However, when the company is reorganized, it needs to conserve cash as far as possible. Therefore, claimants are generally paid in a mixture of cash and securities. This makes it less easy to judge whether they have received their entitlement. For example, each bondholder may be offered $300 in cash and $700 in a new bond which pays no interest for the first 2 years and a low rate of interest thereafter. A bond of this kind in a company that is struggling to survive may not be worth much, but the bankruptcy court usually looks at the face value of the new bonds and may therefore regard the bondholders as paid in full.

Senior creditors who know they are likely to get a raw deal in a reorganization are likely to press for a liquidation. Shareholders and junior creditors prefer a reorganization. They hope that the court will not interpret the pecking order too strictly and that they will receive some crumbs.

Third, although shareholders and junior creditors are at the bottom of the pecking order, they have a secret weapon: they can play for time. Bankruptcies of large companies often take several years before a plan is presented to the court and agreed to by each class of creditor. (The bankruptcy proceedings of the Missouri Pacific Railroad took a total of 22 years.) When they use delaying tactics, the junior claimants are betting on a turn of fortune that will rescue their investment. On the other hand, the senior creditors know that time is working against them, so they may be prepared to accept a smaller payoff as part of the price for getting a plan accepted. Also, prolonged bankruptcy cases are costly. (While their cases are extreme, we've seen that the World-Com and Enron bankruptcies are each likely to generate about $1 billion in legal and administrative costs.) Senior claimants may see their money seeping into lawyers' pockets and therefore decide to settle quickly.

Fourth, while a reorganization plan is being drawn up, the company is allowed to buy goods on credit and borrow money. Postpetition creditors (those who extend credit to a firm already in bankruptcy proceedings) have priority over the old creditors, and their debt may even be secured by assets that are already mortgaged to existing debtholders. This also gives the prepetition creditors an incentive to settle quickly, before their claim on assets is diluted by the new debt.

Finally, profitable companies may file for Chapter 11 bankruptcy to protect themselves against "burdensome" suits. For example, in 1982 Manville Corporation was threatened by 16,000 damage suits alleging injury from asbestos. Manville filed for bankruptcy under Chapter 11, and the bankruptcy judge agreed to put the damage suits on hold until the company was reorganized. This took 6 years. Of course legislators worry that these actions are contrary to the original intent of the bankruptcy acts.

The United States is somewhat unusual in its preference for reorganization over liquidation. In the United Kingdom and other European nations, for example, liquidation is far more prevalent. But practices may converge a bit in the future. In the United States, there is some dismay over the frequent failures of firms reorganized in Chapter 11. And in Europe, there is growing recognition that while liquidation avoids embarrassing and costly serial failures, it also means lost opportunities for successful restructurings that would allow viable firms to remain in business.

SUMMARY

What is the goal of the capital structure decision? What is the financial manager trying to do?

The goal is to maximize the overall market value of all the securities issued by the firm. Think of the financial manager as taking all the firm's real assets and selling them to investors as a package of securities. Some financial managers choose the simplest package possible: all-equity financing. Others end up issuing dozens of types of debt and equity securities. The financial manager must try to find the particular combination that maximizes the market value of the firm. If firm value increases, common stockholders will benefit.

Does firm value increase when more debt is used?

Not necessarily. Modigliani and Miller's (MM's) famous **debt irrelevance proposition** states that firm value can't be increased by changing **capital structure.** Therefore, the proportions of debt and equity financing don't matter. **Financial leverage** does increase the expected rate of return to shareholders, but the risk of their shares increases proportionally. MM show that the extra return and extra risk balance out, leaving shareholders no better or worse off.

Of course, MM's argument rests on simplifying assumptions. For example, it assumes efficient, well-functioning capital markets and ignores taxes and costs of financial distress. But even if these assumptions are incorrect in practice, MM's proposition is important. It exposes logical traps that financial managers sometimes fall into, particularly the idea that debt is "cheap financing" because the explicit cost of debt (the interest rate) is less than the cost of equity. Debt has an implicit cost too, because increased borrowing increases **financial risk** and the cost of equity. When both costs are considered, debt is not cheaper than equity. MM show that if there are no corporate income taxes, the firm's weighted-average cost of capital does not depend on the amount of debt financing.

How do corporate income taxes modify MM's leverage irrelevance proposition?

Debt interest is a tax-deductible expense. Thus borrowing creates an **interest tax shield,** which equals the marginal corporate tax rate T_c times the interest payment $r_{debt} \times D$. Future interest tax shields are usually valued by discounting at the borrowing rate r_{debt}. In the special case of permanent debt,

$$\text{PV tax shield} = \frac{T_c\,(r_{debt} \times D)}{r_{debt}} = T_c D$$

Of course interest tax shields are valuable only for companies that are making profits and paying taxes.

If interest tax shields are valuable, why don't all taxpaying firms borrow as much as possible?

The more they borrow, the higher the odds of financial distress. The **costs of financial distress** can be broken down as follows:

- Direct bankruptcy costs, primarily legal and administrative costs.
- Indirect bankruptcy costs, reflecting the difficulty of managing a company when it is in bankruptcy proceedings.
- Costs of the threat of bankruptcy, such as poor investment decisions resulting from conflicts of interest between debtholders and stockholders.

Suppose I add interest tax shields and costs of financial distress to MM's leverage irrelevance proposition. What's the result?

The **trade-off theory** of optimal capital structure. The trade-off theory says that financial managers should increase debt to the point where the value of additional interest tax shields is just offset by additional costs of possible financial distress.

The trade-off theory says that firms with safe, tangible assets and plenty of taxable income should operate at high debt levels. Less profitable firms, or firms with risky, intangible assets, ought to borrow less.

What's the pecking order theory?

The **pecking order theory** says that firms prefer internal financing (that is, earnings retained and reinvested) over external financing. If external financing is needed, they prefer to issue debt rather than issue new shares. The pecking order theory starts with the observation that managers know more than outside investors about the firm's value and prospects. Investors realize that firms may seek to issue equity when their stock is overvalued and therefore mark down the stock price when an equity issue is announced. Internal financing avoids this problem. If external financing is necessary, debt is the first choice.

The pecking order theory says that the amount of debt a firm issues will depend on its need for external financing. The theory also suggests that financial managers should try to maintain at least some **financial slack,** that is, a reserve of ready cash or unused borrowing capacity.

Is financial slack always valuable?

Not if it leads to slack managers. High debt levels (and the threat of financial distress) can create strong incentives for managers to work harder, conserve cash, and avoid negative-NPV investments.

Is there a rule for finding optimal capital structure?

Sorry, there are no simple answers for capital structure decisions. Debt may be better than equity in some cases, worse in others. But there are at least four dimensions for the financial manager to think about.

- *Taxes.* How valuable are interest tax shields? Is the firm likely to continue paying taxes over the full life of a debt issue? Safe, consistently profitable firms are most likely to stay in a taxpaying position.
- *Risk.* Financial distress is costly even if the firm survives it. Other things equal, financial distress is more likely for firms with high business risk. That is why risky firms typically issue less debt.
- *Asset type.* If distress does occur, the costs are generally greatest for firms whose value depends on intangible assets. Such firms generally borrow less than firms with safe, tangible assets.
- *Financial slack.* How much is enough? More slack makes it easy to finance future investments, but it may weaken incentives for managers. More debt, and therefore less slack, increases the odds that the firm may have to issue stock to finance future investments.

What happens when firms cannot pay their creditors?

A firm that cannot meet its obligations may try to arrange a **workout** with its creditors to enable it to settle its debts. If this is unsuccessful, the firm may file for **bankruptcy,** in which case the business may be liquidated or reorganized. **Liquidation** means that the firm's assets are sold and the proceeds used to pay creditors. **Reorganization** means that the firm is maintained as an ongoing concern and creditors are compensated with securities in the reorganized firm. Ideally, reorganization should be chosen over liquidation when the firm as a going concern is worth more than its liquidation value. However, the conflicting interests of the different parties can result in violations of this principle.

QUIZ

1. **MM's Leverage Irrelevance Proposition.** True or false? MM's leverage irrelevance proposition says:
   a. The value of the firm does not depend on the fraction of debt versus equity financing.
   b. As financial leverage increases, the value of the firm increases by just enough to offset the additional financial risk absorbed by equity.

   c. The cost of equity increases with financial leverage only when the risk of financial distress is high.

   d. If the firm pays no taxes, the weighted-average cost of capital does not depend on the debt ratio.

2. **Effects of Leverage.** Increasing financial leverage can increase both the cost of debt (r_{debt}) and the cost of equity (r_{equity}). How can the overall cost of capital stay constant? (Assume the firm pays no taxes.)

3. **Tax Shields.** What is an interest tax shield? How does it increase the size of the "pie" for after-tax income stockholders? Explain. *Hint:* Construct a simple numerical example showing how financial leverage affects the total cash flow available to debt and equity investors. Be sure to hold pretax operating income constant.

4. **Value of Tax Shields.** Establishment Industries borrows $800 million at an interest rate of 7.6 percent. It expects to maintain this debt level into the far future. What is the present value of interest tax shields? Establishment will pay tax at an effective rate of 35 percent.

5. **Bankruptcy.** True or false?

   a. When a company becomes bankrupt, it is usually in the interests of the equityholders to seek a liquidation rather than a reorganization.

   b. A reorganization plan must be presented for approval by each class of creditor.

   c. The Internal Revenue Service has first claim on the company's assets in the event of bankruptcy.

   d. In a reorganization, creditors may be paid off with a mixture of cash and securities.

   e. When a company is liquidated, one of the most valuable assets to be sold is often the tax-loss carry-forward.

6. **Trade-Off Theory.** What is the trade-off theory of optimal capital structure? How does it define the optimal debt ratio?

7. **Financial Distress.** Give three examples of the types of costs incurred by firms in financial distress.

8. **Pecking Order Theory.** What is the pecking order theory of optimal capital structure? If the theory is correct, what types of firms would you expect to operate at high debt levels?

9. **Financial Slack.** Why is financial slack valuable? *Hint:* What does the pecking order theory say about financial slack? Are there circumstances where too much financial slack might actually reduce the market value of the firm?

10. **Earnings and Leverage.** Suppose that River Cruises, which currently is all-equity-financed, issues $250,000 of debt and uses the proceeds to repurchase 25,000 shares. Assume that the firm pays no taxes and that debt finance has no impact on its market value. Rework Table 15–3 to show how earnings per share and share return now vary with operating income.

11. **Debt Irrelevance.** Suppose an investor is unhappy with River Cruises's decision to borrow $250,000 (see the previous problem). What modifications can she make to her own investment portfolio to offset the effects of the firm's additional borrowing?

12. **Leverage and P/E Ratio.** Calculate the ratio of price to expected earnings for River Cruises both before and after it borrows the $250,000. Why does the P/E ratio fall after the increase in leverage?

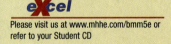

Please visit us at www.mhhe.com/bmm5e or refer to your Student CD

13. **Tax Shields.** Now suppose that the corporate tax is $T_c = .35$. Demonstrate that when River Cruises borrows the $250,000, the combined after-tax income of its debtholders and equityholders increases (compared to all-equity financing) by 35 percent of the firm's interest expense regardless of the state of the economy.

PRACTICE PROBLEMS

14. **Equity Return and Leverage.** The common stock and debt of Northern Sludge are valued at $70 million and $30 million, respectively. Investors currently require a 16 percent return on the common stock and an 8 percent return on the debt. If Northern Sludge issues an additional $10

million of common stock and uses this money to retire debt, what happens to the expected return on the stock? Assume that the change in capital structure does not affect the risk of the debt and that there are no taxes.

15. **Earnings and Leverage.** Reliable Gearing currently is all-equity-financed. It has 10,000 shares of equity outstanding, selling at $100 a share. The firm is considering a capital restructuring. The low-debt plan calls for a debt issue of $200,000 with the proceeds used to buy back stock. The high-debt plan would exchange $400,000 of debt for equity. The debt will pay an interest rate of 10 percent. The firm pays no taxes.

   a. What will be the debt-to-equity ratio after each contemplated restructuring?
   b. If earnings before interest and tax (EBIT) will be either $90,000 or $130,000, what will be earnings per share for each financing mix for both possible values of EBIT? If both scenarios are equally likely, what is expected (i.e., average) EPS under each financing mix? Is the high-debt mix preferable?
   c. Suppose that EBIT is $100,000. What is EPS under each financing mix? Why are they the same in this particular case?

16. **Leverage and Risk Premiums.** Astromet is financed entirely by common stock and has a beta of 1.0. The firm pays no taxes. The stock has a price-earnings multiple of 10 and is priced to offer a 10 percent expected return. The company decides to repurchase half the common stock and substitute an equal value of debt. If the debt yields a *risk-free* 5 percent, calculate

   a. the beta of the common stock after the refinancing.
   b. the required return and risk premium on the common stock before the refinancing.
   c. the required return and risk premium on the common stock after the refinancing.
   d. the required return on the debt.
   e. the required return on the company (i.e., stock and debt combined) after the refinancing.

   Assume that the operating profit of the firm is expected to remain constant. Give

   f. the percentage increase in earnings per share after the refinancing.
   g. the new price-earnings multiple. *Hint:* Has anything happened to the stock price?

17. **Leverage and Capital Costs.** Hubbard's Pet Foods is financed 80 percent by common stock and 20 percent by bonds. The expected return on the common stock is 12 percent, and the rate of interest on the bonds is 6 percent. Assume that the bonds are default-free and that there are no taxes. Now assume that Hubbard's issues more debt and uses the proceeds to retire equity. The new financing mix is 60 percent equity and 40 percent debt. If the debt is still default-free, what happens to the expected rate of return on equity? What happens to the expected return on the package of common stock and bonds?

18. **Leverage and Capital Costs.** "MM totally ignore the fact that as you borrow more, you have to pay higher rates of interest." Explain carefully whether this is a valid objection.

19. **Debt Irrelevance.** What's wrong with the following arguments?

   a. As the firm borrows more and debt becomes risky, both stock- and bondholders demand higher rates of return. Thus by *reducing* the debt ratio we can reduce *both* the cost of debt and the cost of equity, making everybody better off.
   b. Moderate borrowing doesn't significantly affect the probability of financial distress or bankruptcy. Consequently, moderate borrowing won't increase the expected rate of return demanded by stockholders.
   c. A capital investment opportunity offering a 10 percent internal rate of return is an attractive project if it can be 100 percent debt-financed at an 8 percent interest rate.
   d. The more debt the firm issues, the higher the interest rate it must pay. That is one important reason why firms should operate at conservative debt levels.

20. **Leverage and Capital Costs.** A firm currently has a debt-equity ratio of 1/2. The debt, which is virtually riskless, pays an interest rate of 6 percent. The expected rate of return on the equity is 12 percent. What would happen to the expected rate of return on equity if the firm reduced its debt-equity ratio to 1/3? Assume the firm pays no taxes.

21. **Leverage and Capital Costs.** If an increase in the debt-equity ratio makes both debt and equity more risky, how can the cost of capital remain unchanged?

22. **Tax Shields.** Look back to Table 3–2 where we provided a summary 2004 income statement for PepsiCo, Inc. If the tax rate is 35 percent, what is PepsiCo's annual interest tax shield? What is

the present value of the annual tax shield if the company plans to maintain its current debt level indefinitely? Assume a discount rate of 8 percent.

23. **WACC.** Here is Establishment Industries's market-value balance sheet (figures in millions):

Net working capital	$ 550	Debt	$ 800
Long-term assets	$2,150	Equity	$1,900
Value of firm	$2,700		$2,700

The debt is yielding 7 percent, and the cost of equity is 14 percent. The tax rate is 35 percent. Investors expect this level of debt to be permanent.

a. What is Establishment's WACC?

b. Write out a market-value balance sheet assuming Establishment has no debt. Use your answer to Problem 4.

24. **Tax Shields and WACC.** Here are book- and market-value balance sheets of the United Frypan Company:

BOOK-VALUE BALANCE SHEET			
Net working capital	$ 20	Debt	$ 40
Long-term assets	80	Equity	60
	$100		$100

MARKET-VALUE BALANCE SHEET			
Net working capital	$ 20	Debt	$ 40
Long-term assets	140	Equity	120
	$160		$160

Assume that MM's theory holds except for taxes. There is no growth, and the $40 of debt is expected to be permanent. Assume a 35 percent corporate tax rate.

a. How much of the firm's value is accounted for by the debt-generated tax shield?

b. What is United Frypan's after-tax WACC if $r_D = 8\%$ and $r_E = 15\%$?

c. Now suppose that Congress passes a law that eliminates the deductibility of interest for tax purposes after a grace period of 5 years. What will be the new value of the firm, other things equal? Assume an 8 percent borrowing rate.

25. **Bankruptcy.** What are the drawbacks of operating a firm that is close to bankruptcy? Give some examples.

26. **Bankruptcy.** Explain why equity can sometimes have a positive value even when companies petition for bankruptcy.

27. **Costs of Financial Distress.** The Salad Oil Storage Company (SOS) has financed a large part of its facilities with long-term debt. There is a significant risk of default, but the company is not on the ropes yet. Explain

a. why SOS stockholders could lose by investing in a positive-NPV project financed by an equity issue.

b. why SOS stockholders could gain by investing in a highly risky, negative-NPV project.

28. **Financial Distress.** Explain how financial distress can lead to conflicts of interest between debt and equity investors. Then explain how these conflicts can lead to costs of financial distress.

29. **Costs of Financial Distress.** For which of the following firms would you expect the costs of financial distress to be highest? Explain briefly.

a. A computer software company that depends on skilled programmers to produce new products.

b. A shipping company that operates a fleet of modern oil tankers.

30. **Trade-Off Theory.** Smoke and Mirrors currently has EBIT of $25,000 and is all-equity-financed. EBIT is expected to stay at this level indefinitely. The firm pays corporate taxes equal to 35 percent of taxable income. The discount rate for the firm's projects is 10 percent.

   a. What is the market value of the firm?
   b. Now assume the firm issues $50,000 of debt paying interest of 6 percent per year, using the proceeds to retire equity. The debt is expected to be permanent. What will happen to the total value of the firm (debt plus equity)?
   c. Recompute your answer to (b) under the following assumptions: The debt issue raises the probability of bankruptcy. The firm has a 30 percent chance of going bankrupt after 3 years. If it does go bankrupt, it will incur bankruptcy costs of $200,000. The discount rate is 10 percent. Should the firm issue the debt?

31. **Pecking Order Theory.** Alpha Corp. and Beta Corp. both produce turbo encabulators. Both companies' assets and operations are growing at the same rate, and their annual capital expenditures are about the same. However, Alpha Corp. is the more efficient producer and is consistently more profitable. According to the pecking order theory, which company should have the higher debt ratio? Explain.

32. **Financial Slack.** Look back to the Sealed Air example in the box in Section 15.4. What was the value of financial slack to Sealed Air before its restructuring? What does the success of the restructuring say about optimal capital structure? Would you recommend that all firms restructure as Sealed Air did?

CHALLENGE PROBLEMS ᴴᴹ™

33. **Costs of Financial Distress.** Let's go back to the Double-R Nutting Company. Suppose that Double-R's bonds have a face value of $50. Its current *market-value* balance sheet is

Assets		Liabilities and Equity	
Net working capital	$20	Bonds outstanding	$25
Fixed assets	10	Common stock	5
Total assets	$30	Total liabilities and shareholders' equity	$30

   Who would gain or lose from the following maneuvers?

   a. Double-R pays a $10 cash dividend.
   b. Double-R halts operations, sells its fixed assets for $6, and converts net working capital into $20 cash. It invests its $26 in Treasury bills.
   c. Double-R encounters an investment opportunity requiring a $10 initial investment with NPV = $0. It borrows $10 to finance the project by issuing more bonds with the same security, seniority, and so on, as the existing bonds.
   d. Double-R finances the investment opportunity in part (c) by issuing more common stock.

34. **Trade-Off Theory.** Ronald Masulis[14] has analyzed the stock price impact of *exchange offers* of debt for equity or vice versa. In an exchange offer, the firm offers to trade freshly issued securities for seasoned securities in the hands of investors. Thus a firm that wanted to move to a higher debt ratio could offer to trade new debt for outstanding shares. A firm that wanted to move to a more conservative capital structure could offer to trade new shares for outstanding debt securities. Masulis found that debt-for-equity exchanges were good news (stock price increased on announcement) and equity-for-debt exchanges were bad news.

   a. Are these results consistent with the trade-off theory of capital structure?

---

[14] R. W. Masulis, "The Effects of Capital Structure Change on Security Prices: A Study of Exchange Offers," *Journal of Financial Economics* 8 (June 1980), pp. 139–77, and "The Impact of Capital Structure Change on Firm Value," *Journal of Finance* 38 (March 1983), pp. 107–26.

b. Are the results consistent with the evidence that investors regard announcements of (i) stock issues as bad news, (ii) stock repurchases as good news, and (iii) debt issues as no news or, at most, trifling disappointments?

35. **Pecking Order Theory.** Construct a simple example to show that a firm's existing stockholders gain if it can sell overpriced stock to new investors and invest the cash in a zero-NPV project. Who loses from these actions? If investors are aware that managers are likely to issue stock when it is overpriced, what will happen to the stock price when the issue is announced?

36. **Pecking Order Theory.** When companies announce an issue of common stock, the share price typically falls. When they announce an issue of debt, there is typically only a negligible change in the stock price. Can you explain why?

37. **Taxes.** MM's proposition I suggests that in the absence of taxes it makes no difference whether the firm borrows on behalf of its shareholders or whether they borrow directly. However, if there are corporate taxes, this is no longer the case. Construct a simple example to show that with taxes it is better for the firm to borrow than for the shareholders to do so.

38. **Taxes.** MM's proposition I, when modified to recognize corporate taxes, suggests that there is a tax advantage to firm borrowing. If there is a tax advantage to firm borrowing, there is also a tax *disadvantage* to firm lending. Explain why.

STANDARD &POOR'S

1. Go to Market Insight at **www.mhhe.com/edumarketinsight**. Review the Ratio and Profitability reports for one or more of the following companies: UAL Corp. (UAL), Interstate Bakeries (IBCIQ), and Kmart (KM). Are you able to see a trend toward financial distress for these companies? What factors seem to be associated with their financial distress?

2. Go to Market Insight at **www.mhhe.com/edumarketinsight**. In the Excel Analytics section, find the long-term debt ratio for Georgia Pacific (GP) and Microsoft (MSFT). Do the comparative ratios make sense in terms of the trade-off theory of debt policy?

3. Now look at the debt ratio for Merck (MRK). Look as well at Merck's coverage ratios (cash coverage, times interest earned). Does Merck's debt policy seem more consistent with the trade-off or pecking order theory?

SOLUTIONS TO SELF-TEST QUESTIONS

15.1   Price per share will stay at $10, so with $350,000, River Cruises can repurchase 35,000 shares, leaving 65,000 outstanding. The remaining value of equity will be $650,000. Overall firm value stays at $1 million. Shareholders' wealth is unchanged: They start with shares worth $1 million, receive $350,000, and retain shares worth $650,000.

15.2   a.

Data			
Number of shares	25,000		
Price per share	$10		
Market value of shares	$250,000		
Market value of debt	$750,000		

	State of the Economy		
	Slump	**Normal**	**Boom**
Operating income, dollars	75,000	125,000	175,000
Interest, dollars	75,000	75,000	75,000
Equity earnings, dollars	0	50,000	100,000
Earnings per share, dollars	0	2.00	4.00
Return on shares	0%	20%	40%

Every change of $50,000 in operating income leads to a change in the return to equityholders of 20 percent. This is double the swing in equity returns when debt was only $500,000.

b.   The stockholder should lend out $3 for every $1 invested in River Cruises's stock. For example, he could buy one share for $10 and then lend $30. The payoffs are:

	State of the Economy		
	Slump	Normal	Boom
Earnings on one share, dollars	0	2.00	4.00
Plus interest at 10%, dollars	3.00	3.00	3.00
Net earnings, dollars	3.00	5.00	7.00
Return on $40 investment	7.5%	12.5%	17.5%

15.3   Business risk is unaffected by capital structure. As the financing mix changes, whatever equity is outstanding must absorb the fixed business risk of the firm. The less equity, the more risk absorbed per share. Therefore, as capital structure changes, r_{assets} is held fixed while r_{equity} adjusts.

15.4   Wal-Mart's borrowing reduced taxable profits by $996 million. With a tax rate of 35 percent, tax was reduced by $.35 \times \$996 = \$348.6$ million. If the borrowing is permanent, Wal-Mart will save this amount of tax each year. The present value of the tax savings would be $348.6/.06 = $5,810 million.

15.5   In bankruptcy bondholders will receive $2 million less. This lowers the expected cash flow from the bond and reduces its present value. Therefore, the bonds will be priced lower and must offer a higher interest rate. This higher rate is paid by the firm today. It comes out of stockholders' income. Thus common stock value falls.

15.6   The conflicts are costly because they lead to poor investment decisions. The more debt the firm has today, the greater the chance of poor decisions in the future. Investors foresee this possibility and reduce today's market value of the firm.

15.7   The biotech company. Its assets are all intangible. If bankruptcy threatens and the best scientists accept job offers from other firms, there may not be much value remaining for the biotech company's debt and equity investors. On the other hand, bankruptcy would have little or no effect on the value of 50 producing oil wells and of the oil reserves still in the ground.

15.8   The electric utility has the most stable cash flow. It also has the highest reliance on tangible assets that would not be impaired by a bankruptcy. It should have the highest debt ratio. The software firm has the least dependence on tangible assets and the most on assets that have value only if the firm continues as an ongoing concern. It probably also has the most unpredictable cash flows. It should have the lowest debt ratio.

MINICASE

In March 2007 the management team of Londonderry Air (LA) met to discuss a proposal to purchase five shorthaul aircraft at a total cost of $25 million. There was general enthusiasm for the investment, and the new aircraft were expected to generate an annual cash flow of $4 million for 20 years.

The focus of the meeting was on how to finance the purchase. LA had $20 million in cash and marketable securities (see table), but Ed Johnson, the chief financial officer, pointed out that the company needed at least $10 million in cash to meet normal outflow and as a contingency reserve. This meant that there would be a cash deficiency of $15 million, which the firm would need to cover either by the sale of common stock or by additional borrowing. While admitting that the arguments were finely balanced, Mr. Johnson recommended an issue of stock. He pointed out that the airline industry was subject to wide swings in profits and the firm should be careful to avoid the risk of excessive borrowing. He

estimated that in market value terms the long-term debt ratio was about 62 percent and that a further debt issue would raise the ratio to 64 percent.

Mr. Johnson's only doubt about making a stock issue was that investors might jump to the conclusion that management believed the stock was overpriced, in which case the announcement might prompt an unjustified selloff by investors. He stressed therefore that the company needed to explain carefully the reasons for the issue. Also, he suggested that demand for the issue would be enhanced if at the same time LA increased its dividend payment. This would provide a tangible indication of management's confidence in the future.

These arguments cut little ice with LA's chief executive. "Ed," she said, "I know that you're the expert on all this, but everything you say flies in the face of common sense. Why should we want to sell more equity when our stock has fallen over the past year by nearly a fifth? Our stock is currently offering a dividend yield of 6.5 percent, which makes equity an expensive source of capital. Increasing the dividend would simply make it more expensive. What's more, I don't see the point of paying out more money to the stockholders at the same time that we are asking *them* for cash. If we hike the dividend, we will need to increase the amount of the stock issue; so we will just be paying the higher dividend out of the shareholders' own pockets. You're also ignoring the question of dilution. Our equity currently has a book value of $12 a share; it's not playing fair by our existing shareholders if we now issue stock for around $10 a share.

"Look at the alternative. We can borrow today at 5 percent. We get a tax break on the interest, so the after-tax cost of borrowing is .65 × 5 = 3.25 percent. That's about half the cost of equity. We expect to earn a return of 15 percent on these new aircraft. If we can raise money at 3.25 percent and invest it at 15 percent, that's a good deal in my book.

"You finance guys are always talking about risk, but as long as we don't go bankrupt, borrowing doesn't add any risk at all. In any case my calculations show that the debt ratio is only 45 percent, which doesn't sound excessive to me.

"Ed, I don't want to push my views on this—after all, you're the expert. We don't need to make a firm recommendation to the board until next month. In the meantime, why don't you get one of your new business graduates to look at the whole issue of how we should finance the deal and what return we need to earn on these planes?"

Evaluate Mr. Johnson's arguments about the stock issue and dividend payment as well as the reply of LA's chief executive. Who is correct? What is the required rate of return on the new planes?

Summary financial statements for Londonderry Air, 2006 (figures are book values, in millions of dollars)

Balance Sheet			
Bank debt	$ 50	Cash	$ 20
Other current liabilities	20	Other current assets	20
10% bond, due 2026[a]	100	Fixed assets	250
Stockholders' equity[b]	120		
Total liabilities	$290	Total assets	$290
Income Statement			
Gross profit	$57.5		
Depreciation	20.0		
Interest	7.5		
Pretax profit	30.0		
Tax	10.5		
Net profit	19.5		
Dividend	6.5		

[a] The yield to maturity on LA debt currently is 5 percent.
[b] LA has 10 million shares outstanding, with a market price of $10 a share. LA's equity beta is estimated at 1.25, the market risk premium is 8 percent, and the Treasury bill rate is 4 percent.

Payout Policy

RELATED WEB LINKS

www.earnings.com

www.ex-dividend.com Data on recent dividend declarations.

www.cfonews.com Dividend and repurchase announcements.

www.stocksplits.net Information on and calendars of stock splits.

This investor is obviously delighted with her extra cash, but can companies increase share value simply by increasing their dividend payout?
Everett Collection

In this chapter we explain how companies set their payout policy and we discuss the controversial question of how this policy affects value.

Why should you care about these issues? Of course, if you are responsible for deciding on your company's payout, you will want to know how it affects the value of your stock. But there is a more general reason. When we discussed the company's investment decision, we assumed that it was not affected by financing policy. In that case, a good project is a good project, no matter how it is ultimately financed. If payout policy does not affect value, this holds true. But suppose that there is an effect. Then the attractiveness of a project would depend on where the money was coming from. For example, if investors prefer companies with high dividend payouts, then these firms might be reluctant to take on new projects that required them to cut back dividends.

We start the chapter with a discussion of how dividends are paid and how firms repurchase their stock. We then show that in an ideal world, the value of a firm would be independent of its payout policy. This demonstration is in the same spirit as the Modigliani and Miller debt-irrelevance proposition of the previous chapter.

That leads us to look at the real-world complications that might favor one policy over another. These complications include transaction costs, taxes, and the signals that investors might read into the firm's decisions.

After studying this chapter you should be able to:

- Describe how dividends are paid and how companies decide on dividend payments.

- Explain how stock repurchases are used to distribute cash to shareholders.

- Explain why dividends and repurchases may be used to signal the prospects of the firm.

- Explain why payout policy would not affect firm value in an ideal world.

- Show how differences in the tax treatment of dividends and capital gains might affect payout policy.

16.1 How Companies Pay Out Cash to Shareholders

Companies can pay out cash to their shareholders in two ways. They can pay a dividend, or they can buy back some of their outstanding shares. Figure 16–1 shows that, taken together, dividends and share repurchases amount to a high proportion of earnings. For example, between 1999 and 2003 dividend payments by U.S. companies averaged 46 percent of earnings, while repurchases came to a further 35 percent.

Notice that before 1983 stock repurchases were fairly rare, but since then they have become increasingly common. In 2003, a relatively quiet year for repurchases, five U.S. companies each bought back more than $4 billion of stock. Among them were Pfizer ($13 billion), Microsoft ($6.5 billion), and Cisco Systems ($6 billion). Exxon-Mobil is in first place, having spent about $44 billion buying back its stocks since 1980.

In most years dividends are the principal way that corporate America returns cash to its shareholders. Nevertheless, a relatively small proportion of public companies pay a dividend. Some of the remainder have paid dividends in the past but then fell on hard times and were forced to conserve cash. The other group of non-dividend-payers are mostly growth companies. They include such household names as Sun Microsystems, Cisco, and Oracle, as well as many small, rapidly growing firms that have no earnings. When these firms do start to pay out cash to their shareholders, these days they are more likely to start by repurchasing stock.

16.2 The Dividend Payment

Before we look at the choice between dividends and stock repurchase, we need to review how these payments to shareholders take place. We begin with the dividend payment.

cash dividend

Payment of cash by the firm to its shareholders.

In January 2005 Weyerhaeuser's board of directors met to discuss the company's dividends and decided that the company should pay a regular quarterly **cash dividend** of $.40 per share, making a total payment for the year of $1.60. The term *regular* indicates that the directors expected to maintain the payment in the future. If they did not want to give that kind of reassurance, they could have declared both a regular and

FIGURE 16–1 Dividends and stock repurchases in the United States, 1980–2003

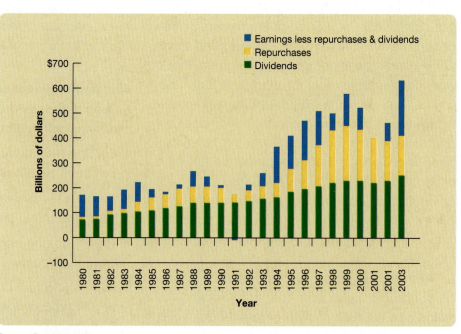

Source: Compustat.

FIGURE 16–2 The key dates for Weyerhaueser's quarterly dividend.

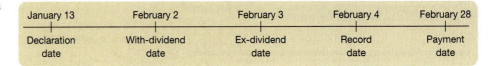

January 13	February 2	February 3	February 4	February 28
Declaration date	With-dividend date	Ex-dividend date	Record date	Payment date

a *special* dividend. Investors realize that special dividends are less likely to be repeated.

Some of Weyerhaeuser's shareholders may have welcomed the cash, but others preferred to reinvest the dividend in the company. To help these investors, Weyerhaeuser offered an automatic dividend reinvestment plan. If a shareholder belonged to this plan, his or her dividends were automatically used to buy additional shares.[1]

Who receives the Weyerhaeuser dividend? That may seem an obvious question but, because shares trade constantly, the firm's record of who owns its shares can never be fully up to date. So Weyerhaeuser announced that it would send a dividend check on February 28 (the *payment date*) to all shareholders recorded in its books on February 4 (the *record date*).

Weyerhaeuser stock could be bought *with dividend* until 2 days before the record date. So if you bought the shares on or before February 2, you could be sure of receiving the dividend. After that it was too late to record the purchase in the company's books, and therefore the share traded **ex-dividend.** Other things equal, the stock is worth more when it is with dividend. Thus when the stock "goes ex," we would expect the stock price to drop by the value of the dividend.

Figure 16–2 illustrates the sequence of the key dividend dates. This sequence is the same whenever companies pay a dividend (though of course the actual dates will differ).

ex-dividend
Without dividend. Buyer of a stock after the ex-dividend date does not receive the most recently declared dividend.

Self-Test 16.1

Mick Milekin buys 100 shares of Junk Bombs, Inc., on Tuesday, June 2. The company has declared a dividend of $1 per share payable on June 30 to shareholders of record as of Friday, June 5. If the ex-dividend date is June 1, is Mick entitled to the dividend? When will the checks go out in the mail?

Some Legal Limitations on Dividends

Suppose that an unscrupulous board decided to sell all the firm's assets and distribute the money as dividends. That would not leave anything in the kitty to pay the firm's debts. Therefore, bondholders often guard against this danger by placing a limit on dividend payments.

State law also helps to protect the firm's creditors against excessive dividend payments. For example, most states prohibit a company from paying dividends if doing so would make the company insolvent.[2] Also, companies are not allowed to pay a dividend if it cuts into legal capital. Legal capital is generally defined as the par value of the outstanding shares.[3]

Stock Dividends and Stock Splits

Weyerhaeuser's dividend was in the form of cash but companies sometimes declare **stock dividends.** For example, the firm could declare a stock dividend of 10 percent. In this case it would send each shareholder 1 additional share for each 10 that are currently owned.

stock dividend
Distribution of additional shares to a firm's stockholders.

---

[1] Often the new shares in an automatic dividend investment plan are issued at a small discount from the market price; the firm offers this sweetener because it saves the underwriting costs of a regular share issue. Sometimes 10 percent or more of total dividends will be reinvested under such plans.

[2] The statutes define insolvency in different ways. In some cases, it just means an inability to meet immediate obligations; in other cases, it means a deficiency of assets compared with all outstanding fixed liabilities.

[3] Where there is no par value, legal capital consists of part or all the receipts from the issue of shares.

Dividend Payments

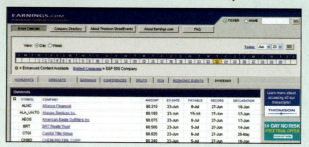

Log on to **www.earnings.com** and click on *Dividends* to find a recent list of dividend declarations. Can you explain what each of the dates means? What is the typical interval between each event?

stock split
Issue of additional shares to firm's stockholders.

A stock dividend is very much like a **stock split.** In both cases the shareholder is given a fixed number of new shares for each one held. For example, in a two-for-one stock split, each investor would receive one additional share for each share already held. The investor ends up with two shares rather than one. A two-for-one stock split is therefore like a 100 percent stock dividend. Both result in a doubling of the number of outstanding shares, but they do not affect the company's assets, profits, or total value.[4]

More often than not, however, the announcement of a stock split does result in a rise in the market price of the stock, even though investors are aware that the company's business is not affected. The reason: Investors take the decision as a signal of management's confidence in the future.[5]

EXAMPLE 16.1 ▶	Stock Dividends and Splits

Amoeba Products has issued 2 million shares currently selling at $15 each. Thus investors place a total market value on Amoeba of $30 million. The company now declares a 50 percent stock dividend. This means that each shareholder will receive one new share for every two shares that are currently held. So the total number of Amoeba shares will increase from 2 million to 3 million. The company's assets are not changed by this paper transaction and are still worth $30 million. The value of each share after the stock dividend is therefore $30/3 = $10.

If Amoeba split its stock three for two, the effect would be the same.[6] In this case two shares would split into three. (Amoeba's motto is "Divide and conquer.") So each shareholder has 50 percent more shares with the same total value. Share price must decline by a third. ◀

16.3 Stock Repurchases

Instead of paying a dividend to its stockholders, the firm can use the cash to repurchase stock. The reacquired shares may be kept in the company's treasury and resold if the company needs money.

---

[4] One survey of managers indicated that 94 percent of splits are motivated by the desire to bring the stock price into an acceptable "trading range." They seem to believe that if the price is too high, investors won't be able to afford to buy a "round lot" of 100 shares. Of course that might be a problem for you or us, but it isn't a worry for the Prudential or GM pension fund. See J. Lakonishok and B. Lev, "Stock Splits and Stock Dividends: Why, Who, and When," *Journal of Finance* 42 (September 1987), pp. 913–932.

[5] The insight that stock splits provide a signal to investors was proposed in E. F. Fama, L. Fisher, M. Jensen, and R. Roll, "The Adjustment of Stock Prices to New Information," *International Economic Review* 10 (February 1969), pp. 1–21. For evidence that companies which split their stock have above-average earnings prospects, see P. Asquith, P. Healy, and K. Palepu, "Earnings and Stock Splits," *Accounting Review* 64 (July 1989), pp. 387–403.

[6] The distinction between stock dividends and stock splits is a technical one. A stock dividend is shown on the balance sheet as a transfer from retained earnings to par value and additional paid-in capital, whereas a split is shown as a proportional reduction in the par value of each share. Neither affects the total book value of stockholders' equity.

stock repurchase
Firm buys back stock from its shareholders.

There are four main ways to implement a **stock repurchase.** By far the most common method is for the firm to announce that it plans to buy its stock in the open market, just like any other investor. However, companies sometimes use a tender offer, where they offer to buy back a stated number of shares at a fixed price. Shareholders can then choose whether to accept this offer. A third procedure is to employ an auction. In this case the firm states a series of prices at which it is prepared to repurchase stock. Shareholders submit offers declaring how many shares they wish to sell at each price, and the company then calculates the lowest price at which it can buy the desired number of shares. Finally, repurchase may take place by direct negotiation with a major shareholder. The most notorious instances are *greenmail* transactions, in which the target of an attempted takeover buys off the hostile bidder by repurchasing any shares that the bidder has acquired. "Greenmail" means that these shares are repurchased at a price that makes the bidder happy to leave the target alone.

Why Repurchases Are Like Dividends

To see why share repurchase is similar to a dividend, look at section A of Table 16–1, which shows the market value of Hewlard Pocket's assets and liabilities. Shareholders hold 100,000 shares worth in total $1 million, so the price per share equals $1 million/100,000 = $10.

Pocket is proposing to pay a dividend of $1 a share. With 100,000 shares outstanding, that amounts to a total payout of $100,000. Section B shows the effect of this dividend payment. The cash account is reduced by $100,000, and the market value of the firm's assets falls to $900,000. Since there are still 900,000 shares outstanding, share price falls to $9. Suppose that before the dividend payment you owned 1,000 shares of Pocket worth $10,000. After the payment you would have $1,000 in cash and 1,000 shares worth $9,000.

Rather than paying out $100,000 as a dividend, Pocket could use the cash to buy back 10,000 shares at $10 each. Section C shows what happens. The firm's assets fall to $900,000, just as in section B, but only 90,000 shares remain outstanding, so the price per share remains at $10. If you owned 1,000 shares before the repurchase, you would own 1 percent of the company. If you then sold 100 of your shares to Pocket, you would still own 1 percent of the company. Your sales would put $1,000 of cash in

TABLE 16–1 Cash dividend versus share repurchase. Hewlard Pocket's market-value balance sheet.

Assets		Liabilities and Shareholders' Equity	
A. Original balance sheet			
Cash	$ 150,000	Debt	$ 0
Other assets	850,000	Equity	1,000,000
Value of firm	$1,000,000	Value of firm	$1,000,000
Shares outstanding = 100,000			
Price per share = $1,000,000/100,000 = $10			
B. After cash dividend			
Cash	$ 50,000	Debt	$ 0
Other assets	850,000	Equity	900,000
Value of firm	$ 900,000	Value of firm	$ 900,000
Shares outstanding = 100,000			
Price per share = $900,000/100,000 = $9			
C. After stock repurchase			
Cash	$ 50,000	Debt	$ 0
Other assets	850,000	Equity	900,000
Value of firm	$ 900,000	Value of firm	$ 900,000
Shares outstanding = 90,000			
Price per share = $900,000/90,000 = $10			

your wallet, and you would keep 900 shares worth $9,000. This is precisely the position that you would have been in if Pocket had paid a dividend.

It is not surprising that a cash dividend and a share repurchase are equivalent transactions. In both cases, the firm pays out some of its cash, which then goes into shareholders' pockets. The assets that are left in the company are the same regardless of whether that cash was used to pay a dividend or to buy back shares.

Self-Test 16.2   **What would Table 16–1 look like if the dividend changes to $1.50 per share and the share repurchase to $150,000?**

The Role of Repurchases

Repurchases are like bumper dividends; they cause large amounts of cash to be paid to investors. But they don't *substitute* for dividends. Most companies that repurchase stock are mature, profitable companies that also pay dividends. When a company announces a repurchase program, it is not making a long-term commitment to distribute more cash. Repurchases are therefore much more volatile than dividends. They tend to mushroom during boom times, as firms accumulate excess cash, and wither in recessions.

Suppose that a company has a large amount of unwanted cash or wishes to change its capital structure by replacing equity with debt. It will usually do so by repurchasing stock rather than by paying out large dividends. For example, consider the case of U.S. banks. In 1997 large bank holding companies paid out just under 40 percent of their earnings as dividends. There were few profitable investment opportunities for the remaining income, but the banks did not want to commit themselves in the long run to any larger dividend payments. They therefore returned the cash to shareholders not by upping the dividend rate but by repurchasing $16 billion of stock.

Shareholders often worry that excess cash will be frittered away on unprofitable ventures. So when firms announce that they will use the cash to repurchase shares, the stock price generally rises. Of course, investors would be less thrilled if the management of their favorite growth company suddenly announced that it could not think of anything better to do with the cash.

Repurchases and Share Valuation

Now here is a question that often causes confusion. We stated in Chapter 6 that the value of a share of stock is equal to the discounted value of the stream of dividends paid on that stock. If companies also hand back cash to their shareholders in the form of repurchases, does our simple dividend discount model still hold?

The answer is yes, but we need to explain why. Suppose that you hold one share of stock. As long as you continue to hold it, you will be entitled to receive any dividend that the company pays. However, if you sell your share either to another investor or to the company itself, you receive cash from the sale, but of course you lose out on any *subsequent* dividends that the company may pay. You can, therefore, value the share either by assuming that you continue to hold it (i.e., discount a continuing stream of dividends) or by assuming that you sell the share back to the company (i.e., discount both the dividend stream *up to the time of sale* and the price at which the stock is sold). As long as the company buys your share at a fair price, the two methods are equivalent.

Here is a simple example: Company X has outstanding 100,000 shares and pays a dividend of $10 a share. Investors expect this dividend to be maintained indefinitely and require a return of 10 percent of their investment. Therefore share price today is

$$PV(\text{share}) = 10/1.10 + 10/(1.10)^2 + \cdots = 10/.10 = \$100$$

Since the dividend stream is not expected to grow, the share price is forecast to remain at $100 after each dividend is paid.

Stock Repurchases

Log on to biz.yahoo.com/bizwk and search for news on recent or planned stock repurchases. What reasons have the companies given for the repurchases? Look up the companies on finance.yahoo.com. Do the repurchase programs appear to be a substitute for dividends?

Now suppose that the company announces that it plans to repurchase 1,000 shares in the market just after it has paid the next dividend. The announcement does not change investors' forecast of future dividends per share. So those shareholders who do not plan to sell their stock back to the company can continue to look forward to dividends of $10 per share each year and will be happy to pay $100 today for the share.

But what about those shareholders who *do* plan to sell their stock? They will receive at the end of the year an expected dividend of $10 plus the $100 that the company must pay to repurchase their stock. The value of the stock today for these shareholders is (10 + 100)/1.10 = $100. Thus, it does not matter whether we consider the cash flows for the shareholder who continues to hold the stock or the cash flows for the shareholder who resells her stock to the company. As long as the company pays a fair price for the share, both methods give the same value. It would, however, be double counting to assume that a shareholder could both sell her share *and* continue to receive dividends.

As long as company X's announcement does not lead investors to revise their view of company prospects, it will not affect today's company value. But after the repurchase has taken place, there will be 1,000 fewer shares outstanding. Since each share is worth $100, the *total* value of the company's stock will fall by 1,000 × $100 = $100,000.

16.4 How Do Companies Decide on the Payout?

What does the board of directors think about when it sets the dividend? To help answer this question, John Lintner held a classic series of interviews with corporate managers about their payout policies.[7] His conclusions can be summarized in four stylized facts:

1. Firms have long-run target dividend-payout ratios. This ratio is the fraction of earnings paid out as dividends.
2. Managers focus more on dividend *changes* than on absolute levels. Thus paying a $2 dividend is an important financial decision if last year's dividend was $1 but no big deal if last year's dividend was $2.
3. Dividend changes follow shifts in long-run sustainable earnings. So even if circumstances appeared to warrant a large dividend increase, managers are likely to move only partway toward their target. As a result, dividends are much more stable than earnings.

---

[7] See J. Lintner, "Distribution of Incomes of Corporations among Dividends, Retained Earnings, and Taxes," *American Economic Review* 46 (May 1956), pp. 97–113. For a more recent survey of payout policies which argues that target payout ratios have become less common, see A. Brav, J. R. Graham, C. R. Harvey, and R. Michaely, "Payout Policy in the 21st Century," *Journal of Financial Economics,* Volume 77, Issue 3, September 2005, pp. 483–527.

4. Managers are reluctant to make dividend changes that may have to be reversed. They are particularly worried about having to cut dividends.

When Lintner conducted his interviews, dividends were effectively the only means of distributing cash. More recent work on payout policy since the dramatic increase in repurchases suggests a fifth stylized fact:

5. Firms repurchase stock when they have accumulated a large amount of unwanted cash or wish to change their capital structure by replacing equity with debt.

The Information Content of Dividends

When companies declare a dividend or decide to repurchase stock, management recognizes that investors will wonder whether the decision provides information about the company's profitability. A firm that reports good earnings and pays a generous dividend is putting its money where its mouth is. Creative accountants may overstate earnings, but dividends require the firm to come up with hard cash. Of course, firms can cheat in the short run by inflating earnings and scraping up cash to pay a generous dividend. But it is hard to cheat in the long run, for a firm that is not making money will not have the cash flow to pay out unless it cuts back on investment or turns to investors for additional debt or equity financing. Since these actions are costly, only firms with sufficient cash flow will find that it pays to signal their good fortune by paying high dividends.

Investors can't read managers' minds, but they do learn from managers' actions. Managers therefore know that when dividends increase, investors will infer their confidence in the firm's cash flow and earnings. Because a high-dividend-payment policy is costly to firms that do not have the cash to support it, dividend increases signal a company's ability to generate sufficient cash to maintain the dividend payments.

It is no surprise, therefore, to find that announcements of dividend cuts are usually taken as bad news (stock price typically falls) and that dividend increases are good news (stock price rises). This is called the **information content of dividends.** For example, Healy and Palepu found that the announcement of a company's first dividend payment resulted in an average rise of 4 percent in its stock price.[8]

This does not mean that investors like dividends for their own sake. A dividend initiation or increase may be welcomed only as a sign that the company is doing well. Even investors who otherwise prefer low-payout policies might find that a cut in the dividend is unwelcome news about the firm's prospects.

Notice that investors do not get excited about the *level* of a company's dividend; they worry about the *change,* which they view as an important indicator of the company's ability to generate cash. The nearby box illustrates how an unexpected change in dividends can cause the stock price to bounce back and forth as investors struggle to interpret its significance.

information content of dividends
Dividend increases send good news about future cash flow and earnings. Dividend cuts send bad news.

Self-Test 16.3

In January 2004 GATX, a specialized leasing company, announced that although earnings for the latest quarter were higher than a year earlier, it was cutting its regular quarterly dividend from $.32 a share to $.20. It pointed out that this new dividend level better reflected current earnings and recovery expectations. The next day, 10 times the normal number of shares changed hands, and the stock price fell by 16 percent. Why would the dividend cut result in such a sharp fall in price?

The Information Content of Share Repurchase

Share repurchases, like dividends, are a way to hand back cash to shareholders. But unlike dividends, share repurchases are frequently a one-off event. So a company that

[8] P. Healy and K. Palepu, "Earnings Information Conveyed by Dividend Initiations and Omissions," *Journal of Financial Economics* 21 (1988), pp. 149–175.

The Dividend Cut Heard 'Round the World

On May 9, 1994, FPL Group, the parent company of Florida Power & Light Company, announced a 32 percent reduction in its quarterly dividend payout, from 62 cents per share to 42 cents. This was the first-ever dividend cut by a healthy utility. A number of utilities had reduced their dividends in the past, but only after cash flow problems—often associated with heavy investment in nuclear plants—had given them no other choice.

In its announcement, FPL stressed that it had studied the situation carefully and that, given the prospect of increased competition in the electric utility industry, the company's high dividend payout ratio (which had averaged 90 percent in the past 4 years) was no longer in the stockholders' best interests. The new policy resulted in a dividend payout of about 60 percent of the prior year's earnings. Management also announced that, starting in 1995, the dividend payout would be reviewed in February instead of May to reinforce the linkage between dividends and annual earnings. In doing so, the company wanted to minimize unintended "signaling effects" from any future changes in the dividend.

At the same time it announced this change in dividend policy, FPL Group's board authorized the repurchase of up to 10 million shares of common stock over the next 3 years. FPL's management said that 4 million shares would be repurchased over the next 12 months, depending on market conditions. In adopting this strategy, the company noted that changes in the U.S. tax code since 1990 had made capital gains more attractive than dividends to shareholders.

Besides providing a more tax-efficient means of distributing excess capital to its stockholders, FPL's substitution of stock repurchases for dividends was also designed to increase the company's financial flexibility in preparation for a new era of deregulation and heightened competition among utilities. Although much of the cash savings from the dividend cut would be returned to investors in the form of stock repurchases, the rest would be used to retire debt at Florida Power & Light and so reduce the company's leverage ratio. This deleveraging and strengthening of FPL's financial condition were intended to prepare the company for an increase in business risk and to provide the financial resources to take advantage of future growth opportunities.

The stock market's initial reaction to FPL's announcement was negative. On the day of the announcement, the company's stock price fell from $31.88 to $27.50, a drop of nearly 14 percent. But as analysts digested the news and considered the reasons for the reduction, they concluded that the action was not a signal of financial distress but rather a strategic decision that would improve the company's long-term financial flexibility and prospects for growth. This view spread throughout the financial community, and FPL's stock began to recover.

On May 31, less than a month after the announcement, FPL's stock closed at $32.17 (adjusted for the quarterly dividend of 42 cents), or about 30 cents higher than the preannouncement price. By the middle of June, at least 15 major brokerage houses had placed FPL's common stock on their "buy" lists. On May 9, 1995—exactly 1 year after the announcement of the cut—FPL's stock price closed at $37.75, giving stockholders a 1-year postannouncement return (including dividends) of 23.8 percent, more than double the 11.2 percent of the S&P Index and well above the 14.2 percent of the S&P utilities index over the same period.

Source: Modified from D. Soter, E. Brigham, and P. Evanson, "The Dividend Cut 'Heard 'Round the World': The Case of FPL," *Journal of Applied Corporate Finance* 9 (Spring 1996), pp. 4–15. Used with permission.

announces a repurchase program is not making a long-term commitment to earn and distribute more cash. The information in the announcement is therefore likely to be different from that of a dividend payment.

Companies repurchase shares when they have accumulated more cash than they can invest profitably or when they wish to substitute debt for equity. Neither circumstance is good news in itself, but shareholders are frequently relieved to see companies paying out the excess cash rather than frittering it away on unprofitable investments. Shareholders also know that firms with large quantities of debt are particularly wary of squandering cash. So announcements of repurchase programs are usually welcome news to investors.

16.5 Why Payout Policy Should Not Matter

The first step toward understanding *payout policy* is to recognize that the phrase means different things to different people. Therefore, we must start by defining what we mean by it.

A firm's payout decision is often intertwined with other financing or investment decisions. Some firms pay out little cash because management is optimistic about the firm's future and wishes to retain earnings for expansion. In this case the payout decision is a by-product of the firm's capital budgeting decision. Another firm might finance capital expenditures largely by borrowing. This frees up cash that can be paid

out to shareholders. In this case the payout decision is a by-product of the borrowing decision.

We wish to isolate payout policy from other problems of financial management. The precise question we should ask is, What is the effect of a change in payout policy, *given the firm's capital budgeting and borrowing decisions?*

Suppose that the firm proposes to increase its dividend. The cash to finance that dividend increase has to come from somewhere. If we fix the firm's investment outlays and borrowing, there is only one possible source—an issue of stock. What if the firm decides to reduce its dividend? In that case it would have extra cash. If investment outlays and borrowing are fixed, there is only one possible way that this cash can be used—to repurchase stock. Thus payout policy involves a trade-off between higher or lower cash dividends and the issue or repurchase of stock.

One nice feature of economics is that it can accommodate not just two but three opposing points of view. And so it is with payout policy. On one side there is a group that believes high dividends increase value. On the other side there is a group that believes high dividends bring high taxes and therefore reduce firm value. And in the center there is a middle-of-the-road party that believes payout policy makes no difference.

Payout Policy Is Irrelevant in Competitive Markets

The middle-of-the-road party was founded in 1961 by Miller and Modigliani (MM)[9]—the same two who showed that in idealized conditions capital structure also is irrelevant.

We can illustrate MM's views about payout policy by considering the Pickwick Paper Company, which had set aside $100 million in cash to construct a new paper mill. But Pickwick's directors now propose to use the $100 million to increase the dividend payment. If Pickwick is to continue to build its new mill, that cash needs to be replaced. If the borrowing is fixed, there is only one place the money can come from, and that is the sale of new shares. The combination of the dividend payment and the new issue of shares leaves Pickwick and its shareholders in exactly the same position they started from. All that has happened is that Pickwick has put an extra $100 million in investors' pockets (the dividend payment) and then taken it out again (the share issue). In other words, Pickwick is simply recycling cash. To suggest that this makes investors better off is like advising the cook to cool the kitchen by leaving the refrigerator door open.

After Pickwick pays the additional dividend and replaces the cash by selling new shares, the company value is unchanged. The old shareholders now have an extra $100 million of cash in their pockets, but they have given up a stake in the firm to those investors who buy the newly issued shares. The new stockholders are putting up $100 million and therefore will demand to receive shares *worth* $100 million. Since the total value of the company is the same, the value of the old stockholders' stake in the company falls by this $100 million. Thus the extra dividend that the old stockholders receive just offsets the loss in the value of the shares that they hold.

Does it make any difference to the old stockholders that they receive an extra dividend payment plus an offsetting capital loss? It might if that were the only way they could get their hands on the cash. But as long as there are efficient capital markets, they can raise cash by selling shares. Thus Pickwick's old shareholders can "cash in" either by persuading the management to pay a higher dividend or by selling some of their shares. In either case there will be the same transfer of value from the old to the new stockholders. Because investors do not need dividends to convert their shares to cash, they will not pay higher prices for firms with higher dividend payouts. In other words, payout policy will have no impact on the value of the firm. This conclusion is known as the **MM dividend-irrelevance proposition.**

MM dividend-irrelevance proposition
Under ideal conditions, the value of the firm is unaffected by dividend policy.

[9] M. H. Miller and F. Modigliani, "Dividend Policy, Growth and the Valuation of Shares," *Journal of Business* 34 (October 1961), pp. 411–433.

The example of the Pickwick Paper Company showed that the firm cannot make shareholders better off simply by increasing the proportion of earnings paid out as dividends. But the same argument also works in reverse: If investment and borrowing are held constant, any *reduction* in dividends must be balanced by a *purchase* of stock. For example, suppose that Old Curiosity Shops has $100 million surplus cash which it had been proposing to pay out to shareholders as a dividend. If Old Curiosity now decides not to pay this dividend, then the surplus cash can be used only to buy back some of the company's shares. The shareholders miss out on $100 million of dividend payments but they receive $100 million from the sale to the company of part of their shareholdings. Thus MM's irrelevance argument holds both for increases in dividends and for reductions. As these examples illustrate, payout policy is a trade-off between cash dividends and the issue or repurchase of common stock. In a perfect capital market, the payout decision would have no impact on firm value.

These examples may seem artificial at first, for we do not observe firms scheduling a stock issue with every dividend payment. But there are many firms that pay dividends and also issue stock from time to time. They could avoid the stock issues by paying lower dividends and retaining more funds in the firm. Many other firms use unwanted cash to repurchase shares. They could instead use the cash to increase the dividend.

Of course our examples of dividend irrelevance have ignored taxes, issue costs, and a variety of other real-world complications. We will turn to these intricacies shortly, but before we do, we note that the crucial assumption in our proof is that the sale or purchase of shares occurs at a fair price. The shares that Pickwick sells to raise $100,000 must actually be worth $100,000; those that Old Curiosity buys for $100,000 must also be worth that figure. In other words, dividend irrelevance assumes efficient capital markets.

EXAMPLE 16.2 ▶ Dividend Irrelevance

The columns labeled "Old Dividend Plan" in Table 16–2 show that Consolidated Pasta is currently expected to pay annual dividends of $10 a share in perpetuity. Shareholders expect a 10 percent rate of return from Consolidated stock, and therefore the value of each share is

$$PV = \frac{10}{1.10} + \frac{10}{(1.10)^2} + \frac{10}{(1.10)^3} + \cdots = \frac{10}{.10} = \$100$$

Consolidated has issued 1 million shares. So the total forecast dividend payment in each year is 1 million × $10 = $10 million, and the total value of Consolidated Pasta equity is 1 million × $100 = $100 million. The president, Al Dente, has read that the value of a share depends on the dividends it pays. That suggests an easy way to keep shareholders happy—increase next year's dividend to $20 per share. That way, he

TABLE 16–2 Consolidated Pasta is currently expected to pay a dividend of $10 million in perpetuity. However, the president is proposing to pay a one-time bumper dividend of $20 million in year 1. To replace the lost cash, the firm will need to issue more shares, and the dividends that will need to be diverted to the new shareholders will exactly offset the effect of the higher dividend in year 1.

	Old Dividend Plan		Revised Dividend Plan	
	Year 1	Year 2 on	Year 1	Year 2 on
Total dividend payments ($ million)	10	10	20	10
Total dividends paid to old shareholders ($ million)	10	10	20	9
Total dividends paid to new shareholders ($ million)	—	—	—	1

Note: New shareholders are putting up $10 million of cash at the end of year 1. Since they require a return of 10 percent, the total dividends paid to the new shares (starting in year 2) must be 10 percent of $10 million, or $1 million.

reasons, share price should rise by the present value of the increase in the first-year dividend to a new value of

$$PV = \frac{20}{1.10} + \frac{10}{(1.10)^2} + \frac{10}{(1.10)^3} + \cdots = \frac{10}{1.10} + \frac{10}{.10} = \$109.91$$

The president's heart is obviously in the right place. Unfortunately, his head isn't. Let's see why.

Consolidated is proposing to pay out an extra $10 million in dividends. It can't do that *and* earn the same profits in the future, unless it also replaces the lost cash by an issue of shares. The new shareholders who provide this cash will require a return of 10 percent on their investment. So Consolidated will need to pay $1 million a year of dividends to the new shareholders ($1 million/$10 million = .10, or 10%). This is shown in the last line of Table 16–2.

As long as the company replaces the extra cash it pays out, it will continue to earn the same profits and to pay out $10 million of dividends each year from year 2. However, $1 million of this total will be needed to satisfy the new shareholders, leaving only $9 million (or $9 a share) for the original shareholders. Now recalculate the value of the original shares under the revised dividend plan:

$$PV = \frac{20}{1.10} + \frac{9}{(1.10)^2} + \frac{9}{(1.10)^3} + \cdots = \frac{11}{1.10} + \frac{9}{.10} = \$100$$

The value of the shares is unchanged. The extra cash dividend in year 1 is exactly offset by the reduction of dividends per share in later years. This reduction is necessary because some of the money paid out as dividends in later years is diverted to the new shareholders.[10] ◀

The Assumptions behind Dividend Irrelevance

Many stockholders and businesspeople find it difficult to accept the suggestion that dividend policy is irrelevant. When faced with MM's argument, they often reply that dividends are cash in hand while capital gains are at best in the bush. It may be true, they say, that the recipient of an extra cash dividend forgoes an equal capital gain, but if the dividend is safe and the capital gain is risky, isn't the stockholder ahead?

It's correct that dividends are more predictable than capital gains. Managers can stabilize dividends but they cannot control stock price. From this it seems a small step to conclude that increased dividends make the firm less risky.[11] But the important point is, once again, that as long as investment policy and borrowing are held constant, a firm's *overall* cash flows are the same regardless of payout policy. The risks borne by *all* the firm's stockholders are likewise fixed by its investment and borrowing policies and unaffected by dividend policy.

If we really believed that existing stockholders are better off by trading a risky asset for cash, then we would also have to argue that the new stockholders—those who trade cash for the newly issued shares—are worse off. But this doesn't make sense: The new stockholders are bearing risk, but they are getting paid for it. They are willing to buy because the new shares are priced to offer an expected return adequate to compensate for the risk.

---

[10] Notice that at the end of year 1, when the new shareholders purchase their shares, the dividend per share they can look forward to receiving will be $9; since this dividend is expected to be a perpetuity, the share price at that time will be $9/.10 = $90. So the new shareholders will receive $10,000,000/$90 = 111,111 shares. Consistent with Table 16–2, the new shareholders therefore will receive total dividend payments of 111,111 × $9 = $1 million and the old shareholders will receive total dividend payments of 1 million × $9 = $9 million. Notice also that after the extra $10 million dividend is paid in year 1, the share price falls to $90, and the value of the shares held by the original shareholders falls by exactly $10 million to $90 million.

[11] In that case one might also argue that interest payments are even more predictable, so a company's risk would be reduced by increasing the proportion of profits paid out as interest. How would you respond to that suggestion?

MM's argument for the irrelevance of dividend policy does not assume a world of certainty; it assumes an efficient capital market. Market efficiency means that the transfers of ownership created by shifts in dividend policy are carried out on fair terms. And since the *overall* value of (old and new) stockholders' equity is unaffected, nobody gains or loses.

16.6 Why Dividends May Increase Firm Value

Market Imperfections

Most economists believe that MM's conclusions are correct, given their assumptions of perfect and efficient capital markets. However, nobody claims their model is an exact description of the so-called real world. Thus the impact of payout policy finally boils down to arguments about imperfections and inefficiencies.

Those who believe that dividends are good argue that some investors have a natural preference for high-payout stocks. For example, some financial institutions are legally restricted from holding stocks lacking established dividend records. Trusts and endowment funds may prefer high-dividend stocks because dividends are regarded as spendable "income," whereas capital gains are "additions to principal," which may not be spent.[12]

In addition, many investors look to their stock portfolios for a steady source of cash to live on. In principle this cash can be generated from stocks paying no dividends at all; the investors can just sell off a small fraction of their holdings from time to time. But that can be inconvenient and lead to heavy transaction costs.

Behavioral psychology may also help to explain why some investors prefer to receive regular dividends rather than sell small amounts of stock. We are all liable to succumb to temptation. Some of us may hanker after fattening foods, while others may be dying for a drink. We could seek to control these cravings by willpower, but that can be a painful struggle. Instead, it may be easier to set simple rules for ourselves ("cut out chocolate," or "wine only with meals"). In just the same way, we may welcome the self-discipline that comes from limiting our spending to dividend income and thereby sidestep the difficult decision of how much we should dip into capital.

All this may well be true, but it does not follow that you can increase the value of *your* firm by increasing the dividend payout. Smart managers already have recognized that there is a clientele of investors who would be prepared to pay a premium for high-payout stocks. There are natural clienteles for high-payout stocks, but it does not follow that any particular firm can benefit by increasing its dividends. The high-dividend clienteles already have plenty of high-dividend stocks to choose from.

You don't hear businesspeople argue that because there is a clientele of car buyers, their company should manufacture cars. So why should you believe that because there is a clientele of investors who like high payouts, your company can increase value by manufacturing a high payout? That clientele was probably satisfied long ago.

Self-Test 16.4 | **Suppose an investor in the Altria Group does not need a regular income. What could she do to offset Altria's "overly generous" payout policy? If there were no trading costs, would she have any reason to care about Altria's dividend payout policy? What if there is a brokerage fee on the purchase of new shares? What if Altria has a dividend reinvestment plan that allows the investor to buy shares at a 5 percent discount?**

---

[12] Most colleges and universities are legally free to spend capital gains from their endowments, but this is rarely done.

16.7 Why Dividends May Reduce Firm Value

The low-dividend creed is simple. Companies can convert dividends into capital gains by shifting their dividend policy. If dividends are taxed more heavily than capital gains, such financial alchemy should be welcomed by any taxpaying investor. Firms should pay the lowest cash dividend they can get away with. Surplus cash should be used to repurchase shares.

Table 16–3 illustrates this. It assumes that dividends are taxed at a rate of 40 percent but that capital gains are taxed at only 20 percent. The stocks of firms A and B are equally risky, and investors demand an expected *after-tax* rate of return of 10 percent on each. Investors expect A to be worth $112.50 per share next year. The share price of B is expected to be only $102.50, but a $10 dividend is also forecast, so the total pretax payoff is the same, $112.50.

Both stocks offer the same pretax dollar payoff. Yet B's stock sells for less than A's. The reason is obvious: Investors are willing to pay more for stock A because its return comes in the form of low-taxed capital gains. After tax, both stocks offer the same 10 percent expected return despite the fact that B's *pretax* return is higher.

Suppose the management of firm B eliminates the $10 dividend and uses the cash to repurchase stock instead. We saw earlier that a stock repurchase is equivalent to a cash dividend but it is treated differently by the tax authorities. Stockholders who sell shares back to their firm pay tax only on any capital gains realized in the sale. By substituting a repurchase for a dividend, B's new policy would reduce the taxes paid by stockholders, and its stock price should rise.

Self-Test 16.5

Look again at Table 16–3. What would happen to the price and pretax rate of return on stock B if the tax on capital gains were eliminated?

Why Pay Any Dividends at All?

If dividends are taxed more heavily than capital gains, why should any firm ever pay a cash dividend? If cash is to be distributed to stockholders, isn't share repurchase the best channel for doing so?

Few would go that far. The Internal Revenue Service has attempted to prevent firms from disguising dividends as repurchases. A firm that eliminates dividends and starts repurchasing stock on a regular basis may find that the IRS would recognize the repurchase program for what it really is and would tax the payments accordingly. That

TABLE 16–3 Effects of a shift in dividend policy when dividends are taxed more heavily than capital gains. The high-payout stock (firm B) must sell at a lower price in order to provide the same after-tax return.

	Firm A	Firm B
Next year's price	$112.50	$102.50
Dividend	$ 0	$ 10.00
Total *pretax* payoff	$112.50	$112.50
Today's stock price	$100	$ 97.78
Capital gain	$ 12.50	$ 4.72
Before-tax rate of return (%)	$\frac{12.5}{100} = .125 = 12.5\%$	$\frac{14.72}{97.78} = .1505 = 15.05\%$
Tax on dividend at 40%	$0	$.40 \times \$10 = \$4.00$
Tax on capital gain at 20%	$.20 \times \$12.50 = \$2.50$	$.20 \times \$4.72 = \$.94$
Total after-tax income (dividends plus capital gains less taxes)	$(0 + 12.50) - 2.50 =$ $10.00	$(10 + 4.72)$ $- (4.00 + .94) = \$9.78$
After-tax rate of return (%)	$\frac{10}{100} = .10 = 10\%$	$\frac{9.78}{97.78} = .10 = 10\%$

FINANCE IN PRACTICE

Microsoft's Payout Bonanza

There is a point at which hoarding money becomes embarrassing. . . . Microsoft, which grew into the world's largest software company . . . and which has been generating cash at the rate of $1 billion a month, passed that point years ago. On July 20, it finally addressed the issue.

Its solution was to give back to its shareholders, in various forms, an unprecedented $75 billion. One dollop, to the tune of $32 billion, will be a one-time dividend to be paid in December. Another will be share buybacks worth $30 billion over four years. The third will be a doubling of Microsoft's ongoing dividend to 32 cents a share annually, payable in quarterly installments. Not bad for a company that has not even turned 30 yet, and that only declared its first dividend in January 2003.

The decision is impressive for the mature analysis by Microsoft of its role in the industry and the prospects for the future that it implies.

Source: Adapted from "An End to Growth?" *The Economist*, July 24, 2004, p. 61.© 2004 The Economist Newspaper Group, Inc. Reprinted with permission. Further reproduction is prohibited. **www.economist.com.** All rights reserved.

is why financial managers seldom announce that they are repurchasing stock to save stockholders taxes; they give some other reason.[13]

Taxation of Dividends and Capital Gains under Current Tax Law

In the United States the case for low dividends was strongest before 1986. The top rate of tax on dividends was then 50 percent, while realized capital gains were taxed at 20 percent.

As we write this in 2005, the top rate of tax on both dividends and capital gains is 15 percent. There is, however, one way that tax law continues to favor capital gains. Taxes on dividends have to be paid immediately, but taxes on capital gains can be deferred until shares are sold and the capital gains are realized. Stockholders can choose when to sell their shares and thus when to pay the capital gains tax.[14] The longer they wait, the less the present value of the capital gains tax liability.[15]

The distinction between dividends and capital gains is less important for financial institutions, many of which operate free of all taxes and therefore have no reason to prefer capital gains to dividends or vice versa. Only corporations have a tax reason to *prefer* dividends. They pay corporate income tax on only 30 percent of any dividends received.[16] Thus the effective tax rate on dividends received by large corporations is 30 percent of 35 percent (the marginal rate of corporate income tax), or 10.5 percent. But they have to pay a 35 percent tax on the full amount of any capital gain.

The implications of these tax rules for payout policy are pretty simple. Capital gains have advantages to many investors, but they are far less advantageous than they were 20 or 30 years ago. Consequently, it is less easy today to make convincing arguments in favor of one kind of payout rather than another.

Look, for example, at the nearby box, which discusses Microsoft's plan to pay out $75 billion of cash to its stockholders. Microsoft opted to split this huge payout between a special dividend and stock repurchases. Would the company have chosen to pay such a large dividend if it still attracted tax of 40 or 50 percent? We doubt it. It seems that today companies can be much more relaxed about differences in the tax treatment of dividends and stock repurchases.

---

[13] They might say, "Our stock is a good investment," or "We want to have the shares available to finance acquisitions of other companies." What do you think of these rationales?

[14] If the stock is willed to your heirs, capital gains escape taxation altogether.

[15] Suppose the discount rate is 8 percent, and an investor in a 15 percent capital gains tax bracket has a $100 capital gain. If the stock is sold today, the capital gains tax will be $15. If sale is deferred 1 year, the tax due on that $100 gain still will be $15, but by virtue of delaying the sale for a year, the present value of the tax falls to $15/1.08 = $13.89. The effective tax rate falls to 13.89 percent. The longer the sale is deferred, the lower the effective tax rate.

[16] Actually, the percentage of dividend income on which tax is paid depends on the firm's ownership share in the company paying the dividend. If the share is less than 20 percent, taxes are paid on 30 percent of dividends received.

445

SUMMARY

How are dividends paid, and how do companies decide on dividend payments?

Dividends come in many forms. The most common is the regular **cash dividend,** but sometimes companies pay a special cash dividend, and sometimes they pay a **stock dividend.** A firm is not free to pay dividends at will. For example, it may have accepted restrictions on dividends as a condition for borrowing money.

Most managers seem to have a target **dividend payout ratio.** But if firms simply applied this target payout rate to each year's earnings, dividends could fluctuate wildly. Managers therefore try to smooth dividends by moving only partway toward the target payout in each year.

How are repurchases used to distribute cash to shareholders?

Companies also pay out money to shareholders by repurchasing their shares. **Stock repurchases** have grown rapidly in recent years, but they do not substitute for dividends. Instead, they are generally used to make major one-off changes to the firm's capital structure, particularly when cash resources have outrun good investment opportunities. Repurchases can be like bumper dividends; they cause large amounts of cash to be paid to investors when the firm buys back their shares.

Why may payout decisions be used by management to signal the prospects of the firm?

A firm that chooses a high-dividend policy without the cash flow to back it up will find that it ultimately has to either cut back on investments or turn to capital markets for additional debt or equity financing. Because this is costly, managers do not increase dividends unless they are confident that the firm is generating enough cash to pay them. This is the principal reason that we say that there is an **information content of dividends**—that is, dividend changes are liable to be interpreted as signals of a change in the firm's prospects.

Investors also seem to welcome the announcement that a company plans to repurchase its stock. If they are worried that the company has more cash than it can profitably employ, they may be pleased to see the cash given back to the shareholders.

Why would payout policy not affect firm value in an ideal world?

If we hold the company's investment policy and capital structure constant, then payout policy is a trade-off between cash dividends and the issue or repurchase of common stock. In an ideally simple and perfect world, the choice would have no effect on market value. This is the **MM dividend-irrelevance proposition.** The controversy centers on the effects of payout policy in our flawed world. A common—though by no means universal—view is that high dividends enhance share price. For example, this could occur if there were unsatisfied clienteles for high-payout stocks.

How might differences in the tax treatment of dividends and capital gains affect dividend policy?

Instead of paying dividends, the company can repurchase its own stock. The Internal Revenue Service taxes shareholders only on the capital gains that they realize as a result of the repurchase.

For many years capital gains were taxed at lower rates than dividend income. If dividend income is seriously tax-disadvantaged, we would expect investors to demand a higher before-tax return on high-payout stocks. Instead of paying high dividends, companies should use the cash to repurchase shares or to reduce the amount of share issues. As we write this in 2005, the personal tax rates on dividends and capital gains are now the same. Capital gains retain the advantage that tax can be deferred until the gains are realized, but it is clear that stock repurchases have lost much of their tax benefit.

QUIZ

1. **Dividend Sequence.** Cash Cow International paid a regular quarterly dividend of $.075 a share.

   a. Connect each of the following dates to the correct term:
May 7	Record date
June 6	Payment date
June 7	Ex-dividend date
June 11	Last with-dividend date
July 2	Declaration date

   b. On one of these dates the stock price is likely to fall by about the value of the dividend. Why?

   c. The stock price in early January was $27. What was the prospective dividend yield?

   d. The earnings per share were forecast at around $1.90. What was the percentage payout rate?

   e. Suppose that the company paid a 10 percent stock dividend. What would be the expected fall in the stock price?

2. **Institutional Background.** True or false? If false, correct the statement.

   a. A company may not generally pay a dividend out of legal capital.

   b. A company may not generally pay a dividend if it is insolvent.

   c. The *effective* tax rate on capital gains can be less than the stated tax rate on such gains.

   d. Corporations are not taxed on dividends received from other corporations.

3. **Splits and Dividends.** Shares in Raven Products are selling for $80 per share. There are 1 million shares outstanding. What will be the share price in each of the following situations? Ignore taxes.

   a. The stock splits five for four.

   b. The company pays a 25 percent stock dividend.

   c. The company repurchases 100,000 shares.

4. **Dividend Irrelevance.** You own 2,000 shares of Patriot Corporation, which is about to raise its dividend from $.75 to $1.00 per share. The share price is currently $100. You would prefer that the dividend remain at its current level. What would you do to offset the effects of the increase in the dividend?

5. **DRIPs.** A firm considers initiating an aggressive dividend reinvestment plan (DRIP) in which it allows its investors to use dividends to buy shares at a discount of 40 percent from current market value. The firm's financial manager argues that the policy will benefit shareholders by giving them the opportunity to buy additional shares at a deep discount and will benefit the firm by providing a source of cash. Is the manager correct?

PRACTICE PROBLEMS

6. **Dividends and Repurchases.** While dividend yields in the United States in the late 1990s were at historically low levels, share repurchases were at historical highs. Was this a coincidence?

7. **Dividend Irrelevance.** Respond to the following comment: "It's all very well saying that I can sell shares to cover cash needs, but that may mean selling at the bottom of the market. If the company pays a regular dividend, investors avoid the risk."

8. **Cash Dividends.** The stock of Payout Corp. will go ex-dividend tomorrow. The dividend will be $0.50 per share, and there are 20,000 shares of stock outstanding. The market-value balance sheet for Payout is shown on the following table.

   a. What price is Payout stock selling for today?

   b. What price will it sell for tomorrow? Ignore taxes.

Assets		Liabilities and Equity	
Cash	$100,000	Equity	$1,000,000
Fixed assets	900,000		

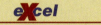

9. **Repurchases.** Now suppose that Payout from Problem 8 announces its intention to repurchase $10,000 worth of stock instead of paying out the dividend.

    a. What effect will the repurchase have on an investor who currently holds 100 shares and sells 1 of those shares back to the company in the repurchase?

    b. Compare the effects of the repurchase to the effects of the cash dividend that you worked out in Problem 8.

10. **Stock Dividend.** Now suppose that Payout again changes its mind and decides to issue a 1 percent stock dividend instead of either issuing the cash dividend or repurchasing 1 percent of the outstanding stock. How would this action affect a shareholder who owns 100 shares of stock? Compare with your answers to Problems 8 and 9.

11. **Dividend Irrelevance.** Suppose Al Dente from Example 16.2 changes his mind and cuts out Consolidated's year-1 dividend entirely, instead spending $10 million to buy back stock. Are shareholders any better or worse off than if Consolidated had paid out $10 million as cash dividends? *Hints:* How many shares will be repurchased? The purchase price at year 1 will be $110.

12. **Dividends and Taxes.** Suppose that the tax rate on dividends is 30 percent and the tax rate on capital gains is zero. Eagle Net Resources is about to pay a $2 per share dividend.

    a. By how much will Eagle Net's share price fall when the stock goes ex-dividend?

    b. Will anything happen to the share price on the payment date when the dividend checks are sent out?

13. **Stock Dividends and Splits.** Suppose that you own 1,000 shares of Nocash Corp. and the company is about to pay a 25 percent stock dividend. The stock currently sells at $100 per share.

    a. What will be the number of shares that you hold and the total value of your equity position after the dividend is paid?

    b. What will happen to the number of shares that you hold and the value of your equity position if the firm splits five for four instead of paying the stock dividend?

14. **Dividends and Taxes.** Good Values, Inc., is all-equity-financed. The total market value of the firm currently is $100,000, and there are 2,000 shares outstanding. Ignore taxes.

    a. The firm has declared a $5 per share dividend. The stock will go ex-dividend tomorrow. At what price will the stock sell today? Tomorrow?

    b. Now assume that the tax rate on dividend income is 30 percent, and the tax rate on capital gains is zero. At what price will the stock sell, taking account of the taxation of dividends?

15. **Repurchases and Taxes.** Now suppose that instead of paying a dividend Good Values (from Problem 14) plans to repurchase $10,000 worth of stock.

    a. What will be the stock price before and after the repurchase?

    b. Suppose an investor who holds 200 shares sells 20 of her shares back to the firm. If there are no taxes on dividends or capital gains, show that she should be indifferent between the repurchase and the dividend.

    c. Show that if dividends are taxed at 30 percent and capital gains are not taxed, the value of the firm is higher if it pursues the share repurchase instead of the dividend.

16. **Dividends and Taxes.** Investors require an after-tax rate of return of 10 percent on their stock investments. Assume that the tax rate on dividends is 30 percent while capital gains escape taxation. A firm will pay a $2 per share dividend 1 year from now, after which it is expected to sell at a price of $20.

    a. Find the current price of the stock.

    b. Find the expected before-tax rate of return for a 1-year holding period.

    c. Now suppose that the dividend will be $3 per share. If the expected after-tax rate of return is still 10 percent, and investors still expect the stock to sell at $20 in 1 year, at what price must the stock now sell?

    d. What is the before-tax rate of return? Why is it now higher than in part (b)?

Please visit us at www.mhhe.com/bmm5e or
refer to your Student CD

17. **Dividends and Taxes.** The expected pretax return on three stocks is divided between dividends and capital gains in the following way:

Stock	Expected Dividend	Expected Capital Gain
A	$ 0	$10
B	5	5
C	10	0

a. If each stock is priced at $100, what are the expected net returns on each stock to (i) a pension fund that does not pay taxes, (ii) a corporation paying tax at 35 percent, and (iii) an individual with an effective tax rate of 15 percent on dividends and 10 percent on capital gains?

b. Suppose that investors pay 50 percent tax on dividends and 20 percent tax on capital gains. If stocks are priced to yield an 8 percent return *after tax,* what would A, B, and C each sell for?

18. **Signaling.** It is well documented that stock prices tend to rise when firms announce an increase in their dividend payouts. How then can it be said that dividend policy is irrelevant?

19. **Dividend Policy.** Here are several assertions about typical corporate dividend policies. Which of them are true? Write out a corrected version of any false statements.

a. Most companies set a target dividend payout ratio.
b. They set each year's dividend equal to the target payout ratio times that year's earnings.
c. Managers and investors seem more concerned with dividend changes than dividend levels.
d. Managers often increase dividends temporarily when earnings are unexpectedly high for a year or two.

20. **Dividend Policy.** For each of the following four groups of companies, state whether you would expect them to distribute a relatively high or low proportion of current earnings and whether you would expect them to have a relatively high or low price-earnings ratio.

a. High-risk companies.
b. Companies that have recently experienced a temporary decline in profits.
c. Companies that expect to experience a decline in profits.
d. "Growth" companies with valuable future investment opportunities.

21. **Dividend Policy.** "Risky companies tend to have lower target payout ratios and more gradual adjustment rates." Explain what is meant by this statement. Why do you think it is so?

CHALLENGE PROBLEM ™

22. **Dividends versus Repurchases.** Big Industries has the following market-value balance sheet. The stock currently sells for $20 a share, and there are 1,000 shares outstanding. The firm will either pay a $1 per share dividend or repurchase $1,000 worth of stock. Ignore taxes.

Assets		Liabilities and Equity	
Cash	$ 2,000	Debt	$ 10,000
Fixed assets	28,000	Equity	20,000

a. What will be the price per share under each alternative (dividend versus repurchase)?
b. If total earnings of the firm are $2,000 a year, find earnings per share under each alternative.
c. Find the price-earnings ratio under each alternative.
d. Adherents of the "dividends-are-good" school sometimes point to the fact that stocks with high-dividend-payout ratios tend to sell at above-average price-earnings multiples. Is this evidence convincing? Discuss this argument with regard to your answers to parts (a) to (c).

STANDARD
&POOR'S

1. Go to Market Insight at **www.mhhe.com/edumarketinsight**. Review the dividend policy of Harley-Davidson (HDI), General Electric (GE), Gateway (GTW), and Hawaiian Electric Industries (HE) in the S&P Stock Reports. Review the dividend yield, dividend payout ratio, and retention rate for each firm. What factors might explain the differences in dividend policies among the companies? Review the Financial Highlights page.

2. Go to Market Insight at **www.mhhe.com/edumarketinsight**. Go to the Industry tab and find three firms in the semiconductor industry and three in the electric utility industry. Now use the Excel Analytics section to find the average dividend-payout ratios of the firms in each industry. What do you conclude from the differences in their average payouts?

SOLUTIONS TO SELF-TEST QUESTIONS

16.1 The ex-dividend date is June 1. Therefore, Mick buys the stock ex-dividend and will not receive the dividend. The checks will be mailed on June 30.

16.2

Assets		Liabilities and Equity	
After cash dividend			
Cash	$ 0	Debt	$ 0
Other assets	850,000	Equity	850,000
Value of firm	$850,000	Value of firm	$850,000

Shares outstanding = 100,000
Price per share = $850,000/100,000 = $8.50

After stock repurchase			
Cash	$ 0	Debt	$ 0
Other assets	850,000	Equity	850,000
Value of firm	$850,000	Value of firm	$850,000

Shares outstanding = 85,000
Price per share = $850,000/85,000 = $10

If a dividend is paid, the stock price falls by the amount of the dividend. If the company instead uses the cash for a share repurchase, the stock price remains unchanged but, with fewer shares left outstanding, the market value of the firm falls by the same amount as it would have if the dividend had been paid. If a shareholder wants to receive the same amount of cash as the firm would have paid as a dividend, he or she must sell shares, and the market value of the remaining stock will be the same as the value had the firm paid a dividend.

16.3 The stock price dropped despite the increase in earnings because investors interpreted the dividend cut as a signal that future earnings would be lower than investors had previously expected. The dividend cut conveyed bad news about the future prospects of the firm.

16.4 An investor who prefers a zero-dividend policy can reinvest any dividends received. This will cause the value of the shares held to be unaffected by payouts. The price drop on the ex-dividend date is offset by the reinvestment of the dividends. However, if the investor had to pay brokerage fees on the newly purchased shares, she would be harmed by a high-payout policy since part of the proceeds of the dividends would go toward paying the broker. On the other hand, if the firm offers a dividend reinvestment plan (DRIP) with a 5 percent discount, she is better off with a high-dividend policy. The DRIP is like a "negative trading cost." She can increase the value of her stock by 5 percent of the dividend just by participating in the DRIP. Of course, her gain is at the expense of shareholders that do not participate in the DRIP.

16.5 The price of the stock will equal the after-tax cash flows discounted by the required (after-tax) rate of return:

$$P = \frac{102.5 + 10 \times (1 - .4)}{1.10} = 98.64$$

Notice that the after-tax proceeds from the stock would increase by the amount that previously went to pay capital gains taxes, $.20 \times \$4.72 = \$.944$. The present value of this tax saving is $\$.944/1.10 = \$.86$. Therefore, the price increases to $\$97.78 + \$.86 = \$98.64$. The pretax rate of return falls to $(102.50 - 98.64 + 10)/98.64 = .1405$, or 14.05 percent, but the after-tax rate of return remains at 10 percent.

MINICASE

George Liu, the CEO of Penn Schumann, was a creature of habit. Every month he and Jennifer Rodriguez, the company's chief financial officer, met for lunch and an informal chat at Pierre's. Nothing was ever discussed until George had finished his favorite *escalope de foie gras chaude*. At their last meeting in March he had then toyed thoughtfully with his glass of Chateau Haut-Brion Blanc before suddenly asking, "What do you think we should be doing about our payout policy?"

Penn Schumann was a large and successful pharmaceutical company. It had an enviable list of highly profitable drugs, many of which had 5 or more further years of patent protection. Earnings in the latest 4 years had increased rapidly, but it was difficult to see that such rates of growth could continue. The company had traditionally paid out about 40 percent of earnings as dividends, though the figure in 2005 was only 35 percent. Penn was spending over $4 billion a year on R&D, but the strong operating cash flow and conservative dividend policy had resulted in a buildup of cash. Penn's recent income statements, balance sheets, and cash-flow statements are summarized in Tables 16–4 to 16–6.

The problem, as Mr. Liu explained, was that Penn's dividend policy was more conservative than that of its main competitors. "Share prices depend on dividends," he said. "If we raise our dividend, we'll raise our share price, and that's the name of the game." Ms. Rodriguez suggested that the real issue was how much cash the

company wanted to hold. The current cash holding was more than adequate for the company's immediate needs. On the other hand, the research staff had been analyzing a number of new compounds with promising applications in the treatment of liver diseases. If this research were to lead to a marketable product, Penn would need to make a large investment. In addition, the company might require cash for possible acquisitions in the biotech field. "What worries me," Ms. Rodriguez said, "is that investors don't give us credit for this and think that we are going to fritter away the cash on negative-NPV investments or easy living. I don't think we should commit to paying out high dividends, but perhaps we could use some of our cash to repurchase stock."

"I don't know where anyone gets the idea that we fritter away cash on easy living," replied Mr. Liu, as he took another sip of

TABLE 16–4 Penn Schumann, Inc., balance sheet (figures in millions of dollars)

	2005	2004
Cash and short-term investments	7,061	5,551
Receivables	2,590	2,214
Inventory	1,942	2,435
Total current assets	11,593	10,200
Property, plant, & equipment	21,088	19,025
Less accumulated depreciation	5,780	4,852
Net fixed assets	15,308	14,173
Total assets	26,901	24,373
Payables	6,827	6,215
Short-term debt	1,557	2,620
Total current liabilities	8,384	8,835
Long-term debt	3,349	3,484
Shareholders' equity	15,168	12,054
Total liabilities and equity	26,901	24,373
Note:		
Shares outstanding, millions	538	516
Market price per share ($)	105	88

TABLE 16–5 Penn Schumann, Inc., income statement (figures in millions of dollars)

Revenue	16,378	13,378
Costs	8,402	7,800
Depreciation	928	850
EBIT	7,048	4,728
Interest	323	353
Tax	1,933	1,160
Net income	4,792	3,215
Dividends	1,678	1,350
Earnings per share ($)	8.91	6.23
Dividends per share ($)	3.12	2.62

TABLE 16–6 Penn Schumann, Inc., statement of cash flows (figures in millions of dollars)

Net income	4,792
Depreciation	928
Decrease (increase) in receivables	(376)
Decrease (increase) in inventories	493
Increase (decrease) in payables	612
Total cash from operations	6,449
Capital expenditures	(2,063)
Increase (decrease) in short-term debt	(1,063)
Increase (decrease) in long-term debt	(135)
Dividends paid	(1,678)
Cash provided by financing activities	(2,876)
Net increase in cash	1,510

wine, "but I like the idea of buying back our stock. We can tell shareholders that we are so confident about the future that we believe buying our own stock is the best investment we can make." He scribbled briefly on his napkin. "Suppose we bought back 50 million shares at $105. That would reduce the shares outstanding to 488 million. Net income last year was nearly $4.8 billion, so earnings per share would increase to $9.84. If the price-earnings multiple stays at 11.8, the stock price should rise to $116. That's an increase of over 10 percent." A smile came over Mr. Liu's face. "Wonderful, he exclaimed, "here comes my *homard à la nage.* Let's come back to this idea over dessert."

Evaluate the arguments of Jennifer Rodriguez and George Liu. Do you think the company is holding too much cash? If you do, how do you think it could be best paid out?

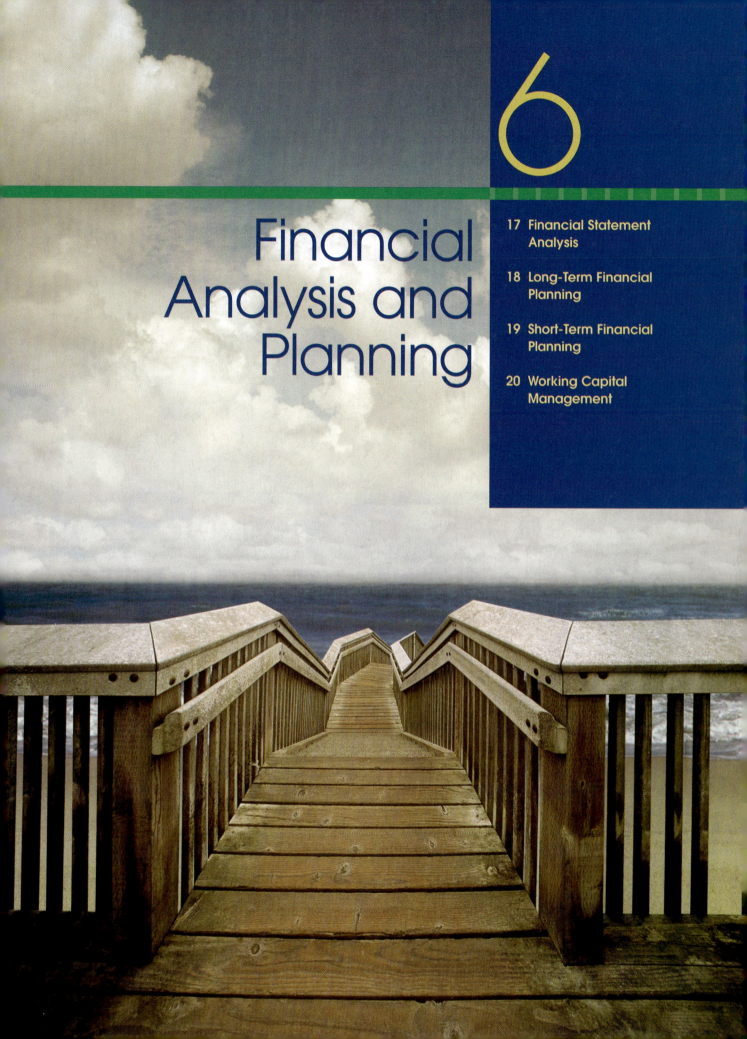

6

Financial Analysis and Planning

Financial Statement Analysis

RELATED WEB LINKS

www.annualreports.com Useful links to financial statements.

www.prars.com Another site with links to financial statements.

www.corporateinformation.com Includes links to financial statements of overseas companies.

www.jaxworks.com Calculates financial ratios.

finance.yahoo.com Contains financial ratio comparisons for companies and industries.

edgarscan.pwcglobal.com Very nice software for comparing financial ratios. Click on *Benchmarking Assistant.*

www.sternstewart.com Articles and data on economic value added.

www.ibm.com/investor/financialguide A guided tour through an annual report.

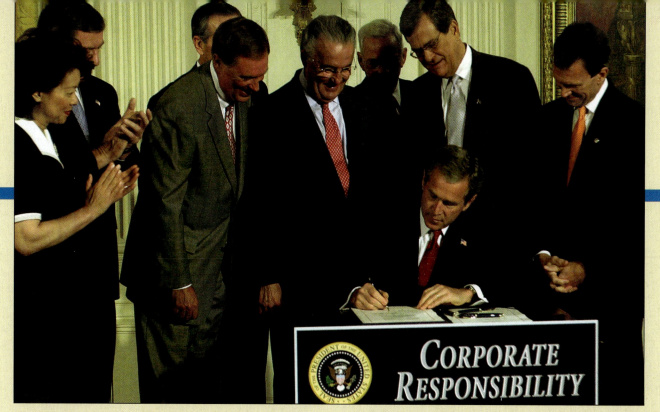

President Bush signs the Sarbanes-Oxley Act, which seeks to ensure that the firm's financial reports accurately represent its financial condition.
© AFP/Getty Images

"Divide and conquer" is the only practical strategy for presenting a complex topic like financial management. That is why we have broken down the financial manager's job into separate areas: capital budgeting, dividend policy, equity financing, and debt policy. Ultimately the financial manager has to consider the combined effects of decisions in each of these areas on the firm as a whole. Therefore, we devote all of Part 6 to financial planning. We begin in this chapter by looking at the analysis of financial statements.

Why do companies provide accounting information? Public companies have a variety of stakeholders: shareholders, bondholders, bankers, suppliers, employees, and management, for example. These stakeholders all need to monitor how well their interests are being served. They rely on the company's periodic financial statements to provide basic information on the profitability of the firm.

In this chapter we look at how you can use financial statements to analyze a firm's overall performance and assess its current financial standing. You may wish to understand the policies of a competitor or the financial health of a customer. Or you may need to check how well your own firm matches up and to determine where there is room for improvement.

We will look at how analysts summarize the large volume of accounting information by calculating some key financial ratios. We will then describe these ratios and look at some interesting relationships among them. Next we will show how the ratios are used and note the limitations of the accounting data on which most ratios are based. Finally, we will look at some measures of firm performance. Some of these are expressed in ratio form; others show how much value the firm's decisions have added.

After studying this chapter you should be able to:

- Calculate and interpret measures of a firm's leverage, liquidity, efficiency, and profitability.

- Use the Du Pont formula to understand the determinants of the firm's return on its assets and equity.

- Evaluate the potential pitfalls of ratios based on accounting data.

- Understand some key measures of firm performance such as market value added and economic value added.

17.1 Financial Ratios

We have all heard stories of whizzes who can take a company's accounts apart in minutes, calculate a few financial ratios, and discover the company's innermost secrets. The truth, however, is that financial ratios are no substitute for a crystal ball. They are just a convenient way to summarize large quantities of financial data and to compare firms' performance. Ratios help you to ask the right questions: They seldom answer them.

We will describe and calculate four types of financial ratios:

- *Leverage ratios* show how heavily the company is in debt.
- *Liquidity ratios* measure how easily the firm can lay its hands on cash.
- *Efficiency* or *turnover ratios* measure how productively the firm is using its assets.
- *Profitability ratios* are used to measure the firm's return on its investments.

We introduced you to PepsiCo's financial statements in Chapter 3. Now let's analyze them. For convenience, Tables 17–1 and 17–3 present again Pepsi's income statement and balance sheet.

The **income statement** summarizes the firm's revenues and expenses and the difference between the two, which is the firm's profit. You can see in Table 17–1 that after deducting the cost of goods sold and other expenses, Pepsi had earnings before interest and taxes (EBIT) of $5,713 million. Of this sum, $167 million was used to pay debt interest (remember interest is paid out of pretax income), and $1,334 was set aside for taxes. The net income belonged to the common stockholders. However, only a part of this income was paid out as dividends, and the remaining $2,883 million was plowed back into the business.[1]

The income statement in Table 17–1 shows the number of dollars that Pepsi earned in 2004. When making comparisons between firms, analysts sometimes calculate a **common-size income statement.** In this case all items in the income statement are expressed as a percentage of revenues. Table 17–2 is Pepsi's common-size income statement. You can see, for example, that the cost of goods sold consumes 41.5 percent of revenues and that selling, general, and administrative expenses absorb a further 34.7 percent.

Whereas the income statement summarizes activity during a period, the **balance sheet** presents a "snapshot" of the firm at a given moment. For example, the balance sheet in Table 17–3 is a snapshot of Pepsi's assets and liabilities at the end of 2004.

income statement
Financial statement that shows the revenues, expenses, and net income of a firm over a period of time.

common-size income statement
Income statement that presents items as a percentage of revenues.

balance sheet
Financial statement that shows the value of the firm's assets and liabilities at a particular time.

TABLE 17–1

CONSOLIDATED INCOME STATEMENT FOR PEPSICO, INC., 2004 (figures in millions of dollars)	
Net sales	$29,261
Cost of goods sold	12,142
Selling, general, & administrative expenses	10,142
Depreciation	1,264
Earnings before interest and income taxes	5,713
Interest expense	167
Taxable income	5,546
Taxes	1,334
Net income	4,212
Allocation of net income	
Dividends	1,329
Addition to retained earnings	2,883

Source: PepsiCo *Annual Report*, 2004.

---

[1] This is in addition to $1,264 million of cash flow earmarked for depreciation.

TABLE 17-2

COMMON-SIZE INCOME STATEMENT OF INCOME FOR PEPSICO, INC., 2004 (all items expressed as percentage of revenues)	
Net sales	100.0
Cost of goods sold	41.5
Selling, general, & administrative expenses	34.7
Depreciation	4.3
Earnings before interest and income taxes	19.5
Interest expense	0.6
Taxable income	19.0
Taxes	4.6
Net income	14.4
Allocation of net income	
Dividends	4.5
Addition to retained earnings	9.9

Source: PepsiCo *Annual Report,* 2004.

As we pointed out in Chapter 3, the accountant lists first the assets that are most likely to be turned into cash in the near future. They include cash itself, short-term securities, receivables (that is, bills that have not yet been paid by the firm's customers), and inventories of raw materials, work in process, and finished goods. These assets are all known as *current assets*. The second main group of assets consists of long-term

TABLE 17-3

CONSOLIDATED BALANCE SHEET FOR PEPSICO, INC., AS OF DECEMBER 31 (millions of dollars)					
Assets	**2004**	**2003**	**Liabilities and Shareholders' Equity**	**2004**	**2003**
Current assets			Current liabilities		
Cash and marketable securities	1,280	820	Debt due for repayment	1,054	591
Receivables	2,999	2,830	Accounts payable	4,594	5,213
Inventories	1,541	1,412	Other current liabilities	1,104	611
Other current assets	2,819	1,868	Total current liabilities	6,752	6,415
Total current assets	8,639	6,930			
			Long-term debt	2,397	1,702
Fixed assets			Deferred income taxes	1,216	1,261
Tangible fixed assets			Other long-term liabilities	4,050	4,075
Property, plant, and equipment	15,930	14,755	Total liabilities	14,415	13,453
Less accumulated depreciation	7,781	6,927	Shareholders' equity:		
Net tangible fixed assets	8,149	7,828	Common stock and other paid-in capital	648	1,833
			Retained earnings	12,924	10,041
Intangible fixed assets			Total shareholders' equity	13,572	11,874
Goodwill	3,909	3,796			
Other intangible assets	1,531	1,587	Total liabilities and shareholders' equity	27,987	25,327
Total intangible assets	5,440	5,383			
Total fixed assets	13,589	13,211			
Other assets	5,759	5,186			
Total assets	27,987	25,327			

Note: Column sums subject to rounding error.
Source: PepsiCo *Annual Report,* 2004.

assets such as buildings, land, machinery, and equipment. Remember that the balance sheet does not show the market value of each asset. Instead, the accountant records the amount that the asset originally cost and then, in the case of plant and equipment, deducts an annual charge for depreciation. Pepsi also owns many valuable assets, such as its brand name, that are *not* shown on the balance sheet.

Pepsi's liabilities show the claims on the firm's assets. These also are classified as current versus long-term. Current liabilities are bills that the company expects to pay in the near future. They include debts that are due to be repaid within the next year and payables (that is, amounts the company owes to its suppliers). In addition to these short-term debts, Pepsi has borrowed money that will not be repaid for several years. These are shown as long-term liabilities.

After taking account of all the firm's liabilities, the remaining assets belong to the common stockholders. The shareholders' equity is simply the total value of the assets less the current and long-term liabilities. It is also equal to the amount that the firm has raised from stockholders ($648 million) plus the earnings that have been retained and reinvested on their behalf ($12,924 million).

common-size balance sheet
Balance sheet that presents items as a percentage of total assets.

Just as it is sometimes useful to provide a common-size income statement, so we can also calculate a **common-size balance sheet.** In this case all items are reexpressed as a percentage of total assets. Table 17–4 is Pepsi's common-size balance sheet. The table shows, for example, that in 2004 cash and marketable securities rose from 3.2 percent of total assets to 4.6 percent.

TABLE 17–4

COMMON-SIZE BALANCE SHEET FOR PEPSICO, INC., AS OF DECEMBER 31 (all items expressed as percentage of total assets)					
Assets	**2004**	**2003**	**Liabilities and Shareholders' Equity**	**2004**	**2003**
Current assets			Current liabilities		
Cash and marketable securities	4.6	3.2	Debt due for repayment	3.8	2.3
Receivables	10.7	11.2	Accounts payable	16.4	20.6
Inventories	5.5	5.6	Other current liabilities	3.9	2.4
Other current assets	10.1	7.4	Total current liabilities	24.1	25.3
Total current assets	30.9	27.4			
			Long-term debt	8.6	6.7
Fixed assets			Deferred income taxes	4.3	5.0
Tangible fixed assets			Other long-term liabilities	14.5	16.1
Property, plant, and equipment	56.9	58.3	Total liabilities	51.5	53.1
Less accumulated depreciation	27.8	27.4	Shareholders' equity		
Net tangible fixed assets	29.1	30.9	Common stock and other paid-in capital	2.3	7.2
			Retained earnings	46.2	39.6
Intangible fixed assets			Total shareholders' equity	48.5	46.9
Goodwill	14.0	15.0			
Other intangible assets	5.5	6.3	Total liabilities and shareholders' equity	100.0	100.0
Total intangible fixed assets	19.4	21.3			
Total fixed assets	48.6	52.2			
Other assets	20.6	20.5			
Total assets	100.0	100.0			

Note: Column sums subject to rounding error.
Source: PepsiCo *Annual Report,* 2004.

Financial Ratios

1. Log on to **www.annualreports.com** to find the latest financial statements for PepsiCo. Prepare simplified summary statements like those in Tables 17–1 to 17–4. Then recalculate Pepsi's financial ratios. What have been the main changes from those shown in these tables? If you owned some of Pepsi's debt, would these changes make you feel more or less happy?

2. Log on to **edgarscan.pwcglobal.com** and use the *Benchmarking Assistant* to enter the name of a large airline company. Find and select some peer airlines, and then graph their financial ratios. How does the company's financial strength stack up compared with other firms in the airline industry?

Source: PriceWaterhouseCoopers' Technology Center.

Leverage Ratios

When a firm borrows money, it promises to make a series of interest payments and then to repay the amount that it has borrowed. If profits rise, the debtholders continue to receive only the fixed interest payment, so all the gains go to the shareholders. Of course, the reverse happens if profits fall. In this case shareholders bear all the pain. If times are sufficiently hard, a firm that has borrowed heavily may not be able to pay its debts. The firm is then bankrupt, and shareholders lose their entire investment. Because debt increases returns to shareholders in good times and reduces them in bad times, it is said to create *financial leverage.* Leverage ratios measure how much financial leverage the firm has taken on.

Debt Ratio   Financial leverage is usually measured by the ratio of long-term debt to total long-term capital. Here "long-term debt" should include not just bonds or other borrowing but also the value of long-term leases.[2] Total long-term capital, sometimes called *total capitalization,* is the sum of long-term debt and shareholders' equity. Thus, for Pepsi,

$$\text{Long-term debt ratio} = \frac{\text{long-term debt}}{\text{long-term debt} + \text{equity}} = \frac{2,397}{2,397 + 13,572} = .15$$

This means that 15 cents of every dollar of long-term capital is in the form of long-term debt. Another way to express leverage is in terms of the company's debt-equity ratio:

$$\text{Long-term debt-equity ratio} = \frac{\text{long-term debt}}{\text{equity}} = \frac{2,397}{13,572} = .18$$

Notice that both these measures make use of book (that is, accounting) values rather than market values.[3] The market value of the company finally determines whether the debtholders get their money back, so you would expect analysts to look at the face amount of the debt as a proportion of the total *market value* of debt and equity. One reason that they don't do this is that market values are often not readily available. Does it matter much? Perhaps not; after all, the market value of the firm includes the value of intangible assets generated by research and development, advertising, staff training, and so on. These assets are not readily salable and, if the company falls on hard times,

---

[2] A lease is a long-term rental agreement and therefore commits the firm to make regular rental payments. As we emphasized in Chapter 13, leases are quite similar to debt.

[3] In the case of leased assets accountants estimate the present value of the lease commitments. In the case of long-term debt they simply show the face value. This can sometimes be very different from present values. For example, the present value of low-coupon debt may be only a fraction of its face value.

the value of these assets may disappear altogether. Thus when banks demand that a borrower keep within a maximum debt ratio, they are usually content to define this debt ratio in terms of book values and to ignore the intangible assets that are not shown in the balance sheet.

Notice also that these measures of leverage take account only of long-term debt. Managers sometimes also define debt to include all liabilities:

$$\text{Total debt ratio} = \frac{\text{total liabilities}}{\text{total assets}} = \frac{14{,}415}{27{,}987} = .52$$

Therefore, Pepsi is financed 52 percent with debt, both long-term and short-term, and 48 percent with equity. We could also say that its ratio of total debt to equity is 14,415/13,572 = 1.06.

Managers sometimes refer loosely to a company's debt ratio, but we have just seen that the debt ratio may be measured in several different ways. For example, Pepsi could be said to have a debt ratio of .15 (the long-term debt ratio) or .52 (the total debt ratio). There is a general point here. There are a variety of ways to define most financial ratios, and there is no law stating how they *should* be defined. So be warned: Don't accept a ratio at face value without understanding how it has been calculated.

Times Interest Earned Ratio Another measure of financial leverage is the extent to which interest obligations are covered by earnings. Banks prefer to lend to firms whose earnings are far in excess of interest payments. Therefore, analysts often calculate the ratio of earnings before interest and taxes (EBIT) to interest payments. For Pepsi,

$$\text{Times interest earned} = \frac{\text{EBIT}}{\text{interest payments}} = \frac{5{,}713}{167} = 34.2$$

Pepsi's profits would need to fall dramatically before they were insufficient to cover the interest payment.

The regular interest payment is a hurdle that companies must keep jumping if they are to avoid default. The *times interest earned ratio* (also called the *interest cover ratio*) measures how much clear air there is between hurdle and hurdler. However, it tells only part of the story. For example, it doesn't tell us whether Pepsi is generating enough cash to repay its debt as it becomes due.

Cash Coverage Ratio We have pointed out that depreciation is deducted when we are calculating the firm's earnings, even though no cash goes out the door. Thus, rather than asking whether *earnings* are sufficient to cover interest payments, it might be more interesting to calculate the extent to which interest is covered by the cash flow from operations. This is measured by the cash coverage ratio. For Pepsi,

$$\text{Cash coverage ratio} = \frac{\text{EBIT} + \text{depreciation}}{\text{interest payments}} = \frac{5{,}713 + 1{,}264}{167} = 41.8$$

Self-Test 17.1

A firm repays $10 million face value of outstanding debt and issues $10 million of new debt with a lower rate of interest. What happens to its long-term debt ratio? What happens to its times interest earned and cash coverage ratios?

Liquidity Ratios

liquidity
Ability to sell an asset for cash at short notice.

If you are extending credit to a customer or making a short-term bank loan, you are interested in more than the company's leverage. You want to know whether it will be able to lay its hands on the cash to repay you. That is why credit analysts and bankers look at several measures of **liquidity.** Liquid assets can be converted into cash quickly and cheaply.

Think, for example, what you would do to meet a large, unexpected bill. You might have some money in the bank or some investments that are easily sold, but you would not find it so simple to convert your old sweaters into cash. Companies likewise own assets with different degrees of liquidity. For example, accounts receivable and inventories of finished goods are generally quite liquid. As inventories are sold and customers pay their bills, money flows into the firm. At the other extreme, real estate may be quite *illiquid*. It can be hard to find a buyer, negotiate a fair price, and close a deal at short notice.

Managers have another reason to focus on liquid assets: The accounting figures are more reliable. The book value of a catalytic cracker may be a poor guide to its true value, but at least you know what cash in the bank is worth.

Liquidity ratios also have some *less* desirable characteristics. Because short-term assets and liabilities are easily changed, measures of liquidity can rapidly become outdated. You might not know what the catalytic cracker is worth, but you can be fairly sure that it won't disappear overnight. Also, companies often choose a slack period for the end of their financial year. For example, retailers may end their financial year in January after the Christmas boom. At these times the companies are likely to have more cash and less short-term debt than during busier seasons.

Net Working Capital to Total Assets Ratio We have seen that current assets are those that the company expects to meet in the near future. The difference between current assets and current liabilities is known as *net working capital*. It roughly measures the company's potential reservoir of cash. Current assets usually exceed current liabilities. For Pepsi,

$$\text{Net working capital} = 8,639 - 6,752 = 1,887$$

Managers often express net working capital as a proportion of total assets. For Pepsi,

$$\frac{\text{Net working capital}}{\text{Total assets}} = \frac{1,887}{27,987} = .07$$

Current Ratio Another measure that serves a similar purpose is the current ratio:

$$\text{Current ratio} = \frac{\text{current assets}}{\text{current liabilities}} = \frac{8,639}{6,752} = 1.28$$

So Pepsi has $1.28 in current assets for every $1 in current liabilities.

Rapid decreases in the current ratio sometimes signify trouble. For example, a firm that drags out its payables by delaying payment of its bills will suffer an increase in current liabilities and a decrease in the current ratio.

Changes in the current ratio can mislead, however. For example, suppose that a company borrows a large sum from the bank and invests it in marketable securities. Current liabilities rise and so do current assets. Therefore, if nothing else changes, net working capital is unaffected but the current ratio changes. For this reason, it is sometimes preferable to net short-term investments against short-term debt when calculating the current ratio.

EXAMPLE 17.1 ▶	Current Ratio

Suppose that Pepsi borrows $1,000 million to invest in marketable securities. Its current assets increase to $9,639 million, while current liabilities increase to $7,752. The current ratio falls from 1.28 to 9,639/7,752 = 1.24. ◀

Quick (or Acid-Test) Ratio Some assets are closer to cash than others. If trouble comes, inventory may not sell at anything above fire-sale prices. (Trouble typically comes *because* the firm can't sell its finished-product inventory for more than production cost.) Thus managers often exclude inventories and other less liquid components of current assets when comparing current assets to current liabilities. They focus instead on cash, marketable securities, and bills that customers have not yet paid. This results in the quick ratio:

$$\text{Quick ratio} = \frac{\text{cash + marketable securities + receivables}}{\text{current liabilities}} = \frac{1{,}280 + 2{,}999}{6{,}752} = .63$$

Self-Test 17.2

a. A firm has $1.2 million in current assets and $1.0 million in current liabilities. If it uses $.5 million of cash to pay off some of its accounts payable, what will happen to the current ratio? What happens to net working capital?
b. A firm uses cash on hand to pay for additional inventories. What will happen to the current ratio? To the quick ratio?

Cash Ratio A company's most liquid assets are its holdings of cash and marketable securities. That is why analysts also look at the cash ratio:

$$\text{Cash ratio} = \frac{\text{cash + marketable securities}}{\text{current liabilities}} = \frac{1{,}280}{6{,}752} = .19$$

A low cash ratio may not matter if the firm can borrow on short notice. Who cares whether the firm has actually borrowed from the bank or whether it has a guaranteed line of credit that lets it borrow whenever it chooses? None of the standard liquidity measures takes the firm's "reserve borrowing power" into account.

Efficiency Ratios

Firms want to use their assets efficiently, and financial analysts want to measure that efficiency. Of course, defining a single measure of "efficiency" for firms that use many inputs and technologies can entail complex and subtle issues, so in practice analysts are usually content to use *turnover* ratios that measure how much the firm produces for every dollar of assets employed. For example, we may look at the sales generated per dollar of assets or at the level of inventory per dollar of goods sold.

Asset Turnover Ratio The asset turnover, or sales-to-assets, ratio shows how hard the firm's assets are being put to use. For Pepsi, each dollar of assets produced $1.10 of sales:

$$\frac{\text{Sales}}{\text{Average total assets}} = \frac{29{,}261}{(27{,}987 + 25{,}327)/2} = 1.10$$

A high ratio compared with other firms in the same industry could indicate that the firm is working close to capacity. It may prove difficult to generate further business without additional investment.

Notice that since the assets are likely to change over the year, we use the *average* of the assets at the beginning and end of the year. Averages are often used when a flow figure (in this case *annual sales*) is compared with a snapshot figure (*total assets*).

Instead of looking at the ratio of sales to *total* assets, managers sometimes look at how hard particular types of capital are being put to use. For example, they might look at the value of sales per dollar invested in fixed assets. Or they might look at the ratio of sales to net working capital.

Thus for Pepsi each dollar of fixed assets generated $2.18 of sales:

$$\frac{\text{Sales}}{\text{Average fixed assets}} = \frac{29{,}261}{(13{,}589 + 13{,}211)/2} = 2.18$$

Average Collection Period The average collection period measures how quickly customers pay their bills. It expresses accounts receivable in terms of daily sales:

$$\text{Average collection period} = \frac{\text{average receivables}}{\text{average daily sales}} = \frac{(2{,}999 + 2{,}830)/2}{29{,}261/365} = 36.4 \text{ days}$$

On average Pepsi's customers pay their bills in about 36 days. A comparatively low figure often indicates an efficient collection department. Sometimes, however, it is the result of an unduly restrictive credit policy, whereby the firm offers credit only to customers that can be relied on to pay promptly.[4]

Inventory Turnover Ratio Managers may also monitor the rate at which the company is turning over its inventories. The financial statements show the cost of inventories rather than what the finished goods will eventually sell for. So we compare the cost of inventories with the cost of goods sold. In Pepsi's case,

$$\text{Inventory turnover} = \frac{\text{cost of goods sold}}{\text{average inventory}} = \frac{12{,}142}{(1{,}541 + 1{,}412)/2} = 8.2$$

Efficient firms turn over their inventory rapidly and don't tie up more capital than they need in raw materials or finished goods. But firms that are living from hand to mouth may also cut their inventories to the bone.

Managers sometimes also look at how many days' sales are represented by inventories. This is equal to the average inventory divided by the daily cost of goods sold:

$$\text{Days' sales in inventories} = \frac{\text{average inventory}}{\text{cost of goods sold}/365} = \frac{(1{,}541 + 1{,}412)/2}{12{,}142/365} = 44.4 \text{ days}$$

You could say that on average Pepsi has sufficient inventories to maintain sales for 44.4 days.[5]

Self-Test 17.3

The average collection period measures the number of days it takes Pepsi to collect its bills. But Pepsi also delays *paying* its own bills. Use the information in Tables 17–1 and 17–3 to calculate the average number of days that it takes the company to pay its bills.

Profitability Ratios

Profitability measures focus on the firm's earnings. Of course, big firms should be expected to generate more profits than smaller ones, so to facilitate comparisons across firms, total earnings are expressed on a per-dollar basis. For example, shareholders want to know how much profit has been generated for each dollar they have invested in the firm. Similarly, profit margin tells us the profit generated by each dollar of sales. Financial analysts employ several profitability measures.

Profit Margin If you want to know the proportion of revenue that finds its way into profits, you look at the profit margin. This is often defined as

$$\text{Profit margin} = \frac{\text{net income}}{\text{sales}} = \frac{4{,}212}{29{,}261} = .144, \text{ or } 14.4\%$$

When companies are partly financed by debt, the profits are divided between the debtholders and the shareholders. We would not want to say that such a firm is less profitable simply because it employs debt finance and pays out part of its profits as interest. Therefore, when we are calculating the profit margin, it makes sense to add back the debt interest to net income. This gives an alternative definition of the profit

---

[4] If possible, it would make sense to divide average receivables by average daily *credit* sales. Otherwise, a low ratio might simply indicate that only a small proportion of sales was made on credit.

[5] This is a loose statement, because it ignores the fact that Pepsi may have more than 44.4 days' supply of some materials and less of others.

margin, which also has wide acceptance and which we will call the *operating* profit margin:

$$\text{Operating profit margin}[6] = \frac{\text{net income} + \text{interest}}{\text{sales}} = \frac{4,212 + 167}{29,261} = .150, \text{ or } 15.0\%$$

Holding everything constant, a firm would naturally prefer a high profit margin. But all else cannot be held constant. A high-price and high-margin strategy typically will result in lower sales. So while Bloomingdales might have a higher margin than JCPenney, it will not necessarily enjoy higher profits. A low-margin but high-volume strategy can be quite successful. We return to this issue later.

Return on Assets (ROA)   Managers often measure the performance of a firm by the ratio of net income to total assets. However, because net income measures profits net of interest expense, this practice makes the apparent profitability of the firm a function of its capital structure. It is better to use net income plus interest because we are measuring the return on *all* the firm's assets, not just the equity investment:[7]

$$\text{Return on assets} = \frac{\text{net income} + \text{interest}}{\text{average total assets}} = \frac{4,212 + 167}{(27,987 + 25,327)/2} = .164, \text{ or } 16.4\%$$

The assets in a company's books are valued on the basis of their original cost (less any depreciation). A high return on assets does not always mean that you could buy the same assets today and get a high return. Nor does a low return imply that the assets could be employed better elsewhere. But it does suggest that you should ask some searching questions.

In a competitive industry firms can expect to earn only their cost of capital. Therefore, a high return on assets is sometimes cited as an indication that the firm is taking advantage of a monopoly position to charge excessive prices. For example, when a public utility commission tries to determine whether a utility is charging a fair price, much of the argument will center on a comparison between the cost of capital and the return that the utility is earning (its ROA).

Return on Equity (ROE)   Another measure of profitability focuses on the return on the shareholders' equity:

$$\text{Return on equity} = \frac{\text{net income}}{\text{average equity}}$$

$$= \frac{4,212}{(13,572 + 11,874)/2} = .331, \text{ or } 33.1\%$$

---

[6] Different analysts may measure profit margin in different ways. For example, some may include interest payments net of the interest tax shield, and so they adjust the numerator in the profit margin to [net income + interest × (1 − tax rate)]. Others use earnings before interest and taxes (EBIT) in the numerator, while still others prefer EBIT(1 − tax rate). Unfortunately, there is no uniformity on which definition is used or preferred. You simply need to be aware that there are differences in practice and be consistent in how you calculate these measures.

[7] This definition of ROA is also misleading if it is used to compare firms with different capital structures. The reason is that firms that pay more interest pay less in taxes. Thus this ratio reflects differences in financial leverage as well as in operating performance. If you want a measure of operating performance alone, we suggest adjusting for leverage by subtracting that part of total income generated by interest tax shields (interest payments × marginal tax rate). This gives the income the firm would earn if it were all-equity-financed. Thus, using a tax rate of 35 percent for Pepsi,

$$\text{Adjusted return on assets} = \frac{\text{net income} + \text{interest} - \text{interest tax shields}}{\text{average total assets}}$$

$$= \frac{4,212 + 167 - (.35 \times 167)}{(27,987 + 25,327)/2} = .162, \text{ or } 16.2\%$$

Payout Ratio The payout ratio measures the proportion of earnings that is paid out as dividends. Thus:

$$\text{Payout ratio} = \frac{\text{dividends}}{\text{earnings}} = \frac{1,329}{4,212} = .316$$

We saw in Section 16.4 that managers don't like to cut dividends because of a short-fall in earnings. Therefore, if a company's earnings are particularly variable, management is likely to play it safe by setting a low average payout ratio.

When earnings fall unexpectedly, the payout ratio is likely to rise temporarily. Likewise, if earnings are expected to rise next year, management may feel that it can pay somewhat more generous dividends than it would otherwise have done.

Earnings not paid out as dividends are retained, or plowed back into the business. The proportion of earnings reinvested in the firm is called the *plowback ratio:*

$$\text{Plowback ratio} = 1 - \text{payout ratio} = \frac{\text{earnings} - \text{dividends}}{\text{earnings}}$$

If you multiply this figure by the return on equity, you can see how rapidly shareholders' equity is growing as a result of plowing back part of its earnings each year. Thus, for Pepsi, earnings plowed back into the firm increased the book value of equity by 22.7 percent:

$$\text{Growth in equity from plowback} = \frac{\text{earnings} - \text{dividends}}{\text{equity}}$$

$$= \frac{\text{earnings} - \text{dividends}}{\text{earnings}} \times \frac{\text{earnings}}{\text{equity}}$$

$$= \text{plowback ratio} \times \text{ROE}$$

$$= .684 \times .331 = .227, \text{ or } 22.7\%$$

If Pepsi can continue to earn 33.1 percent on its book equity and plow back 68.4 percent of earnings, both earnings and equity will grow at 22.7 percent a year.[8]

Is this a reasonable prospect? We saw in Chapter 6 that such high growth rates are unlikely to persist. While Pepsi may continue to grow rapidly for some years to come, such rapid growth will inevitably slow.

17.2 The Du Pont System

Suppose you observe that Pepsi's return on equity has increased substantially in the last few years. You might wonder what explains the improvement. Has the firm put its assets to more efficient use? Has it been able to increase its prices without giving up sales? Or perhaps the increase reflects higher leverage.

To sort these things out, we can decompose ROA and ROE into the product of a series of more fundamental ratios. These ratios help us isolate the separate influences on performance. They also might provide clues as to business strategy. The decomposition of performance measures into component ratios is usually called the **Du Pont system,** in recognition of the chemical company that popularized the procedure.

The first relationship links the return on assets (ROA) with the firm's asset turnover ratio and its operating profit margin:

Du Pont system

A breakdown of ROE and ROA into component ratios.

---

[8] Analysts sometimes refer to this figure as the *sustainable rate of growth.* Notice that, in calculating the sustainable rate of growth, ROE would be better measured by earnings (in Pepsi's case, $4,212 million) as a proportion of equity at the *start* of the year (in Pepsi's case, $11,874 million), rather than the average of the equity at the start and end of the year. We discussed the sustainable rate of growth in Chapter 6, and we will return to it again in Chapter 18.

$$ROA = \frac{\text{net income + interest}}{\text{assets}} = \underset{\substack{\uparrow \\ \text{asset} \\ \text{turnover}}}{\frac{\text{sales}}{\text{assets}}} \times \underset{\substack{\uparrow \\ \text{operating profit} \\ \text{margin}}}{\frac{\text{net income + interest}}{\text{sales}}}$$

All firms would like to earn a higher return on their assets, but their ability to do so is limited by competition. If the expected return on assets is fixed by competition, firms face a trade-off between the turnover ratio and the profit margin. Thus we find that fast-food chains, which have high turnover, also tend to operate on low profit margins. Classy hotels have relatively low turnover ratios but tend to compensate for this with higher margins. Table 17–5 illustrates the trade-off. Both the fast-food chain and the hotel have the same return on assets. However, their profit margins and turnover ratios are entirely different.

Firms often seek to improve their profit margins by acquiring a supplier. The idea is to capture the supplier's profit as well as their own. Unfortunately, unless they have some special skill in running the new business, they are likely to find that any gain in profit margin is offset by a decline in the asset turnover.

A few numbers may help to illustrate this point. Table 17–6 shows the sales, profits, and assets of Admiral Motors and its components supplier Diana Corporation. Both earn a 10 percent return on assets, though Admiral has a lower operating profit margin (20 percent versus Diana's 25 percent). Since all of Diana's output goes to Admiral, Admiral's management reasons that it would be better to merge the two companies. That way the merged company would capture the profit margin on both the auto components and the assembled car.

The bottom line of Table 17–6 shows the effect of the merger. The merged firm does indeed earn the combined profits. Total sales remain at $20 million, however, because all the components produced by Diana are used within the company. With higher profits and unchanged sales, the profit margin increases. Unfortunately, the asset turnover ratio is *reduced* by the merger since the merged firm operates with higher assets. This exactly offsets the benefit of the higher profit margin. The return on assets is unchanged.

We can also break down the return on equity (ROE) into its component parts:

$$ROE = \frac{\text{net income}}{\text{equity}}$$

Therefore,

$$ROE = \underset{\substack{\uparrow \\ \text{leverage} \\ \text{ratio}}}{\frac{\text{assets}}{\text{equity}}} \times \underset{\substack{\uparrow \\ \text{asset} \\ \text{turnover}}}{\frac{\text{sales}}{\text{assets}}} \times \underset{\substack{\uparrow \\ \text{operating profit} \\ \text{margin}}}{\frac{\text{net income + interest}}{\text{sales}}} \times \underset{\substack{\uparrow \\ \text{debt burden}}}{\frac{\text{net income}}{\text{net income + interest}}}$$

Notice that the product of the two middle terms is the return on assets. This depends on the firm's production and marketing skills and is unaffected by the firm's financing mix.[9] However, the first and fourth terms do depend on the debt-equity mix. The first

TABLE 17–5 Fast-food chains and hotels may have a similar return on assets but different asset turnover ratios and profit margins

	Asset Turnover	×	Profit Margin	=	Return on Assets
Fast-food chains	2.0		5%		10%
Hotels	0.5		20		10

---

[9] There is a complication here because the amount of taxes paid depends on the financing mix. It would be better to add back any interest tax shields when calculating the firm's operating profit margin.

TABLE 17–6 Merging with suppliers or customers will generally increase the profit margin, but this will be offset by a reduction in the turnover ratio

	Millions of Dollars			Asset Turnover	Profit Margin	ROA
	Sales	**Profits**	**Assets**			
Admiral Motors	$20	$4	$40	.50	20%	10%
Diana Corp.	8	2	20	.40	25	10
Diana Motors (the merged firm)	20	6	60	.33	30	10

term, assets/equity, which we call the *leverage ratio,* can be expressed as (equity + liabilities)/equity, which equals 1 + total-debt-to-equity ratio. The last term, which we call the *debt burden,* measures the proportion by which interest expense reduces profits.

Suppose that the firm is financed entirely by equity. In this case both the first and the fourth terms are equal to 1.0, and the return on equity is identical to the return on assets. If the firm is leveraged, the first term is greater than 1.0 (assets are greater than equity) and the fourth term is less than 1.0 (part of the profits are absorbed by interest). Thus leverage can either increase or reduce return on equity. In fact, we showed in Section 15.1 that leverage increases ROE when the firm's return on assets is higher than the interest rate on debt.

EXAMPLE 17.2 ▶ Du Pont Analysis for Pepsi

We can link Pepsi's profitability measures to its other financial ratios as follows:

$$\text{ROA} = \text{asset turnover} \times \text{operating profit margin}$$
$$= 1.10 \times .150 = .165$$

$$\text{ROE} = \frac{\text{average assets}}{\text{average equity}} \times \frac{\text{asset}}{\text{turnover}} \times \frac{\text{operating profit}}{\text{margin}} \times \frac{\text{net income}}{\text{net income} + \text{interest}}$$

$$= \frac{(27{,}987 + 25{,}327)/2}{(13{,}572 + 11{,}874)/2} \times 1.10 \times .150 \times \frac{4{,}212}{4{,}212 + 167}$$

$$= .332$$

Aside from negligible rounding error, the results of the ratio decomposition match the values we found above for Pepsi's ROE and ROA. ◀

Self-Test 17.4

a. Sappy Syrup has a profit margin below the industry average, but its ROA equals the industry average. How is this possible?
b. Sappy Syrup's ROA equals the industry average, but its ROE exceeds the industry average. How is this possible?

Other Financial Ratios

Each of the financial ratios that we have described involves accounting data only. But managers also compare accounting numbers with the values that are established in the marketplace. For example, they may compare the total market value of the firm's shares with the book value (the amount that the company has raised from shareholders or reinvested on their behalf). If managers have been successful in adding value for stockholders, the *market-to-book ratio* should be greater than 1.0. In Chapter 6 we also discussed two other ratios that use market-value data, the *price-earnings ratio* and the *dividend yield.* These ratios provide additional measures of how highly the company is valued by investors.

You can probably think of a number of other ratios that could provide useful insights into a company's health. For example, a retail chain might compare its sales per square foot with those of its competitors, a steel producer might look at the cost per ton of steel produced, and an airline might look at revenues per passenger-mile flown. Internet firms have been evaluated on the basis of stock price per "hit" on the Web site.

TABLE 17–7 Summary of financial ratios

Leverage Ratios

$$\text{Long-term debt ratio} = \frac{\text{long-term debt}}{\text{long-term debt} + \text{equity}}$$

$$\text{Long-term debt-equity ratio} = \frac{\text{long-term debt}}{\text{equity}}$$

$$\text{Total debt ratio} = \frac{\text{total liabilities}}{\text{total assets}}$$

$$\text{Times interest earned} = \frac{\text{EBIT}}{\text{interest payments}}$$

$$\text{Cash coverage ratio} = \frac{\text{EBIT} + \text{depreciation}}{\text{interest payments}}$$

Liquidity Ratios

$$\text{NWC to assets} = \frac{\text{net working capital}}{\text{total assets}}$$

$$\text{Current ratio} = \frac{\text{current assets}}{\text{current liabilities}}$$

$$\text{Quick ratio} = \frac{\text{cash} + \text{marketable securities} + \text{receivables}}{\text{current liabilities}}$$

$$\text{Cash ratio} = \frac{\text{cash} + \text{marketable securities}}{\text{current liabilities}}$$

Efficiency Ratios

$$\text{Total asset turnover} = \frac{\text{sales}}{\text{average total assets}}$$

$$\text{Average collection period} = \frac{\text{average receivables}}{\text{average daily sales}}$$

$$\text{Inventory turnover} = \frac{\text{cost of goods sold}}{\text{average inventory}}$$

$$\text{Days' sales in inventories} = \frac{\text{average inventory}}{\text{cost of goods sold}/365}$$

Profitability Ratios

$$\text{Profit margin} = \frac{\text{net income}}{\text{sales}}$$

$$\text{Operating profit margin} = \frac{\text{net income} + \text{interest}}{\text{sales}}$$

$$\text{Return on assets} = \frac{\text{net income} + \text{interest}}{\text{average total assets}}$$

$$\text{Return on equity} = \frac{\text{net income}}{\text{average equity}}$$

$$\text{Payout ratio} = \frac{\text{dividends}}{\text{earnings}}$$

$$\text{Plowback ratio} = 1 - \text{payout ratio}$$

$$\text{Growth in equity from plowback} = \text{plowback ratio} \times \text{ROE}$$

A little thought and common sense should suggest which measures are likely to provide insights into your company's efficiency. See Table 17–7 for a summary of the ratios already introduced.

17.3 Using Financial Ratios

Accounting Principles and Financial Ratios

Accounting rules are designed to provide investors with a fair view of the company's earnings, assets, and liabilities. Accountants are continually revising these rules, but, inevitably, no summary set of numbers can hope to capture the financial position of a large and complex business. So when you calculate financial ratios, it is important to look below the surface and understand some of the limitations in the accounting numbers. Remember our earlier comment that financial ratios are just a starting point and help you to ask the right questions.

Here are a few examples of things that can make simple comparisons of financial ratios misleading:

1. *Goodwill.* The assets shown in Pepsi's 2004 balance sheet include a figure of $5,440 million for "intangibles." The major intangible consists of "goodwill," which is the difference between the amount that Pepsi paid when it acquired several companies and the book value of their assets. If the estimated value of this goodwill ever falls below the amount shown in the balance sheet, the figure in the balance sheet must be adjusted downward and the write-off deducted from that year's earnings. We don't want to debate here whether goodwill is really an asset, but we should warn you about the dangers of comparing ratios of firms whose balance sheets include a substantial goodwill element with those that do not.
2. *Research and development.* Pepsi regularly spends more than $100 million annually on research and development (R&D). Large pharmaceutical companies may spend 50 times this figure. This research and development is an investment that hopefully will pay off in the form of higher future cash flows, but, unlike an investment in plant and equipment, R&D does not show up on the balance sheet. Instead, expenditures on R&D are treated as a current expense. This makes it difficult to compare the profitability of companies with very different levels of expenditure on research and development.
3. *Pensions.* For many firms their largest debts consist of the pension promises that they have made to their employees. In the case of Pepsi the present value of the pensions and postretirement benefits that it has undertaken to pay amounted to about $7.2 billion in 2004. This debt is shown in the notes to the accounts but not in the balance sheet. Instead, balance sheets show a liability only when there are insufficient assets in the pension fund to cover the pension promises. In the case of Pepsi this liability amounted to $1.5 billion in 2004 and in Table 17–4 is lumped in with "other liabilities."

Choosing a Benchmark

We have shown you how to calculate the principal financial ratios for Pepsi. In practice you may not need to calculate all of them, because many measure essentially the same thing. For example, if you know that Pepsi's EBIT is 34.2 times interest payments and that the company is financed 15 percent with long-term debt, the other leverage ratios are of relatively little interest.

Once you have selected and calculated the important ratios, you still need some way of judging whether they are high or low. A good starting point is to compare them with the equivalent figures for the same company in earlier years. For example, you can see in Figure 17–1 that Pepsi's return on assets has generally increased over the past few years. What accounts for this improvement? We know from the Du Pont

FIGURE 17–1 PepsiCo
financial ratios

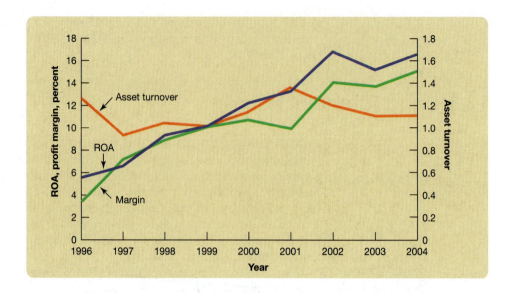

formula that ROA = operating profit margin × asset turnover. The figure shows that for the most part, the improvement in Pepsi's ROA came from improvement in margin. Notice, for example, that after 2001 turnover began a gradual but steady decline, while the profit margin increased substantially. Perhaps Pepsi raised prices during this period (higher margins) even if doing so slowed sales (lower turnover). By and large this strategy seems to have resulted in a higher return on assets.

It is also helpful to compare Pepsi's financial position with that of other firms. However, you would not expect companies in different industries to have similar ratios. For example, a soft-drink manufacturer is unlikely to have the same profit margin as a jeweler or the same leverage as a finance company. It makes sense, therefore, to limit comparison to other firms in the same industry. This is where the common-size balance sheet, which reports all items as a percentage of assets, can facilitate comparisons. Table 17–8 compares the common-size balance sheets of Pepsi and Coca-Cola,

TABLE 17–8

COMMON-SIZE BALANCE SHEETS FOR PEPSICO AND COCA-COLA AS OF DECEMBER 31, 2004 (all items expressed as percentage of total assets)					
Assets	**Pepsi**	**Coke**	**Liabilities and Shareholders' Equity**	**Pepsi**	**Coke**
Current assets			Current liabilities		
Cash and marketable securities	4.6	21.6	Debt due for repayment	3.8	19.2
Receivables	10.7	6.9	Accounts payable	16.4	13.7
Inventories	5.5	4.5	Other current liabilities	3.9	2.1
Other current assets	10.1	5.5	Total current liabilities	24.1	35.0
Total current assets	30.9	38.6			
			Long-term debt	8.6	3.7
Fixed assets			Other long-term liabilities	18.8	10.4
Net tangible assets	29.1	19.4			
Total intangible fixed assets	19.4	12.2	Total liabilities	51.5	49.1
Total fixed assets	48.6	31.7	Shareholders' equity		
Other assets	20.6	29.7	Common stock and other paid-in capital	2.3	18.5
			Retained earnings	46.2	32.3
Total assets	100.0	100.0	Total shareholders' equity	48.5	50.9
			Total liabilities and shareholders' equity	100.0	100.0

TABLE 17–9 Financial ratios for PepsiCo and Coca-Cola, 2004

	PepsiCo	Coca-Cola
Leverage Ratios		
Long-term debt ratio	0.15	0.07
Total debt ratio	0.52	0.49
Times interest earned	34.21	32.74
Cash coverage ratio	41.78	37.30
Liquidity Ratios		
NWC to assets	0.07	0.04
Current ratio	1.28	1.10
Quick ratio	0.63	0.81
Cash ratio	0.19	0.62
Efficiency Ratios		
Asset turnover	1.10	0.75
Fixed asset turnover	2.18	2.19
Collection period (days)	36.36	35.42
Inventory turnover	8.22	5.05
Profitability Ratios		
Operating profit margin (%)	15.0	23.0
Return on assets (%)	16.4	17.2
Return on equity (%)	33.1	32.3

Pepsi's main competitor.[10] We see there that Coke has greater current assets and greater current liabilities than Pepsi. Net working capital for both firms is low: 6.8 percent for Pepsi and 3.6 percent for Coke. Pepsi has a higher proportion of both tangible and intangible fixed assets than Coke. Total leverage is similar for the two firms, as indicated by the similar proportions for total liabilities, but the composition of debt differs considerably. Coke has far more reliance on short-term debt, while Pepsi has issued more long-term debt and other long-term liabilities.

How do these differences translate into financial performance? Table 17–9 compares some key ratios for Coke and Pepsi. As was obvious from the common-size balance sheets, while the composition of leverage differs for the two firms, total leverage is broadly similar, as are interest and cash coverage ratios. Pepsi seems to have a slight advantage in terms of efficiency ratios (compare asset and inventory turnover ratios) but a substantial disadvantage in terms of pricing, as is evident in its considerably lower profit margin. The net result is pretty much a wash. Coke's ROA is slightly higher than Pepsi's, but Pepsi's ROE is slightly higher.

Financial ratios that can be used as benchmarks to evaluate a firm are widely available. A good list of Web resources is at the front of this chapter. You can start with the Market Insight Web site associated with this text: **www.mhhe.com/ edumarketinsight**. Table 17–10 is an excerpt from Reuters Web page (**www. investor.reuters.com**, click on *Ratios*), which provides considerable information. Notice that the site provides both sector benchmarks (for Pepsi, consumer noncyclicals) and industry benchmarks (for Pepsi, nonalcoholic beverages) that one can use to put firm performance in perspective. Financial ratios for industries also are published by the U.S. Department of Commerce (see Table 17–11), Dun & Bradstreet *(Industry Norms and Key Business Ratios),* and the Risk Management Association, or RMA *(Annual Statement Studies).*

---

[10] It might be better to compare Pepsi's ratios with the average values for the entire industry rather than with those of one competitor. Some information on ratios in the food and drink industry is provided in Table 17–10.

TABLE 17–10 Benchmark financial ratios for PepsiCo

Ratios: PEPSICO INC (NYS) **Sector:** Consumer/Noncyclical	**Industry:** Beverages (nonalcoholic)			
	Company	**Industry**	**Sector**	**S&P 500**
Valuation Ratios				
P/E ratio (TTM)	22.35	21.66	20.66	22.06
Price to book (MRQ)	6.68	6.25	7.25	4.04
Price to cash flow (TTM)	17.17	16.85	17.19	15.93
Financial Strength				
Quick ratio (MRQ)	0.95	0.87	0.65	1.21
Current ratio (MRQ)	1.28	1.19	1.26	1.71
LT debt to equity (MRQ)	0.18	0.31	0.77	0.60
Total debt to equity (MRQ)	0.26	0.54	0.97	0.76
Interest coverage (TTM)	31.49	29.74	17.14	12.59
Profitability Ratios (%)				
Operating margin (TTM)	17.97	20.91	17.02	21.97
Net profit margin (TTM)	14.27	17.01	11.49	14.03
Management Effectiveness (%)				
Return on assets (TTM)	15.88	14.96	11.31	7.63
Return on equity (TTM)	32.84	31.06	33.28	20.00
Efficiency				
Receivable turnover (TTM)	9.37	10.08	13.39	10.26
Inventory turnover (TTM)	8.67	7.49	6.75	13.29
Asset turnover (TTM)	1.11	0.92	1.09	0.96

Source: **www.investor.reuters.com,** March 10, 2005.

Notes:
1. TTM = trailing 12 months.
2. MRQ = most recent quarter.

Table 17–11 presents ratios for a sample of major industry groups to give you a feel for some of the differences across industries. You should note that while some ratios such as asset turnover or total debt ratio tend to be relatively stable over time, others such as return on assets or equity will be more sensitive to the state of the economy as profits ebb and flow with the business cycle.

TABLE 17–11 Financial ratios for major industry groups

Industry	LT Debt Assets	Interest Coverage	NWC Assets	Quick Ratio	Asset Turnover	Oper. Profit Margin (%)	Return on Assets (%)	Return on Equity (%)	Payout Ratio
All manufacturing	0.19	4.13	0.07	0.91	0.93	6.88	6.37	15.76	0.31
Food products	0.28	3.65	0.09	0.81	1.37	6.20	8.50	17.80	0.36
Textiles	0.23	2.92	0.20	0.92	1.47	4.35	6.39	8.39	0.23
Petroleum/coal	0.15	3.64	0.04	1.00	1.34	3.31	4.45	18.14	0.25
Chemicals	0.19	4.27	0.00	0.72	0.59	10.37	6.13	7.31	0.33
Drugs	0.25	9.44	0.02	0.76	0.87	13.53	11.72	59.14	0.29
Machinery	0.19	4.64	0.13	1.02	0.89	8.04	7.19	14.82	0.17
Computers/electronic	0.11	4.52	0.14	1.31	0.66	5.30	3.52	10.06	0.20
Transportation equip.	0.17	2.22	0.01	0.72	0.94	3.94	3.69	13.12	0.30
Beverages/tobacco	0.28	5.25	−0.02	0.70	0.63	14.76	9.24	27.62	0.51

Source: U.S. Department of Commerce, *Quarterly Financial Report for Manufacturing, Mining and Trade Corporations,* December 2004.

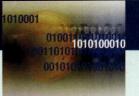

Benchmarking Financial Profiles

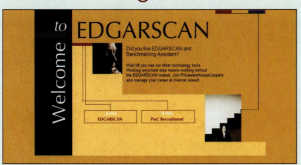

Log on to **edgarscan.pwcglobal.com** and click on *Benchmarking Assistant.* There you can select a company such as PepsiCo and request a list of its peer firms. You can also ask for comparative graphs over time of many key financial statistics. Choose two firms, for example Coca-Cola and PepsiCo or Microsoft and Apple. In what ways are the firms' financial profiles similar? Different?

Self-Test 17.5

Look at the financial ratios shown in Table 17–11. The textiles industry has a higher ratio of net working capital to total assets than manufacturing corporations. It also has a higher asset turnover. What do you think accounts for these differences?

17.4 Measuring Company Performance

market value added

The difference between the market value of the firm's equity and its book value.

The book value of the company's equity is equal to the total amount that the company has raised from its shareholders or retained and reinvested on their behalf. If the company has been successful in adding value, the market value of the equity will be higher than the book value. So investors are likely to smile on the managers of firms that have a high ratio of market-to-book value and to frown on firms whose market value is less than book value. Of course, the market-to-book ratio does not tell you just how much richer the shareholders have become. Take General Electric, for example. At the beginning of 2005, the book value of GE's equity was $101.8 billion, but investors valued its shares at $375.9 billion. The difference between the market value of GE's shares and their book value is often called the **market value added.** GE had added 375.9 − 101.8 = $274.1 billion to the equity capital that it had invested.

The consultancy firm Stern Stewart & Co. publishes an annual ranking of 1,000 firms in terms of their market value added. Table 17–12 shows some of the companies toward the top and bottom of their list. Microsoft heads our sample in terms of market value added. Delta Air Lines is at the bottom: The market value of its shares was barely greater than the amount of shareholders' money invested in the firm.

Measures of company performance that are based on market values have two disadvantages. First, the market value of the company shares reflects investor expectations. Investors placed a high value on Microsoft's shares partly because they believed that its management would *continue* to find profitable investments in the future. Second, market values cannot be used to judge the performance of companies that are privately owned or the performance of divisions or plants that are part of larger companies. Therefore, financial managers also calculate accounting measures of performance.

Think again of how a firm creates value for its investors. It can either invest in new plant and equipment or return the cash to investors, who can then invest the money for themselves by buying stocks and bonds in the capital market. The return that investors could expect to earn if they invested in the capital market is called the *cost of capital.* A firm that earns *more* than the cost of capital makes its investors better off: It is earning them a higher return than they could obtain for themselves. A firm that earns *less*

TABLE 17–12 Measures of company performance, 2005. Companies are ranked by market value added.

	Market-to-Book Ratio	Market Value Added ($ million)	Return on Capital (%)	Cost of Capital (%)	Year-average Capital ($ million)	EVA ($ million)
Microsoft	7.4	204,168	32.9	11.7	31,090	6,456
Wal-Mart	2.9	169,927	13.2	6.2	86,822	5,920
Johnson & Johnson	3.4	135,584	18.1	8.2	57,833	5,682
Intel	4.0	98,189	18.6	13.7	32,394	1,645
Coca-Cola	4.8	83,080	21.3	6.4	21,166	3,116
IBM	2.2	79,894	9.0	11.2	67,369	−1,506
Merck	2.1	37,921	17.9	8.0	36,887	3,705
Dow Chemical	1.0	25,403	5.9	6.5	44,639	−299
Delta Air Lines	1.0	4,090	−1.0	−6.7	27,888	−2,155

Note: Economic value added is the rate of return on capital less the cost of capital times the amount of capital invested; e.g., for Microsoft, EVA = (.329 − .177) × $31,090 million.
Source: Data provided by Stern Stewart & Co.

economic value added or **EVA** (also called **residual income**)
The net profit of a firm or division after deducting the cost of the capital employed.

than the cost of capital makes investors worse off: They could earn a higher expected return simply by investing their cash in the capital market. Naturally, therefore, financial managers are concerned whether the firm's return on its assets exceeds or falls short of the cost of capital. Look, for example, at the third column of Table 17–12, which shows the return on capital[11] for our sample of 12 companies. Microsoft had the highest return at 32.9 percent. Since the cost of capital for Microsoft was 11.7 percent, each dollar invested in Microsoft was earning almost three times the return that investors could have expected by investing in the capital market.

Let us work out how much this amounted to. Microsoft's total capital in 2005 was $31,090 million. With a return of 32.9 percent, it earned profits of .329 × $31,090 = $10,228 million. The total cost of capital employed by Microsoft was .117 × $31,090 = $3,637 million. So after deducting the cost of capital, Microsoft earned $10,228 − $3,637 = $6,591 million. This is called Microsoft's **economic value added,** or **EVA,** a term coined by the consulting firm Stern Stewart, which has done much to develop and promote the concept. (The value of Microsoft's EVA given in Table 17–12 is off by a few percent from the value we've derived because of rounding error in the interest rates.) Another common term for economic value added is **residual income.**

The final column of Table 17–12 shows the economic value added for our sample of large companies. You can see that while Wal-Mart had a far lower return on capital than Intel, it was nevertheless far ahead in terms of EVA. This is partly because Wal-Mart was less risky and investors did not require such a high return, but also because Wal-Mart had far more dollars invested than Intel. Notice that IBM is a laggard in the EVA stakes. Its positive return on capital indicates that the company earns a profit after deducting out-of-pocket costs. But this profit is calculated before deducting the cost of capital. IBM's residual income (or EVA) was negative at −$1,506 million.

Residual income, or EVA, is a better measure of a company's performance than accounting profits. Profits are calculated after deducting all costs *except* the cost of capital. EVA recognizes that companies need to cover their cost of capital before they add value. If a plant or division is not earning a positive EVA, its management is likely to face some pointed questions about whether the assets could be better employed elsewhere or by fresh management. Therefore, a growing number of firms now calculate EVA and tie managers' compensation to it.

This is not the first time that we have encountered EVA. In Chapter 9 we pointed out that managers often ask how far a project's sales could fall before the profits failed to cover the cost of capital. In other words, they define a project as breaking even when its economic value added is zero.

---

[11] Return on capital is closely related to return on assets. It measures profitability per dollar of long-term capital (long-term debt plus shareholders' equity) instead of per dollar of total assets.

17.5 The Role of Financial Ratios

Before concluding, it might be helpful to emphasize the role of accounting measures. Whenever two managers get together to discuss the state of the business, there is a good bet that they will refer to financial ratios. Let's drop in on two conversations.

Conversation 1 The CEO was musing out loud: "How are we going to finance this expansion? Would the banks be happy to lend us the $30 million that we need?"

"I've been looking into that," the financial manager replies. "Our current debt ratio is .3. If we borrow the full cost of the project, the ratio would be about .45. When we took out our last loan from the bank, we agreed that we would not allow our debt ratio to get above .5. So if we borrow to finance this project, we wouldn't have much leeway to respond to possible emergencies. Also, the rating agencies currently give our bonds an investment-grade rating. They too look at a company's leverage when they rate its bonds. I have a table here (Table 17–13) which shows that, when firms are highly leveraged, their bonds receive a lower rating. I don't know whether the rating agencies would downgrade our bonds if our debt ratio increased to .45, but they might. That wouldn't please our existing bondholders, and it could raise the cost of any new borrowing.

"We also need to think about our interest cover, which is beginning to look a bit thin. Debt interest is currently covered three times, and if we borrowed the entire $30 million, interest cover would fall to about two times. Sure, we expect to earn additional profits on the new investment, but it could be several years before they come through. If we run into a recession in the meantime, we could find ourselves short of cash."

"Sounds to me as if we should be thinking about a possible equity issue," concluded the CEO.

Conversation 2 The CEO was not in the best of moods after his humiliating defeat at the company golf tournament by the manager of the packaging division: "I see our stock was down again yesterday," he growled. "It's now selling below book value, and the stock price is only six times earnings. I work my socks off for this company; you would think that our stockholders would show a little more gratitude."

"I think I can understand a little of our shareholders' worries," the financial manager replies. "Just look at our return on assets. It's only 6 percent, well below the cost of capital. Sure we are making a profit, but that profit does not cover the cost of the funds that investors provide. Our economic value added is actually negative. Of course, this doesn't necessarily mean that the assets could be used better elsewhere, but we should certainly be looking carefully at whether any of our divisions should be sold off or the assets redeployed.

TABLE 17–13 Financial ratios and default risk by rating class, long-term debt

	Three-Year (2001–2003) Medians						
	AAA	AA	A	BBB	BB	B	CCC
Operating income/sales (%)	24.6	23.4	18.2	14.7	15.8	13.9	11.4
Free cash flow/sales (%)	14.8	10.9	7.8	5.7	3.9	1.3	(0.9)
EBITDA int. + div. coverage	4.0	3.9	4.1	4.5	3.0	1.7	1.0
Total liabilities/net worth (%)	70.3	123.6	138.8	149.1	194.2	202.7	(208.3)
EBITDA/total assets (%)	22.2	21.2	16.5	13.7	12.9	10.3	7.0
Total debt/market capitalization (%)	0.5	8.1	17.2	27.2	43.2	55.9	80.8
Historical default rate (%)	0.5	1.3	2.3	6.6	19.5	35.8	54.4

Note: EBITDA is earnings before interest, taxes, depreciation, and amortization.
Sources: David Lugg and Wesley E. Chinn, "Credit Stats Final Adjusted Key U.S. Industrial Financial Ratios," August 20, 2004, Standard and Poor's; Brady and Roger J. Bos, "Record Defaults in 2001 the Result of Poor Credit Quality and a Weak Economy," Table 2, Standard and Poor's. Reproduced by permission of Standard & Poor's, a division of The McGraw-Hill Companies, Inc.

"In some ways we're in good shape. We have very little short-term debt, and our current assets are three times our current liabilities. But that's not altogether good news because it also suggests that we may have more working capital than we need. I've been looking at our main competitors. They turn over their inventory 12 times a year compared with our figure of just 8 times. Also, their customers take an average of 45 days to pay their bills. Ours take 67. If we could just match their performance on these two measures, we would release $300 million that could be paid out to shareholders."

"Perhaps we could talk more about this tomorrow," said the CEO. "In the meantime I intend to have a word with the production manager about our inventory levels and with the credit manager about our collections policy. You've also got me thinking about whether we should sell off our packaging division. I've always worried about the divisional manager there. Spends too much time practicing his backswing and not enough worrying about his return on assets."

SUMMARY

www.mhhe.com/bmm5e

What are the standard measures of a firm's leverage, liquidity, efficiency, and profitability? What is the significance of each of these measures?

If you are analyzing a company's financial statements, there is a danger of being overwhelmed by the sheer volume of data contained in the **income statement, balance sheet, and statement of cash flow.** Managers use a few salient ratios to summarize the firm's leverage, liquidity, efficiency, and profitability. They may also combine accounting data with other data to measure the esteem in which investors hold the company or the efficiency with which the firm uses its resources.

Look back at Table 17–7, which summarizes the four categories of financial ratios that we have discussed in this chapter. Remember though that financial analysts define the same ratio in different ways or use different terms to describe the same ratio.

Leverage ratios measure the indebtedness of the firm. Liquidity ratios measure how easily the firm can obtain cash. Efficiency ratios measure how intensively the firm is using its assets. Profitability ratios measure the firm's return on its investments. Be selective in your choice of these ratios. Different ratios often tell you similar things.

Financial ratios crop up repeatedly in financial discussions and arrangements. For example, banks and bondholders commonly place limits on the borrower's leverage ratios. Ratings agencies also look at leverage ratios when they decide how highly to rate the firm's bonds.

How does the Du Pont formula help identify the determinants of the firm's return on its assets and equity?

The **Du Pont system** provides a useful way to link ratios to explain the firm's return on assets and equity. The formula states that the return on equity is the product of the firm's leverage ratio, asset turnover, operating profit margin, and debt burden. Return on assets is the product of the firm's asset turnover and operating profit margin.

What are some potential pitfalls of ratio analysis based on accounting data?

Financial ratio analysis will rarely be useful if practiced mechanically. It requires a large dose of good judgment. Financial ratios seldom provide answers, but they do help you ask the right questions. Moreover, accounting data do not necessarily reflect market values properly, and so must be used with caution. You need a benchmark for assessing a company's financial position. Therefore, we typically compare financial ratios with the company's ratios in earlier years and with the ratios of other firms in the same business.

How do measures such as market value added and economic value added help to assess the firm's performance?

The ratio of the market value of the firm's equity to its book value indicates how far the value of the shareholders' investment exceeds the money that they have contributed. The *difference* between the market and book values is known as **market value added** and measures the number of dollars of value that the company has added.

Managers often compare the company's return on assets with the cost of capital to see whether the firm is earning the return that investors require. It is also useful to deduct the cost of the capital employed from the company's profits to see how much profit the company has earned after all costs. This measure is known as **residual income, economic value added,** or **EVA.** Managers of divisions or plants are often judged and rewarded by their business's economic value added.

QUIZ ℍ™

1. **Calculating Ratios.** Here are simplified financial statements of Phone Corporation from a recent year:

INCOME STATEMENT (figures in millions of dollars)	
Net sales	13,193
Cost of goods sold	4,060
Other expenses	4,049
Depreciation	2,518
Earnings before interest and taxes (EBIT)	2,566
Interest expenses	685
Income before tax	1,881
Taxes	570
Net income	1,311
Dividends	856

BALANCE SHEET (figures in millions of dollars)	End of Year	Start of Year
Assets		
Cash and marketable securities	89	158
Receivables	2,382	2,490
Inventories	187	238
Other current assets	867	932
Total current assets	3,525	3,818
Net property, plant, and equipment	19,973	19,915
Other long-term assets	4,216	3,770
Total assets	27,714	27,503
Liabilities and shareholders' equity		
Payables	2,564	3,040
Short-term debt	1,419	1,573
Other current liabilities	811	787
Total current liabilities	4,794	5,400
Long-term debt and leases	7,018	6,833
Other long-term liabilities	6,178	6,149
Shareholders' equity	9,724	9,121
Total liabilities and shareholders' equity	27,714	27,503

www.mhhe.com/bmm5e

Calculate the following financial ratios:

    a. Long-term debt ratio
    b. Total debt ratio
    c. Times interest earned
    d. Cash coverage ratio
    e. Current ratio
    f. Quick ratio
    g. Operating profit margin
    h. Inventory turnover
    i. Days in inventory
    j. Average collection period
    k. Return on equity
    l. Return on assets
    m. Payout ratio

2. **Gross Investment.** What was Phone Corp.'s gross investment in plant and other equipment?

3. **Market Value Ratios.** If the market value of Phone Corp. stock was $17.2 billion at the end of the year, what was the market-to-book ratio? If there were 205 million shares outstanding, what were earnings per share? The price-earnings ratio?

4. **Common-Size Balance Sheet.** Prepare a common-size balance sheet for Phone Corp. using its balance sheet from Problem 1.

Please visit us at www.mhhe.com/bmm5e or refer to your Student CD

5. **Du Pont Analysis.** Use the data for Phone Corp. to confirm that ROA = asset turnover × operating profit margin.

6. **Du Pont Analysis.** Use the data for Phone Corp. from Problem 1 to

    a. calculate the ROE for Phone Corp.
    b. demonstrate that ROE = leverage ratio × asset turnover ratio × operating profit margin × debt burden.

PRACTICE PROBLEMS

7. **Asset Turnover.** In each case, choose the firm that you expect to have a higher asset turnover ratio.

    a. Economics Consulting Group or Pepsi.
    b. Catalog Shopping Network or Neiman Marcus.
    c. Electric Utility Co. or Standard Supermarkets.

8. **Defining Ratios.** There are no universally accepted definitions of financial ratios, but some of the following ratios make no sense at all. Substitute correct definitions.

    a. Debt-equity ratio $= \dfrac{\text{long-term debt}}{\text{long-term debt} + \text{equity}}$

    b. Return on equity $= \dfrac{\text{EBIT} - \text{tax}}{\text{average equity}}$

    c. Profit margin $= \dfrac{\text{net income} + \text{interest}}{\text{sales}}$

    d. Inventory turnover $= \dfrac{\text{total assets}}{\text{average inventory}}$

    e. Current ratio $= \dfrac{\text{current liabilities}}{\text{current assets}}$

    f. Average collection period $= \dfrac{\text{sales}}{\text{average receivables}/365}$

    g. Quick ratio $= \dfrac{\text{cash} + \text{marketable securities} + \text{receivables}}{\text{current liabilities}}$

9. **Current Liabilities.** Suppose that at year-end Pepsi had unused lines of credit which would have allowed it to borrow a further $300 million. Suppose also that it used this line of credit to

www.mhhe.com/bmm5e

borrow $300 million and invested the proceeds in marketable securities. Would the company have appeared to be (a) more or less liquid, (b) more or less highly leveraged? Calculate the appropriate ratios.

10. **Current Ratio.** How would the following actions affect a firm's current ratio?

    a. Inventory is sold at cost.
    b. The firm takes out a bank loan to pay its accounts due.
    c. A customer pays its accounts receivable.
    d. The firm uses cash to purchase additional inventories.

11. **Liquidity Ratios.** A firm uses $1 million in cash to purchase inventories. What will happen to its current ratio? Its quick ratio?

12. **Receivables.** Chik's Chickens has average accounts receivable of $6,333. Sales for the year were $9,800. What is its average collection period?

13. **Inventory.** Salad Daze maintains an inventory of produce worth $400. Its total bill for produce over the course of the year was $73,000. How old on average is the lettuce it serves its customers?

14. **Inventory Turnover.** If a firm's inventory level of $10,000 represents 30 days' sales, what is the annual cost of goods sold? What is the inventory turnover ratio?

15. **Leverage Ratios.** Lever Age pays an 8 percent coupon on outstanding debt with face value $10 million. The firm's EBIT was $1 million.

    a. What is times interest earned?
    b. If depreciation is $200,000, what is cash coverage?
    c. If the firm must retire $300,000 of debt for the sinking fund each year, what is its "fixed-payment cash-coverage ratio" (the ratio of cash flow to interest plus other fixed debt payments)?

16. **Du Pont Analysis.** Keller Cosmetics maintains an operating profit margin of 5 percent and asset turnover ratio of 3.

    a. What is its ROA?
    b. If its debt-equity ratio is 1.0, its interest payments and taxes are each $8,000, and EBIT is $20,000, what is its ROE?

17. **Du Pont Analysis.** Torrid Romance Publishers has total receivables of $3,000, which represents 20 days' sales. Average total assets are $75,000. The firm's operating profit margin is 5 percent. Find the firm's ROA and asset turnover ratio.

18. **Leverage.** A firm has a long-term debt-equity ratio of .4. Shareholders' equity is $1 million. Current assets are $200,000, and the current ratio is 2.0. The only current liabilities are notes payable. What is the total debt ratio?

19. **Leverage Ratios.** A firm has a debt-to-equity ratio of .5 and a market-to-book ratio of 2.0. What is the ratio of the book value of debt to the market value of equity?

20. **Times Interest Earned.** In the past year, TVG had revenues of $3 million, cost of goods sold of $2.5 million, and depreciation expense of $200,000. The firm has a single issue of debt outstanding with face value of $1 million, market value of $.92 million, and a coupon rate of 8 percent. What is the firm's times interest earned ratio?

21. **Du Pont Analysis.** CFA Corp. has a debt-equity ratio that is lower than the industry average, but its cash coverage ratio is also lower than the industry average. What might explain this seeming contradiction?

22. **Leverage.** Suppose that a firm has both floating-rate and fixed-rate debt outstanding. What effect will a decline in market interest rates have on the firm's times interest earned ratio? On the market-value debt-to-equity ratio? On the basis of these answers, would you say that leverage has increased or decreased?

23. **Interpreting Ratios.** In each of the following cases, explain briefly which of the two companies is likely to be characterized by the higher ratio:

    a. Debt-equity ratio: a shipping company or a computer software company.
    b. Payout ratio: United Foods Inc. or Computer Graphics Inc.
    c. Ratio of sales to assets: an integrated pulp and paper manufacturer or a paper mill.
    d. Average collection period: Regional Electric Power Company or Z-Mart Discount Outlets.
    e. Price-earnings multiple: Basic Sludge Company or Fledgling Electronics.

24. **Using Financial Ratios.** For each category of financial ratios discussed in this chapter, give some examples of who would be likely to examine these ratios and why.

CHALLENGE PROBLEM

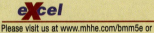

Please visit us at www.mhhe.com/bmm5e or refer to your Student CD

25. **Financial Statements.** As you can see, someone has spilled ink over some of the entries in the balance sheet and income statement of Transylvania Railroad. Can you use the following information to work out the missing entries:

Long-term debt ratio	.4
Times interest earned	8.0
Current ratio	1.4
Quick ratio	1.0
Cash ratio	.2
Return on assets	18%
Return on equity	41%
Inventory turnover	5.0
Average collection period	71.2 days

INCOME STATEMENT
(figures in millions of dollars)

Net sales	•••
Cost of goods sold	•••
Selling, general, and administrative expenses	10
Depreciation	20
Earnings before interest and taxes (EBIT)	•••
Interest expense	•••
Income before tax	•••
Tax	•••
Net income	•••

BALANCE SHEET
(figures in millions of dollars)

	This Year	Last Year
Assets		
Cash and marketable securities	•••	20
Receivables	•••	34
Inventories	•••	26
Total current assets	•••	80
Net property, plant, and equipment	•••	25
Total assets	•••	105
Liabilities and shareholders' equity		
Accounts payable	25	20
Notes payable	30	35
Total current liabilities	•••	55
Long-term debt	•••	20
Shareholders' equity	•••	30
Total liabilities and shareholders' equity	115	105

STANDARD
&POOR'S

Go to Market Insight at **www.mhhe.com/edumarketinsight**.

1. Lowes (LOW) and The Home Depot (HD) have been in a tremendous race for the homeowner's dollar in the last few years. Who is winning? Review the company profiles (also review the industry information under the Home Improvement Retail link), financial highlights, annual ratios, profitability, and monthly valuation data reports. What company performance information supports your view as to which company is winning the race in the home improvement industry? Has the stock market picked a winner in this race?

2. Compare the sources of return on equity (using the Du Pont formula) for Abercrombie & Fitch (ANF) and Gap, Inc. (GPS). Examine both levels and trends in these variables. Review the trends in net profit margin, total asset turnover, and leverage. What factors tend to explain the performance differential between these competing clothing retailers? How has the market reacted to their operating performance?

SOLUTIONS TO SELF-TEST QUESTIONS

17.1 Nothing will happen to the long-term debt ratio computed using book values, since the face values of the old and new debt are equal. However, times interest earned and cash coverage will increase since the firm will reduce its interest expense.

17.2 a. The current ratio starts at 1.2/1.0 = 1.2. The transaction will reduce current assets to $.7 million and current liabilities to $.5 million. The current ratio increases to .7/.5 = 1.4. Net working capital is unaffected: Current assets and current liabilities fall by equal amounts.

b. The current ratio is unaffected, since the firm merely exchanges one current asset (cash) for another (inventories). However, the quick ratio will fall since inventories are not included among the most liquid assets.

17.3 Average daily expenses are (12,142 + 10,142)/365 = $61.1 million. Average accounts payable are (4,594 + 5,213)/2 = 4,903.5 million. The average payment delay is therefore 4,903.5/61.1 = 80 days.

17.4 a. The firm must compensate for its below-average profit margin with an above-average turnover ratio. Remember that ROA is the *product* of operating margin × turnover.

b. If ROA equals the industry average but ROE exceeds the industry average, the firm must have above-average leverage. As long as ROA exceeds the borrowing rate, leverage will increase ROE.

17.5 Textile producers maintain large inventories of goods, specifically the products they stock awaiting sale. This shows up in the high net working capital ratio. Their typical profit margin on sales is relatively low, but they make up for that low margin by turning over goods rapidly. The high asset turnover allows producers to earn an adequate return on assets even with a low profit margin, while competition prevents them from increasing prices and margins to a level that would provide a better ROA.

MINICASE

Burchetts Green had enjoyed the bank training course, but it was good to be starting his first real job in the corporate lending group. Earlier that morning the boss had handed him a set of financial statements for The Hobby Horse Company, Inc. (HH). "Hobby Horse," she said, "has a $45 million loan from us due at the end of September, and it is likely to ask us to roll it over. The company seems to have run into some rough weather recently, and I have asked Furze Platt to go down there this afternoon and see what is happening. It might do you good to go along with her. Before you

go, take a look at these financial statements and see what you think the problems are. Here's a chance for you to use some of that stuff they taught you in the training course."

Mr. Green was familiar with the HH story. Founded in 1990, it had rapidly built up a chain of discount stores selling materials for crafts and hobbies. However, last year a number of new store openings coinciding with a poor Christmas season had pushed the company into loss. Management had halted all new construction and put 15 of its existing stores up for sale.

Mr. Green decided to start with the 6-year summary of HH's balance sheet and income statement (Table 17–14). Then he turned to examine in more detail the latest position (Tables 17–15 and 17–16).

What appear to be the problem areas in HH? Do the financial ratios suggest questions that Ms. Platt and Mr. Green need to address?

TABLE 17–14 Financial highlights for The Hobby Horse Company, Inc., year ending March 31

	2006	2005	2004	2003	2002	2001
Net sales	3,351	3,314	2,845	2,796	2,493	2,160
EBIT	–9	312	256	243	212	156
Interest	37	63	65	58	48	46
Taxes	3	60	46	43	39	34
Net profit	–49	189	145	142	125	76
Earnings per share	–0.15	0.55	0.44	0.42	0.37	0.25
Current assets	669	469	491	435	392	423
Net fixed assets	923	780	753	680	610	536
Total assets	1,592	1,249	1,244	1,115	1,002	959
Current liabilities	680	365	348	302	276	320
Long-term debt	236	159	297	311	319	315
Stockholders' equity	676	725	599	502	407	324
Number of stores	240	221	211	184	170	157
Employees	13,057	11,835	9,810	9,790	9,075	7,825

TABLE 17–15

INCOME STATEMENT FOR THE HOBBY HORSE COMPANY, INC., FOR YEAR ENDING MARCH 31, 2006 (all items in millions of dollars)	
Net sales	3,351
Cost of goods sold	1,990
Selling, general, and administrative expenses	1,211
Depreciation expense	159
Earnings before interest and taxes (EBIT)	–9
Net interest expense	37
Taxable income	–46
Income taxes	3
Net income	–49
Allocation of net income	
Addition to retained earnings	–49
Dividends	0

Note: Column sums subject to rounding error.

TABLE 17–16

CONSOLIDATED BALANCE SHEET FOR THE HOBBY HORSE COMPANY, INC. (figures in millions of dollars)		
Assets	**Mar. 31, 2006**	**Mar. 31, 2005**
Current assets		
Cash and marketable securities	14	72
Receivables	176	194
Inventories	479	203
Total current assets	669	469
Fixed assets		
Property, plant, and equipment (net of depreciation)	1,077	910
Less accumulated depreciation	154	130
Net fixed assets	923	780
Total assets	1,592	1,249
Liabilities and Shareholders' Equity	**Mar. 31, 2006**	**Mar. 31, 2005**
Current liabilities		
Debt due for repayment	484	222
Accounts payable	94	58
Other current liabilities	102	85
Total current liabilities	680	365
Long-term debt	236	159
Stockholders' equity		
Common stock and other paid-in capital	155	155
Retained earnings	521	570
Total stockholders' equity	676	725
Total liabilities and stockholders' equity	1,592	1,249

Note: Column sums subject to rounding error.

Long-Term Financial Planning

RELATED WEB LINKS

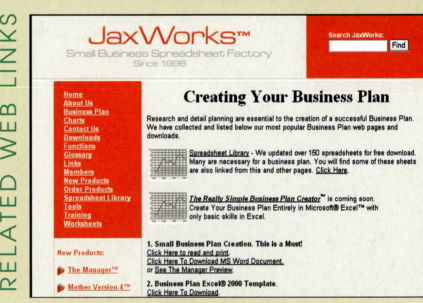

www.planware.org

www.jaxworks.com/bpindex.htm
Useful tools for developing a
business plan.

www.toolkit.cch.com Toolkit for small
businesses.

www.investor.reuters.com

finance.yahoo.com Analyst
estimates of future growth rates.

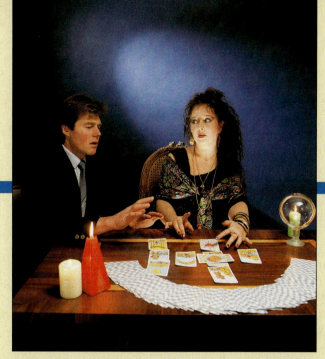

Financial planning? Financial planners don't guess the future, they prepare for it.

© SuperStock

It's been said that a camel looks like a horse designed by a committee. If a firm made every decision piecemeal, it would end up with a financial camel. That is why smart financial managers consider the overall effect of future investment and financing decisions.

Think back to Chapter 1, where we discussed the job of the financial manager. The manager must consider what investments the firm should undertake and how the firm should raise the cash to pay for those investments. By now you know a fair amount about how to make investment decisions that increase shareholder value and about the different securities that the firm can issue. But because new investments need to be paid for, those decisions cannot be made independently. They must add up to a sensible whole. That's why financial planning is needed. The financial plan allows managers to think about the implications of alternative financial strategies and to tease out any inconsistencies in the firm's goals.

Financial planning also helps managers avoid some surprises and consider how they should react to surprises that *cannot* be avoided. In Chapter 9 we stressed that good financial managers insist on understanding what makes projects work and what could go wrong with them. The same approach should be taken when investment and financing decisions are considered as a whole.

Finally, financial planning helps establish goals to motivate managers and provide standards for measuring performance.

We start the chapter by summarizing what financial planning involves, and we describe the contents of a typical financial plan. We then discuss the use of financial models in the planning process. Finally, we examine the relationship between a firm's growth and its need for new financing.

After studying this chapter you should be able to:

- Describe the contents and uses of a financial plan.
- Construct a simple financial planning model.
- Estimate the effect of growth on the need for external financing.

18.1 What Is Financial Planning?

planning horizon
Time horizon for a financial plan.

Firms must plan for both the short term and the long term. Short-term planning rarely looks further ahead than the next 12 months. It seeks to ensure that the firm has enough cash to pay its bills and that short-term borrowing and lending are arranged to the best advantage. We discuss short-term planning in the next chapter.

Here we are concerned with long-term planning, where a typical **planning horizon** is 5 years, although some firms look out 10 years or more. For example, it can take at least 10 years for an electric utility to design, obtain approval for, build, and test a major generating plant.

Long-term financial planning focuses on the firm's long-term goals, the investment that will be needed to meet those goals, and the finance that must be raised. But you can't think about these things without also tackling other important issues. For example, you need to consider possible dividend policies, for the more that is paid out to shareholders, the more the external financing that will be needed. You also need to think about what is an appropriate debt ratio for the firm. A conservative capital structure may mean greater reliance on new share issues. The financial plan is used to enforce consistency in the way that these questions are answered and to highlight the choices that the firm needs to make. Finally, by establishing a set of consistent goals, the plan enables subsequent evaluation of the firm's performance in meeting those goals.

Financial Planning Focuses on the Big Picture

Many of the firm's capital expenditures are proposed by plant managers. But the final budget must also reflect strategic plans made by senior management. Positive-NPV opportunities occur in those businesses where the firm has a real competitive advantage. Strategic plans need to identify such businesses and look to expand them. The plans also seek to identify businesses to sell or liquidate as well as businesses that should be allowed to run down.

Strategic planning involves capital budgeting on a grand scale. In this process, financial planners try to look at the investment by each line of business and avoid getting bogged down in details. Of course, some individual projects are large enough to have significant individual impact. For example, the telecom giant Verizon recently announced its intention to spend billions of dollars to deploy fiber-optic-based broadband technology to its residential customers, and you can bet that this project was explicitly analyzed as part of its long-range financial plan. Normally, however, financial planners do not work on a project-by-project basis. Smaller projects are aggregated into a unit that is treated as a single project.

At the beginning of the planning process the corporate staff might ask each division to submit three alternative business plans covering the next 5 years:

1. A *best-case* or aggressive growth plan calling for heavy capital investment and rapid growth of existing markets.
2. A *normal growth* plan in which the division grows with its markets but not significantly at the expense of its competitors.
3. A plan of *retrenchment* if the firm's markets contract. This is planning for lean economic times.

The plan will contain a summary of capital expenditures, working capital requirements, as well as strategies to raise funds for these investments.

Why Build Financial Plans?

Firms spend considerable energy, time, and resources building elaborate financial plans. What do they get for this investment?

Contingency Planning   Planning is not just forecasting. Forecasting concentrates on the most likely outcomes, but planners need to worry about unlikely events as well as likely ones. If you think ahead about what could go wrong, then you are less likely to ignore the danger signals and you can respond faster to trouble.

Companies have developed a number of ways of asking "what-if" questions about both individual projects and the overall firm. For example, as we saw in Chapter 9, managers often work through the consequences of their decisions under different scenarios. One scenario might envisage high interest rates contributing to a slowdown in world economic growth and lower commodity prices. A second scenario might involve a buoyant domestic economy, high inflation, and a weak currency.

The idea is to formulate responses to inevitable surprises. What will you do, for example, if sales in the first year turn out to be 10 percent below forecast? A good financial plan should help you adapt as events unfold.

Considering Options Planners need to think whether there are opportunities for the company to exploit its existing strengths by moving into a wholly new area. Often they may recommend entering a market for "strategic" reasons—that is, not because the immediate investment has a positive net present value but because it establishes the firm in a new market and creates options for possibly valuable follow-on investments.

For example, Verizon's costly fiber-optic initiative would never be profitable strictly in terms of its current uses, for phone or conventional Internet applications. But the new technology gives Verizon *options* to offer services that may be highly valuable in the future, such as the rapid delivery of an array of home entertainment services. The justification for the huge investment lies in these potential growth options.

Forcing Consistency Financial plans draw out the connections between the firm's plans for growth and the financing requirements. For example, a forecast of 25 percent growth might require the firm to issue securities to pay for necessary capital expenditures, while a 5 percent growth rate might enable the firm to finance capital expenditures by using only reinvested profits.

Financial plans should help to ensure that the firm's goals are mutually consistent. For example, the chief executive might say that she is shooting for a profit margin of 10 percent and sales growth of 20 percent, but financial planners need to think whether the higher sales growth may require price cuts that will reduce profit margin.

Moreover, a goal that is stated in terms of accounting ratios is not operational unless it is translated back into what that means for business decisions. For example, a higher profit margin can result from higher prices, lower costs, or a move into new, high-margin products. Why then do managers define objectives in this way? In part, such goals may be a code to communicate real concerns. For example, a target profit margin may be a way of saying that in pursuing sales growth, the firm has allowed costs to get out of control.

The danger is that everyone may forget the code and the accounting targets may be seen as goals in themselves. No one should be surprised when lower-level managers focus on the goals for which they are rewarded. For example, when Volkswagen set a goal of 6.5 percent profit margin, some VW groups responded by developing and promoting expensive, high-margin cars. Less attention was paid to marketing cheaper models, which had lower profit margins but higher sales volume. In 2002 Volkswagen announced that it would de-emphasize its profit margin goal and would instead focus on return on investment. It hoped that this would encourage managers to get the most profit out of every dollar of invested capital.

18.2 Financial Planning Models

Financial planners often use a financial planning model to help them explore the consequences of alternative financial strategies. These models range from simple models, such as the one presented later in this chapter, to models that incorporate hundreds of equations.

Financial planning models support the financial planning process by making it easier and cheaper to construct forecast financial statements. The models automate an important part of planning that would otherwise be boring, time-consuming, and labor-intensive.

Programming these financial planning models used to consume large amounts of computer time and high-priced talent. These days standard spreadsheet programs such as Microsoft Excel are regularly used to solve complex financial planning problems.

Components of a Financial Planning Model

A completed financial plan for a large company is a substantial document. A smaller corporation's plan would have the same elements but less detail. For the smallest businesses, financial plans may be entirely in the financial managers' heads. The basic elements of the plans will be similar, however, for firms of any size.

Financial plans include three components: inputs, the planning model, and outputs. The relationship among these components is represented in Figure 18–1. Let's look at them in turn.

Inputs The inputs to the financial plan consist of the firm's current financial statements and its forecasts about the future. Usually, the principal forecast is the likely growth in sales, since many of the other variables such as labor requirements and inventory levels are tied to sales. These forecasts are only in part the responsibility of the financial manager. Obviously, the marketing department will play a key role in forecasting sales. In addition, because sales will depend on the state of the overall economy, large firms will seek forecasting help from firms that specialize in preparing macroeconomic and industry forecasts.

The Planning Model The financial planning model calculates the implications of the manager's forecasts for profits, new investment, and financing. The model consists of equations relating output variables to forecasts. For example, the equations can show how a change in sales is likely to affect costs, working capital, fixed assets, and financing requirements. The financial model could specify that the total cost of goods produced may increase by 80 cents for every $1 increase in total sales, that accounts receivable will be a fixed proportion of sales, and that the firm will need to increase fixed assets by 8 percent for every 10 percent increase in sales.

pro formas
Projected or forecast financial statements.

Outputs The output of the financial model consists of financial statements such as income statements, balance sheets, and statements describing sources and uses of cash. These statements are called **pro formas,** which means that they are forecasts based on the inputs and the assumptions built into the plan. Usually the output of financial models also includes many of the financial ratios we discussed in the last chapter. These ratios indicate whether the firm will be financially fit and healthy at the end of the planning period.

Percentage of Sales Models

We can illustrate the basic components of a planning model with a very simple example. In the next section we will start to add some complexity.

FIGURE 18–1 The components of a financial plan

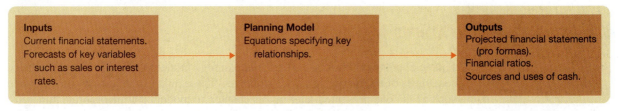

TABLE 18–1 Financial statements of Executive Cheese Company for past year

INCOME STATEMENT	
Sales	$1,200
Costs	1,000
Net income	$ 200

BALANCE SHEET (YEAR-END)			
Assets	$2,000	Debt	$ 800
		Equity	1,200
Total	$2,000	Total	$2,000

percentage of sales models

Planning model in which sales forecasts are the driving variables and most other variables are proportional to sales.

Suppose that Executive Cheese has prepared the simple balance sheet and income statement shown in Table 18–1. The firm's financial planners forecast that total sales next year will increase by 10 percent from this year's level. They expect that costs will be a fixed proportion of sales, so they too will increase by 10 percent. Almost all the forecasts for Executive Cheese are proportional to the forecast of sales. Such models are therefore called **percentage of sales models.** The result is the pro forma, or forecast, income statement in Table 18–2, which shows that next year's income will be $200 × 1.10 = $220.

Executive Cheese has no spare capacity, and in order to sustain this higher level of output, it must increase plant and equipment by 10 percent, or $200. Therefore, the left-hand side of the balance sheet, which lists total assets, must increase to $2,200. What about the right-hand side? The firm must decide how it intends to finance its new assets. Suppose that it decides to maintain a fixed debt-equity ratio. Then both debt and equity would grow by 10 percent, as shown in the pro forma balance sheet in Table 18–2. Notice that this implies that the firm must issue $80 in additional debt. On the other hand, no equity needs to be issued. The 10 percent increase in equity can be accomplished by retaining $120 of earnings.

This raises a question, however. If income is forecast at $220, why does equity increase by only $120? The answer is that the firm must be planning to pay a dividend of $220 – $120 = $100. Notice that this dividend payment is not chosen independently but is a *consequence* of the other decisions. Given the company's need for funds and its decision to maintain the debt-equity ratio, dividend policy is completely determined. Any other dividend payment would be inconsistent with the two conditions that (1) the right-hand side of the balance sheet increase by $200 and (2) both debt and equity increase in the same proportion. For this reason we call dividends the **balancing item,** or *plug.* The balancing item is the variable that adjusts to make the sources of funds equal to the uses.

balancing item

Variable that adjusts to maintain the consistency of a financial plan. Also called *plug.*

Of course, most firms would be reluctant to vary dividends simply because they have a temporary need for cash; instead, they like to maintain a steady progression of dividends. In this case Executive Cheese could commit to some other dividend payment and allow the debt-equity ratio to vary. The amount of debt would therefore become the balancing item.

TABLE 18–2 Pro forma financial statements of Executive Cheese

PRO FORMA INCOME STATEMENT	
Sales	$1,320
Costs	1,100
Net income	$ 220

PRO FORMA BALANCE SHEET (YEAR-END)			
Assets	$2,200	Debt	$ 880
		Equity	1,320
Total	$2,200	Total	$2,200

EXAMPLE 18.1 ▶ Balancing Item

Suppose the firm commits to a dividend level of $180 and raises any extra money it needs by an issue of debt. In this case the amount of debt becomes the balancing item. With the dividend set at $180, retained earnings would be only $40, so the firm would have to issue $160 in new debt to help pay for the additional $200 of assets. Table 18–3, panel A, is the new balance sheet.

Now suppose instead that the firm commits to the $180 dividend but decides that it will issue at most $100 in new debt. In that case, new equity issues become the balancing item. With $40 of earnings retained and $100 of new debt, an additional $60 of equity needs to be raised to support the total addition of $200 to the firm's assets. Table 18–3, panel B, is the resulting balance sheet.   ◀

Is one of these plans better than the others? It's hard to give a simple answer. The choice of dividend payment depends partly on how investors will interpret the decision. If last year's dividend was only $50, investors might regard a dividend payment of $100 as a sign of a confident management; if last year's dividend was $150, investors might not be so content with a payment of $100. The alternative of paying $180 in dividends and making up the shortfall by issuing more debt leaves the company with a debt-equity ratio of 77 percent. That is unlikely to make your bankers edgy, but you may worry about how long you can continue to finance expansion predominantly by borrowing.

Our example shows how experiments with a financial model, including changes in the model's balancing item, can raise important financial questions. But the model does not answer these questions. Financial models ensure *consistency* between growth assumptions and financing plans, but they do not identify the best financing plan.

Self-Test 18.1

Suppose that the firm decides to maintain its debt-equity ratio at 800/1,200 = 2/3. It is committed to increasing assets by 10 percent to support the forecast increase in sales, and it strongly believes that a dividend payment of $180 is in the best interests of the firm. What must be the balancing items? What is the implication for the firm's financing activities in the next year?

An Improved Model

Now that you have grasped the idea behind financial planning models, we can move on to a more sophisticated example.

Table 18–4 shows the financial statements for Executive Fruit Company in 2005. Judging by these figures, the company is ordinary in almost all respects. Its earnings before interest and taxes were 10 percent of sales revenue. Net income was $96,000 after payment of taxes and 10 percent interest on $400,000 of long-term debt. The company paid out two-thirds of its net income as dividends.

Next to each item on the financial statements in Table 18–4 we have entered a comment about the relationship between that variable and sales. In most cases, the comment gives the value of each item as a percentage of sales. This may be useful for forecasting purposes. For example, it would be reasonable to assume that cost of goods

TABLE 18–3 Pro forma balance sheets. *A:* Dividends are fixed, and debt is the balancing item. *B:* Dividends and debt are fixed, and equity issues are the balancing item.

Panel A				Panel B			
Assets	$2,200	Debt	$ 960	Assets	$2,200	Debt	$ 900
		Equity	1,240			Equity	1,300
Total	$2,200	Total	$2,200	Total	$2,200	Total	$2,200

TABLE 18-4 Financial
statements for Executive Fruit
Co., 2005 (figures in
thousands)

INCOME STATEMENT, 2005		
		Comment
Revenue	$ 2,000	
Cost of goods sold	1,800	90% of sales
EBIT	200	Difference = 10% of sales
Interest	40	10% of debt
Earnings before taxes	160	EBIT – interest
State and federal tax	64	40% of (EBIT – interest)
Net income	$ 96	EBIT – interest – taxes
Dividends	$ 64	Payout ratio = ⅔
Retained earnings	$ 32	Net income – dividends
BALANCE SHEET (YEAR-END, 2005)		
Assets		
Net working capital	$ 200	10% of sales
Fixed assets	800	40% of sales
Total assets	$ 1,000	50% of sales
Liabilities and shareholders' equity		
Long-term debt	$ 400	
Shareholders' equity	600	
Total liabilities and shareholders' equity	$ 1,000	Equals total assets

sold will remain at 90 percent of sales even if sales grow by 10 percent next year. Similarly, it is reasonable to assume that net working capital will remain at 10 percent of sales.

On the other hand, the fact that long-term debt was 20 percent of sales in 2005 does not mean that we should assume that this ratio will continue to hold next year. Many alternative financing plans with varying combinations of debt issues, equity issues, and dividend payouts may be considered without affecting the firm's operations.

Now suppose that you are asked to prepare pro forma financial statements for Executive Fruit for 2006. You are told to assume that (1) sales and operating costs are expected to be up 10 percent over 2005, (2) interest rates will remain at their current level, (3) the firm will stick to its traditional dividend policy of paying out two-thirds of earnings, and (4) Executive will need 10 percent more fixed assets and net working capital next year to support the higher sales volume.

In Table 18–5 we present the resulting first-stage pro forma calculations for Executive Fruit. These calculations show what would happen if the size of the firm increases along with projected sales, but at this preliminary stage the plan does not specify a particular mix of new security issues.

Without any security issues, the balance sheet will not balance: Assets increase to $1,100,000, while debt plus shareholders' equity amounts to only $1,036,000. Somehow the firm will need to raise an extra $64,000 to help pay for the increase in assets that is necessary to support the higher projected level of sales in 2006. In this first pass, external financing is the balancing item. Given the firm's growth forecasts and its dividend policy, the financial plan calculates *how much* money the firm needs to raise but does not yet specify how those funds will be raised.

In the second-stage pro forma, the firm must decide on the financing mix that best meets its needs for additional funds. It must choose some combination of new debt or new equity that supports the contemplated acquisition of additional assets. For example, it could issue $64,000 of equity or debt, or it could choose to maintain its long-term debt-equity ratio at two-thirds by issuing both debt and equity.

TABLE 18–5 First-stage pro forma statements for Executive Fruit Co., 2006 (figures in thousands)

PRO FORMA INCOME STATEMENT, 2006		
		Comment
Revenue	$2,200	10% higher
Cost of goods sold	1,980	10% higher
EBIT	220	10% higher
Interest	40	Unchanged
Earnings before taxes	180	EBIT – interest
State and federal tax	72	40% of (EBIT – interest)
Net income	$ 108	EBIT – interest – taxes
Dividends	$ 72	⅔ of net income
Retained earnings	$ 36	Net income – dividends
PRO FORMA BALANCE SHEET (YEAR-END, 2006)		
Assets		
Net working capital	$ 220	10% higher
Fixed assets	880	10% higher
Total assets	$1,100	10% higher
Liabilities and shareholders' equity		
Long-term debt	$ 400	Temporarily held fixed
Shareholders' equity	636	Increased by earnings retained during year
Total liabilities and shareholders' equity	$1,036	Sum of debt plus equity
Required external financing	$ 64	Balancing item or plug (= $1,100 – $1,036)

Table 18–6 shows the second-stage pro forma balance sheet if the required funds are raised by issuing $64,000 of debt. Therefore, in Table 18–6, debt is treated as the balancing item. Notice that while the plan requires the firm to specify a financing plan *consistent* with its growth projections, it does not provide guidance as to the *best* financing mix.

Table 18–7 sets out the firm's sources and uses of funds. It shows that working capital must be increased by $20,000 and fixed assets by $80,000 compared to their level a year earlier. The firm reinvested $36,000 of this year's profits, so $64,000 must be raised in the capital markets. Under the financing plan presented in Table 18–6, the firm borrows the entire $64,000.

We have spared you the trouble of actually calculating the figures necessary for Tables 18–5 and 18–7. The calculations do not take more than a few minutes for this simple example, *provided* you set up the calculations correctly and make no arithmetic

TABLE 18–6 Second-stage pro forma balance sheet for Executive Fruit Co., year-end 2006 (figures in thousands)

		Comment
Assets		
Net working capital	$ 220	10% higher
Fixed assets	880	10% higher
Total assets	$1,100	10% higher
Liabilities and shareholders' equity		
Long-term debt	$ 464	16% higher (new borrowing = $64; this is the balancing item)
Shareholders' equity	$ 636	Increased by retained earnings
Total liabilities and shareholders' equity	$1,100	Again equals total assets

TABLE 18-7 Statement of sources and uses of funds for Executive Fruit, 2006 (figures in thousands)

Sources		Uses	
Retained earnings	$ 36	Investment in working capital	$ 20
New borrowing	64	Investment in fixed assets	80
Total sources	$100	Total uses	$100

mistakes. If that time requirement seems trivial, remember that in reality you probably would be asked for five similar sets of statements covering each year from 2006 to 2010. Probably you would be asked for alternative projections under different assumptions (for example, 5 percent instead of 10 percent growth rate of revenue) or different financial strategies (for example, freezing dividends at their 2005 level of $64,000). This would be far more time-consuming. Moreover, actual plans will have many more line items than this simple one. Building a model and letting the computer toil in your place have obvious attractions.

Figure 18–2 is the spreadsheet we used for the Executive Fruit model. Column E contains the values that appear in Table 18–4. Columns F and G are pro forma statements using the growth rate given in cell B3. The spreadsheet recognizes that additional debt issued in one year will result in increased interest expenses in the following year. For example, interest expense in 2007 is 10 percent of the debt outstanding at the end of 2006.

Column H presents the formulas used to obtain each value in column G. Notice that we assume the firm will maintain its dividend payout ratio at 2/3 and that debt will be the balancing item, increasing in each year by required external financing (row 24). Required external financing in 2006 equals total assets required to support that year's

FIGURE 18-2 Executive Fruit spreadsheet

	A	B	C	D	E	F	G	H
1	**A. Model inputs**				**Base year**			**Formula**
2				*Income Statement*	**2005**	**2006**	**2007**	**for column G**
3	Growth rate	.10		Revenue	2,000	2,200.0	2,420.0	=F3*(1+$B3)
4	Tax rate	0.4		Cost of goods sold	1,800	1980.0	2,178.0	=G3*$B8
5	Interest rate	0.1		EBIT	200	220.0	242.0	=G3-G4
6	NWC/sales ratio	0.1		Interest expense	40	40.0	46.4	=$B$5*F20
7	Fixed assets/sales	0.4		Earnings before taxes	160	180.0	195.6	=G5-G6
8	COGS/sales	0.9		Taxes	64	72.0	78.2	=$B$4*G7
9	Payout ratio	2/3		Net income	96	108.0	117.4	=G7-G8
10				Dividends	64	72.0	78.2	=G9*$B$9
11				Retained earnings	32	36.0	39.1	=G9-G10
12								
13				*Balance Sheet (year end)*				
14				Assets				
15				Net working capital	200	220.0	242.0	=$B$6*G3
16				Fixed assets	800	880.0	968.0	=$B$7*G3
17				Total assets	1,000	1,100.0	1,210.0	=G15+G16
18								
19				Liabilities and equity				
20				Long-term debt (note a)	400	464.0	534.9	=F20+G24
21				Shareholders' equity (note b)	600	636.0	675.1	=F21+G11
22				Total liab. & share. equity	1,000	1,100.0	1,210.0	=G20+G21
23								
24				Required external financing		64.0	70.9	=G17-F17-G11
25								
26								
27	Notes:							
28	(a): Long-term debt, the balancing item, increases by required external financing.							
29	(b): Shareholders' equity equals its value in the previous year plus retained earnings.							

TABLE 18–8 Required external financing for Executive Fruit. Higher growth rates require greater amounts of external capital.

Growth Rate, %	Required External Financing, Thousands of Dollars
0	–32
2	–12.8
3.33	0
5	16
10	64
15	112
20	160

sales (cell F17) minus the previous year's assets (cell E17) minus earnings retained during the year (cell F11). Shareholders' equity (cell F21) equals its previous value plus retained earnings.

Now that the spreadsheet is set up, it is easy to explore the consequences of various assumptions. For example, you can change the assumed growth rate (cell B3) or experiment with different policies, such as changing the dividend-payout ratio or forcing debt or equity finance (or both) to absorb the required external financing.

EXAMPLE 18.2   ▶   What Happens If the Growth Rate Changes?

Let's use the spreadsheet to explore the effect of sales growth on the need for external financing. We can alter the assumed growth rate in cell B3 and see the effect on required external financing in cell F24. For example, we saw in Figure 18–2 that when the growth rate was 10 percent, required external financing was $64,000. In our model, assets are proportional to sales, so as we assume a higher growth rate of sales, assets also increase at a faster rate. The additional funds necessary to pay for those additional assets imply greater external financing.

Table 18–8 shows how required external financing responds to a change in the growth rate. Notice that at a 3.33 percent growth rate, required external financing is zero. At higher growth rates, the firm requires external financing; at lower rates, retained earnings exceed the addition to assets and there is a surplus of funds from internal sources; this shows up as negative required external financing. Later in the chapter, we will explore the limits to internal growth more systematically.   ◀

Self-Test 18.2

a. Suppose that Executive Fruit is committed to a 10 percent growth rate and to paying out two-thirds of its profits as dividends. However, it now also wishes to maintain its debt-equity ratio at ⅔. What are the implications for external financing in 2006?

b. If the company is prepared to reduce dividends paid in 2006 to $60,000, how much external financing would be needed?

18.3 Planners Beware

Pitfalls in Model Design

The Executive Fruit model is still too simple for practical application. You probably have already noticed several ways to improve it. For example, we ignored depreciation of fixed assets. Depreciation is important because it provides a tax shield. If Executive Fruit deducts depreciation before calculating its tax bill, it could plow back more money into new investments and would need to borrow less. We've also simplified the firm's borrowing plans, ignoring short-term debt and assuming that the firm will be able to issue small amounts of long-term debt as needed at a fixed interest rate regardless of changes in its leverage.

FIGURE 18–3 Net working capital as a function of sales. The orange line shows net working capital equal to .10 × sales. The purple line depicts net working capital as $50,000 + .075 × sales, so that NWC increases less than proportionately with sales.

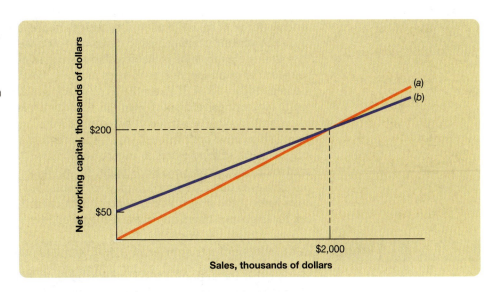

You would certainly want to make these obvious improvements. But beware: There is always the temptation to make a model bigger and more detailed. You may end up with an exhaustive model that is too cumbersome for routine use.

Excessive detail gets in the way of the intended use of corporate planning models, which is to project the financial consequences of a variety of strategies and assumptions. The fascination of detail, if you give in to it, distracts attention from crucial decisions like stock issues and dividend policy and allocation of capital by business area.

The Assumption in Percentage of Sales Models

When forecasting Executive Fruit's capital requirements, we assumed that both fixed assets and working capital increase proportionately with sales. For example, the orange line in Figure 18–3 shows that net working capital is a constant 10 percent of sales.

Percentage of sales models are useful first approximations for financial planning. However, in reality, assets may not be proportional to sales. For example, we will see in Chapter 19 that important components of working capital such as inventories and cash balances will generally rise *less* than proportionately with sales. Suppose that Executive Fruit looks back at past variations in sales and estimates that on average a $1 rise in sales requires only a $.075 increase in net working capital. The purple line in Figure 18–3 shows the level of working capital that would now be needed for

FIGURE 18–4 If factories are operating below full capacity, sales can increase without investment in fixed assets (point A). Beyond some sales level (point B), new capacity must be added.

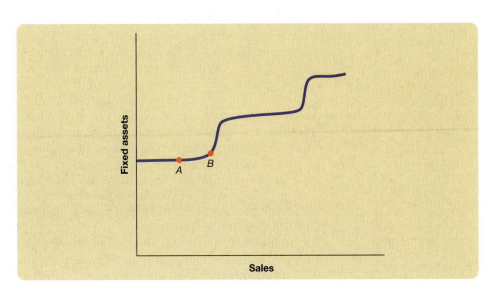

different levels of sales. To allow for this in the Executive Fruit model, we would need to set net working capital equal to ($50,000 + .075 × sales).

A further complication is that fixed assets such as plant and equipment are typically not added in small increments as sales increase. Instead, the picture is more likely to resemble Figure 18–4. If Executive Fruit's factories are operating at less than full capacity (point *A*, for example), then the firm can expand sales without any additional investment in plant. Ultimately, however, if sales continue to increase, say beyond point *B*, Executive Fruit will need to add new capacity. This is shown by the occasional large changes to fixed assets in Figure 18–4. These "lumpy" changes to fixed assets need to be recognized when devising the financial plan. If there is considerable excess capacity, even rapid sales growth may not require big additions to fixed assets. On the other hand, if the firm is already operating at capacity, even small sales growth may call for large investment in plant and equipment.

EXAMPLE 18.3 ▶ Required External Funds and Excess Capacity

Suppose that Carter Tools has $50 million invested in fixed assets and generates sales of $60 million. The company is currently working at 80 percent of capacity. Suppose that a 50 percent increase in sales is forecast. How much investment in fixed assets would be required?

Sales can increase *without* the need for new investments in fixed assets until the company is at 100 percent of capacity. Therefore, sales can increase to $60 million × 100/80 = $75 million before the firm reaches full capacity given its current level of fixed assets. At full capacity, therefore, the ratio of assets to sales would be $50 million/$75 million = ⅔.

The 50 percent increase in forecast sales would imply a sales level of $60 million × 1.5 = $90 million. To support this level of sales, the company needs at least $90 million × ⅔ = $60 million of fixed assets. This calls for a $10 million investment in additional fixed assets. ◀

Self-Test 18.3

Suppose that at its current level of assets and sales, Carter Tools in Example 18.3 is working at 75 percent of capacity.

a. How much can sales expand without any further investment in fixed assets?
b. How much investment in fixed assets would be required to support a 50 percent expansion in sales?

The Role of Financial Planning Models

Models such as the one that we constructed for Executive Fruit help the financial manager to avoid surprises. If the planned rate of growth will require the company to raise external financing, the manager can start planning how best to do so.

We commented earlier that financial planners are concerned about unlikely events as well as likely ones. For example, Executive Fruit's manager may wish to consider how the company's capital requirement would change if profit margins come under pressure and the company generated less cash from its operations. Planning models make it easy to explore the consequences of such events.

However, there are limits to what you can learn from planning models. Although they help to trace through the consequences of alternative plans, they do not tell you which plan is best. For example, we saw that Executive Fruit is proposing to grow its sales and earnings per share. Is that good news for shareholders? Well, not necessarily; it depends on the opportunity cost of the additional capital that the company needs to achieve that growth. In 2006 the company proposes to invest $100,000 in fixed assets and working capital. Table 18–5 showed that this extra investment is expected to generate $12,000 of additional net income, equivalent to a return of 12 percent on the new investment.[1] If the cost of that capital is less than 12 percent, the new investment will have a positive NPV and will add to shareholder wealth. But suppose that the cost of capital is higher at, say, 15 percent. In this case Executive Fruit's investment makes shareholders *worse off,* even though the company is recording steady growth in earnings per share and dividends. Executive Fruit's planning model tells us how much money the firm must raise to fund the planned growth, but it cannot tell us whether that growth contributes to shareholder value. Nor can it tell us whether the company should raise the cash by issuing new debt or equity.

Self-Test 18.4

Which of the following questions will a financial plan help to answer?

a. Is the firm's assumption for asset growth consistent with its plans for debt and equity issues and dividend policy?

b. Will accounts receivable increase in direct proportion to sales?

c. Will the contemplated debt-equity mix maximize the value of the firm?

18.4 External Financing and Growth

Financial *plans* force managers to be consistent in their goals for growth, investments, and financing. The nearby box describes how one company was brought to its knees in part by fundamental inconsistences between its growth strategy and its financing plans.

Financial *models,* such as the one that we have developed for Executive Fruit, can help managers trace through the financial consequences of their growth plans and avoid such disasters. But there is a danger that the complexities of a full-blown financial model can obscure the basic issues. Therefore, managers also use some simple rules of thumb to draw out the relationship between a firm's growth objectives and its requirement for external financing.

Recall that in 2005 Executive Fruit ended the year with $1,000,000 of fixed assets and net working capital, and it had $2,000,000 of sales. In other words, each dollar of sales required $.50 of net assets. The company forecasts that sales in 2006 will increase by $200,000. Therefore, if the ratio of net assets to sales remains constant, assets in 2006 will need to rise by $.50 × $200,000 = $100,000.[2] Part of this increase can be financed by retained earnings, which in 2006 are $36,000. So the amount of external financing needed is

Required external financing = (net assets/sales) × increase in sales − retained earnings
$$= (.50 \times 200,000) - 36,000 = \$64,000$$

Sometimes it is useful to write this calculation in terms of growth rates. Executive Fruit's forecast increase in sales is equivalent to a rise of 10 percent. So, if net assets are a constant proportion of sales, the higher sales volume will also require a 10 percent addition to net assets. Thus

New investment = growth rate × initial assets
$$\$100,000 = .10 \times \$1,000,000$$

Part of the funds to pay for the new assets is provided by retained earnings. The remainder must come from external financing. Therefore,

Required external financing = new investment − retained earnings

= (growth rate × assets) − retained earnings

---

[1] We assume this additional income is a perpetuity.

[2] However, remember our earlier warning that the ratio of net assets to sales may change as the firm grows.

The Collapse of Vivendi: A Failure in Planning

In 1994 39-year-old Jean-Marie Messier became CEO of the French company Generale des Eaux. He immediately set out to transform it from a sleepy water and sewage business into a multinational media and telecommunications group. The company, now renamed Vivendi, entered into a series of major acquisitions, including a $42 billion purchase of Seagram, owner of Universal Studios. To finance its expansion, Vivendi increased its borrowing to $35 billion, and it increased its leverage further by repurchasing 104 million shares for $6.3 billion. Confident that its share price would rise, the company raised the stakes even more by selling a large number of put options on its own stock.

Vivendi's strategy made it very vulnerable to any decline in operating cash flow. As profits began to evaporate, the company faced a severe cash shortage. Its banks were re-luctant to extend further credit, and its bonds were downgraded to junk status. By July 2002 the share price had fallen to less than 10 percent of its level 2 years earlier. With the company facing imminent bankruptcy, M. Messier was ousted and the new management set about slashing costs and selling assets to reduce the debt burden.*

Vivendi's problems were exacerbated by considerable waste and ostentatious extravagance, but its brush with bankruptcy was a result of a lack of financial planning. The company's goals for growth were unsustainable, and it had few options for surviving a decline in operating cash flow.

*The rise and fall of Vivendi is chronicled in J. Johnson and M. Orange, *The Man Who Tried to Buy the World: Jean-Marie Messier and Vivendi Universal* (Portfolio, 2003).

This simple equation highlights that the amount of external financing depends on the firm's projected growth. The faster the firm grows, the more it needs to invest and therefore the more it needs to raise new capital.

In the case of Executive Fruit,

$$\text{Required external financing} = (.10 \times \$1,000,000) - \$36,000$$
$$= \$100,000 - \$36,000 = \$64,000$$

If Executive Fruit's assets remain a constant percentage of sales, then the company needs to raise $64,000 to produce a 10 percent addition to sales.

The sloping line in Figure 18–5 illustrates how required external financing increases with the growth rate. At low growth rates, the firm generates more funds than necessary for expansion. In this sense, its requirement for further external funds is negative. It may choose to use its surplus to pay off some of its debt or buy back its stock. In fact, the vertical intercept in Figure 18–5, at zero growth, is the negative of retained earnings. When growth is zero, no funds are needed for expansion, so all the retained earnings are surplus.

As the firm's projected growth rate increases, more funds are needed to pay for the necessary investments. Therefore, the plot in Figure 18–5 is upward-sloping. For high rates of growth the firm must issue new securities to pay for new investments.

internal growth rate
Maximum rate of growth without external financing.

Where the sloping line crosses the horizontal axis, external financing is zero: The firm is growing as fast as possible without resorting to new security issues. This is called the **internal growth rate.** The growth rate is "internal" because it can be maintained without resorting to additional external sources of capital.

FIGURE 18–5 External financing and growth

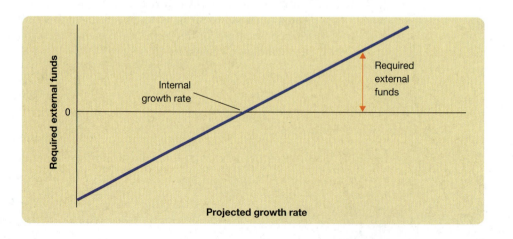

Notice that if we set required external financing to zero, we can solve for the internal growth rate as

$$\textbf{Internal growth rate} = \frac{\textbf{retained earnings}}{\textbf{assets}}$$

Thus the firm's rate of growth without additional external sources of capital will equal the ratio of retained earnings to assets. This means that a firm with a high volume of retained earnings relative to its assets can generate a higher growth rate without needing to raise more capital.

We can gain more insight into what determines the internal growth rate by multiplying the top and bottom of the expression for internal growth by *net income* and *equity* as follows:

$$\textbf{Internal growth rate} = \frac{\textbf{retained earnings}}{\textbf{net income}} \times \frac{\textbf{net income}}{\textbf{equity}} \times \frac{\textbf{equity}}{\textbf{assets}}$$

$$= \textbf{plowback ratio} \times \textbf{return on equity} \times \frac{\textbf{equity}}{\textbf{assets}}$$

A firm can achieve a higher growth rate without raising external capital if (1) it plows back a high proportion of its earnings, (2) it has a high return on equity (ROE), and (3) it has a low debt-to-asset ratio.

EXAMPLE 18.4   ▶   Internal Growth for Executive Fruit

Executive Fruit has chosen a plowback ratio of ⅓. Equity outstanding at the start of 2006 is 600, and outstanding assets are 1,000. Executive Fruit's return on equity[3] is ROE = 16.67 percent, and its ratio of equity to assets is 600/1,000 = .60. If it is unwilling to raise new capital, its maximum growth rate is

$$\text{Internal growth rate} = \text{plowback ratio} \times \text{ROE} \times \frac{\text{equity}}{\text{assets}}$$

$$= \frac{1}{3} \times .1667 \times .60 = .033, \text{ or } 3.33\%$$

Look back at Table 18–8 and you will see that at this growth rate, external financing is in fact zero. This growth rate is much lower than the 10 percent growth Executive Fruit projects, which explains its need for external financing.   ◀

Instead of focusing on the maximum growth rate that can be supported without *any* external financing, firms also may be interested in the growth rate that can be sustained without additional *equity* issues. Of course, if the firm is able to issue enough debt, virtually any growth rate can be financed. It makes more sense to assume that the firm has settled on an optimal capital structure that it will maintain even as equity is augmented by retained earnings. The firm issues only enough debt to keep its debt-equity ratio constant. The **sustainable growth rate** is the highest growth rate the firm can

sustainable growth rate
Steady rate at which a firm can grow without changing leverage; plowback ratio × return on equity.

---

[3] Actually, calculating ROE to find the internal growth rate can be a bit tricky. Executive Fruit is forecasting a growth rate of 10 percent and an ROE of 108/600 = 18 percent, but if it grows more slowly, net income and ROE will be lower. In other words, ROE may depend on the growth rate. We saw in Table 18–8 that a growth rate of 3.33 percent implies external financing of zero; we will choose the ROE corresponding to the internal growth rate of 3.33 percent. If you input .0333 as the growth rate in the Executive Fruit spreadsheet (Figure 18–2), you will find that net income in 2006 is $100,000 while equity outstanding at the beginning of 2006 (end of 2005) is $600,000, which implies an ROE of 100/600 = .1667. Notice that although it is common to calculate ROE by dividing income by either end-of-year or year-average shareholders' equity, neither of those conventions will work in this application. To find the internal growth rate, we need to view ROE as analogous to a rate of return, that is, as income earned *during* the year per dollar of shareholders' equity at the *start* of the year.

Sustainable Growth

Log on to **finance.yahoo.com** and find the profile for any company, for example, IBM. Now click on the word *Sector* in the left-hand column, and you will see some financial ratios for different sectors. What is the sustainable rate of growth for each sector if the firms maintain their plowback ratio and return on equity? (Note: Although Yahoo! does not report the plowback ratio, you can work it out from the P/E and dividend yield.) Do you think that those sectors with a high return on equity can continue to earn such a high return on new investment?

Source: Yahoo! Finance Web site. Reproduced with permission of Yahoo! Inc. © 2005 by Yahoo! Inc. Yahoo! and the Yahoo! logo are trademarks of Yahoo! Inc.

maintain without increasing its financial leverage. It turns out that the sustainable growth rate depends only on the plowback ratio and return on equity:[4]

Sustainable growth rate = plowback ratio × return on equity

You may remember this formula from Chapter 6, where we first used it when we looked at the valuation of the firm and the dividend discount model.

EXAMPLE 18.5 ▶ Sustainable Growth Rate

Executive Suites, Inc., currently has an equity-to-asset ratio of .8. Its ROE is 18 percent. The firm currently reinvests one-third of its earnings back into the firm. Moreover, if it plans to keep leverage unchanged, it will issue an additional 20 cents of debt for every 80 cents of retained earnings. Given this policy, its maximum growth rate is

$$\text{Sustainable growth rate} = \text{plowback ratio} \times \text{ROE}$$
$$= 1/3 \times .18 = .06, \text{ or } 6\%$$

If the firm is willing to plow back a higher proportion of its earnings, it can issue more debt without increasing its leverage. Both the greater reinvested profits and the additional debt issues would allow it to grow more rapidly. You can confirm in the following Self-Test problem [see part (b)] that if the firm increases its plowback ratio, its sustainable growth rate will be higher. ◀

---

[4] Here is a proof:

Required equity issues = growth rate × assets − retained earnings − new debt issues

We find the sustainable growth rate by setting required new equity issues to zero and solving for growth:

$$\text{Sustainable growth rate} = \frac{\text{retained earnings} + \text{new debt issues}}{\text{assets}}$$
$$= \frac{\text{retained earnings} + \text{new debt issues}}{\text{debt} + \text{equity}}$$

However, because both debt and equity are growing at the same rate, new debt issues must equal retained earnings multiplied by the ratio of debt to equity, *D/E*. Therefore, we can write the sustainable growth rate as

$$\text{Sustainable growth rate} = \frac{\text{retained earnings} \times (1 + D/E)}{\text{debt} + \text{equity}}$$
$$= \frac{\text{retained earnings} \times (1 + D/E)}{\text{equity} \times (1 + D/E)} = \frac{\text{retained earnings}}{\text{equity}}$$
$$= \frac{\text{retained earnings}}{\text{net income}} \times \frac{\text{net income}}{\text{equity}} = \text{plowback} \times \text{ROE}$$

Self-Test 18.5 Suppose Executive Suites reduces the dividend payout ratio to 25 percent. Calculate its growth rate assuming (a) that no new debt or equity will be issued and (b) that the firm maintains its debt-to-equity ratio at .25.

SUMMARY

What are the contents and uses of a financial plan?

Most firms take financial planning seriously and devote considerable resources to it. The tangible product of the planning process is a financial plan describing the firm's financial strategy and projecting its future consequences by means of **pro forma** balance sheets, income statements, and statements of sources and uses of funds. The plan establishes financial goals and is a benchmark for evaluating subsequent performance. Usually it also describes why that strategy was chosen and how the plan's financial goals are to be achieved.

Planning, if it is done right, forces the financial manager to think about events that could upset the firm's progress and to devise strategies to be held in reserve for counterattack when unfortunate surprises occur. Planning is more than forecasting, because forecasting deals with the most likely outcome. Planners also have to think about events that may occur even though they are unlikely.

In long-range, or strategic, planning, the **planning horizon** is usually 5 years or more. This kind of planning deals with aggregate decisions; for example, the planner would worry about whether the broadax division should commit to heavy capital investment and rapid growth, but not whether the division should choose machine tool A versus tool B. In fact, planners must be constantly on guard against the fascination of detail, because giving in to it means slighting crucial issues like investment strategy, debt policy, and the choice of a target dividend payout ratio.

The plan is the end result. The process that produces the plan is valuable in its own right. Planning forces the financial manager to consider the combined effects of all the firm's investment and financing decisions. This is important because these decisions interact and should not be made independently.

How are financial planning models constructed?

There is no theory or model that leads straight to *the* optimal financial strategy. Consequently, financial planning proceeds by trial and error. Many different strategies may be projected under a range of assumptions about the future before one strategy is finally chosen. The dozens of separate projections that may be made during this trial-and-error process generate a heavy load of arithmetic and paperwork. Firms have responded by developing corporate planning models to forecast the financial consequences of specified strategies and assumptions about the future. One very simple starting point may be a **percentage of sales model** in which many key variables are assumed to be directly proportional to sales. Planning models are efficient and widely used. But remember that there is not much finance in them. Their primary purpose is to produce accounting statements. The models do not search for the best financial strategy, but only trace out the consequences of a strategy specified by the model user.

What is the effect of growth on the need for external financing?

Higher growth rates will lead to greater need for investments in fixed assets and working capital. The **internal growth rate** is the maximum rate at which the firm can grow if it relies entirely on reinvested profits to finance its growth, that is, the maximum rate of growth without requiring external financing. The **sustainable growth rate** is the rate at which the firm can grow without changing its leverage ratio.

QUIZ HM™

1. **Financial Planning.** True or false? Explain.

   a. Financial planning should attempt to minimize risk.
   b. The primary aim of financial planning is to obtain better forecasts of future cash flows and earnings.
   c. Financial planning is necessary because financing and investment decisions interact and should not be made independently.
   d. Firms' planning horizons rarely exceed 3 years.
   e. Individual capital investment projects are not considered in a financial plan unless they are very large.
   f. Financial planning requires accurate and consistent forecasting.
   g. Financial planning models should include as much detail as possible.

2. **Financial Models.** What are the dangers and disadvantages of using a financial model? Discuss.

3. **Using Financial Plans.** Corporate financial plans are often used as a basis for judging subsequent performance. What can be learned from such comparisons? What problems might arise and how might you cope with such problems?

4. **Growth Rates.** Find the sustainable and internal growth rates for a firm with the following ratios: asset turnover = 1.40; profit margin = 5 percent; payout ratio = 25 percent; equity/assets = .60.

5. **Percentage of Sales Models.** Percentage of sales models usually assume that costs, fixed assets, and working capital all increase at the same rate as sales. When do you think that these assumptions do not make sense? Would you feel happier using a percentage of sales model for short-term or long-term planning?

6. **Relationships among Variables.** Comebaq Computers is aiming to increase its market share by slashing the price of its new range of personal computers. Are costs and assets likely to increase or decrease as a proportion of sales? Explain.

7. **Balancing Items.** What are the possible choices of balancing items when using a financial planning model? Discuss whether some are generally preferable to others.

8. **Financial Targets.** Managers sometimes state a target growth rate for sales or earnings per share. Do you think that either makes sense as a corporate goal? If not, why do you think that managers focus on them?

PRACTICE PROBLEMS HM™

9. **Percentage of Sales Models.** Here are the abbreviated financial statements for Planners Peanuts:

INCOME STATEMENT, 2006	
Sales	$ 2,000
Cost	1,500
Net income	$ 500

BALANCE SHEET, YEAR-END					
	2005	**2006**		**2005**	**2006**
Assets	$ 2,500	$ 3,000	Debt	$ 833	$ 1,000
			Equity	1,667	2,000
Total	$ 2,500	$ 3,000	Total	$ 2,500	$ 3,000

If sales increase by 20 percent in 2007 and the company uses a strict percentage of sales planning model (meaning that all items on the income and balance sheet also increase by 20 percent), what must be the balancing item? What will be its value?

10. **Required External Financing.** If the dividend payout ratio in Problem 9 is fixed at 50 percent, calculate the required total external financing for growth rates in 2007 of 15 percent, 20 percent, and 25 percent.

11. **Feasible Growth Rates.** What is the maximum possible growth rate for Planners Peanuts (see Problem 9) if the payout ratio remains at 50 percent and

    a. no external debt or equity is to be issued.
    b. the firm maintains a fixed debt ratio but issues no equity.

12. **Using Percentage of Sales.** Eagle Sports Supply has the following financial statements. Assume that Eagle's assets are proportional to its sales.

INCOME STATEMENT, 2006	
Sales	$950
Costs	250
Interest	50
Taxes	150
Net income	$500

BALANCE SHEET, YEAR-END					
	2005	**2006**		**2005**	**2006**
Assets	$2,700	$3,000	Debt	$900	$1,000
			Equity	1,800	2,000
Total	$2,700	$3,000	Total	$2,700	$3,000

    a. Find Eagle's required external funds if it maintains a dividend payout ratio of 70 percent and plans a growth rate of 15 percent in 2007.
    b. If Eagle chooses not to issue new shares of stock, what variable must be the balancing item? What will its value be?
    c. Now suppose that the firm plans instead to increase long-term debt only to $1,100 and does not wish to issue any new shares of stock. Why must the dividend payment now be the balancing item? What will its value be?

13. **Feasible Growth Rates.**

    a. What is the internal growth rate of Eagle Sports (see Problem 12) if the dividend payout ratio is fixed at 70 percent and the equity-to-asset ratio is fixed at ⅔?
    b. What is the sustainable growth rate?

14. **Building Financial Models.** How would Executive Fruit's financial model change if the dividend payout ratio were cut to ⅓? Use the revised model to generate a new financial plan for 2006 assuming that debt is the balancing item. Show how the financial statements given in Table 18–6 would change. What would be required external financing?

15. **Required External Financing.** Executive Fruit's financial manager believes that sales in 2006 could rise by as much as 20 percent or by as little as 5 percent.

    a. Recalculate the first-stage pro forma financial statements (Table 18–5) under these two assumptions. How does the rate of growth in revenues affect the firm's need for external funds?
    b. Assume any required external funds will be raised by issuing long-term debt and that any surplus funds will be used to retire such debt. Prepare the completed (second-stage) pro forma balance sheet.

16. **Building Financial Models.** The following tables contain financial statements for Dynastatics Corporation. Although the company has not been growing, it now plans to expand and will increase net fixed assets (that is, assets net of depreciation) by $200,000 per year for the next 5

years and forecasts that the ratio of revenues to total assets will remain at 1.50. Annual depreciation is 10 percent of net fixed assets at the end of the year. Fixed costs are expected to remain at $56,000 and variable costs at 80 percent of revenue. The company's policy is to pay out two-thirds of net income as dividends and to maintain a book debt ratio of 25 percent of total capital.

a. Produce a set of financial statements for 2007. Assume that net working capital will equal 50 percent of fixed assets.
b. Now assume that the balancing item is debt and that no equity is to be issued. Prepare a completed pro forma balance sheet for 2007. What is the projected debt ratio for 2007?

INCOME STATEMENT, 2006
(figures in thousands of dollars)

Revenue	$1,800
Fixed costs	56
Variable costs (80% of revenue)	1,440
Depreciation	80
Interest (8% of beginning-of-year debt)	24
Taxable income	200
Taxes (at 40%)	80
Net income	$ 120
Dividends	$80
Retained earnings	$40

BALANCE SHEET, YEAR-END
(figures in thousands of dollars)

	2006
Assets	
Net working capital	$ 400
Fixed assets	800
Total assets	$ 1,200
Liabilities and shareholders' equity	
Debt	$ 300
Equity	900
Total liabilities and shareholders' equity	$ 1,200

17. **Sustainable Growth.** Plank's Plants had net income of $2,000 on sales of $50,000 last year. The firm paid a dividend of $500. Total assets were $100,000, of which $40,000 was financed by debt.

a. What is the firm's sustainable growth rate?
b. If the firm grows at its sustainable growth rate, how much debt will be issued next year?
c. What would be the maximum possible growth rate if the firm did not issue any debt next year?

18. **Sustainable Growth.** A firm has decided that its optimal capital structure is 100 percent equity financed. It perceives its optimal dividend policy to be a 40 percent payout ratio. Asset turnover is sales/assets = .8, the profit margin is 10 percent, and the firm has a target growth rate of 5 percent.

a. Is the firm's target growth rate consistent with its other goals?
b. If not, by how much does it need to increase asset turnover to achieve its goals?
c. How much would it need to increase the profit margin instead?

19. **Internal Growth.** Go Go Industries is growing at 30 percent per year. It is all-equity-financed and has total assets of $1 million. Its return on equity is 25 percent. Its plowback ratio is 40 percent.

a. What is the internal growth rate?

b. What is the firm's need for external financing this year?

c. By how much would the firm increase its internal growth rate if it reduced its payout ratio to zero?

d. By how much would such a move reduce the need for external financing? What do you conclude about the relationship between dividend policy and requirements for external financing?

20. **Sustainable Growth.** A firm's profit margin is 10 percent, and its asset turnover ratio is .6. It has no debt, has net income of $10 per share, and pays dividends of $4 per share. What is the sustainable growth rate?

21. **Internal Growth.** An all-equity-financed firm plans to grow at an annual rate of at least 10 percent. Its return on equity is 18 percent. What is the maximum possible dividend payout rate the firm can maintain without resorting to additional equity issues?

22. **Internal Growth.** Suppose the firm in the previous question has a debt-equity ratio of ⅓. What is the maximum dividend payout ratio it can maintain without resorting to any external financing?

23. **Internal Growth.** A firm has an asset turnover ratio of 2.0. Its plowback ratio is 50 percent, and it is all-equity-financed. What must its profit margin be if it wishes to finance 10 percent growth using only internally generated funds?

24. **Internal Growth.** If the profit margin of the firm in the previous problem is 6 percent, what is the maximum payout ratio that will allow it to grow at 8 percent without resorting to external financing?

25. **Internal Growth.** If the profit margin of the firm in Problem 23 is 6 percent, what is the maximum possible growth rate that can be sustained without external financing?

26. **Using Percentage of Sales.** The 2006 financial statements for Growth Industries are presented below. Sales and costs in 2007 are projected to be 20 percent higher than in 2006. Both current assets and accounts payable are projected to rise in proportion to sales. The firm is currently operating at full capacity, so it plans to increase fixed assets in proportion to sales. What external financing will be required by the firm? Interest expense in 2007 will equal 10 percent of long-term debt outstanding at the start of the year. The firm will maintain a dividend payout ratio of .40.

INCOME STATEMENT, 2006		
Sales		$200,000
Costs		150,000
EBIT		50,000
Interest expense		10,000
Taxable income		40,000
Taxes (at 35%)		14,000
Net income		$ 26,000
Dividends	10,400	
Retained earnings	15,600	

BALANCE SHEET, YEAR-END, 2006				
Assets			**Liabilities**	
Current assets			Current liabilities	
Cash	$ 3,000		Accounts payable	$ 10,000
Accounts receivable	8,000		Total current liabilities	10,000
Inventories	29,000		Long-term debt	100,000
Total current assets	$ 40,000		Stockholders' equity	
Net plant and equipment	160,000		Common stock plus additional paid-in capital	15,000
			Retained earnings	75,000
Total assets	$200,000		Total liabilities plus stockholders' equity	$200,000

CHALLENGE PROBLEMS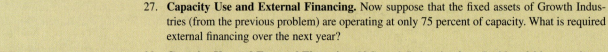

27. **Capacity Use and External Financing.** Now suppose that the fixed assets of Growth Industries (from the previous problem) are operating at only 75 percent of capacity. What is required external financing over the next year?

28. **Capacity Use and External Financing.** If Growth Industries from Problem 26 is operating at only 75 percent of capacity, how much can sales grow before the firm will need to raise any external funds? Assume that once fixed assets are operating at capacity, they will need to grow thereafter in direct proportion to sales.

29. **Internal Growth.** We will see in Chapter 19 that for many firms, cash and inventory needs may grow less than proportionally with sales. When we recognize this fact, will the firm's internal growth rate be higher or lower than the level predicted by the formula

$$\text{Internal growth rate} = \frac{\text{retained earnings}}{\text{assets}}$$

30. **Spreadsheet Problem.** Use a spreadsheet like that in Figure 18–2 to answer the following questions about Executive Fruit:

    a. What would be required external financing if the growth rate is 15 percent and the dividend payout ratio is 60 percent?

    b. Given the assumptions in part (a), what would be the amount of debt and equity issued if the firm wants to maintain its debt-equity ratio at a level of $^2/_3$?

    c. What formulas would you put in cells H20 and H21 (as well as the corresponding cells in columns F and G) of the spreadsheet in Figure 18–2 to maintain the debt-equity ratio at $^2/_3$ while forcing the balance sheet to balance (that is, forcing debt + equity = total assets)?

1. Go to Market Insight at **www.mhhe.com/edumarketinsight**. Calculate and compare Wendy's International (WEN) and McDonald's (MCD) internal growth rates and sustainable growth rates by using recent annual data. (Note that the internal growth rate is calculated by using the earnings reinvested in the firm in the current year, not total retained earnings from the balance sheet.) Use the Annual Ratio Report or the financial statement data. What are the S&P forecasts (Forecasted Values Report) for Wendy's and McDonald's? Are the forecasts supported by the past performance of each firm?

2. Go to Market Insight at **www.mhhe.com/edumarketinsight**. Find the (annual) balance sheet and income statement for American Electric Power (AEP). Suppose the company plans on 4 percent revenue growth over the next year. Under a percentage of sales approach, where assets and costs (except for depreciation) are proportional to sales, find AEP's required external funding over the next year. Assume that it will maintain the same dividend-payout ratio as in the current year and that its average tax rate will be the same next year as it was in the most recent year.

SOLUTIONS TO SELF-TEST QUESTIONS

18.1 Total assets will rise to $2,200. The debt-equity ratio is to be maintained at $^2/_3$. Therefore, debt rises by $80 to $880, and equity rises by $120 to $1,320. Net income will be $220. (See Table 18–2.) If the dividend is fixed at $180, retained earnings will be $40. Therefore, the firm needs to issue $120 – $40 = $80 of new equity and $80 of new debt.

18.2 a. The *total amount* of external financing is unchanged, since the dividend payout is unchanged. The $100,000 increase in total assets will now be financed by a mixture of debt and equity. If the debt-equity ratio is to remain at $^2/_3$, the firm will need to increase equity by $60,000 and debt by $40,000. Since retained earnings already increase shareholders' equity by $32,000, the firm would issue an additional $28,000 of new equity and $40,000 of debt.

  b. If dividends are reduced to $60,000, then the required external funds fall by $4,000 to $60,000.

18.3   a. The company currently runs at 75 percent of capacity given the current level of fixed assets. Sales can increase until the company is at 100 percent of capacity; therefore, sales can increase to $60 million × (100/75) = $80 million.

  b. If sales were to increase by 50 percent to $90 million, new fixed assets would need to be added. The ratio of assets to sales when the company is operating at 100 percent of capacity [from part (a)] is $50 million/$80 million = $\frac{5}{8}$. Therefore, to support sales of $90 million, the company needs at least $90 million × $\frac{5}{8}$ = $56.25 million of fixed assets. This calls for a $6.25 million investment in additional fixed assets.

18.4   a. This question is answered by the planning model. Given assumptions for asset growth, the model will show the need for external financing, and this value can be compared to the firm's plans for such financing.

  b. Such a relationship may be assumed and built into the model. However, the model does not help to determine whether it is a reasonable assumption.

  c. Financial models do not shed light on the best capital structure. They can tell us only whether contemplated financing decisions are consistent with asset growth.

18.5   a. The equity-to-asset ratio is .8. If the payout ratio were reduced to 25 percent, the maximum growth rate assuming no external financing would be .75 × 18 percent × .8 = 10.8 percent.

  b. If the firm also can issue enough debt to maintain its equity-to-asset ratio unchanged, the sustainable growth rate will be .75 × 18 percent = 13.5 percent.

MINICASE

Garnett Jackson, the founder and CEO of Tech Tune-Ups, stared out the window as he finished his customary peanut butter and jelly sandwich, contemplating the dilemma currently facing his firm. Tech Tune-Ups is a start-up firm, offering a wide range of computer services to its clients, including online technical assistance, remote maintenance and backup of client computers through the Internet, and virus prevention and recovery. The firm has been highly successful in the 2 years since it was founded; its reputation for fair pricing and good service is spreading, and Mr. Jackson believes the firm is in a good position to expand its customer base rapidly. But he is not sure that the firm has the financing in place to support that rapid growth.

Tech Tune-Ups' main capital investments are its own powerful computers, and its major operating expense is salary for its consultants. To a reasonably good approximation, both of these factors grow in proportion to the number of clients the firm serves.

Currently, the firm is a privately held corporation. Mr. Jackson and his partners, two classmates from his undergraduate days, have contributed $250,000 in equity capital, largely raised from their parents and other family members. The firm has a line of credit with a bank that allows it to borrow up to $400,000 at an interest rate of 8 percent. So far, the firm has used $200,000 of its credit line. If and when the firm reaches its borrowing limit, it will need to raise equity capital and will probably seek funding from a venture capital firm. The firm is growing rapidly, requiring continual investment in additional computers, and Mr. Jackson is concerned that it is approaching its borrowing limit faster than anticipated.

Mr. Jackson thumbs through past financial statements and estimates that each of the firm's computers, costing $10,000, can support revenues of $80,000 per year but that the salary and benefits paid to each consultant using one of the computers is $70,000. Sales revenue in 2005 was $1.2 million, and sales are expected to grow at a 20 percent annual rate in the next few years. The firm pays taxes at a rate of 35 percent. Its customers pay their bills with an average delay of 3 months, so accounts receivable at any time are usually around 25 percent of that year's sales.

Mr. Jackson and his co-owners receive minimal formal salary from the firm, instead taking 70 percent of profits as a "dividend," which accounts for a substantial portion of their personal incomes. The remainder of the profits are reinvested in the firm. If reinvested profits are not sufficient to support new purchases of computers, the firm borrows the required additional funds using its line of credit with the bank.

Mr. Jackson doesn't think Tech Tune-Ups can raise venture funding until after 2007. He decides to develop a financial plan to determine whether the firm can sustain its growth plans using its line of credit and reinvested earnings until then. If not, he and his partners will have to consider scaling back their hoped-for rate of growth, negotiate with their bankers to increase the line of credit, or consider taking a smaller share of profits out of the firm until further financing can be arranged.

Mr. Jackson wiped the last piece of jelly from the keyboard and settled down to work.

CHAPTER 19

Short-Term Financial Planning

RELATED WEB LINKS

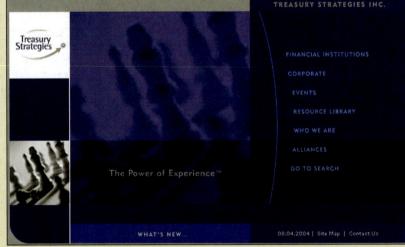

www.treasurystrat.com The resource library on this site contains many articles on short-term management.

www.ny.frb.org/education/addpub/credit.html Primer on bank credit.

www.gecfosolutions.com Information on short-term finance.

www.factors.com Information on factoring.

www.treasuryandrisk.com

www.americanbanker.com

www.intltreasurer.com Articles on short-term financial management.

Short-term financial planning ensures that you have enough cash on hand to pay the bills.
© Bettmann/CORBIS

Much of this book is devoted to long-term financial decisions such as capital budgeting and the choice of capital structure. These decisions are called *long-term* for two reasons. First, they usually involve long-lived assets or liabilities. Second, they are not easily reversed and thus may commit the firm to a particular course of action for several years.

Short-term financial decisions generally involve short-lived assets and liabilities, and usually they are easily reversed. Compare, for example, a 60-day bank loan for $50 million with a $50 million issue of 20-year bonds. The bank loan is clearly a short-term decision. The firm can repay it 2 months later and be right back where it started. A firm might conceivably issue a 20-year bond in January and retire it in March, but it would be extremely inconvenient and expensive to do so. In practice, such a bond issue is a long-term decision, not only because of the bond's 20-year maturity but also because the decision to issue it cannot be reversed on short notice.

A financial manager responsible for short-term financial decisions does not have to look far into the future. The decision to take the 60-day bank loan could properly be based on cash-flow forecasts for the next few months only. The bond issue decision will normally reflect forecast cash requirements 5, 10, or more years into the future.

Short-term financial decisions do not involve many of the difficult conceptual issues encountered elsewhere in this book. In a sense, short-term decisions are easier than long-term decisions—but they are not less important. A firm can identify extremely valuable capital investment opportunities, find the precise optimal debt ratio, follow the perfect dividend policy, and yet founder because no one bothers to raise the cash to pay this year's bills. Hence the need for short-term planning.

We start by showing how long-term financing decisions, introduced in the previous chapter, affect the firm's short-term financial planning problem. Next we review the components of working capital and describe the cash conversion cycle that dictates the types and amount of working capital a firm might maintain. We demonstrate how financial managers forecast month-by-month cash requirements or surpluses and how they develop short-term financing strategies. We conclude with an examination of various sources of short-term finance.

After studying this chapter you should be able to:

- Understand *why* the firm needs to invest in net working capital.

- Show how long-term financing policy affects short-term financing requirements.

- Trace a firm's sources and uses of cash and evaluate its need for short-term borrowing.

- Develop a short-term financing plan that meets the firm's need for cash.

19.1 Links between Long-Term and Short-Term Financing

When formulating a plan, financial or otherwise, you have to choose which factors are central to your decision-making and which are merely distractions. Often, this will depend on your time horizon. For example, at very long horizons such as for retirement planning, you don't think too carefully about when you will need to purchase your next car. At shorter horizons, covering perhaps the next 3 to 5 years, specific big-ticket items such as that potential car purchase need to be accounted for explicitly. At the shortest horizons, your planning might involve details down to the balances you maintain in your checking account.

It is the same with firms. When formulating long-term financial plans such as those considered in the previous chapter, firms may plan year by year. They often will be content with rules of thumb that relate average levels of fixed and short-term assets to annual sales, and not worry so much about seasonal variations in these relationships. When making a long-term plan, for example, the likelihood that accounts receivable rise as sales peak in the Christmas season would be a needless detail that would distract from more important strategic decisions. But such considerations become crucial when firms focus on their near-term needs for cash and working capital. Short-term financing issues are conceptually easier than those involved in capital budgeting, but woe to the firm that takes them for granted.

Moreover, short-term financing needs are tied to the firm's long-term decisions. For example, businesses require capital—that is, money invested in plant, machinery, inventories, accounts receivable, and all the other assets it takes to run a company efficiently. Typically, these assets are not purchased all at once but are obtained gradually over time as the firm grows. The total cost of these assets is called the firm's *total capital requirement.*

When we discussed long-term planning in Chapter 18, we showed how the firm needs to develop a sensible strategy that allows it to finance its long-term goals and weather possible setbacks. But the firm's total capital requirement does not grow smoothly, and the company must be able to meet temporary demands for cash.

Figure 19–1 illustrates the growth in the firm's total capital requirements. The upward-sloping line shows that as the business grows, it is likely to need additional fixed assets and current assets. You can think of this trendline as showing the base level of capital that is required. In addition to this base capital requirement, there may be seasonal fluctuations in the business that require an additional investment in current assets. Thus the wavy line in the illustration shows that the total capital requirement peaks late in each year. In practice, there would also be week-to-week and month-to-month fluctuations in the capital requirement, but these are not shown in Figure 19–1.

The total capital requirement can be met through either long- or short-term financing. When long-term financing does not cover the total capital requirement, the firm

FIGURE 19–1 The firm's total capital requirement grows over time. It also exhibits seasonal variation around the trend.

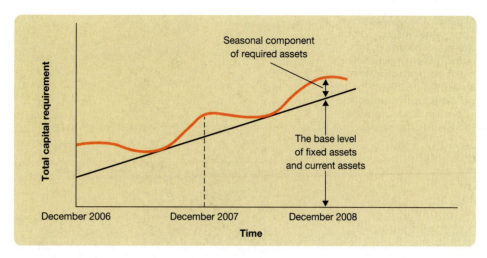

must raise short-term capital to make up the difference. When long-term financing *more* than covers the total capital requirement, the firm has surplus cash available for short-term investment. Thus the difference between the long-term financing raised and the total capital requirement determines whether the firm is a short-term borrower or lender.

The three panels in Figure 19–2 illustrate this. Each depicts a different long-term financing strategy. The "relaxed strategy" in panel *a* implies a permanent short-term cash surplus. This surplus will be invested in marketable securities. The "restrictive" policy illustrated in panel *c* implies a permanent need for short-term borrowing. Finally, panel *b* illustrates an intermediate strategy: The firm has spare cash that it can lend out during the part of the year when total capital requirements are relatively low, but it is a borrower during the rest of the year when capital requirements are relatively high.

What is the *best* level of long-term financing relative to the total capital requirement? It is hard to say. We can make several practical observations, however:

1. *Matching maturities.* Most financial managers attempt to "match maturities" of assets and liabilities. That is, they finance long-lived assets like plant and machinery with long-term borrowing and equity. Short-term assets like inventory and accounts receivable are financed with short-term bank loans or by issuing short-term debt such as commercial paper.
2. *Permanent working capital requirements.* Most firms have a permanent investment in net working capital (current assets less current liabilities). By this we mean that they plan to have at all times a positive amount of working capital. This is financed from long-term sources. This is an extension of the maturity-matching principle. Since the working capital is permanent, it is funded with long-term sources of financing.
3. *The comforts of surplus cash.* Many financial managers would feel more comfortable under the relaxed strategy illustrated in Figure 19–2*a* than the restrictive strategy in panel *c*. Financial managers of firms with a surplus of long-term financing and cash in the bank don't have to worry about finding the money to pay next month's bills. Consider, for example, Microsoft, which in mid-2004 was sitting on a mountain of cash and short-term securities of about $60 billion, far more than it needed to meet seasonal fluctuations in capital requirements. But there are costs to having surplus cash. Holdings of marketable securities are at best a zero-NPV investment for a taxpaying firm.[1] Also, managers of firms with large cash surpluses

---

[1] Why do we say *at best* zero NPV? Not because we worry that the Treasury bills may be overpriced. Instead, we worry that when the firm holds Treasury bills, the interest income is subject to double taxation, first at the corporate level and then again at the personal level when the income is passed through to investors as dividends. The extra layer of taxation can make corporate holdings of Treasury bills a negative-NPV investment even if the bills would provide a fair rate of interest to an individual investor.

FIGURE 19-2 Alternative approaches to long- versus short-term financing: (a) relaxed strategy, where the firm is always a short-term lender; (b) middle-of-the-road policy; (c) restrictive policy, where the firm is always a short-term borrower.

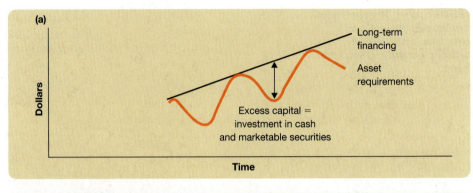

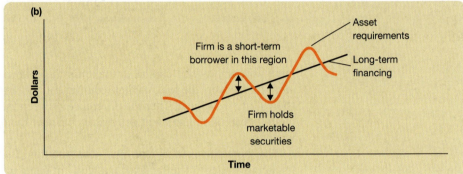

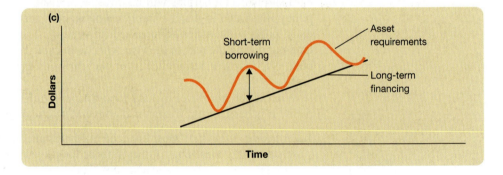

may be tempted to run a less tight ship. The nearby box describes how the fashion company L. A. Gear was able to use its cash to survive 6 years of large losses and to employ a variety of radical, though ultimately unsuccessful, strategies to stave off bankruptcy. For shareholders, it may be best for firms with excess cash to go on a diet and use the money to retire some of their long-term securities. Indeed, we saw in Chapter 16 that Microsoft reduced its cash position by paying a special dividend and repurchasing its stock. By the end of 2004, its cash position had been reduced to about $38 billion.

19.2 Working Capital

Much of short-term financial planning focuses on variation in working capital. Short-term or *current* assets and liabilities such as cash, accounts receivable, inventories, and accounts payable vary considerably as firms move through a cycle in which raw materials are purchased, goods are produced and sold, and customers pay their bills. In order to plan for this variation, it is best to begin by considering the various components of working capital and the factors that determine the level of each component.

The Rise and Fall of L. A. Gear

Fashion company L. A. Gear was one of the stars of the 1980s. Teenie boppers loved its pink sequined sneakers and its silver and gold lamé workout shoes. Investors preferred the 1300 percent growth in the company's stock price in the space of 4 years. But as the company failed to react to changes in fashion during the 1990s, sales and profits fell away rapidly. In January 1998 L. A. Gear filed for Chapter 11 bankruptcy.

The decline of L. A. Gear illustrates how a company's liquid assets can provide the financial slack that allows it to evade market discipline and survive repeated losses. The following table summarizes the changes in L. A. Gear's profitability and its assets:

Sales, income, and assets of L. A. Gear 1989–1996 (figures in $ millions)								
	1989	1990	1991	1992	1993	1994	1995	1996
Sales	617	820	619	430	398	416	297	196
Net income	55	31	–66	–72	–33	–22	–51	–62
Cash & securities	0	3	1	84	28	50	36	34
Receivables	101	156	112	56	73	77	47	24
Inventory	140	161	141	62	110	58	52	33
Current assets	257	338	297	230	220	194	138	93

The first two rows of the table show that after 1990 L. A. Gear's sales declined sharply and the firm produced losses for the rest of its life. The remaining rows show the company's assets. Since L. A. Gear farmed out shoe and clothing production, it had few fixed assets and owned largely cash, receivables, and inventory. As sales declined, two things happened. First, the company was able to reduce its inventory of finished goods. Second, customers paid off their outstanding bills. Thus, despite making steady losses, the company's holdings of cash and short-term securities initially increased.

The following table shows L. A. Gear's capital structure. Notice that after 1991 the company had almost no short-term bank debt, so that it was largely free from the discipline that is exerted whenever a company has to approach its bank for a loan to be renewed. As losses cumulated, common equity dwindled and the debt ratio climbed to 92 percent. Yet even in 1996 the company's cash holdings were over eight times that year's interest payments.

	1989	1990	1991	1992	1993	1994	1995	1996
Bank debt	37	94	20	0	4	1	1	0
Long-term debt	0	0	0	0	50	50	50	50
Preferred stock	0	0	100	100	100	100	108	116
Common equity	168	206	132	88	47	18	–41	–111

Because the company could liquidate its inventories and receivables and had no maturing debt, it was able to survive 6 years of large losses and to try a variety of radical new strategies, including a new emphasis on performance athletic shoes and then on children's shoes. All these strategies were ultimately unsuccessful. A company with large fixed assets that are not so easily liquidated would have found it less easy to survive so long.

Source: The decline of L. A. Gear is chronicled in H. DeAngelo, L. DeAngelo, and K. H. Wruck, "Asset Liquidity, Debt Covenants, and Managerial Discretion in Financial Distress: The Collapse of L. A. Gear," *Journal of Financial Economics* 64 (2002), pp. 3–34.

The Components of Working Capital

Short-term, or *current,* assets and liabilities are collectively known as *working capital.* Table 19–1 gives a breakdown of current assets and liabilities for all manufacturing corporations in the United States in 2004. Total current assets were $1,674 billion and total current liabilities were $1,304 billion.

Current Assets One important current asset is *accounts receivable.* Accounts receivable arise because companies do not usually expect customers to pay for their purchases immediately. These unpaid bills are a valuable asset that companies expect to

TABLE 19–1 Current assets and liabilities, U.S. manufacturing corporations, third quarter 2004 (figures in billions)

Current Assets		Current Liabilities	
Cash	$ 218	Short-term loans	$ 142
Marketable securities	141	Accounts payable	382
Accounts receivable	552	Accrued income taxes	68
Inventories	490	Current payments due on long-term debt	92
Other current assets	273	Other current liabilities	621
Total	$1,674	Total	$1,304

Notes: Net working capital (current assets – current liabilities) = $1,674 – $1,304 = $370 billion. Column sums subject to rounding error.

Source: U.S. Department of Commerce, *Quarterly Financial Report for Manufacturing, Mining and Trade Corporations,* December 2004, **www.census.gov/prod/www/abs/qfr-mm.html.**

be able to turn into cash in the near future. The bulk of accounts receivable consists of unpaid bills from sales to other companies and are known as *trade credit.* The remainder arises from the sale of goods to the final consumer. These are known as *consumer credit.*

Another important current asset is *inventory.* Inventories may consist of raw materials, work in process, or finished goods awaiting sale and shipment. Table 19–1 shows that firms in the United States have about the same amount invested in inventories as in accounts receivable.

The remaining current assets are cash and marketable securities. The cash consists partly of dollar bills, but most of the cash is in the form of bank deposits. These may be *demand deposits* (money in checking accounts that the firm can pay out immediately) and *time deposits* (money in savings accounts that can be paid out only with a delay). The principal marketable security is *commercial paper* (short-term unsecured debt sold by other firms). Other securities include *Treasury bills,* which are short-term debts sold by the United States government, and state and local government securities.

In managing their cash companies face much the same problem you do. There are always advantages to holding large amounts of ready cash—there is less risk of running out of cash and having to borrow more on short notice. On the other hand, there is a cost to holding idle cash balances rather than putting the money to work earning interest.

Current Liabilities We have seen that a company's principal current asset consists of unpaid bills. One firm's credit must be another's debit. Therefore, it is not surprising that a company's principal current liability consists of *accounts payable*—that is, outstanding payments due to other companies.

The other major current liability consists of short-term borrowing. We will have more to say about this later in the chapter.

Working Capital and the Cash Conversion Cycle

net working capital
Current assets minus current liabilities. Often called *working capital.*

The difference between current assets and current liabilities is known as **net working capital,** but financial managers often refer to the difference simply (but imprecisely) as *working capital.* Usually current assets exceed current liabilities—that is, firms have positive net working capital. For U.S. manufacturing companies, current assets are on average nearly 30 percent higher than current liabilities.

To see why firms need net working capital, imagine a small company, Simple Souvenirs, that makes small novelty items for sale at gift shops. It buys raw materials such as leather, beads, and rhinestones for cash, processes them into finished goods like wallets or costume jewelry, and then sells these goods on credit. Figure 19–3 shows the whole cycle of operations.

If you prepare the firm's balance sheet at the beginning of the process, you see cash (a current asset). If you delay a little, you find the cash replaced first by inventories of raw materials and then by inventories of finished goods (also current assets). When the

Working Capital Requirements

Industries differ substantially in the amount of working capital that they need to hold. Which industries would you expect to involve large investments in working capital? Which, small? Now check your answers by looking at the table of working capital requirements by industry sector on Professor Aswath Damodaran's home page, **pages.stern.nyu.edu/~adamodar**.

goods are sold, the inventories give way to accounts receivable (another current asset), and finally, when the customers pay their bills, the firm takes out its profit and replenishes the cash balance.

The components of working capital constantly change with the cycle of operations, but the amount of working capital is fixed. This is one reason why net working capital is a useful summary measure of current assets or liabilities.

Figure 19–4 depicts four key dates in the production cycle that influence the firm's investment in working capital. The firm starts the cycle by purchasing raw materials, but it does not pay for them immediately. This delay is the *accounts payable period.* The firm processes the raw material and then sells the finished goods. The delay between the initial investment in inventories and the sale date is the *inventory period.* Some time after the firm has sold the goods, its customers pay their bills. The delay between the date of sale and the date at which the firm is paid is the *accounts receivable period.*

The top part of Figure 19–4 shows that the *total* delay between initial purchase of raw materials and ultimate payments from customers is the sum of the inventory and accounts receivable periods: First the raw materials must be purchased, processed, and sold, and then the bills must be collected. However, the *net* time that the company is out of cash is reduced by the time it takes to pay its own bills. The length of time between the firm's payment for its raw materials and the collection of payment from the customer is known as the firm's **cash conversion cycle.** To summarize,

cash conversion cycle
Period between firm's payment for materials and collection on its sales.

$$\text{Cash conversion cycle} = (\text{inventory period} + \text{receivables period}) \\ - \text{accounts payable period}$$

The longer the production process, the more cash the firm must keep tied up in inventories. Similarly, the longer it takes customers to pay their bills, the higher the value

FIGURE 19–3 Simple cycle of operations

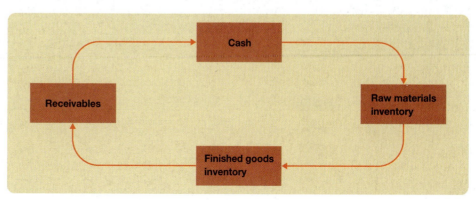

FIGURE 19–4 Cash conversion cycle

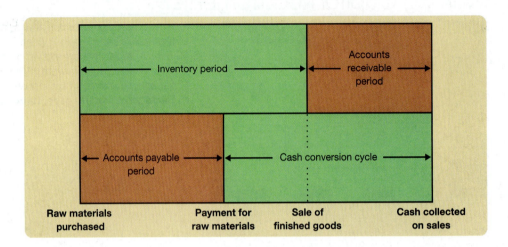

of accounts receivable. On the other hand, if a firm can delay paying for its own materials, it may reduce the amount of cash it needs. In other words, accounts payable reduce net working capital.

In Chapter 17 we showed you how the firm's financial statements can be used to estimate the inventory period, also called *days' sales in inventory:*

$$\text{Inventory period} = \frac{\text{average inventory}}{\text{annual cost of goods sold}/365}$$

The denominator in this equation is the firm's daily output. The ratio of inventory to daily output measures the average number of days from the purchase of the inventories to the final sale.

We can estimate the accounts receivable period and the accounts payable period in a similar way:[2]

$$\text{Accounts receivable period} = \frac{\text{average accounts receivable}}{\text{annual sales}/365}$$

$$\text{Accounts payable period} = \frac{\text{average accounts payable}}{\text{annual cost of goods sold}/365}$$

EXAMPLE 19.1   ▶   Cash Conversion Cycle

Table 19–2 provides the information necessary to compute the cash conversion cycle for manufacturing firms in the United States in 2004. We can use the table to answer four questions. How long on average does it take United States manufacturing firms

TABLE 19–2 These data can be used to calculate the cash conversion cycle for U.S. manufacturing firms (figures in billions)

Income Statement Data		Balance Sheet Data	
	Year Ending, Third Quarter 2004	End of Third Quarter 2003	End of Third Quarter 2004
Sales	$4,951	Inventory $453	$490
Cost of goods sold	4,451	Accounts receivable 500	552
		Accounts payable 335	382

Source: U.S. Department of Commerce, *Quarterly Financial Report for Manufacturing, Mining and Trade Corporations,* December 2004, Tables 1.0 and 1.1.

---

[2] Because inventories are valued at cost, we divide inventory levels by cost of goods sold rather than sales revenue to obtain the inventory period. This way, both numerator and denominator are measured by cost. The same reasoning applies to the accounts payable period. On the other hand, because accounts receivable are valued at product price, we divide average receivables by daily sales revenue to find the receivables period.

to produce and sell their product? How long does it take to collect bills? How long does it take to pay bills? And what is the cash conversion cycle?

The delays in collecting cash are given by the inventory and receivables periods. The delay in paying bills is given by the payables period. The net delay in collecting payments is the cash conversion cycle. We calculate these periods as follows:

$$\text{Inventory period} = \frac{\text{average inventory}}{\text{annual cost of goods sold}/365}$$

$$= \frac{(490 + 453)/2}{4,451/365} = 38.7 \text{ days}$$

$$\text{Receivables period} = \frac{\text{average accounts receivable}}{\text{annual sales}/365}$$

$$= \frac{(552 + 500)/2}{4,951/365} = 38.8 \text{ days}$$

$$\text{Payables period} = \frac{\text{average accounts payable}}{\text{annual cost of goods sold}/365}$$

$$= \frac{(382 + 335)/2}{4,451/365} = 29.4 \text{ days}$$

The cash conversion cycle is

Inventory period + receivables period − payables period
= 38.7 + 38.8 − 29.4 = 48.1 days

It is therefore taking U.S. manufacturing companies an average of almost 7 weeks from the time they lay out money on inventories to collect payment from their customers.   ◀

Self-Test 19.1

a. Suppose U.S. manufacturers are able to reduce average inventory levels to $250 billion and average accounts receivable to $300 billion. By how many days will this reduce the cash conversion cycle?
b. Suppose that with the same level of inventories, accounts receivable, and accounts payable, U.S. manufacturers can increase production and sales by 10 percent. What will be the effect on the cash conversion cycle?

The Working Capital Trade-Off

Of course the cash conversion cycle is not cast in stone. To a large extent it is within management's control. Working capital can be *managed*. For example, accounts receivable are affected by the terms of credit the firm offers to its customers. You can cut the amount of money tied up in receivables by getting tough with customers who are slow in paying their bills. (You may find, however, that in the future they take their business elsewhere.) Similarly, the firm can reduce its investment in inventories of raw materials. (Here the risk is that it may one day run out of inventories and production will grind to a halt.)

These considerations show that investment in working capital has both costs and benefits. For example, the cost of the firm's investment in receivables is the interest that could have been earned if customers had paid their bills earlier. The firm also forgoes interest income when it holds idle cash balances rather than putting the money to work in marketable securities. The cost of holding inventory includes not only the opportunity cost of capital but also storage and insurance costs and the risk of spoilage

carrying costs
Costs of maintaining current assets, including opportunity cost of capital.

shortage costs
Costs incurred from shortages in current assets.

or obsolescence. All of these **carrying costs** encourage firms to hold current assets to a minimum.

While carrying costs discourage large investments in current assets, a low level of current assets makes it more likely that the firm will face **shortage costs.** For example, if the firm runs out of inventory of raw materials, it may have to shut down production. Similarly, a producer holding a small finished goods inventory is more likely to be caught short, unable to fill orders promptly. There are also disadvantages to holding small "inventories" of cash. If the firm runs out of cash, it may have to sell securities and incur unnecessary trading costs. The firm may also maintain too low a level of accounts receivable. If the firm tries to minimize accounts receivable by restricting credit sales, it may lose customers. An important job of the financial manager is to strike a balance between the costs and benefits of current assets, that is, to find the level of current assets that minimizes the sum of carrying costs and shortage costs.

In Chapter 17 we pointed out that in recent years many managers have tried to make their staff more aware of the cost of the capital that is used in the business. So when they review the performance of each part of their business, they deduct the cost of the capital employed from its profits. This measure is known as *residual income* or *economic value added (EVA),* which is the term coined by the consulting firm Stern Stewart. Firms that employ EVA to measure performance have often discovered that they can make large savings on working capital. Herman Miller Corporation, the furniture manufacturer, found that after it introduced EVA, employees became much more conscious of the cash tied up in inventories. One sewing machine operator commented:

> We used to have these stacks of fabric sitting here on the tables until we needed them. . . . We were going to use the fabric anyway, so who cares that we're buying it and stacking it up there? Now no one has excess fabric. They only have stuff we're working on today. And it's changed the way we connect with suppliers, and we're having [them] deliver fabric more often.[3]

The company also started to look at how rapidly customers paid their bills. It found that any time an item was missing from an order, the customer would delay payment until all the pieces had been delivered. When the company cleared up the problem of missing items, it made its customers happier and it collected the cash faster.[4]

We will look more carefully at the costs and benefits of working capital in the next two chapters.

Self-Test 19.2

How will the following affect the size of the firm's optimal investment in current assets?

a. The interest rate rises from 6 to 8 percent.
b. A just-in-time inventory system is introduced that reduces the risk of inventory shortages.
c. Customers pressure the firm for a more lenient credit sales policy.

19.3 Tracing Changes in Cash and Working Capital

Table 19–3 compares 2005 and 2006 year-end balance sheets for Dynamic Mattress Company. Table 19–4 shows the firm's income statement for 2006. Note that Dynamic's cash balance increased from $4 million to $5 million in 2006. What caused this increase? Did the extra cash come from Dynamic Mattress Company's additional long-term borrowing? From reinvested earnings? From cash released by reducing in-

[3] A. Ehrbar, *EVA: The Real Key to Creating Wealth* (New York: John Wiley & Sons, 1998), pp. 130–131.

[4] A. Ehrbar and G. Bennett Stewart III, "The EVA Revolution," *Journal of Applied Corporate Finance* 12 (Summer 1999), pp. 18–31.

TABLE 19–3 Year-end balance sheets for Dynamic Mattress Company (figures in millions)

Assets	2005	2006	Liabilities and Shareholders' Equity	2005	2006
Current assets			Current liabilities		
Cash	$ 4	$ 5	Bank loans	$ 5	$ 0
Marketable securities	0	5	Accounts payable	20	27
Inventory	26	25	Total current liabilities	$25	$ 27
Accounts receivable	25	30	Long-term debt	5	12
Total current assets	$55	$ 65	Net worth (equity and retained earnings)	65	76
Fixed assets			Total liabilities and owners' equity	$95	$115
Gross investment	$56	$ 70			
Less depreciation	16	20			
Net fixed assets	$40	$ 50			
Total assets	$95	$115			

TABLE 19–4 2006 Income statement for Dynamic Mattress Company (figures in millions)

Sales	$ 350
Operating costs	321
Depreciation	4
EBIT	25
Interest	1
Pretax income	24
Tax at 50 percent	12
Net income	$ 12

Note: Dividend = $1 million; retained earnings = $11 million.

ventory? Or perhaps it came from extra credit extended by Dynamic's suppliers. (Note the increase in accounts payable.)

The correct answer? All of the above. There is rarely any point in linking a particular source of funds with a particular use. Instead, financial analysts list the various sources and uses of cash in a statement like the one shown in Table 19–5. The statement shows that Dynamic *generated* cash from the following sources:

1. It issued $7 million of long-term debt.
2. It reduced inventory, releasing $1 million.
3. It increased its accounts payable, in effect borrowing an additional $7 million from its suppliers.
4. By far the largest source of cash was Dynamic's operations, which generated $16 million. Note that the $12 million net income reported in Table 19–4 understates cash flow because depreciation is deducted in calculating income. Depreciation is *not* a cash outlay. Thus it must be added back in order to obtain operating cash flow.

Dynamic *used* cash for the following purposes:

1. It paid a $1 million dividend. (*Note:* The $11 million increase in Dynamic's equity is due to retained earnings: $12 million of equity income less the $1 million dividend.)
2. It repaid a $5 million short-term bank loan.
3. It invested $14 million. This shows up as the increase in gross fixed assets in Table 19–3.
4. It purchased $5 million of marketable securities.
5. It allowed accounts receivable to expand by $5 million. In effect, it lent this additional amount to its customers.

TABLE 19–5 Sources and uses of cash for Dynamic Mattress Company (figures in millions)

Sources	
Issued long-term debt	$ 7
Reduced inventories	1
Increased accounts payable	7
Cash from operations	
Net income	12
Depreciation	4
Total sources	$ 31
Uses	
Repaid short-term bank loan	$ 5
Invested in fixed assets	14
Purchased marketable securities	5
Increased accounts receivable	5
Dividend	1
Total uses	$ 30
Increase in cash balance	$ 1

Self-Test 19.3

How will the following affect *cash* and *net working capital*?

a. The firm takes out a short-term bank loan and uses the funds to pay off some of its accounts payable.
b. The firm uses cash on hand to buy raw materials.
c. The firm repurchases outstanding shares of stock.
d. The firm sells long-term bonds and puts the proceeds in its bank account.

19.4 Cash Budgeting

The financial manager's task is to forecast *future* sources and uses of cash. These forecasts serve two purposes. First, they alert the financial manager to future cash needs. Second, the cash-flow forecasts provide a standard, or budget, against which subsequent performance can be judged.

There are several ways to produce a quarterly cash budget. Many large firms have developed elaborate "corporate models"; others use a spreadsheet program to plan their cash needs. The procedures of smaller firms may be less formal. But no matter what method is chosen, there are three common steps to preparing a cash budget:

Step 1. Forecast the sources of cash. The largest inflow of cash comes from payments by the firm's customers.
Step 2. Forecast uses of cash.
Step 3. Calculate whether the firm is facing a cash shortage or surplus.

The financial *plan* sets out a strategy for investing cash surpluses or financing any deficit.

We will illustrate these issues by continuing the example of Dynamic Mattress.

Forecast Sources of Cash

Most of Dynamic's cash inflow comes from the sale of mattresses. We therefore start with a sales forecast by quarter for 2007:[5]

---

[5] For simplicity, we present a quarterly forecast. However, most firms would forecast by month instead of by quarter. Sometimes weekly or even daily forecasts are made.

Quarter:	First	Second	Third	Fourth
Sales ($ million)	87.5	78.5	116	131

But unless customers pay cash on delivery, sales become accounts receivable before they become cash. Cash flow comes from *collections* on accounts receivable.

Most firms keep track of the average time it takes customers to pay their bills. From this they can forecast what proportion of a quarter's sales is likely to be converted into cash in that quarter and what proportion is likely to be carried over to the next quarter as accounts receivable. This proportion depends on the lags with which customers pay their bills. For example, if customers wait 1 month to pay their bills, then on average one-third of each quarter's bills will not be paid until the following quarter. If the payment delay is 2 months, then two-thirds of quarterly sales will be collected in the following quarter.

Suppose that 80 percent of sales are collected in the immediate quarter and the remaining 20 percent in the next. Panel A of Table 19–6 shows forecast collections under this assumption.

TABLE 19–6 Dynamic Mattress's cash budget for 2007
(figures in millions of dollars)

Please visit us at www.mhhe.com/bmm5e or refer to your Student CD

	A	B	C	D	E
1	Quarter:	First	Second	Third	Fourth
2					
3	A. Accounts Receivable				
4	Receivables (beginning of period)	30.0	32.5	30.7	38.2
5	Sales	87.5	78.5	116.0	131.0
6	Collections				
7	On sales in current period (80%)	70.0	62.8	92.8	104.8
8	On sales in previous period (20%)[a]	15.0	17.5	15.7	23.2
9	Total collections	85.0	80.3	108.5	128.0
10	Receivables (end of period) = Rows 4+5-9	32.5	30.7	38.2	41.2
11					
12	B. Cash Budget				
13	Sources of cash				
14	Collections of accounts receivable (row 9)	85.0	80.3	108.5	128.0
15	Other	1.5	0.0	12.5	0.0
16	Total collections	86.5	80.3	121.0	128.0
17	Uses of cash				
18	Payments of accounts payable	65.0	60.0	55.0	50.0
19	Labor & other expenses	30.0	30.0	30.0	30.0
20	Capital expenses	32.5	1.3	5.5	8.0
21	Taxes, interest, and dividends	4.0	4.0	4.5	5.0
22	Total uses	131.5	95.3	95.0	93.0
23					
24	Net cash inflow = Sources - Uses	-45.0	-15.0	26.0	35.0
25					
26	C. Short-term financing requirements				
27	Cash at start of period	5.0	-40.0	-55.0	-29.0
28	+ Net cash inflow (from row 24)	-45.0	-15.0	26.0	35.0
29	= Cash at end of period[b]	-40.0	-55.0	-29.0	6.0
30	Minimum operating balance	5.0	5.0	5.0	5.0
31	Cumulative financing required[c] (Row 30 - 29)	45.0	60.0	34.0	-1.0
32					
33					

[a] Sales in the fourth quarter of the previous year were $75 million.
[b] Firms cannot literally hold a negative amount of cash. This line shows the amount of cash the firm will have to raise to pay its bills.
[c] A negative sign indicates that no short-term financing is required. Instead the firm has a cash surplus.

In the first quarter, for example, collections from current sales are 80 percent of $87.5 million, or $70 million. But the firm also collects 20 percent of the previous quarter's sales, or $.20 \times \$75$ million = $15 million. Therefore, total collections are $70 million + $15 million = $85 million.

Dynamic started the first quarter with $30 million of accounts receivable. The quarter's sales of $87.5 million were *added* to accounts receivable, but $85 million of collections were *subtracted*. Therefore, as Table 19–6 shows, Dynamic ended the quarter with accounts receivable of $30 million + $87.5 million – $85 million = $32.5 million. The general formula is

Ending accounts receivable = beginning accounts receivable + sales – collections

Panel B of Table 19–6 shows forecast sources and uses of cash for Dynamic Mattress. Collection of receivables is the main source, but it is not the only one. Perhaps the firm plans to dispose of some land or expects a tax refund or payment of an insurance claim. All such items are included as "other" sources. It is also possible that you may raise additional capital by borrowing or selling stock, but we don't want to prejudge that question. Therefore, for the moment we just assume that Dynamic will not raise further long-term finance.

Forecast Uses of Cash

There always seem to be many more uses for cash than there are sources. Panel B of Table 19–6 shows how Dynamic expects to use cash. For simplicity, we condense the uses into four categories:

1. *Payments of accounts payable.* Dynamic has to pay its bills for raw materials, parts, electricity, and so on. The cash-flow forecast assumes all these bills are paid on time, although Dynamic could probably delay payment to some extent. Delayed payment is sometimes called *stretching your payables*. Stretching is one source of short-term financing, but for most firms it is an expensive source, because by stretching they lose discounts given to firms that pay promptly. (This is discussed in more detail in Chapter 20.)
2. *Labor, administrative, and other expenses.* This category includes all other regular business expenses.
3. *Capital expenditures.* Note that Dynamic Mattress plans a major outlay of cash in the first quarter to pay for a long-lived asset.
4. *Taxes, interest, and dividend payments.* This includes interest on currently outstanding long-term debt and dividend payments to stockholders.

The forecast net inflow of cash (sources minus uses) is shown in row 24. Note the large negative figure for the first quarter: a $45 million forecast *outflow.* There is a smaller forecast *outflow* in the second quarter and then substantial cash inflows in the second half of the year.

The Cash Balance

So far, Dynamic Mattress does not know how much it will have to borrow or, for that matter, if it will have to borrow at all. These calculations are presented in panel C, which shows how much financing Dynamic will have to raise if its cash-flow forecasts are right. It starts the year with $5 million in cash. There is a $45 million cash outflow in the first quarter, which in the absence of external financing would create a $40 million cash shortfall at the end of the period (row 29). This deficit is carried to the beginning of the next quarter (cell C27). At the very least, Dynamic must obtain $40 million of additional financing just to cover the forecast cash deficit. This would leave the firm with a forecast cash balance of exactly zero at the start of the second quarter.

However, most financial managers would regard a planned cash balance of zero as driving too close to the edge of the cliff. They establish a *minimum operating cash balance* to absorb unexpected cash inflows and outflows. We assume in Table 19–6 that Dynamic's minimum operating cash balance is $5 million. That means it has to raise $45 million instead of $40 million in the first quarter and $15 million more in the second quarter. Thus its *cumulative* financing requirement is $60 million in the second quarter. Fortunately, this is the peak; the cumulative requirement declines in the third quarter when its $26 million net cash inflow reduces its cumulative financing requirement to $34 million. (Notice that cumulative short-term financing falls by the net cash inflow in that quarter from row 24.) In the final quarter Dynamic is out of the woods. Its $35 million net cash inflow is enough to eliminate short-term financing and actually increase cash balances above the $5 million minimum acceptable balance.

Before moving on, we offer two general observations about this example:

1. The large cash outflows in the first two quarters do not necessarily spell trouble for Dynamic Mattress. In part they reflect the capital investment made in the first quarter: Dynamic is spending $32.5 million, but it should be acquiring an asset worth that much or more. The cash outflows also reflect low sales in the first half of the year; sales recover in the second half.[6] If this is a predictable seasonal pattern, the firm should have no trouble borrowing to help it get through the slow months.
2. Table 19–6 is only a best guess about future cash flows. It is a good idea to think about the *uncertainty* in your estimates. For example, you could undertake a sensitivity analysis, in which you inspect how Dynamic's cash requirements would be affected by a shortfall in sales or by a delay in collections.

Self-Test 19.4

Calculate Dynamic Mattress's quarterly cash receipts, net cash inflow, and cumulative short-term financing required if customers pay for only 60 percent of purchases in the current quarter and pay the remaining 40 percent in the following quarter.

Our next step will be to develop a short-term financing plan that addresses the forecast requirements in the most economical way possible. Before presenting such a plan, however, we should pause briefly to point out that short-term financial planning, like long-term planning, is best done on a computer. The nearby box presents the formula view of the spreadsheet underlying Table 19–6. Examine the entries and note which items are inputs (for example, rows 18 to 21) and which are calculated from equations. The formulas also indicate the links from one panel to another. For example, collections of receivables are calculated in panel A, row 9, and passed through as inputs in panel B, row 14. Similarly, net cash inflow in panel B, row 24, is passed along to panel C, row 28.

Once the spreadsheet is set up, it becomes easy to explore the consequences of many "what-if" questions. For example, Self-Test 19.4 asked you to recalculate the quarterly cash receipts, net cash inflow, and cumulative short-term financing required if the firm's collections on accounts receivable slow down. You can obviously do this by hand, but it is quicker and easier to do it in a spreadsheet—especially when there might be dozens of scenarios that you need to work through!

19.5 A Short-Term Financing Plan

Dynamic's cash budget defines its problem. Its financial manager must find short-term financing to cover the firm's forecast cash requirements. There are dozens of sources of short-term financing, but for simplicity we will consider only two: obtaining bank loans or stretching payables.

---

[6] Maybe people buy more mattresses late in the year when the nights are longer.

Dynamic Mattress's Short-term Plan

	A	B	C	D	E
1	Quarter:	First	Second	Third	Fourth
2					
3	**A. Accounts Receivable**				
4	Receivables (beginning of period)	30	=B10	=C10	=D10
5	Sales	87.5	78.5	116	131
6	Collections				
7	On sales in current period (80%)	=0.8*B5	=0.8*C5	=0.8*D5	=0.8*E5
8	On sales in previous period (20%)	=0.2*75	=0.2*B5	=0.2*C5	=0.2*D5
9	Total collections	=B7+B8	=C7+C8	=D7+D8	=E7+E8
10	Receivables (end of period)	=B4+B5-B9	=C4+C5-C9	=D4+D5-D9	=E4+E5-E9
11					
12	**B. Cash Budget**				
13	**Sources of cash**				
14	Collections of acct receivable	=B9	=C9	=D9	=E9
15	Other	1.5	0	12.5	0
16	Total sources	=B14+B15	=C14+C15	=D14+D15	=E14+E15
17	**Uses**				
18	Payments of accounts payable	65	60	55	50
19	Labor & other expenses	30	30	30	30
20	Capital expenses	32.5	1.3	5.5	8
21	Taxes, interest, and dividends	4	4	4.5	5
22	Total uses	=SUM(B18:B21)	=SUM(C18:C21)	=SUM(D18:D21)	=SUM(E18:E21)
23					
24	**Net cash inflow = Sources - Uses**	=B16-B22	=C16-C22	=D16-D22	=E16-E22
25					
26	**C. Short-term Financing Requirements**				
27	Cash at start of period	5	=B29	=C29	=D29
28	+ Net cash inflow	=B24	=C24	=D24	=E24
29	= Cash at end of period	=B27+B28	=C27+C28	=D27+D28	=E27+E28
30	Minimum operating balance	5	=B30	=C30	=D30
31	Cumulative financing required	=B30-B29	=C30-C29	=D30-D29	=E30-E29
32					
33					

eXcel

Please visit us at www.mhhe.com/bmm5e or refer to your Student CD

We assume that Dynamic can borrow up to $40 million from its bank at an interest rate of 8 percent per year, or 2 percent per quarter. It can borrow and repay the loan whenever it wants to, but it may not exceed its credit limit.

Alternatively, Dynamic can raise capital by putting off paying its bills. The financial manager believes that Dynamic can defer the following amounts in each quarter:

Quarter:	First	Second	Third	Fourth
Amount deferrable ($ million)	52	48	44	40

That is, $52 million can be saved in the first quarter by *not* paying bills in that quarter. (Note that Table 19–6 was prepared assuming these bills *are* paid in the first quarter.) If deferred, these payments *must* be made in the second quarter. Similarly, $48 million of the second quarter's bills can be deferred to the third quarter, and so on.

524

Stretching payables is often costly, however, even if no ill will is incurred.[7] This is because many suppliers offer discounts for prompt payment, so Dynamic loses the discount if it pays late. In this example we assume the lost discount is 5 percent of the amount deferred. In other words, if a $52 million payment is delayed in the first quarter, the firm must pay 5 percent more, or $54.6 million, in the next quarter. This is like borrowing at an annual interest rate of over 20 percent ($1.05^4 - 1 = .216$, or 21.6 percent).

Dynamic Mattress's Financing Plan

With these two options, the short-term financing strategy is obvious: Use the lower-cost bank loan first. Stretch payables only if you can't borrow enough from the bank.

Table 19–7 shows the resulting plan. Panel A (cash requirements) sets out the cash that needs to be raised in each quarter. Panel B (cash raised) describes the various sources of financing the firm plans to use. Panels C and D describe how the firm will use net cash inflows when they turn positive. Panel E keeps track of the bank loan.

In the first quarter the plan calls for borrowing the full amount available from the bank ($40 million). In addition, the firm sells the $5 million of marketable securities it held at the end of 2006. Thus under this plan it raises the necessary $45 million in the first quarter.

In the second quarter, an additional $15 million must be raised to cover the net cash outflow predicted in Table 19–6. In addition, $.8 million must be raised to pay interest on the bank loan. Therefore, the plan calls for Dynamic to maintain its bank borrowing and to stretch $15.8 million in payables. Notice that in the first two quarters, when net cash flow from operations is negative, the firm maintains its cash balance at the minimum acceptable level. Additions to cash balances are zero. Similarly, repayments of outstanding debt are zero. In fact outstanding debt rises in each of these quarters.

In the third and fourth quarters, the firm generates a cash-flow surplus, so the plan calls for Dynamic to pay off its debt. First it pays off stretched payables, as it is required to do, and then it uses any remaining cash-flow surplus to pay down its bank loan. In the third quarter, all of the net cash inflow is used to reduce outstanding short-term borrowing. In the fourth quarter, the firm pays off its remaining short-term borrowing and uses the extra $2.98 million to increase its cash balances.

Self-Test 19.5

Revise Dynamic Mattress's short-term financial plan assuming it can borrow up to $45 million through its bank loan. Assume that the firm will still sell its $5 million of short-term securities in the first quarter.

Evaluating the Plan

Does the plan shown in Table 19–7 solve Dynamic's short-term financing problem? No—the plan is feasible, but Dynamic can probably do better. The most glaring weakness of this plan is its reliance on stretching payables, an extremely expensive financing device. Remember that it costs Dynamic 5 percent *per quarter* to delay paying bills—20 percent per year at simple interest. This first plan should merely stimulate the financial manager to search for cheaper sources of short-term borrowing.

The financial manager would ask several other questions as well. For example:

1. Does Dynamic need a larger reserve of cash or marketable securities to guard against, say, its customers stretching *their* payables (thus slowing down collections on accounts receivable)?

---

[7] In fact, ill will is likely to be incurred. Firms that stretch payments risk being labeled as credit risks. Since stretching is so expensive, suppliers reason that customers will resort to it only when they cannot obtain credit at reasonable rates elsewhere. Suppliers naturally are reluctant to act as the lender of last resort.

TABLE 19–7 Dynamic
Mattress's financing plan
(figures in millions of dollars)

Please visit us at www.mhhe.com/bmm5e or
refer to your Student CD

	A	B	C	D	E
1	Quarter:	First	Second	Third	Fourth
2	**A. Cash requirements**				
3	Cash required for operations[a]	45.00	15.00	-26.00	-35.00
4	Interest on bank loan[b]	0.00	0.80	0.80	0.63
5	Interest on stretched payables[c]	0.00	0.00	0.79	0.00
6	Total cash required	45.00	15.80	-24.41	-34.37
7					
8	**B. Cash raised in quarter**				
9	Bank loan	40.00	0.00	0.00	0.00
10	Stretched payables	0.00	15.80	0.00	0.00
11	Securities sold	5.00	0.00	0.00	0.00
12	Total cash raised	45.00	15.80	0.00	0.00
13					
14	**C. Repayments**				
15	Of stretched payables	0.00	0.00	15.80	0.00
16	Of bank loan	0.00	0.00	8.61	31.39
17					
18	**D. Addition to cash balances**	0.00	0.00	0.00	2.98
19					
20	**E. Bank loan**				
21	Beginning of quarter	0.00	40.00	40.00	31.39
22	End of quarter	40.00	40.00	31.39	0.00

[a] A negative cash requirement implies positive cash flow from operations.

[b] The interest rate on the bank loan is 2 percent per quarter applied to the bank loan outstanding at the start of the quarter. Thus the interest due in the second quarter is .02 × $40 million = $.8 million.

[c] The "interest" cost of the stretched payables is 5 percent of the amount of payment deferred. For example, in the third quarter, 5 percent of the $15.8 million stretched in the second quarter is about $.8 million.

2. Does the plan yield satisfactory current and quick ratios?[8] Its bankers may be worried if these ratios deteriorate.

3. Are there hidden costs to stretching payables? Will suppliers begin to doubt Dynamic's creditworthiness?

4. Does the plan for 2007 leave Dynamic in good financial shape for 2008? (Here the answer is yes, since Dynamic will have paid off all short-term borrowing by the end of the year.)

5. Should Dynamic try to arrange long-term financing for the major capital expenditure in the first quarter? This seems sensible, following the rule of thumb that long-term assets deserve long-term financing. It would also dramatically reduce the need for short-term borrowing. A counterargument is that Dynamic is financing the capital investment *only temporarily* by short-term borrowing. By year-end, the investment is paid for by cash from operations. Thus Dynamic's initial decision not to seek immediate long-term financing may reflect a preference for ultimately financing the investment with retained earnings.

6. Perhaps the firm's operating and investment plans can be adjusted to make the short-term financing problem easier. Is there any easy way of deferring the first quarter's large cash outflow? For example, suppose that the large capital investment in the first quarter is for new mattress-stuffing machines to be delivered and installed in the first half of the year. The new machines are not scheduled to be ready for full-scale use until August. Perhaps the machine manufacturer could be persuaded to accept 60 percent of the purchase price on delivery and 40 percent when the machines are installed and operating satisfactorily.

Short-term financing plans must be developed by trial and error. You lay out one plan, think about it, then try again with different assumptions on financing and investment alternatives. You continue until you can think of no further improvements.

---

[8] These ratios are discussed in Chapter 17.

19.6 Sources of Short-Term Financing

Dynamic solved the greater part of its cash shortage by borrowing from a bank. Banks offer various types of loans and one type may make more sense for you than another. Also, banks are not the only source of short-term borrowing. For example, firms may obtain loans from finance companies, which specialize in lending to businesses and individuals. Unlike banks, finance companies obtain funds through selling securities rather than through deposits. Firms may also raise money by selling their own short-term debt directly to investors. Let's look at some of these alternative sources of short-term financing.

Bank Loans

The simplest and most common source of short-term finance is an unsecured loan from a bank. For example, Dynamic might have a standing arrangement with its bank allowing it to borrow up to $40 million. The firm can borrow and repay whenever it wants so long as it does not exceed the credit limit. This kind of arrangement is called a **line of credit.**

line of credit
Agreement by a bank that a company may borrow at any time up to an established limit.

Lines of credit are typically reviewed annually, and it is possible that the bank may seek to cancel it if the firm's creditworthiness deteriorates. If the firm wants to be sure that it will be able to borrow, it can enter into a *revolving credit agreement* with the bank. Revolving credit arrangements usually last for a few years and formally commit the bank to lending up to the agreed limit. In return the bank will require the firm to pay a commitment fee of around .25 percent on any unused amount.

Most bank loans have durations of only a few months. For example, Dynamic may need a loan to cover a seasonal increase in inventories, and the loan is then repaid as the goods are sold. However, banks also make *term loans,* which last for several years. These term loans sometimes involve huge sums of money, and in this case they may be parceled out among a syndicate of banks. For example, when Vodafone Airtouch needed to borrow $24 billion to help finance its bid for the German telephone company Mannesmann, it engaged 11 banks from around the world to arrange a large syndicate of banks to lend the cash.

Secured Loans

Many short-term loans are unsecured, but more commonly the company may offer assets as security or collateral. Since the bank is lending on a short-term basis, the collateral generally consists of liquid assets such as receivables, inventories, or securities. For example, a firm may decide to borrow short-term money secured by its accounts receivable. When its customers pay their bills, it can use the cash collected to repay the loan. Banks will not usually lend the full value of the assets that are used as security. For example, a firm that puts up $100,000 of receivables as security may find that the bank is prepared to lend only $75,000. The safety margin (or *haircut,* as it is called) is likely to be even larger in the case of loans that are secured by inventory.

Accounts Receivable Financing When a loan is secured by receivables, the firm *assigns* the receivables to the bank. If the firm fails to repay the loan, the bank can collect the receivables from the firm's customers and use the cash to pay off the debt. However, the firm is still responsible for the loan even if the receivables ultimately cannot be collected. The risk of default on the receivables is therefore borne by the firm.

An alternative procedure is to *sell* the receivables at a discount to a financial institution known as a *factor* and let it collect the money. In other words, some companies solve their financing problem by borrowing on the strength of their current assets; others solve it by selling their current assets. Once the firm has sold its receivables, the factor bears all the responsibility for collecting on the accounts. Therefore, the factor plays three roles: It administers collection of receivables, takes responsibility for bad debts, and provides finance.

The Hazards of Secured Bank Lending

The National Safety Council of Australia's Victoria Division had been a sleepy outfit until John Friedrich took over. Under its new management, NSC members trained like commandos and were prepared to go anywhere and do anything. They saved people from drowning, they fought fires, found lost bushwalkers, and went down mines. Their lavish equipment included 22 helicopters, 8 aircraft, and a mini-submarine. Soon the NSC began selling its services internationally.

Unfortunately the NSC's paramilitary outfit cost millions of dollars to run—far more than it earned in revenue. Friedrich bridged the gap by borrowing $A236 million of debt. The banks were happy to lend because the NSC's debt appeared well secured. At one point the company showed $A107 million of receivables (that is, money owed by its customers), which it pledged as security for bank loans. Later checks revealed that many of these customers did not owe the NSC a cent. In other cases banks took comfort in the fact that their loans were secured by containers of valuable rescue gear. There were more than 100 containers stacked around the NSC's main base. Only a handful contained any equipment, but these were the ones that the bankers saw when they came to check that their loans were safe. Sometimes a suspicious banker would ask to inspect a particular container. Friedrich would then explain that it was away on exercise, fly the banker across the country in a light plane, and point to a container well out in the bush. The container would of course be empty, but the banker had no way to know that.

Six years after Friedrich was appointed CEO, his massive fraud was uncovered. But a few days before a warrant could be issued, Friedrich disappeared. Although he was eventually caught and arrested, he shot himself before he could come to trial. Investigations revealed that Friedrich was operating under an assumed name, having fled from his native Germany, where he was wanted by the police. Many rumors continued to circulate about Friedrich. He was variously alleged to have been a plant of the CIA and the KGB, and the NSC was said to have been behind an attempted counter-coup in Fiji. For the banks there was only one hard truth: Their loans to the NSC, which had appeared so well secured, would never be repaid.

Source: Adapted from T. Sykes, *The Bold Riders* (St. Leonards, NSW, Australia: Allen & Unwin, 1994), chap. 7.

EXAMPLE 19.2 ▶ Factoring

To illustrate factoring, suppose that the firm sells its accounts receivable to a factor at a 2 percent discount. This means that the factor pays 98 cents for each dollar of accounts receivable. If the average collection period is 1 month, then in a month the factor should be able to collect $1 for every 98 cents it paid today. Therefore, the implicit interest rate is 2/98 = 2.04 percent per month, which corresponds to an effective annual interest rate of $(1.0204)^{12} - 1 = .274$, or 27.4 percent. ◀

While factoring would appear from this example to be an expensive source of financing for the firm, part of the apparently steep interest rate represents payment for the assumption of default risk as well as for the cost of running the credit operation.

Inventory Financing Banks also lend on the security of inventory, but they are choosy about the inventory they will accept. They want to make sure that they can identify and sell it if you default. Automobiles and other standardized nonperishable commodities are good security for a loan; work in progress and ripe strawberries are poor collateral.

Banks need to monitor companies to be sure they don't sell their assets and run off with the money. Consider, for example, the story of the great salad oil swindle. Fifty-one banks and companies made loans for nearly $200 million to the Allied Crude Vegetable Oil Refining Corporation in the belief that these loans were secured by valuable salad oil. Unfortunately, they did not notice that Allied's tanks contained false compartments which were mainly filled with seawater. When the fraud was discovered, the president of Allied went to jail and the 51 lenders stayed out in the cold looking for their $200 million. The nearby box presents a similar story that illustrates the potential pitfalls of secured lending. Here, too, the loans were not as "secured" as they appeared: The supposed collateral did not exist.

To protect themselves against this sort of risk, lenders often insist on *field warehousing.* An independent warehouse company hired by the bank supervises the inventory pledged as collateral for the loan. As the firm sells its product and uses the revenue to pay back the loan, the bank directs the warehouse company to release the inventory back to the firm. If the firm defaults on the loan, the bank keeps the inventory and sells it to recover the debt.

Commercial Paper

commercial paper
Short-term unsecured notes issued by firms.

When banks lend money, they provide two services. They match up would-be borrowers and lenders, and they check that the borrower is likely to repay the loan. Banks recover the costs of providing these services by charging borrowers on average a higher interest rate than they pay to lenders. These services are less necessary for large, well-known companies that regularly need to raise large amounts of cash. These companies have increasingly found it profitable to bypass the bank and to sell short-term debt, known as **commercial paper,** directly to large investors. Banks have been forced to respond by reducing the interest rates on their loans to blue-chip customers.

In the United States commercial paper has a maximum maturity of 270 days; longer maturities would require registration with the Securities and Exchange Commission. However, most paper matures in 60 days or less. Commercial paper is not secured, but companies generally back their issue of paper by arranging a special backup line of credit with a bank. This guarantees that they can find the money to repay the paper, and the risk of default is therefore small.

Since investors are reluctant to buy paper that does not have the highest credit rating, companies cannot rely on the commerical paper market to provide them with the short-term capital if their credit standing deteriorates. For example, when the rating services downrated the commercial paper of Ford and General Motors, both companies were forced to reduce sharply the amount of paper that they had issued and to rely instead on the long-term debt market. Ford Credit had $42 billion of commerical paper outstanding at the end of 2000; 3 years later it had cut that amount to $6 billion.

19.7 The Cost of Bank Loans

Bank loans often extend for several years. Interest payments on these longer-term loans are sometimes fixed for the term of the loan, but more commonly they are adjusted up or down as the general level of interest rates changes. The most common benchmarks are the London Interbank Offered Rate (LIBOR), the federal funds rate, or the bank's prime rate. The federal funds rate is the rate at which U.S. banks lend reserves to each other. LIBOR is the rate that major international banks charge each other on eurodollar loans, that is, dollar-denominated loans made outside the United States. If the rate is set at "1 percent over LIBOR," the borrower may pay 5 percent in the first 3 months when LIBOR is 4 percent, 6 percent in the next 3 months when LIBOR is 5 percent, and so on.

The interest rate on bank loans of less than a year is almost invariably fixed for the term of the loan. However, you need to be careful when comparing rates on these shorter-term bank loans, for the rates may be calculated in different ways.

Simple Interest (APR)

The interest rate on bank loans frequently is quoted as simple interest, that is, as an annual percentage rate (APR). For example, if the bank quotes an annual rate of 6 percent on a simple interest loan of $100,000 for 1 month, then at the end of the month you would need to repay $100,000 plus 1 month's interest. This interest is calculated as

$$\text{Amount of loan} \times \frac{\text{annual interest rate}}{\text{number of periods in the year}} = \$100,000 \times \frac{.06}{12} = \$500$$

Your total payment at the end of the month would be

$$\text{Repayment of face value } plus \text{ interest} = \$100,000 + \$500 = \$100,500$$

In Chapter 4 you learned to distinguish between simple interest and compound interest. We have just seen that your 6 percent simple interest bank loan costs .5 percent per month. One-half percent per month compounded for 12 months cumulates to $1.005^{12} = 1.0617$. Thus the compound, or *effective,* annual interest rate on the bank loan is 6.17 percent, not the quoted rate of 6 percent.

The general formula for the equivalent compound interest rate on a simple interest loan is

$$\text{Effective annual rate} = \left(1 + \frac{\text{quoted annual interest rate}}{m}\right)^m - 1$$

where the annual interest rate is stated as a fraction (.06 in our example) and m is the number of periods in the year (12 in our example).

Discount Interest

The interest rate on a bank loan is often calculated on a discount basis. Similarly, when companies issue commercial paper, they also usually quote the interest rate as a discount. With a discount interest loan, the bank deducts the interest up front. For example, suppose that you borrow $100,000 on a discount basis for 1 year at 6 percent. In this case the bank hands you $100,000 less 6 percent, or $94,000. Then at the end of the year you repay the bank the $100,000 face value of the loan. This is equivalent to paying interest of $6,000 on a loan of $94,000. The effective interest rate on such a loan is therefore $6,000/$94,000 = .0638, or 6.38 percent.

Now suppose that you borrow $100,000 on a discount basis for 1 *month* at 6 percent. In this case the bank deducts .5 percent up-front interest and hands you $99,500. The monthly rate is $500/$99,500 = .005025 = .5025 percent, and 1 + effective annual rate $= 1.005025^{12} = 1.0620$, which implies an effective annual interest rate of 6.2 percent.

The general formula for the equivalent compound interest rate on a discount interest loan is

$$\text{Effective annual rate on a discount loan} = \left(\frac{1}{1 - \dfrac{\text{quoted annual interest rate}}{m}}\right)^m - 1$$

where the quoted annual interest rate is stated as a fraction (.06 in our example) and m is the number of periods in the year (12 in our example).

Interest with Compensating Balances

Occasionally, bank loans require the firm to maintain some amount of money on balance at the bank. This is called a *compensating balance.* For example, a firm might have to maintain a balance of 20 percent of the amount of the loan. In other words, if the firm borrows $100,000, it gets to use only $80,000, because $20,000 (20 percent of $100,000) must be left on deposit in the bank.

If the compensating balance does not pay interest (or pays a below-market rate of interest), the actual interest rate on the loan is higher than the stated rate. The reason is that the borrower must pay interest on the full amount borrowed but has access to only part of the funds. For example, we calculated above that a firm borrowing $100,000 for 1 month at 6 percent simple interest must pay interest at the end of the month of $500. If the firm gets the use of only $80,000, the effective monthly interest rate is $500/$80,000 = .00625, or .625 percent. This is equivalent to a compound annual interest rate of $1.00625^{12} - 1 = .0776$, or 7.76 percent.

In general, the compound annual interest rate on a loan with compensating balances is

$$\text{Effective annual rate on a loan with compensating balances} = \left(1 + \frac{\text{actual interest paid}}{\text{borrowed funds available}}\right)^m - 1$$

where m is the number of periods in the year (again 12 in our example).

Short-Term Finance and Bank Loans

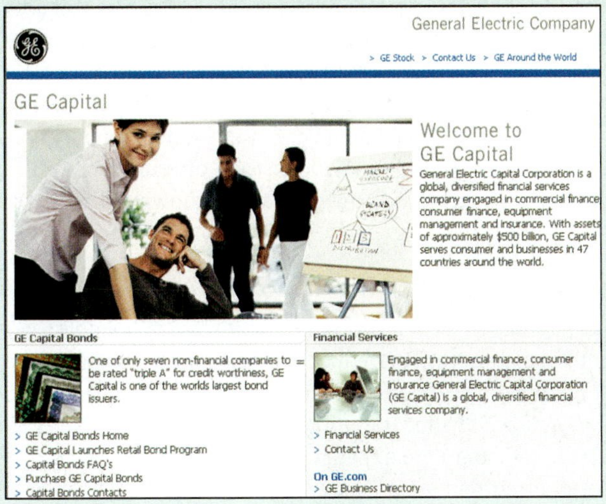

1. GE Capital's Web site, www.gecapital.com, contains a lot of information on types of short-term finance. Suppose that you need to finance your investment in inventory. What are the possible options? Do some make more sense than others?

2. We mentioned that the interest rate on longer term bank loans is not usually fixed for the term of the loan, but is adjusted up or down as the general level of interest rates changes. Often the interest rate is linked to the bank's prime rate or to the London Interbank Offered Rate (LIBOR), which is the interest rate at which major international banks lend to one another. Suppose you are offered the choice between a 3-year loan at the bank's prime rate or at 1 percent above LIBOR. Which would you prefer? Log on to www.bloomberg.com to find current rates.

Self-Test 19.6

Suppose that Dynamic Mattress needs to raise $20 million for 6 months. Bank A quotes a simple interest rate of 7 percent but requires the firm to maintain an interest-free compensating balance of 20 percent. Bank B quotes a simple interest rate of 8 percent but does not require any compensating balances. Bank C quotes a discount interest rate of 7.5 percent and also does not require compensating balances. What is the effective (or compound) annual interest rate on each of these loans?

SUMMARY

Why do firms need to invest in net working capital?

Short-term financial planning is concerned with the management of the firm's short-term, or *current,* assets and liabilities. The most important current assets are cash, marketable securities, inventory, and accounts receivable. The most important current liabilities are bank loans and accounts payable. The difference between current assets and current liabilities is called **net working capital.**

Net working capital arises from lags between the time the firm obtains the raw materials for its product and the time it finally collects its bills from customers. The **cash conversion cycle** is the length of time between the firm's payment for materials and the date that it gets paid by its customers. The cash conversion cycle is partly within management's control. For example, it can choose to have a higher or lower level of inventories. Management needs to trade off the benefits and costs of investing in current assets. Higher investments in current assets entail higher **carrying costs** but lower expected **shortage costs.**

How does long-term financing policy affect short-term financing requirements?

The nature of the firm's short-term financial planning problem is determined by the amount of long-term capital it raises. A firm that issues large amounts of long-term debt or common stock, or that retains a large part of its earnings, may find that it has permanent excess cash. Other firms raise relatively little long-term capital and end up as permanent short-term debtors. Most firms attempt to find a golden mean by financing all fixed assets and part of current assets with equity and long-term debt. Such firms may invest cash surpluses during part of the year and borrow during the rest of the year.

www.mhhe.com/bmm5e

How does the firm's sources and uses of cash relate to its need for short-term borrowing?

The starting point for short-term financial planning is an understanding of sources and uses of cash. Firms forecast their net cash requirement by forecasting collections on accounts receivable, adding other cash inflows, and subtracting all forecast cash outlays. If the forecast cash balance is insufficient to cover day-to-day operations and to provide a buffer against contingencies, you will need to find additional finance. For example, you may borrow from a bank on an unsecured **line of credit,** you may borrow by offering receivables or inventory as security, or you may issue your own short-term notes known as **commercial paper.**

How do firms develop a short-term financing plan that meets their need for cash?

The search for the best short-term financial plan inevitably proceeds by trial and error. The financial manager must explore the consequences of different assumptions about cash requirements, interest rates, limits on financing from particular sources, and so on. Firms are increasingly using computerized financial models to help in this process. Remember the key differences between the various sources of short-term financing—for example, the differences between bank lines of credit and commercial paper. Remember too that firms often raise money on the strength of their current assets, especially accounts receivable and inventories.

QUIZ

1. **Working Capital Management.** Indicate how each of the following six different transactions that Dynamic Mattress might make would affect (i) cash and (ii) net working capital:

   a. Paying out a $2 million cash dividend.
   b. A customer paying a $2,500 bill resulting from a previous sale.
   c. Paying $5,000 previously owed to one of its suppliers.
   d. Borrowing $1 million long-term and investing the proceeds in inventory.
   e. Borrowing $1 million short-term and investing the proceeds in inventory.
   f. Selling $5 million of marketable securities for cash.

2. **Short-Term Financial Plans.** Fill in the blanks in the following statements:

   a. A firm has a cash surplus when its _____ exceeds its _____. The surplus is normally invested in _____.
   b. In developing the short-term financial plan, the financial manager starts with a(n) _____ budget for the next year. This budget shows the _____ generated or absorbed by the firm's operations and also the minimum _____ needed to support these operations. The financial manager may also wish to invest in _____ as a reserve for unexpected cash requirements.

3. **Sources and Uses of Cash.** State how each of the following events would affect the firm's balance sheet. State whether each change is a source or use of cash.

   a. An automobile manufacturer increases production in response to a forecast increase in demand. Unfortunately, the demand does not increase.
   b. Competition forces the firm to give customers more time to pay for their purchases.
   c. The firm sells a parcel of land for $100,000. The land was purchased 5 years earlier for $200,000.
   d. The firm repurchases its own common stock.
   e. The firm pays its quarterly dividend.
   f. The firm issues $1 million of long-term debt and uses the proceeds to repay a short-term bank loan.

4. **Cash Conversion Cycle.** What effect will the following events have on the cash conversion cycle?

   a. Higher financing rates induce the firm to reduce its level of inventory.
   b. The firm obtains a new line of credit that enables it to avoid stretching payables to its suppliers.

   c. The firm factors its accounts receivable.
   d. A recession occurs, and the firm's customers increasingly stretch their payables.

5. **Managing Working Capital.** A new computer system allows your firm to more accurately monitor inventory and anticipate future inventory shortfalls. As a result, the firm feels more able to pare down its inventory levels. What effect will the new system have on working capital and on the cash conversion cycle?

6. **Cash Conversion Cycle.** Calculate the accounts receivable period, accounts payable period, inventory period, and cash conversion cycle for the following firm:

Income statement data:
   Sales   5,000
   Cost of goods sold   4,200

Balance sheet data:

	Beginning of Year	End of Year
Inventory	500	600
Accounts receivable	100	120
Accounts payable	250	290

7. **Cash Conversion Cycle.** What effect will the following have on the cash conversion cycle?

   a. Customers are given a larger discount for cash transactions.
   b. The inventory turnover ratio falls from 8 to 6.
   c. New technology streamlines the production process.
   d. The firm adopts a policy of reducing outstanding accounts payable.
   e. The firm starts producing more goods in response to customers' advance orders instead of producing for inventory.
   f. A temporary glut in the commodity market induces the firm to stock up on raw materials while prices are low.

PRACTICE PROBLEMS

8. **Compensating Balances.** Suppose that Dynamic Sofa (a subsidiary of Dynamic Mattress) has a line of credit with a stated interest rate of 10 percent and a compensating balance of 25 percent. The compensating balance earns no interest.

   a. If the firm needs $10,000, how much will it need to borrow?
   b. Suppose that Dynamic's bank offers to forget about the compensating balance requirement if the firm pays interest at a rate of 12 percent. Should the firm accept this offer? Why or why not?
   c. Redo part (b) assuming the compensating balance pays interest of 4 percent. *Warning:* You cannot use the formula in the chapter for the effective interest rate when the compensating balance pays interest. Think about how to measure the effective interest rate on this loan.

9. **Compensating Balances.** The stated bank loan rate is 8 percent, but the loan requires a compensating balance of 10 percent on which no interest is earned. What is the effective interest rate on the loan? What happens to the effective rate if the compensating balance is doubled to 20 percent?

10. **Factoring.** A firm sells its accounts receivables to a factor at a 1.5 percent discount. The average collection period is 1 month. What is the implicit effective annual interest rate on the factoring arrangement? Suppose the average collection period is 1.5 months. How does this affect the implicit effective annual interest rate?

11. **Discount Loan.** A discount bank loan has a quoted annual rate of 6 percent.

   a. What is the effective rate of interest if the loan is for 1 year and is paid off in one payment at the end of the year?
   b. What is the effective rate of interest if the loan is for 1 month?

12. **Compensating Balances.** A bank loan has a quoted annual rate of 6 percent. However, the borrower must maintain a balance of 25 percent of the amount of the loan, and the balance does not earn any interest.

    a. What is the effective rate of interest if the loan is for 1 year and is paid off in one payment at the end of the year?

    b. What is the effective rate of interest if the loan is for 1 month?

13. **Forecasting Collections.** Here is a forecast of sales by National Bromide for the first 4 months of 2007 (figures in thousands of dollars):

Month:	1	2	3	4
Cash sales	15	24	18	14
Sales on credit	100	120	90	70

On average, 50 percent of credit sales are paid for in the current month, 30 percent in the next month, and the remainder in the month after that. What are expected cash collections in months 3 and 4?

14. **Forecasting Payments.** If a firm pays its bills with a 30-day delay, what fraction of its purchases will be paid for in the current quarter? In the following quarter? What if its payment delay is 60 days?

15. **Short-Term Planning.** Paymore Products places orders for goods equal to 75 percent of its sales forecast in the next quarter. What will be orders in each quarter of the year if the sales forecasts for the next five quarters are:

	Quarter in Coming Year				Following Year
	First	Second	Third	Fourth	First Quarter
Sales forecast	$372	$360	$336	$384	$384

16. **Forecasting Payments.** Calculate Paymore's cash payments to its suppliers under the assumption that the firm pays for its goods with a 1-month delay. Therefore, on average, two-thirds of purchases are paid for in the quarter that they are purchased, and one-third are paid in the following quarter.

17. **Forecasting Collections.** Now suppose that Paymore's customers pay *their* bills with a 2-month delay. What is the forecast for Paymore's cash receipts in each quarter of the coming year? Assume that sales in the last quarter of the previous year were $336.

18. **Forecasting Net Cash Flow.** Assuming that Paymore's labor and administrative expenses are $65 per quarter and that interest on long-term debt is $40 per quarter, work out the net cash inflow for Paymore for the coming year using a table like Table 19–6, Panel B.

19. **Short-Term Financing Requirements.** Suppose that Paymore's cash balance at the start of the first quarter is $40 and its minimum acceptable cash balance is $30. Work out the short-term financing requirements for the firm in the coming year using a table like Table 19–6, Panel C. The firm pays no dividends.

20. **Short-Term Financing Plan.** Now assume that Paymore can borrow up to $100 from a line of credit at an interest rate of 2 percent per quarter. Prepare a short-term financing plan. Use Table 19–7 to guide your answer.

21. **Short-Term Plan.** Recalculate Dynamic Mattress's financing plan (Table 19–7) assuming that the firm wishes to maintain a minimum cash balance of $10 million instead of $5 million. Assume the firm can convince the bank to extend its line of credit to $45 million.

22. **Sources and Uses of Cash.** The accompanying tables show Dynamic Mattress's year-end 2004 balance sheet and its income statement for 2005. Use these tables (and Table 19–3) to work out a statement of sources and uses of cash for 2005.

YEAR-END BALANCE SHEET FOR 2004 (figures in millions of dollars)			
Assets		**Liabilities**	
Current assets		Current liabilities	
Cash	4	Bank loans	4
Marketable securities	2	Accounts payable	15
Inventory	20	Total current liabilities	19
Accounts receivable	22	Long-term debt	5
Total current assets	48	Net worth (equity and retained earnings)	60
Fixed assets			
Gross investment	50		
Less depreciation	14	Total liabilities and net worth	84
Net fixed assets	36		
Total assets	84		

INCOME STATEMENT FOR 2005 (figures in millions of dollars)	
Sales	300
Operating costs	−285
	15
Depreciation	−2
EBIT	13
Interest	−1
Pretax income	12
Tax at 50 percent	−6
Net income	6

Note: Dividend = $1 million, and retained earnings = $5 million.

CHALLENGE PROBLEM ⊞™

Please visit us at www.mhhe.com/bmm5e or refer to your Student CD

23. **Cash Budget.** The following data are from the budget of Ritewell Publishers. Half the company's sales are transacted on a cash basis. The other half are paid for with a 1-month delay. The company pays all of its credit purchases with a 1-month delay. Credit purchases in January were $30, and total sales in January were $180.

	February	March	April
Total sales	200	220	180
Cash purchases	70	80	60
Credit purchases	40	30	40
Labor and administrative expenses	30	30	30
Taxes, interest, and dividends	10	10	10
Capital expenditures	100	0	0

Complete the following cash budget:

	February	March	April
Sources of cash			
Collections on current sales			
Collections on accounts receivable			
Total sources of cash			
Uses of cash			
Payments of accounts payable			
Cash purchases			
Labor and administrative expenses			
Capital expenditures			
Taxes, interest, and dividends			
Total uses of cash			
Net cash inflow			
Cash at start of period	100		
+ Net cash inflow			
= Cash at end of period			
+ Minimum operating cash balance	100	100	100
= Cumulative short-term financing required			

STANDARD
&POOR'S

1. Go to Market Insight at **www.mhhe.com/edumarketinsight**. Wal-Mart Stores and Sears Roebuck & Co. are two retailers at opposite ends of the performance scale. Calculate the net working capital and the cash conversion cycle, discussed in Section 19.2, for each firm. By how much would the investment in working capital fall if each firm could reduce its cash conversion cycle by 1 day? Compare and contrast the level and trend of the "per-employee" ratios for each company. (See the third page of the Profitability Report.) Which company has higher employee efficiency? Use the most recent year-end Balance Sheet Report, Income Statement Report, Annual Ratio Report, and Profitability Report from Market Insight. Based on the Profitability Report, how has the market reacted to the performance differences between the companies?

SOLUTIONS TO SELF-TEST QUESTIONS

19.1 a. The new values for the accounts receivable period and inventory period are

$$\text{Days in inventory} = \frac{250}{4{,}451/365} = 20.5 \text{ days}$$

This is a reduction of 18.2 days from the original value of 38.7 days.

$$\text{Days in receivables} = \frac{300}{4{,}951/365} = 22.1 \text{ days}$$

This is a reduction of 16.7 days from the original value of 38.8 days. The cash conversion cycle falls by a total of 18.2 + 16.7 = 34.9 days.

b. The inventory period, accounts receivable period, and accounts payable period will all fall by a factor of 1.1. (The numerators are unchanged, but the denominators are higher by 10 percent.) Therefore, the conversion cycle will fall from 48.1 days to 48.1/1.10 = 43.7 days.

19.2 a. An increase in the interest rate will increase the cost of carrying current assets. The effect is to reduce the optimal level of such assets.

b. The just-in-time system lowers the expected level of shortage costs and reduces the amount of goods the firm ought to be willing to keep in inventory.

c. If the firm decides that more lenient credit terms are necessary to avoid lost sales, it must then expect customers to pay their bills more slowly. Accounts receivable will increase.

19.3 a. This transaction merely substitutes one current liability (short-term debt) for another (accounts payable). Neither cash nor net working capital is affected.

b. This transaction will increase inventory at the expense of cash. Cash falls but net working capital is unaffected.

c. The firm will use cash to buy back the stock. Both cash and net working capital will fall.

d. The proceeds from the sale will increase both cash and net working capital.

19.4

Quarter:	First	Second	Third	Fourth
Accounts receivable				
Receivables (beginning of period)	30.0	35.0	31.4	46.4
Sales	87.5	78.5	116.0	131.0
Collections*	82.5	82.1	101.0	125.0
Receivables (end of period)	35.0	31.4	46.4	52.4
Cash budget				
Sources of cash				
Collections of accounts receivable	82.5	82.1	101.0	125.0
Other	1.5	0.0	12.5	0.0
Total sources	84.0	82.1	113.5	125.0
Uses				
Payments of accounts payable	65.0	60.0	55.0	50.0
Labor and administrative expenses	30.0	30.0	30.0	30.0
Capital expenses	32.5	1.3	5.5	8.0
Taxes, interest, and dividends	4.0	4.0	4.5	5.0
Total uses	131.5	95.3	95.0	93.0
Net cash inflow	–47.5	–13.2	18.5	32.0
Short-term financing requirements				
Cash at start of period	5.0	–42.5	–55.7	–37.2
+ Net cash inflow	–47.5	–13.2	18.5	32.0
= Cash at end of period	–42.5	–55.7	–37.2	–5.2
Minimum operating balance	5.0	5.0	5.0	5.0
Cumulative short-term financing required	47.5	60.7	42.2	10.2

*Sales in fourth quarter of the previous year totaled $75 million.

19.5 The major change in the plan is the substitution of the extra $5 million of borrowing from the bank in the second quarter and the corresponding reduction in the stretched payables. This substitution is advantageous because the bank loan is a cheaper source of funds. Notice that the cash balance at the end of the year is higher under this plan than in the original plan.

Quarter:	First	Second	Third	Fourth
Cash requirements				
1. Cash required for operations	45	15	−26.0	−35
2. Interest on line of credit	0	0.8	0.9	0.6
3. Interest on stretched payables	0	0	0.5	0
4. Total cash required	45	15.8	−24.6	−34.4
Cash raised				
5. Bank loan	40	5	0	0
6. Stretched payables	0	10.8	0	0
7. Securities sold	5	0	0	0
8. Total cash raised	45	15.8	0	0
Repayments				
9. Of stretched payables	0	0	10.8	0
10. Of bank loan	0	0	13.8	31.2
Increase in cash balances				
11. Addition to cash balances	0	0	0	3.2
Bank loan				
12. Beginning of quarter	0	40	45	31.2
13. End of quarter	40	45	31.2	0

19.6   Bank A: The interest paid on the $20 million loan over the 6-month period will be $20 million × .07/2 = $.7 million. With a 20 percent compensating balance, $16 million is available to the firm. The effective annual interest rate is

$$\text{Effective annual rate on a loan with compensating balances} = \left(1 + \frac{\text{actual interest paid}}{\text{borrowed funds available}}\right)^m - 1$$

$$= \left(1 + \frac{\$.7 \text{ million}}{\$16 \text{ million}}\right)^2 - 1 = .0894, \text{ or } 8.94\%$$

Bank B: The compound annual interest rate on the simple loan is

$$\text{Effective annual rate} = \left(1 + \frac{\text{quoted interest rate}}{m}\right)^m - 1$$

$$= \left(1 + \frac{.08}{2}\right)^2 - 1 = 1.04^2 - 1 = .0816, \text{ or } 8.16\%$$

Bank C: The compound annual interest rate is

$$\text{Effective annual rate on a discount loan} = \left(\frac{1}{1 - \dfrac{\text{annual interest rate}}{m}}\right)^m - 1$$

$$= \left(\frac{1}{1 - \dfrac{.075}{2}}\right)^2 - 1 = \left(\frac{1}{.9625}\right)^2 - 1 = .0794, \text{ or } 7.94\%$$

MINICASE

Capstan Autos operated an East Coast dealership for a major Japanese car manufacturer. Capstan's owner, Sidney Capstan, attributed much of the business's success to its no-frills policy of competitive pricing and immediate cash payment. The business was basically a simple one—the firm imported cars at the beginning of each quarter and paid the manufacturer at the end of the quarter. The revenues from the sale of these cars covered the payment to the manufacturer and the expenses of running the business, as well as providing Sidney Capstan with a good return on his equity investment.

By the fourth quarter of 2009 sales were running at 250 cars a quarter. Since the average sale price of each car was about $20,000, this translated into quarterly revenues of 250 × $20,000 = $5 million. The average cost to Capstan of each imported car was $18,000. After paying wages, rent, and other recurring costs of $200,000 per quarter and deducting depreciation of $80,000, the company was left with earnings before interest and taxes (EBIT) of $220,000 a quarter and net profits of $140,000.

The year 2010 was not a happy year for car importers in the United States. Recession led to a general decline in auto sales, while the fall in the value of the dollar shaved profit margins for many dealers in imported cars. Capstan more than most firms foresaw the difficulties ahead and reacted at once by offering 6 months' free credit while holding the sale price of its cars constant. Wages and other costs were pared by 25 percent to $150,000 a quarter, and the company effectively eliminated all capital expenditures. The policy appeared successful. Unit sales fell by 20 percent to 200 units a quarter, but the company continued to operate at a satisfactory profit (see table).

The slump in sales lasted for 6 months, but as consumer confidence began to return, auto sales began to recover. The company's new policy of 6 months' free credit was proving sufficiently popular that Sidney Capstan decided to maintain the policy. In the third quarter of 2010 sales had recovered to 225 units; by the fourth quarter they were 250 units; and by the first quarter of the next year they had reached 275 units. It looked as if by the second quarter of 2011 the company could expect to sell 300 cars. Earnings before interest and tax were already in excess of their previous high, and Sidney Capstan was able to congratulate himself on weathering what looked to be a tricky period. Over the 18-month period the firm had earned net profits of over half a million dollars, and the equity had grown from just over $1.5 million to about $2 million.

Sidney Capstan was first and foremost a superb salesman and always left the financial aspects of the business to his financial

SUMMARY INCOME STATEMENT
(all figures except unit sales in thousands of dollars)

Year:	2009	2010				2011
Quarter:	4	1	2	3	4	1
1. Number of cars sold	250	200	200	225	250	275
2. Unit price	20	20	20	20	20	20
3. Unit cost	18	18	18	18	18	18
4. Revenues (1 × 2)	5,000	4,000	4,000	4,500	5,000	5,500
5. Cost of goods sold (1 × 3)	4,500	3,600	3,600	4,050	4,500	4,950
6. Wages and other costs	200	150	150	150	150	150
7. Depreciation	80	80	80	80	80	80
8. EBIT (4 − 5 − 6 − 7)	220	170	170	220	270	320
9. Net interest	4	0	76	153	161	178
10. Pretax profit (8 − 9)	216	170	94	67	109	142
11. Tax (.35 × 10)	76	60	33	23	38	50
12. Net profit (10 − 11)	140	110	61	44	71	92

SUMMARY BALANCE SHEETS
(figures in thousands of dollars)

	End of 3rd Quarter 2009	End of 1st Quarter 2011
Cash	10	10
Receivables	0	10,500
Inventory	4,500	5,400
Total current assets	4,510	15,910
Fixed assets, net	1,760	1,280
Total assets	6,270	17,190
Bank loan	230	9,731
Payables	4,500	5,400
Total current liabilities	4,730	15,131
Shareholders' equity	1,540	2,059
Total liabilities	6,270	17,190

www.mhhe.com/bmm5e

manager. However, there was one feature of the financial statements that disturbed Sidney Capstan—the mounting level of debt, which by the end of the first quarter of 2011 had reached $9.7 million. This unease turned to alarm when the financial manager phoned to say that the bank was reluctant to extend further credit and was even questioning its current level of exposure to the company.

Mr. Capstan found it impossible to understand how such a successful year could have landed the company in financial difficulties. The company had always had good relationships with its bank, and the interest rate on its bank loans was a reasonable 8 percent a year (or about 2 percent a quarter). Surely, Mr. Capstan reasoned, when the bank saw the projected sales growth for the rest of 2011, it would realize that there were plenty of profits to enable the company to start repaying its loans.

Mr. Capstan kept coming back to three questions: Was his company really in trouble? Could the bank be right in its decision to withhold further credit? And why was the company's indebtedness increasing when its profits were higher than ever?

Working Capital Management

RELATED WEB LINKS

www.federalreserve.gov
www.ny.frb.org
www.stlouisfed.org Information on money market rates.
www.nacha.org
www.gtnews.com
www.phoenixhecht.com Information on cash management and payment systems.
www.simba.org Devoted to best practices in inventory management.
www.treasuryandrisk.com
www.americanbanker.com
www.intltreasurer.com Online publications on short-term financial management.

www.nacm.org
www.creditworthy.com Resources and information on credit management.
www.dnb.com
www.equifax.com
www.experian.com
www.transunion.com Sites of major credit evaluation firms.
www.myfico.com
www.fairisaac.com Information and analytics concerning credit ratings.
www.jaxworks.com/calc2.htm Calculate Z scores at this site.
www.moodyskmv.com Credit analysis tools.

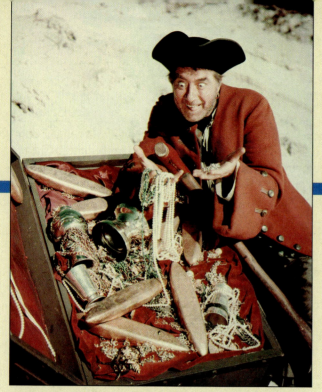

Not the right way to manage cash. Why hoard cash when you could invest it? Still, you need some cash on hand to pay bills. What's the right cash inventory?

The Kobal Collection/Walt Disney Productions

Most of this book is devoted to long-term financial decisions such as capital budgeting and the choice of capital structure. In the previous chapter, we started our analysis of short-term planning decisions by looking at how firms ensure that they have enough cash to pay their bills. It is now time to look more closely at the management of short-term assets and liabilities, known collectively as *working capital.*

There are four principal types of current assets. All need to be managed. We begin with accounts receivable. Companies frequently sell goods on credit, so it may be weeks or even months before they receive payment. The unpaid bills show up in the balance sheet as accounts receivable. We will explain how the company's credit manager sets the terms of payment, decides which customers should be offered credit, and ensures that they pay promptly.

The second major short-term asset is inventory. To do business, firms need reserves of raw materials, work in progress, and finished goods. But these inventories can be expensive to store, and they tie up capital. Inventory management involves a trade-off between these costs and benefits. In manufacturing companies, the production manager is most likely to make this judgment without direct input from the financial manager. Therefore, we spend less time on this topic than on the management of the other components of working capital.

Our next task is to discuss the firm's cash balances. The first problem is to decide how much cash the firm should retain and, therefore, how much can be invested in interest-bearing securities. The second is to ensure that cash payments are handled efficiently. You want to collect payments as quickly as possible and put them to work earning interest. We will describe some of the techniques that firms use to move money around efficiently.

Finally, we describe some of the firm's choices for how to invest excess funds in a variety of short-term securities, which are the fourth major component of working capital.

After reading this chapter you should be able to:

- Measure the implicit interest rate on credit sales.

- Decide whether it makes sense to grant credit to customers.

- Cite the costs and benefits of holding inventories and cash balances.

- Describe the methods firms use to manage cash efficiently.

- Compare alternatives for investing excess funds over short horizons.

20.1 Accounts Receivable and Credit Policy

trade credit

Bills awaiting payment from one company to another.

consumer credit

Bills awaiting payment from final customer to a company.

We start our tour of current assets with the firm's accounts receivable. When one company sells goods to another, it does not usually expect to be paid immediately. The unpaid bills, or **trade credit,** compose the bulk of accounts receivable. The remainder is made up of **consumer credit,** bills awaiting payment by the final customer.

Credit management involves the following five steps:

1. You must establish the terms of sale on which you propose to sell your goods. For example, how long will you give customers to pay their bills? Will you offer a discount for immediate payment?
2. You must decide what evidence you require that the customer owes you money. For example, is a signed receipt enough, or do you insist on a formal IOU?
3. You must determine which customers are likely to pay their bills. This is called *credit analysis.*
4. You must decide on credit policy. How much credit will you extend to each customer? How much risk are you prepared to take on marginally creditworthy prospects?
5. Finally, you have to collect the money when it becomes due. This is called *collection policy.* How do you keep track of payments and pursue slow payers?

We discuss these topics in turn.

Terms of Sale

terms of sale

Credit, discount, and payment terms offered on a sale.

Whenever you sell goods, you need to set the **terms of sale.** For example, if you are supplying goods to a wide variety of irregular customers, you may require cash on delivery (COD). And if you are producing goods to the customer's specification or incurring heavy delivery costs, then it may be sensible to ask for cash before delivery (CBD).

In many other cases, payment is not made until after delivery, so the buyer receives *credit.* Each industry seems to have its own typical credit arrangements. These arrangements have a rough logic. For example, the seller will naturally demand earlier payment if its customers are financially less secure, if their accounts are small, or if the goods are perishable or quickly resold.

When you buy goods on credit, the supplier will state a final payment date. To encourage you to pay *before* the final date, it is common to offer a cash discount for prompt settlement. For example, a manufacturer may require payment within 30 days but offer a 5 percent discount to customers who pay within 10 days. These terms would be referred to as 5/10, net 30:

5	/	10,	net 30
↑		↑	↑
percent discount for early payment		number of days that discount is available	number of days before payment is due

Similarly, if a firm sells goods on terms of 2/30, net 60, customers receive a 2 percent discount for payment within 30 days or else must pay in full within 60 days. If the terms are simply net 30, then customers must pay within 30 days of the invoice date and no discounts are offered for early payment.

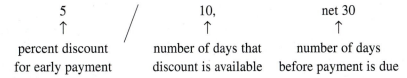

Self-Test 20.1   Suppose that a firm sells goods on terms of 2/10, net 20. On May 1 you buy goods from the company with an invoice value of $20,000. How much would you need to pay if you took the cash discount? What is the latest date on which the cash discount is available? By what date should you pay for your purchase if you decide not to take the cash discount?

For many items that are bought regularly, it is inconvenient to require separate payment for each delivery. A common solution is to pretend that all sales during the month in fact occur at the end of the month (EOM). Thus goods may be sold on terms of 8/10, *EOM,* net 60. This allows the customer a cash discount of 8 percent if the bill is paid within 10 days of the end of the month; otherwise, the full payment is due within 60 days of the invoice date.

A firm that buys on credit is in effect borrowing from its supplier. It saves cash today but will have to pay later. This is an implicit loan from the supplier. Of course, if it is free, a loan is always worth having. But if you pass up a cash discount, then the loan may prove to be very expensive. For example, a customer who buys on terms of 3/10, net 30, may decide to forgo the cash discount and pay on the thirtieth day. The customer obtains an extra 20 days' credit by deferring payment from 10 to 30 days after the sale but pays about 3 percent more for the goods. This is equivalent to borrowing money at a rate of 74.3 percent a year. To see why, consider an order of $100. If the firm pays within 10 days, it gets a 3 percent discount and pays only $97. If it waits the full 30 days, it pays $100. The extra 20 days of credit increase the payment by the fraction 3/97 = .0309, or 3.09 percent. Therefore, the implicit interest charged to extend the trade credit is 3.09 percent *per 20 days.* There are 365/20 = 18.25 twenty-day periods in a year, so the effective annual rate of interest on the loan is $(1.0309)^{18.25} - 1 = .743$, or 74.3 percent.

The general formula for calculating the implicit annual interest rate for customers who do not take the cash discount is

$$\text{Effective annual rate} = \left(1 + \frac{\text{discount}}{\text{discounted price}}\right)^{365/\text{extra days credit}} - 1$$

The discount divided by the discounted price is the percentage increase in price paid by a customer who forgoes the discount. In our example, with terms of 3/10, net 30, the percentage increase in price is 3/97 = .0309, or 3.09 percent. This is the per-period implicit rate of interest. The period of the loan is the number of extra days of credit that you can obtain by forgoing the discount. In our example, this is 20 days. To annualize this rate, we compound the per-period rate by the number of periods in a year.

Of course any firm that delays payment beyond day 30 gains a cheaper loan but damages its reputation for creditworthiness.

EXAMPLE 20.1 ▶ Trade Credit Rates

What is the implied interest rate on the trade credit if the discount for early payment is 5/10, net 60?

The cash discount in this case is 5 percent and customers who choose not to take the discount receive an extra 60 − 10 = 50 days credit. So the effective annual interest is

$$\text{Effective annual rate} = \left(1 + \frac{\text{discount}}{\text{discounted price}}\right)^{365/\text{extra days credit}} - 1$$

$$= \left(1 + \frac{5}{95}\right)^{365/50} - 1 = .454, \text{ or } 45.4\%$$

In this case the customer who does not take the discount is effectively borrowing money at an annual interest rate of 45.4 percent. ◀

You might wonder why the effective interest rate on trade credit is typically so high. At such steep effective rates, most purchasers will choose to pay early and receive the discount. Those who don't are probably strapped for cash. It makes sense to charge these firms a high rate of interest.

Self-Test 20.2   **What would be the effective annual interest rate in Example 20.1 if the terms of sale were 5/10, net 50? Why is the rate higher?**

Credit Agreements

open account
Agreement whereby sales are made with no formal debt contract.

The terms of sale define the amount of any credit but not the nature of the contract. Repetitive sales are almost always made on **open account** and involve only an implicit contract. There is simply a record in the seller's books and a receipt signed by the buyer.

Sometimes you might want a clear commitment from the buyer before you deliver the goods. In this case the common procedure is to arrange a *commercial draft*. This is simply jargon for an order to pay.[1] It works as follows: The seller prepares a draft ordering payment by the customer and sends this draft to the customer's bank. If immediate payment is required, the draft is termed a *sight draft;* otherwise, it is known as a *time draft*. Depending on whether it is a sight or a time draft, the customer either tells the bank to pay up or acknowledges the debt by adding the word "accepted" and a signature. Once accepted, a time draft is like a postdated check and is called a *trade acceptance*. This trade acceptance is then forwarded to the seller, who holds it until the payment becomes due.

If the customer's credit is shaky, the seller may ask the customer to arrange for his or her bank to accept the time draft. In this case, the bank guarantees the customer's debt, and the draft is called a *banker's acceptance*. Banker's acceptances are often used in overseas trade. They are actively bought and sold in the money market, the market for short-term high-quality debt.

If you sell goods to a customer who proves unable to pay, you cannot get your goods back. You simply become a general creditor of the company, in common with other unfortunates. You can avoid this situation by making a *conditional sale,* so that ownership of the goods remains with the seller until full payment is made. The conditional sale is common in Europe. In the United States it is used only for goods that are bought on installment. In this case, if the customer fails to make the agreed number of payments, then the equipment can be immediately repossessed by the seller.

Credit Analysis

credit analysis
Procedure to determine the likelihood a customer will pay its bills.

There are a number of ways to find out whether customers are likely to pay their debts, that is, to carry out **credit analysis.** The most obvious indication is whether they have paid promptly in the past. Prompt payment is usually a good omen, but beware of the customer who establishes a high credit limit on the basis of small payments and then disappears, leaving you with a large unpaid bill.

If you are dealing with a new customer, you will probably check with a credit agency. Dun & Bradstreet, which is by far the largest of these agencies, provides credit ratings on several million domestic and foreign firms. In addition to its rating service, Dun & Bradstreet provides on request a full credit report on a potential customer.

Credit agencies usually report the experience that other firms have had with your customer, but you can also get this information by contacting those firms directly or through a credit bureau.

Your bank can also make a credit check. It will contact the customer's bank and ask for information on the customer's average bank balance, access to bank credit, and general reputation.

In addition to checking with your customer's bank, it might make sense to check what everybody else in the financial community thinks about your customer's credit

---

[1] For example, a check is an example of a draft. Whenever you write a check, you are ordering the bank to make a payment.

standing. Does that sound expensive? Not if your customer is a public company. You just look at the Moody's or Standard & Poor's rating for the customer's bonds.[2] You can also compare prices of these bonds with the prices of other firms' bonds. (Of course the comparisons should be between bonds of similar maturity, coupon, and so on.)

If you don't like relying on the judgment of others, you can do your own homework. Ideally this would involve a detailed analysis of the company's business prospects and financing, but this is usually too expensive. Therefore, credit analysts concentrate on the company's financial statements, using rough rules of thumb to judge whether the firm is a good credit risk. The rules of thumb are based on *financial ratios.* Chapter 17 described how these ratios are calculated and interpreted.

Numerical Credit Scoring   Analyzing credit risk is like detective work. You have a lot of clues—some important, some fitting into a neat pattern, others contradictory. You must weigh these clues to come up with an overall judgment.

When the firm has a small, regular clientele, the credit manager can easily handle the process informally and make a judgment about what are often termed the *five Cs of credit:*

1. The customer's *character.*
2. The customer's *capacity* to pay.
3. The customer's *capital.*
4. The *collateral* provided by the customer.[3]
5. The *condition* of the customer's business.

When the company is dealing directly with consumers or with a large number of small trade accounts, some streamlining is essential. In these cases it may make sense to use a scoring system to prescreen credit applications.

For example, if you apply for a credit card or a bank loan, you will be asked about your job, home, and financial position. The information that you provide is used to calculate an overall credit score. Applicants who do not make the grade on the score are likely to be refused credit or subjected to more detailed analysis.

Banks and the credit departments of industrial firms also use mechanical credit scoring systems to cut the costs of assessing commercial credit applications. One bank claimed that by introducing a credit scoring system, it cut the cost of reviewing loan applications by two-thirds.

Firms use several statistical techniques to separate the creditworthy sheep from the impecunious goats. One common method employs *multiple discriminant analysis* to produce a measure of solvency called a *Z score.* For example, a study by Edward Altman suggested the following relationship between a firm's financial ratios and its creditworthiness (*Z*):[4]

$$Z = 3.3 \frac{\text{EBIT}}{\text{total assets}} + 1.0 \frac{\text{sales}}{\text{total assets}} + .6 \frac{\text{market value of equity}}{\text{total book debt}}$$

$$+ 1.4 \frac{\text{retained earnings}}{\text{total assets}} + 1.2 \frac{\text{working capital}}{\text{total assets}}$$

This equation did a good job at distinguishing the bankrupt and nonbankrupt firms. Of the former, 94 percent had *Z* scores *less* than 2.7 before they went bankrupt. In

---

[2] We described bond ratings in Chapter 5, Section 5.2.

[3] For example, the customer can offer bonds as collateral. These bonds can then be seized by the seller if the customer fails to pay.

[4] EBIT is earnings before interest and taxes. E. I. Altman, "Financial Ratios, Discriminant Analysis and the Prediction of Corporate Bankruptcy," *Journal of Finance* 23 (September 1968), pp. 589–609.

Credit Scoring: What Your Lender Won't Tell You

To hear bankers tell it, credit scoring is the best thing to happen to small-business borrowers since the invention of compound interest. Forget haggling over things like how well your business is doing or what your competitors are up to. Just hand in some predetermined data about yourself and your company, let the computer crunch the numbers, and voilà: Out comes a "credit score" that predicts the chances that you'll actually pay off the loan. Score high enough, and you get approved, sometimes within minutes.

Scoring is already ubiquitous in consumer lending, and 22 of the 25 biggest players in the small-business loan market use the system, according to Fair, Isaac & Co., a pioneer in the development of credit-scoring software. Almost any loan of $50,000 or less issued by a national financial services company will have gone through a credit-scoring system.

Credit-scoring models assign points for up to 20 factors. The more points you get, the better credit risk you represent. The best-known credit-scoring models are provided by Fair, Isaac. The score on its Small Business Scoring Service ranges from 50 to 350, with most small businesses falling into the 150 to 250 area. While lenders set their own cutoff points, if you score above 220, that's generally good, while scores below 170 are considered high risk.

The overriding factor in a small-business credit score is your personal credit history. Specifically, the system looks at whether you pay your personal bills on time. The later you pay, the fewer points you get, and the more bills you pay late, the more your score gets knocked down.

The next key input is how much credit you've already got access to and balances on your accounts. If lines of credit are maxed out, lenders worry that there is little room to maneuver if the business runs into trouble. Other major red flags include bankruptcies, debts turned over to a collection agency, liens, and even overdue child-support payments. You can even get penalized for shopping too hard for credit.

Finally, specific business characteristics are weighed. They include the size of the company, its age, the industry in which it does business, and whether it's a corporation, partnership, or sole proprietorship. A sole prop gets fewer points than a partnership, and a partnership gets fewer points than a corporation. After all, if you're a sole proprietor and you get hit by a bus, all bets are off on your business. By the same token, a manufacturer gets higher points than bars or restaurants because it's less likely to go under quickly.

Source: V. M. Kahn, "Credit Scoring: What Your Lender Won't Tell You," *BusinessWeek*, May 22, 2000, p. F30. Reprinted from the May 22, 2000, issue of *BusinessWeek* magazine by special permission. © 2000 The McGraw-Hill Companies, Inc.

contrast, 97 percent of the nonbankrupt firms had Z scores *above* this level.[5] You can find an example of Z-score analysis at **www.jaxworks.com/zscore3.htm**.

EXAMPLE 20.2 ▶	Credit Scoring

Consider a firm with the following financial ratios:

$$\frac{\text{EBIT}}{\text{total assets}} = .12 \qquad \frac{\text{sales}}{\text{total assets}} = 1.4 \qquad \frac{\text{market equity}}{\text{book debt}} = .9$$

$$\frac{\text{retained earnings}}{\text{total assets}} = .4 \qquad \frac{\text{working capital}}{\text{total assets}} = .12$$

The firm's Z score is thus

$$(3.3 \times .12) + (1.0 \times 1.4) + (.6 \times .9) + (1.4 \times .4) + (1.2 \times .12) = 3.04$$

This score is above the cutoff level for predicting bankruptcy, and thus would be considered favorable in terms of evaluating the firm's creditworthiness. ◀

The nearby box describes how statistical scoring systems similar to the Z score can provide timely first-cut estimates of creditworthiness. These assessments can streamline the credit decision and free up labor for other, less mechanical tasks.

The Credit Decision

credit policy
Standards set to determine the amount and nature of credit to extend to customers.

You have taken the first three steps toward an effective credit operation. In other words, you have fixed your terms of sale; you have decided whether to sell on open account or to ask your customers to sign an IOU; and you have established a procedure for estimating the probability that each customer will pay up. Your next step is to decide on **credit policy.**

---

[5] This equation was fitted with hindsight. The equation did slightly less well when used to *predict* bankruptcies after 1965.

Credit Analysis

Source: Dun & Bradstreet Web site.

1. When credit managers need a credit check on a small business, they often look up the Dun & Bradstreet report on the company. You can see a sample Comprehensive Report by logging on to www.dnb.com and clicking on *Products and Services* and then *Risk Management Solutions.* On the basis of this report, would you be prepared to extend credit to this company? Why or why not?
2. Credit scoring is widely used to rate applicants for personal loans. You can estimate your own credit rating with the *Credit Analyzer* on finance.yahoo.com. You can find the Analyzer using the Credit Reports link. Try varying some of the inputs and see how your credit rating changes. Would the rating change if in the past you had shopped around to find the best source for a loan? Now log on to www.myfico.com and find out how other credit applicants compare and what difference your score makes to the interest rate that you are likely to pay on a loan.

If there is no possibility of repeat orders, the credit decision is relatively simple. Figure 20–1 summarizes your choice. On the one hand, you can refuse credit and pass up the sale. In this case you make neither profit nor loss. The alternative is to offer credit. If you offer credit and the customer pays, you benefit by the profit margin on the sale. If the customer defaults, you lose the cost of the goods delivered. The decision to offer credit depends on the probability of payment. You should grant credit if the expected profit from doing so is greater than the profit from refusing.

Suppose that the probability that the customer will pay up is p. If the customer does pay, you receive additional revenues (REV) and you deliver goods that you incurred costs to produce; your net gain is the present value of REV – COST. Unfortunately, you can't be certain that the customer will pay; there is a probability $(1 - p)$ of default. Default means you receive nothing but still incur the additional costs of the delivered goods. The *expected profit*[6] from the two sources of action is therefore as follows:

Action	Expected Profit
Refuse credit:	0
Grant credit:	$p \times PV(REV - COST) - (1 - p) \times PV(COST)$

You should grant credit if the expected profit from doing so is positive.

FIGURE 20–1 If you refuse credit, you make neither profit nor loss. If you offer credit, there is a probability p that the customer will pay and you will make REV – COST and there is a probability $(1 - p)$ that the customer will default and you will lose COST.

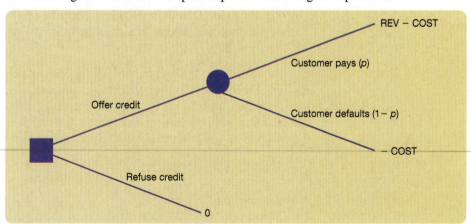

[6] Notice that we use the present values of costs and revenues. This is because there sometimes are significant lags between costs incurred and revenues generated. Also, while we follow convention in referring to the "expected profit" of the decision, it should be clear that our equation for expected profit is in fact the net present value of the decision to grant credit. As we emphasized in Chapter 1, the manager's task is to add value, not to maximize accounting profits.

EXAMPLE 20.3   ▶   The Credit Decision

Consider the case of the Cast Iron Company. On each nondelinquent sale Cast Iron receives revenues with a present value of $1,200 and incurs costs with a present value of $1,000. Therefore, the company's expected profit if it offers credit is

$$p \times \text{PV(REV} - \text{COST)} - (1 - p) \times \text{PV(COST)} = p \times 200 - (1 - p) \times 1,000$$

If the probability of collection is 5/6, Cast Iron can expect to break even:

$$\text{Expected profit} = 5/6 \times 200 - (1 - 5/6) \times 1,000 = 0$$

Thus Cast Iron's policy should be to grant credit whenever the chances of collection are better than 5 out of 6.   ◀

In this last example, the net present value of granting credit is positive if the probability of collection exceeds 5/6. In general, this break-even probability can be found by setting the net present value of granting credit equal to zero and solving for p. It turns out that the formula for the break-even probability is simply the ratio of the present value of costs to revenues:

$$p \times \text{PV(REV} - \text{COST)} - (1 - p) \times \text{PV(COST)} = 0$$

Break-even probability of collection, then, is

$$p = \frac{\text{PV(COST)}}{\text{PV(REV)}}$$

and the break-even probability of *default* is

$$(1 - p) = 1 - \text{PV(COST)/PV(REV)} = \text{PV(PROFIT)/PV(REV)}$$

In other words, the break-even probability of default is simply the profit margin on each sale. If the default probability is larger than the profit margin, you should not extend credit.

Think what this implies. Companies that operate on low profit margins should be cautious about granting credit to high-risk customers. Firms with high margins can afford to deal with more doubtful ones.

Self-Test 20.3   **What is the break-even probability of collection if the present value of the revenues from the sale is $1,100 rather than $1,200? Why does the break-even probability increase? Use your answer to decide whether firms that sell high-profit-margin or low-margin goods should be more willing to issue credit.**

So far we have ignored the possibility of repeat orders. But one of the reasons for offering credit today is that you may get yourself a good, regular customer.

Suppose Cast Iron has been asked to extend credit to a new customer. You can find little information on the firm, and you believe that the probability of payment is no better than .8. If you grant credit, the expected profit on this order is

$$\text{Expected profit on initial order} = p \times \text{PV(REV} - \text{COST)} - (1 - p) \times \text{PV(COST)}$$
$$= (.8 \times 200) - (.2 \times 1,000) = -\$40$$

You decide to refuse credit.

This is the correct decision *if* there is no chance of a repeat order. But now consider future periods. If the customer does pay up, there will be a reorder next year. Having paid once, the customer will seem less of a risk. For this reason, any repeat order is very profitable.

Think back to Chapter 9, and you will recognize that the credit decision bears many similarities to our earlier discussion of real options. By granting credit now, the firm retains the option to grant credit on an entire sequence of potentially profitable repeat sales. This option can be very valuable and can tilt the decision toward granting credit. Even a dubious prospect may warrant some initial credit if there is a chance that the company will develop into a profitable steady customer.

EXAMPLE 20.4 ▶ Credit Decisions with Repeat Orders

To illustrate, let's look at an extreme case. Suppose that if a customer pays up on the first sale, you can be *sure* you will have a regular and completely reliable customer. In this case, the value of such a customer is not the profit on one order but an entire stream of profits from repeat purchases. For example, suppose that the customer will make one purchase each year from Cast Iron. If the discount rate is 10 percent and the profit on each order is $200 a year, then the present value of an indefinite stream of business from a good customer is not $200 but $200/.10 = $2,000. There is a probability p that Cast Iron will secure a good customer with a value of $2,000. There is a probability of $(1 - p)$ that the customer will default, resulting in a loss of $1,000. So, once we recognize the benefits of securing a good and permanent customer, the expected profit from granting credit is

$$\text{Expected profit} = (p \times 2,000) - (1 - p) \times 1,000$$

This is positive for any probability of collection above .33. Thus the break-even probability falls from 5/6 to 1/3. If one sale may lead to profitable repeat sales, the firm should be inclined to grant credit on the initial purchase. ◀

Self-Test 20.4 How will the break-even probability vary with the discount rate? Try a rate of 20 percent in Example 20.4. What is the intuition behind your answer?

Of course, real-life situations are generally far more complex than our simple examples. Customers are not all good or all bad. Many pay late consistently; you get your money, but it costs more to collect and you lose a few months' interest. And estimating the probability that a customer will pay up is far from an exact science. Then there is uncertainty about repeat sales. There may be a good chance that the customer will give you further business, but you can't be sure of that and you can't know for how long she or he will continue to buy from you.

Like almost all financial decisions, credit allocation involves a strong dose of judgment. Our examples are intended as reminders of the issues involved rather than as cookbook formulas. Here are the basic things to remember:

1. *Maximize profit.* As credit manager your job is not to minimize the number of bad accounts; it is to maximize profits. You are faced with a trade-off. The best that can happen is that the customer pays promptly; the worst is default. In the one case the firm receives the full additional revenues from the sale less the additional costs; in the other it receives nothing and loses the costs. You must weigh the chances of these alternative outcomes. If the margin of profit is high, you are justified in a liberal credit policy; if it is low, you cannot afford many bad debts.
2. *Concentrate on the dangerous accounts.* You should not expend the same effort on analyzing all credit decisions. If an application is small or clear-cut, your decision should be largely routine; if it is large or doubtful, you may do better to move straight to a detailed credit appraisal. Most credit managers don't make credit decisions on an order-by-order basis. Instead, they set a credit limit for each customer. The sales representative is required to refer the order for approval only if the customer exceeds this limit.
3. *Look beyond the immediate order.* Sometimes it may be worth accepting a relatively poor risk as long as there is a likelihood that the customer will grow into a regular

and reliable buyer. (This is why credit card companies are eager to sign up college students even though few students can point to an established credit history.) New businesses must be prepared to incur more bad debts than established businesses because they have not yet formed relationships with low-risk customers. This is part of the cost of building up a good customer list.

Collection Policy

It would be nice if all customers paid their bills by the due date. But they don't, and since you may also "stretch" your payables, from time to time, you can't altogether blame them.

Slow payers impose two costs on the firm. First, they require the firm to spend more resources in collecting payments. They also force the firm to invest more in working capital. Recall from Chapter 17 that accounts receivable are proportional to the average collection period (also known as days' sales in receivables):

$$\text{Accounts receivable} = \text{daily sales} \times \text{average collection period}$$

When your customers stretch payables, you end up with a longer collection period and a greater investment in accounts receivable. Thus you must establish a **collection policy.**

collection policy
Procedures to collect and monitor receivables.

The credit manager keeps a record of payment experiences with each customer. In addition, the manager monitors overdue payments by drawing up a schedule of the aging of receivables. The **aging schedule** classifies accounts receivable by the length of time they are outstanding. This may look roughly like Table 20–1. The table shows that customer A, for example, is fully current: There are no bills outstanding for more than a month. Customer Z, however, might present problems, as there are $15,000 in bills that have been outstanding for more than 3 months.

aging schedule
Classification of accounts receivable by time outstanding.

Self-Test 20.5 Suppose a customer who buys goods on terms 1/10, net 45, always forgoes the cash discount and pays on the 45th day after sale. If the firm typically buys $10,000 of goods a month, spread evenly over the month, what will the aging schedule look like?

When a customer is in arrears, the usual procedure is to send a *statement of account* and to follow this at intervals with increasingly insistent letters, telephone calls, or fax messages. If none of these has any effect, most companies turn the debt over to a collection agency or an attorney.

Large firms can reap economies of scale in record keeping, billing, and so on, but the small firm may not be able to support a fully fledged credit operation. However, it can obtain some scale economies by farming out part of the job to a *factor.* The factor and its client firm agree on credit limits for each customer, and the client notifies each customer that the factor has purchased the debt (i.e., the trade credit). The factor then takes on the responsibility (and risk) of collecting the bills and pays the invoice value

TABLE 20–1 An aging schedule of receivables

Customer's Name	Less than 1 Month	1–2 Months	2–3 Months	More than 3 Months	Total Owed
A	$ 10,000	$ 0	$ 0	$ 0	$ 10,000
B	8,000	3,000	0	0	11,000
•	•	•	•	•	•
•	•	•	•	•	•
•	•	•	•	•	•
Z	5,000	4,000	6,000	15,000	30,000
Total	$200,000	$40,000	$15,000	$43,000	$298,000

to the client minus a fee of 1 or 2 percent. Aside from gaining the economies that come from specializing in collection for a large number of manufacturers, factors see many more transactions than any single firm and so may be better placed to judge the creditworthiness of each customer.

There is always a potential conflict of interest between the collection department and the sales department. Sales representatives commonly complain that they no sooner win new customers than the collection department frightens them off with threatening letters. The collection manager, on the other hand, bemoans the fact that the sales force is concerned only with winning orders and does not care whether the goods are subsequently paid for. This conflict is another example of the agency problem introduced in Chapter 1. Good collection policy balances conflicting goals. The company wants cordial relations with its customers. It also wants them to pay their bills on time.

There are instances of cooperation between sales managers and the financial managers who worry about collections. For example, the specialty chemicals division of a major pharmaceutical company actually made a business loan to an important customer that had been suddenly cut off by its bank. The pharmaceutical company bet that it knew its customer better than the customer's bank did—and the pharmaceutical company was right. The customer arranged alternative bank financing, paid back the pharmaceutical company, and became an even more loyal customer. It was a nice example of financial management supporting sales.

It is not common for suppliers to make business loans in this way, but they lend money *indirectly* whenever they allow a delay in payment. Trade credit can be an important source of funds for indigent customers that cannot obtain a bank loan. But that raises an important question: If the bank is unwilling to lend, does it make sense for you, the supplier, to continue to extend trade credit? Here are two possible reasons that it may make sense: First, as in the case of our pharmaceutical company, you may have more information than the bank about the customer's business. Second, you need to look beyond the immediate transaction and recognize that your firm may stand to lose some profitable future sales if the customer goes out of business.[7]

20.2 Inventory Management

The second important current asset is *inventory*. Inventories may consist of raw materials, work in process, or finished goods awaiting sale and shipment. Firms are not obliged to carry these inventories. For example, they could buy materials day by day, as needed. But then they would pay higher prices for ordering in small lots, and they would risk production delays if the materials were not delivered on time. They can avoid that risk by ordering more than the firm's immediate needs. Similarly, firms could do away with inventories of finished goods by producing only what they expect to sell tomorrow. But this also could be a dangerous strategy. A producer with only a small inventory of finished goods is more likely to be caught short and unable to fill orders if demand is unexpectedly high. Moreover, a large inventory of finished goods may allow longer, more economical production runs.

But there are also costs to holding inventories that must be set against these benefits. These are called *carrying costs*. For example, money tied up in inventories does not earn interest; storage and insurance must be paid for; and there may be a risk of spillage or obsolescence. Therefore, production managers need to strike a sensible balance between the benefits of holding inventory and the costs.

---

[7] Of course, banks also need to recognize the possibility of continuing business from the firm. The question therefore is whether suppliers have a *greater* stake in the firm's continuing prosperity. For some evidence on the determinants of the supply and demand for trade credit, see M. A. Petersen and R. G. Rajan, "Trade Credit: Theories and Evidence," *Review of Financial Studies* 10 (Fall 1997), pp. 661–692.

Part Six Financial Analysis and Planning

Several mathematical models of optimal inventory management have been developed that attempt to derive the best trade-off between carrying costs, ordering costs, and the potential costs that would be incurred by running out of inventory. These models offer the following lessons:

1. Carrying costs include both the cost of storing goods and the cost of capital tied up in inventory.
2. Optimal inventory levels are lower when carrying costs are high, and they are higher when the cost of restocking inventories is high. This makes sense. If order costs are high, you will want to make larger and therefore less frequent orders, even at the expense of somewhat higher average carrying costs.
3. Average inventory levels are higher when there is more uncertainty about sales and the flow of goods out of inventory.
4. Optimal levels of inventories do not rise in direct proportion to sales. As sales increase, the inventory level rises, but less than proportionately.

Corporations today get by with lower levels of inventory than they used to. Thirty years ago, inventories held by U.S. companies accounted for 12 percent of firm assets. Today the figure is little more than half that.

just-in-time approach
System of inventory management that requires minimal inventories of materials and very frequent deliveries by suppliers.

One way that companies have reduced inventory levels is by moving to a **just-in-time approach.** Just-in-time was pioneered by Toyota in Japan. Toyota keeps inventories of auto parts to a minimum by ordering supplies only as they are needed. Thus deliveries of components to its plants are made throughout the day at intervals as short as 1 hour. Toyota is able to operate successfully with such low inventories only because it has a set of plans to ensure that strikes, traffic snarl-ups, or other hazards don't halt the flow of components and bring production to a standstill. Many companies in the United States have learned from Toyota's example. Thirty years ago Ford used to turn over its inventories about 5 times a year; today that figure is over 20 times.

Firms are also finding that they can reduce their inventories of finished goods by producing their goods to order. For example, Dell Computer discovered that it did not need to keep a large stock of finished machines. Its customers are able to use the Internet to specify what features they want on their PC. The computer is then assembled to order and shipped to the customer.[8]

20.3 Cash Management

Short-term securities pay interest; cash doesn't. So why do corporations and individuals hold billions of dollars in cash and demand deposits? Why, for example, don't you take all *your* cash and invest it in interest-bearing securities? The answer of course is that cash gives you more *liquidity* than do securities. You can use it to buy things. It is hard enough to get New York cab drivers to give you change for a $20 bill, but try asking them to split a Treasury bill.

When you have only a small proportion of your wealth in cash, a little extra can be extremely useful; when you have a substantial holding, any additional liquidity is not worth much. Therefore, as financial manager you want to hold cash balances up to the point where the marginal value of the liquidity is equal to the value of the interest forgone.

In choosing between cash and short-term securities, the financial manager faces a task like that of the production manager. After all, cash is just another raw material that you need to do business, and there are costs and benefits to holding large "inventories" of cash. If the cash were invested in securities, it would earn interest. On the other hand, you can't use those securities to pay the firm's bills. If you had to sell them every

---

[8] These examples of just-in-time and build-to-order production are taken from T. Murphy, "JIT When ASAP Isn't Good Enough," *Ward's Auto World,* May 1999, pp. 67–73; R. Schreffler, "Alive and Well," *Ward's Auto World,* May 1999, pp. 73–77; "A Long March: Mass Customization," *The Economist,* July 14, 2001, pp. 63–65.

Cash Management

Log on to the Web page of a major bank such as the Bank of New York (www.bankofny.com) or Bank of America (www.bankofamerica.com). How do these banks help corporations to manage their cash?

Source: The Bank of New York Web site.

time you needed to pay a bill, you could incur heavy transaction costs. The financial manager must trade off the cost of keeping an inventory of cash (the lost interest) against the benefits (the saving on transaction costs).

For very large firms, the transaction costs of buying and selling securities are trivial compared with the opportunity cost of holding idle cash balances. Suppose that the interest rate is 4 percent per year, or roughly 4/365 = .011 percent per day. Then the daily interest earned on $1 million is .00011 × $1,000,000 = $110. Even at a cost of $50 per transaction, which is generous, it pays to buy Treasury bills today and sell them tomorrow rather than to leave $1 million idle overnight.

A corporation such as Wal-Mart with about $300 billion of annual sales has an average daily cash flow of $300,000,000,000/365, or more than $800 million. Firms of this size end up buying or selling securities once a day, every day, unless by chance they have only a small positive cash balance at the end of the day.

Why do such firms hold any significant amounts of cash? For two reasons. First, cash may be left in non-interest-bearing accounts to compensate banks for the services they provide. Second, large corporations may have literally hundreds of accounts with dozens of different banks. It is often less expensive to leave idle cash in some of these accounts than to monitor each account daily and make daily transfers between them.

One major reason for the proliferation of bank accounts is decentralized management. You cannot give a subsidiary operating freedom to manage its own affairs without giving it the right to spend and receive cash.

Good cash management nevertheless implies some degree of centralization. You cannot maintain your desired inventory of cash if all the subsidiaries in the group are responsible for their own private pools of cash. And you certainly want to avoid situations in which one subsidiary is investing its spare cash at 8 percent while another is borrowing at 10 percent. It is not surprising, therefore, that even in highly decentralized companies there is generally central control over cash balances and bank relations.

Payment Systems

Most small face-to-face purchases are made with dollar bills. But you probably would not want to use cash to buy a new car or to make a purchase over the Internet. There are a variety of ways that you can pay for larger purchases or send payments to another location. Some of the more important payment methods are set out in Table 20–2.

Look now at Figure 20–2. You can see that there are large differences in the ways that people around the world pay for their purchases. For example, checks are almost unknown in Germany, the Netherlands, and Sweden. Most payments in these countries are made by debit cards or credit transfer. By contrast, Americans love to write checks. Each year U.S. individuals and firms make about 37 billion payments by check.

What happens to the checks that you write? Suppose, for example, that you renew your auto insurance by writing a check for $600, which you mail to your insurance company. A day or so later the insurance company receives your check and deposits it

TABLE 20-2 Small face-to-face purchases are commonly paid for in cash, but here are some of the other ways that you can pay your bills.

Check   When you write a check, you are instructing your bank to pay a specified sum on demand to the particular firm or person named on the check.

Credit card   A credit card, such as a Visa card or MasterCard, gives you a line of credit that allows you to make purchases up to a stated limit. At the end of each month, either you pay the credit card company for these purchases or you will be charged interest on any outstanding balance.

Charge card (or **travel and entertainment card)**   A charge card may look like a credit card and you can spend money with it like a credit card. But with a charge card the day of reckoning comes at the end of each month, when you must pay for all purchases that you have made. In other words, you must pay off your entire balance every month.

Debit card   A debit card allows you to have your purchases from a store charged directly to your bank account. The deduction is usually made electronically and is immediate. Often, debit cards may also be used to make withdrawals from a cash machine (ATM).

Credit transfer   With a credit transfer you ask your bank to set up a standing order to make a regular set payment to a supplier. For example, standing orders are often used to make regular fixed mortgage payments.

Direct debit   A direct debit is an instruction to your bank to allow a company to collect varying amounts from your account, as long as you have been given advance notice of the collection amounts and dates. For example, an electric utility company may ask you to set up a direct debit that allows it to receive automatic payment of your electricity bills from your bank account.

in its bank account. But this money isn't available to the company immediately. The company's bank won't actually have the money in hand until it sends the check to your bank and receives payment. Since the bank has to wait, it makes the insurance company wait too—usually 1 or 2 business days. Until the check has been presented and cleared, that $600 will continue to sit in your bank account.

Checks that have been mailed but not yet cleared are known as *float*. In our example, float provided you with an extra $600 in your bank account while the check went first to the insurance company, then to the company's bank, and finally to your own bank. This may make float seem like a marvelous invention, but unfortunately it can also work in reverse. Every time someone writes *you* a check, you have to wait several days after depositing it before you may spend the money.

Speeding Up Collections

Float is the child of delay. Anything that your insurance company can do to lessen that delay will increase its usable cash balances (and reduce yours). You probably have come across attempts by companies to reduce float in your financial transactions. For

FIGURE 20-2 Percentages of total volume of transactions paid for without cash.

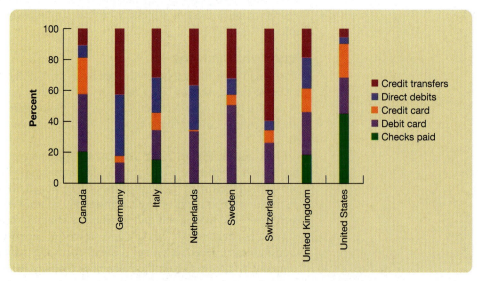

FINANCE IN PRACTICE

How Laidlaw Restructured Its Cash Management

The Canadian company Laidlaw Inc. has more than 4,000 facilities throughout America, operating school bus services, ambulance services, and Greyhound coaches. During the 1990s the company expanded rapidly through acquisition, and its number of banking relationships multiplied until it had 1,000 separate bank accounts with more than 200 different banks. The head office had no way of knowing how much cash was stashed away in these accounts until the end of each quarter, when it was able to construct a consolidated balance sheet.

To economize on the use of cash, Laidlaw's financial manager sought to cut the company's average float from 5 days to 2. At the same time management decided to consolidate cash management at five key banks. This enabled cash to be zero-balanced to a single account for each division and swept daily to Laidlaw's disbursement bank. Because the head office could obtain daily reports of the company's cash position, cash forecasting was improved and the company could reduce its cash needs still further.

Source: Cash management at Laidlaw is described in G. Mann and S. Hutchinson, "Driving Down Working Capital: Laidlaw's Story," *Canadian Treasurer Magazine,* August/September 1999.

---

example, some stores now encourage you to pay bills with your bank debit card. The payment is immediately debited from your bank account, which eliminates the float that you would enjoy if you paid by check or credit card. Similarly, many companies now arrange direct debits with their customers. For instance, if you have a student loan, you may be encouraged to authorize the lender to take the payment automatically from your bank account each month. You save the work of writing regular checks. The lender avoids the labor-intensive process of handling thousands of checks and saves the few days of float during which your checks would have been processed through the banking system.

Firms that receive a large volume of checks have devised a number of ways to make sure that the cash becomes available as quickly as possible. One way to speed up collections is by a method known as **concentration banking.** In this case, customers in a particular area make payments to a local branch office rather than to company headquarters. The local branch office then deposits the checks into a local bank account. Surplus funds are transferred to a *concentration account* at one of the company's principal banks.

concentration banking
System whereby customers make payments to a regional collection center, which then transfers funds to a principal bank.

Concentration banking allows the company to gain quicker use of its funds in two ways. First, because the branch office is nearer to the customer, the mailing time is reduced. Second, because the customers are local, the chances are that they have local bank accounts and therefore the time taken to clear their checks is also reduced. Another advantage is that concentration banking brings many small balances together in one large central balance, which can then be invested in interest-paying assets through a single transaction.

lock-box system
System whereby customers send payments to a post-office box, and a local bank collects and processes checks.

Concentration banking is often combined with a **lock-box system.** In this case, the company rents a locked post-office box in each principal region. All customers within a region are instructed to send their payments to the post-office box. The local bank then takes on the administrative chore of emptying the box (as often as several times a day) and depositing the checks in the company's local account. Surplus funds are transferred periodically to one of the company's principal banks. For a look at how a real company implemented some of these techniques to reduce float, see the nearby Finance in Practice Box.

How many collection points do you need if you use a lock-box system or concentration banking? The answer depends on where your customers are and on the speed of the U.S. mail.

EXAMPLE 20.5 ▶ Lock-Box Systems

Suppose that you are thinking of opening a lock box. The local bank shows you a map of mail delivery times. From that and knowledge of your customers' locations, you come up with the following data:

Average number of daily payments to lock box = 150
Average size of payment   = $1,200
Rate of interest *per day*   = .02 percent
Saving in mailing time   = 1.2 days
Saving in processing time   = .8 day

On this basis, the lock box would reduce collection float by

150 items per day × $1,200 per item × (1.2 + .8) days saved = $360,000

Invested at .02 percent per day, that gives a daily return of

$$.0002 \times \$360,000 = \$72$$

The bank's charge for operating the lock-box system depends on the number of checks processed. Suppose that the bank charges $.26 per check. That works out to 150 × $.26 = $39 per day. You are ahead by $72 – $39 = $33 per day, plus whatever your firm saves from not having to process the checks itself. ◄

Our example assumes that the company has only two choices. It can do nothing, or it can operate the lock box. But maybe there is some other lock-box location, or some mixture of locations, that would be still more effective. Of course, you can always find this out by working through all possible combinations, but many banks have computer programs that find the best locations for lock boxes.[9]

Self-Test 20.6

How will the following conditions affect the price that a firm should be willing to pay for a lock-box service?

a. The average size of its payments increases.
b. The number of payments per day increases (with no change in average size of payments).
c. The interest rate increases.
d. The average mail time saved by the lock-box system increases.
e. The processing time saved by the lock-box system increases.

Recent changes in federal law have also helped to speed up collections. The Check Clearing for the 21st Century Act, usually known as "Check 21," allows banks to send digital images of checks to one another rather than sending the checks themselves. As the new technology becomes more widespread, there will be ever-fewer cargo planes and trucks crisscrossing the country to take bundles of checks from one bank to another, and it will be possible to clear checks in hours.

Electronic Funds Transfer

Throughout the world the use of checks is on the decline. For consumers they are being replaced by debit or credit cards, while many recurring payments are increasingly settled by credit transfer or direct debit (see Table 20–2). Most payments between companies in the United States are now made electronically. Many of these payments involve huge sums of money. Consequently, while electronic funds transfer accounts for only a small proportion of the *number* of transactions, it accounts for 95 percent of the *value* of transactions.

Large-value electronic payments within the United States go through the *Fedwire* system. Fedwire is operated by the Federal Reserve and connects more than 10,000 fi-

---

[9] These usually involve linear programming. Linear programming is an efficient method of hunting through the possible solutions to find the optimal one.

nancial institutions in the United States to the Fed and so to each other. Suppose bank A wires the Fed to transfer $1 million from its account with the Fed to the account of bank B. Bank A's account is immediately reduced by $1 million, and bank B's is increased at the same time.

Fedwire is used to make high-value payments. Bulk payments such as wages, dividends, and payments to suppliers generally travel through the *Automated Clearinghouse (ACH)* system. The company simply needs to provide a computer file of instructions to its bank, which then debits the company's account and forwards the payments to the ACH system.

Electronic payment systems have several advantages:

- Record keeping and routine transactions are easy to automate when money moves electronically.
- The marginal cost of transactions is very low. For example, a transfer using Fedwire typically costs about $10, while it costs only a few cents to make each ACH payment.
- Float is reduced. For example, cash managers at Occidental Petroleum found that one plant was paying out about $8 million a month several days early to avoid any risk of late fees if checks were delayed in the mail. The solution was obvious: The plant's managers switched to paying large bills electronically; that way they could ensure payments arrived exactly on time.

International Cash Management

Cash management in domestic firms is child's play compared with that in large multinational corporations operating in dozens of different countries, each with its own currency, banking system, and legal structure.

A single centralized cash management system is an unattainable ideal for these companies, although they are edging toward it. For example, suppose that you are treasurer of a large multinational company with operations throughout Europe. You could allow the separate businesses to manage their own cash, but that would be costly and would almost certainly result in each one accumulating little hoards of cash. The solution is to set up a regional system. In this case the company establishes a local concentration account with a bank in each country. Any surplus cash is swept daily into central multicurrency accounts in London or another European banking center. This cash is then invested in marketable securities or used to finance any subsidiaries that have a cash shortage.

Payments can also be made out of the regional center. For example, to pay wages in each European country, the company just needs to send its principal bank a computer file with details of the payments to be made. The bank then finds the least costly way to transfer the cash from the company's central accounts and arranges for the funds to be credited on the correct day to the employees in each country.

Most large multinationals have several banks in each country, but the more banks they use, the less control they have over their cash balances. So development of regional cash management systems favors banks that can offer a worldwide branch network. These banks can also afford the high costs of setting up computer systems for handling cash payments and receipts in different countries.

20.4 Investing Idle Cash: The Money Market

money market

Market for short-term financial assets.

When firms have excess funds, they can invest the surplus in a variety of securities in the **money market,** the market for short-term financial assets. Larger firms usually invest directly in these securities. However, smaller firms often park their spare cash in a money market mutual fund, which holds a portfolio of money market investments.

Only fixed-income securities with maturities less than 1 year are considered to be part of the money market. In fact, however, most instruments in the money market have considerably shorter maturity. Limiting maturity has two advantages for the cash manager. First, short-term securities entail little interest rate risk. Recall from Chapter 5 that price risk due to interest rate fluctuations increases with maturity. Very short-term securities, therefore, have almost no interest rate risk. Second, it is far easier to gauge the risk of default over short horizons. One need not worry as much about deterioration in financial strength over a 90-day horizon as over the 30-year life of a bond. These considerations imply that high-quality money market securities are a safe "parking spot" to keep idle balances until they are converted back to cash.

Most money market securities are also highly marketable or *liquid,* meaning that it is easy and cheap to sell the asset for cash. This property, too, is an attractive feature of securities used as temporary investments until cash is needed.

Some of the important instruments of the money market are:

Treasury bills. Treasury bills are issued weekly by the U.S. government and mature in 4 weeks, 3 months, or 6 months. They are the safest and most liquid money market instrument.

Commercial paper. This is the short-term, usually unsecured, debt of large and well-known companies. While maturities can range up to 270 days before registration with the SEC is required, most commercial paper is issued with maturities of less than 2 months. Because there is no active trading in commercial paper, it has low marketability. Therefore, it would not be an appropriate investment for a firm that could not hold it until maturity. Both Moody's and Standard & Poor's rate commercial paper in terms of the default risk of the issuer.

Certificates of deposit. CDs are time deposits at banks, usually in denominations greater than $100,000. Unlike demand deposits (checking accounts), time deposits cannot be withdrawn from the bank on demand: The bank pays interest and principal only at the maturity of the deposit. However, short-term CDs (with maturities less than 3 months) are actively traded, so a firm can easily sell the security if it needs cash.

Repurchase agreements. Also known as *repos,* repurchase agreements are, in effect, collateralized loans. A government bond dealer sells Treasury securities to an investor, with an agreement to repurchase them at a later date at a higher price. The increase in price serves as implicit interest, so the investor in effect is lending money to the dealer, first giving money to the dealer and later getting it back with interest. The bills serve as collateral for the loan: If the dealer fails, and cannot buy back the bill, the investor can keep it. Repurchase agreements are usually very short-term, with maturities of only a few days.

In the last chapter, we saw that interest rates on short-term loans (loans of less than 1 year) are often quoted on a so-called *discount basis.* For example, a $95,000 loan might require repayment of $100,000 in 1 year. On a discount basis, the rate would be *quoted* as the discount from face value, in this case 5 percent. The actual interest rate is a bit higher than this. You pay interest of $5,000 on a $95,000 loan, so the interest rate is $5,000/$95,000 = .0526, or 5.26 percent. You should be aware that rates in the money market also are typically quoted on a discount basis.

EXAMPLE 20.6 ▶ **Money Market Rates**

A Treasury bill with face value $100,000 and maturity 6 months is sold for $98,000. The rate on this bill on a discount basis would be quoted as 4 percent. The actual discount from face value is 2 percent semiannually, or 4 percent on an annualized basis. Notice also that money market rates are annualized using simple, not compound, interest. The *effective* annual rate on this half-year investment can be found by solving

$$98,000 \times (1 + r)^{1/2} = 100,000$$

which implies that $r = .0412$, or 4.12 percent. ◀

Yields on Money Market Investments

When we value long-term debt, it is important to take account of default risk. Almost anything may happen in 30 years, and even today's most respectable company may get into trouble eventually. Therefore, corporate bonds offer higher yields than Treasury bonds.

Short-term debt is not risk-free either. When California was mired in the energy crisis of 2001, Southern California Edison and Pacific Gas and Electric were forced to suspend payments on nearly $1 billion of maturing commercial paper. However, such examples are exceptions; in general, the danger of default is less for money market securities issued by corporations than for corporate bonds. There are two reasons for this. First, as we pointed out above, the range of possible outcomes is smaller for short-term investments. Even though the distant future may be clouded, you can usually be confident that a particular company will survive for at least the next month. Second, for the most part only well-established companies can borrow in the money market. If you are going to lend money for just a few days, you can't afford to spend too much time in evaluating the loan. Thus, you will consider only blue-chip borrowers.

Despite the high quality of money market investments, there are often significant differences in yield between corporate and U.S. government securities. Why is this? One answer is the risk of default. Another is that the investments have different degrees of liquidity, or "moneyness." Investors like Treasury bills because they are easily turned into cash on short notice. Securities that cannot be converted so quickly and cheaply into cash need to offer relatively high yields.

During times of market turmoil investors may place a higher value on having ready access to cash. On these occasions the yield on illiquid securities can increase dramatically. This happened in the fall of 1998 when a large hedge fund, Long Term Capital Management (LTCM), came close to collapse.[10] Fearful that LTCM would be forced to liquidate its huge positions, investors shrank from illiquid securities, and there was a "flight to quality." The spread between the yields on commercial paper and Treasury bills rose to about 120 basis points (1.2 percent), almost four times its level at the beginning of the year.

The International Money Market

In addition to the domestic money market, there is also an international market for short-term dollar investments, which is known as the *eurodollar* market. Eurodollars have nothing to do with the euro, the currency of the European Monetary Union (EMU). They are simply dollars deposited in a bank in Europe. For example, suppose that an American oil company buys crude oil from an Arab sheik and pays for it with a $1 million check drawn on JP Morgan Chase. The sheik then deposits the check with his account at Barclays Bank in London. As a result, Barclays has an asset in the form of a $1 million credit in its account with JP Morgan Chase. It also has an offsetting liability in the form of a dollar deposit. Since that dollar deposit is placed in Europe, it is called a eurodollar deposit.[11]

Just as there is both a domestic U.S. money market and a eurodollar market, so there is both a domestic Japanese money market and a market in London for euroyen. So if a U.S. corporation wishes to make a short-term investment in yen, it can deposit the yen with a bank in Tokyo or it can make a euroyen deposit in London. Similarly, there is both a domestic money market in the euro area as well as a money market for euros in London. And so on.

---

[10] Hedge funds specialize in making positive investments in securities that are believed to be underpriced, while selling short those that appear overvalued. The story of LTCM is told in R. Lowenstein, *When Genius Failed: The Rise and Fall of Long Term Capital Management* (New York: Random House, 2000), and N. Dunbar, *Inventing Money: The Story of Long Term Capital Management and the Legends behind It* (New York: Wiley, 2000).

[11] The sheik could equally well deposit the check with the London branch of a U.S. bank or a Japanese bank. He would still have made a eurodollar deposit.

Major international banks in London lend dollars to one another at the *London Interbank Offered Rate* (LIBOR). Similarly, they lend yen to each other at the yen LIBOR interest rate, and they lend euros at the euro interbank offered rate, or Euribor. These interest rates are used as a benchmark for pricing many types of short-term loans in the United States and in other countries. For example, a corporation in the United States may issue a floating-rate note with interest payments tied to dollar LIBOR.

SUMMARY

What are the usual steps in credit management?

The first step in credit management is to set normal **terms of sale.** This means that you must decide the length of the payment period and the size of any cash discounts. In most industries these conditions are fairly standardized.

Your second step is to decide the form of the contract with your customer. Most domestic sales are made on **open account.** In this case the only evidence that the customer owes you money is the entry in your ledger and a receipt signed by the customer. Sometimes, you may require a more formal commitment before you deliver the goods. For example, the supplier may arrange for the customer to provide a trade acceptance.

The third task is to assess each customer's creditworthiness. When you have made an assessment of the customer's credit standing, the fourth step is to establish sensible credit policy. Finally, once the credit policy is set, you need to establish a collection policy to identify and pursue slow payers.

How do we measure the implicit interest rate on credit?

The effective interest rate for customers who buy goods on credit rather than taking the discount for quicker payment is

$$\left(1 + \frac{\text{discount}}{\text{discounted price}}\right)^{365/\text{extra days credit}} - 1$$

When does it make sense to ask the customer for a formal IOU?

When a customer places a large order, and you want to eliminate the possibility of any subsequent disputes about the existence, amount, and scheduled payment date of the debt, a formal IOU such as a signed commercial draft may be appropriate.

How do firms assess the probability that a customer will pay?

Credit analysis is the process of deciding which customers are likely to pay their bills. There are various sources of information: your own experience with the customer, the experience of other creditors, the assessment of a credit agency, a check with the customer's bank, the market value of the customer's securities, and an analysis of the customer's financial statements. Firms that handle a large volume of credit information often use a formal system for combining the various sources into an overall credit score.

How do firms decide whether it makes sense to grant credit to a customer?

Credit policy refers to the decision to extend credit to a customer. The job of the credit manager is not to minimize the number of bad debts; it is to maximize profits. This means that you need to weigh the odds that the customer will pay, providing you with a profit, against the odds that the customer will default, resulting in a loss. Remember not to be too shortsighted when reckoning the expected profit. It is often worth accepting the marginal applicant if there is a chance that the applicant may become a regular and reliable customer.

If credit is granted, the next problem is to set a **collection policy.** This requires tact and judgment. You want to be firm with the truly delinquent customer, but you don't want to offend the good one by writing demanding letters just because a check has been delayed in the mail. You will find it easier to spot troublesome accounts if you keep a careful **aging schedule** of outstanding accounts.

What are the costs and benefits of holding inventories and cash?

The benefit of higher inventory levels is the reduction in order costs associated with re-stocking and the reduced chances of running out of material. The costs are the carrying costs, which include the cost of space, insurance, spoilage, and the opportunity cost of the capital tied up in inventory. Cash provides liquidity, but it doesn't pay interest. Securities pay interest, but you can't use them to buy things. As financial manager you want to hold cash up to the point where the incremental or marginal benefit of liquidity is equal to the cost of holding cash, that is, the interest that you could earn on securities.

What is float, and why can it be valuable?

The cash shown in the company ledger is not the same as the available balance in its bank account. When you write a check, it takes time before your bank balance is adjusted downward. During this time your available balance at the bank will be larger than your company's ledger balance. When you deposit a check, there is a delay before it gets credited to your bank account. This reduces your available balance compared to your ledger balance. Your net float is the difference between the balance in your company ledger and the balance recognized by your bank. If you can predict how long it will take checks to clear, you may be able to "play the float" and get by on a smaller cash balance. The interest you can thereby earn on the net float is a source of value.

What are some tactics to increase net float?

You can manage the float by speeding up collections. One way to do this is by **concentration banking.** Customers make payments to a regional office, which then pays the checks into a local bank account. Surplus funds are transferred from the local account to a concentration bank. A related technique is **lock-box banking.** In this case customers send their payments to a local post-office box. A local bank empties the box at regular intervals and clears the checks. Concentration banking and lock-box banking reduce mailing time and the time required to clear checks. As check clearing speeds up, for example, because of changes such as those introduced by the Check 21 Act, these techniques presumably will become less important. Similarly, as the trend toward electronic payments progresses, these delays in clearing payments will continue to fall even without sophisticated cash management strategies.

Where do firms invest excess funds until they are needed to pay bills?

Firms can invest idle cash in the **money market,** the market for short-term financial assets. These assets tend to be short-term, low risk, and highly liquid, making them ideal instruments in which to invest funds for short periods of time before cash is needed.

QUIZ

1. **Trade Credit Rates.** Company X sells on a 1/20, net 60, basis. Customer Y buys goods with an invoice of $1,000.

   a. How much can company Y deduct from the bill if it pays on day 20?
   b. How many extra days of credit can company Y receive if it passes up the cash discount?
   c. What is the effective annual rate of interest if Y pays on the due date rather than day 20?

2. **Terms of Sale.** Complete the following passage by selecting the appropriate terms from the following list (some terms may be used more than once): *acceptance, open, commercial, trade, the United States, his or her own, draft, account, bank, banker's, the customer's.*

   Most goods are sold on _____ _____. In this case the only evidence of the debt is a record in the seller's books and a signed receipt. An alternative is for the seller to arrange a(n) _____ _____ ordering payment by the customer. In order to obtain the goods, the customer must acknowledge this order and sign the document. This signed acknowledgment is known as a(n) _____ _____. Sometimes the seller may also ask _____ _____ bank to sign the document. In this case it is known as a(n) _____ _____.

3. **Terms of Sale.** Indicate which firm of each pair you would expect to grant shorter or longer credit periods:

a. One firm sells hardware; the other sells bread.

b. One firm's customers have an inventory turnover ratio of 10; the other's customers have turnover of 15.

c. One firm sells mainly to electric utilities; the other to fashion boutiques.

4. **Payment Lag.** The lag between purchase date and the date at which payment is due is known as the *terms lag.* The lag between the due date and the date on which the buyer actually pays is termed the *due lag,* and the lag between the purchase and actual payment dates is the *pay lag.* Thus

$$\text{Pay lag} = \text{terms lag} + \text{due lag}$$

State how you would expect the following events to affect each type of lag:

a. The company imposes a service charge on late payers.

b. A recession causes customers to be short of cash.

c. The company changes its terms from net 10 to net 20.

5. **Trade Credit Rates.** A firm currently offers terms of sale of 3/20, net 40. What effect will the following actions have on the implicit interest rate charged to customers that pass up the cash discount? State whether the implicit interest rate will increase or decrease.

a. The terms are changed to 4/20, net 40.

b. The terms are changed to 3/30, net 40.

c. The terms are changed to 3/20, net 30.

6. **Float.** On January 25, Coot Company has $250,000 deposited with a local bank. On January 27, the company writes and mails checks of $20,000 and $60,000 to suppliers. At the end of the month, Coot's financial manager deposits a $45,000 check received from a customer in the morning mail and picks up the end-of-month account summary from the bank. The manager notes that only the $20,000 payment of the 27th has cleared the bank. What is the company's ledger balance with its bank? What is the company's net float?

7. **Float.** Most banks now allow you to pay your bills over the Internet. You log on to your account to tell the bank which payments it should send out on your behalf. Whereas most banks charge you for writing paper checks, they do not charge for this Internet bill-paying service and, in fact, do not even charge you for their cost of postage. Why are the banks willing to provide this service to you for no fee?

8. **Float.** General Products writes checks that average $20,000 daily. These checks take an average of 6 days to clear. It receives payments that average $22,000 daily. It takes 3 days before these checks are available to the firm.

a. Calculate the firm's net float due to payment delays.

b. What would be General Products's annual savings if it could obtain access to the payments it receives within 2 days? The interest rate is 6 percent per year.

9. **Lock Boxes.** Anne Teak, the financial manager of a furniture manufacturer, is considering operating a lock-box system. She forecasts that 400 payments a day will be made to lock boxes with an average payment size of $2,000. The bank's charge for operating the lock boxes is $.40 a check. The interest rate is .015 percent per day.

a. If the lock box saves 2 days in collection float, is it worthwhile to adopt the system?

b. What minimum reduction in the time to collect and process each check is needed to justify use of the lock-box system?

10. **Cash Management.** Complete the passage that follows by choosing the appropriate terms from the following list: *lock-box banking. Fedwire, concentration banking.*

Firms can increase their cash resources by speeding up collections. One way to do this is to arrange for payments to be made to regional offices which pay the checks into local banks. This is known as _____. Surplus funds are then transferred from the local bank to one of the company's main banks. Transfers can be made electronically through the _____ system. Another technique is to arrange for a local bank to collect the checks directly from a post office. This is known as _____.

PRACTICE PROBLEMS

11. **Trade Credit and Receivables.** A firm offers terms of 3/15, net 30. Currently, two-thirds of all customers take advantage of the trade discount; the remainder pay bills at the due date.

    a. What will be the firm's typical value for its accounts receivable period? (See Chapter 19, Section 19.1, for a review of the accounts receivable period.)
    b. What is the average investment in accounts receivable if annual sales are $20 million?
    c. What would likely happen to the firm's accounts receivable period if it changed its terms to 4/15, net 30?

12. **Terms of Sale.** Microbiotics currently sells all of its frozen dinners cash on delivery but believes it can increase sales by offering supermarkets 1 month of free credit. The price per carton is $50, and the cost per carton is $40.

    a. If unit sales will increase from 1,000 cartons to 1,060 per month, should the firm offer the credit? The interest rate is 1 percent per month, and all customers will pay their bills.
    b. What if the interest rate is 1.5 percent per month?
    c. What if the interest rate is 1.5 percent per month but the firm can offer the credit only as a special deal to new customers, while old customers will continue to pay cash on delivery?

13. **Credit Decision/Repeat Sales.** Locust Software sells computer training packages to its business customers at a price of $101. The cost of production (in present value terms) is $96. Locust sells its packages on terms of net 30 and estimates that about 7 percent of all orders will be uncollectible. An order comes in for 20 units. The interest rate is 1 percent per month.

    a. Should the firm extend credit if this is a one-time order? The sale will not be made unless credit is extended.
    b. What is the break-even probability of collection?
    c. Now suppose that if a customer pays this month's bill, it will place an identical order in each month indefinitely and can be safely assumed to pose no risk of default. Should credit be extended?
    d. What is the break-even probability of collection in the repeat-sales case?

14. **Credit Decision.** Look back at Example 20.3. Cast Iron's costs have increased from $1,000 to $1,050. Assuming there is no possibility of repeat orders, and that the probability of successful collection from the customer is $p = .95$, answer the following:

    a. Should Cast Iron grant or refuse credit?
    b. What is the break-even probability of collection?

15. **Credit Analysis.** Financial ratios were described in Chapter 17. If you were the credit manager, to which financial ratios would you pay most attention?

16. **Credit Decision.** The Branding Iron Company sells its irons for $60 apiece wholesale. Production cost is $50 per iron. There is a 25 percent chance that a prospective customer will go bankrupt within the next half-year. The customer orders 1,000 irons and asks for 6 months' credit. Should you accept the order? Assume an 8 percent per year discount rate, no chance of a repeat order, and that the customer will pay either in full or not at all.

17. **Credit Policy.** As treasurer of the Universal Bed Corporation, Aristotle Procrustes is worried about his bad debt ratio, which is currently running at 6 percent. He believes that imposing a more stringent credit policy might reduce sales by 5 percent and reduce the bad debt ratio to 4 percent. If the cost of goods sold is 80 percent of the selling price, should Mr. Procrustes adopt the more stringent policy?

18. **Credit Decision/Repeat Sales.** Surf City sells its network browsing software for $15 per copy to computer software distributors and allows its customers 1 month to pay their bills. The cost of the software is $10 per copy. The industry is very new and unsettled, however, and the probability that a new customer granted credit will go bankrupt within the next month is 25 percent. The firm is considering switching to a cash-on-delivery credit policy to reduce its exposure to defaults on trade credit. The discount rate is 1 percent per month.

    a. Should the firm switch to a cash-on-delivery policy? If it does so, its sales will fall by 40 percent.

b. How would your answer change if a customer that is granted credit and pays its bills can be expected to generate repeat orders with negligible likelihood of default for each of the next 6 months? Similarly, customers that pay cash also will generate on average 6 months of repeat sales.

19. **Credit Policy.** A firm currently makes only cash sales. It estimates that allowing trade credit on terms of net 30 would increase monthly sales from 100 to 110 units per month. The price per unit is $101, and the cost (in present value terms) is $80. The interest rate is 1 percent per month.

a. Should the firm change its credit policy?
b. Would your answer to (a) change if 5 percent of all customers will fail to pay their bills under the new credit policy?
c. What if 5 percent of only the *new* customers fail to pay their bills? The current customers take advantage of the 30 days of free credit but remain safe credit risks.

20. **Lock Boxes.** Sherman's Sherbet currently takes about 6 days to collect and deposit checks from customers. A lock-box system could reduce this time to 4 days. Collections average $15,000 daily. The interest rate is .02 percent per day.

a. By how much will the lock-box system reduce float?
b. What is the daily interest savings of the system?
c. Suppose the lock-box service is offered for a fixed monthly fee instead of payment per check. What is the maximum monthly fee that Sherman's should be willing to pay for this service? (Assume a 30-day month.)

21. **Lock Boxes.** The financial manager of JAC Cosmetics is considering opening a lock box in Pittsburgh. Checks cleared through the lock box will amount to $300,000 per month. The lock box will make cash available to the company 3 days earlier.

a. Suppose that the bank offers to run the lock box for a $25,000 compensating balance. Is the lock box worthwhile?
b. Suppose that the bank offers to run the lock box for a fee of $.10 per check cleared instead of a compensating balance. What must the average check size be for the fee alternative to be less costly? Assume an interest rate of 6 percent per year.
c. Why did you need to know the interest rate to answer (b) but not to answer (a)?

22. **Collection Policy.** Major Manufacturing currently has one bank account located in New York to handle all of its collections. The firm keeps a compensating balance of $300,000 to pay for these services (see Section 19.7). It is considering opening a bank account with West Coast National Bank to speed up collections from its many California-based customers. Major estimates that the West Coast account would reduce collection time by 1 day on the $1 million a day of business that it does with its California-based customers. If it opens the account, it can reduce the compensating balance with its New York bank to $200,000 since it will do less business in New York. However, West Coast also will require a compensating balance of $200,000. Should Major open the new account?

23. **Cash Management.** Suppose that the rate of interest increases from 4 to 8 percent per year. Would firms' cash balances go up or down relative to sales? Explain.

CHALLENGE PROBLEMS

24. **Credit Analysis.** Use the data in Example 20.3. Now suppose, however, that 10 percent of Cast Iron's customers are slow payers and that slow payers have a probability of 30 percent of defaulting on their bills. If it costs $5 to determine whether a customer has been a prompt or slow payer in the past, should Cast Iron undertake such a check? *Hint:* What is the expected savings from the credit check? It will depend on both the probability of uncovering a slow payer and the savings from denying these payers credit.

25. **Credit Analysis.** Look back at the previous problem, but now suppose that if a customer defaults on a payment, you can eventually collect about half the amount owed to you. Will you be more or less tempted to pay for a credit check once you account for the possibility of partial recovery of debts?

26. **Credit Policy.** Jim Khana, the credit manager of Velcro Saddles, is reappraising the company's credit policy. Velcro sells on terms of net 30. Cost of goods sold is 85 percent of sales. Velcro classifies customers on a scale of 1 to 4. During the past 5 years, the collection experience was as follows:

Classification	Defaults as Percentage of Sales	Average Collection Period in Days for Nondefaulting Accounts
1	0	45
2	2	42
3	10	50
4	20	85

The average interest rate was 15 percent. What conclusions (if any) can you draw about Velcro's credit policy? Should the firm deny credit to any of its customers? What other factors should be taken into account before changing this policy?

27. **Credit Analysis.** Galenic, Inc., is a wholesaler for a range of pharmaceutical products. Before deducting any losses from bad debts, Galenic operates on a profit margin of 5 percent. For a long time the firm has employed a numerical credit scoring system based on a small number of key ratios. This has resulted in a bad debt ratio of 1 percent.

Galenic has recently commissioned a detailed statistical study of the payment record of its customers over the past 8 years and, after considerable experimentation, has identified five variables that could form the basis of a new credit scoring system. On the evidence of the past 8 years, Galenic calculates that for every 10,000 accounts it would have experienced the following default rates:

Credit Score under Proposed System	Number of Accounts		
	Defaulting	Paying	Total
Better than 80	60	9,100	9,160
Worse than 80	40	800	840
Total	100	9,900	10,000

By refusing credit to firms with a poor credit score (worse than 80) Galenic calculates that it would reduce its bad debt ratio to 60/9,160, or just under .7 percent. While this may not seem like a big deal, Galenic's credit manager reasons that this is equivalent to a decrease of one-third in the bad debt ratio and would result in a significant improvement in the profit margin.

a. What is Galenic's current profit margin, allowing for bad debts?
b. Assuming that the firm's estimates of default rates are right, how would the new credit scoring system affect profits?
c. Why might you suspect that Galenic's estimates of default rates will not be realized in practice?
d. Suppose that one of the variables in the proposed new scoring system is whether the customer has an existing account with Galenic (new customers are more likely to default). How would this affect your assessment of the proposal? *Hint:* Think about repeat sales.

Go to Market Insight at **www.mhhe.com/edumarketinsight**.

STANDARD
&POOR'S

1. Look at the financial statements of Ann Taylor Stores (ANN) and Buckle, Inc. (BKE), two fashion-clothing retailers. Compare the inventory level and turnover of each. What might explain the differences you uncover?

2. Check out the recent performance of two very nice coffee shops with attached free reading rooms: Barnes & Noble, Inc. (BKS), and Borders Group (BGP). These firms are sometimes characterized as "inventory businesses." Why? How does their inventory management compare?

3. Compare and contrast the accounts receivable turnover and days' sales outstanding for Peets Coffee & Tea, Inc. (PEET), and Harrahs Entertainment, Inc. (HET). Read the business description for information that may explain the level of each company's investment in accounts receivables.

4. Calculate the Z score for General Motors (GM) over the last 3 years. You can find GM's relevant ratios in the Excel Analytics section. What do you think has happened to its bond rating over this period?

SOLUTIONS TO SELF-TEST QUESTIONS

20.1 To get the cash discount, you have to pay the bill within 10 days, that is, by May 11. With the 2 percent discount, the amount that needs to be paid by May 11 is $20,000 × .98 = $19,600. If you forgo the cash discount, you do not have to pay your bill until May 21, but on that date, the amount due is $20,000.

20.2 The cash discount in this case is 5 percent, and customers who choose not to take the discount receive an extra 50 − 10 = 40 days credit. So the effective annual interest is

$$\text{Effective annual rate} = \left(1 + \frac{\text{discount}}{\text{discounted price}}\right)^{365/\text{extra days credit}} - 1$$

$$= \left(1 + \frac{5}{95}\right)^{365/40} - 1 = .597, \text{ or } 59.7\%$$

In this case the customer who does not take the discount is effectively borrowing money at an annual interest rate of 59.7 percent. This is higher than the rate in Example 20.1 because fewer days of credit are obtained by forfeiting the discount.

20.3 The present value of costs is still $1,000. Present value of revenues is now $1,100. The break-even probability is defined by

$$p \times 100 - (1 - p) \times 1,000 = 0$$

which implies that $p = .909$. The break-even probability is higher because the profit margin is now lower. The firm cannot afford as high a bad debt ratio as before since it is not making as much on its successful sales. We conclude that high-margin goods will be offered with more liberal credit terms.

20.4 The higher the discount rate the less important are future sales. Because the present value of repeat sales is lower, the break-even probability on the initial sale is higher. For instance, we saw that the break-even probability was 1/3 when the discount rate was 10 percent. When the discount rate is 20 percent, the present value of a perpetual flow of repeat sales falls to $200/.20 = $1,000, and the break-even probability increases to 1/2:

$$1/2 \times \$1,000 - 1/2 \times \$1,000 = 0$$

20.5 The customer pays bills 45 days after the invoice date. Because goods are purchased daily, at any time there will be bills outstanding with "ages" ranging from 1 to 45 days. At any time, the customer will have 30 days' worth of purchases, or $10,000, outstanding for a period of up to 1 month and have 15 days' worth of purchases, or $5,000, outstanding for between 1 month and 45 days. The aging schedule will appear as follows:

Age of Account	Amount
< 1 month	$10,000
1–2 months	5,000

20.6 The benefit of the lock-box system, and the price the firm should be willing to pay for the system, is higher when:
   a. Payment size is higher (since interest is earned on more funds).
   b. Payments per day are higher (since interest is earned on more funds).
   c. The interest rate is higher (since the cost of float is higher).
   d. Mail time saved is higher (since more float is saved).
   e. Processing time saved is higher (since more float is saved).

MINICASE

George Stamper, a credit analyst with Micro-Encapsulators Corp. (MEC), needed to respond to an urgent e-mail request from the southeast sales office. The local sales manager reported that she had an opportunity to clinch an order from Miami Spice (MS) for 50 encapsulators at $10,000 each. She added that she was particularly keen to secure this order since MS was likely to have a continuing need for 50 encapsulators a year and could therefore prove a very valuable customer. However, orders of this size to a new customer generally required head office agreement, and it was therefore George's responsibility to make a rapid assessment of MS's creditworthiness and to approve or disapprove the sale.

Mr. Stamper knew that MS was a medium-sized company with a patchy earnings record. After growing rapidly in the 1980s, MS had encountered strong competition in its principal markets and earnings had fallen sharply. Mr. Stamper was not sure exactly to what extent this was a bad omen. New management had been brought in to cut costs, and there were some indications that the worst was over for the company. Investors appeared to agree with this assessment, for the stock price had risen to $5.80 from its low of $4.25 the previous year. Mr. Stamper had in front of him MS's latest financial statements, which are summarized in Table 20–3. He rapidly calculated a few key financial ratios and the company's Z score.

Mr. Stamper also made a number of other checks on MS. The company had a small issue of bonds outstanding, which were rated B by Moody's. Inquiries through MEC's bank indicated that MS had unused lines of credit totaling $5 million but had entered into discussions with its bank for a renewal of a $15 million bank loan that was due to be repaid at the end of the year. Telephone calls to MS's other suppliers suggested that the company had recently been 30 days late in paying its bills.

Mr. Stamper also needed to take into account the profit that the company could make on MS's order. Encapsulators were sold on standard terms of 2/30, net 60. So if MS paid promptly, MEC would receive additional revenues of $50 \times \$9,800 = \$490,000$. However, given MS's cash position, it was more than likely that it would forgo the cash discount and would not pay until sometime after the 60 days. Since interest rates were about 8 percent, any such delays in payment would reduce the present value to MEC of the revenues. Mr. Stamper also recognized that there were production and transportation costs in filling MS's order. These worked out at $475,000, or $9,500 a unit. Corporate profits were taxed at 35 percent.

TABLE 20–3 Miami Spice: Summary financial statements (figures in millions of dollars)

	2006	2005
Assets		
Current assets		
Cash and marketable securities	5.0	12.2
Accounts receivable	16.2	15.7
Inventories	27.5	32.5
Total current assets	48.7	60.4
Fixed assets		
Property, plant, and equipment	228.5	228.1
Less accumulated depreciation	129.5	127.6
Net fixed assets	99.0	100.5
Total assets	147.7	160.9
Liabilities and Shareholders' Equity		
Current liabilities		
Debt due for repayment	22.8	28.0
Accounts payable	19.0	16.2
Total current liabilities	41.8	44.2
Long-term debt	40.8	42.3
Shareholders' equity		
Common stock*	10.0	10.0
Retained earnings	55.1	64.4
Total shareholders' equity	65.1	74.4
Total liabilities and shareholders' equity	147.7	160.9
Income Statement		
Revenue	149.8	134.4
Cost of goods sold	131.0	124.2
Other expenses	1.7	8.7
Depreciation	8.1	8.6
Earnings before interest and taxes	9.0	– 7.1
Interest expense	5.1	5.6
Income taxes	1.4	– 4.4
Net income	2.5	– 8.3
Allocation of net income		
Addition to retained earnings	1.5	– 9.3
Dividends	1.0	1.0

*10 million shares, $1 par value.

QUESTIONS

1. What can you say about Miami Spice's creditworthiness?
2. What is the break-even probability of default? How is it affected by the delay before MS pays its bills?
3. How should George Stamper's decision be affected by the possibility of repeat orders?

7

Special Topics

Mergers, Acquisitions, and Corporate Control

RELATED WEB LINKS

SourceMedia

Mergers&Acquisitions Report

Covering M&A, distressed situations and other corporate restructurings

HOME | ABOUT US | EDITORIAL | CONTACT | August 29, 2005

LOGIN NOW
SUBSCRIBE NOW
FREE TRIAL

NEWS UPDATES
WEEKLY HEADLINES
FOR SUBSCRIBERS ONLY

DEALFLOW ALERT
INDUSTRY TRENDS
BANKRUPTCY/ DISTRESSED
BANKER/ FIRM UPDATES
LEGAL/ REGULATORY
NEWS
M&A DATABASE
US Public M&A Activity
Private Targets
Divestitures
Withdrawn Deals
Smallcap Summary
Completed Transactions
SEARCH ARCHIVES

News Updates

Redstone Raises Midway Stake Yet Again
Judy Radler Cohen
(Login For Full Story)
Today, Sumner Redstone filed yet again on $1.35 billion market cap Midway Games Inc. Now the chairman and chief executive officer of Viacom Inc. owns 85.75% of Midway.

Polymer Group Climbs Down from the Block
Joshua Hamerman
(Login For Full Story)
Polymer Group Inc. (PGI) has crossed a sale off its list of strategic alternatives. And the $285 million market cap plastic products maker is no longer retaining JPMorgan to assist with a strategic review.

Lee Enterprises Plans New Deal Debt
Mark Cecil
(Login For Full Story)
Fresh off a large deal, newspaper publisher Lee Enterprises Inc. filed a hefty shelf registration as it looks to a future of small dealmaking.

The monthly publication you need now more than ever.

Mergers&Acquisitions

www.cfonews.com

money.cnn.com/news For news on current merger activity.

www.mergerstat.com Articles and some data on merger activity.

biz.yahoo.com/me Merger calendar at Yahoo! Finance.

www.mareport.com Online newsletter covering mergers, acquisitions, and restructurings.

www.corporateaffiliations.com Who owns whom; allows a trial subscription.

Procter & Gamble agrees to buy Gillette in a $57 billion deal. Management of both firms is obviously delighted with the deal, but mergers can often end in tears.

Associated Press/AP

In recent years the scale and pace of merger activity have been remarkable. For example, Table 21–1 lists just a few of the more important mergers of 2004 and 2005. All these mergers were between two U.S. companies, but many of the largest mergers have involved firms in different countries. These cross-border mergers include such giant combinations as BP and Amoco ($48 billion), Daimler and Chrysler ($38 billion), and Vodafone and Mannesmann ($203 billion). During periods of intense merger activity financial managers spend considerable time either searching for firms to acquire or worrying whether some other firm is about to take over their company.

When one company buys another, it is making an investment, and the basic principles of capital investment decisions apply. You should go ahead with the purchase if it makes a net contribution to shareholders' wealth. But mergers are often awkward transactions to evaluate, and you have to be careful to define benefits and costs properly.

Many mergers are arranged amicably, but in other cases one firm will make a hostile takeover bid for the other. We describe the principal techniques of modern merger warfare, and since the threat of hostile takeovers has stimulated corporate restructurings and leveraged buyouts (LBOs), we describe them too and attempt to explain why these deals have generated rewards for investors. We close with a look at who gains and loses from mergers, and we discuss whether mergers are beneficial on balance.

After studying this chapter you should be able to:

- Describe ways that companies change their ownership or management.

- Explain why it may make sense for companies to merge.

- Estimate the gains and costs of mergers to the acquiring firm.

- Describe takeover defenses.

- Summarize the evidence on whether mergers increase efficiency and on how the gains from mergers are distributed between shareholders of the acquired and acquiring firms.

- Explain some of the motivations for leveraged and management buyouts of the firm.

21.1 The Market for Corporate Control

The shareholders are the owners of the firm. But most shareholders do not feel like the boss, and with good reason. Try buying a share of General Motors stock and marching into the boardroom for a chat with your employee, the chief executive officer.

The *ownership* and *management* of large corporations are almost always separated. Shareholders do not directly appoint or supervise the firm's managers. They elect the board of directors, who act as their agents in choosing and monitoring the managers of the firm. Shareholders have a direct say in very few matters. Control of the firm is in the hands of the managers, subject to the general oversight of the board of directors.

This system of governance creates potential *agency costs*. Agency costs occur when managers or directors take actions adverse to shareholders' interests.

The temptation to take such actions may be ever-present, but there are many forces and constraints working to keep managers' and shareholders' interests in line. As we pointed out in Chapter 1, managers' paychecks in large corporations are almost always tied to the profitability of the firm and the performance of its shares. Boards of directors take their responsibilities seriously—they may face lawsuits if they don't—and therefore are reluctant to rubber-stamp obviously bad financial decisions.

But what ensures that the board has engaged the most talented managers? What happens if managers are inadequate? What if the board of directors is derelict in monitoring the performance of managers? Or what if the firm's managers are fine but resources of the firm could be used more efficiently by merging with another firm? Can we count on managers to pursue arrangements that would put them out of jobs?

These are all questions about *the market for corporate control*, the mechanisms by which firms are matched up with management teams and owners who can make the most of the firm's resources. You should not take a firm's current ownership and management for granted. If it is possible for the value of the firm to be enhanced by changing management or by reorganizing under new owners, there will be incentives for someone to make a change.

TABLE 21-1 Some important recent mergers

Acquiring Company	Selling Company	Payment, (Billions of Dollars)
JP Morgan Chase	Bank One Corp.	58.8
Procter & Gamble	Gillette Co.	57.0
Bank of America Corp.	FleetBoston Financial Corp.	49.3
Cingular Wireless	AT&T Wireless Services Inc.	41.0
Sprint Corp.	Nextel Communications Inc.	35.2
Johnson & Johnson	Guidant Corp.	25.4
Chevron Corp.	Unocal Corp.	18.3
Anthem Inc.	WellPoint Health Networks Inc.	16.4
SBC Corp.	AT&T Corp.	16.0
Verizon	MCI	8.5

Source: *Mergers and Acquisitions*, various issues.

There are four ways to change the management of a firm. These are (1) a successful proxy contest in which a group of stockholders votes in a new group of directors, who then pick a new management team; (2) the purchase of one firm by another in a merger or acquisition; (3) a leveraged buyout of the firm by a private group of investors; and (4) a divestiture, in which a firm either sells part of its operations to another company or spins it off as an independent firm.

We will review briefly each of these methods.

Method 1: Proxy Contests

Shareholders elect the board of directors to keep watch on management and replace unsatisfactory managers. If the board is lax, shareholders are free to elect a different board. In theory this ensures that the corporation is run in the best interests of shareholders.

In practice things are not so clear-cut. Ownership in large corporations is widely dispersed. Usually even the largest single shareholder holds only a small fraction of the shares. Most shareholders have little notion who is on the board or what the members stand for. Management, on the other hand, deals directly with the board and has a personal relationship with its members. In many corporations, management sits on the committee that nominates candidates for the board. It is not surprising that some boards seem less than aggressive in forcing managers to run a lean, efficient operation and to act primarily in the interests of shareholders.

When a group of investors believe that the board and its management team should be replaced, they can launch a **proxy contest.** A *proxy* is the right to vote another shareholder's shares. In a proxy contest, the dissident shareholders attempt to obtain enough proxies to elect their own slate to the board of directors. Once the new board is in control, management can be replaced and company policy changed. A proxy fight is therefore a direct contest for control of the corporation.

Successful proxy contests are rare. One reason is that they can cost millions of dollars. Dissidents who engage in proxy fights must use their own money, but management can use the corporation's funds and lines of communications with shareholders to defend itself.

The SEC has proposed new rules that would make it easier to mount a proxy fight, but in the meantime shareholders have found that simply voting against the reelection of existing directors can send a powerful signal. When Disney shareholders voted 43 percent of the shares against the reelection of Michael Eisner, the company's autocratic chairman, he heard the message and resigned the next day.

Institutional shareholders such as large pension funds have become more aggressive in pressing for managerial accountability and have been able to gain concessions from firms without initiating proxy contests. For example, firms have agreed to split the jobs of chief executive officer and chairman of the board of directors. This ensures that an outsider is responsible for keeping watch over the company. Also, more firms now bar corporate insiders from serving on the committee that nominates candidates to the board. Perhaps as a result of shareholder pressure, boards also seem to be getting more aggressive. For example, outside directors were widely credited for hastening the replacement of top management at Hewlett-Packard, Boeing, and Office Depot.

Method 2: Mergers and Acquisitions

Poorly performing managers face a greater risk from acquisition than from proxy contests. If the management of one firm observes another firm underperforming, it can try to acquire the business and replace the poor managers with its own team. In practice, corporate takeovers are the arenas where contests for corporate control are usually fought.

There are three ways for one firm to acquire another. One possibility is to *merge* the two companies into one, in which case the acquiring company assumes *all* the assets

proxy contest

Takeover attempt in which outsiders compete with management for shareholders' votes. Also called *proxy fight.*

and *all* the liabilities of the other. The acquired firm ceases to exist, and its former shareholders receive cash and/or securities in the acquiring firm. In many mergers there is a clear acquiring company, whose management then runs the enlarged firm. Sometimes a merger is presented as a "merger of equals," but even in these cases one firm's management usually comes out on top.

A **merger** must have the approval of at least 50 percent of the shareholders of each firm.[1] Shareholders are not always satisfied that the proposed merger is in their best interests. For example, when Hewlett-Packard wished to merge with Compaq Computer, the Hewlett family led a shareholders' revolt. The merger was eventually approved by shareholders, but only by a wafer-thin majority.

A second alternative is for the acquiring firm to buy the target firm's stock in exchange for cash, shares, or other securities. The acquired firm may continue to exist as a separate entity, but it is now owned by the acquirer. The approval and cooperation of the target firm's managers are generally sought, but even if they resist, the acquirer can attempt to purchase a majority of the outstanding shares. By offering to buy shares directly from shareholders, the acquiring firm can bypass the target firm's management altogether. The offer to purchase stock is called a **tender offer.** If the tender offer is successful, the buyer obtains control and can, if it chooses, toss out incumbent management.

The third approach is to buy the target firm's assets. In this case ownership of the assets needs to be transferred, and payment is made to the selling firm rather than directly to its stockholders. Usually, the target firm sells only some of its assets, but occasionally it sells *all* of them. In this case, the selling firm continues to exist as an independent entity, but it becomes an empty shell—a corporation engaged in no business activity.

The terminology of mergers and acquisitions (M&A) can be confusing. These phrases are used loosely to refer to any kind of corporate combination or takeover. But strictly speaking, *merger* means the combination of all the assets and liabilities of two firms. The purchase of the stock or assets of another firm is an **acquisition.**

Method 3: Leveraged Buyouts

Sometimes a group of investors takes over a firm by means of a **leveraged buyout,** or **LBO.** The LBO group takes the firm private and its shares no longer trade in the securities markets. Usually a considerable proportion of LBO financing is borrowed, hence the term *leveraged* buyout.

If the investor group is led by the management of the firm, the takeover is called a **management buyout,** or **MBO.** In this case, the firm's managers actually buy the firm from the shareholders and continue to run it. They become owner-managers. We will discuss LBOs and MBOs later in the chapter.

Method 4: Divestitures, Spin-Offs, and Carve-Outs

In the market for corporate control, fusion—mergers and acquisitions—gets the most publicity. But fission—the divestiture of assets or entire businesses—can be just as important. Often one firm may sell part of its business to another firm. For example, in 2005 IBM announced that it was selling its struggling PC business to China's Lenovo Group for $1.25 billion.

Instead of selling part of their operations, companies sometimes *spin off* a business by separating it from the parent firm and distributing to their shareholders the stock in the newly independent company. For example, in 2005 Viacom announced plans to create a separate company from its MTV cable networks and Paramount film studio, leaving its television and radio operations with the existing company. Viacom's shareholders ended up with shares in each company.

merger
Combination of two firms into one, with the acquirer assuming assets and liabilities of the target firm.

tender offer
Takeover attempt in which outsiders directly offer to buy the stock of the firm's shareholders.

acquisition
Takeover of a firm by purchase of that firm's common stock or assets.

leveraged buyout (LBO)
Acquisition of the firm by a private group using substantial borrowed funds.

management buyout (MBO)
Acquisition of the firm by its own management in a leveraged buyout.

---

[1] Corporate charters and state laws sometimes specify a higher percentage.

How Palm Was Carved and Spun

When 3Com acquired U.S. Robotics in 1997, it also became the owner of Palm, a small start-up business developing handheld computers. It was a lucky purchase, for over the next 3 years the Palm Pilot came to dominate the market for handheld computers. But as Palm began to take up an increasing amount of management time, 3Com concluded that it needed to return to its knitting and focus on its basic business of selling computer network systems. It therefore announced that it would carve out 5 percent of its holding of Palm through an initial public offering. At the same time it published plans to spin off the remaining 95 percent of Palm shares later in 2000 by giving 3Com shareholders about 1.5 Palm shares for each 3Com share that they owed.

The Palm carve-out occurred at close to the peak of the high-tech boom and got off to a dazzling start. The shares were issued in the IPO at $38 each. On the first day of trading the stock price touched $165 before closing at $95. Therefore, anyone owning a share of 3Com stock could look forward later in the year to receiving about 1.5 shares of Palm worth 1.5 × 95 = $142.50. But apparently 3Com's shareholders were not fully convinced that their newfound wealth was for real, for on the same day 3Com's stock price closed at $82, or more than $60 a share *less* than the market value of the shares in Palm that they were due to receive.*

Three years after 3Com spun off its holding in Palm, Palm itself entered the spin-off business by giving shareholders stock in PalmSource, a subsidiary that was responsible for developing and licensing the Palm operating system. The remaining business, renamed palmOne, would focus on making mobile gadgets. The company gave three reasons for its decision to split into two. First, like 3Com's management, Palm's management believed that the company would benefit from clarity of focus and mission. Second, it argued that shareholder value could "be enhanced if investors could evaluate and choose between both businesses separately, thereby attracting new and different investors." Finally, it seemed that Palm's rivals were reluctant to buy software from a company that competed with them in making handheld hardware.

*This difference would seem to present an arbitrage opportunity. An investor who bought 1 share of 3Com and sold short 1.5 shares of Palm would receive an immediate cash flow of $60 *and* own 3Com's other assets for free. The difficulty in executing this arbitrage is explored in O. A. Lamont and R. H. Thaler, "Can the Market Add and Subtract? Mispricing in Tech Stock Carve-Outs," *Journal of Political Economy* 111 (April 2003), pp. 227–268.

Carve-outs are similar to spin-offs except that shares in the new company are not given to existing stockholders but, instead, are sold in a public offering. Sometimes companies carve out a small proportion of the company to establish a market in the subsidiary and subsequently spin off the remainder of the shares. The nearby box describes how the computer company, Palm, was first carved and then spun.

The most frequent motive for spin-offs is improved efficiency. Companies sometimes refer to a business as being a "poor fit." By spinning off a poor fit, the management of the parent company can concentrate on its main activity. If each business must stand on its own feet, there is no risk that funds will be siphoned off from one in order to support unprofitable investments in the other. Moreover, if the two parts of the business are independent, it is easy to see the value of each and to reward managers accordingly.

21.2 Sensible Motives for Mergers

We now look more closely at mergers and acquisitions and consider when they do and do not make sense. Mergers are often categorized as *horizontal, vertical,* or *conglomerate.* A horizontal merger is one that takes place between two firms in the same line of business; the merged firms are former competitors. Most of the mergers around the turn of the century were of this type. For example, there have been a large number of bank mergers, such as the combination of JPMorgan Chase and BankOne. Other headline-grabbing horizontal mergers have brought together telecom companies, such as SBC and AT&T, and oil companies, such as Chevron and Unocal.

These horizontal mergers may be blocked if they are thought to be anticompetitive or create too much market power. For example, the decline in defense spending led to a number of mergers between aerospace companies, until by 1998 there remained just three giant companies—Boeing, Lockheed Martin, and Raytheon—plus several smaller ones, including Northrup Grumman. When Lockheed Martin and Northrup Grumman announced plans to get together, the antitrust regulators decided that this was a merger too far. In the face of this opposition, the two companies broke off their engagement.

A *vertical merger* involves companies at different stages of production. The buyer expands back toward the source of raw materials or forward in the direction of the ultimate consumer. Thus, a soft-drink manufacturer might buy a sugar producer (expanding backward) or a fast-food chain as an outlet for its product (expanding forward). Walt Disney's acquisition of the ABC television network was an example of a vertical merger. Disney planned to use the network to show its movies to huge audiences.

A *conglomerate merger* involves companies in unrelated lines of business. For example, before it went belly up in 1999, the Korean conglomerate, Daewoo, had nearly 400 different subsidiaries and 150,000 employees. It built ships in Korea, manufactured microwaves in France, TVs in Mexico, cars in Poland, fertilizers in Vietnam, and managed hotels in China and a bank in Hungary. No U.S. company is as diversified as Daewoo, but in the 1960s and 1970s it was common in the United States for unrelated businesses to merge. However, the number of conglomerate mergers declined in the 1980s. In fact much of the action in the 1980s came from breaking up the conglomerates that had been formed 10 to 20 years earlier.

Self-Test 21.1

Are the following hypothetical mergers horizontal, vertical, or conglomerate?

a. IBM acquires Dell Computer.
b. Dell Computer acquires Safeway (a supermarket chain).
c. Safeway acquires Campbell Soup.
d. Campbell Soup acquires IBM.

We have already seen that one motive for a merger is to replace the existing management team. If this motive is important, one would expect that poorly performing firms would tend to be targets for acquisition; this seems to be the case.[2]

Of course, not all acquisitions that are intended to improve management end up doing so. Hubris, excessive belief in one's own ability, has led many managers into unsuccessful acquisitions. Take the case of Jean-Marie Messier, the CEO of Vivendi, whom we first encountered in Chapter 18. Messier attempted to turn Vivendi into "the world's preferred creator and provider of entertainment, education, and personalized services to customers anywhere, at any time, and across all distribution platforms and devices." Vivendi entered into a series of major acquisitions, including the purchase of Seagram, which in turn owned Universal Studios. Messier's ambitions earned him the nickname "J6M," which, spelled out, stood for "Jean-Marie Messier, *moi-même, maitre du monde*"—"myself, master of the world." Ultimately, however, profits collapsed, the firm faced imminent bankruptcy, and Messier was ousted.[3]

Changing management, whether for better or worse, is not the only reason that firms make acquisitions. Many mergers and acquisitions are motivated by possible gains in efficiency from combining operations. These mergers create *synergies*. By this we mean that the two firms are worth more together than apart. A merger adds value only if synergies, better management, or other changes make the two firms worth more together than apart.

It would be convenient if we could say that certain types of mergers are usually successful and other types fail. Unfortunately, there are no such simple generalizations. Many mergers that appear to make sense nevertheless fail because managers cannot handle the complex task of integrating two firms with different production processes, pay structures, and accounting methods. Moreover, the value of most businesses depends on *human* assets—managers, skilled workers, scientists, and engineers. If these

[2] For example, Palepu found that investors in firms that were subsequently acquired earned relatively low rates of return for several years before the merger. See K. Palepu, "Predicting Takeover Targets: A Methodological and Empirical Analysis," *Journal of Accounting and Economics* 8 (March 1986), pp. 3–36.

[3] The rise and fall of Vivendi is chronicled in J. Johnson and M. Orange, *The Man Who Tried to Buy the World: Jean-Marie Messier and Vivendi Universal* (Portfolio, 2003).

people are not happy in their new roles in the merged firm, the best of them will leave. Beware of paying too much for assets that go down in the elevator and out to the parking lot at the close of each business day.

Consider the $38 billion merger between Daimler-Benz and Chrysler. Although it was hailed as a model for consolidation in the auto industry, the early years were bedeviled by conflicts between two very different cultures:

> German management-board members had executive assistants who prepared detailed position papers on any number of issues. The Americans didn't have assigned aides and formulated their decisions by talking directly to engineers or other specialists. A German decision worked its way through the bureaucracy for final approval at the top. Then it was set in stone. The Americans allowed midlevel employees to proceed on their own initiative, sometimes without waiting for executive-level approval.
>
> . . . Cultural integration also was proving to be a slippery commodity. The yawning gap in pay scales fueled an undercurrent of tension. The Americans earned two, three, and, in some cases, four times as much as their German counterparts. But the expenses of U.S. workers were tightly controlled compared with the German system. Daimler-side employees thought nothing of flying to Paris or New York for a half-day meeting, then capping the visit with a fancy dinner and a night in an expensive hotel. The Americans blanched at the extravagance.[4]

These observations illustrate the difficulties in realizing the benefits of merger. There are also occasions when the merger does achieve the intended synergies, but the buyer nevertheless loses because it pays too much. For example, the buyer may overestimate the value of stale inventory or underestimate the costs of renovating old plant and equipment, or it may overlook the warranties on a defective product.

With these caveats in mind, we will now consider some possible sources of synergy.

Economies of Scale

Just as most of us believe that we would be happier if only we were a little richer, so managers always seem to believe their firm would be more competitive if only it were just a little bigger. They hope for *economies of scale,* that is, the opportunity to spread fixed costs across a larger volume of output. The banking industry provides many examples. As a result of bank regulation, the United States had too many small, local banks. When these regulations were relaxed, some banks grew by systematically buying up other banks and streamlining their operations. When JPMorgan Chase and Bank One, two of the country's largest banks, merged in 2004, they forecast cost savings of $3 billion before tax by 2007. The savings would come from consolidating operations and eliminating redundant costs. Beware of overly optimistic predictions of cost savings, however. The nearby box tells the story of one bank merger that resulted in a spectacular debacle rather than the predicted synergies.

These economies of scale are the natural goal of horizontal mergers. But they have been claimed in conglomerate mergers, too. The architects of these mergers have pointed to the economies that come from sharing central services such as accounting, financial control, and top-level management.

Economies of Vertical Integration

Large industrial companies commonly like to gain as much control and coordination as possible over the production process by expanding back toward the output of the raw material and forward to the ultimate consumer. One way to achieve this is to merge with a supplier or a customer. Consider Du Pont's purchase of an oil company, Conoco. This was vertical integration because petroleum is the ultimate raw material for much of Du Pont's chemical production.

Do not assume that more vertical integration is necessarily better than less. Carried to extremes, it is absurdly inefficient. For example, before the Polish economy was restructured, LOT, the Polish state airline, found itself raising pigs to make sure that its

---

[4] Bill Vlasic and Bradley A. Stertz, "Taken for a Ride," *BusinessWeek,* June 5, 2000. Reprinted with special permission © 2000 The McGraw-Hill Companies, Inc.

Those Elusive Synergies

When three of Japan's largest banks combined to form Mizuho Bank, it brought together assets of $1.5 trillion, more than twice those of the world leader Deutsche Bank. The name "Mizuho" means "rich rice harvest," and the bank's management forecast that the merger would create a rich harvest of synergies. In a message to shareholders, the bank president claimed that the merger would create "a comprehensive financial services group that will surge forward in the 21st century." He predicted that the bank would "lead the new era through cutting-edge comprehensive financial services . . . by exploiting to the fullest extent the Group's enormous strengths, which are backed by a powerful customer base and state-of-the-art financial and information technologies." The cost of putting the banks together was forecast at ¥130 billion, but management predicted future benefits of ¥466 billion a year.

Within a few months of the announcement reports began to emerge of squabbles between the three partners. One problem area was IT. Each of the three merging banks had a different supplier for its computer system. At first it was proposed to use just one of these three systems, but then the banks decided to connect the three different systems together by using "relay" computers.

Three years after the initial announcement the new company opened for business on April 1, 2002. Five days later, computer glitches resulted in a spectacular foul-up. Some 7,000 of the bank's cash machines did not work; 60,000 accounts were debited twice for the same transaction; and millions of bills went unpaid. *The Economist* reported that 2 weeks later Tokyo Gas, the biggest gas company, was still missing ¥2.2 billion in payments and the top telephone company, NTT, which was looking for ¥12.7 billion, was forced to send its customers receipts marked with asterisks in place of figures, since it did not know which of about 760,000 bills had been paid.

One of the objects behind the formation of Mizuho was to exploit economies in its IT systems. The launch fiasco illustrated dramatically that it is easier to predict such merger synergies than to realize them.

Source: The creation of Mizuho Bank and its launch problems are described in "Undispensable: A Fine Merger Yields One Fine Mess," *The Economist,* April 27, 2002.

employees had fresh meat on their tables. (Of course, in a centrally managed economy it may prove necessary to grow your own meat, since you can't be sure you'll be able to buy it.)

Vertical integration has fallen out of fashion recently. Many companies are finding it more efficient to *outsource* many of their activities. For example, back in the 1950s and 1960s, General Motors was thought to have a cost advantage over its competitors because it produced a greater fraction of its components in-house. By the 1990s Ford and Chrysler had the advantage. They could buy the parts more cheaply from outside suppliers. This was partly because the outside suppliers tended to use nonunion labor. But it also appears that manufacturers have more bargaining power when they are dealing with independent suppliers rather than with another part of the corporate family. In 1998 GM decided to spin off Delphi, its automotive parts division, as a separate company. After the spin-off, GM continued to buy parts from Delphi in large volumes, but it negotiated the purchases at arm's length.

Combining Complementary Resources

Many small firms are acquired by large firms that can provide the missing ingredients necessary for the firm's success. The small firm may have a unique product but lack the engineering and sales organization necessary to produce and market it on a large scale. The firm could develop engineering and sales talent from scratch, but it may be quicker and cheaper to merge with a firm that already has ample talent. The two firms have *complementary resources*—each has what the other needs—so it may make sense for them to merge. Also the merger may open up opportunities that neither firm would pursue otherwise. Federal Express's purchase of Caliber System, a trucking company, is an example. Federal Express specializes in shipping packages by air, mostly for overnight delivery. Caliber's RMS subsidiary moves nonexpress packages by truck. RMS greatly increases Federal Express's capability to move packages on the ground. At the same time, RMS-originated business can move easily on the Federal Express system when rapid or distant delivery is essential.

Mergers as a Use for Surplus Funds

Suppose that your firm is in a mature industry. It is generating a substantial amount of cash, but it has few profitable investment opportunities. Ideally such a firm should distribute the surplus cash to shareholders by increasing its dividend payment or by repurchasing its shares. Unfortunately, energetic managers are often reluctant to shrink their firm in this way.

If the firm is not willing to purchase its own shares, it can instead purchase someone else's. Thus firms with a surplus of cash and a shortage of good investment opportunities often turn to mergers *financed by cash* as a way of deploying their capital.

Firms that have excess cash and do not pay it out or redeploy it by acquisition often find themselves targets for takeover by other firms that propose to redeploy the cash for them. During the oil price slump of the early 1980s, many cash-rich oil companies found themselves threatened by takeover. This was not because their cash was a unique asset. The acquirers wanted to capture the companies' cash flow to make sure it was not frittered away on negative-NPV oil exploration projects. We return to this *free-cash-flow* motive for takeovers later in the chapter.

21.3 Dubious Reasons for Mergers

The benefits that we have described so far all make economic sense. Other arguments sometimes given for mergers are more dubious. Here are two.

Diversification

We have suggested that the managers of a cash-rich company may prefer to see that cash used for acquisitions. That is why we often see cash-rich firms in stagnant industries merging their way into fresh woods and pastures new. But what about diversification as an end in itself? It is obvious that diversification reduces risk. Isn't that a gain from merging?

The trouble with this argument is that diversification is easier and cheaper for the stockholder than for the corporation. Why should firm A buy firm B to diversify when the shareholders of firm A can buy shares in firm B to diversify their own portfolios? It is far easier and cheaper for individual investors to diversify than it is for firms to combine operations.

The Bootstrap Game

During the 1960s some conglomerate companies made acquisitions that offered no evident economic gains. Nevertheless, the conglomerates' aggressive strategy produced several years of rising earnings per share. To see how this can happen, let us look at the acquisition of Muck and Slurry by the well-known conglomerate World Enterprises.

EXAMPLE 21.1 ▶ The Bootstrap Game

The position before the merger is set out in the first two columns of Table 21–2. Notice that because Muck and Slurry has relatively poor growth prospects, its stock sells at a lower price-earnings ratio than World Enterprises (line 3). The merger, we assume, produces no economic benefits, so the firms should be worth exactly the same together as apart. The value of World Enterprises after the merger is therefore equal to the sum of the separate values of the two firms (line 6).

Since World Enterprises stock is selling for double the price of Muck and Slurry stock (line 2), World Enterprises can acquire the 100,000 Muck and Slurry shares for 50,000 of its own shares. Thus World will have 150,000 shares outstanding after the merger.

World's total earnings double as a result of the acquisition (line 5), but the number of shares increases by only 50 percent. Its earnings *per share* rise from $2.00 to $2.67. We call this a *bootstrap effect* because there is no real gain created by the merger and

TABLE 21–2 Impact of merger on market value and earnings per share of World Enterprises

	World Enterprises (before merger)	Muck and Slurry	World Enterprises (after acquiring Muck and Slurry)
1. Earnings per share	$2	$2	$2.67
2. Price per share	$40	$20	$40
3. Price-earnings ratio	20	10	15
4. Number of shares	100,000	100,000	150,000
5. Total earnings	$200,000	$200,000	$400,000
6. Total market value	$4,000,000	$2,000,000	$6,000,000
7. Current earnings per dollar invested in stock (line 1 divided by line 2)	$.05	$.10	$.067

Note: When World Enterprises purchases Muck and Slurry, there are no gains. Therefore, total earnings and total market value should be unaffected by the merger. But earnings *per share* increase. World Enterprises issues only 50,000 of its shares (priced at $40) to acquire the 100,000 Muck and Slurry shares (priced at $20).

no increase in the two firms' combined value. Since World's stock price is unchanged by the acquisition of Muck and Slurry, the price-earnings ratio falls (line 3).

Before the merger, $1 invested in World Enterprises bought 5 cents of current earnings and rapid growth prospects. On the other hand, $1 invested in Muck and Slurry bought 10 cents of current earnings but slower growth prospects. If the *total* market value is not altered by the merger, then $1 invested in the merged firm gives World shareholders 6.7 cents of immediate earnings but slower growth than before the merger. Muck and Slurry shareholders get lower immediate earnings but faster growth. Neither side gains or loses *provided* that everybody understands the deal.

Financial manipulators sometimes try to ensure that the market does *not* understand the deal. Suppose that investors are fooled by the exuberance of the president of World Enterprises and mistake the 33 percent postmerger increase in earnings per share for *sustainable* growth. If they do, the price of World Enterprises stock rises and the shareholders of both companies receive something for nothing. ◀

You should now see how to play the bootstrap game. Suppose that you manage a company enjoying a high price-earnings ratio. The reason it is high is that investors anticipate rapid growth in future earnings. You achieve this growth not by capital investment, product improvement, or increased operating efficiency but by purchasing slow-growing firms with low price-earnings ratios. The long-run result will be slower growth and a depressed price-earnings ratio, but in the short run earnings per share can increase dramatically. If this fools investors, you may be able to achieve the higher earnings per share without suffering a decline in your price-earnings ratio. But in order to *keep* fooling investors, you must continue to expand by merger *at the same compound rate*. Obviously you cannot do this forever; one day expansion must slow down or stop. Then earnings growth will cease, and your house of cards will fall. Buying a firm with a lower P/E ratio can increase earnings per share. But the increase should not result in a higher share price. The short-term increase in earnings should be offset by lower future earnings growth.

Self-Test 21.2

Suppose that Muck and Slurry has even worse growth prospects than in our example and its share price is only $10. Recalculate the effects of the merger in this case. You should find that earnings per share increase by a greater amount, since World Enterprises can now buy the same *current* earnings for fewer shares.

21.4 Evaluating Mergers

If you are given the responsibility for evaluating a proposed merger, you must think hard about the following two questions:

1. Is there an overall economic gain to the merger? In other words, is the merger value-enhancing? Are the two firms worth more together than apart?
2. Do the terms of the merger make my company and its shareholders better off? There is no point in merging if the cost is too high and all the economic gain goes to the other company.

Answering these deceptively simple questions is rarely easy. Some economic gains can be nearly impossible to quantify, and complex merger financing can obscure the true terms of the deal. But the basic principles for evaluating mergers are not too difficult.

Mergers Financed by Cash

We will concentrate on a simple numerical example. Your company, Cislunar Foods, is considering acquisition of a smaller food company, Targetco. Cislunar is proposing to finance the deal by purchasing all of Targetco's outstanding stock for $19 per share. Some financial information on the two companies is given in the left and center columns of Table 21–3.

Question 1 Why would Cislunar and Targetco be worth more together than apart? Suppose that operating costs can be reduced by combining the companies' marketing, distribution, and administration. Revenues can also be increased in Targetco's region. The rightmost column of Table 21–3 contains projected revenues, costs, and earnings for the two firms operating together: annual operating costs postmerger will be $2 million less than the sum of the separate companies' costs, and revenues will be $2 million more. Therefore, projected earnings increase by $4 million.[5] We will assume that the increased earnings are the only synergy to be generated by the merger.

The economic gain to the merger is the present value of the extra earnings. If the earnings increase is permanent (a level perpetuity) and the cost of capital is 20 percent,

$$\text{Economic gain} = \text{PV(increased earnings)} = \frac{4}{.20} = \$20 \text{ million}$$

This additional value is the basic motivation for the merger.

TABLE 21–3 Cislunar Foods is considering an acquisition of Targetco. The merger would increase the companies' combined earnings by $4 million.

	Cislunar Foods	**Targetco**	**Combined Companies**	
Revenues	$ 150	$20	$172	(+2)
Operating costs	118	16	132	(-2)
Earnings	$ 32	$ 4	$ 40	(+4)
Cash	$ 55	$ 2.5		
Other assets' book value	185	17.0		
Total assets	$ 240	$19.5		
Price per share	$ 48	$16		
Number of shares	10.0	2.5		
Market value	$ 480	$40		

Note: Figures in millions except price per share.

---

[5] To keep things simple, the example ignores taxes and assumes that both companies are all-equity-financed. We also ignore the interest income that could have been earned by investing the cash used to finance the merger.

Question 2   What are the terms of the merger? What is the cost to Cislunar and its shareholders?

Targetco's management and shareholders will not consent to the merger unless they receive at least the stand-alone value of their shares. They can be paid in cash or by new shares issued by Cislunar. In this case we are considering a cash offer of $19 per Targetco share, $3 per share over the prior share price. Targetco has 2.5 million shares outstanding, so Cislunar will have to pay out $47.5 million, a premium of $7.5 million over Targetco's prior market value. On these terms, Targetco stockholders will capture $7.5 million out of the $20 million gain from the merger. That ought to leave $12.5 million for Cislunar.

This is confirmed in the Cash Purchase column of Table 21–4. Start at the *bottom* of the column, where the total market value of the merged firms is $492.5 million. This is derived as follows:

Cislunar market value prior to merger	$480 million
Targetco market value	40
Present value of gain to merger	20
Less Cash paid out to Targetco shareholders	–47.5
Postmerger market value	$492.5 million

The postmerger share price for Cislunar will be $49.25, an increase of $1.25 per share. There are 10 million shares now outstanding, so the total increase in the value of Cislunar shares is $12.5 million.

Now let's summarize. The merger makes sense for Cislunar for two reasons. First, the merger adds $20 million of overall value. Second, the terms of the merger give only $7.5 million of that $20 million overall gain to Targetco's stockholders, leaving $12.5 million for Cislunar. You could say that the *cost* of acquiring Targetco is $7.5 million, the difference between the cash payment and the value of Targetco as a separate company:

$$\text{Cost} = \text{cash paid out} - \text{Targetco value} = \$47.5 - 40 = \$7.5 \text{ million}$$

Of course the Targetco stockholders are ahead by $7.5 million. *Their gain is your cost.* As we've already seen, Cislunar stockholders come out $12.5 million ahead. This is the merger's NPV for Cislunar:

$$\text{NPV} = \text{economic gain} - \text{cost} = \$20 - 7.5 = \$12.5 \text{ million}$$

Writing down the economic gain and cost of a merger in this way separates the motive for the merger (the economic gain, or value added) from the terms of the merger (the *division* of the gain between the two merging companies).

Self-Test 21.3

Killer Shark Inc. makes a surprise cash offer of $22 a share for Goldfish Industries. Before the offer, Goldfish was selling for $18 a share. Goldfish has 1 million shares outstanding. What must Killer Shark believe about the present value of the improvement it can bring to Goldfish's operations?

TABLE 21–4 Financial forecasts after the Cislunar-Targetco merger. The left column assumes a cash purchase at $19 per Targetco share. The right column assumes Targetco stockholders receive one new Cislunar share for every three Targetco shares.

	Cash Purchase	Exchange of Shares
Earnings	$ 40	$ 40
Cash	$ 10	$ 57.5
Other assets' book value	202	202
Total assets	$212	$259.5
Price per share	$ 49.25	$ 49.85
Number of shares	10.0	10.833
Market value	$492.5	$540

Note: Figures in millions except price per share.

Mergers Financed by Stock

What if Cislunar wants to conserve its cash for other investments and therefore decides to pay for the Targetco acquisition with new Cislunar shares? The deal calls for Targetco shareholders to receive one Cislunar share in exchange for every three Targetco shares.

It's the same merger, but the financing is different. The right column of Table 21–4 works out the consequences. Again, start at the *bottom* of the column. Note that the market value of Cislunar's shares after the merger is $540 million, $47.5 million higher than in the cash deal, because that cash is kept rather than paid out to Targetco shareholders. On the other hand, there are more shares outstanding, since 833,333 new shares have to be issued in exchange for the 2.5 million Targetco shares (a 1-to-3 ratio). Therefore, the price per share is 540/10.833 = $49.85, which is 60 cents higher than in the cash offer.

Why do Cislunar stockholders do better from the share exchange? The economic gain from the merger is the same, but the Targetco stockholders capture less of it. They get 833,333 shares at $49.85, or $41.5 million, a premium of only $1.5 million over Targetco's prior market value:

$$\text{Cost} = \text{value of shares issued} - \text{Targetco value}$$
$$= \$41.5 - 40 = \$1.5 \text{ million}$$

The merger's NPV to Cislunar's original shareholders is

$$\text{NPV} = \text{economic gain} - \text{cost} = 20 - 1.5 = \$18.5 \text{ million}$$

Note that Cislunar stock rises by $1.85 from its prior value. The total increase in value for Cislunar's original shareholders, who retain 10 million shares, is $18.5 million.

Evaluating the terms of a merger can be tricky when there is an exchange of shares. The target company's shareholders will retain a stake in the merged firms, so you have to figure out what the firm's shares will be worth *after* the merger is announced and its benefits appreciated by investors. Notice that we started with the total market value of Cislunar and Targetco postmerger, took account of the merger terms (833,333 new shares issued), and worked back to the postmerger share price. Only then could we work out the division of the merger gains between the two companies.

There is a key distinction between cash and stock for financing mergers. If cash is offered, the cost of the merger is not affected by the size of the merger gains. If stock is offered, the cost depends on the gains because the gains show up in the postmerger share price, and these shares are used to pay for the acquired firm.

Stock financing also mitigates the effects of over- or undervaluation of either firm. Suppose, for example, that A overestimates B's value as a separate entity, perhaps because it has overlooked some hidden liability. Thus A makes too generous an offer. Other things equal, A's stockholders are better off if it is a stock rather than a cash offer. With a stock offer, the inevitable bad news about B's value will fall partly on B's former stockholders.

Self-Test 21.4 Suppose Targetco shareholders demand 1 Cislunar share for every 2.5 Targetco shares. Otherwise they will not accept the merger. Under these revised terms, is the merger still a good deal for Cislunar?

A Warning

The cost of a merger is the premium the acquirer pays for the target firm over its value as a separate company. If the target is a public company, you can measure its separate value by multiplying its stock price by the number of outstanding shares. Watch out, though: If investors expect the target to be acquired, its stock price may overstate the company's separate value. The target company's stock price may already have risen in anticipation of a premium to be paid by an acquiring firm.

Another Warning

Some companies begin their merger analyses with a forecast of the target firm's future cash flows. Any revenue increases or cost reductions attributable to the merger are included in the forecasts, which are then discounted back to the present and compared with the purchase price:

$$\text{Estimated net gain} = \text{DCF valuation of target including merger benefits}$$
$$- \text{cash required for acquisition}$$

This is a dangerous procedure. Even the brightest and best-trained analyst can make large errors in valuing a business. The estimated net gain may come up positive not because the merger makes sense, but simply because the analyst's cash-flow forecasts are too optimistic. On the other hand, a good merger may not be pursued if the analyst fails to recognize the target's potential as a stand-alone business.

A better procedure *starts* with the target's current and stand-alone market value and concentrates instead on the *changes* in cash flow that would result from the merger. Always ask why the two firms should be worth more together than apart. Remember, *you add value only if you can generate additional economic benefits*—some competitive edge that other firms can't match and that the target firm's managers can't achieve on their own.

It makes sense to keep an eye on the value that investors place on the gains from merging. If A's stock price falls when the deal is announced, investors are sending a message that the merger benefits are doubtful *or* that A is paying too much for these benefits.

21.5 Merger Tactics

In recent years, most mergers have been agreed upon by both parties, but occasionally, an acquirer goes over the heads of the target firm's management and makes a *tender offer* directly to its stockholders. The management of the target firm may advise shareholders to accept the tender, or it may attempt to fight the bid in the hope that the acquirer will either raise its offer or throw in the towel.

The rules of merger warfare are largely set by federal and state laws[6] and the courts act as referee to see that contests are conducted fairly. We will look at one recent contest that illustrates the tactics and weapons employed. Outside the English-speaking countries hostile takeovers once were rare. But the world is changing, and there have recently been a number of high-profile takeover battles involving European companies.

EXAMPLE 21.2 ▶	Oracle Bids for PeopleSoft

These days hostile takeover bids are relatively uncommon, particularly in high-tech industries where an acrimonious takeover battle may cause many of the target's most valued staff to leave. Investors were therefore startled in June 2003 when the software giant Oracle Corp. announced a $5.1 billion cash tender offer for its rival PeopleSoft. The offer price of $16 a share was only a very modest 6 percent above the recent price of PeopleSoft stock. PeopleSoft's CEO angrily rejected the bid as dramatically undervaluing the business and accused Oracle of trying to disrupt PeopleSoft's business and to thwart its recently announced plan to merge with its smaller rival J.D. Edwards & Co. PeopleSoft immediately filed a suit claiming that Oracle's management had engaged in "acts of unfair trade practices" and had "disrupted PeopleSoft's customer relationships." In another suit J.D. Edwards claimed that Oracle had wrongly "interfered with its proposed merger with PeopleSoft" and demanded $1.7 billion in compensatory damages.

---

[6] The principal federal act regulating takeovers is the Williams Act of 1968.

TABLE 21-5 Some key dates in the Oracle/PeopleSoft takeover battle

Date	Event
June 6, 2003	Oracle offers cash of $16 a share for PeopleSoft stock, a premium of 6 percent.
June 18, 2003	Oracle increases offer to $19.50 a share.
February 4, 2004	Oracle raises offer to $26 a share.
February 26, 2004	Justice Department files suit to block deal. Oracle announces plans to appeal.
May 16, 2004	Oracle *reduces* offer to $21 a share.
September 9, 2004	Oracle wins appeal in a federal court against Department of Justice antitrust ruling.
September 27, 2004	Hearing begins in Delaware court on Oracle's request to overturn PeopleSoft's poison pill.
November 1, 2004	Oracle raises offer to $24 a share. Accepted by 61% of PeopleSoft shares.
November 23, 2004	Oracle announces plans to mount a proxy fight by naming four nominees for PeopleSoft's board.
December 13, 2004	Oracle raises offer to $26.50 a share. Accepted by PeopleSoft's board.

poison pill

Measure taken by a target firm to avoid acquisition; for example, the right for existing shareholders to buy additional shares at an attractive price if a bidder acquires a large holding.

Oracle's bid was the opening salvo in a battle that was to last 18 months. Some of the key dates in this battle are set out in Table 21–5. PeopleSoft had several defenses at its disposal. First, it had in place a **poison pill,** which would allow it to flood the market with additional shares if a predator acquired 20 percent of the stock. Second, the company instituted a customer-assurance program that offered customers money-back guarantees if an acquirer were to reduce customer support. At one point in the takeover battle the potential liability under this program reached nearly $1.6 billion. Third, elections to the PeopleSoft board were staggered, so different directors came up for reelection in different years. This meant that it would take two annual meetings to replace a majority of PeopleSoft's board.

Oracle not only had to overcome PeopleSoft's defenses but also had to clear possible antitrust roadblocks. Connecticut's attorney general instituted an antitrust action to block Oracle's bid, in part to protect his state's considerable investment in PeopleSoft software, and announced that he was seeking to assemble a coalition of other states and customers as well. Then an investigation of the deal by the U.S. Department of Justice ruled that the deal was anticompetitive. Normally such an objection is enough to kill a deal, but Oracle was persistent and successfully appealed the ruling in a federal court.

While these battles were being fought out, Oracle revised its offer four times. It upped its offer first to $19.50 and then to $26 a share. Then, in an effort to put pressure on PeopleSoft shareholders, Oracle *reduced* its offer to $21 a share, citing a drop of 28 percent in the price of PeopleSoft's shares. Six months later it raised the offer again to $24 a share, warning investors that it would walk away if the offer was not accepted by PeopleSoft's board or a majority of the PeopleSoft shareholders.

Sixty-one percent of PeopleSoft's shareholders indicated that they wished to accept this last offer, but before Oracle could gain control of PeopleSoft, it still needed the company to get rid of the poison pill and customer-assurance scheme. That meant putting pressure on PeopleSoft's management, which had continued to reject every approach. Oracle tried two tactics. First, it initiated a proxy fight to change the composition of PeopleSoft's board. Second, it filed a suit in a Delaware court alleging that PeopleSoft's management had breached its fiduciary duty by trying to thwart Oracle's offer and not giving it "due consideration." The lawsuit asked the court to require that PeopleSoft dismantle its takeover defenses, including the poison-pill plan and the customer-assurance program.

PeopleSoft's CEO had at one point said that he "could imagine no price nor combination of price and other conditions to recommend accepting the offer." But with 61 percent of PeopleSoft's shareholders wishing to take up Oracle's latest offer, it was becoming less easy for the company to keep saying no, and many observers were starting to question whether PeopleSoft's management was acting in the shareholders' interest. If management showed itself deaf to shareholders' interests, the court could well rule in favor of Oracle or disgruntled shareholders might vote to change the composition of the PeopleSoft board. PeopleSoft's directors therefore decided to be less intransigent and testified at the Delaware trial that they would consider negotiating with Oracle if it were to offer $26.50 or $27 a share. This was the breakthrough that Oracle was looking for. It upped its offer immediately to $26.50 a share, PeopleSoft lifted its defenses, and within a month 97 percent of PeopleSoft's shareholders had agreed to the bid. After 18 months of punch and counterpunch the battle for People-Soft was over.   ◄

What are the lessons? First, the example illustrates some of the stratagems of merger warfare. Firms like PeopleSoft that are worried about being taken over usually prepare their defenses in advance. Often they will persuade shareholders to agree to **shark-repellent** changes to the corporate charter. For example, the charter may be amended to require that any merger must be approved by a *supermajority* of 80 percent of the shares rather than the normal 50 percent.

shark repellent
Amendment to a
company charter made to
forestall takeover attempts.

Firms frequently deter potential bidders by devising poison pills, which make the company unappetizing. For example, the poison pill may give existing shareholders the right to buy the company's shares at half-price as soon as a bidder acquires more than 15 percent of the shares. The bidder is not entitled to the discount. Thus the bidder resembles Tantalus—as soon as it has acquired 15 percent of the shares, control is lifted away from its reach.

The battle for PeopleSoft illustrates the strength of poison pills and other takeover defenses. Oracle's offensive still gained ground, but with great expense and at a very slow pace. But eventually the pressure on PeopleSoft's management became overwhelming. Unless it could demonstrate that it was acting in the shareholders' interests, it risked having the poison pill removed by the court. The second reason that the company carved in was the increasing pressure from its shareholders, including some large institutions, who wished to accept Oracle's offer.

21.6 Leveraged Buyouts

Leveraged buyouts, or *LBOs,* differ from ordinary acquisitions in two ways. First, a large fraction of the purchase price is debt-financed. Some, perhaps all, of this debt is junk, that is, below investment grade. Second, the shares of the LBO no longer trade on the open market. The remaining equity in the LBO is privately held by a small group of (usually institutional) investors and is known as *private equity.* When this group is led by the company's management, the acquisition is called a *management buyout (MBO).* Many LBOs are in fact MBOs.

In the 1970s and 1980s many management buyouts were arranged for unwanted divisions of large, diversified companies. Smaller divisions outside the companies' main lines of business often lacked top management's interest and commitment, and divisional management chafed under corporate bureaucracy. Many such divisions flowered when spun off as MBOs. Their managers, pushed by the need to generate cash for debt service and encouraged by a substantial personal stake in the business, found ways to cut costs and compete more effectively.

During the 1980s private-equity activity shifted to buyouts of entire businesses, including large, mature public corporations. The largest, most dramatic, and best-documented LBO of them all was the $25 billion takeover of RJR Nabisco in 1988 by Kohlberg Kravis Roberts (KKR). The players, tactics, and controversies of LBOs are writ large in this case.

EXAMPLE 21.3 ▶	RJR Nabisco[7]

On October 28, 1988, the board of directors of RJR Nabisco revealed that Ross Johnson, the company's chief executive officer, had formed a group of investors prepared to buy all the firm's stock for $75 per share in cash and take the company private. Johnson's group was backed up and advised by Shearson Lehman Hutton, the investment bank subsidiary of American Express.

RJR's share price immediately moved to about $75, handing shareholders a 36 percent gain over the previous day's price of $56. At the same time RJR's bonds fell, since it was clear that existing bondholders would soon have a lot more company.

Johnson's offer lifted RJR onto the auction block. Once the company was in play, its board of directors was obliged to consider other offers, which were not long coming. Four days later, a group of investors led by LBO specialists Kohlberg Kravis Roberts bid $90 per share, $79 in cash plus preferred stock valued at $11.

The bidding finally closed on November 30, some 32 days after the initial offer was revealed. In the end it was Johnson's group against KKR. KKR offered $109 per share, after adding $1 per share (roughly $230 million) at the last hour. The KKR bid was $81 in cash, convertible subordinated debentures valued at about $10, and preferred shares valued at about $18. Johnson's group bid $112 in cash and securities.

But the RJR board chose KKR. True, Johnson's group had offered $3 per share more, but its security valuations were viewed as "softer" and perhaps overstated. Also, KKR's planned asset sales were less drastic; perhaps their plans for managing the business inspired more confidence. Finally, the Johnson group's proposal contained a management compensation package that seemed extremely generous and had generated an avalanche of bad press.

But where did the merger benefits come from? What could justify offering $109 per share, about $25 billion in all, for a company that only 33 days previously had been selling for $56 per share?

KKR and other bidders were betting on two things. First, they expected to generate billions of additional dollars from interest tax shields, reduced capital expenditures, and sales of assets not strictly necessary to RJR's core businesses. Asset sales alone were projected to generate $5 billion. Second, they expected to make those core businesses significantly more profitable, mainly by cutting back on expenses and bureaucracy. Apparently there was plenty to cut, including the RJR "Air Force," which at one point operated 10 corporate jets.

In the year after KKR took over, new management was installed. This group sold assets and cut back operating expenses and capital spending. There were also layoffs. As expected, high interest charges meant a net loss of $976 million for 1989, but pretax operating income actually increased, despite extensive asset sales, including the sale of RJR's European food operations.

While management was cutting costs and selling assets, prices in the junk bond market were rapidly declining, implying much higher future interest charges for RJR and stricter terms on any refinancing. In mid-1990 KKR made an additional equity investment, and later that year the company announced an offer of cash and new shares in exchange for $753 million of junk bonds. By 1993 the burden of debt had been reduced from $26 billion to $14 billion. For RJR, the world's largest LBO, it seemed that high debt was a temporary, not permanent, virtue.   ◀

---

[7] The story of the RJR Nabisco buyout is reconstructed by B. Burrough and J. Helyar in *Barbarians at the Gate: The Fall of RJR Nabisco* (New York: Harper & Row, 1990) and is the subject of a movie with the same title.

Barbarians at the Gate?

The buyout of RJR crystallized views on LBOs, the junk bond market, and the takeover business. For many it exemplified all that was wrong with finance in the 1980s, especially the willingness of "raiders" to carve up established companies, leaving them with enormous debt burdens, basically in order to get rich quick.

There was plenty of confusion, stupidity, and greed in the LBO business. Not all the people involved were nice. On the other hand, LBOs generated enormous increases in market value, and most of the gains went to selling stockholders, not raiders. For example, the biggest winners in the RJR Nabisco LBO were the company's stockholders.

We should therefore consider briefly where these gains may have come from before we try to pass judgment on LBOs. There are several possibilities.

The Junk Bond Markets LBOs and debt-financed takeovers may have been driven by artificially cheap funding from the junk bond markets. With hindsight it seems that investors in junk bonds underestimated the risks of default. Default rates climbed painfully between 1989 and 1991, yields rose dramatically, and new issues dried up. For a while junk-financed LBOs disappeared from the scene.

Leverage and Taxes As we explained in Chapter 15, borrowing money saves taxes. But taxes were not the main driving force behind LBOs. The value of interest tax shields was just not big enough to explain the observed gains in market value.

Of course, if interest tax shields were the main motive for LBOs' high debt, then LBO managers would not be so concerned to pay off debt. We saw that this was one of the first tasks facing RJR Nabisco's new management.

Other Stakeholders It is possible that the gain to the selling stockholders is just someone else's loss and that no value is generated overall. Therefore, we should look at the total gain to *all* investors in an LBO, not just the selling stockholders.

Bondholders are the obvious losers. The debt they thought was well-secured may turn into junk when the borrower goes through an LBO. We noted how market prices of RJR Nabisco debt fell sharply when Ross Johnson's first LBO offer was announced. But again, the value losses suffered by bondholders in LBOs are not nearly large enough to explain stockholder gains.

Leverage and Incentives Managers and employees of LBOs work harder and often smarter. They have to generate cash to service the extra debt. Moreover, managers' personal fortunes are riding on the LBO's success. They become owners rather than organization men or women.

It is hard to measure the payoff from better incentives, but there is some evidence of improved operating efficiency in LBOs. Kaplan, who studied 48 management buyouts between 1980 and 1986, found average increases in operating income of 24 percent over the following 3 years. Ratios of operating income and net cash flow to assets and sales increased dramatically. He observed cutbacks in capital expenditures but not in employment. Kaplan suggests that these operating changes "are due to improved incentives rather than layoffs or managerial exploitation of shareholders through inside information."[8]

Free Cash Flow The free-cash-flow theory of takeovers is basically that mature firms with a surplus of cash will tend to waste it. This contrasts with standard finance theory, which says that firms with more cash than positive-NPV investment opportunities should give the cash back to investors through higher dividends or share repurchases. But we see firms like RJR Nabisco spending on corporate luxuries and questionable capital investments. One benefit of LBOs is to put such companies on a diet and force them to pay out cash to service debt.

---

[8] S. Kaplan, "The Effects of Management Buyouts on Operating Performance and Value," *Journal of Financial Economics* 24 (October 1989), pp. 217–254.

The free-cash-flow theory predicts that mature, "cash cow" companies will be the most likely targets of LBOs. We can find many examples that fit the theory, including RJR Nabisco. The theory says that the gains in market value generated by LBOs are just the present values of the future cash flows that would otherwise have been frittered away.[9]

We do not endorse the free-cash-flow theory as the sole explanation for LBOs. We have mentioned several other plausible rationales, and we suspect that most LBOs are driven by a mixture of motives. Nor do we say that all LBOs are beneficial. On the contrary, there are many mistakes and even soundly motivated LBOs can be dangerous, as the bankruptcies of Campeau, Revco, National Gypsum, and many other highly leveraged companies prove. However, we do take issue with those who portray LBOs *simply* as Wall Street barbarians breaking up the traditional strengths of corporate America. In many cases LBOs have generated true gains.

The buyout of RJR Nabisco illustrates how during the merger boom of the 1980s even very large companies were not immune from attack by a rival management team. What made such attacks possible was the ability of the bidder to finance the takeover with large amounts of junk bonds. But by the end of the decade the merger environment had changed. Many of the obvious targets had disappeared and the battle for RJR Nabisco highlighted the increasing cost of victory. Institutions were reluctant to increase their holdings of junk bonds. Moreover, the market for these bonds had depended to a remarkable extent on one individual, Michael Milken, of the investment bank Drexel Burnham Lambert. By the late 1980s Milken and his employer were in trouble. Milken was indicted by a grand jury on 98 counts and was subsequently sentenced to jail. Drexel filed for bankruptcy, but by that time the junk bond market was moribund and the finance for highly leveraged buyouts had largely dried up.[10] Finally, in reaction to the perceived excesses of the merger boom, the state legislatures and the courts began to lean against hostile takeovers.

Eventually, LBO activity began to recover. Today's buyouts are generally smaller and not leveraged as aggressively as the deals of the 1980s. But the volume of LBO deals is still impressive. Recent deals include the $11.3 billion buyout of SunGard Data Systems Inc., a $6.6 billion buyout of Toys "R" Us Inc., and a $4.4 billion buyout of PanAmSat.

21.7 The Benefits and Costs of Mergers

Merger activity comes in waves and is concentrated in a relatively small number of industries. This urge to merge frequently seems to be prompted by deregulation and by changes in technology or the pattern of demand. Take the merger wave of the 1990s, for example. Deregulation of telecoms and banking earlier in the decade led to a spate of mergers in both industries that has continued to the present. Elsewhere, the decline in military spending brought about a number of mergers between defense companies until the Department of Justice decided to call a halt. And in the entertainment industry the prospective advantages from controlling both content and distribution led to mergers between such giants as AOL and Time Warner.

There are undoubtedly good acquisitions and bad acquisitions, but economists find it hard to agree on whether acquisitions are beneficial *on balance*. In general, shareholders of the target firm make a healthy gain. For example, one study found that following the announcement of the bid, the stock price of the target company jumped

---

[9] The free-cash-flow theory's chief proponent is Michael Jensen. See M. C. Jensen, "The Eclipse of the Public Corporation," *Harvard Business Review* 67 (September–October 1989), pp. 61–74, and "The Agency Costs of Free Cash Flow, Corporate Finance and Takeovers," *American Economic Review* 76 (May 1986), pp. 323–329.

[10] For a history of the role of Milken in the development of the junk bond market, see C. Bruck, *The Predator's Ball: The Junk Bond Raiders and the Man Who Staked Them* (New York: Simon and Schuster, 1988).

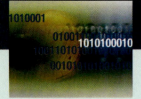
Mergers

Look at a recent example of a merger announcement, and log on to the Web site of the acquiring company. What reasons does the acquirer give for buying the target? How does it intend to pay for the target—with cash, shares, or a mixture of the two? Can you work out how much the target's shareholders will gain from the offer? Is it more or less than would be the case for an average merger? Now log on to **finance.yahoo.com** and find out what happened to the stock price of the acquiring company when the merger was announced. Were shareholders pleased with the announcement?

Source: Yahoo! Finance Web site. Reproduced with permission of Yahoo! Inc. © 2005 by Yahoo! Inc. Yahoo! and the Yahoo! logo are trademarks of Yahoo! Inc.

by 16 percent on average.[11] On the other hand, it appears that investors expected the acquiring companies to just about break even, for the price of their shares fell by .7 percent. The value of the total package—buyer plus seller—increased by 1.8 percent. Of course, these are averages; selling shareholders, for example, have sometimes obtained much higher returns. When IBM took over Lotus Corporation, it paid a premium of 100 percent, or about $1.7 billion, for Lotus stock.

Since buyers roughly break even and sellers make substantial gains, it seems that there are positive overall benefits from mergers. But not everybody is convinced. Some believe that investors analyzing mergers pay too much attention to short-term earnings gains and don't notice that these gains are at the expense of long-term prospects.

Since we can't observe how companies would have fared in the absence of a merger, it is difficult to measure the effects on profitability. However, several studies of merger activity suggest that mergers *do* seem to improve real productivity. For example, Healy, Palepu, and Ruback examined 50 large mergers between 1979 and 1983 and found an average increase in the companies' pretax returns of 2.4 percentage points.[12] They argue that this gain came from generating a higher level of sales from the same assets. There was no evidence that the companies were mortgaging their long-term futures by cutting back on long-term investments; expenditures on capital equipment and research and development tracked the industry average.

If you are concerned with public policy toward mergers, you do not want to look only at their impact on the shareholders of the companies concerned. For instance, we have already seen that in the case of RJR Nabisco some part of the shareholders' gain was at the expense of the bondholders and the Internal Revenue Service (through the enlarged interest tax shield). The acquirer's shareholders may also gain at the expense of the target firm's employees, who in some cases are laid off or are forced to take pay cuts after takeovers.

Perhaps the most important effect of acquisition is felt by the managers of companies that are not taken over. For example, one effect of LBOs was that the managers of even the largest corporations could not feel safe from challenge. Perhaps the threat of takeover spurs the whole of corporate America to try harder. Unfortunately, we don't know whether on balance the threat of merger makes for more active days or sleepless nights.

---

[11] See G. Andrade, M. Mitchell, and E. Stafford, "New Evidence and Perspectives on Mergers," *Journal of Economic Perspectives* 15 (Spring 2001), pp. 103–120.

[12] See P. Healy, K. Palepu, and R. Ruback, "Does Corporate Performance Improve after Mergers?" *Journal of Financial Economics* 31 (April 1992), pp. 135–175. The study examined the pretax returns of the merged companies relative to industry averages.

The threat of takeover may be a spur to inefficient management, but it is also costly. The companies need to pay for the services provided by the investment bankers, lawyers, and accountants. In addition, mergers can soak up large amounts of management time and effort. When a company is planning a takeover, it can be difficult to give as much attention as one should to the firm's existing business.

Even if the gains to the community exceed these costs, one wonders whether the same benefits could not be achieved more cheaply another way. For example, are leveraged buyouts necessary to make managers work harder? Perhaps the problem lies in the way that many corporations reward and penalize their managers. Perhaps many of the gains from takeover could be captured by linking management compensation more closely to performance.

SUMMARY

In what ways do companies change the composition of their ownership or management?

If the board of directors fails to replace an inefficient management, there are four ways to effect a change: (1) Shareholders may engage in a **proxy contest** to replace the board; (2) the firm may be acquired by another; (3) the firm may be purchased by a private group of investors in a leveraged buyout; or (4) it may sell off part of its operations to another company. There are three ways for one firm to acquire another: (1) It can **merge** all the assets and liabilities of the target firm into those of its own company; (2) it can buy the stock of the target; or (3) it can buy the individual assets of the target. The offer to buy the stock of the target firm is called a **tender offer.** The purchase of the stock or assets of another firm is called an **acquisition.**

Why may it make sense for companies to merge?

A merger may be undertaken in order to replace an inefficient management. But sometimes two businesses may be more valuable together than apart. Gains may stem from economies of scale, economies of vertical integration, the combination of complementary resources, or redeployment of surplus funds. We don't know how frequently these benefits occur, but they do make economic sense. Sometimes mergers are undertaken to diversify risks or artificially increase growth of earnings per share. These motives are dubious.

How should the gains and costs of mergers to the acquiring firm be measured?

A merger generates an economic gain if the two firms are worth more together than apart. The *gain* is the difference between the value of the merged firm and the value of the two firms run independently. The *cost* is the premium that the buyer pays for the selling firm over its value as a separate entity. When payment is in the form of shares, the value of this payment naturally depends on what those shares are worth after the merger is complete. You should go ahead with the merger if the gain exceeds the cost.

What are some takeover defenses?

Mergers are often amicably negotiated between the management and directors of the two companies; but if the seller is reluctant, the would-be buyer can decide to make a tender offer for the stock. We sketched some of the offensive and defensive tactics used in takeover battles. These defenses include **shark repellents** (changes in the company charter meant to make a takeover more difficult to achieve) and **poison pills** (measures that make takeover of the firm more costly).

What are some of the motivations for leveraged and management buyouts of the firm?

In a **leveraged buyout (LBO)** or **management buyout (MBO),** all public shares are repurchased and the company "goes private." LBOs tend to involve mature businesses with ample cash flow and modest growth opportunities. LBOs and other debt-financed takeovers are driven by a mixture of motives, including (1) the value of interest tax shields; (2) transfers of value from bondholders, who may see the value of their bonds fall as the firm piles up more debt; and (3) the opportunity to create better incentives for managers and employees, who have a personal stake in the company. In addition, many LBOs have

www.mhhe.com/bmm5e

been designed to force firms with surplus cash to distribute it to shareholders rather than plowing it back. Investors feared such companies would otherwise channel free cash flow into negative-NPV investments.

Do mergers increase efficiency, and how are the gains from mergers distributed between shareholders of the acquired and acquiring firms?

We observed that when the target firm is acquired, its shareholders typically win: Target firms' shareholders earn abnormally large returns. The bidding firm's shareholders roughly break even. This suggests that the typical merger generates positive net benefits, but competition among bidders and active defense by management of the target firm pushes most of the gains toward selling shareholders.

QUIZ

1. **Merger Motives.** Which of the following motives for mergers make economic sense?

   a. Merging to achieve economies of scale.
   b. Merging to reduce risk by diversification.
   c. Merging to redeploy cash generated by a firm with ample profits but limited growth opportunities.
   d. Merging to increase earnings per share.

2. **Merger Motives.** Explain why it might make good sense for Northeast Heating and Northeast Air Conditioning to merge into one company.

3. **Empirical Facts.** True or false?

   a. Sellers almost always gain in mergers.
   b. Buyers almost always gain in mergers.
   c. Firms that do unusually well tend to be acquisition targets.
   d. Merger activity in the United States varies dramatically from year to year.
   e. On average, mergers produce substantial economic gains.
   f. Tender offers require the approval of the selling firm's management.
   g. The cost of a merger is always independent of the economic gain produced by the merger.

4. **Merger Tactics.** Connect each term to its correct definition or description:

   A. LBO
   B. Poison pill
   C. Tender offer
   D. Shark repellent
   E. Proxy contest

   1. Attempt to gain control of a firm by winning the votes of its stockholders.
   2. Changes in corporate charter designed to deter unwelcome takeover.
   3. Shareholders are issued rights to buy shares if bidder acquires large stake in the firm.
   4. Offer to buy shares directly from stockholders.
   5. Company or business bought out by private investors, largely debt-financed.

5. **Merger Facts.** True or false?

   a. One of the first tasks of an LBO's financial manager is to pay down debt.
   b. The cost of a merger is affected by the size of the merger gains when the merger is financed with cash.
   c. Targets for LBOs in the 1980s tended to be profitable companies in mature industries with limited investment opportunities.

PRACTICE PROBLEMS

6. **Merger Gains.** Acquiring Corp. is considering a takeover of Takeover Target Inc. Acquiring has 10 million shares outstanding, which sell for $40 each. Takeover Target has 5 million shares outstanding, which sell for $20 each. If the merger gains are estimated at $25 million, what is the highest price per share that Acquiring should be willing to pay to Takeover Target shareholders?

7. **Mergers and P/E Ratios.** If Acquiring Corp. from Problem 6 has a price-earnings ratio of 12 and Takeover Target has a P/E ratio of 8, what should be the P/E ratio of the merged firm? Assume in this case that the merger is financed by an issue of new Acquiring Corp. shares. Takeover Target will get one Acquiring share for every two Takeover Target shares held.

8. **Merger Gains and Costs.** Velcro Saddles is contemplating the acquisition of Pogo Ski Sticks, Inc. The values of the two companies as separate entities are $20 million and $10 million, respectively. Velcro Saddles estimates that by combining the two companies, it will reduce marketing and administrative costs by $500,000 per year in perpetuity. Velcro Saddles is willing to pay $14 million cash for Pogo. The opportunity cost of capital is 8 percent.

   a. What is the gain from merger?
   b. What is the cost of the cash offer?
   c. What is the NPV of the acquisition under the cash offer?

9. **Stock versus Cash Offers.** Suppose that instead of making a cash offer as in Problem 8, Velcro Saddles considers offering Pogo shareholders a 50 percent holding in Velcro Saddles.

   a. What is the value of the stock in the merged company held by the original Pogo shareholders?
   b. What is the cost of the stock alternative?
   c. What is its NPV under the stock offer?

10. **Merger Gains.** Immense Appetite, Inc., believes that it can acquire Sleepy Industries and improve efficiency to the extent that the market value of Sleepy will increase by $5 million. Sleepy currently sells for $20 a share, and there are 1 million shares outstanding.

    a. Sleepy's management is willing to accept a cash offer of $25 a share. Can the merger be accomplished on a friendly basis?
    b. What will happen if Sleepy's management holds out for an offer of $28 a share?

11. **Mergers and P/E Ratios.** Castles in the Sand currently sells at a price-earnings multiple of 10. The firm has 2 million shares outstanding, and sells at a price per share of $40. Firm Foundation has a P/E multiple of 8, has 1 million shares outstanding, and sells at a price per share of $20.

    a. If Castles acquires the other firm by exchanging one of its shares for every two of Firm Foundation's, what will be the earnings per share of the merged firm?
    b. What should be the P/E of the new firm if the merger has no economic gains? What will happen to Castles's price per share? Show that shareholders of neither Castles nor Firm Foundation realize any change in wealth.
    c. What will happen to Castles's price per share if the market does not realize that the P/E ratio of the merged firm ought to differ from Castles's premerger ratio?
    d. How are the gains from the merger split between shareholders of the two firms if the market is fooled as in part (c)?

12. **Stock versus Cash Offers.** Sweet Cola Corp. (SCC) is bidding to take over Salty Dog Pretzels (SDP). SCC has 3,000 shares outstanding, selling at $50 per share. SDP has 2,000 shares outstanding, selling at $17.50 a share. SCC estimates the economic gain from the merger to be $15,000.

    a. If SDP can be acquired for $20 a share, what is the NPV of the merger to SCC?
    b. What will SCC sell for when the market learns that it plans to acquire SDP for $20 a share? What will SDP sell for? What are the percentage gains to the shareholders of each firm?

Please visit us at www.mhhe.com/bmm5e or refer to your Student CD

Please visit us at www.mhhe.com/bmm5e or refer to your Student CD

Please visit us at www.mhhe.com/bmm5e or refer to your Student CD

c. Now suppose that the merger takes place through an exchange of stock. On the basis of the premerger prices of the firms, SCC sells for $50, so instead of paying $20 cash, SCC issues .40 of its shares for every SDP share acquired. What will be the price of the merged firm?

d. What is the NPV of the merger to SCC when it uses an exchange of stock? Why does your answer differ from part (a)?

CHALLENGE PROBLEMS

13. **Bootstrap Game.** The Muck and Slurry merger has fallen through (see Section 21.3). But World Enterprises is determined to report earnings per share of $2.67. It therefore acquires the Wheelrim and Axle Company. You are given the following facts:

	World Enterprises	Wheelrim and Axle	Merged Firm
Earnings per share	$2	$2.50	$2.67
Price per share	$40	$25	____
Price-earnings ratio	20	10	____
Number of shares	100,000	200,000	____
Total earnings	$200,000	$500,000	____
Total market value	$4,000,000	$5,000,000	____

Once again there are no gains from merging. In exchange for Wheelrim and Axle shares, World Enterprises issues just enough of its own shares to ensure its $2.67 earnings per share objective.

a. Complete the above table for the merged firm.

b. How many shares of World Enterprises are exchanged for each share of Wheelrim and Axle?

c. What is the cost of the merger to World Enterprises?

d. What is the change in the total market value of those World Enterprises shares that were outstanding before the merger?

Please visit us at www.mhhe.com/bmm5e or refer to your Student CD

14. **Merger Gains and Costs.** As treasurer of Leisure Products, Inc., you are investigating the possible acquisition of Plastitoys. You have the following basic data:

	Leisure Products	Plastitoys
Forecast earnings per share	$5	$1.50
Forecast dividend per share	$3	$.80
Number of shares	1,000,000	600,000
Stock price	$90	$20

You estimate that investors currently expect a steady growth of about 6 percent in Plastitoys's earnings and dividends. You believe that Leisure Products could increase Plastitoys's growth rate to 8 percent per year, without any additional capital investment required.

a. What is the gain from the acquisition?

b. What is the cost of the acquisition if Leisure Products pays $25 in cash for each share of Plastitoys?

c. What is the cost of the acquisition if Leisure Products offers one share of Leisure Products for every three shares of Plastitoys?

d. How would the cost of the cash offer and the share offer alter if the expected growth rate of Plastitoys were not increased by the merger?

STANDARD
&POOR'S

Go to Market Insight at **www.mhhe.com/edumarketinsight**.

1. Hewlett-Packard purchased Compaq Computer in 2002. Go to the *Excel Analytics* section for HP and examine its financial ratios to see whether the merger created any obvious synergies. Examine various measures of operational efficiency (e.g., turnover ratios, output per employee) as well as evidence from market prices (e.g., price-earnings ratios).

2. Suppose that Southern Company (SO), an electric utility, purchased the biotech firm Amgen (AMGN) by exchanging Southern stock for Amgen stock. There would be no meaningful synergies since the firms are in wholly different industries, so suppose that the combined market value of the merged firm would be just the sum of the market values of both firms taken individually. Use data from *Excel Analytics* for each firm to compute what would happen to Southern's price-earnings ratio.

SOLUTIONS TO SELF-TEST QUESTIONS

21.1   a. Horizontal merger. IBM is in the same industry as Dell Computer.
       b. Conglomerate merger. Dell Computer and Safeway are in different industries.
       c. Vertical merger. Safeway is expanding backward to acquire one of its suppliers, Campbell Soup.
       d. Conglomerate merger. Campbell Soup and IBM are in different industries.

21.2   Given current earnings of $2 a share and a share price of $10, Muck and Slurry would have a market value of $1,000,000 and a price-earnings ratio of only 5. It can be acquired for only half as many shares of World Enterprises, 25,000 shares. Therefore, the merged firm will have 125,000 shares outstanding and earnings of $400,000, resulting in earnings per share of $3.20, higher than the $2.67 value in the third column of Table 21–2.

21.3   The cost of the merger is $4 million: the $4 per share premium offered to Goldfish shareholders times 1 million shares. If the merger has positive NPV to Killer Shark, the gain must be greater than $4 million.

21.4   Yes. Look again at Table 21–4. Total market value is still $540, but Cislunar will have to issue 1 million shares to complete the merger. Total shares in the merged firm will be 11 million. The postmerger share price is $49.09, so Cislunar and its shareholders still come out ahead.

MINICASE

McPhee Food Halls operated a chain of supermarkets in the west of Scotland. The company had had a lackluster record, and since the death of its founder in late 2001, it had been regarded as a prime target for a takeover bid. In anticipation of a bid, McPhee's share price moved up from £4.90 in March to a 12-month high of £5.80 on June 10, despite the fact that the London stock market index as a whole was largely unchanged.

Almost nobody anticipated a bid coming from Fenton, a diversified retail business with a chain of clothing and department stores. Though Fenton operated food halls in several of its department stores, it had relatively little experience in food retailing. Fenton's management had, however, been contemplating a merger with McPhee for some time. The managers not only felt that they could make use of McPhee's food retailing skills within their department stores, but they also believed that better management and inventory control in McPhee's business could result in cost savings worth £10 million.

Fenton's offer of 8 Fenton shares for every 10 McPhee shares was announced after the market close on June 10. Since McPhee had 5 million shares outstanding, the acquisition would add an additional 5 × (8/10) = 4 million shares to the 10 million Fenton shares that were already outstanding. While Fenton's management believed that it would be difficult for McPhee to mount a successful takeover defense, the company and its investment bankers privately agreed that the company could afford to raise the offer if it proved necessary.

Investors were not persuaded of the benefits of combining a supermarket with a department store company, and on June 11 Fenton's shares opened lower and drifted down £.10 to close the day at £7.90. McPhee's shares, however, jumped to £6.32 a share.

Fenton's financial manager was due to attend a meeting with the company's investment bankers that evening, but before doing so, he decided to run the numbers once again. First he reestimated the gain and cost of the merger. Then he analyzed that day's fall in Fenton's stock price to see whether investors believed there were any gains to be had from merging. Finally, he decided to revisit the issue of whether Fenton could afford to raise its bid at a later stage. If the effect was simply a further fall in the price of Fenton stock, the move could be self-defeating.

International Financial Management

RELATED WEB LINKS

BANK OF ENGLAND

Search

About the Bank   Monetary Policy   Banknotes   Markets   Financial Stability   Publications   Statistics   Education

Welcome to the Central Bank of the United Kingdom

What We Do

The Bank sets interest rates to keep inflation low, issues banknotes and works to maintain a stable financial system. More

Current Highlights

» Speech by the Governor - Wyoming, USA
» Speech by Charlie Bean - Wyoming, USA
» MPC Minutes - August 2005
» Inflation Report - August 2005

The Financial System

A safe and stable financial system is essential to the economy. The Bank assesses risks to the stability of the financial system and works to strengthen the way it operates. More

Interest Rates and Inflation

Interest rates influence spending and saving in the economy and the prices we pay for goods and services. Low inflation helps to maintain a stable economy and the value of our money. More

Inflation Report Press Conference August 2005 Click here for Webcast

Banknotes

The Bank issues the banknotes that we use in our daily lives. Confidence in the currency is vital to the economy. More

www.federalreserve.gov

www.ny.frb.org

www.stlouisfed.org

www.oecd.org

www.bankofengland.co.uk

www.ecb.int   Analysis and data for economies around the world.

www.exchangerate.com

www.x-rates.com

www.oanda.com

www.economist.com/markets/currency/map.cfm   Exchange rate data.

www.corporateinformation.com

www.emgmkts.com

www.securities.com   Information about corporations and economies around the world.

www.cia.gov/cia/publications/factbook

www.prsgroup.com   Country profiles and political risk analysis.

www.riskcenter.com   A site devoted to risk analysis and management, with many international applications.

McDonald's does business around the world. What new issues does international business raise for the financial manager?

© Getty Images

Thus far we have talked principally about doing business at home. But many companies have substantial overseas interests. Of course, the objectives of international financial management are still the same. You want to buy assets that are worth *more* than they cost, and you want to pay for them by issuing liabilities that are worth *less* than the money raised. But when you try to apply these criteria to an international business, you come up against some new wrinkles.

You must, for example, know how to deal with more than one currency. Therefore we open this chapter with a look at foreign exchange markets.

The financial manager must also remember that interest rates differ from country to country. For example, in early 2005, the short-term interest rate was 3.25 percent in the United States, 2.1 percent in the euro countries, and less than .1 percent in Japan. We will discuss the reasons for these differences in interest rates, along with some of the implications for financing overseas operations.

Exchange rate fluctuations can knock companies off course and transform black ink into red. We will therefore discuss how firms can protect themselves against exchange risks.

We will also discuss how international companies decide on capital investments. How do they choose the discount rate? You'll find that the basic principles of capital budgeting are the same as those for domestic projects, but there are a few pitfalls to watch for.

After studying this chapter you should be able to:

- Understand the difference between spot and forward exchange rates.

- Understand the basic relationships between spot exchange rates, forward exchange rates, interest rates, and inflation rates.

- Formulate simple strategies to protect the firm against exchange rate risk.

- Perform an NPV analysis for projects with cash flows in foreign currencies.

22.1　Foreign Exchange Markets

An American company that imports goods from France may need to exchange its dollars for euros in order to pay for its purchases. An American company exporting to France may *receive* euros, which it sells in exchange for dollars. Both firms must make use of the foreign exchange market, where currencies are traded.

The foreign exchange market has no central marketplace. All business is conducted by computer and telephone. The principal dealers are the large commercial banks, and any corporation that wants to buy or sell currency usually does so through a commercial bank.

Turnover in the foreign exchange markets is huge. In London alone about $750 billion of currency changes hands each day. That is equivalent to an annual turnover of $188 trillion ($188,000,000,000,000). New York and Tokyo together account for a further $660 billion of turnover per day. Compare this with trading volume of the New York Stock Exchange, where less than $60 billion of stock typically changes hands on any given day.

Suppose you ask someone the price of bread. He may tell you that you can buy two loaves for a dollar, or he may say that one loaf costs 50 cents. Similarly, if you ask a foreign exchange dealer to quote you a price for Ruritanian francs, she may tell you that you can buy 2 francs for a dollar *or* that 1 franc costs $.50. The first quote (the number of francs that you can buy for a dollar) is known as an *indirect quote* of the **exchange rate.** The second quote (the number of dollars that it costs to buy 1 franc) is known as a *direct quote.* Of course, both quotes provide the same information. If you can buy 2 francs for a dollar, then you can easily calculate that the cost of 1 franc is $1/2.0 = \$.50$.

Now look at Table 22–1, which has been adapted from the daily table of exchange rates in the London *Financial Times.* The first column of figures in the table shows the exchange rate for a number of countries on January 20, 2005. By custom, the prices of most currencies are expressed as indirect quotes. Thus you can see that you could buy 11.2365 Mexican pesos for 1 dollar. However, to make things confusing, the price of the euro and the British pound are generally expressed as *direct* quotes. So Table 22–1 shows that it cost $1.2952 to buy 1 euro (€1).

exchange rate

Amount of one currency needed to purchase one unit of another.

TABLE 22–1 Spot and forward exchange rates

	Quotation*	Spot Rate	Forward Rate		
			1 Month	3 Months	1 Year
Europe					
EMU (euro)	Direct	1.2952	1.2956	1.2969	1.3069
Sweden (krona)	Indirect	6.9786	6.9756	6.9674	6.9078
Switzerland (franc)	Indirect	1.1919	1.1901	1.1861	1.1651
United Kingdom (pound)	Direct	1.8704	1.8668	1.8607	1.8412
Americas					
Canada (dollar)	Indirect	1.2333	1.2334	1.2330	1.2282
Mexico (peso)	Indirect	11.2365	11.2985	11.4145	11.8775
Pacific/Africa					
Hong Kong (dollar)	Indirect	7.7989	7.7858	7.7626	7.6681
Japan (yen)	Indirect	103.155	102.935	102.465	99.930
South Africa (rand)	Indirect	6.0813	6.1071	6.1552	6.3518
South Korea (won)	Indirect	1032.50	1033.35	1033.85	1030.95

*Direct quotation: number of dollars per unit of foreign currency; *indirect quotation:* units of foreign currency per dollar.
Source: *Financial Times,* January 21, 2005.

| EXAMPLE 22.1 ▶ | A Yen for Trade |

How many yen will it cost a Japanese importer to purchase $1,000 worth of oranges from a California farmer? How many dollars will it take for that farmer to buy a Japanese DVD player priced in Japan at 30,000 yen (¥)?

The exchange rate is ¥103.155 per dollar. The $1,000 of oranges will require the Japanese importer to come up with $1,000 × (¥103.155/$) = ¥103,155. The DVD player will require the American importer to come up with ¥30,000/(¥103.155/$) = $290. ◀

Self-Test 22.1

Use the exchange rates in Table 22–1. How many euros can you buy for 1 dollar (an indirect quote)? How many dollars can you buy for 1 yen (a direct quote)?

spot rate of exchange
Exchange rate for an immediate transaction.

The exchange rates in the first column of figures in Table 22–1 are the prices of currency for immediate delivery. These are known as spot rates of exchange. For example, the **spot rate of exchange** for Mexican pesos is pesos 11.2365/$. In other words, it costs 11.2365 Mexican pesos to buy 1 dollar.

Many countries allow their currencies to float, so that the exchange rate fluctuates from day to day, and from minute to minute. When the currency increases in value, meaning that you need less of the foreign currency to buy 1 dollar, the currency is said to *appreciate*. When you need more of the currency to buy 1 dollar, the currency is said to *depreciate*.

Self-Test 22.2

Table 22–1 shows the exchange rate for the Swiss franc on January 20, 2005. The previous day, the spot rate of exchange for the Swiss franc was SFr1.1827/$. Thus on January 20, you could buy more Swiss francs for your dollar than 1 day earlier. Did the Swiss franc appreciate or depreciate?

Some countries try to avoid fluctuations in the value of their currency and seek instead to maintain a fixed exchange rate. But fixed rates seldom last forever. If everybody tries to sell the currency, eventually the country will be forced to allow the currency to depreciate. When this happens, exchange rates can change dramatically. For example, when Argentina gave up trying to fix its exchange rate in December 2001, the value of the Argentinian peso fell by over 70 percent in a few months.

These fluctuations in exchange rates can get companies into hot water. For example, suppose you have agreed to buy a shipment of Japanese DVD players for ¥100 million and to make the payment when you take delivery of the players at the end of 12 months. You could wait until the 12 months have passed and then buy 100 million yen at the spot exchange rate. If the spot rate is unchanged at ¥103.155/$, then the players will cost you ¥100 million/(¥103.155/$) = $969,415. But you are taking a risk by waiting, for the yen may become more expensive. For example, if the yen appreciates to ¥100/$, then you will have to pay out ¥100 million/(¥100/$) = $1 million.

forward exchange rate
Exchange rate for a future transaction.

You can avoid exchange rate risk and fix your dollar cost by "buying the yen forward," that is, by arranging *now* to buy yen in the future. A foreign exchange *forward contract* is an agreement to trade at a future date a given amount of currency at an exchange rate agreed to *today*. The **forward exchange rate** is the price of currency for delivery at some time in the future. The last three columns in Table 22–1 show 1-month, 3-month, and 1-year forward exchange rates. For example, the 1-year forward rate for the yen is quoted at 99.93 yen per dollar. If you buy 100 million yen forward, you don't pay anything today; you simply fix today the price which you will pay for your yen in the future. At the end of the year you receive your 100 million yen and hand over ¥100 million/(¥99.93/$) = $1,000,700 in payment.

Notice that if you buy Japanese yen forward, you get fewer yen for your dollar than if you buy spot. In this case, the yen is said to trade at a forward *premium* relative to the dollar. Expressed as a percentage, the 1-year forward premium is

$$\frac{103.155 - 99.93}{99.93} \times 100 = 3.23\%$$

You could also say that the dollar was selling at a *forward discount* of about 3.23 percent.[1]

A forward purchase or sale is a made-to-order transaction between you and the bank. It can be for any currency, any amount, and any delivery day. You could buy, say, 99,999 Vietnamese dong or Haitian gourdes for a year and a day forward as long as you can find a bank ready to deal. Most forward transactions are for 6 months or less, but banks are prepared to buy or sell the major currencies for up to 10 years forward.

There is also an organized market for currency for future delivery known as the currency *futures* market. Futures contracts are highly standardized versions of forward contracts—they exist only for the main currencies, they are for specified amounts, and choice of delivery dates is limited. The advantage of this standardization is that there is a very low-cost market in currency futures. Huge numbers of contracts are bought and sold daily on the futures exchanges.

When you buy a forward or futures contract, you are committed to taking delivery of the currency. As an alternative, you can take out an *option* to buy or sell currency in the future at a price that is fixed today. Made-to-measure currency options can be bought from the major banks, and standardized options are traded on the options exchanges. We discuss futures, forwards, and options in more detail in Chapters 23 and 24.

Self-Test 22.3

A skiing vacation in Switzerland costs SFr1,500.

a. How many dollars does that represent? Use the exchange rates in Table 22–1.
b. Suppose that the dollar depreciates by 10 percent relative to the Swiss franc, so each dollar buys 10 percent fewer Swiss francs than before. What will be the new value of the indirect exchange rate?
c. If the Swiss vacation continues to cost the same number of Swiss francs, what will happen to the cost in dollars?
d. If the tour company that is offering the vacation keeps the price fixed in dollars, what will happen to the number of Swiss francs that it will receive?

22.2 Some Basic Relationships

The financial manager of an international business must cope with fluctuations in exchange rates and must be aware of the distinction between spot and forward exchange rates. She must also recognize that two countries may have different interest rates. To

---

[1] Here is a minor point that sometimes causes confusion. To calculate the forward premium, we divide by the *forward* rate as long as the exchange quotes are *indirect*. If you use *direct* quotes, the correct formula is

$$\text{Forward premium} = \frac{\text{forward rate} - \text{spot rate}}{\text{spot rate}}$$

In our example, the corresponding direct quote for spot yen is $1/103.155 = .009694$, while the direct forward quote is $1/99.93 = .010007$. Substituting these rates in our revised formula gives

$$\text{Forward premium} = \frac{.010007 - .009694}{.009694} = .0323, \text{ or } 3.23\%$$

The two methods give the same answer.

FIGURE 22–1 Some simple theories linking spot and forward exchange rates, interest rates, and inflation rates.

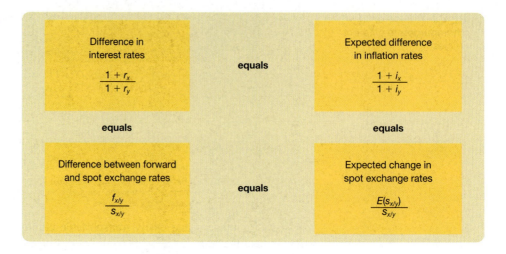

develop a consistent international financial policy, the financial manager needs to understand how exchange rates are determined and why one country may have a lower interest rate than another. Here are four questions that managers need to consider:

1. Why do interest rates in different countries differ?
2. What explains the difference between the forward exchange rate and the spot rate?
3. What is the relationship between the spot exchange rate today and the expected exchange rate at some future date?
4. How do different rates of inflation in two countries affect each country's interest rate as well as the exchange rate between the currencies of those countries?

These are complex issues, but as a first cut we suggest that you think of spot and forward exchange rates, interest rates, and inflation rates as being linked as shown in Figure 22–1. Let's explain.

Exchange Rates and Inflation

Consider first the relationship between changes in the exchange rate and inflation rates (the two boxes on the right in Figure 22–1). The idea here is simple: If country X suffers a higher rate of inflation than country Y, then the value of X's currency will decline relative to Y's. The decline in value shows up in the spot exchange rate for X's currency.

But let's slow down and consider why changes in inflation and spot interest rates are linked. Think first about the prices of the *same* good or service in two different countries and currencies.

Suppose you notice that gold can be bought in New York for $400 an ounce and sold in Mexico City for 5,000 pesos an ounce. If there are no restrictions on the import of gold, you could be onto a good thing. You buy gold for $400 and put it on the first plane to Mexico City, where you sell it for 5,000 pesos. Then (using the exchange rates from Table 22–1) you can exchange your 5,000 pesos for 5,000/11.2365 = $445. You have made a gross profit of $45 an ounce. Of course, you have to pay transportation and insurance costs out of this, but there should still be something left over for you.

You returned from your trip with a surefire profit. But surefire profits don't exist—not for long. As others notice the disparity between the price of gold in Mexico and the price in New York, the price will be forced down in Mexico and up in New York until the profit opportunity disappears. This ensures that the dollar price of gold is about the same in the two countries.[2]

---

[2] Activity of this kind is known as *arbitrage*. The arbitrageur makes a riskless profit by noticing discrepancies in prices.

TABLE 22-2 Price of Big Mac hamburgers in different currencies

Country	Local Price Converted to U.S. Dollars	Country	Local Price Converted to U.S. Dollars
Canada	2.60	Philippines	1.42
China	1.26	Russia	1.49
Denmark	4.97	South Africa	2.44
Euro area	3.75	Switzerland	5.46
Japan	2.50	United Kingdom	3.61
Mexico	2.12	United States	3.00

Gold is a standard and easily transportable commodity, but to some degree you might expect that the same forces would be acting to equalize the domestic and foreign prices of other goods. Those goods that can be bought more cheaply abroad will be imported, and that will force down the price of the domestic product. Similarly, those goods that can be bought more cheaply in the United States will be exported, and that will force down the price of the foreign product.

law of one price
Theory that prices of goods in all countries should be equal when translated to a common currency.

This conclusion is often called the **law of one price.** Just as the price of goods in Safeway must be roughly the same as the price of goods in A&P, so the price of goods in Mexico when converted into dollars must be roughly the same as the price in the United States:

$$\text{Dollar price of goods in USA} = \frac{\text{peso price of goods in Mexico}}{\text{number of pesos per dollar}}$$

$$\$400 = \frac{\text{peso price of gold in Mexico}}{11.2365}$$

$$\text{Price of gold in Mexico} = \$400 \times (\text{peso } 11.2365/\$) = 4{,}495 \text{ pesos}$$

No one who has compared prices in foreign stores with prices at home really believes that the law of one price holds exactly. Look at the first column of Table 22–2, which shows the local price of a Big Mac in different countries converted into dollars. You can see that the price varies considerably across countries. For example, Big Macs were 82 percent more expensive in Switzerland than in the United States, but they were less than half the price in China.[3]

This suggests a possible way to make a quick buck. Why don't you buy a hamburger-to-go in China for $1.26 and take it for resale to Switzerland, where the price in dollars is $5.46? The answer, of course, is that the gain would not cover the costs. The law of one price works very well for commodities like gold where transportation costs are relatively small; it works far less well for Big Macs and very badly indeed for haircuts and appendectomies, which cannot be transported at all.

EXAMPLE 22.2 ▶   The Beer Standard

There are very few McDonald's branches in Africa, so we can't use Big Macs to test the law of one price there. But barley beer is a common and relatively homogeneous product throughout Africa. So we can test the law of one price using the beer standard.

Table 22–3 shows the price of a bottle of beer in several African countries expressed in local currencies and converted into South African rand using the spot exchange rate. For example, beer in Kenya cost 41.25 shillings; at an exchange rate of 10.27 Kenyan shillings per rand, this is equivalent to a price of 41.25/10.27 = 4.02 rand. This is 1.75 times the cost of beer in South Africa; for the costs to be equal, the shilling would need

---

[3] Of course, it could also be that Big Macs come with a bigger smile in Switzerland. If the quality of the hamburgers or the service differs, we are not comparing like with like.

TABLE 22–3 The price of a beer in different countries

Country	Beer Prices		Actual Rand Exchange Rate, March 1999	Under(–)/Over(+) Valuation against the Rand, %
	In Local Currency	In Rand		
South Africa	Rand2.30	2.30		
Botswana	Pula2.20	2.94	0.75	28
Ghana	Cedi1,200	3.17	379.10	38
Kenya	Shilling41.25	4.02	10.27	75
Malawi	Kwacha18.50	2.66	6.96	16
Mauritius	Rupee15.00	3.72	4.03	62
Namibia	N$2.50	2.50	1.00	9
Zambia	Kwacha1,200	3.52	340.68	53
Zimbabwe	Z$9.00	1.46	6.15	–36

to depreciate by 75 percent to a new exchange rate of $10.27 \times 1.75 = 17.9$ shillings per rand. Therefore, we might say that this comparison suggests the shilling is 75 percent overvalued against the rand. ◀

purchasing power parity (PPP)

Theory that the cost of living in different countries is equal and that exchange rates adjust to offset inflation differentials across countries.

A weaker version of the law of one price is known as **purchasing power parity,** or **PPP.** PPP states that although some goods may cost different amounts in different countries, the *general* cost of living should be the same in any two countries. Purchasing power parity implies that the relative costs of living in two countries will not be affected by differences in their inflation rates. Instead, the different inflation rates in local currencies will be offset by changes in the exchange rate between the two currencies.

For example, between 1999 and 2004, prices in Turkey rose 4.7 times. As prices in Turkey increased, Turkish exporters would have found it impossible to sell their goods if the exchange rate had not also changed. But, of course, the exchange rate did adjust. In fact, by the end of the period the lira bought about 60 percent less foreign currency than before.

In Figure 22–2 we have plotted the relative change in purchasing power for a sample of countries against the change in the exchange rate. Turkey is toward the bottom left-hand corner. You can see that although the relationship is far from exact, large differences in inflation rates are generally accompanied by an offsetting change in the exchange rate. In fact, if you have to make a long-term forecast of the exchange rate, it is very difficult to do much better than to assume that it will offset the effect of any differences in the inflation rates.

If purchasing power parity holds, then your forecast of the difference in inflation rates is also your best forecast of the change in the spot rate of exchange. For example, suppose you need a forecast of the exchange rate for the South African rand (R). Purchasing power parity would imply that you should focus on the difference between inflation rates in South Africa and the United States:

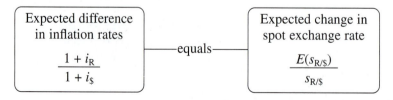

Let's check that this makes sense. Table 22–1 shows that the exchange rate for the South African rand in early 2005 was R6.0813/$. If the cost of living was the same in

FIGURE 22-2 A decline in the exchange rate and a decline in a country's purchasing power usually go hand in hand. In this diagram, each point represents the experience of a different country between 1999 and 2004.

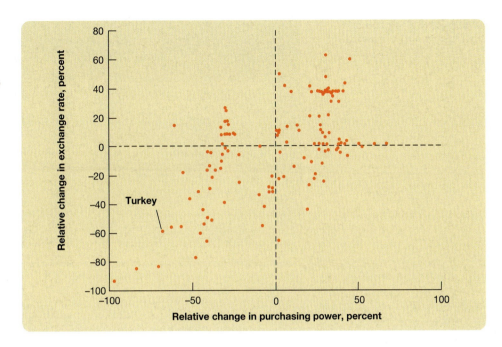

the United States and South Africa, then 6.0813 rands bought the same bundle of goods and services as 1 dollar. Economists were forecasting that inflation in 2005 would be about 5 percent in South Africa and 2 percent in the United States. So at the end of the year, based on these inflation rates, R6.0813 × 1.05 will buy the same quantity of goods as $1 × 1.02. Equivalently, $1 will have the same purchasing power as R6.0813 × 1.05/1.02. Purchasing power parity, therefore, implies that this is the expected exchange rate at the end of 2005. Therefore,[4]

$$\begin{array}{l} \text{Expected spot} \\ \text{exchange rate (R/\$)} \end{array} = \begin{array}{l} \text{Current spot} \\ \text{rate (R/\$)} \end{array} \times \frac{1 + \text{expected South African inflation}}{1 + \text{expected U.S. inflation}}$$

$$= \text{R6.0813/\$} \times 1.05/1.02 = \text{R6.2602/\$}$$

Notice that since inflation is expected to be higher in South Africa, the rand is forecast to depreciate. If inflation were expected to be higher in the United States, then the dollar would be forecast to depreciate.

Self-Test 22.4

Suppose that gold currently costs $440 an ounce in the United States and £240 an ounce in Great Britain.

a. What must be the pound/dollar exchange rate?
b. Suppose that gold prices rise by 2 percent in the United States and by 5 percent in Great Britain. What will be the price of gold in the two currencies at the end of the year? What must be the exchange rate at the end of the year?
c. Show that at the end of the year each dollar buys about 3 percent more pounds, as predicted by PPP.

Inflation and Interest Rates

One-year interest rates in 2005 were about $7\frac{7}{8}$ percent in South Africa and 3.25 percent in the United States. Why?

---

[4] A warning: Notice that the relationships in Figure 22–1 all apply to *indirect* exchange rates, i.e., foreign currency per dollar. Some exchange rates such as the pound/U.S. dollar and euro/U.S. dollar exchange rates are conventionally expressed as direct rates. To use our formulas, you must first convert the quoted rates to indirect rates.

The answer lies in the distinction that we made in Chapter 4 between nominal and real rates of interest. Bank deposits usually promise you a fixed nominal rate of interest, but they don't promise what that money will buy. If you invested 100 rand for a year at an interest rate of 7⅞ percent, you would have 7⅞ percent more rands at the end of the year than you did at the start. But you might not be 7⅞ percent better off. Some of the gain would be needed to compensate for inflation.

The nominal rate of interest in 2005 was much lower in the United States, but then so was the inflation rate. The real rates of interest were much closer to each other than the nominal rates. There is a general law at work here. Just as water always flows downhill, so capital always flows where returns are greatest. But it is the *real* returns that concern investors, not the *nominal* returns. Two countries may have different nominal interest rates but the same expected real interest rate.

If expected real interest rates are the same everywhere, then differences in the nominal interest rate must reflect differences in expected inflation rates. This conclusion is often called the **international Fisher effect,** after the economist Irving Fisher.

international Fisher effect
Theory that real interest rates in all countries should be equal, with differences in nominal rates reflecting differences in expected inflation.

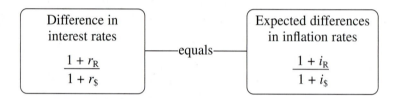

In other words, capital market equilibrium requires that real interest rates be the same in any two countries.

EXAMPLE 22.3 ▶ International Fisher Effect

If the nominal interest rate in South Africa is 7⅞ = 7.875 percent and the expected inflation is 5 percent, then

$$r_R(\text{real}) = \frac{1 + r_R}{E(1 + i_R)} - 1 = \frac{1.07875}{1.05} - 1 = .027, \text{ or } 2.7\%$$

In the United States, where the nominal interest rate is about 3.25 percent and the expected inflation rate is about 2 percent,

$$r_\$(\text{real}) = \frac{1 + r_\$}{E(1 + i_\$)} - 1 = \frac{1.0325}{1.02} - 1 = .012, \text{ or } 1.2\%$$

The real interest rate is higher in South Africa than in the United States, but the difference in the real rates is less than half the difference in nominal rates.   ◀

How similar are real interest rates around the world? It is hard to say, because we cannot directly observe *expected* inflation. In Figure 22–3 we have plotted the average interest rate in each of 42 countries against the inflation that in fact occurred. You can see that the countries with the highest interest rates generally had the highest inflation rates.

Self-Test 22.5

American investors can invest $1,000 at an interest rate of 3.25 percent. Alternatively, they can convert those funds to 6,979 Swedish krona at the current exchange rate and invest at 2 percent in Sweden. If the expected inflation rate in the United States is 2 percent, what must be investors' forecast of the inflation rate in Sweden?

FIGURE 22–3 Countries with the highest interest rates generally have the highest subsequent inflation rates. In this diagram, each point represents a different country.

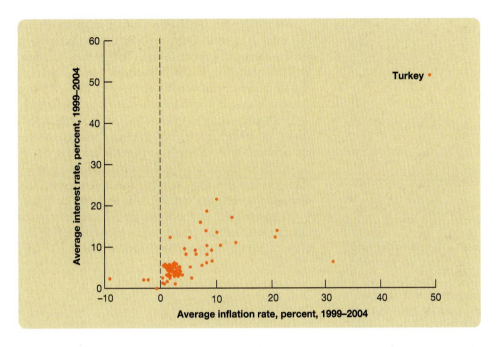

Interest Rates and Exchange Rates

You are an investor with $1 million to invest for 1 year. The interest rate in South Africa is 7.875 percent, and in the United States it is 3.25 percent. Is it better to make a South African rand loan or a U.S. dollar loan?

The answer seems obvious: Isn't it better to earn an interest rate of 7.875 percent than 3.25 percent? But appearances may be deceptive. If you lend in South Africa, you first need to convert your $1 million into rands. When the loan is repaid at the end of the year, you need to convert your rands back into U.S. dollars. Of course, you don't know what the exchange rate will be at the end of the year, but you can fix the future value of your rands by selling them forward. If the forward rate of exchange is sufficiently low, you may do just as well keeping your money in the United States.

Let's use the data from Table 22–1 to check which loan is the better deal:

- *U.S. dollar loan.* The rate of interest on a U.S. dollar loan is 3.25 percent. Therefore, at the end of the year, you get $1,000,000 \times 1.0325 = \$1,032,500$.
- *South African rand loan.* The current rate of exchange (from Table 22–1) is R6.0813/$. Therefore, you can convert your $1,000,000 into R6,081,300. The interest rate on a rand loan is $7\frac{7}{8} = 7.875$ percent, so at the end of the year you will have $6,081,300 \times 1.07875 = $ R6,560,202. Of course, you don't know what the exchange rate will be at the end of the year. But that doesn't matter. You can nail down the rate at which you convert your rands back into U.S. dollars. The 1-year forward exchange rate is R6.3518/$. Therefore, by selling the R6,560,202 forward, you make sure that you will get R6,560,202/(R6.3518/$) = $1,032,810.

Thus the two investments offer almost exactly the same rate of return. They have to—they are both risk-free. If the domestic interest rate were different from the "covered" foreign rate, you would have a money machine: You could borrow in the market with the lower rate and lend in the market with the higher rate.

A difference in interest rates must be offset by a difference between spot and forward exchange rates. If the risk-free interest rate in country X is higher than that in country Y, then country X's currency will buy less of Y's in a forward transaction than in a spot transaction.

When you lend South African rands, you gain because you get a higher interest rate. But you lose because you sell the rands forward for fewer dollars than you have to pay for them today. The interest rate differential is

$$\frac{1 + r_R}{1 + r_\$} = \frac{1.07875}{1.0325} = 1.0448$$

and the differential between the forward and spot exchange rates is virtually identical:

$$\frac{f_{R/\$}}{s_{R/\$}} = \frac{\text{R}6.3518/\$}{\text{R}6.0813/\$} = 1.0445$$

interest rate parity
Theory that forward premium equals interest rate differential.

Interest rate parity theory says that the interest rate differential must equal the differential between the forward and spot exchange rates. Thus

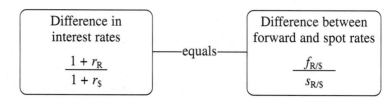

EXAMPLE 22.4 ▶ What If Interest Rate Parity Does *Not* Hold?

Suppose the 1-year forward rate on the rand is not R6.3518/$ but is instead R6.10/$. The following table lays out a strategy that enables you to take advantage of the mispricing:

	Cash Flow Now	Cash Flow in 1 Year
Borrow $1 million for 1 year at dollar interest rate of 3.25%. Convert the proceeds of the dollar loan into rands at the spot exchange rate of R6.0813/$.	+ $1 million × (R6.0813/$) = +R6,081,300	−$1 million × 1.0325 = −$1,032,500
Invest the rands in South Africa at the interest rate of 7.875%.	− R6,081,300	+ R6,081,300 × 1.07875 = +R6,560,202
Sell forward the rands that you will receive in 1 year. The forward exchange rate is R6.10/$.	0	−R6,560,202 + R6,560,202/(R6.10/$) = −R6,560,202 + $1,075,443
Total	0	+$42,943

Notice that your profit is risk-free and that you don't need to invest any of your own funds (your initial net cash flow was zero). Risk-free strategies like these that take advantage of misalignments in two prices (here, the spot and forward exchange rates) are called *arbitrage* strategies. It's too bad that, in practice, arbitrage opportunities are rare. ◀

Self-Test 22.6

Look at the exchange rates in Table 22–1. Does the Swiss franc sell at a forward premium or discount on the dollar? Does this suggest that the interest rate in Switzerland is higher or lower than in the United States? Use the interest rate parity relationship to estimate the 1-year interest rate in Switzerland. Assume the U.S. interest rate is 3.25 percent.

Whereas the other relationships shown in Figure 22–1 tend to hold approximately, interest rate parity almost always holds with great precision. This should not be

surprising in light of Example 22.4, which shows that there will be easy opportunities for riskless arbitrage whenever parity is violated. In fact, foreign currency dealers set the forward exchange rate by looking at the difference between the interest rates on deposits in different currencies.

Interest rate parity also holds an important lesson for managers. International capital markets and currency markets function well and offer no free lunches. You can't assume that it is cheaper to borrow in a currency with a low nominal rate of interest. If you hedge your exchange rate exposure, interest rate parity implies that the all-in cost of borrowing will be the same in any currency. If you don't hedge, exchange rate movements can easily offset the apparent advantage of a low interest rate opportunity.

Self-Test 22.7

Starlight Corporation borrows 100 million Japanese yen at an apparently attractive interest rate of 1 percent, when the exchange rate between the yen and the U.S. dollar is ¥103.155/$. Suppose that 1 year later, when Starlight has to repay its loan, the exchange rate is ¥98.20/$. Calculate in U.S. dollars the amount that Starlight borrows and the amounts that it pays in interest and principal (assume annual interest payments). What is the effective U.S. dollar interest rate that Starlight has paid on the loan?

The Forward Rate and the Expected Spot Rate

If you buy rands forward, you get more rands for your U.S. dollar than if you buy them spot. So the rand is selling at a forward discount. Now let us think how this discount is related to expected changes in spot rates of exchange.

The 1-year forward rate for the rand is R6.3518/$. Would you sell rands at this rate if you expected the rand to rise in value? Probably not. You would be tempted to wait until the end of the year and get a better price in the spot market. If other traders felt the same way, nobody would sell rands forward and everybody would want to buy. The result would be that the number of rands that you could get for your dollar in the forward market would fall. Similarly, if traders expected the rand to fall sharply in value, they might be reluctant to *buy* forward and, in order to attract buyers, the number of rands that you could buy for a U.S. dollar in the forward market would need to rise.[5]

expectations theory of exchange rates

Theory that expected spot exchange rate equals the forward rate.

This is the reasoning behind the **expectations theory of exchange rates,** which predicts that the forward rate equals the expected future spot exchange rate: $f_{R/\$} = E(s_{R/\$})$. Equivalently, we can say that the *percentage* difference between the forward rate and today's spot rate is equal to the expected *percentage* change in the spot rate:

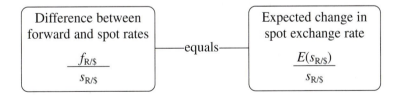

This is the final leg of our quadrilateral in Figure 22–1.

The expectations theory of forward rates does not imply that managers are perfect forecasters. Sometimes the *actual* future spot rate will turn out to be above the previous forward rate. Sometimes it will fall below. But if the theory is correct, we should find that *on the average* the forward rate is equal to the future spot rate.

---

[5] This reasoning ignores risk. If a forward purchase reduces your risk sufficiently, you *might* be prepared to buy forward even if you expected to pay more as a result. Similarly, if a forward sale reduces risk, you *might* be prepared to sell forward even if you expected to receive less as a result.

Exchange Rates

Source: OzForex Web site.

1. There are plenty of good sites that show current and past spot rates of exchange. For example, for current spot rates, look at **finance.yahoo.com**. Forward rates are less easy to come by, but you can find forward rates for a limited set of currencies at the OzForex Web site, **www.ozforex.com.au**, or the New York Fed site, **www.ny.frb.org** (look for the link to *Markets*). Can you deduce from these whether the interest rate is higher in the United States than in Europe or Japan (warning: look out for the difference between direct and indirect quotes)? Here is a trickier problem: Can you work out from these rates whether Japan has a higher interest rate than Europe?

2. The Organization for Economic Cooperation and Development (OECD) provides data on nominal and effective (i.e., real) exchange rates. Log on to **www.oecd.org** and click on *Statistics* and then *Finance*. You need the tables on interest rates and exchange rates. Look at the effective exchange rate for the dollar against other currencies. Has the dollar been appreciating or declining in real terms? Is this helping or hurting U.S. exporters? Which country has experienced the sharpest fall in the real value of its currency?

How well does the expectations theory explain the level of forward rates? Scholars who have studied exchange rates have found that forward rates typically exaggerate the likely change in the spot rate. When the forward rate appears to predict a sharp rise in the spot rate, the forward rate tends to overestimate the rise in the spot rate. Conversely, when the forward rate appears to predict a fall in the currency, it tends to overestimate this fall.[6] This finding is *not* consistent with the expectations theory. Instead it seems that companies are sometimes prepared to give up return in order to *buy* forward currency and other times they are prepared to give up return in order to *sell* forward currency. Almost half the time the forward rate *overstates* the likely future spot rate and half the time it *understates* the likely spot rate. This is important news for the financial manager; it means that a company which always covers its foreign exchange commitments by buying or selling currency in the forward market does not have to pay a premium to avoid exchange rate risk: *On average,* the forward price at which it agrees to exchange currency will equal the eventual spot exchange rate, no better but no worse.

We should, however, warn you that the forward rate does not tell you very much about the future spot rate. For example, when the forward rate appears to suggest that the spot rate is likely to appreciate, you will find that the spot rate is about equally likely to head off in the opposite direction.

22.3 Hedging Exchange Rate Risk

Firms with international operations are subject to exchange rate risk. As exchange rates fluctuate, the dollar value of their revenues or expenses also fluctuates. It is useful to distinguish two types of exchange rate risk: *transaction risk* and *economic risk.* Transaction risk arises when the firm agrees to pay or receive a known amount of foreign currency. For example, our importer of DVD players was committed to pay ¥100 million at the end of 12 months. If the value of the yen appreciates rapidly over this period, those players will cost more dollars than the importer expected.

Transaction risk is easily identified and hedged. For every yen our importer is committed to pay, for example, she can buy 1 yen forward. If she buys ¥100 million

---

[6] Many researchers have even found that, when the forward rate predicts a rise, the spot rate is more likely to fall, and vice versa. For a readable discussion of this puzzling finding, see K. A. Froot and R. H. Thaler, "Anomalies: Foreign Exchange," *Journal of Political Economy* 4 (1990), pp. 179–192.

forward, the importer fixes the entire dollar cost of the DVD players and avoids the risk of an appreciation of the yen.

Of course, it is possible that the yen will *depreciate* over the year, in which case the importer would regret that she did not wait to buy the yen more cheaply in the spot market. Unfortunately, you cannot both have your cake and eat it. By fixing the dollar cost of the DVD players, the importer forfeits the chance of pleasant, as well as unpleasant, surprises.

Is there any other way the importer could hedge against exchange rate loss? Of course. She could borrow dollars, convert them into yen today, put the proceeds in a Japanese bank deposit, and withdraw the ¥100 million at the end of the year to pay her bill. Interest rate parity tells us that the cost of buying yen forward is exactly the same as the cost of borrowing dollars, buying yen in the spot market, and leaving them on deposit.

What is the cost of protection against currency risk? You sometimes hear managers say that it is equal to the difference between the forward rate and *today's* spot rate. This is wrong. If our importer did not hedge, she would pay the spot price for yen when the payment is due at the end of the year. Therefore, the cost of hedging is the difference between the forward rate and the expected spot rate when payment is due.

Hedge or speculate? We generally vote for hedging. First, it makes life simpler for the firm and allows it to concentrate on its own business. Second, it does not cost much. (In fact, the cost is zero if the forward rate equals the expected spot rate, as our simple theories imply.) Third, the foreign exchange market seems reasonably efficient, at least for the major currencies. Speculation should be a zero-sum game unless financial managers have superior information to that of the pros who make the market.

Even if a firm neither owes nor is owed foreign currency, it still may be affected by currency fluctuations. Consider, for example, the competitive position of foreign auto producers such as Volkswagen or Toyota when the value of the U.S. dollar fell dramatically in 2003 and 2004. These firms faced a difficult choice between maintaining the dollar price of their product, thus accepting a reduced price in their home currencies, or raising the dollar price and becoming less competitive against U.S. producers such as Ford and GM. *Economic exposure* to the exchange rate arises because exchange rate fluctuations affect the competitive position of the firm.

Firms with overseas sales can protect themselves against economic risk in two ways. They may hedge in the financial markets, either by borrowing in a foreign currency or by selling the currency forward. For example, if Volkswagen has borrowed some of its funds in U.S. dollars, then if the dollar falls, the pressure on its profits will be offset in part by a reduction in the number of euros needed to service this debt. Alternatively, firms may construct overseas production facilities. If it becomes cheaper to produce overseas, some production may be shifted to the foreign plant. For example, Toyota now produces many of its cars in the United States.

22.4 International Capital Budgeting

Net Present Value Analysis

KW Corporation is an American firm manufacturing flat-packed kit wardrobes. Its export business has risen to the point that it is considering establishing a small manufacturing operation overseas in Narnia. KW's decision to invest overseas should be based on the same criteria as a decision to invest in the United States—that is, the company needs to forecast the incremental cash flows from the project, discount the cash flows at the opportunity cost of capital, and accept those projects with a positive NPV.

Suppose KW's Narnian facility is expected to generate the following cash flows *in Narnian leos (L):*

Year:	0	1	2	3	4	5
Cash flow (millions of leos)	−7.6	2.0	2.5	3.0	3.5	4.0

The interest rate in the United States is 5 percent. KW's financial manager estimates that the company requires an additional expected return of 10 percent to compensate for the risk of the project, so the opportunity cost of capital for the project is $5 + 10 = 15$ percent.

Notice that KW's opportunity cost of capital is stated in terms of the return on a dollar-denominated investment, but the cash flows are given in leos. A project that offers a 15 percent expected return in leos could fall far short of offering the required return in dollars if the value of the leo is expected to decline. Conversely, a project that offers an expected return of less than 15 percent in leos may be worthwhile if the leo is likely to appreciate.

You cannot compare the project's return measured in one currency with the return that you require from investing in another currency. If the opportunity cost of capital is measured as a dollar-denominated return, consistency demands that the forecast cash flows should also be stated in dollars.

To translate the leo cash flows into dollars, KW needs a forward leo/dollar exchange rate. Where does this come from? Forward exchange rates for longer than a year are not usually quoted in the financial press. We suggest using the simple interest rate parity relationships. For example, suppose that the financial manager looks in the newspaper and finds that the current exchange rate is 2 leos to the dollar ($s_{L/\$} = 2.0$), while the interest rate is 5 percent in the United States ($r_\$ = .05$) and 10 percent in Narnia ($r_L = .10$). Thus the manager sees right away that the leo is likely to sell at a forward discount of 5 percent a year. For example, the 1-year forward rate is

$$\frac{\text{Forward}}{\text{rate for year 1}} = \frac{\text{spot rate}}{\text{in year 0}} \times \frac{\text{interest rate}}{\text{differential}}$$

$$= 2.00 \times \frac{1.10}{1.05} = L2.095/\$$$

The implied forward exchange rates for each year of the project are calculated in a similar way as follows:

Year	Forward Exchange Rate		
0	Spot exchange rate = L2.00/$		
1	$2.00 \times (1.10/1.05)$	= L2.095/$	
2	$2.00 \times (1.10/1.05)^2$	= L2.195/$	
3	$2.00 \times (1.10/1.05)^3$	= L2.300/$	
4	$2.00 \times (1.10/1.05)^4$	= L2.409/$	
5	$2.00 \times (1.10/1.05)^5$	= L2.524/$	

The financial manager can use these forward exchange rates to convert the leo cash flows into dollars:

Year:	0	1	2	3	4	5
Cash flow ($ million)	$-\dfrac{7.6}{2.00}$	$\dfrac{2.0}{2.095}$	$\dfrac{2.5}{2.195}$	$\dfrac{3.0}{2.300}$	$\dfrac{3.5}{2.409}$	$\dfrac{4.0}{2.524}$
	= −$3.8	= $.95	= $1.14	= $1.30	= $1.45	= $1.58

INTERNET INSIDER

Political Risk

Address http://www.prsgroup.com/icrg/icrg.html

THE PRS GROUP

The PRS Group

International
Country Risk Guide

Country Reports

Financial, political and economic risk ratings for 140 countries

Source: The PRS Group Web site.

Log on to **www.prsgroup.com**, and click on *Intl. Country Risk Guide* for updated estimates of the political risk of different countries. For which characteristics does the USA score well? For which does it score badly?

Now the manager discounts these dollar cash flows at the 15 percent dollar cost of capital:

$$NPV = -3.8 + \frac{.95}{1.15} + \frac{1.14}{1.15^2} + \frac{1.30}{1.15^3} + \frac{1.45}{1.15^4} + \frac{1.58}{1.15^5}$$

$$= \$.36 \text{ million, or } \$360,000$$

Notice that the manager discounted cash flows at 15 percent, not the United States risk-free interest rate of 5 percent. The cash flows are risky, so a risk-adjusted interest rate is appropriate. The positive NPV tells the manager that the project is worth undertaking; it increases shareholder wealth by $360,000.

Notice also that the firm does *not* have to forecast the future leo/dollar exchange rate to translate its leo cash flows into dollar equivalents. It instead uses the forward exchange rates implied by the interest rate differential in the two countries. No currency forecast is needed, because the company can hedge its foreign exchange exposure. If it does hedge, for example, by selling leos forward, then its leo cash flows will be brought back into dollars at precisely the forward exchange rates implied by the interest rate differential. The decision to accept or reject the project therefore is separate from the firm's outlook on the future leo/dollar exchange rate.

What if the management actually expects the leo to appreciate rather than depreciate? Should it use its own forecasts of the future exchange rate instead of the forward exchange rates implied by interest rate parity? No! For a project to be attractive, it must be able to stand on its own, based on *hedged* cash flows. It would be foolish for a firm to accept a poor project just because it forecasts an improvement in the exchange rate. If management is confident in its predictions of future exchange rates, it would be better to speculate on the currency directly rather than use a negative-NPV project to gain exposure to the currency. (Of course, before it does this, management ought to think very carefully about why it believes its exchange rate forecast is superior to the market's. After all, KW's comparative advantage is presumably in manufacturing furniture, not in exchange rate speculation.)

Self-Test 22.8

Suppose that the nominal interest rate in Narnia is 3 percent rather than 10 percent. The spot exchange rate is still L2.00/$ and the expected leo cash flows on KW's project are also the same as before.

a. What do you deduce about the likely difference in the inflation rates in Narnia and the United States?

b. Would you now be able to buy more or less leos in the forward market than the spot market?

c. Do you think that the NPV of KW's project will now be higher or lower than the figure we calculated above? Check your answer by calculating NPV under this new assumption.

Political Risk

So far we have focused on the management of exchange rate risk, but managers also worry about political risk. By this they mean the threat that a government will change the rules of the game—that is, break a promise or understanding—after the investment is made. Of course, political risks are not confined to overseas investments. Businesses in every country are exposed to the risk of unanticipated actions by governments or the courts. But in some parts of the world foreign companies are particularly vulnerable.

A number of consultancy services offer analyses of political and economic risks and draw up country rankings.[7] For example, Table 22.4 is an extract from the March 2005 political risk rankings provided by the PRS Group. You can see that each country is scored on 12 separate dimensions. Finland comes top of the class overall, while Haiti languishes at the bottom.

Some managers dismiss political risk as an act of God, like a hurricane or earthquake. But the most successful multinational companies structure their business to reduce political risk. Foreign governments are not likely to expropriate a local business if it cannot operate without the support of its parent. For example, the foreign subsidiaries of American computer manufacturers or pharmaceutical companies would have relatively little value if they were cut off from the know-how of their parents. Such operations are much less likely to be expropriated than, say, a mining operation that can be operated as a stand-alone venture.

We are not recommending that you turn your silver mine into a pharmaceutical company, but you may be able to plan your overseas manufacturing operations to improve your bargaining position with foreign governments. For example, Ford has integrated its overseas operations so that the manufacture of components, subassemblies, and complete automobiles is spread across plants in a number of countries. None of these plants would have much value on its own, and Ford can switch production between plants if the political climate in one country deteriorates.

Multinational corporations have also devised financing arrangements to help keep foreign governments honest. For example, suppose your firm is contemplating an investment of $500 million to reopen the San Tomé silver mine in Costaguana with modern machinery, smelting equipment, and shipping facilities.[8] The Costaguanan government agrees to invest in roads and other infrastructure and to take 20 percent of the silver produced by the mine in lieu of taxes. The agreement is to run for 25 years.

The project's NPV on these assumptions is quite attractive. But what happens if a new government comes into power 5 years from now and imposes a 50 percent tax on "any precious metals exported from the Republic of Costaguana"? Or changes the government's share of output from 20 to 50 percent? Or simply takes over the mine "with fair compensation to be determined in due course by the Minister of Natural Resources of the Republic of Costaguana"?

No contract can absolutely restrain sovereign power. But you can arrange project financing to make these acts as painful as possible for the foreign government. For example, you might set up the mine as a subsidiary corporation, which then borrows a large fraction of the required investment from a consortium of major international banks. If your firm guarantees the loan, make sure the guarantee stands only if the Costaguanan government honors its contract. The government will be reluctant to break the contract if that causes a default on the loans and undercuts the country's credit standing with the international banking system.

The Cost of Capital for Foreign Investment

We did not say how KW arrived at a 15 percent dollar discount rate for its Narnian project. That depends on the risk of overseas investment and the reward that investors

---

[7] For a discussion of these services see C. Erb, C. R. Harvey, and T. Viskanta, "Political Risk, Financial Risk, and Economic Risk," *Financial Analysts Journal* 52 (1996), pp. 28–46. Campbell Harvey's Web page (**www.duke.edu/~charvey**) is also a useful source of information on political risk.

[8] The early history of the San Tomé mine is described in Joseph Conrad's *Nostromo*.

TABLE 22-4 Political risk scores for a sample of countries

	A	B	C	D	E	F	G	H	I	J	K	L	Total
Maximum score	12	12	12	12	12	6	6	6	6	6	6	4	100
Country													
Finland	9.5	9.5	12.0	11.0	11.5	6.0	6.0	6.0	6.0	6.0	6.0	4.0	93.5
Luxembourg	10.0	9.5	12.0	12.0	11.5	5.0	6.0	6.0	6.0	5.0	6.0	4.0	93.0
Sweden	8.5	10.0	12.0	11.0	11.5	5.0	5.5	6.0	6.0	5.0	6.0	4.0	90.5
Canada	10.0	8.5	12.0	12.0	11.0	4.0	6.0	6.0	6.0	3.5	6.0	4.0	89.0
Switzerland	9.0	10.5	11.5	12.0	11.5	4.5	6.0	5.0	5.0	4.0	6.0	4.0	89.0
United Kingdom	8.5	10.5	12.0	10.0	8.5	4.5	6.0	6.0	6.0	4.0	6.0	4.0	86.0
Japan	10.0	8.0	11.5	11.5	9.5	3.5	5.0	5.5	5.0	5.5	5.0	4.0	84.0
Singapore	11.0	9.0	12.0	10.5	10.0	4.5	5.0	4.5	5.0	6.0	2.0	4.0	83.5
United States	10.0	8.5	11.5	10.5	8.0	5.0	4.0	5.5	5.0	5.0	5.5	4.0	82.5
Germany	7.5	7.0	12.0	11.0	10.0	4.5	6.0	6.0	5.0	4.0	5.0	4.0	82.0
France	9.5	8.0	12.0	9.5	9.0	3.0	5.0	4.0	5.0	3.5	5.0	3.0	76.5
China	11.0	7.0	7.5	11.5	11.0	2.0	3.0	5.0	4.5	5.0	1.0	2.0	70.5
Russia	11.5	6.5	9.0	9.0	9.5	2.0	4.5	5.5	4.0	3.0	3.0	1.0	68.5
India	9.0	3.5	9.5	8.5	9.5	2.0	4.0	2.5	4.0	2.5	6.0	3.0	64.0
Indonesia	8.5	3.5	6.0	7.5	11.0	1.0	2.5	1.0	2.0	2.0	4.5	2.0	51.5
Myanmar	9.0	4.0	3.5	8.0	8.5	1.0	0.0	6.0	3.0	3.0	0.0	1.0	47.0
Somalia	5.0	1.0	2.5	5.5	4.0	1.0	1.0	3.0	2.0	2.0	1.0	0.0	28.0
Haiti	2.5	0.0	0.0	2.0	6.0	1.0	0.0	6.0	1.0	4.0	0.0	0.0	22.5

Key:
A Government stability
B Socioeconomic conditions
C Investment profile
D Internal conflict
E External conflict
F Corruption
G Military in politics
H Religious tensions
I Law and order
J Ethnic tensions
K Democratic accountability
L Bureaucracy quality

Source: PRS Group, "International Country Risk Guide," **www.prsgroup.com,** March 2005.

require for taking this risk. These are issues on which few economists can agree, but we will tell you where we stand.[9]

Remember that the risk of an investment cannot be considered in isolation; it depends on the securities that the investor holds in his or her portfolio. For example, suppose KW's shareholders invest mainly in companies that do business in the United States. They would find that the value of KW's Narnian venture was relatively unaffected by fluctuations in the value of United States shares. So an investment in the Narnian furniture business would appear to be a relatively low-risk project to KW's shareholders. That would not be true of a Narnian company, whose shareholders are already exposed to the fortunes of the Narnian market. To them an investment in the Narnian furniture business might seem a relatively high-risk project. They would therefore demand a higher return *(measured in dollars)* than KW's shareholders.

Avoiding Fudge Factors

We certainly don't pretend that we can put a precise figure on the cost of capital for foreign investment. But you can see that we disagree with the frequent practice of *automatically* increasing the domestic cost of capital when foreign investment is considered. We suspect that managers mark up the required return for foreign investment because it is more costly to manage an operation in a foreign country and to cover the

---

[9] Why don't economists agree? One fundamental reason is that economists have never been able to agree on what makes one country different from another. Is it just that they have different currencies? Or is it that their citizens have different tastes? Or is it that they are subject to different regulations and taxes? The answer affects the relationship among security prices in different countries.

risk of expropriation, foreign exchange restrictions, or unfavorable tax changes. A fudge factor is added to the discount factor to cover these costs.

We think managers should leave the discount rate alone and reduce expected cash flows instead. For example, suppose that KW is expected to earn L2.5 million in the first year *if no penalties are placed on the operations of foreign firms.* Suppose also that there is a 20 percent chance that KW's cash flow may be expropriated without compensation. The *expected* cash flow is not L2.5 million but .8 × 2.5 million = L2 million.

The end result may be the same if you pretend that the expected cash flow is L2.5 million but add a fudge factor to the discount rate. Nevertheless, adjusting cash flows brings management's assumptions about "political risks" out in the open for scrutiny and sensitivity analysis.

SUMMARY

What is the difference between spot and forward exchange rates?	The **exchange rate** is the amount of one currency needed to purchase one unit of another currency. The **spot rate of exchange** is the exchange rate for an immediate transaction. The **forward rate** is the exchange rate for a forward transaction, that is, a transaction at a specified future date.

What are the basic relationships between spot exchange rates, forward exchange rates, interest rates, and inflation rates?

To produce order out of chaos, the international financial manager needs some model of the relationships between exchange rates, interest rates, and inflation rates. Four very simple theories prove useful:

- In its strict form, **purchasing power parity** states that $1 must have the same purchasing power in every country. You only need to take a vacation abroad to know that this doesn't square well with the facts. Nevertheless, *on average,* changes in exchange rates tend to match differences in inflation rates and, if you need a long-term forecast of the exchange rate, it is difficult to do much better than to assume that the exchange rate will offset the effect of any differences in the inflation rates.
- In an open world capital market *real* rates of interest would have to be the same. Thus differences in *nominal* interest rates result from differences in expected inflation rates. This **international Fisher effect** suggests that firms should not simply borrow where interest rates are lowest. Those countries are also likely to have the lowest inflation rates and the strongest currencies.
- **Interest rate parity theory** states that the interest differential between two countries must be equal to the difference between the forward and spot exchange rates. In the international markets, arbitrage ensures that parity almost always holds.
- The **expectations theory of exchange rates** tells us that the forward rate equals the expected spot rate (though it is very far from being a perfect forecaster of the spot rate).

What are some simple strategies to protect the firm against exchange rate risk?

Our simple theories about forward rates have two practical implications for the problem of hedging overseas operations. First, the expectations theory suggests that hedging exchange risk is on average costless. Second, there are two ways to hedge against exchange risk: One is to buy or sell currency forward; the other is to lend or borrow abroad. Interest rate parity tells us that the cost of the two methods should be the same.

How do we perform an NPV analysis for projects with cash flows in foreign currencies?

Overseas investment decisions are no different in principle from domestic decisions. You need to forecast the project's cash flows and then discount them at the opportunity cost of capital. But it is important to remember that if the opportunity cost of capital is stated in dollars, the cash flows must also be converted to dollars. This requires a forecast of foreign

www.mhhe.com/bmm5e

www.mhhe.com/bmm5e

exchange rates. We suggest that you rely on the simple parity relationships and use the interest rate differential to produce these forecasts. In international capital budgeting the return that shareholders require from foreign investments must be estimated. Adding a premium for the "extra risks" of overseas investment is not a good solution.

QUIZ

1. **Exchange Rates.** Use Table 22–1 to answer these questions:
   a. How many euros can you buy for $100? How many dollars can you buy for 100 euros?
   b. How many Swiss francs can you buy for $100? How many dollars can you buy for 100 Swiss francs?
   c. If the British pound depreciates with respect to the dollar, will the exchange rate quoted in Table 22–1 increase or decrease?
   d. Is a United States or a Canadian dollar worth more?

Please visit us at www.mhhe.com/bmm5e or refer to your Student CD

2. **Exchange Rate Relationships.** Look at Table 22–1.
   a. How many Japanese yen do you get for your dollar?
   b. What is the 1-year forward rate for the yen?
   c. Is the yen at a forward discount or premium on the dollar?
   d. Calculate the annual percentage discount or premium on the yen.
   e. If the interest rate on dollars is 3.4 percent, what do you think is the interest rate on yen?
   f. According to the expectations theory, what is the expected spot rate for the yen in 1 year's time?
   g. According to purchasing power parity, what is the expected difference in the rate of price inflation in the United States and Japan?

3. **Exchange Rate Relationships.** Define each of the following theories in a sentence or simple equation:
   a. Interest rate parity theory.
   b. Expectations theory of forward rates.
   c. Law of one price.
   d. International Fisher effect (relationship between interest rates in different countries).

4. **International Capital Budgeting.** Which of the following items do you need if you do all your capital budgeting calculations in your own currency?

   Forecasts of future exchange rates.
   Forecasts of the foreign inflation rate.
   Forecasts of the domestic inflation rate.
   Foreign interest rates.
   Domestic interest rates.

5. **Foreign Currency Management.** Rosetta Stone, the treasurer of International Reprints, Inc., has noticed that the interest rate in Japan is below the rates in most other countries. She is therefore suggesting that the company should make an issue of Japanese yen bonds. What considerations ought she first take into account?

6. **Hedging Exchange Rate Risk.** An importer in the United States is due to take delivery of silk scarves from Europe in 6 months. The price is fixed in euros. Which of the following transactions could eliminate the importer's exchange risk?
   a. Buy euros forward.
   b. Sell euros forward.
   c. Borrow euros, buy dollars at the spot exchange rate.
   d. Sell euros at the spot exchange rate, lend dollars.

PRACTICE PROBLEMS

7. **Currency Risk.** Sanyo produces audio and video consumer goods and exports a large fraction of its output to the United States under its own name and the Fisher brand name. It prices its products in yen, meaning that it seeks to maintain a fixed price in terms of yen. Suppose the yen moves from ¥103.155/$ to ¥97/$. What currency risk does Sanyo face? How can it reduce its exposure?

8. **Managing Exchange Rate Risk.** A firm in the United States is due to receive payment of 1 million Australian dollars in 8 years' time. It would like to protect itself against a decline in the value of the Australian dollar but finds it difficult to arrange a forward sale for such a long period. Is there any other way that it can protect itself?

9. **Interest Rate Parity.** The following table shows interest rates and exchange rates for the U.S. dollar and Mexican peso. The spot exchange rate is 11.2365 pesos per dollar. Complete the missing entries:

	1 Month	1 Year
Dollar interest rate (annually compounded)	2.5%	3.3
Peso interest rate (annually compounded)	9.5%	——
Forward pesos per dollar	——	11.88

Hint: When calculating the 1-month forward rate, remember to translate the annual interest rate into a monthly interest rate.

10. **Exchange Rate Risk.** An American investor buys 100 shares of London Enterprises at a price of £50 when the exchange rate is $1.60/£. A year later the shares are selling at £52. No dividends have been paid.

   a. What is the rate of return to an American investor if the exchange rate is still $1.60/£?
   b. What if the exchange rate is $1.70/£?
   c. What if the exchange rate is $1.50/£?

11. **Interest Rate Parity.** Look at Table 22–1. If the 3-month interest rate on dollars is 3.5 percent (effective annual rate), what do you think is the 3-month sterling (U.K.) interest rate? Explain what would happen if the rate were substantially above your figure. *Hint:* In your calculations remember to convert the annually compounded interest rate into a rate for 3 months.

12. **Expectations Theory.** Table 22–1 shows the 1-year forward rate on the Canadian dollar.

   a. Is the Canadian dollar at a forward discount or a premium on the U.S. dollar?
   b. What is the annualized *percentage* discount or premium?
   c. If you have no other information about the two currencies, what is your best guess about the spot rate in 1 year?
   d. Suppose that you expect to receive 100,000 Canadian dollars in 1 year. How many U.S. dollars is this likely to be worth?

13. **Interest Rate Parity.** Suppose the interest rate on 1-year loans in the United States is 3 percent while in the United Kingdom the interest rate is 5 percent. The spot exchange rate is $1.87/£ and the 1-year forward rate is $1.84/£. In what country would you choose to borrow? To lend? Can you profit from this situation?

14. **Purchasing Power Parity.** Suppose that the inflation rate in the United States is 4 percent and in Canada it is 5 percent. What would you expect is happening to the exchange rate between the United States and Canadian dollars?

15. **Cross Rates.** Look at Table 22–1. How many Swiss francs can you buy for $1? How many yen can you buy? What rate do you think a Japanese bank would quote for buying or selling Swiss francs? Explain what would happen if it quoted a rate that was substantially less than your figure.

eXcel

Please visit us at www.mhhe.com/bmm5e or refer to your Student CD

Please visit us at www.mhhe.com/bmm5e or
refer to your Student CD

16. **International Capital Budgeting.** Suppose that you do use your own views about exchange rates when valuing an overseas investment proposal. Specifically, suppose that you believe that the leo will depreciate by 2 percent per year. Recalculate the NPV of KW's project.

17. **Currency Risk.** You have bid for a possible export order that would provide a cash inflow of €1 million in 6 months. The spot exchange rate is $1.29/€, and the 1-year forward rate is $1.31/€. There are two sources of uncertainty: (1) The euro could appreciate or depreciate, and (2) you may or may not receive the export order. Illustrate in each case the profits or losses that you would make if you sell €1 million forward by filling in the following table. Assume that the exchange rate in 1 year will be either $1.25/€ or $1.35/€.

	Total Profit/Loss	
Spot Rate	**Receive Order**	**Lose Order**
$1.25/€	_____	_____
$1.35/€	_____	_____

18. **Managing Currency Risk.** General Gadget Corp. (GGC) is a U.S.-based multinational firm that makes electrical coconut scrapers. These gadgets are made only in the United States using local inputs. The scrapers are sold mainly to Asian and West Indian countries where coconuts are grown.

   a. If GGC sells scrapers in Trinidad, what is the currency risk faced by the firm?
   b. In what currency should GGC borrow funds to pay for its investment in order to mitigate its foreign exchange exposure?
   c. Suppose that GGC begins manufacturing its products in Trinidad using local (Trinidadian) inputs and labor. How does this affect its exchange rate risk?

19. **Currency Risk.** If investors recognize the impacts of inflation and exchange rate changes on a firm's cash flows, changes in exchange rates should be reflected in stock prices. How would the stock price of each of the following Swiss companies be affected by an unanticipated appreciation in the Swiss franc of 10 percent, only 2 percent of which could be justified by comparing Swiss inflation to that in the rest of the world?

   a. *Swiss Air:* More than two-thirds of its employees are Swiss. Most revenues come from international fares set in U.S. dollars.
   b. *Nestlé:* Fewer than 5 percent of its employees are Swiss. Most revenues are derived from sales of consumer goods in a wide range of countries with competition from local producers.
   c. *Union Bank of Switzerland:* Most employees are Swiss. All non–Swiss franc monetary positions are fully hedged.

CHALLENGE PROBLEM

Please visit us at www.mhhe.com/bmm5e or
refer to your Student CD

20. **International Capital Budgeting.** An American firm is evaluating an investment in Mexico. The project costs 500 million pesos, and it is expected to produce an income of 250 million pesos a year in real terms for each of the next 3 years. The expected inflation rate in Mexico is 7 percent a year, and the firm estimates that an appropriate discount rate for the project would be about 8 percent above the risk-free rate of interest. Calculate the net present value of the project in U.S. dollars. Exchange rates are given in Table 22–1. The interest rate is about 8.9 percent in Mexico and 3 percent in the United States.

Go to Market Insight at www.mhhe.com/edumarketinsight.

STANDARD
&POOR'S

You can purchase shares of many foreign firms on the New York Stock Exchange through securities called American Depository Receipts. One such firm is Kepco-Korea Electric Power (KEP). Find the company's sales in U.S. dollars from the company profile page. Suppose that the South Korean won, currently at about 1,000 to a U.S. dollar, depreciates by 10 percent to 1,100 to a dollar. If the firm's revenues and costs are relatively fixed in terms of won, what will happen to their values in U.S. dollars as reported by Market Insight? What might happen to KEP's stock price on the NYSE?

SOLUTIONS TO SELF-TEST QUESTIONS

22.1 Direct quote: \$1.2952/€
Indirect quote: 1/1.2952 = €.7721/\$.
Indirect quote: ¥103.155/\$
Direct quote: \$1/¥103.155 = \$.009694/¥

22.2 The dollar buys more Swiss francs, so the franc has depreciated with respect to the dollar.

22.3 a. 1,500/1.1919 = \$1,258.
b. Indirect exchange rate: \$1 = .9 × 1.1919 = 1.0727 francs.
c. 1,500/1.0727 = \$1,398. The dollar price increases.
d. 1,258 × 1.0727 = 1,350 francs. The firm receives 10 percent fewer francs, reflecting the 10 percent decline in the value of each dollar.

22.4 a. £240 = \$440. Therefore £1 = 440/240 = \$1.8333.
b. In the United States, price = \$440 × 1.02 = \$448.80. In Great Britain, price = £240 × 1.05 = £252. The new exchange rate = \$448.80/£252 = \$1.781/£.
c. Initially \$1 buys 1/1.8333 = £.5454. At the end of the year, \$1 buys 1/1.781 = £.5615, which is about 3 percent higher than the original value of £.5454.

22.5 The real interest rate in the United States is 1.0325/1.02 − 1 = .0123, or 1.23 percent. If the real rate is the same in Sweden, then expected inflation must be (1 + nominal rate)/(1 + real rate) − 1 = 1.020/1.0123 − 1 = .0076 = 0.76 percent.

22.6 The Swiss franc is at a forward premium (that is, you get fewer francs for \$1 in the forward market). This implies that interest rates in Switzerland are lower than in the United States. The interest rate in the United States is 3.25 percent. Interest rate parity states

$$\frac{1 + r_{franc}}{1 + r_\$} = \frac{f_{franc/\$}}{s_{franc/\$}}$$

Therefore $r_{franc} = 1.0325 \times \dfrac{1.1651}{1.1919} - 1 = .0093$, or 0.93%

22.7 Starlight borrows ¥100 million in 2005. It pays ¥1 million in interest after 1 year, when it also repays the loan. Cash flows in dollars are:

2005: $\dfrac{+\,100\ million}{103.155} = +\$969,415$

2006:   Interest $= \dfrac{1\ million}{98.2} = \$10,183$

Principal $= \dfrac{100\ million}{98.2} = 1,018,330$

Total   \$1,028,513

To find the effective dollar interest rate, solve

$$969,415 \times (1 + r_\$) = 1,028,513$$

$$r_\$ = \frac{1,028,513}{969,415} - 1 = .0610,\ or\ = 6.10\%$$

22.8 a. The lower interest rate in Narnia than in the United States suggests that forecast inflation is lower in Narnia than in the U.S. If real interest rates are the same in the two countries, then the difference in inflation rates is about 5 − 3 = 2 percent.

b. The lower interest rate in Narnia than in the United States suggests that you can buy fewer leos for your dollar in the forward market.

c. Since KW can now expect to change its leo cash flows into more dollars than before, the project's NPV is increased. Forecast exchange rates will be as follows:

Year	Forecast Exchange Rate
0	Spot exchange rate = L2.00/$
1	$2.00 \times (1.03/1.05) = L1.962/\$$
2	$2.00 \times (1.03/1.05)^2 = L1.925/\$$
3	$2.00 \times (1.03/1.05)^3 = L1.888/\$$
4	$2.00 \times (1.03/1.05)^4 = L1.852/\$$
5	$2.00 \times (1.03/1.05)^5 = L1.817/\$$

The expected dollar cash flows from the project are

Year:	0	1	2	3	4	5
Cash flow ($, million)	$\dfrac{-7.6}{2.00}$	$\dfrac{2.0}{1.962}$	$\dfrac{2.5}{1.925}$	$\dfrac{3.0}{1.888}$	$\dfrac{3.5}{1.852}$	$\dfrac{4.0}{1.817}$
	= −$3.8	= $1.02	= $1.30	= $1.59	= $1.89	= $2.20

Discounting these dollar cash flows at the 15 percent *dollar* cost of capital gives

$$NPV = -3.8 + \frac{1.02}{1.15} + \frac{1.30}{1.15^2} + \frac{1.59}{1.15^3} + \frac{1.89}{1.15^4} + \frac{2.20}{1.15^5}$$

$$= \$1.29 \text{ million, or } \$1,290,000$$

MINICASE

"Jumping jackasses! Not another one!" groaned George Luger. This was the third memo that he had received that morning from the CEO of VCR Importers. It read as follows:

From: CEO's Office

To: Company Treasurer

George,

I have been looking at some of our foreign exchange deals and they don't seem to make sense.

First, we have been buying yen forward to cover the cost of our imports. You have explained that this insures us against the risk that the dollar may depreciate over the next year, but it is incredibly expensive insurance. Each dollar buys only 99.930 yen when we buy forward, compared with the current spot rate of 103.155 yen to the dollar. We could save a fortune by buying yen as and when we need them rather than buying them forward.

Another possibility has occurred to me. If we are worried that the dollar may depreciate (or do I mean "appreciate"?), why don't we buy yen at the low spot rate of ¥103.155 to the dollar and then put them on deposit until we have to pay for the VCRs? That way we can make sure that we get a good rate for our yen.

I am also worried that we are missing out on some cheap financing. We are paying about 6 percent to borrow dollars for one year, but Ben Hur was telling me at lunch that we could get a one-year yen loan for about 2 percent. I find that a bit surprising, but if that's the case, why don't we repay our dollar loans and borrow yen instead?

Perhaps we could discuss these ideas at next Wednesday's meeting. I would be interested in your views on the matter.

Jill Edison

Options

RELATED WEB LINKS

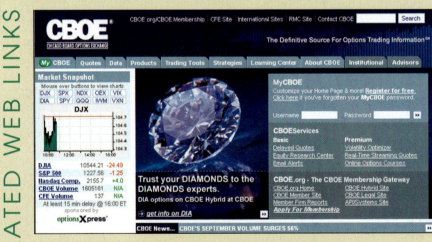

www.cboe.com

www.iseoptions.com

www.euronext.com   Web sites of major options exchanges.

finance.yahoo.com

www.pcquote.com   Includes option quotes.

www.numa.com

www.fintools.com

www.optionscentral.com

www.pmpublishing.com

www.nceo.org   National Center for Employee Ownership, with information on employee stock options.

Just another day on the options exchange. But why does the financial manager of an industrial company need to understand options?
© Getty Images

When the Chicago Board Options Exchange (CBOE) was established in 1973, few observers guessed what a success it would be. Today the CBOE trades options to buy or sell more than 33 billion shares of stock in almost 1,500 companies each year, while its younger rival, the International Securities Exchange (ISE), trades options on a further 36 billion shares. In addition to trading options on individual stocks, you can now trade options on stock indexes, bonds, commodities, and foreign exchange.

You will see that options can be valuable tools for managing the risk characteristics of an investment portfolio. But why should the financial manager of an industrial company read further? There are several reasons. First, most capital budgeting projects have options embedded in them that allow the company to expand at a future date or to bail out. These options allow the company to profit if things go well but give downside protection when they don't.

Second, many of the securities that firms issue include an option. For example, companies often issue convertible bonds. The holder has the op-

tion to exchange the bond for common stock. Some corporate bonds also contain a call provision, meaning that the issuer has the option to buy back the bond from the investor.

Finally, managers routinely use currency, commodity, and interest rate options to protect the firm against a variety of risks. (We will have more to say about this in Chapter 24.)

In one chapter we can provide you with only a brief introduction to options. Our first goal is to explain how options work and how option value is determined. Then we will tell you how to recognize some of the options that crop up in capital investment proposals and in company financing.

After studying this chapter you should be able to:

- Calculate the payoff to buyers and sellers of call and put options.

- Understand the determinants of option values.

- Recognize options in capital investment proposals.

- Identify options that are provided in financial securities.

23.1 Calls and Puts

call option
Right to buy an asset at a specified exercise price on or before the expiration date.

A **call option** gives its holder the right to buy stock for a fixed *exercise price* (also called the *strike price*) on or before a specified expiration date.[1] For example, if you buy a call option on Google stock with an expiration date in January and an exercise price of $180, you have the right to buy the stock at a price of $180 any time until January.

You need not exercise a call option; it will be profitable to do so only if the share price exceeds the exercise price. If it does not, the option will be left unexercised and will be valueless. But suppose that when the option expires, Google shares are selling above the exercise price, say, at $220. In this case you will choose to exercise your option to pay $180 for shares worth $220. Your payoff will equal the difference between the $220 for which you can sell the shares and the $180 that you pay when you exercise the option. More generally, when the stock price is greater than the exercise price, the payoff from your call option is equal to the difference between the stock price and the exercise price.

In summary, the value of the call option at expiration is as follows:

Stock Price at Expiration	Value of Call at Expiration
Greater than exercise price	Stock price – exercise price
Less than exercise price	Zero

Of course, that payoff is not all profit: You have to pay for the option. The price of the call is known as the option *premium.* Option buyers pay the premium for the right to exercise later. Your *profit* equals the ultimate payoff to the call option (which may be zero) minus the initial premium.

EXAMPLE 23.1 ▶   Call Options on Google

In March 2005 a call option on Google stock with a January 2006 expiration and an exercise price of $180 per share sold for $27. If you had bought this call, you would have had the right to purchase Google stock for $180 at any time until the option expired in January. The price of Google in March was $180. If the stock price had not risen by January, the option would not have been worth exercising and you would have wasted your investment of $27. On the other hand, even a relatively modest rise in the stock price could give you a rich profit on your option. For example, if Google sold in January for $220, the proceeds from exercising the call would be

Proceeds = stock price – exercise price = $220 – $180 = $40

and the net profit on the call would be

Profit = proceeds – original investment = $40 – $27 = $13

In 10 months, you would have earned a return of $13/$27 = .48, or 48 percent.   ◀

put option
Right to sell an asset at a specified exercise price on or before the expiration date.

Whereas a call option gives you the right to buy a share of stock, a **put option** gives you the right to *sell* it for the exercise price. If you own a put on a share of stock and the stock price turns out to be greater than the exercise price, you will not want to exercise your option to sell the shares for the exercise price. The put will be left unexercised and will expire valueless. But if the stock price turns out to be less than the exercise price, it will pay to buy the share in the market at the low price and then exercise

[1] In some cases, the option can be exercised only on one particular day, and it is then conventionally known as a *European call;* in other cases, it can be exercised on or before that day, and it is known as an *American call.*

your option to sell it for the exercise price. The put would then be worth the difference between the exercise price and the stock price.

EXAMPLE 23.2 ▶ Put Options on Google

In March 2005 it cost $23.30 to buy a put option on Google stock with a January 2006 expiration and an exercise price of $180. Suppose that Google is selling for $140 when the put option expires. Then if you hold the put, you can buy a share of stock in the market for $140 and exercise your right to sell it for $180. The put will be worth $180 − $140 = $40. Because you paid $23.30 for the put originally, your net profit is $40 − $23.30 = $16.70. As a put buyer, your worry is that the stock price will rise above the $180 exercise price. If that happens, you will let the put option expire worthless and you will lose the $23.30 that you originally paid for it. ◀

In general, the value of the put option at expiration is as follows:

Stock Price at Expiration	Value of Put at Expiration
Greater than exercise price	Zero
Less than exercise price	Exercise price − stock price

Table 23–1 shows how the value of Google calls and puts is affected by the level of the stock price on the expiration date. You can see that once the stock price is above the exercise price, the call value rises dollar for dollar with the stock price, and once the stock price is below the exercise price, the put value rises a dollar for each dollar *decrease* in the stock price. Figure 23–1 plots the values of each option on the expiration date.

Table 23–2 shows the prices of nine options on Google stock in March 2005. Notice that for any particular expiration call options are worth more when the exercise price is lower, while puts are worth more when the exercise price is higher. This makes sense: You would rather have the right to buy at a low price and the right to sell at a high price. Notice also that for any particular exercise price the longer-dated options are the most valuable. This also makes sense. An option that expires in January 2007 gives you everything that a shorter-dated option offers and more. Naturally, you would be prepared to pay for the chance to keep your options open for as long as possible.

Self-Test 23.1

a. What will be the proceeds and net profits (i.e., net of the option premium) to an investor who purchases the September-expiration Google call options with exercise price of $180 if the stock price at expiration is $150? What if the stock price at expiration is $230? Use the data in Table 23–2.
b. Now answer part (a) for an investor who purchases a September-expiration Google put option with exercise price $180.

Selling Calls and Puts

The traded options that you see quoted in the financial pages are not sold by the companies themselves but by other investors. If one investor buys an option on Google

TABLE 23–1 How the value of a Google option on its expiration date varies with the price of the stock on that date (exercise price = $180)

Stock Price:	$140	$160	$180	$200	$220
Call value	0	0	0	$20	$40
Put value	$40	$20	0	0	0

FIGURE 23–1 Values of call options and put options on Google stock on option expiration date (exercise price = $180)

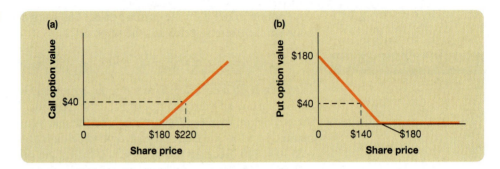

stock, some other investor must be on the other side of the bargain. We will look now at the position of the investor who sells an option.[2]

We have already seen that the January-expiration Google calls with an exercise price of $180 are trading at $27. Thus if you *sell* the January call option on Google stock, the buyer pays you $27. However, in return you promise to sell Google shares at a price of $180 to the call buyer if he decides to exercise his option. The option seller's obligation to *sell* Google is just the other side of the coin to the option holder's right to *buy* the stock. The buyer pays the option premium for the right to exercise; the seller *receives* the premium but may be required at a later date to deliver the stock for an exercise price that is less than the market price of the stock. If the share price is below the exercise price of $180 when the option expires in January, holders of the call will not exercise their option and you, the seller, will have no further liability. However, if the price of Google is greater than $180, it will pay the buyer to exercise and you must give up your shares for $180 each. You lose the difference between the share price and the $180 that you receive from the buyer.

Suppose that Google's stock price turns out to be $220. In this case the buyer will exercise the call option and will pay $180 for stock that can be resold for $220. The buyer therefore has a payoff of $40. Of course, that positive payoff for the buyer means a negative payoff for you the seller, for you are obliged to sell Google stock worth $220 for only $180. This $40 loss more than wipes out the $27 that you were originally paid for selling the option.

In general, the seller's loss is the buyer's gain, and vice versa. Figure 23–2a shows the payoffs to the call option seller. Note that this figure is just Figure 23–1a drawn upside down.

The position of an investor who sells the Google put option can be shown in just the same way by standing Figure 23–1b on its head. The put *buyer* has the right to sell a share for $180; so the *seller* of the put has agreed to pay $180 for the share if the put buyer should demand it. Clearly the seller will be safe as long as the share price re-

TABLE 23–2 Examples of options on Google shares in March 2005, when Google stock was selling for $180

Expiration Date	Exercise Price	Call Price	Put Price
September 2005	$160	$32.00	$ 9.60
	180	19.60	17.90
	200	11.20	29.10
January 2006	160	37.20	14.10
	180	27.00	23.30
	200	18.00	33.60
January 2007	160	51.10	21.50
	180	41.20	30.30
	200	32.00	41.60

Source: **finance.yahoo.com.**

---

[2] The option seller is known as the *writer.*

Option Prices

Source: Yahoo! Finance Web site. Reproduced with permission of Yahoo! Inc. © 2005 by Yahoo! Inc. Yahoo! and the Yahoo! logo are trademarks of Yahoo! Inc.

You can find option prices on finance.yahoo.com. Enter the company symbol and then click on *Options*. Try looking up option prices for Dell Computer (DELL) and Pfizer (PFE). Does the price of calls increase or decrease with (a) exercise price, (b) time to expiration? Would your answer be the same for puts? Can you explain why or why not?

FIGURE 23–2 Payoffs to sellers of call and put options on Google stock (exercise price = $180)

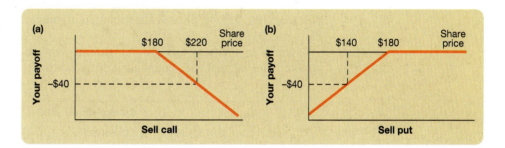

mains above $180 but his payoff will be negative if the share price falls below this figure. The worst thing that can happen to the put seller is for the stock to be worthless. The seller would then be obliged to pay $180 for a worthless stock. The payoff to the seller would be –$180. Note that the advantage always lies with the option buyer, and the obligation lies with the seller. Therefore, the buyer must pay the seller to acquire the option.

Table 23–3 summarizes the rights and obligation of buyers and sellers of calls and puts.

Self-Test 23.2

a. What will be the proceeds and net profits to an investor who sells the September-expiration Google call options with exercise price of $180 if the stock price at expiration is $150? What if the stock price at expiration is $230? Use the data in Table 23–2.

b. Now answer part (a) for an investor who sells a September-expiration Google put option with exercise price $180.

Financial Alchemy with Options

Options can be used to modify the risk characteristics of a portfolio. Suppose, for example, that you are generally optimistic about Google's prospects but you perceive enough risk that a large investment in the stock would cause you sleepless nights. Here is a strategy that might appeal to you: Buy the stock, but also buy a put option on the stock with exercise price $180. If the stock price rises from its current level of $180,

TABLE 23–3 Rights and obligations of various option positions

	Buyer	Seller
Call option	Right to buy asset	Obligation to sell asset
Put option	Right to sell asset	Obligation to buy asset

629

FIGURE 23–3 Payoff to protective put strategy. If the ultimate stock price exceeds $180, the put is valueless but you own the stock. If it is less than $180, you can sell the stock for the exercise price.

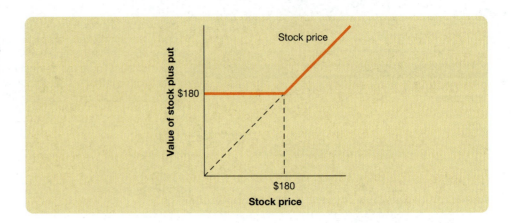

your put turns out to be worthless but you win on the stock investment. If the stock price falls, your losses are limited, since the put gives you the right to sell your stock for the $180 exercise price. Thus the value of your stock-plus-put position cannot be less than $180.

Here is another way to view your overall position. You hold the stock and the put option. The value of each component of the portfolio will be as follows:

	Stock Price < $180	**Stock Price ≥ $180**
Value of stock	Stock price	Stock price
Value of put option	$180 – stock price	0
Total value	$180	Stock price

No matter how far the stock price falls, the total value of your portfolio cannot fall below the $180 exercise price.

The value of your position when the option expires is graphed in Figure 23–3. You have downside protection at $180, but still share in potential gains on the stock. This strategy is called a *protective put,* because the put option gives protection against losses. Of course, such protection is not free. Look again at Table 23–2 and you will find the cost of such protection. "Stock price insurance" at a level of $180 between March 2005 and January 2006 cost $23.30 per share; this was the price of a put option with exercise price $180 and January expiration.

Some More Option Magic
Look again at Figure 23–3, which shows the possible payoffs at maturity from holding both a share of Google stock and a put option to sell it for $180. Does this picture look somewhat familiar? It should. Turn back to panel (a) of Figure 23–2, which shows the payoffs from holding a call option on Google stock with an exercise price of $180. The only difference between the two sets of payoffs is that the combination of the stock and put option always provides exactly $180 more than the call option. In other words, regardless of the final stock price, holding the stock plus a put option gives the same payoff as an alternative strategy of buying a call option plus investing the present value of $180 in a bank deposit.

Think what happens if you follow this second strategy. If the stock price is below $180 when the option expires, your call option will be valueless but you will still have $180 in the bank. On the other hand, if the stock price rises above $180, you will take your money out of the bank, use it to exercise the call, and own the stock. The following table confirms that this second investment package gives you exactly the same payoffs as you get from holding the stock and a put option:

	Payoffs at Maturity	
	Stock price < $180	Stock price > $180
Call option	Zero	Stock price—$180
Bank deposit paying $180	$180	$180
Total value	$180	Stock price

If you plan to hold each of these packages until the options expire, the packages must sell for the same price today. This gives us a fundamental relationship between the value of a call and the value of a put:[3]

Value of stock + value of put = value of call + present value of exercise price

This basic relationship between share price, call and put values, and the present value of the exercise price is called *put-call parity*.

Self-Test 23.3

A 1-year *call* option on Witterman stock with an exercise price of $60 costs $8.05. The stock price is $55 and the interest rate on a bank deposit is 4 percent. What is the value of a 1-year *put* option on Witterman with an exercise price of $60?

23.2 What Determines Option Values?

In Table 23–2 we set out the prices of different Google options. But we said nothing about how the market values of options are determined. It is time that we did so.

Upper and Lower Limits on Option Values

We know what an option is worth when it expires. Consider, for example, the option to buy Google stock at $180. If the stock price is below $180 at the expiration date, the call will be worthless; if the stock price is above $180, the call will be worth the value of the stock minus the $180 exercise price. The relationship is depicted by the heavy orange line in Figure 23–4.

Even before expiration, the price of the option can never remain *below* the heavy orange line in Figure 23–4. For example, if our option were priced at $10 and the stock at $220, it would pay any investor to buy the option, exercise it for an additional $180, and then sell the stock for $220. That would give a "money machine" with a profit of $220 – ($10 + $180) = $30. Money machines can't last. The demand for options from investors using this strategy would quickly force the option price up at least to the heavy orange line in the figure. The heavy orange line is therefore a lower limit on the market price of the option. Thus

$$\text{Lower limit on value of call option} = \text{the greater of } zero \text{ or } (stock\ price - exercise\ price)$$

The diagonal purple line in Figure 23–4, which is the plot of the stock price, is the *upper* limit to the option price. Why? Because the stock itself gives a higher final payoff whatever happens. If when the option expires the stock price ends up above the exercise price, the option is worth the stock price *less* the exercise price. If the stock price ends up below the exercise price, the option is worthless but the stock's owner still has

---

[3] This relationship assumes that the two options have the same exercise price and maturity. Note that the present value of the exercise price is simply the amount that you would need to set aside in a bank deposit in order to receive the exercise price at maturity.

FIGURE 23–4 Value of a call before its expiration date (dashed line). The value depends on the stock price. The call is always worth more than its value if exercised now (heavy orange line). It is never worth more than the stock price itself (purple line).

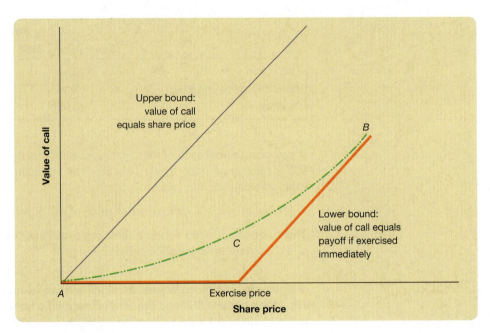

a valuable security. Thus the extra payoff to holding the stock rather than the option is as follows:

Stock Price at Expiration	Stock Payoff	Option Payoff	Extra Payoff from Holding Stock rather than Option
Greater than $180	Stock price	Stock price – $180	$180
Less than or equal to $180	Stock price	$0	Stock price

The Determinants of Option Value

The option price must lie between the upper and lower limits in Figure 23–4. In fact, the price will lie on a curved, upward-sloping line like the dashed curve shown in the figure. This line begins its travels where the upper and lower bounds meet (at zero). Then it rises, gradually becoming parallel to the lower bound. This line tells us an important fact about option values: Given the exercise price, *the value of a call option increases as the stock price increases.*

That should be no surprise. Owners of call options clearly hope for the stock price to rise and are happy when it does. But let us look more carefully at the shape and location of the dashed line. Three points, *A, B,* and *C,* are marked on the dashed line. As we explain each point, you will see why the option price has to behave as the dashed line predicts.

Point A   *When the stock is worthless, the option is worthless.* A stock price of zero means that there is no possibility the stock will ever have any future value.[4] If so, the option is sure to expire unexercised and worthless, and it is worthless today.

Point B   *When the stock price becomes very high, the option price approaches the stock price less the present value of the exercise price.* Notice that the dashed line representing the option price in Figure 23–4 eventually becomes parallel to the ascending heavy orange line representing the lower bound on the option price. The reason is as

---

[4] If a stock can be worth something in the future, then investors will pay *something* for it today, although possibly a very small amount.

follows. The higher the stock price, the greater the odds that the option will eventually be exercised. If the stock price is high enough, exercise becomes a virtual certainty; the probability that the stock price will fall below the exercise price before the option expires becomes trivial.

If you own an option that you know will be exchanged for a share of stock, you effectively own the stock now. The only difference is that you don't have to pay for the stock (by handing over the exercise price) until later, when formal exercise occurs. In these circumstances, buying the call is equivalent to buying the stock now with deferred payment and delivery. The value of the call is therefore equal to the stock price less the present value of the exercise price.[5]

This brings us to another important point about options. Investors who acquire stock by way of a call option are buying on "installment credit." They pay the purchase price of the option today, but they do not pay the exercise price until they actually exercise the option. The delay in payment is particularly valuable if interest rates are high and the option has a long maturity. Thus *the value of a call option increases with both the rate of interest and the time to expiration.*

Self-Test 23.4   How would the value of a put option be affected by an increase in the exercise price? Explain.

Point C   *The option price always exceeds its minimum value* (except at expiration or when stock price is zero). We have seen that the dashed and heavy lines in Figure 23–4 coincide when stock price is zero (point *A*), but elsewhere the lines diverge; that is, the option price must exceed the minimum value given by the heavy orange line. You can see why by examining point *C*.

At point *C,* the stock price exactly equals the exercise price. The option therefore would be worthless if it expired today. However, suppose that the option will not expire until 3 months hence. Of course we do not know what the stock price will be at the expiration date. There is roughly a 50 percent chance that it will be higher than the exercise price, and a 50 percent chance that it will be lower. The possible payoffs to the option are therefore:

Outcome	Payoff
Stock price rises	Stock price – exercise price
(50% probability)	(option is exercised)
Stock price falls	Zero
(50% probability)	(option expires worthless)

If there is some chance of a positive payoff, and if the worst payoff is zero, then the option must be valuable. That means the option price at point *C* exceeds its lower bound, which at point *C* is zero. In general, the option price will exceed the lower bound as long as there is time left before expiration.

One of the most important determinants of the *height* of the dashed curve (that is, of the difference between actual and lower-bound value) is the likelihood of substantial movements in the stock price. An option on a stock whose price is unlikely to change by more than 1 or 2 percent is not worth much; an option on a stock whose price may halve or double is very valuable.

---

[5] We assume here that the stock pays no dividends until after the option expires. If dividends were paid, you *would* care about when you get to own the stock because the option holder misses out on any dividends.

1010001
01001
10011010
00101

INTERNET INSIDER
1010100010

Option Valuation

1. How do option prices change as volatility or the time to expiration changes? A nice way to find out is to log on to Professor Campbell Harvey's home page on **www.duke.edu/~charvey** and look under *Java Finance Tools*, and then *Option Pricer*.

2. Several Web sites contain calculators that use the Black-Scholes formula for valuing options. For example. you could log on to the *Education* pages of the ISE's Web site at **www.iseoptions.com** or to **www.numa.com**. Try valuing a call option on Dell Computer or Pfizer. The inputs are the same as in our simple valuation example (see nearby box), except that instead of putting in the spread of possible stock prices, you must put in the standard deviation of stock returns. You can find estimates of the standard deviation for Dell and Pfizer in Table 10–6. How different are the values you obtain from the prices shown on **finance.yahoo.com**? What happens to the option values if you change the standard deviation? Can you explain?

For example, suppose that a call option has an exercise price of $180 and the stock price will be either $160 or $200 when the option expires. The possible payoffs to the option are as follows:

Stock price at expiration	$160	$200
Call value at expiration	0	$20

Now suppose that the value of the stock when the option expires can be $140 or $220. The *average* of the possible stock prices is the same as before, but the volatility is greater. In this case the payoffs to the call are:

Stock price at expiration	$140	$220
Call value at expiration	0	$40

A comparison of the two cases highlights the valuable asymmetry that options offer. If the stock price turns out to be below the exercise price when the option expires, the option is valueless regardless of whether the shortfall is a cent or a dollar. However, the option holder reaps all the benefits of stock price advances. Thus in our example the option is worth only $20 if the stock price reaches $200, but it is worth $40 if the stock price rises to $220. Therefore, volatility helps the option holder.

The probability of large stock price changes during the remaining life of an option depends on two things: (1) the variability of the stock price *per unit of time* and (2) the length of time until the option expires. Other things equal, you would like to hold an option on a volatile stock. Given volatility, you would like to hold an option with a long life ahead of it, since that longer life means that there is more opportunity for the stock price to change. The value of an option increases with both the variability of the share price and the time to expiration.

It's a rare person who can keep all these properties straight at first reading. Therefore, we have summed them up in Table 23–4.

TABLE 23–4 What the price of a call option depends on

If the following variables *increase*, . . .	. . . the value of a call option will
Stock price	Increase
Exercise price	Decrease
Interest rate	Increase
Time to expiration	Increase
Volatility of stock price	Increase

A Simple Option-Valuation Model

It is March 2005 and you are contemplating the purchase of a call option on Google stock. The call has a January 2007 exercise date and an exercise price of $180. Google's stock price is also currently $180, so the option will be valueless unless the stock price appreciates over the next 22 months. The outlook for Google stock is uncertain, and all you know is that at the end of the 22 months the price will either fall by a third to $120 or rise by 50 percent to $270. Finally we assume that the rate of interest on a bank loan is 4 percent a year, or about 7.5 percent for 22 months.

The following table depicts the outlook for three alternative investments:

Google Stock		Call Option		Bank Loan	
March	January	March	January	March	January
$180 ⟨ $270 / $120		? ⟨ $90 / $0		$100 ⟨ $107.50 / $107.50	

The first investment is Google stock. Its current price is $180, but the price could rise to $270 or fall to $120. The second investment is the call option. When the call expires in January, the option will be valueless if the stock price falls to $120, and it will be worth $270 – $180 = $90 if the stock price rises to $270. We don't know (yet) what the call is worth today, so for the time being we put a question mark against the March value. Our third investment is a bank loan at an interest rate of 7.5 percent for 22 months. The payoff on a $100 bank loan is $107.50 no matter what happens to the price of Google stock.

Consider now two investment strategies. The first (strategy A) is to buy 10 call options. The second (strategy B) is to buy six Google shares and to borrow the present value of $720 from the bank. Table 23–5 shows the possible payoffs from the two strategies. Notice that when you borrow from the bank, you receive a *positive* cash flow now but have a *negative flow* when the loan is repaid in January.

You can see that *regardless of whether the stock price falls to $120 or rises to $270,* the payoffs from the two strategies are identical. To put it another way, you can exactly replicate an investment in call options by a combination of a bank loan and an investment in the stock.* If two investments give the same payoffs in all circumstances, then their value must be the same today. In other words, the cost of buying 10 call options must be exactly the same as borrowing PV($720) from the bank and buying six Google shares:

$$\text{Price of 10 calls} = \$1{,}080 - \$670 = \$410$$

$$\text{Price of 1 call} = \frac{\$410}{10} = \$41$$

Presto! You have just valued a call option.†

---

* The only tricky part in valuing the Google option was to work out the number of shares that were needed to replicate the call option. Fortunately, there is a simple formula which says that the number of shares needed is equal to

$$\frac{\text{Spread of possible option prices}}{\text{Spread of possible stock prices}} = \frac{\$90 - \$0}{\$270 - \$120} = .6$$

To replicate one call option, you need to buy .6 of a share. To replicate 10 calls, you need to buy six shares of stock.
† Notice that the actual price of the Google call in March 2005 was $41.20, close to our simple estimate of the option's value.

TABLE 23–5 It is possible to replicate the payoffs from Google call options by borrowing to invest in Google stock

	Cash Flow in March 2005	Payoff in January 2007 if Stock Price Equals	
		$120	$270
Strategy A			
Buy 10 calls	?	$ 0	+ $900
Strategy B			
Buy six shares	–$1,080	+$720	+$1,620
Borrow PV($720)	+ $670	–$720	– $720
	– $410	$ 0	+ $900

Note: PV($720) paid 22 months from now is $720/1.075 = $670.

Self-Test 23.5 Rework our numerical example for a put option with an exercise price of $180. Show that put options also are more valuable when the stock price is more volatile.

Option-Valuation Models

If you want to value an option, you need to go beyond the qualitative statements of Table 23–4; you need an exact option-valuation model—a formula that you can plug numbers into and come up with a figure for option value.

Using the Black-Scholes Formula

You may like to try your hand at using the Black-Scholes option-pricing formula to value the Google option. A number of Web sites include a Black-Scholes calculator (see, for example, www.numa.com, and look for the options calculator). But it takes only a few moments to construct your own Excel program to calculate Black-Scholes values. The following spreadsheet shows how you do it. First, type in the formulas shown on the right side of the spreadsheet in cells E2 to E8. Now enter the data for the Google January 2007 call in cells B2 to B6. Notice that the values for the standard deviation and interest rate are entered as decimals.* On past evidence, the standard deviation of Google's annual returns has been about 35 percent, so we enter the standard deviation in cell B2 as .35, not 35. The last two lines of the output column show that the Black-Scholes formula gives a value of $39.16 for the Google call option, close to its market price in March 2005. (Don't worry about the other lines of output.)

Please visit us at www.mhhe.com/bmm5e or refer to your Student CD

	A	B	C	D	E	F	G	H	I	J
1	INPUTS			OUTPUTS			FORMULA FOR OUTPUT IN COLUMN E			
2	Standard deviation (annual)	0.35		PV(Ex. Price)	167.512		B6/(1+B4)^B3			
3	Maturity (in years)	1.833		d1	0.389		(LN(B5/E2)+(0.5*B2^2)*B3)/(B2*SQRT(B3))			
4	Risk-free rate (effective annual rate)	0.04		d2	-0.085		E3-B2*SQRT(B3)			
5	Stock price	180		N(d1)	0.651		NORMSDIST(E3)			
6	Exercise price	180		N(d2)	0.466		NORMSDIST(E4)			
7				B/S call value	39.156		B5*E5 - E2*E6			
8				B/S put value	26.668		E2*(1-E6) - B5*(1-E5)			

* Chapter 10 described how to calculate standard deviations. Notice also that in cell E2, we compute the present value of the exercise price by treating the interest rate as an effective annual yield. You should be aware, however, that many Black-Scholes calculators require that the interest rate be expressed as a continuously compounded rate. See Chapter 4, Table 4–8, if you need a review of continuous compounding.

Valuing complex options is a high-tech business and well beyond the scope of this book. Our aim here is not to make you into instant option whizzes, but we can illustrate the basics of option valuation by walking you through an example. The trick to option valuation is to find a combination of borrowing and an investment in the stock that exactly replicates the option. The nearby box illustrates a simple version of one of these option-valuation models.

This model achieves simplicity by assuming that the share price can take on only two values at the expiration date of the option. This assumption is clearly unrealistic, but it turns out that the same approach can be generalized to allow for a large number of possible future share prices rather than just the two values in our example.

In 1973 Fischer Black, Myron Scholes, and Robert Merton came up with a formula which showed that even when share prices are changing continuously, you can still replicate an option by a series of levered investments in the stock. The Black-Scholes formula is regularly used by option traders, investment bankers, and financial managers to value a wide variety of options. Scholes and Merton shared the 1997 Nobel Prize in economics for their work on the development of this formula.[6] The box on this page shows you how to set up a Black-Scholes calculator in Excel.

Today, there are many ever-more-sophisticated variants on the Black-Scholes formula that can better capture some aspect of real-life markets. As computer power continues to increase, these models can be made more complex and increasingly accurate.

Self-Test 23.6

Use the nearby Finance in Practice box as a model to help you answer this question. Suppose that the price of Disney stock is $30 and could either double to $60 or halve to $15 over the next 3 months. Show that the following two strategies have exactly the same payoffs regardless of whether the stock price rises or falls: *Strategy A*—Buy three call options with an exercise price of $30; *Strategy B*—Buy two shares and borrow the present value of $30. What is your cash outflow today if you follow Strategy B? What does this tell you about the value of three call options? Assume that the interest rate is 1 percent per 3 months.

---

[6] Fischer Black passed away in 1995.

Allegheny Acquires a Real Option

Allegheny Corporation acquired open gas-fired power plants in Mississippi and Tennessee. These plants were expected to sit idle most of the year and, when operating, to produce electricity at a cost at least 50 percent higher than the most efficient state-of-the-art facilities. Allegheny's decision to build these power plants resulted from a sophisticated application of real options analysis.

The firm observed that electricity prices in an increasingly free energy market can be wildly volatile. For example, during some power shortages in the Midwest during the hot summer months the cost of 1 megawatt-hour of electricity has increased briefly from a typical level of $40 to several thousand dollars. The option to obtain additional energy in these situations obviously would be quite valuable.

Allegheny concluded that it would pay to acquire some cheap power plants, even if they were relatively high-cost electricity producers. Most of the time, the plants will sit idle, with market prices for electricity below the marginal cost of production. But every so often, when electricity prices spike, the plants can be fired up to produce electricity—at a great profit. Even if they operate only a few weeks a year, they can be positive-NPV investments.

These plants are in effect call options on electrical power. The options are currently out of the money, but the possibility that power prices will increase makes these calls worth more than their price. The decision to build them therefore makes the firm more valuable.

23.3 Spotting the Option

In our discussion so far we may have given you the impression that financial managers are concerned only with traded options to buy or sell shares. But once you have learned to recognize the different kinds of options, you will find that they are everywhere. Unfortunately, they rarely come with a large label attached. Often the trickiest part of the problem is to identify the option.

We will start by looking briefly at options on real assets and then turn to options on financial assets. You should find that you have already encountered many of these options in earlier chapters.

Options on Real Assets

In Chapter 9 we pointed out that the capital investment projects that you accept today may affect the opportunities you have tomorrow. Today's capital budgeting decisions need to recognize these future opportunities.

Other things equal, a capital investment project that generates new opportunities is more valuable than one that doesn't. A flexible project—one that doesn't commit management to a fixed operating strategy—is more valuable than an inflexible one. When a project is flexible or generates new opportunities for the firm, it is said to contain **real options.**

real options

Options to invest in, modify, or dispose of a capital investment project.

If you look out for real options, you'll find them almost everywhere. The nearby Finance in Practice box provides an illustration of a firm that took real options into account in an important capital budgeting decision. In Chapter 9 we looked at several ways that companies may build future flexibility into a project. Here is a brief reminder of two types of real options that we introduced in that chapter.

The Option to Expand   Many capital investment proposals include an option to expand in the future. For instance, some of the world's largest oil reserves are found in the tar sands of Athabasca, Canada. Unfortunately, the cost of extracting oil is substantially higher than the current market price and almost certainly higher than most people's estimate of the likely price in the future. Yet oil companies have been prepared to pay considerable sums for these tracts of barren land. The reason? Ownership of the tar sands gives the companies an option. If prices remain below the cost of extraction, the Athabasca sands will remain undeveloped. But if prices rise above the cost of extraction those land purchases could prove very valuable. Thus, ownership gives the companies a real option—a call option to extract the oil.

The Option to Abandon   Suppose that you need a new plant ready to produce turboencabulators in 3 years. You have a choice of designs. If design A is chosen construction must start immediately. Design B is more expensive but you can wait a year before breaking ground.

If you know with certainty that the plant will be needed, you should opt for design A. But suppose that there is some possibility that demand for turboencabulators will fall off and that in a year's time you will decide the plant is not required. Then design B may be preferable because it gives you the option to bail out at low cost any time during the next 12 months.

You can think of the option to abandon as a put option. The exercise price of the put is the amount that you could recover if you abandon the project. The abandonment option makes design B more attractive by limiting the downside exposure; the worst outcome is that you receive the project's salvage value. The more uncertain is the need for the new plant, the more valuable is the downside protection offered by the option to abandon.

Self-Test 23.7

A real estate developer buys 70 acres of land in a rural area, planning to build a subdivision on the land if and when the population from the city begins to expand into the area. If population growth is less than anticipated, the developer believes that the land can be sold to a country club that would build a golf course on the property.

a. In what way does the possibility of sale to the country club provide a put option to the developer?
b. What is the exercise price of the option? The asset value?
c. How does the golf course option increase the NPV of the land project to the developer?

Options on Financial Assets

When companies issue securities, they often include an option in the package. Here are a few examples of the options that are associated with new financing.

warrant
Right to buy shares from a company at a stipulated price before a set date.

Warrants   A **warrant** is a long-term call option on the company's stock. Unlike the Google option that we considered earlier, a warrant is issued by the company. The company sells the warrant; the investor buys it. For example, in 2002 American Community Bancshares, a North Carolina bank, needed to raise new equity capital. It did so by selling a package of common stock and warrants. Each warrant gave its owner the right to buy one share of the company's stock for $10.50 at any time before the end of April 2005. At the time, the stock price was only $8.90. So the price would need to rise by more than $1.60, or 18 percent, before the warrants were "in the money." As it turned out, the warrant holders were in luck, for the stock price when the options expired was $14.50 making the warrants worth $14.50 − $10.50 = $4 each.

Warrants are often given to underwriters as part of their compensation for managing an issue of securities. At other times they may be issued when a firm becomes bankrupt; the bankruptcy court offers the firm's bondholders warrants in the reorganized company as part of the settlement. When a company issues a bond, it will sometimes add some warrants as a "sweetener." Since these warrants are valuable to investors, they are prepared to pay a higher price for a package of bonds and warrants than for the bond on its own. Managers sometimes look with delight at this higher price, forgetting that in return the company has incurred a liability to sell its shares to the warrant holders at what with hindsight may turn out to be a low price.

Warrants also have become an ever-increasing (and ever-more controversial) part of firms' employee compensation packages, especially for upper management. The following box discusses these grants, which, while technically warrants, are more commonly referred to as stock options.

convertible bond
Bond that the holder may exchange for a specified amount of security.

Convertible Bonds The **convertible bond** is a close relative of the bond-warrant package. It allows the bondholder to exchange the bond for a given number of shares of common stock. Therefore, it is a package of a straight bond and a call option. The exercise price of the call option is the value of the "straight bond" (that is, a bond that is not convertible). It will be profitable to convert if the value of the stock to which the investor is entitled exceeds the value of the straight bond.

The owner of a convertible bond owns a bond and a call option on the firm's stock. So does the owner of a package of a bond and a warrant. However, there are differences, the most important being that a convertible bond's owner must give up the bond to exercise the option. The owner of a package of bonds and warrants exercises the warrants for cash and keeps the bond.

EXAMPLE 23.3 ▶	Convertible Bonds

In early 2005 Corning issued $297 million of 3.5 percent convertible bonds maturing in 2008. Each of these bonds can be converted before maturity into 103.4 shares of Corning stock. In other words, the owner of the convertible has the option to return the bond to Corning and receive 103.4 shares in exchange. The number of shares that are received for each bond is called the bond's *conversion ratio*. The conversion ratio of the Corning bond is 103.4.

In order to receive 103.4 shares of Corning stock, you must surrender bonds with a face value of $1,000. Therefore, to receive *one* share, you have to surrender a face amount of $1,000/103.4 = $9.67. This figure is called the *conversion price*. Anybody who originally bought the bond at $1,000 in order to convert into 103.4 shares paid the equivalent of $9.67 a share.

As we write this in April 2005, Corning's stock price is $11.13. So if investors were obliged to convert their bond today, their investment would be worth $103.4 \times \$11.13 = \$1,150.84$. This figure is called the bond's *conversion value*. Of course, investors do not need to convert immediately. They obviously hope that Corning's stock price will zoom up and make conversion very profitable. But they have the comfort of knowing that if the stock price zooms down, they can choose not to convert and simply hold on to the bond. The value of the bond if it could not be converted is known as its *bond value*. If Corning's bond could not be converted, it would probably be worth about $930 in April 2005.   ◀

Since the owner of the convertible always has the option *not* to convert, bond value establishes a lower bound, or floor, to the price of a convertible. Of course, this floor is not completely flat. If the firm falls on hard times, the bond may not be worth much. In the extreme case where the firm becomes worthless, the bond is also worthless.

When the firm does well, conversion value exceeds bond value. In this case the investor would choose to convert if forced to make an immediate choice. Bond value exceeds conversion value when the firm does poorly. In these circumstances the investor would hold on to the bonds if forced to choose. Convertible holders do not have to make a now-or-never choice for or against conversion. They can wait and then, with the benefit of hindsight, take whatever course turns out to give them the highest payoff. Thus a convertible is always worth more than both its bond value and its conversion value (except when time runs out at the bond's maturity).

We stated earlier that it is useful to think of a convertible bond as a package of a straight bond and an option to buy the common stock in exchange for the straight bond. The value of this call option is equal to the difference between the convertible's market price and its bond value.

Valuing Employee Stock Options

In 2004 Intel granted options to its directors, management, and employees to buy about 115 million shares of the company's stock. The exercise price was set at the market price at the time of the grant. Presumably Intel believed that these options provided an incentive for everyone to work together to maximize share value and encouraged them to stay with the company.

Employee stock options are valuable and therefore are an expense just like salaries and wages. The Financial Ac-

counting Standards Board (FASB) requires that companies recognize this fact. Its Statement 123 stipulates that companies must use an option-valuation model, such as the Black-Scholes model, to estimate the fair value of any option grants and then deduct this value when calculating profits. The FASB rule became compulsory only in 2005. Had it been operative in 2004, Intel's net income would have been reduced by 17 percent, or $1,271 million.

Self-Test 23.8

a. What would be the conversion value of the Corning convertible bond if the stock price rose to $20? What would happen to its conversion price?
b. Suppose that a straight (nonconvertible) bond issued by Corning had been priced to yield 5 percent. What would be the bond value of the 3.5 percent convertibles in 2005? (Assume annual coupon payments.)

---

callable bond
Bond that may be repurchased by the issuer before maturity at specified call price.

Callable Bonds   Unlike warrants and convertibles, which give the *investor* an option, a **callable bond** gives an option to the *issuer.* A company that issues a callable bond has an option to buy the bond back at the stated exercise or "call" price. Therefore, you can think of a callable bond as a *package* of a straight bond (a bond that is not callable) and a call option held by the issuer.

The option to call the bond is obviously attractive to the issuer. If interest rates decline and bond prices rise, the company has the opportunity to repurchase the bond at a fixed call price. Therefore, the option to call the bond puts a ceiling on the bond price. We examined callable bond pricing in Chapter 5.

Of course, when the company issues a callable bond, investors are aware of this ceiling on the bond price and will pay less for a callable bond than for a straight bond. The difference between the value of a straight bond and a callable bond with the same coupon rate and maturity is the value of the call option that investors have given to the company:

Value of callable bond = value of straight bond – value of the issuer's call option

---

Self-Test 23.9

"Puttable bonds" allow the investor to redeem the bond at face value or let the bond remain outstanding until maturity. Suppose a 20-year puttable bond is issued with the investor allowed after 5 years to redeem the bond at face value.

a. On what asset is the option written? (What asset do the option holders have the right to sell?)
b. What is the exercise price of the option?
c. In what circumstances will the option be exercised?
d. Does the put option make the bond more or less valuable?

SUMMARY

What is the payoff to buyers and sellers of call and put options?

There are two basic types of options. A **call option** is the right to buy an asset at a specific exercise price on or before the exercise date. A **put** is the right to sell an asset at a specific exercise price on or before the exercise date. The payoff to a call is the value of the asset minus the exercise price if the difference is positive, and zero otherwise. The payoff to a put is the exercise price minus the value of the asset if the difference is positive, and zero otherwise. The payoff to the seller of an option is the negative of the payoff to the option buyer.

What are the determinants of option values?

The value of a call option depends on the following considerations:

- To exercise the call option you must pay the exercise price. Other things equal, the less you are obliged to pay, the better. Therefore, the value of the option is higher when the exercise price is low relative to the stock price.
- Investors who buy the stock by way of a call option are buying on installment credit. They pay the purchase price of the option today but they do not pay the exercise price until they exercise the option. The higher the rate of interest and the longer the time to expiration, the more this "free credit" is worth.
- No matter how far the stock price falls, the owner of the call cannot lose more than the price of the call. On the other hand, the more the stock price rises above the exercise price, the greater the profit on the call. Therefore, the option holder does not lose from increased variability if things go wrong, but gains if they go right. The value of the option increases with the variability of stock returns. Of course the longer the time to the final exercise date, the more opportunity there is for the stock price to vary.

What options may be present in capital investment proposals?

The importance of building flexibility into investment projects (discussed in Chapter 9) can be reformulated in the language of options. For example, many capital investments provide the flexibility to expand capacity in the future if demand turns out to be unusually buoyant. They are in effect providing the firm with a call option on the extra capacity. Firms also think about alternative uses for their assets if things go wrong. The option to abandon a project is a put option; the put's exercise price is the value of the project's assets if shifted to an alternative use. The ability to expand or to abandon are both examples of **real options.**

What options may be provided in financial securities?

Many of the securities that firms issue contain an option. For example, a **warrant** is nothing but a long-term call option issued by the firm. **Convertible bonds** give the investor the option to buy the firm's stock in exchange for the value of the underlying bond. Unlike warrants and convertibles, which give an option to the investor, **callable bonds** give the option to the issuing firm. If interest rates decline and the value of the underlying bond rises, the firm can buy the bonds back at a specified exercise price.

QUIZ

1. **Option Payoffs.** Turn back to Table 23–2, which lists prices of various Google options. Use the data in the table to calculate the payoff and the profits for investments in each of the following September maturity options, assuming that the stock price on the expiration date is $180.

   a. Call option with exercise price of $160.
   b. Put option with exercise price of $160.
   c. Call option with exercise price of $180.
   d. Put option with exercise price of $180.
   e. Call option with exercise price of $200.
   f. Put option with exercise price of $200.

2. **Option Payoffs.** Redo the preceding problem assuming the stock price on the expiration date is (a) $190; (b) $170.

3. **Determinants of Option Value.** Look at the data in Table 23–2.

   a. What is the price of a call option with an exercise price of $180 and expiration in January 2006? What if expiration is in January 2007?

FIGURE 23–5 **See Quiz Problem 5.**

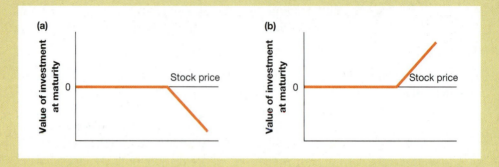

b. Why do you think the January 2007 calls cost more than the January 2006 calls?

c. Is the same true of put options? Why?

4. **Option Contracts.** Fill in the blanks by choosing the appropriate terms from the following list: *call, exercise, put.*

A(n) _____ option gives its owner the opportunity to buy a stock at a specific price which is generally called the _____ price. A(n) _____ option gives its owner the opportunity to sell stock at a specified _____ price.

5. **Option Payoffs.** Note Figure 23–5*a* and 23–5*b*. Match each figure with one of the following positions:

a. Call buyer

b. Call seller

c. Put buyer

d. Put seller

6. **Puts versus Calls.** "The buyer of a call and the seller of a put both hope that the stock price will rise. Therefore the two positions are identical." Is the speaker correct? Illustrate with a simple example or diagram.

7. **Hedging with Options.** Suppose that you hold a share of stock and a put option on that share with an exercise price of $100. What is the value of your portfolio when the option expires if

a. the stock price is below $100?

b. the stock price is above $100?

PRACTICE PROBLEMS

8. **Option Portfolios.** Mixing options and securities can often create interesting payoffs. For each of the following combinations show what the payoff would be when the option expires if (i) the stock price is below the exercise price, and (ii) the stock price is above the exercise price. Assume that each option has the same exercise price and expiration date.

a. Buy a call and invest the present value of the exercise price in a bank deposit.

b. Buy a share and a put option on the share.

c. Buy a share, buy a put option on the share, and sell a call option on the share.

d. Buy a call option and a put option on the share.

9. **Option Portfolios.** Look at Figure 23–6, which shows the possible future payoffs in January 2006 from a particular package of investments.

a. What package of investments would provide you with this set of payoffs?

b. How much would the package have cost you in March 2005? (See Table 23–2.)

c. In what circumstances might it make sense to invest in this package? Incidentally, this package of investments is known as a "straddle" by option buffs.

10. **Option Values.** What is the lower bound to the price of a call option? What is the upper bound?

11. **Option Values.** What is a call option worth if

a. the stock price is zero?

b. the stock price is extremely high relative to the exercise price?

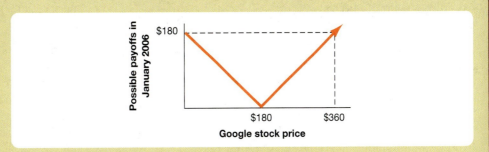

FIGURE 23–6 This strategy provides a payoff of $0 if the Google stock price remains at $180 and a payoff of $180 if Google's stock price either falls to zero or rises to $360. See Practice Problem 9.

12. **Option Valuation.** Table 23–2 shows call options on Google stock with the same exercise date in September and with exercise prices $160, $180, and $200. Notice that the price of the middle call option (with exercise price $180) is less than halfway between the prices of the other two calls (with exercise prices $160 and $200). Suppose that this were not the case. For example, suppose that the price of the middle call were the average of the prices of the other two calls. Show that if you sell two of the middle calls and use the proceeds to buy one each of the other calls, your proceeds in September may be positive but cannot be negative despite the fact that your net outlay today is zero. What can you deduce from this example about option pricing?

13. **Put Prices.** How does the price of a *put* option respond to the following changes, other things equal? Does the put price go up or down?

   a. Stock price increases.
   b. Exercise price is increased.
   c. Risk-free interest rate increases.
   d. Expiration date of the option is extended.
   e. Volatility of the stock price falls.
   f. Time passes, so the option's expiration date comes closer.

14. **Option Values.** As manager of United Bedstead you own substantial executive stock options. These options entitle you to buy the firm's shares during the next 5 years at a price of $100 a share. The plant manager has just outlined two alternative proposals to reequip the plant. Both proposals have the same net present value but one is substantially riskier than the other. At first you are undecided which to choose, but then you remember your stock options. How might these influence your choice?

15. **Real and Financial Options.** Fill in the blanks:

   a. An oil company acquires mining rights to a silver deposit. It is not obliged to mine the silver, however. The company has effectively acquired a _____ option, where the exercise price is the cost of opening the mine and extracting the silver.
   b. Some preferred shareholders have the right to redeem their shares at par value after a specified date. (If they hand over their shares, the firm sends them a check equal to the shares' par value.) These shareholders have a _____ option.
   c. A firm buys a standard machine with a ready secondhand market. The secondhand market gives the firm a _____ option.

16. **Real Options.** What is the option in each of the following cases. Is it a call or a put?

   a. Western Telecom commits to production of digital switching equipment specifically designed for the European market. As a stand-alone venture, the project has a negative NPV, but it is justified by the need for a strong market position in the rapidly growing, and potentially very profitable, market.
   b. Western Telecom vetoes a fully integrated automated production line for the new digital switches. It will rely on standard, less expensive equipment even though the automated production line would be more efficient overall using the specialized equipment, according to a discounted cash-flow calculation.

17. **Real Options.** Describe each of the following situations in the language of options.

   a. Drilling rights to undeveloped heavy crude oil in southern California. Development and production of the oil now is a negative-NPV endeavor. The break-even price is $80 per barrel, versus a spot price of $60. However, the decision to develop can be put off for up to 5 years.
   b. A restaurant producing net cash flows, after all out-of-pocket expenses, of $700,000 per year. There is no upward or downward trend in the cash flows, but they fluctuate. The real estate occupied by the restaurant is owned, and it could be sold for $5 million.

18. **Real Options.** Price support systems for various agricultural products have allowed farmers to sell their crops to the government for a specified "support price." What kind of option has the government given to the farmers? What is the exercise price?

19. **Hidden Options.** Some investment management contracts give the portfolio manager a bonus proportional to the amount by which a portfolio return exceeds a specified threshold.

    a. In what way is this an implicit call option on the portfolio?
    b. Can you think of a way in which such contracts can lead to incentive problems? For example, what happens to the value of the prospective bonus if the manager invests in high-volatility stocks?

20. **Hidden Options.** The Rank and File Company is considering a stock issue to raise $50 million. An underwriter offers to guarantee the success of the issue by buying any unwanted stock at the $25 issue price. The underwriter's fee is $2 million.

    a. What kind of option does Rank and File acquire if it accepts the underwriter's offer?
    b. What determines the value of the option?

21. **Hidden Options.**

    a. Some banks have offered their customers an unusual type of time deposit. The deposit does not pay any interest if the market falls, but instead the depositor receives a proportion of any rise in the Standard & Poor's Index. What implicit option do the investors hold? How should the bank invest the money in order to protect itself against the risk of offering this deposit?
    b. You can also make a deposit with a bank that does not pay interest if the market index rises but makes an increasingly large payment as the market index *falls*. How should the bank protect itself against the risk of offering this deposit?

22. **Loan Guarantees.** The FDIC insures bank deposits. If a bank's assets are insufficient to pay off all depositors, the FDIC will contribute enough money to ensure that all depositors can be paid off in full. (We ignore the $100,000 maximum coverage on each account.) In what way is this guarantee of deposits the provision of a put option by the FDIC? *Hint:* Write out the funds the FDIC will have to contribute when bank assets are less than deposits owed to depositors. What is the exercise price of the put option?

23. **Real Options.** After dramatic increases in oil prices in the 1970s, the U.S. government funded several projects to create synthetic oil or natural gas from abundant U.S. supplies of coal and oil shale. Although the cost of producing such synthetic fuels at the time was greater than the price of oil, it was argued that the projects still could be justified for their insurance value since the cost of synthetic fuel would be essentially fixed while the price of oil was risky. Evaluate the synthetic fuel program as an option on fuel sources. Is it a call or a put option? What is the exercise price? How would uncertainty in the future price of oil affect the amount the United States should have been willing to spend on such projects?

Please visit us at www.mhhe.com/bmm5e or refer to your Student CD

24. **Arbitrage Opportunities.**

    a. Circular File stock is selling for $25 a share. You see that call options on the stock with exercise price of $20 are selling at $3. What should you do? What will happen to the option price as investors identify this opportunity?
    b. Now you observe that put options on Circular File with exercise price $30 are selling for $4. What should you do?

25. **Convertible Bonds.** A 10-year maturity convertible bond with a 6 percent coupon on a company with a bond rating of Aaa is selling for $1,050. Each bond can be exchanged for 20 shares, and the stock price currently is $50 per share. Other Aaa-rated bonds with the same maturity would sell at a yield to maturity of 8 percent. What is the value of the bondholders' call option? Why is the bond selling for more than the value of the shares it can be converted into?

CHALLENGE PROBLEMS

26. **Option Portfolios.** Repeat the three parts of question 9 except that now the problem is to devise a package of investments with the payoffs shown in Figure 23–7. This package of investments is known as a "butterfly."

FIGURE 23–7 This strategy provides a total payoff of $20 if the stock price is $180 and a payoff of zero if the stock price is either (a) $160 or less or (b) $200 or more. See Practice Problem 26.

Please visit us at www.mhhe.com/bmm5e or refer to your Student CD

27. **Option Pricing.** Look again at the Google call option that we valued in Section 23.2. Suppose that by the end of January 2007 the price of Google stock could rise to $360 or fall to $90. Everything else is unchanged from our example.

    a. What would be the value of the Google call at the end of January 2007 if the stock price is $360? If it is $90?

    b. Show that a strategy of buying 3 calls provides exactly the same payoffs as borrowing the present value of $180 from the bank and buying two shares.

    c. What is the net cash flow in March 2005 from the policy of borrowing PV($180) and buying two shares?

    d. What does this tell you about the value of the call option?

    e. Why is the value of the call option different from the value that we calculated in Section 23.2? What does this tell you about the relationship between the value of a call and the volatility of the share price?

28. **Option Pricing.** Look once more at the Google call option that we valued in Section 23.2. Suppose (just suppose) that the interest rate on bank loans is zero. Recalculate the value of the Google call option. What does this tell you about the relationship between interest rates and the value of a call?

Go to Market Insight at **www.mhhe.com/edumarketinsight**.

STANDARD &POOR'S

1. Look back at the January 2006 expiration Google call and put options, discussed in Examples 23.1 and 23.2 of the chapter. Use the Monthly Adjusted Prices to determine whether these options were ever in the money.

2. Find IBM's most recent income statement. What was the value that IBM assigned to the stock options it granted its employees in the most recent year?

SOLUTIONS TO SELF-TEST QUESTIONS

23.1 a. The call with exercise price $180 costs $19.60. If the stock price at the expiration date is $150, the call expires valueless and the investor loses the entire $19.60. If the stock price is $230, the value of the call is $230 – $180 = $50, and the investor's profit is $50 – $19.60 = $30.40.

    b. The put costs $17.90. If the stock price at expiration is $150, the put value is $180 – $150 = $30, and the investor's profit is $30 – $17.90 = $12.10. If the stock price is $230, the value of the put is zero, and the investor's loss is the price paid for the put, $17.90.

23.2 a. The call seller receives $19.60 for writing the call. If the stock price at expiration is $150, the call expires valueless and the investor keeps the entire $19.60 as a profit. If the stock price is $230, the value of the call is $230 – $180 = $50. In other words, the option seller must deliver a stock worth $230 for an exercise price of only $180. The investor's net profit is $19.60 – $50 = –$30.40. The call seller will clear a positive net profit as long as the stock price remains below $199.60.

b. The put seller receives $17.90 for writing the put. If the stock price at expiration is $150, the put value is $180 − $150 = $30. In other words, the put option seller must pay an exercise price of $180 to buy a stock worth only $150. The put seller's loss is $30 − $17.90 = $12.10. If the stock price is $230, the final value of the put is zero, and the investor's profit is the price originally received for the put, $17.90.

23.3   Put-call parity states that value of stock + value of put = value of call + present value of exercise price. Therefore, in the case of Witterman

$$\$55 + \text{value of put} = \$8.05 + \frac{\$60}{1.04}$$

and value of put = $8.05 + $57.69 − $55 = $10.74.

23.4   The value of a put option is higher when the exercise price is higher. You would be willing to pay more for the right to sell a stock at a high price than the right to sell it at a low price.

23.5   First consider the payoff to the put holder in the lower volatility scenario:

Stock price	$160	$200
Put value	$ 20	0

In the higher volatility scenario, the value of the stock can be $140 or $220. Now the payoff to the put is

Stock price	$140	$220
Put value	$40	0

The expected value of the payoff of the put doubles.

23.6   The payoffs are as follows:

		Payoff in 3 Months if Stock Price Equals	
	Cash Flow Today	**$15**	**$60**
Strategy A	?	$ 0	+$ 90
Buy three calls			
Strategy B			
Buy two shares	−$60	+$ 30	+$120
Borrow PV($30)	+ 29.70	− 30	− 30
	−$30.30	$ 0	+$ 90

Note: PV($30) at an interest rate of 1 percent for 3 months is 30/1.01 = $29.70.

The initial net cash outflow from strategy B is $30.30. Since the three calls offer the same payoffs in the future, they must also cost $30.30. One call is worth 30.30/3 = $10.10.

23.7   a. The developer has the option to sell the potential housing development to the country club. This abandonment option is like a put that guarantees a minimum payoff from the investment.
b. The exercise price of the option is the price at which it can be sold to the country club. The asset value is the present value of the project if maintained as a housing development. If this value is less than the value as a golf course, the project will be sold.
c. The abandonment option increases NPV by placing a lower bound on the possible payoffs from the project.

23.8   a. Conversion value = 103.4 × $20 = $2,068.
Conversion price = $1,000/103.4 = $9.67 (unchanged).
b. Bond value = $35 × 3-year annuity factor at 5% + $1,000 × 3-year PV factor at 5%
= $95.31 + $863.84 = $959.15.

23.9 a. In 5 years, the bond will be a 15-year maturity bond. The bondholder can sell the bond back to the firm at face value. The bondholder therefore has a put option to sell a 15-year bond for face value even if interest rates have risen and the bond would otherwise sell below face value.

   b. The exercise price is the face value of the bond.

   c. The bondholder will sell the bond back to the company if interest rates increase or the company's credit deteriorates.

   d. More valuable. The bondholder now has the right, but not the obligation, to sell the bond at face value in 5 years.

CHAPTER

24

Risk Management

RELATED WEB LINKS

www.cme.com

www.cbot.com

www.nymex.com

www.euronext.com

www.lme.com   Web sites of major futures exchanges.

www.bis.org

www.isda.org   For statistics on the derivative markets.

www.commoditytrader.net   Extensive quotes on commodities, futures, and other derivatives.

www.appliedderivatives.com

www.erivativesreview.com

www.futuresmag.com

www.risk.net   Journals specializing in derivatives.

Risk management does not mean avoiding risk.
It means deciding what risks to take.

© Joaquin Palting/Getty Images

We often assume that risk is beyond our control. A business is exposed to unpredictable changes in raw material costs, tax rates, technology, and a long list of other variables. There's nothing the manager can do about it.

This is not wholly true. To some extent a manager can *select* which risks to accept. For example, in the last chapter we saw that companies can consciously affect the risk of an investment by building in flexibility. A company that reduces the cost of bailing out of a project by using standardized equipment is taking less risk than a similar firm that uses specialized equipment with no alternative uses. In this case the option to resell the equipment serves as an insurance policy.

Sometimes, rather than building flexibility into the project, companies accept the risk but then use financial instruments to offset it. This practice of taking offsetting risks is known as *hedging.* In this chapter we will explain how hedging works and we will describe some of the specialized financial instruments that have been devised to help manage risk. These instruments include options, futures, forwards, and swaps. Each of these instruments provides a payoff that depends on the price of some underlying commodity or financial asset. Because their payoffs derive from the prices of other assets, they are often known collectively as *derivative instruments (or derivatives* for short).[1]

After reading this chapter you should be able to:

- Understand why companies hedge to reduce risk.

- Use options, futures, and forward contracts to devise simple hedging strategies.

- Explain how companies can use swaps to change the risk of securities that they have issued.

---

[1] Derivatives often conjure up an image of wicked speculators. Derivative instruments attract their share of speculators, some of whom may be wicked, but they are also used by sober and prudent businesspeople who simply want to reduce risk.

24.1 Why Hedge?

In this chapter we will explain *how* companies use derivatives to hedge the risks of their business. But first we should give some of the reasons *why* they do it.

Surely, the answer to this question is obvious. Isn't less risk always better than more? Well, not necessarily. Even if hedging is costless, transactions undertaken *solely* to reduce risk are unlikely to add value. There are two basic reasons for this:

- *Reason 1: Hedging is a zero-sum game.* A company that hedges a risk does not eliminate it. It simply passes the risk on to someone else. For example, suppose that a heating-oil distributor agrees with a refiner to buy all of next winter's heating-oil deliveries at a fixed price. This contract is a zero-sum game, because the refiner loses what the distributor gains and vice versa. If next winter's price of heating oil turns out to be unusually high, the distributor wins from having locked in a below-market price but the refiner is forced to sell below market. Conversely, if the price of heating oil is unusually *low,* the refiner wins because the distributor is forced to buy at the high fixed price. Of course, neither party knows next winter's price at the time that the deal is struck, but they consider the range of possible prices and negotiate terms that are fair (zero NPV) on both sides of the bargain.
- *Reason 2: Investors' do-it-yourself alternative.* Companies cannot increase the value of their shares by undertaking transactions that investors can easily do on their own. We came across this idea when we discussed whether leverage increases company value, and we met it again when we came to dividend policy. It also applies to hedging. For example, when the shareholders in our heating-oil distributor invested in the company, they were presumably aware of the risks of the business. If they did not want to be exposed to the ups and downs of energy prices, they could have protected themselves in several ways. Perhaps they own shares in both the distributor and the refiner and do not care whether one wins at the other's expense.

  Of course, shareholders can adjust their exposure only when companies keep investors fully informed of the transactions that they have made. For example, when a group of European central banks announced in 1999 that they would limit their sales of gold, the gold price immediately shot up. Investors in gold-mining shares rubbed their hands at the prospect of rising profits. But when they discovered that some mining companies had protected themselves against price fluctuations and would *not* benefit from the price rise, the hand-rubbing turned to hand-wringing.

  Some stockholders of these gold-mining companies wanted to make a bet on rising gold prices; others didn't. But all of them gave the same message to management. The first group said, "Don't hedge! I'm happy to bear the risk of fluctuating gold prices, because I think gold prices will increase." The second group said, "Don't hedge! I'd rather do it myself."

We have seen that although hedging reduces risk, this doesn't in itself increase firm value. So when does it make sense to hedge? Sometimes hedging is worthwhile because it makes financial planning easier and reduces the odds of an embarrassing cash shortfall. A shortfall might mean only an unexpected trip to the bank, but on other occasions the firm might have to forgo worthwhile investments, and in extreme cases the shortfall could trigger bankruptcy. Why not reduce the odds of these awkward outcomes with a hedge?

We saw in our discussion of debt policy in Chapter 15 that financial distress can result in indirect as well as direct costs to a firm. Costs of financial distress arise from disruption to normal business operations as well as from the effect that financial distress has on the firm's investment decisions. The better the risk management policies, the less chance that the firm will incur these costs of distress. As a side benefit, better risk management increases the firm's debt capacity.

In some cases hedging also makes it easier to decide whether an operating manager deserves a stern lecture or a pat on the back. Suppose that your export division shows a 50 percent decline in profits when the dollar unexpectedly strengthens against other currencies. How much of that decrease is due to the exchange rate shift and how much to poor management? If the company had protected itself against the effect of exchange rate changes, it's probably bad management. If it wasn't protected, you have to make a judgment with hindsight, probably by asking, "What would profits have been *if* the firm had hedged against exchange rate movements?"

Finally, hedging extraneous events can help focus the operating manager's attention. We know we shouldn't worry about events outside our control, but most of us do anyway. It's naive to expect the manager of the export division not to worry about exchange rate movements if his bottom line and bonus depend on them. The time spent worrying could be better spent if the company hedged itself against such movements.

A sensible risk strategy needs answers to the following questions:

- *What are the major risks that the company faces and what are the possible consequences?* Some risks are scarcely worth a thought, but there are others that might bankrupt the company.
- *Is the company being paid for taking these risks?* Managers are not paid to avoid all risks, but if they can reduce their exposure to risks for which there are no compensating rewards, they can afford to place larger bets when the odds are stacked in their favor.
- *Can the company take any measures to reduce the probability of a bad outcome or to limit its impact?* For example, most businesses install alarm and sprinkler systems to prevent damage from fire and invest in backup facilities in case damage does occur.
- *Can the company purchase fairly priced insurance to offset any losses?* Insurance companies have some advantages in bearing risk. In particular, they may be able to spread the risk across a portfolio of different insurers.
- *Can the company use derivatives, such as options or futures, to hedge the risk?* In the remainder of this chapter we explain when and how derivatives may be used.

24.2 Reducing Risk with Options

In the last chapter we introduced you to put and call options. Managers regularly buy options on currencies, interest rates, and commodities to limit their downside risk. Many of these options are traded on options exchanges, but often they are simply private deals between the corporation and a bank.

Petrochemical Parfum, Inc., is concerned about potential increases in the price of heavy crude oil, which is one of its major inputs. To protect itself against such increases Petrochemical buys 6-month call options to purchase 1,000 barrels of crude oil at an exercise price of $40. These options might cost $1 per barrel.

If the price of crude is above the $40 exercise price when the options expire, Petrochemical will exercise the options and will receive the difference between the oil price and the exercise price. If the oil price falls below the exercise price, the options will expire worthless. The net cost of oil will therefore be:

	Oil Price, Dollars per Barrel		
	$35	**$40**	**$45**
Cost of 1,000 barrels	$35,000	$40,000	$45,000
– Payoff on call options	0	0	5,000
Net cost	$35,000	$40,000	$40,000

You can see that by buying options Petrochemical protects itself against increases in the oil price while continuing to benefit from oil price decreases. If prices fall, it can discard its call option and buy its oil at the market price. If oil prices rise, however, it can exercise its call option to purchase oil for $40 a barrel. Therefore, options create an attractive asymmetry. Of course, this asymmetry comes at a price—the $1,000 cost of the options.

Consider now the problem of Onnex, Inc., which supplies Petrochemical with crude oil. Its problem is the mirror image of Petrochemical's; it loses when oil prices fall and gains when oil prices rise.

Onnex wants to lock in a minimum price of oil but still benefit from rising oil prices. It can do so by purchasing *put* options that give it the right to *sell* oil at an exercise price of $40 per barrel. If oil prices fall, it will exercise the put. If they rise, it will discard the put and sell oil at the market price:

	Oil Price, Dollars per Barrel		
	$35	**$40**	**$45**
Revenue from 1,000 barrels	$35,000	$40,000	$45,000
+ Payoff on put option	5,000	0	0
Total revenues	$40,000	$40,000	$45,000

If oil prices rise, Onnex reaps the benefit. But if oil prices fall below $40 a barrel the payoff of the put option exactly offsets the revenue shortfall. As a result, Onnex realizes total revenues of at least $40 a barrel, which is the exercise price of the put option.

Once again, you don't get something for nothing. The price that Onnex pays for insurance against a fall in the price of oil is the cost of the put option. Similarly, the price that Petrochemical paid for insurance against a rise in the price of oil was the cost of the call option. Options provide protection against adverse price changes for a fee—the option premium.

Notice that both Petrochemical and Onnex use options to insure against an adverse move in oil prices. But the options do not remove all uncertainty. For example, Onnex may be able to sell oil for much more than the exercise price of the option.

Figure 24–1 illustrates the nature of Onnex's insurance strategy. Panel *a* shows the revenue derived from selling the 1,000 barrels of oil. The firm is currently exposed to oil price risk: As prices fall, so will the firm's revenue. But, as panel *b* illustrates, the payoff on a put option to sell 1,000 barrels rises as oil prices fall below $40 a barrel, and therefore it can offset the firm's exposure. Panel *c* shows the firm's total revenues after it buys the put option. For prices below $40 per barrel, revenues are $40,000. But revenues rise $1,000 for every dollar that oil prices rise above $40. The profile in panel *c* should be familiar to you: Think back to the protective put strategy we first saw in Section 23.1. In both cases, the put provides a floor on the value of the overall position.

Self-Test 24.1   **Draw three graphs like those in Figure 24–1 to illustrate how Petrochemical puts a ceiling on its costs by purchasing call options on oil.**

24.3 Futures Contracts

futures contract
Exchange-traded promise to buy or sell an asset in the future at a prespecified price.

Suppose you are a wheat farmer. You are optimistic about next year's wheat crop, but still you can't sleep. You are worried that when the time comes to sell the wheat, prices may have fallen through the floor. The cure for insomnia is to sell wheat *futures*. In this case, you agree to deliver so many bushels of wheat in (say) September at a price that is set today. Do not confuse this **futures contract** with an option, where the holder

FIGURE 24-1 Onnex can buy put options to place a floor on its overall revenues.

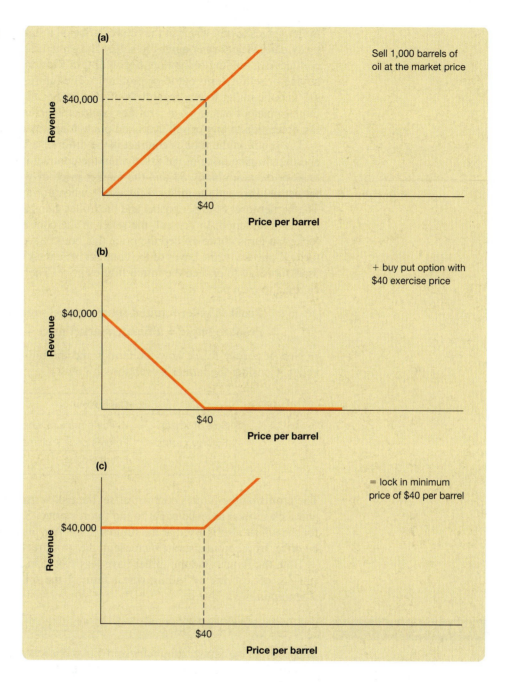

has a *choice* whether to make delivery; your futures contract is a firm promise to deliver wheat at a fixed selling price.

A miller is in the opposite position. She needs to *buy* wheat after the harvest. If she would like to fix the price of this wheat ahead of time, she can do so by *buying* wheat futures. In other words, she agrees to take delivery of wheat in the future at a price that is fixed today. The miller also does not have an option; if she still holds the futures contract when it matures, she is obliged to take delivery.

Let's suppose the farmer and the miller strike a deal. They enter a futures contract. What happens? First, no money changes hands when the contract is initiated.[2] The

---

[2] Actually, each party will be required to set up a margin account to guarantee performance on the contract. Despite this, the futures contract still may be considered as essentially requiring no money down. First, the amount of margin is small. Second, it may be posted in interest-bearing securities, so that the parties to the trade need not suffer opportunity cost from placing assets in the margin account.

miller agrees to buy wheat at the futures price on a stated *future* date (the contract maturity date). The farmer agrees to sell at the same price and date. Second, the futures contract is a binding obligation, not an option. Options give the right to buy or sell *if* buying or selling turns out to be profitable. The futures contract *requires* the farmer to sell and the miller to buy regardless of who profits and who loses. Just remember, no money changes hands when a futures contract is entered into. The contract is a binding obligation to buy or sell at a fixed price at contract maturity.

The profit on the futures contract is the difference between the initial futures price and the ultimate price of the asset when the contract matures. For example, if the futures price is originally $3 and the market price of wheat turns out to be $3.40, the farmer delivers and the miller receives the wheat for a price $.40 below market value. The farmer loses $.40 per bushel and the miller gains $.40 per bushel as a result of the futures transaction. In general, the seller of the contract benefits if the price initially locked in turns out to exceed the price that could have been obtained at contract maturity. Conversely, the buyer of the contract benefits if the ultimate market price of the asset turns out to exceed the initial futures price. Therefore, the profits on the futures contract to each party are

Profit to seller = initial futures price – ultimate market price

Profit to buyer = ultimate market price – initial futures price

Now it is easy to see how the farmer and the miller can both use the contract to hedge. Consider the farmer's overall cash flows:

Cash Flow	
Sale of wheat	Ultimate price of wheat
Futures profits	Futures price – ultimate price of wheat
Total	Futures price

The profits on the futures contract offset the risk surrounding the sales price of wheat and lock in total revenue equal to the futures price. Similarly, the miller's all-in cost for the wheat also is fixed at the futures price. Any increase in the cost of wheat will be offset by a commensurate increase in the profit realized on the futures contract.

Both the farmer and the miller have less risk than before. The farmer has hedged (that is, offset) risk by selling wheat futures; the miller has hedged risk by buying wheat futures.[3]

EXAMPLE 24.1 ▶   Hedging with Futures

Suppose that the farmer originally sold 5,000 bushels of September wheat futures at a price of $3 a bushel. In September, when the futures contract matures, the price of wheat is only $2.50 a bushel. The farmer buys back the wheat futures at $2.50 just before maturity, giving him a profit of $.50 a bushel on the sale and subsequent repurchase. At the same time he sells his wheat at the spot price of $2.50 a bushel. His total receipts are therefore $3 a bushel:

Profit on sale and repurchase of futures	$ .50
Sale of wheat at the September spot price	2.50
Total receipts	$3.00

You can see that the futures contract has allowed the farmer to lock in total proceeds of $3 a bushel.   ◀

---

[3] Neither has eliminated all risk. For example, the farmer still has quantity risk. He does not know for sure how many bushels of wheat he will produce.

FIGURE 24-2 The farmer
can use wheat futures to
hedge the value of the crop.
See Example 24.1.

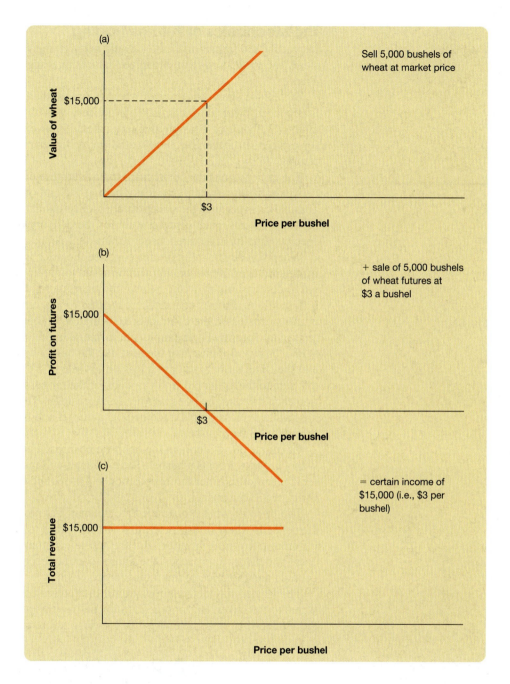

Figure 24–2 illustrates how the futures contract enabled the farmer in Example 24.1 to hedge his position. Panel *a* shows how the value of 5,000 bushels of wheat varies with the spot price of wheat. The value rises by $5,000 for every dollar increase in wheat prices. Panel *b* is the profit on a futures contract to deliver 5,000 bushels of wheat at a futures price of $3 per bushel. The profit will be zero if the ultimate price of wheat equals the original futures price, $3. The profit on the contract to deliver at $3 rises by $5,000 for every dollar the price of wheat *falls* below $3. The exposures to the price of wheat depicted in panels *a* and *b* obviously cancel out. Panel *c* shows that the total value of the 5,000 bushels plus the futures position is unaffected by the ultimate price of wheat, and equals $3 × 5,000 = $15,000. In other words, the farmer has locked in proceeds of $3 per bushel, equal to the original futures price.

The Mechanics of Futures Trading

In practice the farmer and miller would not sign the futures contract face-to-face. Instead, each would go to an organized futures exchange such as the Chicago Board of Trade.

Table 24–1 shows the price of wheat futures at the Chicago Board of Trade in April 2005, when the price for immediate delivery was about $3.20 a bushel. Notice that there is a choice of possible delivery dates. If, for example, you were to sell wheat for delivery in December, you would get a higher price than by selling September futures.

The miller would not be prepared to buy futures contracts if the farmer were free to deliver half-rotten wheat to a leaky barn at the end of a cart track. Futures trading is possible only because the contracts are highly standardized. For example, in the case of wheat futures, each contract calls for the delivery of 5,000 bushels of wheat of a specified quality at a warehouse in Chicago, Toledo, or Burns Harbor.

When you buy or sell a futures contract, the price is fixed today, but payment is not made until later. However, you will be asked to put up some cash or securities as *margin* to demonstrate that you are able to honor your side of the bargain.

In addition, futures contracts are *marked to market*. This means that each day any profits or losses on the contract are calculated; you pay the exchange any losses and receive any profits. For example, our farmer agreed to deliver 5,000 bushels of wheat at $3 a bushel. Suppose that the next day the price of wheat futures increases to $3.05 a bushel. The farmer now has a loss on his sale of $5,000 \times \$.05 = \$250$ and must pay this sum to the exchange. You can think of the farmer as buying back his futures position each day and then opening up a new position. Thus after the first day the farmer has realized a loss on his trade of $.05 a bushel and now has an obligation to deliver wheat for $3.05 a bushel.

Of course our miller is in the opposite position. The rise in futures price leaves her with a *profit* of 5 cents a bushel. The exchange will therefore pay her this profit. In effect the miller sells her futures position at a profit and opens a new contract to take delivery at $3.05 a bushel.

The price of wheat for immediate delivery is known as the *spot price*. When the farmer sells wheat futures, the price that he agrees to take for his wheat may be very different from the spot price. But the future eventually becomes the present. As the date for delivery approaches, the futures contract becomes more and more like a spot contract and the price of the futures contract snuggles up to the spot price.

The farmer may decide to wait until the futures contract matures and then deliver wheat to the buyer. But in practice such delivery is rare, for it is more convenient for the farmer to buy back the wheat futures just before maturity.[4]

TABLE 24–1 The price of wheat futures at the Chicago Board of Trade on April 4, 2005

Delivery Date	Price per Bushel
July 2005	$3.25
September 2005	3.32
December 2005	3.40
March 2006	3.48
May 2006	3.47
July 2006	3.43
December 2006	3.53

Source: The Chicago Board of Trade Web site, **www.cbot.com.**

---

[4] In the case of some of the financial futures described later, you cannot deliver the asset. At maturity the buyer simply receives (or pays) the difference between the spot price and the price at which he or she has agreed to purchase the asset.

Self-Test 24.2

Suppose that 2 days after taking out the futures contracts the price of September wheat increases to $3.20 a bushel. What additional payments will be made by or to the farmer and the miller? What will be their remaining obligation at the end of this second day?

Commodity and Financial Futures

We have shown how the farmer and the miller can both use wheat futures to hedge their risk. It is also possible to trade futures in a wide variety of other commodities, such as sugar, soybean oil, pork bellies, orange juice, crude oil, and copper.

Commodity prices can bounce up and down like a bungee jumper. For example, in December 2000 the price of a ton of cocoa hit a low of $674. Two years later the price had more than tripled to $2,400. For a large buyer of cocoa, such as Hershey, these price fluctuations could knock the company badly off course. Hershey therefore reduces its exposure to movements in cocoa and sugar prices by hedging with commodity futures.

For many firms, the wide fluctuations in interest rates and exchange rates have become at least as important a source of risk as changes in commodity prices. You can use *financial futures* to hedge against these risks.

Financial futures are similar to commodity futures, but instead of placing an order to buy or sell a commodity at a future date, you place an order to buy or sell a financial asset at a future date. You can use financial futures to protect yourself against fluctuations in short- and long-term interest rates, exchange rates, and the level of share prices.

Financial futures have been a remarkable success. Figure 24–3 shows the explosive growth of trading on the Chicago Board of Trade. While financial futures barely registered in 1980, they now dominate the market. Table 24–2 lists some of the more popular financial futures contracts.

Self-Test 24.3

You plan to issue long-term bonds in 9 months but are worried that interest rates may have increased in the meantime. How could you use financial futures to protect yourself against a general rise in interest rates?

FIGURE 24–3 Trading on the Chicago Board of Trade has come to be dominated by financial futures and options.

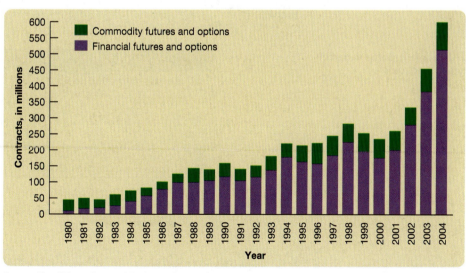

Source: The Chicago Board of Trade Web site, **www.cbot.com.**

INTERNET INSIDER

Futures Exchanges

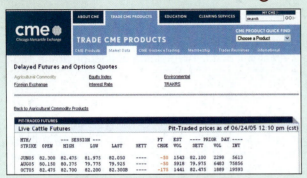

1. Log on to the Web site for the Chicago Mercantile Exchange on **www.cme.com** and click on *About CME* to find out how trading is conducted on the floor of the exchange. What new futures contracts have begun to trade in the last year or so? Who do you think would be the main buyers and sellers of these contracts? Look under *Market Data* at the latest quotes for (say) live-cattle futures. What is the longest maturity for this contract? Is there more trading in the near-term or the far-term contract? Does it cost more to buy live cattle for delivery in the next few months or for delivery in the more distant future? Click on *Education,* and learn more about how futures work. One other thing: We mentioned that it is very difficult to predict which new futures contracts will succeed and which will fail. Here is a chance to see what has happened to weather futures (see page 662). Have they proved to be popular, or have they ceased to trade?

2. The Chicago Board of Trade's Web site is **www.cbot.com**. You will find here similar material to that provided by the CME, and you can use it to answer similar questions. If you have the time, look at both sites; if you have to choose one, we suggest that you look at the CME.

24.4 Forward Contracts

Each day billions of dollars of futures contracts are bought and sold. We have seen that this liquidity is possible only because futures contracts are standardized. Futures contracts mature on a limited number of dates each year (take another look at the wheat contract in Table 24–1), and the contract size is standardized. For example, a contract may call for delivery of 5,000 bushels of wheat, 100 ounces of gold, or 62,500 British pounds. If the terms of a futures contract do not suit your particular needs, you may be able to buy or sell a **forward contract.**

forward contract
Agreement to buy or sell an asset in the future at an agreed price.

Forward contracts are custom-tailored futures contracts.[5] You can write a forward contract with any maturity date for delivery of any quantity of goods. For example, suppose that you know that you will need to pay out yen in 3 months' time. You can fix today the price that you will pay for the yen by arranging with your bank to buy yen forward. At the end of the 3 months, you pay the agreed sum and take delivery of the yen.

TABLE 24-2 Some financial futures contracts

Contract	Principal Exchange
U.S. Treasury notes and bonds	CBT
Eurodollar deposits	IMM
Standard & Poor's Index	IMM
Euro	IMM
Yen	IMM
German government bonds (Bunds)	Eurex

Key to abbreviations:
CBT   Chicago Board of Trade
IMM   International Monetary Market (at the Chicago Mercantile Exchange)

---

[5] One difference between forward and futures contracts is that forward contracts are not marked to market. Thus with a forward contract you settle up any profits or losses when the contract matures.

EXAMPLE 24.2 ▶	Forward Contracts

Computer Parts Inc. has ordered memory chips from its supplier in Japan. The bill for ¥53 million must be paid on July 27. The company can arrange with its bank today to buy this number of yen forward for delivery on July 27 at a forward price of ¥110 per dollar. Therefore, on July 27, Computer Parts pays the bank $53 million/(¥110/$) = $481,818 and receives ¥53 million, which it can use to pay its Japanese supplier. By committing forward to exchange $481,818 for ¥53 million, its dollar costs are locked in. Notice that if the firm had not used the forward contract to hedge and the dollar had depreciated over this period, the firm would have had to pay a greater amount of dollars. For example, if the dollar had depreciated to ¥100/dollar, the firm would have had to exchange $530,000 for the ¥53 million necessary to pay its bill. The firm could have used a futures contract to hedge its foreign exchange exposure, but standardization of futures would not allow for delivery of precisely ¥53 million on precisely July 27. ◀

The most active trading in forwards is in foreign currencies, but in recent years companies have increasingly entered into forward rate agreements that allow them to fix in advance the interest rate at which they borrow or lend.

24.5 Swaps

Suppose Computer Parts from Example 24.2 decides to produce memory chips instead of purchasing them from outside suppliers. It has issued $100 million in floating-rate bonds to help finance the construction of a new plant. (Recall from Chapter 13 that floating-rate loans make interest payments that go up and down with the general level of interest rates. The coupon payments on the bonds are tied to a specific short-term interest rate.) But the financial manager is concerned that interest rates are becoming more volatile, and she would like to lock in the firm's interest expenses. One approach would be to buy back the floating-rate bonds and replace them with a new issue of fixed-rate debt. But it is costly to issue new debt to the public; in addition, buying back the outstanding bonds in the market will result in considerable trading costs.

A better approach to hedge out its interest rate exposure is for the firm to enter an interest rate **swap.** The firm will pay or "swap" a fixed payment for another payment that is tied to the level of interest rates. Thus if rates do rise, increasing the firm's interest expense on its floating-rate debt, its cash flow from the swap agreement will rise as well, offsetting its exposure.

Suppose the firm pays the LIBOR rate on its floating-rate bonds. (Recall that LIBOR, or London Interbank Offer Rate, is the interest rate at which banks borrow from each other in the eurodollar market. It is the most frequently used short-term interest rate in the swap market.) The firm's interest expense each year therefore equals the LIBOR rate times $100 million. It would like to transform this obligation into one that will not fluctuate with interest rates.

Suppose that current rates in the swaps market are "LIBOR for 5 percent fixed." This means that Computer Parts can enter into a swap agreement to *pay* 5 percent on "notional principal" of $100 million to a swap dealer and *receive* payment of the LIBOR rate on the same amount of notional principal. The dealer and the firm are called *counterparties* in the swap. The firm pays the dealer .05 × $100 million and receives LIBOR × $100 million. The firm's *net* cash payment to the dealer is therefore (.05 − LIBOR) × $100 million. (If LIBOR exceeds 5 percent, the firm receives money from the dealer; if it is less than 5 percent, the firm pays money to the dealer.) Figure 24–4 illustrates the cash flows paid by Computer Parts and the swap dealer.

Table 24–3 shows Computer Parts's net payments for three possible interest rates. The total payment on the bond-with-swap agreement equals $5 million regardless of

swap
Arrangement by two counterparties to exchange one stream of cash flows for another.

FIGURE 24–4 Interest rate swap. Computer Parts currently pays the LIBOR rate on its outstanding bonds (the arrow on the left). If the firm enters a swap to pay a fixed rate of 5 percent and receive a floating rate of LIBOR, its exposure to LIBOR will cancel out and its net cash outflow will be a fixed rate of 5 percent.

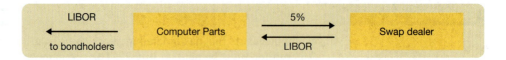

the interest rate. The swap has transformed the floating-rate bond into synthetic fixed-rate debt with an effective coupon rate of 5 percent. The firm has thus hedged away its interest rate exposure without actually having to replace its floating-rate bonds with fixed-rate bonds. Swaps offer a much cheaper way to "rearrange the balance sheet."[6]

There are many other applications of interest rate swaps. A portfolio manager who is holding a portfolio of long-term bonds but is worried that interest rates might increase, causing a capital loss on the portfolio, can enter a swap to pay a fixed rate and receive a floating rate, thereby converting the holdings into a synthetic floating-rate portfolio (see Self-Test 24.4). Or a pension fund manager might identify some money market securities that are paying excellent yields compared with other comparable-risk short-term securities. However, the manager might believe that such short-term assets are inappropriate for the portfolio. The fund can hold these high-yielding securities and enter a swap in which it receives a fixed rate and pays a floating rate. It thus captures the benefit of the advantageous *relative* yields on these securities but still establishes a portfolio with the fixed interest rate risk characteristic of long-term bonds.

Self-Test 24.4 Consider the portfolio manager who is holding a $100 million portfolio of long-term 5 percent coupon bonds and wishes to reduce price risk by transforming the holdings into a synthetic floating-rate portfolio. Assume that the portfolio currently pays a 5 percent fixed rate and that swap dealers currently offer terms of 5 percent fixed for LIBOR. What swap would the manager establish? Show the total income on the fund in a table like Table 24–3, and illustrate the cash flows in a diagram like Figure 24–4.

There are many variations on the interest rate swap. For example, currency swaps allow firms to exchange a series of payments in dollars (which may be tied to a fixed or floating rate) for a series of payments in another currency (which also may be tied to a fixed or floating rate). These swaps can therefore be used to manage exposure to exchange rate fluctuations.

TABLE 24–3 An interest rate swap can transform floating-rate bonds into synthetic fixed-rate bonds

| | LIBOR Rate | | |
	4.5%	5.0%	5.5%
Interest paid on floating-rate bonds (= LIBOR × $100 million)	$4,500,000	$5,000,000	$5,500,000
+ Cash payment on swap [= (.05 – LIBOR) × notional principal of $100 million]	500,000	0	–500,000
Total payment	$5,000,000	$5,000,000	$5,000,000

[6] You might wonder what's in this arrangement for the swap dealer. The dealer will profit by charging a bid-ask spread. Since the dealer pays LIBOR in return for 5 percent in this swap, it might search for another trader who wishes to receive a fixed rate and pay LIBOR. The dealer will pay a 4.9 percent rate to that trader in return for the LIBOR rate. So the dealer pays a fixed rate and receives floating with one trader but pays floating and receives fixed with the other. Its net cash flow is thus fixed and equal to .1 percent of notional principal.

TABLE 24–4 Cash flows from Possum's dollar loan and currency swap (figures in millions)

	Year 0		Years 1–4		Year 5	
	$	**SFr**	**$**	**SFr**	**$**	**SFr**
1. Issue dollar loan	+10		−.5		−10.5	
2. Arrange currency swap						
a. Possum receives $	−10		+.5		+10.5	
b. Possum pays SFr	___	+20	___	−1.2	___	−21.2
3. Net cash flow	0	+20	0	−1.2	0	−21.2

EXAMPLE 24.3 ► Currency Swaps

Suppose that the Possum Company wishes to borrow Swiss francs (SFr) to help finance its European operations. Since Possum is better known in the United States, the financial manager believes that the company can obtain more attractive terms on a dollar loan than on a Swiss franc loan. Therefore, the company borrows $10 million for 5 years at 5 percent in the United States. At the same time Possum arranges with a swap dealer to trade its future dollar liability for Swiss francs. Under this arrangement the dealer agrees to pay Possum sufficient dollars to service its dollar loan, and in exchange Possum agrees to make a series of annual payments in Swiss francs to the dealer.

Possum's cash flows are set out in Table 24–4. Line 1 shows that when Possum takes out its dollar loan, it promises to pay annual interest of $.5 million and to repay the $10 million that it has borrowed. Lines 2a and 2b show the cash flows from the swap, assuming that the spot exchange rate for Swiss francs is $1 = SFr2. Possum hands over to the dealer the $10 million that it borrowed and receives in exchange 2 × $10 million = SFr20 million. In each of the next 4 years the dealer pays Possum $.5 million, which it uses to pay the annual interest on its loan. In year 5 the dealer pays Possum $10.5 million to cover both the final year's interest and the repayment of the loan. In return for these future dollar receipts, Possum agrees to pay the dealer SFr1.2 million in each of the next 4 years and SFr21.2 million in year 5.

The combined effect of Possum's two steps (line 3) is the conversion of its 5 percent dollar loan into a 6 percent Swiss franc loan. The device that makes this possible is the currency swap. ◄

Self-Test 24.5

Suppose that the spot exchange rate had been $1 = SFr3 and that Swiss interest rates were 8 percent. Recalculate the Swiss franc cash flows that the dealer would agree to (line 2b of Table 24–4) and Possum's net cash flows (line 3).

24.6 Innovation in the Derivatives Market

Almost every day some new derivative contract seems to be invented. At first there may be just a few private deals between a bank and its customers, but if the contract proves popular, one of the futures exchanges may try to muscle in on the business.

Derivatives dealers try to identify the major risks that face businesses and then design a contract that will allow them to lay off these risks. For example, a major hazard for many financial institutions is the possibility that a large customer will get into difficulties and default on its debts. Credit derivatives offer a way for the lender to insure against such a default. The provider of the insurance promises to pay out if the borrower defaults on its debts and in return charges a premium for taking on the risk. The market for credit derivatives has grown very rapidly in recent years.

INTERNET INSIDER

Trading in Derivatives

Every 3 years the Bank for International Settlements undertakes a survey of derivatives trading which is available on its Web site **www.bis.org** under *Regular Publications*. Which are the most important types of derivative contract? Which have been growing most rapidly? Why? Who do you think would find them useful?

Farmers, electric utilities, and soft-drink sellers all worry about the weather. So, wouldn't it be nice if they could stop worrying and hedge themselves against bad weather? Well, now they can do so, either by entering into a private deal with a derivative firm or by dealing in weather futures and options on the Chicago Mercantile Exchange.

It seems to be very difficult to predict which new contracts will succeed and which will bomb. By the time you read this, weather contracts may have been forgotten, and everyone will be talking about the new growth market in _____ derivatives. Perhaps you can help fill in the missing word.

24.7 Is "Derivative" a Four-Letter Word?

Our earlier examples of the farmer and the miller showed how derivatives—futures, options, or swaps, for example—can be used to reduce business risk. However, if you were to copy the farmer and sell wheat futures without an offsetting holding of wheat, you would not be *reducing* risk; you would be *speculating*.

A successful futures market needs speculators who are prepared to take on risk and provide the farmer and the miller with the protection they need. For example, if an excess of farmers wished to sell wheat futures, the price of futures would be forced down until enough speculators were tempted to buy in the hope of a profit. If there is a surplus of millers wishing to buy wheat futures, the reverse will happen. The price will be forced up until speculators are drawn in to sell.

Speculation may be necessary to a thriving derivatives market, but it can get companies into serious trouble. For example, for 10 years, a Japanese trading company, Sumitomo Corporation, used the futures market to place huge bets on the price of copper; its chief trader, known in the business simply as "Mr. Copper," was lauded for his contributions to firm profits. However, in June 1996 the copper market was battered by the revelation that the man with the Midas touch had managed to hide losses amounting to about $2 billion.

Sumitomo has plenty of company. In 1995 Baring Brothers, a blue-chip British merchant bank, became insolvent. The reason: Nick Leeson, a trader in its Singapore office, had lost $1.4 billion speculating in futures on the Japanese stock market index. The same year Daiwa Bank reported that a bond trader in its New York office had managed to hide losses over 11 years of $1.1 billion. In 2004 Allied Irish Banks just failed to join the billion-dollar club when it reported a loss of $750 million from trading in foreign exchange derivatives.

The nearby Finance in Practice box discusses another billion-dollar debacle. In this case, Metallgesellschaft claimed to be using futures markets to hedge, but it still managed to lose well over $1 billion. Whether the firm really was hedging, however, is a matter that is subject to debate.

Do these horror stories mean that firms should ban the use of derivatives? Of course not. But they do illustrate that derivatives need to be used with care. Speculation is foolish unless you have reason to believe that the odds are stacked in your favor. If you are not better informed than the highly paid professionals in banks and other institutions, you should use derivatives for hedging, not for speculation.

662

Meltdown at Metallgesellschaft

Metallgesellschaft AG was one of Germany's most respected companies, with more than 20,000 employees and revenues of some $10 billion. Its 251 subsidiaries were engaged in engineering, mining, financial services, and commodities trading, and its major shareholders included such blue-chip German companies as Deutsche Bank, Daimler-Benz, and Allianz.

However, in 1993 Metallgesellschaft was nearly brought to its knees by losses of $1.4 billion from trading in oil futures. The problem arose in one of its U.S. subsidiaries, MGRM. MGRM offered its customers firm price guarantees for up to 10 years on any oil that they agreed to buy. These guarantees proved very popular, so by the end of 1993 the company had entered into long-term contracts to supply 160 million barrels of oil worth more than $3 billion.

There was only one problem. MGRM did not own the oil that it had promised to deliver and would therefore have to buy it from the major oil companies. If the price of oil rose above the price that customers had agreed to pay, MGRM would make a loss on every barrel of oil that it had sold. The apparent solution was for MGRM to hedge its exposure by buying oil futures. This would fix the price at which the company could buy oil when it needed to deliver it. The company would have liked to buy oil futures that matured on the same dates as it was obliged to deliver the oil, but, unfortunately, most futures trading takes place in contracts that mature within a year. MGRM's solution was to buy short-term oil futures and to replace them when they matured.

During the second half of 1993 oil prices fell by 25 percent, and MGRM's contracts to deliver oil at a predetermined price looked increasingly attractive. However, at the same time the company started to pile up large losses on its purchases of oil futures. This was not in itself a cause for concern. If MGRM was truly hedged, the profits on the oil contracts should have exactly offset the losses on the futures.

So what went wrong? One view is that management focused on the accumulating losses on the futures positions and failed to recognize the gains on the oil contracts. When the losses became sufficiently large, management's nerve cracked and it sold out of its futures positions at the wrong time. Moreover, because MGRM's futures positions were marked to market, the company had to find the cash each day to cover the losses on these positions. This problem of financing the hedge may have contributed to management's decision to abandon its strategy.

Other commentators are less convinced that all would have come right if only management had not panicked. They argue that the company's strategy of hedging long-term liabilities with short-term futures was fundamentally flawed. The problem was that MGRM could not predict the price at which it would be able to replace each futures contract when it matured. If the price of the new future was below that of the maturing one, MGRM would make a profit from the trade. But unfortunately for MGRM, the reverse proved to be the case, so the company incurred a loss each time it replaced the maturing futures contract with a new one.

While financial experts continued to debate the cause of MGRM's losses, the company's bankers struggled to put together a rescue package. A massive $1.9 billion loan from 150 international banks was needed to keep the company from foundering.

SUMMARY

Why do companies hedge to reduce risk?

Fluctuations in commodity prices, interest rates, or exchange rates can make planning difficult and can throw companies badly off course. Financial managers therefore look for opportunities to manage these risks, and a number of specialized instruments have been invented to help them. These are collectively known as *derivative instruments*.

How can options, futures, and forward contracts be used to devise simple hedging strategies?

In the last chapter we introduced you to put and call options. **Options** are often used by firms to limit their downside risk. For example, if you own an asset and have the option to sell it at the current price, then you have effectively insured yourself against loss.

Futures contracts are agreements made today to buy or sell an asset in the future. The price is fixed today, but the final payment does not occur until the delivery date. Futures contracts are highly standardized and are traded on organized exchanges. Commodity futures allow firms to fix the future price that they pay for a wide range of agricultural commodities, metals, and oil. Financial futures help firms to protect themselves against unforeseen movements in interest rates, exchange rates, and stock prices.

Forward contracts are equivalent to tailor-made futures contracts. For example, firms often enter into forward agreements with a bank to buy or sell foreign exchange or to fix the interest rate on a loan to be made in the future.

www.mhhe.com/bmm5e

| How can companies use swaps to change the risk of securities that they have issued? | **Swaps** allow firms to exchange one series of future payments for another. For example, the firm might agree to make a series of regular payments in one currency in return for receiving a series of payments in another currency. |

QUIZ

1. **Risk Management.** Large businesses spend millions of dollars annually on insurance. Why? Should they insure against all risks or does insurance make more sense for some risks than others?

2. **Hedging.**
   a. An investor currently holding $1 million in long-term Treasury bonds becomes concerned about increasing volatility in interest rates. She decides to hedge her risk by using Treasury bond futures contracts. Should she buy or sell such contracts?
   b. The treasurer of a corporation that will be issuing bonds in 3 months also is concerned about interest rate volatility and wants to lock in the price at which he could sell 8 percent coupon bonds. How would he use Treasury bond futures contracts to hedge his firm's position?

3. **Commodity Futures.** What commodity futures are traded on futures exchanges? Who do you think could usefully reduce risk by buying each of these contracts? Who do you think might wish to sell each contract?

4. **Hedging.** "The farmer does not avoid risk by selling wheat futures. If wheat prices stay above $3.40 a bushel, then he will actually have lost by selling wheat futures at $3.40." Is this a fair comment?

5. **Marking to Market.** Suppose that in the 5 days following a farmer's sale of September wheat futures at a futures price of $3.83 the futures price is:

Day	1	2	3	4	5
Price	$3.83	$3.89	$3.70	$3.50	$3.60

   At the end of day 5 the farmer decides to quit wheat farming and buys back his futures contract. What payments are made between the farmer and the exchange on each day? What is the total payment over the 5 days? Would the total payment be any different if the contract was not marked to market?

6. **Futures versus Spot Positions.** What do you think are the advantages of holding futures rather than the underlying commodity? What do you think are the disadvantages?

PRACTICE PROBLEMS

7. **Hedging with Futures versus Puts.** A gold-mining firm is concerned about short-term volatility in its revenues. Gold currently sells for $430 an ounce, but the price is volatile and could fall as low as $400 or rise as high as $460 in the next month. The company will bring 1,000 ounces to the market next month.

   a. What will be total revenues if the firm remains unhedged for gold prices of $400, $430, and $460 an ounce?
   b. The futures price of gold for 1-month-ahead delivery is $440. What will be the firm's total revenues at each gold price if the firm enters a 1-month futures contract to deliver 1,000 ounces of gold?
   c. What will total revenues be if the firm buys a 1-month put option to sell gold for $430 an ounce? The puts cost $3 per ounce.

8. **Hedging with Calls.** A large dental lab plans to purchase 1,000 ounces of gold in 1 month. Assume again that gold prices can be $400, $430, or $460 an ounce.

   a. What will total expenses be if the firm purchases call options on 1,000 ounces of gold with an exercise price of $430 an ounce? The options cost $5 per ounce.
   b. What will total expenses be if the firm purchases call options on 1,000 ounces of gold with an exercise price of $420 an ounce? These options cost $10 per ounce.

9. **Forward Contract.** Assume that the 1-year interest rate is 6 percent and the 2-year interest rate is 7 percent. You approach a bank and ask at what rate the bank will promise to make a 1-year loan in 12 months' time. The bank offers to make a forward commitment to lend to you at 12 percent. Would you accept the offer? Can you think of a simple, cheaper alternative?

10. **Hedging Project Risk.** Your firm has just tendered for a contract in Japan. You won't know for 3 months whether you get the contract but if you do, you will receive a payment of ¥10 million 1 year from now. You are worried that if the yen declines in value, the dollar value of this payment will be less than you expect and the project could even show a loss. Discuss the possible ways that you could protect the firm against a decline in the value of the yen. Illustrate the possible outcomes if you do get the contract and if you don't.

11. **Hedging with Futures.** Show how Petrochemical Parfum (see Section 24.2) can also use futures contracts to protect itself against a rise in the price of crude oil. Show how the payoffs would vary if the oil price is $35, $40, or $45 a barrel. Assume the futures price is $40 per barrel. What are the advantages and disadvantages for Petrochemical of using futures rather than options to reduce risk? Repeat the exercise for Onnex.

12. **Futures Contracts.** Look in *The Wall Street Journal* at the prices of gold futures. What is the date of the most distant contract? Suppose that you buy 100 ounces of gold futures for this date. When do you receive the gold? When do you pay for it? Is the futures price higher or lower than the current spot price? Can you suggest why?

13. **Hedging Currency Risk.** When the euro strengthened in 2002–2005, German luxury car manufacturers found it increasingly difficult to compete in the U.S. market. How could they have hedged themselves against this risk? Would a company that was hedged have been in a better position to compete? Explain why or why not.

14. **Swaps.** What is a currency swap? An interest rate swap? Give one example of how each might be used.

Please visit us at www.mhhe.com/bmm5e or refer to your Student CD

CHALLENGE PROBLEM ✛™

Please visit us at www.mhhe.com/bmm5e or refer to your Student CD

15. **Swaps.** Firms A and B face the following borrowing rates for a 5-year fixed-rate debt issue in U.S. dollars or euros:

	U.S. Dollars	Euros
Firm A	8%	6%
Firm B	6%	5%

Suppose that A wishes to borrow U.S. dollars and B wishes to borrow euros. Show how a swap could be used to reduce the borrowing costs of each company. Assume a spot exchange rate of 1 euro to the dollar.

Go to Market Insight at **www.mhhe.com/edumarketinsight**. The packaged foods and meats industry (use *Industry* link) is made up of companies that buy commodities and package and/or transform them into food for retail customers. Review the list of companies (*Industry Constituents*) in the industry, and review the company profile of one firm of interest to you. Link to that company's home page, investor relations, and SEC filings. Review the latest 10K filing or annual report for management's discussion of risk management activities.

1. What areas of risk does the firm manage with derivative contracts?

2. Given the company's products and the commodities they are derived from, what futures and options contracts would make most sense for hedging price risk? Review the list of futures and options contracts traded on exchanges. (See *Currencies, Agricultural,* etc., links at **www.site-by-site.com/usa/optfut.htm**.)

SOLUTIONS TO SELF-TEST QUESTIONS

24.1   See Figure 24–5.

FIGURE 24–5 Petrochemical puts a ceiling on its costs

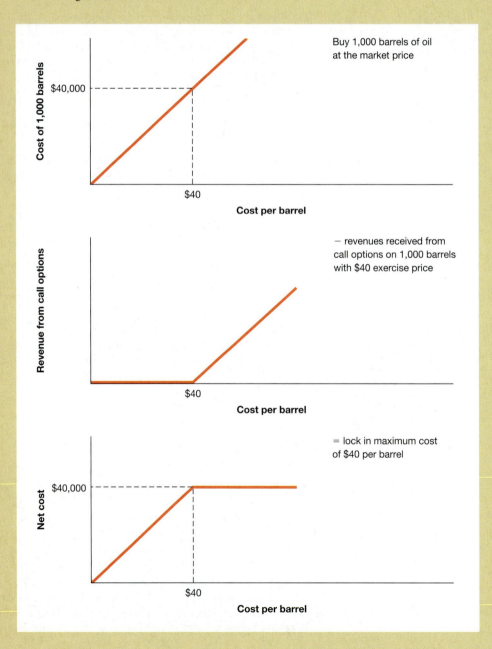

24.2   The farmer has a further loss of 15 cents a bushel ($3.20 – $3.05) and will be required to pay this amount to the exchange. The miller has a further profit of 15 cents per bushel and will receive this from the exchange. The farmer is now committed to delivering wheat in September for $3.20 per bushel, and the miller is committed to paying $3.20 per bushel.

24.3   You sell long-term bond futures with a delivery date of 9 months. Suppose, for example, that you agree to deliver long-term bonds in 9 months at a price of 100. If interest rates rise, the price of the bond futures will fall to (say) 95. (Remember that when interest rates rise, bond prices fall.) In this case the profit that you make on your bond futures offsets the lower price that the firm is likely to receive on the sale of its own bonds. Conversely, if interest rates fall, the company will make a loss on its futures position but will receive a higher price for its own bonds.

24.4   The manager should enter a swap to pay a 5 percent fixed rate and receive LIBOR on notional principal of $100 million. The cash flows will then rise in tandem with the LIBOR rate:

	LIBOR Rate		
	4.5%	**5.0%**	**5.5%**
Interest received on fixed-rate bonds (= .05 × $100 million)	$5,000,000	$5,000,000	$5,000,000
+ Cash flow on swap [= (LIBOR − .05) × notional principal of $100 million]	−500,000	0	+500,000
Total payment	$4,500,000	$5,000,000	$5,500,000

The diagram describing the cash flows of each party to the swap is as follows:

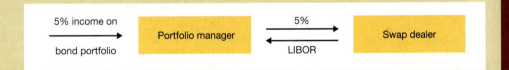

The manager nets a cash flow proportional to the LIBOR rate.

24.5   The following table shows revised cash flows from Possum's dollar loan and currency swap (figures in millions):

	Year 0		Years 1–4		Year 5	
	$	**SFr**	**$**	**SFr**	**$**	**SFr**
1. Issue dollar loan	+10		−.5		−10.5	
2. Arrange currency swap						
a. Possum receives $	−10		+.5		+10.5	
b. Possum pays SFr		+30		−2.4		−32.4
3. Net cash flow	0	+30	0	−2.4	0	−32.4

Notice that in exchange for $10 million today the dealer is now prepared to pay SFr30 million. Since the Swiss interest rate is now 8 percent, the dealer will expect to earn .08 × 30 = SFr2.4 million interest on its Swiss franc outlay.

Conclusion

8

25 What We Do and Do Not Know about Finance

What We Do and Do Not Know about Finance

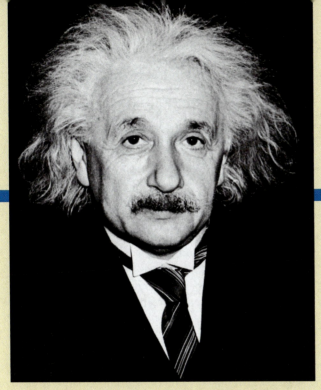

Too bad Einstein didn't tackle the unsolved problems of finance. But he would have grasped the six most important ideas in finance.

© Bettmann/CORBIS

We began this book with the claim that finance is important, interesting, and challenging. We hope that you have come to agree. Now it is time to sum up. We begin this chapter with a very brief recap of the six most important ideas in finance. By now, these should be second nature to you.

Of course, there are still many puzzles that remain to be worked out. We will give you our list of the seven most important unsolved problems in finance.

We have tried to provide you with the essentials of finance, but it would be a dull subject if you could learn all that there is to know in one book. Therefore, we provide a short road map of the important topics that you may encounter in more advanced finance classes.

T. S. Eliot wrote, "To make an end is to make a beginning. The end is where we start from." We hope that the end of this book is also the beginning for you of a growing study of finance.

25.1 What We Do Know: The Six Most Important Ideas in Finance

What would you say if you were asked to name the six most important ideas in finance? Here is our list.

Net Present Value (Chapter 4)

When you wish to know the value of a used car, you look at prices in the second-hand car market. Similarly, when you wish to know the value of a future cash flow, you look at prices quoted in the capital markets, where claims to future cash flows are traded (remember, those highly paid investment bankers are just secondhand cash-flow dealers). If you can buy cash flows for your shareholders at a cheaper price than they would have to pay in the capital market, you have increased the value of their investment.

This is the simple idea behind *net present value* (NPV). When we calculate a project's NPV, we are asking whether the project is worth more than it costs. We are estimating its value by calculating what its cash flows would be worth if a claim on them were offered separately to investors and traded in the capital markets.

This is why we calculate NPV by discounting future cash flows at the opportunity cost of capital—that is, at the expected rate of return offered by securities having the same degree of risk as the project. In well-functioning capital markets, all equivalent-risk assets are priced to offer the same expected return. By discounting at the opportunity cost of capital, we calculate the price at which investors in the project could expect to earn that rate of return.

Like most good ideas, the net present value rule is obvious when you think about it. But notice what an important idea it is. The NPV rule allows thousands of shareholders, who may have vastly different levels of wealth and attitudes toward risk, to participate in the same enterprise and to delegate its operation to a professional manager. They give the manager one simple instruction: "Maximize net present value."

Risk and Return (Chapters 10 and 11)

Some people say that modern finance is all about the capital asset pricing model. That's nonsense. If the capital asset pricing model had never been invented, our advice to financial managers would be essentially the same. The attraction of the model is that it gives us a manageable way of thinking about the required return on a risky investment.

Again, it is an attractively simple idea. There are two kinds of risks—those that you can diversify away and those that you can't. The only risks people care about are the ones that they can't get rid of—the nondiversifiable ones.

You can measure the *nondiversifiable,* or *market,* risk of an investment by the extent to which the value of the investment is affected by a change in the *aggregate* value of all the assets in the economy. This is called the *beta* of the investment. The required return on an asset increases in line with its beta.

Many people are worried by some of the rather strong assumptions behind the capital asset pricing model, or they are concerned about the difficulties of estimating a project's beta. They are right to be worried about these things. One day, we will have much better theories than we do now, but we are prepared to bet that these more sophisticated theories will retain the two crucial ideas behind the capital asset pricing model:

- Investors don't like risk and require a higher return to compensate.
- The risk that matters is the risk that investors cannot get rid of.

Efficient Capital Markets (Chapter 5)

The third fundamental idea is that security prices accurately reflect available information and respond rapidly to new information as soon as it becomes *available*. This *efficient-market theory* comes in three flavors, corresponding to different definitions of "available information." The weak form (or random-walk theory) says that prices reflect all the information in past prices; the semistrong form says that prices reflect all publicly available information; and the strong form holds that prices reflect all acquirable information.

Don't misunderstand the efficient-market idea. It doesn't say that there are no taxes or costs; it doesn't say that there aren't some clever people and some stupid ones. It merely implies that competition in capital markets is very tough—there are no money machines, and security prices reflect the true underlying values of assets on the basis of the best information available to investors.

MM's Irrelevance Propositions (Chapters 15 and 16)

The irrelevance propositions of Modigliani and Miller (MM) imply that you can't increase value through financing policies unless these policies also increase the total cash flow available to investors. Financing decisions that simply repackage the same cash flows don't add value.

Financial managers often ask how much their company should borrow. MM's response is that as long as borrowing does not alter the *total* cash flow generated by the firm's assets, it does not affect firm value.

Miller and Modigliani used a similar argument to show that dividend policy does not affect value unless it affects the total cash flow available to present and future shareholders. A firm that pays you an increased dividend and gets the cash back by selling more shares is simply putting cash in one of your pockets and taking it out of another.

The same ideas can be run in reverse. Just as splitting up the cash flows doesn't add value, neither does combining different cash-flow streams. This implies that you can't increase value by putting two whole companies together unless you thereby increase total cash flow. Thus there are no benefits to mergers solely for diversification.

Option Theory (Chapter 23)

In everyday conversation we often use the word "option" as synonymous with "choice" or "alternative"; thus we speak of someone as *having a number of options*. In finance an *option* refers specifically to the opportunity to trade in the future on terms that are fixed today. Smart managers know that it is often worth paying today for the option to buy or sell an asset tomorrow.

We saw in Chapters 9 and 23 that companies are willing to pay extra for capital projects that give them future flexibility. Also, many securities provide the company or the investor with options. For example, a convertible bond gives the owner an option to exchange the bond for shares.

Managers spend much more time thinking about options than they used to. This is partly because they increasingly use options to help limit risk. Also, managers and economists are more aware that many assets contain disguised real options. For example, the opportunity to abandon a project and recover its salvage value is a put option.

If options are so prevalent, it is important to know how to value them. One of the great finance developments of recent years was the discovery by Black, Scholes, and Merton of a formula to value options. We reviewed briefly the determinants of option value in Chapter 23.

Agency Theory

A modern corporation is a team effort involving many players, including management, employees, shareholders, and bondholders. The members of this corporate team are bound together by a series of formal and informal contracts to ensure that they pull together.

For a long time economists assumed that all players acted for the common good. But in the last 20 years we have learned a lot about the possible conflicts of interest and how companies try to overcome such conflicts. These ideas are collectively known as *agency theory*.

Although we didn't allocate a separate chapter to agency theory, the theory has helped us to think about such questions as these:

- How can an entrepreneur persuade venture capital investors to join in his or her enterprise? (Chapter 14)
- What are the reasons for all the fine print in bond agreements? (Chapter 15)
- Are mergers, acquisitions, and LBOs simply attempts to "rip off" other players, or do they change management's incentives to maximize company value? (Chapter 21)

Are these six ideas exciting theories or plain common sense? Call them what you will, they are basic to the financial manager's job. If after reading this book you really understand these ideas and know how to apply them, you have learned a great deal.

25.2 What We Do Not Know: Seven Unsolved Problems in Finance

Since the unknown is never exhausted, the list of what we do not know about finance could go on forever. Here are seven unsolved problems that seem ripe for productive research.

What Determines Project Risk and Present Value?

A good capital investment is one that has a positive NPV. We have talked at some length about how to calculate NPV, but we have given you very little guidance about how to find positive-NPV projects, except to say in Chapter 9 that projects have positive NPVs when the firm can earn above-normal rates of return. But why do some companies earn superior returns while others in the same industry do not?

Here is a related question: Why are some real assets risky and others relatively safe? In Chapter 11 we suggested a few reasons for differences in project betas—differences in operating leverage, for example, or in the extent to which a project's cash flows respond to the performance of the national economy. These are useful clues, but we have as yet no general procedure for estimating project betas. Assessing project risk is therefore still largely a seat-of-the-pants matter.

Risk and Return—Have We Missed Something?

In 1848 John Stuart Mill wrote, "Happily there is nothing in the laws of value which remains for the present or any future writer to clear up; the theory is complete." Economists today are not so sure about that. For example, the capital asset pricing model is an enormous step toward understanding the effect of risk on the value of an asset, but there are many puzzles left, some statistical and some theoretical.

The statistical problems arise because the capital asset pricing model is hard to prove or disprove conclusively. It appears that average returns from low-beta stocks are too high (that is, higher than the capital asset pricing model predicts), and those from high-beta stocks are too low. But this could be a problem with the way the tests are conducted and not with the model itself.

We also described the puzzling discovery that expected returns appear to be related to firm size and to the ratio of the book value of the stock to its market value. Of course, these findings could be just a coincidence—an accidental result that is unlikely to be repeated. But if they are not a coincidence, the capital asset pricing model cannot be the whole truth. Perhaps firm size and the book-to-market ratio are related to some other variable x that, along with beta, truly determines the expected returns demanded by investors. But we cannot yet identify variable x and prove that it matters.

Meanwhile, work is proceeding on the theoretical front to relax the simple assumptions underlying the capital asset pricing model. Here is one example: Suppose that you love fine wine. It may make sense for you to buy shares in a grand cru chateau, even if that soaks up a large fraction of your personal wealth and leaves you with a relatively undiversified portfolio. However, you are *hedged* against a rise in the price of fine wine: Your hobby will cost you more in a bull market for wine, but your stake in the chateau will make you correspondingly richer. Thus you are holding a relatively undiversified portfolio for a good reason. We would not expect you to demand a premium for bearing that portfolio's undiversifiable risk.

In general, if two people have different tastes, it may make sense for them to hold different portfolios. You may hedge your consumption needs with an investment in winemaking, whereas somebody else may do better to invest in Baskin-Robbins.[1] The capital asset pricing model isn't rich enough to deal with such a world. It assumes that all investors have similar tastes; the "hedging motive" does not enter, and therefore they hold the same portfolio of risky assets. Merton has extended the capital asset pricing model to accommodate the hedging motive.[2] If enough investors are attempting to hedge against the same thing, this model implies a more complicated risk-return relationship. However, it is not yet clear who is hedging against what, so the model remains difficult to test.

Are There Important Exceptions to the Efficient-Market Theory?

The efficient-market theory is very persuasive, but no theory is perfect—there must be exceptions.

Some of the apparent exceptions could simply be coincidences, for the more that researchers study stock performance, the more strange coincidences they are likely to find. For example, there is evidence that daily returns around new moons have been roughly double those around full moons.[3] It seems difficult to believe that this is anything other than a chance relationship—fun to read about but not a concern for serious investors or financial managers. But not all exceptions can be dismissed so easily. We saw that the stocks of firms that announce unexpectedly good earnings continue to perform well for a couple of months after the announcement date. Some scholars believe that this may mean that the stock market is inefficient and investors have consistently been slow to react to earnings announcements. Of course, we can't expect investors never to make mistakes. If they have been slow to react in the past, it will be interesting to see whether they learn from their mistake and price the stocks more efficiently in the future.

Some researchers believe that the efficient-market theory ignores important aspects of human behavior. For example, psychologists find that people place too much emphasis on recent events when they are predicting the future. We don't yet know how far such behavioral observations can help us to understand apparent anomalies.

During the dot-com boom of the late 1990s stock prices rose to astronomical levels. The NASDAQ Composite Index rose 580 percent from the beginning of 1995 to its peak in March 2000 and then fell by nearly 80 percent. Maybe such extreme price movements can be explained by standard valuation techniques. However, others argue that stock prices are liable to speculative bubbles, where investors are caught up in a

[1] In practice, such hedging is more easily said than done. Baskin-Robbins is part of Pernod Ricard, which of course also produces fine wines.

[2] See R. Merton, "An Intertemporal Capital Asset Pricing Model," *Econometrica* 41 (1973), pp. 867–887.

[3] K. Yuan, L. Zheng, and Q. Zhu, "Are Investors Moonstruck? Lunar Phases and Stock Returns," working paper, University of Michigan, September 2001.

whirl of irrational exuberance. Now it may well be true that some of us are liable to become overexcited, but why don't professional investors bail out of the overpriced stocks? Perhaps they would do so if it were their own money at stake, but maybe there is something in the way that their performance is measured and rewarded that encourages them to run with the herd.

These are important questions. Much more research is needed before we have a full understanding of why asset prices sometimes seem to get so out of line with what appears to be their discounted future payoffs.

How Can We Explain Capital Structure?

Modigliani and Miller's article about capital structure emphasized that the value of a firm depends on real variables—the goods it produces, the prices it charges, and the costs that it incurs. Financing decisions merely affect the way that the cash flows are packaged for distribution to investors. What goes into the package is more important than the package itself.

Does it really not matter how much your firm borrows? We have come across several reasons why it *may* matter. Tax is one possibility. Debt provides a corporate tax shield, and this tax shield may more than compensate for any extra personal tax that the investor has to pay on debt interest. Perhaps managers are concerned with potential bankruptcy costs. Perhaps differences in capital structure reflect differences in the relative importance of growth opportunities. So far, none of these possibilities has been either proved relevant or definitely excluded.

The upshot of the matter is that we still don't have an accepted, coherent theory of capital structure. It is not for want of argument on the subject.

How Can We Resolve the Dividend Controversy?

We spent all of Chapter 16 on dividend policy without being able to resolve the dividend controversy. Many people believe dividends are good; others believe they are bad and repurchases are good; and still others believe that, as long as the firm's investment decisions are unaffected, the payout decision is largely irrelevant. If pressed, we largely take the middle view, but we can't be dogmatic about it.

We don't mean to disparage existing research; rather, we say that more is needed. Whether future research will change anybody's mind is another matter. The problem is to disentangle several possible reasons that payout policy *may* matter. The recent change in the U.S. tax law that lowered the tax rate on dividends to that on capital gains may provide useful evidence that allows this to be done.

The problem is to disentangle several possible reasons that dividend policy *may* matter. For example, a firm that pays dividends rather than repurchase stock is likely to land its shareholders with heavier tax bills. On the other hand, a commitment to pay regular dividends may also provide a signal of the company's prosperity; in effect, the company that pays dividends is putting its money where its mouth is.

Twenty years ago companies that wished to distribute cash to their shareholders almost always did so by declaring a dividend. But since that time the volume of stock repurchases has mushroomed, while an increasing number of companies have chosen not to pay any dividends. This means that we now have two questions to answer: How do companies decide on the amount to pay out to shareholders? and Why do they sometimes distribute cash by buying back stock rather than paying dividends?

How Can We Explain Merger Waves?

There are many plausible reasons why two firms might wish to merge. If you single out a *particular* merger, it is usually possible to think up a reason why that merger could make sense. But that leaves us with a special hypothesis for each merger. What we need is a *general* hypothesis to explain merger waves. For example, everybody seemed to be merging in 2000 and nobody 2 years later. Why?

We can think of other instances of financial fashions. For example, from time to time there are hot new-issue periods when there seems to be an endless supply of speculative new issues and an insatiable demand for them. In recent years economists have been developing new theories of speculative bubbles. Perhaps such theories will help to explain these mystifying financial fashions.

What Is the Value of Liquidity?

Unlike Treasury bills, cash pays no interest. On the other hand, cash provides more liquidity than Treasury bills. The value of this liquidity declines as you hold increasing amounts of cash. When you have only a small proportion of your assets in cash, a little extra can be extremely useful; when you have a substantial holding, any additional liquidity is not worth much. Unfortunately, we don't really understand how to value the liquidity service of cash, and therefore we can't say how much cash is enough or how readily the firm should be able to raise it. In our chapters on working capital management we largely finessed these questions by speaking vaguely of the need to ensure an "adequate" liquidity reserve.

A better knowledge of liquidity would also help us to understand how corporate bonds are priced. We already know part of the reason that corporate bonds sell for lower prices than Treasury bonds—corporate bonds are risky. However, the differences between the prices of corporate bonds and Treasury bonds are too large to be explained just by the possibility that the company will default. It seems likely that the price difference is partly due to the fact that corporate bonds are less liquid than Treasury bonds. But until we know how to price differences in liquidity, we can't really say much more than this.

Investors seem to value liquidity much more highly at some times than at others. When liquidity suddenly dries up, asset prices can become very volatile. This happened in 1998 when Long-Term Capital Management (LTCM), a large hedge fund, collapsed.[4] Since its formation 4 years earlier LTCM had generated high returns by buying large positions in "cheap" illiquid assets and selling "expensive" liquid assets. LTCM, therefore, served as a supplier of liquidity to other investors. When Russia defaulted on its debt in 1998, there was a rush by investors to get out of illiquid assets. As the value of LTCM's holdings declined, its banks demanded additional protection for their loans and LTCM was forced to unwind its positions in a market that was already short of liquidity. Eventually, the New York Fed encouraged a group of institutions to rescue LTCM, but not before there had been very sharp swings in asset prices.

That concludes our list of unsolved problems. We have given you the seven uppermost in our minds. If there are others that you find more interesting and challenging, by all means construct your own list and start thinking about it.

25.3 A Final Word

We titled this chapter "What We Do and Do Not Know about Finance." We should perhaps have added a third section, "What We Know about Finance but Haven't Told You." After all, this book is an introduction to finance and there are plenty of topics that we have only skimmed over. Here are some examples:

- Investment decisions always have side effects on financing—every dollar has to be raised somehow. Sometimes these side effects may be important. For instance, if the project allows the company to issue more debt, it may bring with it valuable tax shields. How can companies allow for these financing side effects when evaluating new investment projects? We touched on this issue in Chapter 12 when we showed you how to calculate the weighted-average cost of capital, but there is a huge body of knowledge about how best to allow for financing side effects in project valuation.

---

[4] **Hedge funds** attempt to buy underpriced securities and to sell short overpriced ones. They are typically organized as partnerships and owned by a small number of institutions or wealthy individuals.

- We stressed in Chapter 13 the wide variety of claims that companies can sell to raise money. We described the principal ones, but there are others that we largely ignored. Leasing is an example. Companies lease assets rather than buy them because it is convenient and because in some circumstances there can be tax advantages. A lot is now known about how to value leases.
- Treasurers of large corporations worry about fluctuations in exchange rates, interest rates, and commodity prices. Various tools—including options, futures, forwards, and swaps—have been invented to help managers hedge against these risks. Many of the best brains in finance have been applied to devising and valuing these new instruments. We only touched on the problem of option valuation and said nothing at all about valuing futures. It's an exciting area and there is no shortage of books and articles to help you learn more.

QUIZ

If you have reached this far, you deserve a break. So we haven't provided any heavyweight problems at the end of this chapter. Instead we have included a quiz of the "Trivial Pursuit" variety. You don't need to know the answers to be a financial wizard, and for the most part they are not to be found in earlier chapters. However, they may help you to impress your friends at smart dinner parties.[5]

1. What do these countries' currencies have in common?
   - Australia
   - Canada
   - Hong Kong
   - New Zealand
   - Singapore
   - Taiwan
   - United States

   [Score 10]

2. What do the following countries' currencies have in common?
   - Belgium
   - Finland
   - Ireland
   - Greece
   - Portugal

   [Score 10]

3. Government bonds are known by a variety of names. In which countries are the following government bonds issued?
   - Bunds
   - JGBs
   - Gilts
   - OATs
   - Tesobonos

   [Score 2 for each correct answer]

4. Each of these indexes measures stock market performance in a different country. What are the countries?
   - CAC Index
   - DAX Index

---

[5] The answers are given on pages 681–682.

- FTSE Index
- Hang Seng Index
- Nikkei Index

[Score 2 for each correct answer]

5. Where is each of these futures markets located?
- CME
- Eurex
- LME
- NYMEX
- SIMEX

[Score 2 for each correct answer]

6. Name the company:

   a. Headquartered in Houston, it filed for Chapter 11 bankruptcy in 2001 amid accusations that it had falsified its accounts.
   b. In 2001 this large conglomerate announced, and later canceled, plans to break itself up. Its chief executive was subsequently charged with tax evasion.
   c. In 2003 this Italian food company collapsed. It appeared that €3.8 billion, said to be held by the company in its Cayman Islands bank account, did not exist.
   d. In 2002 this telecoms company admitted to inflating its profits by booking more than $3.6 billion of expenses as capital expenditures.

[Score 2.5 for each correct answer]

7. Match the acquiring firms with the acquired.

Acquiring Firms	Acquired Firms
Unicredit	Mannesmann
Procter & Gamble	Bank One
Vodafone	Gillette
JPMorgan Chase	Warner Lambert
Pfizer	HVB

[Score 2 for each correct answer]

8. To which country does each of the following banks belong?
- ING
- Banesto
- Barclays Bank
- Commerzbank
- Mizuho Bank

[Score 2 for each correct answer]

9. In which state are the major U.S. corporations commonly incorporated?
- Alabama
- California
- Delaware
- Illinois
- Maryland

[Score 10]

10. Spot the "odd one out."
- Butterfly
- Odd lot
- Straddle
- Vertical spread

[Score 10]

11. What do the following abbreviations stand for?
    - CD
    - LBO
    - MTN
    - OTC
    - SEC

    [Score 2 for each correct answer]

12. Spot the "odd one out."
    - Delta Airlines
    - United Airlines
    - Southwest Airlines
    - Eastern Airlines
    - Pan Am

    [Score 10]

13. Match up the following events and dates:
    - 1963   The first financial futures contract was traded in Chicago.
    - 1972   The first swap was arranged (between the World Bank and IBM).
    - 1973   The first eurobond was issued (by the Italian company Autostrade).
    - 1981   The first traded options market was formed in the United States.
    - 1997   The U.S. Treasury first issued indexed bonds.

    [Score 2 for each correct answer]

14. Match each of the following Asian countries with its currency:
    - China   Baht
    - South Korea   Dong
    - Mongolia   Tugrik
    - Thailand   Won
    - Vietnam   Yuan

    [Score 2 for each correct answer]

15. In which year did the United States stock market decline by 43 percent?
    - 1931
    - 1939
    - 1987

    [Score 10]

16. Brokers on the New York Stock Exchange often refer to stocks by their nicknames. To which stocks do the following nicknames refer?
    - Big Blue
    - Ketchup
    - Mickey Mouse
    - Timber

    [Score 2.5 for each correct answer]

17. Each of the following organizations made large losses from trading. Match each firm with a major cause of the loss.
    - Barings   Copper futures
    - Metallgesellschaft   Nikkei index futures
    - Allied Irish Bank   Oil futures
    - Procter & Gamble   Currencies
    - Sumitomo Corporation   Swaps

    [Score 2 for each correct answer]

18. What do the following professors of finance have in common?
    - Harry Markowitz   • Robert Merton
    - Merton Miller   • Myron Scholes
    - William Sharpe

    [Score 10]

19. Match each of the following individuals with one of the quotations.

- Bernie Cornfeld   a. "Do you sincerely want to be rich?"
- Gordon Gecko   b. "Where are the customers' yachts?"
- John Maynard Keynes   c. "Believing that fundamental conditions of the country are sound . . . my son and I have for some days been purchasing sound common stocks."
- John D. Rockefeller   d. The stock market "is, so to speak, a game of Snap, of Old Maid, of Musical Chairs—a pastime in which he is a victor who says Snap neither too soon nor too late, who passes the Old Maid to his neighbor before the game is over, who secures a chair for himself when the music stops."
- Fred Schwed   e. "Greed is good."

[Score 2 for each correct answer]

20. International bond issues are often known by nicknames. For example, an international bond issued in Southeast Asia is known as a "dragon bond." What is the common term for a bond issued by a foreign company in the bond market of each of the following countries?

- Japan
- Netherlands
- Spain
- United Kingdom
- United States

[Score 2 for each correct answer]

ANSWERS TO QUIZ

1. Each of their currencies is called the dollar.

2. They are all members of the European Monetary Union (EMU) and therefore all use the euro.

3. Bunds = Germany
   JGBs (Japanese Government Bonds) = Japan
   Gilts = United Kingdom
   OATs (Obligations Assimilables du Trésor) = France
   Tesobonos = Mexico

4. CAC Index = France
   DAX Index = Germany
   FTSE Index = United Kingdom
   Hang Seng Index = Hong Kong
   Nikkei Index = Japan

5. CME (Chicago Mercantile Exchange) = Chicago
   Eurex = Frankfurt
   LME (London Metal Exchange) = London
   NYMEX (New York Mercantile Exchange) = New York
   SIMEX (Singapore International Monetary Exchange) = Singapore

6. a. Enron
   b. Tyco International
   c. Parmalat
   d. WorldCom

7. Unicredit   HVB
   Procter & Gamble   Gillette
   Vodafone   Mannesmann
   JPMorgan Chase   Bank One
   Pfizer   Warner Lambert

8. ING = Netherlands
    Banesto = Spain
    Barclays Bank = United Kingdom
    Commerzbank = Germany
    Mizuho Bank = Japan

9. Delaware

10. "Odd lot" refers to an order to buy or sell fewer than 100 shares. The other terms all refer to combinations of options.

11. CD = certificate of deposit
    LBO = leveraged buyout
    MTN = medium-term note
    OTC = over-the-counter
    SEC = Securities and Exchange Commission

12. Southwest is the only one of these airlines that has not been through Chapter 11 bankruptcy proceedings.

13. 1963   The first eurobond was issued (by the Italian company Autostrade).
    1972   The first financial futures contract was traded in Chicago.
    1973   The first traded options market was formed in the United States.
    1981   The first swap was arranged (between the World Bank and IBM).
    1997   The U.S. Treasury first issued indexed bonds.

14. China = Yuan
    South Korea = Won
    Mongolia = Tugrik
    Thailand = Baht
    Vietnam = Dong

15. 1931

16. Big Blue = IBM
    Ketchup = Heinz
    Mickey Mouse = Disney
    Timber = Weyerhaeuser

17. Barings   Nikkei index futures
    Metallgesellschaft   Oil futures
    Allied Irish Bank   Currencies
    Procter & Gamble   Swaps
    Sumitomo Corporation   Copper futures

18. Each received the Nobel Prize for his contribution to financial economics.

19. Bernie Cornfeld   (head of Investors' Overseas Services in address to the fund sales force) = a
    Gordon Gecko   (in the movie *Wall Street*) = e
    John Maynard Keynes   (writing in *The General Theory of Employment, Interest and Money,* 1936) = d
    John D. Rockefeller   (at the start of the 1929 Great Crash) = c
    Fred Schwed   (in a 1940 book of that title) = b

20. Japan = Samurai bond
    Netherlands = Rembrandt bond
    Spain = Matador bond
    United Kingdom = Bulldog bond
    United States = Yankee bond

If you scored:

0–50	You weren't trying.
51–80	Not bad.
81–120	You are probably going to be an investment banker.
121–160	You are probably an investment banker *already*.
161–200	You probably cheated.

APPENDIX TABLE A–1 Future value of $1 after t years = $(1 + r)^t$

Number of Years	1%	2%	3%	4%	5%	6%	7%	8%	9%	10%	11%	12%	13%	14%	15%
								Interest Rate per Year							
1	1.0100	1.0200	1.0300	1.0400	1.0500	1.0600	1.0700	1.0800	1.0900	1.1000	1.1100	1.1200	1.1300	1.1400	1.1500
2	1.0201	1.0404	1.0609	1.0816	1.1025	1.1236	1.1449	1.1664	1.1881	1.2100	1.2321	1.2544	1.2769	1.2996	1.3225
3	1.0303	1.0612	1.0927	1.1249	1.1576	1.1910	1.2250	1.2597	1.2950	1.3310	1.3676	1.4049	1.4429	1.4815	1.5209
4	1.0406	1.0824	1.1255	1.1699	1.2155	1.2625	1.3108	1.3605	1.4116	1.4641	1.5181	1.5735	1.6305	1.6890	1.7490
5	1.0510	1.1041	1.1593	1.2167	1.2763	1.3382	1.4026	1.4693	1.5386	1.6105	1.6851	1.7623	1.8424	1.9254	2.0114
6	1.0615	1.1262	1.1941	1.2653	1.3401	1.4185	1.5007	1.5869	1.6771	1.7716	1.8704	1.9738	2.0820	2.1950	2.3131
7	1.0721	1.1487	1.2299	1.3159	1.4071	1.5036	1.6058	1.7138	1.8280	1.9487	2.0762	2.2107	2.3526	2.5023	2.6600
8	1.0829	1.1717	1.2668	1.3686	1.4775	1.5938	1.7182	1.8509	1.9926	2.1436	2.3045	2.4760	2.6584	2.8526	3.0590
9	1.0937	1.1951	1.3048	1.4233	1.5513	1.6895	1.8385	1.9990	2.1719	2.3579	2.5580	2.7731	3.0040	3.2519	3.5179
10	1.1046	1.2190	1.3439	1.4802	1.6289	1.7908	1.9672	2.1589	2.3674	2.5937	2.8394	3.1058	3.3946	3.7072	4.0456
11	1.1157	1.2434	1.3842	1.5395	1.7103	1.8983	2.1049	2.3316	2.5804	2.8531	3.1518	3.4785	3.8359	4.2262	4.6524
12	1.1268	1.2682	1.4258	1.6010	1.7959	2.0122	2.2522	2.5182	2.8127	3.1384	3.4985	3.8960	4.3345	4.8179	5.3503
13	1.1381	1.2936	1.4685	1.6651	1.8856	2.1329	2.4098	2.7196	3.0658	3.4523	3.8833	4.3635	4.8980	5.4924	6.1528
14	1.1495	1.3195	1.5126	1.7317	1.9799	2.2609	2.5785	2.9372	3.3417	3.7975	4.3104	4.8871	5.5348	6.2613	7.0757
15	1.1610	1.3459	1.5580	1.8009	2.0789	2.3966	2.7590	3.1722	3.6425	4.1772	4.7846	5.4736	6.2543	7.1379	8.1371
16	1.1726	1.3728	1.6047	1.8730	2.1829	2.5404	2.9522	3.4259	3.9703	4.5950	5.3109	6.1304	7.0673	8.1372	9.3576
17	1.1843	1.4002	1.6528	1.9479	2.2920	2.6928	3.1588	3.7000	4.3276	5.0545	5.8951	6.8660	7.9861	9.2765	10.7613
18	1.1961	1.4282	1.7024	2.0258	2.4066	2.8543	3.3799	3.9960	4.7171	5.5599	6.5436	7.6900	9.0243	10.5752	12.3755
19	1.2081	1.4568	1.7535	2.1068	2.5270	3.0256	3.6165	4.3157	5.1417	6.1159	7.2633	8.6128	10.1974	12.0557	14.2318
20	1.2202	1.4859	1.8061	2.1911	2.6533	3.2071	3.8697	4.6610	5.6044	6.7275	8.0623	9.6463	11.5231	13.7435	16.3665
25	1.2824	1.6406	2.0938	2.6658	3.3864	4.2919	5.4274	6.8485	8.6231	10.8347	13.5855	17.0001	21.2305	26.4619	32.9190
30	1.3478	1.8114	2.4273	3.2434	4.3219	5.7435	7.6123	10.0627	13.2677	17.4494	22.8923	29.9599	39.1159	50.9502	66.2118
40	1.4889	2.2080	3.2620	4.8010	7.0400	10.2857	14.9745	21.7245	31.4094	45.2593	65.0009	93.0510	132.7816	188.8835	267.8635
50	1.6446	2.6916	4.3839	7.1067	11.4674	18.4202	29.4570	46.9016	74.3575	117.3909	184.5648	289.0022	450.7359	700.2330	1083.657

APPENDIX TABLE A–1 Future value of $1 after t years $= (1 + r)^t$ **(concluded)**

Number of Years	Interest Rate per Year														
	16%	17%	18%	19%	20%	21%	22%	23%	24%	25%	26%	27%	28%	29%	30%
1	1.1600	1.1700	1.1800	1.1900	1.2000	1.2100	1.2200	1.2300	1.2400	1.2500	1.2600	1.2700	1.2800	1.2900	1.3000
2	1.3456	1.3689	1.3924	1.4161	1.4400	1.4641	1.4884	1.5129	1.5376	1.5625	1.5876	1.6129	1.6384	1.6641	1.6900
3	1.5609	1.6016	1.6430	1.6852	1.7280	1.7716	1.8158	1.8609	1.9066	1.9531	2.0004	2.0484	2.0972	2.1467	2.1970
4	1.8106	.8739	1.9388	2.0053	2.0736	2.1436	2.2153	2.2889	2.3642	2.4414	2.5205	2.6014	2.6844	2.7692	2.8561
5	2.1003	2.1924	2.2878	2.3864	2.4883	2.5937	2.7027	2.8153	2.9316	3.0518	3.1758	3.3038	3.4360	3.5723	3.7129
6	2.4364	2.5652	2.6996	2.8398	2.9860	3.1384	3.2973	3.4628	3.6352	3.8147	4.0015	4.1959	4.3980	4.6083	4.8268
7	2.8262	3.0012	3.1855	3.3793	3.5832	3.7975	4.0227	4.2593	4.5077	4.7684	5.0419	5.3288	5.6295	5.9447	6.2749
8	3.2784	3.5115	3.7589	4.0214	4.2998	4.5950	4.9077	5.2389	5.5895	5.9605	6.3528	6.7675	7.2058	7.6686	8.1573
9	3.8030	4.1084	4.4355	4.7854	5.1598	5.5599	5.9874	6.4439	6.9310	7.4506	8.0045	8.5948	9.2234	9.8925	10.6045
10	4.4114	4.8068	5.2338	5.6947	6.1917	6.7275	7.3046	7.9259	8.5944	9.3132	10.0857	10.9153	11.8059	12.7614	13.7858
11	5.1173	5.6240	6.1759	6.7767	7.4301	8.1403	8.9117	9.7489	10.6571	11.6415	12.7080	13.8625	15.1116	16.4622	17.9216
12	5.9360	6.5801	7.2876	8.0642	8.9161	9.8497	10.8722	11.9912	13.2148	14.5519	16.0120	17.6053	19.3428	21.2362	23.2981
13	6.8858	7.6987	8.5994	9.5964	10.6993	11.9182	13.2641	14.7491	16.3863	18.1899	20.1752	22.3588	24.7588	27.3947	30.2875
14	7.9875	9.0075	10.1472	11.4198	12.8392	14.4210	16.1822	18.1414	20.3191	22.7374	25.4207	28.3957	31.6913	35.3391	39.3738
15	9.2655	10.5387	11.9737	13.5895	15.4070	17.4494	19.7423	22.3140	25.1956	28.4217	32.0301	36.0625	40.5648	45.5875	51.1859
16	10.7480	12.5303	14.1290	16.1715	18.4884	21.1138	24.0856	27.4462	31.2426	35.5271	40.3579	45.7994	51.9230	58.8079	66.5417
17	12.4677	14.4265	16.6722	19.2441	22.1861	25.5477	29.3844	33.7588	38.7408	44.4089	50.8510	58.1652	66.4614	75.8621	86.5042
18	14.4625	16.8790	19.6733	22.9005	26.6233	30.9127	35.8490	41.5233	48.0386	55.5112	64.0722	73.8698	85.0706	97.8622	112.4554
19	16.7765	19.7484	23.2144	27.2516	31.9480	37.4043	43.7358	51.0737	59.5679	69.3889	80.7310	93.8147	108.8904	126.2422	146.1920
20	19.4608	23.1056	27.3930	32.4294	38.3376	45.2593	53.3576	62.8206	73.8641	86.7362	101.7211	119.1446	139.3797	162.8524	190.0496
25	40.8742	50.6578	62.6686	77.3881	95.3962	117.3909	144.2101	176.8593	216.5420	264.6978	323.0454	393.6344	478.9049	581.7585	705.6410
30	85.8499	111.0647	143.3706	184.6753	237.3763	304.4816	389.7579	497.9129	634.8199	807.7936	1,025.927	1,300.504	1,645.505	2,078.219	2,619.996
40	378.7212	533.8687	750.3783	1,051.668	1,469.772	2,048.400	2,847.038	3,946.430	5,455.913	7,523.164	10,347.18	14,195.44	19,426.69	26,520.91	36,118.86
50	1,670.704	2,566.215	3,927.357	5,988.914	9,100.438	13,780.61	20,796.56	31,279.20	46,890.43	70,064.92	104,358.4	154,948.0	229,349.9	338,443.0	497,929.2

APPENDIX TABLE A-2 Discount factors: Present value of $1 to be received after t years $= 1/(1 + r)^t$

Number of Years	Interest Rate per Year														
	1%	2%	3%	4%	5%	6%	7%	8%	9%	10%	11%	12%	13%	14%	15%
1	0.9901	0.9804	0.9709	0.9615	0.9524	0.9434	0.9346	0.9259	0.9174	0.9091	0.9009	0.8929	0.8850	0.8772	0.8696
2	0.9803	0.9612	0.9426	0.9246	0.9070	0.8900	0.8734	0.8573	0.8417	0.8264	0.8116	0.7972	0.7831	0.7695	0.7561
3	0.9706	0.9423	0.9151	0.8890	0.8638	0.8396	0.8163	0.7938	0.7722	0.7513	0.7312	0.7118	0.6931	0.6750	0.6575
4	0.9610	0.9238	0.8885	0.8548	0.8227	0.7921	0.7629	0.7350	0.7084	0.6830	0.6587	0.6355	0.6133	0.5921	0.5718
5	0.9515	0.9057	0.8626	0.8219	0.7835	0.7473	0.7130	0.6806	0.6499	0.6209	0.5935	0.5674	0.5428	0.5194	0.4972
6	0.9420	0.8880	0.8375	0.7903	0.7462	0.7050	0.6663	0.6302	0.5963	0.5645	0.5346	0.5066	0.4803	0.4556	0.4323
7	0.9327	0.8706	0.8131	0.7599	0.7107	0.6651	0.6227	0.5835	0.5470	0.5132	0.4817	0.4523	0.4251	0.3996	0.3759
8	0.9235	0.8535	0.7894	0.7307	0.6768	0.6274	0.5820	0.5403	0.5019	0.4665	0.4339	0.4039	0.3762	0.3506	0.3269
9	0.9143	0.8368	0.7664	0.7026	0.6446	0.5919	0.5439	0.5002	0.4604	0.4241	0.3909	0.3606	0.3329	0.3075	0.2843
10	0.9053	0.8203	0.7441	0.6756	0.6139	0.5584	0.5083	0.4632	0.4224	0.3855	0.3522	0.3220	0.2946	0.2697	0.2472
11	0.8963	0.8043	0.7224	0.6496	0.5847	0.5268	0.4751	0.4289	0.3875	0.3505	0.3173	0.2875	0.2607	0.2366	0.2149
12	0.8874	0.7885	0.7014	0.6246	0.5568	0.4970	0.4440	0.3971	0.3555	0.3186	0.2858	0.2567	0.2307	0.2076	0.1869
13	0.8787	0.7730	0.6810	0.6006	0.5303	0.4688	0.4150	0.3677	0.3262	0.2897	0.2575	0.2292	0.2042	0.1821	0.1625
14	0.8700	0.7579	0.6611	0.5775	0.5051	0.4423	0.3878	0.3405	0.2992	0.2633	0.2320	0.2046	0.1807	0.1597	0.1413
15	0.8613	0.7430	0.6419	0.5553	0.4810	0.4173	0.3624	0.3152	0.2745	0.2394	0.2090	0.1827	0.1599	0.1401	0.1229
16	0.8528	0.7284	0.6232	0.5339	0.4581	0.3936	0.3387	0.2919	0.2519	0.2176	0.1883	0.1631	0.1415	0.1229	0.1069
17	0.8444	0.7142	0.6050	0.5134	0.4363	0.3714	0.3166	0.2703	0.2311	0.1978	0.1696	0.1456	0.1252	0.1078	0.0929
18	0.8360	0.7002	0.5874	0.4936	0.4155	0.3503	0.2959	0.2502	0.2120	0.1799	0.1528	0.1300	0.1108	0.0946	0.0808
19	0.8277	0.6864	0.5703	0.4746	0.3957	0.3305	0.2765	0.2317	0.1945	0.1635	0.1377	0.1161	0.0981	0.0829	0.0703
20	0.8195	0.6730	0.5537	0.4564	0.3769	0.3118	0.2584	0.2145	0.1784	0.1486	0.1240	0.1037	0.0868	0.0728	0.0611
25	0.7798	0.6095	0.4776	0.3751	0.2953	0.2330	0.1842	0.1460	0.1160	0.0923	0.0736	0.0588	0.0471	0.0378	0.0304
30	0.7419	0.5521	0.4120	0.3083	0.2314	0.1741	0.1314	0.0994	0.0754	0.0573	0.0437	0.0334	0.0256	0.0196	0.0151
40	0.6717	0.4529	0.3066	0.2083	0.1420	0.0972	0.0668	0.0460	0.0318	0.0221	0.0154	0.0107	0.0075	0.0053	0.0037
50	0.6080	0.3715	0.2281	0.1407	0.0872	0.0543	0.0339	0.0213	0.0134	0.0085	0.0054	0.0035	0.0022	0.0014	0.0009

APPENDIX TABLE A-2 Discount factors: Present value of $1 to be received after t years = $1/(1 + r)^t$ **(concluded)**

Number of Years	16%	17%	18%	19%	20%	21%	22%	23%	24%	25%	26%	27%	28%	29%	30%
											Interest Rate per Year				
1	0.8621	0.8547	0.8475	0.8403	0.8333	0.8264	0.8197	0.8130	0.8065	0.8000	0.7937	0.7874	0.7813	0.7752	0.7692
2	0.7432	0.7305	0.7182	0.7062	0.6944	0.6830	0.6719	0.6610	0.6504	0.6400	0.6299	0.6200	0.6104	0.6009	0.5917
3	0.6407	0.6244	0.6086	0.5934	0.5787	0.5645	0.5507	0.5374	0.5245	0.5120	0.4999	0.4882	0.4768	0.4658	0.4552
4	0.5523	0.5337	0.5158	0.4987	0.4823	0.4665	0.4514	0.4369	0.4230	0.4096	0.3968	0.3844	0.3725	0.3611	0.3501
5	0.4761	0.4561	0.4371	0.4190	0.4019	0.3855	0.3700	0.3552	0.3411	0.3277	0.3149	0.3027	0.2910	0.2799	0.2693
6	0.4104	0.3898	0.3704	0.3521	0.3349	0.3186	0.3033	0.2888	0.2751	0.2621	0.2499	0.2383	0.2274	0.2170	0.2072
7	0.3538	0.3332	0.3139	0.2959	0.2791	0.2633	0.2486	0.2348	0.2218	0.2097	0.1983	0.1877	0.1776	0.1682	0.1594
8	0.3050	0.2848	0.2660	0.2487	0.2326	0.2176	0.2038	0.1909	0.1789	0.1678	0.1574	0.1478	0.1388	0.1304	0.1226
9	0.2630	0.2434	0.2255	0.2090	0.1938	0.1799	0.1670	0.1552	0.1443	0.1342	0.1249	0.1164	0.1084	0.1011	0.0943
10	0.2267	0.2080	0.1911	0.1756	0.1615	0.1486	0.1369	0.1262	0.1164	0.1074	0.0992	0.0916	0.0847	0.0784	0.0725
11	0.1954	0.1778	0.1619	0.1476	0.1346	0.1228	0.1122	0.1026	0.0938	0.0859	0.0787	0.0721	0.0662	0.0607	0.0558
12	0.1685	0.1520	0.1372	0.1240	0.1122	0.1015	0.0920	0.0834	0.0757	0.0687	0.0625	0.0568	0.0517	0.0471	0.0429
13	0.1452	0.1299	0.1163	0.1042	0.0935	0.0839	0.0754	0.0678	0.0610	0.0550	0.0496	0.0447	0.0404	0.0365	0.0330
14	0.1252	0.1110	0.0985	0.0876	0.0779	0.0693	0.0618	0.0551	0.0492	0.0440	0.0393	0.0352	0.0316	0.0283	0.0254
15	0.1079	0.0949	0.0835	0.0736	0.0649	0.0573	0.0507	0.0448	0.0397	0.0352	0.0312	0.0277	0.0247	0.0219	0.0195
16	0.0930	0.0811	0.0708	0.0618	0.0541	0.0474	0.0415	0.0364	0.0320	0.0281	0.0248	0.0218	0.0193	0.0170	0.0150
17	0.0802	0.0693	0.0600	0.0520	0.0451	0.0391	0.0340	0.0296	0.0258	0.0225	0.0197	0.0172	0.0150	0.0132	0.0116
18	0.0691	0.0592	0.0508	0.0437	0.0376	0.0323	0.0279	0.0241	0.0208	0.0180	0.0156	0.0135	0.0118	0.0102	0.0089
19	0.0596	0.0506	0.0431	0.0367	0.0313	0.0267	0.0229	0.0196	0.0168	0.0144	0.0124	0.0107	0.0092	0.0079	0.0068
20	0.0514	0.0433	0.0365	0.0308	0.0261	0.0221	0.0187	0.0159	0.0135	0.0115	0.0098	0.0084	0.0072	0.0061	0.0053
25	0.0245	0.0197	0.0160	0.0129	0.0105	0.0085	0.0069	0.0057	0.0046	0.0038	0.0031	0.0025	0.0021	0.0017	0.0014
30	0.0116	0.0090	0.0070	0.0054	0.0042	0.0033	0.0026	0.0020	0.0016	0.0012	0.0010	0.0008	0.0006	0.0005	0.0004
40	0.0026	0.0019	0.0013	0.0010	0.0007	0.0005	0.0004	0.0003	0.0002	0.0001	0.0001	0.0001	0.0001	0.0000	0.0000
50	0.0006	0.0004	0.0003	0.0002	0.0001	0.0001	0.0000	0.0000	0.0000	0.0000	0.0000	0.0000	0.0000	0.0000	0.0000

APPENDIX TABLE A–3 Annuity table: Present value of $1 per year for each of t years $= 1/r - 1/(r(1 + r)^t)$

Number of Years	Interest Rate per Year														
	1%	2%	3%	4%	5%	6%	7%	8%	9%	10%	11%	12%	13%	14%	15%
1	0.9901	0.9804	0.9709	0.9615	0.9524	0.9434	0.9346	0.9259	0.9174	0.9091	0.9009	0.8929	0.8850	0.8772	0.8696
2	1.9704	1.9416	1.9135	1.8861	1.8594	1.8334	1.8080	1.7833	1.7591	1.7355	1.7125	1.6901	1.6681	1.6467	1.6257
3	2.9410	2.8839	2.8286	2.7751	2.7232	2.6730	2.6243	2.5771	2.5313	2.4869	2.4437	2.4018	2.3612	2.3216	2.2832
4	3.9020	3.8077	3.7171	3.6299	3.5460	3.4651	3.3872	3.3121	3.2397	3.1699	3.1024	3.0373	2.9745	2.9137	2.8550
5	4.8534	4.7135	4.5797	4.4518	4.3295	4.2124	4.1002	3.9927	3.8897	3.7908	3.6959	3.6048	3.5172	3.4331	3.3522
6	5.7955	5.6014	5.4172	5.2421	5.0757	4.9173	4.7665	4.6229	4.4859	4.3553	4.2305	4.1114	3.9975	3.8887	3.7845
7	6.7282	6.4720	6.2303	6.0021	5.7864	5.5824	5.3893	5.2064	5.0330	4.8684	4.7122	4.5638	4.4226	4.2883	4.1604
8	7.6517	7.3255	7.0197	6.7327	6.4632	6.2098	5.9713	5.7466	5.5348	5.3349	5.1461	4.9676	4.7988	4.6389	4.4873
9	8.5660	8.1622	7.7861	7.4353	7.1078	6.8017	6.5152	6.2469	5.9952	5.7590	5.5370	5.3282	5.1317	4.9464	4.7716
10	9.4713	8.9826	8.5302	8.1109	7.7217	7.3601	7.0236	6.7101	6.4177	6.1446	5.8892	5.6502	5.4262	5.2161	5.0188
11	10.3676	9.7868	9.2526	8.7605	8.3064	7.8869	7.4987	7.1390	6.8052	6.4951	6.2065	5.9377	5.6869	5.4527	5.2337
12	11.2551	10.5753	9.9540	9.3851	8.8633	8.3838	7.9427	7.5361	7.1607	6.8137	6.4924	6.1944	5.9176	5.6603	5.4206
13	12.1337	11.3484	10.6350	9.9856	9.3936	8.8527	8.3577	7.9038	7.4869	7.1034	6.7499	6.4235	6.1218	5.8424	5.5831
14	13.0037	12.1062	11.2961	10.5631	9.8986	9.2950	8.7455	8.2442	7.7862	7.3667	6.9819	6.6282	6.3025	6.0021	5.7245
15	13.8651	12.8493	11.9379	11.1184	10.3797	9.7122	9.1079	8.5595	8.0607	7.6061	7.1909	6.8109	6.4624	6.1422	5.8474
16	14.7179	13.5777	12.5611	11.6523	10.8378	10.1059	9.4466	8.8514	8.3126	7.8237	7.3792	6.9740	6.6039	6.2651	5.9542
17	15.5623	14.2919	13.1661	12.1657	11.2741	10.4773	9.7632	9.1216	8.5436	8.0216	7.5488	7.1196	6.7291	6.3729	6.0472
18	16.3983	14.9920	13.7535	12.6593	11.6896	10.8276	10.0591	9.3719	8.7556	8.2014	7.7016	7.2497	6.8399	6.4674	6.1280
19	17.2260	15.6785	14.3238	13.1339	12.0853	11.1581	10.3356	9.6036	8.9501	8.3649	7.8393	7.3658	6.9380	6.5504	6.1982
20	18.0456	16.3514	14.8775	13.5903	12.4622	11.4699	10.5940	9.8181	9.1285	8.5136	7.9633	7.4694	7.0248	6.6231	6.2593
25	22.0232	19.5235	17.4131	15.6221	14.0939	12.7834	11.6536	10.6748	9.8226	9.0770	8.4217	7.8431	7.3300	6.8729	6.4641
30	25.8077	22.3965	19.6004	17.2920	15.3725	13.7648	12.4090	11.2578	10.2737	9.4269	8.6938	8.0552	7.4957	7.0027	6.5660
40	32.8347	27.3555	23.1148	19.7928	17.1591	15.0463	13.3317	11.9246	10.7574	9.7791	8.9511	8.2438	7.6344	7.1050	6.6418
50	39.1961	31.4236	25.7298	21.4822	18.2559	15.7619	13.8007	12.2335	10.9617	9.9148	9.0417	8.3045	7.6752	7.1327	6.6605

APPENDIX TABLE A-3 Annuity table: Present value of $1 per year for each of t years = $1/r - 1/(r(1 + r)^t)$ **(concluded)**

Number of Years	Interest Rate per Year														
	16%	17%	18%	19%	20%	21%	22%	23%	24%	25%	26%	27%	28%	29%	30%
1	0.8621	0.8547	0.8475	0.8403	0.8333	0.8264	0.8197	0.8130	0.8065	0.8000	0.7937	0.7874	0.7813	0.7752	0.7692
2	1.6052	1.5852	1.5656	1.5465	1.5278	1.5095	1.4915	1.4740	1.4568	1.4400	1.4235	1.4074	1.3916	1.3761	1.3609
3	2.2459	2.2096	2.1743	2.1399	2.1065	2.0739	2.0422	2.0114	1.9813	1.9520	1.9234	1.8956	1.8684	1.8420	1.8161
4	2.7982	2.7432	2.6901	2.6386	2.5887	2.5404	2.4936	2.4483	2.4043	2.3616	2.3202	2.2800	2.2410	2.2031	2.1662
5	3.2743	3.1993	3.1272	3.0576	2.9906	2.9260	2.8636	2.8035	2.7454	2.6893	2.6351	2.5827	2.5320	2.4830	2.4356
6	3.6847	3.5892	3.4976	3.4098	3.3255	3.2446	3.1669	3.0923	3.0205	2.9514	2.8850	2.8210	2.7594	2.7000	2.6427
7	4.0386	3.9224	3.8115	3.7057	3.6046	3.5079	3.4155	3.3270	3.2423	3.1611	3.0833	3.0087	2.9370	2.8682	2.8021
8	4.3436	4.2072	4.0776	3.9544	3.8372	3.7256	3.6193	3.5179	3.4212	3.3289	3.2407	3.1564	3.0758	2.9986	2.9247
9	4.6065	4.4506	4.3030	4.1633	4.0310	3.9054	3.7863	3.6731	3.5655	3.4631	3.3657	3.2728	3.1842	3.0997	3.0190
10	4.8332	4.6586	4.4941	4.3389	4.1925	4.0541	3.9232	3.7993	3.6819	3.5705	3.4648	3.3644	3.2689	3.1781	3.0915
11	5.0286	4.8364	4.6560	4.4865	4.3271	4.1769	4.0354	3.9018	3.7757	3.6564	3.5435	3.4365	3.3351	3.2388	3.1473
12	5.1971	4.9884	4.7932	4.6105	4.4392	4.2784	4.1274	3.9852	3.8514	3.7251	3.6059	3.4933	3.3868	3.2859	3.1903
13	5.3423	5.1183	4.9095	4.7147	4.5327	4.3624	4.2028	4.0530	3.9124	3.7801	3.6555	3.5381	3.4272	3.3224	3.2233
14	5.4675	5.2293	5.0081	4.8023	4.6106	4.4317	4.2646	4.1082	3.9616	3.8241	3.6949	3.5733	3.4587	3.3507	3.2487
15	5.5755	5.3242	5.0916	4.8759	4.6755	4.4890	4.3152	4.1530	4.0013	3.8593	3.7261	3.6010	3.4834	3.3726	3.2682
16	5.6685	5.4053	5.1624	4.9377	4.7296	4.5364	4.3567	4.1894	4.0333	3.8874	3.7509	3.6228	3.5026	3.3896	3.2832
17	5.7487	5.4746	5.2223	4.9897	4.7746	4.5755	4.3908	4.2190	4.0591	3.9099	3.7705	3.6400	3.5177	3.4028	3.2948
18	5.8178	5.5339	5.2732	5.0333	4.8122	4.6079	4.4187	4.2431	4.0799	3.9279	3.7861	3.6536	3.5294	3.4130	3.3037
19	5.8775	5.5845	5.3162	5.0700	4.8435	4.6346	4.4415	4.2627	4.0967	3.9424	3.7985	3.6642	3.5386	3.4210	3.3105
20	5.9288	5.6278	5.3527	5.1009	4.8696	4.6567	4.4603	4.2786	4.1103	3.9539	3.8083	3.6726	3.5458	3.4271	3.3158
25	6.0971	5.7662	5.4669	5.1951	4.9476	4.7213	4.5139	4.3232	4.1474	3.9849	3.8342	3.6943	3.5640	3.4423	3.3286
30	6.1772	5.8294	5.5168	5.2347	4.9789	4.7463	4.5338	4.3391	4.1601	3.9950	3.8424	3.7009	3.5693	3.4466	3.3321
40	6.2335	5.8713	5.5482	5.2582	4.9966	4.7596	4.5439	4.3467	4.1659	3.9995	3.8458	3.7034	3.5712	3.4481	3.3332
50	6.2463	5.8801	5.5541	5.2623	4.9995	4.7616	4.5452	4.3477	4.1666	3.9999	3.8461	3.7037	3.5714	3.4483	3.3333

APPENDIX TABLE A-4 Annuity table: Future value of $1 per year for each of t years $= ((1 + r)^t - 1)/r$

Number of Years	Interest Rate per Year														
	1%	2%	3%	4%	5%	6%	7%	8%	9%	10%	11%	12%	13%	14%	15%
1	1.0000	1.0000	1.0000	1.0000	1.0000	1.0000	1.0000	1.0000	1.0000	1.0000	1.0000	1.0000	1.0000	1.0000	1.0000
2	2.0100	2.0200	2.0300	2.0400	2.0500	2.0600	2.0700	2.0800	2.0900	2.1000	2.1100	2.1200	2.1300	2.1400	2.1500
3	3.0301	3.0604	3.0909	3.1216	3.1525	3.1836	3.2149	3.2464	3.2781	3.3100	3.3421	3.3744	3.4069	3.4396	3.4725
4	4.0604	4.1216	4.1836	4.2465	4.3101	4.3746	4.4399	4.5061	4.5731	4.6410	4.7097	4.7793	4.8498	4.9211	4.9934
5	5.1010	5.2040	5.3091	5.4163	5.5256	5.6371	5.7507	5.8666	5.9847	6.1051	6.2278	6.3528	6.4803	6.6101	6.7424
6	6.1520	6.3081	6.4684	6.6330	6.8019	6.9753	7.1533	7.3359	7.5233	7.7156	7.9129	8.1152	8.3227	8.5355	8.7537
7	7.2135	7.4343	7.6625	7.8983	8.1420	8.3938	8.6540	8.9228	9.2004	9.4872	9.7833	10.0890	10.4047	10.7305	11.0668
8	8.2857	8.5830	8.8923	9.2142	9.5491	9.8975	10.2598	10.6366	11.0285	11.4359	11.8594	12.2997	12.7573	13.2328	13.7268
9	9.3685	9.7546	10.1591	10.5828	11.0266	11.4913	11.9780	12.4876	13.0210	13.5795	14.1640	14.7757	15.4157	16.0853	16.7858
10	10.4622	10.9497	11.4639	12.0061	12.5779	13.1808	13.8164	14.4866	15.1929	15.9374	16.7220	17.5487	18.4197	19.3373	20.3037
11	11.5668	12.1687	12.8078	13.4864	14.2068	14.9716	15.7836	16.6455	17.5603	18.5312	19.5614	20.6546	21.8143	23.0445	24.3493
12	12.6825	13.4121	14.1920	15.0258	15.9171	16.8699	17.8885	18.9771	20.1407	21.3843	22.7132	24.1331	25.6502	27.2707	29.0017
13	13.8093	14.6803	15.6178	16.6268	17.7130	18.8821	20.1406	21.4953	22.9534	24.5227	26.2116	28.0291	29.9847	32.0887	34.3519
14	14.9474	15.9739	17.0863	18.2919	19.5986	21.0151	22.5505	24.2149	26.0192	27.9750	30.0949	32.3926	34.8827	37.5811	40.5047
15	16.0969	17.2934	18.5989	20.0236	21.5786	23.2760	25.1290	27.1521	29.3609	31.7725	34.4054	37.2797	40.4175	43.8424	47.5804
16	17.2579	18.6393	20.1569	21.8245	23.6575	25.6725	27.8881	30.3243	33.0034	35.9497	39.1899	42.7533	46.6717	50.9804	55.7175
17	18.4304	20.0121	21.7616	23.6975	25.8404	28.2129	30.8402	33.7502	36.9737	40.5447	44.5008	48.8837	53.7391	59.1176	65.0751
18	19.6147	21.4123	23.4144	25.6454	28.1324	30.9057	33.9990	37.4502	41.3013	45.5992	50.3959	55.7497	61.7251	68.3941	75.8364
19	20.8109	22.8406	25.1169	27.6712	30.5390	33.7600	37.3790	41.4463	46.0185	51.1591	56.9395	63.4397	70.7494	78.9692	88.2118
20	22.0190	24.2974	26.8704	29.7781	33.0660	36.7856	40.9955	45.7620	51.1601	57.2750	64.2028	72.0524	80.9468	91.0249	102.4436
25	28.2432	32.0303	36.4593	41.6459	47.7271	54.8645	63.2490	73.1059	84.7009	98.3471	114.4133	133.3339	155.6196	181.8708	212.7930
30	34.7849	40.5681	47.5754	56.0849	66.4388	79.0582	94.4608	113.2832	136.3075	164.4940	199.0209	241.3327	293.1992	356.7868	434.7451
40	48.8864	60.4020	75.4013	95.0255	120.7998	154.7620	199.6351	259.0565	337.8824	442.5926	581.8261	767.0914	1,013.704	1,342.025	1,779.0903
50	64.4632	84.5794	112.7969	152.6671	209.3480	290.3359	406.5289	573.7702	815.0836	1,163.909	1,668.771	2,400.018	3,459.507	4,994.521	7,217.7163

APPENDIX TABLE A–4 Annuity table: Future value of \$1 per year for each of t years $= ((1 + r)^t - 1)/r$ **(concluded)**

Number of Years							Interest Rate per Year								
	16%	17%	18%	19%	20%	21%	22%	23%	24%	25%	26%	27%	28%	29%	30%
1	1.0000	1.0000	1.0000	1.0000	1.0000	1.0000	1.0000	1.0000	1.0000	1.0000	1.0000	1.0000	1.0000	1.0000	1.0000
2	2.1600	2.1700	2.1800	2.1900	2.2000	2.2100	2.2200	2.2300	2.2400	2.2500	2.2600	2.2700	2.2800	2.2900	2.3000
3	3.5056	3.5389	3.5724	3.6061	3.6400	3.6741	3.7084	3.7429	3.7776	3.8125	3.8476	3.8829	3.9184	3.9541	3.9900
4	5.0665	5.1405	5.2154	5.2913	5.3680	5.4457	5.5242	5.6038	5.6842	5.7656	5.8480	5.9313	6.0156	6.1008	6.1870
5	6.8771	7.0144	7.1542	7.2966	7.4416	7.5892	7.7396	7.8926	8.0484	8.2070	8.3684	8.5327	8.6999	8.8700	9.0431
6	8.9775	9.2068	9.4420	9.6830	9.9299	10.1830	10.4423	10.7079	10.9801	11.2588	11.5442	11.8366	12.1359	12.4423	12.7560
7	11.4139	11.7720	12.1415	12.5227	12.9159	13.3214	13.7396	14.1708	14.6153	15.0735	15.5458	16.0324	16.5339	17.0506	17.5828
8	14.2401	14.7733	15.3270	15.9020	16.4991	17.1189	17.7623	18.4300	19.1229	19.8419	20.5876	21.3612	22.1634	22.9953	23.8577
9	17.5185	18.2847	19.0859	19.9234	20.7989	21.7139	22.6700	23.6690	24.7125	25.8023	26.9404	28.1287	29.3692	30.6639	32.0150
10	21.3215	22.3931	23.5213	24.7089	25.9587	27.2738	28.6574	30.1128	31.6434	33.2529	34.9449	36.7235	38.5926	40.5564	42.6195
11	25.7329	27.1999	28.7551	30.4035	32.1504	34.0013	35.9620	38.0388	40.2379	42.5661	45.0306	47.6388	50.3985	53.3178	56.4053
12	30.8502	32.8239	34.9311	37.1802	39.5805	42.1416	44.8737	47.7877	50.8950	54.2077	57.7386	61.5013	65.5100	69.7800	74.3270
13	36.7862	39.4040	42.2187	45.2445	48.4966	51.9913	55.7459	59.7788	64.1097	68.7596	73.7506	79.1066	84.8529	91.0161	97.6250
14	43.6720	47.1027	50.8180	54.8409	59.1959	63.9095	69.0100	74.5280	80.4961	86.9495	93.9258	101.4654	109.6117	118.4108	127.9125
15	51.6595	56.1101	60.9653	66.2607	72.0351	78.3305	85.1922	92.6694	100.8151	109.6868	119.3465	129.8611	141.3029	153.7500	167.2863
16	60.9250	66.6488	72.9390	79.8502	87.4421	95.7799	104.9345	114.9834	126.0108	138.1085	151.3766	165.9236	181.8677	199.3374	218.4722
17	71.6730	78.9792	87.0680	96.0218	105.9306	116.8937	129.0201	142.4295	157.2534	173.6357	191.7345	211.7230	233.7907	258.1453	285.0139
18	84.1407	93.4056	103.7403	115.2659	128.1167	142.4413	158.4045	176.1883	195.9942	218.0446	242.5855	269.8882	300.2521	334.0074	371.5180
19	98.6032	110.2846	123.4135	138.1664	154.7400	173.3540	194.2535	217.7116	244.0328	273.5558	306.6577	343.7580	385.3227	431.8696	483.9734
20	115.3797	130.0329	146.6280	165.4180	186.6880	210.7584	237.9893	268.7853	303.6006	342.9447	387.3887	437.5726	494.2131	558.1118	630.1655
25	249.2140	292.1049	342.6035	402.0425	471.9811	554.2422	650.9551	764.6054	898.0916	1,054.791	1,238.636	1,454.201	1,706.803	2,002.616	2,348.803
30	530.312	647.439	790.948	966.712	1,181.882	1,445.151	1,767.081	2,160.491	2,640.916	3,227.174	3,942.026	4,812.977	5,873.231	7,162.824	8,729.985
40	2,360.76	3,134.52	4,163.21	5,529.83	7,343.86	9,749.52	12,936.54	17,154.05	22,728.80	30,088.66	39,792.98	52,572.00	69,377.46	91,447.96	120,392.9
50	10,435.65	15,089.50	21,813.09	31,515.34	45,497.19	65,617.20	94,525.28	135,992.2	195,372.6	280,255.7	401,374.5	573,877.9	819,103.1	1,167,041	1,659,761

Chapter 1

1. Investment decisions: Build a new factory; conduct research to develop a new drug. Financing decisions: Take out a bank loan; issue shares of stock to raise funds.

2. Unlike proprietorships, corporations are legally distinct from their owners, and so they have limited liability and pay taxes on their earnings. Shares of public corporations trade in stock markets, unlike those of private corporations.

6. a. financial
    b. financial
    c. real
    d. real
    e. real
    f. financial
    g. real
    h. financial

10. Managers who are more securely entrenched in their positions are more able to pursue their own interests.

19. The contingency arrangement aligns the interests of the lawyer and the client.

26. If you know that you will engage in business with another party on a repeated basis, you will be less likely to take advantage of your business partner should the opportunity to do so arise.

Chapter 2

4. Options markets, foreign exchange markets, futures markets, commodity markets, money market.

5. Buy shares in a mutual fund.

10. Look up the price of gold in commodity markets, and compare it to $2,500/6 = $416.67/ounce.

14. a. False
     b. False
     c. True
     d. False
     e. False
     f. False

18. These funds collect money from small investors and invest the money in the stock or bonds of large corporations, thus channeling funds from individuals to corporations. The advantages of mutual funds for individuals are diversification, professional investment management, and record keeping.

22. a. Find the rate of return available on other riskless investments, e.g., 1-year maturity U.S. Treasury notes.
     b. The opportunity cost is 20%, the same expected rate of return available on other investments of comparable risk.

Chapter 3

1.

Assets		Liabilities and Shareholders' Equity	
Cash	$ 10,000	Accounts payable	$ 17,000
Receivables	22,000	Long-term debt	170,000
Inventory	200,000		
Store and property	100,000	Shareholders' equity	145,000
Total assets	$332,000	Liabilities and shareholders' equity	$332,000

5. a. Taxes = $2,635
       Average tax rate = 13.2%
       Marginal tax rate = 15%
    b. Taxes = $9,165
       Average tax rate = 18.3%
       Marginal tax rate = 25%
    c. Taxes = $85,999
       Average tax rate = 28.7%
       Marginal tax rate = 33%
    d. Taxes = $1,030,470
       Average tax rate = 34.3%
       Marginal tax rate = 35%

9. Dividends = $600,000

10. Total taxes are reduced by $2,000.

11. a. Book value = $200,000
        Market value = $50,200,000
     b. Price per share = $25.10
        Book value per share = $.10

12.

Sales	$10,000
Cost of goods sold	6,500
G & A expenses	1,000
Depreciation expense	1,000
EBIT	1,500
Interest expense	500
Taxable income	1,000
Taxes (35%)	350
Net income	$ 650

Cash flow = net income + depreciation = $1,650

15. Cash flow will be $3,000 less than profits.

17. a. Cash flow = $3.95 million
        Net income = $1.95 million
     b. CF increases by $.35 million
        NI decreases by $.65 million
     c. Positive impact. Investors should care more about cash flow than book income.
     d. Both CF and NI decrease by $.65 million.

20. a. 2005: Equity = 890 − 650 = 240
    2006: Equity = 1,040 − 810 = 230
    b. 2005: NWC = 90 − 50 = 40
    2006: NWC = 140 − 60 = 80
    c. Taxable income = 1,950 − 1,030 − 350 − 240 = 330
    Taxes paid = .35 × 330 = 115.50
    d. Cash flow from operations = 524.50
    e. Gross investment = 450
    f. Other current liabilities increased by 45.

22. Net working capital decreased by 50.

24. Earnings per share in 2005 = $1.70
    Earnings per share in 2006 = $1.52

28. Price per share = $6,650,000/500,000 = $13.30

Chapter 4

1. a. 46.32
   b. 21.45
   c. 67.56
   d. 45.64

3. $100 × (1.04)^{113} = $8,409
   $100 × (1.08)^{113} = $598,252

5. PV = $548.47

7.

	Discount Rate	PV of 10-Year, $1,000 Annuity	PV of 15-Year, $800 Annuity
a.	5%	$7,722	$8,304
b.	20%	4,192	3,740

9. PV = 796.56

10. a. $t = 23.36$
    b. $t = 11.91$
    c. $t = 6.17$

11. Effective annual rate
    a. 12.68%
    b. 8.24%
    c. 10.25%

13. $n = 11.9$ years

15. EAR = 67.77%

20. The PV for the quarterback is $11.37 million. The PV for the receiver is $11.58 million.

24. a. EAR = 6.78%
    b. PMT = 573.14

26. a. $r = 11.11\%$
    b. $r = 1/(1 − d) − 1 = d/(1 − d)$

28. APR = 19.19%

30. The value of the lease payments is $38,132. It is cheaper to lease the truck.

34. a. PMT = 277.41
    b. PMT = 247.69

35. $66,703.25

37. $79,079

46. $100 × e^{.10 × 8} = $222.55
    $100 × e^{.08 × 10} = $222.55

47. $n = 44.74$ months

48. The present value of your payments is $736. The present value of your receipts is $931. This is a good deal.

50. $r = 8\%$

53. a. The present value of the payoff is $1,117. This is a good deal.
    b. PV is $771. This is a bad deal.

60. $3,231

62. $2,964.53

66. a. Nominal rate = 3%
    b. Nominal rate = 7.12%
    c. Nominal rate = 9.18%

68. a. $79.38
    b. $91.51
    c. Real interest rate = 4.854%
    d. $91.51/(1.04854)^3 = $79.38

70. a. $228,107
    b. $13,950

71. 24 years

72. Inflation = 1,099% per year

77. $.8418

78. $2,653.87

Chapter 5

1. a. Coupon rate remains unchanged.
   b. Price will fall.
   c. Yield to maturity increases.
   d. Current yield increases.

3. Bond price = $1,142.86

4. Coupon rate = 8%
   Current yield = 8.42%
   Yield to maturity = 9.12%

9. Rate of return on both bonds = 10%

10. a. Price will be $1,000.
    b. Rate of return = −1.82%
    c. Real return = −4.68%

11. a. Bondholder receives $80 per year.
    b. Price = $1,065.15
    c. The bond will sell for $1,136.03.

12. a. 8.97%
    b. 8%
    c. 7.18%

16. 20 years

18. a. Price = $641.01
    b. $r = 12.87\%$

19. a. Yield to maturity = 6.5%
    b. Rate of return = 20.41%

22. a. 9.89%
    b. 8%
    c. 6.18%

25. a. 3.92%
    b. 1.92%
    c. 0
    d. −1.85%

Chapter 6

3. a. $66.67
    b. $66.67
    c. Dividend yield = 12%
       Capital gains yield = 0

6. a. 14%
    b. $P_0 = \$24$

11. a. $DIV_1 = \$1.04$
       $DIV_2 = \$1.0816$
       $DIV_3 = \$1.1249$
    b. $P_0 = \$13$
    c. $P_3 = \$14.62$
    d. Your payments are:

	Year 1	Year 2	Year 3
DIV	1.04	1.0816	1.1249
Sales price			14.6232
Total cash flow	1.04	1.0816	15.7481
PV of cash flow	0.9286	0.8622	11.2092
Sum of PV = $13			

13. a. $P_0 = \$31.50$
    b. $P_0 = \$45$

16. $P_0 = \$33.33$

18. a. (i)   Reinvest 0% of earnings.
              $P_0 = \$40$
       (ii) Reinvest at 40%.
              $P_0 = \$40$
       (iii) Reinvest at 60%.
              $P_0 = \$40$
    b. (i)   Reinvest at 0%.
              $P_0 = \$40$
       (ii) Reinvest at 40%.
              $P_0 = 51.43$
              PVGO = $11.43
       (iii) Reinvest at 60%.
              $P_0 = \$80$
              PVGO = $40
    c. In part (a), the return on reinvested earnings was equal to the discount rate.
       In part (b), the return on reinvested earnings was greater than the discount rate.

19. a. $P_0 = \$18.10$
    b. $DIV_1/P_0 = 5.52\%$

21. a. 6%
    b. $35
    c. $10
    d. 11.67
    e. 8.33

23. a. P/E = 33.33/4 = 8.33
    b. P/E increases to 10.

25. a. $P_0 = \$125$
    b. Assets in place = $80
       PVGO = $45

28. a. Market-to-book ratio = $800/$200 = 4
    b. Market-to-book ratio = ½

29. $16.59

40. a. $P_0 = \$52.80$
    b. $P_1 = \$57.14$
    c. Return = 12%

42. a. Expected return = 8%
    b. PVGO = $16.67
    c. $P_0 = \$106.22$

Chapter 7

1. Both projects are worth pursuing.

3. $NPV_A = \$23.86$ and $NPV_B = \$24.59$. Choose B.

5. No.

7. Project A has a payback period of 2.5 years. Project B has a payback period of 2 years.

11. .2680

13. $IRR_A = 25.7\%$
    $IRR_B = 20.7\%$

14. NPV = –$197.7. Reject.

15. a. $r = 0$ implies NPV = $15,750.
       $r = 50\%$ implies NPV = $4,250.
       $r = 100\%$ implies NPV = 0.
    b. IRR = 100%

17. $NPV_{9\%} = \$2,139.28$ and $NPV_{14\%} = -\$1,444.54$. The IRR is 11.81%.

20. NPV must be negative.

22. a.

Project	Payback
A	3
B	2
C	3

    b. Only B
    c. All three projects
    d.

Project	NPV
A	−1,011
B	3,378
C	2,405

    e. False

26. a. If $r = 2\%$, choose A.
    b. If $r = 12\%$, choose B.

27. $22,638

29. b. At 5% NPV = –$.443
    c. At 20% NPV = $.840
       At 40% NPV = –$.634

30. a. The equivalent annual cost of owning and operating Econo-cool is $252.53. The equivalent annual cost of Luxury Air is $234.21.
    b. Luxury Air.
    c. Econo-cool equivalent annual cost is $229.14. Luxury Air equivalent annual cost is $193.72.

33. a. The equivalent cost of owning and operating the new machine is $4,466. The old machine costs $5,000 a year to operate. You should replace.
    b. If $r = 12\%$, do not replace.

Chapter 8

3. $2.3 million

5. Increase in net cash flow = $106 million

6.

Revenue	$160,000
Rental costs	30,000
Variable costs	50,000
Depreciation	10,000
Pretax profit	$ 70,000
Taxes (35%)	24,500
Net income	$ 45,500

8. Cash flow = $3,300

10. Cash flow = $56,250

11. a.

Year	Depreciation	Book Value (end of year)
1	8,000	32,000
2	12,800	19,200
3	7,680	11,520
4	4,608	6,912
5	4,608	2,304
6	2,304	0

b. After-tax proceeds are $18,332.

17. Cash flow = $3.70585 million

18. a. Incremental operating CF = $1,300 in years 1 to 6
Net after-tax cash flow at time 0 = –$4,800
b. NPV = –4,800 + 1,300 × annuity factor (16%, 6 years) = –$9.84
c. NPV = $137.09

21. a. Initial investment = $53,000
b.

Year	Cash Flow ($000)
1	20.9
2	17.3
3	13.7
4	10.1

c. NPV = – $4,377
d. IRR = 7.50%

23. NPV = –10,894. Don't buy.

24. Equivalent annual (net-of-tax) capital costs:
Quick and Dirty: $2.075 million
Do-It-Right: $1.891 million
Choose Do-It-Right.

26. NPV = –$349,773

28. Net present value = –$.182

30. c. NPV = $28.35 million
IRR = 31.33%

Chapter 9

1. Variable costs = $.50 per burger
Fixed costs = $2.5 million

4. a. $1.836 million
$5.509 million
b. $544,588
c. $1.95 million

5. a. NPV = $5.6 million
b. NPV = $2.9 million
c. NPV = $6.8 million
d. Price = $1.59 per jar

8. $1.50

11. Accounting break-even is unaffected. NPV break-even increases.

12. CF break-even is less than zero-profit break-even sales level.

14. a. Accounting break-even sales level is $6,400 per year. NPV break-even sales level is $7,166.
b. Accounting break-even is unchanged. NPV break-even is $7,578.

15. a. Accounting break-even increases.
b. NPV break-even falls.
c. MACRS makes the project more attractive.

17. NPV will be negative.

20. DOL = 1

23. a. Average CF = 0
b. Average CF = $15,000

26. a. Expected NPV = –$681,728. The firm will reject the project.
b. Expected NPV = $69,855. The project is now worth pursuing.

Chapter 10

1. Return = 15%
Dividend yield = 5%
Capital gains yield = 10%

3. a. Rate of return = 0
Real rate = –3.85%
b. Rate of return = 5%
Real rate = 0.96%
c. Rate of return = 10%
Real rate = 5.77%

5.

Asset Class	Real Rate
Treasury bills	1.46%
Treasury bonds	2.73
Common stock	8.98

9. a.

Year	Risk Premium
2000	–16.78
2001	–14.80
2002	–22.51
2003	30.62
2004	11.42
Average	–2.41

b. Average risk premium = –2.41%
c. Standard deviation = 18.47%

15. The bankruptcy lawyer

17. b. $r_{stock} = 13\%$
    $r_{bonds} = 8.4\%$
    Standard deviation (stocks) = 9.8%
    Standard deviation (bonds) = 3.2%

19. Our estimate of "normal" risk premiums will fall.

21. a. General Steel
    b. Club Med

23. Sassafras is *not* a risky investment to a diversified investor. Its return is better when the economy enters a recession. In contrast, the Leaning Tower of Pita has returns that are positively correlated with the rest of the economy.

Chapter 11

1. a. False
   b. False
   c. False
   d. True
   e. True

3. It is not well diversified.

7. Required return = $r_f + \beta(r_m - r_f)$ = 14.75%
   Expected return = 16%
   The security is underpriced.

9. a. GE, which has the lowest beta of 0.97.
   b. GE, with standard deviation of 24.3%.
   c. $\beta = 1.28$
   d. The portfolio beta = 1.53
      Portfolio standard deviation = 30.6%
   e. Ford: $r = 14.72\%$
      GE: $r = 11.76\%$
      Microsoft: $r = 16.24\%$

11. a. $\beta_A = 1.2$
       $\beta_D = .75$
    b. $r_m = 12\%$
       $r_A = 14\%$
       $r_D = 9\%$
    c. $r = r_f + \beta(r_m - r_f)$
       $r_A = 13.6\%$
       $r_D = 10\%$
    d. Stock A

13. NPV = –$25.29

15. $P_1 = \$52.625$

19. $400,000

21.

Company	Cost of Capital
Cisco	19.91%
Citigroup	14.17
Merck	7.03
Disney	13.05

23. $\beta = 4/7 = .571$

25. a. False
    b. True
    c. False
    d. True
    e. False

26. $r = r_f + \beta(r_m - r_f)$ = 12%
    The 11% expected return is unattractive relative to its risk.

Chapter 12

1. 4.87%

4. 13.75%

8. The cost of equity capital is 11.2%.
   WACC = 8.74%

11. WACC = 12.4%

16.

	Dollars	Percent
Bonds	$ 9.36 million	30.3%
Preferred stock	1.50 million	4.9
Common stock	20.00 million	64.8
Total	$30.86 million	100.0%

17. 11.36%

18. The IRR is less than the WACC of firms in the computer industry. Reject the project.

19. a. $r = 16\%$
    b. Weighted-average beta = .72
    c. WACC = 10.56%
    d. Discount rate = 10.56%
    e. $r = 18\%$

Chapter 13

1. a. 60,000 shares issued
   b. Outstanding shares = 58,000
   c. 40,000

3. a. funded
   b. Eurobond
   c. subordinated
   d. sinking fund
   e. call
   f. prime rate
   g. floating rate
   h. private placement, public issue
   i. lease
   j. convertible
   k. warrant

6. a. 100 votes
   b. 1,000 votes

7. a. 200,001 shares
   b. 80,000 shares

9. Par value of common shares = $400,000
   Additional paid-in capital = $1,600,000
   Retained earnings = $500,000

12. Similarity: The firm promises to make specified payments. Advantage of income bonds: Interest payments are tax-deductible expenses.

Chapter 14

1. a. Subsequent issue
   b. Bond issue
   c. Bond issue

3. a. A large issue
   b. A bond issue
   c. Private placements

4. Less underwriter risk; less signaling effect from debt; easier to value.

7. a. 10%
   b. Average return = 3.94%
   c. I have suffered the winner's curse.

10. No

12. 12% of the value of funds raised.

14. a. Net proceeds of public issue = $9,770,000
       Net proceeds of private placement = $9,970,000
    b. The public issue
    c. The private placement can be custom-tailored, and its terms can be more easily renegotiated.

15. a. $12.5 million
    b. $5.80 per share

17. a. $10
    b. $18.333
    c. $8.333
    d. 200 rights

Chapter 15

4. $280 million

12. P/E = 10/1.25 = 8 (no leverage)
    P/E = 10/1.33 = 7.5 (leveraged)

15. a. Low-debt plan: D/E = .25
       High-debt plan: D/E = .67
    b.

	Low-Debt Plan		High-Debt Plan	
EPS	8.75	13.75	8.33	15.00
Expected EPS	$11.25		$11.67	

    c.

	Low-Debt	High-Debt
EPS	10	10

17. r_{equity} = 14%

23. a. 11.2%
    b. Without the tax shield, the value of equity would fall by $280 million. E falls to 1,900 − 280 = 1,620. Market-value balance sheet:

Assets	Liabilities and Equity	
2,420	Debt	0
	Equity	2,420

24. a. PV tax shield = $14
    b. PV tax shield = $4.47. Values of firm falls by $14 − $4.47 = $9.53, from $160 to $150.47.

25. Distorted investment decisions, impeded relations with other firms and creditors.

33. a. Stockholders gain; bondholders lose.
    b. Bondholders gain; stockholders lose.
    c. Bondholders lose; stockholders gain.
    d. Original stockholders lose; bondholders gain.

Chapter 16

1. a. May 7:   Declaration date
      June 6:   Last with-dividend date
      June 7:   Ex-dividend date
      June 11:   Record date
      July 2:   Payment date
   b. The ex-dividend date, June 7.
   c. Dividend yield = 1.1%
   d. Payout ratio = 15.8%
   e. New stock price = $24.55

3. a. Price = $64
   b. Price = $64
   c. Price = $80, unchanged

9. a. No effect on total wealth.
   b. Identical to position after the stock repurchase.

11. No impact on wealth.

12. a. The after-tax dividend, $1.40.
    b. No

13. a. 1,250 shares. Value of equity remains at $100,000.
    b. Same effect as the stock dividend.

14. a. $50
    b. $48.50

16. a. Price = $19.45
    b. Before-tax return = 13.1%
    c. Price = $20.09
    d. Before-tax return = 14.5%

17. a.

Stock	Pension	Corporation	Individual
A	10.00%	6.50%	9.00%
B	10.00	7.73	8.75
C	10.00	8.95	8.50

    b.

Stock	Price
A	$100
B	$ 81.25
C	$ 62.50

22. a. $20 per share.
    b. If the firm pays a dividend, EPS = $2. If the firm does the repurchase, EPS = $2.105.
    c. If the dividend is paid, the P/E ratio = 9.5. If the stock is repurchased, the P/E ratio = 9.5.

Chapter 17

1. a. Long-term debt ratio = .42
   b. Total debt ratio = .65
   c. Times interest earned = 3.75
   d. Cash coverage ratio = 7.42
   e. Current ratio = .74
   f. Quick ratio = .52
   g. Operating profit margin = .15
   h. Inventory turnover = 19.11
   i. Days sales in inventory = 19.10
   j. Average collection period = 67.39 days
   k. ROE = .14
   l. ROA = .072
   m. payout ratio = .65

2. Gross investment = 2,576

4. Balance sheet for Phone Corp.:

	Common Size (% amounts)	
	End of Year	Start of Year
Assets		
Cash and marketable securities	0.32%	0.57%
Receivables	8.59	9.05
Inventories	0.67	0.87
Other current assets	3.13	3.39
Total current assets	12.72%	13.88%
Net property, plant, and equipment	72.07	72.41
Other long-term assets	15.21	13.71
Total assets	100.00%	100.00%
Liabilities and Shareholders' Equity		
Payables	9.25%	11.05%
Short-term debt	5.12	5.72
Other current liabilities	2.93	2.86
Total current liabilities	17.30%	19.63%
Long-term debt and leases	25.32	24.84
Other long-term liabilities	22.29	22.36
Shareholders' equity	35.09	33.16
Total liabilities and shareholders' equity	100.00%	100.00%

6. a. ROE = 13.9%

 b. $\frac{\text{Assets}}{\text{Equity}} \times \frac{\text{sales}}{\text{assets}} \times \frac{\text{net income} + \text{interest}}{\text{sales}}$

 $\times \frac{\text{net income}}{\text{net income} + \text{interest}}$

 $= \frac{27,608.5}{9,422} \times \frac{13,193}{27,608.5} \times \frac{1,311 + 685}{13,193}$

 $\times \frac{1,311}{1,311 + 685} = .139$

8. a. Debt-equity ratio = $\frac{\text{long-term debt}}{\text{equity}}$

 b. Return on equity = $\frac{\text{net income}}{\text{average equity}}$

 c. Profit margin = $\frac{\text{net income} + \text{interest}}{\text{sales}}$

 d. Inventory turnover = $\frac{\text{cost of goods sold}}{\text{average inventory}}$

 e. Current ratio = $\frac{\text{current assets}}{\text{current liabilities}}$

 f. Average collection period = $\frac{\text{average receivables}}{\text{average daily sales}}$

 g. Quick ratio

 $= \frac{\text{cash} + \text{marketable securities} + \text{accounts receivable}}{\text{current liabilities}}$

11. The current ratio is unaffected. The quick ratio falls.

13. Days sales in inventory = 2

15. a. Times interest earned = 1.25
 b. Cash coverage ratio = 1.5
 c. Fixed-payment coverage = 1.09

17. Total sales = $54,750
 Asset turnover = .73
 ROA = 3.65%

19. $\frac{\text{Book debt}}{\text{Book equity}} = .5$

 $\frac{\text{Market equity}}{\text{Book equity}} = 2$

 $\frac{\text{Book debt}}{\text{Market equity}} = \frac{.5}{2} = .25$

21. Perhaps the firm has a lower ROA than its competitors; perhaps it pays a higher interest rate on its debt.

23. a. The shipping company
 b. United Foods
 c. The paper mill
 d. The power company
 e. Fledgling Electronics

Chapter 18

1. a. False
 b. False
 c. True
 d. False
 e. True
 f. True
 g. False

6. Sales revenue will increase less than proportionally to output; costs and assets will increase roughly in proportion to output. Costs and assets will increase as a proportion of sales.

9. The balancing item is dividends. Dividends must be $200.

11. a. Internal growth rate = 10%
 b. Sustainable growth rate = 15%

13. a. Internal growth rate = 5.56%
 b. Sustainable growth rate = 8.33%

15. a.

Income Statement	20% growth
Revenue	2,400
Cost of goods sold	2,160
EBIT	240
Interest expense	40
Earnings before taxes	200
State and federal taxes	80
Net income	120
Dividends	80
Retained earnings	40

Balance Sheet	
Assets	
Net working capital	240
Fixed assets	960
Net assets	1,200
Liabilities and Shareholders' Equity	
Long-term debt	400
Shareholders' equity	640
Total liabilities and shareholders' equity	1,040
Required external financing	160

b.

Second-Stage Pro Forma Balance Sheet	
Assets	
Net working capital	240
Fixed assets	960
Net assets	1,200
Liabilities and Shareholders' Equity	
Long-term debt	560
Shareholders' equity	640
Total liabilities and shareholders' equity	1,200

17. a. $g = .025$
 b. Issue $1,000 in new debt.
 c. 1.5%

19. a. Internal growth rate = 10%
 b. External financing = $200,000
 c. Internal growth rate = 25%
 d. External financing = $50,000

21. Payout ratio can be at most .44.

23. Profit margin = 10%

25. $g = 12\%$

27. Required external financing is zero.

29. Higher

Chapter 19

1.

	Cash	Net Working Capital
a.	$2 million decline	$2 million decline
b.	$2,500 increase	Unchanged
c.	$5,000 decline	Unchanged
d.	Unchanged	$1 million increase
e.	Unchanged	Unchanged
f.	$5 million increase	Unchanged

2. a. Long-term financing, total capital requirement, marketable securities.
 b. Cash, cash, cash balance, marketable securities.

5. Lower inventory period and cash conversion cycle; reduce net working capital.

7. a. Cash conversion cycle falls.
 b. Cash conversion cycle increases.
 c. Cash conversion cycle falls.
 d. Cash conversion cycle increases.
 e. Cash conversion cycle falls.
 f. Cash conversion cycle increases.

9. Effective rate = 8.89%. If the compensating balance is 20%, the effective rate is 10%.

11. a. 6.38%
 b. 6.20%

15. The order is .75 times the following quarter's sales forecast:

Quarter	Order
1	270
2	252
3	288
4	288

17.

Quarter	Collections
1	348
2	368
3	352
4	352

19.

		Quarter		
	First	Second	Third	Fourth
Cash at start of period	$40	$10	$15	–$14
Net cash inflow (from problem 18)	–30	+5	–29	–41
= Cash at end of period	10	15	–14	–55
Minimum operating cash balance	30	30	30	30
Cumulative short-term financing required (minimum cash balance minus cash at end of period)	$20	$15	$44	$85

21.

	Quarter			
	First	Second	Third	Fourth
Cash requirements				
1. Cash required for operations	$45	$15	–$26	–$35
2. Interest on line of credit	0	0.9	0.9	0.7
3. Interest on stretched payables	0	0	0.8	0
4. Total cash required	$45	$15.9	–$24.3	–$34.3
Cash raised				
5. Line of credit (bank loan)	$45	$ 0	$0	$0
6. Stretched payables	0	15.9	0	0
7. Securities sold	5	0	0	0
8. Total cash raised	$50	$15.9	$0	$0
Repayments				
9. Of stretched payables	0	0	$15.9	0
10. Of line of credit (bank loan)	0	0	8.4	34.3
Increase in cash balances				
11. Addition to cash balances	$ 5	$0	$0	$0
Line of credit (bank loan)				
12. Beginning of quarter	$ 0	$45	$45	$36.6
13. End of quarter	45	45	36.6	2.3

22.

Sources of Cash	
Sale of marketable securities	2
Increase in bank loans	1
Increase in accounts payable	5
Cash from operations:	
Net income	6
Depreciation	2
Total	16
Uses of Cash	
Increase in inventories	6
Increase in accounts receivable	3
Investment in fixed assets	6
Dividend paid	1
Total	16
Change in cash balance	0

23.

	February	March	April
Sources of cash			
Collections on current sales	$ 100	$110	$ 90
Collections on accounts receivable	90	100	110
Total sources of cash	$ 190	$210	$200
Uses of cash			
Payments of accounts payable	$ 30	$ 40	$ 30
Cash purchases	70	80	60
Labor and administrative expenses	30	30	30
Capital expenditures	100	0	0
Taxes, interest, and dividends	10	10	10
Total uses of cash	$ 240	$ 160	$ 130
Net cash inflow (sources – uses)	–$ 50	+$ 50	+$ 70
Cash at start of period	$ 100	$ 50	$100
+ Net cash inflow	–50	+50	+70
= Cash at end of period	$ 50	$100	$170
Minimum operating cash balance	$ 100	$ 100	$ 100
Cumulative short-term financing required (minimum cash balance minus cash at end of period)	$ 50	$ 0	–$ 70

Chapter 20

1. a. $10
   b. 40 days
   c. 9.6%

4. a. Due lag and pay lag fall.
   b. Due lag and pay lag increase.
   c. Terms lag and pay lag increase.

6. Ledger balance = $215,000
   Net float = $15,000

8. a. Checks not yet cleared   = $120,000
      Collections not yet available = $\underline{66,000}$
      Net float   = $54,000
   b. Annual interest earnings = $1,320
      Present value of earnings = $22,000

11. a. 20 days
    b. $1.096 million
    c. Average days in receivables will fall.

13. a. The expected profit from a sale is –3. Do not extend credit.
    b. $p = .96$
    c. The present value of a sale, net of default, is positive, $365.28.
    d. $p = 19.35\%$

14. a. The expected profit of a sale is positive, $90.
    b. $p = .875$

19. a. Yes
    b. Credit should not be advanced.
    c. Net benefit from advancing credit = $50.

20. a. $30,000
    b. $6
    c. $180

22. Yes

23. Cash balances fall relative to sales.

24. PV(REV) = $1,200
    PV(COST) = $1,000
    Slow payers have a 70% probability of paying their bills. The expected profit of a sale to a slow payer is therefore .70($1,200 – $1,000) – .30($1,000) = –$160.
    Expected savings = $16. The credit check costs $5, so it is cost effective.

26. Sell only to groups 1, 2, and 3.

Chapter 21

1. a. Economies of scale is a valid reason.
   b. Diversification is not a valid reason.
   c. Possibly a valid reason.
   d. The bootstrap strategy is not a valid reason.

2. By merging, the firms can even out the workload over the year.

4. LBO: 5
   Poison pill: 3
   Tender offer: 4
   Shark repellent: 2
   Proxy contest: 1

6. $25 per share

8. a. $6.25 million
   b. $4 million
   c. NPV = $2.25 million

12. a. NPV = $10,000
    b. SCC will sell for $53.33; SDP will sell for $20.
    c. Price = $52.63
    d. NPV = $7,890

13. a. Total market value = $4,000,000 + 5,000,000 = $9,000,000
       Total earnings = $200,000 + 500,000 = $700,000
       Number of shares = 262,172
       Price per share = $9,000,000/262,172 = $34.33
       Price-earnings ratio = 34.33/2.67 = 12.9
    b. .81 share
    c. $567,365
    d. $567,365

Chapter 22

1. a. 77.21 euros; $129.52
   b. 119.19 Swiss francs; $83.90
   c. Direct exchange rate will decrease and indirect exchange rate will increase.
   d. U.S. dollar is worth more.

3. a. $\dfrac{1 + r_x}{1 + r_\$} = \dfrac{f_{x/\$}}{s_{x/\$}}$

   b. $\dfrac{f_{x/\$}}{s_{x/\$}} = \dfrac{E(s_{x/\$})}{s_{x/\$}}$

   c. $\dfrac{E(1 + i_x)}{E(1 + i_\$)} = \dfrac{E(s_{x/\$})}{s_{x/\$}}$

   d. $\dfrac{1 + r_x}{1 + r_\$} = \dfrac{E(1 + i_x)}{E(1 + i_\$)}$

4. Foreign inflation rate
   Future exchange rates
   Domestic interest rates

6. a

8. Borrow the present value of 1 million Australian dollars, sell them for U.S. dollars in the spot market, and invest the proceeds in an 8-year U.S. dollar loan. In 8 years, it can repay the Australian loan with the anticipated Australian dollar payment.

10. a. 4%
    b. 10.5%
    c. –2.5%

11. 5.68%

14. Canadian dollar should be depreciating relative to the U.S. dollar.

16. Net present value = $.72 million

18. a. Depreciation of Trinidadian dollars
    b. Borrow in Trinidad.
    c. Its exposure is mitigated.

Chapter 23

1.

		Payoff	Profit
a.	Call option, $X = 160$	20	–12.00
b.	Put option, $X = 160$	0	–9.60
c.	Call option, $X = 180$	0	–19.60
d.	Put option, $X = 180$	0	–17.90
e.	Call option, $X = 200$	0	–11.20
f.	Put option, $X = 200$	20	–9.10

3. a. The January 2006 call costs $27. The January 2007 call costs $41.20.
   b. More uncertainty about the stock price in 2007.
   c. This is true of puts as well.

5. Figure 23.7a represents a call seller; Figure 23.7b represents a call buyer.

7. a. The exercise price of the put option.
   b. The value of the stock.

10. Lower bound is either zero or the stock price minus the exercise price, whichever is greater. The upper bound is the stock price.

14. You will be more tempted to choose the high-risk proposal.

16. a. Call option to pursue a project.
    b. Put option to sell the equipment.

18. Put option with exercise price equal to support price.

20. a. Option to put (sell) the stock to the underwriter.
    b. Volatility of the stock value; the length of the period for which the underwriter guarantees the issue; the interest rate; the price at which the underwriter is obligated to buy the stock; and the market value of the stock.

22. Put option on the bank assets with exercise price equal to the deposits owed to bank customers.

24. a. Buy a call option for $3. Exercise the call to purchase stock. Pay the $20 exercise price. Sell the share for $25.
    b. Buy a share and put option. Exercise the put. Riskless profit equals $1.

28. Call price = $36.

Chapter 24

1. Both activities eliminate the firm's exposure to a particular source of risk.

4. No

6. Advantages: liquidity, no storage costs, no spoilage. Disadvantages: no income or benefits that could accrue from holding asset in portfolio.

7.

	Gold Price		
	$400	**$430**	**$460**
a. Sales	$400,000	$430,000	$460,000
Futures contract cash flow	40,000	10,000	–20,000
b. Total revenues	$440,000	$440,000	$440,000
c. Sales	$400,000	$430,000	$460,000
+ Put option payoff	30,000	0	0
– Put option cost	–3,000	–3,000	–3,000
Total revenues	$427,000	$427,000	$457,000

9. Reject its offer.

11. The futures price for oil is $40 per barrel. Petrochemical will take a long position to hedge its cost of buying oil. Onnex will take a short position to hedge its revenue from selling oil.

	Oil Price ($ per barrel)		
	$35	**$40**	**$45**
Cost for Petrochemical:			
Cash flow to buy 1,000 barrels	–35,000	–40,000	–45,000
+ Cash flow on long futures position	– 5,000	0	5,000
Total cash flow	–40,000	–40,000	–40,000
Revenue for Onnex:			
Revenue from 1,000 barrels	$35,000	$40,000	$45,000
+ Cash flow on short futures position	5,000	0	– 5,000
Total cash flow	$40,000	$40,000	$40,000

The benefit of futures is the ability to lock in a riskless position without paying any money. The benefit of the option hedge is that you benefit if prices move in one direction without losing if they move in the other direction. However, this asymmetry comes at a price: the cost of the option.

12. The futures price is greater than the spot price for gold. This reflects the fact that the futures contract ensures your receipt of the gold without tying up your money now. The difference between the spot price and the futures price reflects compensation for the time value of money. Another way to put it is that the spot price must be lower than the futures price to compensate investors who buy and store gold for the opportunity cost of their funds until the futures maturity date.

14. A currency swap is an agreement to exchange a series of payments in one currency for a given series of payments in another currency. An interest rate swap is an exchange of a series of fixed payments for a series of payments that are linked to market interest rates.

A

acquisition Takeover of a firm by purchase of that firm's common stock or assets.

additional paid-in capital Difference between issue price and par value of stock. Also called *capital surplus.*

agency problems Managers, acting as agents for stockholders, may act in their own interests rather than maximizing value.

aging schedule Classification of accounts receivable by time outstanding.

annual percentage rate (APR) Interest rate that is annualized using simple interest.

annuity Equally spaced level stream of cash flows with a finite maturity.

annuity due Level stream of cash flows starting immediately.

annuity factor Present value of a $1 annuity.

authorized share capital Maximum number of shares that the company is permitted to issue.

average tax rate Total taxes owed divided by total income.

B

balance sheet Financial statement that shows the value of the firm's assets and liabilities at a particular time.

balancing item Variable that adjusts to maintain the consistency of a financial plan. Also called *plug.*

bankruptcy The reorganization or liquidation of a firm that cannot pay its debts.

beta Sensitivity of a stock's return to the return on the market portfolio.

bond Security that obligates the issuer to make specified payments to the bondholder.

book rate of return Accounting income divided by book value. Also called *accounting rate of return.*

book value Net worth of the firm according to the balance sheet.

break-even analysis Analysis of the level of sales at which the project breaks even.

C

call option Right to buy an asset at a specified exercise price on or before the expiration date.

callable bond Bond that may be repurchased by the firm before maturity at a specified call price.

capital asset pricing model (CAPM) Theory of the relationship between risk and return which states that the expected risk premium on any security equals its beta times the market risk premium.

capital budget List of planned investment projects.

capital budgeting decision Decision to invest in tangible or intangible assets.

capital markets Markets for long-term financing.

capital rationing Limit set on the amount of funds available for investment.

capital structure The mix of long-term debt and equity financing.

CAPM See *capital asset pricing model.*

carrying costs Costs of maintaining current assets, including opportunity cost of capital.

cash conversion cycle Period between firm's payment for materials and collection on its sales.

cash dividend Payment of cash by the firm to its shareholders.

CEO Acronym for chief executive officer.

CFO See *chief financial officer.*

chief financial officer (CFO) Oversees the treasurer and controller and sets overall financial strategy.

collection policy Procedures to collect and monitor receivables.

commercial paper Short-term unsecured notes issued by firms.

common-size balance sheet Balance sheet that presents items as a percentage of total assets.

common-size income statement Income statement that presents items as a percentage of revenues.

common stock Ownership shares in a publicly held corporation.

company cost of capital Expected rate of return demanded by investors in a company, determined by the average risk of the company's securities.

compound interest Interest earned on interest.

concentration banking System whereby customers make payments to a regional collection center which transfers funds to a principal bank.

constant-growth dividend discount model Version of the dividend discount model in which dividends grow at a constant rate.

consumer credit Bills awaiting payment from final customer to a company.

controller Officer responsible for budgeting, accounting, and taxes.

convertible bond Bond that the holder may exchange for a specified amount of another security.

corporation Business organized as a separate legal entity owned by stockholders.

cost of capital Minimum acceptable rate of return on capital investment.

costs of financial distress Costs arising from bankruptcy or distorted business decisions before bankruptcy.

coupon The interest payments paid to the bondholder.

coupon rate Annual interest payment as a percentage of face value.

credit analysis Procedure to determine the likelihood a customer will pay its bills.

credit policy Standards set to determine the amount and nature of credit to extend to customers.

cumulative voting Voting system in which all the votes one shareholder is allowed to cast can be cast for one candidate for the board of directors.

current yield Annual coupon payments divided by bond price.

D

decision tree Diagram of sequential decisions and possible outcomes.

default premium The additional yield on a bond investors require for bearing credit risk.

default risk The risk that a bond issuer may default on its bonds. Also called *credit risk.*

degree of operating leverage (DOL) Percentage change in profits given a 1 percent change in sales.

depreciation tax shield Reduction in taxes attributable to depreciation.

discount factor Present value of a $1 future payment.

discount rate Interest rate used to compute present values of future cash flows.

diversification Strategy designed to reduce risk by spreading the portfolio across many investments.

dividend   Periodic cash distribution from the firm to its shareholders.

dividend discount model   Discounted cash-flow model which states that today's stock price equals the present value of all expected future dividends.

dividend-payout ratio   Percentage of earnings paid out as dividends.

Dow Jones Industrial Average   Index of the investment performance of a portfolio of 30 "blue-chip" stocks.

Du Pont system   A breakdown of ROE and ROA into component ratios.

E

economic break-even point   Minimum level of sales needed to cover all costs including the cost of capital.

economic value added (EVA)   Income that is measured after deduction of the cost of capital.

effective annual interest rate   Interest rate that is annualized using compound interest.

efficient markets   Markets in which prices reflect all available information.

equivalent annual annuity   The cash flow per period with the same present value as the cost of buying and operating a machine.

eurobond   Bond that is marketed internationally.

eurodollars   Dollars held on deposit in a bank outside the United States.

EVA   See *economic value added*.

exchange rate   Amount of one currency needed to purchase one unit of another.

ex-dividend   Without the dividend. Buyer of a stock after the ex-dividend date does not receive the most recently declared dividend.

expectations theory of exchange rates   Theory that expected spot exchange rate equals the forward rate.

F

face value   Payment at the maturity of the bond. Also called *par value* or *maturity value*.

financial assets   Claims to the income generated by real assets. Also called *securities*.

financial deficit   Difference between cash the companies need and the amount generated internally.

financial institution   A bank, insurance company, or similar financial intermediary.

financial intermediary   An organization that raises money from many investors and provides financing to individuals, corporations, or other organizations.

financial leverage   Debt financing to amplify the effects of changes in operating income on the returns to stockholders.

financial markets   Markets in which securities are issued and traded.

financial risk   Risk to shareholders resulting from the use of debt.

financial slack   Ready access to cash or debt financing.

financing decision   The form and amount of financing of a firm's investments.

fixed costs   Costs that do not depend on the level of output.

fixed-income market   Market for debt securities.

floating-rate security   Security paying dividends or interest that vary with short-term interest rates.

flotation costs   The costs incurred when a firm issues new securities to the public.

forex   Abbreviation for foreign exchange; also abbreviated *fx*.

forward contract   Agreement to buy or sell an asset in the future at an agreed price.

forward exchange rate   Exchange rate agreed today for a future transaction.

fundamental analysts   Analysts who attempt to find mispriced securities by analyzing fundamental information, such as accounting data and business prospects.

funded debt   Debt with more than 1 year remaining to maturity.

future value   Amount to which an investment will grow after earning interest.

futures contract   Exchange-traded promise to buy or sell an asset in the future at a prespecified price.

fx   Abbreviation for foreign exchange; also abbreviated *forex*.

G

GAAP   See *generally accepted accounting principles*.

general cash offer   Sale of securities open to all investors by an already-public company.

generally accepted accounting principles (GAAP)   Procedures for preparing financial statements.

I

income statement   Financial statement that shows the revenues, expenses, and net income of a firm over a period of time.

inflation   Rate at which prices as a whole are increasing.

information content of dividends   Dividend increases send good news about future cash flow and earnings. Dividend cuts send bad news.

initial public offering (IPO)   First offering of stock to the general public.

interest rate parity   Theory that forward premium equals interest rate differential.

interest tax shield   Tax savings resulting from deductibility of interest payments.

internal growth rate   Maximum rate of growth without external financing.

internal rate of return (IRR)   Discount rate at which project NPV = 0.

internally generated funds   Cash reinvested in the firm; depreciation plus earnings not paid out as dividends.

international Fisher effect   Theory that real interest rates in all countries should be equal, with differences in nominal rates reflecting differences in expected inflation.

investment grade   Bonds rated Baa or above by Moody's or BBB or above by Standard & Poor's.

IPO   See *initial public offering*.

IRR   See *internal rate of return*.

issued shares   Shares that have been issued by the company.

J

junk bond   Bond with a rating below Baa or BBB.

just-in-time approach   System of inventory management that requires minimum inventories of materials and very frequent deliveries by suppliers.

L

law of one price   Theory that prices of goods in all countries should be equal when translated to a common currency.

lease   Long-term rental agreement.

leveraged buyout (LBO) Acquisition of a firm by a private group using substantial borrowed funds.

limited liability The owners of the corporation are not personally responsible for its obligations.

line of credit Agreement by a bank that a company may borrow at any time up to an established limit.

liquidation Sale of bankrupt firm's assets.

liquidation value Net proceeds that could be realized by selling the firm's assets and paying off its creditors.

liquidity Ability to sell an asset for cash at short notice.

lock-box system System whereby customers send payments to a post-office box and a local bank collects and processes checks.

M

majority voting Voting system in which each director is voted on separately.

management buyout (MBO) Acquisition of the firm by its own management in a leveraged buyout.

M&A Abbreviation for mergers and acquisitions.

marginal tax rate Additional taxes owed per dollar of additional income.

market index Measure of the investment performance of the overall market.

market portfolio Portfolio of all assets in the economy. In practice a broad stock market index is used to represent the market.

market risk Economywide (macroeconomic) sources of risk that affect the overall stock market. Also called *systematic risk.*

market risk premium Risk premium of market portfolio. Difference between market return and return on risk-free Treasury bills.

market value added The difference between the market value of firm's equity and its book value.

market-value balance sheet Financial statement that uses the market value of all assets and liabilities.

maturity premium Extra average return from investing in long- versus short-term Treasury securities.

merger Combination of two firms into one, with the acquirer assuming assets and liabilities of the target firm.

MM dividend-irrelevance proposition Under ideal conditions the value of the firm is unaffected by dividend policy.

MM's proposition I (debt irrelevance proposition) The value of a firm is unaffected by its capital structure.

MM's proposition II The required rate of return on equity increases as the firm's debt-equity ratio increases.

Modified Accelerated Cost Recovery System (MACRS) Depreciation method that allows higher tax deductions in early years and lower deductions later.

money market Market for short-term financing (less than 1 year).

mutual fund An investment company that pools the savings of many investors and invests in a portfolio of securities.

mutually exclusive projects Two or more projects that cannot be pursued simultaneously.

N

net present value (NPV) Present value of cash flows minus investment.

net working capital Current assets minus current liabilities.

net worth Book value of common stockholders' equity plus preferred stock.

nominal interest rate Rate at which money invested grows.

NPV See *net present value.*

NYSE New York Stock Exchange.

O

open account Agreement whereby sales are made with no formal debt contract.

operating leverage Degree to which costs are fixed.

operating risk (business risk) Risk in firm's operating income.

opportunity cost Benefit or cash flow forgone as a result of an action.

opportunity cost of capital Expected rate of return given up by investing in a project.

outstanding shares Shares that have been issued by the company and are held by investors.

P

par value Value of security shown in the company's accounts.

payback period Time until cash flows recover the initial investment in the project.

payout ratio Fraction of earnings paid out as dividends.

P/E See *price-earnings multiple.*

pecking order theory Firms prefer to issue debt rather than equity if internal finance is insufficient.

pension fund Investment plan set up by an employer to provide for employees' retirement.

percentage of sales model Planning model in which sales forecasts are the driving variables and most other variables are proportional to sales.

perpetuity Stream of level cash payments that never ends.

planning horizon Time horizon for a financial plan.

plowback ratio Fraction of earnings retained by the firm.

poison pill Measure taken by a target firm to avoid acquisition; for example, the right for existing shareholders to buy additional shares at an attractive price if a bidder acquires a large holding.

preferred stock Stock that takes priority over common stock in regard to dividends.

present value (PV) Value today of a future cash flow.

present value of growth opportunities (PVGO) Net present value of a firm's future investments.

price-earnings (P/E) multiple Ratio of stock price to earnings per share.

primary market Market for the sale of new securities by corporations.

prime rate Benchmark interest rate charged by banks.

private placement Sale of securities to a limited number of investors without a public offering.

pro formas Projected or forecast financial statements.

profitability index Ratio of net present value to initial investment.

project cost of capital Minimum acceptable expected rate of return on a project given its risk.

prospectus Formal summary that provides information on an issue of securities.

protective covenant Restriction on a firm to protect bondholders.

proxy contest Takeover attempt in which outsiders compete with management for shareholders' votes. Also called *proxy fight.*

purchasing power parity (PPP) Theory that the cost of living in different countries is equal, and exchange rates adjust to offset inflation differentials across countries.

put option   Right to sell an asset at a specified exercise price on or before the expiration date.

PV See *present value.*

R

random walk   Security prices change randomly, with no predictable trends or patterns.

rate of return   Total income per period per dollar invested.

real assets   Assets used to produce goods and services.

real interest rate   Rate at which the purchasing power of an investment increases.

real options   Options to invest in, modify, or dispose of a capital investment project.

real value of $1   Purchasing power-adjusted value of a dollar.

reorganization   Restructuring of financial claims on failing firm to allow it to keep operating.

residual income   Also called economic value added or EVA. Profit minus cost of capital employed.

restructuring   Process of changing the firm's capital structure without changing its assets.

retained earnings   Earnings not paid out as dividends.

rights issue   Issue of securities offered only to current stockholders.

risk premium   Expected return in excess of risk-free return as compensation for risk.

S

S&P   Abbreviation for Standard & Poor's stock market index.

scenario analysis   Project analysis given a particular combination of assumptions.

seasoned offering   Sale of securities by a firm that is already publicly traded.

secondary market   Market in which previously issued securities are traded among investors.

secured debt   Debt that has first claim on specified collateral in the event of default.

security market line   Relationship between expected return and beta.

sensitivity analysis   Analysis of the effects on project profitability of changes in sales, costs, and so on.

shark repellent   Amendments to a company charter made to forestall takeover attempts.

shelf registration   A procedure that allows firms to file one registration statement for several issues of the same security.

shortage costs   Costs incurred from shortages in current assets.

simple interest   Interest earned only on the original investment; no interest is earned on interest.

simulation analysis   Estimation of the probabilities of different possible outcomes, e.g., from an investment project.

sinking fund   Fund established to retire debt before maturity.

spot rate of exchange   Exchange rate for an immediate transaction.

spread   Difference between public offer price and price paid by underwriter.

stakeholder   Anyone with a financial interest in the firm.

Standard & Poor's Composite Index   Index of the investment performance of a portfolio of 500 large stocks. Also called the *S&P 500.*

standard deviation   Square root of variance. Another measure of volatility.

statement of cash flows   Financial statement that shows the firm's cash receipts and cash payments over a period of time.

stock dividend   Distribution of additional shares to a firm's stockholders.

stock repurchase   Firm buys back stock from its shareholders.

stock split   Issue of additional shares to firm's stockholders.

straight-line depreciation   Constant depreciation for each year of the asset's accounting life.

subordinated debt   Debt that may be repaid in bankruptcy only after senior debt is paid.

sunk costs   Costs that have been incurred and cannot be recovered.

sustainable growth rate   Steady rate at which a firm can grow without changing leverage; return on equity × plowback ratio.

swap   Arrangement by two counterparties to exchange one stream of cash flows for another.

T

technical analysts   Investors who attempt to identify undervalued stocks by searching for patterns in past prices.

tender offer   Takeover attempt in which outsiders directly offer to buy the stock of the firm's shareholders.

terms of sale   Credit, discount, and payment terms offered on a sale.

trade credit   Bills awaiting payment from one company to another.

trade-off theory   Debt levels are chosen to balance interest tax shields against the costs of financial distress.

treasurer   Manager responsible for financing, cash management, and relationships with banks and other financial institutions.

treasury stock   Stock that has been repurchased by the company and held in its treasury.

U

underpricing   Issuing securities at an offering price set below the true value of the security.

underwriter   Firm that buys an issue of securities from a company and resells it to the public.

unique risk   Risk factors affecting only that firm. Also called *diversifiable risk.*

V

variable costs   Costs that change as the level of output changes.

variance   Average value of squared deviations from mean. A measure of volatility.

venture capital   Money invested to finance a new firm.

W

WACC   See *weighted-average cost of capital.*

warrant   Right to buy shares from a company at a stipulated price before a set date.

weighted-average cost of capital (WACC)   Expected rate of return on a portfolio of all the firm's securities, adjusted for tax savings due to interest payments.

workout   Agreement between a company and its creditors establishing the steps the company must take to avoid bankruptcy.

Y

yield curve   Graph of the relationship between time to maturity and yield to maturity.

yield to maturity   Interest rate for which the present value of the bond's payments equals the price.

Subject Index

Capital Budgeting

Operating Leverage (9.3)

The degree of operating leverage, DOL, is the sensitivity of profits to changes in sales:

$$\text{DOL} = \frac{\text{percentage change in profits}}{\text{percentage change in sales}} = 1 + \frac{\text{fixed costs}}{\text{profits}}$$

Break-Even Point (9.3)

The sales revenue necessary for the firm to break even (in terms of accounting profits) is

$$\text{Break-even revenue} = \frac{\text{fixed costs including depreciation}}{\text{additional profit from each additional dollar of sales}}$$

Risk and Return

Measures of Risk and Return (10.3, 11.1)

Mean or expected return = probability-weighted average of possible outcomes
Variance $= \sigma^2 =$ mean of squared deviations around the mean
Standard deviation $= \sigma = \sqrt{\text{Variance}}$
Beta $= \beta =$ Expected increase in stock return for an extra 1 percent increase in the return on the market index

Capital Asset Pricing Model (11.2)

The expected rate of return on a risky security equals the rate of return on risk-free assets plus a risk premium that depends on the security beta:

$$r = r_f + \beta(r_m - r_f)$$

Capital Structure

Weighted-Average Cost of Capital (12.2)

$$\text{WACC} = \frac{D}{V} \times r_{\text{debt}}(1 - T_c) + \frac{E}{V} \times r_{\text{equity}}$$

where T_c is the corporate tax rate, D is debt, E is equity, and $V = D + E$

Return on Assets (15.1)

Return on assets equals the weighted average of the returns of the firm's outstanding securities:

$$r_{\text{assets}} = r_{\text{debt}}\frac{D}{V} + r_{\text{equity}}\frac{E}{V}$$

(assuming no taxes)

Value of Interest Tax Shields (15.2)

If a firm maintains a fixed amount of debt in perpetuity, then the present value of the tax savings equals $T_c \times \text{Debt}$

DuPont Formulas (17.2)

$$\text{Return on assets} = \text{asset turnover} \times \text{profit margin}$$

$$\text{Return on equity} = \frac{\text{asset}}{\text{equity}} \times \text{asset turnover} \times \text{profit margin} \times \text{debt burden}$$